THE ALMANAC OF AMERICAN EMPLOYERS 2020

The Only Guide to America's Hottest, Fastest-Growing Major Corporations

Jack W. Plunkett

Published by:
Plunkett Research®, Ltd., Houston, Texas
www.plunkettresearch.com

THE ALMANAC OF AMERICAN EMPLOYERS 2020

Editor and Publisher:
Jack W. Plunkett

Executive Editor and Database Manager:
Martha Burgher Plunkett

Senior Editor and Researchers:
Isaac Snider

Editors, Researchers and Assistants:
Jeremy Amorin
Michael Cappelli
Annie Paynter
Anoosh Saidi
Jorden Smith
Gina Sprenkel

Information Technology Manager:
Rebeca Tijiboy

Digital Production:
Uriel Rios

Special Thanks to:
U.S. Department of Labor
Bureau of Labor Statistics
U.S. Department of Commerce
Bureau of Economic Analysis, National Technical Information Service

Plunkett Research®, Ltd.
P. O. Drawer 541737, Houston, Texas 77254 USA
Phone: 713.932.0000 Fax: 713.932.7080
www.plunkettresearch.com

Copyright © 2019, Plunkett Research®, Ltd. All rights reserved. Except as provided for below, you may not copy, resell, reproduce, distribute, republish, download, display, post, or transmit any portion of this book in any form or by any means, including, but not limited to, electronic, mechanical, photocopying, recording, or otherwise, without the express prior written permission of Plunkett Research, Ltd. Additional copyrights are held by other content providers, including, in certain cases, Morningstar, Inc. The information contained herein is proprietary to its owners and it is not warranted to be accurate, complete or timely. Neither Plunkett Research, Ltd. nor its content providers are responsible for any damages or losses arising from any use of this information. Market and industry statistics, company revenues, profits and other details may be estimates. Financial information, company plans or status, and other data can change quickly and may vary from those stated here. **Past performance is no guarantee of future results**.

Plunkett Research®, Ltd.
P. O. Drawer 541737
Houston, Texas 77254-1737
Phone: 713.932.0000, Fax: 713.932.7080 www.plunkettresearch.com

ISBN13 # 978-1-62831-546-2 (eBook Edition # 978-1-62831-854-8)

Limited Warranty and Terms of Use:

Users' publications in static electronic format containing any portion of the content of this book (and/or the content of any related Plunkett Research, Ltd. online service to which you are granted access, hereinafter collectively referred to as the "Data") or Derived Data (that is, a set of data that is a derivation made by a User from the Data, resulting from the applications of formulas, analytics or any other method) may be resold by the User only for the purpose of providing third-party analysis within an established research platform under the following conditions: (However, Users may not extract or integrate any portion of the Data or Derived Data for any other purpose.)

a) Users may utilize the Data only as described herein. b) User may not export more than an insubstantial portion of the Data or Derived Data, c) Any Data exported by the User may only be distributed if the following conditions are met:

i) Data must be incorporated in added-value reports or presentations, either of which are part of the regular services offered by the User and not as stand-alone products.
ii) Data may not be used as part of a general mailing or included in external websites or other mass communication vehicles or formats, including, but not limited to, advertisements.
iii) Except as provided herein, Data may not be resold by User.

"Insubstantial Portions" shall mean an amount of the Data that (1) has no independent commercial value, (2) could not be used by User, its clients, Authorized Users and/or its agents as a substitute for the Data or any part of it, (3) is not separately marketed by the User, an affiliate of the User or any third-party source (either alone or with other data), and (4) is not retrieved by User, its clients, Authorized Users and/or its Agents via regularly scheduled, systematic batch jobs.

LIMITED WARRANTY; DISCLAIMER OF LIABILITY: While Plunkett Research, Ltd. ("PRL") has made an effort to obtain the Data from sources deemed reliable, PRL makes no warranties, expressed or implied, regarding the Data contained herein. This book and its Data are provided to the End-User "AS IS" without warranty of any kind. No oral or written information or advice given by PRL, its employees, distributors or representatives will create a warranty or in any way increase the scope of this Limited Warranty, and the Customer or End-User may not rely on any such information or advice. Customer Remedies: PRL's entire liability and your exclusive remedy shall be, at PRL's sole discretion, either (a) return of the price paid, if any, or (b) repair or replacement of a book that does not meet PRL's Limited Warranty and that is returned to PRL with sufficient evidence of or receipt for your original purchase.

NO OTHER WARRANTIES: TO THE MAXIMUM EXTENT PERMITTED BY APPLICABLE LAW, PRL AND ITS DISTRIBUTORS DISCLAIM ALL OTHER WARRANTIES AND CONDITIONS, EITHER EXPRESSED OR IMPLIED, INCLUDING, BUT NOT LIMITED TO, IMPLIED WARRANTIES OR CONDITIONS OF MERCHANTABILITY, FITNESS FOR A PARTICULAR PURPOSE, TITLE AND NON-INFRINGEMENT WITH REGARD TO THE BOOK AND ITS DATA, AND THE PROVISION OF OR FAILURE TO PROVIDE SUPPORT SERVICES. LIMITATION OF LIABILITY: TO THE MAXIMUM EXTENT PERMITTED BY APPLICABLE LAW, IN NO EVENT SHALL PRL BE LIABLE FOR ANY SPECIAL, INCIDENTAL OR CONSEQUENTIAL DAMAGES WHATSOEVER (INCLUDING, WITHOUT LIMITATION, DAMAGES FOR LOSS OF BUSINESS PROFITS, BUSINESS INTERRUPTION, ABILITY TO OBTAIN OR RETAIN EMPLOYMENT OR REMUNERATION, ABILITY TO PROFITABLY MAKE AN INVESTMENT, OR ANY OTHER PECUNIARY LOSS) ARISING OUT OF THE USE OF, OR RELIANCE UPON, THE BOOK OR DATA, OR THE INABILITY TO USE THIS DATA OR THE FAILURE OF PRL TO PROVIDE SUPPORT SERVICES, EVEN IF PRL HAS BEEN ADVISED OF THE POSSIBILITY OF SUCH DAMAGES. IN ANY CASE, PRL'S ENTIRE LIABILITY SHALL BE LIMITED TO THE AMOUNT ACTUALLY PAID BY YOU FOR THE BOOK.

THE ALMANAC OF AMERICAN EMPLOYERS 2020

CONTENTS

Introduction	1
How To Use This Book	3
Chapter 1: Major Trends Affecting Job Seekers	7
1) U.S. Job Market Overview	8
2) Cost Control Remains a Major Concern at Employers/Consolidation Through Mergers Continues	9
3) Unemployment Is Down to Extremely Low Levels	9
4) The Sharing & Gig Economy's Effect on Employment, Work Life and Careers	10
5) Technology Continues to Create Sweeping Changes in the Workplace	11
6) Continued Growth in Outsourcing, Including Supply Chain and Logistics Services	12
7) Offshoring, Reshoring and the Rebound in American Manufacturing	13
8) Older Americans Will Delay Retirement and Work Longer/Many Employers Find Older Employees Desirable	13
9) Employment Sectors that Will Offer an Above-Average Number of Job Opportunities	14
Chapter 2: Statistics	17
U.S. Employment Overview: 2018-2019	18
U.S. Civilian Labor Force: 1997-July 2019	19
Employment by Major Industry Sector: 2006, 2016 & Projected 2026	20
Number of People Employed and Unemployed, U.S.: July 2018 vs. July 2019	21
U.S. Labor Force Ages 16 to 24 Years Old by School Enrollment, Educational Attainment, Sex, Race & Ethnicity: October 2018	22
Medical Care Benefits in the U.S.: Access, Participation and Take-Up Rates, March 2018	23
Retirement Benefits in the U.S.: Access, Participation and Take-Up Rates, March 2018	24
Top 30 U.S. Occupations by Numerical Change in Job Growth: 2016-2026	25
Top 30 U.S. Fastest Growing Occupations: 2016-2026	26
Occupations with the Largest Expected Employment Increases, U.S.: 2016-2026	27
Occupations with the Fastest Expected Decline, U.S.: 2016-2026	28
Chapter 3: Research: 7 Keys for Job Seekers	29
1) Financial Stability	29
2) Growth Plans	29
3) Research and Development Programs	29
4) Product Launch and Production	29
5) Marketing and Distribution Methods	29
6) Employee Benefits	30
7) Quality of Work Factors	30
Other Considerations	30
Chapter 4: Important Contacts for Job Seekers	37
Addresses, Telephone Numbers and Internet Sites	

Continued on the next page

Continued from the previous page

Chapter 5: **THE AMERICAN EMPLOYERS 500:**
    Who They Are and How They Were Chosen — **65**
    Index of Companies Within Industry Groups — **67**
    Alphabetical Index — **84**
    Index of U.S. Headquarters Location by State — **87**

Individual Data Profiles on each of THE AMERICAN EMPLOYERS 500 — **91**

Additional Indexes
    Index of Firms Noted as Hot Spots for Advancement for Women & Minorities — **588**
    Index of Subsidiaries, Brand Names and Selected Affiliations — **590**

INTRODUCTION

THE ALMANAC OF AMERICAN EMPLOYERS is an easy-to-use solution to what would otherwise be a complicated problem: How can you tell, among America's giant companies, which firms are most likely to be hiring? Among those firms, which are the best to work for? No other source provides this book's easy-to-understand comparisons of growth, treatment of employees, salaries, benefits, pension plans, profit sharing and many other items of great importance to job seekers.

Especially helpful is the way in which THE ALMANAC OF AMERICAN EMPLOYERS enables readers with no business background to readily compare the growth potential and benefit plans of large employers. You'll see the mid-term financial record of each firm, along with the impact of earnings, sales and growth plans on each company's potential to provide employment opportunities.

Information is presented in a way that addresses the differing interests of individual employees. You'll find separate listings for dozens of categories of data that you may want to consider. While this book is aimed primarily at job seekers, it will also be of tremendous value to researchers, marketing executives and personnel professionals. THE ALMANAC OF AMERICAN EMPLOYERS is the premier guide to the most successful employers in the nation, their policies and their performance.

THE ALMANAC OF AMERICAN EMPLOYERS is your opportunity to gain valuable knowledge in a matter of minutes. Five hundred of the biggest, most successful corporate employers in America are analyzed in this book. Tens of thousands of pieces of information, gathered from a wide variety of sources, have been researched for these corporations and are presented here in a form that can be easily understood by job seekers of all types.

Thanks to THE ALMANAC OF AMERICAN EMPLOYERS' exclusive data system, potentially confusing considerations have been reduced to simple groups of focused data. By scanning the data groups and the long list of unique indexes, you can find the right employers to fit your personal needs.

The AMERICAN EMPLOYERS 500 are among the best major growth companies to work for in America. Which companies offer the best benefits, are the biggest employers or earn the most profits? Where are these companies operating? All of these things and more are made easy for the reader to determine.

Thousands of observations are made that will be of great interest to prospective employees. For many of the firms, you'll find comments about such items as plans for growth, increases or decreases in the number of employees and charitable programs. You'll also find notes about corporate culture and special programs for the convenience of employees, such as health and recreation facilities, on-site child care, job training or career paths. Finally, you'll find basic information on each company, including the home office address and telephone number; regional, national and international locations; a description of the business; and a list of selected subsidiaries and trade names. In addition, you will find fax numbers and Internet addresses.

Whether you are currently employed by one of these corporate giants or are considering applying for a job with one, you will be able to see how each company compares with the others, even if you don't have the slightest understanding of accounting, finance or employee benefits.

Whatever your purpose for researching corporate employers, you'll find this book to be an indispensable guide. Nonetheless, as is true with all resources, this volume has limitations that the reader should be aware of:

- Financial data and other corporate information can change quickly. A book of this type can be no more current than the data that was available as of the time of editing. Consequently, the financial picture, management and ownership of the firm(s) you are studying may have changed since the date of this book. For example, this almanac includes the most up-to-date sales figures and profits available to the editors as of mid-2019. This means that we have typically used corporate financial data as of the end of 2018.

- Corporate mergers, changes in corporate financial ratings or stability, acquisitions and downsizing are occurring at a very rapid rate. Such events may have created significant change, subsequent to the publishing of this book, within a company you are studying.

- Some of the companies in THE AMERICAN EMPLOYERS 500 are so large in scope and in variety of business endeavors conducted within a parent organization that we have been unable to completely list all subsidiaries, affiliations, divisions and activities within a firm's corporate structure.

- This volume is intended to be a general guide to major employers in numerous industries. That means that researchers should look to this book for an overview and, when conducting in-depth research, should contact the specific corporations and related industry associations in question for the very latest changes and data. Where possible, we have listed contact information, telephone numbers and Internet addresses for pertinent companies, government agencies and industry associations so that the reader may get further details without unnecessary delay.

- We have used exhaustive efforts to locate and fairly present accurate and complete data. However, when using this book or any other source for business and industry information, the reader should use caution and due diligence by conducting further research where it seems appropriate. We wish you success in your endeavors, and we trust that your experience with this book will be both satisfactory and productive.

- To obtain the best results and to best understand the fields in the company profiles, you should first read the chapter titled "How to Use This Book."

Good luck in your job search. Be patient, do your research and use this book as an important start in the right direction.

Jack W. Plunkett
Houston, Texas
September 2019

HOW TO USE THIS BOOK

Dozens of excellent books already exist to help you choose a career, write a resume, apply for a job and so on. That is not the purpose of THE ALMANAC OF AMERICAN EMPLOYERS. Instead, this book's job is to help you sort through America's giant corporate employers to determine which may be the best for you, or to see how your current employer compares to others. Whether you are entering the job market and looking for your first position, or you are thinking about switching companies in mid-career to find more promising vistas, this book will be a valuable guide.

The two primary sections of the book are devoted first to general information for job seekers (trends analysis and advice on conducting employer research, along with resources, statistics and contacts), followed by the "Individual Data Listings" for THE AMERICAN EMPLOYERS 500. If time permits, you should begin your research in the front chapters of this book. Also, you will find lengthy indexes in Chapter 5 and in the back of the book.

GENERAL INFORMATION FOR JOB SEEKERS

Chapter 1: Major Trends Affecting Job Seekers. This chapter presents an encapsulated view of the major trends in business and the economy that are creating rapid changes in the employment picture at large corporations.

Chapter 2: Statistics. This chapter presents in-depth statistics on employment by education level, sex and race, along with unemployment rates, the fastest-growing occupations and more.

Chapter 3: Research—7 Keys for Job Seekers. This chapter provides a definitive list of items that job seekers should look for when conducting research into major corporate employers.

Chapter 4: Important Contacts for Job Seekers. This chapter covers contacts for important government agencies, professional societies, industry associations, job banks, reference sources and more. Included are Internet sites and contact addresses for a wide variety of job search uses.

THE AMERICAN EMPLOYERS 500

Chapter 5: THE AMERICAN EMPLOYERS 500: Who They Are and How They Were Chosen.

The companies compared in this book were chosen from nearly all industries, on a nationwide basis. They were individually chosen from the largest U.S. employers, based on selected types of business and industry sectors. For a complete description, see Chapter 5.

Individual Data Listings:

Look at one of the companies in THE AMERICAN EMPLOYERS 500's Individual Data Listings. You'll find the following information fields:

Company Name:

The company profiles are in alphabetical order by company name. If you don't find the company you are seeking, it may be a subsidiary or division of one of the firms covered in this book. Try looking it up in the Index by Subsidiaries, Brand Names and Selected Affiliations in the back of the book.

Industry Code:

Industry Group Code: An NAIC code used to group companies within like segments.

Types of Business:

A listing of the primary types of business specialties conducted by the firm.

Brands/Divisions/Affiliations:

Major brand names, operating divisions or subsidiaries of the firm, as well as major corporate affiliations—such as another firm that owns a significant portion of the company's stock. A complete Index by Subsidiaries, Brand Names and Selected Affiliations is in the back of the book.

Contacts:

The names and titles up to 27 top officers of the company are listed, including human resources contacts.

Growth Plans/ Special Features:

Listed here are observations regarding the firm's strategy, hiring plans, plans for growth and product development, along with general information regarding a company's business and prospects.

Financial Data:

Revenue (2018 or the latest fiscal year available to the editors, plus up to five previous years): This figure represents consolidated worldwide sales from all operations. These numbers may be estimates.

R&D Expense (2018 or the latest fiscal year available to the editors, plus up to five previous years): This figure represents expenses associated with the research and development of a company's goods or services. These numbers may be estimates.

Operating Income (2018 or the latest fiscal year available to the editors, plus up to five previous years): This figure represents the amount of profit realized from annual operations after deducting operating expenses including costs of goods sold, wages and depreciation. These numbers may be estimates.

Operating Margin % (2018 or the latest fiscal year available to the editors, plus up to five previous years): This figure is a ratio derived by dividing operating income by net revenues. It is a measurement of a firm's pricing strategy and operating efficiency. These numbers may be estimates.

SGA Expense (2018 or the latest fiscal year available to the editors, plus up to five previous years): This figure represents the sum of selling, general and administrative expenses of a company, including costs such as warranty, advertising, interest, personnel, utilities, office space rent, etc. These numbers may be estimates.

Net Income (2018 or the latest fiscal year available to the editors, plus up to five previous years): This figure represents consolidated, after-tax net profit from all operations. These numbers may be estimates.

Operating Cash Flow (2018 or the latest fiscal year available to the editors, plus up to five previous years): This figure is a measure of the amount of cash generated by a firm's normal business operations. It is calculated as net income before depreciation and after income taxes, adjusted for working capital. It is a prime indicator of a company's ability to generate enough cash to pay its bills. These numbers may be estimates.

Capital Expenditure (2018 or the latest fiscal year available to the editors, plus up to five previous years): This figure represents funds used for investment in or improvement of physical assets such as offices, equipment or factories and the purchase or creation of new facilities and/or equipment. These numbers may be estimates.

EBITDA (2018 or the latest fiscal year available to the editors, plus up to five previous years): This figure is an acronym for earnings before interest, taxes, depreciation and amortization. It represents a company's financial performance calculated as revenue minus expenses (excluding taxes, depreciation and interest), and is a prime indicator of profitability. These numbers may be estimates.

Return on Assets % (2018 or the latest fiscal year available to the editors, plus up to five previous years): This figure is an indicator of the profitability of a company relative to its total assets. It is calculated by dividing annual net earnings by total assets. These numbers may be estimates.

Return on Equity % (2018 or the latest fiscal year available to the editors, plus up to five previous years): This figure is a measurement of net income as a percentage of shareholders' equity. It is also called the rate of return on the ownership interest. It is a vital indicator of the quality of a company's operations. These numbers may be estimates.

Debt to Equity (2018 or the latest fiscal year available to the editors, plus up to five previous years): A ratio of the company's long-term debt to its shareholders' equity. This is an indicator of the overall financial leverage of the firm. These numbers may be estimates.

Address:
The firm's full headquarters address, the headquarters telephone, plus toll-free and fax numbers where available. Also provided is the internet address.

Stock Ticker, Exchange: When available, the unique stock market symbol used to identify this firm's common stock for trading and tracking purposes is indicated. Where appropriate, this field may contain "private" or "subsidiary" rather than a ticker symbol. If the firm is a publicly-held company headquartered outside of the U.S., its international ticker and exchange are given.

Total Number of Employees: The approximate total number of employees, worldwide, as of the end of 2018 (or the latest data available to the editors).

Parent Company: If the firm is a subsidiary, its parent company is listed.

Salaries/Bonuses:
(The following descriptions generally apply to U.S. employers only.)

Highest Executive Salary: The highest executive salary paid, typically a 2018 amount (or the latest year available to the editors) and typically paid to the Chief Executive Officer.

Highest Executive Bonus: The apparent bonus, if any, paid to the above person.

Second Highest Executive Salary: The next-highest executive salary paid, typically a 2018 amount (or the latest year available to the editors) and typically paid to the President or Chief Operating Officer.

Second Highest Executive Bonus: The apparent bonus, if any, paid to the above person.

Other Thoughts:
Estimated Female Officers or Directors: It is difficult to obtain this information on an exact basis, and employers generally do not disclose the data in a public way. However, we have indicated what our best efforts reveal to be the apparent number of women who either are in the posts of corporate officers or sit on the board of directors. There is a wide variance from company to company.

Hot Spot for Advancement for Women/Minorities: A "Y" in appropriate fields indicates "Yes." These are firms that appear either to have posted a substantial number of women and/or minorities to high posts or that appear to have a good record of going out of their way to recruit, train, promote and retain women or minorities. (See the Index of Hot Spots For Women and Minorities in the back of the book.) This information may change frequently and can be difficult to obtain and verify. Consequently, the reader should use caution and conduct further investigation where appropriate.

Chapter 1

MAJOR TRENDS AFFECTING JOB SEEKERS

Major trends sweeping through business and the economy that affect job seekers of all types:
1) U.S. Job Market Overview
2) Cost Control Remains a Major Concern at Employers/Consolidation Through Mergers Continues
3) Unemployment Is Down to Extremely Low Levels
4) The Sharing & Gig Economy's Effect on Employment, Work Life and Careers
5) Technology Continues to Create Sweeping Changes in the Workplace
6) Continued Growth in Outsourcing, Including Supply Chain and Logistics Services
7) Offshoring, Reshoring and the Rebound in American Manufacturing
8) Older Americans Will Delay Retirement and Work Longer/Many Employers Find Older Employees Desirable
9) Employment Sectors that Will Offer an Above-Average Number of Job Opportunities:

Employment Sectors that Will Offer an Above-Average Number of Job Opportunities:
- Biotechnology
- Child Care/Children's Products
- Consulting, including Technology Consulting
- Consumer Products
- Cosmetics
- Cybersecurity, Digital Customer ID Tools, Online Payment Tools
- Elder Care, Home Health Care, Nursing Homes and Assisted Living Communities
- Electronic Games, Games for Smartphones
- Energy Conservation Products and Services
- Health Care Services
- Health Care Products
- Health Care Technology, Including Electronic Health Records
- Health Foods, Organic Foods, Enhanced Foods
- Home Building
- Hotels
- Insurance
- Internet Services, Server Hosting, Cloud Computing
- Internet of Things: Connected Devices, Remote Wireless Sensors and their Networks, Machine to Machine Communications
- Online Search Services & Social Media, with Advertising Revenues
- Online-based Business and Consumer Sales and Services, including E-Commerce
- Outsourcing, Including Outsourced Business and Computer Services
- Pets: Services and Products
- Pharmaceuticals (Drugs)
- Restaurants
- Retailing—Basic, Including Drugstores and Supermarkets
- Robotics and Factory Automation
- Software—Artificial Intelligence
- Software—Business
- Software—Data Analytics
- Software—Mobile Apps
- Software-as-a-Service (SaaS)
- Solar Energy Cells Installation & Maintenance
- Supply Chain Services That Create Cost-Savings
- Water Filtration and Conservation Equipment
- Wireless and Cellular Communications

1) U.S. Job Market Overview

Job seekers in 2020 should see strong hiring and rising wages, if the low unemployment rates seen in late 2019 continue, and if confidence is reasonably high among both consumers and business leaders. As of 2019, The U.S. was enjoying very robust economic growth, and the unemployment rate was extremely low. Wages were responding by rising in virtually all industries, and there were significant shortages of workers in fields ranging from trucking to retailing to computer technology.

Job seekers who want good positions with good pay must be extremely well prepared for the process of seeking a job. A large part of the preparation requires meaningful research into prospective employers and the industries in which they operate. The fact remains that several million Americans consider themselves underemployed, and many of them will be looking for better jobs. Competition for the most desirable positions will remain fierce. Many companies receive hundreds or even thousands of resumes for every job opening. Simply sending in a resume and hoping for the best is nowhere near enough for a successful job search.

The good news is that a select set of employers and growth companies will offer superb job opportunities. Sectors such as cloud computing and health care will continue to grow and hire. A few companies with exciting new technologies or cost-saving services will see terrific growth. Salesforce.com, a highly innovative provider of online business services, has been a good example.

Solid companies that do a terrific job of providing the day-to-day needs of consumers and business will continue to hire—Costco, Amazon.com and Southwest Airlines are good examples. Other industry sectors that fall into this category include insurance firms, such as USAA and The Progressive Corporation, along with online services and apps that provide efficient or new ways for consumers and businesses to make purchases, gather data or view entertainment and news.

Growing numbers of consumers prefer to buy from firms that sell goods and services online, offering savings of time, money and car travel. This boosts companies like Amazon.com that offer low prices combined with deep selections and great customer service. Virtually all major retailers, including giants like Wal-Mart and Home Depot, are working hard to provide better online services and choices to their customers. Even major supermarkets are enabling online ordering and many offer home delivery.

The travel industry has been enjoying tremendous growth in revenues over the past few years. Airlines are in much better financial shape than they were in the recent pastHotels are enjoying high occupancy rates. Meanwhile, travel has become one of the most successful sectors at selling products and services via the internet, creating vast numbers of new job opportunities.

Americans who find themselves in the market for a job will need to understand the changes surging through the economy in order to determine which companies to pursue and which to avoid. The U.S. employment market has evolved dramatically, and job seekers must be both knowledgeable and nimble in order to position themselves to find promising careers. There will be excellent opportunities for those who are diligent in seeking top employers in most business sectors.

Economic Factors Affecting the Job Market

Business Productivity: Productivity growth has been positive in recent years, but the increases have been very modest. That is, business can be produced—whether it is goods or services—by utilizing fewer workers than before. This will be extremely beneficial to the U.S. economy in the long run. Productivity is boosted by new technologies (such as the use of robotics or artificial intelligence), improved management methods and other factors, sometimes as simple as reorganizing the staff and redesigning the workflow to increase output. (It can also receive a quick boost from restrained corporate hiring.) If rising productivity occurs along with rapidly rising sales and profits, then the job market improves.

Corporate Revenues: A trend of rising revenues encourages hiring.

Corporate Profits: When profits increase sharply, companies are inclined to increase both investment and hiring. Hiring is strongest when corporate revenues, and accompanying profits, show significant growth, encouraging executives to forecast an extended period of increased demand for their products and services.

It is vital for the job seeker to use the best reference tools possible in order to seek out employers that offer a reasonable balance of financial stability, opportunities for advancement and good pay. Excellent job opportunities always exist if you know where to look.

Thousands of companies will need significant numbers of new hires. In particular, companies that offer products or services that save time and/or money will prosper—for example, many types of companies that offer services that help businesses operate more efficiently, will be hiring. Meanwhile, large companies that are not increasing their overall numbers of employees will nonetheless be hiring on a regular basis due to normal attrition—that is, the loss of employees due to retirement, relocation or other personal circumstances. Massive companies like Walgreen's or Kroger typically need to hire tens of thousands of workers yearly due to normal attrition. At the same time, hiring will be fueled by the massive numbers of Americans who are turning retirement age and either quitting work or reducing their hours through part-time work. This trend boosts the need for new hires.

2) Cost Control Remains a Concern at Employers/Consolidation Through Mergers Continues

For most firms, executives have been focusing on cost control as a means to boost profits and financial stability. Employee costs have been targeted as well, as employers seek to boost the overall productivity of their work forces. Often, companies merge with others in order to seek operating efficiencies or gain access to needed capital. Financing is readily available for large corporate mergers and acquisitions, and the number of mergers has been high. A consolidation of companies via a merger may enable the firms to combine customer bases, administrative staff, sales offices and production facilities, while cutting employees who hold duplicated jobs, in hopes of thereby creating more efficient, more profitable firms. Mergers may be spurred by economic difficulties and falling profits, or they may involve large firms seeking to acquire companies that bring advantages that may boost growth and accelerate profits. For example, online leaders Amazon, Facebook and Google have acquired numerous firms in order to bring in new technologies.

Even in a period of vibrant economic growth, good managers continue to seek ways to control costs, including payroll costs. Because they face tough, global competition, manufacturing firms are frequently involved in such mergers. Good jobs in the U.S. manufacturing sector can be found, despite intense competition from manufacturers in China and other offshore markets. Overall, U.S. factories are running with fewer people per unit of output, thanks to immense investments in factory automation and robotics.

A small, but significant, number of firms are "reshoring" some of their manufacturing, by making products at American plants that were previously manufactured in overseas facilities. Even the American textile industry, which was hit hard by layoffs and bankruptcies during the late 1900s, is enjoying a modest rebound. This is positive, but it is not leading to large numbers of job openings.

Some of the statistical loss in manufacturing employment has been exaggerated by the fact that many firms now outsource a good deal of their non-manufacturing operations to services companies. For example, many computer departments, company cafeterias, distribution centers and engineering needs are now outsourced to companies that specialize in such work, thus dramatically reducing the number of in-house jobs at manufacturing firms. This is the long term trend of outsourcing in action.

Also, companies in both manufacturing and service sectors have caught on to management by teams, vastly enhanced supply chain technology (such as the use of the internet for ordering and tracking components), along with networked management, distribution and manufacturing systems, which all add up to the fact that fewer mid-management, white-collar types are needed to communicate with the people doing the day-to-day work. Production workers have been encouraged to communicate among themselves. In many cases, workers are taking on unprecedented responsibilities, setting their own goals and schedules, tracking costs and output, thereby boosting profits. Historically, these were the tasks of middle managers. Today, vast numbers of those management jobs have been eliminated. Businesses without factories are also undergoing re-engineering and leaps in productivity, often through the streamlining of processes through the use of better computers and software.

3) Unemployment Is Down To Extremely Low Levels

By the end of June 2019, the unemployment rate in America was 3.7%, down from 4.4% two years earlier. This low unemployment rate is encouraging some people to re-enter the workforce who had previously become discouraged and stopped looking for work.

Many job seekers will be able to find satisfying positions if they apply themselves to the job hunt, make sure their resumes and self-marketing skills are in superb shape, network effectively and do thorough research. Even with low unemployment numbers, the number of people applying for each job opening is often high. Consequently, it is vital for a job seeker to understand how to best apply for a job online, how to conduct research that will help him or her to shine during an interview and how to create an effective list of prospective employers.

It is also important for job seekers to face the fact that locale has a lot to do with the unemployment rate. There is wide variance in the unemployment rate from state to state and city to city.

> *Internet Research Tip:*
> The latest rankings of states by unemployment rate can be found at the Bureau of Labor Statistics, www.bls.gov.

4) The Sharing & Gig Economy's Effect on Employment, Work Life and Careers

The sharing economy is disrupting the nature of work, employment and entrepreneurship. Most sharing/gig economy workers are working as independent, contract workers, not employees. This means that they do not qualify for company-provided benefits such as health coverage or retirement plans. Many of them conduct work for two or more sharing economy firms. That is, a worker might drive for Uber at night, do installations for TaskRabbit on weekends and shop for Instacart on weekdays. They may vary the schedule according to the demand level, which can be constantly monitored via smartphone.

In one-on-one interviews, Plunkett Research has found that many sharing/gig workers consider themselves to be "entrepreneurs." While they may not have created a new company that employs others or makes products, they nonetheless work for themselves, independently, using their own tools or vehicles and setting their own schedules. In that regard, they are literally running a business, in the same way that a one-man plumbing shop is a business. Traditional new business formation has been weak in the U.S., which is a startling change. In particular, formation of businesses that intend to hire employees and pay wages (as opposed to one-person enterprises) has been extremely weak.

At Plunkett Research, we believe that the weakness in small business startups is fueled by the ease of finding independent work in the sharing/gig economy, with little or no capital or risk involved and the prospect of immediate income. In addition, working independently in this manner generally requires no specialized education, and no licensing beyond a drivers' license. This type of work also lends itself very well to people, such as retirees or students, who only want to work part-time, or who want a part-time sideline in addition to a regular job. One study (MBO Partners) found that 49% of part-time independent workers also had a full-time traditional job.

A McKinsey Global Institute study, published in 2016, estimated that 20% to 30% (162 million people) of the working-age population in the US and the EU16 were engaged in independent work of one type or another—about 30% of this group were working in this manner out of necessity and would prefer traditional jobs. The study also found that about 15% (24 million people) of the "independent workforce" was already using such digital platforms as Uber or Etsy. That percentage will grow. People who intentionally chose the independent work life showed extremely high levels of satisfaction with their work life as compared to traditional workers.

MBO Partners publishes an annual report "The State of Independence in America," that studies the independent worker market. It found that 75% of independent workers state they are taking this career path in order to "be my own boss," while 74% listed the "flexibility" of such as career as a top incentive. This clearly is an alternative path to the benefits of traditional entrepreneurship. MBO estimated the 2018 level of independent workers in the U.S. at 41.8 million, and forecasts that number to grow to 47.8 million by 2023. (Their total includes three categories of independent worker: full-time, part-time and occasional. Many of these people have multiple jobs.)

There is a significant debate underway in many nations as to whether or not people working as Uber drivers, Instacart shoppers and similar agents are actually employees, rather than contract workers. Legislative reform may well be attempted on large scale in this regard. In some cases, class action lawsuits have been filed by the contract workers. If governments rule that such workers are employees, it would have a massive effect on the business models of sharing economy firms. In the U.S., for example, it would mean that firms were subject to paying payroll taxes such as Social Security, and were subject to very high levels of labor, safety, health and anti-discrimination laws. This debate will likely continue for many years to come, and may well lead to legal reform in some nations. Another outcome may be the formation of contractor workers' unions or union-like organizations that might demand better pay or working conditions. The "Independent Drivers Guild" now exists in New York City, representing tens of thousands of local Uber drivers, but not quite acting as a true labor union.

As of September 2019, the state of California appeared close to passing landmark legislation that would require firms, such as Uber and Lyft, that rely on gig (contract) workers to consider these workers to be classified as employees. This would create massive changes within gig-based companies of all types. Multiple laws and regulations that protect employees and regulate the ways in which firms must treat them would come into play, such as minimum wage, unemployment coverage, employer's liability, OSHA, EEOC and a long list of additional rules. Unions are extremely excited at the prospect of unionizing the gig industry's hundreds of thousands of California workers. If the bill is passed, it could take effect as early as January 1, 2019. Uber, Lyft and food delivery firm DoorDash vowed to invest a joint $90 million to put a ballot in front of voters in 2020, aimed at overturning the law.

5) Technology Continues to Create Sweeping Changes in the Workplace

Technology has introduced vast changes throughout industries of all types, greatly boosting productivity and reallocating (or eliminating) workers. A major cause of change for employees, and therefore job seekers, is the tidal wave of new technologies that continues to revolutionize the workplace at all levels. Prospering companies are using new ways to communicate with customers, automate back-office tasks and factory operations, and push ahead with research and development. There is a never-ending stream of technological innovation. For example, employers long ago harnessed the power of networked desktop computers. Today, they are rapidly adopting the use of mobile computing devices such as tablets, internet-based telephone systems (VOIP and unified communication systems), voice-recognition software, cloud computing and video conferencing technologies.

The trend of using new practices and technologies while cutting layers of management is largely about communication. This is true whether it is communication between the top offices and the factory floor, communication with customers, communication between the computers in one corporate office with those in another, or communication from the sales department to the warehouse and the supply chain.

These new technologies mean continuous retraining for much of the workforce. Job seekers who want the best posts must have the training and skills that will let them utilize new technologies effectively. Hundreds of thousands of jobs are remaining unfilled at many companies because of a shortage of technically qualified people. Workforce training is a critical need nationwide.

Jobs in America are shifting to new categories of work based on technologies that didn't exist a few decades ago. For example, the job title "social media manager" emerged in recent years. Services firms, as well as manufacturers, are placing more and more employees in recently created technical and service positions, while many of the tasks once performed in-house are now provided by outsourced services providers. In the telecommunications industry, digital technology has completely changed the list of job titles while enabling phone service providers to reduce the ratio of employees to customers. In the meantime, hundreds of thousands of jobs have been created at cellular telephone companies. Now, internet-based telephony, competition from cable providers, fiber to the premises and wireless networks such as Wi-Fi and LTE continue to force telecommunications firms to evolve.

Another excellent example: Retailing, shipping and warehousing are undergoing a technology revolution due to the introduction of Radio Frequency Identification Tags (RFID). This breakthrough in inventory management is based on the placement of digitized product data within product packaging, combined with the use of special sensors in stores and warehouses that can automatically read that data. These sensors can alert a central inventory management system of product movement and the need to restock inventory. From loading docks to shelves to cash registers to parking lots, RFID sensors will eventually track the movement of each pallet or individual item. Many bar codes will eventually be replaced by RFIDs. RFID can even eliminate the need to scan each item at checkout in a retail store. Checkout stations will be equipped with sensors that read RFID-based data such as product code and price, and then automatically calculate purchase totals. Benefits can include less shoplifting and few inventory errors. Another benefit is that firms will be able to reduce overall inventory thanks to better tracking.

As online ordering, tracking and inventory management continue to become more sophisticated and cost-effective, purchasing executives at firms of all types and sizes will accelerate the use of internet-based systems for management of their supply chains. There are significant opportunities here for e-commerce services and software companies. Likewise, there is great promise for third-party logistics (3PL) companies that combine the power of internet-based information with strategically located warehouses to fulfill the inventory needs of manufacturers. Robots are being used to a rapidly growing extent in picking inventory within warehouses prior to shipment. Amazon.com is a leader in this regard.

Manufacturing is undergoing its own technology revolution. This is often referred to as factory automation. Advanced technology used with great success on the factory floor includes computer-driven machine tools that require highly skilled operators, along with robotic assemblers that are capable of working nonstop, 24/7 to create and assemble parts into finished goods.

Over the mid-term, massive changes in business and industry will be caused through rapid adoption of processes and systems based on artificial intelligence (AI). AI enables software to identify patterns in digital data, as well as in images such as digital photos/video of people, places and things. AI and a process known as machine learning means that more and more task that are currently handled by humans will be processed by computers. It remains to be seen how quickly, and to what extent, this will have broad effects on the workplace and hiring.

6) Continued Growth in Outsourcing, Including Supply Chain and Logistics Services

Part of the re-engineering process at employers has been a boom in "outsourcing," or the use of outside specialty firms to do chores that firms formerly performed through in-house departments. One of the largest fields of outsourcing growth has long been in computer departments. IBM and Accenture are among the global leaders in this area. Cloud computing (the use of outsourced, remote servers to run computer functions) is the latest major trend in this regard.

However, many other business functions are commonly outsourced. ServiceMaster takes over janitorial tasks, building management and maintenance functions for giant corporate office campuses and industrial facilities. Another company outsources all of the food warehousing and distribution for nationwide restaurant chains. Why? Because it can run trucks and warehouses more efficiently while its clients concentrate on running restaurants.

While the 1960s, '70s and '80s saw many firms frantically trying to do all tasks in-house, recent trends are quite different. As a period noted for rising productivity and efficiency, the 1990s and 2000s combined were an era of specialization and focus. Companies may do a better job by focusing on their core tasks, while allowing outside firms to provide support and maintenance needs. That trend will continue to be powerful over the long term. Outsourcing, which rapidly gained popularity, will persist in leading the way to higher efficiency and profits. Many outsourced services companies continue to grow, and they will create (and displace) large numbers of jobs.

One of the fastest-growing fields in outsourcing has been supply chain and logistics management. Companies offering services in this field include giant transportation companies like UPS. "Supply chain" refers to the entire set of providers of supplies and services that are involved in creating and delivering a component or end product. For example, for an automobile manufacturer like Ford, the supply chain includes companies that make tires, batteries, interior components and engine parts, as well as the trucks and trains that ship these parts and the warehouses that hold them. This supply chain supports Ford's own manufacturing and assembly plants. At the end of Ford's business chain lie the automobile dealers that receive completed cars and deliver them to the end customers. Another example: For a clothing store chain like The Gap, the supply chain includes clothing designers, clothing manufacturers and the warehouses and transportation systems that deliver completed clothes to the stores. The Gap's supply chain is located across dozens of nations.

Logistics is the art of moving goods through the supply chain. Supply chains are so complex and so critical to a company's operations that there are countless ways to automate, improve efficiencies and cut costs. Many manufacturers and retailers are outsourcing all or part of their logistics needs to firms that specialize in creating efficiencies and saving costs. Logistics and supply chain companies have been growing rapidly over the past several years, and creating large numbers of jobs. A concept you should be familiar with is Third Party Logistics ("3PL"), a system whereby a specialist firm in logistics provides a variety of transportation, warehousing and logistics-related services to its clients. These tasks were previously performed in-house by the client. When 3PL services are provided within the client's own facilities, it can also be referred to as "Insourcing." In other words, you might find yourself working for UPS at a site within a distribution company that has no other ties to UPS.

Robotics and Artificial Intelligence (AI) are already having a significant effect on the way that warehouses and distribution centers are operated, including those of outsourced 3PL (third party logistics) companies. This means higher capital investment, but lower overall management and manpower requirements.

7) Offshoring, Reshoring and the Rebound in American Manufacturing

Competition from workers in such nations as Mexico, Indonesia, Thailand and, in particular, China, has been fierce. For several decades, America's manufacturing employment was declining while a vast amount of manufacturing has been sent overseas by U.S. firms.

Today, however, some U.S. industries are experiencing reshoring, or the practice of moving formerly offshored tasks back to America. As wages rise in countries such as China and India, a number of manufacturers are rethinking offshoring, taking into account higher productivity rates among American workers.

This is not to say that vast numbers of manufacturing jobs are going to return to America. Many of the newest factories are relying on advanced technologies instead of large workforces. Robots and artificial intelligence are driving today's most modern factories. An additional, informal classification of robots is collaborative robots, or "cobots." This refers to robots that work closely alongside human workers, with the intent of making repetitive tasks easier and faster to complete.

Another factor fueling reshoring is energy costs, which continue to be lower in the U.S. than in many other countries. Savings through low energy costs can be further augmented by increased manufacturing efficiency. This is due to the growing adoption of robotics. 3-D printing (additive manufacturing) is another technology that is significantly lowering prototyping and product design costs.

While lower employee wages have been a factor in some offshoring, proximity to growing foreign markets is another. Giant multinational companies ranging from Apple to Kraft to General Motors find that a vast portion of their business now lies overseas, often in the rapidly-growing, emerging nations. Many of the world's largest companies find that they need to have local operations throughout the world.

Globalization has a profound effect on Americans—consumer prices become lower, while the U.S. job market changes considerably. Consumer goods are quite inexpensive due to the vast variety of items the U.S. imports from other nations, and prices for many categories of these goods have declined dramatically. Americans can purchase consumer electronics like DVD players and color televisions at extremely low prices, and the price of many types of apparel is much lower thanks to globalization. For example, over 90% of the shoes sold in America are manufactured in low cost nations, especially China.

More than ever before, the world is one vast marketplace. Globalization of business supply chains is a strong trend today and will grow even stronger in the future. Consider the rapid globalization of the automobile industry. The entire global automobile sector is dominated by only a handful of companies, including Toyota, GM, Ford, Daimler, Honda, Volkswagen and Nissan, as well as the increasingly successful Korean automakers Kia and Hyundai. Car manufacturers in China are becoming more dominant as well. Car manufacturers commonly have engineering teams collaborating from offices in multiple nations, while parts and components may be imported from a wide variety of suppliers in various countries to undergo final assembly at home.

American companies in many industry sectors have been merging and consolidating on a global basis at a rapid clip. That consolidation will continue. One benefit is that U.S. firms can enter into foreign markets through international acquisitions.

U.S. firms hold leadership positions in several key product and service sectors vital to the rest of the world, including health technology, computers, e-commerce, software and entertainment of all types. The message is clear: global trade and export markets are extremely vital to the health of American business and industry.

A growing middle class in India, China and other emerging nations has been creating demand for goods exported from the U.S., including consumer products bearing desirable brands, as well as luxury automobiles. Also, U.S.-based firms have been enjoying great success in franchising and licensing their methods to startup businesses in China, India and elsewhere, in everything from hotels to fast food to services. American brands such as Nike and Buick are big sellers in China.

8) Older Americans Will Delay Retirement and Work Longer/Many Employers Find Older Employees Desirable

Certain large employers, particularly national retail chains, have discovered that older workers provide a terrific pool of potential employees. This may be positive for older workers, but to younger job seekers it means more competition for work.

Many members of the immense Baby Boom generation are not planning to retire any time soon. This trend is accelerated by the fact that today's senior citizens will enjoy much longer life spans than earlier generations. Many will continue to work simply because they want to remain active, contributing members of society.

The phrase "Baby Boomer" generally refers to the 78 million Americans born from 1946 to 1964. The term evolved to describe the children of soldiers and war industry workers who were involved in World War II. When those veterans and workers returned to civilian life, they started or added to families in large numbers. As a result, this generation is one of the largest demographic segments in the U.S. Baby Boomers make more than 20% of the U.S. population.

Not long ago, 2011 marked the year when millions began turning traditional retirement age (65). As Baby Boomers continue to age, America will be experiencing extremely rapid growth in the senior portion of the population. Many Baby Boomers will leave their traditional, long-term jobs and turn to part-time work. Others will continue in their full-time jobs as long as possible.

By the early 2000s, many employers were already developing human resources strategies aimed at hiring or retaining older workers. On the lower end of the pay scale, retailers like Home Depot, a firm that has been known to need tens of thousands of new hires each year, have found older people to be ideal employees. They have knowledge that is extremely useful for providing advice and service to shoppers. They are experienced workers who understand the need to show up on time.

On the higher end of the employment scale, older workers with long-term experience in scientific and engineering tasks will be vital in keeping the gears of business and industry turning. During the 2000s boom, when the airline industry saw good growth, rules were altered in the U.S. to enable commercial airline pilots to keep flying until age 65, instead of facing forced retirement at age 60 as they had in the past.

Industrial firms are dealing with this challenge along two lines: First, how to document and pass along the immense treasure of work-related knowledge that these employees have, and second, how to keep these employees interested in working later into their lives.

9) Employment Sectors that Will Offer an Above-Average Number of Job Opportunities

Job seekers should remain aware of the fact that certain industries will have above-average likelihood to offer job openings. This is due to a number of circumstances, including shifts in consumer tastes and requirements, normal employee turnover and attrition, structural changes within industries, global economic conditions and national policies and priorities.

Below is a list of industries particularly recommended to job seekers.

Employment Sectors that Will Offer an Above-Average Number of Job Opportunities:
- Biotechnology
- Child Care/Children's Products
- Consulting, including Technology Consulting
- Consumer Products
- Cosmetics
- Cybersecurity, Digital Customer ID Tools, Online Payment Tools
- Elder Care, Home Health Care, Nursing Homes and Assisted Living Communities
- Electronic Games, Games for Smartphones
- Energy Conservation Products and Services
- Health Care Services
- Health Care Products
- Health Care Technology, Including Electronic Health Records
- Health Foods, Organic Foods, Enhanced Foods
- Home Building
- Hotels
- Insurance
- Internet Services, Server Hosting, Cloud Computing
- Internet of Things: Connected Devices, Remote Wireless Sensors and their Networks, Machine to Machine Communications
- Online Search Services & Social Media, with Advertising Revenues
- Online-based Business and Consumer Sales and Services, including E-Commerce
- Outsourcing, Including Outsourced Business and Computer Services
- Pets: Services and Products
- Pharmaceuticals (Drugs)
- Restaurants
- Retailing—Basic, Including Drugstores and Supermarkets

- Robotics and Factory Automation
- Software—Artificial Intelligence
- Software—Business
- Software—Data Analytics
- Software—Mobile Apps
- Software-as-a-Service (SaaS)
- Solar Energy Cells Installation & Maintenance
- Supply Chain Services That Create Cost-Savings
- Water Filtration and Conservation Equipment
- Wireless and Cellular Communications

Chapter 2

STATISTICS

Contents:	
U.S. Employment Overview: 2018-2019	**18**
U.S. Civilian Labor Force: 1997-July 2019	**19**
Employment by Major Industry Sector: 2006, 2016 & Projected 2026	**20**
Number of People Employed and Unemployed, U.S.: July 2018 vs. July 2019	**21**
U.S. Labor Force Ages 16 to 24 Years Old by School Enrollment, Educational Attainment, Sex, Race & Ethnicity: October 2018	**22**
Medical Care Benefits in the U.S.: Access, Participation and Take-Up Rates, March 2018	**23**
Retirement Benefits in the U.S.: Access, Participation and Take-Up Rates, March 2018	**24**
Top 30 U.S. Occupations by Numerical Change in Job Growth: 2016-2026	**25**
Top 30 U.S. Fastest Growing Occupations: 2016-2026	**26**
Occupations with the Largest Expected Employment Increases, U.S.: 2016-2026	**27**
Occupations with the Fastest Expected Decline, U.S.: 2016-2026	**28**

U.S. Employment Statistics Overview: 2018-2019
(Labor Counts In Thousands; Seasonally Adjusted)

	Jul-18	May-19	Jun-19	Jul-19
Civilian Labor Force, Total	162,209	162,646	162,981	163,351
Employed	155,964	156,758	157,005	157,288
Unemployed	6,245	5,888	5,975	6,063
Persons 16 Years of Age and Over, Not in Labor Force	95,633	96,215	96,057	95,874
Unemployment Rate, 16 years and over	3.9%	3.6%	3.7%	3.7%
Adult Men (20 years and over)	3.4%	3.3%	3.3%	3.4%
Adult Women (20 years and over)	3.6%	3.5%	3.6%	3.7%
Teenagers (16 to 19 years)	13.1%	12.7%	12.7%	12.8%
White	3.3%	3.3%	3.3%	3.3%
Black or African American	6.6%	6.2%	6.0%	6.0%
Asian	3.1%	2.5%	2.1%	2.8%
Hispanic or Latino	4.5%	4.2%	4.3%	4.5%
Average Hourly Earnings, Private Industry	$27.11	$27.82	$27.90	$27.98
Weekly Earnings, Private Industry	$935.30	$957.01	$959.76	$959.71
Average Work Week, Private Industry (Hours)	34.5	34.4	34.4	34.3
Employment by Selected Industry (Over-the-month change, in thousands)				
Total nonfarm	178.0	62	193	164
Total private	173.0	81	179	148
Goods-producing	38.0	5	29	15
Mining and logging	-1.0	2	-1	-5
Construction	19.0	1	18	4
Manufacturing	20.0	2	12	16
Private service-providing	135.0	76	150	133
Wholesale trade	14.4	5	-1	7
Retail trade	2.3	-12	-7	-4
Transportation and warehousing	8.0	3	21	0
Utilities	-2.9	1	1	0
Information	1.0	9	14	-10
Financial activities	5.0	5	3	18
Professional and business services	37.0	21	38	38
Education and health services	48.0	34	57	66
Health care and social assistance	37.2	28	45	50
Leisure and hospitality	35.0	12	7	10
Other services	-12.0	-3	17	8
Government	5.0	-19	14	16

Source: U.S. Bureau of Labor Statistics
Plunkett Research,® Ltd.
www.plunkettresearch.com

U.S. Civilian Labor Force: 1997-July 2019

(Persons 16 & Older; In Thousands)

Year	Civilian Workforce Level
1997	136,297
1998	137,673
1999	139,368
2000	142,583
2001	143,734
2002	144,863
2003	146,510
2004	147,401
2005	149,320
2006	151,428
2007	153,124
2008	154,287
2009	154,142
2010	153,889
2011	153,617
2012	154,975
2013	155,389
2014	155,922
2015	157,130
2016	159,187
2017	160,320
2018	162,075
Jul-19	163,351

Note: The civilian labor force consists of employed and unemployed people actively seeking work, but it does not include any Armed Forces personnel.

Source: U.S. Bureau of Labor Statistics

Plunkett Research,® Ltd.

www.plunkettresearch.com

Employment by Major Industry Sector: 2006, 2016 & Projected 2026

Industry Sector	Employment (in Thousands)			Change (in Thousands)		Percent Distribution			Compound Annual Rate of Change	
	2006	2016	2026	2006-16	2016-26	2006	2016	2026	2006-16	2016-26
Total[1]	148,988.2	156,063.8	167,582.3	7,075.7	11,518.5	100.0	100.0	100.0	0.5	0.7
Nonagriculture wage & salary[2]	137,190.9	144,979.3	155,724.8	7,788.4	10,745.5	92.1	92.9	92.9	0.6	0.7
Goods-producing, excluding agriculture	22,466.7	19,685.2	19,904.2	-2,781.5	219.0	15.1	12.6	11.9	-1.3	0.1
Mining	619.7	626.1	716.9	6.4	90.8	0.4	0.4	0.4	0.1	1.4
Construction	7,691.2	6,711.0	7,575.7	-980.2	864.7	5.2	4.3	4.5	-1.4	1.2
Manufacturing	14,155.8	12,348.1	11,611.7	-1,807.7	-736.4	9.5	7.9	6.9	-1.4	-0.6
Services-providing	114,724.2	125,294.1	135,820.6	10,569.9	10,526.5	77.0	80.3	81.0	0.9	0.8
Utilities	548.5	556.2	559.6	7.7	3.4	0.4	0.4	0.3	0.1	0.1
Wholesale trade	5,904.6	5,867.0	6,012.8	-37.6	145.8	4.0	3.8	3.6	-0.1	0.2
Retail trade	15,353.2	15,820.4	16,232.7	467.2	412.3	10.3	10.1	9.7	0.3	0.3
Transportation & warehousing	4,469.6	4,989.1	5,353.4	519.5	364.3	3.0	3.2	3.2	1.1	0.7
Information	3,037.9	2,772.3	2,824.8	-265.6	52.5	2.0	1.8	1.7	-0.9	0.2
Financial activities	8,366.6	8,284.8	8,764.6	-81.8	479.8	5.6	5.3	5.2	-0.1	0.6
Professional & business services	17,566.2	20,135.6	22,295.3	2,569.4	2,159.7	11.8	12.9	13.3	1.4	1.0
Educational services	2,900.9	3,559.7	4,066.2	658.8	506.5	1.9	2.3	2.4	2.1	1.3
Health care & social assistance	15,253.3	19,056.3	23,054.6	3,803.0	3,998.3	10.2	12.2	13.8	2.3	1.9
Leisure & hospitality	13,109.7	15,620.4	16,939.4	2,510.7	1,319.0	8.8	10.0	10.1	1.8	0.8
Other services	6,240.5	6,409.4	6,761.4	168.9	352.0	4.2	4.1	4.0	0.3	0.5
Federal government	2,732.0	2,795.0	2,739.2	63.0	-55.8	1.8	1.8	1.6	0.2	-0.2
State & local government	19,241.2	19,427.9	20,216.6	186.7	788.7	12.9	12.4	12.1	0.1	0.4
Agriculture, forestry, fishing & hunting[3]	2,111.2	2,351.5	2,345.4	240.3	-6.1	1.4	1.5	1.4	1.1	0.0
Agriculture wage & salary	1,218.6	1,501.0	1,518.0	282.4	17.0	0.8	1.0	0.9	2.1	0.1
Agriculture self-employed & unpaid family workers	892.6	850.5	827.5	-42.1	-23.0	0.6	0.5	0.5	-0.5	-0.3
Nonagriculture self-employed & unpaid family workers	9,686.0	8,733.0	9,512.1	-953.0	779.1	6.5	5.6	5.7	-1.0	0.9

[1] Employment data for wage and salary workers are from the BLS Current Employment Statistics survey, which counts jobs, whereas self-employed, unpaid family workers, and agriculture, forestry, fishing, and hunting are from the Current Population Survey (household survey), which counts workers.

[2] Includes wage and salary data from the Current Employment Statistics survey, except private households, which is from the Current Populations Survey. Logging workers are excluded.

[3] Includes agriculture, forestry, fishing, and hunting data from the Current Population Survey, except logging, which is from Current Employment Statistics survey. Government wage and salary workers are excluded.

Source: U.S. Bureau of Labor Statistics

Plunkett Research,® Ltd.

www.plunkettresearch.com

Number of People Employed and Unemployed, U.S.: July 2018 vs. July 2019

(Persons 16 & Older; Numbers In Thousands; Not Seasonally Adjusted)

Occupation	Employed		Unemployed		Unemp. Rates (%)	
	Jul-18	Jul-19	Jul-18	Jul-19	Jul-18	Jul-19
Total*	**157,004**	**158,385**	**6,730**	**6,556**	**4.1**	**4.0**
Management, professional and related	61,433	63,394	1,539	1,591	2.4	2.4
Management, business and financial operations	25,739	26,877	511	492	1.9	1.8
Professional and related	35,694	36,517	1,028	1,099	2.8	2.9
Service	27,887	27,975	1,508	1,319	5.1	4.5
Sales and office	34,025	33,686	1,431	1,274	4.0	3.6
Sales and related	16,023	15,998	662	523	4.0	3.2
Office and administrative support	18,003	17,688	769	751	4.1	4.1
Natural resources, construction and maintenance	15,005	14,705	589	640	3.8	4.2
Farming, fishing and forestry	1,285	1,211	97	61	7.0	4.8
Construction and extraction	8,527	8,545	373	406	4.2	4.5
Installation, maintenance and repair	5,193	4,948	119	174	2.2	3.4
Production, transportation and material moving	18,654	18,625	850	903	4.4	4.6
Production	8,466	8,415	366	362	4.1	4.1
Transportation and material moving	10,188	10,209	484	541	4.5	5.0

* Persons with no previous work experience and persons whose last job was in the Armed Forces are included in the unemployed total.

Note: Updated population controls are introduced annually with the release of January data.

Source: U.S. Bureau of Labor Statistics
Plunkett Research,® Ltd.
www.plunkettresearch.com

U.S. Labor Force Ages 16 to 24 Years Old by School Enrollment, Educational Attainment, Sex, Race & Ethnicity: October 2018

(Numbers in Thousands, Latest Year Available)	Civilian non-institutional population	Total in Labor Force	Percent of Populace	Employed Total	Employed Percent of Populace	Unemployed Number	Unemployed Rate (%)	Not in Labor Force
Total, 16 to 24 years	37,962	20,829	54.9	19,120	50.4	1,709	8.2	17,134
Educational Attainment								
Enrolled in school	21,698	7,962	36.7	7,429	34.2	533	6.7	13,735
Enrolled in high school[1]	9,435	2,137	22.7	1,912	20.3	225	10.5	7,298
Men	4,970	1,037	20.9	919	18.5	118	11.4	3,933
Women	4,465	1,100	24.6	993	22.2	107	9.7	3,365
White	6,860	1,654	24.1	1,495	21.8	159	9.6	5,207
Black or African American	1,416	240	16.9	199	14.1	40	16.8	1,176
Asian	449	52	11.5	47	10.6	4	-	398
Hispanic or Latino ethnicity	2,193	360	16.4	307	14.0	53	14.8	1,833
Enrolled in college	12,263	5,825	47.5	5,517	45.0	308	5.3	6,437
Enrolled in 2-year college	3,008	1,663	55.3	1,564	52.0	99	6.0	1,345
Enrolled in 4-year college	9,254	4,162	45.0	3,953	42.7	209	5.0	5,092
Full-time students	10,641	4,472	42.0	4,227	39.7	246	5.5	6,168
Part-time students	1,622	1,353	83.4	1,290	79.6	63	4.6	269
Men	5,644	2,535	44.9	2,385	42.3	150	5.9	3,110
Women	6,618	3,290	49.7	3,132	47.3	159	4.8	3,328
White	8,913	4,494	50.4	4,285	48.1	209	4.7	4,420
Black or African American	1,683	793	47.1	734	43.6	59	7.4	890
Asian	1,082	306	28.2	283	26.1	23	7.4	777
Hispanic or Latino ethnicity	2,482	1,303	52.5	1,256	50.6	47	3.6	1,179
Not enrolled in school	16,264	12,866	79.1	11,691	71.9	1,175	9.1	3,398
16 to 19 years	3,231	2,127	65.8	1,799	55.7	328	15.4	1,104
20 to 24 years	13,033	10,740	82.4	9,892	75.9	847	7.9	2,294
Sex								
Men	8,492	6,886	81.1	6,252	73.6	634	9.2	1,606
Less than a high school diploma	1,212	767	63.3	646	53.3	121	15.7	445
High school graduates, no college[2]	4,209	3,393	80.6	3,067	72.9	325	9.6	817
Some college or associate degree	1,894	1,643	86.8	1,527	80.6	116	7.1	251
Bachelor's degree and higher[3]	1,177	1,084	92.1	1,012	86.0	72	6.6	93
Women	7,772	5,980	76.9	5,438	70.0	541	9.1	1,792
Less than a high school diploma	953	514	54.0	451	47.3	63	12.3	439
High school graduates, no college[2]	3,118	2,271	72.8	1,980	63.5	291	12.8	847
Some college or associate degree	2,090	1,703	81.5	1,615	77.3	88	5.2	387
Bachelor's degree and higher[3]	1,612	1,492	92.6	1,393	86.5	99	6.6	120
Race								
White	12,057	9,634	79.9	8,900	73.8	735	7.6	2,423
Black or African American	2,547	1,934	75.9	1,644	64.5	290	15.0	613
Asian	734	549	74.8	480	65.4	69	12.6	185
Hispanic or Latino ethnicity	4,049	3,093	76.4	2,815	69.5	277	9.0	956

Note: Detail for the above race groups (White, Black or African American, and Asian) do not sum to totals because data are not presented for all races. Persons whose ethnicity is identified as Hispanic or Latino may be of any race. Updated population controls are introduced annually with the release of January data. Dash indicates no data or data that do not meet publication criteria (values not shown where base is less than 75,000).

[1] Includes a small number of persons who are in grades below high school. [2] Includes persons with a high school diploma or equivalent. [3] Includes persons with bachelor's, master's, professional, and doctoral degrees.

Source: U.S. Bureau of Labor Statistics

Plunkett Research,® Ltd.

www.plunkettresearch.com

Medical Care Benefits in the U.S.: Access, Participation and Take-Up Rates, March 2018

(All workers = 100 percent)

Characteristics	Private Industry			State/Local Government		
	Access	Participation	Take-up Rate[1]	Access	Participation	Take-up Rate[1]
All workers	69%	50%	72%	89%	70%	79%
Worker Characteristics						
Management, professional and related	87%	66%	76%	92%	72%	78%
Service	42%	26%	62%	81%	64%	79%
Sales and office	66%	45%	69%	89%	74%	84%
Natural resources, construction and maintenance	73%	57%	78%	95%	75%	79%
Production, transportation and material moving	77%	56%	73%	84%	67%	79%
Full time	86%	63%	73%	99%	79%	80%
Part time	21%	11%	54%	27%	19%	70%
Union	94%	77%	81%	95%	74%	78%
Nonunion	66%	47%	71%	84%	68%	81%
Wage percentiles[2]						
Lowest 25 percent	35%	20%	58%	72%	57%	79%
Lowest 10 percent	24%	12%	49%	60%	47%	78%
Second 25 percent	72%	51%	70%	93%	75%	80%
Third 25 percent	86%	64%	75%	97%	78%	80%
Highest 25 percent	92%	72%	78%	95%	74%	77%
Highest 10 percent	93%	74%	79%	93%	75%	80%
Establishment Characteristics						
1 to 99 workers	55%	39%	70%	85%	68%	80%
1 to 49 workers	51%	36%	71%	82%	66%	80%
50 to 99 workers	69%	48%	69%	89%	70%	79%
100 workers or more	85%	62%	73%	90%	71%	79%
100 to 499 workers	83%	59%	71%	86%	67%	78%
500 workers or more	88%	68%	76%	92%	73%	80%

Note: For this table, a worker with access to medical care benefits is defined as having an employer-provided medical plan available for use, regardless of the worker's decision to enroll or participate in the plan. Farm and private household workers, the self-employed and Federal government workers are excluded from the survey.

[1] The take-up rate is a rounded estimate of the percentage of workers with access to a plan who participate in the plan.
[2] Surveyed occupations are classified into wage categories based on the average wage for the occupation, which may include workers with earnings both above and below the threshold. The categories were formed using percentile estimates generated using data from the National Compensation Survey publication, "Employer Costs for Employee Compensation - March 2018."

Source: U.S. Bureau of Labor Statistics
Plunkett Research,® Ltd.
www.plunkettresearch.com

Retirement Benefits in the U.S.: Access, Participation and Take-Up Rates, March 2018

(All workers = 100 percent)

Characteristics	Private Industry			State/Local Government		
	Access	Participation	Take-up Rate[1]	Access	Participation	Take-up Rate[1]
All workers	68%	51%	76%	91%	83%	90%
Worker Characteristics						
Management, professional and related	83%	72%	86%	94%	84%	90%
Service	44%	24%	55%	84%	78%	92%
Sales and office	71%	52%	73%	91%	82%	90%
Natural resources, construction and maintenance	62%	47%	76%	97%	91%	93%
Production, transportation and material moving	71%	54%	76%	90%	82%	91%
Full time	77%	61%	79%	99%	90%	91%
Part time	39%	22%	56%	45%	39%	86%
Union	92%	82%	88%	97%	88%	90%
Nonunion	65%	48%	74%	86%	78%	90%
Wage percentiles[2]						
Lowest 25 percent	44%	22%	51%	78%	70%	90%
Lowest 10 percent	32%	13%	42%	68%	59%	88%
Second 25 percent	67%	49%	72%	94%	86%	91%
Third 25 percent	79%	65%	82%	98%	89%	90%
Highest 25 percent	87%	77%	89%	97%	87%	90%
Highest 10 percent	88%	80%	90%	95%	85%	89%
Establishment Characteristics						
1 to 99 workers	53%	37%	70%	87%	83%	94%
1 to 49 workers	49%	34%	70%	85%	80%	94%
50 to 99 workers	66%	46%	70%	89%	85%	95%
100 workers or more	85%	67%	79%	93%	83%	89%
100 to 499 workers	83%	61%	74%	91%	83%	92%
500 workers or more	88%	77%	87%	93%	82%	88%

Note: Benefits may include defined benefit pension plans as well as defined contribution retirement plans. Workers are considered as having access or as participating if they have access to or participate in at least one of these plan types. Farm and private household workers, the self-employed and Federal government workers are excluded from the survey.

[1] The take-up rate is a rounded estimate of the percentage of workers with access to a plan who participate in the plan.

[2] Surveyed occupations are classified into wage categories based on the average wage for the occupation, which may include workers with earnings both above and below the threshold. The categories were formed using percentile estimates generated using wage data for March 2018.

Source: U.S. Bureau of Labor Statistics
Plunkett Research,® Ltd.
www.plunkettresearch.com

Top 30 U.S. Occupations by Numerical Change in Job Growth: 2016-2026

(By Thousands of Employees)

Occupation	Employment		Change, 2016-26		Median annual wage, 2018*
	2016	2026	Number	Percent	
Total, all occupations	156,063.8	167,582.3	11,518.6	7.4	$38,640
Personal care aides	2,016.1	2,793.8	777.6	38.6	$24,020
Combined food preparation and serving workers, including fast food	3,452.2	4,032.1	579.9	16.8	$21,250
Registered nurses	2,955.2	3,393.2	438.1	14.8	$71,730
Home health aides	911.5	1,342.7	431.2	47.3	$24,200
Software developers, applications	831.3	1,086.6	255.4	30.7	$103,620
Janitors and cleaners, except maids and housekeeping cleaners	2,384.6	2,621.2	236.5	9.9	$26,110
General and operations managers	2,263.1	2,468.3	205.2	9.1	$100,930
Laborers and freight, stock, and material movers, hand	2,628.4	2,828.1	199.7	7.6	$28,260
Medical assistants	634.4	818.4	183.9	29.0	$33,610
Waiters and waitresses	2,600.5	2,783.0	182.5	7.0	$21,780
Nursing assistants	1,510.3	1,683.7	173.4	11.5	$28,540
Construction laborers	1,216.7	1,367.1	150.4	12.4	$35,800
Cooks, restaurant	1,231.9	1,377.2	145.3	11.8	$26,530
Accountants and auditors	1,397.7	1,537.6	139.9	10.0	$70,500
Market research analysts and marketing specialists	595.4	733.7	138.3	23.2	$63,120
Customer service representatives	2,784.5	2,920.8	136.3	4.9	$33,750
Landscaping and groundskeeping workers	1,197.9	1,333.1	135.2	11.3	$29,000
Medical secretaries	574.2	703.2	129.0	22.5	$35,760
Management analysts	806.4	921.6	115.2	14.3	$83,610
Maintenance and repair workers, general	1,432.6	1,545.1	112.5	7.9	$38,300
Teacher assistants	1,308.1	1,417.6	109.5	8.4	$26,970
Financial managers	580.4	689.0	108.6	18.7	$127,990
Heavy and tractor-trailer truck drivers	1,871.7	1,980.1	108.4	5.8	$43,680
Elementary school teachers, except special education	1,410.9	1,514.9	104.1	7.4	$58,230
Stock clerks and order fillers	2,008.6	2,109.6	100.9	5.0	$25,700
Teachers and instructors, all other	993.9	1,091.8	98.0	9.9	$30,850
Receptionists and information clerks	1,053.7	1,149.2	95.5	9.1	$29,140
Sales representatives, services, all other	983.0	1,077.9	94.9	9.7	$54,550
Business operations specialists, all other	1,023.9	1,114.3	90.3	8.8	$70,530
Licensed practical and licensed vocational nurses	724.5	813.4	88.9	12.3	$46,240

* Data are from the Occupational Employment Statistics program, U.S. Bureau of Labor Statistics. Wage data cover non-farm wage and salary workers and do not cover the self-employed, owners and partners in unincorporated firms, or household workers.

Source: U.S. Bureau of Labor Statistics
Plunkett Research,® Ltd.
www.plunkettresearch.com

Top 30 U.S. Fastest Growing Occupations: 2016-2026

(Employment in Thousands)

Occupation	Employment		Change, 2016-26		Median annual wage, 2018*
	2016	2026	Number	Percent	
Total, all occupations	156,063.8	167,582.3	11,518.6	7.4	$38,640
Solar photovoltaic installers	11.3	23.1	11.8	104.9	$42,680
Wind turbine service technicians	5.8	11.3	5.6	96.3	$54,370
Home health aides	911.5	1,342.7	431.2	47.3	$24,200
Personal care aides	2,016.1	2,793.8	777.6	38.6	$24,020
Physician assistants	106.2	145.9	39.6	37.3	$108,610
Nurse practitioners	155.5	211.6	56.1	36.1	$107,030
Statisticians	37.2	49.8	12.6	33.8	$87,780
Physical therapist assistants	88.3	115.8	27.4	31.0	$58,040
Software developers, applications	831.3	1,086.6	255.4	30.7	$103,620
Mathematicians	3.1	4.0	0.9	29.7	$101,900
Physical therapist aides	52.0	67.2	15.3	29.4	$26,240
Bicycle repairers	12.4	16.1	3.6	29.3	$28,960
Medical assistants	634.4	818.4	183.9	29.0	$33,610
Genetic counselors	3.1	4.0	0.9	29.0	$80,370
Occupational therapy assistants	39.3	50.7	11.4	28.9	$60,220
Information security analysts	100.0	128.5	28.5	28.5	$98,350
Physical therapists	239.8	306.9	67.1	28.0	$87,930
Operations research analysts	114.0	145.3	31.3	27.4	$83,390
Forest fire inspectors and prevention specialists	1.7	2.2	0.5	26.6	$39,600
Massage therapists	160.3	202.4	42.1	26.3	$41,420
Health specialties teachers, postsecondary	233.5	294.0	60.6	25.9	$97,370
Derrick operators, oil and gas	11.1	13.9	2.8	25.7	$46,120
Roustabouts, oil and gas	50.0	62.4	12.4	24.8	$37,580
Occupational therapy aides	7.5	9.3	1.8	24.7	$28,160
Phlebotomists	122.7	152.8	30.1	24.5	$34,480
Nonfarm animal caretakers	241.5	300.0	58.5	24.2	$23,760
Rotary drill operators, oil and gas	16.7	20.8	4.0	24.2	$53,800
Nursing instructors and teachers, postsecondary	67.9	84.2	16.3	24.0	$73,490
Occupational therapists	130.4	161.4	31.0	23.8	$84,270
Service unit operators, oil, gas, and mining	41.4	51.1	9.7	23.4	$47,860

* Data are from the Occupational Employment Statistics program, U.S. Bureau of Labor Statistics. Wage data cover non-farm wage and salary workers and do not cover the self-employed, owners and partners in unincorporated firms, or household workers.

Source: U.S. Bureau of Labor Statistics
Plunkett Research,® Ltd.
www.plunkettresearch.com

Occupations with the Largest Expected Employment Increases, U.S.: 2016-2026

(By Increase in Number Employed, in Thousands)

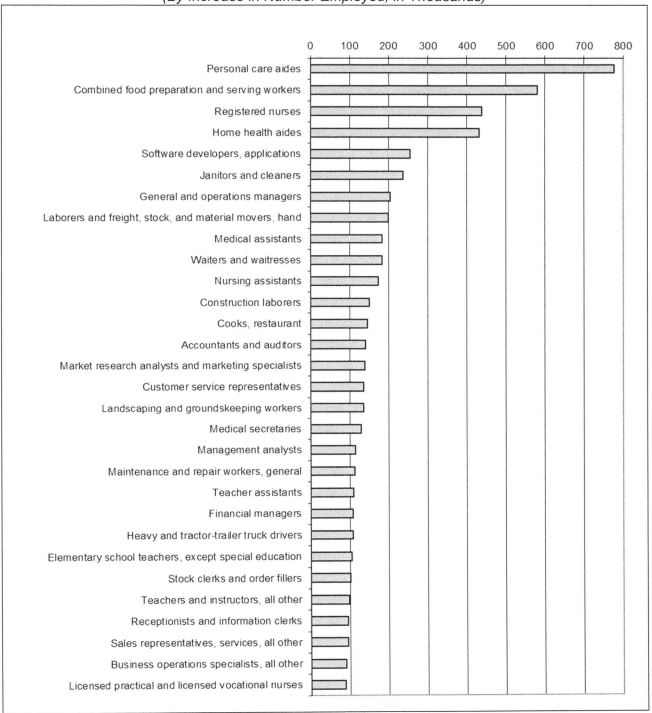

Source: U.S. Bureau of Labor Statistics
Plunkett Research,® Ltd.
www.plunkettresearch.com

Occupations with the Fastest Expected Decline, U.S.: 2016-2026

(In Thousands)

Occupation	Employment 2016	Employment 2026	Change, 2016-26 Number	Change, 2016-26 Percent	Median Annual Wage, 2018*
Total, all occupations	156,063.8	167,582.3	11,518.6	7.4	38,640
Locomotive firers	1.2	0.3	-0.9	-78.6	63,820
Respiratory therapy technicians	10.8	4.7	-6.1	-56.3	51,210
Parking enforcement workers	9.4	6.1	-3.3	-35.3	39,840
Word processors and typists	74.9	50.1	-24.8	-33.1	39,750
Watch repairers	1.8	1.2	-0.5	-29.7	39,910
Electronic equipment installers and repairers, motor vehicles	12.1	9.0	-3.1	-25.6	35,590
Foundry mold and coremakers	12.5	9.5	-3.0	-24.0	35,430
Pourers and casters, metal	8.4	6.5	-2.0	-23.4	37,730
Computer operators	51.5	39.7	-11.8	-22.8	45,840
Telephone operators	9.1	7.0	-2.0	-22.6	37,240
Mine shuttle car operators	1.5	1.2	-0.3	-21.9	56,340
Electromechanical equipment assemblers	45.7	35.9	-9.8	-21.4	—
Data entry keyers	203.8	160.6	-43.3	-21.2	32,170
Postmasters and mail superintendents	14.2	11.2	-3.0	-20.9	75,970
Electrical and electronic equipment assemblers	218.9	173.3	-45.6	-20.8	—
Coil winders, tapers, and finishers	14.1	11.2	-2.9	-20.7	34,400
Grinding and polishing workers, hand	26.6	21.1	-5.4	-20.5	29,550
Timing device assemblers and adjusters	0.8	0.6	-0.2	-20.1	34,650
Switchboard operators, including answering service	93.2	74.7	-18.5	-19.9	29,420
Prepress technicians and workers	34.6	27.7	-6.9	-19.9	40,410
Drilling and boring machine tool setters, operators, and tenders, metal and plastic	12.3	9.9	-2.4	-19.5	38,020
Textile knitting and weaving machine setters, operators, and tenders	22.2	17.9	-4.3	-19.3	29,160
Milling and planing machine setters, operators, and tenders, metal and plastic	17.6	14.2	-3.4	-19.3	43,590
Forging machine setters, operators, and tenders, metal and plastic	19.2	15.5	-3.7	-19.2	38,900
Legal secretaries	194.7	157.5	-37.1	-19.1	46,360
Photographic process workers and processing machine operators	26.9	22.0	-4.9	-18.1	29,180
Textile bleaching and dyeing machine operators and tenders	11.3	9.2	-2.0	-18.1	28,780
Aircraft structure, surfaces, rigging, and systems assemblers	41.8	34.5	-7.3	-17.4	53,340
Executive secretaries and executive administrative assistants	685.3	566.2	-119.2	-17.4	59,340
Engine and other machine assemblers	38.0	31.5	-6.5	-17.2	44,380

* Data are from the Occupational Employment Statistics program, U.S. Bureau of Labor Statistics. Wage data cover non-farm wage and salary workers and do not cover the self-employed, owners and partners in unincorporated firms, or household workers.

Source: U.S. Bureau of Labor Statistics
Plunkett Research,® Ltd.
www.plunkettresearch.com

Chapter 3

RESEARCH: 7 KEYS FOR JOB SEEKERS

How to use your library, college placement office, the internet and other resources to become well-informed about a company and its industry <u>before</u> you ask for an interview

Research is the key to finding appropriate job openings, targeting the best possible employers and performing well when you go to job interviews. Learn what's unique about a company compared to other firms in its industry. Learn why it's prospering–or why it isn't. Where is this company going? Is it favored by stock investors? Is it privately-owned by a family, or has it been acquired by private equity investors who plan to resell it over the mid-term? What are its hottest-selling products and services? Is it investing in research and new facilities so that it may prosper in the future? Also, as many people who have been laid off from failing firms have learned the hard way, determining a company's level of financial stability can be one of the most important factors in making a career decision.

The more you're willing to dig deep at the library or your college's career planning office, and the more adept you are at using the internet for research, the better your chances of success in a job search. If you are willing to ask questions of knowledgeable businesspeople and of employees who currently work for your target employers, you will enhance your job search even further. The two secrets to successful job research are tenacity and focus. Know what to look for and where to find it.

Once you've landed an interview, you should research both the prospective employer and its industry even further. In this manner, you'll know what questions to ask before you agree to take the job, and you'll present yourself as a knowledgeable potential hire who is truly interested in the company and its business.

Here are the seven keys for research that can lead you to a great employer:

1) Financial Stability
Check bond ratings, credit ratings, debt level, growth in sales and growth in profits, along with the views of stock analysts and business journalists.

2) Growth Plans
Look for new plants, stores or offices to be opened; new technologies, products or divisions to be launched; or plans for strategic acquisitions. (See 3, 4 and 5 below.) Is the employer's growth strategy focused primarily on offshoring work to overseas locations or outsourcing work to outside services providers? Or, does it have a balanced growth strategy that will create good opportunities in its American operations?

3) Research and Development Programs
If the company is a major manufacturer or a technology-based firm, then you should investigate how it invests in R&D (research and development). Is its research and development budget growing? For many types of companies, research is a vital investment in the future.

4) Product Launch and Production
Does the company have the ability to successfully launch new products and services (see 5 below) or to invest in and utilize cutting-edge technologies needed to maintain a competitive edge?

5) Marketing and Distribution Methods
Does the firm utilize an in-house sales force? Does it work through outside dealers and distribution partners? What are its advertising methods? Is it increasing its market share, or are competitors taking customers away? Is the company growing its international sales? Is it adept at using the internet as a powerful sales tool? Is it successful at selling into vital international markets?

6) Employee Benefits
Are wealth-building benefit plans offered? Will the company match all or part of your deposits to a 401(k) savings plan? Check for tuition reimbursement, pension plans, profit sharing, stock ownership plans, discount stock purchase plans, stock options or performance-based bonuses.

7) Quality-of-Work Factors
Does the company offer continual training, wellness programs, child care, elder care support, promote-from-within policies, flexible work schedules, performance reviews, product discounts or on-site health clubs? Is it a corporate culture that fits your lifestyle?

As a serious job seeker, you should conduct in-depth research and make detailed notes about these key factors for each firm you are considering. Then compare each company's finances, plans and programs to others in the same industry. You'll begin to see what makes some firms outstanding and why those outstanding companies are the best places to make a career investment.

Your research goal should be twofold: <u>First</u>, determine whether this is a firm you want to work for. Are the salaries and benefits appealing? Are layoffs likely? Is it planning to expand its workforce in lower-cost nations like India and then lay off U.S. employees? Is the firm growing steadily? A growing company will offer opportunities for you to advance when it launches new locations, services, technologies or product lines. <u>Second</u>, develop a personal understanding of both the company and its industry so you can better sell yourself as a potential employee.

Other Considerations:

Women and Minorities:
Certain industries have a greater tendency to offer advancement opportunities for women or minorities. Historically, the banking and insurance segments have tended to promote both women and minorities, as have retailing, electric utilities, apparel, consumer goods, packaged food and beverages, education, publishing and telephone companies.

Some technology companies have been terrific places for women who want to advance, and many tech companies, such as Hewlett-Packard, IBM, Yahoo, Xerox and eBay, have been known to post women to CEO spots.

Black Enterprise magazine publishes an annual list of the "Power in the Boardroom: Registry of Black Corporate Board Members," (see www.blackenterprise.com). Meanwhile, the Executive Leadership Council, www.elcinfo.com, a Washington, D.C.-based nonprofit group that conducts programs aimed at filling more executive posts with African Americans, has a unique statistic to report. Its membership is composed of senior-level black executives who have jobs that are no more than three levels below the CEO spot at *Fortune 500* companies. When the group was founded in 1986, it had only a handful of members. Today, its membership is comprised of hundreds of people employed in high-level executive jobs at major corporations (about one-third of them are women).

The Hispanic Association on Corporate Responsibility (www.hacr.org) promotes Hispanic advancement in the areas of employment, procurement, philanthropy and governance. Another nonprofit agency, National Hispanic Corporate Achievers (hispanicachievers.org), provides an educational forum for Hispanics working for *Fortune 1000* companies.

Tips on Using Business Magazines, Newspapers and Trade Journals to Find Job Leads and Do Employer Research

Many job seekers overlook the tremendous advantages offered by industry magazines (called "trade journals") and other publications when conducting research.

Industry-specific trade journals frequently have classified ads in the back that list job openings. An example of a great magazine to study is *American Banker,* which can be found at major libraries. Additional information is available at www.americanbanker.com.

Journalists at trade journals and business newspapers continuously interview industry-leading executives regarding their companies' growth plans. New projects and company expansion plans described in these articles provide terrific job leads.

You can also get great contact information from these publications. Read the latest business stories about companies and industries that interest you and you will learn vital information. Best of all, you can glean from stories and interviews the names and titles of executives who lead projects, divisions and subsidiaries.

There are literally hundreds of these trade journals—at least one for each industry sector and sometimes dozens covering the largest industries.

Other great resources include business newspapers such as the *Dallas/Ft. Worth Business Journal*, *The Wall Street Journal*, the business pages of major newspapers like *The New York Times* and publications written for major investors like *Investor's Business Daily*. At www.bizjournals.com, you can gain access to news stories from business journals from all over the U.S.

Quality-of-Life Benefits:
Many companies offer benefits that help employees balance their personal and professional lives. The concept is that employees who are healthy and comfortable with their personal and family lives make better, more productive employees. To that end, many companies include fitness programs and family services such as

extended maternity leaves and child care or elder care, whether on-site or off-site in the form of referral services. Other popular family-friendly benefits include flextime, flexible benefits spending accounts, adoption assistance and telecommuting. In many cases, benefits are listed on employers' web sites.

Work-Life has become a popular phrase for family-friendly benefits and programs among major employers such as Intel, Abbott Laboratories, Baxter International and Aramark. For additional information, you can study such organizations at WorldatWork (formerly the Alliance for Work-Life Progress) site at www.worldatwork.org.

Growth Potential and Job Stability:

A firm's growth potential should be among your top priorities. Companies are always trying to maintain or increase productivity, or the ratio of revenues per employee. If a company's sales are sliding, or if it is running out of cash, the job picture starts to collapse. A little extra research into a company's finances and true potential for growth might save you from a future layoff.

Of course, employers sometimes must resort to layoffs due to conditions outside of their control. The devastating economic recession that officially ran from late 2007 through early 2009 led to millions of layoffs in America.

As a job seeker, you're forced to look out for your own best interests while you sort through thousands of potential employers in dozens of industries. This means that good research is vital. For example, if you put salary at the top of your list, you may have the wrong priorities. From time to time, some of the highest-paying firms have been among those cutting the largest numbers of employees. If you are looking for job stability, your biggest challenge is to pick companies that are more likely to hire now and less likely to have layoffs in the future. That's why a firm's growth outlook should be one of your guiding lights.

However, the goal is *internal* growth caused by expanding sales. Generally less appealing are firms that post a quick spike in growth through big mergers. (In many cases, merged companies lay off people who suddenly find themselves filling jobs duplicated in newly consolidated offices. Also, companies that grow excessively through acquisitions may be taking on loads of debt that can become hard to handle later. However, there are occasional exceptions to this rule, where firms are enjoying soaring demand for products or services and find it difficult to hire quickly enough to keep up.) Companies that are growing rapidly through internal expansion include those opening new stores, distribution centers or offices, developing exciting new products, moving into new markets (including international markets) and creating hot new technologies, retail formats or services. Those types of expansion frequently mean great career opportunities, including the chance for rapid job promotion.

If you're tenacious, you can find opportunities where others will find only rejection. Identifying real prospects for growth takes more than a quick glance.

Here's an extremely important point for you to remember: You should also look for opportunities in growing divisions that serve special niches, even when the company as a whole is cutting jobs. For example, a firm's online division may be growing, even while its traditional business units are shrinking.

Additional key factors for strong corporate growth, and thereby the best job prospects, include:

1) Companies or divisions with a growing share of a promising market.

Management's ability to anticipate or create change in the marketplace makes for a growing company with great prospects. For example, Sam Walton revolutionized the department store business by realizing that consumers want everyday low prices on name-brand merchandise. He created Wal-Mart, while competitor Sears suffered by maintaining an old-fashioned policy of special sales events on private-label goods. Wal-Mart rapidly became one of the largest creators of new jobs in the private sector. Sears was forced to close multiple stores and slash its employee ranks.

Microsoft made its way to the top with unique products serving a soaring market when it developed highly functional software for personal computers. The software giant created thousands of millionaire employees through the immense increase in the value of its stock plans. HEB, an innovative grocer in Texas, has evolved continually over the decades, constantly introducing improvements to store layouts, and even creating an exciting new HEB Marketplace concept that is a retail industry leader. HEB has large numbers of job openings of many types on a continuous basis.

The point to these stories is that you shouldn't invest your career in a company with mediocre prospects. With perseverance, you can target your own list of employers that are posting growth due to competitive advantages or growing market demand. Your best bets are companies taking reasonable risks in order to move ahead. Those risks may include investments in advertising, research and development, new technology, improved techniques on the manufacturing floor, testing of new products and the opening of new retail store formats. For example, Chico's FAS stores scored a hit by filling a niche in the women's apparel market, and Genentech became a leader in the biotechnology field by risking vast amounts on research. Also, don't overlook the potential of the export market—many American firms find much of their growth by creating products and services that enjoy demand overseas as well as in the U.S.

2) Sales and profits: past and present.

The companies most likely to move along at a good clip are those with an exciting mid-term history. Firms with an average annual growth in sales of 10% to 15% or more over the past several years are generally very promising. Many small and mid-size firms grow at much faster rates and find themselves hiring continuously.

3) Beware of fads.

Unfortunately, a few companies post meteoric growth in businesses that turn out to be mere fads. The restaurant industry suffers from this problem on a regular basis. In recent years, companies selling bagels, frozen yogurt, rotisserie chicken and the like enjoyed impressive, nationwide growth only to collapse like a house of cards a couple of years later.

How to Find and Use Expert Opinions:

Superior sources used by sophisticated job researchers include reports written by: 1) analysts; 2) professional researchers and executives; and 3) journalists at business magazines and industry-specific web sites. Many major libraries have large collections of industry-specific "trade magazines" that can give you vital clues that competing job seekers will overlook. Virtually every industry is covered by one or two major websites and trade magazines that will give you leads to growing companies. Many articles in these resources contain the names of executives you may want to contact. Also, some trade magazines publish help-wanted ads in the back. It's easy to do an online search for trade magazines and industry-specific websites, and many of them are filled with extremely useful information. For example, a recent search on Google for "pet industry trade magazine" quickly turned up leads to the top magazines for that sector.

Next, move on to reports from experts. Marketing and investment professionals are looking for some of the same clues you should use as a job seeker, and reports written by full-time analysts who cover specific companies or industries can help you find firms that are growing and hiring. Search the internet for white papers, industry reports and studies that cover your industry of interest.

Professionally written market research can be found at Marketresearch.com, www.marketresearch.com. This market research broker charges varying fees for access to the reports. However, many of the reports are reasonably priced, and the insight you gain into industries, markets and leading companies can be extremely helpful. Web sites such as this offer the ability to search for reports by a wide variety of criteria, including company name and industry.

Internet Research Tip:
Be sure to create Google "Alerts" to follow your targeted employers and profession. Google will email results to you daily.

By going to the "more" link at the top of the Google home page, and then selecting "even more" from the drop-down list, you can access Google's "Alerts" tool. Here you can arrange to receive email updates on topics of your choice. For example, you can set a general alert about an industry or locale: sales jobs in California, for example. Or something like: opportunities in the American wireless industry. Or even: sales jobs at automobile dealers.

You can use alerts to track specific jobs or employers. For example: openings at Intel. Or: regional sales manager opening Los Angeles. Finally, don't forget that you may want to put a search phrase within quotes to get an exact match to part of your phrase. For example: "loan officer" wanted.

Other Basic Resources:

Annual Reports/10-Ks/S-1s: Companies that sell their stocks to the public, including most of the firms covered in this book, publish annual reports that contain a wealth of information. Annual reports and 10-Ks cover yearly results, financial statements, management practices and other vital information for publicly held firms. S-1s provide the same type of information on companies that are selling stock to the public for the first time. You can find copies of these reports at large libraries. Online, the best place to acquire this information is at typically at the "Investors" tab on the website of the company you are researching. Alternately, try the site of the U.S. Securities and Exchange Commission. They have a user-friendly service that enables you to search for companies and access their financial reports at www.sec.gov. (Look for the "Filings & Forms" section, and then see "Search for Company Filings.") Look especially at the five-year "summary financial statement" in the back of these reports. Also, look for growth in sales and earnings. If these are falling, dig deeper to find out why. Faltering sales or profits can lead to layoffs or to a merger with another firm (which could result in deep job cuts).

Also, you can find a wealth of financial information on publicly-traded firms at Yahoo! Finance, http://finance.yahoo.com.

See Chapter 4, "Important Contacts for Job Seekers," for additional places to get basic corporate data.

Tips on Utilizing Financial Documents Filed by Publicly Held Firms

(Access these documents at the Securities Exchange Commission, www.sec.gov.)

10-K (also called Annual Report on Form 10-K): This is an annual filing required by federal law. It follows a standard format. Information includes a complete description of the business, risk factors, historical financial data and much more. It is vital reading for job seekers. You will find that these documents are written in dry, legal language, but they contain a wealth of information.

DEF 14A Proxy Statement: This is an annual document that gives shareholders certain options to consider at their annual meeting. It names the firm's board of directors and top management. It also gives the dollar value and description of salaries, bonuses, pension plans, stock options and other benefits enjoyed by the company's five highest-paid officers. Job seekers can learn a great deal about a firm's management, pay and benefits from this document. Included is a list of the people or organizations that own more than 5% of the company's stock.

S-1: This is a new registration document for companies that are going public for the first time. In other words, they are creating an IPO (initial public offering). The information includes all of the data found in the 10-K and proxy statement filed annually by companies that have been public for more than one year.

10-Q: This is a quarterly report detailing a company's latest sales, profits and balance sheet.

Press Releases: Most mid-size to large companies issue a continual stream of press releases about new products, technologies and locations; new executive appointments; community activities and a wide variety of other company developments. The best place to find these is online, at the "News" tab on the company's own web site. You can also search popular business press release services such as www.prnewswire.com and www.businesswire.com.

More Ways to Research an Employer's Financial Stability and Growth Plans:

1) Check out its bond rating.

There's no sense in trying to become a financial analyst on your own. Use internet searches to look for the bond ratings of potential employers. These ratings are based on a company's ability to pay principal and interest when due. If you're considering a major corporation with a bond rating of less than BB (an indicator that a company's debt is riskier than "investment grade"), you should do a lot more investigating before you continue chasing a job at that company.

2) Talk to vendors and current employees.

Talk to employees who work for the employer, or talk to people who do business with it. No one knows what's really going on better than people who are on the scene. If there are problems that are not yet known by the media, or if there are exciting new developments that have not yet been announced, you may find out a lot just by asking around. While you're at it, ask about corporate culture—how well are employees treated?

Popular Job-Search Internet Sites

CareerBuilder	www.careerbuilder.com
Monster	www.monster.com
Indeed	www.indeed.com

Tips on Finding Information on Privately Held Employers

Our subscription service, Plunkett Research Online, and our printed Plunkett's industry almanacs, are among the world's most highly regarded sources of profiles of privately-held companies. Check with your library to see if you have access to these tools.

Study back-issue indexes and archives to major newspapers to see what journalists are reporting about a prospective private employer. Many libraries have recent issues of *The Wall Street Journal, The New York Times* and other important business newspapers. At major public and university libraries, you may be able to access online databases like ProQuest. These databases have excellent search engines that lead you into online archives of the best publications, including *The Wall Street Journal*, as well as many trade magazines and local business journals.

For smaller firms, go online and try American Journalism Review at www.newslink.org, where you'll be able to search news sites including hometown newspapers across the nation. Likewise, search local business newspapers at www.bizjournals.com, where you'll find links to dozens of major business weeklies like the *Houston Business Journal*.

Finally, consider investing in a credit report. If you really want reassurance, go to Experian SmartBusinessReports, www.smartbusinessreports.com. You can use its links to order a credit report on the employer. These reports are reasonably priced, and they can help you determine whether the company is paying its bills on time or has other problems. This could be vital in helping you determine whether to accept a job at a privately-held firm.

3) Use Internet search engines.

Look up your firm and industry in an internet search engine such as Google. (You may need to click on "News" instead of relying on a general web search.) There, you may find unusual articles that were recently written about a company's product breakthroughs, treatment of women or minorities, human interest stories, training programs or stories written from other unique slants.

4) Study other business books and guides.

Search at a library or at an online bookseller like Amazon.com for recent books regarding major companies. For example, if you want to apply to biotech leader Genentech for a job, don't fail to read *The Billion Dollar Molecule: One Company's Quest for the Perfect Drug*. With a little research, you can turn up many other excellent books about specific companies, from banks like Bank of America to publishers like Gannett.

Great Places for Industry Research

Plunkett Research, www.plunkettresearch.com. Go to the specific industry of your choice to see an overview of trends and statistics. At our subscription service, www.plunkettresearchonline.com, subscribers have access to thousands of pages of industry analysis, statistics, contacts and company profiles, along with multiple search and export tools.

Vault.com, www.vault.com. This site publishes insights about careers with hundreds of leading firms.

---

5) Explore industry-specific web sites.

In particular, study the leading industry associations for the sector in which you want to work. You will find listings of hundreds of the most important organizations, professional societies and resources, personally selected by our editors, in the almanacs published by Plunkett Research, Ltd., and in the contacts databases at Plunkett Research Online.

6) Research benefits and pension plans.

For additional information about corporate pension plans, start with the government agency charged with protecting and regulating pensions: the Pension Benefit Guaranty Corporation, 1200 K St. NW, Washington, D.C. 20005-4026, 202-326-4000, www.pbgc.gov. They can answer certain questions over the telephone.

The U.S. Department of Labor publishes a useful site titled Consumer Information on Retirement Plans, https://www.dol.gov/general/topic/retirement/consumerinfpension.

The Social Security Administration, 800-772-1213, www.ssa.gov, can provide you with information regarding your potential Social Security benefits.

NOTE: Generally, employees covered by wealth-building benefit plans do not fully own ("vest in") funds contributed on their behalf by the employer until as many as five years of service with that employer have passed. All pension plans are voluntary—that is, employers are not obligated to offer pensions.

Pension Plans: The type and generosity of these plans vary widely from firm to firm. Caution: Some employers refer to plans as "pension" or "retirement" plans when they are actually 401(k) savings plans that require a contribution by the employee.

Defined Benefit Pension Plans: Pension plans that do not require a contribution from the employee are infrequently offered. However, a few companies, particularly larger employers in high-profit-margin industries, offer defined benefit pension plans where the employee is guaranteed to receive a set pension benefit upon retirement. The amount of the benefit is determined by the years of service with the company and the employee's salary during the later years of employment. The longer a person works for the employer, the higher the retirement benefit. These defined benefit plans are funded entirely by the employer. The benefits, up to a reasonable limit, are guaranteed by the Federal Government's Pension Benefit Guaranty Corporation. These plans are not portable—if you leave the company, you cannot transfer your benefits into a different plan. Instead, upon retirement you will receive the benefits that vested during your service with the company. If your employer offers a pension plan, it must give you a "summary plan description" within 90 days of the date you join the plan. You can also request a "summary annual report" of the plan, and once every 12 months you may request an "individual benefit statement" accounting of your interest in the plan.

Defined Contribution Plans: These are quite different. They do not guarantee a certain amount of pension benefit. Instead, they set out circumstances under which the employer will make a contribution to a plan on your behalf. The most common example is the 401(k) savings plan. Pension benefits are not guaranteed under these plans.

Cash Balance Pension Plans: These plans were recently invented. They are hybrid plans—part defined benefit and part defined contribution. Many employers have converted their older defined benefit plans into cash balance plans. The employer makes deposits (or credits a given amount of money) on the employee's behalf, usually based on a percentage of pay. Employee accounts grow based on a predetermined interest benchmark, such as the interest rate on Treasury Bonds. There are some advantages to these plans, particularly for younger workers: a) The benefits, up to a reasonable limit, are guaranteed by the Pension Benefit Guaranty Corporation. b) Benefits are portable—they can be moved to another plan when the employee changes companies. c) Younger workers and those who spend a shorter number of years with an employer may receive higher benefits than they would under a traditional defined benefit plan.

ESOP Stock Plan (Employees' Stock Ownership Plan): This type of plan is becoming rare, but it can be of great value to employees. Typically, the plan borrows money from a bank and uses those funds to purchase a large block of the corporation's stock. The corporation makes contributions to the plan over a period of time, and the stock purchase loan is eventually paid off. The value of the plan grows significantly as long as the market price of the stock holds up. Qualified employees are allocated a share of the plan based on their length of service and their level of salary. Under federal regulations, participants in ESOPs are allowed to diversify their account holdings in set percentages that rise as the employee ages and gains years of service with the company. In this manner, not all of the employee's assets are tied up in the employer's stock.

Savings Plan, 401(k): Under this type of plan, employees make a tax-deferred deposit into an account. In the best plans, the company makes annual matching donations to the employees' accounts, typically in some proportion to deposits made by the employees themselves. A good plan will match one-half of employee deposits of up to 6% of wages. For example, an employee earning $50,000 yearly might deposit $3,000 (6%) into the plan. The company will match one-half of the employee's deposit, or $1,500. The plan grows on a tax-deferred basis, similar to an IRA. A very generous plan will match 100% of employee deposits. However, some plans do not call for the employer to make a matching deposit at all. Other plans call for a matching contribution to be made at the discretion of the firm's board of directors. Actual terms of these plans vary widely from firm to firm. Generally, these savings plans allow employees to deposit as much as 15% of salary into the plan on a tax-deferred basis. However, the portion that the company uses to calculate its matching deposit is generally limited to a maximum of 6%. Employees should take care to diversify the holdings in their 401(k) accounts, and most people should seek professional guidance or investment management for their accounts. (Note: when profits are down, many employers exercise their right to suspend their contributions to 401(k)s. Employees may continue to make contributions, but they will not be matched by the employer in these cases.)

Stock Purchase Plan: Qualified employees may purchase the company's common stock at a price below its market value under a specific plan. Typically, the employee is limited to investing a small percentage of wages in this plan. The discount may range from 5% to 15%. Some of these plans allow for deposits to be made through regular monthly payroll deductions. However, new accounting rules for corporations, along with other factors, are leading many companies to curtail these plans—dropping the discount allowed, cutting the maximum yearly stock purchase or otherwise making the plans less generous or appealing.

Profit Sharing: Qualified employees are awarded an annual amount equal to some portion of a company's profits. In a very generous plan, the pool of money awarded to employees would be 15% of profits. Typically, this money is deposited into a long-term retirement account. Caution: Some employers refer to plans as "profit sharing" when they are actually 401(k) savings plans. True profit sharing plans are rarely offered.

Plunkett Research Online and Plunkett's Industry Reference Books:

1) Internet-Based Services: Plunkett Research Online is a reference service that is subscribed to by the nation's leading university placement offices, libraries and information offices. You can use it to filter prospective employers by location, industry, size and more. You can then export contact information for those companies into spreadsheets or text files. In addition, you can use the site to research the latest editions of our industry analysis. Many additional tools for job seekers are included. For an extensive online tour, see www.plunkettresearch.com.

2) Plunkett's Industry Almanacs: Plunkett Research also publishes industry-specific almanacs for the world's most vital industries. They are available in both printed and eBook editions. These are top-notch resources for job seekers.

Industry-Specific Books from Plunkett Research:

- Plunkett's Advertising & Branding Industry Almanac
- Plunkett's Aerospace, Aircraft, Satellites & Drones Industry Almanac
- Plunkett's Airline, Hotel & Travel Industry Almanac
- Plunkett's Almanac of Middle Market Companies
- Plunkett's Apparel, Shoes & Textiles Industry Almanac
- Plunkett's Artificial Intelligence (AI) & Machine Learning Industry Almanac
- Plunkett's Automobile Industry Almanac
- Plunkett's Banking, Mortgages & Credit Industry Almanac
- Plunkett's Biotech, Pharmaceuticals & Genetics Industry Almanac
- Plunkett's Chemicals, Coatings & Plastics Industry Almanac
- Plunkett's Computers, Hardware & Software Industry Almanac
- Plunkett's Consulting Industry Almanac
- Plunkett's Consumer Products, Cosmetics, Hair & Personal Services Industry Almanac
- Plunkett's E-Commerce & Internet Business Almanac
- Plunkett's Education, EdTech and MOOCs Industry Almanac
- Plunkett's Energy Industry Almanac
- Plunkett's Engineering & Research Industry Almanac
- Plunkett's Entertainment. Movie, Publishing & Media Industry Almanac
- Plunkett's Food Industry Almanac
- Plunkett's Games, Apps & Social Media Industry Almanac

- Plunkett's Green Technology Industry Almanac
- Plunkett's Health Care Industry Almanac
- Plunkett's Insurance Industry Almanac
- Plunkett's Internet of Things (IoT) & Data Analytics Industry Almanac
- Plunkett's Investment & Securities Industry Almanac
- Plunkett's Manufacturing, Automation & Robotics Industry Almanac
- Plunkett's Outsourcing & Offshoring Industry Almanac
- Plunkett's Real Estate & Construction Industry Almanac
- Plunkett's Solar Power, Wind Power & Renewable Energy Industry Almanac
- Plunkett's Restaurant & Hospitality Industry Almanac
- Plunkett's Retail Industry Almanac
- Plunkett's Sharing & Gig Economy, Freelance Workers & On-Demand Delivery Almanac
- Plunkett's Sports & Recreation Industry Almanac
- Plunkett's Telecommunications Industry Almanac
- Plunkett's Transportation, Supply Chain & Logistics Industry Almanac
- Plunkett's Wireless & Cellular Telephone Industry Almanac

Publications from Plunkett Research Written Especially for Job Seekers:

- The Almanac of American Employers
- Plunkett's Companion to the Almanac of American Employers

Our books will give you in-depth coverage of specific industries and the leading firms in those industries, along with trends and developments in technology and services. You will find these books in public and academic libraries, college placement offices, human resources offices, corporate libraries and government agency libraries. For sample chapters and additional details, you can preview as well as purchase these books at www.plunkettresearch.com.

The Almanac of American Employers provides profiles and detailed listings of 500 hand-picked, U.S. employers of 2,500 employees or more in size

Plunkett's Companion to The Almanac of American Employers is our book that provides profiles on 500 additional, rapidly growing corporate employers. This companion book covers smaller firms than those in the main volume of *The Almanac of American Employers*.

Chapter 4

IMPORTANT CONTACTS FOR JOB SEEKERS

Contents:

1) Accountants & CPAs Associations
2) Advertising/Marketing Associations
3) Aerospace & Defense Industry Associations
4) Airline & Air Cargo Industry Associations
5) Alternative Energy-Ethanol
6) Alternative Energy-Solar
7) Alternative Energy-Wind
8) Banking Industry Associations
9) Biotechnology & Biological Industry Associations
10) Booksellers Associations
11) Broadcasting, Cable, Radio & TV Associations
12) Careers-Airlines/Flying
13) Careers-Apparel
14) Careers-Banking
15) Careers-Biotech
16) Careers-Coatings
17) Careers-Computers/Technology
18) Careers-Contract & Freelance
19) Careers-First Time Jobs/New Grads
20) Careers-General Job Listings
21) Careers-Health Care
22) Careers-Job Listings for Seniors
23) Careers-Job Listings Hong Kong, China, Singapore, Asia
24) Careers-Job Reference Tools
25) Careers-Restaurants
26) Careers-Science
27) Careers-Sports
28) Careers-Video Games Industry
29) Chemicals Industry Associations
30) Communications Professional Associations
31) Computer & Electronics Industry Associations
32) Consulting Industry Associations
33) Consulting Industry Resources
34) Corporate Information Resources
35) Disabling Conditions
36) Electronic Health Records/Continuity of Care Records
37) Energy Associations-Electric Power
38) Energy Associations-Natural Gas
39) Energy Associations-Other
40) Energy Associations-Petroleum, Exploration, Production, etc.
41) Engineering, Research & Scientific Associations
42) Entertainment & Amusement Associations-General
43) Film & Theater Associations
44) Fitness Industry Associations
45) Food Industry Associations, General
46) Food Industry Resources, General
47) Food Processor Industry Associations
48) Food Service Industry Associations
49) Games Industry Associations
50) Grocery Industry Associations
51) Health & Nutrition Associations
52) Health Care Business & Professional Associations
53) Health Insurance Industry Associations
54) Hearing & Speech
55) Hotel/Lodging Associations
56) Human Resources Industry Associations
57) Industry Research/Market Research
58) Insurance Industry Associations
59) Insurance Industry Associations-Agents & Brokers
60) Magazines, Business & Financial
61) MBA Resources
62) Online Recruiting & Employment ASPs & Solutions
63) Outsourcing Industry Associations
64) Pensions, Benefits & 401(k) Associations
65) Pensions, Benefits & 401(k) Resources
66) Pharmaceutical Industry Associations (Drug Industry)
67) Pilots Associations
68) Printers & Publishers Associations
69) Real Estate Industry Associations
70) Recording & Music Associations
71) Satellite Industry Associations
72) Satellite-Related Professional Organizations
73) Securities Industry Associations
74) Software Industry Associations

75)	Stocks & Financial Markets Data
76)	Telecommunications Industry Associations
77)	Temporary Staffing Firms
78)	Testing Resources
79)	Textile & Fabric Industry Associations
80)	Travel Business & Professional Associations
81)	Travel Industry Associations
82)	U.S. Government Agencies
83)	Water Technologies & Resources
84)	Wireless & Cellular Industry Associations
85)	Writers, Photographers & Editors Associations

1) Accountants & CPA Associations

American Institute of CPAs (AICPA)
1211 Ave. of the Americas
New York, NY 10036-8775 US
Phone: 212-596-6200
Fax: 800-362-5066
Toll Free: 888-777-7077
E-mail Address: service@aicpa.org
Web Address: www.aicpa.org
American Institute of CPAs (AICPA) represents nearly 370,000 members in 128 countries involved in the accounting profession. Its web site provides information and news for CPAs, news from the organization and a search for accounting firms.

Council of Petroleum Accountants Societies, Inc. (COPAS)
445 Union Blvd., Ste. 207
Lakewood, CO 80228 USA
Phone: 303-300-1131
Toll Free: 877-992-6727
Web Address: www.copas.org
The Council of Petroleum Accountants Societies, Inc. (COPAS) provides a forum for discussing and solving the variety of problems related to accounting for oil and gas. COPAS also provides valuable educational materials related to oil and gas accounting.

International Accounting Standards Board (IASB)
30 Cannon St.
London, EC4M 6XH UK
Phone: 44-20-7246-6410
Fax: 44-20-7246-6411
E-mail Address: info@ifrs.org
Web Address: www.ifrs.org
The International Accounting Standards Board (IASB) website hosts an electronic subscription service to the International Financial Reporting (IFRS) Standards as well access to IFRS summaries.

2) Advertising/Marketing Associations

4A's (American Association of Advertising Agencies)
1065 Ave. of the Americas, Fl. 16
New York, NY 10018 USA
Phone: 212-682-2500
Web Address: www.aaaa.org
The 4A's (American Association of Advertising Agencies) is the national trade association representing the advertising agency industry in the U.S.

Advertising Women of New York (AWNY)
28 W. 44th St., Ste. 912
New York, NY 10036 USA
Phone: 212-221-7969
E-mail Address: lynn.branigan@awny.org
Web Address: www.awny.org
Advertising Women of New York (AWNY) provides a forum for personal and professional growth, serves as a catalyst for the advancement of women in the communications field and promotes and supports philanthropic endeavors through the AWNY Foundation. The web site also provides content from Women Executives in Public Relations (WERP), such as its a dynamic job board.

American Institute of Graphic Arts (AIGA)
233 Broadway, Fl. 17
New York, NY 10279 USA
Phone: 212-807-1990
Web Address: www.aiga.org
The American Institute of Graphic Arts (AIGA) strives to further excellence in communication design, both as a strategic tool for business and as a cultural force.

American Marketing Association (AMA)
130 E. Randolph St., Fl. 22
Chicago, IL 60601 USA
Phone: 312-542-9000
Fax: 312-542-9001
Toll Free: 800-262-1150
Web Address: www.ama.org
The American Marketing Association (AMA) serves marketing professionals in both business and education and serves all levels of marketing practitioners, educators and students.

Cable & Telecommunications Association for Marketing (CTAM)
120 Waterfront St., Ste. 200
National Harbor, MD 20745 USA
Phone: 301-485-8900
Fax: 301-560-4964
E-mail Address: info@ctam.com
Web Address: www.ctam.com
The Cable & Telecommunications Association for Marketing (CTAM) is dedicated to the discipline and development of consumer marketing excellence in cable television, new media and telecommunications services.

Direct Marketing Association (DMA)
1120 Ave. of the Americas
New York, NY 10036-6700 USA
Phone: 212-768-7277
Web Address: thedma.org
The Direct Marketing Association (DMA) is the oldest and largest trade association for users and suppliers in the direct, database and interactive marketing fields.

3) Aerospace & Defense Industry Associations

American Institute of Aeronautics and Astronautics (AIAA)
12700 Sunrise Valley Dr., Ste. 200
Reston, VA 20191-5807 USA
Phone: 703-264-7500
Fax: 703-264-7551
Toll Free: 800-639-2422
E-mail Address: custserv@aiaa.org
Web Address: www.aiaa.org
The American Institute of Aeronautics and Astronautics (AIAA) is a nonprofit society aimed at advancing the arts, sciences and technology of aeronautics and astronautics. The institute represents the U.S. in the International Astronautical Federation and the International Council on the Aeronautical Sciences.

4) Airline & Air Cargo Industry Associations

International Air Transport Association (IATA)
800 Place Victoria
P.O. Box 113
Montreal, QC H4Z 1M1 Canada
Phone: 514-874-0202
Web Address: www.iata.org
The International Air Transport Association (IATA) represents about 260 airlines in order to offer the highest standards of passenger and cargo service.

5) Alternative Energy-Ethanol

Renewable Fuels Association (RFA)
425 3rd St. SW, Ste. 1150
Washington, DC 20024 USA
Phone: 202-289-3835
Fax: 202-289-7519
Web Address: www.ethanolrfa.org
The Renewable Fuels Association (RFA) is a trade organization representing the ethanol industry. It publishes a wealth of useful information, including a listing of biorefineries and monthly U.S. fuel ethanol production and demand.

6) Alternative Energy-Solar

Solar Energy Industries Association (SEIA)
600 14th St. NW, Ste. 400
Washington, DC 20005 USA
Phone: 202-682-0556
E-mail Address: info@seia.org
Web Address: www.seia.org
Established in 1974, the Solar Energy Industries Association is the American trade association of the solar energy industry. Among its operations is a web site that provides news for the solar energy industry, links to related products and companies and solar energy statistics.

7) Alternative Energy-Wind

American Wind Energy Association (AWEA)
1501 M St. NW, Ste. 1000
Washington, DC 20005 USA
Phone: 202-383-2500
Fax: 202-383-2505
Web Address: www.awea.org
The American Wind Energy Association (AWEA) promotes wind energy as a clean source of electricity worldwide. Its website provides excellent resources for research, including an online library, discussions of legislation, and descriptions of wind technologies.

8) Banking Industry Associations

American Bankers Association (ABA)
1120 Connecticut Ave. NW
Washington, DC 20036 USA
Toll Free: 800-226-5377
E-mail Address: custserv@aba.com
Web Address: www.aba.com
The American Bankers Association (ABA) represents banks of all sizes on issues of national importance for financial institutions and their customers. The site offers financial information and solutions, financial news and member access to further advice and content.

9) Biotechnology & Biological Industry Associations

Biotechnology Industry Organization (BIO)
1201 Maryland Ave. SW, Ste. 900
Washington, DC 20024 USA
Phone: 202-962-9200
Fax: 202-488-6301
E-mail Address: info@bio.org
Web Address: www.bio.org
The Biotechnology Industry Organization (BIO) represents members involved in the research and development of health care, agricultural, industrial and environmental biotechnology products. BIO has both small and large member organizations.

10) Booksellers Associations

American Booksellers Association, Inc.
333 Westchester Ave., Ste. S202
White Plains, NY 10604 USA
Phone: 914-406-7500
Fax: 914-417-4013
Toll Free: 800-637-0037
E-mail Address: info@bookweb.org
Web Address: www.bookweb.org
The American Booksellers Association is a nonprofit association representing independent bookstores in the United States.

11) Broadcasting, Cable, Radio & TV Associations

Academy of Television Arts and Sciences
5220 Lankershim Blvd.
North Hollywood, CA 91601-3109 USA
Phone: 818-754-2800
Web Address: www.emmys.tv
The Academy of Television Arts and Sciences is a nonprofit corporation devoted to the advancement of telecommunications arts and sciences and to fostering creative leadership in the telecommunications industry. It is one of three organizations that administer the Emmy Awards. It is responsible for prime time Emmys.

Alliance for Women in Media
1760 Old Meadow Rd., Ste. 500
McLean, VA 22102 USA
Phone: 703-506-3290
Fax: 703-506-3266
E-mail Address: info@allwomeninmedia.org
Web Address: www.allwomeninmedia.org/
The Alliance for Women in Media, formerly the American Women in Radio and Television (AWRT), founded in 1951, is a national nonprofit organization dedicated to advancing the role of women in electronic media and related fields.

Association of America's Public Television Stations (APTS)
2100 Crystal Dr., Ste. 700
Arlington, VA 22202 USA
Phone: 202-654-4200
Fax: 202-654-4236
E-mail Address: skarp@apts.org
Web Address: www.apts.org
The Association of America's Public Television Stations (APTS) is a nonprofit membership organization formed to support the continued growth and development of strong and financially sound noncommercial television service for the American public.

Broadcast Education Association (BEA)
1771 N St. NW
Washington, DC 20036-2891 USA
Phone: 202-429-3935
Fax: 202-775-2981
E-mail Address: tbailey@nab.org
Web Address: www.beaweb.org
The Broadcast Education Association (BEA) is the professional association for professors, industry professionals and graduate students interested in teaching and research related to electronic media and multimedia enterprises.

National Academy of Television Arts and Sciences
1697 Broadway, Ste. 404
New York, NY 10019 USA
Phone: 212-586-8424
Fax: 212-246-8129
E-mail Address: ppillitteri@emmyonline.tv
Web Address: www.emmyonline.org
The National Academy of Television Arts and Sciences is dedicated to the advancement of the arts and sciences of television and the promotion of creative leadership for artistic, educational and technical achievements within the television industry. It is responsible for awarding the Emmy Awards.

National Association of Broadcasters (NAB)
1771 N St. NW
Washington, DC 20036 USA
Phone: 202-429-5300
Toll Free: 800-622-3976
E-mail Address: nab@nab.org

Web Address: www.nab.org
The National Association of Broadcasters (NAB) represents broadcasters for radio and television. The organization also provides benefits to employees of member companies and to individuals and companies that provide products and services to the electronic media industries.

National Association of Television Program Executives (NATPE)
5757 Wilshire Blvd., Penthouse 10
Los Angeles, CA 90036-3681 USA
Phone: 310-857-1601
E-mail Address: jpbommel@natpe.org
Web Address: www.natpe.org
The National Association of Television Program Executives (NATPE) is the leading association for content professionals in the global television industry. It is dedicated to the growth of video content development, creations, production, financing and distribution across various platforms by providing education and networking opportunities to its members.

National Cable and Telecommunications Association (NCTA)
25 Massachusetts Ave. NW, Ste. 100
Washington, DC 20001-1413 USA
Phone: 202-222-2300
Fax: 202-222-2514
E-mail Address: info@ncta.com
Web Address: www.ncta.com
The National Cable and Telecommunications Association (NCTA) is the principal trade association of the cable television industry in the United States. It represents cable operators as well as over 200 cable program networks that produce TV shows.

Radio Television Digital News Association (RTDNA)
529 14th St. NW, Ste. 1240
Washington, DC 20045 USA
Fax: 202-223-4007
E-mail Address: mikec@rtdna.org
Web Address: www.rtdna.org
The Radio Television Digital News Association (RTDNA), formerly the Radio-Television News Directors Association (RTNDA), is the world's largest professional organization exclusively committed to professionals in electronic journalism.

Screen Actor's Guild, American Federation of Television and Radio Artists (SAG-AFTRA)
5757 Wilshire Blvd., Fl. 7
Los Angeles, CA 90036-3600 USA
Phone: 323-634-8100
Fax: 323-549-6792
Toll Free: 855-724-2387
E-mail Address: sagaftrainfo@sagaftra.org
Web Address: www.sagaftra.org
The Screen Actors Guild, American Federation of Television and Radio Artists (SAG-AFTRA), a product of the merger of the Screen Actors Guild (SAG) and the American Federation of Television and Radio Artists (AFTRA), is a national labor union representing actors and other professional performers and broadcasters in television, radio, sound recordings, non-broadcast/industrial programming and new technologies such as interactive programming and CD-ROMs.

Screen Actors Guild-American Federation of Television and Radio Artists (SAG-AFTRA)
5757 Wilshire Blvd., Fl. 7
Los Angeles, CA 90036-3600 USA
Phone: 323-634-8100
Fax: 323-549-6792
Toll Free: 855-724-2387
E-mail Address: sagaftrainfo@sagaftra.org
Web Address: www.sagaftra.org
The Screen Actors Guild-American Federation of Television and Radio Artists (SAG-AFTRA), a product of the merger of the Screen Actors Guild (SAG) and the American Federation of Television and Radio Artists (AFTRA), is a national labor union representing actors and other professional performers and broadcasters in television, radio, sound recordings, non-broadcast/industrial programming and new technologies such as interactive programming and CD-ROMs.

Women in Cable & Telecommunications (WICT)
14555 Avion Pkwy., Ste. 250
Chantilly, VA 20151 USA
Phone: 703-234-9810
Fax: 703-817-1595
E-mail Address: tgibson@wict.org
Web Address: www.wict.org
Women in Cable & Telecommunications (WICT) exists to advance the position and influence of women in media through leadership programs and services at both the national and local level.

12) Careers-Airlines/Flying

Aviation/Aerospace/Defense Jobs Page
920 Morgan St., Ste. T
Des Moines, IA 50309 USA
Fax: 515-243-5384
Toll Free: 800-292-7731
E-mail Address: customerservice@nationjob.com
Web Address: www.nationjob.com/aviation
The Aviation/Aerospace Jobs Page, a division of NationJob, Inc., features detailed aviation and aerospace job listings and company profiles.

AviationJobSearch.com
7955 NW 12th St., Ste. 401
Miami, FL 33126 USA
Phone: 786-433-7120 ext. 203
Fax: 305-716-4064
E-mail Address: info@aviationjobsearch.com
Web Address: www.aviationjobsearch.com
AviationJobSearch.com lists jobs related to the airline industry.

Avjobs, Inc.
9609 S. University Blvd., Unit 630830
Littleton, CO 80163-3032 USA
Phone: 303-683-2322
Fax: 303-683-5239
E-mail Address: info@avjobs.com
Web Address: www.avjobs.com
Avjobs, Inc. is a group of employers dedicated to helping individuals obtain aviation, airline, aerospace and airport careers.

Flightdeck Recruitment Ltd.
15 High St., W. Mersea
Colchester, Essex CO5 8QA UK
E-mail Address: contact@flightdeckrecruitment.com
Web Address: www.flightdeckrecruitment.com
Flightdeck Recruitment Ltd. provides a link between aviation recruiters who are looking for flight deck crew and pilots or flight engineers who are seeking employment.

13) Careers-Apparel

24 Seven Fashion Recruitment
120 Wooster St., Fl. 4
New York, NY 10012 USA
Phone: 212-966-4426
Fax: 212-966-2313
E-mail Address: newyork@24seventalent.com
Web Address: www.24seventalent.com
24 Seven Fashion Recruitment is an employment agency serving the fashion, beauty, entertainment, advertising, marketing and retail industries.

Fashion Career Center
950 Tower Ln., Fl. 6

Foster City, CA 94404 USA
Web Address: www.fashioncareercenter.com
The Fashion Career Center site provides employees and employers with a place to meet and access information about employment in the fashion industry. The FashionCareerCenter.com web site offers links to fashion jobs and fashion schools, as well as offering fashion career advice.

14) Careers-Banking

National Banking & Financial Service Network (NBFSN)
3075 Brickhouse Ct.
Virginia Beach, VA 23452-6860 USA
Phone: 757-463-5766
Fax: 757-340-0826
E-mail Address: smurrell@nbn-jobs.com
Web Address: www.nbn-jobs.com/
The National Banking & Financial Service Network (NBFSN) is made up of recruiting firms in the banking and financial services marketplace. The web site provides job listings.

15) Careers-Biotech

BiotechEmployment.com
E-mail Address: jobs@Biotechemployment.com
Web Address: www.biotechemployment.com
BiotechEmployment.com is an online resource for job seekers in biotechnology. The site's features include resume posting, job search agents and employer profiles. It is part of the eJobstores.com, Inc., which includes the Health Care Job Store sites.

Chase Group (The)
10975 Grandview Dr., Ste. 100
Overland Park, KS 66210 USA
Phone: 913-663-3100
Fax: 913-663-3131
E-mail Address: chase@chasegroup.com
Web Address: www.chasegroup.com
The Chase Group is an executive search firm specializing in biomedical and pharmaceutical placement.

16) Careers-Coatings

CoatingsJobs.com
Web Address: www.coatingsjobs.com
CoatingsJobs.com connects coatings industry job seekers and employers. The web site offers job postings, resume postings, information for job seekers and an employment newsletter.

17) Careers-Computers/Technology

ComputerJobs.com, Inc.
1995 N. Park Pl., Ste. 375
Atlanta, GA 30339 USA
Toll Free: 800-850-0045
Web Address: www.computerjobs.com
ComputerJobs.com, Inc. is an employment web site that offers users a links to computer-related job opportunities organized by skill and market.

Dice.com
12150 Meredith Dr.
Urbandale, IA 50323 USA
Phone: 515-280-1144
Fax: 515-280-1452
Toll Free: 888-321-3423
E-mail Address: techsupport@dice.com
Web Address: www.dice.com
Dice.com provides free employment services for IT jobs. The site includes advanced job searches by geographic location and category, availability announcements and resume postings, as well as employer profiles, a recruiter's page and career links. It is maintained by Dice Holdings, Inc., a publicly traded company.

Institute for Electrical and Electronics Engineers (IEEE) Job Site
445 Hoes Ln.
Piscataway, NJ 08855-1331 USA
Phone: 732-981-0060
Toll Free: 800-678-4333
E-mail Address: candidatejobsite@ieee.org
Web Address: careers.ieee.org
The Institute for Electrical and Electronics Engineers (IEEE) Job Site provides a host of employment services for technical professionals, employers and recruiters. The site offers job listings by geographic area, a resume bank and links to employment services.

Pencom Systems, Inc.
152 Remsen St.
Brooklyn, NY 11201 USA
Phone: 718-923-1111
Fax: 718-923-6065
E-mail Address: tom@pencom.com
Web Address: www.pencom.com
Pencom Systems, Inc., an open system recruiting company, hosts a career web site geared toward high-technology and scientific professionals, featuring an interactive salary survey, career advisor, job listings and technology resources. Its focus is the financial services industry within the New York City area.

18) Careers-Contract & Freelance

Guru.com
5001 Baum Blvd., Ste. 760
Pittsburgh, PA 15213 USA
Toll Free: 888-678-0136
Web Address: www.guru.com
Guru.com provides contract job access for freelancers and contract workers, in fields ranging from interior design to architecture, marketing and web design, among others. Employers can post projects, and freelancers can offer bids on prospective jobs. Many tools are provided to enable freelancers to be completely informed about the scope of the work needed.

19) Careers-First Time Jobs/New Grads

CollegeGrad.com, Inc.
950 Tower Ln., Fl. 6
Foster City, CA 94404 USA
E-mail Address: info@quinstreet.com
Web Address: www.collegegrad.com
CollegeGrad.com, Inc. offers in-depth resources for college students and recent grads seeking entry-level jobs.

MonsterCollege
444 N. Michigan Ave., Ste. 600
Chicago, IL 60611 USA
E-mail Address: info@college.monster.com
Web Address: www.college.monster.com
MonsterCollege provides information about internships and entry-level jobs, as well as career advice and resume tips, to recent college graduates.

National Association of Colleges and Employers (NACE)
62 Highland Ave.
Bethlehem, PA 18017-9085 USA
Phone: 610-868-1421
E-mail Address: customer_service@naceweb.org
Web Address: www.naceweb.org
The National Association of Colleges and Employers (NACE) is a premier U.S. organization representing college placement offices and corporate recruiters who focus on hiring new grads.

20) Careers-General Job Listings

6FigureJobs
25 3rd St., Ste. 230
Stamford, CT 06905 USA
Phone: 203-326-8777

Toll Free: 800-605-5154
E-mail Address: info@6figurejobs.com
Web Address: www.6figurejobs.com
6FigureJobs offers executives a database of high-level positions. Membership is free for qualified individuals.

CareerBuilder, Inc.
200 N La Salle St., Ste. 1100
Chicago, IL 60601 USA
Phone: 773-527-3600
Fax: 773-353-2452
Toll Free: 800-891-8880
Web Address: www.careerbuilder.com
CareerBuilder, Inc. focuses on the needs of companies and also provides a database of job openings. The site has over 1 million jobs posted by 300,000 employers, and receives an average 23 million unique visitors monthly. The company also operates online career centers for 140 newspapers and 9,000 online partners. Resumes are sent directly to the company, and applicants can set up a special e-mail account for job-seeking purposes. CareerBuilder is primarily a joint venture between three newspaper giants: The McClatchy Company, Gannett Co., Inc. and Tribune Company.

CareerOneStop
Toll Free: 877-872-5627
E-mail Address: info@careeronestop.org
Web Address: www.careeronestop.org
CareerOneStop is operated by the employment commissions of various state agencies. It contains job listings in both the private and government sectors, as well as a wide variety of useful career resources and workforce information. CareerOneStop is sponsored by the U.S. Department of Labor.

Careers Organization (The)
4300 Horton St.
Emeryville, CA 94608 USA
Phone: 510-761-5805
Web Address: www.careers.org
The Career Organization is an online career resource center with links to jobs and other career-related web sites, as well as information regarding colleges and online degree programs.

CollegeRecruiter.com
3109 W. 50 St., Ste. 121
Minneapolis, MN 55410-2102 USA
Phone: 952-848-2211
Web Address: www.collegerecruiter.com
CollegeRecruiter.com provides college students with internship, part-time and summer job listings. Recent graduates can search for career opportunities by category and location.

ContractJobHunter
C. E. Publications, Inc.
P.O. Box 3006
Bothell, WA 98041-3006 USA
Phone: 425-806-5200
Fax: 425-806-5585
E-mail Address: staff@cjhunter.com
Web Address: cjhunter.com
ContractJobHunter is a web-based version of the magazine Contract Employment Weekly Online. It posts job listings and links to contract firms in the engineering, IT and technical fields. Libraries for reference materials and resume writing guidelines are also offered. The site is a service of C. E. Publications, Inc.

eFinancialCareers
1040 Ave. of the Americas, Ste. 16B
New York, NY 10018 USA
Phone: 212-370-8502
Web Address: www.efinancialcareers.com
eFinancialCareers.com provides employment listings in the finance industry, as well as job tools such as salary surveys, resume writing assistance and industry news. It is owned DHI Group, Inc.

EmploymentGuide
4460 Corporation Ln., Ste. 317
Virginia Beach, VA 23462 USA
Toll Free: 877-876-4039
Web Address: www.employmentguide.com
EmploymentGuide offers general career resources along with lists of position openings, company profiles and a resume database. It also circulates a free print publication.

EscapeArtist International
300 Caye Financial Center, Coconut Dr.
P.O. Box 11
San Pedro, Belize
Web Address: www.escapeartist.com
EscapeArtist.com provides job searches for overseas positions, as well as international working condition resources and immigration information. It's an online resource offering information, analysis and insights for international expat community in areas of business opportunities, employment, asset protection, investments and international real estate.

ExecuNet, Inc.
295 Westport Ave.
Norwalk, CT 06851 USA
Toll Free: 800-637-3126
E-mail Address: member.services@execunet.com
Web Address: www.execunet.com
ExecuNet, Inc. is an executive career management information and contact service. It's a private career network for executives at the senior level offering career advancement, recruitment, coaching and advisory and peer networking opportunities.

HigherEdJobs.com
328 Innovation Blvd., Ste. 300
State College, PA 16803 USA
Phone: 814-861-3080
Fax: 814-861-3082
E-mail Address: sales@HigherEdJobs.com
Web Address: www.higheredjobs.com
HigherEdJobs.com lists job vacancies in colleges and universities.

IMDiversity, Inc.
201 St. Charles Ave., Ste. 2502
New Orleans, LA 70170 USA
Phone: 281-265-2472
Fax: 281-265-2476
E-mail Address: admin@indiversity.com
Web Address: www.imdiversity.com
IMDiversity, Inc. provides job listings and career development information for minorities in the U.S., with a particular focus on African Americans, Asian Americans and Pacific Islanders, Latino/Hispanic Americans, Native Americans and women.

Indeed.com
6433 Champion Grandview Way, Bldg. 1
Austin, TX 78750 USA
Web Address: www.indeed.com
Indeed.com provides extensive lists of jobs of all types, with links directly to the employers. It covers over 60 countries, including the U.S., Canada, India, Mexico.

Job Search USA
E-mail Address: contactjsu@jobsearchusa.org
Web Address: www.jobsearchusa.org
Job Search USA is a major job posting site that contains job opportunities classified by a variety of keywords.

Jobs in Logistics
Toll Free: 877-562-7678
Web Address: www.jobsinlogistics.com
Jobs in Logistics is an online job board, which provides contacts for job seekers in the transportation, manufacturing, freight forwarding, warehousing, purchasing, inventory management and logistics fields.

JobSearchUSA.org
Web Address: www.jobsearchusa.org

Founded in 2006, Job Search USA is an all-purpose job search web site offering job listings from various organizations including not for profits, small businesses, corporations and educational institutions. Job Search USA was developed from the concept of integrating the best features, design practices and privacy principles of the leading US job search websites.

LaborMarketInfo (LMI)
Employment Development Dept.
P.O. Box 826880, MIC 57
Sacramento, CA 94280-0001 USA
Phone: 916-262-2162
Fax: 916-262-2352
Web Address: www.labormarketinfo.edd.ca.gov
LaborMarketInfo (LMI) provides job seekers and employers a wide range of resources, namely the ability to find, access and use labor market information and services. It provides statistics for employment demographics on both a local and regional level, as well as career searching tools for California residents. The web site is sponsored by California's Employment Development Office.

MediaBistro.com
825 Eighth Ave., Fl. 29
New York, NY 10019 USA
E-mail Address: support@mediabistro.com
Web Address: www.mediabistro.com
MediaBistro.com provides news and information on current events relating to the media industry. It also offers an array of employment resources, including job listings within the industry.

Monster Worldwide, Inc.
622 Third Ave., Fl. 39
New York, NY 10017 USA
Phone: 212-351-7000
Fax: 646-658-0540
E-mail Address: ir@monster.com
Web Address: www.monster.com
Monster Worldwide, Inc., parent company of Monster.com, provides online career and personnel services. The firm operates in over 40 countries.

MyResumeAgent.com
24 Railroad St.
Kennedy Information, LLC
Keene, NH 03431 USA
Phone: 603-357-8104
Toll Free: 800-531-0007
E-mail Address: customerservice@kennedyinfo.com
Web Address: www.myresumeagent.com
MyResumeAgent.com allows senior-level professionals to have their resumes sent to executive placement firms for a fee. The site is owned by Kennedy Information, Inc.

NationJob, Inc.
920 Morgan St., Ste. T
Des Moines, IA 50309 USA
Fax: 515-243-5384
Toll Free: 888-292-7731
E-mail Address: customerservice@nationjob.com
Web Address: www.nationjob.com
NationJob.com is an online job search portal. The web site allows users to search through listings or develop a profile of the ideal job based on the criterion of location, industry, salary; and, if they provide an e-mail address, wait for appropriate listings to be sent to them through the firm's PJScout feature.

NETSHARE, Inc.
359 Bel Marin Keys, Ste. 24
Novato, CA 94949 USA
Toll Free: 800-241-5642
E-mail Address: netshare@netshare.com
Web Address: www.netshare.com
Netshare provides access to exclusive listings of executive jobs that pay $100,000 and up.

Net-Temps, Inc.
55 Middlesex St., Ste. 220
North Chelmsford, MA 01863 USA
Fax: 978-251-7250
Toll Free: 800-307-0062
E-mail Address: service@net-temps.com
Web Address: www.net-temps.com
Net-Temps, Inc. offers a web site, operated by professional career consultants, that features job listings and job seeking tips.

Recruiters Online Network
E-mail Address: rossi.tony@comcast.net
Web Address: www.recruitersonline.com
The Recruiters Online Network provides job postings from thousands of recruiters, Careers Online Magazine, a resume database, as well as other career resources.

USAJOBS
USAJOBS Program Office
1900 E St. NW, Ste. 6500
Washington, DC 20415-0001 USA
Phone: 818-934-6600
Web Address: www.usajobs.gov
USAJOBS, a program of the U.S. Office of Personnel Management, is the official job site for the U.S. Federal Government. It provides a comprehensive list of U.S. government jobs, allowing users to search for employment by location; agency; type of work; or by senior executive positions. It also has special employment sections for individuals with disabilities, veterans and recent college graduates; an information center, offering resume and interview tips and other information; and allows users to create a profile and post a resume.

21) Careers-Health Care

Health Care Source
100 Sylvan Rd., Ste. 100
Woburn, MA 01801 USA
Phone: 781-368-1033
Fax: 800-829-6600
Toll Free: 800-869-5200
E-mail Address: solutions@healthcaresource.com
Web Address: www.healthcaresource.com
Health Care Source is a leading provider of talent management, recruitment and employment services for healthcare providers. It offers a comprehensive suite of solutions, which includes features, such as applicant tracking and onboarding, recruitment optimization, reference checking, behavioral assessments, merit planning, employee performance and eLearning courseware among others.

MedicalWorkers.com
Web Address: www.medicalworkers.com
MedicalWorkers.com is an employment site for medical and health care professionals.

MedJump.com
E-mail Address: info@medjump.com
Web Address: www.medjump.com
MedJump.com is dedicated to empowering health care and medical-related professionals with the necessary tools to market their abilities and skills.

Medzilla, Inc.
P.O. Box 1710
Marysville, WA 98270 USA
Phone: 360-657-5681
Fax: 425-279-5427
E-mail Address: info@medzilla.com
Web Address: www.medzilla.com
Medzilla, Inc.'s web site offers job searches, salary surveys, a search agent and information on employment in the biotech, pharmaceuticals, healthcare and science sectors.

Monster Career Advice-Healthcare
133 Boston Post Rd.
Weston, MA 02493 USA
Phone: 978-461-8000
Fax: 978-461-8100
Toll Free: 800-666-7837

Web Address: career-advice.monster.com/Healthcare/job-category-3975.aspx
Monster Career Advice-Healthcare, a service of Monster Worldwide, Inc., provides industry-related articles, job listings, job searches and search agents for the medical field.

NationJob Network-Medical and Health Care Jobs Page
920 Morgan St., Ste. T
Des Moines, IA 50309 USA
Fax: 515-243-5384
Toll Free: 800-292-7731
E-mail Address: customerservice@nationjob.com
Web Address: www.nationjob.com/medical
The NationJob Network-Medical and Health Care Jobs Page offers information and listings for health care employment.

Nurse-Recruiter.com
15500 SW Jay St., Ste. 26760
Beaverton, OR 97006-6018 USA
Toll Free: 877-562-7966
Web Address: www.nurse-recruiter.com
Nurse-Recruiter.com is an online job portal devoted to bringing health care employers and the nursing community together.

PracticeLink
415 2nd Ave.
Hinton, WV 25951 USA
Toll Free: 800-776-8383
E-mail Address: helpdesk@practicelink.com
Web Address: www.practicelink.com
PracticeLink, one of the largest physician employment web sites, is a free service with over 1.7 million page views each month. There are more than 5,000 hospitals, medical groups, private practices and health systems, posting over 20,000 physician job opportunities on the web site.

RPh on the Go USA, Inc.
8001 N. Lincoln Ave., Ste. 800
Skokie, IL 60077 USA
Phone: 847-588-7170
Fax: 847-588-7060
Toll Free: 800-553-7359
Web Address: www.rphonthego.com
RPh on the Go USA, Inc. places temporary and permanent qualified professionals in the pharmacy community. This pharmacy staffing firm offers access to more than 160,000 pharmacy professionals and matches the right pharmacy personnel to help meet clients' needs.

22) Careers-Job Listings for Seniors

Dinosaur Exchange
Sutherland House
1759, London Rd.
Leigh-on-Sea, Essex SS9 @RZ UK
Phone: 44-1702--470531
E-mail Address: CustomerSupport@dinosaur-exchange.com
Web Address: www.dinosaur-exchange.com
Dinosaur Exchange, opened in 2003, is a job forum for the elderly, which allows seniors to post resumes and be contacted by employers. Dino-X Ltd. owns and operates the web site.

Employment Network for Retired Government Experts (ENRGE)
Zavala, Inc.
P.O. Box 1532
N. Falmouth, MA 02556 USA
Phone: 508-564-4140
Web Address: www.enrge.us
The Employment Network for Retired Government Experts (ENRGE) helps government employees to remain active in their professions after retirement. ENERGE is the business name of Zavala, Inc.

Senior Job Bank
NHC Group, Inc.
P.O. Box 508
Marlborough, MA 01752 USA
Toll Free: 866-562-2627
E-mail Address: publisher@seniorjobbank.org
Web Address: www.seniorjobbank.org
The Senior Job Bank web site offers an easy, effective and free method for senior citizens to find occasional, part-time, flexible, temporary or full-time jobs. The site is owned and managed by NHC Group, Inc.

Seniors4Hire.org
7071 Warner Ave. F466
Huntington Beach, CA 92647 USA
Phone: 714-848-0996
Fax: 714-848-5445
Toll Free: 800-906-7107
E-mail Address: info@seniors4hire.org
Web Address: www.seniors4hire.org
Seniors4Hire.org is an online career center with job postings, employment resources and information on community service employment programs for older workers, retirees and senior citizens. The site is owned and operated by The Forward Group.

YourEncore
20 N. Meridian St., Ste. 800
Indianapolis, IN 46204 USA
Phone: 317-226-9301
Fax: 317-226-9312
E-mail Address: info@yourencore.com
Web Address: www.yourencore.com
YourEncore is a program that seeks to employ retirees by matching them with member companies. The web site utilizes retirees mainly in the areas of engineering, science and product development.

23) Careers-Job Listings Hong Kong, China, Singapore, Asia

CareerJet
Web Address: www.careerjet.hk
CareerJet provides excellent search tools leading to job listings in Hong Kong, China and throughout Asia.

Careers@Gov
Web Address: www.careers.gov.sg
Careers@Gov is the government-sponsored job search site within Singapore.

CT Good Jobs
Web Address: www.ctgoodjobs.hk
CT Good Jobs provides easy to use job listings. It also offers online communities in such areas as retail, human resources and finance.

HeadHunt
Web Address: www.headhunt.com.sg/
HeadHunt bills itself as an executive job search site for Singapore.

JobMarket
Web Address: www.jobmarket.com.hk
JobMarket features a very detailed advanced search option.

JobsCentral Singapore
Web Address: http://jobscentral.com.sg/
JobsCentral Singapore is maintained by CareerBuilder.

jobsDB
Web Address: http://hk.jobsdb.com/hk
jobsDB provides well organized job listings in Hong Kong, Indonesia, Malaysia, Philippines, Singapore, Thailand and China.

JobStreet
Web Address: www.jobstreet.sg
JobStreet is an extensive job search site focused in positions within Singapore.

Monster Hong Kong
Web Address: www.monster.com.hk/
Monster Hong Kong provides easy online access to thousands of jobs in Hong Kong, Macau, Mainland China and Taiwan.

Monster Singapore
Web Address: www.monster.com.sg/
Monster Singapore is specific to the Singapore area.

Recruit
Web Address: www.recruit.com.hk
Recruit provides job news, job tips employer new and job listings in the Hong Kong area.

Singapore Jobs Online
Web Address: www.singaporejobsonline.com/
Singapore Jobs Online enables job searches within Singapore for a wide variety of job categories.

STJobs
Web Address: www.stjobs.sg/site/index
STJobs is an extensive web site offering job search within Singapore and the surrounding area.

24) Careers-Job Reference Tools

CareerXroads (CXR)
7 Clark Ct.
Kendall Park, NJ 08824-1810 USA
Phone: 732-821-6652
E-mail Address: mmc@careerxroads.com
Web Address: www.careerxroads.com
CareerXroads (CXR) publishes an annual guide on job and resume web sites. It was cofounded by Gerry Crispin and Mark Mehler.

Job-Hunt.org
186 Main St.
NETability, Inc.
Marlborough, MA 01752 USA
Phone: 508-624-6261
E-mail Address: info@job-hunt.org
Web Address: www.job-hunt.org
Job-Hunt.org, rather than collecting resumes or posting job vacancies, offers a vast list of job listing web sites and links to helpful job search tools. It is owned by NETability, Inc.

jobipedia.org
E-mail Address: info@jobipedia.org
Web Address: www.jobipedia.org
jobipedia.org is a public service provided by the HR Policy Association to help new entrants into the workforce find jobs. Every answer you read on jobipedia was written by someone from a large employer who actually hires employees for a living.

MBA Career Services Council (CSC)
P.O. Box 47478
Tampa, FL 33646-7478 USA
Phone: 813-220-3191
Fax: 813-319-4952
E-mail Address: execdirector@mbacsc.org
Web Address: www.mbacsc.org
The MBA Career Services Council (CSC) is a global professional association for individuals in the field of MBA career services and those that recruit directly from graduate management programs.

Vault.com, Inc.
132 W. 31st St., Fl. 17
New York, NY 10001 USA
Fax: 212-366-6117
Toll Free: 800-535-2074
E-mail Address: customerservice@vault.com
Web Address: www.vault.com
Vault.com, Inc. is a comprehensive career web site for employers and employees, with job postings and valuable information on a wide variety of industries. Its features and content are largely geared toward MBA degree holders.

What Color is Your Parachute?
E-mail Address: rnbolles@jobhuntersbible.com
Web Address: www.jobhuntersbible.com
The What Color is Your Parachute? official web site, JobHuntersBible.com, is based on the Job-Hunting on the Internet chapter of Richard (Dick) Bolle's best-selling book. Designed to aid job hunters and career changers who want to use the Internet as part of their job search, the site provides links to job listing, resume, career counseling, contacts and research sites.

25) Careers-Restaurants

FoodService.com
24 W. Camelback Rd., Ste. 104
Phoenix, AZ 85013 USA
Phone: 602-381-3663
Web Address: www.foodservice.com
FoodService.com, managed and run by Food Service Interactive, LLC, offers web site design and job search services for the food service industry.

Resources in Food, Inc. (RIF)
417 S Lincolnway, Ste. B
North Aurora, IL 60542 USA
Phone: 630-801-0469
Fax: 630-357-7548
Toll Free: 877-743-1100
E-mail Address: jgrimm@rifood.com
Web Address: www.rifood.com
Resources in Food (RIF) provides professional management placement for the hospitality, food manufacturing, food services, restaurants and wholesale grocery industry.

26) Careers-Science

Chem Jobs
730 E. Cypress Ave.
Monrovia, CA 91016 USA
Phone: 626-930-0808
Fax: 626-930-0102
E-mail Address: info@chemindustry.com
Web Address: www.chemjobs.net
Chem Jobs is a leading Internet site for job seekers in chemistry and related fields, with a particular focus on chemists, biochemists, pharmaceutical scientists and chemical engineers. The web site is powered by Chemindustry.com.

New Scientist Jobs
Quadrant House
Sutton
Surrey, SM2 5AS UK
Phone: 781-734-8770
E-mail Address: nssales@newscientist.com
Web Address: jobs.newscientist.com
New Scientist Jobs is a web site produced by the publishers of New Scientist Magazine that connects jobseekers and employers in the bioscience fields. The site includes a job search engine and a free-of-charge e-mail job alert service.

Science Careers
Phone: 202-312-6375
Web Address: jobs.sciencecareers.org
Science Careers is a web site that contains many useful categories of links, including employment newsgroups, scientific journals, hob postings and placement agencies. It also links to sites containing information regarding internship and fellowship opportunities for high school students, undergrads, graduates, doctoral and post-doctoral students.

27) Careers-Sports

Jobs in Sports
106 Calendar Ave., Ste. 184
LaGrange, IL 60525 USA
Web Address: www.jobsinsports.com
Jobs in Sports is an employment web site that provides job listings in areas including sports marketing, sports media, sales, health and fitness, computers and

administration, as well as other job resources.

Sports Careers
Web Address: www.sportscareers.com
Sports Careers offers a range of services to help individuals and employers in the sports industry, including job listings, a resume bank, industry contacts and salary information.

Sports Job Board
Web Address: www.sportsjobboard.com
The Sports Job Board is an employment web site for the sports industry.

WomenSportsJobs.com
Women's Sport Services, LLC
P.O. Box 11
Huntington Beach, CA 92648 USA
Phone: 714-848-1201
Fax: 714-848-5111
E-mail Address: Feedback@WSServices.com
Web Address: www.womensportsjobs.com
WomenSportsJobs.com is an employment web site specializing in jobs for women in the sports industry. The site is managed by Women's Sport Services, LLC.

Work in Sports LLC
7335 E. Chauncey Ln., Ste. 115
Phoenix, AZ 85054 USA
Phone: 480-905-7221
Fax: 480-905-7231
Web Address: www.workinsports.com
Work in Sports LLC is an online employment resource for the sports industry that posts hundreds of jobs on its web site.

28) Careers-Video Games Industry

GameJobs
Web Address: www.gamejobs.com
GameJobs.com is independently owned and operated by the Crest Group, LLC, the managers of the Entertainment Consumers Association (ECA), a non-profit membership association. It offers both employers and job seekers in the interactive entertainment industry access to online tools and resources, such as post resume and job openings to accomplish their respective goals.

Video Game Jobs-About.com Career Planning
Web Address: http://careerplanning.about.com/od/occupations/a/videogamecareer.htm
A useful page on About.com that contains advice and links for people interested in working in the video games industry.

29) Chemicals Industry Associations

American Chemical Society (ACS)
1155 16th St. NW
Washington, DC 20036 USA
Phone: 202-872-4600
Toll Free: 800-227-5558
E-mail Address: help@acs.org
Web Address: www.acs.org
The American Chemical Society (ACS) is a nonprofit organization aimed at promoting the understanding of chemistry and chemical sciences. It represents a wide range of disciplines including chemistry, chemical engineering and other technical fields.

30) Communications Professional Associations

Association for Women In Communications (AWC)
1717 E Republic Rd., Ste. A
Springfield, MO 65804 USA
Phone: 417-886-8606
Fax: 417-886-3685
E-mail Address: members@womcom.org
Web Address: www.womcom.org
The Association for Women In Communications (AWC) is a professional organization that works for the advancement of women across all communications disciplines by recognizing excellence, promoting leadership and positioning its members at the forefront of the communications industry.

Health and Science Communications Association (HeSCA)
P.O. Box 31323
Omaha, NE 68132 USA
Phone: 402-915-5373
E-mail Address: hesca@hesca.org
Web Address: hesca.net
The Health and Science Communications Association (HeSCA) is an organization of communications professionals committed to sharing knowledge and resources in the health sciences arena.

Health Industry Business Communications Council (HIBCC)
2525 E. Arizona Biltmore Cir., Ste. 127
Phoenix, AZ 85016 USA
Phone: 602-381-1091
Fax: 602-381-1093
E-mail Address: info@hibcc.org
Web Address: www.hibcc.org
The Health Industry Business Communications Council (HIBCC) seeks to facilitate electronic communications by developing appropriate standards for information exchange among all health care trading partners.

International Association of Business Communicators (IABC)
155 Montgomery St., Ste. 1210
San Francisco, CA 94111 USA
Phone: 415-544-4700
Fax: 415-544-4747
Toll Free: 800-776-4222
Web Address: www.iabc.com
The International Association of Business Communicators (IABC) is the leading resource for effective business communication practices.

31) Computer & Electronics Industry Associations

Electronics Technicians Association international (ETA International)
5 Depot St.
Greencastle, IN 46135 USA
Phone: 765-653-8262
Fax: 765-653-4287
Toll Free: 800-288-3824
E-mail Address: eta@eta-i.org
Web Address: www.eta-i.org
The Electronics Technicians Association International (ETA International) is a nonprofit professional association for electronics technicians worldwide. The organization provides recognized professional credentials for electronics technicians.

Semiconductor Industry Association (SIA)
1101 K St. NW, Ste. 450
Washington, DC 20005 USA
Phone: 202-446-1700
Fax: 202-216-9745
Toll Free: 866-756-0715
Web Address: www.semiconductors.org
The Semiconductor Industry Association (SIA) is a trade association representing the semiconductor industry in the U.S. Through its coalition of more than 60 companies, SIA members represent roughly 80% of semiconductor production in the U.S. The coalition aims to advance the competitiveness of the chip industry and shape public policy on issues particular to the industry.

32) Consulting Industry Associations

Association of Internal Management Consultants (AIMC)
720 North Collier Blvd., Ste. 201
Marco Island, FL 34145 USA
Phone: 239-642-0580
Web Address: www.aimc.org
The Association of Internal Management Consultants (AIMC) is a professional association representing in-house management consultants. Members work in for-profit corporations, government agencies, educational institutions and nonprofit organizations.

Association of Management Consulting Firms (AMCF)
370 Lexington Ave., Ste. 2209
New York, NY 10017 USA
Phone: 212-262-3055
Fax: 212-262-3054
E-mail Address: info@amcf.org
Web Address: www.amcf.org
The Association of Management Consulting Firms (AMCF) is a recognized leader in promoting the management consulting industry. AMCF represents a diverse list of international members, from large, multinational companies to small, regional firms.

Institute of Management Consultants USA (IMC)
631 U.S. Highway One, Ste. 400
North Palm Beach, FL 33408 USA
Phone: 561-472-0833
Toll Free: 800-837-7321
Web Address: www.imcusa.org
The Institute of Management Consultants USA (IMC) certifies management consultants in accordance with the strict international standards of the International Council of Management Consulting Institutes.

Investment Management Consultant Association (IMCA)
5619 DTC Pkwy., Ste. 500
Greenwood Village, CO 80111 USA
Phone: 303-770-3377
Fax: 303-770-1812
E-mail Address: imca@imca.org
Web Address: www.imca.org
The Investment Management Consultant Association (IMCA) provides information and communication for investment management consultants.

33) Consulting Industry Resources

Consulting Magazine
120 Broadway, Fl.5
New York, NY 10271 USA
Phone: 877-256-2472
Web Address: www.consultingmag.com
Consulting Magazine is a leading online publication for the consulting industry, and features information on consulting careers, thought leadership and corporate strategies. The web site is owned and operated by ALM Media, LLC.

34) Corporate Information Resources

bizjournals.com
120 W. Morehead St., Ste. 400
Charlotte, NC 28202 USA
Toll Free: 866-853-3661
E-mail Address: gmurchison@bizjournals.com
Web Address: www.bizjournals.com
Bizjournals.com is the online media division of American City Business Journals, the publisher of dozens of leading city business journals nationwide. It provides access to research into the latest news regarding companies both small and large. The organization maintains 42 websites and 64 print publications and sponsors over 700 annual industry events.

Business Wire
101 California St., Fl. 20
San Francisco, CA 94111 USA
Phone: 415-986-4422
Fax: 415-788-5335
Toll Free: 800-227-0845
E-mail Address: info@businesswire.com
Web Address: www.businesswire.com
Business Wire offers news releases, industry- and company-specific news, top headlines, conference calls, IPOs on the Internet, media services and access to tradeshownews.com and BW Connect On-line through its informative and continuously updated web site.

Edgar Online, Inc.
11200 Rockville Pike, Ste. 310
Rockville, MD 20852 USA
Phone: 301-287-0300
Fax: 301-287-0390
Toll Free: 888-870-2316
Web Address: www.edgar-online.com
Edgar Online, Inc. is a gateway and search tool for viewing corporate documents, such as annual reports on Form 10-K, filed with the U.S. Securities and Exchange Commission.

PR Newswire Association LLC
350 Hudson St., Ste. 300
New York, NY 10014-4504 USA
Fax: 800-793-9313
Toll Free: 800-776-8090
E-mail Address: MediaInquiries@prnewswire.com
Web Address: www.prnewswire.com
PR Newswire Association LLC provides comprehensive communications services for public relations and investor relations professionals, ranging from information distribution and market intelligence to the creation of online multimedia content and investor relations web sites. Users can also view recent corporate press releases from companies across the globe. The Association is owned by United Business Media plc.

Silicon Investor
E-mail Address: si.admin@siliconinvestor.com
Web Address: www.siliconinvestor.com
Silicon Investor is focused on providing information about technology companies. Its web site serves as a financial discussion forum and offers quotes, profiles and charts.

35) Disabling Conditions

Job Accommodation Network (JAN)
P.O. Box 6080
Morgantown, WV 26506-6080 USA
Phone: 304-293-7186
Fax: 304-293-5407
Toll Free: 800-526-7234
E-mail Address: jan@askjan.org
Web Address: askjan.org
The Job Accommodation Network (JAN) is a free consulting service that provides guidance and information about job accommodations, the Americans with Disabilities Act and the employability of people with disabilities.

36) Electronic Health Records/Continuity of Care Records

American Health Information Management Association (AHIMA)
233 N. Michigan Ave., Fl. 21
Chicago, IL 60601-5809 USA
Phone: 312-233-1100
Fax: 312-233-1090
Toll Free: 800-335-5535
Web Address: www.ahima.org
The American Health Information Management Association (AHIMA) is a professional association that consists health information management professionals who work throughout the health care industry.

American Medical Informatics Association (AMIA)
4720 Montgomery Ln., Ste. 500
Bethesda, MD 20814 USA
Phone: 301-657-1291
Fax: 301-657-1296
Web Address: www.amia.org
The American Medical Informatics Association (AMIA) is a membership organization of individuals, institutions and corporations dedicated to developing and using information technologies to improve health care.

College of Healthcare Information Management Executives (CHIME)
710 Avis Dr., Ste. 200
Ann Arbor, MI 48108 USA
Phone: 734-665-0000
Fax: 734-665-4922
E-mail Address: staff@cio-chime.org
Web Address: www.cio-chime.org
College of Healthcare Information Management Executives (CHIME) was formed with the dual objective of serving the professional development needs of health care CIOs and advocating the more effective use of information management within health care.

Healthcare Information and Management Systems Society (HIMSS)
33 W Monroe St., Ste. 1700
Chicago, IL 60603-5616 USA
Phone: 312-664-4467
Fax: 312-664-6143
Web Address: www.himss.org
The Healthcare Information and Management Systems Society (HIMSS) provides leadership in the optimal use of technology, information and management systems for the betterment of health care.

37) Energy Associations- Electric Power

American Public Power Association (APPA)
2451 Crystal Dr., Ste. 1000
Arlington, VA 22202-4804 USA
Phone: 202-467-2900
E-mail Address: info@PublicPower.org
Web Address: www.publicpower.org
The American Public Power Association (APPA) is a nonprofit service organization for the country's community-owned electric utilities, dedicated to advancing the public policy interests of its members and their consumers.

Edison Electric Institute (EEI)
701 Pennsylvania Ave. NW
Washington, DC 20004-2696 USA
Phone: 202-508-5000
E-mail Address: feedback@eei.org
Web Address: www.eei.org
The Edison Electric Institute (EEI) is an association of U.S. shareholder-owned electric companies as well as worldwide affiliates and industry associates. Its web site provides energy news and a link to Electric Perspectives magazine.

Women's International Network of Utility Professionals (WINUP)
P.O. Box 64
Grove City, OH 43123-0064 USA
Phone: 614-738-0603
E-mail Address: winup@att.net
Web Address: www.winup.org
The Women's International Network of Utility Professionals (WINUP) provides networking and support for women in the utility industry.

38) Energy Associations- Natural Gas

American Gas Association (AGA)
400 N. Capitol St. NW, Ste. 450
Washington, DC 20001 USA
Phone: 202-824-7000
Web Address: www.aga.org
The American Gas Association (AGA) represents a large number of natural gas providers, advocating for these companies and providing a broad range of programs and services for members.

39) Energy Associations-Other

American Association of Blacks in Energy
1625 K St. NW, Ste. 450
Washington, DC 20006 USA
Phone: 202-371-9530
Fax: 202-371-9218
E-mail Address: info@aabe.org
Web Address: www.aabe.org
The American Association of Blacks in Energy is dedicated to ensuring the input of African Americans and other minorities in discussions and developments of energy policies, regulations, research and development technologies and environmental issues.

40) Energy Associations- Petroleum, Exploration, Production, etc.

American Association of Professional Landmen (AAPL)
800 Fournier St.
Fort Worth, TX 76102 USA
Phone: 817-847-7700
Fax: 817-847-7704
E-mail Address: aapl@landman.org
Web Address: www.landman.org
The American Association of Professional Landmen (AAPL) promotes the highest standards of performance for all land professionals and seeks to advance their stature and to encourage sound stewardship of energy and mineral resources.

American Petroleum Institute (API)
1220 L St. NW
Washington, DC 20005-4070 USA
Phone: 202-682-8000
Web Address: www.api.org
American Petroleum Institute (API) represents U.S. oil and gas industries and its web site includes in-depth sections for energy consumers and energy professionals.

Independent Petroleum Association of America (IPAA)
1201 15th St. NW, Ste. 300
Washington, DC 20005 USA
Phone: 202-857-4722
Fax: 202-857-4799
E-mail Address: nkirby@ipaa.org
Web Address: www.ipaa.org
The Independent Petroleum Association of America (IPAA) provides a forum for the exploration and production segment of the independent oil and natural gas business. It also provides information on the domestic exploration and production industry.

International Association of Drilling Contractors (IADC)
10370 Richmond Ave., Ste. 760
Houston, TX 77042 USA
Phone: 713-292-1945
Fax: 713-292-1946
E-mail Address: info@iadc.org
Web Address: www.iadc.org
The International Association of Drilling Contractors (IADC) represents the worldwide oil and gas drilling industry and promotes commitment to safety, preservation of the environment and advances in drilling technology.

41) Engineering, Research & Scientific Associations

American Association of Petroleum Geologists (AAPG)
1444 S. Boulder Ave.
Tulsa, OK 74119 USA
Phone: 918-584-2555
Fax: 918-560-2665
Toll Free: 800-364-2274
Web Address: www.aapg.org

The American Association of Petroleum Geologists (AAPG) is an international geological organization that supports educational and scientific programs and projects related to geosciences.

American Institute of Chemical Engineers (AIChE)
120 Wall St., Fl. 23
New York, NY 10005-4020 USA
Phone: 203-702-7660
Fax: 203-775-5177
Toll Free: 800-242-4363
Web Address: www.aiche.org
The American Institute of Chemical Engineers (AIChE) provides leadership in advancing the chemical engineering profession. The organization, which is comprised of more than 50,000 members from over 100 countries, provides informational resources to chemical engineers.

American Society for Healthcare Engineering (ASHE)
155 N. Wacker Dr., Ste. 400
Chicago, IL 60606 USA
Phone: 312-422-3800
Fax: 312-422-4571
E-mail Address: ashe@aha.org
Web Address: www.ashe.org
The American Society for Healthcare Engineering (ASHE) is the advocate and resource for continuous improvement in the health care engineering and facilities management professions. It is devoted to professionals who design, build, maintain and operate hospitals and other healthcare facilities.

American Society of Agricultural and Biological Engineers (ASABE)
2950 Niles Rd.
St. Joseph, MI 49085 USA
Phone: 269-429-0300
Fax: 269-429-3852
Toll Free: 800-371-2723
E-mail Address: hq@asabe.org
Web Address: www.asabe.org
The American Society of Agricultural and Biological Engineers (ASABE) is a nonprofit professional and technical organization interested in engineering knowledge and technology for food and agriculture and associated industries.

American Society of Civil Engineers (ASCE)
1801 Alexander Bell Dr.
Reston, VA 20191-4400 USA
Phone: 703-295-6300
Toll Free: 800-548-2723
Web Address: www.asce.org
The American Society of Civil Engineers (ASCE) is a leading professional organization serving civil engineers. It ensures safer buildings, water systems and other civil engineering works by developing technical codes and standards.

American Society of Safety Engineers (ASSE)
520 N. Northwest Hwy
Park Ridge, IL 60068 USA
Phone: 847-699-2929
E-mail Address: customerservice@asse.org
Web Address: www.asse.org
The American Society of Safety Engineers (ASSE) is the world's oldest and largest professional safety organization. It manages, supervises and consults on safety, health and environmental issues in industry, insurance, government and education.

Association of Federal Communications Consulting Engineers (AFCCE)
P.O. Box 19333
Washington, DC 20036 USA
Web Address: www.afcce.org
The Association of Federal Communications Consulting Engineers (AFCCE) is a professional organization of individuals who regularly assist clients on technical issues before the Federal Communications Commission (FCC).

Institute of Industrial Engineers (IIE)
3577 Parkway Ln., Ste. 200
Norcross, GA 30092 USA
Phone: 770-449-0460
Fax: 770-441-3295
Toll Free: 800-494-0460
E-mail Address: cs@iienet.org
Web Address: www.iienet2.org
The Institute of Industrial Engineers (IIE) is an international, non-profit association dedicated to the education, development, training and research in the field of industrial engineering.

National Society of Professional Engineers (NSPE)
1420 King St.
Alexandria, VA 22314-2794 USA
Fax: 703-836-4875
Toll Free: 888-285-6773
Web Address: www.nspe.org
The National Society of Professional Engineers (NSPE) represents individual engineering professionals and licensed engineers across all disciplines. NSPE serves approximately 45,000 members and has more than 500 chapters.

Society of Automotive Engineers (SAE)
755 W. Big Beaver, Ste. 1600
Troy, MA 48084 USA
Phone: 248-273-2455
Fax: 248-273-2494
Toll Free: 877-606-7323
E-mail Address: automotive_hq@sae.org
Web Address: www.sae.org
The Society of Automotive Engineers (SAE) is a resource for technical information and expertise used in designing, building, maintaining and operating self-propelled vehicles for use on land, sea, air or space.

Society of Broadcast Engineers, Inc. (SBE)
9102 N. Meridian St., Ste. 150
Indianapolis, IN 46260 USA
Phone: 317-846-9000
E-mail Address: jporay@sbe.org
Web Address: www.sbe.org
The Society of Broadcast Engineers (SBE) exists to increase knowledge of broadcast engineering and promote its interests, as well as to continue the education of professionals in the industry.

Society of Cable Telecommunications Engineers (SCTE)
140 Philips Rd.
Exton, PA 19341-1318 USA
Fax: 610-884-7237
Toll Free: 800-542-5040
E-mail Address: scte@scte.org
Web Address: www.scte.org
The Society of Cable Telecommunications Engineers (SCTE) is a nonprofit professional association dedicated to advancing the careers and serving the industry of telecommunications professionals by providing technical training, certification and information resources.

Society of Hispanic Professional Engineers (SHPE)
13181 Crossroads Pkwy. N., Ste. 450
City of Industry, CA 91746 USA
Phone: 323-725-3970
Fax: 323-725-0316
E-mail Address: shpenational@shpe.org
Web Address: oneshpe.shpe.org
The Society of Hispanic Professional Engineers (SHPE) is a national nonprofit organization that promotes Hispanics in science, engineering and math.

Society of Manufacturing Engineers (SME)
One SME Dr.
Dearborn, MI 48121 USA
Phone: 313-425-3000
Fax: 313-425-3400
Toll Free: 800-733-4763
E-mail Address: communications@sme.org
Web Address: www.sme.org

The Society of Manufacturing Engineers (SME) is a leading professional organization serving engineers in the manufacturing industries.

Society of Motion Picture and Television Engineers (SMPTE)
3 Barker Ave., Fl. 5
White Plains, NY 10601 USA
Phone: 914-761-1100
Fax: 914-761-3115
E-mail Address: marketing@smpte.org
Web Address: www.smpte.org
The Society of Motion Picture and Television Engineers (SMPTE) is the leading technical society for the motion imaging industry. The firm publishes recommended practice and engineering guidelines, as well the SMPTE Journal.

Society of Women Engineers (SWE)
230 N La Salle St., Ste. 1675
Chicago, IL 60601 USA
Toll Free: 877-793-4636
E-mail Address: hq@swe.org
Web Address: societyofwomenengineers.swe.org
The Society of Women Engineers (SWE) is a nonprofit educational and service organization of female engineers.

SPIE
1000 20th St.
Bellingham, WA 98225-6705 USA
Phone: 360-676-3290
Fax: 360-647-1445
Toll Free: 888-504-8171
E-mail Address: customerservice@spie.org
Web Address: www.spie.org
SPIE is a nonprofit technical society aimed at the advancement and dissemination of knowledge in optics, photonics and imaging.

42) Entertainment & Amusement Associations-General

International Association of Amusement Parks and Attractions (IAAPA)
1448 Duke St.
Alexandria, VA 22314 USA
Phone: 703-836-4800
Fax: 703-836-4801
E-mail Address: iaapa@iaapa.org
Web Address: www.iaapa.org
The International Association of Amusement Parks and Attractions (IAAPA) is dedicated to the preservation and prosperity of the amusement industry.

International Special Events Society (ISES)
330 N. Wabash Ave., Ste. 2000
Chicago, IL 60611-4267 USA
Phone: 312-321-6853
Fax: 312-673-6953
Toll Free: 800-688-4737
E-mail Address: info@ises.com
Web Address: www.ises.com
The International Special Events Society (ISES) is comprised of over 7,200 professionals in over 38 countries representing special event planners and producers (from festivals to trade shows), caterers, decorators, florists, destination management companies, rental companies, special effects experts, tent suppliers, audio-visual technicians, event and convention coordinators, balloon artists, educators, journalists, hotel sales managers, specialty entertainers, convention center managers, and many more professional disciplines.

43) Film & Theater Associations

Academy of Motion Picture Arts and Sciences (AMPAS)
8949 Wilshire Blvd.
Beverly Hills, CA 90211-1972 USA
Phone: 310-247-3000
Fax: 310-859-9619
Web Address: www.oscars.org
The Academy of Motion Picture Arts and Sciences (AMPAS) is a professional honorary organization, founded to advance the arts and sciences of motion pictures. Besides hosting the Academy Awards and selecting the winners of the Oscars, AMPAS organizes smaller events highlighting the art of filmmaking, including lectures and seminars, and is currently building the Academy Museum of Motion Pictures.

Alliance of Motion Picture and Television Producers (AMPTP)
15301 Ventura Blvd., Bldg. E
Sherman Oaks, CA 91403 USA
Phone: 818-995-3600
Web Address: www.amptp.org
The Alliance of Motion Picture and Television Producers (AMPTP) is the primary trade association with respect to labor issues in the motion picture and television industry.

American Cinema Editors, Inc. (ACE)
100 Universal City Plz.
Verna Fields Bldg. 2282, Rm. 190
Universal City, CA 91608 USA
Phone: 818-777-2900
E-mail Address: amercinema@earthlink.net
Web Address: www.ace-filmeditors.org
American Cinema Editors (ACE) is an honorary society of motion picture editors that seeks to advance the art and science of the editing profession.

American Society of Cinematographers (ASC)
1782 N. Orange Dr.
Hollywood, CA 90028 USA
Phone: 323-969-4333
Fax: 323-882-6391
Toll Free: 800-448-0145
E-mail Address: office@theasc.com
Web Address: www.theasc.com
The American Society of Cinematographers (ASC) is a trade association for cinematographers in the motion picture industry.

Art Directors Guild (ADG)
11969 Ventura Blvd., Fl. 2
Studio City, CA 91604 USA
Phone: 818-762-9995
Fax: 818-760-4847
E-mail Address: nick@artdirectors.org
Web Address: www.artdirectors.org
The Art Directors Guild (ADG) represents the creative talents that conceive and manage the background and settings for most films and television projects.

Association of Cinema and Video Laboratories (ACVL)
Phone: 805-427-2620
E-mail Address: peterbulcke@hotmail.com
Web Address: www.acvl.org
The Association of Cinema and Video Laboratories (ACVL) is an international organization whose members are pledged to the highest possible standards of service to the film and video industries.

Independent Film & Television Alliance (IFTA)
10850 Wilshire Blvd., Fl. 9
Los Angeles, CA 90024-4311 USA
Phone: 310-446-1000
Fax: 310-446-1600
E-mail Address: info@ifta-online.org
Web Address: www.ifta-online.org
The Independent Film & Television Alliance (IFTA), formerly the American Film Marketing Association (AFMA), is a trade association whose mission is to provide the independent film and television industry with high-quality, market-oriented services and worldwide representation.

International Alliance of Theatrical Stage Employees (IATSE)
207 W. 25th St., Fl. 4
New York, NY 10001 USA

Phone: 212-730-1770
Fax: 212-730-7809
E-mail Address: webmaster@iatse-intl.org
Web Address: www.iatse-intl.org
The International Alliance of Theatrical Stage Employees (IATSE) is the labor union representing technicians, artisans and crafts workers in the entertainment industry, including live theater, film and television production and trade shows.

International Animated Film Society (ASIFA-Hollywood)
2114 W. Burbank Blvd.
Burbank, CA 91506 USA
Phone: 818-842-8330
E-mail Address: info@asifa-hollywood.org
Web Address: www.asifa-hollywood.org
International Animated Film Society (ASIFA-Hollywood) is a nonprofit organization dedicated to the advancement of the art of animation.

International Documentary Association (IDA)
3470 Wilshire Blvd., Ste. 980
Los Angeles, CA 90010 USA
Phone: 213-232-1660
Fax: 213-232-1669
E-mail Address: michael@documentary.org
Web Address: www.documentary.org
The International Documentary Association (IDA) is a nonprofit member service organization, providing publications, benefits and a public forum to its members for issues regarding nonfiction film, video and multimedia.

Motion Picture Association of America (MPAA)
15301 Ventura Blvd., Bldg. E
Sherman Oaks, CA 91403 USA
Phone: 818-995-6600
Fax: 818-285-4403
E-mail Address: ContactUs@mpaa.org
Web Address: www.mpaa.org
The Motion Picture Association of America (MPAA) serves as the voice and advocate of the U.S. motion picture, home video and television industries.

Motion Picture Editors Guild (MPEG)
7715 Sunset Blvd., Ste. 200
Hollywood, CA 90046 USA
Phone: 323-876-4770
Fax: 323-876-0861
Toll Free: 800-705-8700
E-mail Address: social@editorsguild.com
Web Address: www.editorsguild.com
The Motion Picture Editors Guild's (MPEG) web site provides an online directory of editors, a discussion forum and links to related magazines and other organizations that serve the motion picture industry.

Producers Guild of America, Inc. (PGA)
8530 Wilshire Blvd., Ste. 400
Beverly Hills, CA 90211 USA
Phone: 310-358-9020
Fax: 310-358-9520
E-mail Address: info@producersguild.org
Web Address: www.producersguild.org
The Producers Guild of America, Inc. (PGA) is a nonprofit organization for career professionals who initiate, create, coordinate, supervise and control all aspects of the motion picture and television production processes.

Women In Film (WIF)
6100 Wilshire Blvd., Ste. 710
Los Angeles, CA 90048 USA
Phone: 323-935-2211
Fax: 323-935-2212
E-mail Address: info@wif.org
Web Address: www.wif.org
Women In Film (WIF) strives to empower, promote and mentor women in the entertainment, communication and media industries through a network of contacts, educational programs and events.

44) Fitness Industry Associations

American Fitness Professionals and Associates (AFPA)
1601 Long Beach Blvd.
P.O. Box 214
Ship Bottom, NJ 08008 USA
Phone: 609-978-7583
Fax: 609-978-7582
Toll Free: 800-494-7782
E-mail Address: afpa@afpafitness.com
Web Address: www.afpafitness.com
American Fitness Professionals and Associates (AFPA) offers health and fitness professionals certification programs, continuing education courses, home correspondence courses and regional conventions.

45) Food Industry Associations, General

Institute of Food Technologies (IFT)
525 W. Van Buren, Ste. 1000
Chicago, IL 60607 USA
Phone: 312-782-8424
Fax: 312-782-8348
Toll Free: 800-438-3663
E-mail Address: info@ift.org
Web Address: www.ift.org
The Institute of Food Technologies (IFT) is devoted to the advancement of the science and technology of food through the exchange of knowledge. The site also provides information and resources for job seekers in the food industry. Members work in food science, food technology and related professions in industry, academia and government.

46) Food Industry Resources, General

Food Manufacturing
199 E. Badger Rd., Ste. 101
Madison, WI 53713 USA
Phone: 973-920-7761
E-mail Address: abmprogrequests@advantagemedia.com
Web Address: www.foodmanufacturing.com
Food Manufacturing is a trade magazine for companies and employees in the food manufacturing industry. It is published by Advantage Business Media.

47) Food Processor Industry Associations

Grocery Manufacturers Association (GMA)
1350 I St. NW, Ste. 300
Washington, DC 20005 USA
Phone: 202-639-5900
Fax: 202-639-5932
E-mail Address: info@gmaonline.org
Web Address: www.gmaonline.org
The Grocery Manufacturers Association (GMA), formerly the National Food Products Association (NFPA), is the voice of the food, beverage and consumer products industry on scientific and public policy issues involving food safety, food security, nutrition, technical and regulatory matters and consumer affairs.

National Frozen and Refrigerated Foods Association (NFRA)
4755 Linglestown Rd., Ste. 300
Harrisburg, PA 17112 USA
Phone: 717-657-8601
Fax: 717-657-9862
E-mail Address: info@nfraweb.org
Web Address: www.nfraweb.org
The National Frozen and Refrigerated Foods Association (NFRA) promotes the sales and consumption of refrigerated and frozen foods through education, research, training, sales planning and menu development, providing a forum for industry dialogue. It represents manufacturers, sales agents, suppliers, local associations, retailers, wholesalers, distributors and logistic providers

involved in the frozen and refrigerated food industry.

48) Food Service Industry Associations

International Flight Services Association (IFSA)
1100 Fry Rd., Ste. 300
Atlanta, GA 30342 USA
Phone: 404-303-2969
E-mail Address: ifsa@kellencompany.com
Web Address: www.ifsanet.com
The International Flight Services Association (IFSA), formerly the International Inflight Food Service Association, informs the public with respect to educational and career opportunities within the multi-billion-dollar inflight and railway food service industry. IFSA is managed by the Kellen Company.

49) Games Industry Associations

Entertainment Software Association (ESA)
575 7th St. NW, Ste. 300
Washington, DC 20004 USA
Phone: 202-223-2400
E-mail Address: esa@theesa.com
Web Address: www.theesa.com
The Entertainment Software Association (ESA) is a U.S. trade association for companies that publish video and computer games for consoles, personal computers and the Internet. The ESA owns the E3 Media & Business Summit, a major invitation-only annual trade show for the video game industry.

Fantasy Sports & Gaming Association (FSGA)
600 N. Lake Shore Dr.
Chicago, IL 60611 USA
Phone: 312-771-7019
E-mail Address: megan@fsga.org
Web Address: www.fsga.org
The Fantasy Sports & Gaming Association (FSGA), formerly the Fantasy Sports Trade Association, was founded in 1997 to provide a forum for interaction between companies in a unique and growing fantasy sports industry. FSGA represents more than 300 member companies.

Game Manufacturers Association (GAMA)
240 N. Fifth St., Ste. 340
Columbus, OH 43215 USA
Phone: 614-255-4500
Fax: 614-255-4499
E-mail Address: ed@gama.org
Web Address: www.gama.org
The Game Manufacturers Association (GAMA) is an international non-profit trade association serving the hobby games industry. It hosts two annual events, the GAMA Trade Show and Origins Game Fair, and publishes a quarterly information newsletter, GAMATimes.

International Game Developers Association (IGDA)
19 Mantua Rd.
Mt. Royal, NJ 08061 USA
Phone: 856-423-2990
Web Address: www.igda.org
The International Game Developers Association (IGDA) represents members involved in the video game production industry. The firm aims to promote professional development within the gaming industry and advocates for issues that affect the game developer community, including anti-censorship issues.

50) Grocery Industry Associations

National Grocers Association (NGA)
1005 N. Glebe Rd., Ste. 250
Arlington, VA 22201-5758 USA
Phone: 703-516-0700
Fax: 703-516-0115
E-mail Address: feedback@nationalgrocers.org
Web Address: www.nationalgrocers.org
The National Grocers Association (NGA) is a national trade association representing retail and wholesale grocers that comprise the independent sector of the food distribution industry.

51) Health & Nutrition Associations

Academy of Nutrition and Dietetics
120 S. Riverside Plz., Ste. 2190
Chicago, IL 60606-6995 USA
Phone: 312-899-0040
Toll Free: 800-877-1600
E-mail Address: foundation@eatright.org
Web Address: www.eatright.org
The Academy of Nutrition and Dietetics, formerly known as the American Dietetic Association (ADA) is the world's largest organization of food and nutrition professionals, with nearly 65,000 members. In addition to services for its professional members, this organization's web site offers consumers a respected source for food and nutrition information.

52) Health Care Business & Professional Associations

Advanced Medical Technology Association (AdvaMed)
701 Pennsylvania Ave. NW, Ste. 800
Washington, DC 20004-2654 USA
Phone: 202-783-8700
Fax: 202-783-8750
E-mail Address: info@advamed.org
Web Address: www.advamed.org
The Advanced Medical Technology Association (AdvaMed) strives to be the advocate for a legal, regulatory and economic climate that advances global health care by assuring worldwide access to the benefits of medical technology.

American Academy of Nursing (AAN)
1000 Vermont Ave., Ste. 910
Washington, DC 20005 USA
Phone: 202-777-1170
E-mail Address: info@aannet.org
Web Address: www.aannet.org
The American Academy of Nursing (AAN) works to enhance nursing profession by advancing health policy and practice and generate, synthesize and disseminate nursing knowledge.

American Association of Medical Assistants (AAMA)
20 N. Wacker Dr., Ste. 1575
Chicago, IL 60606 USA
Phone: 312-899-1500
Fax: 312-899-1259
Toll Free: 800-228-2262
Web Address: www.aama-ntl.org
The American Association of Medical Assistants (AAMA) seeks to promote the professional identity and stature of its members and the medical assisting profession through education and credentialing.

American College of Health Care Administrators (ACHCA)
1101 Connecticut Ave. NW, Ste. 450
Washington, DC 20036 USA
Phone: 202-536-5120
Fax: 866-874-1585
E-mail Address: wodonnell@achca.org
Web Address: www.achca.org
The American College of Health Care Administrators (ACHCA) offers educational programming, professional certification and career development opportunities for health care administrators.

American College of Healthcare Executives (ACHE)
1 N. Franklin St., Ste. 1700
Chicago, IL 60606-3529 USA

Phone: 312-424-2800
Fax: 312-424-0023
E-mail Address: contact@ache.org
Web Address: www.ache.org
The American College of Healthcare Executives (ACHE) is an international professional society of health care executives that offers certification and educational programs.

American Dental Association (ADA)
211 E. Chicago Ave.
Chicago, IL 60611-2678 USA
Phone: 312-440-2500
Web Address: www.ada.org
The American Dental Association (ADA) is a nonprofit professional association of dentists committed to enhancing public's oral health with a focus on ethics, science and professional advancement.

American Medical Technologists (AMT)
10700 W. Higgins Rd., Ste. 150
Rosemont, IL 60018 USA
Phone: 847-823-5169
Fax: 847-823-0458
E-mail Address: mail@americanmedtech.org
Web Address: www.americanmedtech.org
American Medical Technologists (AMT) is a nationally and internationally recognized nonprofit certification agency and professional membership association representing allied health professionals. Its members include laboratory health professionals, as well as medical and dental office professionals.

American Medical Women's Association (AMWA)
12100 Sunset Hills Rd., Ste. 130
Reston, VA 20190 USA
Phone: 703-234-4069
Fax: 703-435-4390
Toll Free: 866-564-2483
E-mail Address: associatedirector@amwa-doc.org
Web Address: www.amwa-doc.org
The American Medical Women's Association (AMWA) is an organization of women physicians and medical students dedicated to serving as the unique voice for women's health and the advancement of women in medicine.

American Occupational Therapy Association, Inc. (AOTA)
4720 Montgomery Ln., Ste. 200
Bethesda, MD 20814-3449 USA
Phone: 301-652-6611
Fax: 301-652-7711
Toll Free: 800-377-8555
Web Address: www.aota.org
The American Occupational Therapy Association, Inc. (AOTA) advances the quality, availability, use and support of occupational therapy through standard-setting, advocacy, education and research on behalf of its members and the public.

American Organization of Nurse Executives (AONE)
800 10th St. NW
Two City Ctr., Ste. 400
Washington, DC 20001 USA
Phone: 312-422-2800
E-mail Address: aone@aha.org
Web Address: www.aone.org
The American Organization of Nurse Executives (AONE) is a national organization focused on advancing nursing practice and patient care through leadership, professional development, advocacy and research.

American Public Health Association (APHA)
800 I St. NW
Washington, DC 20001-3710 USA
Phone: 202-777-2742
Fax: 202-777-2534
Web Address: www.apha.org
The American Public Health Association (APHA) is an association of individuals and organizations working to improve the public's health and to achieve equity in health status for all.

American School Health Association (ASHA)
7918 Jones Branch Dr., Ste. 300
McLean, VA 22102 USA
Phone: 703-506-7675
Fax: 703-506-3266
E-mail Address: info@ashaweb.org
Web Address: www.ashaweb.org
The American School Health Association (ASHA) advocates high-quality school health instruction, health services and a healthy school environment.

Dental Trade Alliance (DTA)
4350 N. Fairfax Dr., Ste. 220
Arlington, VA 22203 USA
Phone: 703-379-7755
Fax: 703-931-9429
Web Address: www.dentaltradealliance.org
The Dental Trade Alliance (DTA) represents dental manufacturers, dental dealers and dental laboratories.

Health Industry Distributors Association (HIDA)
310 Montgomery St.
Alexandria, VA 22314-1516 USA
Phone: 703-549-4432
Fax: 703-549-6495
E-mail Address: rowan@hida.org
Web Address: www.hida.org
The Health Industry Distributors Association (HIDA) is the international trade association representing medical products distributors.

Healthcare Financial Management Association (HFMA)
3 Westbrook Corp. Ctr., Ste. 600
Westchester, IL 60154 USA
Phone: 708-531-9600
Fax: 708-531-0032
Toll Free: 800-252-4362
E-mail Address: memberservices@hfma.org
Web Address: www.hfma.org
The Healthcare Financial Management Association (HFMA) is one of the nation's leading personal membership organizations for health care financial management executives and leaders.

Medical Device Manufacturers Association (MDMA)
1333 H St., Ste. 400 W.
Washington, DC 20005 USA
Phone: 202-354-7171
Web Address: www.medicaldevices.org
The Medical Device Manufacturers Association (MDMA) is a national trade association that represents independent manufacturers of medical devices, diagnostic products and health care information systems.

Medical Group Management Association (MGMA)
104 Inverness Terrace E.
Englewood, CO 80112-5306 USA
Phone: 303-799-1111
Toll Free: 877-275-6462
E-mail Address: support@mgma.com
Web Address: www.mgma.com
Medical Group Management Association (MGMA) is one of the nation's principal voices for medical group practice. It represents over 33,000 administrators and executives in 18,000 healthcare organizations in which 385,000 physicians practice.

National Association of Health Services Executives (NAHSE)
1050 Connecticut Ave. NW, Fl. 5
Washington, DC 20036 USA
Phone: 202-772-1030
Fax: 202-772-1072
Web Address: www.nahse.org
The National Association of Health Services Executives (NAHSE) is a nonprofit association of black health care executives who promote the advancement and development of black health care leaders and elevate the quality of health

care services rendered to minority and underserved communities.

Regulatory Affairs Professionals Society (RAPS)
5635 Fishers Ln., Ste. 550
Rockville, MD 20852 USA
Phone: 301-770-2920
Fax: 301-841-7956
E-mail Address: raps@raps.org
Web Address: www.raps.org
The Regulatory Affairs Professionals Society (RAPS) is an international professional society representing the health care regulatory affairs profession and individual professionals worldwide.

53) Health Insurance Industry Associations

America's Health Insurance Plans (AHIP)
601 Pennsylvania Ave. NW
S. Bldg., Ste. 500
Washington, DC 20004 USA
Phone: 202-778-3200
Fax: 202-331-7487
E-mail Address: ahip@ahip.org
Web Address: www.ahip.org
America's Health Insurance Plans (AHIP) is a prominent trade association representing the health care insurance community. Its members offer health and supplemental benefits through employer-sponsored coverage, the individual insurance market, and public programs such as Medicare and Medicaid.

54) Hearing & Speech

Hearing Industries Association (HIA)
1444 I St. NW, Ste. 700
Washington, DC 20005 USA
Phone: 202-449-1090
Fax: 202-216-9646
E-mail Address: mjones@bostrom.com
Web Address: www.hearing.org
The Hearing Industries Association (HIA) represents and unifies the many aspects of the hearing industry.

55) Hotel/Lodging Associations

American Hotel and Lodging Association
1250 I St., NW, Ste. 1100
Washington, DC 20005-3931 USA
Phone: 202-289-3100
Fax: 202-289-3199
E-mail Address: informationcenter@ahla.com
Web Address: www.ahla.com
The American Hotel and Lodging Association is a federation of state lodging associations throughout the U.S.

56) Human Resources Industry Associations

Association for Talent Development (ATD) (The)
1640 King St.
Alexandria, VA 22313-1443 USA
Phone: 703-683-8100
Fax: 703-299-8723
Toll Free: 800-628-2783
E-mail Address: customercare@td.org
Web Address: www.td.org
The Association for Talent Development (ATD), formerly American Society for Training & Development (ASTD) is dedicated to those professionals in the fields of training and development. It provides resources such as research, analysis, benchmarking, online information, books and other publications to training and development professional, educators and students. Additionally, the association brings professional together in conferences, workshops and online, while also offering professional development opportunities, certificate programs and Certified Professional in Learning and Performance (CPLP) credential.

HR Policy Association
1100 13th St., Ste. 850
Washington, DC 20005 USA
Phone: 202-789-8670
Fax: 202-789-0064
E-mail Address: info@hrpolicy.org
Web Address: www.hrpolicy.org
HR Policy Association is a public policy organization of chief human resource officers from major employers. The association brings together HR professionals at the highest level of corporations to discuss changes in public policy, and to lay out a vision and advocate for competitive workplace initiatives that promote job growth and employment security.

Society for Human Resource Management (SHRM)
1800 Duke St.
Alexandria, VA 22314 USA
Phone: 703-548-3440
Fax: 703-535-6490
Toll Free: 800-283-7476
E-mail Address: shrm@shrm.org
Web Address: www.shrm.org
The Society for Human Resource Management (SHRM) addresses the interests and needs of HR professionals through advocacy, publications, research and other resource materials. The organization has 575 affiliate chapters, both in the U.S. and internationally, serving over 5,000 members in approximately 160 countries.

57) Industry Research/Market Research

Forrester Research
60 Acorn Park Dr.
Cambridge, MA 02140 USA
Phone: 617-613-5730
Toll Free: 866-367-7378
E-mail Address: press@forrester.com
Web Address: www.forrester.com
Forrester Research is a publicly traded company that identifies and analyzes emerging trends in technology and their impact on business. Among the firm's specialties are the financial services, retail, health care, entertainment, automotive and information technology industries.

MarketResearch.com
11200 Rockville Pike, Ste. 504
Rockville, MD 20852 USA
Phone: 240-747-3093
Fax: 240-747-3004
Toll Free: 800-298-5699
E-mail Address: customerservice@marketresearch.com
Web Address: www.marketresearch.com
MarketResearch.com is a leading broker for professional market research and industry analysis. Users are able to search the company's database of research publications including data on global industries, companies, products and trends.

Plunkett Research, Ltd.
P.O. Drawer 541737
Houston, TX 77254-1737 USA
Phone: 713-932-0000
Fax: 713-932-7080
E-mail Address: customersupport@plunkettresearch.com
Web Address: www.plunkettresearch.com
Plunkett Research, Ltd. is a leading provider of market research, industry trends analysis and business statistics. Since 1985, it has served clients worldwide, including corporations, universities, libraries, consultants and government agencies. At the firm's web site, visitors can view product information and pricing and access a large amount of basic market information on industries such as financial services, InfoTech, e-commerce, health care and biotech.

58) Insurance Industry Associations

American Insurance Association (AIA)
2101 L St. NW, Ste.400
Washington, DC 20037 USA
Phone: 202-828-7100
Fax: 202-293-1219
E-mail Address: jbrodt@aiadc.org
Web Address: www.aiadc.org
The American Insurance Association (AIA) is a leading property and casualty insurance trade organization, representing companies that offer all types of property and casualty insurance.

59) Insurance Industry Associations-Agents & Brokers

Council of Insurance Agents & Brokers (CIAB)
701 Pennsylvania Ave. NW, Ste. 750
Washington, DC 20004 USA
Phone: 202-783-4400
Fax: 202-783-4410
E-mail Address: ciab@ciab.com
Web Address: www.ciab.com
The Council of Insurance Agents & Brokers (CIAB) is an association for commercial insurance and employee benefits intermediaries in the U.S. and abroad.

Independent Insurance Agents & Brokers of America, Inc. (IIABA)
127 S. Peyton St.
Alexandria, VA 22314 USA
Fax: 703-683-7556
Toll Free: 800-221-7917
E-mail Address: info@iiaba.org
Web Address: www.independentagent.com
Independent Insurance Agents & Brokers of America (IIABA) represents its over 300,000 members who are independent insurance agents and brokers.

Professional Insurance Agents (PIA)
25 Chamberlain St.
P.O. Box 997
Glenmont, NY 12077-0997 USA
Fax: 888-225-6935
Toll Free: 800-424-4244
E-mail Address: pia@pia.org
Web Address: www.piaonline.org
Professional Insurance Agents (PIA) is a group of voluntary, membership-based trade associations representing professional, independent property and casualty insurance agents.

60) Magazines, Business & Financial

Bloomberg Businessweek Online
731 Lexington Ave.
New York, NY 10022 USA
Phone: 212-318-2000
Fax: 917-369-5000
Web Address: www.businessweek.com
Business Week Online offers an investor service, global business advice, technology news, small business guides, career information, business school advice, daily news briefs and more.

Forbes Online
60 5th Ave.
New York, NY 10011 USA
Phone: 212-620-2200
E-mail Address: customerservice@forbes.com
Web Address: www.forbes.com
Forbes Online offers varied stock information, news and commentary on business, technology and personal finance, as well as financial calculators and advice.

Fortune
1271 Ave. of the Americas
Rockefeller Ctr.
New York, NY 10020-1393 USA
Phone: 212-522-8528
Web Address: http://fortune.com/
Fortune, one of the world's premiere business magazines, contains news, business profiles and information on investing, careers, small business, technology and other details of U.S. and international business. Fortune is a publication of Cable News Network (CNN), a Time Warner company.

Investor's Business Daily (IBD)
12655 Beatrice St.
Los Angeles, CA 90066 USA
Phone: 310-448-6000
Toll Free: 800-831-2525
Web Address: www.investors.com
Investor's Business Daily (IBD) offers subscribers information and articles on the stock market, educational resources, advice from analyst William O'Neil, personal portfolios and updates on events and workshops.

Wall Street Journal Online (The)
1211 Ave. of the Americas
New York, NY 10036 USA
Phone: 609-514-0870
Toll Free: 800-568-7625
E-mail Address: support@wsj.com
Web Address: www.wsj.com
The outstanding resources of The Wall Street Journal are available online for a nominal fee.

61) MBA Resources

MBA Depot
Web Address: www.mbadepot.com
MBA Depot is an online community and information portal for MBAs, potential MBA program applicants and business professionals.

62) Online Recruiting & Employment ASPs & Solutions

Hrsoft
2200 Lucien Way, Ste. 201
Maitland, FL 32751 USA
Phone: 407-475-5500
Fax: 407-475-5502
Toll Free: 866-953-8800
E-mail Address: Michael.Noland@HRsoft.com
Web Address: www.hrsoft.com
HRsoft, formerly Workstream, Inc., creates workforce management solutions through a combination of technology and services designed to integrate an organization.

Insala
2005 NE Green Oaks Blvd., Ste. 110
Arlington, TX 76006 USA
Phone: 817-355-0939
Fax: 817-355-0746
E-mail Address: info@insala.com
Web Address: www.insala.com
Insala provides job search software solutions for the outplacement industry.

Kenexa
650 E. Swedesford Rd., Fl. 2
Wayne, PA 19087 USA
Phone: 877-971-9171
Fax: 610-971-9181
Toll Free: 800-391-9557
E-mail Address: contactus@kenexa.com
Web Address: www.kenexa.com
Kenexa is a back-end recruiting and job-posting service that is used by many companies in building a workforce. Products and services include recruitment software solutions, talent consulting and recruitment process management.

63) Outsourcing Industry Associations

International Association of Outsourcing Professionals (IAOP)
2600 South Rd., Ste. 44-240

Poughkeepsie, NY 12601 USA
Phone: 845-452-0600
Fax: 845-452-6988
E-mail Address: memberservices@iaop.org
Web Address: www.iaop.org
The International Association of Outsourcing Professionals (IAOP) represents outsourcing leaders and experts from companies of all sizes and industries around the world.

64) Pensions, Benefits & 401(k) Associations

Plan Sponsor Council of America (PSCA)
20 N. Wacker Dr., Ste. 3164
Chicago, IL 60606 USA
Phone: 312-419-1863
Fax: 312-419-1864
E-mail Address: psca@psca.org
Web Address: www.psca.org
The Plan Sponsor Council of America (PSCA), formerly the Profit Sharing/401(k) Council of America (PSCA). is a national nonprofit association of 1,200 companies and their 6 million employees. The group expresses its members' interests to federal policymakers and offers practical, cost-effective assistance with profit sharing and 401(k) plan design, administration, investment, compliance and communication. Its web site offers a thorough glossary, statistics and educational material.

65) Pensions, Benefits & 401(k) Resources

Employee Benefits Security Administration (EBSA)
200 Constitution Ave. NW
Washington, DC 20210 USA
Toll Free: 866-444-3272
Web Address: www.dol.gov/ebsa
The Employee Benefits Security Administration (EBSA) is a division of the U.S. Department of Labor, whose web site features a wealth of benefits information for both employers and employees. Included are the answers to such questions as to how a company's bankruptcy will affect its employees and what one should know about pension rights.

Pension Benefit Guarantee Corporation (PBGC)
1200 K St. NW, Ste. 9429
Washington, DC 20005-4026 USA
Phone: 202-326-4000
Fax: 202-326-4047
Toll Free: 800-400-7242
E-mail Address: webmaster@pbgc.gov
Web Address: www.pbgc.gov
The Pension Benefit Guarantee Corporation (PBGC) is a U.S. Government agency that guarantees a portion of the retirement incomes of about 41 million American workers in about 24,000 private defined benefit pension plans. Its web site contains information regarding this guarantee, along with information on retirement planning and links to several related organizations.

66) Pharmaceutical Industry Associations (Drug Industry)

American Pharmacists Association (AphA)
2215 Constitution Ave. NW
Washington, DC 20037 USA
Phone: 202-628-4410
Fax: 202-783-2351
Toll Free: 800-237-4410
E-mail Address: infocenter@aphanet.org
Web Address: www.pharmacist.com
American Pharmaceutical Association (APhA), formerly American Pharmaceutical Association is a national professional society that provides news and information to pharmacists. Its membership includes over 62,000 practicing pharmacists, pharmaceutical scientists, student pharmacists and pharmacy technicians.

Pharmaceutical Research and Manufacturers of America (PhRMA)
950 F St. NW, Ste. 300
Washington, DC 20004 USA
Phone: 202-835-3400
Web Address: www.phrma.org
Pharmaceutical Research and Manufacturers of America (PhRMA) represents the nation's leading research-based pharmaceutical and biotechnology companies.

67) Pilots Associations

Airline Pilots Association (ALPA)
1625 Massachusetts Ave NW
Washington, DC 20036 USA
Phone: 703-689-2270
E-mail Address: media@alpa.org
Web Address: www.alpa.org
The Airline Pilots Association (ALPA) is an association for professional airline pilots in the United States, in Canada and internationally. ALPA provides airline safety, security, pilot assistance, representation and advocacy to its members.

68) Printers & Publishers Associations

Epicomm
1800 Diagonal Rd., Ste. 320
Alexandria, VA 22314-2862 USA
Phone: 703-836-9200
Web Address: http://epicomm.org
Epicomm is a non-profit business management association formed in 2014, through the merger of the National Association of Printers & Lithographers (NAPL), National Association of Quick Printers (NAQP) and the Association of Marketing Service Providers (AMSP). It represents the interests of graphic communications industry in the U.S.

In-Plant Printing and Mailing Association (IPMA)
105 S. Jefferson, Ste. B-4
Kearney, MO 64060 USA
Phone: 816-903-4762
Fax: 816-902-4766
E-mail Address: ipmainfo@ipma.org
Web Address: www.ipma.org
The In-Plant Printing and Mailing Association (IPMA), formerly the International Publishing Management Association, is an exclusive not-for-profit organization dedicated to assisting in-house corporate publishing and distribution professionals.

MPA-The Association of Magazine Media
810 7th Ave., Fl. 24
New York, NY 10019 USA
Phone: 212-872-3700
E-mail Address: mpa@magazine.org
Web Address: www.magazine.org
MPA-The Association of Magazine Media (formerly the Magazine Publishers of America, Inc.) is the industry association for consumer magazines in all formats, including printed, mobile and online.

Newspaper Association of America (NAA)
4401 Wilson Blvd., Ste. 900
Arlington, VA 22203-1867 USA
Phone: 571-366-1000
Fax: 571-366-1195
E-mail Address: membsvc@naa.org
Web Address: www.naa.org
The Newspaper Association of America (NAA) is a nonprofit organization representing the newspaper industry.

69) Real Estate Industry Associations

Institute of Real Estate Management (IREM)
430 N. Michigan Ave.
Chicago, IL 60611 USA
Fax: 800-338-4736
Toll Free: 800-837-0706
E-mail Address: getinfo@irem.org
Web Address: www.irem.org
The Institute of Real Estate Management (IREM) seeks to educate real estate managers, certify their competence and professionalism, serve as an advocate on issues affecting the real estate management industry and enhance its members' professional competence so they can better identify and meet the needs of those who use their services.

NAREC
6348 N. Milwaukee Ave., Ste. 103
Chicago, IL 60606 USA
Phone: 773-283-6362
E-mail Address: info@narec.org
Web Address: narec.org
NAREC, formerly PeerSpan and, prior to that, the National Association of Real Estate Companies, is composed of representatives of publicly and privately owned real estate companies, significant subsidiaries of publicly owned companies and public accounting firms.

National Association of Real Estate Brokers (NAREB)
9831 Greenbelt Rd., Ste. 309
Lanham, MD 20706 USA
Phone: 301-552-9340
Fax: 301-552-9216
E-mail Address: info@nareb.com
Web Address: www.nareb.com
The National Association of Real Estate Brokers (NAREB) is a national trade organization dedicated to bringing together the nation's minority professionals in the real estate industry.

National Association of Realtors (NAR)
430 N. Michigan Ave.
Chicago, IL 606-4087 USA
Toll Free: 800-874-6500
Web Address: www.realtor.org
The National Association of Realtors (NAR) is composed of realtors involved in residential and commercial real estate as brokers, salespeople, property managers, appraisers and counselors and in other areas of the industry. NAR also sponsors Realtor.com, operated by Move, Inc.

Women's Council of Realtors (WCR)
430 N. Michigan Ave.
Chicago, IL 60611 USA
Fax: 312-329-3290
Toll Free: 800-245-8512
E-mail Address: wcr@wcr.org
Web Address: www.wcr.org
The Women's Council of Realtors (WCR) is a community of women real estate professionals. It promotes the professional growth of its members through networking, leadership development, resources, infrastructure and accessibility

70) Recording & Music Associations

American Federation of Musicians (AFM)
1501 Broadway, Ste. 600
New York, NY 10036 USA
Phone: 212-869-1330
Fax: 212-764-6134
Web Address: www.afm.org
The American Federation of Musicians (AFM) is the largest union in the world for music professionals, serving musicians throughout the U.S. and Canada.

American Society of Composers, Authors & Publishers (ASCAP)
1900 Broadway
New York, NY 10023-7142 USA
Phone: 212-621-6000
Fax: 212-621-8453
Web Address: www.ascap.com
American Society of Composers, Authors & Publishers (ASCAP) is a membership association of U.S. composers, songwriters and publishers of every kind of music, with hundreds of thousands of members worldwide.

Content Delivery & Storage Association (CDSA)
39 N. Bayles Ave.
Port Washington, NY 11050 USA
Phone: 516-767-6720
Fax: 516-883-5793
E-mail Address: mporter@CDSAonline.org
Web Address: www.cdsaonline.org
The Content Delivery & Storage Association (CDSA), formerly the International Recording Media Association, is a worldwide trade association for organizations involved in every facet of recording media, including entertainment, information and software content storage. CDSA is under the management of the Media & Entertainment Services Alliance (MESA).

International Association of Audio Information Services (IAAIS)
Toll Free: 800-280-5325
E-mail Address: Stuart.Holland@state.mn.us
Web Address: www.iaais.org
International Association of Audio Information Services (IAAIS) is an organization that provides audio access to information for people who are print-disabled.

Music Publisher's Association of the United States (MPA)
243 5th Ave., Ste. 236
New York, NY 10016 USA
Phone: 212-327-4044
E-mail Address: admin@mpa.org
Web Address: mpa.org
The Music Publisher's Association of the United States (MPA) serves as a forum for publishers to deal with the music industry's vital issues and is actively involved in supporting and advancing compliance with copyright law, combating copyright infringement and exploring the need for further reform.

Recording Industry Association of America (RIAA)
1025 F St. NW, Fl. 10
Washington, DC 20004 USA
Phone: 202-775-0101
Web Address: www.riaa.com
The Recording Industry Association of America (RIAA) is the trade group that represents the U.S. recording industry.

Society of Professional Audio Recording Services (SPARS)
Fax: 214-722-1442
Toll Free: 800-771-7727
E-mail Address: info@spars.com
Web Address: www.spars.com
The Society of Professional Audio Recording Services (SPARS) is an organization for members of the recording industry to share practical business information about audio and multimedia facility ownership, management and operations.

Songwriters Guild of America
5120 Virginia Way, Ste. C22
Brentwood, TN 37027 USA
Phone: 615-742-9945
Fax: 615-630-7501
Toll Free: 800-524-6742
Web Address: www.songwritersguild.com
The Songwriters Guild of America is the nation's largest and oldest songwriters' organization, providing its members with information and programs to further their careers and understanding of the music industry.

71) Satellite Industry Associations

Satellite Broadcasting & Communications Association (SBCA)
1100 17th St. NW, Ste. 1150
Washington, DC 20036 USA
Phone: 202-349-3620
Fax: 202-349-3621
Toll Free: 800-541-5981
E-mail Address: info@sbca.org
Web Address: www.sbca.com
The Satellite Broadcasting & Communications Association (SBCA) is the national trade organization representing all segments of the satellite consumer services industry in America.

72) Satellite-Related Professional Organizations

Society of Satellite Professionals International (SSPI)
250 Park Ave., Fl. 7
The New York Information Technology Ctr.
New York, NY 10177 USA
Phone: 212-809-5199
Fax: 212-825-0075
E-mail Address: rbell@sspi.org
Web Address: www.sspi.org
The Society of Satellite Professionals International (SSPI) is a nonprofit member-benefit society that serves satellite professionals worldwide.

73) Securities Industry Associations

North American Securities Administrators Association, Inc. (NASAA)
750 First St. NE, Ste. 1140
Washington, DC 20002 USA
Phone: 202-737-0900
Fax: 202-783-3571
E-mail Address: ri@nasaa.org
Web Address: www.nasaa.org
The North American Securities Administrators Association (NASAA) is the oldest international organization committed to investor protection. Its web site provides information on franchising and raising capital, as well as state blue sky securities laws and resources for small investment advisors.

Securities Industry and Financial Markets Association (SIFMA)
120 Broadway, Fl. 35
New York, NY 10271-0080 USA
Phone: 212-313-1200
Fax: 212-313-1301
E-mail Address: inquiry@sifma.org
Web Address: www.sifma.org
The Securities Industry and Financial Markets Association (SIFMA), formed by the merger of the Securities Industry Association (SIA) and the Bond Market Association, brings together the shared interests of more than 650 securities and bond industry firms to accomplish common goals.

74) Software Industry Associations

Software & Information Industry Association (SIIA)
1090 Vermont Ave. NW, Fl. 6
Washington, DC 20005-4095 USA
Phone: 202-289-7442
Fax: 202-289-7097
Web Address: www.siia.net
The Software & Information Industry Association (SIIA) is a principal trade association for the software and digital content industry.

75) Stocks & Financial Markets Data

Reuters.com
3 Times Sq.
New York, NY 10036 USA
Phone: 646-223-6890
Web Address: www.reuters.com
Reuters.com, a service of Thomson Reuters, offers information on business and world markets, political and international news and company-specific stock information.

Yahoo! Finance
701 1st Ave.
Yahoo! Inc.
Sunnyvale, CA 94089 USA
Phone: 408-349-3300
Web Address: finance.yahoo.com
Yahoo! Finance provides a wealth of links and a supreme search guide. Users can find just about any financial information concerning both U.S. and world markets. Tax, insurance information, financial news and community research can be conducted through this site, as can searches for other aspects of the financial world.

76) Telecommunications Industry Associations

CompTel
900 17th St. NW, Ste. 400
Washington, DC 20006 USA
Phone: 202-296-6650
E-mail Address: gnorris@comptel.org
Web Address: www.comptel.org
CompTel is a trade organization representing voice, data and video communications service providers and their supplier partners. Members are supported through education, networking, policy advocacy and trade shows.

National Association of Telecommunications Officers and Advisors (NATOA)
3213 Duke St., Ste. 695
Alexandria, VA 22314 USA
Phone: 703-519-8035
Fax: 703-997-7080
E-mail Address: info@natoa.org
Web Address: www.natoa.org
The National Association of Telecommunications Officers and Advisors (NATOA) works to support and serve the telecommunications industry's interests and the needs of local governments.

Telecommunications Industry Association (TIA)
1320 N. Courthouse Rd., Ste. 200
Arlington, VA 22201 USA
Phone: 703-907-7700
Fax: 703-907-7727
E-mail Address: smontgomery@tiaonline.org
Web Address: www.tiaonline.org
The Telecommunications Industry Association (TIA) is a leading trade association in the information, communications and entertainment technology industry. TIA focuses on market development, trade promotion, trade shows, domestic and international advocacy, standards development and enabling e-business.

United States Telecom Association (USTelecom)
607 14th St. NW, Ste. 400
Washington, DC 20005 USA
Phone: 202-326-7300
Fax: 202-315-3603
E-mail Address: membership@ustelecom.org
Web Address: www.ustelecom.org
The United States Telecom Association (USTelecom) is a trade association representing service providers and suppliers for the telecom industry.

77) Temporary Staffing Firms

Adecco
Saegereistrasse 10
Glattbrugg, CH-8152 Switzerland
Phone: 41-44-878-88-88

Fax: 41-44-829-88-06
E-mail Address: press.office@adecco.com
Web Address: www.adecco.com
Adecco maintains human resources and staffing services offices in 70 countries. It provides temporary and permanent personnel.

Advantage Resourcing, Inc.
220 Norwood Park S.
Norwood, MA 02062 USA
Phone: 781-251-8000
Toll Free: 800-343-4314
E-mail Address: M
Web Address: www.hirethinking.com
Advantage Resourcing, Inc., formerly Radia Holdings, Inc., provides integrated human resources services throughout Japan, North America, Europe and Australia. It is one of the largest staffing providers, with over 350 branches and satellite offices.

Allegis Group
7301 Parkway Dr.
Hanover, MD 21076 USA
Toll Free: 800-927-8090
Web Address: www.allegisgroup.com
The Allegis Group provides technical, professional and industrial recruiting and staffing services. Allegis specializes in information technology staffing services. The firm operates in the United Kingdom, Germany and The Netherlands as Aerotek and TEKsystems, and in India as Allegis Group India. Aerotek provides staffing solutions for aviation, engineering, automotive and scientific personnel markets.

CDI Corporation
1717 Arch St., Fl. 35
Philadelphia, PA 19103-2768 USA
Phone: 215-636-1240
E-mail Address: vince.webb@cdicorp.com
Web Address: www.cdicorp.com
CDI Corporation specializes in engineering and information technology staffing services. Company segments include CDI IT Solutions, specializing in information technology; CDI Engineering Solutions, specializing in engineering outsourcing services; AndersElite Limited, operating in the United Kingdom and Australia; and MRINetwork, specializing in executive recruitment.

Express Employment Professionals
9701 Boardwalk Blvd.
Oklahoma City, OK 73162 USA
Phone: 405-840-5000
Toll Free: 888-923-3797
Web Address: www.expresspros.com
Express Employment Professionals operates through a network of over 550 locations in the United States, Canada, South Africa and Australia. Services include temporary and flexible staffing, evaluation and direct hire, professional and contract staffing, human resource services and online payroll processing (U.S. only).

Glotel Inc.
8700 W. Bryn Mawr Ave., Ste. 400N
Chicago, IL 60631 USA
Phone: 312-612-7480
E-mail Address: info@glotelinc.com
Web Address: www.glotel.com
Glotel is a global technology staffing and managed projects solutions company specializing in the placement of contract and permanent personnel within all areas of technology. Glotel has a network of offices throughout Europe, the U.S. and Asia-Pacific.

Harvey Nash
110 Bishopgate
London, EC2N 4AY UK
Phone: 44-20-7333-0033
Fax: 44-20-7333-0032
E-mail Address: richard.ashcroft@harveynash.com
Web Address: www.harveynash.com
Harvey Nash provides professional recruitment, interim executive leadership services and outsourcing services. The firm specializes in information technology staffing on a permanent and contract basis in US, UK and Europe. It also offers outsourcing services including offshore software development services, information technology systems management, workforce risk management and managed services for network administration.

Hays plc
250 Euston Rd.
London, NW1 2AF UK
Phone: 44-20-7383-2266
Fax: 44-20-7388-4367
E-mail Address: customerservice@hays.com
Web Address: www.hays.com
Hays plc is a global leader in specialist recruitment. It places professional candidates in permanent, temporary and interim positions across numerous fields, including accountancy and finance; education; health care; IT and telecom; manufacturing and engineering; pharmaceuticals; professional services; retail, sales and marketing; and support services.

Hudson Highland Group, Inc.
1325 Avenue of the Americas, Fl. 12
New York, NY 10019 USA
Phone: 212-351-7400
Fax: 212-351-7401
Web Address: www.hudson.com
Hudson Highland Group, Inc. provides permanent recruitment, contract and human resources consulting and inclusion solutions. Services range from single placements to total outsourced solutions. The company employs professionals serving clients and candidates in 20 countries.

Kelly Services, Inc.
999 W. Big Beaver Rd.
Troy, MI 48084-4782 USA
Phone: 248-362-4444
E-mail Address: kfirst@kellyservices.com
Web Address: www.kellyservices.com
Kelly Services is a workforce solutions company offering a wide range of outsourcing and consulting services, as well as quality staffing on a temporary, temporary-to-hire and direct-hire basis both locally and worldwide.

Kforce, Inc.
1001 E. Palm Ave.
Tampa, FL 33605 USA
Toll Free: 800-395-5575
E-mail Address: internalstaffing@kforce.com
Web Address: www.kforce.com
Kforce, Inc. is one of America's largest temporary placement firms, with more than 70 offices in 44 cities across the U.S. It specializes in employees for the following types of jobs: finance and accounting, scientific, technology, health care, clinical research, mortgages, title insurance and real estate.

Labor Ready, Inc.
1015 A St.
Tacoma, WA 98402 USA
Phone: 253-383-9101
Fax: 877-733-0399
Toll Free: 877-733-0430
E-mail Address: customercare@laborready.com
Web Address: www.laborready.com
Labor Ready, Inc. specializes in temporary staffing in construction, manufacturing, hospitality services, transportation, landscaping, warehousing, retail and more with almost 700 branches throughout the U.S., Canada and Puerto Rico.

Manpower, Inc.
100 Manpower Pl.
Milwaukee, WI 53212 USA
Phone: 414-961-1000

Fax: 414-906-7822
E-mail Address:
Britt.Zarling@manpowergroup.com
Web Address: www.manpower.com
One of the largest temporary staffing providers in the world, Manpower places approximately 2 million workers annually in a variety of positions around the world.

Michael Page International plc
Page House, 1 Dashwood Lang Rd.
Addlestone, Weybridge
Surrey, KT15 2QW UK
Phone: 44-207-831-2000
Web Address: www.michaelpage.co.uk
Michael Page International is one of the world's leading professional recruitment consultancies specializing in the placement of candidates in permanent, contract, temporary and interim positions. The Group has operations in the US, UK, Continental Europe, Asia-Pacific and a regional presence in France and Australia. In the US, the firm's focus is on the areas of financial services, supply chain, executive searches, marketing, legal and administrative support.

Pasona Group Inc. (Japan)
Otemachi 2-6-4 Chiyoda-ku
Tokyo, 100-8228 Japan
Web Address: www.pasonagroup.co.jp
Pasona, Inc. provides personnel services, ranging from temporary staffing/contracting, placement/recruiting and outplacement to outsourcing and training.

Randstad USA
2015 S. Park Pl.
Atlanta, GA 30339 USA
Phone: 770-937-7000
Fax: 770-937-7100
Toll Free: 877-922-2468
E-mail Address: info@us.randstad.com
Web Address: www.us.randstad.com
Randstad provides staffing services in the office, industrial, technical, creative and professional markets. It specializes in temporary and permanent staffing; recruitment and consultant services; and human resource services. It operates in 83 countries, primarily in Europe, Asia and the U.S. Brands include Capac, Yacht, and Tempo-Team.

Robert Half International Inc. (RHI)
2884 Sand Hill Rd.
Menlo Park, CA 94025 USA
Phone: 650-234-6000
E-mail Address: webmaster@rhi.com
Web Address: www.rhi.com
Robert Half International Inc. (RHI) specializes in accounting and finance positions. It also places workers in administrative, information technology, legal, advertising and marketing positions on temporary or permanent bases.

Robert Walters plc
11 Slingsby Pl.
St. Martin's Courtyard
London, WC2E 9AB UK
Phone: 44-20-7379-3333
Fax: 44-20-7509-8714
E-mail Address:
london@robertwalters.com
Web Address: www.robertwalters.com
Robert Walters PLC is a professional recruitment specialist, outsourcing and human resource consultant. The firm provides services for the temporary, contract and permanent placement of individuals in the sectors of finance, operations, legal, information technology, marketing and administration support. It has offices in 24 countries including the US.

Spherion Corporation
33625 Cumberland Blvd., Ste. 600
Atlanta, GA 30339 USA
Phone: 954-308-6266
E-mail Address: gailferro@spherion.com
Web Address: www.spherion.com
Spherion Corp., a subsidiary of SFN Group, provides temporary staffing, recruitment and employee consulting, primarily in administrative, clerical, customer service and light industrial fields.

Synergie SA (France)
11 Ave. du Colonel Bonnet
Paris, 75016 France
Phone: 44-14-90-20
Fax: 45-25-97-10
Web Address: www.synergie.fr
Synergie provides human resource management services that include temporary placement, consulting and training. The firm is most active in France, but also operates through a network of 550 agencies in throughout Europe and Canada.

Tempstaff Co., Ltd. (Japan)
Shinjuku Maynds Twr. 2-1-1
Yoyogi, Shibuya-ku
Tokyo, 151-0053 Japan
Phone: 81-3-5350-1212
Web Address: www.tempstaff.co.jp
Tempstaff Co., Ltd. provides temporary and permanent placement and recruiting and outsourcing services. It has 263 offices in Japan and 12 overseas offices located in Los Angeles, Seattle, Shanghai, Suzhou, Guangzhou, Hong Kong, Taiwan, Korea, Singapore and Indonesia.

Volt Information Sciences, Inc.
1133 Ave. of the Americas, Fl. 15
New York, NY 10036 USA
Phone: 212-704-2400
Web Address: www.volt.com
Volt Information Sciences, Inc. provides temporary staffing services, professional search, managed services programs, vendor management systems and recruitment process outsourcing, as well as a wealth of additional support services, in North and South America, Europe and Asia through approximately 400 locations.

78) Testing Resources

CPP, Inc.
1055 Joaquin Rd., Ste. 200
Mountain View, CA 94043 USA
Phone: 650-969-8901
Fax: 650-969-8608
Toll Free: 800-624-1765
E-mail Address: custserv@cpp.com
Web Address: www.cpp.com
CPP, Inc. (formerly known as Consulting Psychologists Press) publishes the Meyers-Briggs Type Indicator, Strong Inventory Test and other psychological assessment-related products. CPP also provides information about the tests and, through division Davies-Black Publishing, offers business-related books and services, including those covering career management and leadership development.

79) Textile & Fabric Industry Associations

International Textile and Apparel Association (ITAA)
P.O. Box 70687
Knoxville, TN 37938-0687 USA
Phone: 865-992-1535
E-mail Address: info@itaaonline.org
Web Address: www.itaaonline.org
The International Textile and Apparel Association (ITAA) is a nonprofit educational and scientific corporation dedicated to providing opportunities to scholars in the retail, textile and apparel industries.

80) Travel Business & Professional Associations

American Society of Travel Agents (ASTA)
1101 King St., Ste. 200
Alexandria, VA 22314 USA
Phone: 703-739-2782
Toll Free: 800-275-2782
E-mail Address: askasta@asta.org

Web Address: www.asta.org
The American Society of Travel Agents (ASTA) is one of the world's largest associations of travel professionals.

Association of Corporate Travel Executives (ACTE)
515 King St., Ste. 440
Alexandria, VA 22314 USA
Phone: 703-683-5322
Fax: 703-683-2720
E-mail Address: info@acte.org
Web Address: www.acte.org
The Association of Corporate Travel Executives (ACTE) serves the specialized travel interests of corporate purchasers and travel service suppliers from nearly 50 countries.

Association of Retail Travel Agents (ARTA)
4320 North Miller Rd.
c/o Travel Destinations, Inc.
Scottsdale, AZ 85251-3606 USA
Fax: 866-743-2087
Toll Free: 866-369-8969
Web Address: www.arta.travel
The Association of Retail Travel Agents (ARTA) is one of the largest nonprofit associations in North America to exclusively represent travel agents.

Association of Travel Marketing Executives (ATME)
P.O. Box 3176
West Tisbury, MA 02575 USA
Phone: 508-693-0550
Fax: 508-693-0115
E-mail Address: kzern@atme.org
Web Address: www.atme.org
The Association of Travel Marketing Executives (ATME) is a global professional association of senior-level travel marketing executives dedicated to providing cutting-edge information, education and opportunities for meaningful networking with peers.

National Society of Minorities in Hospitality
6933 Commons Plz., Ste. 537
Chesterfield, VA 23832 USA
Phone: 703-549-9899
Fax: 703-997-7795
E-mail Address: hq@nsmh.org
Web Address: www.nsmh.org
The National Society of Minorities in Hospitality strives to establish a working relationship between the hospitality industry and minority students.

Network of Executive Women in Hospitality, Inc. (NEWH)
P.O. Box 322
Shawano, WI 54166 USA
Fax: 800-693-6394
Toll Free: 800-593-6394
Web Address: www.newh.org
The Network of Executive Women in Hospitality, Inc. (NEWH) brings together professionals from all facets of the hospitality industry by providing opportunities for education, professional development and networking. Although primarily a U.S.-based organization, NEWH does have international chapters in Toronto and London.

Society of Incentive and Travel Executives
401 N. Michigan Ave.
Chicago, IL 60611-4267 USA
Phone: 312-321-5148
Fax: 312-527-6783
E-mail Address: site@siteglobal.com
Web Address: www.site-intl.org
The Society of Incentive and Travel Executives is a worldwide organization of business professionals dedicated to the recognition and development of motivational and performance improvement strategies in the travel industry.

81) Travel Industry Associations

Destination Marketing Association International
2025 M St. NW, Ste. 500
Washington, DC 20036 USA
Phone: 202-296-7888
Fax: 202-296-7889
E-mail Address: info@destinationmarketing.org
Web Address: www.destinationmarketing.org
The Destination Marketing Association International, formerly the International Association of Convention & Visitor Bureaus, strives to enhance the professionalism, effectiveness and image of destination management organizations worldwide. Its members include professionals, industry partners, students and educators from roughly 15 countries.

International Association of Conference Centers (IACC)
243 N. Lindbergh Blvd.
St. Louis, MO 63141 USA
Phone: 314-993-8575
Fax: 314-993-8919
E-mail Address: info@iacconline.org
Web Address: www.iacconline.com
The International Association of Conference Centers (IACC) is a nonprofit, facilities-based organization founded to promote a greater awareness and understanding of the unique features of conference centers around the world.

National Tour Association (NTA)
101 Prosperous Pl., Ste. 350
Lexington, KY 40509 USA
Phone: 859-264-6540
Fax: 859-266-6570
Toll Free: 800-682-8886
E-mail Address: NTAwashington@gmail.com
Web Address: www.ntaonline.com
The National Tour Association (NTA) is an association for travel professionals who have an interest in the packaged travel sector of the industry.

U.S. Travel Association
1100 New York Ave. NW, Ste. 450
Washington, DC 20005-3934 USA
Phone: 202-408-8422
Fax: 202-408-1255
E-mail Address: feedback@ustravel.org
Web Address: www.ustravel.org
The U.S. Travel Association is the result of a merger between the Travel Industry Association (TIA) and the Travel Business Roundtable. It is a nonprofit association that represents and speaks for the common interests and concerns of all components of the U.S. travel industry.

82) U.S. Government Agencies

Bureau of Economic Analysis (BEA)
4600 Silver Hill Rd.
Washington, DC 20233 USA
Phone: 301-278-9004
E-mail Address: customerservice@bea.gov
Web Address: www.bea.gov
The Bureau of Economic Analysis (BEA), an agency of the U.S. Department of Commerce, is the nation's economic accountant, preparing estimates that illuminate key national, international and regional aspects of the U.S. economy.

Bureau of Labor Statistics (BLS)
2 Massachusetts Ave. NE
Washington, DC 20212-0001 USA
Phone: 202-691-5200
Fax: 202-691-7890
Toll Free: 800-877-8339
E-mail Address: blsdata_staff@bls.gov
Web Address: stats.bls.gov
The Bureau of Labor Statistics (BLS) is the principal fact-finding agency for the Federal Government in the field of labor economics and statistics. It is an independent national statistical agency that collects, processes, analyzes and disseminates statistical data to the American public, U.S. Congress, other

federal agencies, state and local governments, business and labor. The BLS also serves as a statistical resource to the Department of Labor.

Equal Employment Opportunity Commission (EEOC)
131 M St. NE
Washington, DC 20507-0100 USA
Phone: 202-663-4900
Fax: 202-633-4679
Toll Free: 800-669-4000
E-mail Address: info@eeoc.gov
Web Address: www.eeoc.gov
The Equal Employment Opportunity Commission (EEOC) is a Federal Government agency focused on practices and programs that foster equal opportunity at work and elsewhere. Its web site features details about various protective laws regarding employment. It also provides information on how to file a discrimination claim.

FedStats Web Address: fedstats.sites.usa.gov/
FedStats compiles information for statistics from over 100 U.S. federal agencies. Visitors can sort the information by agency, geography and topic, as well as perform searches.

National Labor Relations Board (NLRB)
1015 Half Street SE
Washington, DC 20570-0001 USA
Phone: 2002-273-1000
Toll Free: 866-667-6572
Web Address: www.nlrb.gov
The National Labor Relations Board (NLRB) provides case reports on labor disputes, searchable by company or union.

U.S. Census Bureau
4600 Silver Hill Rd.
Washington, DC 20233-8800 USA
Phone: 301-763-4636
Toll Free: 800-923-8282
E-mail Address: pio@census.gov
Web Address: www.census.gov
The U.S. Census Bureau is the official collector of data about the people and economy of the U.S. Founded in 1790, it provides official social, demographic and economic information. In addition to the Population & Housing Census, which it conducts every 10 years, the U.S. Census Bureau numerous other surveys annually.

U.S. Department of Commerce (DOC)
1401 Constitution Ave. NW
Washington, DC 20230 USA
Phone: 202-482-2000
E-mail Address: TheSec@doc.gov
Web Address: www.commerce.gov
The U.S. Department of Commerce (DOC) regulates trade and provides valuable economic analysis of the economy.

U.S. Department of Labor (DOL)
200 Constitution Ave. NW
Washington, DC 20210 USA
Phone: 202-693-4676
Toll Free: 866-487-2365
Web Address: www.dol.gov
The U.S. Department of Labor (DOL) is the government agency responsible for labor regulations.

U.S. Securities and Exchange Commission (SEC)
100 F St. NE
Washington, DC 20549 USA
Phone: 202-942-8088
Toll Free: 800-732-0330
E-mail Address: help@sec.gov
Web Address: www.sec.gov
The U.S. Securities and Exchange Commission (SEC) is a nonpartisan, quasi-judicial regulatory agency responsible for administering federal securities laws. These laws are designed to protect investors in securities markets and ensure that they have access to disclosure of all material information concerning publicly traded securities. Visitors to the web site can access the EDGAR database of corporate financial and business information.

83) Water Technologies & Resources

American Water Resources Association (AWRA)
P.O. Box 1626
Middleburg, VA 20118 USA
Phone: 540-687-8390
Fax: 540-687-8395
E-mail Address: info@awra.org
Web Address: www.awra.org
The American Water Resources Association (AWRA) represents the interests of professionals involved in water resources and provides a platform for education, research, information exchange on water related issues.

84) Wireless & Cellular Industry Associations

Cellular Telecommunications & Internet Association (CTIA)
1400 16th St. NW, Ste. 600
Washington, DC 20036 USA
Phone: 202-785-0081
Web Address: www.ctia.org
The Cellular Telecommunications & Internet Association (CTIA) is an international nonprofit membership organization that represents a variety of wireless communications sectors including cellular service providers, manufacturers, wireless data and Internet companies. CTIA's industry committees study spectrum allocation, homeland security, taxation, safety and emerging technology.

Wireless Communications Association International (WCAI)
1333 H St. NW, Ste. 700 W
Washington, DC 20005-4754 USA
Phone: 202-452-7823
Web Address: www.wcai.com
The Wireless Communications Association International (WCAI) is a nonprofit trade association representing the wireless broadband industry.

85) Writers, Photographers & Editors Associations

American Society of Journalists and Authors, Inc. (ASJA)
355 Lexington Ave., Fl. 15
New York, NY 10017 USA
Phone: 212-997-0947
Web Address: www.asja.org
The American Society of Journalists and Authors (ASJA) is one of the nation's leading organizations of independent nonfiction writers.

American Society of Magazine Editors (ASME)
757 Third Ave., Fl. 11
New York, NY 10017 USA
Phone: 212-872-3700
E-mail Address: mpa@magazine.org
Web Address: www.magazine.org/asme
The American Society of Magazine Editors (ASME) is a professional organization for editors of print and online magazines. ASME is part of the Magazine Publishers of America (MPA).

American Society of News Editors (ASNE)
209 Reynolds Journalism Institute
Missouri School of Journalism
Columbia, MO 65211 USA
Phone: 573-884-2405
Fax: 573-884-3824
Web Address: www.asne.org
The American Society of News Editors (ASNE) is an association that brings together editors of daily newspapers and people directly involved with developing content for daily newspapers.

Association of Opinion Journalists
801 Third St. South
c/o The Poynter Institute
St. Petersburg, FL 33701 USA
Phone: 518-454-5472
E-mail Address: AOJ@poynter.org
Web Address: https://aoj.wildapricot.org/
The Association of Opinion Journalists, formerly known as The National Conference of Editorial Writers (NCEW) strives to stimulate the conscience and improve the quality of opinion writing.

International Women's Writing Guild (IWWG)
274 Madison Ave., Ste. 1202
New York, NY 10016 USA
Phone: 917-720-6959
E-mail Address: iwwgquestions@gmail.com
Web Address: www.iwwg.com
The International Women's Writing Guild (IWWG) is a network for the personal and professional empowerment of women through writing.

Media Communications Association International (MCAI)
c/o MCA-I Chapter
P.O. Box 5135
Madison, WI 53705-0135 USA
Phone: 888-899-6224
E-mail Address: m_k_schaefer@yahoo.com
Web Address: www.mca-i.org
The Media Communications Association International (MCAI) is the leading global community for media communications professionals seeking to drive the convergence of communications and technology for the growth of the profession.

National Association of Hispanic Journalists (NAHJ)
1050 Connecticut Ave. NW, Fl. 10
Washington, DC 20036 USA
Phone: 202-662-7145
E-mail Address: nahj@nahj.org
Web Address: www.nahj.org
The National Association of Hispanic Journalists (NAHJ) is dedicated to the recognition and professional advancement of Hispanics in the news industry.

National Association of Science Writers, Inc. (NASW)
P.O. Box 7905
Berkley, CA 94707 USA
Phone: 510-647-9500
Web Address: www.nasw.org
The National Association of Science Writers (NASW) exists to foster the dissemination of accurate information regarding science through all media devoted to informing the public.

National Federation of Press Women (NFPW)
200 Little Falls St., Ste. 405
Falls Church, VA 22046 USA
Phone: 703-237-9804
Fax: 703-237-9808
E-mail Address: presswomen@aol.com
Web Address: www.nfpw.org
The National Federation of Press Women (NFPW) is an organization of professional journalists and communicators.

National Writers Union (NWU)
256 W. 38th St., Ste. 703
New York, NY 10018 USA
Phone: 212-254-0279
Fax: 212-254-0673
E-mail Address: nwu@nwu.org
Web Address: www.nwu.org
The National Writers Union (NWU) is a labor union that represents freelance writers in all genres, formats and media. It is committed to improving the economic and working conditions of freelance writers.

Society of Children's Book Writers and Illustrators (SCBWI)
4727 Wilshire Blvd., Ste. 301
Los Angeles, CA 90010 USA
Phone: 323-782-1010
Fax: 323-782-1892
E-mail Address: scbwi@scbwi.org
Web Address: www.scbwi.org
The Society of Children's Book Writers and Illustrators (SCBWI) serves people who write, illustrate or share a vital interest in children's literature, including publishers, librarians, booksellers and agents.

Chapter 5

THE AMERICAN EMPLOYERS 500: WHO THEY ARE AND HOW THEY WERE CHOSEN

Note: financial data given for each of the AMERICAN EMPLOYERS 500 firms is for the year ended December 31, 2018 or the latest figures available to the editors. Telephone numbers, addresses, contact names, Internet addresses and other vital facts were collected in the fall of 2019.

The companies chosen to be listed in THE ALMANAC OF AMERICAN EMPLOYERS are not the same as the "Fortune 500" or any other list of corporations. The AMERICAN EMPLOYERS 500 were chosen specifically for their likelihood to provide new job openings to the greatest number of employees. Complete information about each firm can be found in the "Individual Data Listings," beginning about the middle of this book. They are in alphabetical order.

THE AMERICAN EMPLOYERS 500 includes companies from all parts of the United States and from nearly all industry segments: selected financial services firms, retailers, service companies, wholesalers and distributors, and others, as well as industrial companies, technology firms and manufacturers.

Simply stated, the list contains 500 of the largest, most successful employers in the United States today. In particular, the list contains companies that we have hand-selected to have qualities that we feel will be of greatest interest to job seekers of today who are looking for opportunities to obtain employment with major corporations.

In order to make this reference guide as useful as possible, we are selecting companies for this list by focusing on the type of business, the industry sector served and a company's competitive advantage. To a lesser extent, we are also considering the most recent year's financial performance. We consider industry sector to be a major factor, because some sectors may not offer good career prospects today. Consequently, we have deleted some well-known companies due to the state of their particular markets.

To be included in our list, the firms were selected based on the following criteria:

1) U.S.-based companies. (However, a small number of companies may be subsidiaries of foreign-based firms. Also, a small number of the firms are major U.S. employers that utilize headquarters addresses in other nations.)

2) 2,500 employees or more.

3) These are almost exclusively for-profit companies. However, a small number are major, non-profit health care companies.

4) Selected Type of Business and/or Industry Sector. Companies were chosen based on our analysis of the business potential of their products, services and industrial sectors in light of today's economic conditions and the effects of globalization and technological changes.

The companies were chosen in this manner for the following reasons:

500 COMPANIES so there is a broad base among which to make comparisons and from which you can study potential employers.

LARGER EMPLOYERS (2,500 or more employees) so the information can pertain to as many employees as reasonably possible, and so the companies ranked will tend to create large numbers of job openings. Also, large companies historically have offered significantly higher wages, better benefits and better training than small employers.

FOR-PROFIT so that job seekers using THE ALMANAC OF AMERICAN EMPLOYERS can choose positions in the profit-seeking, private sector, where incentive plans may be available to motivate and reward them, such as profit sharing, stock ownership, bonuses, stock options and the high pay and prestige of top executive posts.

COMPANIES THAT OPERATE IN PROMISING BUSINESS SECTORS because:
1) Companies that are stable or enjoying growing business are much more likely to have job openings. Corporate stability is more important to job seekers today than ever before due to the wave of layoffs and downsizing that continues to sweep through the U.S. (See Chapter 1, "Major Trends Affecting Job Seekers.")
2) These companies are much more likely to offer advancement opportunities. Current employees will benefit from promote-from-within policies when new plants, new stores, new product lines or new offices are opened.

Obviously, some companies are better to work for than others, depending on what you value. Creating this annual list is an arduous task. Generally, our results are very good, but we do occasionally select a company that soon develops problems or announces a layoff. The world of business constantly goes through major changes, and unforeseen events often occur. Nonetheless, it is not easy for a firm to be selected for the AMERICAN EMPLOYERS 500, and the mere presence of a company on the list can be taken as evidence that it has excelled in many ways. To start with, it has to have generated enough business to employ thousands of people–never a simple task. Also, many of these firms are among the dominant companies in their industries.

INDEX OF COMPANIES WITHIN INDUSTRY GROUPS

The industry codes shown below are based on the 2012 NAIC code system (NAIC is used by many analysts as a replacement for older SIC codes because NAIC is more specific to today's industry sectors, see www.census.gov/NAICS). Companies are given a primary NAIC code, reflecting the main line of business of each firm.

Industry Group/Company	Industry Code	2018 Sales	2018 Profits
Advertising Agencies and Marketing Services			
BBDO Worldwide	541810	2,821,500,000	
Interpublic Group of Companies Inc	541810	9,714,400,256	618,899,968
McCann Worldgroup	541810	5,500,000,000	
Omnicom Group Inc	541810	15,290,200,064	1,326,400,000
Advertising, Public Relations and Marketing Services			
Acosta Inc	541800	3,910,000,000	
Alliance Data Systems Corporation	541800	7,791,200,256	963,100,032
Valassis Communications Inc	541800	2,341,000,000	
Agricultural Equipment or Machinery (Farm Implement) Manufacturing			
Deere & Company (John Deere)	333111	37,021,298,688	2,368,399,872
Aircraft Components, Parts, Assemblies, Interiors and Systems Manufacturing (Aerospace)			
Spirit AeroSystems Holdings Inc	336413	7,222,000,128	617,000,000
TransDigm Group Incorporated	336413	3,811,126,016	957,062,016
Aircraft Engine and Engine Parts Manufacturing			
United Technologies Corporation	336412	66,501,001,216	5,269,000,192
Aircraft Manufacturing (Aerospace), including Passenger Airliners and Military Aircraft,			
General Dynamics Corporation	336411	36,193,001,472	3,344,999,936
Gulfstream Aerospace Corporation	336411	8,977,500,000	
Lockheed Martin Corporation	336411	53,761,998,848	5,046,000,128
Northrop Grumman Corporation	336411	30,094,999,552	3,228,999,936
Textron Inc	336411	13,971,999,744	1,222,000,000
Airlines, Scheduled Passenger Air Transportation			
Alaska Air Group Inc	481111	8,264,000,000	437,000,000
American Airlines Group Inc	481111	44,541,001,728	1,412,000,000
Delta Air Lines Inc	481111	44,437,999,616	3,935,000,064
JetBlue Airways Corporation	481111	7,657,999,872	188,000,000
Southwest Airlines Co	481111	21,965,000,704	2,464,999,936
Spirit Airlines Inc	481111	3,323,034,112	155,748,992
United Continental Holdings Inc	481111	41,302,999,040	2,128,999,936
Aluminum Production, Alumina Refining and Aluminum Form Production			
Alcoa Corporation	331313	13,402,999,808	227,000,000
Ambulatory Health Care Services, Other			
Magellan Health Inc	621999	7,314,150,912	24,181,000
Ambulatory, Outpatient Surgical Clinics, Urgent Care and Emergency Centers			
AMSURG Corporation	621493	3,200,000,000	
Apparel and Clothing Brands, Designers, Importers and Distributors			
HanesBrands Inc	424300	6,803,955,200	553,084,032

Industry Group/Company	Industry Code	2018 Sales	2018 Profits
Asset Management			
BlackRock Inc	523920	14,197,999,616	4,304,999,936
Fidelity Investments Financial Services	523920	20,400,000,000	6,300,000,000
T Rowe Price Group Inc	523920	5,372,599,808	1,837,500,032
TIAA	523920	41,052,100,000	
Automobile (Car) and Light Truck Dealers (New)			
Group 1 Automotive Inc	441110	11,601,357,824	157,772,000
Hendrick Automotive Group	441110	9,427,756,576	
Larry H Miller Group of Companies	441110	5,159,425,257	
Lithia Motors Inc	441110	11,821,400,064	265,700,000
Penske Automotive Group Inc	441110	22,785,099,776	471,000,000
Automobile (Car) and Light Truck Dealers (Used)			
CarMax Inc	441120	17,120,208,896	664,112,000
DriveTime Automotive Group Inc	441120	1,764,000,000	
Automobile (Car) and Other Motor Vehicle Wholesale Distribution			
JM Family Enterprises Inc	423110	16,300,000,000	
Automobile (Car) and Truck Brake System Manufacturing			
WABCO Holdings Inc	336340	3,831,000,064	394,100,000
Automobile (Car) and Truck Gasoline Engine and Engine Parts Manufacturing			
BorgWarner Inc	336310	10,529,599,488	930,700,032
Automobile (Car) and Truck Parts, Components and Systems Manufacturing, Including Gasoline Engines, Interiors and Electronics,			
Cummins Inc	336300	23,771,000,832	2,140,999,936
Dana Incorporated	336300	8,143,000,064	427,000,000
Federal-Mogul LLC	336300	8,190,000,000	
Gentex Corporation	336300	1,834,063,744	437,883,104
Lear Corporation	336300	21,148,499,968	1,149,799,936
LKQ Corporation	336300	11,876,673,536	480,118,016
Modine Manufacturing Company	336300	2,103,100,032	22,200,000
Tenneco Inc	336300	11,763,000,320	55,000,000
Automobile (Car) Manufacturing (incl. Autonomous or Self-Driving)			
Ford Motor Company	336111	160,338,001,920	3,676,999,936
General Motors Company (GM)	336111	147,049,005,056	8,014,000,128
Hyundai Motor America	336111	13,689,800,000	-295,529,000
Mercedes-Benz USA LLC	336111	48,171,422,250	
Automobile (Car) Parts Stores			
Advance Auto Parts Inc	441310	9,580,554,240	423,847,008
O Reilly Automotive Inc	441310	9,536,428,032	1,324,487,040
Automobile (Car) Rental			
Avis Budget Group Inc	532111	9,123,999,744	165,000,000
Dollar Thrifty Automotive Group Inc	532111	1,620,000,000	
Enterprise Holdings Inc	532111	24,100,000,000	
Automobile (Car) Reservations (e.g. Uber), Car Sharing, Sharing Economy, Ticket Offices, Time Share and Vacation Club Rentals and Specialty Reservation Services			
Lyft Inc	561599	2,156,615,936	-911,334,976

Industry Group/Company	Industry Code	2018 Sales	2018 Profits
Uber Technologies Inc	561599	11,269,999,616	997,000,000
Building Material Dealers			
BMC Stock Holdings Inc	444190	3,682,447,872	119,738,000
Burial Casket Manufacturing			
Matthews International Corporation	339995	1,602,579,968	107,371,000
Cable TV Programming, Cable Networks and Subscription Video			
Discovery Inc	515210	10,552,999,936	614,000,000
Netflix Inc	515210	15,794,340,864	1,211,241,984
Walt Disney Company (The)	515210	59,434,000,384	12,597,999,616
Candy and Chocolate Manufacturing (From Cocao Beans)			
Hershey Company (The)	311351	7,791,069,184	1,177,561,984
Mars Incorporated	311351	37,931,250,000	
Car Repair (Repair and Maintenance of Automobiles and Trucks)			
Monro Muffler Brake Inc	811100	1,127,815,040	63,935,000
Carpets (Carpeting and Floor Coverings) and Rugs Mills and Manufacturing			
Mohawk Industries Inc	314110	9,983,634,432	861,704,000
Casino Hotels and Casino Resorts			
Las Vegas Sands Corp (The Venetian)	721120	13,729,000,448	2,412,999,936
Wynn Resorts Limited	721120	6,717,660,160	572,430,016
Chips (Tortilla, Potato and Corn), Popcorn and Pretzel Manufacturing			
Frito-Lay North America Inc	311919	16,578,450,000	4,566,600,000
Cloud, Data Processing, Business Process Outsourcing (BPO) and Internet Content Hosting Services			
Automatic Data Processing Inc (ADP)	518210	13,325,800,448	1,620,800,000
GoDaddy Inc	518210	2,660,100,096	77,100,000
Coffee Shops, Doughnut Shops, Ice Cream Parlors, Canteens and Snack Bars			
Starbucks Corporation	722515	24,719,499,264	4,518,300,160
Commercial Banks (Banking)			
Bank of America Corporation	522110	91,247,001,600	28,146,999,296
Bank of New York Mellon Corporation	522110	15,985,999,872	4,265,999,872
BB&T Corporation	522110	11,557,999,616	3,236,999,936
Capital One Financial Corporation	522110	27,172,999,168	6,015,000,064
Citigroup Inc	522110	72,854,003,712	18,044,999,680
Cullen-Frost Bankers Inc	522110	1,309,177,984	454,918,016
JP Morgan Chase & Co Inc	522110	109,028,999,168	32,473,999,360
US Bancorp (US Bank)	522110	22,520,999,936	7,096,000,000
Commercial Real Estate Investment and Operations, Including Office Buildings, Shopping Centers, Industrial Properties and Related REITs			
Jones Lang LaSalle Incorporated	531120	16,318,400,512	484,500,000
Computer and Data Systems Design, Consulting and Integration Services			
Accenture LLP	541512	17,800,000,000	
CACI International Inc	541512	4,467,859,968	301,171,008
Cognizant Technology Solutions Corporation	541512	16,124,999,680	2,100,999,936

Industry Group/Company	Industry Code	2018 Sales	2018 Profits
Concentrix Corporation	541512	2,463,151,000	
MAXIMUS Inc	541512	2,392,236,032	220,751,008
Sapient Corporation	541512	1,765,050,000	
Science Applications International Corporation (SAIC)	541512	4,454,000,128	179,000,000
Computer Disks (Discs) and Drives, including Magnetic and Optical Storage Media Manufacturing			
Dell EMC	334112	28,000,000,000	
Computer Manufacturing, Including PCs, Laptops, Mainframes and Tablets			
Dell Technologies Inc	334111	78,660,001,792	-3,728,000,000
Computer Networking & Related Equipment Manufacturing (may incl. Internet of Things, IoT)			
Cisco Systems Inc	334210A	49,329,999,872	110,000,000
Juniper Networks Inc	334210A	4,647,499,776	566,899,968
Computer Peripherals and Accessories, including Printers, Monitors and Terminals Manufacturing			
NCR Corporation	334118	6,405,000,192	-88,000,000
Computer Software, Accounting, Banking & Financial			
Concur Technologies Inc	511210Q	1,767,980,000	2,043,960
Intuit Inc	511210Q	5,964,000,256	1,211,000,064
Jack Henry & Associates Inc	511210Q	1,536,603,008	376,660,000
Workday Inc	511210Q	2,143,049,984	-321,222,016
Computer Software, Business Management & ERP			
BMC Software Inc	511210H	2,000,000,000	
Microsoft Corporation	511210H	110,360,002,560	16,570,999,808
Oracle Corporation	511210H	39,830,999,040	3,824,999,936
Oracle NetSuite	511210H	914,550,000	
SAS Institute Inc	511210H	3,300,000,000	
Computer Software, Electronic Games, Apps & Entertainment			
Activision Blizzard Inc	511210G	7,500,000,256	1,812,999,936
Disney Parks, Experiences and Products (DPEP)	511210G	24,947,000,000	6,001,000,000
Computer Software, Healthcare & Biotechnology			
Allscripts Healthcare Solutions Inc	511210D	1,749,961,984	412,334,016
Cerner Corporation	511210D	5,366,325,248	630,059,008
Epic Systems Corporation	511210D	2,890,000,000	
Computer Software, Multimedia, Graphics & Publishing			
Adobe Systems Inc	511210F	9,030,007,808	2,590,774,016
Computer Software, Network Management, System Testing, & Storage			
Citrix Systems Inc	511210B	2,973,903,104	575,667,008
F5 Networks Inc	511210B	2,161,406,976	453,688,992
ServiceNow Inc	511210B	2,608,816,128	-26,704,000
VMware Inc	511210B	7,921,999,872	570,000,000
Computer Software, Operating Systems, Languages & Development Tools, Artificial Intelligence (AI)			
Red Hat Inc	511210I	2,920,461,056	258,803,008
Computer Software, Product Lifecycle, Engineering, Design & CAD			
Cadence Design Systems Inc	511210N	2,138,022,016	345,776,992

Industry Group/Company	Industry Code	2018 Sales	2018 Profits
National Instruments Corporation	511210N	1,359,132,032	155,056,992
Synopsys Inc	511210N	3,121,058,048	432,518,016
Computer Software, Sales & Customer Relationship Management			
SalesForce.com Inc	511210K	10,480,012,288	127,478,000
Computer Software, Security & Anti-Virus			
McAfee LLC	511210E	2,815,050,000	
Symantec Corporation	511210E	4,833,999,872	1,138,000,000
Computers, Peripherals, Software and Accessories Distribution			
Anixter International Inc	423430	8,400,200,192	156,300,000
Arrow Electronics Inc	423430	29,676,767,232	716,195,008
Avnet Inc	423430	19,036,891,136	-156,424,000
CDW Corporation	423430	16,240,499,712	643,000,000
Ingram Micro Inc	423430	50,436,670,000	352,186,000
SYNNEX Corporation	423430	20,053,764,096	300,598,016
Tech Data Corporation	423430	36,775,010,304	116,641,000
Connectors for Electronics Manufacturing			
Belden Inc	334417	2,585,368,064	160,894,000
Molex LLC	334417	4,150,000,000	
Construction and Mining (except Oil Well) Machinery and Equipment Wholesale Distribution			
Fastenal Company	423810	4,965,100,032	751,900,032
Construction Equipment and Machinery Manufacturing			
Hillenbrand Inc	333120	1,770,099,968	76,600,000
Terex Corporation	333120	5,125,000,192	113,700,000
Construction of Telecommunications Lines and Systems & Electric Power Lines and Systems			
American Tower Corporation (REIT)	237130	7,440,099,840	1,236,400,000
Crown Castle International Corp	237130	5,423,000,064	671,000,000
Dycom Industries Inc	237130	1,411,347,968	68,835,000
Quanta Services Inc	237130	11,171,423,232	293,345,984
Consulting Services, Human Resources			
Aon Hewitt	541612	6,200,000,000	
Mercer LLC	541612	4,745,300,000	
Contract Electronics Manufacturing Services (CEM) and Printed Circuits Assembly			
Jabil Inc	334418	22,095,415,296	86,330,000
Sanmina Corporation	334418	7,110,130,176	-95,533,000
Couriers, Express, Gig Economy, and Overnight Delivery			
FedEx Corporation	492110	65,450,000,384	4,572,000,256
United Parcel Service Inc (UPS)	492110	71,861,002,240	4,791,000,064
CPA Firms (Certified Public Accountants), Accounting			
Deloitte LLP	541211	19,897,000,000	
EY LLP	541211	15,600,000,000	
Grant Thornton LLP	541211	1,790,000,000	
KPMG LLP	541211	11,100,000,000	
PricewaterhouseCoopers (PwC)	541211	41,280,000,000	
Credit Bureaus and Credit Rating Agencies			
Moody's Corporation	561450	4,442,699,776	1,309,600,000

Industry Group/Company	Industry Code	2018 Sales	2018 Profits
Credit Card Processing, Online Payment Processing, EFT, ACH and Clearinghouses			
American Express Company	522320	28,864,999,424	6,920,999,936
Fiserv Inc	522320	5,823,000,064	1,187,000,064
FleetCor Technologies Inc	522320	2,433,491,968	811,483,008
Heartland Payment Systems Inc	522320	2,717,400,000	
MasterCard Inc	522320	14,949,999,616	5,858,999,808
PayPal Holdings Inc	522320	15,450,999,808	2,056,999,936
Visa Inc	522320	20,608,999,424	10,300,999,680
Cruise Lines			
Carnival Corporation	483112	18,880,999,424	3,152,000,000
Norwegian Cruise Line Holdings Ltd (NCL)	483112	6,055,126,016	954,843,008
Royal Caribbean Cruises Ltd	483112	9,493,849,088	1,811,042,048
Department Stores (except Discount Department Stores)			
Nordstrom Inc	452111	15,477,999,616	437,000,000
Dialysis Centers			
DaVita Healthcare Partners Inc	621492	11,404,851,200	159,394,000
Direct Selling			
Mary Kay Inc	454390	3,250,000,000	
Discount Department Stores			
Kohls Corporation	452112	19,094,999,040	859,000,000
Distributors of Telecommunications Equipment, Telephones, Cellphones and Electronics Components (Wholesale Distribution)			
Brightstar Corporation	423690	10,500,000,000	
Electric Motor and Power & Motor Generator Manufacturing			
Regal-Beloit Corporation	335312	3,645,600,000	231,200,000
Electric Wiring Device Manufacturing			
Hubbell Incorporated	335931	4,481,699,840	360,200,000
Electrical Contractors and Other Wiring Installation Contractors			
EMCOR Group Inc	238210	8,130,631,168	283,531,008
Rosendin Electric Inc	238210	2,000,000,000	
Electricity Control Panels, Circuit Breakers and Power Switches Equipment (Switchgear) Manufacturing			
Broadcom Inc	335313	20,848,001,024	12,259,000,320
Littelfuse Inc	335313	1,718,467,968	164,564,992
Engineered Wood Member (except Truss) Manufacturing			
Boise Cascade Company	321213	4,995,290,112	20,477,000
Engineering Services, Including Civil, Mechanical, Electronic, Computer and Environmental Engineering			
Black & Veatch Holding Company	541330	3,450,000,000	
Burns & McDonnell Inc	541330	2,586,000,000	
Factory Automation, Robots (Robotics) Industrial Process, Thermostat, Flow Meter and Environmental Quality Monitoring and Control Manufacturing (incl. Artificial Intelligence, AI)			
Ametek Inc	334513	4,845,872,128	777,932,992
Emerson Electric Co	334513	17,408,000,000	2,203,000,064
Rockwell Automation Inc	334513	6,665,999,872	535,500,000

Industry Group/Company	Industry Code	2018 Sales	2018 Profits
Roper Technologies Inc	334513	5,191,199,744	944,400,000
Family Clothing, Apparel and Accessories Stores			
Ross Stores Inc	448140	14,134,731,776	1,362,753,024
TJX Companies Inc (T.J. Maxx)	448140	35,864,662,016	2,607,948,032
Fiber Optic Cable, Connectors and Related Products Manufacturing			
Amphenol Corporation	335921	8,201,999,872	1,204,999,936
CommScope Holding Company Inc	335921	4,568,506,880	140,216,992
Financial Data Publishing - Print & Online			
Bloomberg LP	511120A	10,000,000,000	
FactSet Research Systems Inc	511120A	1,350,145,024	267,084,992
Flour, Grain & Corn Milling and Cooking Oils (Including Vegetable, Canola, Olive, Peanut & Soy) Manufacturing			
Archer-Daniels-Midland Company (ADM)	311200	64,341,000,192	1,810,000,000
Bunge Limited	311200	45,743,001,600	267,000,000
Cargill Incorporated	311200	114,695,000,000	3,103,000,000
Food Service Contractors			
Aramark Corporation	722310	15,789,632,512	567,884,992
HMSHost Corporation	722310	3,500,000,000	
Sodexo Inc	722310	9,900,000,000	
Fossil Fuel Electric Power Generation			
Berkshire Hathaway Energy Company	221112	19,787,000,000	2,591,000,000
DTE Energy Company	221112	14,211,999,744	1,120,000,000
Duke Energy Corporation	221112	24,521,000,960	2,665,999,872
FirstEnergy Corporation	221112	11,260,999,680	1,348,000,000
Funeral Homes and Funeral Services			
Service Corporation International Inc	812210	3,190,173,952	447,208,000
General Grocery Products Distributors (Groceries Wholesale Distribution, Excluding Meats, Frozen Foods and Vegetables)			
C&S Wholesale Grocers Inc	424410	32,025,000,000	
SYSCO Corporation	424410	58,727,325,696	1,430,765,952
United Natural Foods Inc	424410	10,226,682,880	165,670,000
Hardware Stores			
Tractor Supply Company	444130	7,911,046,144	532,356,992
Hazardous Waste Collection			
Stericycle Inc	562112	3,485,900,032	-244,700,000
Health Insurance and Medical Insurance Underwriters (Direct Carriers), including Group Health, Supplemental Health and HMOs			
Aetna Inc	524114	61,500,000,000	4,000,000,000
AFLAC Incorporated	524114	21,688,999,936	2,920,000,000
Amerigroup Corporation	524114	11,500,000,000	
Anthem Inc	524114	92,104,998,912	3,750,000,128
Blue Shield of California	524114	20,632,000,000	413,000,000
Centene Corporation	524114	60,116,000,768	900,000,000
Cigna Corporation	524114	48,568,999,936	2,636,999,936
Health Care Service Corporation (HCSC)	524114	35,900,000,000	
Humana Inc	524114	56,911,998,976	1,683,000,064
Molina Healthcare Inc	524114	18,765,000,704	707,000,000

Industry Group/Company	Industry Code	2018 Sales	2018 Profits
UnitedHealth Group Inc	524114	224,871,006,208	11,985,999,872
Unum Group	524114	11,598,499,840	523,400,000
WellCare Health Plans Inc	524114	20,414,099,456	439,800,000
Heavy Construction, Including Civil Engineering-Construction, Major Construction Projects, Land Subdivision, Infrastructure, Utilities, Highways and Bridges			
Bechtel Group Inc	237000	25,500,000,000	
Fluor Corporation	237000	19,166,599,168	224,832,992
Jacobs Engineering Group Inc	237000	14,984,645,632	163,431,008
KBR Inc	237000	4,912,999,936	281,000,000
Heavy Duty Truck (including Buses) Manufacturing			
Oshkosh Corporation	336120	7,705,500,160	471,900,000
Highway, Street, Tunnel & Bridge Construction (Infrastructure)			
AECOM	237310	20,155,512,832	136,468,000
Tutor Perini Corporation	237310	4,454,662,144	83,436,000
Home Centers, Building Materials			
Home Depot Inc (The)	444110	100,904,001,536	8,629,999,616
Lowe's Companies Inc	444110	68,619,001,856	3,447,000,064
Menard Inc	444110	10,950,000,000	
Home Health Care Services			
Chemed Corporation	621610	1,782,648,064	205,544,000
Envision Healthcare Corporation	621610	8,500,000,000	
LHC Group Inc	621610	1,809,963,008	63,574,000
Hospitals, General Medical and Surgical			
AdventHealth	622110	10,000,000,000	
Advocate Aurora Health	622110	9,213,406,000	38,416,000
Ascension	622110	23,158,956,000	2,374,986,000
Baylor Scott & White Health	622110	994,075,691	
BJC HealthCare	622110	5,300,000,000	
Cleveland Clinic Foundation (The)	622110	8,900,000,000	266,000,000
Community Health Systems Inc	622110	14,154,999,808	-788,000,000
Fairview Health Services	622110	5,600,000,000	96,700,000
HCA Healthcare Inc	622110	46,677,000,192	3,787,000,064
Houston Methodist	622110	4,000,000,000	
Kaiser Permanente	622110	79,700,000,000	2,500,000,000
LifePoint Health Inc	622110	7,400,000,000	
Mayo Clinic	622110	12,600,000,000	706,000,000
MedStar Health	622110	5,800,000,000	
Providence St Joseph Health	622110	24,428,000,000	-445,000,000
Spectrum Health	622110	6,004,223,000	285,582,000
Sutter Health Inc	622110	12,700,000,000	-200,000,000
Trinity Health	622110	18,345,405,000	949,130,000
Universal Health Services Inc	622110	10,772,278,272	779,705,024
Hospitals, Psychiatric and Substance Abuse			
Acadia Healthcare Company Inc	622210	3,012,442,112	-175,750,000
Hospitals, Specialty			
Select Medical Holdings Corporation	622310	5,081,257,984	137,840,000

Industry Group/Company	Industry Code	2018 Sales	2018 Profits
Hotels, Motels, Inns and Resorts (Lodging and Hospitality)			
Hilton Worldwide Holdings Inc	721110	8,906,000,384	764,000,000
Hyatt Hotels Corporation	721110	4,473,999,872	769,000,000
Kimpton Hotel & Restaurant Group LLC	721110	1,300,000,000	
Loews Hotels Holding Corporation	721110	1,422,750,000	
Marriott International Inc	721110	20,757,999,616	1,907,000,064
Ritz-Carlton Hotel Company LLC (The)	721110	2,415,000,000	
Wyndham Destinations Inc	721110	3,931,000,064	672,000,000
Household Dishwasher, Disposal, Trash Compactor and Water Heater Manufacturing			
AO Smith Corporation	335228	3,187,899,904	444,200,000
Housewares, including Linen, Bath, Kitchen and Cookware			
Bed Bath & Beyond Inc	442299	12,349,300,736	424,857,984
Container Store Inc (The)	442299	857,228,032	19,428,000
Industrial Equipment and Machinery Distribution			
WW Grainger Inc	423830	11,221,000,192	782,000,000
Industrial Machinery Manufacturing, Other			
Illinois Tool Works Inc	333249	14,768,000,000	2,563,000,064
Insurance Agencies, Risk Management Consultants and Insurance Brokers			
Arthur J Gallagher & Co	524210	6,934,000,128	633,500,032
Brown & Brown Inc	524210	2,009,857,024	344,255,008
Hub International Limited	524210	2,000,000,000	
Marsh & McLennan Companies Inc	524210	14,949,999,616	1,650,000,000
Insurance Claims Administration and Services			
athenahealth Inc	524292	1,300,000,000	
Internet Search Engines, Online Publishing, Sharing, Gig and Consumer Services, Online Radio, TV and Entertainment Sites and Social Media			
Alphabet Inc (Google)	519130	136,818,999,296	30,735,998,976
CoStar Group Inc	519130	1,191,832,064	238,334,000
Cox Automotive Inc	519130	7,780,500,000	
Facebook Inc	519130	55,837,999,104	22,112,000,000
IAC/InterActiveCorp	519130	4,262,892,032	626,961,024
LinkedIn Corporation	519130	5,300,000,000	
Match Group Inc	519130	1,729,849,984	477,939,008
Zillow Inc	519130	1,333,554,048	-119,858,000
Investment Banking, and Related Stock Brokerage and Investment Services			
Goldman Sachs Group Inc (The)	523110	33,415,999,488	10,458,999,808
Legg Mason Inc	523110	3,140,322,048	285,075,008
Merrill Lynch & Co Inc	523110	15,900,000,000	
Morgan Stanley	523110	37,714,001,920	8,748,000,256
Raymond James Financial Inc	523110	7,181,929,984	856,694,976
Stifel Financial Corp	523110	2,982,914,048	393,968,000
Iron and Steel Mills and Ferroalloy Manufacturing			
United States Steel Corporation	331110	14,177,999,872	1,115,000,064
Janitorial Services			
ABM Industries Incorporated	561720	6,442,200,064	97,800,000

Industry Group/Company	Industry Code	2018 Sales	2018 Profits
Laboratory Instruments and Lab Equipment Manufacturing			
Waters Corporation	334516	2,419,929,088	593,793,984
Landscaping Services			
ServiceMaster Company LLC (The)	561730	1,900,000,000	-41,000,000
Life Insurance and Annuity Underwriters (Direct Carriers)			
Hartford Financial Services Group Inc (The)	524113	18,954,999,808	1,807,000,064
John Hancock Financial	524113	8,599,500,000	
Lincoln National Corporation	524113	16,423,999,488	1,640,999,936
MassMutual Financial Group	524113	32,484,000,000	-716,000,000
Mutual of Omaha Companies (The)	524113	9,347,200,000	277,300,000
New York Life Insurance Company	524113	43,425,300,000	880,000,000
Northwestern Mutual Life Insurance Company (The)	524113	28,482,000,000	783,000,000
Principal Financial Group Inc	524113	14,237,200,384	1,546,499,968
Prudential Financial Inc	524113	62,991,998,976	4,073,999,872
Linen Supply			
Cintas Corporation	812331	6,476,632,064	842,585,984
Management Consulting and General Business Consulting (including Human Resources)			
AT Kearney Inc	541610	1,300,000,000	
Bain & Company Inc	541610	3,800,000,000	
Booz Allen Hamilton Holding Corporation	541610	6,171,852,800	305,111,008
Boston Consulting Group Inc (The, BCG)	541610	7,500,000,000	
FTI Consulting Inc	541610	2,027,876,992	150,611,008
McKinsey & Company Inc	541610	10,000,000,000	
Oliver Wyman Group	541610	2,033,700,000	
Strategy&	541610	1,400,000,000	
Market Research, Business Intelligence and Opinion Polling			
Gartner Inc	541910	3,975,453,952	122,456,000
Nielsen Holdings plc	541910	6,514,999,808	-712,000,000
Medical Diagnostics, Reagents, Assays and Test Kits Manufacturing			
Bio-Rad Laboratories Inc	325413	2,289,414,912	365,614,016
Illumina Inc	325413	3,332,999,936	826,000,000
PerkinElmer Inc	325413	2,777,996,032	237,927,008
Medical Equipment and Supplies Manufacturing			
3M Company	339100	32,764,999,680	5,349,000,192
Baxter International Inc	339100	11,127,000,064	1,624,000,000
Becton, Dickinson and Company	339100	15,982,999,552	311,000,000
Boston Scientific Corporation	339100	9,822,999,552	1,671,000,064
Cooper Companies Inc (The)	339100	2,532,800,000	139,900,000
Dentsply Sirona Inc	339100	3,986,299,904	-1,011,000,000
Edwards Lifesciences Corporation	339100	3,722,800,128	722,200,000
Hill-Rom Holdings Inc	339100	2,848,000,000	252,400,000
Stryker Corporation	339100	13,601,000,448	3,552,999,936
Zimmer Biomet Holdings Inc	339100	7,932,899,840	-379,200,000
Medical Imaging and Electromedical (Medical Devices) Equipment, including MRI, Ultrasound, Pacemakers, EKG and CAT			
IDEXX Laboratories Inc	334510	2,213,242,112	377,031,008

Industry Group/Company	Industry Code	2018 Sales	2018 Profits
Philips Healthcare	334510	20,726,700,000	1,254,740,000
ResMed Inc	334510	2,340,196,096	315,588,000
Varian Medical Systems Inc	334510	2,919,099,904	149,900,000
Medical Laboratories			
Laboratory Corporation of America Holdings	621511	11,333,399,552	883,699,968
Quest Diagnostics Incorporated	621511	7,530,999,808	736,000,000
Medical, Dental and Hospital Equipment and Supplies (Medical Devices) Wholesale Distribution			
Henry Schein Inc	423450	13,201,994,752	535,880,992
Thermo Fisher Scientific Inc	423450	24,358,000,640	2,937,999,872
Metal Can Manufacturing			
Ball Corporation	332431	11,635,000,320	454,000,000
Crown Holdings Inc	332431	11,150,999,552	439,000,000
Missile (Aerospace Defense) and Space Vehicle Manufacturing			
Raytheon Company	336414	27,057,999,872	2,908,999,936
Mobile, Modular & Prefabricated Homes and Buildings Manufacturing			
Clayton Homes Inc	321992	6,046,000,000	911,000,000
Mortgage Brokers and Loan Brokers			
Quicken Loans Inc	522310	4,305,000,000	
Motion Picture, Movies, Films, Television (TV) Programming and Video Production			
Walt Disney Studios (The)	512110	9,500,000,000	
New Home Builders (Production, For-Sale Home Builders)			
DR Horton Inc	236117	16,067,999,744	1,460,300,032
Lennar Corporation	236117	20,571,631,616	1,695,831,040
NVR Inc	236117	7,175,266,816	797,196,992
PulteGroup Inc	236117	10,188,331,008	1,022,022,976
Toll Brothers Inc	236117	7,143,258,112	748,150,976
Nuclear Electric Power Generation			
Exelon Corporation	221113	35,984,998,400	2,010,000,000
Nursing Care Facilities (Skilled Nursing Facilities)			
Kindred Healthcare LLC	623110	6,335,828,890	
Oil and Gas Exploration & Production			
Chevron Corporation	211111	158,901,993,472	14,823,999,488
ConocoPhillips Company	211111	36,416,999,424	6,256,999,936
Exxon Mobil Corporation (ExxonMobil)	211111	279,331,995,648	20,839,999,488
Shell Oil Company	211111	9,000,000,000	
Oil and Gas Field Services			
Schlumberger Limited	213112	32,814,999,552	2,138,000,000
Online Sales, B2C Ecommerce, Sharing Economy Platforms			
Amazon.com Inc	454111	232,886,992,896	10,072,999,936
Chewy Inc (Chewy.com)	454111	2,104,286,976	-338,056,992
Qurate Retail Inc	454111	14,069,999,616	916,000,000
Wayfair LLC	454111	6,779,173,888	-504,080,000
Paints and Coatings Manufacturing			
PPG Industries Inc	325510	15,374,000,128	1,340,999,936
RPM International Inc	325510	5,321,643,008	337,769,984

Industry Group/Company	Industry Code	2018 Sales	2018 Profits
Sherwin-Williams Company (The)	325510	17,534,492,672	1,108,745,984
Paper Bag and Coated and Treated Paper Manufacturing			
Sonoco Products Company	322220	5,390,938,112	313,560,000
Payroll Services			
Paychex Inc	541214	3,380,900,096	933,699,968
Personal Care Products; Consumer Products; Cosmetics and Makeup; Fragrances and Perfumes; and Hair Care Products Manufacturing			
Estee Lauder Companies Inc (The)	325620	13,683,000,320	1,108,000,000
Procter & Gamble Company (The)	325620	66,831,998,976	9,749,999,616
Revlon Inc	325620	2,564,499,968	-294,200,000
Pet and Pet Supplies Stores			
PetSmart Inc	453910	9,912,500,000	
Petrochemicals Manufacturing			
Chevron Phillips Chemical Company LLC	325110	11,310,000,000	2,069,000,000
ExxonMobil Chemical Company Inc	325110	35,500,000,000	3,351,000,000
Lubrizol Corporation (The)	325110	6,800,000,000	
Westlake Chemical Corporation	325110	8,634,999,808	996,000,000
Petroleum Refineries			
Koch Industries Inc	324110	115,500,000,000	105,000,000
Marathon Petroleum Corporation	324110	96,503,996,416	2,780,000,000
Phillips 66	324110	111,460,999,168	5,594,999,808
Valero Energy Corporation	324110	117,033,000,960	3,121,999,872
Pharmaceuticals and Druggists' Merchandise Distributors			
AmerisourceBergen Corporation	424210	167,939,637,248	1,658,404,992
Cardinal Health Inc	424210	136,808,996,864	256,000,000
McKesson Corporation	424210	208,356,999,168	67,000,000
Pharmaceuticals, Biopharmaceuticals, Generics and Drug Manufacturing			
Abbott Laboratories	325412	30,577,999,872	2,368,000,000
AbbVie Inc	325412	32,753,000,448	5,687,000,064
Amgen Inc	325412	23,747,000,320	8,393,999,872
Biogen Inc	325412	13,452,900,352	4,430,700,032
Bristol-Myers Squibb Company	325412	22,560,999,424	4,920,000,000
Celgene Corporation	325412	15,281,000,448	4,046,000,128
Eli Lilly and Company	325412	24,555,700,224	3,232,000,000
Genentech Inc	325412	20,000,000,000	
Johnson & Johnson	325412	81,580,998,656	15,297,000,448
Merck & Co Inc	325412	42,294,001,664	6,220,000,256
Pfizer Inc	325412	53,646,999,552	11,153,000,448
Pharmacies and Drug Stores			
CVS Health Corporation	446110	194,579,005,440	-594,000,000
Walgreens Boots Alliance Inc	446110	131,537,002,496	5,024,000,000
Physicians (except Mental Health Specialists)			
Team Health Holdings Inc	621111	4,500,000,000	
Pipeline Transportation of Natural Gas			
Enterprise Products Partners LP	486210	36,534,198,272	4,172,400,128

Industry Group/Company	Industry Code	2018 Sales	2018 Profits
Plastic Product Manufacturing, Miscellaneous, Including Trash Containers, Household Items			
Owens Corning	326199	7,056,999,936	545,000,000
Plastics (Including Packaging Materials, Pipe, Laminated & Unlaminated Film & Sheet, Foam and Bottles) Product Manufacturing			
Berry Global Group Inc	326100	7,869,000,192	496,000,000
Plastics Material and Resin Manufacturing			
Celanese Corporation	325211	7,154,999,808	1,207,000,064
Huntsman Corporation	325211	9,379,000,320	337,000,000
Pottery, Ceramics and Plumbing Fixture Manufacturing			
Kohler Company	327110	7,000,000,000	
Poultry (Including Chicken, Duck & Turkey) Processing and Packaging			
Tyson Foods Inc	311615	40,051,998,720	3,024,000,000
Power-Driven Handtool Manufacturing			
Stanley Black & Decker Inc	333991	13,982,400,512	605,200,000
Pressed and Blown Glass and Glassware (except Glass Packaging Containers) Manufacturing			
Corning Incorporated	327212	11,290,000,384	1,066,000,000
Primary Battery Manufacturing			
Spectrum Brands Holdings Inc	335912	3,145,900,032	768,300,032
Property and Casualty (P&C) Insurance Underwriters (Direct Carriers)			
American Financial Group Inc	524126	7,150,000,128	530,000,000
American International Group Inc (AIG)	524126	47,480,999,936	-6,000,000
AmTrust Financial Services Inc	524126	6,000,000,000	
Berkshire Hathaway Inc (Holding Co)	524126	225,382,006,784	4,020,999,936
GEICO Corporation	524126	33,363,000,000	2,449,000,000
Liberty Mutual Group Inc	524126	41,568,000,000	2,160,000,000
Progressive Corporation (The)	524126	31,978,999,808	2,615,300,096
Safeco Insurance Company of America	524126	1,840,000,000	
State Farm Insurance Companies	524126	81,700,000,000	8,800,000,000
Travelers Companies Inc (The)	524126	30,282,000,384	2,523,000,064
USAA	524126	31,367,800,000	2,291,900,000
W R Berkley Corporation	524126	7,718,717,952	640,748,992
Pump and Pumping Equipment Manufacturing			
Graco Inc	333911	1,653,292,032	341,054,016
Radar, Navigation, Sonar, Space Vehicle Guidance, Flight Systems and Marine Instrument Manufacturing			
Collins Aerospace	334511	16,634,000,000	2,303,000,000
Trimble Inc	334511	3,108,400,128	282,800,000
Radio, Television and Other Electronics Stores			
Best Buy Co Inc	443142	42,150,998,016	1,000,000,000
Railroad Cars, Subways, Trams, Trolleys, Engines and Locomotives Manufacturing			
Trinity Industries Inc	336510	2,509,100,032	159,300,000
Real Estate Agents & Brokers			
CBRE Group Inc	531210	21,340,088,320	1,063,219,008

Industry Group/Company	Industry Code	2018 Sales	2018 Profits
Reconstituted Wood Products Manufacturing			
Patrick Industries Inc	321219	2,263,060,992	119,832,000
Recreational Vehicle (RV) Trailer and Camper Manufacturing			
Thor Industries Inc	336214	8,328,908,800	430,151,008
Restaurants, Fast-Food, Pizza Delivery, Takeout and Family			
Buffalo Wild Wings Inc	722513	2,100,000,000	
Chick-fil-A Inc	722513	10,200,000,000	
Darden Restaurants Inc	722513	8,080,099,840	596,000,000
In-N-Out Burgers Inc	722513	984,900,000	
McDonald's Corporation	722513	21,025,200,128	5,924,299,776
Restaurants, Full-Service, Sit Down			
Brinker International Inc	722511	3,135,417,088	125,882,000
Retirement Communities and Assisted Living Facilities for the Elderly			
Brookdale Senior Living Inc	623310	4,531,425,792	-528,257,984
Sawmills			
Weyerhaeuser Company	321113	7,475,999,744	748,000,000
Scientific Research and Development (R&D) in Life Sciences, Medical Devices, Biotechnology and Pharmaceuticals (Drugs)			
Charles River Laboratories International Inc	541711	2,266,096,128	226,372,992
IQVIA Holdings Inc	541711	10,412,000,256	259,000,000
PAREXEL International Corporation	541711	2,221,000,000	
Pharmaceutical Product Development LLC	541711	1,400,000,000	
PRA Health Sciences Inc	541711	2,871,921,920	153,904,992
Securities Brokerage, Discount Brokers and Online Stock Brokers			
Charles Schwab Corporation (The)	523120	9,943,000,064	3,507,000,064
Edward D Jones & Co LP	523120	7,500,000,000	
TD Ameritrade Holding Corporation	523120	5,342,000,128	1,472,999,936
Semiconductor and Solar Cell Manufacturing, Including Chips, Memory, LEDs, Transistors and Integrated Circuits, Artificial Intelligence (AI), & Internet of Things (IoT)			
Advanced Micro Devices Inc (AMD)	334413	6,474,999,808	337,000,000
Diodes Inc	334413	1,213,988,992	104,021,000
Intel Corporation	334413	70,848,004,096	21,052,999,680
Qualcomm Incorporated	334413	22,731,999,232	-4,864,000,000
Texas Instruments Inc (TI)	334413	15,783,999,488	5,580,000,256
Semiconductor Manufacturing Equipment and Systems (Including Etching, Wafer Processing & Surface Mount) Manufacturing			
Applied Materials Inc	333242	17,252,999,168	3,312,999,936
Lam Research Corporation	333242	11,076,998,144	2,380,680,960
Shoe and Footwear Brands, Designers, Importers and Distributors			
Nike Inc	424340	36,396,998,656	1,932,999,936
Soap and Other Detergent Manufacturing			
Clorox Company (The)	325611	6,124,000,256	823,000,000

Industry Group/Company	Industry Code	2018 Sales	2018 Profits
Soft Drinks (Including Bottled Carbonated and Flavored Water, Bottled Coffee & Tea, Sodas, Pop and Energy Drinks) Manufacturing			
Coca-Cola Bottling Co Consolidated	312111	4,625,363,968	-19,930,000
PepsiCo Inc	312111	64,661,000,192	12,515,000,320
Solid Waste Collection, Treatment, Disposal and Recycling			
Republic Services Inc	562111	10,040,899,584	1,036,899,968
Specialty Chemicals Manufacturing, Including Frangrances, Silicones, Biodiesel and Enzymes,			
DowDupont Inc	325199	85,976,997,888	3,844,000,000
Spices, Seasonings, Salad Dressing, Mayonnaise, Mustard, Catsup and Condiments Manufacturing			
McCormick & Company Incorporated	311940	5,408,900,096	933,400,000
Sporting Goods Stores			
Academy Sports & Outdoors Ltd	451110	4,900,000,000	
Cabela's Inc	451110	4,410,000,000	
REI (Recreational Equipment Inc)	451110	2,781,909,000	46,753,000
Supermarkets and Grocery (except Convenience) Stores			
Albertsons Companies LLC	445110	62,920,830,000	
HEB Grocery Company LP	445110	25,000,000,000	
Kroger Co (The)	445110	122,662,002,688	1,907,000,064
Publix Super Markets Inc	445110	36,395,716,608	2,381,167,104
Safeway Inc	445110	37,600,000,000	
Trader Joe's Company Inc	445110	13,912,500,000	
Whole Foods Market Inc	445110	16,831,500,000	
Talent Agencies, Agents and Managers for Athletes and Entertainers			
Endeavor LLC	711410	3,613,478,000	231,304,000
Telecommunications, Telephone and Network Equipment Manufacturing, including PBX, Routers, Switches, Internet of Things (IoT), and Handsets Manufacturing			
ARRIS International plc	334210	6,742,640,128	113,740,000
Telephone, Internet Access, Broadband, Data Networks, Server Facilities and Telecommunications Services Industry			
AT&T Inc	517110	170,755,997,696	19,370,000,384
CenturyLink Inc	517110	23,442,999,296	-1,732,999,936
Charter Communications Inc	517110	43,633,999,872	1,230,000,000
Comcast Corporation	517110	94,506,999,808	11,731,000,320
Cox Communications Inc	517110	12,000,000,000	
EchoStar Corporation	517110	2,091,362,944	-40,475,000
Rackspace Hosting Inc	517110	2,000,000,000	
Verizon Communications Inc	517110	130,862,997,504	15,527,999,488
Television Broadcasting			
CBS Corporation	515120	14,513,999,872	1,960,000,000
Cox Enterprises Inc	515120	20,750,000,000	
Disney Media Networks	515120	23,800,000,000	
NBCUniversal Media LLC	515120	35,761,000,000	5,279,000,000
Temporary Staffing, Help and Employment Agencies			
Kelly Services Inc	561320	5,513,900,032	22,900,000
Robert Half International Inc	561320	5,800,270,848	434,288,000

Industry Group/Company	Industry Code	2018 Sales	2018 Profits
Third-Party Logistics (3PL), Supply Chain and Freight Forwarding			
CH Robinson Worldwide Inc	488510	16,631,172,096	664,505,024
Expeditors International of Washington Inc	488510	8,138,364,928	618,198,976
XPO Logistics Inc	488510	17,279,000,576	422,000,000
Tire and Tube Wholesale Distribution			
American Tire Distributors Inc	423130	5,565,000,000	
Tire Stores			
Discount Tire Company	441320	4,784,850,000	
Title Insurance Underwriters (Direct Carriers)			
Fidelity National Financial Inc	524127	7,593,999,872	628,000,000
Travel Agencies and Room or Accommodation Sharing Services			
Airbnb Inc	561510	3,598,000,000	
Booking Holdings Inc	561510	14,526,999,552	3,998,000,128
Expedia Group Inc	561510	11,223,000,064	406,000,000
Sabre Corporation	561510	3,866,956,032	337,531,008
Truck, Utility Trailer and RV (Recreational Vehicle) Rental and Leasing			
AMERCO (U-Haul)	532120	3,601,114,112	790,582,976
Penske Corporation	532120	27,000,000,000	
Ryder System Inc	532120	8,409,214,976	273,297,984
Trucking and Freight—Long Distance, Full Truckload (FTL)			
JB Hunt Transport Services Inc	484121	8,614,874,112	489,584,992
Trucking and Freight—Long Distance, Less Than Truckload (LTL)			
Old Dominion Freight Line Inc	484122	4,043,695,104	605,667,968
Veterinary Services			
VCA Inc	541940	3,000,000,000	
Warehouse Clubs and Super Stores			
Costco Wholesale Corporation	452910	141,575,995,392	3,134,000,128
PriceSmart Inc	452910	3,166,702,080	74,328,000
Walmart Inc	452910	500,343,013,376	9,861,999,616
Waste Collection, Recycling, Treatment and Remediation Services			
Waste Management Inc	562000	14,913,999,872	1,924,999,936
Wet Corn Milling			
Ingredion Incorporated	311221	6,288,999,936	443,000,000
Wine Manufacturing (including Wineries with Vineyards)			
Constellation Brands Inc	312130	7,584,999,936	2,318,899,968
Wireless Communications and Radio and TV Broadcasting Equipment Manufacturing, including Cellphones (Handsets) and Internet of Things (IoT)			
Apple Inc	334220	265,594,994,688	59,531,001,856
Harris Corporation	334220	6,182,000,128	718,000,000
Wireless Telecommunications Carriers (except Satellite)			
AT&T Mobility LLC	517210	71,344,000,000	21,723,000,000
T-Mobile US Inc	517210	43,309,998,080	2,888,000,000
United States Cellular Corporation	517210	3,967,000,064	150,000,000

Industry Group/Company	Industry Code	2018 Sales	2018 Profits
Women's Clothing, Apparel and Accessories Stores			
Ascena Retail Group Inc	448120	6,578,299,904	-39,700,000
Victoria's Secret	448120	7,375,000,000	462,000,000

ALPHABETICAL INDEX

3M Company
Abbott Laboratories
AbbVie Inc
ABM Industries Incorporated
Academy Sports & Outdoors Ltd
Acadia Healthcare Company Inc
Accenture LLP
Acosta Inc
Activision Blizzard Inc
Adobe Systems Inc
Advance Auto Parts Inc
Advanced Micro Devices Inc (AMD)
AdventHealth
Advocate Aurora Health
AECOM
Aetna Inc
AFLAC Incorporated
Airbnb Inc
Alaska Air Group Inc
Albertsons Companies LLC
Alcoa Corporation
Alliance Data Systems Corporation
Allscripts Healthcare Solutions Inc
Alphabet Inc (Google)
Amazon.com Inc
AMERCO (U-Haul)
American Airlines Group Inc
American Express Company
American Financial Group Inc
American International Group Inc (AIG)
American Tire Distributors Inc
American Tower Corporation (REIT)
Amerigroup Corporation
AmerisourceBergen Corporation
Ametek Inc
Amgen Inc
Amphenol Corporation
AMSURG Corporation
AmTrust Financial Services Inc
Anixter International Inc
Anthem Inc
AO Smith Corporation
Aon Hewitt
Apple Inc
Applied Materials Inc
Aramark Corporation
Archer-Daniels-Midland Company (ADM)
ARRIS International plc
Arrow Electronics Inc
Arthur J Gallagher & Co
Ascena Retail Group Inc
Ascension
AT Kearney Inc
AT&T Inc
AT&T Mobility LLC
athenahealth Inc
Automatic Data Processing Inc (ADP)
Avis Budget Group Inc
Avnet Inc
Bain & Company Inc
Ball Corporation
Bank of America Corporation
Bank of New York Mellon Corporation
Baxter International Inc
Baylor Scott & White Health
BB&T Corporation
BBDO Worldwide
Bechtel Group Inc
Becton, Dickinson and Company
Bed Bath & Beyond Inc
Belden Inc
Berkshire Hathaway Energy Company
Berkshire Hathaway Inc (Holding Co)
Berry Global Group Inc
Best Buy Co Inc
Biogen Inc
Bio-Rad Laboratories Inc
BJC HealthCare
Black & Veatch Holding Company
BlackRock Inc
Bloomberg LP
Blue Shield of California
BMC Software Inc
BMC Stock Holdings Inc
Boise Cascade Company
Booking Holdings Inc
Booz Allen Hamilton Holding Corporation
BorgWarner Inc
Boston Consulting Group Inc (The, BCG)
Boston Scientific Corporation
Brightstar Corporation
Brinker International Inc
Bristol-Myers Squibb Company
Broadcom Inc
Brookdale Senior Living Inc
Brown & Brown Inc
Buffalo Wild Wings Inc
Bunge Limited
Burns & McDonnell Inc
C&S Wholesale Grocers Inc
Cabela's Inc
CACI International Inc
Cadence Design Systems Inc
Capital One Financial Corporation
Cardinal Health Inc
Cargill Incorporated
CarMax Inc
Carnival Corporation
CBRE Group Inc
CBS Corporation
CDW Corporation
Celanese Corporation
Celgene Corporation
Centene Corporation
CenturyLink Inc
Cerner Corporation
CH Robinson Worldwide Inc
Charles River Laboratories International Inc
Charles Schwab Corporation (The)
Charter Communications Inc
Chemed Corporation
Chevron Corporation
Chevron Phillips Chemical Company LLC
Chewy Inc (Chewy.com)
Chick-fil-A Inc
Cigna Corporation
Cintas Corporation
Cisco Systems Inc
Citigroup Inc
Citrix Systems Inc
Clayton Homes Inc
Cleveland Clinic Foundation (The)
Clorox Company (The)
Coca-Cola Bottling Co Consolidated
Cognizant Technology Solutions Corporation
Collins Aerospace
Comcast Corporation
CommScope Holding Company Inc
Community Health Systems Inc
Concentrix Corporation
Concur Technologies Inc
ConocoPhillips Company
Constellation Brands Inc
Container Store Inc (The)
Cooper Companies Inc (The)
Corning Incorporated
CoStar Group Inc
Costco Wholesale Corporation
Cox Automotive Inc
Cox Communications Inc
Cox Enterprises Inc
Crown Castle International Corp
Crown Holdings Inc
Cullen-Frost Bankers Inc
Cummins Inc
CVS Health Corporation
Dana Incorporated
Darden Restaurants Inc
DaVita Healthcare Partners Inc
Deere & Company (John Deere)
Dell EMC
Dell Technologies Inc
Deloitte LLP
Delta Air Lines Inc
Dentsply Sirona Inc
Diodes Inc
Discount Tire Company
Discovery Inc
Disney Media Networks
Disney Parks, Experiences and Products (DPEP)
Dollar Thrifty Automotive Group Inc
DowDupont Inc
DR Horton Inc
DriveTime Automotive Group Inc
DTE Energy Company
Duke Energy Corporation
Dycom Industries Inc
EchoStar Corporation
Edward D Jones & Co LP
Edwards Lifesciences Corporation
Eli Lilly and Company
EMCOR Group Inc
Emerson Electric Co
Endeavor LLC
Enterprise Holdings Inc
Enterprise Products Partners LP
Envision Healthcare Corporation
Epic Systems Corporation
Estee Lauder Companies Inc (The)

Exelon Corporation
Expedia Group Inc
Expeditors International of Washington Inc
Exxon Mobil Corporation (ExxonMobil)
ExxonMobil Chemical Company Inc
EY LLP
F5 Networks Inc
Facebook Inc
FactSet Research Systems Inc
Fairview Health Services
Fastenal Company
Federal-Mogul LLC
FedEx Corporation
Fidelity Investments Financial Services
Fidelity National Financial Inc
FirstEnergy Corporation
Fiserv Inc
FleetCor Technologies Inc
Fluor Corporation
Ford Motor Company
Frito-Lay North America Inc
FTI Consulting Inc
Gartner Inc
GEICO Corporation
Genentech Inc
General Dynamics Corporation
General Motors Company (GM)
Gentex Corporation
GoDaddy Inc
Goldman Sachs Group Inc (The)
Graco Inc
Grant Thornton LLP
Group 1 Automotive Inc
Gulfstream Aerospace Corporation
HanesBrands Inc
Harris Corporation
Hartford Financial Services Group Inc (The)
HCA Healthcare Inc
Health Care Service Corporation (HCSC)
Heartland Payment Systems Inc
HEB Grocery Company LP
Hendrick Automotive Group
Henry Schein Inc
Hershey Company (The)
Hillenbrand Inc
Hill-Rom Holdings Inc
Hilton Worldwide Holdings Inc
HMSHost Corporation
Home Depot Inc (The)
Houston Methodist
Hub International Limited
Hubbell Incorporated
Humana Inc
Huntsman Corporation
Hyatt Hotels Corporation
Hyundai Motor America
IAC/InterActiveCorp
IDEXX Laboratories Inc
Illinois Tool Works Inc
Illumina Inc
Ingram Micro Inc
Ingredion Incorporated
In-N-Out Burgers Inc
Intel Corporation

Interpublic Group of Companies Inc
Intuit Inc
IQVIA Holdings Inc
Jabil Inc
Jack Henry & Associates Inc
Jacobs Engineering Group Inc
JB Hunt Transport Services Inc
JetBlue Airways Corporation
JM Family Enterprises Inc
John Hancock Financial
Johnson & Johnson
Jones Lang LaSalle Incorporated
JP Morgan Chase & Co Inc
Juniper Networks Inc
Kaiser Permanente
KBR Inc
Kelly Services Inc
Kimpton Hotel & Restaurant Group LLC
Kindred Healthcare LLC
Koch Industries Inc
Kohler Company
Kohls Corporation
KPMG LLP
Kroger Co (The)
Laboratory Corporation of America Holdings
Lam Research Corporation
Larry H Miller Group of Companies
Las Vegas Sands Corp (The Venetian)
Lear Corporation
Legg Mason Inc
Lennar Corporation
LHC Group Inc
Liberty Mutual Group Inc
LifePoint Health Inc
Lincoln National Corporation
LinkedIn Corporation
Lithia Motors Inc
Littelfuse Inc
LKQ Corporation
Lockheed Martin Corporation
Loews Hotels Holding Corporation
Lowe's Companies Inc
Lubrizol Corporation (The)
Lyft Inc
Magellan Health Inc
Marathon Petroleum Corporation
Marriott International Inc
Mars Incorporated
Marsh & McLennan Companies Inc
Mary Kay Inc
MassMutual Financial Group
MasterCard Inc
Match Group Inc
Matthews International Corporation
MAXIMUS Inc
Mayo Clinic
McAfee LLC
McCann Worldgroup
McCormick & Company Incorporated
McDonald's Corporation
McKesson Corporation
McKinsey & Company Inc
MedStar Health
Menard Inc

Mercedes-Benz USA LLC
Mercer LLC
Merck & Co Inc
Merrill Lynch & Co Inc
Microsoft Corporation
Modine Manufacturing Company
Mohawk Industries Inc
Molex LLC
Molina Healthcare Inc
Monro Muffler Brake Inc
Moody's Corporation
Morgan Stanley
Mutual of Omaha Companies (The)
National Instruments Corporation
NBCUniversal Media LLC
NCR Corporation
Netflix Inc
New York Life Insurance Company
Nielsen Holdings plc
Nike Inc
Nordstrom Inc
Northrop Grumman Corporation
Northwestern Mutual Life Insurance Company (The)
Norwegian Cruise Line Holdings Ltd (NCL)
NVR Inc
O Reilly Automotive Inc
Old Dominion Freight Line Inc
Oliver Wyman Group
Omnicom Group Inc
Oracle Corporation
Oracle NetSuite
Oshkosh Corporation
Owens Corning
PAREXEL International Corporation
Patrick Industries Inc
Paychex Inc
PayPal Holdings Inc
Penske Automotive Group Inc
Penske Corporation
PepsiCo Inc
PerkinElmer Inc
PetSmart Inc
Pfizer Inc
Pharmaceutical Product Development LLC
Philips Healthcare
Phillips 66
PPG Industries Inc
PRA Health Sciences Inc
PriceSmart Inc
PricewaterhouseCoopers (PwC)
Principal Financial Group Inc
Procter & Gamble Company (The)
Progressive Corporation (The)
Providence St Joseph Health
Prudential Financial Inc
Publix Super Markets Inc
PulteGroup Inc
Qualcomm Incorporated
Quanta Services Inc
Quest Diagnostics Incorporated
Quicken Loans Inc
Qurate Retail Inc
Rackspace Hosting Inc

Raymond James Financial Inc
Raytheon Company
Red Hat Inc
Regal-Beloit Corporation
REI (Recreational Equipment Inc)
Republic Services Inc
ResMed Inc
Revlon Inc
Ritz-Carlton Hotel Company LLC (The)
Robert Half International Inc
Rockwell Automation Inc
Roper Technologies Inc
Rosendin Electric Inc
Ross Stores Inc
Royal Caribbean Cruises Ltd
RPM International Inc
Ryder System Inc
Sabre Corporation
Safeco Insurance Company of America
Safeway Inc
SalesForce.com Inc
Sanmina Corporation
Sapient Corporation
SAS Institute Inc
Schlumberger Limited
Science Applications International Corporation (SAIC)
Select Medical Holdings Corporation
Service Corporation International Inc
ServiceMaster Company LLC (The)
ServiceNow Inc
Shell Oil Company
Sherwin-Williams Company (The)
Sodexo Inc
Sonoco Products Company
Southwest Airlines Co
Spectrum Brands Holdings Inc
Spectrum Health
Spirit AeroSystems Holdings Inc
Spirit Airlines Inc
Stanley Black & Decker Inc
Starbucks Corporation
State Farm Insurance Companies
Stericycle Inc
Stifel Financial Corp
Strategy&
Stryker Corporation
Sutter Health Inc
Symantec Corporation
SYNNEX Corporation
Synopsys Inc
SYSCO Corporation
T Rowe Price Group Inc
TD Ameritrade Holding Corporation
Team Health Holdings Inc
Tech Data Corporation
Tenneco Inc
Terex Corporation
Texas Instruments Inc (TI)
Textron Inc
Thermo Fisher Scientific Inc
Thor Industries Inc
TIAA
TJX Companies Inc (T.J. Maxx)
T-Mobile US Inc

Toll Brothers Inc
Tractor Supply Company
Trader Joe's Company Inc
TransDigm Group Incorporated
Travelers Companies Inc (The)
Trimble Inc
Trinity Health
Trinity Industries Inc
Tutor Perini Corporation
Tyson Foods Inc
Uber Technologies Inc
United Continental Holdings Inc
United Natural Foods Inc
United Parcel Service Inc (UPS)
United States Cellular Corporation
United States Steel Corporation
United Technologies Corporation
UnitedHealth Group Inc
Universal Health Services Inc
Unum Group
US Bancorp (US Bank)
USAA
Valassis Communications Inc
Valero Energy Corporation
Varian Medical Systems Inc
VCA Inc
Verizon Communications Inc
Victoria's Secret
Visa Inc
VMware Inc
W R Berkley Corporation
WABCO Holdings Inc
Walgreens Boots Alliance Inc
Walmart Inc
Walt Disney Company (The)
Walt Disney Studios (The)
Waste Management Inc
Waters Corporation
Wayfair LLC
WellCare Health Plans Inc
Westlake Chemical Corporation
Weyerhaeuser Company
Whole Foods Market Inc
Workday Inc
WW Grainger Inc
Wyndham Destinations Inc
Wynn Resorts Limited
XPO Logistics Inc
Zillow Inc
Zimmer Biomet Holdings Inc

INDEX OF U.S. HEADQUARTERS LOCATION BY STATE

To help you locate members of THE AMERICAN EMPLOYERS 500 geographically, the city and state of the headquarters of each company are in the following index.

ARIZONA
Avnet Inc; Phoenix
Discount Tire Company; Scottsdale
DriveTime Automotive Group Inc; Tempe
GoDaddy Inc; Scottsdale
Magellan Health Inc; Scottsdale
PetSmart Inc; Phoenix
Republic Services Inc; Phoenix

ARKANSAS
JB Hunt Transport Services Inc; Lowell
Tyson Foods Inc; Springdale
Walmart Inc; Bentonville

CALIFORNIA
Activision Blizzard Inc; Santa Monica
Adobe Systems Inc; San Jose
Advanced Micro Devices Inc (AMD); Santa Clara
AECOM; Los Angeles
Airbnb Inc; San Francisco
Alphabet Inc (Google); Mountain View
Amgen Inc; Thousand Oaks
Apple Inc; Cupertino
Applied Materials Inc; Santa Clara
Bechtel Group Inc; San Francisco
Bio-Rad Laboratories Inc; Hercules
Blue Shield of California; San Francisco
Broadcom Inc; San Jose
Cadence Design Systems Inc; San Jose
CBRE Group Inc; Los Angeles
Charles Schwab Corporation (The); San Francisco
Chevron Corporation; San Ramon
Cisco Systems Inc; San Jose
Clorox Company (The); Oakland
Concentrix Corporation; Freemont
Cooper Companies Inc (The); Pleasanton
Disney Media Networks; Burbank
Disney Parks, Experiences and Products (DPEP); Burbank
Edwards Lifesciences Corporation; Irvine
Endeavor LLC; Beverly Hills
Facebook Inc; Menlo Park
Genentech Inc; South San Francisco
Hyundai Motor America; Fountain Valley
Illumina Inc; San Diego
Ingram Micro Inc; Irvine
In-N-Out Burgers Inc; Irvine
Intel Corporation; Santa Clara
Intuit Inc; Mountain View
Jacobs Engineering Group Inc; Dallas
Juniper Networks Inc; Sunnyvale
Kaiser Permanente; Oakland
Kimpton Hotel & Restaurant Group LLC; San Francisco
Lam Research Corporation; Fremont
LinkedIn Corporation; Mountain View
Lyft Inc; San Francisco
McAfee LLC; Santa Clara
Molina Healthcare Inc; Long Beach
Netflix Inc; Los Gatos
Oracle Corporation; Redwood City
Oracle NetSuite; San Mateo
PayPal Holdings Inc; San Jose
PriceSmart Inc; San Diego
Qualcomm Incorporated; San Diego
ResMed Inc; San Diego
Robert Half International Inc; Menlo Park
Rosendin Electric Inc; San Jose
Ross Stores Inc; Dublin
Safeway Inc; Pleasanton
SalesForce.com Inc; San Francisco
Sanmina Corporation; San Jose
ServiceNow Inc; Santa Clara
Sutter Health Inc; Sacramento
Symantec Corporation; Mountain View
SYNNEX Corporation; Fremont
Synopsys Inc; Mountain View
Trader Joe's Company Inc; Monrovia
Trimble Inc; Sunnyvale
Tutor Perini Corporation; Sylmar
Uber Technologies Inc; San Francisco
Varian Medical Systems Inc; Palo Alto
VCA Inc; Los Angeles
Visa Inc; San Francisco
VMware Inc; Palo Alto
Walt Disney Company (The); Burbank
Walt Disney Studios (The); Burbank
Workday Inc; Pleasanton

COLORADO
Arrow Electronics Inc; Centennial
Ball Corporation; Broomfield
DaVita Healthcare Partners Inc; Denver
EchoStar Corporation; Englewood
Qurate Retail Inc; Englewood

CONNECTICUT
Aetna Inc; Hartford
Amphenol Corporation; Wallingford
Booking Holdings Inc; Norwalk
Charter Communications Inc; Stamford
Cigna Corporation; Bloomfield
EMCOR Group Inc; Norwalk
FactSet Research Systems Inc; Norwalk
Gartner Inc; Stamford
Hartford Financial Services Group Inc (The); Hartford
Hubbell Incorporated; Shelton
Stanley Black & Decker Inc; New Britain
Terex Corporation; Westport
United Technologies Corporation; Farmington
W R Berkley Corporation; Greenwich
XPO Logistics Inc; Greenwich

DISTRICT OF COLUMBIA
FTI Consulting Inc; Washington

FLORIDA
Acosta Inc; Jacksonville
AdventHealth; Altamonte Springs
Brightstar Corporation; Miami
Brown & Brown Inc; Daytona Beach
Carnival Corporation; Miami
Chewy Inc (Chewy.com); Dania Beach
Citrix Systems Inc; Fort Lauderdale
Collins Aerospace; West Palm Beach
Darden Restaurants Inc; Orlando
Dycom Industries Inc; Palm Beach Gardens
Fidelity National Financial Inc; Jacksonville
Harris Corporation; Melbourne
Jabil Inc; St. Petersburg
JM Family Enterprises Inc; Deerfield Beach
Lennar Corporation; Miami
Norwegian Cruise Line Holdings Ltd (NCL); Miami
Publix Super Markets Inc; Lakeland
Raymond James Financial Inc; St. Petersburg
Roper Technologies Inc; Sarasota
Royal Caribbean Cruises Ltd; Miami
Ryder System Inc; Miami
Spirit Airlines Inc; Miramar
Tech Data Corporation; Clearwater
WellCare Health Plans Inc; Tampa
Wyndham Destinations Inc; Orlando

GEORGIA
AFLAC Incorporated; Columbus
ARRIS International plc; Suwanee
AT&T Mobility LLC; Atlanta
BMC Stock Holdings Inc; Atlanta
Chick-fil-A Inc; Atlanta
Cox Automotive Inc; Atlanta
Cox Communications Inc; Atlanta
Cox Enterprises Inc; Atlanta
Delta Air Lines Inc; Atlanta
FleetCor Technologies Inc; Norcross
Gulfstream Aerospace Corporation; Savannah
Heartland Payment Systems Inc; Atlanta
Home Depot Inc (The); Atlanta
Mercedes-Benz USA LLC; Sandy Springs
Mohawk Industries Inc; Calhoun
NCR Corporation; Atlanta
PulteGroup Inc; Atlanta
United Parcel Service Inc (UPS); Atlanta

IDAHO
Albertsons Companies LLC; Boise
Boise Cascade Company; Boise

ILLINOIS
Abbott Laboratories; Abbott Park
AbbVie Inc; North Chicago
Accenture LLP; Chicago
Advocate Aurora Health; Downers Grove

Allscripts Healthcare Solutions Inc; Chicago
Anixter International Inc; Glenview
Aon Hewitt; Chicago
Archer-Daniels-Midland Company (ADM); Chicago
Arthur J Gallagher & Co; Rolling Meadows
AT Kearney Inc; Chicago
Baxter International Inc; Deerfield
CDW Corporation; Lincolnshire
Deere & Company (John Deere); Moline
Exelon Corporation; Chicago
Grant Thornton LLP; Chicago
Health Care Service Corporation (HCSC); Chicago
Hill-Rom Holdings Inc; Chicago
Hub International Limited; Chicago
Hyatt Hotels Corporation; Chicago
Illinois Tool Works Inc; Glenview
Ingredion Incorporated; Westchester
Jones Lang LaSalle Incorporated; Chicago
Littelfuse Inc; Chicago
LKQ Corporation; Chicago
McDonald's Corporation; Chicago
Molex LLC; Lisle
State Farm Insurance Companies; Bloomington
Stericycle Inc; Lake Forest
Tenneco Inc; Lake Forest
United Continental Holdings Inc; Chicago
United States Cellular Corporation; Chicago
Walgreens Boots Alliance Inc; Deerfield
WW Grainger Inc; Lake Forest

INDIANA
Anthem Inc; Indianapolis
Berry Global Group Inc; Evansville
Cummins Inc; Columbus
Eli Lilly and Company; Indianapolis
Hillenbrand Inc; Batesville
Patrick Industries Inc; Elkhart
Thor Industries Inc; Elkhart
Zimmer Biomet Holdings Inc; Warsaw

IOWA
Berkshire Hathaway Energy Company; Des Moines
Principal Financial Group Inc; Des Moines

KANSAS
Black & Veatch Holding Company; Overland Park
Koch Industries Inc; Wichita
Spirit AeroSystems Holdings Inc; Wichita

KENTUCKY
Humana Inc; Louisville
Kindred Healthcare LLC; Louisville

LOUISIANA
CenturyLink Inc; Monroe
LHC Group Inc; Lafayette

MAINE
IDEXX Laboratories Inc; Westbrook

MARYLAND
Discovery Inc; Silver Spring
GEICO Corporation; Chevy Chase
HMSHost Corporation; Bethesda
Legg Mason Inc; Baltimore
Lockheed Martin Corporation; Bethesda
Marriott International Inc; Bethesda
McCormick & Company Incorporated; Hunt Valley
MedStar Health; Columbia
Ritz-Carlton Hotel Company LLC (The); Bethesda
Sodexo Inc; Gaithersburg
T Rowe Price Group Inc; Baltimore

MASSACHUSETTS
American Tower Corporation (REIT); Boston
athenahealth Inc; Watertown
Bain & Company Inc; Boston
Biogen Inc; Cambridge
Boston Consulting Group Inc (The, BCG); Boston
Boston Scientific Corporation; Marlborough
Charles River Laboratories International Inc; Wilmington
Dell EMC; Hopkinton
Fidelity Investments Financial Services; Boston
John Hancock Financial; Boston
Liberty Mutual Group Inc; Boston
MassMutual Financial Group; Springfield
PAREXEL International Corporation; Waltham
PerkinElmer Inc; Waltham
Philips Healthcare; Andover
Raytheon Company; Waltham
Sapient Corporation; Boston
Thermo Fisher Scientific Inc; Waltham
TJX Companies Inc (T.J. Maxx); Framingham
Waters Corporation; Milford
Wayfair LLC; Boston

MICHIGAN
BorgWarner Inc; Auburn Hills
DowDupont Inc; Midland
DTE Energy Company; Detroit
Federal-Mogul LLC; Southfield
Ford Motor Company; Dearborn
General Motors Company (GM); Detroit
Gentex Corporation; Zeeland
Kelly Services Inc; Troy
Lear Corporation; Southfield
Penske Automotive Group Inc; Bloomfield Hills
Penske Corporation; Bloomfield Hills
Quicken Loans Inc; Detroit
Spectrum Health; Grand Rapids
Stryker Corporation; Kalamazoo
Trinity Health; Livonia
Valassis Communications Inc; Livonia
WABCO Holdings Inc; Auburn Hills

MINNESOTA
3M Company; St. Paul
Best Buy Co Inc; Richfield
Buffalo Wild Wings Inc; Minneapolis
Cargill Incorporated; Minneapolis
CH Robinson Worldwide Inc; Eden Prairie
Fairview Health Services; Minneapolis
Fastenal Company; Winona
Graco Inc; Minneapolis
Mayo Clinic; Rochester
UnitedHealth Group Inc; Minnetonka
US Bancorp (US Bank); Minneapolis

MISSOURI
Ascension; St. Louis
Belden Inc; St. Louis
BJC HealthCare; St. Louis
Burns & McDonnell Inc; Kansas City
Centene Corporation; St. Louis
Cerner Corporation; North Kansas City
Edward D Jones & Co LP; Des Peres
Emerson Electric Co; St. Louis
Enterprise Holdings Inc; St. Louis
Jack Henry & Associates Inc; Monett
O Reilly Automotive Inc; Springfield
Stifel Financial Corp; St. Louis

NEBRASKA
Berkshire Hathaway Inc (Holding Co); Omaha
Cabela's Inc; Sidney
Mutual of Omaha Companies (The); Omaha
TD Ameritrade Holding Corporation; Omaha

NEVADA
AMERCO (U-Haul); Reno
Las Vegas Sands Corp (The Venetian); Las Vegas
Wynn Resorts Limited; Las Vegas

NEW HAMPSHIRE
C&S Wholesale Grocers Inc; Keene

NEW JERSEY
Ascena Retail Group Inc; Mahwah
Automatic Data Processing Inc (ADP); Roseland
Avis Budget Group Inc; Parsippany
Becton, Dickinson and Company; Franklin Lakes
Bed Bath & Beyond Inc; Union
Celgene Corporation; Summit
Cognizant Technology Solutions Corporation; Teaneck
Johnson & Johnson; New Brunswick
Merck & Co Inc; Kenilworth
Prudential Financial Inc; Newark
Quest Diagnostics Incorporated; Secaucus

NEW YORK
ABM Industries Incorporated; New York
American Express Company; New York
American International Group Inc (AIG); New York
AmTrust Financial Services Inc; New York
Bank of New York Mellon Corporation; New York
BBDO Worldwide; New York
BlackRock Inc; New York
Bloomberg LP; New York
Bristol-Myers Squibb Company; New York
Bunge Limited; White Plains
CBS Corporation; New York
Citigroup Inc; New York
Constellation Brands Inc; Victor
Corning Incorporated; Corning
Deloitte LLP; New York
Estee Lauder Companies Inc (The); New York
EY LLP; New York
Goldman Sachs Group Inc (The); New York
Henry Schein Inc; Melville
IAC/InterActiveCorp; New York
Interpublic Group of Companies Inc; New York
JetBlue Airways Corporation; Long Island City
JP Morgan Chase & Co Inc; New York
KPMG LLP; New York
Loews Hotels Holding Corporation; New York
Marsh & McLennan Companies Inc; New York
MasterCard Inc; Purchase
McCann Worldgroup; New York
McKinsey & Company Inc; New York
Mercer LLC; New York
Merrill Lynch & Co Inc; New York
Monro Muffler Brake Inc; Rochester
Moody's Corporation; New York
Morgan Stanley; New York
NBCUniversal Media LLC; New York
New York Life Insurance Company; New York
Nielsen Holdings plc; New York
Oliver Wyman Group; New York
Omnicom Group Inc; New York
Paychex Inc; Rochester
PepsiCo Inc; Purchase
Pfizer Inc; New York
PricewaterhouseCoopers (PwC); New York
Revlon Inc; New York
Strategy&; New York
TIAA; New York
Travelers Companies Inc (The); New York
Verizon Communications Inc; New York

NORTH CAROLINA
Advance Auto Parts Inc; Raleight
American Tire Distributors Inc; Huntersville
Bank of America Corporation; Charlotte
BB&T Corporation; Winston-Salem
Coca-Cola Bottling Co Consolidated; Charlotte
CommScope Holding Company Inc; Hickory
Dentsply Sirona Inc; Charlotte
Duke Energy Corporation; Charlotte
HanesBrands Inc; Winston-Salem
Hendrick Automotive Group; Charlotte
IQVIA Holdings Inc; Durham
Laboratory Corporation of America Holdings; Burlington
Lowe's Companies Inc; Mooresville
Old Dominion Freight Line Inc; Thomasville
Pharmaceutical Product Development LLC; Wilmington
PRA Health Sciences Inc; Raleigh
Red Hat Inc; Raleigh
SAS Institute Inc; Cary

OHIO
American Financial Group Inc; Cincinnati
Cardinal Health Inc; Dublin
Chemed Corporation; Cincinnati
Cintas Corporation; Cincinnati
Cleveland Clinic Foundation (The); Cleveland
Dana Incorporated; Maumee
FirstEnergy Corporation; Akron
Kroger Co (The); Cincinnati
Lubrizol Corporation (The); Wickliffe
Marathon Petroleum Corporation; Findlay
Owens Corning; Toledo
Procter & Gamble Company (The); Cincinnati
Progressive Corporation (The); Mayfield Village
RPM International Inc; Medina
Sherwin-Williams Company (The); Cleveland
TransDigm Group Incorporated; Cleveland
Victoria's Secret; Reynoldsburg

OKLAHOMA
Dollar Thrifty Automotive Group Inc; Tulsa

OREGON
Lithia Motors Inc; Medford
Nike Inc; Beaverton

PENNSYLVANIA
Alcoa Corporation; Pittsburge
AmerisourceBergen Corporation; Chesterbrook
Ametek Inc; Berwyn
Aramark Corporation; Philadelphia
Comcast Corporation; Philadelphia
Crown Holdings Inc; Yardley
Hershey Company (The); Hershey
Lincoln National Corporation; Radnor
Matthews International Corporation; Pittsburgh
PPG Industries Inc; Pittsburgh
Select Medical Holdings Corporation; Mechanicsburg
Toll Brothers Inc; Horsham
United States Steel Corporation; Pittsburgh
Universal Health Services Inc; King Of Prussia

RHODE ISLAND
CVS Health Corporation; Woonsocket
Textron Inc; Providence
United Natural Foods Inc; Providence

SOUTH CAROLINA
Sonoco Products Company; Hartsville

TENNESSEE
Acadia Healthcare Company Inc; Franklin
AMSURG Corporation; Nashville
Brookdale Senior Living Inc; Brentwood
Clayton Homes Inc; Maryville
Community Health Systems Inc; Franklin
Envision Healthcare Corporation; Nashville
FedEx Corporation; Memphis
HCA Healthcare Inc; Nashville
LifePoint Health Inc; Brentwood
ServiceMaster Company LLC (The); Memphis
Team Health Holdings Inc; Knoxville
Tractor Supply Company; Brentwood
Unum Group; Chattanooga

TEXAS
Academy Sports & Outdoors Ltd; Katy
Alliance Data Systems Corporation; Plano
American Airlines Group Inc; Fort Worth
AT&T Inc; Dallas
Baylor Scott & White Health; Dallas
BMC Software Inc; Houston
Brinker International Inc; Dallas
Celanese Corporation; Irving
Chevron Phillips Chemical Company LLC; The Woodlands
ConocoPhillips Company; Houston
Container Store Inc (The); Coppell
Crown Castle International Corp; Houston
Cullen-Frost Bankers Inc; San Antonio
Dell Technologies Inc; Round Rock
Diodes Inc; Plano
DR Horton Inc; Arlington
Enterprise Products Partners LP; Houston
Exxon Mobil Corporation (ExxonMobil); Irving
ExxonMobil Chemical Company Inc; Spring
Fluor Corporation; Irving
Frito-Lay North America Inc; Plano
Group 1 Automotive Inc; Houston
HEB Grocery Company LP; San Antonio
Houston Methodist; Houston
Huntsman Corporation; The Woodlands
KBR Inc; Houston
Mary Kay Inc; Dallas
Match Group Inc; Dallas
McKesson Corporation; Irving
National Instruments Corporation; Austin

Phillips 66; Houston
Quanta Services Inc; Houston
Rackspace Hosting Inc; San Antonio
Sabre Corporation; Southlake
Schlumberger Limited; Houston
Service Corporation International Inc; Houston
Shell Oil Company; Houston
Southwest Airlines Co; Dallas
SYSCO Corporation; Houston
Texas Instruments Inc (TI); Dallas
Trinity Industries Inc; Dallas
USAA; San Antonio
Valero Energy Corporation; San Antonio
Waste Management Inc; Houston
Westlake Chemical Corporation; Houston
Whole Foods Market Inc; Austin

UTAH
Larry H Miller Group of Companies; Sandy

VIRGINIA
Amerigroup Corporation; Virginia Beach
Booz Allen Hamilton Holding Corporation; McLean
CACI International Inc; Arlington
Capital One Financial Corporation; McLean
CarMax Inc; Richmond
General Dynamics Corporation; Falls Church
Hilton Worldwide Holdings Inc; McLean
Mars Incorporated; McLean
MAXIMUS Inc; Reston
Northrop Grumman Corporation; Falls Church
NVR Inc; Reston
Science Applications International Corporation (SAIC); Reston

WASHINGTON
Alaska Air Group Inc; Seattle
Amazon.com Inc; Seattle
Concur Technologies Inc; Bellevue
CoStar Group Inc; Northwest
Costco Wholesale Corporation; Issaquah
Expedia Group Inc; Bellevue
Expeditors International of Washington Inc; Seattle
F5 Networks Inc; Seattle
Microsoft Corporation; Redmond
Nordstrom Inc; Seattle
Providence St Joseph Health; Renton
REI (Recreational Equipment Inc); Kent
Safeco Insurance Company of America; Seattle
Starbucks Corporation; Seattle
T-Mobile US Inc; Bellevue
Weyerhaeuser Company; Seattle
Zillow Inc; Seattle

WISCONSIN
AO Smith Corporation; Milwaukee
Epic Systems Corporation; Verona
Fiserv Inc; Brookfield
Kohler Company; Kohler
Kohls Corporation; Menomonee Falls
Menard Inc; Eau Claire
Modine Manufacturing Company; Racine
Northwestern Mutual Life Insurance Company (The); Milwaukee
Oshkosh Corporation; Oshkosh
Regal-Beloit Corporation; Beloit
Rockwell Automation Inc; Milwaukee
Spectrum Brands Holdings Inc; Middleton

Individual Data
Profiles
On Each Of
The AMERICAN EMPLOYERS 500

3M Company

www.3m.com

NAIC Code: 339100

TYPES OF BUSINESS:
Health Care Products
Specialty Materials & Textiles
Industrial Products
Safety, Security & Protection Products
Display & Graphics Products
Consumer & Office Products
Electronics & Communications Products
Fuel Cell Technology

BRANDS/DIVISIONS/AFFILIATES:
3M Purification Inc
Thinsulate
Scotch
Command
Filtrete
Scott Safety

CONTACTS:
Note: Officers with more than one job title may be intentionally listed here more than once.

Michael Roman, CEO
Jon Lindekugel, Senior VP, Divisional
Theresa Reinseth, Chief Accounting Officer
John Banovetz, Chief Technology Officer
Joaquin Delgado, Executive VP, Divisional
Julie Bushman, Executive VP, Divisional
Michael Vale, Executive VP, Divisional
Mojdeh Poul, Executive VP, Divisional
Ashish Khandpur, Executive VP, Divisional
Paul Keel, Executive VP, Divisional
James Bauman, Executive VP, Divisional
Ivan Fong, General Counsel
Inge Thulin, President
Eric Hammes, Senior VP, Divisional
Kristen Ludgate, Senior VP, Divisional
Denise Rutherford, Senior VP, Divisional

GROWTH PLANS/SPECIAL FEATURES:

3M Company is involved in the research, manufacturing and marketing of a variety of products. Its operations are organized in five segments: industrial, safety and graphics, electronics and energy, healthcare and consumer. The industrial segment serves the automotive, electronics, appliance, paper, printing, food, beverage and construction markets. Its major industrial products include Thinsulate acoustic insulation and 3M paint finishing and detail products. Also, 3M Purification, Inc. provides a line of filtration products. The safety and graphics segment serves a range of markets, with major product offerings including personal protection, traffic safety, border and civil security solutions, commercial graphics sheeting, architectural surface and lighting solutions, cleaning products and roofing granules for asphalt shingles. The electronics and energy segment serves customers with telecommunications networks, electrical products, power generation and distribution and infrastructure protection. Major products include LCD computers and televisions, hand-held mobile devices, notebook PCs and automotive displays. The healthcare segment serves medical clinics, hospitals, pharmaceuticals, dental and orthodontic practitioners, health information systems and food manufacturing and testing. Products include medical and surgical supplies, skin health, infection prevention, inhalation and transdermal drug delivery systems. The consumer segment serves markets such as consumer retail, office retail, home improvement and building maintenance. Major products include the Scotch tape, Command adhesive and Filtrete filtration family lines of products.

The company offers employees medical and dental insurance, domestic partner benefits, tuition reimbursement, flexible spending accounts, disability coverage, 401(k) and adoption assistance.

FINANCIAL DATA:
Note: Data for latest year may not have been available at press time.

In U.S. $	2018	2017	2016	2015	2014	2013
Revenue	32,765,000,000	31,657,000,000	30,109,000,000	30,274,000,000	31,821,000,000	30,871,000,000
R&D Expense	1,821,000,000	1,850,000,000	1,735,000,000	1,763,000,000	1,770,000,000	1,715,000,000
Operating Income	6,660,000,000	7,234,000,000	7,223,000,000	6,946,000,000	7,135,000,000	6,666,000,000
Operating Margin %		.23%	.24%	.23%	.22%	.22%
SGA Expense	7,602,000,000	6,572,000,000	6,111,000,000	6,182,000,000	6,469,000,000	6,384,000,000
Net Income	5,349,000,000	4,858,000,000	5,050,000,000	4,833,000,000	4,956,000,000	4,659,000,000
Operating Cash Flow	6,439,000,000	6,240,000,000	6,662,000,000	6,420,000,000	6,626,000,000	5,817,000,000
Capital Expenditure	1,577,000,000	1,373,000,000	1,420,000,000	1,461,000,000	1,493,000,000	1,665,000,000
EBITDA	8,838,000,000	9,414,000,000	8,726,000,000	8,407,000,000	8,576,000,000	8,078,000,000
Return on Assets %		.14%	.15%	.15%	.15%	.14%
Return on Equity %		.44%	.46%	.39%	.32%	.27%
Debt to Equity		1.051	1.041	0.752	0.518	0.25

CONTACT INFORMATION:
Phone: 651 733-1110
Fax: 651 733-9973
Toll-Free: 800-364-3577
Address: 3M Center, St. Paul, MN 55144 United States

STOCK TICKER/OTHER:
Stock Ticker: MMM
Exchange: NYS
Employees: 93,516
Fiscal Year Ends: 12/31
Parent Company:

SALARIES/BONUSES:
Top Exec. Salary: $1,269,200
Bonus: $
Second Exec. Salary: $1,049,976
Bonus: $

OTHER THOUGHTS:
Estimated Female Officers or Directors: 7
Hot Spot for Advancement for Women/Minorities: Y

Sales, profits and employees may be estimates. Financial information, benefits and other data can change quickly and may vary from those stated here.

Abbott Laboratories

NAIC Code: 325412

www.abbott.com

TYPES OF BUSINESS:
Nutritional Products Manufacturing
Immunoassays
Diagnostics
Consumer Health Products
Medical & Surgical Devices
Generic Pharmaceutical Products
LASIK Devices

BRANDS/DIVISIONS/AFFILIATES:
Similac
Ensure
Pedialyte
Jevity
Freego
Cephea Valve Technologies Inc

CONTACTS:
Note: Officers with more than one job title may be intentionally listed here more than once.

Miles White, CEO
Jaime Contreras, Senior VP, Divisional
Brian Yoor, CFO
Robert Funck, Chief Accounting Officer
Robert Ford, COO
Andrew Lane, Executive VP, Divisional
Stephen Fussell, Executive VP, Divisional
John Capek, Executive VP, Divisional
Brian Blaser, Executive VP, Divisional
Daniel Salvadori, Executive VP, Divisional
Hubert Allen, Executive VP
Roger Bird, Senior VP, Divisional
Jared Watkin, Senior VP, Divisional
Sharon Bracken, Senior VP, Divisional
Sammy Karam, Senior VP, Divisional

GROWTH PLANS/SPECIAL FEATURES:

Abbott Laboratories develops, manufactures and sells healthcare products and technologies, marketed in over 150 countries. The firm operates in four product segments: established pharmaceuticals, diagnostics, nutritional and cardiovascular and neuromodulation products. The established pharmaceuticals segment includes a broad line of branded generic pharmaceuticals manufactured worldwide and marketed and sold outside the U.S. in emerging markets. These products are primarily sold directly to wholesalers, distributors, government agencies, healthcare facilities, pharmacies and independent retailers from Abbott-owned distribution centers and public warehouses. This segment's principal therapeutic offerings include gastroenterology, women's health, cardiovascular, metabolic, pain, central nervous system, respiratory and vaccination products. The diagnostics segment includes a line of diagnostic systems and tests manufactured, marketed and sold worldwide. These products are primarily marketed and sold directly to blood banks, hospitals, commercial laboratories, clinics, physicians' offices, government agencies, alternate care testing sites and plasma protein therapeutic companies from Abbot-owned distribution centers, public warehouses and third-party distributors. This segment's products include: core laboratory systems in the areas of immunoassay, clinical chemistry, hematology and transfusions; molecular diagnostics systems; point of care systems; rapid diagnostic systems; and informatics and automation solutions for use in laboratories. The nutritional segment offers a line of pediatric and adult nutritional products manufactured, marketed and sold worldwide. This segment's products include: various forms of prepared infant formula and follow-on formula; adult and other pediatric nutritional products; and nutritional products used in enteral feeding in healthcare institutions. Brands include Similac, Ensure, Pedialyte, Jevity and Freego, among many others. In January 2019, Abbott purchased Cephea Valve Technologies, Inc., which is developing a less-invasive replacement heart valve for people with mitral valve disease.

Abbott offers comprehensive insurance benefits and employee assistance programs.

FINANCIAL DATA:
Note: Data for latest year may not have been available at press time.

In U.S. $	2018	2017	2016	2015	2014	2013
Revenue	30,578,000,000	27,390,000,000	20,853,000,000	20,405,000,000	20,247,000,000	21,848,000,000
R&D Expense	2,300,000,000	2,235,000,000	1,422,000,000	1,405,000,000	1,345,000,000	1,452,000,000
Operating Income	3,650,000,000	1,726,000,000	3,185,000,000	2,867,000,000	2,599,000,000	2,629,000,000
Operating Margin %		.06%	.15%	.14%	.13%	.12%
SGA Expense	9,744,000,000	9,117,000,000	6,672,000,000	6,785,000,000	6,530,000,000	6,936,000,000
Net Income	2,368,000,000	477,000,000	1,400,000,000	4,423,000,000	2,284,000,000	2,576,000,000
Operating Cash Flow	6,300,000,000	5,570,000,000	3,203,000,000	2,966,000,000	3,675,000,000	3,324,000,000
Capital Expenditure	1,394,000,000	1,135,000,000	1,121,000,000	1,110,000,000	1,077,000,000	1,145,000,000
EBITDA	6,977,000,000	6,156,000,000	3,197,000,000	4,818,000,000	4,216,000,000	4,397,000,000
Return on Assets %		.01%	.03%	.11%	.05%	.05%
Return on Equity %		.02%	.07%	.21%	.10%	.10%
Debt to Equity		0.881	1.007	0.277	0.158	0.135

CONTACT INFORMATION:
Phone: 847 937-6100   Fax: 847 937-1511
Toll-Free:
Address: 100 Abbott Park Rd., Abbott Park, IL 60064-6400 United States

STOCK TICKER/OTHER:
Stock Ticker: ABT
Employees: 75,000
Parent Company:

Exchange: NYS
Fiscal Year Ends: 12/31

SALARIES/BONUSES:
Top Exec. Salary: $1,900,000   Bonus: $
Second Exec. Salary: $796,057   Bonus: $

OTHER THOUGHTS:
Estimated Female Officers or Directors: 5
Hot Spot for Advancement for Women/Minorities: Y

Sales, profits and employees may be estimates. Financial information, benefits and other data can change quickly and may vary from those stated here.

AbbVie Inc

NAIC Code: 325412

www.abbvie.com

TYPES OF BUSINESS:
Pharmaceuticals Manufacturing

BRANDS/DIVISIONS/AFFILIATES:
HUMIRA
IMBRUVICA
VIEKIRA PAK
AndroGel
Lupron
Duopa
KALETRA

CONTACTS:
Note: Officers with more than one job title may be intentionally listed here more than once.

Richard Gonzalez, CEO
Robert Michael, CFO
Brian Durkin, Chief Accounting Officer
Laura Schumacher, Chief Legal Officer
Azita Saleki-Gerhardt, Executive VP, Divisional
William Chase, Executive VP, Divisional
Timothy Richmond, Executive VP
Henry Gosebruch, Executive VP
Carlos Alban, Other Executive Officer
Michael Severino, President
Jeffrey Stewart, Senior VP, Divisional
Nicholas Donoghoe, Senior VP, Divisional

GROWTH PLANS/SPECIAL FEATURES:

AbbVie, Inc. is a global biopharmaceutical manufacturing and research firm. The company's core areas of focus include immunology, kidney disease, liver disease, neuroscience, renal disease, Crohn's disease, hepatitis C, endometriosis, thyroid disease, Parkinson's disease, oncology and women's health. AbbVie investigates both small and large molecule approaches, and its research efforts are partnered with external collaborations across industry, academia and healthcare authorities. The firm's leading drugs include HUMIRA, a biologic therapy; IMBRUVICA, an oral therapy that inhibits a protein called Bruton's tyrosine kinase for the treatment of lymphoma-related issues and more; VIEKIRA PAK, an all-oral, short-course interferon-free therapy; AndroGel, a testosterone replacement therapy; Lupron, a product for the palliative treatment of advanced prostate cancer, endometriosis and central precocious puberty; Duopa, an intestinal gel for advanced Parkinson's; and KALETRA, a prescription anti-HIV 1 medicine that maintains viral suppression in people with HIV-1. The company operates research centers in Abbott Park and North Chicago, Illinois; Redwood City, South San Francisco and Sunnyvale, California; Worcester and Cambridge, Massachusetts; and Ludwigshafen, Germany. Its products are sold in more than 75 nations worldwide. In June 2019, Abbvie agreed to acquire Allergan PLC in a cash and stock transaction valued at $63 billion.

Benefits for U.S. employees include on-site fitness centers or health club memberships, sports and recreation clubs and wellness programs. Time off includes 11 paid holidays per year. Other perks include Work-Life balance programs, adoption assistance and mothers at work programs. Eligible employees may participate in both a 401(k) savings plan and a pension plan.

FINANCIAL DATA:
Note: Data for latest year may not have been available at press time.

In U.S. $	2018	2017	2016	2015	2014	2013
Revenue	32,753,000,000	28,216,000,000	25,638,000,000	22,859,000,000	19,960,000,000	18,790,000,000
R&D Expense	10,753,000,000	5,309,000,000	4,566,000,000	4,435,000,000	3,649,000,000	3,193,000,000
Operating Income	6,383,000,000	9,592,001,000	9,383,999,000	7,537,000,000	3,411,000,000	5,664,000,000
Operating Margin %		.34%	.37%	.33%	.17%	.30%
SGA Expense	7,399,000,000	6,275,000,000	5,855,000,000	6,387,000,000	7,724,000,000	5,352,000,000
Net Income	5,687,000,000	5,309,000,000	5,953,000,000	5,144,000,000	1,774,000,000	4,128,000,000
Operating Cash Flow	13,427,000,000	9,959,999,000	7,041,000,000	7,535,000,000	3,549,000,000	6,267,000,000
Capital Expenditure	638,000,000	529,000,000	479,000,000	532,000,000	612,000,000	491,000,000
EBITDA	8,310,000,000	10,378,000,000	10,120,000,000	8,200,000,000	3,584,000,000	6,528,000,000
Return on Assets %		.08%	.10%	.13%	.06%	.15%
Return on Equity %		1.09%	1.38%	1.81%	.57%	1.05%
Debt to Equity		6.073	7.86	7.412	6.065	3.182

CONTACT INFORMATION:
Phone: 847-932-7900 Fax:
Toll-Free: 800-255-5162
Address: 1 N. Waukegan Rd., North Chicago, IL 60064 United States

SALARIES/BONUSES:
Top Exec. Salary: $1,650,000 Bonus: $
Second Exec. Salary: $1,100,605 Bonus: $

STOCK TICKER/OTHER:
Stock Ticker: ABBV Exchange: NYS
Employees: 30,000 Fiscal Year Ends: 12/31
Parent Company:

OTHER THOUGHTS:
Estimated Female Officers or Directors:
Hot Spot for Advancement for Women/Minorities:

ABM Industries Incorporated

NAIC Code: 561720

www.abm.com

TYPES OF BUSINESS:
Janitorial Services
Parking Facilities
Maintenance Personnel
Security Services
Lighting Services
Billing & Accounting Services
Supplier Management
Energy Efficiency Technology

BRANDS/DIVISIONS/AFFILIATES:
ABM
ABM Building Value
ABM Greencare
MPower
Linc Service
OmniServ
TEGG

CONTACTS:
Note: Officers with more than one job title may be intentionally listed here more than once.

Scott Salmirs, CEO
Diego Scaglione, CFO
Sudhakar Kesavan, Chairman of the Board
Dean Chin, Chief Accounting Officer
Scott Giacobbe, COO
Andrea Newborn, Executive VP
Andrew Block, Executive VP
Rene Jacobsen, President, Divisional

GROWTH PLANS/SPECIAL FEATURES:

ABM Industries Incorporated, operating through its subsidiaries, is one of the country's largest facility services providers. The company operates through six segments: business and industry (B&I), aviation, technology and manufacturing (T&M), education, technical solutions, and healthcare. B&I is the firm's largest segment, and encompasses janitorial, facilities engineering, and parking services for commercial real estate properties and entertainment venues. This division also provides vehicle maintenance and other services to rental car providers. The aviation segment supports airlines and airports with services ranging from parking and janitorial to passenger assistance, catering logistics, air cabin maintenance and transportation. The T&M segment provides janitorial, facilities engineering and parking services for industrial, manufacturing, high-tech and emerging industries. The education segment delivers janitorial, custodial, landscaping/grounds, facilities engineering and parking services for public school districts, private schools, colleges and universities. The technical solutions segment specializes in mechanical and electrical services, which can also be leveraged for cross-selling across all of ABM's industry groups, domestically and internationally. Last, the healthcare segment offers janitorial, facilities engineering, clinical engineering, food/nutrition, laundry/linen, parking, guest services and patient transportation services at traditional hospitals and non-acute facilities. ABM holds various service marks, trademarks and trade names for its activities and businesses, including ABM, ABM Building Value, ABM Greencare, MPower, Linc Service, OmniServ and TEGG.

ABM Industries offers dental, medical, vision, disability, life, AD&D and business travel accident insurance; workers compensation insurance; 401(k) and employee stock plans; and various employee assistance programs.

FINANCIAL DATA:
Note: Data for latest year may not have been available at press time.

In U.S. $	2018	2017	2016	2015	2014	2013
Revenue	6,442,200,000	5,453,600,000	5,144,700,000	4,897,800,000	5,032,800,000	4,809,281,000
R&D Expense						
Operating Income	190,800,000	104,200,000	106,200,000	73,600,000	128,600,000	119,025,000
Operating Margin %		.02%	.02%	.02%	.03%	.02%
SGA Expense	438,000,000	436,600,000	390,100,000	390,000,000	363,900,000	348,274,000
Net Income	97,800,000	3,800,000	57,200,000	76,300,000	75,600,000	72,900,000
Operating Cash Flow	320,900,000	5,600,000	83,500,000	145,300,000	120,700,000	135,313,000
Capital Expenditure	50,900,000	57,200,000	44,000,000	26,500,000	37,400,000	32,593,000
EBITDA	254,300,000	176,200,000	119,800,000	139,600,000	192,400,000	185,734,000
Return on Assets %		.00%	.03%	.04%	.04%	.04%
Return on Equity %		.00%	.06%	.08%	.08%	.08%
Debt to Equity		0.844	0.275	0.157	0.33	0.343

CONTACT INFORMATION:
Phone: 212 297-0200 Fax: 212 297-0375
Toll-Free:
Address: One Liberty Plaza, 7/Fl, New York, NY 10006 United States

STOCK TICKER/OTHER:
Stock Ticker: ABM
Employees: 140,000
Parent Company:

Exchange: NYS
Fiscal Year Ends: 10/31

SALARIES/BONUSES:
Top Exec. Salary: $975,000 Bonus: $
Second Exec. Salary: $550,000 Bonus: $

OTHER THOUGHTS:
Estimated Female Officers or Directors: 4
Hot Spot for Advancement for Women/Minorities: Y

Academy Sports & Outdoors Ltd

www.academy.com

NAIC Code: 451110

TYPES OF BUSINESS:
Sporting Goods Stores
Apparel
Footwear
Outdoor Sports Gear
Hunting Licenses

BRANDS/DIVISIONS/AFFILIATES:
KKR & Co LP (Kohlberg Kravis Roberts & Co)

CONTACTS: Note: Officers with more than one job title may be intentionally listed here more than once.
Ken Hicks, CEO
Michael Mullican, CFO
Steven P. Lawrence, Exec. Pres., Retail Oper.
Steven P. Lawrence, Chief Merchandising Officer
Beth Menuer, Exec. VP-Footwear
Robert Frennea, Exec. VP-Apparel
Kevin Chapman, Exec. VP-Stores

GROWTH PLANS/SPECIAL FEATURES:
Academy Sports & Outdoors, Ltd., owned by KKR & Co LP, is one of the largest sporting goods retailers in the U.S. The company operates over 250 stores throughout 16 states including Alabama, Arkansas, Florida, Georgia, Illinois, Indiana, Kansas, Kentucky, Louisiana, Mississippi, Missouri, North Carolina, Oklahoma, South Carolina, Tennessee and Texas. Its retail operations also include a full e-commerce retail store. Academy Sports offers a broad selection of sporting equipment, apparel and footwear. The stores, which range in size from 50,000 to 100,000 square feet, are laid out in a racetrack format with soft goods on the inside, including branded and private label athletic and casual apparel; and hard goods, such as camping, hunting, fishing, marine, footwear and fitness and sporting goods on the outside. The company distributes merchandise to its stores from its distribution centers located in Katy, Texas and Twiggs County, Georgia. The center utilizes radio frequency identification devices (RFID), automated inventory and replenishment systems and a state-of-the-art warehouse management system to smoothly operate its large processing and inventory space. In 2018, Academy Sports opened 17 new stores throughout the U.S.

The company offers its employees a 401(k) plan; medical, dental and vision insurance; life insurance; short- and long-term disability benefits; tuition reimbursement; merchandise discounts; bereavement leave; continuing education benefits; and business travel accident insurance.

FINANCIAL DATA: Note: Data for latest year may not have been available at press time.

In U.S. $	2018	2017	2016	2015	2014	2013
Revenue	4,900,000,000	4,700,000,000	4,600,000,000	4,500,000,000	4,000,000,000	3,700,000,000
R&D Expense						
Operating Income						
Operating Margin %						
SGA Expense						
Net Income						
Operating Cash Flow						
Capital Expenditure						
EBITDA						
Return on Assets %						
Return on Equity %						
Debt to Equity						

CONTACT INFORMATION:
Phone: 281-646-5200   Fax: 281-646-5000
Toll-Free: 888-922-2336
Address: 1800 N. Mason Rd., Katy, TX 77449 United States

STOCK TICKER/OTHER:
Stock Ticker: Private   Exchange:
Employees: 23,000   Fiscal Year Ends: 02/28
Parent Company: KKR & Co LP (Kohlberg Kravis Roberts & Co)

SALARIES/BONUSES:
Top Exec. Salary: $ Bonus: $
Second Exec. Salary: $ Bonus: $

OTHER THOUGHTS:
Estimated Female Officers or Directors: 1
Hot Spot for Advancement for Women/Minorities:

Sales, profits and employees may be estimates. Financial information, benefits and other data can change quickly and may vary from those stated here.

Acadia Healthcare Company Inc

www.acadiahealthcare.com

NAIC Code: 622210

TYPES OF BUSINESS:
Psychiatric and Substance Abuse Hospitals
Residential Treatment Facilities
Behavioral Health Care Centers

BRANDS/DIVISIONS/AFFILIATES:
Partnerships in Care (PiC)

CONTACTS:
Note: Officers with more than one job title may be intentionally listed here more than once.

Debra Osteen, CEO
David Duckworth, CFO
Reeve Waud, Chairman of the Board
Ronald Fincher, COO
Christopher Howard, Executive VP

GROWTH PLANS/SPECIAL FEATURES:
Acadia Healthcare Company, Inc. provides inpatient behavioral healthcare services via 583 facilities with approximately 18,100 licensed beds in 40 U.S. states, the U.K. and Puerto Rico. Acadia provides psychiatric and chemical dependency services in a variety of settings, including psychiatric hospitals, residential treatment centers, outpatient clinics and therapeutic school-based programs. Treatment specializes in helping children, teenagers and adults suffering from mental health disorders and/or alcohol and drug addiction. Acadia operates through four types of facilities: acute inpatient psychiatric facilities, residential treatment centers, outpatient community-based services and specialty. Acute inpatient psychiatric facilities help stabilize patients that are either a threat to themselves or to others, and have 24-hour observation, daily intervention and residential treatment centers. Residential treatment centers treat patients with behavioral disorders in a non-hospital setting, and balance therapy activities with social, academic and other activities. Certain residential treatment centers provide group home and therapeutic foster care programs. Outpatient community-based services are usually divided between children and adolescents (7-18 years of age) and young children (three months to six years old). Community-based programs provide therapeutic treatment to minors who have clinically-defined emotional, psychiatric or chemical dependency disorders while enabling the youth to remain at home and within their community. Specialty treatment facilities include residential recovery facilities, eating disorder facilities and comprehensive treatment centers (CTCs) for addictive disorders, co-occurring mental disorders and detoxification. Acadia's U.K. operations work under the Partnerships in Care (PiC) name.

FINANCIAL DATA:
Note: Data for latest year may not have been available at press time.

In U.S. $	2018	2017	2016	2015	2014	2013
Revenue	3,012,442,000	2,836,316,000	2,810,914,000	1,794,492,000	1,004,601,000	713,408,000
R&D Expense						
Operating Income	378,236,000	413,615,000	396,819,000	284,239,000	159,113,000	115,845,000
Operating Margin %		.15%	.14%	.16%	.16%	.16%
SGA Expense	2,120,876,000	1,947,864,000	1,966,436,000	1,239,957,000	702,167,000	499,901,000
Net Income	-175,750,000	199,835,000	6,143,000	112,554,000	83,040,000	42,579,000
Operating Cash Flow	414,080,000	399,577,000	361,478,000	240,403,000	115,286,000	65,562,000
Capital Expenditure	359,845,000	315,234,000	348,229,000	302,669,000	136,421,000	77,033,000
EBITDA	537,068,000	556,625,000	531,922,000	347,789,000	191,780,000	132,935,000
Return on Assets %		.03%	.00%	.03%	.05%	.04%
Return on Equity %		.08%	.00%	.09%	.12%	.09%
Debt to Equity		1.246	1.501	1.304	1.214	1.252

CONTACT INFORMATION:
Phone: 615 861-6000 Fax: 615 261-9685
Toll-Free:
Address: 6100 Tower Circle, Ste. 1000, Franklin, TN 37067 United States

STOCK TICKER/OTHER:
Stock Ticker: ACHC
Employees: 40,400
Parent Company:

Exchange: NAS
Fiscal Year Ends: 12/31

SALARIES/BONUSES:
Top Exec. Salary: $1,124,500   Bonus: $
Second Exec. Salary: $689,520   Bonus: $

OTHER THOUGHTS:
Estimated Female Officers or Directors:
Hot Spot for Advancement for Women/Minorities:

Accenture LLP

NAIC Code: 541512

www.accenture.com/us-en

TYPES OF BUSINESS:
IT Consulting
Computer Operations Outsourcing
Supply Chain Technologies
Technology Research
Software Development
Human Resources Consulting
Management Consulting
Research and Development

BRANDS/DIVISIONS/AFFILIATES:
Accenture plc

CONTACTS:
Note: Officers with more than one job title may be intentionally listed here more than once.

Pierre Nanterme, CEO
Jo Deblaere, COO
David P. Rowland, CFO
Amy Fuller, Chief Marketing and Communications Officer
Ellyn J. Shook, Chief Leadership and Human Resources Officer
Paul Daugherty, Chief Technology Officer
Pierre Nanterme, Chmn.

GROWTH PLANS/SPECIAL FEATURES:

Accenture, LLP, the U.S. subsidiary of Accenture plc, is a leading provider of management consulting, technology and outsourcing services, with operations in over 30 American cities. The firm delivers services through five operating groups: communications, media and technology; financial services; health and public service; products; and resources. Accenture's communications, media and technology group offers technology, consulting and systems integration to the electronics, communications, high tech, software, platform and media companies. Its financial services group provides consulting, regulatory, growth and outsourcing strategies to the insurance, capital markets and banking industries. The firm's health and public service group works with local, state, provincial and national governments and healthcare providers to deliver better social, economic and health outcomes to the people they serve. Its products group serves interconnected consumer-relevant industries to increase digital presence and help enhance performance in different aspects of everyday business functions. The company's resources group works with the chemicals, energy, natural resources and utilities industries. Additionally, Accenture offers management consulting services in finance and enterprise performance, operations, technology, IT security consulting/outsourcing, cloud computing, business, risk management, sales and growth customer services, strategy, sustainability and talent and organization.

Accenture offers its employees medical, dental, long-term disability, life and AD&D coverage; nurselines; legal coverage; a profit sharing plan; a 401(k) savings plan; and adoption assistance.

FINANCIAL DATA:
Note: Data for latest year may not have been available at press time.

In U.S. $	2018	2017	2016	2015	2014	2013
Revenue	17,800,000,000	16,290,842,000	15,653,000,000	14,209,387,000	12,796,847,000	12,035,847,000
R&D Expense						
Operating Income						
Operating Margin %						
SGA Expense						
Net Income						
Operating Cash Flow						
Capital Expenditure						
EBITDA						
Return on Assets %						
Return on Equity %						
Debt to Equity						

CONTACT INFORMATION:
Phone: 312-693-0161   Fax: 312-693-0507
Toll-Free: 877-889-9009
Address: 161 N. Clark St., Chicago, IL 60601 United States

SALARIES/BONUSES:
Top Exec. Salary: $ Bonus: $
Second Exec. Salary: $ Bonus: $

STOCK TICKER/OTHER:
Stock Ticker: Subsidiary
Employees: 180,000
Parent Company: Accenture plc

Exchange:
Fiscal Year Ends: 08/31

OTHER THOUGHTS:
Estimated Female Officers or Directors:
Hot Spot for Advancement for Women/Minorities: Y

Sales, profits and employees may be estimates. Financial information, benefits and other data can change quickly and may vary from those stated here.

Acosta Inc

www.acosta.com

NAIC Code: 541800

TYPES OF BUSINESS:
Marketing Services
Consumer Packaged Goods Sales Research
Retail Sales Support
Integrated Marketing Solutions
Outsourcing
Retail Services

BRANDS/DIVISIONS/AFFILIATES:
Acosta Sales & Marketing
Acosta Marketing Group

CONTACTS:
Note: Officers with more than one job title may be intentionally listed here more than once.

Alejandro Rodriguez Bas, CEO
Steve Kremser, Chief Strategy & Transformation Officer
Matt Laurie, Interim CFO
Ned Peverley, Exec. VP-Retail Strategy & Oper.
Claudia Saenz Amlie, Chief Human Resources Officer
Darin Pickett, Chief Client Officer
Reece Alford, General Counsel
Brian King, Chief Strategy Officer
Vilma Consuegra, VP-Corp. Comm.
Woody Norris, Pres., Client Dev.
Jack Parker, Pres., Grocery Channel Sales
Brian Baldwin, Pres., Strategic Channel Sales
Aidan Tracey, Pres., Acosta Mktg. Group
Gary R. Chartrand, Chmn.

GROWTH PLANS/SPECIAL FEATURES:
Acosta, Inc., which does business as Acosta Sales & Marketing, is an outsourced sales and marketing agency. Founded in 1927 as single-location food broker L.T. Acosta Company, Inc., the firm serves consumer packaged goods companies and retail groups through offices across the U.S. and Canada. Acosta's client roster includes over 60% of the No. 1 and No. 2 grocery store brands. On behalf of its consumer packaged goods clients, the company offers direct sales of new and existing items to retailers such as Safeway and Kroger. As part of this process, Acosta provides services such as the negotiation of volume and price levels. For retail clients, the firm provides in-store stocking services. It seeks to ensure optimal shelf space location and exposure of its customer's brands in order to maximize the sale of their products. Acosta Marketing Group offers enhanced integrated marketing services including buyer trend reports and customer analytics.

Acosta offers its employees medical, vision and dental insurance; a prescription drug plan; life, disability and AD&D insurance; a 401(k) retirement plan; tuition assistance; gym membership; and cell phone, new car and new computer discounts.

FINANCIAL DATA:
Note: Data for latest year may not have been available at press time.

In U.S. $	2018	2017	2016	2015	2014	2013
Revenue	3,910,000,000	3,800,000,000	3,375,000,000	3,300,000,000	3,300,000,000	3,214,322,800
R&D Expense						
Operating Income						
Operating Margin %						
SGA Expense						
Net Income						
Operating Cash Flow						
Capital Expenditure						
EBITDA						
Return on Assets %						
Return on Equity %						
Debt to Equity						

CONTACT INFORMATION:
Phone: 904-281-9800 Fax: 904-281-9966
Toll-Free:
Address: 6600 Corporate Center Pkwy., Jacksonville, FL 32216 United States

STOCK TICKER/OTHER:
Stock Ticker: Private
Employees: 35,000
Parent Company: Carlyle Group (The)

Exchange:
Fiscal Year Ends: 07/31

SALARIES/BONUSES:
Top Exec. Salary: $ Bonus: $
Second Exec. Salary: $ Bonus: $

OTHER THOUGHTS:
Estimated Female Officers or Directors: 2
Hot Spot for Advancement for Women/Minorities: Y

Sales, profits and employees may be estimates. Financial information, benefits and other data can change quickly and may vary from those stated here.

Activision Blizzard Inc

www.activisionblizzard.com

NAIC Code: 0

TYPES OF BUSINESS:
Electronic Games, Apps & Entertainment
League-Based, Live Gaming Competition
Apps
TV Distribution of Gaming Events
Merchandising
Licensing Game Content for Movies
Licensing Content to Comic Books

BRANDS/DIVISIONS/AFFILIATES:
Activision Publishing Inc
Blizzard Entertainment Inc
King Digital Entertainment
Call of Duty
World of Warcraft
Overwatch
Activision Blizzard Studios
Activision Blizzard Distribution

CONTACTS:
Note: Officers with more than one job title may be intentionally listed here more than once.

Riccardo Zacconi, CEO, Subsidiary
Robert Kotick, CEO
Dennis Durkin, CFO
Brian Kelly, Chairman of the Board
Stephen Wereb, Chief Accounting Officer
Christopher Walther, Chief Legal Officer
Collister Johnson, COO
Brian Stolz, Other Executive Officer

GROWTH PLANS/SPECIAL FEATURES:

Activision Blizzard, Inc. is a leading international publisher and developer of subscription-based massively multiplayer online role-playing games (MMORPGs) and other PC-based, console, handheld and mobile games. The firm develops and distributes content and services across all major gaming platforms, including video game consoles, personal computers (PCs) and mobile devices. Activision operates through four business segments: Activision Publishing, Inc.; Blizzard Entertainment, Inc.; King Digital Entertainment; and other. Activision Publishing is a developer and publisher of interactive software products and entertainment content, particularly in console gaming. Key product franchises include: Call of Duty and Destiney. Blizzard Entertainment develops and publishes interactive software products and entertainment content, particularly in PC gaming. Its content is primarily delivered through retail channels or digital downloads, including subscriptions, full-game sales and in-game purchases. This division's key product franchises include World of Warcraft, a subscription-based MMORPG; StarCraft, a real-time strategy PC franchise; Diablo, an action-role-playing franchise; Hearthstone, an online collectible card franchise; Heroes of the Storm, a free-to-play team brawler; and Overwatch, a team-based, first-person shooter. In addition, Overwatch League sells tickets to fans who watch teams competing at live events or via TV broadcasting. King Digital develops and publishes interactive entertainment content and services, particularly on mobile platforms such as Android and iOS, but distributes its content and services on online social platforms as well. King's games are free. Its product franchises include Candy Crush, Farm Heroes and Bubble Witch. Last, the other segment includes: Activision Blizzard Studios, which creates original film and television content based on the company's library of globally-recognized intellectual properties, including the animated TV series Skylanders Academy; and Activision Blizzard Distribution, consisting of operations in Europe that provide warehousing, logistics and sales distribution services to third-party publishers of interactive entertainment software.

FINANCIAL DATA:
Note: Data for latest year may not have been available at press time.

In U.S. $	2018	2017	2016	2015	2014	2013
Revenue	7,500,000,000	7,017,000,000	6,608,000,000	4,664,000,000	4,408,000,000	4,583,000,000
R&D Expense	1,101,000,000	1,069,000,000	958,000,000	646,000,000	571,000,000	584,000,000
Operating Income	1,988,000,000	1,309,000,000	1,412,000,000	1,319,000,000	1,183,000,000	1,372,000,000
Operating Margin %		.19%	.21%	.28%	.27%	.30%
SGA Expense	1,894,000,000	2,138,000,000	1,844,000,000	1,114,000,000	1,129,000,000	1,096,000,000
Net Income	1,813,000,000	273,000,000	966,000,000	892,000,000	835,000,000	1,010,000,000
Operating Cash Flow	1,790,000,000	2,213,000,000	2,155,000,000	1,192,000,000	1,292,000,000	1,264,000,000
Capital Expenditure	131,000,000	155,000,000	136,000,000	111,000,000	107,000,000	74,000,000
EBITDA	2,986,000,000	2,508,000,000	2,562,000,000	1,813,000,000	1,535,000,000	1,692,000,000
Return on Assets %		.02%	.06%	.06%	.06%	.07%
Return on Equity %		.03%	.11%	.12%	.12%	.11%
Debt to Equity		0.464	0.536	0.506	0.598	0.705

CONTACT INFORMATION:
Phone: 310 255-2000　　Fax: 310 255-2100
Toll-Free:
Address: 3100 Ocean Park Blvd., Santa Monica, CA 90405 United States

STOCK TICKER/OTHER:
Stock Ticker: ATVI　　Exchange: NAS
Employees: 9,600　　Fiscal Year Ends: 12/31
Parent Company:

SALARIES/BONUSES:
Top Exec. Salary: $1,330,194　　Bonus: $1,200,000
Second Exec. Salary: $871,476　　Bonus: $1,000,000

OTHER THOUGHTS:
Estimated Female Officers or Directors:
Hot Spot for Advancement for Women/Minorities:

Sales, profits and employees may be estimates. Financial information, benefits and other data can change quickly and may vary from those stated here.

Adobe Systems Inc

www.adobe.com

NAIC Code: 0

TYPES OF BUSINESS:
Computer Software, Multimedia, Graphics & Publishing
Document Management Software
Photo Editing & Management Software
Graphic Design Software

BRANDS/DIVISIONS/AFFILIATES:
Adobe Experience Cloud
Adobe LiveCycle
Adobe Connect
Marketo Inc

CONTACTS: Note: Officers with more than one job title may be intentionally listed here more than once.
Shantanu Narayen, CEO
John Murphy, CFO
Mark Garfield, Chief Accounting Officer
Ann Lewnes, Chief Marketing Officer
Abhay Parasnis, Chief Technology Officer
John Warnock, Co-Founder
Charles Geschke, Director
Matthew Thompson, Executive VP, Divisional
Donna Morris, Executive VP, Divisional
Scott Belsky, Executive VP, Divisional
Dana Rao, Executive VP
Bryan Lamkin, Executive VP
Bradley Rencher, Executive VP

GROWTH PLANS/SPECIAL FEATURES:
Adobe Systems, Inc. is one of the largest software companies in the world. The company operates in three segments, namely digital media, digital experience and publishing, with a current focus on investing in digital media and digital experience, its two strategic growth areas. Digital media provides products, services and solutions that enable individuals, teams and enterprises to create, publish and promote their content anywhere. Its customers include content creators, web designers, app developers and digital media professional, as well as management in marketing departments and agencies, companies and publishers. Customers also include workers who create, collaborate and distribute documents. The digital experience segment provides solutions and services for creating, managing, executing, measuring and optimizing digital marketing and advertising campaigns across multiple channels. Its customers include marketers, advertisers, agencies, publishers, merchandisers, web analysts, marketing executives, information management executives, product development executives and sales and support executives. This division processes more than 180 trillion data transactions in a given year with its analytics products, which provides customers with a data platform that can be used to gain insight and optimize digital experiences through the Adobe Experience Cloud. By combining the creativity of the digital media business and the science of the digital experience offerings, Adobe helps customers more efficiently and effectively make, manage, measure and monetize their content across all channels. Last, the publishing segment contains legacy products and services that address diverse market opportunities such as eLearning solutions, technical document publishing, web application development and high-end printing. This division offers Adobe LiveCycle, an enterprise document and forms platform; and Adobe Connect, a web conferencing platform. In October 2018, Adobe acquired Marketo, Inc., a revenue performance management company, for $4.75 billion, its largest transaction to date.

Adobe offers employees comprehensive benefits.

FINANCIAL DATA: Note: Data for latest year may not have been available at press time.

In U.S. $	2018	2017	2016	2015	2014	2013
Revenue	9,030,008,000	7,301,505,000	5,854,430,000	4,795,511,000	4,147,065,000	4,055,240,000
R&D Expense	1,537,812,000	1,224,059,000	975,987,000	862,730,000	844,353,000	826,631,000
Operating Income	2,840,369,000	2,168,095,000	1,492,094,000	904,654,000	432,568,000	449,220,000
Operating Margin %		.30%	.25%	.19%	.10%	.11%
SGA Expense	3,365,727,000	2,822,298,000	2,487,907,000	2,215,161,000	2,195,640,000	2,140,578,000
Net Income	2,590,774,000	1,693,954,000	1,168,782,000	629,551,000	268,395,000	289,985,000
Operating Cash Flow	4,029,304,000	2,912,853,000	2,199,728,000	1,469,502,000	1,287,482,000	1,151,686,000
Capital Expenditure	266,579,000	178,122,000	203,805,000	184,936,000	148,332,000	188,358,000
EBITDA	3,229,610,000	2,538,040,000	1,837,115,000	1,277,438,000	734,698,000	744,876,000
Return on Assets %		.12%	.10%	.06%	.03%	.03%
Return on Equity %		.21%	.16%	.09%	.04%	.04%
Debt to Equity		0.222	0.256	0.272	0.134	0.223

CONTACT INFORMATION:
Phone: 408 536-6000   Fax: 408 536-6799
Toll-Free: 800-833-6687
Address: 345 Park Ave., San Jose, CA 95110 United States

SALARIES/BONUSES:
Top Exec. Salary: $545,769   Bonus: $1,250,000
Second Exec. Salary: $1,000,000   Bonus: $

STOCK TICKER/OTHER:
Stock Ticker: ADBE
Employees: 15,706
Parent Company:

Exchange: NAS
Fiscal Year Ends: 11/30

OTHER THOUGHTS:
Estimated Female Officers or Directors: 5
Hot Spot for Advancement for Women/Minorities: Y

Advance Auto Parts Inc

NAIC Code: 441310

www.advanceautoparts.com

TYPES OF BUSINESS:
Auto Parts & Accessories Stores
Online Sales

BRANDS/DIVISIONS/AFFILIATES:
Advance Auto Parts
Carquest
Worldpac
Autopart International

CONTACTS:
Note: Officers with more than one job title may be intentionally listed here more than once.

Thomas Greco, CEO
Jeffrey Shepherd, CFO
Jeffrey Smith, Chairman of the Board
Andrew Page, Chief Accounting Officer
Natalie Schechtman, Executive VP, Divisional
Robert Cushing, Executive VP, Divisional
Reuben Slone, Executive VP, Divisional
Michael Broderick, Executive VP, Divisional
Tammy Finley, Executive VP

GROWTH PLANS/SPECIAL FEATURES:

Advance Auto Parts, Inc. is a leading specialty retailer of automotive aftermarket parts, accessories, batteries and maintenance items. The firm primarily operates in the U.S. and serves both do-it-yourself (DIY) and commercial customers. It operates in a single segment comprised of the company's store and branch operations. Advance Auto serves its customers through a variety of channels ranging from brick-and-mortar store locations to self-service eCommerce sites. The company operates under the following store names: Advance Auto Parts, consisting of 4,912 stores that average 7,500 square feet in size; Carquest, consisting of 1,250 stores that average 7,600 square feet in size; Worldpac, consisting of 150 stores that average 28,000 square feet in size; and Autopart International, consisting of 185 stores that offer approximately 41,000 SKUs. Primary categories of products offered by the company include: parts such as alternators, batteries, belts, hoses, brakes, brake pads, chassis parts, climate control parts, clutches, drive shafts, engines, engine parts, ignition parts, lighting, radiators, starters, spark plugs, wires, steering and alignment parts, transmissions, water pumps and windshield wiper blades; accessories such as air fresheners, auto paint, anti-theft devices, emergency road kits, floor mats, ice scrapers, mirrors, seat and steering wheel covers and vent shades; chemicals such as antifreeze, brake and power steering fluids, car wash fluids, car waxes, Freon, fuel additives and windshield washer fluid; and oil such as transmission fluid and other automotive petroleum products. The company's stores are primarily located in the U.S., and are also located throughout Canada, Puerto Rico and the Virgin Islands.

The firm offers employees comprehensive benefits, 401(k) and retirement options, as well as a variety to employee assistance programs.

FINANCIAL DATA:
Note: Data for latest year may not have been available at press time.

In U.S. $	2018	2017	2016	2015	2014	2013
Revenue	9,580,554,000	9,373,784,000	9,567,679,000	9,737,018,000	9,843,862,000	6,493,814,000
R&D Expense						
Operating Income	604,275,000	570,212,000	787,598,000	825,780,000	851,710,000	660,318,000
Operating Margin %		.06%	.08%	.08%	.09%	.10%
SGA Expense	3,615,138,000	3,514,837,000	3,468,317,000	3,596,992,000	3,601,903,000	2,591,828,000
Net Income	423,847,000	475,505,000	459,622,000	473,398,000	493,825,000	391,758,000
Operating Cash Flow	811,028,000	600,805,000	500,874,000	689,642,000	708,991,000	545,250,000
Capital Expenditure	193,715,000	189,758,000	259,559,000	234,747,000	228,446,000	195,757,000
EBITDA	850,036,000	828,320,000	1,057,132,000	1,087,772,000	1,139,495,000	870,811,000
Return on Assets %		.06%	.06%	.06%	.07%	.08%
Return on Equity %		.15%	.17%	.21%	.28%	.29%
Debt to Equity		0.306	0.358	0.493	0.817	0.694

CONTACT INFORMATION:
Phone: 540-362-4911 Fax:
Toll-Free: 877-238-2623
Address: 2635 East Millbrook Rd., Raleight, NC 27604 United States

STOCK TICKER/OTHER:
Stock Ticker: AAP
Employees: 74,000
Parent Company:

Exchange: NYS
Fiscal Year Ends: 12/31

SALARIES/BONUSES:
Top Exec. Salary: $1,100,008 Bonus: $
Second Exec. Salary: $515,491 Bonus: $

OTHER THOUGHTS:
Estimated Female Officers or Directors: 3
Hot Spot for Advancement for Women/Minorities: Y

Advanced Micro Devices Inc (AMD)

NAIC Code: 334413

www.amd.com

TYPES OF BUSINESS:
Microprocessors
Semiconductors
Chipsets
Wafer Manufacturing
Multimedia Graphics

BRANDS/DIVISIONS/AFFILIATES:
AMD
AMD Athlon
AMD Geode
FirePro
LiquidVR
Ryzen
Sempron
Turion

CONTACTS: Note: Officers with more than one job title may be intentionally listed here more than once.
Lisa Su, CEO
Devinder Kumar, CFO
Darla Smith, Chief Accounting Officer
Mark Papermaster, Chief Technology Officer
John Caldwell, Director
Sandeep Chennakeshu, Executive VP, Divisional
Forrest Norrod, General Manager, Divisional
Darren Grasby, Other Executive Officer
Harry Wolin, Senior VP

GROWTH PLANS/SPECIAL FEATURES:

Advanced Micro Devices, Inc. (AMD) is a global semiconductor company that provides processing products for the computing, graphics and consumer electronics markets. The company's x86 microprocessors are primarily offered as standalone devices or as incorporated into an accelerated processing unit (APU), chipsets, discrete/integrated graphics processing units (GPUs) and professional GPUs. A microprocessor is an integrated circuit (IC) that serves as the CPU of a computer, and generally consists of hundreds of millions or billions of transistors that process date in a serial fashion, and control other devices in the system, acting as the brain of the computer. A GPU is a programmable logic chip that helps render images, animations and video. An APU is a processing unit that integrates a CPU and a GPU onto one chip, along with other special-purpose components. This integration enhances system performance by offloading selected tasks to the best-suited component (the CPU of GPU) to optimize component use, increasing the speed of data flow via shared memory while also improving energy efficiency. AMD's server and embedded processors and semi-custom system-on-a-chip (SoC) products and technology are utilized in game consoles. AMD also license portions of its intellectual property. Trademarks of the firm include AMD, AMD Athlon, AMD Geode, AMD Opteron, AMD Phenom, EPYC, FirePro, FreeSync, LiquidVR, Radeon, Ryzen, Sempron and Turion, as well as combinations of these.

FINANCIAL DATA: Note: Data for latest year may not have been available at press time.

In U.S. $	2018	2017	2016	2015	2014	2013
Revenue	6,475,000,000	5,329,000,000	4,272,000,000	3,991,000,000	5,506,000,000	5,299,000,000
R&D Expense	1,434,000,000	1,160,000,000	1,008,000,000	947,000,000	1,072,000,000	1,201,000,000
Operating Income	451,000,000	204,000,000	-382,000,000	-352,000,000	149,000,000	85,000,000
Operating Margin %		.03%	-.11%	-.09%	.03%	.03%
SGA Expense	562,000,000	511,000,000	460,000,000	482,000,000	604,000,000	674,000,000
Net Income	337,000,000	43,000,000	-497,000,000	-660,000,000	-403,000,000	-83,000,000
Operating Cash Flow	34,000,000	68,000,000	90,000,000	-226,000,000	-98,000,000	-148,000,000
Capital Expenditure	163,000,000	113,000,000	77,000,000	96,000,000	95,000,000	84,000,000
EBITDA	621,000,000	339,000,000	-159,000,000	-319,000,000	-18,000,000	339,000,000
Return on Assets %		.01%	-.15%	-.19%	-.10%	-.02%
Return on Equity %		.08%	-248.50%		-1.10%	-.15%
Debt to Equity		2.169	3.45		10.882	3.673

CONTACT INFORMATION:
Phone: 408 749-4000   Fax:
Toll-Free:
Address: 2485 Augustine Dr., Santa Clara, CA 95054 United States

SALARIES/BONUSES:
Top Exec. Salary: $961,057   Bonus: $
Second Exec. Salary: $587,015   Bonus: $

STOCK TICKER/OTHER:
Stock Ticker: AMD
Employees: 9,100
Parent Company:

Exchange: NAS
Fiscal Year Ends: 12/31

OTHER THOUGHTS:
Estimated Female Officers or Directors: 3
Hot Spot for Advancement for Women/Minorities: Y

Sales, profits and employees may be estimates. Financial information, benefits and other data can change quickly and may vary from those stated here.

AdventHealth

www.adventhealth.com

NAIC Code: 622110

TYPES OF BUSINESS:
General Medical and Surgical Hospitals
Nursing Homes
Home Health Care Services

BRANDS/DIVISIONS/AFFILIATES:
Seventh-day Adventist Church

CONTACTS: Note: Officers with more than one job title may be intentionally listed here more than once.
Terry D. Shaw, CEO
Paul C. Rathbun, CFO
Olesea Azevedo, Chief Human Resources Officer
Brent G. Snyder, CIO/Exec. VP
Robert R. Henderschedt, Sr. VP-Admin.
Jeffrey S. Bromme, Chief Legal Officer
Sandra K. Johnson, VP-Bus. Dev., Risk Mgmt. & Compliance
Womack H. Rucker, Jr., VP-Corp. Rel.
Lewis Seifert, Sr. VP-Finance
Amanda Brady, Chief Acct. Officer
Amy L. Zbaraschuk, VP-Finance
T.L. Trimble, VP-Legal Svcs.
Ted Hamilton, VP-Medical Mission
Carlene Jamerson, Sr. VP
John Brownlow, Sr. VP-Managed Care
Celeste M. West, VP-Supply Chain Mgmt.

GROWTH PLANS/SPECIAL FEATURES:
AdventHealth is sponsored by the Seventh-day Adventist Church and is one of the largest nonprofit Protestant healthcare organizations in the U.S. The firm operates 60 hospitals in several states and multiple affiliated extended care centers within the long-term care division. The company serves millions of patients annually through its more than 80,000 caregivers. Adventist Health's services span bariatric/weight care, behavioral health, cancer, children's care, diabetes, digestive, emergency/urgent, heart/vascular, home care, hospice care, imaging services, lab services, men's health, mother and baby care, neurology/neurosurgical care, orthopedic, pain, primary care, senior care, skilled nursing, sleep care, spine, sports medicine, rehab, surgical care, transplant care, wellness care, women's health and wound care. The firm is guided by its Christian mission, combining disease treatment, preventative medicine, education and advocacy of a wholesome lifestyle. Hospitals within the health group provide a wide range of free or reduced-price services in their communities, including free medical vans and community clinics, free screening and education programs, debt forgiveness, abuse shelters and programs for the homeless and jobless.

FINANCIAL DATA: Note: Data for latest year may not have been available at press time.

In U.S. $	2018	2017	2016	2015	2014	2013
Revenue	10,000,000,000	9,699,947,345	9,651,689,000	9,116,187,000	7,955,000,000	7,597,799,000
R&D Expense						
Operating Income						
Operating Margin %						
SGA Expense						
Net Income		229,800,000	89,559,000	-131,403,000	600,000,000	578,818,000
Operating Cash Flow						
Capital Expenditure						
EBITDA						
Return on Assets %						
Return on Equity %						
Debt to Equity						

CONTACT INFORMATION:
Phone: 407-357-1000 Fax:
Toll-Free:
Address: 900 Hope Way, Altamonte Springs, FL 32714 United States

STOCK TICKER/OTHER:
Stock Ticker: Nonprofit Exchange:
Employees: 80,000 Fiscal Year Ends: 12/31
Parent Company:

SALARIES/BONUSES:
Top Exec. Salary: $ Bonus: $
Second Exec. Salary: $ Bonus: $

OTHER THOUGHTS:
Estimated Female Officers or Directors: 6
Hot Spot for Advancement for Women/Minorities: Y

Sales, profits and employees may be estimates. Financial information, benefits and other data can change quickly and may vary from those stated here.

Advocate Aurora Health

www.advocateaurorahealth.org

NAIC Code: 622110

TYPES OF BUSINESS:
General Medical and Surgical Hospitals
Clinics & Outpatient Centers
Home Health Care
Physician Groups

BRANDS/DIVISIONS/AFFILIATES:
Advocate BroMenn Medical Center
Advocate Christ Medical Center
Advocate Condell Medical Center
Advocate Good Samaritan Hospital
Advocate Good Shepherd Hospital
Advocate Illinois Masonic Medical Center
Advocate Lutheran General Hospital
Advocate Trinity Hospital

CONTACTS:
Note: Officers with more than one job title may be intentionally listed here more than once.

Jim Skogsbergh, CEO
Bill Santulli, COO
Dominic Nakis, CFO
Kelly Jo Golson, CMO
Kevin Brady, Chief Human Resources Officer
Lee Sacks, Chief Medical Officer
Bobbie Byrne, CIO
Gail D. Hasbrouck, General Counsel
Scott Powder, Sr. VP-Strategic Planning & Growth
Dominic Nakis, Treasurer
Lee Sacks, CEO-Advocate Physician Partners
James R. Dan, Pres., Advocate Medical Group
Kathie Bender Schwich, Sr. VP-Mission & Spiritual Care

GROWTH PLANS/SPECIAL FEATURES:

Advocate Aurora Health, a product of the merger between Advocate Health Care and Aurora Health Care, is a nonprofit healthcare network providing acute care and outpatient services in Illinois. The company's operations have over 784,000 patient portal users, with 500 Outpatient locations, 63 Walgreen's Clinics and 28 hospitals. Advocate-branded hospitals include BroMenn Medical Center, Christ Medical Center, Condell Medical Center, Dreyer, Eureka Hospital, Good Samaritan Hospital, Good Shepherd Hospital, Illinois Masonic Medical Center, Lutheran General Hospital, Sherman Hospital, South Suburban Hospital and Trinity Hospital. Its children's hospital is Advocate Children's Hospital, with campuses located at Oak Lawn and Park Ridge. Advocate's outpatient facilities include sites run by its physician groups as well as Advocate Medical Campus Southwest, Advocate Occupational Health, Midwest Center for Day Surgery, Naperville Surgical Center and Tinley Woods Surgery Center. The company utilizes an Electronic Intensive Care Unit program (eICU) that links real-time monitoring from all adult ICU beds in Advocate's hospitals to a central command center staffed by physicians. Advocate sponsors community outreach programs such as school-based health centers; free and reduced cost clinics; nutritional services; and educational programs. The firm is also affiliated with several medical schools and serves as one of the leading trainers of primary care physicians in Illinois.

Advocate's employees receive benefits including medical, dental and vision plans; education assistance; life and disability insurance; and adoption assistance.

FINANCIAL DATA:
Note: Data for latest year may not have been available at press time.

In U.S. $	2018	2017	2016	2015	2014	2013
Revenue	9,213,406,000	6,233,413,000	5,587,420,000	5,329,562,000	5,231,393,000	4,940,000,000
R&D Expense						
Operating Income						
Operating Margin %						
SGA Expense						
Net Income	38,416,000	811,343,000	597,604,000	78,605,000	369,607,000	765,300,000
Operating Cash Flow						
Capital Expenditure						
EBITDA						
Return on Assets %						
Return on Equity %						
Debt to Equity						

CONTACT INFORMATION:
Phone: 630-572-9393   Fax:
Toll-Free:
Address: 3075 Highland Pkwy., Ste. 600, Downers Grove, IL 60515 United States

STOCK TICKER/OTHER:
Stock Ticker: Nonprofit
Employees: 70,000
Parent Company:

Exchange:
Fiscal Year Ends: 12/31

SALARIES/BONUSES:
Top Exec. Salary: $ Bonus: $
Second Exec. Salary: $ Bonus: $

OTHER THOUGHTS:
Estimated Female Officers or Directors: 3
Hot Spot for Advancement for Women/Minorities: Y

Sales, profits and employees may be estimates. Financial information, benefits and other data can change quickly and may vary from those stated here.

AECOM

NAIC Code: 237310

www.aecom.com

TYPES OF BUSINESS:
Engineering & Design Services
Transportation Projects
Environmental Projects
Power & Mining Support
Consulting
Economic Development Consulting

BRANDS/DIVISIONS/AFFILIATES:

GROWTH PLANS/SPECIAL FEATURES:
AECOM designs, builds, finances and operates infrastructure assets for governments, businesses and organizations in more than 150 countries. The firm provides planning, consulting, architectural and engineering design services to clients in major end markets such as transportation, facilities, environmental, energy, water and government markets. AECOM also provides: construction services, such as building, energy, infrastructure and industrial construction; and program and facilities management and maintenance, training, logistics, consulting, technical assistance and systems integration and IT services primarily for the U.S. government, but also for national governments around the world. Based in the U.S., the firm has additional offices in New York, London, Moscow, Hong Kong, Abu Dhabi and Brisbane.

CONTACTS:
Note: Officers with more than one job title may be intentionally listed here more than once.

Lara Poloni, CEO, Geographical
Daniel Tishman, CEO, Subsidiary
Michael Burke, CEO
Randall Wotring, COO
W. Rudd, Executive VP
Carla Christofferson, Executive VP
Mary Finch, Executive VP
John Vollmer, President, Divisional
Daniel McQuade, President, Divisional
Fredrick Werner, President, Divisional
Steve Morriss, President, Geographical
Chuan-Sheng Chiao, President, Geographical

FINANCIAL DATA: Note: Data for latest year may not have been available at press time.

In U.S. $	2018	2017	2016	2015	2014	2013
Revenue	20,155,510,000	18,203,400,000	17,410,820,000	17,989,880,000	8,356,783,000	8,153,495,000
R&D Expense						
Operating Income	514,862,000	550,411,000	527,736,000	421,213,000	322,268,000	352,670,000
Operating Margin %		.03%	.03%	.02%	.04%	.04%
SGA Expense	135,787,000	133,309,000	115,088,000	113,975,000	80,908,000	97,318,000
Net Income	136,468,000	339,390,000	96,109,000	-154,845,000	229,854,000	239,243,000
Operating Cash Flow	774,553,000	696,654,000	814,155,000	764,433,000	360,625,000	408,598,000
Capital Expenditure	113,279,000	86,354,000	191,386,000	69,426,000	62,852,000	52,117,000
EBITDA	712,573,000	939,123,000	782,447,000	747,422,000	451,024,000	474,917,000
Return on Assets %		.02%	.01%	-.02%	.04%	.04%
Return on Equity %		.09%	.03%	-.06%	.11%	.11%
Debt to Equity		0.926	1.116	1.305	0.43	0.539

CONTACT INFORMATION:
Phone: 213 593-8000   Fax: 213 593-8730
Toll-Free:
Address: 1999 Avenue of the Stars, Ste. 2600, Los Angeles, CA 90067 United States

STOCK TICKER/OTHER:
Stock Ticker: ACM
Employees: 87,000
Parent Company:

Exchange: NYS
Fiscal Year Ends: 09/30

SALARIES/BONUSES:
Top Exec. Salary: $1,354,812   Bonus: $
Second Exec. Salary: $731,925   Bonus: $20,000

OTHER THOUGHTS:
Estimated Female Officers or Directors: 6
Hot Spot for Advancement for Women/Minorities: Y

Aetna Inc

NAIC Code: 524114

www.aetna.com

TYPES OF BUSINESS:
Insurance-Medical & Health
Long-Term Care Insurance
Group Insurance
Pension Products
Dental Insurance
Disability Insurance
Life Insurance

BRANDS/DIVISIONS/AFFILIATES:
CVS Health Corporation

CONTACTS:
Note: Officers with more than one job title may be intentionally listed here more than once.

Mark Bertolini, CEO
Shawn Guertin, CFO
Francis Soistman, Executive VP, Divisional
Margaret McCarthy, Executive VP, Divisional
Richard Jelinek, Executive VP, Divisional
Thomas Sabatino, Executive VP
Karen Lynch, Pres.

GROWTH PLANS/SPECIAL FEATURES:

Aetna, Inc. is a healthcare benefits company, providing a broad range of health insurance products and services to individuals, employers, healthcare professionals, producers and others. These products and services include medical, pharmacy, dental, behavioral health, group life and disability plans and Medicaid. Aetna operates in three segments: health care, group insurance and large case pensions. Health care products include medical insurance plans & products, pharmacy benefits management, dental, behavioral health and vision plans offered on both an insured basis and an employee-funded basis. This division's medical plans include point of service, health maintenance organization, preferred provider organization, health savings accounts and indemnity benefits. Group insurance products primarily include life insurance, including group term life insurance coverage and accidental death and dismemberment coverage; disability insurance, including short- and long-term disability; and long-term care insurance products, including the cost of care in private home settings, adult day care, assisted living or nursing facilities. The large case pensions segment primarily manages retirement products for tax-qualified pension plans. In November 2018, CVS Health Corporation completed its $70 billion acquisition if Aetna. Aetna continues to operate as a separate unit.

Employee benefits include medical, dental and vision coverage; flexible spending accounts; life and AD&D insurance; short- and long-term disability; employee assistance programs; 401(k) & employee stock purchase plan; and tuition assistance.

FINANCIAL DATA:
Note: Data for latest year may not have been available at press time.

In U.S. $	2018	2017	2016	2015	2014	2013
Revenue	61,500,000,000	60,535,001,088	63,154,999,296	60,336,500,736	56,976,900,096	47,294,599,168
R&D Expense						
Operating Income						
Operating Margin %						
SGA Expense						
Net Income	4,000,000,000	1,904,000,000	2,271,000,064	2,390,200,064	2,040,800,000	1,913,600,000
Operating Cash Flow						
Capital Expenditure						
EBITDA						
Return on Assets %						
Return on Equity %						
Debt to Equity						

CONTACT INFORMATION:
Phone: 860 273-0123 Fax:
Toll-Free: 800-872-3862
Address: 151 Farmington Ave., Hartford, CT 06156 United States

SALARIES/BONUSES:
Top Exec. Salary: $ Bonus: $
Second Exec. Salary: $ Bonus: $

STOCK TICKER/OTHER:
Stock Ticker: Subsidiary
Employees: 49,500
Parent Company: CVS Health Corporation

Exchange:
Fiscal Year Ends: 12/31

OTHER THOUGHTS:
Estimated Female Officers or Directors: 8
Hot Spot for Advancement for Women/Minorities: Y

Sales, profits and employees may be estimates. Financial information, benefits and other data can change quickly and may vary from those stated here.

AFLAC Incorporated

NAIC Code: 524114

www.aflac.com

TYPES OF BUSINESS:
Insurance-Supplemental & Specialty Health
Life Insurance
Cancer Insurance
Long-Term Care Insurance
Accident & Disability Insurance
Vision Plans
Dental Plans

BRANDS/DIVISIONS/AFFILIATES:
Aflac Life Insurance Japan
One Day Pay

GROWTH PLANS/SPECIAL FEATURES:
AFLAC Incorporated provides supplemental insurance to more than 50 million people through its subsidiaries in Japan and the U.S. In short, the firm pays cash when policyholders get sick or injured. Aflac Life Insurance Japan is the leading provider of medical and cancer insurance in Japan, where it insures one in four households. Through its One Day Pay initiative in the U.S. (for eligible claims), AFLAC can process, approve and electronically send funds to claimants for quick access to cash in one business day. AFLAC helps protect its customers from asset loss, income loss and supplemental medical expenses. In the U.S., AFLAC is a leader in voluntary insurance sales at the work site, including short-term disability, life insurance, accident insurance, cancer coverage, critical illness coverage, hospital intensive care, hospital indemnity, dental care and vision care. Aflac Japan's revenues accounted for 70% of the company's total 2018 revenues, with Aflac U.S. accounting for the remaining 30%..

CONTACTS:
Note: Officers with more than one job title may be intentionally listed here more than once.

Daniel Amos, CEO
James Daniels, CFO, Divisional
June Howard, Chief Accounting Officer
Masatoshi Koide, COO, Divisional
Eric Kirsch, Executive VP, Subsidiary
Frederick Crawford, Executive VP
Audrey Tillman, Executive VP
Koji Ariyoshi, Executive VP
Richard Williams, Executive VP
Albert Riggieri, Other Corporate Officer
Teresa White, President, Divisional
Charles Lake, President, Subsidiary
Max Broden, Senior VP

FINANCIAL DATA:
Note: Data for latest year may not have been available at press time.

In U.S. $	2018	2017	2016	2015	2014	2013
Revenue	21,689,000,000	21,600,000,000	22,380,000,000	20,845,000,000	22,606,000,000	23,827,000,000
R&D Expense						
Operating Income						
Operating Margin %						
SGA Expense						
Net Income	2,920,000,000	4,604,000,000	2,659,000,000	2,533,000,000	2,951,000,000	3,158,000,000
Operating Cash Flow	6,014,000,000	6,128,000,000	5,987,000,000	6,776,000,000	6,550,000,000	10,547,000,000
Capital Expenditure						
EBITDA						
Return on Assets %		.03%	.02%	.02%	.02%	.03%
Return on Equity %		.20%	.14%	.14%	.18%	.21%
Debt to Equity		0.215	0.262	0.283	0.288	0.335

CONTACT INFORMATION:
Phone: 706 323-3431   Fax:
Toll-Free: 800-235-2667
Address: 1932 Wynnton Rd., Columbus, GA 31999 United States

SALARIES/BONUSES:
Top Exec. Salary: $1,441,100   Bonus: $
Second Exec. Salary: $725,000   Bonus: $

STOCK TICKER/OTHER:
Stock Ticker: AFL   Exchange: NYS
Employees: 10,212   Fiscal Year Ends: 12/31
Parent Company:

OTHER THOUGHTS:
Estimated Female Officers or Directors: 8
Hot Spot for Advancement for Women/Minorities: Y

Airbnb Inc

www.airbnb.com

NAIC Code: 561510

TYPES OF BUSINESS:
Online Homestay Reservations
Room Rental Reservations
Tour Booking Online
Restaurant Reservations
Luxury Accommodations Booking

BRANDS/DIVISIONS/AFFILIATES:
Airbnb.com
Airbnb for Business
Airbnb Experiences
Beyond by Airbnb
Airbnb Plus
Airbnb Citizen

CONTACTS: Note: Officers with more than one job title may be intentionally listed here more than once.
Brian Chesky, CEO
Belinda Johnson, COO
Dave Stephenson, CFO
Joe Gebbia, Chief Product Officer
Aristotle Balogh, CTO

GROWTH PLANS/SPECIAL FEATURES:

Airbnb, Inc., founded in 2008, operates an online booking site for travelers and those who offer guest accommodation space. Through Airbnb.com, members who are willing to let travelers stay in their homes, guest houses, hotels, resort properties and other accommodations can post their information, including pricing, photos and amenities. In turn, travelers may search within a market for places to stay. Airbnb offers nearly 5 million listings spanning over 191 countries and 81,000 cities. Members are encouraged to write reviews describing the positive or negative aspects of their stays. These reviews are partially encouraged so that renters and travelers may view profiles and feedback before committing to a guest stay. The company offers booking of tours, restaurant reservations and events in addition to lodging options. Airbnb Experiences, the tour and event booking offering, offers more than 15,000 experiences run in more than 1,000 markets around the world. Beyond by Airbnb offers luxury trips and Airbnb Plus offers luxury accommodations. Airbnb for Business allows employees and employers to book business travel for co-workers. Airbnb also runs Airbnb Citizen, a platform for Airbnb to offer advice and stories to those who rent through Airbnb. Airbnb charges room owners a 3% host fee and an additional guest service fee that ranges between 0% to 20%, and is calculated using a variety of factors. The firm sets standards for cleanliness, communication and cancellations and offers a mobile app to facilitate guest/host communication. The firm has a goal of achieving $10 billion in yearly revenues by 2020, and a goal of serving 1 billion guests yearly by 2028.

About 41% of employees are women.

FINANCIAL DATA: Note: Data for latest year may not have been available at press time.

In U.S. $	2018	2017	2016	2015	2014	2013
Revenue	3,598,000,000	2,570,000,000	1,624,000,000	908,000,000	515,000,000	264,000,000
R&D Expense						
Operating Income						
Operating Margin %						
SGA Expense						
Net Income		93,000,000				
Operating Cash Flow						
Capital Expenditure						
EBITDA						
Return on Assets %						
Return on Equity %						
Debt to Equity						

CONTACT INFORMATION:
Phone: 415-728-0000 Fax:
Toll-Free:
Address: 888 Brannan St., Fl. 4, San Francisco, CA 94107 United States

STOCK TICKER/OTHER:
Stock Ticker: Private
Employees: 4,227
Parent Company:

Exchange:
Fiscal Year Ends: 12/31

SALARIES/BONUSES:
Top Exec. Salary: $ Bonus: $
Second Exec. Salary: $ Bonus: $

OTHER THOUGHTS:
Estimated Female Officers or Directors:
Hot Spot for Advancement for Women/Minorities: Y

Alaska Air Group Inc

NAIC Code: 481111

www.alaskaair.com

TYPES OF BUSINESS:
Airlines
Air Cargo

BRANDS/DIVISIONS/AFFILIATES:
Alaska Airlines Inc
Horizon Air Industries Inc

CONTACTS: Note: Officers with more than one job title may be intentionally listed here more than once.
Benito Minicucci, CEO, Subsidiary
Gary Beck, CEO, Subsidiary
Bradley Tilden, CEO
Brandon Pedersen, CFO
Christopher Berry, Chief Accounting Officer
Shane Tackett, Executive VP, Subsidiary
Kyle Levine, General Counsel
Andrew Harrison, Other Executive Officer
Andrea Schneider, Vice President, Subsidiary
Diana Rakow, Vice President, Subsidiary

GROWTH PLANS/SPECIAL FEATURES:
Alaska Air Group, Inc., through its operating subsidiaries Alaska Airlines, Inc. (Alaska) and Horizon Air Industries, Inc. (Horizon) provides airline services. Alaska and Horizon operate as separate airlines, but together, they fly to 115 destinations with over 1,200 daily departures through its network that spans the U.S., Mexico, Canada and Costa Rica. Via global airline partners, Alaska Air provides its guests with a network of more than 900 destinations worldwide. The company is organized into three segments: mainline, regional and Horizon. The mainline segment includes scheduled air transportation on Alaska's Boeing or Airbus jet aircraft for passengers and cargo throughout the U.S., and in parts of Canada, Mexico and Costa Rica. The regional segment includes Horizon's and other third-party carriers' scheduled air transportation for passengers across a shorter distance within the U.S. under capacity purchase agreements. The Horizon segment includes the capacity sold to Alaska under capacity purchase agreements, and typically encompasses crew, ownership and maintenance costs. Alaska and its regional partners flew 46 million guests in 2018. During 2018, the Virgin America brand was merged with/into Alaska.

Both Alaska and Horizon airlines offer employee benefits such as flight privileges, personal time off, health coverage, a 401(k) plan, a profit sharing plan and performance rewards.

FINANCIAL DATA: Note: Data for latest year may not have been available at press time.

In U.S. $	2018	2017	2016	2015	2014	2013
Revenue	8,264,000,000	7,933,000,000	5,931,000,000	5,598,000,000	5,368,000,000	5,156,000,000
R&D Expense						
Operating Income	730,000,000	1,378,000,000	1,466,000,000	1,298,000,000	962,000,000	838,000,000
Operating Margin %		.17%	.25%	.23%	.18%	.16%
SGA Expense	326,000,000	357,000,000	225,000,000	211,000,000	199,000,000	179,000,000
Net Income	437,000,000	1,034,000,000	814,000,000	848,000,000	605,000,000	508,000,000
Operating Cash Flow	1,195,000,000	1,590,000,000	1,386,000,000	1,584,000,000	1,030,000,000	981,000,000
Capital Expenditure	960,000,000	1,026,000,000	678,000,000	831,000,000	694,000,000	566,000,000
EBITDA	1,056,000,000	1,665,000,000	1,738,000,000	1,640,000,000	1,297,000,000	1,121,000,000
Return on Assets %		.10%	.10%	.13%	.10%	.09%
Return on Equity %		.31%	.30%	.37%	.29%	.29%
Debt to Equity		0.608	0.902	0.237	0.323	0.372

CONTACT INFORMATION:
Phone: 206 392-5040   Fax:
Toll-Free: 800-252-7522
Address: 19300 International Blvd., Seattle, WA 98188 United States

STOCK TICKER/OTHER:
Stock Ticker: ALK
Employees: 19,112
Parent Company:

Exchange: NYS
Fiscal Year Ends: 12/31

SALARIES/BONUSES:
Top Exec. Salary: $563,846   Bonus: $
Second Exec. Salary: $500,385   Bonus: $

OTHER THOUGHTS:
Estimated Female Officers or Directors: 13
Hot Spot for Advancement for Women/Minorities: Y

Albertsons Companies LLC

NAIC Code: 445110

www.albertsons.com

TYPES OF BUSINESS:
Grocery Stores/Supermarkets
Pharmacy
Fuel Centers
Home Delivery
Online Services

BRANDS/DIVISIONS/AFFILIATES:
Cerberus Capital Management
Kimco Realty
SUPERVALU
Safeway
Vons
Tom Thumb
Randalls
Pavilions

CONTACTS:
Note: Officers with more than one job title may be intentionally listed here more than once.

Jim Donald, CEO
Susan Morris, Exec. VP-COO
Robert Dimond, CFO
Shane Sampson, Chief Mktg. & Merchandising Officer
Andrew J. Scoggin, Exec. VP-Human Resources
Anuj Dhanda, CIO
Shane Dorcheus, Pres., Southwest Div.
Wayne Denningham, Pres., Southern
Dennis Bassler, Pres., Northwest Div.
Susan Morris, Pres., Intermountain Div.
Bob Miller, Chmn.

GROWTH PLANS/SPECIAL FEATURES:

Albertsons Companies, LLC is one of the largest U.S. based retailers of food and drugs. The firm operates more than 2,350 stores in 35 states under 20 well-known banners, including Albertsons, Safeway, Vons, Jewel-Osco, Shaw's, Acme, Tom Thumb, Randalls, United Supermarkets, Pavilions, Star Market, Haggen and Carrs. The firm operates in many metropolitan areas in the U.S. Most stores contain pharmacies and some have an adjacent fuel center. The firm serves, on average, 34 million customers every week. The pharmacy services offered by Albertsons include health screenings, immunizations and a pharmacy products discount card as well as drug interaction information provided through its website. More than 1,775 pharmacies are located in-store, serving approximately 5.5 million patients annually. The company also operates 24 strategically located distribution centers and 19 manufacturing facilities. Albertsons is owned by a consortium led Cerberus Capital Management and includes Kimco Realty and grocery chain SUPERVALU.

The company offers employees a benefit package that includes health and wellness plans.

FINANCIAL DATA:
Note: Data for latest year may not have been available at press time.

In U.S. $	2018	2017	2016	2015	2014	2013
Revenue	62,920,830,000	59,924,600,000	59,678,200,000	58,734,000,000	27,198,600,000	20,054,700,000
R&D Expense						
Operating Income						
Operating Margin %						
SGA Expense						
Net Income		46,300,000	-373,300,000	-502,200,000	-1,225,200,000	1,732,600,000
Operating Cash Flow						
Capital Expenditure						
EBITDA						
Return on Assets %						
Return on Equity %						
Debt to Equity						

CONTACT INFORMATION:
Phone: 208-395-6200 Fax: 208-395-6349
Toll-Free: 877-932-7948
Address: 250 Parkcenter Blvd., Boise, ID 83706 United States

SALARIES/BONUSES:
Top Exec. Salary: $ Bonus: $
Second Exec. Salary: $ Bonus: $

STOCK TICKER/OTHER:
Stock Ticker: Private Exchange:
Employees: 275,000 Fiscal Year Ends: 01/31
Parent Company: Cerberus Capital Management

OTHER THOUGHTS:
Estimated Female Officers or Directors: 1
Hot Spot for Advancement for Women/Minorities:

Alcoa Corporation

www.alcoa.com

NAIC Code: 331313

TYPES OF BUSINESS:
Primary & Fabricated Aluminum
Bauxite Mining
Vinyl Siding
Industrial Fasteners
Building & Construction Materials

BRANDS/DIVISIONS/AFFILIATES:
Alcoa World Alumina and Chemicals

CONTACTS:
Note: Officers with more than one job title may be intentionally listed here more than once.

Roy Harvey, CEO
Michael Morris, Chairman of the Board
Molly Beerman, Chief Accounting Officer
Leigh Ann Fisher, Chief Administrative Officer
John Slaven, Chief Strategy Officer
William Oplinger, Executive VP
Jeffrey Heeter, Executive VP
Garret Dixon, President, Divisional
Michael Parker, President, Divisional
Timothy Reyes, President, Divisional

GROWTH PLANS/SPECIAL FEATURES:

Alcoa Corporation is a global industry leader in the production of bauxite, alumina, and aluminum, with a strong portfolio of value-added cast and rolled products, as well as substantial energy assets. The company is active in all major aspects of the aluminum industry, including bauxite mining, alumina refining, aluminum smelting and fabrication, recycling and technology. Alcoa is a global company with 40 operating locations across 10 countries. The firm's operations consist of three reportable segments: bauxite, alumina and aluminum. The bauxite and alumina segments primarily consist of a series of affiliated operating entities held in Alcoa World Alumina and Chemicals, a global, unincorporated joint venture between Alcoa and Alumina Limited. The aluminum segment consists of Alco's aluminum smelting, casting and rolling businesses, along with the majority of the energy business. Aluminum metal is produced by refining alumina oxide from bauxite into alumina, which is then smelted into aluminum and can be cast and rolled into many shapes and forms. Alumina is an intermediary product. Joint ventures of Alcoa include: Alcoa World Alumina and Chemicals, which has a number of affiliated entities that own, operate or have an interest in bauxite mines and alumina refineries, as well as certain aluminum smelters in seven countries; and a Ma'aden-afilated joint venture owns and operates a bauxite mine with a capacity of 4 million bone dry metric tons per year (mtpy), an alumina factory with a capacity of 1.8 million mtpy, an aluminum smelter with a capacity of ingot, slab and billet of 740,000 million mtpy, and a rolling mill with a capacity of 380,000 million mtpy.

Employee benefits include health coverage, life insurance, disability, coverage for domestic partners, savings plans, retirement programs and tuition assistance.

FINANCIAL DATA:
Note: Data for latest year may not have been available at press time.

In U.S. $	2018	2017	2016	2015	2014	2013
Revenue	13,403,000,000	11,652,000,000	9,318,000,000	11,199,000,000	13,147,000,000	12,573,000,000
R&D Expense	31,000,000	32,000,000	33,000,000	69,000,000	95,000,000	86,000,000
Operating Income	1,972,000,000	1,496,000,000	187,000,000	958,000,000	1,052,000,000	15,000,000
Operating Margin %		.13%	.02%	.09%	.08%	.00%
SGA Expense	579,000,000	284,000,000	359,000,000	353,000,000	383,000,000	406,000,000
Net Income	227,000,000	217,000,000	-400,000,000	-863,000,000	-256,000,000	-2,909,000,000
Operating Cash Flow	448,000,000	1,224,000,000	-311,000,000	875,000,000	842,000,000	452,000,000
Capital Expenditure	399,000,000	405,000,000	404,000,000	391,000,000	444,000,000	567,000,000
EBITDA	2,452,000,000	2,015,000,000	799,000,000	713,000,000	1,200,000,000	-1,416,000,000
Return on Assets %		.01%	-.02%	-.03%	-.01%	
Return on Equity %		.04%	-.05%	-.06%	-.02%	
Debt to Equity		0.307	0.252	0.022	0.03	

CONTACT INFORMATION:
Phone: 412-315-2900 Fax:
Toll-Free:
Address: 201 Isabella St., Ste. 500, Pittsburge, PA 15212-5858 United States

STOCK TICKER/OTHER:
Stock Ticker: AA
Employees: 14,000
Parent Company:

Exchange: NYS
Fiscal Year Ends: 12/31

SALARIES/BONUSES:
Top Exec. Salary: $966,667 Bonus: $
Second Exec. Salary: $630,208 Bonus: $

OTHER THOUGHTS:
Estimated Female Officers or Directors: 4
Hot Spot for Advancement for Women/Minorities: Y

Sales, profits and employees may be estimates. Financial information, benefits and other data can change quickly and may vary from those stated here.

Alliance Data Systems Corporation

www.alliancedata.com

NAIC Code: 541800

TYPES OF BUSINESS:
Marketing Services
Credit Services
Transaction Services

BRANDS/DIVISIONS/AFFILIATES:
LoyaltyOne
AIR MILES
Epsilon
BrandLoyalty Group BV
World Financial Capital Bank
World Financial Network National Bank

CONTACTS:
Note: Officers with more than one job title may be intentionally listed here more than once.

Melisa Miller, CEO
Timothy King, CFO
Robert Minicucci, Chairman of the Board
Laura Santillan, Chief Accounting Officer
Joseph Motes, Chief Administrative Officer
Bryan Kennedy, Executive VP
Bryan Pearson, Executive VP
Charles Horn, Vice Chairman

GROWTH PLANS/SPECIAL FEATURES:

Alliance Data Systems Corporation (ADS) is a provider of data-driven and transaction-based marketing and customer loyalty services. The company's products and services are operated through three segments: LoyaltyOne, Epsilon, and card services. The LoyaltyOne segment, which includes the Canadian AIR MILES Reward Program, provides loyalty marketing services, including consumer data, customer-centric retail strategies, direct-to-consumer marketing and loyalty consulting services. Approximately 170 brand name sponsors participate in the AIR MILES program, including Shell Canada, Jean Coutu, RONA, Amex Bank of Canada, Sobeys Inc. and Bank of Montreal. . Epsilon provides integrated direct marketing solutions that combine database marketing technology and analytics with a broad range of direct marketing services. The firm uses cooperative databases containing consumer transactional data from multi-channel marketers to develop customer acquisition and retention strategies. The card services segment manages over 160 private label credit cards for various retailers. Its operations include account origination, transaction processing, customer care and collections services for the company's private label and other retail credit card programs. Wholly-owned BrandLoyalty Group BV designs, implements, conducts and evaluates innovative and tailor-made loyalty programs for grocers worldwide. Primary subsidiaries in this segment are World Financial Network National Bank and World Financial Capital Bank. ADS' client base includes companies in the retail, financial services, hospitality, telecommunications and healthcare markets. In April 2019, ADS agreed to sell its marketing-services business to Publicis Groupe S.A. for $4.4 billion.

The firm offers its employees medical, dental and vision insurance; a 401(k); disability coverage; life, auto and home insurance; flexible spending accounts; an employee stock purchase program; tuition reimbursement; an employee assistance program; prepaid legal services; and adoption assistance.

FINANCIAL DATA:
Note: Data for latest year may not have been available at press time.

In U.S. $	2018	2017	2016	2015	2014	2013
Revenue	7,791,200,000	7,719,400,000	7,138,100,000	6,439,746,000	5,302,940,000	4,319,063,000
R&D Expense						
Operating Income	1,894,300,000	1,645,500,000	1,265,500,000	1,326,423,000	1,098,467,000	1,098,912,000
Operating Margin %		.21%	.18%	.20%	.23%	.25%
SGA Expense	172,700,000	166,300,000	143,200,000	138,483,000	141,468,000	109,115,000
Net Income	963,100,000	788,700,000	515,800,000	596,541,000	506,293,000	496,170,000
Operating Cash Flow	2,754,900,000	2,609,600,000	2,088,400,000	1,705,841,000	1,344,159,000	1,003,492,000
Capital Expenditure	199,800,000	225,400,000	207,100,000	191,683,000	158,694,000	135,376,000
EBITDA	2,381,600,000	2,143,100,000	1,777,600,000	1,754,000,000	1,411,549,000	1,315,031,000
Return on Assets %		.03%	.02%	.03%	.03%	.04%
Return on Equity %		.45%	.24%	.25%	.31%	.72%
Debt to Equity		7.231	6.093	5.043	3.394	7.014

CONTACT INFORMATION:
Phone: 214 494-3000 Fax:
Toll-Free:
Address: 7500 Dallas Pkwy., Ste. 700, Plano, TX 75024 United States

SALARIES/BONUSES:
Top Exec. Salary: $1,150,000 Bonus: $
Second Exec. Salary: $666,592 Bonus: $

STOCK TICKER/OTHER:
Stock Ticker: ADS
Employees: 17,000
Parent Company:

Exchange: NYS
Fiscal Year Ends: 12/31

OTHER THOUGHTS:
Estimated Female Officers or Directors: 5
Hot Spot for Advancement for Women/Minorities: Y

Allscripts Healthcare Solutions Inc

www.allscripts.com

NAIC Code: 0

TYPES OF BUSINESS:
Computer Software, Healthcare & Biotechnology
Interactive Education Services
Clinical Software
Electronic Records Systems
Care Management Software

BRANDS/DIVISIONS/AFFILIATES:
Sunrise
Paragon
Allscripts TouchWorks EHR
Allscripts Professional EHR
Veradigm
FollowMyHealth
Allscripts CareInMotion
2bPrecise

CONTACTS: Note: Officers with more than one job title may be intentionally listed here more than once.

Paul Black, CEO
Dennis Olis, CFO
Brian Farley, Chief Administrative Officer
Michael Klayko, Director
Lisa Khorey, Executive VP
Richard Poulton, President

GROWTH PLANS/SPECIAL FEATURES:

Allscripts Healthcare Solutions, Inc. provides clinical software, connectivity and information solutions that physicians and healthcare providers use to improve service delivery. The firm provides software solutions to physicians, hospitals, governments, health systems, health plans, life-sciences companies, retail clinics, retail pharmacies, pharmacy benefit managers, insurance companies, employer wellness clinics, post-acute organizations, consumers and lab companies. Allscripts' solutions enable clinical, financial and operational efficiencies while helping patients deepen their engagement in their own care. The company's electronic health records (EHR) solutions are built on an open platform with advanced clinical decision support via analysis and insights. EHR brands include Sunrise, Paragon, Allscripts TouchWorks EHR and Allscripts Professional EHR. Payer and life sciences solutions include the Veradigm brand of integrated data systems and services, which combine data-driven clinical insights with actionable tools for clinical workflow, research, analytics and media. Consumer solutions include the FollowMyHealth platform, for patient engagement via telehealth and remote patient monitoring. Financial management solutions support revenue cycle, claims management, budgeting and analytic functions for healthcare organizations. These tools can help change clinician behavior to improve patient flow, increase quality, advance outcomes, optimize referral networks, decrease leakage and reduce costs. Population health management solutions includes Allscripts CareInMotion, a community-connected population health management platform that delivers care coordination, connectivity, data aggregation and analytics. 2bPrecise is a precision medicine solution for enabling a personalized approach regarding diagnostic, therapeutic and preventive interventions. Allscripts offers customizable professional and managed service offerings, from hosting, consulting, optimization and managed IT services to revenue cycle services.

Allscripts offers its employees medical, dental and vision insurance; flex spending accounts; a 401(k); adoption assistance; and education assistance.

FINANCIAL DATA: Note: Data for latest year may not have been available at press time.

In U.S. $	2018	2017	2016	2015	2014	2013
Revenue	1,749,962,000	1,806,342,000	1,549,899,000	1,386,393,000	1,377,873,000	1,373,061,000
R&D Expense	268,409,000	220,219,000	187,906,000	184,791,000	192,821,000	199,751,000
Operating Income	-21,420,000	41,917,000	64,421,000	33,427,000	-36,798,000	-116,147,000
Operating Margin %		.02%	.04%	.02%	-.03%	-.08%
SGA Expense	450,967,000	486,271,000	392,865,000	339,175,000	358,681,000	419,599,000
Net Income	412,334,000	-152,609,000	2,884,000	-2,226,000	-66,453,000	-104,026,000
Operating Cash Flow	67,891,000	279,415,000	269,004,000	211,579,000	103,496,000	80,987,000
Capital Expenditure	144,617,000	185,271,000	137,982,000	67,586,000	67,099,000	116,156,000
EBITDA	256,398,000	96,398,000	220,523,000	191,544,000	133,402,000	50,956,000
Return on Assets %		-.05%	-.01%	.00%	-.03%	-.04%
Return on Equity %		-.17%	-.02%	.00%	-.05%	-.08%
Debt to Equity		1.373	1.059	0.435	0.427	0.414

CONTACT INFORMATION:
Phone: 866 358-6869   Fax:
Toll-Free: 800-654-0889
Address: 222 Merchandise Mart Plz., Ste. 2024, Chicago, IL 60654 United States

STOCK TICKER/OTHER:
Stock Ticker: MDRX
Employees: 7,500
Parent Company:

Exchange: NAS
Fiscal Year Ends: 12/31

SALARIES/BONUSES:
Top Exec. Salary: $1,030,000   Bonus: $
Second Exec. Salary: $630,000   Bonus: $

OTHER THOUGHTS:
Estimated Female Officers or Directors: 2
Hot Spot for Advancement for Women/Minorities: Y

Sales, profits and employees may be estimates. Financial information, benefits and other data can change quickly and may vary from those stated here.

Alphabet Inc (Google)

NAIC Code: 519130

www.google.com

TYPES OF BUSINESS:
Search Engine-Internet
Paid Search Listing Advertising Services
Online Software and Productivity Tools
Online Video and Photo Services
Travel Booking
Web Analytical Tools
Venture Capital
Online Ad Exchanges

BRANDS/DIVISIONS/AFFILIATES:
DV 360
AdX
Android
Analytics 360
DoubleClick
YouTube
Google Ad Manager
AdMob

CONTACTS:
Note: Officers with more than one job title may be intentionally listed here more than once.

Sundar Pichai, CEO, Subsidiary
Larry Page, CEO
Ruth Porat, CFO
John Hennessy, Chairman of the Board
Amie OToole, Chief Accounting Officer
David Drummond, Chief Legal Officer
Sergey Brin, Director

GROWTH PLANS/SPECIAL FEATURES:

Alphabet, Inc. owns a collection of businesses, the largest of which is Google, LLC, an information company offering a leading online search and advertising platform. Google is the leader in the online search and advertising business. Alphabet states that its primary job is to make the internet available to as many people as possible, and does this by tailoring hardware and software experiences that suit the needs of emerging markets, mainly through Android and Chrome. Google's core products include Search, Android, Maps, Chrome, YouTube, GooglePlay and Gmail, each of which have more than 1 billion monthly active users. Within Google, Alphabet's investments in machine learning are what enable the firm to continually innovate and build Google products, making them smarter and more useful over time. Machine learning also dramatically improves the energy efficiency of the company's data centers. For advertisers, Google offers a full suite of tools to bid on and analyze the results of online ads, both fixed and mobile. These include DoubleClick, the Google Ad Manager, Google AdMob and Analytics 360. Alphabet's other businesses include Access, Calico, CapitalG, GV, Nest, Verily, Waymo and X, all of which are not primarily engaged in the company's main internet offerings. Across these businesses, machine learning has the capability of doing things like helping self-driving cars better detect and respond to others on the road, or aiding clinicians in detecting diabetic retinopathy. Therefore, these firms utilize technology to try and solve big problems across many industries. They are early-stage businesses with the goal to become thriving ones in the medium- to long-term.

Employee perks at the main campus include on-site wellness, fitness, massage and health care facilities; along with free cafes, snacks and micro-kitchens. Other benefits for qualified employees include generous savings plans, training programs and flexible schedules.

FINANCIAL DATA:
Note: Data for latest year may not have been available at press time.

In U.S. $	2018	2017	2016	2015	2014	2013
Revenue	136,819,000,000	110,855,000,000	90,272,000,000	74,989,000,000	66,001,000,000	59,825,000,000
R&D Expense	21,419,000,000	16,625,000,000	13,948,000,000	12,282,000,000	9,831,999,000	7,952,000,000
Operating Income	31,392,000,000	28,882,000,000	23,716,000,000	19,360,000,000	16,496,000,000	13,966,000,000
Operating Margin %		.26%	.26%	.26%	.25%	.23%
SGA Expense	24,459,000,000	19,765,000,000	17,470,000,000	15,183,000,000	13,982,000,000	12,049,000,000
Net Income	30,736,000,000	12,662,000,000	19,478,000,000	16,348,000,000	14,444,000,000	12,920,000,000
Operating Cash Flow	47,971,000,000	37,091,000,000	36,036,000,000	26,024,000,000	22,376,000,000	18,659,000,000
Capital Expenditure	26,630,000,000	13,471,000,000	11,198,000,000	10,151,000,000	15,847,000,000	8,806,000,000
EBITDA	44,062,000,000	34,217,000,000	30,418,000,000	24,818,000,000	22,339,000,000	18,518,000,000
Return on Assets %		.07%	.12%	.11%	.12%	.13%
Return on Equity %		.09%	.15%	.14%	.15%	.16%
Debt to Equity		0.026	0.028	0.017	0.031	0.026

CONTACT INFORMATION:
Phone: 650 253-0000   Fax: 650 253-0001
Toll-Free:
Address: 1600 Amphitheatre Pkwy., Mountain View, CA 94043 United States

STOCK TICKER/OTHER:
Stock Ticker: GOOG
Employees: 72,053
Parent Company:

Exchange: NAS
Fiscal Year Ends: 12/31

SALARIES/BONUSES:
Top Exec. Salary: $1,250,000   Bonus: $
Second Exec. Salary: $650,000   Bonus: $

OTHER THOUGHTS:
Estimated Female Officers or Directors: 3
Hot Spot for Advancement for Women/Minorities: Y

Sales, profits and employees may be estimates. Financial information, benefits and other data can change quickly and may vary from those stated here.

Amazon.com Inc

NAIC Code: 454111

www.amazon.com

TYPES OF BUSINESS:
Online Retailing and Related Services
Robotics
Cloud Computing Services
Logistics Services
Retail Supermarkets & Grocery Delivery
Online Household Goods Retail
Online Auto & Industrial Retail
E-Commerce Support & Hosting

BRANDS/DIVISIONS/AFFILIATES:
Amazon Web Services (AWS)
Amazon Marketplace
Amazon Prime
Echo
Whole Foods Market
Amazon Go

CONTACTS:
Note: Officers with more than one job title may be intentionally listed here more than once.

Andrew Jassy, CEO, Divisional
Jeffrey Wilke, CEO, Divisional
Jeffrey Bezos, CEO
Brian Olsavsky, CFO
Shelley Reynolds, Chief Accounting Officer
David Zapolsky, General Counsel
Jeffrey Blackburn, Senior VP, Divisional

GROWTH PLANS/SPECIAL FEATURES:

Amazon.com, Inc. is an internet consumer-shopping site that offers millions of new, used, refurbished and collectible items in categories such as books, movies, music and games, electronics and computers, home and garden, toys, children's goods, grocery, apparel and jewelry, health and beauty, sports, outdoors, digital downloads, tools and auto and industrial. The company, which serves more than 50 million members, operates in three segments: North America (which generates about 60% of annual revenue), international (33%) and Amazon Web Services (AWS) (7%), which offers computing, storage, database and other service offerings globally for start-ups, enterprises, government agencies and academic institutions. The Amazon Marketplace and Merchants programs allow third parties to integrate their products on Amazon websites and provide related fulfillment and advertising services to third-party merchants; allow customers to shop for products owned by third parties using Amazon's features and technologies; and enable customers to complete transactions that include multiple sellers in a single checkout process. Amazon Prime memberships afford members a host of perks including free two-day shipping, streaming music and video, delivery from participating restaurants and much more. The company also sells proprietary electronic devices, including eReaders, tablets, TVs and phones; as well as the Echo personal digital assistant. The firm serves authors and independent publishers with Kindle Direct Publishing, an online platform that lets independent authors and publishers choose a 70% royalty option and make their books available in the Kindle Store. Subsidiary Whole Foods Market is a supermarket chain featuring foods without artificial preservatives, colors, flavors, sweeteners and hydrogenated fats, with stores throughout the U.S and internationally. During 2018, Amazon opened Amazon Go stores, the first in Seattle, which uses cameras and sensors to detect items that a shopper purchases. The firm plans to open as many as 3,000 Amazon Go locations throughout the U.S. by 2021.

FINANCIAL DATA:
Note: Data for latest year may not have been available at press time.

In U.S. $	2018	2017	2016	2015	2014	2013
Revenue	232,887,000,000	177,866,000,000	135,987,000,000	107,006,000,000	88,988,000,000	74,452,000,000
R&D Expense	28,837,000,000	22,620,000,000	16,085,000,000	12,540,000,000	9,275,000,000	6,565,000,000
Operating Income	12,421,000,000	4,106,000,000	4,186,000,000	2,233,000,000	178,000,000	745,000,000
Operating Margin %		.02%	.03%	.02%	.00%	.01%
SGA Expense	18,150,000,000	13,743,000,000	9,665,000,000	7,001,000,000	5,884,000,000	4,262,000,000
Net Income	10,073,000,000	3,033,000,000	2,371,000,000	596,000,000	-241,000,000	274,000,000
Operating Cash Flow	30,723,000,000	18,434,000,000	16,443,000,000	11,920,000,000	6,842,000,000	5,475,000,000
Capital Expenditure	13,427,000,000	11,955,000,000	6,737,000,000	4,589,000,000	4,893,000,000	3,444,000,000
EBITDA	28,019,000,000	16,132,000,000	12,492,000,000	8,308,000,000	4,845,000,000	3,900,000,000
Return on Assets %		.03%	.03%	.01%	-.01%	.01%
Return on Equity %		.13%	.15%	.05%	-.02%	.03%
Debt to Equity		1.369	0.789	1.06	1.163	0.532

CONTACT INFORMATION:
Phone: 206 266-1000
Fax:
Toll-Free:
Address: 410 Terry Ave. N., Seattle, WA 98109 United States

SALARIES/BONUSES:
Top Exec. Salary: $175,000   Bonus: $
Second Exec. Salary: $175,000   Bonus: $

STOCK TICKER/OTHER:
Stock Ticker: AMZN
Employees: 341,400
Parent Company:

Exchange: NAS
Fiscal Year Ends: 12/31

OTHER THOUGHTS:
Estimated Female Officers or Directors: 3
Hot Spot for Advancement for Women/Minorities: Y

AMERCO (U-Haul)

NAIC Code: 532120

www.amerco.com

TYPES OF BUSINESS:

Truck Rental & Leasing Services
Moving & Storage Services & Supplies
Property & Casualty Insurance
Life Insurance
Annuities
Self-Storage Properties
Propane Tank Refilling
Car Sharing Services

BRANDS/DIVISIONS/AFFILIATES:

U-Haul International Inc
Amerco Real Estate Company
Repwest Insurance Company
Oxford Life Insurance Company
Uhaul.com
Safemove
Safetow
Safestor

CONTACTS: Note: Officers with more than one job title may be intentionally listed here more than once.

Jason Berg, CFO
Edward Shoen, Chairman of the Board
Samuel Shoen, Director
Laurence Derespino, General Counsel
Mark Haydukovich, President, Subsidiary
John Taylor, President, Subsidiary
Carlos Vizcarra, President, Subsidiary
Douglas Bell, President, Subsidiary

GROWTH PLANS/SPECIAL FEATURES:

AMERCO is a holding company operating through four primary subsidiaries: U-Haul International, Inc.; Amerco Real Estate Company; Repwest Insurance Company; and Oxford Life Insurance Company. Accordingly, the firm has three reportable business segments: moving and storage, property and casualty insurance and life insurance. Moving and storage consists of U-Haul, with its rental equipment fleet of trucks, trailers and tow dollies offered at 1,790 company operated locations and 20,000 independent dealer outlets. It also provides furniture pads, utility dollies and hand trucks; sells a wide selection of moving supplies; and offers protection packages for moving and storage. U-Haul owns more than 160,000 trucks, 118,000 trailers and 42,000 towing devices. The firm's Uhaul.com online reservation portal allows its self-storage customers to make reservations, access all U-Haul storage centers and affiliate partners. This segment is also operated by Amerco Real Estate Company, which manages 632,000 rentable rooms comprising 55.2 million square feet of rentable storage space located in North America. The property and casualty insurance segment, operated by Repwest Insurance Company, provides loss adjusting and claims handling for U-Haul through regional offices across North America. This segment also underwrites components of the Safemove, Safetow, Safestor and Safestor Mobile protection packages to U-Haul customers. The life insurance segment, operated by Oxford Life Insurance Company, provides life and health insurance products primarily to the senior market through the direct writing and reinsuring of life insurance, Medicare supplement and annuity policies.

FINANCIAL DATA: Note: Data for latest year may not have been available at press time.

In U.S. $	2018	2017	2016	2015	2014	2013
Revenue	3,601,114,000	3,421,767,000	3,275,656,000	3,074,531,000	2,835,252,000	
R&D Expense						
Operating Income	568,905,000	742,263,000	866,814,000	663,024,000	630,214,000	
Operating Margin %	.16%	.22%	.26%	.22%	.22%	
SGA Expense						
Net Income	790,583,000	398,424,000	489,001,000	356,741,000	342,391,000	
Operating Cash Flow	936,328,000	1,020,061,000	1,041,063,000	808,190,000	709,504,000	
Capital Expenditure	1,363,745,000	1,419,505,000	1,509,154,000	1,111,899,000	999,365,000	
EBITDA	1,315,521,000	1,219,839,000	1,252,972,000	1,008,244,000	919,832,000	
Return on Assets %	.08%	.05%	.07%	.06%	.06%	
Return on Equity %	.26%	.16%	.24%	.21%	.25%	
Debt to Equity	1.031	1.245	1.194	1.163	1.272	

CONTACT INFORMATION:

Phone: 775-688-6300   Fax: 775 688-6338
Toll-Free:
Address: 5555 Kietzke Ln., Ste. 100, Reno, NV 89511 United States

STOCK TICKER/OTHER:

Stock Ticker: UHAL
Employees: 28,300
Parent Company:

Exchange: NAS
Fiscal Year Ends: 03/31

SALARIES/BONUSES:

Top Exec. Salary: $675,004   Bonus: $215,000
Second Exec. Salary: $410,777   Bonus: $200,000

OTHER THOUGHTS:

Estimated Female Officers or Directors: 1
Hot Spot for Advancement for Women/Minorities:

American Airlines Group Inc

NAIC Code: 481111

www.usairways.com

TYPES OF BUSINESS:
Airline
Air Freight

BRANDS/DIVISIONS/AFFILIATES:
American Airlines Inc
Piedmont Airlines Inc
Envoy Aviation Group Inc
PSA Airlines Inc
American Eagle

CONTACTS:
Note: Officers with more than one job title may be intentionally listed here more than once.

W. Parker, CEO
Derek Kerr, CFO
Maya Leibman, Chief Information Officer
Elise Eberwein, Executive VP, Divisional
Stephen Johnson, Executive VP, Divisional
Robert Isom, President

GROWTH PLANS/SPECIAL FEATURES:

American Airlines Group, Inc. operates one of the largest air carriers in the U.S. Its subsidiaries include American Airlines, Inc.; Piedmont Airlines, Inc.; Envoy Aviation Group, Inc.; and PSA Airlines, Inc. The company offers 6,800 flights per day from its hubs in Charlotte, Chicago, Dallas/Fort Worth, Los Angeles, Miami, New York, Philadelphia, Phoenix and Washington, D.C. The firm transports passengers to more than 365 destinations in 61 countries (as of July 2019). American Airlines' wholly-owned regional airline subsidiaries and third-party regional carriers operate under the brand name American Eagle. American Eagle is a network of seven regional carriers that operate under a codeshare and service agreement with American. Together they operate 615 regional aircraft, servicing millions of passengers. The cargo division of the firm provides a wide range of freight and mail services, with facilities and interline connections available across the globe. American and US Airways are members of the oneworld alliance whose members and members-elect serve more than 1,000 destinations with 14,250 daily flights to over 150 countries. In July 2019, American Airlines received final approval from the U.S. Department of Transportation for a joint business agreement with Qantas, which together can jointly offer more products that will better serve customers flying between the U.S. and Australia and New Zealand.

US Airways provides employees with auto, home, accident, health, long-term care and critical illness insurance; a 401(k); identity theft protection; travel privileges; employee assistance programs; business resource groups; domestic partner programs; paid vacation; and days off.

FINANCIAL DATA:
Note: Data for latest year may not have been available at press time.

In U.S. $	2018	2017	2016	2015	2014	2013
Revenue	44,541,000,000	42,207,000,000	40,180,000,000	40,990,000,000	42,650,000,000	26,743,000,000
R&D Expense						
Operating Income	3,405,000,000	4,612,000,000	6,007,000,000	7,284,000,000	5,073,000,000	1,966,000,000
Operating Margin %		.11%	.15%	.18%	.12%	.07%
SGA Expense	1,889,000,000	1,838,000,000	1,670,000,000	1,727,000,000	1,851,000,000	1,312,000,000
Net Income	1,412,000,000	1,919,000,000	2,676,000,000	7,610,000,000	2,882,000,000	-1,834,000,000
Operating Cash Flow	3,533,000,000	4,744,000,000	6,524,000,000	6,249,000,000	3,080,000,000	675,000,000
Capital Expenditure	3,745,000,000	5,971,000,000	5,731,000,000	6,151,000,000	5,311,000,000	3,114,000,000
EBITDA	5,099,000,000	6,154,000,000	7,108,000,000	7,105,000,000	5,612,000,000	-304,000,000
Return on Assets %		.04%	.05%	.17%	.07%	-.06%
Return on Equity %		.50%	.57%	1.99%		
Debt to Equity		5.734	5.942	3.253	8.014	

CONTACT INFORMATION:
Phone: 817-963-1234 Fax:
Toll-Free:
Address: 4333 Amon Carter Blvd., Fort Worth, TX 76155 United States

STOCK TICKER/OTHER:
Stock Ticker: AAL
Employees: 128,900
Parent Company:

Exchange: NAS
Fiscal Year Ends: 12/31

SALARIES/BONUSES:
Top Exec. Salary: $722,329 Bonus: $
Second Exec. Salary: $626,421 Bonus: $

OTHER THOUGHTS:
Estimated Female Officers or Directors: 7
Hot Spot for Advancement for Women/Minorities: Y

American Express Company

www.americanexpress.com

NAIC Code: 522320

TYPES OF BUSINESS:
Credit Card Processing and Issuing
Travel-Related Services
Lending & Financing
Transaction Services
Bank Holding Company
International Banking Services
Expense Management
Magazine Publishing

BRANDS/DIVISIONS/AFFILIATES:
American Express Travel Related Services Co Inc
American Express Global Business Travel

CONTACTS:
Note: Officers with more than one job title may be intentionally listed here more than once.

Stephen Squeri, CEO
Jeffrey Campbell, CFO
Richard Petrino, Chief Accounting Officer
Marc Gordon, Chief Information Officer
Laureen Seeger, Chief Legal Officer
Elizabeth Rutledge, Chief Marketing Officer
Denise Pickett, Chief Risk Officer
Michael ONeill, Other Executive Officer
Paul Fabara, President, Divisional
Anre Williams, President, Divisional
Douglas Buckminster, President, Divisional
Anna Marrs, President, Divisional

GROWTH PLANS/SPECIAL FEATURES:
American Express Company (AmEx), a bank holding company, is a leading global payments and travel firm. Its principal products are charge and credit payment card products and travel-related services. The firm primarily operates through subsidiary American Express Travel Related Services Company, Inc. AmEx's business is organized into three main segments: global consumer services, global commercial services and global merchant & network services. Together, these segment offer a range of products and services that include: charge card, credit card and other payment and financing products; merchant acquisition and processing, servicing and settlement, and point-of-sale marketing and information products and services for merchants; network services; other fee services, such as fraud prevention services and the design and operation of customer loyalty programs; expense management products and services; and travel-related services. AmEx's products and serves are sold globally to diverse customer groups through various channels, including mobile and online applications, third-party vendors and business partners, direct mail, telephone, in-house sales teams and direct response advertising. Business travel-related services are offered through the firm's non-consolidated joint venture, American Express Global Business Travel. In May 2019, AmEx agreed to acquire Resy, the digital restaurant reservation booking and management platform, expanding AmEx's digital dining, access and experiences capabilities.

FINANCIAL DATA:
Note: Data for latest year may not have been available at press time.

In U.S. $	2018	2017	2016	2015	2014	2013
Revenue	28,865,000,000	24,424,000,000	25,411,000,000	24,804,000,000	34,292,000,000	32,974,000,000
R&D Expense						
Operating Income						
Operating Margin %						
SGA Expense	11,720,000,000	8,751,000,000	9,211,000,000	8,430,000,000	17,551,000,000	16,837,000,000
Net Income	6,921,000,000	2,736,000,000	5,408,000,000	5,163,000,000	5,885,000,000	5,359,000,000
Operating Cash Flow	8,930,000,000	13,540,000,000	8,224,000,000	10,972,000,000	10,990,000,000	8,547,000,000
Capital Expenditure	1,310,000,000	1,062,000,000	1,375,000,000	1,341,000,000	1,195,000,000	1,006,000,000
EBITDA						
Return on Assets %		.02%	.03%	.03%	.04%	.03%
Return on Equity %		.14%	.26%	.24%	.29%	.28%
Debt to Equity		3.062	2.292	2.325	2.803	2.838

CONTACT INFORMATION:
Phone: 212 640-2000 Fax: 212 640-2458
Toll-Free: 800-528-4800
Address: 200 Vesey St., World Financial Ctr., New York, NY 10285 United States

SALARIES/BONUSES:
Top Exec. Salary: $1,487,500 Bonus: $5,850,000
Second Exec. Salary: $1,000,000 Bonus: $4,900,000

STOCK TICKER/OTHER:
Stock Ticker: AXP
Employees: 56,400
Parent Company:

Exchange: NYS
Fiscal Year Ends: 12/31

OTHER THOUGHTS:
Estimated Female Officers or Directors: 4
Hot Spot for Advancement for Women/Minorities: Y

American Financial Group Inc

www.afginc.com

NAIC Code: 524126

TYPES OF BUSINESS:
Insurance, Direct Property & Casualty
Long-Term Care Insurance
Annuities
Supplemental Health Insurance
Specialty Insurance
Multi-Peril Crop & Crop Hail Insurance
Car Insurance
Commercial Real Estate

BRANDS/DIVISIONS/AFFILIATES:
Great American Insurance Group
Great American Life Insruance Company
Annuity Investors Life Insurance Company

CONTACTS:
Note: Officers with more than one job title may be intentionally listed here more than once.

Karl Grafe, Assistant General Counsel
Joseph Consolino, CFO
Michelle Gillis, Chief Administrative Officer
Carl Lindner, Co-CEO
S. Lindner, Co-CEO
John Berding, Director
Vito Peraino, General Counsel

GROWTH PLANS/SPECIAL FEATURES:

American Financial Group, Inc. (AFG) is an insurance holding company that, through subsidiary Great American Insurance Group, is engaged primarily in property and casualty insurance. The company focuses on specialized commercial products for businesses, as well as the sale of fixed, fixed-indexed and variable-indexed annuities in the retail, financial institutions, registered investment advisor and education markets. Property and casualty insurance products include a range of commercial coverages through more than 30 niche insurance businesses that make up Great American Insurance Group. This division's specialized products include, but are not limited to, property and transportation insurance for marine, agriculture and commercial automobile sectors; specialty casualty insurance such as executive/professional liability, umbrella/excess liability, excess and surplus, general liability, targeted programs and workers' compensation; and specialty financial products such as fidelity and surety coverage, as well as lease and loan coverage. AFG sells traditional fixed and fixed-indexed annuities in the retail, financial institutions and education markets through independent producers, as well as through direct relationships with certain financial institutions. This division's operations are conducted primarily through subsidiaries: Great American Life Insurance Company (GALIC) and Annuity Investors Life Insurance Company (AILIC). As of December 31, 2018, AFG had approximately 536,000 annuity policies in force. Annuities are long-term retirement savings instruments that benefit from income accruing on a tax-deferred basis. Annuity contracts are generally classified as either fixed rate (including fixed-indexed) or variable.

The firm offers employees medical, dental, vision, disability and life coverage; paid time off; and onsite fitness centers.

FINANCIAL DATA:
Note: Data for latest year may not have been available at press time.

In U.S. $	2018	2017	2016	2015	2014	2013
Revenue	7,150,000,000	6,865,000,000	6,498,000,000	6,145,000,000	5,713,000,000	5,092,000,000
R&D Expense						
Operating Income						
Operating Margin %						
SGA Expense						
Net Income	530,000,000	475,000,000	649,000,000	352,000,000	452,000,000	471,000,000
Operating Cash Flow	2,083,000,000	1,804,000,000	1,150,000,000	1,357,000,000	1,222,000,000	760,000,000
Capital Expenditure						
EBITDA						
Return on Assets %		.01%	.01%	.01%	.01%	.01%
Return on Equity %		.09%	.14%	.07%	.10%	.10%
Debt to Equity		0.244	0.261	0.222	0.217	0.199

CONTACT INFORMATION:
Phone: 513 579-2121 Fax: 513 412-0200
Toll-Free:
Address: 301 E. 4th St., Cincinnati, OH 45202 United States

STOCK TICKER/OTHER:
Stock Ticker: AFG
Employees: 7,000
Parent Company:

Exchange: NYS
Fiscal Year Ends: 12/31

SALARIES/BONUSES:
Top Exec. Salary: $1,234,615 Bonus: $
Second Exec. Salary: $1,234,615 Bonus: $

OTHER THOUGHTS:
Estimated Female Officers or Directors: 3
Hot Spot for Advancement for Women/Minorities: Y

Sales, profits and employees may be estimates. Financial information, benefits and other data can change quickly and may vary from those stated here.

American International Group Inc (AIG)

www.aig.com

NAIC Code: 524126

TYPES OF BUSINESS:
Insurance, Direct Property & Casualty
Life Insurance
Commercial Insurance
Property Insurance

BRANDS/DIVISIONS/AFFILIATES:
American Home Assurance Company
Lexington Insurance Company
AIG General Insurance Company Ltd
AIG Europe Limited
American General Life Insurance Company
Variable Annuity Life Insurance Company (The)
United States Life Insurance Company (The)
Validus Re

CONTACTS: Note: Officers with more than one job title may be intentionally listed here more than once.
Peter Zaffino, CEO, Divisional
Naohiro Mouri, Executive VP
Kevinm Hogan, CEO, Divisional
Brian Duperreault, CEO
Mark Lyons, CFO
Douglas Steenland, Chairman of the Board
John Repko, Chief Information Officer
Douglas Dachille, Chief Investment Officer
Alessandrea Quane, Chief Risk Officer
Seraina Macia, Executive VP
Thomas Leonardi, Executive VP, Divisional
Thomas Leonardi, Executive VP, Divisional
Lucy Fato, Executive VP

GROWTH PLANS/SPECIAL FEATURES:
American International Group, Inc. (AIG) is an international insurance organization serving customers in more than 100 countries. The company serves more than 88% of companies included in the Fortune Global 500 and demonstrates strength via its $65 billion in shareholders' equity. AIG distributes insurance products and services across the geographic regions of the Americas (the U.S., Canada, Mexico, South America, the Caribbean and Bermuda), Asia Pacific (Japan, China, Korea, Singapore, Malaysia, Thailand, Australia, Indonesia and others) and EMEA (the U.K., Continental Europe, Russian Federation, India, Middle East and Africa). AIG primarily operates through two segments: General Insurance and Life and Retirement. General Insurance is a leading provider of insurance products and services for commercial and personal insurance customers. It includes one of the world's most far-reaching property casualty networks. Operating companies within this segment include: National Union Fire Insurance Company of Pittsburgh, Pa.; American Home Assurance Company; Lexington Insurance Company; AIG General Insurance Company, Ltd.; AIG Asia Pacific Insurance, Pte, Ltd.; and AIG Europe Limited. Life and Retirement is a franchise that brings together a broad portfolio of life insurance, retirement and institutional products offered through an extensive, multichannel distribution network. Operating companies within this segment include: American General Life Insurance Company; The Variable Annuity Life Insurance Company and The United States Life Insurance Company in the City of New York. In December 2018, subsidiary AIG Life Limited completed the acquisition of Ellipse from Munich Re. In June 2019, the firm consolidated its reinsurance operations, including Validus Re, AlphaCat and Talbot Treaty into AIG Re.

FINANCIAL DATA: Note: Data for latest year may not have been available at press time.

In U.S. $	2018	2017	2016	2015	2014	2013
Revenue	47,481,000,000	49,570,000,000	52,357,000,000	58,385,000,000	64,407,000,000	68,704,000,000
R&D Expense						
Operating Income						
Operating Margin %						
SGA Expense	9,302,000,000	9,107,000,000	10,989,000,000	12,686,000,000	13,138,000,000	
Net Income	-6,000,000	-6,084,000,000	-849,000,000	2,196,000,000	7,529,000,000	9,085,000,000
Operating Cash Flow	61,000,000	-8,585,000,000	2,383,000,000	2,877,000,000	5,007,000,000	5,865,000,000
Capital Expenditure						
EBITDA						
Return on Assets %		-.01%	.00%	.00%	.01%	.02%
Return on Equity %		-.09%	-.01%	.02%	.07%	.09%
Debt to Equity		0.485	0.405	0.327	0.292	0.415

CONTACT INFORMATION:
Phone: 212 770-7000   Fax: 212 344-6828
Toll-Free: 877-638-4244
Address: 180 Maiden Ln., New York, NY 10038 United States

STOCK TICKER/OTHER:
Stock Ticker: AIG
Employees: 56,400
Parent Company:

Exchange: NYS
Fiscal Year Ends: 12/31

SALARIES/BONUSES:
Top Exec. Salary: $1,250,000   Bonus: $2,396,867
Second Exec. Salary: $1,600,000   Bonus: $

OTHER THOUGHTS:
Estimated Female Officers or Directors: 10
Hot Spot for Advancement for Women/Minorities: Y

Sales, profits and employees may be estimates. Financial information, benefits and other data can change quickly and may vary from those stated here.

American Tire Distributors Inc

www.atd-us.com

NAIC Code: 423130

TYPES OF BUSINESS:
Tires & Related Products, Distribution

BRANDS/DIVISIONS/AFFILIATES:
American Tire Distributors Holdings Inc
ATDOnline
TireBuyer.com

CONTACTS:
Note: Officers with more than one job title may be intentionally listed here more than once.

Stuart Schuette, CEO
Michael Gaither, General Counsel
Phillip Marrett, Exec. VP-Product Planning & Positioning
Daniel Brown, Pres., Tire Pros

GROWTH PLANS/SPECIAL FEATURES:
American Tire Distributors, Inc. (ATD) is one of the nation's largest suppliers of tires and wheels as well as tools and other automotive service equipment. The company serves the replacement tire market through approximately 140 distribution centers in Canada and the U.S., and a fleet of 1,500 delivery vehicles, delivering products to approximately 80,000 customers. ATD distributes more than 40 million replacement tires each year. ATD offers its tire retailers and service shop clients various tires for passenger vehicles and light trucks, tractor-trailers, buses, farm machinery and specialty and recreational vehicles. The company carries brands including Michelin, Continental, BFGoodrich and Bridgestone. Its wheel division offers rims in a range of sizes for passenger vehicles and light trucks. The firm maintains ATDOnline, which offers dealers access to prices, availability and the ability to place orders 24 hours a day, seven days a week; and TireBuyer.com, where customers can buy tires and wheels as well as choose a dealer location for installation. TireBuyer.com also allows potential purchasers to view tires and wheels on their particular vehicle, using the website's 3D visualizer. ATD operates as a subsidiary of American Tire Distributors Holdings, Inc. In December 2018, ATD announced that it had successfully completed its financial recapitalization and emerged from Chapter 11 bankruptcy protection.

FINANCIAL DATA:
Note: Data for latest year may not have been available at press time.

In U.S. $	2018	2017	2016	2015	2014	2013
Revenue	5,565,000,000	5,300,000,000	5,000,000,000	4,800,000,000	5,030,698,000	3,839,269,000
R&D Expense						
Operating Income						
Operating Margin %						
SGA Expense						
Net Income			-92,256,933	-95,800,000	-94,599,999	-6,357,000
Operating Cash Flow						
Capital Expenditure						
EBITDA						
Return on Assets %						
Return on Equity %						
Debt to Equity						

CONTACT INFORMATION:
Phone: 704-992-2000 Fax: 704-992-1384
Toll-Free: 800-222-1167
Address: 12200 Herbert Wayne Ct., Ste. 150, Huntersville, NC 28070 United States

STOCK TICKER/OTHER:
Stock Ticker: Subsidiary Exchange:
Employees: 5,000 Fiscal Year Ends: 01/04
Parent Company: American Tire Distributors Holdings Inc

SALARIES/BONUSES:
Top Exec. Salary: $ Bonus: $
Second Exec. Salary: $ Bonus: $

OTHER THOUGHTS:
Estimated Female Officers or Directors:
Hot Spot for Advancement for Women/Minorities:

American Tower Corporation (REIT)

NAIC Code: 237130

www.americantower.com

TYPES OF BUSINESS:
Cellular Service Antenna Towers
Antenna Site Leasing
Radio & TV Broadcast Towers
Network Development & Consulting
Antenna Site Leasing

BRANDS/DIVISIONS/AFFILIATES:
American Towers LLC
SpectraSite Communications LLC
American Tower International Inc

CONTACTS:
Note: Officers with more than one job title may be intentionally listed here more than once.

James Taiclet, CEO
Thomas Bartlett, CFO
Robert Meyer, Chief Accounting Officer
Edmund DiSanto, Chief Administrative Officer
William Hess, Executive VP
Steven Vondran, Executive VP
Olivier Puech, Executive VP
Amit Sharma, Executive VP

GROWTH PLANS/SPECIAL FEATURES:
American Tower Corporation (AMT) is a global real estate investment trust (REIT) and an independent owner, operator and developer of multitenant communications real estate. AMT's primary business is the leasing of space on communications sites to wireless service providers, radio and television broadcast companies, wireless data providers, government agencies and municipalities, and tenants in other industries. The firm also offers tower-related services in the U.S., such as site acquisition, zoning, permitting and structural analysis. AMT's principal domestic operating subsidiaries are American Towers, LLC and SpectraSite Communications, LLC. International operations are conducted through American Tower International, Inc., which in turn conducts operations through its various international subsidiaries and joint ventures. As of December 31, 2018, AMT's communications real estate portfolio consisted of 170,686 communications sites spread throughout North America (U.S. and Mexico), Asia, Europe/Middle East/Africa and Latin America. In March 2019, AMT agreed to acquire Eaton Towers Holding Limited, which owns and operates approximately 5,500 communications sites across five African markets.

FINANCIAL DATA:
Note: Data for latest year may not have been available at press time.

In U.S. $	2018	2017	2016	2015	2014	2013
Revenue	7,440,100,000	6,663,900,000	5,785,668,000	4,771,516,000	4,100,048,000	3,361,407,000
R&D Expense						
Operating Income	1,905,000,000	1,998,400,000	1,853,029,000	1,612,789,000	1,486,922,000	1,214,305,000
Operating Margin %		.30%	.32%	.34%	.36%	.36%
SGA Expense	733,200,000	637,000,000	543,395,000	497,835,000	446,542,000	415,545,000
Net Income	1,236,400,000	1,238,900,000	956,425,000	685,074,000	824,910,000	551,333,000
Operating Cash Flow	3,748,300,000	2,925,600,000	2,703,604,000	2,183,052,000	2,134,589,000	1,599,047,000
Capital Expenditure	913,200,000	803,600,000	682,505,000	728,753,000	974,404,000	724,532,000
EBITDA	4,092,100,000	3,722,800,000	3,369,783,000	2,712,059,000	2,451,222,000	1,801,673,000
Return on Assets %		.04%	.03%	.02%	.04%	.03%
Return on Equity %		.18%	.13%	.11%	.21%	.16%
Debt to Equity		3.113	2.705	2.566	3.468	4.077

CONTACT INFORMATION:
Phone: 617 375-7500   Fax: 617 375-7575
Toll-Free: 877-282-7483
Address: 116 Huntington Ave., Boston, MA 02116 United States

SALARIES/BONUSES:
Top Exec. Salary: $1,100,000   Bonus: $
Second Exec. Salary: $766,500   Bonus: $

STOCK TICKER/OTHER:
Stock Ticker: AMT
Employees: 4,507
Parent Company:

Exchange: NYS
Fiscal Year Ends: 12/31

OTHER THOUGHTS:
Estimated Female Officers or Directors: 3
Hot Spot for Advancement for Women/Minorities: Y

Amerigroup Corporation

www.amerigroup.com/

NAIC Code: 524114

TYPES OF BUSINESS:
Managed Health Care

BRANDS/DIVISIONS/AFFILIATES:
Anthem Inc

CONTACTS:
Note: Officers with more than one job title may be intentionally listed here more than once.

Felicia F. Norwood, Exec. VP-Anthem
Richard C. Zoretic, Exec. VP
Mary T. McCluskey, Exec. VP
Jack Young, VP
Ken Aversa, Sr. VP-Customer Svc. Oper., Medicaid, WellPoint
Georgia Dodds Foley, Chief Compliance Officer, Medicaid, WellPoint
John E. Little, Interim Sr. VP-Gov't Affairs, WellPoint
Aileen McCormick, CEO-Western Region, Medicaid, WellPoint

GROWTH PLANS/SPECIAL FEATURES:
Amerigroup Corporation is the state-sponsored program services division of health benefits company Anthem, Inc. These programs include Medicaid, Family Care and the Children's Health Insurance Program (CHIP), across all states. Amerigroup also offers Medicare plans in Arizona, New Jersey, New Mexico, Tennessee, Texas and Washington. The firm reduces costs for families and state governments by combining social and behavioral health services to help members obtain health care. Amerigroup's provider networks consist of: hospitals; and physicians, including primary care physicians, specialists and ancillary providers. The company connects members to the services and supports they need for physical health, mental health and substance abuse. It addresses members' psychosocial needs and goals for housing, education/employment, transportation and meaningful participation in the community. Amerigroup works with individuals with intellectual and developmental disabilities, children and youth in foster care, individuals with mental health and substance abuse needs, individuals who need long-term services and support, and children with special needs.

FINANCIAL DATA:
Note: Data for latest year may not have been available at press time.

In U.S. $	2018	2017	2016	2015	2014	2013
Revenue	11,500,000,000	11,000,000,000	10,500,000,000	10,000,000,000	9,625,000,000	9,125,000,000
R&D Expense						
Operating Income						
Operating Margin %						
SGA Expense						
Net Income						
Operating Cash Flow						
Capital Expenditure						
EBITDA						
Return on Assets %						
Return on Equity %						
Debt to Equity						

CONTACT INFORMATION:
Phone: 757 490-6900 Fax:
Toll-Free: 800-600-4441
Address: 4425 Corporation Ln., Virginia Beach, VA 23462 United States

SALARIES/BONUSES:
Top Exec. Salary: $ Bonus: $
Second Exec. Salary: $ Bonus: $

STOCK TICKER/OTHER:
Stock Ticker: Subsidiary Exchange:
Employees: 8,000 Fiscal Year Ends: 12/31
Parent Company: Anthem Inc

OTHER THOUGHTS:
Estimated Female Officers or Directors: 3
Hot Spot for Advancement for Women/Minorities: Y

Sales, profits and employees may be estimates. Financial information, benefits and other data can change quickly and may vary from those stated here.

AmerisourceBergen Corporation

www.amerisourcebergen.com

NAIC Code: 424210

TYPES OF BUSINESS:
Drug Distribution
Pharmacy Management & Consulting Services
Packaging Solutions
Information Technology
Healthcare Equipment

BRANDS/DIVISIONS/AFFILIATES:
AmerisourceBergen Consulting Services
MWI
World Courier
Dymaxium

CONTACTS:
Note: Officers with more than one job title may be intentionally listed here more than once.

Steven Collis, CEO
Lazarus Krikorian, Chief Accounting Officer
Gina Clark, Chief Administrative Officer
Kathy Gaddes, Chief Compliance Officer
Dale Danilewitz, Chief Information Officer
John Chou, Chief Legal Officer
James Cleary, Executive VP
Robert Mauch, Executive VP

GROWTH PLANS/SPECIAL FEATURES:

AmerisourceBergen Corporation is one of the largest wholesale distributors of pharmaceutical products and services to a wide variety of health care providers and pharmacies. The firm offers brand name and generic pharmaceuticals, supplies and equipment and serves the U.S., Canada and selected global markets. The company's operations are divided into two segments: pharmaceutical distribution services (PDS) and other. PDS provides drug distributes a comprehensive offering of brand-name, specialty brand-name and generic pharmaceuticals, over-the-counter healthcare products, home healthcare supplies and equipment, outsourced compounded sterile preparations and related services to a wide variety of healthcare providers, including acute care hospitals and health systems, independent and chain retail pharmacies, mail order pharmacies, medical clinics, long-term care and alternate site pharmacies and other customers. Through a number of operating businesses, the PDS reportable segment provides pharmaceutical distribution (including plasma and other blood products, injectible pharmaceuticals, vaccines and other specialty pharmaceutical products) and additional services to physicians who specialize in a variety of disease states, especially oncology, and to other healthcare providers, including hospitals and dialysis clinics. Additionally, the PDS provides data analytics, outcomes research and additional services for biotechnology and pharmaceutical manufacturers. The other segment oversees: AmerisourceBergen Consulting Services (ABCS), which provides commercialization support services such as reimbursement support programs, outcomes research, contract field staffing, patient assistance and copay assistance programs; MWI, a leading animal health distribution company in the U.S. and in the U.K.; and World Courier, which is a global specialty transportation and logistics provider for the biopharmaceutical industry serving more than 50 countries. In May 2019, AmerisourceBergen acquired Dymaxium, a market access partner specializing in the exchange of evidence and information between payers and life science companies through its FormularyDecisions.com platform.

Employee benefits include health care, retirement, life insurance and disability protection.

FINANCIAL DATA:
Note: Data for latest year may not have been available at press time.

In U.S. $	2018	2017	2016	2015	2014	2013
Revenue	167,939,600,000	153,143,800,000	146,849,700,000	135,961,800,000	119,569,100,000	87,959,170,000
R&D Expense						
Operating Income	1,564,896,000	1,974,742,000	1,726,723,000	1,330,094,000	1,201,623,000	988,454,000
Operating Margin %		.01%	.01%	.01%	.01%	.01%
SGA Expense	2,496,995,000	2,166,825,000	2,161,905,000	1,923,381,000	1,589,174,000	1,334,203,000
Net Income	1,658,405,000	364,484,000	1,427,929,000	-134,887,000	276,484,000	433,707,000
Operating Cash Flow	1,411,388,000	1,504,138,000	3,178,497,000	3,920,379,000	1,463,153,000	788,125,000
Capital Expenditure	336,411,000	466,397,000	464,616,000	231,585,000	264,457,000	202,450,000
EBITDA	1,877,172,000	1,499,260,000	1,927,425,000	625,735,000	943,864,000	1,070,299,000
Return on Assets %		.01%	.05%	-.01%	.01%	.03%
Return on Equity %		.17%	1.03%	-.10%	.13%	.18%
Debt to Equity		1.661	1.688	5.514	1.02	0.602

CONTACT INFORMATION:
Phone: 610 727-7000 Fax: 610 647-0141
Toll-Free: 800-829-3132
Address: 1300 Morris Dr., Chesterbrook, PA 19087 United States

SALARIES/BONUSES:
Top Exec. Salary: $1,240,000 Bonus: $
Second Exec. Salary: $710,000 Bonus: $

STOCK TICKER/OTHER:
Stock Ticker: ABC
Employees: 19,000
Parent Company:

Exchange: NYS
Fiscal Year Ends: 09/30

OTHER THOUGHTS:
Estimated Female Officers or Directors: 7
Hot Spot for Advancement for Women/Minorities: Y

Sales, profits and employees may be estimates. Financial information, benefits and other data can change quickly and may vary from those stated here.

Ametek Inc

NAIC Code: 334513

www.ametek.com

TYPES OF BUSINESS:
Monitoring, Testing, Calibration and Display Electronic Device Manufacturing
Electromechanical Device Manufacturing

BRANDS/DIVISIONS/AFFILIATES:
FMH Aerospace
Arizona Instrument
SoundCom Systems
Motec GmbH
Telular
Forza Silicon
Spectro Scientific

CONTACTS:
Note: Officers with more than one job title may be intentionally listed here more than once.

David Zapico, CEO
William Burke, CFO
Thomas Montgomery, Chief Accounting Officer
Ronald Oscher, Chief Administrative Officer
Tony Ciampitti, President, Divisional
Timothy Jones, President, Divisional
John Hardin, President, Divisional
Thomas Marecic, President, Divisional

GROWTH PLANS/SPECIAL FEATURES:
Ametek, Inc. is a manufacturer of electronic instruments and electromechanical devices, with operations across the globe. The company markets its products through two operating groups: the electronic instruments group (EIG) and the electromechanical group (EMG). EIG builds monitoring, testing, calibration and display devices for the process, aerospace, industrial and power markets. The group makes significant use of distributors and sales representatives in marketing its products as well as direct sales in some of its more technically sophisticated products. EMG is a supplier of electromechanical devices. EMG produces highly engineered electromechanical connectors for hermetic (moisture-proof) applications, specialty metals for niche markets and brushless air-moving motors, blowers and heat exchangers. AMETEK owns numerous unexpired U.S. patents and foreign patents, including counterparts of its more important U.S. patents, in the major industrial countries of the world. The firm has 150 operating facilities in 25 states and 30 foreign countries. In 2018, the firm acquired FMH Aerospace, a provider of complex, highly-engineered solutions; Arizona Instrument, a provider of differentiated, high-precision moisture and gas measurement instruments; SoundCom Systems, a designer, integrator, installer and supporter of clinical workflow and communication systems for healthcare facilities, educational institutions and corporations; Motc GmbH, a provider of integrated vision systems serving the mobile machine vision market; Telular, a provider of communication solutions for logistics management, tank monitoring and security applications; Forza Silicon, a designer and producer of high-performance imaging sensors used in medical, defense, commercial and industrial applications; and Spectro Scientific, a provider of machine condition monitoring solutions for critical assets in high-value industrial applications.

FINANCIAL DATA:
Note: Data for latest year may not have been available at press time.

In U.S. $	2018	2017	2016	2015	2014	2013
Revenue	4,845,872,000	4,300,170,000	3,840,087,000	3,974,295,000	4,021,964,000	3,594,136,000
R&D Expense						
Operating Income	1,075,540,000	915,094,000	801,897,000	907,716,000	898,586,000	815,079,000
Operating Margin %		.21%	.21%	.23%	.22%	.23%
SGA Expense	584,022,000	533,645,000	462,970,000	448,592,000	462,637,000	398,177,000
Net Income	777,933,000	681,470,000	512,158,000	590,859,000	584,460,000	516,999,000
Operating Cash Flow	925,518,000	833,259,000	756,835,000	672,540,000	725,962,000	660,659,000
Capital Expenditure	82,076,000	75,074,000	63,280,000	69,083,000	71,327,000	63,314,000
EBITDA	1,269,415,000	1,077,985,000	967,123,000	1,047,635,000	1,023,344,000	917,024,000
Return on Assets %		.09%	.07%	.09%	.10%	.09%
Return on Equity %		.19%	.16%	.18%	.18%	.18%
Debt to Equity		0.463	0.633	0.478	0.441	0.364

CONTACT INFORMATION:
Phone: 610 647-2121 Fax:
Toll-Free:
Address: 1100 Cassatt Rd., Berwyn, PA 19312-1177 United States

STOCK TICKER/OTHER:
Stock Ticker: AME
Employees: 15,700
Parent Company:

Exchange: NYS
Fiscal Year Ends: 12/31

SALARIES/BONUSES:
Top Exec. Salary: $1,200,000 Bonus: $528,000
Second Exec. Salary: $575,000 Bonus: $86,250

OTHER THOUGHTS:
Estimated Female Officers or Directors:
Hot Spot for Advancement for Women/Minorities:

Sales, profits and employees may be estimates. Financial information, benefits and other data can change quickly and may vary from those stated here.

Amgen Inc

www.amgen.com

NAIC Code: 325412

TYPES OF BUSINESS:
Drugs-Diversified
Oncology Drugs
Nephrology Drugs
Inflammation Drugs
Neurology Drugs

BRANDS/DIVISIONS/AFFILIATES:
ENBREL
Neulasta
Prolia
Aranesp
XGEVA
Sensipar
EPOGEN
AMG 520/CNP520

CONTACTS: Note: Officers with more than one job title may be intentionally listed here more than once.
Robert Bradway, CEO
David Meline, CFO
Murdo Gordon, Executive VP, Divisional
David Reese, Executive VP, Divisional
Esteban Santos, Executive VP, Divisional
Cynthia Patton, Other Executive Officer
Lori Johnston, Senior VP, Divisional
David Piacquad, Senior VP, Divisional
Jonathan Graham, Senior VP

GROWTH PLANS/SPECIAL FEATURES:
Amgen, Inc. is a global biotechnology medicines company that discovers, develops, manufactures and markets human therapeutics based on cellular and molecular biology. Amgen's current (April 2019) pipeline products in Phase 3 include: AMG 520/CNP520, a small molecule inhibitor for the prevention of Alzheimer's disease; ENBREL, a fusion protein that inhibits tumor necrosis factor for rheumatoid arthritis; EVENITY, a humanized monoclonal antibody that inhibits the action of sclerostin for post-menopausal osteoporosis and male osteoporosis; IMLYGIC, an oncolytic immunotherapy for patients with mid- to late-stage metastatic melanoma and other cancer types; KYPROLIS, a proteasome inhibitor for multiple myeloma; omecamtiv mecarbil, a small molecule activator of cardiac myosin for the treatment of chronic heart failure; and tezepelumab, a human monoclonal antibody that inhibits the action of thymic stromal lymphopoietin for severe asthma and atopic dermatitis. During 2018, Amgen's largest marketed product was ENBREL (22%), which is used in indications for the treatment of adult patients with types of rheumatoid arthritis and psoriasis. Neulasta was the second largest marketed product (20%), and is a pegylated protein used to help reduce the chance of infection due to low white blood cell count in patients with certain types of cancer. Other leading products include Prolia, Aranesp, XGEVA, Sensipar/Mimpara, and EPOGEN. Amgen's product sales to three large wholesalers, AmerisourceBergen Corporation, McKesson Corporation and Cardinal Health, Inc., each individually accounted for more than 10% of total revenues in 2016, 2017 and 2018. On a combined basis, they accounted for 98% of U.S. gross product sales, and 84% of worldwide gross revenue (in 2018).

Amgen offers its employees health, disability and life insurance; paid time off; home and auto insurance; tuition reimbursement; childcare services; telecommuting options; and recreation/fitness classes.

FINANCIAL DATA: Note: Data for latest year may not have been available at press time.

In U.S. $	2018	2017	2016	2015	2014	2013
Revenue	23,747,000,000	22,849,000,000	22,991,000,000	21,662,000,000	20,063,000,000	18,676,000,000
R&D Expense	3,737,000,000	3,562,000,000	3,840,000,000	4,070,000,000	4,297,000,000	4,083,000,000
Operating Income	10,263,000,000	9,973,000,000	9,794,000,000	8,470,000,000	6,191,000,000	5,867,000,000
Operating Margin %		.44%	.43%	.39%	.31%	.31%
SGA Expense	5,332,000,000	4,870,000,000	5,062,000,000	4,846,000,000	4,699,000,000	5,184,000,000
Net Income	8,394,000,000	1,979,000,000	7,722,000,000	6,939,000,000	5,158,000,000	5,081,000,000
Operating Cash Flow	11,296,000,000	11,177,000,000	10,354,000,000	9,077,000,000	8,555,000,000	6,291,000,000
Capital Expenditure	738,000,000	664,000,000	837,000,000	649,000,000	1,003,000,000	693,000,000
EBITDA	12,883,000,000	12,856,000,000	12,528,000,000	11,181,000,000	8,748,000,000	7,573,000,000
Return on Assets %		.03%	.10%	.10%	.08%	.08%
Return on Equity %		.07%	.27%	.26%	.22%	.25%
Debt to Equity		1.355	1.011	1.044	1.172	1.341

CONTACT INFORMATION:
Phone: 805 447-1000　　Fax: 805 447-1010
Toll-Free: 800-772-6436
Address: 1 Amgen Center Dr., Thousand Oaks, CA 91320 United States

STOCK TICKER/OTHER:
Stock Ticker: AMGN
Employees: 19,200
Parent Company:

Exchange: NAS
Fiscal Year Ends: 12/31

SALARIES/BONUSES:
Top Exec. Salary: $330,769　　Bonus: $2,000,000
Second Exec. Salary: $1,566,000　　Bonus: $

OTHER THOUGHTS:
Estimated Female Officers or Directors: 4
Hot Spot for Advancement for Women/Minorities: Y

Sales, profits and employees may be estimates. Financial information, benefits and other data can change quickly and may vary from those stated here.

Amphenol Corporation

www.amphenol.com

NAIC Code: 335921

TYPES OF BUSINESS:
Cables & Connectors
Fiber Optic Cable

BRANDS/DIVISIONS/AFFILIATES:

CONTACTS: *Note: Officers with more than one job title may be intentionally listed here more than once.*
Richard Norwitt, CEO
Craig Lampo, CFO
Martin Loeffler, Director
Lance DAmico, General Counsel
Zachary Raley, General Manager, Divisional
Luc Walter, General Manager, Divisional
William Doherty, General Manager, Divisional
Martin Booker, General Manager, Divisional
Richard Gu, General Manager, Divisional
David Silverman, Senior VP, Divisional
Jean-Luc Gavelle, Vice President
Dieter Ehrmanntraut, Vice President

GROWTH PLANS/SPECIAL FEATURES:
Amphenol Corporation is a leading global designer, manufacturer and marketer of electrical, electronic and fiber optic connectors, interconnect systems and coaxial and flat-ribbon cable. The company has two operating segments: interconnect products and assemblies, and cable products and solutions. Interconnect products and assemblies include connectors, which when attached to an electrical, electronic or fiber optic cable; a printed circuit board; or other device, facilitate transmission of power or signal. Value-add systems generally consist of a system of cable, flexible circuits or printed circuit boards and connectors for linking electronic equipment. The cable products and solutions segment primarily designs, manufacturers and markets cable, value-added products and components for use primarily in the broadband communications and information technology markets as well as certain applications in other markets. Amphenol's products are intended for eight primary end markets: automotive, which accounted for 18% of its 2018 sales; broadband communications, 5%; commercial aerospace, 4%; industrial, 19%; information technology and data communications, 19%; military, 10%; mobile devices, 17%; and mobile networks, 8%. During 2018, non-U.S. markets constituted approximately 73% of Amphenol's net sales, with China generating about 32% total net sales. Amphenol has international manufacturing and assembly facilities in the Americas, Europe, Asia, Australia and Africa.

FINANCIAL DATA: *Note: Data for latest year may not have been available at press time.*

In U.S. $	2018	2017	2016	2015	2014	2013
Revenue	8,202,000,000	7,011,300,000	6,286,400,000	5,568,700,000	5,345,500,000	4,614,669,000
R&D Expense						
Operating Income	1,695,400,000	1,431,600,000	1,241,800,000	1,110,400,000	1,048,700,000	902,796,000
Operating Margin %		.20%	.20%	.20%	.20%	.20%
SGA Expense	959,500,000	878,300,000	798,200,000	669,100,000	645,100,000	548,038,000
Net Income	1,205,000,000	650,500,000	822,900,000	763,500,000	709,100,000	635,672,000
Operating Cash Flow	1,112,700,000	1,144,200,000	1,077,600,000	1,030,500,000	880,900,000	769,050,000
Capital Expenditure	310,600,000	226,600,000	190,800,000	172,100,000	209,100,000	158,448,000
EBITDA	1,989,800,000	1,671,500,000	1,430,700,000	1,292,700,000	1,221,000,000	1,046,680,000
Return on Assets %		.07%	.10%	.11%	.11%	.11%
Return on Equity %		.17%	.24%	.25%	.25%	.24%
Debt to Equity		0.888	0.717	0.869	0.919	0.501

CONTACT INFORMATION:
Phone: 203 265-8900 Fax: 203 265-8516
Toll-Free: 877-267-4366
Address: 358 Hall Ave., Wallingford, CT 06492 United States

STOCK TICKER/OTHER:
Stock Ticker: APH
Employees: 62,000
Parent Company:

Exchange: NYS
Fiscal Year Ends: 12/31

SALARIES/BONUSES:
Top Exec. Salary: $1,130,000 Bonus: $
Second Exec. Salary: $600,000 Bonus: $

OTHER THOUGHTS:
Estimated Female Officers or Directors: 1
Hot Spot for Advancement for Women/Minorities:

Sales, profits and employees may be estimates. Financial information, benefits and other data can change quickly and may vary from those stated here.

AMSURG Corporation

www.amsurg.com

NAIC Code: 621493

TYPES OF BUSINESS:
Practice-Based Ambulatory Surgery Centers
Physician Services

BRANDS/DIVISIONS/AFFILIATES:
Envision Healthcare Corporation

CONTACTS: Note: Officers with more than one job title may be intentionally listed here more than once.
Phillip A. Clendenin, Pres.
Steven Geringer, Chairman of the Board
Thomas Sloan, CFO
Sandy Clingan Smith, VP-ASC Mktg.
Katie Lamb, VP-Human Resources
Eric Thrailkill, CIO
Phillip Clendenin, Executive VP, Divisional
Robert Coward, Other Executive Officer
Christopher Holden, President
Kevin Eastridge, Senior VP, Divisional

GROWTH PLANS/SPECIAL FEATURES:
AMSURG Corporation, a subsidiary of Envision Healthcare Corporation, is a leading physician-centric surgical center and physician services firm. The company operates in two business segments: ambulatory services and physician services. Ambulatory services acquire, develop and operate ambulatory surgery centers (ASCs) in partnerships with physicians. This segment operates more than 260 ASCs and one surgical hospital in 35 states and the District of Columbia, in partnership with approximately 2,000 physicians. The typical size of a single-specialty ASC is 3,000 to 6,000 square feet; and the size of a multi-specialty ASC is approximately 8,000 to 12,000 square feet. Each center has two or three operating/procedure rooms with areas for reception, preparation, recovery and administration. Each surgery center is specifically tailored to meet the needs of physician partners. The physician services segment provides outsourced physician services in multiple specialties to hospitals, ASCs and other healthcare facilities, primarily in the areas of anesthesiology, radiology, children's services and emergency medicine.

Employee benefits include medical, vision and dental coverage; a flexible spending account; a health savings account; life and AD&D insurance; short- and long-term disability; long-term care insurance; a 401(k); a wellness program; and employee discounts.

FINANCIAL DATA: Note: Data for latest year may not have been available at press time.

In U.S. $	2018	2017	2016	2015	2014	2013
Revenue	3,200,000,000	3,000,000,000	2,800,000,000	2,566,884,096	1,621,949,056	1,079,342,976
R&D Expense						
Operating Income						
Operating Margin %						
SGA Expense						
Net Income				162,947,008	53,701,000	72,703,000
Operating Cash Flow						
Capital Expenditure						
EBITDA						
Return on Assets %						
Return on Equity %						
Debt to Equity						

CONTACT INFORMATION:
Phone: 615 665-1283 Fax: 615 665-0755
Toll-Free: 800-945-2301
Address: 1A Burton Hills Blvd., Nashville, TN 37215 United States

SALARIES/BONUSES:
Top Exec. Salary: $ Bonus: $
Second Exec. Salary: $ Bonus: $

STOCK TICKER/OTHER:
Stock Ticker: Subsidiary   Exchange:
Employees: 10,500   Fiscal Year Ends: 12/31
Parent Company: Envision Healthcare Corporation

OTHER THOUGHTS:
Estimated Female Officers or Directors: 2
Hot Spot for Advancement for Women/Minorities: Y

Sales, profits and employees may be estimates. Financial information, benefits and other data can change quickly and may vary from those stated here.

AmTrust Financial Services Inc

www.amtrustgroup.com

NAIC Code: 524126

TYPES OF BUSINESS:
Specialty Property & Casualty Insurance
Underwrites Insurance Policies
Specialty Risk & Extended Warranty
Property and Casualty Insurance

BRANDS/DIVISIONS/AFFILIATES:
Stone Point Capital LLC
Evergreen Parent LP
AmTrust Title
Republic Group
Agent Alliance Reinsurance
AmTrust International
AmTrust Specialty Risk
AmTrust E&S Insurance Services

CONTACTS: *Note: Officers with more than one job title may be intentionally listed here more than once.*
Barry Zyskind, CEO
Ariel Gorelik, Exec. VP-Operations
Adam Karkowsky, CFO
Chaya Cooperberg, Exec. VP-Human Resources
Michael Saxon, Executive VP, Divisional
Stephen Ungar, General Counsel
David Saks, Other Executive Officer
Barry Zyskind, Chmn.

GROWTH PLANS/SPECIAL FEATURES:
AmTrust Financial Services, Inc. is a multinational insurance holding company based in New York. The firm offers specialty property and casualty insurance products, including workers' compensation, business owner's policy (BOP), general liability and extended service and warranty coverage such as specialty risk coverages, equipment management, financial warranty, consumer electronics and automotive warranty. Industries served by AmTrust Financial include financial institutions, nonprofits, restaurants and transportation. The company's website provides links to claims, payments, loss control, premium audits and more. The firm's brands include AmTrust Title, Republic Group, Agent Alliance Reinsurance, AmTrust International, AmTrust Specialty Risk, AmTrust E&S Insurance Services, AmTrust Europe, AmTrust Underwriters and All Insurance Management Limited. Through its subsidiaries and affiliates, the company does business in more than 30 countries worldwide. In November 2018, AmTrust merged with Evergreen Parent, LP, an entity formed by private equity funds managed by Stone Point Capital LLC, together with the Karfunkel-Zyskind Family. Evergreen Parent acquired approximately 45% of the shares that the Karfunkel-Zyskind Family and certain of its affiliates and related parties did not own or control.

FINANCIAL DATA: *Note: Data for latest year may not have been available at press time.*

In U.S. $	2018	2017	2016	2015	2014	2013
Revenue	6,000,000,000	5,816,586,752	5,467,314,176	4,727,443,968	4,156,881,920	2,695,162,112
R&D Expense						
Operating Income						
Operating Margin %						
SGA Expense						
Net Income		-348,888,992	410,985,984	503,593,984	447,014,016	290,863,008
Operating Cash Flow						
Capital Expenditure						
EBITDA						
Return on Assets %						
Return on Equity %						
Debt to Equity						

CONTACT INFORMATION:
Phone: 212 220-7120   Fax: 212 704-6288
Toll-Free:
Address: 59 Maiden Ln., Fl. 43, New York, NY 10038 United States

STOCK TICKER/OTHER:
Stock Ticker: Private   Exchange: NAS
Employees: 8,000   Fiscal Year Ends: 12/31
Parent Company: Stone Point Capital LLC

SALARIES/BONUSES:
Top Exec. Salary: $ Bonus: $
Second Exec. Salary: $ Bonus: $

OTHER THOUGHTS:
Estimated Female Officers or Directors: 1
Hot Spot for Advancement for Women/Minorities:

Anixter International Inc

NAIC Code: 423430

www.anixter.com

TYPES OF BUSINESS:
Wire & Cable Distribution
C Class Inventory Component Distribution
Connectivity Parts Distribution

BRANDS/DIVISIONS/AFFILIATES:

CONTACTS:
Note: Officers with more than one job title may be intentionally listed here more than once.

William Galvin, CEO
Theodore Dosch, CFO
Samuel Zell, Chairman of the Board
Ilaria Mocciaro, Chief Accounting Officer
Scott Ramsbottom, Chief Information Officer
Rodney Smith, Executive VP, Divisional
Robert Graham, Executive VP, Divisional
William Geary, Executive VP, Divisional
Orlando McGee, Executive VP, Divisional
Justin Choi, Executive VP

GROWTH PLANS/SPECIAL FEATURES:

Anixter International, Inc. is a leading global distributor of data, voice, video and security network communication products and one of the largest North American distributors of specialty wire and cable products. With approximately 310 sales and warehouse locations in over 50 countries, the firm sells nearly 600,000 products, such as transmission media (copper and fiber optic cable) and connectivity, support, supply and security surveillance products as well as C-class inventory components (small parts used in manufacturing such as nuts and bolts) to original equipment manufacturers (OEMs). These products, used to connect personal computers, peripheral equipment, mainframe equipment, security equipment and various networks to each other, are incorporated into enterprise networks, physical security networks, central switching offices, web hosting sites and remote transmission sites. In addition, Anixter provides industrial wire and cable products, including electrical and electronic wire and cable, control and instrumentation cable and coaxial cable, used in a wide variety of maintenance, repair and construction-related applications.

FINANCIAL DATA:
Note: Data for latest year may not have been available at press time.

In U.S. $	2018	2017	2016	2015	2014	2013
Revenue	8,400,200,000	7,927,400,000	7,622,800,000	6,190,500,000	6,445,500,000	6,226,500,000
R&D Expense						
Operating Income	309,700,000	313,100,000	285,300,000	267,800,000	360,900,000	356,500,000
Operating Margin %		.04%	.04%	.04%	.06%	.06%
SGA Expense						
Net Income	156,300,000	109,000,000	120,500,000	127,600,000	194,800,000	200,500,000
Operating Cash Flow	137,700,000	183,800,000	278,800,000	91,900,000	104,200,000	334,500,000
Capital Expenditure	42,400,000	41,100,000	32,600,000	28,600,000	40,300,000	32,200,000
EBITDA	368,500,000	376,600,000	341,700,000	295,900,000	378,600,000	373,500,000
Return on Assets %		.03%	.03%	.03%	.06%	.07%
Return on Equity %		.08%	.10%	.11%	.18%	.20%
Debt to Equity		0.855	1.067	1.393	1.066	0.814

CONTACT INFORMATION:
Phone: 224-521-8000   Fax: 224-521-8100
Toll-Free: 800-323-8167
Address: 2301 Patriot Blvd., Glenview, IL 60026 United States

SALARIES/BONUSES:
Top Exec. Salary: $712,500   Bonus: $
Second Exec. Salary: $650,000   Bonus: $

STOCK TICKER/OTHER:
Stock Ticker: AXE
Employees: 8,900
Parent Company:

Exchange: NYS
Fiscal Year Ends: 12/31

OTHER THOUGHTS:
Estimated Female Officers or Directors: 2
Hot Spot for Advancement for Women/Minorities: Y

Anthem Inc

NAIC Code: 524114

www.antheminc.com

TYPES OF BUSINESS:
Health Insurance
Health Maintenance Organizations (HMOs)
Point-of-Service Plans
Dental and Vision Plans
Plan Management (ASO) for Self-Insured Organizations
Prescription Plans
Wellness Programs
Medicare Administrative Services

BRANDS/DIVISIONS/AFFILIATES:
Blue Cross and Blue Shield Association
Americas 1st Choice
CareMore
Freedom Health
HealthSun
Optimum HealthCare
Simply Healthcare
UniCare

CONTACTS:
Note: Officers with more than one job title may be intentionally listed here more than once.

Gail Boudreaux, CEO
John Gallina, CFO
Elizabeth Tallett, Chairman of the Board
Ronald Penczek, Chief Accounting Officer
Gloria McCarthy, Chief Administrative Officer
Thomas Zielinski, Executive VP
Leah Stark, Executive VP
Felicia Norwood, Executive VP
Prakash Patel, Executive VP
Peter Haytaian, Executive VP

GROWTH PLANS/SPECIAL FEATURES:

Anthem, Inc. is a health benefits company, serving approximately 40 million medical members through its affiliated health plans (as of mid-2019). The firm is an independent licensee of the Blue Cross and Blue Shield Association, an association of independent health benefit plans, and also serves customers throughout the country under the America's 1st Choice, Amerigroup, Aspire Health, CareMore, Freedom Health, HealthLink, HealthSun, Optimum HealthCare, Simply Healthcare and UniCare brands. Anthem is licensed to conduct insurance operations in all 50 U.S. states and the District of Columbia through its subsidiaries. Anthem offers a broad spectrum of network-based managed care plans to large group, small group, individual, Medicaid and Medicare markets. Managed care plans include preferred provider organizations (PPOs), health maintenance organizations (HMOs), point-of-service (POS) plans, traditional indemnity plans and other hybrid plans. The firm also offers hospital only and limited benefit products, as well as an array of managed care services to self-funded customers, including claims processing, stop loss insurance, actuarial services, provider network access, medical cost management, disease management, wellness programs and other administrative services. Anthem provides specialty and other insurance products and services such as dental, vision, life and disability benefits, radiology benefit management and analytics-driven personal healthcare. The firm provides services to the federal government in connection with the Federal Employee Program (FEP). In mid-2019, Anthem agreed to acquire Beacon Health Options, a behavioral health organization.

Anthem offers comprehensive health benefits, retirement plans and a variety of employee assistance programs.

FINANCIAL DATA:
Note: Data for latest year may not have been available at press time.

In U.S. $	2018	2017	2016	2015	2014	2013
Revenue	92,105,000,000	90,039,400,000	84,863,000,000	79,156,500,000	73,874,100,000	71,023,500,000
R&D Expense						
Operating Income						
Operating Margin %						
SGA Expense	14,020,000,000	12,649,600,000	12,557,900,000	12,534,800,000	11,748,400,000	9,952,900,000
Net Income	3,750,000,000	3,842,800,000	2,469,800,000	2,560,000,000	2,569,700,000	2,489,700,000
Operating Cash Flow	3,827,000,000	4,184,800,000	3,204,500,000	4,116,000,000	3,369,300,000	3,052,300,000
Capital Expenditure	1,208,000,000	799,500,000	583,600,000	638,200,000	714,600,000	646,500,000
EBITDA						
Return on Assets %		.06%	.04%	.04%	.04%	.04%
Return on Equity %		.15%	.10%	.11%	.10%	.10%
Debt to Equity		0.656	0.572	0.665	0.583	0.548

CONTACT INFORMATION:
Phone: 317 488-6000   Fax:
Toll-Free: 800-331-1476
Address: 220 Virginia Ave., Indianapolis, IN 46204 United States

STOCK TICKER/OTHER:
Stock Ticker: ANTM
Employees: 53,000
Parent Company:

Exchange: NYS
Fiscal Year Ends: 12/31

SALARIES/BONUSES:
Top Exec. Salary: $1,400,000   Bonus: $
Second Exec. Salary: $814,904   Bonus: $

OTHER THOUGHTS:
Estimated Female Officers or Directors: 1
Hot Spot for Advancement for Women/Minorities: Y

Sales, profits and employees may be estimates. Financial information, benefits and other data can change quickly and may vary from those stated here.

AO Smith Corporation

NAIC Code: 335228

www.aosmith.com

TYPES OF BUSINESS:
Water Heaters
Water Boilers
Solar Water Heating Systems

BRANDS/DIVISIONS/AFFILIATES:
AO Smith
American
GSW
Reliance
State
Takagi
US Craftmaster
Water-Right Inc

CONTACTS:
Note: Officers with more than one job title may be intentionally listed here more than once.

William Vallett, CEO, Subsidiary
Ajita Rajendra, CEO
John Kita, CFO
Daniel Kempken, Chief Accounting Officer
Peter Martineau, Chief Information Officer
Robert Heideman, Chief Technology Officer
James Stern, Executive VP
Kevin Wheeler, General Manager, Geographical
Wei Ding, General Manager, Subsidiary
Paul Dana, President, Subsidiary
Wilfridus Brouwer, President, Subsidiary
Charles Lauber, Senior VP, Divisional
Mark Petrarca, Senior VP, Divisional

GROWTH PLANS/SPECIAL FEATURES:

A.O. Smith Corporation is a manufacturer of water heating equipment serving a diverse mix of residential, commercial and industrial end markets. The firm markets its products under the brand names AO Smith, American, GSW, John Wood, Reliance, Hague, State, Takagi, U.S. Craftmaster, Lochinvar and Aquasana. The company operates in two segments: North America and rest of the world. The North America segment markets products mainly in the U.S. In addition, it manufactures and markets specialty commercial condensing and non-condensing boilers and water system tanks. The rest of the world segment does business in China, Europe and India. It manufactures and markets water treatment products, primarily for Asia. Both segments manufacture and market comprehensive lines of residential gas, gas tankless and electric water heaters. The firm's residential and commercial water heaters come in sizes ranging from two and a half-gallon (point-of-use) models to 4,000 gallon models with varying efficiency ranges. It offers electric, natural gas and liquid propane models as well as solar tank units. Typical applications include restaurants, hotels and motels, office buildings, laundries, car washes and small businesses. The company's commercial and residential boilers come in capacities ranging from 40,000 British Thermal Units (BTUs) to 6.0 million BTUs. The boilers are used in hospitals, schools, hotels and other large commercial buildings. Other products include expansion tanks, commercial solar water heating systems, swimming pool and spa heaters and related products and parts. During 2019, A.O. Smith acquired Water-Right, Inc., a Wisconsin-based water treatment company, including all its subsidiaries, real estate and sister company Mineral-Right, Inc.

FINANCIAL DATA:
Note: Data for latest year may not have been available at press time.

In U.S. $	2018	2017	2016	2015	2014	2013
Revenue	3,187,900,000	2,996,700,000	2,685,900,000	2,536,500,000	2,356,000,000	2,153,800,000
R&D Expense						
Operating Income	551,700,000	520,500,000	460,400,000	399,100,000	287,200,000	249,300,000
Operating Margin %		.17%	.17%	.16%	.12%	.12%
SGA Expense	753,800,000	718,200,000	658,900,000	610,700,000	572,100,000	524,500,000
Net Income	444,200,000	296,500,000	326,500,000	282,900,000	207,800,000	169,700,000
Operating Cash Flow	448,900,000	326,400,000	446,600,000	344,400,000	263,900,000	279,600,000
Capital Expenditure	85,200,000	94,200,000	80,700,000	72,700,000	86,100,000	97,700,000
EBITDA	638,100,000	601,000,000	534,900,000	472,900,000	352,200,000	301,800,000
Return on Assets %		.10%	.12%	.11%	.08%	.07%
Return on Equity %		.19%	.22%	.20%	.15%	.13%
Debt to Equity		0.244	0.209	0.164	0.152	0.134

CONTACT INFORMATION:
Phone: 414 359-4000 Fax:
Toll-Free:
Address: 11270 W. Park Pl., Milwaukee, WI 53224-9508 United States

STOCK TICKER/OTHER:
Stock Ticker: AOS
Employees: 15,500
Parent Company:

Exchange: NYS
Fiscal Year Ends: 12/31

SALARIES/BONUSES:
Top Exec. Salary: $900,000 Bonus: $
Second Exec. Salary: $900,000 Bonus: $

OTHER THOUGHTS:
Estimated Female Officers or Directors:
Hot Spot for Advancement for Women/Minorities:

Sales, profits and employees may be estimates. Financial information, benefits and other data can change quickly and may vary from those stated here.

Aon Hewitt

NAIC Code: 541612

www.aon.com/human-capital-consulting

TYPES OF BUSINESS:
Human Resources Consulting
Human Resources Outsourcing
Employee Benefits Consulting

BRANDS/DIVISIONS/AFFILIATES:
Aon plc

CONTACTS: *Note: Officers with more than one job title may be intentionally listed here more than once.*
Greg Case, CEO-Aon plc

GROWTH PLANS/SPECIAL FEATURES:
Aon Hewitt is the human capital consulting division of Aon plc. The company's primary goal is to reduce people-related management issues through assessment, succession planning and organizational design. With operations in the U.S., Canada, the U.K., Europe, South Africa, Latin America and the Asia Pacific, Aon Hewitt provides companies with consulting services, benefit administration and human resource business process outsourcing (BPO). Through its consulting services, Aon Hewitt advises large multi-national and mid-size companies on developing strategies to attract and retain talent, such as incentive programs, health insurance and compensation packages; manages personal risk, such as investment initiatives; and implements effective organizational structures. The benefits administration segment advises employers regarding the structure, funding and administration of employee benefit programs, which attract, retain and motivate employees. Human resource BPO services provides clients with assistance in process improvement and design, leadership, organization and human capital development and change management. The firm matches the specific workforce and business needs of a given company with an appropriate business strategy in order to make the most efficient and effective working environment possible. The firm handles client companies of all types and needs, from global corporations and organizations to small businesses operating in a single county.

FINANCIAL DATA: *Note: Data for latest year may not have been available at press time.*

In U.S. $	2018	2017	2016	2015	2014	2013
Revenue	6,200,000,000	6,000,000,000	5,845,000,000	4,820,000,000	4,264,000,000	4,057,000,000
R&D Expense						
Operating Income						
Operating Margin %						
SGA Expense						
Net Income						
Operating Cash Flow						
Capital Expenditure						
EBITDA						
Return on Assets %						
Return on Equity %						
Debt to Equity						

CONTACT INFORMATION:
Phone: 847-295-5000 Fax:
Toll-Free:
Address: 4 Overlook Point, Chicago, IL 60069-4302 United States

STOCK TICKER/OTHER:
Stock Ticker: Subsidiary
Employees: 29,000
Parent Company: Aon plc

Exchange:
Fiscal Year Ends: 12/31

SALARIES/BONUSES:
Top Exec. Salary: $ Bonus: $
Second Exec. Salary: $ Bonus: $

OTHER THOUGHTS:
Estimated Female Officers or Directors: 1
Hot Spot for Advancement for Women/Minorities: Y

Apple Inc

NAIC Code: 334220

www.apple.com

TYPES OF BUSINESS:
Electronics Design and Manufacturing
Software
Computers and Tablets
Retail Stores
Smartphones
Online Music Store
Apps Store
Home Entertainment Software & Systems

BRANDS/DIVISIONS/AFFILIATES:
iPhone
iPad
Apple Watch
Apple TV
iOS
watchOS
HomePod
AirPods

CONTACTS:
Note: Officers with more than one job title may be intentionally listed here more than once.

Timothy Cook, CEO
Luca Maestri, CFO
Arthur Levinson, Chairman of the Board
Chris Kondo, Chief Accounting Officer
Jeffery Williams, COO
Katherine Adams, General Counsel
Angela Ahrendts, Senior VP, Divisional
Deirdre O'Brien, Senior VP, Divisional

GROWTH PLANS/SPECIAL FEATURES:

Apple, Inc. designs, manufactures and markets personal computers, portable digital music players and mobile communication devices and sells a variety of related software, services, peripherals and networking applications. The company's products and services include iPhone, iPad, Mac, Apple Watch, Apple TV; a portfolio of consumer and professional software applications; iOS, macOS, watchOS and tvOS operating systems; iCloud, Apple Pay and a variety of accessory, service and support offerings. iPhone is the company's line of smartphones based on its iOS operating system. iCloud stores music, photos, contacts, calendars, mail, documents and more, keeping them up-to-date and available across multiple iOS devices, Mac and Windows personal computers and Apple TV. Other products include apple-branded and third-party accessories; the HomePod wireless speaker; AirPods wireless headphone; and iPod touch, a flash memory-based digital music and medial player that works with the iTunes store, App Store, iBooks store and Apple Music (collectively referred to as digital content and services) for purchasing and playing digital content and apps. The firm has more than 500 brick and mortar stores in 24 countries, but also sells its products worldwide through online stores and direct sales force, as well as through third-party cellular network carriers, wholesalers, retailers and value-added resellers. During 2018, Apple agreed acquired Texture, a digital magazine subscription service by Next Issue Media, LLC, which gives users unlimited access to their favorite titles for a monthly subscription fee. That December, Apple announced a major expansion of its operations in Austin, including a $1 billion new campus, with plans to establish new sites in Seattle, San Diego and Culver City. Apple added 6,000 jobs in America in 2018, with plans to create 20,000 jobs in the U.S. by 2023.

Apple offers employees comprehensive health benefits, retirement plans and various employee assistance programs.

FINANCIAL DATA:
Note: Data for latest year may not have been available at press time.

In U.S. $	2018	2017	2016	2015	2014	2013
Revenue	265,595,000,000	229,234,000,000	215,639,000,000	233,715,000,000	182,795,000,000	170,910,000,000
R&D Expense	14,236,000,000	11,581,000,000	10,045,000,000	8,067,000,000	6,041,000,000	4,475,000,000
Operating Income	70,898,000,000	61,344,000,000	60,024,000,000	71,230,000,000	52,503,000,000	48,999,000,000
Operating Margin %		.27%	.28%	.30%	.29%	.29%
SGA Expense	16,705,000,000	15,261,000,000	14,194,000,000	14,329,000,000	11,993,000,000	10,830,000,000
Net Income	59,531,000,000	48,351,000,000	45,687,000,000	53,394,000,000	39,510,000,000	37,037,000,000
Operating Cash Flow	77,434,000,000	63,598,000,000	65,824,000,000	81,266,000,000	59,713,000,000	53,666,000,000
Capital Expenditure	13,313,000,000	12,795,000,000	13,548,000,000	11,488,000,000	9,813,000,000	9,076,000,000
EBITDA	87,046,000,000	76,569,000,000	73,333,000,000	84,505,000,000	61,813,000,000	57,048,000,000
Return on Assets %		.14%	.15%	.20%	.18%	.19%
Return on Equity %		.37%	.37%	.46%	.34%	.31%
Debt to Equity		0.725	0.588	0.448	0.26	0.137

CONTACT INFORMATION:
Phone: 408 996-1010   Fax: 408 974-2483
Toll-Free: 800-692-7753
Address: One Apple Park Way, Cupertino, CA 95014 United States

SALARIES/BONUSES:
Top Exec. Salary: $3,000,000   Bonus: $
Second Exec. Salary: $1,000,000   Bonus: $

STOCK TICKER/OTHER:
Stock Ticker: AAPL
Employees: 132,000
Parent Company:

Exchange: NAS
Fiscal Year Ends: 09/30

OTHER THOUGHTS:
Estimated Female Officers or Directors:
Hot Spot for Advancement for Women/Minorities:

Sales, profits and employees may be estimates. Financial information, benefits and other data can change quickly and may vary from those stated here.

Applied Materials Inc

NAIC Code: 333242

www.appliedmaterials.com

TYPES OF BUSINESS:
Semiconductor Manufacturing Equipment
LCD Display Technology Equipment
Automation Software
Energy Generation & Conversion Technologies

BRANDS/DIVISIONS/AFFILIATES:

CONTACTS:
Note: Officers with more than one job title may be intentionally listed here more than once.

Gary Dickerson, CEO
Daniel Durn, CFO
James Morgan, Chairman Emeritus
Charles Read, Chief Accounting Officer
Omkaram Nalamasu, Chief Technology Officer
Thomas Iannotti, Director
Thomas Larkins, General Counsel
Ali Salehpour, Senior VP
Steve Ghanayem, Senior VP, Divisional
Prabu Raja, Senior VP, Divisional
Ginetto Addiego, Senior VP, Divisional

GROWTH PLANS/SPECIAL FEATURES:

Applied Materials, Inc. (AMI), a global leader in the semiconductor industry, provides manufacturing equipment, services and software to the global semiconductor, flat panel display, solar photovoltaic (PV) and related industries. AMI operates in three segments: semiconductor systems, applied global services and display and adjacent markets. The semiconductor systems division develops, manufactures and sells a range of manufacturing equipment used to fabricate semiconductor chips or integrated circuits. Technologies found in this segment are transistor and interconnect, patterning and packaging, and imaging and process control. The applied global services segment provides integrated solutions to optimize equipment and fab performance and productivity, including spares, upgrades, services, remanufactured earlier generation equipment and factory automation software for semiconductor, display and other products. Its services encompass the following components: fabrication services, automation systems and software, sub-fabrication systems and equipment, parts programs and abatement control systems. The display and adjacent market segment is comprised of products for manufacturing liquid crystal displays (LCDs), organic light-emitting diodes (OLEDs), and other display technologies for TVs, personal computers (PCs), tablets, smart phones, and other consumer-oriented devices as well as equipment for flexible substrates. The segment offers a variety of technologies and products, including: array testing, defect review, chemical vapor deposition, physical vapor deposition and flexible technologies.

The company offers employees medical, life, AD&D, disability and business travel accident insurance; flexible spending accounts; an employee assistance program; health appraisals; a 401(k) plan; a stock purchase plan; and credit union membership.

FINANCIAL DATA:
Note: Data for latest year may not have been available at press time.

In U.S. $	2018	2017	2016	2015	2014	2013
Revenue	17,253,000,000	14,537,000,000	10,825,000,000	9,659,000,000	9,072,000,000	7,509,000,000
R&D Expense	2,019,000,000	1,774,000,000	1,540,000,000	1,451,000,000	1,428,000,000	1,320,000,000
Operating Income	4,796,000,000	3,868,000,000	2,152,000,000	1,618,000,000	1,525,000,000	769,000,000
Operating Margin %		.27%	.20%	.17%	.17%	.10%
SGA Expense	1,002,000,000	890,000,000	819,000,000	883,000,000	890,000,000	902,000,000
Net Income	3,313,000,000	3,434,000,000	1,721,000,000	1,377,000,000	1,072,000,000	256,000,000
Operating Cash Flow	3,787,000,000	3,609,000,000	2,466,000,000	1,163,000,000	1,800,000,000	623,000,000
Capital Expenditure	622,000,000	345,000,000	253,000,000	215,000,000	241,000,000	197,000,000
EBITDA	5,385,000,000	4,336,000,000	2,557,000,000	2,072,000,000	1,918,000,000	855,000,000
Return on Assets %		.20%	.12%	.10%	.09%	.02%
Return on Equity %		.41%	.23%	.18%	.14%	.04%
Debt to Equity		0.567	0.436	0.439	0.247	0.275

CONTACT INFORMATION:
Phone: 408 727-5555   Fax: 408 727-9943
Toll-Free:
Address: 3050 Bowers Ave., Santa Clara, CA 95052 United States

STOCK TICKER/OTHER:
Stock Ticker: AMAT   Exchange: NAS
Employees: 16,700   Fiscal Year Ends: 10/31
Parent Company:

SALARIES/BONUSES:
Top Exec. Salary: $1,000,000   Bonus: $
Second Exec. Salary: $600,000   Bonus: $250,000

OTHER THOUGHTS:
Estimated Female Officers or Directors: 2
Hot Spot for Advancement for Women/Minorities: Y

Sales, profits and employees may be estimates. Financial information, benefits and other data can change quickly and may vary from those stated here.

Aramark Corporation

NAIC Code: 722310

www.aramark.com

TYPES OF BUSINESS:
Food Service Contractor
Facilities Management
Uniforms & Career Apparel Rental
Parks & Resorts Concessions & Facilities
Health Care Support Services
Apparel Manufacturing
Clinical Equipment Maintenance

BRANDS/DIVISIONS/AFFILIATES:

CONTACTS:
Note: Officers with more than one job title may be intentionally listed here more than once.

Eric Foss, CEO
Stephen Bramlage, CFO
Lynn McKee, Executive VP, Divisional
Stephen Reynolds, Executive VP

GROWTH PLANS/SPECIAL FEATURES:

Aramark Corporation is a global provider of food, facilities and uniform services. Active in 19 countries, the company's core market is the United States. Aramark operates its business in three segments: food and support services United States (FSS United States), food and support services international (FSS international) and uniform and career apparel (uniform). FSS United States generates 64% of total sales, and FSS international generates 23%. Both serve clients in four principal sectors: education, including colleges, universities, public school districts and private schools; healthcare, including hospitals and nursing homes; business/industry, including office parks/buildings, manufacturing plants, corporate cafeterias, mining operations and oil/gas drilling operations; and sports, leisure and corrections, including professional/collegiate stadiums and arenas, concert venues, national/state parks, convention/civic centers and correctional facilities. To these sectors, Aramark offers dining services, catering, food service management, facilities management, nutrition services, convenience stores, custodial services, grounds keeping, energy management, vending, drinking water filtration, restaurants, clinical equipment maintenance, environmental services, laundry/linen distribution, housekeeping management and much more. The uniform segment provides uniforms and other garments including work clothes and ancillary items such as mats and shop towels in the U.S., Puerto Rico, Canada and Japan. Its clients use uniforms for a variety of reasons, including establishing corporate identity, projecting a professional image and for protection purposes. This division operates approximately 3,900 routes, delivering uniforms and generating 13% of total sales. Aramark is owned by a group of investors affiliated with Goldman Sachs Capital Partners, CCMP Capital Advisors, J.P. Morgan Partners, Thomas H. Lee Partners LP and Warburg Pincus, LLC, as well as approximately 250 senior management personnel. In September 2018, Aramark agreed to sell its healthcare technologies business to TRIMEDX for $300 million.

Aramark offers medical, dental, vision, life and disability insurance; and pension and employee assistance plans.

FINANCIAL DATA:
Note: Data for latest year may not have been available at press time.

In U.S. $	2018	2017	2016	2015	2014	2013
Revenue	15,789,630,000	14,604,410,000	14,415,830,000	14,329,140,000	14,832,910,000	13,945,660,000
R&D Expense						
Operating Income	826,137,000	808,057,000	746,314,000	627,938,000	564,563,000	514,474,000
Operating Margin %		.06%	.05%	.04%	.04%	.04%
SGA Expense	377,129,000	299,170,000	283,342,000	316,740,000	382,851,000	227,902,000
Net Income	567,885,000	373,923,000	287,806,000	235,946,000	148,956,000	69,356,000
Operating Cash Flow	1,047,351,000	1,053,387,000	806,640,000	683,036,000	398,159,000	695,907,000
Capital Expenditure	628,604,000	552,729,000	512,532,000	524,384,000	545,194,000	392,932,000
EBITDA	1,421,106,000	1,314,849,000	1,241,862,000	1,132,290,000	1,085,700,000	1,058,390,000
Return on Assets %		.03%	.03%	.02%	.01%	.01%
Return on Equity %		.16%	.14%	.13%	.11%	.08%
Debt to Equity		2.111	2.417	2.768	3.117	6.372

CONTACT INFORMATION:
Phone: 215-238-3000 Fax: 215-238-3333
Toll-Free: 800-272-6275
Address: 1101 Market St., Aramark Tower, Philadelphia, PA 19107 United States

STOCK TICKER/OTHER:
Stock Ticker: ARMK
Employees: 270,000
Parent Company:

Exchange: NYS
Fiscal Year Ends: 09/30

SALARIES/BONUSES:
Top Exec. Salary: $1,700,004 Bonus: $
Second Exec. Salary: $700,227 Bonus: $

OTHER THOUGHTS:
Estimated Female Officers or Directors: 1
Hot Spot for Advancement for Women/Minorities:

Sales, profits and employees may be estimates. Financial information, benefits and other data can change quickly and may vary from those stated here.

Archer-Daniels-Midland Company (ADM)

www.adm.com

NAIC Code: 311200

TYPES OF BUSINESS:

Food Processing-Oilseeds, Corn & Wheat
Agricultural Services
Nutraceuticals
Transportation Services
Biodiesel
Natural Plastics
Chocolate
Corn Syrups

BRANDS/DIVISIONS/AFFILIATES:

Crosswind Industries inc
Probiotics International Limited
Rodelle Inc
Neovia
Almidones Mexicanos SA
Edibles Oils Limited
Red Star Yeast Company LLC
Hungrana Ltd

CONTACTS: *Note: Officers with more than one job title may be intentionally listed here more than once.*

Thuy-Nga Vo, Assistant Secretary
Gregory Morris, Pres., Divisional
Juan Luciano, CEO
Ray Young, CFO
John Stott, Chief Accounting Officer
Kristy Folkwein, Chief Information Officer
Stefano Rettore, Chief Risk Officer
Todd Werpy, Chief Technology Officer
D. Findlay, General Counsel
Benjamin Bard, Other Executive Officer
Patricia Logan, Other Executive Officer
Ismael Roig, Other Executive Officer
Pierre Duprat, President, Divisional
Christopher Cuddy, President, Divisional
Vincent Macciocchi, President, Divisional
Joseph Taets, President, Divisional

GROWTH PLANS/SPECIAL FEATURES:

Archer-Daniels-Midland Company (ADM) produces food and beverage ingredients, and other products made from a variety of agricultural products. ADM's products include natural flavors and colors, health and nutrition products, vegetable oil, corn sweeteners, flour, animal feed, and biofuels. The company has an extensive global grain elevator and transportation network to procure, store, clean and transport agricultural commodities such as oilseeds, corn, wheat, milo, oats and barley, as well as products derived from those inputs. Wholly-owned Crosswind Industries, Inc. manufactures contract and private label treats and foods as well as specialty ingredients; Probiotics International Limited, which provides supplements for human, pet and production-animal uses in the U.K.; Rodelle, Inc. a premium originator, processor and supplier of vanilla products; and Neovia, a French-based global provider of value-added nutrition solutions, with 72 production facilities and a presence in 25 countries. Joint ventures of ADM include: a 50% interest in Almidones Mexicanos SA, which operates a wet corn milling plant in Mexico; a 50% interest in Edible Oils Limited, which procures, packages and sells edible oils in the U.K.; a 40% stake in Red Star Yeast Company LLC, which produces and sells fresh and dry yeast in the U.S. and Canada; a 50% interest in Aston Foods and Food Ingredients, which produces starches and sweeteners in Russia; and a 50% interest in Hungrana Ltd., which operates a wet corn milling plant in Hungary. Moreover, ADM wholly-owns Eaststarch CV, which operates wet corn milling plants in Bulgaria, Hungary, Slovakia and Turkey.

Employee benefits include medical, prescription, dental and vision coverage; and 401(k), stock & pension plans.

FINANCIAL DATA: *Note: Data for latest year may not have been available at press time.*

In U.S. $	2018	2017	2016	2015	2014	2013
Revenue	64,341,000,000	60,828,000,000	62,346,000,000	67,702,000,000	81,201,000,000	89,804,000,000
R&D Expense						
Operating Income	2,016,000,000	1,513,000,000	1,639,000,000	2,010,000,000	2,861,000,000	2,130,000,000
Operating Margin %		.02%	.03%	.03%	.04%	.02%
SGA Expense	2,165,000,000	1,993,000,000	2,045,000,000	2,010,000,000	1,907,000,000	1,759,000,000
Net Income	1,810,000,000	1,595,000,000	1,279,000,000	1,849,000,000	2,248,000,000	1,342,000,000
Operating Cash Flow	-4,784,000,000	2,211,000,000	1,475,000,000	2,481,000,000	4,962,000,000	5,226,000,000
Capital Expenditure	842,000,000	1,049,000,000	882,000,000	1,125,000,000	894,000,000	913,000,000
EBITDA	3,365,000,000	2,863,000,000	3,015,000,000	3,474,000,000	4,361,000,000	3,346,000,000
Return on Assets %		.04%	.03%	.04%	.05%	.03%
Return on Equity %		.09%	.07%	.10%	.11%	.07%
Debt to Equity		0.362	0.379	0.323	0.284	0.265

CONTACT INFORMATION:

Phone: 312-634-8100   Fax:
Toll-Free: 800-637-5843
Address: 77 West Wacker Dr., Ste. 4600, Chicago, IL 60601 United States

STOCK TICKER/OTHER:

Stock Ticker: ADM
Employees: 31,800
Parent Company:

Exchange: NYS
Fiscal Year Ends: 12/31

SALARIES/BONUSES:

Top Exec. Salary: $1,300,008   Bonus: $
Second Exec. Salary: $825,048   Bonus: $

OTHER THOUGHTS:

Estimated Female Officers or Directors: 4
Hot Spot for Advancement for Women/Minorities: Y

ARRIS International plc

NAIC Code: 334210

www.arris.com/company/regions/us/

TYPES OF BUSINESS:
Communications Equipment-Cable Systems
Optical & Radio Frequency Transmission Equipment
Internet Access Products
Support & Testing Products
Motorola Home Business

BRANDS/DIVISIONS/AFFILIATES:

CONTACTS: Note: Officers with more than one job title may be intentionally listed here more than once.
David Potts, CFO
Robert Stanzione, Chairman of the Board
Philip Baldock, Chief Information Officer
Bruce McClelland, Director
Stephen McCaffery, Managing Director, Divisional
Daniel Whalen, President, Divisional
Timothy OLoughlin, President, Divisional
Daniel Rabinovitsj, President, Divisional
Lawrence Robinson, President, Divisional
James Brennan, Senior VP, Divisional
Victoria Brewster, Senior VP, Divisional
Patrick Macken, Senior VP

GROWTH PLANS/SPECIAL FEATURES:
ARRIS International plc provides entertainment, communications and networking technology on a global scale. The company's offerings combine hardware, software and services to enable advanced video experiences and constant connectivity. ARRIS operates through three segments: customer premises equipment (CPE); network & cloud (N&C); and enterprise networks. CPE products are divided into two categories: broadband equipment, which includes DSL (digital subscriber line) and cable modems, and broadband gateways; and video equipment, including set-top boxes and video gateways. N&C products are divided into two categories: networks, which include a cable modem termination system, a converged cable access platform, a passive optical network, video systems and access technologies; and software and services, which includes software products that enable providers to securely deliver content and advertising services across multi-screen devices on and off their networks, network management products that collect information from the broadband network and apply analytics, customer experience management solutions, global professional services and global technical services. Last, the enterprise networks segment provides campus network Ethernet switches for next-generation and campus IP networks, Wi-Fi access points, smart wireless services/software, mobile apps, system management and system control products. As of January 31, 2019, ARRIS' intellectual property portfolio consists of approximately 5,009 issued patents (both U.S. and foreign), not including the firm's 1,280 current patent protection applications pending (U.S. and foreign). In February 2019, ARRIS agreed to acquire CommScope Holding Company, Inc.

FINANCIAL DATA: Note: Data for latest year may not have been available at press time.

In U.S. $	2018	2017	2016	2015	2014	2013
Revenue	6,742,640,128	6,614,391,808	6,829,117,952	4,798,331,904	5,322,920,960	3,620,901,888
R&D Expense						
Operating Income						
Operating Margin %						
SGA Expense						
Net Income	113,740,000	92,027,000	18,100,000	92,181,000	327,211,008	-48,760,000
Operating Cash Flow						
Capital Expenditure						
EBITDA						
Return on Assets %						
Return on Equity %						
Debt to Equity						

CONTACT INFORMATION:
Phone: 678 473-2000   Fax:
Toll-Free:
Address: 3871 Lakefield Dr., Suwanee, GA 30024 United States

STOCK TICKER/OTHER:
Stock Ticker: ARRS
Employees: 7,020
Parent Company:

Exchange: NAS
Fiscal Year Ends: 12/31

SALARIES/BONUSES:
Top Exec. Salary: $ Bonus: $
Second Exec. Salary: $ Bonus: $

OTHER THOUGHTS:
Estimated Female Officers or Directors: 2
Hot Spot for Advancement for Women/Minorities:

Arrow Electronics Inc

NAIC Code: 423430

www.arrow.com

TYPES OF BUSINESS:
Electronic Components-Distributor
Computer Products-Distributor
Technical Support Services
Supply Chain Services
Design Services
Materials Planning
Assembly Services
Inventory Management

BRANDS/DIVISIONS/AFFILIATES:
eInfochips

CONTACTS:
Note: Officers with more than one job title may be intentionally listed here more than once.

Michael Long, CEO
Christopher Stansbury, CFO
Richard Seidlitz, Chief Accounting Officer
Vincent Melvin, Chief Information Officer
Gregory Tarpinian, Chief Legal Officer
Mary Morris, Chief Strategy Officer
Matthew Anderson, Other Executive Officer
Chuck Kostalnick, Other Executive Officer
Gretchen Zech, Other Executive Officer
Sean Kerins, President, Divisional
Andy King, President, Divisional

GROWTH PLANS/SPECIAL FEATURES:
Arrow Electronics, Inc. is a global provider of products, services and solutions to industrial and commercial users of electronic components and enterprise computing software. Products and solutions include materials planning, new product design services, programming and assembly services, inventory management, reverse logistics, electronics asset disposition (EAD) and a variety of online supply chain tools. Arrow serves as a supply channel partner for over 100,000 original equipment manufacturers (OEMs), contract manufacturers and commercial customers through a global network of over 300 sales facilities and 45 distribution centers located in 53 countries, serving over 80 countries. Its operations are divided into two segments: global enterprise computing solutions (ECS), representing 32% of sales, and the global components business, 68%. The global ECS segment distributes enterprise IT products, such as servers, software and storage devices, as well as midrange computing products, services and solutions to value added retailers (VARs) in North America and Europe, the Middle East and Africa (EMEA). This segment also provides unified communications products and related services in North America. The global components business segment distributes electronics components and related products to customers in North and South America, EMEA and the Asia-Pacific. Its sales consist of semiconductors; passive, electro-mechanical and interconnect products, such as capacitors, resistors, potentiometers, power supplies, relays, switches and connectors; and computing, memory and other products. The company maintains an aggressive growth strategy based on acquiring competitors and complementary businesses and has completed 16 strategic acquisitions in the last three years. In January 2018, the firm acquired eInfochips, a leading design and managed services company.

FINANCIAL DATA:
Note: Data for latest year may not have been available at press time.

In U.S. $	2018	2017	2016	2015	2014	2013
Revenue	29,676,770,000	26,812,510,000	23,825,260,000	23,282,020,000	22,768,670,000	21,357,290,000
R&D Expense						
Operating Income	1,204,607,000	1,040,744,000	932,141,000	893,247,000	880,098,000	786,150,000
Operating Margin %		.04%	.04%	.04%	.04%	.04%
SGA Expense	2,309,921,000	2,162,996,000	2,052,863,000	1,986,249,000	1,959,749,000	1,873,638,000
Net Income	716,195,000	401,962,000	522,750,000	497,726,000	498,045,000	399,420,000
Operating Cash Flow	272,690,000	124,557,000	355,806,000	655,079,000	673,301,000	450,691,000
Capital Expenditure	155,336,000	203,949,000	164,695,000	154,800,000	122,505,000	116,162,000
EBITDA	1,310,528,000	1,011,697,000	1,025,307,000	983,338,000	955,366,000	827,793,000
Return on Assets %		.03%	.04%	.04%	.04%	.03%
Return on Equity %		.09%	.12%	.12%	.12%	.10%
Debt to Equity		0.592	0.611	0.575	0.50	0.533

CONTACT INFORMATION:
Phone: 300 824-4000   Fax:
Toll-Free:
Address: 9201 E. Dry Creek Rd., Centennial, CO 80112 United States

SALARIES/BONUSES:
Top Exec. Salary: $1,200,000   Bonus: $
Second Exec. Salary: $600,000   Bonus: $

STOCK TICKER/OTHER:
Stock Ticker: ARW
Employees: 18,700
Parent Company:

Exchange: NYS
Fiscal Year Ends: 12/31

OTHER THOUGHTS:
Estimated Female Officers or Directors: 4
Hot Spot for Advancement for Women/Minorities: Y

Sales, profits and employees may be estimates. Financial information, benefits and other data can change quickly and may vary from those stated here.

Arthur J Gallagher & Co

NAIC Code: 524210

www.ajg.com

TYPES OF BUSINESS:
Insurance Brokerage & Management
Risk Management Services
Employee Benefit Services
Investment Operations
Claims Management
Information Management
Insurance Software
Reinsurance

BRANDS/DIVISIONS/AFFILIATES:
Novick Group Inc (The)
Gillis Ellis & Baker Inc
Fullerton Health Corporate Services (Aus)
Adjusting Associates LLP
RGA Group
Serna Insurance Agency

CONTACTS:
Note: Officers with more than one job title may be intentionally listed here more than once.
J. Gallagher, CEO
Douglas Howell, CFO
Christopher Mead, Chief Marketing Officer
Richard Cary, Controller
Walter Bay, General Counsel
Thomas Gallagher, President, Divisional
Scott Hudson, President, Divisional
William Ziebell, Vice President
Susan Pietrucha, Vice President
Joel Cavaness, Vice President

GROWTH PLANS/SPECIAL FEATURES:

Arthur J. Gallagher & Co. and its subsidiaries provide insurance brokerage, third-party claims settlement and administration services to clients in the U.S. and abroad, with Gallagher's brokers, agents and administrators acting as intermediaries between insurers and their customers. The firm operates in three business segments: brokerage, risk management and corporate. The brokerage segment, accounting for 61% of the firm's revenues, is comprised of retail and wholesale brokerage operations. Retail operations focus on property/casualty, employer-provided health and welfare insurance and retirement planning on behalf of middle market commercial, industrial, public, religious and nonprofit clients, while wholesale brokers assist the retail brokers and other non-Gallagher brokers in placing specialized and hard-to-place insurance coverage. The risk management segment (14% of revenues) provides contract claim settlement and administration services for clients that self-insure some or all of their property/casualty coverage and for insurance companies choosing to outsource some or all of their property/casualty claims departments. Gallagher markets its risk management services primarily to Fortune 1000 companies, larger middle market companies, nonprofit organizations and public entities. The corporate segment (25% of revenues) manages the firm's clean energy and tax-advantaged investments and venture capital funds. The majority of the company's revenues are generated in the U.S., with the remaining coming out of the U.K., Australia, Canada, the Caribbean and New Zealand. During 2019, Gallagher made many acquisitions, including: The Novick Group, Inc.; Gillis, Ellis & Baker, Inc.; Fullerton Health Corporate Services (Aust) Pty Ltd.; Adjusting Associates LLP; RGA Group; and Serna Insurance Agency.

Employees are offered medical, dental and vision coverage; AD&D; flexible spending account; short- and long-term disability; a 401(k); educational assistance; and an employee stock purchase plan.

FINANCIAL DATA:
Note: Data for latest year may not have been available at press time.

In U.S. $	2018	2017	2016	2015	2014	2013
Revenue	6,934,000,000	6,159,600,000	5,594,800,000	5,392,400,000	4,626,500,000	3,179,600,000
R&D Expense						
Operating Income	627,400,000	533,100,000	498,800,000	437,100,000	373,900,000	326,300,000
Operating Margin %		.08%	.09%	.08%	.08%	.10%
SGA Expense						
Net Income	633,500,000	463,100,000	414,400,000	356,800,000	303,400,000	268,600,000
Operating Cash Flow	765,100,000	854,200,000	622,100,000	652,600,000	402,300,000	349,900,000
Capital Expenditure	124,400,000	129,200,000	217,800,000	99,000,000	81,500,000	93,600,000
EBITDA	1,036,800,000	888,000,000	817,500,000	730,700,000	615,300,000	503,200,000
Return on Assets %		.04%	.04%	.03%	.04%	.04%
Return on Equity %		.12%	.11%	.10%	.11%	.14%
Debt to Equity		0.656	0.596	0.57	0.658	0.396

CONTACT INFORMATION:
Phone: 630 773-3800   Fax: 630 285-4000
Toll-Free:
Address: 2850 Golf Rd., Rolling Meadows, IL 60008 United States

STOCK TICKER/OTHER:
Stock Ticker: AJG
Employees: 24,800
Parent Company:

Exchange: NYS
Fiscal Year Ends: 12/31

SALARIES/BONUSES:
Top Exec. Salary: $1,250,000   Bonus: $
Second Exec. Salary: $900,000   Bonus: $

OTHER THOUGHTS:
Estimated Female Officers or Directors: 3
Hot Spot for Advancement for Women/Minorities: Y

Ascena Retail Group Inc

www.ascenaretail.com

NAIC Code: 448120

TYPES OF BUSINESS:
Women's Apparel, Retail
Teen Fashion Stores
Fashion Accessories
Private-Label Credit Cards

BRANDS/DIVISIONS/AFFILIATES:
Justice
Lane Bryant
maurices
Catherines
LOFT
Ann Taylor

CONTACTS:
Note: Officers with more than one job title may be intentionally listed here more than once.

Gary Muto, CEO
Robb Giammatteo, CFO
Carrie Teffner, Chairman of the Board
Daniel Lamadrid, Chief Accounting Officer
Jonathan Pershing, Executive VP

GROWTH PLANS/SPECIAL FEATURES:

Ascena Retail Group, Inc. operates a national chain of value-priced specialty stores offering in-season, moderate to better quality apparel and accessories. The company has approximately 4,000 stores throughout the U.S., Puerto Rico and Canada. It operates in segments based on a brand-oriented approach: Premium Fashion, Value Fashion, Plus Fasion and Kids Fashion. The Premium Fashion segment consists of the Ann Taylor and LOFT brands. Ann Taylor includes 304 specialty retail and outlet stores and direct channel operations. Ann Taylor is polished, modern feminine classics with an iconic style point of view for every aspect of her life. LOFT includes 672 specialty retail and outlet stores, direct channel operations and certain licensed franchises in international territories. LOFT offers modern, feminine and versatile clothing for a wide range of women. The Value Fashion segment consists of the maurices brand. The maurices segment includes 972 specialty retail and outlet stores and e-commerce operations, offering up-to-date fashion for women in their 20s and 30s. The Plus Fashion segment consists of the Lane Bryant and Catherines brands. Lane Bryant includes 779 specialty retail and outlet stores and e-commerce operations and is a widely-recognized brand name in plus-size fashion. Catherines includes 348 specialty retail stores and e-commerce operations and sells plus-size fashion to women 45 years and older who shop in the moderate price range and are concerned with comfort, fit and value. The Kids Fashion segment, which consists of the Justice brand, includes 847 specialty retail and outlet stores, e-commerce operations and licensed franchises internationally, offering fashionable apparel to girls ages 6-12, designed for an energetic lifestyle. In May 2019, Ascena Retail Group announced that it would be closing all its approximately 650 Dressbarn stores in order to focus on its more profitable brands.

FINANCIAL DATA:
Note: Data for latest year may not have been available at press time.

In U.S. $	2018	2017	2016	2015	2014	2013
Revenue	6,578,300,000	6,649,800,000	6,995,400,000	4,802,900,000	4,790,600,000	4,714,900,000
R&D Expense						
Operating Income	118,200,000	131,900,000	171,200,000	103,200,000	257,800,000	299,900,000
Operating Margin %		.02%	.02%	.02%	.05%	.06%
SGA Expense	3,317,800,000	3,342,800,000	3,398,800,000	2,347,800,000	2,208,600,000	2,172,200,000
Net Income	-39,700,000	-1,067,300,000	-11,900,000	-236,800,000	133,400,000	151,300,000
Operating Cash Flow	273,900,000	343,600,000	445,400,000	431,300,000	374,700,000	450,000,000
Capital Expenditure	186,300,000	269,700,000	366,500,000	312,500,000	477,500,000	290,900,000
EBITDA	387,000,000	-927,100,000	453,700,000	-16,400,000	403,600,000	432,400,000
Return on Assets %		-.23%	.00%	-.08%	.04%	.05%
Return on Equity %		-.80%	-.01%	-.15%	.08%	.10%
Debt to Equity		2.244	1.063	0.235	0.099	0.087

CONTACT INFORMATION:
Phone: 551-777-6700   Fax:
Toll-Free:
Address: 933 MacArthur Blvd., Mahwah, NJ 07430 United States

STOCK TICKER/OTHER:
Stock Ticker: ASNA   Exchange: NAS
Employees: 64,000   Fiscal Year Ends: 07/31
Parent Company:

SALARIES/BONUSES:
Top Exec. Salary: $1,016,026   Bonus: $
Second Exec. Salary: $1,000,000   Bonus: $

OTHER THOUGHTS:
Estimated Female Officers or Directors: 2
Hot Spot for Advancement for Women/Minorities: Y

Ascension

NAIC Code: 622110

ascension.org

TYPES OF BUSINESS:
General Medical and Surgical Hospitals
Acute Care Hospitals
Rehabilitation Hospitals
Psychiatric Hospitals
Pharmacy Management

BRANDS/DIVISIONS/AFFILIATES:
Ascension At Home
Ascension Care Management
Ascension Global Mission
Ascension Investment Management LLC
Ascension Leader Institute
Ascension Living
Ascension Technologies
Ascention Ventures

CONTACTS:
Note: Officers with more than one job title may be intentionally listed here more than once.

Joe Impicciche, CEO
Craig Cordola, COO
Robert J. Henkel, Pres.
Elizabeth Foshage, CFO
Ziad Haydar, Chief Medical Officer
Christine Kocot McCoy, General Counsel
Patricia A. Maryland, Pres., Health Care Oper.
Eric S. Engler, Sr. VP-Strategic Planning & Dev.
Jon Glaudemans, Chief Advocacy & Communications Officer
Ann Espoito, Sr. VP
Bonnie Phipps, CEO., St. Agnes HealthCare
Susan L. Davis, New York
Scott Caldwell, Chief Supply Chain Officer

GROWTH PLANS/SPECIAL FEATURES:

Ascension is a faith-based, nonprofit healthcare organization in the U.S. Its headquarters are in St. Louis, Missouri, and the network is comprised of more than 150 hospitals in 21 states and Washington D.C. Ascension has more than 2,600 sites of care and more than 50 senior care facilities. Ascension's medical group has a clinical care model that utilizes a care team that supports its providers and patients via seamless care delivery, transitions of care, disease management and case management. Services offered at Ascension's sites of care include behavioral health, counseling, support groups, child development, early childhood education, dental care, health education, wellness, exercise, disease management programs, legal and social services, (rent and utility assistance, and food pantries) and senior services. Ascension At Home helps support patients as they transition from acute care facilities to their homes. Ascension Care Management is a population health engagement company that offers a range of customizable healthcare services to three primary groups: providers, members and payers. Ascension Global Mission supports international efforts that improve the health and well-being of poor and vulnerable populations in developing countries. Ascension Investment Management, LLC manages investment portfolios for Ascension. Ascension Leader Institute provides continued education and training. Ascension Living provides holistic, person-centered care and support to meet the physical, mental and spiritual needs of seniors. Ascension Risk Services manages commercial and self-insured risk management functions. Ascension Technologies is a healthcare information technology services organization, leveraging technology to create collaborative solutions for everyday health decisions. Ascension Ventures is a venture fund focused on the medical device, healthcare technology and healthcare services sectors. In September 2019, Allegan Healthcare Group, Inc. joined Ascension Michigan.

Ascension offers comprehensive benefits, retirement options and a variety of employee assistance programs.

FINANCIAL DATA:
Note: Data for latest year may not have been available at press time.

In U.S. $	2018	2017	2016	2015	2014	2013
Revenue	23,158,956,000	22,713,753,000	21,900,000,000	20,538,803,000	19,901,657,000	16,537,000,000
R&D Expense						
Operating Income						
Operating Margin %						
SGA Expense						
Net Income	2,374,986,000	1,861,183,000	477,700,000	562,596,000	1,803,615,000	451,000,000
Operating Cash Flow						
Capital Expenditure						
EBITDA						
Return on Assets %						
Return on Equity %						
Debt to Equity						

CONTACT INFORMATION:
Phone: 314-733-8000 Fax: 314-733-8013
Toll-Free:
Address: 101 S. Hanley Rd., Ste. 450, St. Louis, MO 63105 United States

STOCK TICKER/OTHER:
Stock Ticker: Nonprofit
Employees: 156,000
Parent Company:

Exchange:
Fiscal Year Ends: 06/30

SALARIES/BONUSES:
Top Exec. Salary: $ Bonus: $
Second Exec. Salary: $ Bonus: $

OTHER THOUGHTS:
Estimated Female Officers or Directors: 9
Hot Spot for Advancement for Women/Minorities: Y

Sales, profits and employees may be estimates. Financial information, benefits and other data can change quickly and may vary from those stated here.

AT Kearney Inc

www.atkearney.com

NAIC Code: 541610

TYPES OF BUSINESS:
Management Consulting
Technology Consulting
Retail Consulting
Government Consulting
Manufacturing Consulting
Transportation Consulting
Supply Chain Consulting
Industry Research & Publications

BRANDS/DIVISIONS/AFFILIATES:
Global Business Policy Council

GROWTH PLANS/SPECIAL FEATURES:
A.T. Kearney, Inc. is a global consulting firm involved in a wide variety of industries. It works alongside clients to create bespoke, collaborative, analytical and entrepreneurial solutions. A.T. Kearney specializes in transformation services, mergers/acquisitions, digital, procurement, operations/performance, strategy, top-line, analytics, leadership, change, organization and Global Business Policy Council services and solutions. The Global Business Policy Council was designed to give a select companies prescient information on global market trends. Industries served by the company include energy, chemicals, metals, mining, public sector, financial services, health, aerospace, defense, communications, media, technology, infrastructure, transportation, travel, private equity, industrial goods, automotive consumer goods and retail. A.T. Kearney maintains offices in major business centers in over 40 countries.

CONTACTS:
Note: Officers with more than one job title may be intentionally listed here more than once.

Alex Liu, Managing Officer
Christine Laurens, CFO
Abby Klanecky, CMO
Stephen Parker, Chief Human Resources Officer
Daniel Mahler, Head-The Americas
Luca Rossi, Head-EMEA
Laura Gurski, Head-Global Practices
Alex Liu, Chmn.
John Kurtz, Head-Asia Pacific

FINANCIAL DATA:
Note: Data for latest year may not have been available at press time.

In U.S. $	2018	2017	2016	2015	2014	2013
Revenue	1,300,000,000	1,100,000,000	1,120,000,000	1,150,000,000	1,100,000,000	1,135,000,000
R&D Expense						
Operating Income						
Operating Margin %						
SGA Expense						
Net Income						
Operating Cash Flow						
Capital Expenditure						
EBITDA						
Return on Assets %						
Return on Equity %						
Debt to Equity						

CONTACT INFORMATION:
Phone: 312-648-0111 Fax: 312-223-6200
Toll-Free:
Address: 227 W. Monroe St., Chicago, IL 60606 United States

STOCK TICKER/OTHER:
Stock Ticker: Private
Employees: 3,600
Parent Company:

Exchange:
Fiscal Year Ends: 12/31

SALARIES/BONUSES:
Top Exec. Salary: $ Bonus: $
Second Exec. Salary: $ Bonus: $

OTHER THOUGHTS:
Estimated Female Officers or Directors: 1
Hot Spot for Advancement for Women/Minorities:

Sales, profits and employees may be estimates. Financial information, benefits and other data can change quickly and may vary from those stated here.

AT&T Inc

NAIC Code: 517110

www.att.com

TYPES OF BUSINESS:
Local Telephone Service
Wireless Telecommunications
Long-Distance Telephone Service
Corporate Telecom, Backbone & Wholesale Services
Internet Access
Entertainment & Television via Internet
Satellite TV
VOIP

BRANDS/DIVISIONS/AFFILIATES:
Home Box Office Inc (HBO)
Turner Broadcasting System Inc
Warner Bros Entertainment Inc
Time Warner Inc
AlienVault Inc

CONTACTS:
Note: Officers with more than one job title may be intentionally listed here more than once.

Brian Lesser, CEO, Divisional
John Stankey, CEO, Subsidiary
John Donovan, CEO, Subsidiary
Lori Lee, CEO, Subsidiary
Randall Stephenson, CEO
John Stephens, CFO
David Huntley, Chief Compliance Officer
David McAtee, General Counsel
William Blase, Senior Executive VP, Divisional

GROWTH PLANS/SPECIAL FEATURES:
AT&T, Inc. is one of the world's largest providers of diversified telecommunications services. The company and its subsidiaries offers communications, digital entertainment services and products to consumers in the U.S., Mexico and Latin America, as well as to businesses and other providers of telecommunications services worldwide. AT&T also owns and operates three regional sports networks. Services and products include wireless communications, data/broadband and internet services, digital video services, local and long-distance telephone services, telecommunications equipment, managed networking and wholesale services. The company operates through four business segments: communication, generating revenues greater than $150 billion; media business, $31 billion; international, $8 billion; and advertising & analytics business. The communications segment provides mobile, broadband, video and other communications services to over 100 million U.S.-based consumers and nearly 3.5 million companies, ranging from the smallest business to nearly all the Fortune 1000, with highly secure, smart solutions. The media business segment consists of the operations of Home Box Office, Inc. (HBO); Turner Broadcasting System, Inc. (Turner); and Warner Bros Entertainment, Inc. Together these firms create premium content, operate one of the largest TV and film studios and own a vast library of entertainment. The international business provides mobile service in Mexico to consumers and businesses, plus pay-tv services across 11 countries in South America and the Caribbean. The advertising & analytics business segment provides marketers with advanced solutions using valuable customer insights from AT&T's TV, mobile and broadband services, combined with extensive ad inventory from Turner and AT&T's pay-tv services. In June 2018, the firm acquired media company Time Warner, Inc. In August of the same year, AT&T, to create a cybersecurity solutions business division, acquired AlienVault, Inc., a developer of commercial and open source solutions to manage cyber-attacks. In January 2019, the firm sold its data center colocation operations to Brookfield Infrastructure.

FINANCIAL DATA:
Note: Data for latest year may not have been available at press time.

In U.S. $	2018	2017	2016	2015	2014	2013
Revenue	170,756,000,000	160,546,000,000	163,786,000,000	146,801,000,000	132,447,000,000	128,752,000,000
R&D Expense						
Operating Income	26,142,000,000	23,863,000,000	24,708,000,000	24,785,000,000	13,866,000,000	30,479,000,000
Operating Margin %		.15%	.15%	.17%	.10%	.24%
SGA Expense	36,765,000,000	34,917,000,000	36,347,000,000	32,954,000,000	39,697,000,000	28,414,000,000
Net Income	19,370,000,000	29,450,000,000	12,976,000,000	13,345,000,000	6,224,000,000	18,249,000,000
Operating Cash Flow	43,602,000,000	39,151,000,000	39,344,000,000	35,880,000,000	31,338,000,000	34,796,000,000
Capital Expenditure	20,758,000,000	20,647,000,000	21,516,000,000	19,218,000,000	21,199,000,000	20,944,000,000
EBITDA	61,260,000,000	45,826,000,000	50,569,000,000	46,828,000,000	31,846,000,000	50,112,000,000
Return on Assets %		.07%	.03%	.04%	.02%	.07%
Return on Equity %		.22%	.11%	.13%	.07%	.20%
Debt to Equity		0.894	0.923	0.966	0.88	0.762

CONTACT INFORMATION:
Phone: 210 821-4105 Fax:
Toll-Free:
Address: 208 S. Akard St., Dallas, TX 75202 United States

STOCK TICKER/OTHER:
Stock Ticker: T
Employees: 268,000
Parent Company:

Exchange: NYS
Fiscal Year Ends: 12/31

SALARIES/BONUSES:
Top Exec. Salary: $1,058,333 Bonus: $5,000,000
Second Exec. Salary: $2,058,333 Bonus: $2,000,000

OTHER THOUGHTS:
Estimated Female Officers or Directors: 4
Hot Spot for Advancement for Women/Minorities: Y

Sales, profits and employees may be estimates. Financial information, benefits and other data can change quickly and may vary from those stated here.

AT&T Mobility LLC

NAIC Code: 517210

www.att.com/wireless/

TYPES OF BUSINESS:
Mobile Phone and Wireless Services
Wireless Data Services
Cell Phone Services

BRANDS/DIVISIONS/AFFILIATES:
AT&T Inc

GROWTH PLANS/SPECIAL FEATURES:
AT&T Mobility, LLC, a wholly-owned subsidiary of AT&T, Inc., is a leading wireless telecommunications service provider predominantly serving the U.S. The company provides wireless voice and data services to approximately 143 million subscribers, including consumer and wholesale. AT&T Mobility offers a comprehensive range of nationwide wireless voice and data communications services in a variety of pricing plans, including postpaid and prepaid service plans. Overall, the firm covers approximately 400 million North American people through its advanced 4G LTE network. AT&T Mobility recently (2018) dropped its roaming restrictions on Unlimited Plans, allowing customers to roam in Canada and Mexico without limits. It is also currently working on test deployments of 5G wireless, and may deploy it in 2018.

CONTACTS: Note: Officers with more than one job title may be intentionally listed here more than once.
Ralph de la Vega, Pres.
Randall Stephenson, Chmn.-Corporate

FINANCIAL DATA: Note: Data for latest year may not have been available at press time.

In U.S. $	2018	2017	2016	2015	2014	2013
Revenue	71,344,000,000	71,090,000,000	72,587,000,000	73,705,000,000	73,992,000,000	69,899,000,000
R&D Expense						
Operating Income						
Operating Margin %						
SGA Expense						
Net Income	21,723,000,000	20,204,000,000	20,743,000,000	19,803,000,000	17,121,000,000	17,848,000,000
Operating Cash Flow						
Capital Expenditure						
EBITDA						
Return on Assets %						
Return on Equity %						
Debt to Equity						

CONTACT INFORMATION:
Phone: 404-236-7895　Fax:
Toll-Free:
Address: 1025 Lenox Park Blvd., Atlanta, GA 30319 United States

STOCK TICKER/OTHER:
Stock Ticker: Subsidiary
Employees: 20,000
Parent Company: AT&T Inc

Exchange:
Fiscal Year Ends: 12/31

SALARIES/BONUSES:
Top Exec. Salary: $　Bonus: $
Second Exec. Salary: $　Bonus: $

OTHER THOUGHTS:
Estimated Female Officers or Directors:
Hot Spot for Advancement for Women/Minorities:

Sales, profits and employees may be estimates. Financial information, benefits and other data can change quickly and may vary from those stated here.

athenahealth Inc

NAIC Code: 524292

www.athenahealth.com

TYPES OF BUSINESS:
Outsourced Health Reimbursement Services
Patient Information Management
Billing & Collection Services for Health Care Providers
Automated Messaging

BRANDS/DIVISIONS/AFFILIATES:
Veritas Capital
Evergreen Coast Capital
Virence Health Technologies

GROWTH PLANS/SPECIAL FEATURES:
Athenahealth, Inc. is a provider of network-enables services and mobile applications for medical groups and health systems. Services provided by the company include electronic health records, medical billing, patient engagement, population health, care coordination, medical order transmission and medical decision support. In February 2019, athenahealth was taken private by Veritas Capital and Evergreen Coast Capital, for $5.47 billion. The firm was combined with Veritas' Virence Health Technologies but continues to operate under the athenahealth brand.

athenahealth offers comprehensive benefits to its employees.

CONTACTS:
Note: Officers with more than one job title may be intentionally listed here more than once.

Bob Segert, CEO
Matthew Levesque, Sr.VP-Operations
Jeffrey Immelt, Chairman of the Board
William J. Conway, Chief Sales Officer
Fran Lawler, Chief Human Resources Officer
Stephen Kahane, Other Corporate Officer
Kyle Armbrester, Other Executive Officer
Jonathan Porter, Other Executive Officer
Bob Segert, Chmn.

FINANCIAL DATA:
Note: Data for latest year may not have been available at press time.

In U.S. $	2018	2017	2016	2015	2014	2013
Revenue	1,300,000,000	1,220,300,032	1,082,899,968	924,728,000	752,598,976	595,003,008
R&D Expense						
Operating Income						
Operating Margin %						
SGA Expense						
Net Income		53,100,000	21,000,000	14,027,000	-3,119,000	2,594,000
Operating Cash Flow						
Capital Expenditure						
EBITDA						
Return on Assets %						
Return on Equity %						
Debt to Equity						

CONTACT INFORMATION:
Phone: 617 402-1000 Fax: 617 402-1099
Toll-Free: 800-981-5084
Address: 311 Arsenal St., Watertown, MA 02472 United States

STOCK TICKER/OTHER:
Stock Ticker: Private
Employees: 5,305
Parent Company: Veritas Capital

Exchange:
Fiscal Year Ends: 12/31

SALARIES/BONUSES:
Top Exec. Salary: $ Bonus: $
Second Exec. Salary: $ Bonus: $

OTHER THOUGHTS:
Estimated Female Officers or Directors: 1
Hot Spot for Advancement for Women/Minorities:

Sales, profits and employees may be estimates. Financial information, benefits and other data can change quickly and may vary from those stated here.

Automatic Data Processing Inc (ADP)

NAIC Code: 518210

www.adp.com

TYPES OF BUSINESS:
Data Processing Services
Business Outsourcing Solutions
Information Services
Payroll Processing

BRANDS/DIVISIONS/AFFILIATES:
ADP TotalSource
RUN Powered by ADP
ADP Vantage HCM
ADP GlobalView HCM
ADP Workforce Now

CONTACTS:
Note: Officers with more than one job title may be intentionally listed here more than once.

Carlos Rodriguez, CEO
Maria Black, Pres., Divisional
Kathleen Winters, CFO
Brock Albinson, Chief Accounting Officer
John Jones, Director
Michael Bonarti, General Counsel
Dermot OBrien, Other Executive Officer
Sreeni Kutam, Other Executive Officer
Don McGuire, President, Divisional
Thomas Perrotti, President, Divisional
John Ayala, President, Divisional
Douglas Politi, President, Divisional
Deborah Dyson, President, Divisional
Michael Eberhard, Treasurer
Stuart Sackman, Vice President, Divisional
Donald Weinstein, Vice President, Divisional

GROWTH PLANS/SPECIAL FEATURES:

Automatic Data Processing, Inc. (ADP) is one of the world's largest providers of cloud-based human capital management (HCM) solutions to employers, as well as business outsourcing services, analytics and compliance expertise. The company serves approximately 740,000 clients in more than 110 countries. ADP operates in two segments: employer services and professional employer organization (PEO) services. The employer services segment offers a comprehensive range of business outsourcing and HCM solutions including payroll services, benefits administration, talent management, human resource management, time and attendance management, insurance services, retirement services and compliance services. Integrated HCM solutions include RUN Powered by ADP, a software platform for managing small business payroll, HR management and tax compliance administration; ADP Vantage HCM, a solution for multinational corporations; ADP Workforce Now, a flexible HCM solution for mid-sized and large businesses; and ADP GlobalView HCM, a solution for mid-sized and large businesses to standardize their HCM strategies. The PEO services segment, which operates as ADP TotalSource, provides small and medium sized businesses with comprehensive employment administration outsourcing solutions (through a co-employment relationship) including employee recruitment, payroll, payroll tax filing, human resources guidance, 401(k) plan administration, benefits administration, compliance services, health and workers' compensation coverage and other supplemental benefits for employees. ADP TotalSource has approximately 12,000 clients in all 50 states; the businesses it serves have a combined total of 530,000 worksite employees.

Employee benefits in the U.S. include medical, dental and vision insurance; health care and dependent care flexible spending accounts; life, AD&D and disability coverage; a pension and 401(k) plan; a stock purchase and stock option plan; auto & home insurance programs; tuition reimbursement; and a scholarship program.

FINANCIAL DATA:
Note: Data for latest year may not have been available at press time.

In U.S. $	2018	2017	2016	2015	2014	2013
Revenue	13,325,800,000	12,379,800,000	11,667,800,000	10,938,500,000	12,206,500,000	11,310,100,000
R&D Expense						
Operating Income	2,511,700,000	2,326,800,000	2,190,500,000	2,014,000,000	2,222,700,000	2,039,900,000
Operating Margin %		.19%	.19%	.18%	.18%	.18%
SGA Expense	2,971,500,000	2,783,200,000	2,637,000,000	2,496,900,000	2,762,400,000	2,620,600,000
Net Income	1,620,800,000	1,733,400,000	1,492,500,000	1,452,500,000	1,515,900,000	1,405,800,000
Operating Cash Flow	2,515,200,000	2,125,900,000	1,859,900,000	1,905,600,000	1,821,400,000	1,577,200,000
Capital Expenditure	470,800,000	470,600,000	386,000,000	335,500,000	367,700,000	282,900,000
EBITDA	2,651,400,000	2,927,200,000	2,579,500,000	2,355,100,000	2,616,900,000	2,410,400,000
Return on Assets %		.04%	.04%	.04%	.05%	.04%
Return on Equity %		.41%	.32%	.25%	.24%	.23%
Debt to Equity		0.503	0.448	0.002	0.002	0.002

CONTACT INFORMATION:
Phone: 973 974-5000   Fax: 973 974-5390
Toll-Free: 800-225-5237
Address: 1 ADP Blvd., Roseland, NJ 07068 United States

SALARIES/BONUSES:
Top Exec. Salary: $1,055,000   Bonus: $
Second Exec. Salary: $693,600   Bonus: $

STOCK TICKER/OTHER:
Stock Ticker: ADP
Employees: 57,000
Parent Company:

Exchange: NAS
Fiscal Year Ends: 06/30

OTHER THOUGHTS:
Estimated Female Officers or Directors: 1
Hot Spot for Advancement for Women/Minorities: Y

Avis Budget Group Inc

NAIC Code: 532111

www.avisbudgetgroup.com

TYPES OF BUSINESS:
Automobile Rental
Franchising
Truck Rental

BRANDS/DIVISIONS/AFFILIATES:
Avis
Budget
ZipCar
Payless
Apex
Maggiore
FranceCars
Turiscar Group

CONTACTS: Note: Officers with more than one job title may be intentionally listed here more than once.
Larry De Shon, CEO
John North, CFO
Leonard Coleman, Chairman of the Board
David Calabria, Chief Accounting Officer
Michael Tucker, Chief Compliance Officer
Edward Linnen, Executive VP
Joseph Ferraro, President, Divisional
Mark Servodidio, President, Divisional
Cathleen DeGenova, Vice President, Divisional

GROWTH PLANS/SPECIAL FEATURES:

Avis Budget Group, Inc. (ABG) operates in the global vehicle rental industry through Avis, Budget, Zipcar, Payless, Apex, Maggiore and FranceCars. Avis is a rental car supplier to the premium commercial and leisure segments of the travel industry. Budget is a rental car supplier to the price-conscious segments of the travel industry. Its fleet of approximately 19,000 Budget trucks are rented through a network of approximately 925 dealer-operated and 450 company-operated locations throughout the U.S. Zipcar operates a membership-based car sharing network present in more than 500 cities and towns and on more than 600 college campuses across the U.S., Canada, Europe and Central America. Payless is a rental car supplier comprised of 280 vehicle rental locations worldwide. Apex operates in New Zealand and Australia via 25 locations. Maggiore operates in Italy through 140 rental locations. The FranceCars operates one of the largest light commercial vehicle fleets in France from more than 70 rental locations. On average, ABG's operations include approximately 11,000 car and truck rental locations throughout the world, with a fleet of more than 620,000 vehicles. Annually, it completes more than 39 million vehicle rental transactions worldwide. The company operates in two segments: Americas, which provides vehicle rentals and ancillary products and services throughout the Americas and the Caribbean, and operates the car sharing business in these markets; and International, which provides and licenses ABG's brands to third parties for vehicle rentals and ancillary products and services primarily in Europe, the Middle East, Asia, Australia and New Zealand, and operates the car sharing business in select markets. In October 2018, Avis Budget acquired Turiscar Group, a car rental company in Portugal.

The company offers its employees medical, dental and vision coverage; life insurance; flexible spending accounts; short-and long-term disability, AD&D; and 401(k).

FINANCIAL DATA: Note: Data for latest year may not have been available at press time.

In U.S. $	2018	2017	2016	2015	2014	2013
Revenue	9,124,000,000	8,848,000,000	8,659,000,000	8,502,000,000	8,485,000,000	7,937,000,000
R&D Expense						
Operating Income	830,000,000	776,000,000	843,000,000	974,000,000	978,000,000	881,000,000
Operating Margin %		.09%	.10%	.11%	.11%	.11%
SGA Expense	1,220,000,000	1,120,000,000	1,134,000,000	1,093,000,000	1,080,000,000	1,019,000,000
Net Income	165,000,000	361,000,000	163,000,000	313,000,000	245,000,000	16,000,000
Operating Cash Flow	2,609,000,000	2,648,000,000	2,629,000,000	2,584,000,000	2,579,000,000	2,253,000,000
Capital Expenditure	12,820,000,000	11,735,000,000	12,651,000,000	12,127,000,000	12,057,000,000	11,051,000,000
EBITDA	2,999,000,000	2,891,000,000	2,896,000,000	2,920,000,000	2,903,000,000	2,419,000,000
Return on Assets %		.02%	.01%	.02%	.01%	.00%
Return on Equity %		.91%	.49%	.57%	.34%	.02%
Debt to Equity		11.019	24.557	12.526	7.771	6.467

CONTACT INFORMATION:
Phone: 973 496-4700 Fax: 212 413-1924
Toll-Free:
Address: 6 Sylvan Way, Parsippany, NJ 07054 United States

SALARIES/BONUSES:
Top Exec. Salary: $1,100,000 Bonus: $
Second Exec. Salary: $650,000 Bonus: $

STOCK TICKER/OTHER:
Stock Ticker: CAR Exchange: NAS
Employees: 30,000 Fiscal Year Ends: 12/31
Parent Company:

OTHER THOUGHTS:
Estimated Female Officers or Directors: 2
Hot Spot for Advancement for Women/Minorities:

Avnet Inc

NAIC Code: 423430

www.avnet.com

TYPES OF BUSINESS:
Components-Distributor
Marketing Services
Supply Chain Advisory Services

BRANDS/DIVISIONS/AFFILIATES:
Premier Farnell Ltd
element14

CONTACTS: Note: Officers with more than one job title may be intentionally listed here more than once.
William Amelio, CEO
Thomas Liguori, CFO
Rodney Adkins, Chairman of the Board
Kenneth Jacobson, Chief Accounting Officer
Kevin Summers, Chief Information Officer
MaryAnn Miller, Other Corporate Officer
Therese Bassett, Other Executive Officer
Peter Bartolotta, Other Executive Officer
Michael O'Neill, Other Executive Officer
Philip Gallagher, President, Divisional

GROWTH PLANS/SPECIAL FEATURES:

Avnet, Inc. is one of the world's largest value-added distributors of electronic components. The firm creates a link in the technology supply chain that connects electronic component manufacturers with a global customer base primarily comprised of original equipment manufacturers (OEMs), electronic manufacturing services (EMS) providers and original design manufacturers (ODMs). Avnet operates through two primary groups: electronic components and Premier Farnell Ltd. Both groups have operations in the Americas, Europe, the Middle East, Africa, Asia, Australia and New Zealand. The electronics components group markets and sells semiconductors, electronic components and other integrated components from leading electronic component manufacturers. These products and services cater to a diverse customer base, serving end-markets such as automotive, communications, computer hardware/peripherals, industrial, manufacturing, medical equipment and defense and aerospace. Premier Farnell globally distributes a comprehensive portfolio of electronic components, typically in small order quantities, primarily to support design engineers, maintenance and test engineers, makers and entrepreneurs as they develop technology products. Premier Farnell operates element14, an online engineering community of more than 500,000 active user members from which purchasers and engineers can access peers, experts, technical information and proprietary tools in relation to the latest products, services and development software. In December 2018, Avnet announced that it will acquire Softweb Solutions, Inc., a privately held software and Artificial Intelligence company that delivers innovative software solutions for Internet of Things applications and systems designed to increase efficiency, speed time to market, and help businesses transform.

Avnet employees receive life, AD&D, disability, travel accident, medical, dental and vision insurance; flexible spending accounts; a pension plan; a 401(k); an employee stock purchase plan; and tuition reimbursement.

FINANCIAL DATA: Note: Data for latest year may not have been available at press time.

In U.S. $	2018	2017	2016	2015	2014	2013
Revenue	19,036,890,000	17,439,960,000	26,219,280,000	27,924,660,000	27,499,650,000	25,458,920,000
R&D Expense						
Operating Income	557,081,000	598,815,000	866,987,000	918,478,000	884,563,000	775,482,000
Operating Margin %		.03%	.03%	.03%	.03%	.03%
SGA Expense	1,970,103,000	1,770,627,000	2,170,524,000	2,274,642,000	2,341,168,000	2,204,319,000
Net Income	-156,424,000	525,278,000	506,531,000	571,913,000	545,604,000	450,073,000
Operating Cash Flow	253,485,000	-368,691,000	224,315,000	583,883,000	237,418,000	696,197,000
Capital Expenditure	155,873,000	120,397,000	147,548,000	174,374,000	123,242,000	97,379,000
EBITDA	482,474,000	572,455,000	896,043,000	955,949,000	943,138,000	777,594,000
Return on Assets %		.05%	.05%	.05%	.05%	.04%
Return on Equity %		.11%	.11%	.12%	.12%	.11%
Debt to Equity		0.334	0.285	0.351	0.248	0.281

CONTACT INFORMATION:
Phone: 480 643-2000   Fax: 480 643-7370
Toll-Free: 800-409-1483
Address: 2211 South 47th St., Phoenix, AZ 85034 United States

STOCK TICKER/OTHER:
Stock Ticker: AVT
Employees: 15,700
Parent Company:

Exchange: NAS
Fiscal Year Ends: 06/30

SALARIES/BONUSES:
Top Exec. Salary: $1,000,000   Bonus: $
Second Exec. Salary: $211,538   Bonus: $350,000

OTHER THOUGHTS:
Estimated Female Officers or Directors: 2
Hot Spot for Advancement for Women/Minorities: Y

Sales, profits and employees may be estimates. Financial information, benefits and other data can change quickly and may vary from those stated here.

Bain & Company Inc

NAIC Code: 541610

www.bain.com

TYPES OF BUSINESS:
Management Consulting
Technology Consulting
Merger & Acquisition Consulting
Analytics
Digital Media Strategies

BRANDS/DIVISIONS/AFFILIATES:
Results Delivery
Bain Media Lab

CONTACTS:
Note: Officers with more than one job title may be intentionally listed here more than once.

Leonard C. Banos, CFO
Erika Serow, CMO
Dave Johnson, Managing Dir.-The Americas
Dale Cottrell, Managing Dir.-Asia Pacific
Paul Meehan, Managing Dir.-EMEA

GROWTH PLANS/SPECIAL FEATURES:

Bain & Company, Inc. is a global provider of management consulting services. The firm advises clients on their most critical issues and opportunities, including strategy, marketing, organization, operations, information technology (IT), digital transformation, digital strategy, advanced analytics, transformations, sustainability, corporate finance and mergers and acquisitions, across all industries and geographies. Bain & Company's approach to change management is through its Results Delivery platform, which helps clients measure and manage risk and overcome the odds to realize results. The company has worked with the majority of the Global 500, as well as major regional and local organizations, nonprofits and private equity funds representing 75% of global equity capital. Bain & Company operates through more than 55 offices located in 36 countries worldwide. In April 2019, Bain & Company announced the formation of Bain Media Lab, a business that will feature a portfolio of digital products and related services that combine breakthrough technologies with powerful data sets.

The firm tends to hire college graduates with either liberal arts degrees, MBA degrees or both. Positions often involve extensive travel and sometimes major relocation, the costs of which are reimbursed by Bain.

FINANCIAL DATA:
Note: Data for latest year may not have been available at press time.

In U.S. $	2018	2017	2016	2015	2014	2013
Revenue	3,800,000,000	2,700,000,000	2,500,000,000	2,300,000,000	2,100,000,000	2,086,000,000
R&D Expense						
Operating Income						
Operating Margin %						
SGA Expense						
Net Income						
Operating Cash Flow						
Capital Expenditure						
EBITDA						
Return on Assets %						
Return on Equity %						
Debt to Equity						

CONTACT INFORMATION:
Phone: 617-572-2000 Fax: 617-572-2427
Toll-Free:
Address: 131 Dartmouth St., Boston, MA 02116 United States

STOCK TICKER/OTHER:
Stock Ticker: Private Exchange:
Employees: 8,000 Fiscal Year Ends: 12/31
Parent Company:

SALARIES/BONUSES:
Top Exec. Salary: $ Bonus: $
Second Exec. Salary: $ Bonus: $

OTHER THOUGHTS:
Estimated Female Officers or Directors: 1
Hot Spot for Advancement for Women/Minorities:

Sales, profits and employees may be estimates. Financial information, benefits and other data can change quickly and may vary from those stated here.

Ball Corporation

NAIC Code: 332431

www.ball.com

TYPES OF BUSINESS:
Metal Can Manufacturing
Civil Space Systems
Defense Systems
Commercial Space Systems
Metal Food and Household Products Packaging
Radio Frequency and Microwave Technology
Metal Beverage Packaging

BRANDS/DIVISIONS/AFFILIATES:

CONTACTS: Note: Officers with more than one job title may be intentionally listed here more than once.
John Hayes, CEO
Scott Morrison, CFO
Nate Carey, Chief Accounting Officer
Daniel Fisher, COO, Geographical
Charles Baker, General Counsel
Robert Strain, President, Subsidiary
Lisa Pauley, Senior VP, Divisional
Jeffrey Knobel, Treasurer

GROWTH PLANS/SPECIAL FEATURES:
Ball Corporation is a leading manufacturer of metal packaging for the food and beverage, personal care and household products industries. It also supplies aerospace and other technologies and services to governmental and commercial customers within Ball's aerospace segment. The firm's packaging businesses are responsible for 90% of the company's net sales, with the remaining 10% by the aerospace business. Ball's largest product line is aluminum beverage containers; but the company also produces aerosol containers, extruded aluminum aerosol containers and aluminum slugs. The packaging products are primarily sold to large multinational beverage, personal care and household products companies, including The Coca-Cola Company and its affiliated bottlers, Anheuser-Busch InBev nv/sa, Molson Coors Brewing Company and Unilever NV. The aerospace business designs, develops and manufactures innovative aerospace systems for civil, commercial and national cyber security aerospace markets. It produces spacecraft, instruments and sensors, radio frequency systems and components, data exploitation solutions and a variety of advanced aerospace technologies and products that enable deep space missions.

FINANCIAL DATA: Note: Data for latest year may not have been available at press time.

In U.S. $	2018	2017	2016	2015	2014	2013
Revenue	11,635,000,000	10,983,000,000	9,061,000,000	7,997,000,000	8,570,000,000	8,468,100,000
R&D Expense						
Operating Income	1,126,000,000	1,023,000,000	800,000,000	799,900,000	919,100,000	874,200,000
Operating Margin %		.09%	.09%	.10%	.11%	.10%
SGA Expense	478,000,000	514,000,000	512,000,000	451,300,000	466,500,000	418,600,000
Net Income	454,000,000	374,000,000	263,000,000	280,900,000	470,000,000	406,800,000
Operating Cash Flow	1,566,000,000	1,478,000,000	194,000,000	1,006,700,000	1,012,500,000	839,000,000
Capital Expenditure	816,000,000	556,000,000	606,000,000	527,900,000	390,800,000	378,300,000
EBITDA	1,636,000,000	1,528,000,000	807,000,000	774,200,000	1,086,400,000	1,067,300,000
Return on Assets %		.02%	.02%	.03%	.06%	.05%
Return on Equity %		.10%	.11%	.25%	.42%	.35%
Debt to Equity		1.654	2.128	4.039	2.898	2.652

CONTACT INFORMATION:
Phone: 303 469-3131 Fax: 303 460-2127
Toll-Free:
Address: 10 Longs Peak Dr., Broomfield, CO 80021 United States

SALARIES/BONUSES:
Top Exec. Salary: $288,360 Bonus: $2,154,000
Second Exec. Salary: $1,299,013 Bonus: $

STOCK TICKER/OTHER:
Stock Ticker: BLL
Employees: 18,450
Parent Company:

Exchange: NYS
Fiscal Year Ends: 12/31

OTHER THOUGHTS:
Estimated Female Officers or Directors: 2
Hot Spot for Advancement for Women/Minorities: Y

Plunkett Research, Ltd.

Bank of America Corporation

NAIC Code: 522110

www.bankofamerica.com

TYPES OF BUSINESS:
Banking
Asset Management
Investment & Brokerage Services
Mortgages
Credit Cards
Insurance Agency

BRANDS/DIVISIONS/AFFILIATES:

CONTACTS:
Note: Officers with more than one job title may be intentionally listed here more than once.

Brian Moynihan, CEO
Sheri Bronstein, Other Executive Officer
Paul Donofrio, CFO
Rudolf Bless, Chief Accounting Officer
Andrea Smith, Chief Administrative Officer
Geoffrey Greener, Chief Risk Officer
Catherine Bessant, Chief Technology Officer
Thomas Montag, COO
David Leitch, General Counsel
Dean Athanasia, President, Divisional
Kathleen Knox, President, Subsidiary
Andrew Sieg, President, Subsidiary

GROWTH PLANS/SPECIAL FEATURES:

Bank of America Corporation is a bank holding and a financial holding company, through which its subsidiaries provide a diversified range of related services on a global basis. The company operates through four primary business segments: consumer banking, global wealth and investment management (GWIM), global banking and global markets. Consumer banking provides deposit and lending services, as well as small business client management services, consumer and small business credit card services, debit card services, consumer vehicle lending and home loan options. GWIM offers Merrill Lynch branded global wealth management, as well as U.S. trust services and private wealth management services. Global banking offers investment banking, global corporate banking, global commercial banking and business banking services. The global markets segment offers fixed income and equity market products. Other activities by Bank of America include asset and liability management (ALM), equity investments, international consumer cards, merchant services, liquidating services, residual expense allocation services and more.

The company offers its employees benefits including tuition and adoption reimbursement; medical, dental and vision insurance plans; employee assistance programs; and health care and dependent care flexible spending accounts.

FINANCIAL DATA: *Note: Data for latest year may not have been available at press time.*

In U.S. $	2018	2017	2016	2015	2014	2013
Revenue	91,247,000,000	87,352,000,000	83,701,000,000	82,246,000,000	83,117,000,000	86,041,000,000
R&D Expense						
Operating Income						
Operating Margin %						
SGA Expense	45,911,000,000	47,154,000,000	46,408,000,000	47,962,000,000	65,324,000,000	58,623,000,000
Net Income	28,147,000,000	18,232,000,000	17,906,000,000	15,888,000,000	4,833,000,000	11,431,000,000
Operating Cash Flow	39,520,000,000	10,403,000,000	18,306,000,000	27,730,000,000	26,739,000,000	92,817,000,000
Capital Expenditure					1,160,000,000	521,000,000
EBITDA						
Return on Assets %		.01%	.01%	.01%	.00%	.00%
Return on Equity %		.07%	.07%	.06%	.02%	.05%
Debt to Equity		0.929	0.996	1.012	1.085	1.138

CONTACT INFORMATION:
Phone: 704 386-5681 Fax:
Toll-Free: 800-432-1000
Address: 100 N. Tryon St., Charlotte, NC 28255 United States

STOCK TICKER/OTHER:
Stock Ticker: BAC Exchange: NYS
Employees: 204,000 Fiscal Year Ends: 12/31
Parent Company:

SALARIES/BONUSES:
Top Exec. Salary: $833,333 Bonus: $11,250,000
Second Exec. Salary: $1,250,000 Bonus: $7,700,000

OTHER THOUGHTS:
Estimated Female Officers or Directors: 8
Hot Spot for Advancement for Women/Minorities: Y

Sales, profits and employees may be estimates. Financial information, benefits and other data can change quickly and may vary from those stated here.

Bank of New York Mellon Corporation

www.bnymellon.com

NAIC Code: 522110

TYPES OF BUSINESS:
Asset Management & Securities Services
Investment & Wealth Management
Private Banking
Shareowner Services
Broker-Dealer Services
Issuer Services
Treasury Services

BRANDS/DIVISIONS/AFFILIATES:
Bank of New York Mellon (The)
BNY Mellon National Association
Bank of New York Mellon Trust Company, NA (The)
BNY Mellon Trust of Delaware
BNY Mellon Investment Servicing Trust Co
BNY Mellon Trust Company of Illinois
Pershing LLC

CONTACTS: Note: Officers with more than one job title may be intentionally listed here more than once.
Lester Owens, Sr. VP
Roman Regelman, Other Corporate Officer
Hani Kablawi, CEO, Divisional
Francis Salla, CEO, Divisional
Mitchell Harris, CEO, Divisional
Thomas Gibbons, CEO, Divisional
Charles Scharf, CEO
Michael Santomassimo, CFO
Kurtis Kurimsky, Chief Accounting Officer
Bridget Engle, Chief Information Officer
James Wiener, Chief Risk Officer
J. Mccarthy, General Counsel
Akash Shah, Other Corporate Officer
Monique Herena, Other Exec. Officer

GROWTH PLANS/SPECIAL FEATURES:

Bank of New York Mellon Corporation (BNYM) is a global investment company providing asset management and securities services for individual investors, institutions and corporations in 35 countries and more than 100 markets. In addition, BNYM offers financial solutions for individuals, including investment and wealth management, private banking and shareowner services. The company works with consultants and advisors to help them select the services that best meet their customers' needs. The firm has two principal banking subsidiaries: The Bank of New York Mellon and BNY Mellon, National Association (NA), which provide trust and custody activities, investment management services, banking services and various securities-related activities. Additionally, the firm has four other U.S. bank and/or trust company subsidiaries concentrating on trust products and services across the nation: The Bank of New York Mellon Trust Company NA, BNY Mellon Trust of Delaware, BNY Mellon Investment Servicing Trust Company and BNY Mellon Trust Company of Illinois. Most of the asset management businesses are direct or indirect non-bank subsidiaries of BNY Mellon. Through Pershing, LLC, the firm offers broker-dealer and advisor services. Pershing is a provider of clearing, execution and financial business solutions to institutional and retail financial organizations and independent registered investment advisors. BNYM's issuer service offerings include global corporate trust services, depositary receipt services and shareowner services. The company also offers treasury services. BNYM has approximately $1.8 trillion in assets under management and $35.5 trillion in assets under administration or custody. Customers include corporations, foundations, governments, unions, endowments, mutual funds and high-net-worth individuals.

Employees are offered medical, vision and dental health plans; life insurance; and an array of retirement plans varying by location.

FINANCIAL DATA: Note: Data for latest year may not have been available at press time.

In U.S. $	2018	2017	2016	2015	2014	2013
Revenue	15,986,000,000	15,124,000,000	14,832,000,000	14,813,000,000	15,264,000,000	14,548,000,000
R&D Expense						
Operating Income						
Operating Margin %						
SGA Expense	6,373,000,000	6,201,000,000	5,978,000,000	6,104,000,000	6,113,000,000	6,336,000,000
Net Income	4,266,000,000	4,090,000,000	3,547,000,000	3,158,000,000	2,567,000,000	2,111,000,000
Operating Cash Flow	5,996,000,000	4,641,000,000	6,246,000,000	4,127,000,000	4,484,000,000	-642,000,000
Capital Expenditure	1,108,000,000	1,197,000,000	825,000,000	601,000,000	791,000,000	609,000,000
EBITDA						
Return on Assets %		.01%	.01%	.01%	.01%	.01%
Return on Equity %		.11%	.10%	.09%	.07%	.06%
Debt to Equity		0.742	0.694	0.607	0.565	0.552

CONTACT INFORMATION:
Phone: 212 495-1784   Fax:
Toll-Free:
Address: 240 Greenwich St., New York, NY 10286 United States

SALARIES/BONUSES:
Top Exec. Salary: $1,250,000   Bonus: $
Second Exec. Salary: $650,000   Bonus: $

STOCK TICKER/OTHER:
Stock Ticker: BK
Employees: 52,000
Parent Company:

Exchange: NYS
Fiscal Year Ends: 12/31

OTHER THOUGHTS:
Estimated Female Officers or Directors: 6
Hot Spot for Advancement for Women/Minorities: Y

Sales, profits and employees may be estimates. Financial information, benefits and other data can change quickly and may vary from those stated here.

Plunkett Research, Ltd. 155

Baxter International Inc

www.baxter.com

NAIC Code: 339100

TYPES OF BUSINESS:
Medical Equipment Manufacturing
Supplies-Intravenous & Renal Dialysis Systems
Medication Delivery Products & IV Fluids
Biopharmaceutical Products
Plasma Collection & Processing
Vaccines
Software
Contract Research

BRANDS/DIVISIONS/AFFILIATES:
RECOTHROM
PREVELEAK

CONTACTS:
Note: Officers with more than one job title may be intentionally listed here more than once.

Jose Almeida, CEO
James Saccaro, CFO
Brian Stevens, Chief Accounting Officer
Sean Martin, General Counsel
Andrew Frye, President, Geographical
Giuseppe Accogli, President, Geographical
Cristiano Franzi, President, Geographical
Scott Pleau, Senior VP, Divisional
Jeanne Mason, Senior VP, Divisional

GROWTH PLANS/SPECIAL FEATURES:

Baxter International, Inc., through its subsidiaries, provides a broad portfolio of essential healthcare products. These offerings include: acute and chronic dialysis therapies; sterile intravenous (IV) solutions; infusion systems and devices; parenteral nutrition therapies; inhaled anesthetics; generic injectable pharmaceuticals; and surgical hemostat and sealant products. In addition, Baxter's renal portfolio addresses the needs of patients with kidney failure or kidney disease. This portfolio includes innovative technologies and therapies for peritoneal dialysis, in-center and home hemodialysis, continuous renal replacement therapy, multi-organ extracorporeal support therapy, and additional dialysis services. Baxter's scientists are currently pursuing a range of next-generation monitors, dialyzers, devices, dialysis solutions and connectivity technology for home patients. Baxter manufactures its products in over 20 countries, and sells them in more than 100 countries. The majority of the firm's revenues (approximately 60%) are generated outside the U.S., with an international presence including operations in Europe (Eastern and Central Europe), the Middle East, Africa, Asia-Pacific, Latin America and Canada. Each of these regions provide a wide range of essential healthcare products across the company's entire portfolio. Baxter maintains approximately 50 manufacturing facilities worldwide. In March 2018, the firm acquired two hemostat and sealant products from Mallinckrodt plc: RECOTHROM, a stand-alone recombinant thrombin; and PREVELEAK, a surgical sealant used in vascular reconstruction.

FINANCIAL DATA:
Note: Data for latest year may not have been available at press time.

In U.S. $	2018	2017	2016	2015	2014	2013
Revenue	11,127,000,000	10,561,000,000	10,163,000,000	9,968,000,000	16,671,000,000	15,259,000,000
R&D Expense	655,000,000	617,000,000	647,000,000	603,000,000	1,421,000,000	1,246,000,000
Operating Income	1,599,000,000	1,258,000,000	724,000,000	449,000,000	2,707,000,000	2,668,000,000
Operating Margin %		.12%	.07%	.05%	.16%	.17%
SGA Expense	2,617,000,000	2,587,000,000	2,739,000,000	3,094,000,000	4,029,000,000	3,681,000,000
Net Income	1,624,000,000	717,000,000	4,965,000,000	968,000,000	2,497,000,000	2,012,000,000
Operating Cash Flow	2,096,000,000	1,837,000,000	1,654,000,000	1,647,000,000	3,215,000,000	3,198,000,000
Capital Expenditure	681,000,000	634,000,000	719,000,000	911,000,000	1,898,000,000	1,525,000,000
EBITDA	2,571,000,000	2,063,000,000	5,843,000,000	1,333,000,000	3,611,000,000	3,527,000,000
Return on Assets %		.04%	.27%	.04%	.10%	.09%
Return on Equity %		.08%	.58%	.11%	.30%	.26%
Debt to Equity		0.385	0.335	0.445	0.937	0.96

CONTACT INFORMATION:
Phone: 847 948-2000   Fax: 847 948-2964
Toll-Free: 800-422-9837
Address: 1 Baxter Pkwy., Deerfield, IL 60015 United States

STOCK TICKER/OTHER:
Stock Ticker: BAX
Employees: 48,000
Parent Company:

Exchange: NYS
Fiscal Year Ends: 12/31

SALARIES/BONUSES:
Top Exec. Salary: $1,300,000   Bonus: $
Second Exec. Salary: $714,485   Bonus: $

OTHER THOUGHTS:
Estimated Female Officers or Directors: 6
Hot Spot for Advancement for Women/Minorities: Y

Sales, profits and employees may be estimates. Financial information, benefits and other data can change quickly and may vary from those stated here.

Baylor Scott & White Health

www.bswhealth.com

NAIC Code: 622110

TYPES OF BUSINESS:
General Medical and Surgical Hospitals
Long-Term Care
Retirement & Nursing Homes
Retail Pharmacies
Rehabilitation Services

BRANDS/DIVISIONS/AFFILIATES:
Baylor Health Care System
Scott & White Healthcare
MyBSWHealth
FollowMyHealth

CONTACTS:
Note: Officers with more than one job title may be intentionally listed here more than once.

James H. (Jim) Hinton, CEO
Pete McCanna, Pres.
Penny Cermak, CFO
Nikki Moll, Sr. VP-Mktg. & Communications
John Lacy, Chief Human Resources Officer
Matthew Chambers, CIO
Ross McKnight, Chmn.

GROWTH PLANS/SPECIAL FEATURES:
Baylor Scott & White Health is a non-profit healthcare system in Texas, and born from the 2013 combination of Baylor Health Care System and Scott & White Healthcare. Today, Baylor Scott & White includes 50 hospitals, more than 1,000 patient care sites and over 7,800 active physicians. The firm provides full-range, inpatient, outpatient, rehabilitation and emergency medical services, serving more than 7.4 million patients each year. Specialties include allergy, anesthesiology, back and neck care, behavioral and psychological health, breast imaging, cancer care, dentistry, diabetes, ear/nose/throat, genetics, heart/vascular, hospice, infectious diseases, kidney disease, lung care, men's health, neuroscience, pediatric care, pharmacy, rheumatology, sleep disorders, surgical services, transplants, urology, weight loss surgery and more. Appointments can be made by phone and online, and patient registration and billing can also be completed online. MyBSWHealth and FollowMyHealth enable patients to access their personal health records, set or change appointments, view test results and communicate with providers from any computer, tablet or smartphone device. Insurance products are available including a variety of health plans as well as dental and life insurance.

FINANCIAL DATA:
Note: Data for latest year may not have been available at press time.

In U.S. $	2018	2017	2016	2015	2014	2013
Revenue	994,075,691	946,738,753	938,248,557	877,345,140		
R&D Expense						
Operating Income						
Operating Margin %						
SGA Expense						
Net Income		-16,448,684	7,205,412	-17,805,755		
Operating Cash Flow						
Capital Expenditure						
EBITDA						
Return on Assets %						
Return on Equity %						
Debt to Equity						

CONTACT INFORMATION:
Phone: 254-724-2111   Fax:
Toll-Free: 844-279-3627
Address: 3500 Gaston Ave., Dallas, TX 75246-2017 United States

STOCK TICKER/OTHER:
Stock Ticker: Nonprofit   Exchange:
Employees: 47,000   Fiscal Year Ends:
Parent Company:

SALARIES/BONUSES:
Top Exec. Salary: $ Bonus: $
Second Exec. Salary: $ Bonus: $

OTHER THOUGHTS:
Estimated Female Officers or Directors:
Hot Spot for Advancement for Women/Minorities:

Sales, profits and employees may be estimates. Financial information, benefits and other data can change quickly and may vary from those stated here.

BB&T Corporation

www.bbt.com

NAIC Code: 522110

TYPES OF BUSINESS:
Banking
Mortgages
Consumer Loans
Commercial Loans
Investment Services
Securities Lending
Insurance
Leasing

BRANDS/DIVISIONS/AFFILIATES:
Branch Bank and Trust Company
BB&T Equipment Finance Corporation
BB&T Investment Services Inc
BB&T Insurance Services Inc
CRC Insurance Services Inc
Crump Life Insurance Services Inc
BB&T Commercial Equipment Capital Corp
McGriff Seibels & Williams Inc

CONTACTS:
Note: Officers with more than one job title may be intentionally listed here more than once.

Kelly King, CEO
W. Bradley, Other Corporate Officer
Daryl Bible, CFO
William Yates, Chairman, Subsidiary
Cynthia Powell, Chief Accounting Officer
Jimmy Godwin, Chief Credit Officer
Barbara Duck, Chief Information Officer
Clarke Starnes, Chief Risk Officer
Christopher Henson, COO
Robert Johnson, General Counsel
Donta Wilson, Other Executive Officer
Brantley Standridge, President, Divisional
David Weaver, President, Divisional

GROWTH PLANS/SPECIAL FEATURES:

BB&T Corporation is a financial holding company that conducts most of its operations through its commercial bank subsidiary, Branch Bank and Trust Company, and other nonbank subsidiaries. Services include those for community banking, residential mortgage banking, dealer financial services, specialized lending, insurance services and financial services. BB&T's largest subsidiary, Branch Bank, provides banking and trust services for retail and commercial clients including small and mid-size businesses, public agencies, local governments and individuals, through 2,049 offices. Branch Bank's principal operating subsidiaries include: BB&T Equipment Finance Corporation, providing loan and lease financing to commercial and small businesses; BB&T Investment Services, Inc., offering non-deposit investment alternatives; BB&T Insurance Services, Inc., offering property and casualty, life, health, employee benefits, commercial general liability, surety, title and other insurance products; CRC Insurance Services, Inc., a nationwide wholesale insurance broker; Grandbridge Real Estate Capital, LLC which arranges and services commercial mortgage loans; Crump Life Insurance Services, Inc., a nationwide wholesale insurance broker; BB&T Commercial Equipment Capital Corp., providing branch banking and trust options; and McGriff, Seibels & Williams, Inc., providing insurance products on an agency basis to large commercial clients. BB&T's non-bank subsidiaries include: BB&T Securities, LLC, a registered investment banking and full-service brokerage firm; Regional Acceptance Corporation, specializing in indirect financing for consumer purchases of primarily mid-model and late-model used automobiles; and Sterling Capital Management, LLC, providing a full range of investment strategies, including domestic and international equity, alternative investment products and strategies and fixed income investing. In mid-2018, BB&T acquired Regions Insurance Group from Regions Financial Corporation. In 2019, the firm announced plans to acquire SunTrust Banks, Inc. for about $28.1 billion in stock, and to rename itself Truist Financial Corp.

Employee benefits include 401(k) and pension options; medical, vision and dental coverage; disability, life and AD&D insurance; health savings account; and wellness program.

FINANCIAL DATA:
Note: Data for latest year may not have been available at press time.

In U.S. $	2018	2017	2016	2015	2014	2013
Revenue	11,558,000,000	11,317,000,000	10,935,000,000	9,863,999,000	9,501,000,000	9,846,000,000
R&D Expense						
Operating Income						
Operating Margin %						
SGA Expense	4,851,000,000	4,676,000,000	4,661,000,000	4,150,000,000	3,918,000,000	3,887,000,000
Net Income	3,237,000,000	2,394,000,000	2,426,000,000	2,084,000,000	2,151,000,000	1,679,000,000
Operating Cash Flow	4,349,000,000	4,635,000,000	2,672,000,000	2,915,000,000	3,258,000,000	5,339,000,000
Capital Expenditure						
EBITDA						
Return on Assets %		.01%	.01%	.01%	.01%	.01%
Return on Equity %		.08%	.09%	.08%	.10%	.08%
Debt to Equity		0.889	0.819	0.962	1.073	1.066

CONTACT INFORMATION:
Phone: 336 733-2000   Fax:
Toll-Free: 800-226-5228
Address: 200 W. 2nd St., Winston-Salem, NC 27101 United States

SALARIES/BONUSES:
Top Exec. Salary: $1,091,125   Bonus: $
Second Exec. Salary: $710,500   Bonus: $

STOCK TICKER/OTHER:
Stock Ticker: BBT   Exchange: NYS
Employees: 37,500   Fiscal Year Ends: 12/31
Parent Company:

OTHER THOUGHTS:
Estimated Female Officers or Directors: 3
Hot Spot for Advancement for Women/Minorities: Y

BBDO Worldwide

NAIC Code: 541810

www.bbdo.com

TYPES OF BUSINESS:
Advertising Agency
Marketing Services
Communications Services

BRANDS/DIVISIONS/AFFILIATES:
Omnicom Group Inc
Proximity Worldwide

CONTACTS:
Note: Officers with more than one job title may be intentionally listed here more than once.

Andrew Robertson, CEO
St. John Walsh, Exec. VP
John Osborn, CEO/Pres., BBDO New York
Chris Thomas, Chmn.

GROWTH PLANS/SPECIAL FEATURES:

BBDO Worldwide is the lead agency network of the Omnicom Group, Inc. and one of the largest agency networks worldwide. The firm provides advertising, marketing and communications planning and execution through an extensive network of 289 offices in 81 countries across the globe. The company's network is structured geographically, and includes North America, with offices in Canada and the U.S.; Middle East & Africa, with offices in Egypt, Kenya, Kuwait, Lebanon, Nigeria, Saudi Arabia, South Africa, Tunisia, Turkey and the United Arab Emirates; Asia, with offices in Bangladesh, China, Hong Kong, India, Indonesia, Japan, Kazakhstan, Korea, Malaysia, Pakistan, Philippines, Singapore, Sri Lanka, Taiwan, Thailand and Vietnam; Latin America, with offices in Argentina, Bolivia, Brazil, Chile, Colombia, Costa Rica, Dominican Republic, Ecuador, El Salvador, Guatemala, Honduras, Mexico, Nicaragua, Peru, Puerto Rico and Venezuela; Europe, with offices in Austria, Belgium, Bulgaria, Croatia, Cyprus, Czech Republic, Estonia, France, Germany, Great Britain, Greece, Ireland, Israel, Italy, Lithuania, Macedonia, Netherlands, Poland, Portugal, Russia, Serbia, Slovak Republic, Spain, Sweden, Switzerland and Ukraine; and Australia and New Zealand. Within these geographic arms, the lead agency's activity is supported by a range of subsidiary regional agencies that possess strategic expertise and long-standing histories within those markets. Proximity Worldwide, BBDO's spun-off global customer relationship and direct marketing network, provides additional support. A select number of clients utilize BBDO's services on a global basis. The company's current clients include The Economist, VISA, Foot Locker, GE, Bacardi, Hungry Jack's, Macy's and Pedigree, among many others. The agency is well-established in developing and delivering campaigns in television, radio, print and interactive and new media formats.

FINANCIAL DATA:
Note: Data for latest year may not have been available at press time.

In U.S. $	2018	2017	2016	2015	2014	2013
Revenue	2,821,500,000	2,745,000,000	2,636,000,000	2,250,000,000		
R&D Expense						
Operating Income						
Operating Margin %						
SGA Expense						
Net Income						
Operating Cash Flow						
Capital Expenditure						
EBITDA						
Return on Assets %						
Return on Equity %						
Debt to Equity						

CONTACT INFORMATION:
Phone: 212-459-5000 Fax:
Toll-Free:
Address: 1285 Ave. of the Americas, New York, NY 10019 United States

STOCK TICKER/OTHER:
Stock Ticker: Subsidiary   Exchange:
Employees: 15,000   Fiscal Year Ends: 12/31
Parent Company: Omnicom Group Inc

SALARIES/BONUSES:
Top Exec. Salary: $ Bonus: $
Second Exec. Salary: $ Bonus: $

OTHER THOUGHTS:
Estimated Female Officers or Directors:
Hot Spot for Advancement for Women/Minorities:

Bechtel Group Inc

www.bechtel.com

NAIC Code: 237000

TYPES OF BUSINESS:
Heavy Construction
Civic Engineering
Outsourcing
Financial Services
Atomic Propulsion Systems Engineering
Airport Construction
Electric Power Plant Construction
Nuclear Power Plant Construction

BRANDS/DIVISIONS/AFFILIATES:

CONTACTS: Note: Officers with more than one job title may be intentionally listed here more than once.
Brendan Bechtel, CEO
Jack Futcher, COO
Catherine Hunt Ryan, CFO
Justin Zaccaria, Chief Human Resources Officer
Michael Bailey, General Counsel
Charlene Wheeless, Head-Corp. Affairs
Anette Sparks, Controller
Steve Katzman, Pres., Asia
Jose Ivo, Pres., Americas
Charlene Wheeless, Head-Sustainability Svcs.
Michael Wilkinson, Head-Risk Mgmt.
Brendan Bechtel, Chmn.
David Welch, Pres., EMEA

GROWTH PLANS/SPECIAL FEATURES:

Bechtel Group, Inc. is one of the world's largest engineering companies. The privately-owned firm offers engineering, construction and project management services, with a broad project portfolio including road and rail systems, airports and seaports, nuclear power plants, petrochemical facilities, mines, defense and aerospace facilities, environmental cleanup projects, telecommunication networks, pipelines and oil fields development. Bechtel has four main business units: infrastructure; nuclear, security and environmental; oil, gas and chemicals; and mining and metals. The infrastructure segment oversees projects pertaining to hydroelectric power plants, ports, harbors, bridges, airports and airport systems, commercial and light-industrial buildings, wireless sites, railroads, rapid-transit and rail systems. The nuclear, security and environmental includes missile defense infrastructure, scientific and national security facility operations, environmental restoration and recovery, commercial and U.S. navy nuclear reactor services and chemical weapons dematerialization projects. The oil, gas and chemicals segment offers integrated design, procurement, construction and project management of oil, gas and natural gas facilities. The mining and metal segment encompasses mining and metal projects across six continents, including procurement, construction, engineering and solutions for mining of coal, ferrous, industrial and nonferrous metals. The firm has participated in such notable endeavors as the construction of the Hoover Dam, the creation of the Bay Area Rapid Transit system in San Francisco, the massive James Bay Hydroelectric Project in Quebec and the quelling of oil field fires in Kuwait following the Persian Gulf War. Bechtel also constructed the Trans-Alaska Oil Pipeline, covering 800 miles between the Prudhoe Bay oil field and Valdez.

The firm offers employees benefits including medical, dental and vision coverage; short- and long-term disability; flexible spending accounts; an employee assistance program; life insurance; and a 401(k) plan.

FINANCIAL DATA: Note: Data for latest year may not have been available at press time.

In U.S. $	2018	2017	2016	2015	2014	2013
Revenue	25,500,000,000	25,900,000,000	32,900,000,000	32,300,000,000	37,200,000,000	39,400,000,000
R&D Expense						
Operating Income						
Operating Margin %						
SGA Expense						
Net Income						
Operating Cash Flow						
Capital Expenditure						
EBITDA						
Return on Assets %						
Return on Equity %						
Debt to Equity						

CONTACT INFORMATION:
Phone: 415-768-1234   Fax: 415-768-9038
Toll-Free:
Address: 50 Beale St., San Francisco, CA 94105-1895 United States

STOCK TICKER/OTHER:
Stock Ticker: Private
Employees: 58,000
Parent Company:

Exchange:
Fiscal Year Ends: 12/31

SALARIES/BONUSES:
Top Exec. Salary: $ Bonus: $
Second Exec. Salary: $ Bonus: $

OTHER THOUGHTS:
Estimated Female Officers or Directors: 4
Hot Spot for Advancement for Women/Minorities: Y

Sales, profits and employees may be estimates. Financial information, benefits and other data can change quickly and may vary from those stated here.

Becton, Dickinson and Company

www.bd.com

NAIC Code: 339100

TYPES OF BUSINESS:
Medical Equipment-Injection/Infusion
Drug Delivery Systems
Infusion Therapy Products
Diabetes Care Products
Surgical Products
Microbiology Products
Diagnostic Products
Consulting Services

BRANDS/DIVISIONS/AFFILIATES:
BD Medical
BD Life Sciences
BD Interventional
V Muller

CONTACTS:
Note: Officers with more than one job title may be intentionally listed here more than once.

Vincent Forlenza, CEO
Roland Goette, Executive VP
Christopher Reidy, CFO
Charles Bodner, Chief Accounting Officer
James Borzi, Executive VP, Divisional
Betty Larson, Executive VP, Divisional
Samrat Khichi, Executive VP
Alberto Mas, Executive VP
Patrick Kaltenbach, Executive VP
Simon Campion, Executive VP
James Lim, Executive VP
Thomas Polen, President
Gary DeFazio, Secretary

GROWTH PLANS/SPECIAL FEATURES:

Becton, Dickinson and Company (BD) is a global medical technology company engaged in the development, manufacture and sale of medical supplies, devices, laboratory equipment and diagnostic products. These offerings are primarily used by healthcare institutions, life science researchers, clinical laboratories, the pharmaceutical industry and the general public. The company operates in three worldwide business segments: BD Medical, BD Life Sciences and BD Interventional. BD Medical's principal product lines include a broad range of medication delivery solutions, medication maangement solutions, diabetes care solutions and pharmaceutical systems. BD Life Sciences offers products for safe collection and transport of diagnostics specimens, and instruments and reagent systems to detect infectious diseases, healthcare-associated infections and cancers. This division produces research and clinical tools that facilitate the study of cells, and the components of cells, to gain a better understanding of normal and disease processes. This information is used to aid the discovery and development of new drugs and vaccines, among other purposes. Last, the BD Interventional segment provides vascular, urology, oncology and surgical specialty products intended to be used once and then discarded or are either temporarily or permanently implanted. V. Muller-trademarked surgical laparoscopic instrumentation products are an exception to these temporary offerings. Manufacturing operations outside the U.S. include Bosnia/Herzegovina, Brazil, Canada, China, Dominican Republic, France, Germany, Hungary, India, Ireland, Israel, Italy, Japan, Malaysia, Mexico, Netherlands, Singapore, Spain and the U.K. Products are marketed and distributed in the U.S. and internationally through distribution channels, and directly to end-users by BD and independent sales representatives.

The firm offers employees medical, dental, vision and prescription drug coverage, as well as a variety of employee assistance programs and perks.

FINANCIAL DATA:
Note: Data for latest year may not have been available at press time.

In U.S. $	2018	2017	2016	2015	2014	2013
Revenue	15,983,000,000	12,093,000,000	12,483,000,000	10,282,000,000	8,446,000,000	8,054,000,000
R&D Expense	1,006,000,000	774,000,000	828,000,000	632,000,000	550,000,000	494,000,000
Operating Income	2,241,000,000	1,833,000,000	2,158,000,000	1,500,000,000	1,606,000,000	1,255,000,000
Operating Margin %		.15%	.17%	.15%	.19%	.16%
SGA Expense	4,015,000,000	2,925,000,000	3,005,000,000	2,563,000,000	2,145,000,000	2,422,000,000
Net Income	311,000,000	1,100,000,000	976,000,000	695,000,000	1,185,000,000	1,293,000,000
Operating Cash Flow	2,865,000,000	2,550,000,000	2,559,000,000	1,730,000,000	1,746,000,000	1,505,000,000
Capital Expenditure	895,000,000	727,000,000	718,000,000	633,000,000	653,000,000	588,000,000
EBITDA	3,857,000,000	2,585,000,000	2,576,000,000	2,001,000,000	2,219,000,000	1,849,000,000
Return on Assets %		.03%	.04%	.04%	.10%	.11%
Return on Equity %		.10%	.13%	.11%	.23%	.28%
Debt to Equity		1.442	1.382	1.587	0.746	0.746

CONTACT INFORMATION:
Phone: 201 847-6800 Fax:
Toll-Free: 800-284-6845
Address: 1 Becton Dr., Franklin Lakes, NJ 07417 United States

STOCK TICKER/OTHER:
Stock Ticker: BDX Exchange: NYS
Employees: 50,928 Fiscal Year Ends: 09/30
Parent Company:

SALARIES/BONUSES:
Top Exec. Salary: $216,667 Bonus: $2,000,000
Second Exec. Salary: $450,000 Bonus: $1,051,343

OTHER THOUGHTS:
Estimated Female Officers or Directors: 6
Hot Spot for Advancement for Women/Minorities: Y

Sales, profits and employees may be estimates. Financial information, benefits and other data can change quickly and may vary from those stated here.

Bed Bath & Beyond Inc

NAIC Code: 442299

www.bedbathandbeyond.com

TYPES OF BUSINESS:
Linens & Housewares, Retail
Small Appliances
Home Accessories
Health & Beauty Care
Baby & Toddler Merchandise

BRANDS/DIVISIONS/AFFILIATES:
Bed Bath & Beyond
buybuy BABY
Christmas Tree Shops
Cost Plus World Market
One Kings Lane
PersonalizationMall.com
Wamsutta
Artisanal Kitchen Supply

CONTACTS: *Note: Officers with more than one job title may be intentionally listed here more than once.*

Robyn D'Elia, CFO
Patrick Gaston, Chairman of the Board
Susan Lattmann, Chief Administrative Officer
Warren Eisenberg, Co-Chairman Emeritus
Leonard Feinstein, Co-Chairman Emeritus
Eugene Castagna, COO
Matthew Fiorilli, Senior VP, Divisional

GROWTH PLANS/SPECIAL FEATURES:

Bed Bath & Beyond, Inc. (BBB) is one of the nation's largest operators of domestic superstores, with approximately 1,552 stores in 50 states as well as Washington D.C., Canada and Puerto Rico. In connection with BBB's retail services, its service marks include: Bed Bath & Beyond, buybuy BABY, Christmas Tree Shops, and That!, Harmon, Face Values, Cost Plus, World Market, Cost Plus World Market, Of a Kind, One Kings Lane, PersonalizationMall.com, PMall, Chef Central and Decorist. Together, these stores sell a wide assortment of domestic merchandise and home furnishings. Domestic merchandise includes categories such as bed linens and related items, bath items and kitchen textiles. Home furnishing include categories such as kitchen and tabletop items, fine tabletop, basic housewares, general home furnishings, consumables and certain juvenile products. Proprietary brands of BBB include Wamsutta, Real Simple, SALT and Artisanal Kitchen Supply. On an ongoing basis, BBB tests new merchandise categories and adjusts the categories of merchandise carried in-store and online, and may add new product categories or expand its merchandise assortment as appropriate. BBB purchases its merchandise in the U.S., the majority from domestic sources and the balance from importers. It purchases a small amount of merchandise directly from overseas sources. The company buys from approximately 11,100 suppliers.

FINANCIAL DATA: *Note: Data for latest year may not have been available at press time.*

In U.S. $	2018	2017	2016	2015	2014	2013
Revenue	12,349,300,000	12,215,760,000	12,103,890,000	11,881,180,000	11,503,960,000	
R&D Expense						
Operating Income	761,321,000	1,135,210,000	1,414,903,000	1,554,293,000	1,614,587,000	
Operating Margin %	.06%	.09%	.12%	.13%	.14%	
SGA Expense	3,681,694,000	3,441,140,000	3,205,407,000	3,065,486,000	2,950,995,000	
Net Income	424,858,000	685,108,000	841,489,000	957,474,000	1,022,290,000	
Operating Cash Flow	859,689,000	1,041,788,000	1,012,184,000	1,185,848,000	1,383,186,000	
Capital Expenditure	375,793,000	373,574,000	328,395,000	330,637,000	317,180,000	
EBITDA	1,074,428,000	1,426,124,000	1,688,850,000	1,793,486,000	1,833,396,000	
Return on Assets %	.06%	.10%	.13%	.15%	.16%	
Return on Equity %	.15%	.26%	.32%	.29%	.25%	
Debt to Equity	0.517	0.549	0.586	0.547		

CONTACT INFORMATION:
Phone: 908 688-0888   Fax: 908 810-8813
Toll-Free: 800-462-3966
Address: 650 Liberty Ave., Union, NJ 07083 United States

SALARIES/BONUSES:
Top Exec. Salary: $6,048,851   Bonus: $
Second Exec. Salary: $3,582,885   Bonus: $

STOCK TICKER/OTHER:
Stock Ticker: BBBY   Exchange: NAS
Employees: 65,000   Fiscal Year Ends: 02/28
Parent Company:

OTHER THOUGHTS:
Estimated Female Officers or Directors: 1
Hot Spot for Advancement for Women/Minorities:

Sales, profits and employees may be estimates. Financial information, benefits and other data can change quickly and may vary from those stated here.

Belden Inc

www.belden.com

NAIC Code: 334417

TYPES OF BUSINESS:
Cable & Wire Connectors Manufacturing
Electronic Products
Broadcasting Equipment
Aerospace & Automotive Electronics
Enclosures

BRANDS/DIVISIONS/AFFILIATES:

CONTACTS:
Note: Officers with more than one job title may be intentionally listed here more than once.

John Stroup, CEO
Doug Zink, Chief Accounting Officer
Henk Derksen, CFO
Douglas Zink, Chief Accounting Officer
Dhrupad Trivedi, Chief Technology Officer
Roel Vestjens, Executive VP, Divisional
Glenn Pennycook, Executive VP, Divisional
Brian Anderson, General Counsel
Dean McKenna, Senior VP, Divisional
Ross Rosenberg, Senior VP, Divisional
Leo Kulmaczewski, Senior VP, Divisional
Paul Turner, Senior VP, Divisional

GROWTH PLANS/SPECIAL FEATURES:

Belden, Inc. is an innovative signal transmission solutions company operating through two business segments: enterprise solutions and industrial solutions. Enterprise solutions provides in-network infrastructure solutions, as well as cabling and connectivity solutions for broadcast, commercial audio/video and security applications. This division serves customers in markets such as healthcare, education, financial, government and corporate enterprises, as well as end-markets, including sport venues, broadcast studios and academic campuses and facilities. Enterprise product lines include copper cable and related connectivity solutions, fiber cable and related connectivity solutions, and racks and enclosures. These products are used in applications such as local area networks, data centers, access control and building automation. The industrial solutions segment provides high-performance networking components and machine connectivity products. These products include physical network and fieldbus infrastructure components and on-machine connectivity systems customized to end-user and original equipment manufacturer (OEM) needs. They are used in applications such as network and fieldbus infrastructure, sensor and actuator connectivity; and power, control and data transmission. Belden has manufacturing facilities in the U.S., and manufacturing and other operating facilities in Brazil, China, India, Japan, Mexico and St. Kitts, as well as in various countries in Europe. Nearly half of the firm's 2018 sales were to customers outside the U.S.

FINANCIAL DATA:
Note: Data for latest year may not have been available at press time.

In U.S. $	2018	2017	2016	2015	2014	2013
Revenue	2,585,368,000	2,388,643,000	2,356,672,000	2,309,222,000	2,308,265,000	2,069,193,000
R&D Expense	140,585,000	134,330,000	140,601,000	148,311,000	113,914,000	83,277,000
Operating Income	243,080,000	234,690,000	247,784,000	138,783,000	159,164,000	192,340,000
Operating Margin %		.10%	.11%	.06%	.07%	.09%
SGA Expense	525,918,000	461,022,000	494,224,000	527,288,000	487,945,000	378,009,000
Net Income	160,894,000	93,210,000	128,003,000	66,204,000	74,449,000	103,313,000
Operating Cash Flow	289,220,000	255,300,000	314,794,000	236,410,000	194,028,000	164,601,000
Capital Expenditure	97,847,000	64,261,000	53,974,000	54,969,000	45,459,000	40,209,000
EBITDA	391,712,000	384,340,000	393,377,000	289,125,000	265,864,000	294,595,000
Return on Assets %		.02%	.03%	.02%	.02%	.04%
Return on Equity %		.04%	.10%	.08%	.09%	.13%
Debt to Equity		1.088	1.109	2.124	2.187	1.631

CONTACT INFORMATION:
Phone: 314 854-8000
Fax: 314 854-8001
Toll-Free: 800-235-3361
Address: 1 N. Brentwood Blvd., 15/Fl, St. Louis, MO 63105 United States

STOCK TICKER/OTHER:
Stock Ticker: BDC
Employees: 8,400
Parent Company:

Exchange: NYS
Fiscal Year Ends: 12/31

SALARIES/BONUSES:
Top Exec. Salary: $893,750   Bonus: $
Second Exec. Salary: $570,221   Bonus: $

OTHER THOUGHTS:
Estimated Female Officers or Directors: 2
Hot Spot for Advancement for Women/Minorities: Y

Sales, profits and employees may be estimates. Financial information, benefits and other data can change quickly and may vary from those stated here.

Berkshire Hathaway Energy Company

www.berkshirehathawayenergyco.com/

NAIC Code: 221112

TYPES OF BUSINESS:

Utilities-Electricity & Natural Gas
Pipelines
Wind Generation
Hydroelectric Generation
Thermal Solar Generation
Real Estate Brokerage
Solar Power

BRANDS/DIVISIONS/AFFILIATES:

Berkshire Hathaway Inc
PacifiCorp
MidAmerican Energy Company
NV Energy Inc
Northern Powergrid
Northern Natural Gas Company
Kern River Gas Transmission Company
BHE Renewables

CONTACTS:
Note: Officers with more than one job title may be intentionally listed here more than once.

William J. Fehrman, CEO
Patrick J. Goodman, CFO
Maureen E. Sammon, Chief Admin. Officer
Douglas L. Anderson, General Counsel
Gregory Edward Abel, Chmn.

GROWTH PLANS/SPECIAL FEATURES:

Berkshire Hathaway Energy Company generates, transmits, stores, distributes and supplies energy through its subsidiaries to roughly 8.8 million customers. The company has 10 primary subsidiaries. PacifiCorp serves roughly 1.9 million customers, operating in two business units: Rocky Mountain Power, which delivers electricity in Wyoming, Utah and Idaho; and Pacific Power, delivering electricity in Oregon, Washington and California. MidAmerican Energy Company generates, transmits and sells electricity to 1.6 million customers, supplying natural gas to customers in Illinois, Nebraska, Iowa and South Dakota. NV Energy, Inc. has approximately 1.36 million customers in Nevada, serving approximately 90% of the state with electricity. Northern Powergrid offers 3.9 million users electricity in the Northeastern part of England. Northern Natural Gas Company owns a 14,700-mile interstate natural gas pipeline system extending from Texas to the upper Midwest, serving 81 utility companies. Kern River Gas Transmission Company owns 1,700 miles of interstate pipeline and delivers natural gas to Nevada, Utah and California. BHE Renewables' 4,083 megawatts total capacity of owned and under construction clean energy includes: 1,536 MW solar; 1,365 MW wind; 338 MW geothermal; and 138 MW hydro. AltaLink is the largest regulated transmission company with an 81,850-square-mile (212,000 square kilometers) service area, supplying electricity to more than 85% of the population in Alberta. BHE U.S. Transmission provides transmission solutions for wholesale customers, owning more than 1,000 miles of lines. Last, HomeServices of America, Inc. is a leading U.S. residential real estate brokerage firm, with over 840 sales offices throughout the country. Berkshire Hathaway Energy is a wholly-owned subsidiary of Berkshire Hathaway, Inc.

The company offers employees medical, dental, vision, disability and life insurance; a 401(k) plan; a profit sharing plan; and various employee assistance programs.

FINANCIAL DATA:
Note: Data for latest year may not have been available at press time.

In U.S. $	2018	2017	2016	2015	2014	2013
Revenue	19,787,000,000	18,614,000,000	17,422,000,000	17,880,000,000	17,614,000,000	12,743,000,000
R&D Expense						
Operating Income						
Operating Margin %						
SGA Expense						
Net Income	2,591,000,000	2,910,000,000	2,570,000,000	2,400,000,000	2,711,000,000	1,806,000,000
Operating Cash Flow						
Capital Expenditure						
EBITDA						
Return on Assets %						
Return on Equity %						
Debt to Equity						

CONTACT INFORMATION:
Phone: 515-242-3022 Fax:
Toll-Free:
Address: 666 Grand Ave., Des Moines, IA 50306-0657 United States

STOCK TICKER/OTHER:
Stock Ticker: Subsidiary
Employees: 23,000
Parent Company: Berkshire Hathaway Inc

Exchange:
Fiscal Year Ends: 12/31

SALARIES/BONUSES:
Top Exec. Salary: $ Bonus: $
Second Exec. Salary: $ Bonus: $

OTHER THOUGHTS:
Estimated Female Officers or Directors: 1
Hot Spot for Advancement for Women/Minorities:

Berkshire Hathaway Inc (Holding Co)
www.berkshirehathaway.com

NAIC Code: 524126

TYPES OF BUSINESS:
Insurance--Property & Casualty, Specialty, Surety
Retail Operations
Foodservice Operations
Building Products & Services
Apparel & Footwear
Technology Training
Manufactured Housing & RVs
Business Jet Flexible Ownership Services

BRANDS/DIVISIONS/AFFILIATES:
GEICO Corporation
Berkshire Hathaway Reinsurance Group
Berkshire Hathaway Primary Group
Burlington Northern Santa Fe
Berkshire Hathaway Energy Company
Precision Castparts Corp
Clayton Homes Inc
McLane Company Inc

CONTACTS:
Note: Officers with more than one job title may be intentionally listed here more than once.

Warren Buffett, CEO
Marc Hamburg, CFO
Daniel Jaksich, Chief Accounting Officer
Charles Munger, Director
Gregory Abel, Director
Ajit Jain, Director

GROWTH PLANS/SPECIAL FEATURES:
Berkshire Hathaway, Inc. is a holding company that owns subsidiaries engaged in diverse business activities, most importantly insurance and reinsurance. Berkshire provides property and casualty insurance and reinsurance, as well as life, accident and health reinsurance, through U.S. and foreign businesses. The company conducts its insurance underwriting business through three subsidiary divisions. First, GEICO Corporation mainly provides private passenger auto insurance to individuals in all 50 U.S. states and Washington, D.C. Second, Berkshire Hathaway Reinsurance Group underwrites excess-of-loss and quota-share reinsurance for insurers and reinsurers. Third, Berkshire Hathaway Primary Group offers insurance for property and casualty. Other businesses and subsidiaries include, but are not limited to: Burlington Northern Santa Fe, which operates a leading railroad system in North America through BNSF Railway Company; Berkshire Hathaway Energy Company, a global energy company with subsidiaries that generate, transmit, store, distribute and supply energy; Precision Castparts Corp., which manufactures complex metal components and products and provides high-quality investment castings, forgings, fasteners/fastener systems and aerostructures for critical aerospace and power/energy applications; Clayton Homes, Inc., a housing company utilizing manufactured, modular and site build methods; McLane Company, Inc., which provides wholesale distribution services in all 50 states to customers that include convenience stores, discount retailers, wholesale clubs, drug stores, military bases, quick service restaurants and casual dining restaurants; FlightSafety International, Inc., a provider of professional aviation training services; XTRA Corporation, a transportation equipment lessor operating under the XTRA Lease brand name; and See's Candies, which produces boxed chocolates and other confectionery products, operating approximately 250 retail and discount stores primarily in California and other western states.

FINANCIAL DATA:
Note: Data for latest year may not have been available at press time.

In U.S. $	2018	2017	2016	2015	2014	2013
Revenue	225,382,000,000	242,137,000,000	223,604,000,000	210,821,000,000	194,673,000,000	182,150,000,000
R&D Expense						
Operating Income						
Operating Margin %						
SGA Expense	18,238,000,000	18,181,000,000	18,217,000,000	15,309,000,000	13,721,000,000	11,917,000,000
Net Income	4,021,000,000	44,940,000,000	24,074,000,000	24,083,000,000	19,872,000,000	19,476,000,000
Operating Cash Flow	37,400,000,000	45,776,000,000	32,535,000,000	31,491,000,000	32,010,000,000	27,704,000,000
Capital Expenditure	14,537,000,000	11,708,000,000	12,954,000,000	16,082,000,000	15,185,000,000	11,087,000,000
EBITDA						
Return on Assets %		.07%	.04%	.04%	.04%	.04%
Return on Equity %		.14%	.09%	.10%	.09%	.10%
Debt to Equity		0.223	0.352	0.322	0.33	0.321

CONTACT INFORMATION:
Phone: 402 346-1400   Fax: 402 346-3375
Toll-Free:
Address: 3555 Farnam St., Omaha, NE 68131 United States

SALARIES/BONUSES:
Top Exec. Salary: $16,000,000   Bonus: $2,000,000
Second Exec. Salary: $16,000,000   Bonus: $2,000,000

STOCK TICKER/OTHER:
Stock Ticker: BRK.A   Exchange: NYS
Employees: 367,700   Fiscal Year Ends: 12/31
Parent Company:

OTHER THOUGHTS:
Estimated Female Officers or Directors:

Hot Spot for Advancement for Women/Minorities:

Sales, profits and employees may be estimates. Financial information, benefits and other data can change quickly and may vary from those stated here.

Berry Global Group Inc

www.berryplastics.com

NAIC Code: 326100

TYPES OF BUSINESS:
Injection Molded Packaging
Open-Top Containers
Closures
Consumer Products
Plastic Housewares
Thermoforming

BRANDS/DIVISIONS/AFFILIATES:
Berry Global Inc

CONTACTS:
Note: Officers with more than one job title may be intentionally listed here more than once.

Thomas Salmon, CEO
Mark Miles, CFO
James Till, Chief Accounting Officer
Jason Greene, Chief Legal Officer
Curtis Begle, President, Divisional
Jean-Marc Galvez, President, Divisional
Michael Hill, President, Divisional

GROWTH PLANS/SPECIAL FEATURES:

Berry Global Group, Inc., operating through Berry Global, Inc., is a leading manufacturer of non-woven, flexible and rigid products that are used every day within the consumer and industrial end markets. Berry operates through manufacturing and distribution facilities in the U.S., Canada, Mexico, Belgium, France, Spain, the U.K., Italy, Germany, Brazil, Argentina, Colombia, Malaysia, India, China and the Netherlands. Berry operates through three business segments: engineered materials; health, hygiene and specialties; and consumer packaging. The engineered materials segment comprises the following product groups: stretch and shrink films, manufacturing both hand and machine-wrap stretch films and custom shrink films used to prepare products and packages for storage and shipping; converter films, manufacturing sealant and barrier films for flexible packaging converters companies; institutional can liners, manufacturing trash-can liners and food bags for offices, restaurants, schools, hospitals, hotels and other customer markets; tape products, manufacturing cloth and foil tape products; food and consumer films, manufacturing printed film products for the fresh bakery, tortilla, deli and frozen vegetable markets; retail bags, manufacturing polyethylene-based film products to end users in the retail markets; and PVC films, manufacturing polyvinyl chloride films used to wrap meats, poultry and produce. The health, hygiene and specialties segment comprises three product groups: health, manufacturing medical garment materials, surgical drapes, household cleaning wipes and face masks; hygiene, manufacturing components for baby diapers and other absorbent hygiene products; and specialty, manufacturing products and components for corrosion protection. Last, the consumer packaging segment manufactures containers, lightweight polypropylene cups and lids, child-resistant closures and overcaps, bottles, prescription vials and a line of extruded and laminate tubes. Berry's primary raw material is plastic resin, but other materials used include butyl rubber, adhesives, paper, linerboard, rayon, polyester fiber and foil.

FINANCIAL DATA:
Note: Data for latest year may not have been available at press time.

In U.S. $	2018	2017	2016	2015	2014	2013
Revenue	7,869,000,000	7,095,000,000	6,489,000,000	4,881,000,000	4,958,000,000	4,647,000,000
R&D Expense						
Operating Income	797,000,000	756,000,000	613,000,000	421,000,000	346,000,000	400,000,000
Operating Margin %		.11%	.09%	.09%	.07%	.09%
SGA Expense	480,000,000	494,000,000	531,000,000	357,000,000	320,000,000	307,000,000
Net Income	496,000,000	340,000,000	236,000,000	86,000,000	62,000,000	57,000,000
Operating Cash Flow	1,004,000,000	975,000,000	857,000,000	637,000,000	530,000,000	464,000,000
Capital Expenditure	336,000,000	269,000,000	288,000,000	180,000,000	215,000,000	239,000,000
EBITDA	1,274,000,000	1,239,000,000	1,124,000,000	663,000,000	646,000,000	670,000,000
Return on Assets %		.04%	.04%	.02%	.01%	.01%
Return on Equity %		.55%	2.91%			
Debt to Equity		5.578	26.358			

CONTACT INFORMATION:
Phone: 812 424-2904 Fax:
Toll-Free:
Address: 101 Oakley St., Evansville, IN 47710 United States

SALARIES/BONUSES:
Top Exec. Salary: $973,077 Bonus: $
Second Exec. Salary: $569,000 Bonus: $

STOCK TICKER/OTHER:
Stock Ticker: BERY
Employees: 24,000
Parent Company:

Exchange: NYS
Fiscal Year Ends: 09/26

OTHER THOUGHTS:
Estimated Female Officers or Directors:
Hot Spot for Advancement for Women/Minorities:

Sales, profits and employees may be estimates. Financial information, benefits and other data can change quickly and may vary from those stated here.

Best Buy Co Inc

NAIC Code: 443142

www.bestbuy.com

TYPES OF BUSINESS:
Consumer Electronics Stores
Retail Music & Video Sales
Personal Computers
Office Supplies
Cell Phones and Accessories
Appliances
Cameras
Consumer Electronics Installation & Service

BRANDS/DIVISIONS/AFFILIATES:
bestbuy.com
Best Buy Direct
Best Buy Express
Geek Squad
Magnolia
Pacific Kitchen and Home
bestbuy.ca
bestbuy.com.mx

CONTACTS:
Note: Officers with more than one job title may be intentionally listed here more than once.

Corie Barry, CEO
Hubert Joly, Chairman of the Board
Mathew Watson, Chief Accounting Officer
Todd Hartman, Chief Compliance Officer
Michael Mohan, COO
Brian Tilzer, Other Executive Officer
Kamy Scarlett, Other Executive Officer

GROWTH PLANS/SPECIAL FEATURES:

Best Buy Co., Inc. is a leading provider of technology products, services and solutions. The company offers these products and solutions through Best Buy stores, Geek Squad agents, eCommerce channels and mobile apps. Retail operations are located in the U.S., Canada and Mexico. Best Buy Co. operates its business through two segments: domestic and international. The domestic segment is comprised of the U.S. operations, including brand names such as Best Buy, bestbuy.com, Best Buy Direct, Best Buy Express, Geek Squad, GreatCall, Magnolia and Pacific Kitchen and Home. The international segment is comprised of all operations in Canada and Mexico, including brand names such as Best Buy, Best Buy Express, Geek Squad and the domain names bestbuy.ca and bestbuy.com.mx. Both segment's development of merchandise and service offerings, pricing and promotions, procurement and supply chain, online and mobile application operations, marketing and advertising and labor deployment across all channels are centrally managed. The company has field operations that support retail teams from corporate as well as regional office locations. Best Buy's merchandise and services consist of the following: consumer electronics, including digital imaging, health/fitness, home automation, home theater and portable audio devices; computing and mobile phones, including computers, laptops, tablets, eReaders, mobile phones, networking and wearables; entertainment, including drones, gaming hardware/software, movies, music, technology toys, virtual reality and other software; appliances, including dishwashers, laundry, ovens, refrigerators, blenders, coffee makers and much more; and services, including consultation, delivery, design, educational classes, installation, memberships, protection plans, repair, set-up and tech support.

Employee benefits include medical, dental, vision, life and disability insurance; 401(k); and various assistance programs.

FINANCIAL DATA:
Note: Data for latest year may not have been available at press time.

In U.S. $	2018	2017	2016	2015	2014	2013
Revenue	42,151,000,000	39,403,000,000	39,528,000,000	40,339,000,000	42,410,000,000	
R&D Expense						
Operating Income	1,853,000,000	1,893,000,000	1,573,000,000	1,455,000,000	1,299,000,000	
Operating Margin %	.04%	.05%	.04%	.04%	.03%	
SGA Expense	8,023,000,000	7,547,000,000	7,618,000,000	7,592,000,000	8,391,000,000	
Net Income	1,000,000,000	1,228,000,000	897,000,000	1,233,000,000	532,000,000	
Operating Cash Flow	2,141,000,000	2,545,000,000	1,322,000,000	1,935,000,000	1,094,000,000	
Capital Expenditure	688,000,000	582,000,000	649,000,000	561,000,000	547,000,000	
EBITDA	2,575,000,000	2,542,000,000	2,047,000,000	2,133,000,000	1,903,000,000	
Return on Assets %	.07%	.09%	.06%	.08%	.04%	
Return on Equity %	.24%	.27%	.19%	.27%	.13%	
Debt to Equity	0.225	0.281	0.306	0.316	0.404	

CONTACT INFORMATION:
Phone: 612 291-1000   Fax: 612 292-4001
Toll-Free:
Address: 7601 Penn Ave. S., Richfield, MN 55423 United States

SALARIES/BONUSES:
Top Exec. Salary: $1,275,000   Bonus: $
Second Exec. Salary: $892,308   Bonus: $

STOCK TICKER/OTHER:
Stock Ticker: BBY   Exchange: NYS
Employees: 125,500   Fiscal Year Ends: 02/28
Parent Company:

OTHER THOUGHTS:
Estimated Female Officers or Directors: 5
Hot Spot for Advancement for Women/Minorities: Y

Biogen Inc

NAIC Code: 325412

www.biogen.com

TYPES OF BUSINESS:
Drugs-Immunology, Neurology & Oncology
Autoimmune & Inflammatory Disease Treatments
Drugs-Multiple Sclerosis
Drugs-Cancer

BRANDS/DIVISIONS/AFFILIATES:
TECFIDERA
AVONEX
PLEGRIDY
SPINRAZA
FUMADERM
RITUXAN
GAZYVA
OCREVUS

CONTACTS:
Note: Officers with more than one job title may be intentionally listed here more than once.

Michel Vounatsos, CEO
Jeffrey Capello, CFO
Gregory Covino, Chief Accounting Officer
Alfred Sandrock, Chief Medical Officer
Stelios Papadopoulos, Director
Michael Ehlers, Executive VP, Divisional
Paul McKenzie, Executive VP, Divisional
Kenneth Dipietro, Executive VP, Divisional
Adriana Karaboutis, Executive VP, Divisional
Chirfi Guindo, Executive VP
Ginger Gregory, Executive VP
Susan Alexander, Executive VP

GROWTH PLANS/SPECIAL FEATURES:
Biogen, Inc. is a biotechnology company focused on discovering, developing, manufacturing and marketing therapies for people living with serious neurological and neurodegenerative diseases. The company's core growth areas in relation to these diseases include multiple sclerosis (MS), neuroimmunology, Alzheimer's disease, dementia, movement disorders, and neuromuscular disorders such as spinal muscular atrophy (SMA) and amyotrophic lateral sclerosis (ALS). Biogen announced plans to invest in emerging growth areas such as pain, ophthalmology, neuropsychiatry and acute neurology, as well as discovering potential treatments for rare and genetic disorders. The firm also manufactures and commercializes biosimilars of advanced biologics. Biogen's marketed products include: TECFIDERA, AVONEX, PLEGRIDY, TYSABRI, ZINBRYTA and FAMPRYA for the treatment of MS; SPINRAZA for the treatment of SMA; and FUMADERM for the treatment of severe plaque psoriasis. In addition, the company has certain business and financial rights with respect to: RITUXAN for the treatment of non-Hodgkin's lymphoma, chronic lymphocytic leukemia (CLL) and other conditions; GAZYVA for the treatment of CLL and follicular lymphoma; OCREVUS for the treatment of primary progressive MS and relapsing MS and other potential anti-CD20 therapies under a collaboration agreement with Genentech, Inc., which is wholly-owned by Roche Group. In March 2019, Biogen agreed to sell its large-scale biologics manufacturing site in Hillerod, Denmark to Fujifilm Corporation; and agreed to acquire Nightstar Therapeutics, which is focused on adeno-associated virus-based gene therapeutics for inherited retinal disorders.

Biogen offers employees medical, dental and vision insurance; tuition reimbursement; flexible spending accounts; and an employee assistance program.

FINANCIAL DATA:
Note: Data for latest year may not have been available at press time.

In U.S. $	2018	2017	2016	2015	2014	2013
Revenue	13,452,900,000	12,273,900,000	11,448,800,000	10,763,800,000	9,703,324,000	6,932,199,000
R&D Expense	2,597,200,000	2,253,600,000	1,973,300,000	2,012,800,000	1,893,422,000	1,444,053,000
Operating Income	6,000,800,000	5,527,800,000	5,653,100,000	5,014,900,000	3,916,763,000	2,490,064,000
Operating Margin %		.44%	.49%	.47%	.40%	.36%
SGA Expense	2,106,300,000	1,935,500,000	1,947,900,000	2,113,100,000	2,232,342,000	1,712,051,000
Net Income	4,430,700,000	2,539,100,000	3,702,800,000	3,547,000,000	2,934,784,000	1,862,341,000
Operating Cash Flow	6,187,700,000	4,551,000,000	4,522,400,000	3,716,100,000	2,942,115,000	2,345,078,000
Capital Expenditure	886,100,000	1,962,800,000	727,700,000	643,000,000	287,751,000	3,509,000,000
EBITDA	7,116,800,000	6,460,600,000	5,875,700,000	5,463,200,000	4,664,283,000	3,044,219,000
Return on Assets %		.11%	.17%	.21%	.22%	.17%
Return on Equity %		.21%	.34%	.35%	.30%	.24%
Debt to Equity		0.471	0.536	0.696	0.054	0.069

CONTACT INFORMATION:
Phone: 617-679-2000   Fax: 619 679-2617
Toll-Free:
Address: 225 Binney St., Cambridge, MA 02142 United States

SALARIES/BONUSES:
Top Exec. Salary: $519,231   Bonus: $1,500,000
Second Exec. Salary: $491,827   Bonus: $1,170,177

STOCK TICKER/OTHER:
Stock Ticker: BIIB
Employees: 7,400
Parent Company:

Exchange: NAS
Fiscal Year Ends: 12/31

OTHER THOUGHTS:
Estimated Female Officers or Directors: 4
Hot Spot for Advancement for Women/Minorities: Y

Bio-Rad Laboratories Inc

www.bio-rad.com

NAIC Code: 325413

TYPES OF BUSINESS:
Clinical Diagnostics Products
Medical Equipment
Analytical Instruments
Laboratory Devices
Biomaterials
Imaging Products
Assays
Software

BRANDS/DIVISIONS/AFFILIATES:

CONTACTS:
Note: Officers with more than one job title may be intentionally listed here more than once.

Norman Schwartz, CEO
Ilan Daskal, CFO
James Stark, Chief Accounting Officer
Andrew Last, COO
Michael Crowley, Executive VP, Divisional
Timothy Ernst, Executive VP
Giovanni Magni, Executive VP
Annette Tumolo, Executive VP
John Hertia, Executive VP
Ronald Hutton, Executive VP

GROWTH PLANS/SPECIAL FEATURES:

Bio-Rad Laboratories, Inc. supplies the research, healthcare and analytical chemistry markets with a broad range of life science research and clinical diagnostic products and systems. These are used to separate complex chemical and biological materials and to identify, analyze and purify components. Bio-Rad operates in two segments: clinical diagnostics and life science. The clinical diagnostics division encompasses an array of technologies incorporated into a variety of tests used to detect, identify and quantify substances in blood or other body fluids and tissues. The test results are used as aids for medical diagnosis, detection, evaluation, monitoring and treatment of diseases and other conditions. This division is known for diabetes monitoring products, quality control systems, blood virus testing, blood typing, toxicology, genetic disorders products, molecular pathology and Internet-based software. The firm's life science division develops, manufactures and markets more than 6,000 products for applications including electrophoresis, image analysis, molecular detection, chromatography, gene transfer, sample preparation and amplification. Products include a range of laboratory instruments, apparatuses and consumables used for research in genomics, proteomics and food safety. The life science division provides its services to universities, medical schools, pharmaceutical manufacturers, industrial research organizations, food testing laboratories, government agencies and biotechnology researchers. In April 2019, Bio-Rad announced that it received 510(k) clearance from the U.S. Food and Drug Administration (FDA) for its IH-500 product, an automated random access system for blood typing and screening.

FINANCIAL DATA:
Note: Data for latest year may not have been available at press time.

In U.S. $	2018	2017	2016	2015	2014	2013
Revenue	2,289,415,000	2,160,153,000	2,068,172,000	2,019,441,000	2,175,044,000	2,132,694,000
R&D Expense	199,196,000	250,301,000	205,864,000	192,972,000	220,333,000	210,952,000
Operating Income	189,172,000	128,156,000	115,499,000	166,708,000	149,984,000	169,456,000
Operating Margin %		.06%	.06%	.08%	.07%	.08%
SGA Expense	834,783,000	808,942,000	816,724,000	761,990,000	808,200,000	798,070,000
Net Income	365,614,000	122,249,000	28,125,000	113,093,000	88,845,000	77,790,000
Operating Cash Flow	285,494,000	103,885,000	216,433,000	186,210,000	273,312,000	175,476,000
Capital Expenditure	129,828,000	115,127,000	141,571,000	113,372,000	136,478,000	113,698,000
EBITDA	674,721,000	268,419,000	206,402,000	299,339,000	303,588,000	320,856,000
Return on Assets %		.03%	.01%	.03%	.03%	.02%
Return on Equity %		.04%	.01%	.05%	.04%	.04%
Debt to Equity		0.148	0.168	0.175	0.199	0.199

CONTACT INFORMATION:
Phone: 510 724-7000   Fax: 510 741-5817
Toll-Free: 800-424-6723
Address: 1000 Alfred Nobel Dr., Hercules, CA 94547 United States

STOCK TICKER/OTHER:
Stock Ticker: BIO
Employees: 8,250
Parent Company:

Exchange: NYS
Fiscal Year Ends: 12/31

SALARIES/BONUSES:
Top Exec. Salary: $942,468   Bonus: $
Second Exec. Salary: $495,657   Bonus: $

OTHER THOUGHTS:
Estimated Female Officers or Directors: 3
Hot Spot for Advancement for Women/Minorities: Y

Sales, profits and employees may be estimates. Financial information, benefits and other data can change quickly and may vary from those stated here.

BJC HealthCare

NAIC Code: 622110

www.bjc.org

TYPES OF BUSINESS:
General Medical and Surgical Hospitals
Home Health Services
Physical Rehab Center
Physician Groups
Long-Term Health Care
Occupational Health Services
Hospice Services
Teaching Hospitals

BRANDS/DIVISIONS/AFFILIATES:
Barnes-Jewish Hospital
St Louis Children's Hospital
BJC Home Care Services
BarnesCare
BJC Community Health Services
BJC Employee Assistance Program
BJC Hospice

CONTACTS: Note: Officers with more than one job title may be intentionally listed here more than once.
Richard J. Liekweg, CEO
Nick Barto, Sr. VP
June McAllister Fowler, Sr. VP-Mktg. & Communications
John r. Beatty, Sr. VP
Jerry Fox, Chief Information Officer
Michael A. DeHaven, General Counsel
Robert W. Cannon, Group Pres., Strategic Planning
June McAllister Fowler, VP-Corp. & Public Comm.
Larry Tracy, Pres., Barnes-Jewish St. Peters Hospital
JoAnn M. Shaw, Chief Learning Officer
Richard J. Liekweg, VP
Lee F. Fetter, Group Pres., Clinical Quality
Robert W. Cannon, Group Pres., Supply Chain Oper.

GROWTH PLANS/SPECIAL FEATURES:
BJC HealthCare is a nonprofit healthcare organization primarily serving the areas of St. Louis, Missouri, mid-Missouri and southern Illinois. The firm operates 15 hospitals as well as long-term care facilities, physician offices and rehabilitation and imaging centers. BJC has over 4,300 physicians and over 3,400 staffed beds. Two of the company's hospitals, Barnes-Jewish Hospital and St. Louis Children's Hospital, are ranked highly among America's elite medical centers and teaching hospitals. Both are affiliated with Washington University in St. Louis' School of Medicine. The company's services include inpatient and outpatient care, primary care, community health, workplace health, home health, mental health, rehabilitation, long-term care and hospice. BJC Home Care Services offers patients in Missouri and Illinois a wide range of in-home services, including skilled nursing, adult and pediatric supportive care, rehabilitation therapy, respiratory care, infusion therapy and hospice services. Through BarnesCare, an occupational medicine service, BJC provides occupational health services to the St. Louis metropolitan business community. The company provides a variety of preventive and early detection services for employers and community members through its BJC Community Health Services program, which includes screenings, wellness coaching and other services. The BJC Employee Assistance Program assists in the identification and resolution of health, behavioral and productivity problems. BJC Hospice provides support for terminally ill adults and children, and their families.

FINANCIAL DATA: Note: Data for latest year may not have been available at press time.

In U.S. $	2018	2017	2016	2015	2014	2013
Revenue	5,300,000,000	5,000,000,000	4,800,000,000	4,300,000,000	4,100,000,000	4,000,000,000
R&D Expense						
Operating Income						
Operating Margin %						
SGA Expense						
Net Income						
Operating Cash Flow						
Capital Expenditure						
EBITDA						
Return on Assets %						
Return on Equity %						
Debt to Equity						

CONTACT INFORMATION:
Phone: 314-286-2000 Fax: 314-286-2060
Toll-Free:
Address: 4901 Forest Park Ave., St. Louis, MO 63108 United States

STOCK TICKER/OTHER:
Stock Ticker: Nonprofit
Employees: 31,510
Parent Company:

Exchange:
Fiscal Year Ends: 12/31

SALARIES/BONUSES:
Top Exec. Salary: $ Bonus: $
Second Exec. Salary: $ Bonus: $

OTHER THOUGHTS:
Estimated Female Officers or Directors: 5
Hot Spot for Advancement for Women/Minorities: Y

Sales, profits and employees may be estimates. Financial information, benefits and other data can change quickly and may vary from those stated here.

Black & Veatch Holding Company

www.bv.com

NAIC Code: 541330

TYPES OF BUSINESS:
Heavy & Civil Engineering, Construction
Infrastructure & Energy Services
Environmental & Hydrologic Engineering
Consulting Services
IT Services
Power Plant Engineering and Construction
LNG and Gas Processing Plant Engineering
Climate Change Services

BRANDS/DIVISIONS/AFFILIATES:
Atonix Digital

CONTACTS: Note: Officers with more than one job title may be intentionally listed here more than once.
Steven L. Edwards, CEO
Martin G. Travers, Pres.
Ken Williams, CFO
John Janchar, Pres.-Telecommunications
Stephanie Hasenbos-Case, Chief Human Resources Officer
Barbie Bigelow, Sr. VP
James R. Lewis, Chief Admin. Officer
Timothy W. Triplett, General Counsel
Cindy Wallis-Lage, Pres., Water
O.H. Oskvig, CEO-Energy Business
William R. Van Dyke, Pres., Federal Svcs.
Steven L. Edwards, Chmn.
Hoe Wai Cheong, Sr. VP-Water-Asia Pacific
John E. Murphy, Pres., Construction & Procurement

GROWTH PLANS/SPECIAL FEATURES:
Black & Veatch Holding Company (B&V) is an employee-owned engineering, procurement, consulting and construction company, with more than 100 offices worldwide. The company specializes in the following markets: banking/finance, connected communities, data centers, governments, mining, oil/gas, power, chemicals, smart cities, telecommunications, transportation and water. B&V divides its service offerings into 11 categories. Asset management services span from single asset evaluation to enterprise optimization and efficiency, with specific services including: ISO 55000 assessment and implementation, enterprise asset management system implementation or optimization, capital prioritization and risk management. Consulting services include advanced metering infrastructure, operations, investment, infrastructure transactions, utility rates and regulatory support. Data analytic services includes software subsidiary Atonix Digital, which focuses on cloud-based software development, sales and delivery. EPC & Design services include design engineering, procurement and expediting, construction and construction management, quality control/quality assurance, startup and training. Engineering ensures project performance in relation to power generation, power delivery, oil/gas, water supply challenges and integrated broadband/telecommunications. Procurement provides proposal support, global sourcing, procurement management, evaluation, contract administration and more. Construction services include solutions in regards to power, water, telecommunications, non-union shops and more. Operations services include preparation of facility-specific operations manuals, process control optimization/troubleshooting, on-site technical support for facility startup/commissioning, assessments, lab design and equipment specification. Physical and cybersecurity services help secure the volume of connected physical assets and networks across wide geographies and applications. Program and construction management services offers a comprehensive approach that includes managing entire systems, improving project delivery and managing construction. Last, sustainability services include the adoption of smart technology and innovative resource management solutions such as Internet of Things (IoT), spanning enterprise, environment and utility segments.

FINANCIAL DATA: Note: Data for latest year may not have been available at press time.

In U.S. $	2018	2017	2016	2015	2014	2013
Revenue	3,450,000,000	3,400,000,000	3,200,000,000	3,030,000,000	3,600,000,000	3,560,000,000
R&D Expense						
Operating Income						
Operating Margin %						
SGA Expense						
Net Income						
Operating Cash Flow						
Capital Expenditure						
EBITDA						
Return on Assets %						
Return on Equity %						
Debt to Equity						

CONTACT INFORMATION:
Phone: 913-458-2000　　Fax: 913-458-2934
Toll-Free:
Address: 11401 Lamar Ave., Overland Park, KS 66211 United States

STOCK TICKER/OTHER:
Stock Ticker: Private
Employees: 10,000
Parent Company:

Exchange:
Fiscal Year Ends: 12/31

SALARIES/BONUSES:
Top Exec. Salary: $　　Bonus: $
Second Exec. Salary: $　　Bonus: $

OTHER THOUGHTS:
Estimated Female Officers or Directors: 4
Hot Spot for Advancement for Women/Minorities: Y

Sales, profits and employees may be estimates. Financial information, benefits and other data can change quickly and may vary from those stated here.

BlackRock Inc

NAIC Code: 523920

www.blackrock.com

TYPES OF BUSINESS:
Investment Management
Risk Management Services
Investment System Services

BRANDS/DIVISIONS/AFFILIATES:
Aladdin
iShares
BlackRock Solutions
BlackRock Investment Institute

CONTACTS: Note: Officers with more than one job title may be intentionally listed here more than once.
Laurence Fink, CEO
Jeffrey Smith, Other Corporate Officer
Marc Comerchero, Chief Accounting Officer
Christopher Meade, Chief Legal Officer
Robert Goldstein, COO
Robert Kapito, Director
Mark McCombe, Other Corporate Officer
J. Kushel, Other Corporate Officer
Rachel Lord, Other Corporate Officer
Mark Wiedman, Other Corporate Officer
Geraldine Buckingham, Other Corporate Officer

GROWTH PLANS/SPECIAL FEATURES:
BlackRock, Inc. and its subsidiaries form one of the largest investment management firms in the U.S., with $6.288 trillion worth of assets under management as of 2018. The company manages offices in 30 countries which serve clients in over 100 countries. The firm acts as a fiduciary on behalf of institutional and individual investors worldwide through a variety of fixed income, cash management, equity and balanced and alternative investment accounts and funds. The company also provides risk management, investment system outsourcing and financial advisory services. BlackRock's Aladdin platform is an operating system for investment managers that combines risk analytics with portfolio management, trading and operations tools. Its clients include a diverse group of taxable, tax-exempt and official institutions, retail investors and high-net-worth individuals globally. Institutional clients include pension funds, official institutions, foundations, endowments and charities, insurance companies, banks, sub-advisory relationships and private banks. Products are offered directly through intermediaries that include open-end and closed-end mutual funds, iShares exchange-traded funds (ETFs), collective investment funds and separate accounts. The firm also offers risk management, investment systems and advisory services to institutional investors through its BlackRock Solutions (BRS) product line. The firm's global platform, BlackRock Investment Institute, leverages its expertise in markets, asset classes and client segments to produce information that makes the company's portfolio managers better investors.

The company offers employees health care, disability and life coverage; retirement benefits; and tuition assistance.

FINANCIAL DATA: Note: Data for latest year may not have been available at press time.

In U.S. $	2018	2017	2016	2015	2014	2013
Revenue	14,198,000,000	12,491,000,000	11,155,000,000	11,401,000,000	11,081,000,000	10,180,000,000
R&D Expense						
Operating Income	5,598,000,000	5,272,000,000	4,646,000,000	4,664,000,000	4,524,000,000	3,857,000,000
Operating Margin %		.42%	.42%	.41%	.40%	.38%
SGA Expense	1,557,000,000	1,462,000,000	1,301,000,000	1,380,000,000	1,403,000,000	1,540,000,000
Net Income	4,305,000,000	4,970,000,000	3,172,000,000	3,345,000,000	3,294,000,000	2,932,000,000
Operating Cash Flow	3,075,000,000	3,828,000,000	2,154,000,000	3,004,000,000	3,081,000,000	3,642,000,000
Capital Expenditure	204,000,000	155,000,000	119,000,000	221,000,000	66,000,000	94,000,000
EBITDA	5,782,000,000	5,722,000,000	4,894,000,000	5,053,000,000	4,905,000,000	4,475,000,000
Return on Assets %		.02%	.01%	.01%	.01%	.01%
Return on Equity %		.16%	.11%	.12%	.12%	.11%
Debt to Equity		0.158	0.169	0.173	0.304	0.276

CONTACT INFORMATION:
Phone: 212 810-5300 Fax: 212 754-3123
Toll-Free:
Address: 40 E. 52nd St., New York, NY 10022 United States

STOCK TICKER/OTHER:
Stock Ticker: BLK
Employees: 13,000
Parent Company:

Exchange: NYS
Fiscal Year Ends: 12/31

SALARIES/BONUSES:
Top Exec. Salary: $1,500,000 Bonus: $7,750,000
Second Exec. Salary: $1,250,000 Bonus: $6,250,000

OTHER THOUGHTS:
Estimated Female Officers or Directors: 5
Hot Spot for Advancement for Women/Minorities: Y

Bloomberg LP

www.bloomberg.com

NAIC Code: 0

TYPES OF BUSINESS:
Financial Data and News Publishing
Magazine Publishing
Management Software
Multimedia Presentation Services
Broadcast Television
Radio Broadcasting
Electronic Exchange Systems
Economic Data

BRANDS/DIVISIONS/AFFILIATES:
Bloomberg Terminal
Bloomberg Tradebook
Bloomberg Briefs
Bloomberg Indexes
Bloomberg Government
Bloomberg New Energy Finance Limited
Bloomberg Business
RegTek.Solutions

CONTACTS:
Note: Officers with more than one job title may be intentionally listed here more than once.

Michael Bloomberg, CEO
Jason Schechter, Chief Communications Officer
Matthew Winkler, Editor-in-Chief, Bloomberg News
Thomas Secunda, Vice Chmn.
Peter Grauer, Chmn.

GROWTH PLANS/SPECIAL FEATURES:

Bloomberg LP is an information services, news and media company, serving the financial services industry, government offices and agencies, corporations and news organizations. The company operates in five segments: communications, financial products, industry products, media and media services. Communications provides press announcements involving Bloomberg through its worldwide press contact centers, including the Americas, Europe/Middle East/Africa and Asia Pacific. Financial products is comprised of the Bloomberg Terminal, a platform for financial professionals who need real-time data, news and analytics to make fast and informed decisions; and the Bloomberg Tradebook, a global agency broker that provides anonymous direct market access and algorithmic trading to more than 125 global liquidity venues across 40+ countries. This division also includes Bloomberg Briefs, Bloomberg Indexes, Bloomberg SEF (swap execution facility) and Bloomberg Institute. Industry products include Bloomberg Government, a web-based information service for professionals who interact with the federal government; Bloomberg Law/BNA and Bloomberg Big Law for legal, tax and regulatory professionals; and Bloomberg New Energy Finance Limited for decision-makers in the energy system. Media delivers business and political news through Bloomberg Business, Bloomberg Politics, Bloomberg View, Bloomberg Television, Bloomberg Radio, Bloomberg Mobile Apps and news bureaus. Media Services includes advertising and media distribution services. Bloomberg LP's news and analytics solutions allow enterprise customers to access, integrate, distribute and manage data and information across organizations. In August 2019, Bloomberg acquired RegTek.Solutions, a provider of global regulatory reporting software solutions.

FINANCIAL DATA:
Note: Data for latest year may not have been available at press time.

In U.S. $	2018	2017	2016	2015	2014	2013
Revenue	10,000,000,000	9,658,000,000	9,400,000,000	9,184,000,000	9,000,000,000	8,275,000,000
R&D Expense						
Operating Income						
Operating Margin %						
SGA Expense						
Net Income						
Operating Cash Flow						
Capital Expenditure						
EBITDA						
Return on Assets %						
Return on Equity %						
Debt to Equity						

CONTACT INFORMATION:
Phone: 212-318-2000 Fax: 917-369-5000
Toll-Free:
Address: 731 Lexington Ave., New York, NY 10022 United States

SALARIES/BONUSES:
Top Exec. Salary: $ Bonus: $
Second Exec. Salary: $ Bonus: $

STOCK TICKER/OTHER:
Stock Ticker: Private   Exchange:
Employees: 20,000   Fiscal Year Ends: 12/31
Parent Company:

OTHER THOUGHTS:
Estimated Female Officers or Directors: 8
Hot Spot for Advancement for Women/Minorities: Y

Sales, profits and employees may be estimates. Financial information, benefits and other data can change quickly and may vary from those stated here.

Blue Shield of California

NAIC Code: 524114

www.blueshieldca.com

TYPES OF BUSINESS:
Insurance-Medical & Health, HMOs & PPOs
Managed Care
Life Insurance
Dental Insurance

BRANDS/DIVISIONS/AFFILIATES:
Blue Cross and Blue Shield Association
Blue Shield of California Life & Health Insurance
Blue Shield of California Foundation

CONTACTS:
Note: Officers with more than one job title may be intentionally listed here more than once.

Paul Markovich, CEO
Sandra Clarke, CFO
Jeff Robertson, Sr. VP
Mary O'Hara, Chief Human Resources Officer
Marcus Thygeson, Chief Health Officer
Michael Mathias, CIO
Seth A. Jacobs, General Counsel
Steve Shivinsky, VP-Corp. Comm.
Tom Brophy, VP-Finance & Treas. Svcs.
Ed Cymerys, Chief Actuary
Juan Davila, Exec. VP-Health Care Quality & Affordability
Rob Geyer, Sr. VP-Customer Quality
Kirsten Gorsuch, Sr. VP-External Affairs
Doug Busch, Chmn.

GROWTH PLANS/SPECIAL FEATURES:

Blue Shield of California (BSC) is a nonprofit mutual benefit corporation and a member of the Blue Cross Blue Shield Association, serving approximately 4 million members. The firm offers insurance plans including health maintenance organizations (HMOs) and preferred provider organizations (PPOs), as well as dental and Medicare supplemental through its offices in California. BSC works with HMO physicians and specialists, PPO physicians and specialists, HMO hospitals and PPO hospitals. The company also offers executive medical reimbursement, life and vision insurance and short-term health plans through Blue Shield of California Life & Health Insurance Company (Blue Shield Life). The Blue Shield of California Foundation provides charitable contributions and conducts research and supports programs with an emphasis on domestic violence prevention and medical technology assessments. BSC also offers plans for self-employed California workers not covered by employer-sponsored health plans, as well as low cost PPO plans for individuals. The company offers an enhanced small group dental benefit for pregnant women to reduce risks of periodontal disease and pregnancy gingivitis and is expanding dental coverage options with four new dental PPO plans for small groups.

The firm offers employees medical, dental and vision coverage; life insurance; disability insurance; tuition reimbursement; flexible spending accounts; discounts on entertainment and chiropractic and massage therapy; income protection benefits; a 401(k) savings plan; and a pension.

FINANCIAL DATA:
Note: Data for latest year may not have been available at press time.

In U.S. $	2018	2017	2016	2015	2014	2013
Revenue	20,632,000,000	17,684,000,000	17,598,000,000	14,836,000,000	13,349,000,000	11,000,000,000
R&D Expense						
Operating Income						
Operating Margin %						
SGA Expense						
Net Income	413,000,000	296,000,000	67,000,000	115,000,000	162,000,000	171,000,000
Operating Cash Flow						
Capital Expenditure						
EBITDA						
Return on Assets %						
Return on Equity %						
Debt to Equity						

CONTACT INFORMATION:
Phone: 415-229-5000   Fax: 800-329-2742
Toll-Free: 888-800-2742
Address: 315 Montgomery St., San Francisco, CA 94104 United States

STOCK TICKER/OTHER:
Stock Ticker: Nonprofit   Exchange:
Employees: 6,800   Fiscal Year Ends: 12/31
Parent Company:

SALARIES/BONUSES:
Top Exec. Salary: $ Bonus: $
Second Exec. Salary: $ Bonus: $

OTHER THOUGHTS:
Estimated Female Officers or Directors: 14
Hot Spot for Advancement for Women/Minorities: Y

BMC Software Inc

www.bmc.com

NAIC Code: 0

TYPES OF BUSINESS:
Computer Software, Mainframe Related
Systems Management Software
e-Business Software
Consulting & Training Services

BRANDS/DIVISIONS/AFFILIATES:
KKR & Co LP

CONTACTS:
Note: Officers with more than one job title may be intentionally listed here more than once.

Peter Leav, CEO
Steve Solcher, CFO
Dan Streetman, Exec. VP-Global Mktg. & Sales
Hollie Castro, Sr. VP-Admin.
Patrick K. Tagtow, General Counsel
Steve Goddard, Sr. VP-Bus. Oper.
Ken Berryman, Sr. VP-Strategy & Corp. Dev.
Ann Duhon, Mgr.-Comm.
Derrick Vializ, VP-Investor Rel.
T. Cory Bleuer, Chief Acct. Officer
Patrick K. Tagtow, Chief Compliance Officer
Paul Avenant, Sr. VP-Solutions

GROWTH PLANS/SPECIAL FEATURES:
BMC Software, Inc. is a software vendor company that provides system management, service management and automation solutions primarily for large companies. Its software products span mainframe systems, IT service management, cloud management, IT operations, workload automation and IT automation. BMC's solutions are grouped into six categories: multi-cloud management, security and compliance, artificial intelligence and machine learning, automation and DevOps, IT optimization and service management. Multi-cloud management solutions include multi-cloud cost control, asset visibility, cloud performance management, automation across clouds, cloud security, cloud migration and services management across clouds. Security and compliance solutions include building a SecOps strategy, ensuring GDPR compliance, remediating vulnerabilities and managing policies and compliance. AI & machine learning solutions include cognitive service management, AI application to IT, big data insights, and acceleration via self-managing mainframe. Automation and DevOps solutions include automating workloads, file transfers, application deployment and data centers. IT optimization solutions cover IT infrastructure, cloud spend, applications performance, mainframe costs and database performance. Last, service management solutions offer transformation, modernization, IT asset visibility and digital workplace enhancement. During 2018, BMC was acquired by KKR & Co. LP; and BMC agreed to acquire assets of CorreLog, Inc., a provider of real-time security management to mainframe customers.

FINANCIAL DATA:
Note: Data for latest year may not have been available at press time.

In U.S. $	2018	2017	2016	2015	2014	2013
Revenue	2,000,000,000	2,500,000,000	2,300,000,000	2,250,000,000	2,205,000,000	2,201,000,000
R&D Expense						
Operating Income						
Operating Margin %						
SGA Expense						
Net Income						
Operating Cash Flow						
Capital Expenditure						
EBITDA						
Return on Assets %						
Return on Equity %						
Debt to Equity						

CONTACT INFORMATION:
Phone: 713 918-8800
Fax: 713 918-8000
Toll-Free: 800-841-2031
Address: 2101 Citywest Blvd., Houston, TX 77042 United States

STOCK TICKER/OTHER:
Stock Ticker: Subsidiary
Employees: 9,000
Parent Company: KKR & Co LP
Exchange:
Fiscal Year Ends: 03/31

SALARIES/BONUSES:
Top Exec. Salary: $
Bonus: $
Second Exec. Salary: $
Bonus: $

OTHER THOUGHTS:
Estimated Female Officers or Directors: 2
Hot Spot for Advancement for Women/Minorities: Y

BMC Stock Holdings Inc

NAIC Code: 444190

www.buildwithbmc.com

TYPES OF BUSINESS:
Building Materials & Hardware Stores, Retail
Building & Construction Services

BRANDS/DIVISIONS/AFFILIATES:
BMC
Ready-Frame
BMC Design
BMC Timber Truss
Building Materials Holding Corp

CONTACTS:
Note: Officers with more than one job title may be intentionally listed here more than once.

David Flitman, CEO
James Major, CFO
David Bullock, Director
Mike Farmer, Executive VP, Divisional
Lisa Hamblet, Executive VP, Divisional
Timothy Johnson, Executive VP

GROWTH PLANS/SPECIAL FEATURES:
BMC Stock Holdings, Inc. (formerly Building Materials Holding Corp.) is a diversified lumber and building materials distributor and solutions provider that sells to new construction, repair and remodeling contractors. The company carries a wide range of products via operations in 18 U.S. states. Its primary products include lumber, lumber sheet goods, millwork, doors, flooring, windows, structural components (engineered wood products, trusses and wall panels) and other exterior products. BMC's solution-based services include design, product specification, installation and installation management services. The firm also offers a broad range of products sourced through a network of suppliers, which together with various solution-based services, represent approximately 50% of the construction cost of a typical new home. BMC serves its customers from 149 locations, which include 101 distribution and retail operations, 48 millwork fabrication operations, 51 structural components fabrication operations and 8 flooring operations. Brands of the company include BMC, Ready-Frame, BMC Design and BMC Timber Truss. In February 2018, BMC announced that it will acquire the business of W.E. Shone Co., a leading supplier of building materials in Delaware.

FINANCIAL DATA:
Note: Data for latest year may not have been available at press time.

In U.S. $	2018	2017	2016	2015	2014	2013
Revenue	3,682,448,000	3,365,968,000	3,093,743,000	1,576,746,000	1,295,716,000	1,197,037,000
R&D Expense						
Operating Income	174,301,000	116,944,000	111,004,000	35,241,000	18,953,000	11,342,000
Operating Margin %		.03%	.04%	.02%	.01%	.01%
SGA Expense	680,273,000	619,546,000	571,799,000	306,843,000	279,717,000	254,935,000
Net Income	119,738,000	57,425,000	30,880,000	-4,831,000	10,419,000	-4,635,000
Operating Cash Flow	210,025,000	93,934,000	106,888,000	743,000	16,941,000	-40,264,000
Capital Expenditure	55,174,000	63,278,000	38,067,000	31,319,000	43,306,000	7,448,000
EBITDA	246,337,000	176,080,000	143,957,000	37,621,000	32,454,000	13,694,000
Return on Assets %		.04%	.02%	-.01%	.03%	-.02%
Return on Equity %		.08%	.05%	-.01%	.08%	-.08%
Debt to Equity		0.487	0.537	0.67	0.682	0.51

CONTACT INFORMATION:
Phone: 678-222-1219   Fax: 678-222-1316
Toll-Free:
Address: Two Lakeside Commons, 980 Hammond Drive NE, Ste 500, Atlanta, GA 30328 United States

STOCK TICKER/OTHER:
Stock Ticker: BMCH
Employees: 9,000
Parent Company:

Exchange: NAS
Fiscal Year Ends: 12/31

SALARIES/BONUSES:
Top Exec. Salary: $559,444   Bonus: $375,000
Second Exec. Salary: $561,635   Bonus: $

OTHER THOUGHTS:
Estimated Female Officers or Directors: 2
Hot Spot for Advancement for Women/Minorities:

Boise Cascade Company

NAIC Code: 321213

www.bc.com

TYPES OF BUSINESS:
Lumber Products, Manufacturing
Engineered Wood Products
Wholesale Building Materials Distribution
Packaging & Newsprint
Cottonwood Fiber Farming

BRANDS/DIVISIONS/AFFILIATES:
American Lumber Distributors

CONTACTS: Note: Officers with more than one job title may be intentionally listed here more than once.
Thomas Corrick, CEO
Wayne Rancourt, CFO
Thomas Carlile, Chairman of the Board
Kelly Hibbs, Chief Accounting Officer
Nathan Jorgensen, COO
Nick Stokes, Executive VP, Divisional
Mike Brown, Executive VP, Divisional
Jill Twedt, General Counsel
Erin Nuxoll, Senior VP, Divisional
Rich Viola, Senior VP, Divisional
Thomas Hoffmann, Vice President, Divisional
Frank Elfering, Vice President, Divisional

GROWTH PLANS/SPECIAL FEATURES:
Boise Cascade Company is a major vertically-integrated wood products manufacturer and building materials distributor with operations throughout the U.S, as well as one facility in Canada. The company operates through two business segments: wood products and building materials distribution. The wood products segment manufactures laminated veneer lumber (LVL), I-joists and laminated beams, which are structural products used in applications where extra strength and consistent quality are required. I-joists are used primarily in residential and commercial flooring and roofing systems and other structural applications. This division operates six engineered wood product (EWP) facilities, nine plywood and veneer plants, five sawmills and one particleboard plant. Wood fiber is the primary raw material used in Boise Cascade's wood products operations. The building materials distribution segment sells a broad line of building materials, including oriented strand board (OSB), plywood, lumber, siding, composite decking, metal products, insulation, roofing and EWP. This division operates a nationwide network of more than 30 building materials distribution facilities, as well as a single truss manufacturing plant. During 2019, Boise Cascade acquired American Lumber Distributors, which is based in Birmingham, Alabama.

The firm offers its employees health, medical, prescription drug, dental and vision coverage; flexible spending accounts; 16-31 days paid-time off; life, AD&D and long-term disability insurance; a 401(k) plan with a 4% employer match; a wellness program; and an employee assistance program.

FINANCIAL DATA: Note: Data for latest year may not have been available at press time.

In U.S. $	2018	2017	2016	2015	2014	2013
Revenue	4,995,290,000	4,431,991,000	3,911,215,000	3,633,415,000	3,573,732,000	3,273,496,000
R&D Expense						
Operating Income	85,353,000	141,153,000	79,578,000	103,189,000	145,549,000	98,757,000
Operating Margin %		.03%	.02%	.03%	.04%	.03%
SGA Expense	456,948,000	390,423,000	361,382,000	322,733,000	312,662,000	290,772,000
Net Income	20,477,000	82,957,000	38,254,000	52,182,000	80,009,000	116,936,000
Operating Cash Flow	163,611,000	151,567,000	151,907,000	80,331,000	101,843,000	33,427,000
Capital Expenditure	79,987,000	75,450,000	83,583,000	87,526,000	61,217,000	45,751,000
EBITDA	197,232,000	225,279,000	144,920,000	160,411,000	198,406,000	138,384,000
Return on Assets %		.05%	.03%	.04%	.07%	.12%
Return on Equity %		.13%	.07%	.10%	.17%	.43%
Debt to Equity		0.65	0.755	0.644	0.612	0.667

CONTACT INFORMATION:
Phone: 208-384-6161　　Fax: 208-384-7189
Toll-Free:
Address: 1111 W. Jefferson St., Ste. 300, Boise, ID 83702-5389 United States

STOCK TICKER/OTHER:
Stock Ticker: BCC　　Exchange: NYS
Employees: 6,190　　Fiscal Year Ends: 12/31
Parent Company:

SALARIES/BONUSES:
Top Exec. Salary: $854,615　　Bonus: $
Second Exec. Salary: $499,885　　Bonus: $

OTHER THOUGHTS:
Estimated Female Officers or Directors: 1
Hot Spot for Advancement for Women/Minorities:

Sales, profits and employees may be estimates. Financial information, benefits and other data can change quickly and may vary from those stated here.

Booking Holdings Inc

www.bookingholdings.com

NAIC Code: 561510

TYPES OF BUSINESS:
Online Retail-Travel Services
Auction-Based Travel Sales
Online Financial Services
Commission-Based Travel Bookings (Travel Agency Model)

BRANDS/DIVISIONS/AFFILIATES:
Priceline.com
Booking.com
Name Your Own Price
Priceline Group Inc
RentalCars.com
OpenTable
KAYAK
FareHarbor

CONTACTS: Note: Officers with more than one job title may be intentionally listed here more than once.
Gillian Tans, CEO, Subsidiary
Glenn Fogel, CEO
David Goulden, CFO
Jeffery Boyd, Chairman of the Board
Sue DEmic, Chief Accounting Officer
Peter Millones, Executive VP

GROWTH PLANS/SPECIAL FEATURES:

Booking Holdings, Inc., formerly Priceline Group, Inc., is a leading online travel company that offers a broad range of travel services, including airline tickets, hotel rooms, car rentals, vacation packages, cruises and destination services primarily through its proprietary Priceline.com, KAYAK.com, Booking.com, Agoda.com, RentalCars.com and OpenTable.com websites. Within the U.S., the firm offers customers the ability to purchase travel services in a traditional, price-disclosed manner or the opportunity to use the Name Your Own Price service, which allows customers to make offers on travel goods and services at discounted prices. To make an offer, a customer specifies the origin and destination of the trip, the dates on which the customer wishes to depart and return, the price the customer is willing to pay and the customer's valid credit card to guarantee the offer. The company enables customers to make hotel reservations on a worldwide basis, primarily under the Booking.com and Agoda.com brands internationally, and primarily under the Priceline.com brand in the U.S. These operations offer consumers an array of accommodations such as hotels, bed and breakfasts, hostels, apartments, vacation rentals and other properties. Through subsidiary RentalCars.com, the company offers retail price-disclosed rental car reservations through approximately 49,000 locations. OpenTable is the company's brand for booking online restaurant reservations, and primarily operates in the U.S. Its international business represents approximately 88% of the company's gross bookings and contributes more than 94% of Priceline's consolidated operating income. Subsidiary KAYAK Software Corporation provides a price comparison service allowing consumers to search and compare prices for travel services. In April 2018, Booking Holdings acquired FareHarbor, a local activities and experiences booking software provider. In December, the firm acquired HotelsCombined, a hotel metasearch site. HotelsCombined will be added to KAYAK's portfolio of brands.

Employee benefits include medical, life, AD&D, disability and dental coverage; 401(k) with company match; tuition reimbursement; an employee assistance plan; flexible spending accounts; and travel agent discount benefits.

FINANCIAL DATA: Note: Data for latest year may not have been available at press time.

In U.S. $	2018	2017	2016	2015	2014	2013
Revenue	14,527,000,000	12,681,080,000	10,743,010,000	9,223,987,000	8,441,971,000	6,793,306,000
R&D Expense	233,000,000	189,344,000	142,393,000	113,617,000	97,498,000	71,890,000
Operating Income	5,341,000,000	4,537,992,000	3,847,013,000	3,258,907,000	3,073,312,000	2,412,414,000
Operating Margin %		.36%	.36%	.35%	.36%	.36%
SGA Expense	8,527,000,000	7,340,435,000	6,016,151,000	4,946,789,000	4,205,500,000	3,113,607,000
Net Income	3,998,000,000	2,340,765,000	2,134,987,000	2,551,360,000	2,421,753,000	1,892,663,000
Operating Cash Flow	5,338,000,000	4,662,036,000	3,924,697,000	3,102,231,000	2,914,397,000	2,301,436,000
Capital Expenditure	442,000,000	287,805,000	268,383,000	173,915,000	131,504,000	84,445,000
EBITDA	5,530,000,000	5,015,072,000	3,230,273,000	3,561,043,000	3,285,621,000	2,497,801,000
Return on Assets %		.10%	.11%	.16%	.19%	.22%
Return on Equity %		.22%	.23%	.29%	.31%	.35%
Debt to Equity		0.783	0.631	0.70	0.449	0.253

CONTACT INFORMATION:
Phone: 203-2998000 Fax:
Toll-Free:
Address: 800 Connecticut Ave., Norwalk, CT 06854 United States

STOCK TICKER/OTHER:
Stock Ticker: BKNG
Employees: 18,500
Parent Company:

Exchange: NAS
Fiscal Year Ends:

SALARIES/BONUSES:
Top Exec. Salary: $500,000   Bonus: $500,000
Second Exec. Salary: $750,000   Bonus: $

OTHER THOUGHTS:
Estimated Female Officers or Directors: 1
Hot Spot for Advancement for Women/Minorities: Y

Sales, profits and employees may be estimates. Financial information, benefits and other data can change quickly and may vary from those stated here.

Booz Allen Hamilton Holding Corporation

www.boozallen.com

NAIC Code: 541610

TYPES OF BUSINESS:
Strategy Consulting
Engineering & IT Consulting
Supply Chain Management
Industry Research & Publications
War Gaming & Strategic Simulation

BRANDS/DIVISIONS/AFFILIATES:
Carlyle Group (The)

CONTACTS:
Note: Officers with more than one job title may be intentionally listed here more than once.

Horacio Rozanski, CEO
Lloyd Howell, CFO
Ralph Shrader, Chairman of the Board
Nancy Laben, Chief Legal Officer
Gary Labovich, Executive VP
Kristine Anderson, Executive VP
Christopher Ling, Executive VP
Karen Dahut, Executive VP
Joseph Mahaffee, Executive VP
Angela Messer, Executive VP
Susan Penfield, Executive VP
Elizabeth Thompson, Executive VP

GROWTH PLANS/SPECIAL FEATURES:

Booz Allen Hamilton Holding Corporation (BAH), founded in 1914, provides management and technology consulting, engineering, analytics, digital solutions, mission operations and cyber expertise to U.S. and international governments, major corporations and nonprofit organizations. Specific markets served by BAH include civil government, commercial, defense, intelligence, international, energy, resources, utilities, financial services, health, homeland security, law enforcement and transportation. In addition, BAH is currently (May 2019) engaged in incubating and developing digital, cyber, artificial intelligent (AI) and immersive solutions in order to solve future problems via technology, software and other solutions for its clients. Investment firm, The Carlyle Group, maintains a majority interest in the company.

The company offers employees dental, medical and vision insurance; life insurance; medical flexible spending accounts; tuition assistance; an employee assistance program; and health and wellness programs.

FINANCIAL DATA:
Note: Data for latest year may not have been available at press time.

In U.S. $	2018	2017	2016	2015	2014	2013
Revenue	6,171,853,000	5,804,284,000	5,405,738,000	5,274,770,000	5,478,693,000	
R&D Expense						
Operating Income	520,085,000	484,247,000	444,584,000	458,822,000	460,611,000	
Operating Margin %	.08%	.08%	.08%	.09%	.08%	
SGA Expense	2,719,909,000	2,568,511,000	2,319,592,000	2,159,439,000	2,229,642,000	
Net Income	305,111,000	252,490,000	294,094,000	232,569,000	232,188,000	
Operating Cash Flow	369,143,000	382,277,000	249,234,000	309,958,000	332,718,000	
Capital Expenditure	78,437,000	53,919,000	66,635,000	36,041,000	20,905,000	
EBITDA	579,668,000	533,742,000	511,813,000	520,410,000	531,144,000	
Return on Assets %	.09%	.08%	.10%	.08%	.07%	
Return on Equity %	.54%	.51%	.98%	1.28%	1.15%	
Debt to Equity	3.165	2.563	3.634	8.414	9.236	

CONTACT INFORMATION:
Phone: 703 902-5000 Fax: 703 902-3333
Toll-Free:
Address: 8283 Greensboro Dr., McLean, VA 22102 United States

STOCK TICKER/OTHER:
Stock Ticker: BAH Exchange: NYS
Employees: 23,300 Fiscal Year Ends:
Parent Company: Carlyle Group (The)

SALARIES/BONUSES:
Top Exec. Salary: $1,500,000 Bonus: $
Second Exec. Salary: $1,025,000 Bonus: $

OTHER THOUGHTS:
Estimated Female Officers or Directors: 4
Hot Spot for Advancement for Women/Minorities: Y

BorgWarner Inc

NAIC Code: 336310

www.borgwarner.com

TYPES OF BUSINESS:
Gasoline Engine and Engine Parts Manufacturing
Motor Vehicle Transmissions
Power Train Parts
Turbochargers
Cooling Systems
Chain Systems
Industrial Equipment

BRANDS/DIVISIONS/AFFILIATES:

CONTACTS:
Note: Officers with more than one job title may be intentionally listed here more than once.

Frederic Lissalde, CEO
Kevin Nowlan, CFO
Alexis Michas, Chairman of the Board
Thomas McGill, Chief Accounting Officer
Tonit Calaway, Chief Legal Officer
Brady Ericson, Chief Strategy Officer
Joseph Fadool, General Manager, Subsidiary
Joel Wiegert, General Manager, Subsidiary
Martin Fischer, General Manager, Subsidiary
Stefan Demmerle, General Manager, Subsidiary
Robin Kendrick, General Manager, Subsidiary
Anthony Hensel, Vice President, Divisional

GROWTH PLANS/SPECIAL FEATURES:

BorgWarner, Inc. manufactures and sells engineered systems and components, designed to improve fuel efficiency, air quality and vehicle stability, to original equipment manufacturers (OEMs) of passenger cars, SUVs, trucks, commercial transportation products and industrial equipment worldwide. BorgWarner's products fall into two operating segments: engine and drivetrain. The engine segment develops and manufactures products to improve fuel economy, reduce emissions and enhance performance. These products include combustion, hybrid and electric propulsion systems. Its technologies include turbo chargers, eBoosters, timing systems, emissions systems, thermal systems, gasoline ignition technology, cabin heaters, battery heaters and battery charging. The drivetrain segment develops and manufactures products to improve fuel economy, reduce emissions and enhance performance in combustion, hybrid and electric vehicles. This division's technologies include rotating electrical components, power electronics, clutching systems, control modules and all-wheel drive systems. Its mechanical products include friction, mechanical and controls products for automatic transmissions; and torque management products for all-wheel-drive vehicles. Rotating electrical components include starter motors, alternators and electric motors for hybrid and electric vehicles. BorgWarner operates manufacturing and technical facilities at 68 locations in 16 U.S. locations, nine in China, eight in Germany, seven in South Korea, four each in India and Mexico, three each in Brazil, Japan and the U.K., two in Italy, and one each in Canada, France, Hungary, Ireland, Poland, Portugal, Spain, Sweden and Thailand.

FINANCIAL DATA: Note: Data for latest year may not have been available at press time.

In U.S. $	2018	2017	2016	2015	2014	2013
Revenue	10,529,600,000	9,799,300,000	9,071,000,000	8,023,200,000	8,305,100,000	7,436,600,000
R&D Expense						
Operating Income	1,291,800,000	1,221,900,000	1,119,800,000	1,016,400,000	1,064,800,000	918,800,000
Operating Margin %		.12%	.12%	.13%	.13%	.12%
SGA Expense	945,700,000	898,500,000	817,500,000	687,700,000	702,400,000	645,600,000
Net Income	930,700,000	439,900,000	118,500,000	609,700,000	655,800,000	624,300,000
Operating Cash Flow	1,126,500,000	1,180,300,000	1,035,700,000	867,900,000	801,800,000	718,800,000
Capital Expenditure	546,600,000	560,000,000	500,600,000	577,300,000	563,000,000	417,800,000
EBITDA	1,685,900,000	1,541,900,000	666,500,000	1,307,400,000	1,346,900,000	1,202,900,000
Return on Assets %		.05%	.01%	.08%	.09%	.09%
Return on Equity %		.13%	.03%	.17%	.18%	.19%
Debt to Equity		0.566	0.635	0.598	0.198	0.287

CONTACT INFORMATION:
Phone: 248 754-9200   Fax:
Toll-Free:
Address: 3850 Hamlin Rd., Auburn Hills, MI 48326 United States

SALARIES/BONUSES:
Top Exec. Salary: $1,108,945   Bonus: $
Second Exec. Salary: $946,235   Bonus: $

STOCK TICKER/OTHER:
Stock Ticker: BWA
Employees: 27,000
Parent Company:

Exchange: NYS
Fiscal Year Ends: 12/31

OTHER THOUGHTS:
Estimated Female Officers or Directors: 4
Hot Spot for Advancement for Women/Minorities: Y

Sales, profits and employees may be estimates. Financial information, benefits and other data can change quickly and may vary from those stated here.

Boston Consulting Group Inc (The, BCG)

NAIC Code: 541610

www.bcg.com

TYPES OF BUSINESS:
Management Consulting
Marketing Consulting
Corporate Strategy Research

BRANDS/DIVISIONS/AFFILIATES:

CONTACTS: Note: Officers with more than one job title may be intentionally listed here more than once.
Rich Lesser, CEO
Paul Tranter, Chief of Staff
Debbie Simpson, CFO
Jeremy Barton, General Counsel
Miki Tsusaka, Sr. Partner
Sharon Marcil, Sr. Partner
Matthew Krentz, Sr. Partner
Hans-Paul Burkner, Chmn.
Vaishali Rastogi, Partner

GROWTH PLANS/SPECIAL FEATURES:

The Boston Consulting Group, Inc. (BCG) is a global management consulting firm as well as a world-leading advisor on business strategy. BCG partners with clients from the private, public and nonprofit sectors in all regions to identify their highest-value opportunities, address critical challenges and transform their enterprises. The company's capabilities include big data, advanced analytics, diversity/inclusion, growth, marketing, sales, people/organization, procurement, strategy, transformation, restructuring, change management, enablement, innovation, product development, mergers/acquisitions, post-merger integration, smart simplicity, sustainability, corporate development, finance, globalization, manufacturing, operations, pricing, social impact and technology/digital. Industries served by BCG include automotive, mobility, biopharmaceuticals, consumer products, education, energy, environment, engineered products, infrastructure, financial institutions, health care payers/providers/services, insurance, media, entertainment, medical devices, technology, metals, mining, principal investors, private equity, process industrial materials, building materials, public sector, retail, technology industries, telecommunications, transportation, travel and tourism. BCG has offices in more than 90 cities in 50 countries.

FINANCIAL DATA: Note: Data for latest year may not have been available at press time.

In U.S. $	2018	2017	2016	2015	2014	2013
Revenue	7,500,000,000	6,300,000,000	5,600,000,000	5,000,000,000	4,200,000,000	3,710,000,000
R&D Expense						
Operating Income						
Operating Margin %						
SGA Expense						
Net Income						
Operating Cash Flow						
Capital Expenditure						
EBITDA						
Return on Assets %						
Return on Equity %						
Debt to Equity						

CONTACT INFORMATION:
Phone: 617-973-1200 Fax: 617-973-1399
Toll-Free:
Address: 1 Exchange Pl., Fl. 30 & 31, Boston, MA 02109 United States

STOCK TICKER/OTHER:
Stock Ticker: Private
Employees: 18,500
Parent Company:

Exchange:
Fiscal Year Ends: 12/31

SALARIES/BONUSES:
Top Exec. Salary: $ Bonus: $
Second Exec. Salary: $ Bonus: $

OTHER THOUGHTS:
Estimated Female Officers or Directors: 4
Hot Spot for Advancement for Women/Minorities: Y

Sales, profits and employees may be estimates. Financial information, benefits and other data can change quickly and may vary from those stated here.

Boston Scientific Corporation

www.bostonscientific.com

NAIC Code: 339100

TYPES OF BUSINESS:
Supplies-Surgery
Interventional Medical Products
Catheters
Guide wires
Stents
Oncology Research

BRANDS/DIVISIONS/AFFILIATES:
Millipede Inc

CONTACTS:
Note: Officers with more than one job title may be intentionally listed here more than once.

Michael Mahoney, CEO
Eric Thepaut, Pres., Geographical
Daniel Brennan, CFO
Jodi Eddy, Chief Information Officer
Ian Meredith, Chief Medical Officer
Edward Mackey, Executive VP, Divisional
Joseph Fitzgerald, Executive VP
David Pierce, Executive VP
Kevin Ballinger, Executive VP
Desiree Ralls-Morrison, General Counsel
Jonathan Monson, Other Corporate Officer
Arthur Butcher, President, Divisional
Jeffrey Mirviss, President, Divisional
Maulik Nanavaty, President, Divisional
Warren Wang, President, Geographical
John Sorenson, Senior VP, Divisional
Wendy Carruthers, Senior VP, Divisional

GROWTH PLANS/SPECIAL FEATURES:

Boston Scientific Corporation is a global developer, manufacturer and marketer of medical devices used in a broad range of interventional medical specialties. The firm comprises seven core businesses organized into three segments: cardiovascular, rhythm management and MedSurg. The cardiovascular segment has two business units: the interventional cardiology business develops and manufactures technologies for diagnosing and treating coronary artery disease and other cardiovascular disorders, including structural heart conditions; and the peripheral interventions business develops and manufactures products to diagnose and treat peripheral arterial diseases, including a broad line of medical devices used in percutaneous transluminal angioplasty (PTA) and peripheral vascular diseases, as well as products to diagnose, treat and ease various forms of cancer. The rhythm management segment has three business units: the cardiac rhythm management business develops and manufactures a variety of implantable devices that monitor the heart and deliver electricity to treat cardiac abnormalities; the electrophysiology business develops and manufactures less-invasive medical technologies used in the diagnosis and treatment of rate and rhythm disorders of the heart, including a broad portfolio of therapeutic and diagnostic catheters and a variety of equipment used in the electrophysiology lab; and the neuromodulation business develops and manufactures devices to treat various neurological movement disorders and manage chronic pain. Last, the MedSurg segment has three business units: the endoscopy business develops and manufactures devices to diagnose and treat a range of gastrointestinal and pulmonary conditions with innovative, less-invasive technologies; the urology and pelvic health business develops and manufactures devices to treat various urological and pelvic conditions for both male and female anatomies; and the neuromodulation business develops and manufactures devices to treat various neurological movement disorders and manage chronic pain. In December 2018, Boston Scientific acquired the remaining shares of Millipede, Inc.

The firm offers comprehensive health benefits and employee assistance programs.

FINANCIAL DATA:
Note: Data for latest year may not have been available at press time.

In U.S. $	2018	2017	2016	2015	2014	2013
Revenue	9,823,000,000	9,048,001,000	8,386,000,000	7,477,000,000	7,380,000,000	7,143,000,000
R&D Expense	1,113,000,000	997,000,000	920,000,000	876,000,000	817,000,000	861,000,000
Operating Income	1,659,000,000	1,531,000,000	1,319,000,000	990,000,000	902,000,000	884,000,000
Operating Margin %		.17%	.16%	.13%	.12%	.12%
SGA Expense	3,569,000,000	3,294,000,000	3,099,000,000	2,873,000,000	2,902,000,000	2,674,000,000
Net Income	1,671,000,000	104,000,000	347,000,000	-239,000,000	-119,000,000	-121,000,000
Operating Cash Flow	310,000,000	1,426,000,000	972,000,000	600,000,000	1,269,000,000	1,082,000,000
Capital Expenditure	316,000,000	319,000,000	376,000,000	247,000,000	259,000,000	245,000,000
EBITDA	2,557,000,000	2,006,000,000	1,225,000,000	403,000,000	432,000,000	790,000,000
Return on Assets %		.01%	.02%	-.01%	-.01%	-.01%
Return on Equity %		.02%	.05%	-.04%	-.02%	-.02%
Debt to Equity		0.544	0.805	0.898	0.598	0.648

CONTACT INFORMATION:
Phone: 508 683-4000 Fax: 508 647-2200
Toll-Free: 888-272-1001
Address: 300 Boston Scientific Way, Marlborough, MA 01752-1234 United States

STOCK TICKER/OTHER:
Stock Ticker: BSX
Employees: 27,000
Parent Company:

Exchange: NYS
Fiscal Year Ends: 12/31

SALARIES/BONUSES:
Top Exec. Salary: $1,234,630 Bonus: $
Second Exec. Salary: $639,958 Bonus: $

OTHER THOUGHTS:
Estimated Female Officers or Directors: 5
Hot Spot for Advancement for Women/Minorities: Y

Sales, profits and employees may be estimates. Financial information, benefits and other data can change quickly and may vary from those stated here.

Brightstar Corporation

www.brightstar.com

NAIC Code: 423690

TYPES OF BUSINESS:
Telecommunication Supply Chain & Distribution Services
Wireless Device & Accessories Distribution
Wireless Device Manufacturing
Supply Chain, Marketing and Retail Consultation

BRANDS/DIVISIONS/AFFILIATES:
SoftBank Group Corp
Brightstar India

GROWTH PLANS/SPECIAL FEATURES:
Brightstar Corporation, a wholly-owned subsidiary of SoftBank Group Corp., distributes and manages telecommunication devices and accessories globally. The firm serves carrier, retail and enterprise customers across 57 countries worldwide and process over 80 million devices annually. Brightstar operates at every stage of the device lifecycle to provide an integrated experience with its customer's business, from the moment it is manufactured to the time it is traded in and remarketed. For businesses, Brightstar also operates at every stage of the device lifecycle in order to provide integrated services that link seamlessly. This infrastructure enables businesses to better serve their customers by providing end-to-end service. Majority-owned Brightstar India (a joint venture with Bharti Enterprises) assists with distribution across India.

CONTACTS: Note: Officers with more than one job title may be intentionally listed here more than once.
Paul S. Galant, CEO
Arturo A. Osorio, Pres.
Dennis J. Strand, Pres., Brightstar Financial Svcs.
Joe Kalinoski, CFO
Catherine Smith, Sr. VP
Bela Lainck, Pres., Buy-Back & Trade-In Solutions
Rafael M. de Guzman, III, VP-Strategy
Oscar J. Fumagali, Chief Treas. Officer
Oscar J. Rojas, Pres., Brightstar Latin America
Arturo A. Osorio, Pres., Asia Pacific, Middle East & Africa
Jeff Gower, Pres., Brightstar U.S. & Canada
David Leach, CEO-eSecuritel
Michael Singer, Sr. VP-Global Strategy & New Bus. Dev.
Ramon Colomina, Pres., Supply Chain Solutions

FINANCIAL DATA: Note: Data for latest year may not have been available at press time.

In U.S. $	2018	2017	2016	2015	2014	2013
Revenue	10,500,000,000	10,000,000,000	7,750,000,000	7,600,000,000	7,200,000,000	7,228,000,000
R&D Expense						
Operating Income						
Operating Margin %						
SGA Expense						
Net Income						
Operating Cash Flow						
Capital Expenditure						
EBITDA						
Return on Assets %						
Return on Equity %						
Debt to Equity						

CONTACT INFORMATION:
Phone: 305-421-6000 Fax:
Toll-Free:
Address: 9725 NW 117th Ave., #105, Miami, FL 33178 United States

STOCK TICKER/OTHER:
Stock Ticker: Subsidiary Exchange:
Employees: 9,000 Fiscal Year Ends: 12/31
Parent Company: SoftBank Group Corp

SALARIES/BONUSES:
Top Exec. Salary: $ Bonus: $
Second Exec. Salary: $ Bonus: $

OTHER THOUGHTS:
Estimated Female Officers or Directors: 1
Hot Spot for Advancement for Women/Minorities:

Sales, profits and employees may be estimates. Financial information, benefits and other data can change quickly and may vary from those stated here.

Brinker International Inc

NAIC Code: 722511

www.brinker.com

TYPES OF BUSINESS:
Casual Dining Restaurants

BRANDS/DIVISIONS/AFFILIATES:
Chili's Grill and Bar
Maggiano's Little Italy

CONTACTS:
Note: Officers with more than one job title may be intentionally listed here more than once.

Wyman Roberts, CEO
Joseph Taylor, CFO
Joseph Depinto, Director
Steve Provost, Executive VP, Subsidiary
Kelly Baltes, Executive VP, Subsidiary
Wade Allen, Other Executive Officer
Rick Badgley, Other Executive Officer
Charles Lousignont, Senior VP, Divisional

GROWTH PLANS/SPECIAL FEATURES:

Brinker International, Inc. owns, develops, operates and franchises over 1,685 casual dining restaurant chains primarily in 49 U.S. states, Washington DC and two U.S. territories under two brands, Chili's Grill & Bar and Maggiano's Little Italy. Chili's Grill & Bar serves a variety of fresh Tex-Mex lunch and dinner items, and also offers a To-Go menu (which is available online). Entree selections for Chili's range in price from approximately $6 to $18.99. All company-owned Chili's restaurants are outfitted with Ziosk multi-functional table top tablets that provide entertainment, ordering, guest survey and pay-at-the-table capabilities. Maggiano's Little Italy is a classic Italian-American restaurant, featuring individual and family style menus and extensive banquet facilities. Entree selections for Maggiano's range in price from approximately $13.95 to $47.95. Brinker International's growth plans include expansion through franchises and joint ventures, most revolving around Chili's Grill & Bar. In particular, it plans to focus its international growth in emerging markets. As of June 2018, of the firm's 1685+ restaurants, more than 415 are located outside mainland U.S. including the territories of Guam and Puerto Rico, and the countries of Bahrain, Canada, Chile, Costa Rica, Dominican Republic, Ecuador, Egypt, El Salvador, Germany, Guatemala, Honduras, India, Indonesia, Japan, Jordan, Kuwait, Lebanon, Malaysia, Mexico, Morocco, Oman, Panama, Peru, Philippines, Qatar, Saudi Arabia, Singapore, South Korea, Taiwan, Tunisia and United Arab Emirates. During 2018, Brinker International entered into new development agreements for development in China.

The firm offers employees medical, dental, vision, life and short-term disability insurance; prescription discounts; flexible spending accounts; an employee assistance program; 401(k); discounts at company restaurants; and reimbursement programs.

FINANCIAL DATA:
Note: Data for latest year may not have been available at press time.

In U.S. $	2018	2017	2016	2015	2014	2013
Revenue	3,135,417,000	3,150,837,000	3,257,489,000	3,002,278,000	2,905,452,000	2,846,098,000
R&D Expense						
Operating Income	254,325,000	272,123,000	331,254,000	316,460,000	291,112,000	272,633,000
Operating Margin %		.08%	.10%	.11%	.10%	.10%
SGA Expense	136,012,000	132,819,000	127,593,000	133,467,000	132,094,000	134,538,000
Net Income	125,882,000	150,823,000	200,745,000	196,694,000	154,039,000	163,359,000
Operating Cash Flow	284,451,000	312,886,000	394,700,000	368,611,000	359,842,000	290,688,000
Capital Expenditure	101,281,000	102,573,000	112,788,000	140,262,000	161,066,000	131,531,000
EBITDA	382,532,000	416,452,000	475,329,000	458,525,000	380,460,000	390,914,000
Return on Assets %		.10%	.14%	.13%	.10%	.11%
Return on Equity %					1.45%	.71%
Debt to Equity					13.191	5.223

CONTACT INFORMATION:
Phone: 972 980-9917 Fax: 972 770-9593
Toll-Free:
Address: 6820 LBJ Freeway, Dallas, TX 75240 United States

STOCK TICKER/OTHER:
Stock Ticker: EAT
Employees: 58,478
Parent Company:

Exchange: NYS
Fiscal Year Ends: 06/30

SALARIES/BONUSES:
Top Exec. Salary: $1,000,000 Bonus: $
Second Exec. Salary: $540,962 Bonus: $

OTHER THOUGHTS:
Estimated Female Officers or Directors: 3
Hot Spot for Advancement for Women/Minorities: Y

Sales, profits and employees may be estimates. Financial information, benefits and other data can change quickly and may vary from those stated here.

Bristol-Myers Squibb Company

NAIC Code: 325412

www.bms.com

TYPES OF BUSINESS:
Drugs-Diversified
Medical Imaging Products
Nutritional Products

BRANDS/DIVISIONS/AFFILIATES:
Opdivo
Eliquis
Orencia

CONTACTS:
Note: Officers with more than one job title may be intentionally listed here more than once.

Giovanni Caforio, CEO
Charles Bancroft, CFO
Adam Dubow, Chief Compliance Officer
Paul von Autenried, Chief Information Officer
Thomas Lynch, Chief Scientific Officer
Christopher Boerner, Executive VP
Sandra Leung, General Counsel
Ann Judge, Other Executive Officer
Louis Schmukler, President, Divisional
John Elicker, Senior VP, Divisional
Paul Biondi, Senior VP, Divisional
Karen Santiago, Senior VP

GROWTH PLANS/SPECIAL FEATURES:

Bristol-Myers Squibb Company (BMS) discovers, develops, licenses, manufactures, markets, distributes and sells biopharmaceutical products on a global basis. BMS focuses on discovering, developing and delivering transformational medicines for patients facing serious diseases such as cancer, as well as inflammatory, immunologic or cardiovascular diseases. The company manufactures its products in the U.S., Puerto Rico and in four foreign countries, with 56% of 2018 revenues being derived from the U.S., 25% from Europe and 19% from the rest of the world. The firm's pharmaceutical products include chemically-synthesized or small molecule drugs and products produced from biological processes (biologics). Small molecule drugs are typically administered orally, and biologics are typically administered through injections or by intravenous infusion. Just a few of BMS' products include: Opdivo (nivolumab), a fully-human monoclonal antibody used to treat several anti-cancer indications; Eliquis (apixaban), an oral Factor Xa inhibitor targeted at stroke prevention in adult patients with non-valvular atrial fibrillation (NVAF); and Orencia (abatacept), a fusion protein for adult patients with moderately-to-severely active rheumatoid arthritis and psoriatic arthritis (PsA), as well as for reducing signs and symptoms in certain pediatric patients with moderately-to-severely active polyarticular juvenile idiopathic arthritis (JIA). The company's products are primarily sold to wholesalers, retail pharmacies, hospitals, government entities and the medical profession. Pipeline categories in current (early-2019) stages of development include oncology, immunoscience, cardiovascular and fibrotic diseases.

BMS offers employees medical and dental insurance; pension and 401(k) plans; short- and long-term disability coverage; travel accident insurance; an employee assistance plan; and adoption assistance.

FINANCIAL DATA:
Note: Data for latest year may not have been available at press time.

In U.S. $	2018	2017	2016	2015	2014	2013
Revenue	22,561,000,000	20,776,000,000	19,427,000,000	16,560,000,000	15,879,000,000	16,385,000,000
R&D Expense	6,345,000,000	6,411,000,000	4,940,000,000	5,920,000,000	4,534,000,000	3,731,000,000
Operating Income	5,118,000,000	3,450,000,000	4,539,000,000	1,730,000,000	1,714,000,000	2,931,000,000
Operating Margin %		.17%	.23%	.10%	.11%	.18%
SGA Expense	4,551,000,000	4,849,000,000	5,002,000,000	5,001,000,000	5,699,000,000	5,104,000,000
Net Income	4,920,000,000	1,007,000,000	4,457,000,000	1,565,000,000	2,004,000,000	2,563,000,000
Operating Cash Flow	5,940,000,000	5,275,000,000	2,850,000,000	1,832,000,000	3,148,000,000	3,545,000,000
Capital Expenditure	951,000,000	1,055,000,000	1,215,000,000	820,000,000	526,000,000	537,000,000
EBITDA	6,788,000,000	6,116,000,000	6,464,000,000	2,637,000,000	3,051,000,000	3,853,000,000
Return on Assets %		.03%	.14%	.05%	.06%	.07%
Return on Equity %		.07%	.29%	.11%	.13%	.18%
Debt to Equity		0.594	0.353	0.459	0.488	0.527

CONTACT INFORMATION:
Phone: 212 546-4000   Fax: 212 546-4020
Toll-Free:
Address: 430 E. 29th St., 14/Fl, New York, NY 10016 United States

SALARIES/BONUSES:
Top Exec. Salary: $1,637,500   Bonus: $
Second Exec. Salary: $1,027,212   Bonus: $

STOCK TICKER/OTHER:
Stock Ticker: BMY   Exchange: NYS
Employees: 25,000   Fiscal Year Ends: 12/31
Parent Company:

OTHER THOUGHTS:
Estimated Female Officers or Directors: 4
Hot Spot for Advancement for Women/Minorities: Y

Broadcom Inc

NAIC Code: 335313

www.broadcom.com

TYPES OF BUSINESS:
Electrical Switches, Sensors, MEMS, Optomechanicals
Analog Interface Components
Optoelectronics
LEDs

BRANDS/DIVISIONS/AFFILIATES:
CA Technologies

CONTACTS: Note: Officers with more than one job title may be intentionally listed here more than once.
Hock Tan, CEO
Thomas Krause, CFO
Kirsten Spears, Chief Accounting Officer
Henry Samueli, Chief Technology Officer
Bryan Ingram, General Manager, Divisional
Mark Brazeal, Other Executive Officer
Charles Kawwas, Other Executive Officer

GROWTH PLANS/SPECIAL FEATURES:
Broadcom, Inc. designs, develops and supplies a broad range of semiconductor and infrastructure software solutions, with a focus on connectivity technologies. The firm's applications include data center, enterprise storage, broadband, wired networking, wireless communications, mobile communications, industrial, automotive and software solutions. Broadcom's products are vast, and include wireless embedded solutions, radio frequency components, storage adapters, controllers, integrated circuits, fiber channel networking, broadband:CPE-gateway/infrastructure/set-top box, embedded processors, network processors, ethernet connectivity, switches, bridges, modules, components, light-emitting-diodes (LEDs), displays, motion control encoders, optocouplers, optical sensors, custom silicon, mainframe software and enterprise software. In November 2018, the firm acquired CA Technologies, a producer of software used in corporate IT infrastructure. The following December, Broadcom sold Veracode, Inc., a provider of cloud-based application security software solutions and services acquired in the CA Technologies transaction, to Thoma Bravo, LLC, a leading private equity investment firm, in an all-cash transaction valued at $950 million.

FINANCIAL DATA: Note: Data for latest year may not have been available at press time.

In U.S. $	2018	2017	2016	2015	2014	2013
Revenue	20,848,000,000	17,636,000,000	13,240,000,000	6,824,000,000	4,269,000,000	2,520,000,000
R&D Expense	3,768,000,000	3,292,000,000	2,674,000,000	1,049,000,000	695,000,000	398,000,000
Operating Income	5,368,000,000	2,666,000,000	587,000,000	1,769,000,000	578,000,000	554,000,000
Operating Margin %		.15%	.04%	.26%	.14%	.22%
SGA Expense	1,056,000,000	787,000,000	806,000,000	486,000,000	407,000,000	222,000,000
Net Income	12,259,000,000	1,692,000,000	-1,739,000,000	1,364,000,000	263,000,000	552,000,000
Operating Cash Flow	8,880,000,000	6,551,000,000	3,411,000,000	2,318,000,000	1,175,000,000	722,000,000
Capital Expenditure	635,000,000	1,069,000,000	723,000,000	593,000,000	409,000,000	236,000,000
EBITDA	9,254,000,000	7,016,000,000	2,520,000,000	2,620,000,000	1,077,000,000	756,000,000
Return on Assets %		.03%	-.06%	.13%	.04%	.18%
Return on Equity %		.09%	-.15%	.34%	.09%	.21%
Debt to Equity		0.859	0.698	0.828	1.401	0.00

CONTACT INFORMATION:
Phone: 408-433-8000 Fax:
Toll-Free:
Address: 1320 Ridder Park Dr., San Jose, CA 95131 United States

SALARIES/BONUSES:
Top Exec. Salary: $1,121,154 Bonus: $
Second Exec. Salary: $497,924 Bonus: $200,000

STOCK TICKER/OTHER:
Stock Ticker: AVGO
Employees: 15,700
Parent Company:

Exchange: NAS
Fiscal Year Ends: 10/31

OTHER THOUGHTS:
Estimated Female Officers or Directors: 5
Hot Spot for Advancement for Women/Minorities: Y

Brookdale Senior Living Inc

www.brookdaleliving.com

NAIC Code: 623310

TYPES OF BUSINESS:
Assisted Living Facilities
Retirement Communities
Assisted Living Communities
Continued Care Retirement Communities (CCRCs)
Managed Facilities

BRANDS/DIVISIONS/AFFILIATES:

CONTACTS: Note: Officers with more than one job title may be intentionally listed here more than once.
Lucinda Baier, CEO
Steven E. Swain, CFO
Lee Wielansky, Chairman of the Board
Dawn Kussow, Chief Accounting Officer
H. Kaestner, Executive VP, Divisional
Mary Patchett, Executive VP, Divisional
George Hicks, Executive VP, Divisional
Chad White, Executive VP
Ryan Wilson, Other Executive Officer
Anthony Mollica, President, Divisional

GROWTH PLANS/SPECIAL FEATURES:
Brookdale Senior Living, Inc. is one of the largest senior living facility operators in the U.S. It operates 892 owned, leased or managed senior living facilities in 45 states that can serve approximately 84,000 residents (as of December 31, 2018). Brookdale operates independent living, assisted living and dementia-care communities, as well as continuing care retirement centers (CCRCs). The facilities strive to offer residents a home-like setting and typically feature assistance with daily living, multiple forms of therapy and various home health services. Brookdale offers a full spectrum of care options, including independent living, personalized assisted living, rehabilitation and skilled nursing. It operates memory care communities, which are freestanding assisted living communities designed for residents with Alzheimer's disease and other dementias. Through the firm's ancillary services programs, it also offers a range of home health, hospice and outpatient therapy services to residents of many Brookdale communities and to seniors living outside of Brookdale communities. The company maintains its own culinary arts institute, which offers a training ground for chefs and dining staff. Owned communities generated the largest share (44.7%) of 2018 revenues, followed by leased communities (42.6%), and 12.7% from health care services. Brookdale generated 81.5% of 2018 revenue from private pay customers, with the remainder from government reimbursement programs (primarily Medicare).

FINANCIAL DATA: Note: Data for latest year may not have been available at press time.

In U.S. $	2018	2017	2016	2015	2014	2013
Revenue	4,531,426,000	4,747,116,000	4,976,980,000	4,960,608,000	3,831,706,000	2,891,966,000
R&D Expense						
Operating Income	66,625,000	176,586,000	232,535,000	-22,870,000	-7,964,000	144,179,000
Operating Margin %		.04%	.05%	.00%	.00%	.05%
SGA Expense	553,789,000	595,167,000	687,044,000	738,153,000	604,097,000	461,277,000
Net Income	-528,258,000	-571,419,000	-404,397,000	-457,477,000	-148,990,000	-3,584,000
Operating Cash Flow	203,961,000	366,664,000	365,732,000	292,366,000	242,652,000	366,121,000
Capital Expenditure	225,473,000	213,887,000	333,647,000	411,051,000	304,245,000	257,527,000
EBITDA	149,513,000	219,936,000	506,583,000	570,768,000	451,781,000	405,308,000
Return on Assets %		-.07%	-.04%	-.04%	-.02%	.00%
Return on Equity %		-.32%	-.18%	-.17%	-.08%	.00%
Debt to Equity		2.966	2.806	2.52	2.08	2.385

CONTACT INFORMATION:
Phone: 615 221-2250 Fax: 615 221-2289
Toll-Free: 866-785-9025
Address: 111 Westwood Place, Ste. 400, Brentwood, TN 37027 United States

STOCK TICKER/OTHER:
Stock Ticker: BKD
Employees: 77,600
Parent Company:

Exchange: NYS
Fiscal Year Ends: 12/31

SALARIES/BONUSES:
Top Exec. Salary: $950,000 Bonus: $
Second Exec. Salary: $550,000 Bonus: $

OTHER THOUGHTS:
Estimated Female Officers or Directors: 1
Hot Spot for Advancement for Women/Minorities:

Brown & Brown Inc

NAIC Code: 524210

www.bbinsurance.com

TYPES OF BUSINESS:
Insurance-Property & Casualty
Risk Management Services
Professional Liability Insurance
Third-Party Administration & Consulting
Managed Care & Utilization Management Services
Reinsurance
Life Insurance
Health Insurance

BRANDS/DIVISIONS/AFFILIATES:
Yozell Associates
LSI Lender Services LLC
Innovative Risk Solutions Inc
WBR Insurance LLC
Twinbrook Insruance Brokerage Inc
United Development Systems Inc
ALMEA Insurance Inc
MEDVAL LLC

CONTACTS:
Note: Officers with more than one job title may be intentionally listed here more than once.

R. Watts, CFO
J. Brown, Chairman of the Board
James Hays, Director
Robert Lloyd, Executive VP
Julie Ryan, Executive VP
J. Penny, Other Executive Officer
Anthony Strianese, President, Divisional
Chris Walker, President, Divisional
J. Brown, President

GROWTH PLANS/SPECIAL FEATURES:

Brown & Brown, Inc. is a diversified insurance agency, wholesale brokerage, insurance programs and service organization. The firm markets and sells insurance products and services, primarily in the property, casualty and employee benefit areas. The company operates through 286 locations in 42 states, as well as international offices in the U.K., Bermuda, Canada and the Cayman Islands. It operates through four segments: retail, wholesale brokerage, national programs and services. The retail segment provides a range of insurance products and services to commercial, public entity, professional and individual customers. The wholesale brokerage division markets and sells excess and surplus commercial and personal insurance and reinsurance, primarily through independent agents and brokers. The national programs division consists of two units: professional programs, which provides professional liability and related package products for certain medical, financial, real estate and law professionals; and special programs, which markets targeted products and services designated for specific industries, trade groups, public entities and market niches. The services division provides clients with third-party claims administration, consulting for the workers' compensation insurance markets, comprehensive medical utilization management services and Medicare Secondary Payer statute compliance-related services. The retail division generates the majority (51.8%) of the company's revenue, followed by the national programs division (24.6%), the wholesale brokerage division (14.2%), and the services division (9.4%). During 2019, Brown & Brown acquired Yozell Associates; LSI Lender Services, LLC; Innovative Risk Solutions, Inc.; WBR Insurance, LLC; Twinbrook Insurance Brokerage, Inc.; United Development Systems, Inc.; ALMEA Insurance, Inc.; MEDVAL, LLC; Cossio Insurance Agency; Austin & Austin Insurance Services, Inc.; and CKP Insurance, LLC, among others.

FINANCIAL DATA:
Note: Data for latest year may not have been available at press time.

In U.S. $	2018	2017	2016	2015	2014	2013
Revenue	2,009,857,000	1,857,270,000	1,762,787,000	1,656,951,000	1,567,460,000	1,355,503,000
R&D Expense						
Operating Income	501,090,000	493,455,000	469,418,000	443,187,000	424,773,000	375,944,000
Operating Margin %		.27%	.27%	.27%	.27%	.28%
SGA Expense				15,513,000	19,363,000	22,603,000
Net Income	344,255,000	399,630,000	257,491,000	243,318,000	206,896,000	217,112,000
Operating Cash Flow	567,529,000	441,975,000	375,158,000	411,848,000	385,019,000	389,374,000
Capital Expenditure	41,520,000	24,192,000	17,765,000	18,375,000	24,923,000	16,366,000
EBITDA	612,420,000	596,182,000	570,646,000	550,118,000	471,993,000	459,466,000
Return on Assets %		.07%	.05%	.05%	.05%	.06%
Return on Equity %		.16%	.11%	.11%	.10%	.11%
Debt to Equity		0.331	0.431	0.502	0.545	0.189

CONTACT INFORMATION:
Phone: 386 252-9601 Fax: 386 239-7252
Toll-Free:
Address: 220 S. Ridgewood Ave., Daytona Beach, FL 32114 United States

STOCK TICKER/OTHER:
Stock Ticker: BRO
Employees: 8,297
Parent Company:

Exchange: NYS
Fiscal Year Ends: 12/31

SALARIES/BONUSES:
Top Exec. Salary: $1,000,000 Bonus: $
Second Exec. Salary: $600,000 Bonus: $

OTHER THOUGHTS:
Estimated Female Officers or Directors: 3
Hot Spot for Advancement for Women/Minorities: Y

Buffalo Wild Wings Inc

NAIC Code: 722513

www.buffalowildwings.com

TYPES OF BUSINESS:
Limited-Service Restaurants

BRANDS/DIVISIONS/AFFILIATES:
Roark Capital Group
Inspire Brands Inc
Arby's Restaurant Group Inc
Jammin Jalapeno
Thai Curry
Desert Heat
Blazin
Buffalito

CONTACTS:
Note: Officers with more than one job title may be intentionally listed here more than once.

Lyle Tick, Pres.
John Bowie, COO
Alexander Ware, CFO
Seth Freeman, CMO
Emily Decker, General Counsel
Lee Patterson, Senior VP, Divisional
Andrew Block, Senior VP, Divisional

GROWTH PLANS/SPECIAL FEATURES:

Buffalo Wild Wings, Inc. is the owner, operator and franchisor of Buffalo Wild Wings Grill & Bar restaurants. The company operates more than 1,230 restaurants located in the U.S., Canada, Mexico, the Middle East, Philippines, Panama and Vietnam. The restaurants' proprietary item is its Buffalo, New York-style chicken wings served with any of its 21 signature sauces, including Jammin' Jalapeno and Thai Curry; and five signature seasonings, such as Sweet BBQ, Desert Heat, Buffalo and Blazin. Orders can range from 6 wings to 100, with larger orders available for parties. Additionally, the company's menu also features items such as chicken tenders, salads, Wild Flatbreads, sandwiches, popcorn shrimp, specialty hamburgers, wraps, Buffalito soft tacos and appetizers, which are made to order and are available for dine-in and take-out. The restaurants are geared toward both sports fans and families, and designed to make guests feel as if they were in an actual sports stadium. Most restaurants have major sporting events displayed on projection screens, as well as approximately 60 additional televisions either broadcasting various sporting events, or providing the capability to play Buzztime Trivia or other video games. A typical size is approximately 6,200-6,500 square feet. Buffalo Wild Wings restaurants feature anywhere from 20-30 domestic, imported and craft beers on tap, and also sell bottled beers, wines and liquor. Restaurant operations generally are open on a daily basis from 11am-1am, with franchising agreements requiring franchisees to operate the establishments for at least twelve hours a day. During 2018, Buffalo Wild Wings was acquired by Arby's Restaurant Group, Inc., which is part of the Inspire Brands, Inc. family of restaurants and backed by private equity firm, Roark Capital Group.

FINANCIAL DATA:
Note: Data for latest year may not have been available at press time.

In U.S. $	2018	2017	2016	2015	2014	2013
Revenue	2,100,000,000	2,000,000,000	1,986,792,960	1,812,722,048	1,516,222,976	1,266,718,976
R&D Expense						
Operating Income						
Operating Margin %						
SGA Expense						
Net Income			94,745,000	95,069,000	94,094,000	71,554,000
Operating Cash Flow						
Capital Expenditure						
EBITDA						
Return on Assets %						
Return on Equity %						
Debt to Equity						

CONTACT INFORMATION:
Phone: 952 593-9943
Fax: 952 593-9787
Toll-Free: 800-499-9586
Address: 5500 Wayzata Blvd., Ste. 1600, Minneapolis, MN 55416 United States

STOCK TICKER/OTHER:
Stock Ticker: Private
Exchange:
Employees: 37,200
Fiscal Year Ends: 12/31
Parent Company: Roark Capital Management LLC

SALARIES/BONUSES:
Top Exec. Salary: $
Bonus: $
Second Exec. Salary: $
Bonus: $

OTHER THOUGHTS:
Estimated Female Officers or Directors: 5
Hot Spot for Advancement for Women/Minorities: Y

Bunge Limited

NAIC Code: 311200

www.bunge.com

TYPES OF BUSINESS:
Crop Production, Soybeans
Oils & Shortening
Oilseed Processing
Ingredients & Prepared Foods
Fertilizer
Milling

BRANDS/DIVISIONS/AFFILIATES:
IOI Loders Croklaan

CONTACTS:
Note: Officers with more than one job title may be intentionally listed here more than once.

Gregory Heckman, CEO
Thomas Boehlert, CFO
Kathleen Hyle, Chairman of the Board
J. Simmons, Chief Accounting Officer
Robert Coviello, Chief Strategy Officer
David Kabbes, Executive VP, Divisional
Deborah Borg, Executive VP
Pierre Mauger, Other Executive Officer
Raul Padilla, President, Divisional
Brian Zachman, President, Divisional
Christos Dimopoulous, President, Divisional

GROWTH PLANS/SPECIAL FEATURES:
Bunge Limited is a food and agribusiness involved in the farm-to-consumer food chain. Through its facilities in North and South America, the company manufactures fertilizer and animal feed for farmers; transports oilseeds and grains to markets worldwide; processes oilseeds to produce meal for the livestock industry and oil for food processing, food service and biofuel industries; produces bottled oils, mayonnaise, margarines and other food products for consumers; and mills wheat and corn for food processors, bakeries, brewers and other commercial customers. The company divides its operations into five segments: Agribusiness, Edible Oil Products, Sugar and Bioenergy, Milling Products and Fertilize. The Agribusiness segment is characterized by both inputs and outputs being agricultural commodities and thus high volume and low margin. Additionally, the segment invests in biodiesel producers throughout the U.S., Argentina and Europe. The Edible Oil Products segment involves the processing, production and marketing of products derived from vegetable oils. The Sugar and Bioenergy segment involves sugarcane growing and milling in Brazil, sugar trading and merchandising in various countries, as well as sugarcane-based ethanol production and corn-based ethanol investments and related activities. The Milling Products segment involves the processing, production and marketing of products derived primarily from wheat and corn. The fertilizer division produces, blends and distributes solid and liquid nitrogen, phosphate and potash (NPK) fertilizers throughout South America, with assets and operations primarily located in Argentina. In 2018, Bunge completed its acquisition of a 70% ownership interest in IOI Loders Croklaan from IOI Corporation Berhad; sold its 49.9% stake in SB Renewables Oils, a facility specializing in the production of algae ingredients, such as Omega 3 rich oil, for aquaculture and animal feed, to Corbin nv, its former joint venture partner; and completed the sale of its international sugar trading operations to Wilmar Sugar Pte.

FINANCIAL DATA:
Note: Data for latest year may not have been available at press time.

In U.S. $	2018	2017	2016	2015	2014	2013
Revenue	45,743,000,000	45,794,000,000	42,679,000,000	43,455,000,000	57,161,000,000	61,347,000,000
R&D Expense						
Operating Income	843,000,000	319,000,000	1,124,000,000	1,258,000,000	930,000,000	1,201,000,000
Operating Margin %		.01%	.03%	.03%	.02%	.02%
SGA Expense	1,423,000,000	1,445,000,000	1,286,000,000	1,435,000,000	1,691,000,000	1,559,000,000
Net Income	267,000,000	160,000,000	745,000,000	791,000,000	515,000,000	306,000,000
Operating Cash Flow	-1,264,000,000	1,006,000,000	1,904,000,000	610,000,000	1,399,000,000	2,225,000,000
Capital Expenditure	493,000,000	662,000,000	784,000,000	649,000,000	839,000,000	1,042,000,000
EBITDA	1,417,000,000	1,102,000,000	1,777,000,000	1,854,000,000	1,688,000,000	1,945,000,000
Return on Assets %		.01%	.04%	.04%	.02%	.01%
Return on Equity %		.02%	.12%	.11%	.06%	.02%
Debt to Equity		0.644	0.476	0.51	0.368	0.347

CONTACT INFORMATION:
Phone: 914 684-2800   Fax: 914 684-3499
Toll-Free:
Address: 50 Main St., White Plains, NY 10606 United States

SALARIES/BONUSES:
Top Exec. Salary: $1,300,000   Bonus: $
Second Exec. Salary: $978,731   Bonus: $

STOCK TICKER/OTHER:
Stock Ticker: BG   Exchange: NYS
Employees: 32,000   Fiscal Year Ends: 12/31
Parent Company:

OTHER THOUGHTS:
Estimated Female Officers or Directors: 2
Hot Spot for Advancement for Women/Minorities:

Burns & McDonnell Inc

www.burnsmcd.com

NAIC Code: 541330

TYPES OF BUSINESS:
Engineering Services
Construction
Consulting
Environmental Consulting
Architecture & Design
Energy Transmission

BRANDS/DIVISIONS/AFFILIATES:

CONTACTS:
Note: Officers with more than one job title may be intentionally listed here more than once.
Ray Kowalik, CEO
Mark Taylor, CFO
Mark Taylor, Treas.
Don Greenwood, Pres., Construction
Ray Kowalik, VP
John Nobles, Pres., Process & Industrial

GROWTH PLANS/SPECIAL FEATURES:
Burns & McDonnell, Inc. is a family of companies that provide engineering, architectural, construction, environmental and consulting services across an array of industries on a global scale. Aviation services span every facility and every service related to the customer's commercial or private operation, including airfields, architecture, infrastructure, technology, security, cogeneration, commissioning, construction, environmental, code consulting, and wastewater/stormwater collection. Chemicals, oil and gas services include biorefining, business consulting, construction, electric power generation/exploration/production, industrial cogeneration, water/wastewater, facilities, midstream, pipeline, Tier 3 compliance and unmanned aerial systems/unmanned aerial vehicles (UAS/UAV). Commercial, retail and institutional services consist of planning, design and construction for project success, covering air quality/noise, architecture, business consulting, construction, commissioning, data/switch centers, federal/military, food/beverage, green buildings, mission-critical, smart buildings and more. Environmental services include air quality/noise, coal combustion residuals management, constructed wetland treatment systems, decommissioning/demolition, emerging contaminants, compliance, engineering, health and safety, studies, permitting, mitigation and much more. Government, military and municipal services include aircraft beddowns, airfields, architecture, cybersecurity, power transmission/distribution, planning, intelligent sea ports, technology and more. Manufacturing and industrial services include solutions for controlling costs and optimizing systems and processes. Power services include solutions for building business into the future, such as electric vehicles (EVs), energy storage/transmission/distribution, gas turbines, microgrids, nuclear, plant decommissioning and smart energy. Telecommunications services include backup systems, communication shelters, automation, EVs, fiber, local area networks, SCADA systems and much more. Transportation services include planning, designing and constructing ways to keep traffic flowing while saving time and money. Last, water services include water treatment, supply and systems solutions, erosion/sediment control and water program management.

FINANCIAL DATA:
Note: Data for latest year may not have been available at press time.

In U.S. $	2018	2017	2016	2015	2014	2013
Revenue	2,586,000,000	2,450,000,000	2,400,000,000	2,700,000,000	2,645,000,000	2,300,000,000
R&D Expense						
Operating Income						
Operating Margin %						
SGA Expense						
Net Income						
Operating Cash Flow						
Capital Expenditure						
EBITDA						
Return on Assets %						
Return on Equity %						
Debt to Equity						

CONTACT INFORMATION:
Phone: 816-333-9400   Fax: 816-822-3028
Toll-Free:
Address: 9400 Ward Pkwy., Kansas City, MO 64114 United States

SALARIES/BONUSES:
Top Exec. Salary: $ Bonus: $
Second Exec. Salary: $ Bonus: $

STOCK TICKER/OTHER:
Stock Ticker: Private
Employees: 7,000
Parent Company:

Exchange:
Fiscal Year Ends: 12/31

OTHER THOUGHTS:
Estimated Female Officers or Directors:
Hot Spot for Advancement for Women/Minorities:

Sales, profits and employees may be estimates. Financial information, benefits and other data can change quickly and may vary from those stated here.

C&S Wholesale Grocers Inc

www.cswg.com

NAIC Code: 424410

TYPES OF BUSINESS:
Wholesale Food Distribution
Warehousing
Wholesale Food Distribution
Produce
Meat
Health & Beauty Aids
Dairy Products
Fresh/Frozen Bakery Items

BRANDS/DIVISIONS/AFFILIATES:

CONTACTS: Note: Officers with more than one job title may be intentionally listed here more than once.
Mike Duffy, CEO
Kevin McNamara, CFO
Joe Cavaliere, Chief Commercial Officer
Asad Husain, Chief Human Resources Officer
George Dramalis, CIO
Mike Newbold, Chief Admin. Officer
Bruce Johnson, Chief Organization Effectiveness Officer
Peter Fiore, Exec. VP-Distribution Services
Rick Cohen, Chmn.
Bob Palmer, Exec. VP-Procurement & Sales

GROWTH PLANS/SPECIAL FEATURES:
C&S Wholesale Grocers, Inc. provides grocery retailers with warehousing, distribution and logistics service solutions. C&S delivers food and non-food items to approximately 14,000 stores in 15 states, including supermarket chains, independent supermarkets, mass marketers and wholesale clubs. It also distributes to military bases and retail stores. The company supplies over 170,000 items including private label products, such as produce, meat, dairy products, delicatessen products, frozen products, tobacco, beauty items and candy. The company's warehouse locations include facilities in Maryland, Alabama, Vermont, New York, Pennsylvania, California, Florida, Indiana, Louisiana, Hawaii, Massachusetts, New Hampshire, South Carolina, New Jersey and Connecticut. C&S has customers that include Giant of Carlisle, Giant of Landover, Safeway, Stop & Shop and Target. Through its subsidiaries and affiliates, C&S provides licensing trademark services and automated warehouse technologies to retail grocery stores and assists large food manufacturers in developing logistical solutions.

FINANCIAL DATA: Note: Data for latest year may not have been available at press time.

In U.S. $	2018	2017	2016	2015	2014	2013
Revenue	32,025,000,000	30,500,000,000	30,000,000,000	29,000,000,000	25,900,000,000	24,200,000,000
R&D Expense						
Operating Income						
Operating Margin %						
SGA Expense						
Net Income						
Operating Cash Flow						
Capital Expenditure						
EBITDA						
Return on Assets %						
Return on Equity %						
Debt to Equity						

CONTACT INFORMATION:
Phone: 603-354-7000 Fax:
Toll-Free:
Address: 7 Corporate Dr., Keene, NH 03431 United States

STOCK TICKER/OTHER:
Stock Ticker: Private
Employees: 14,000
Parent Company:

Exchange:
Fiscal Year Ends: 09/30

SALARIES/BONUSES:
Top Exec. Salary: $ Bonus: $
Second Exec. Salary: $ Bonus: $

OTHER THOUGHTS:
Estimated Female Officers or Directors:
Hot Spot for Advancement for Women/Minorities:

Cabela's Inc

www.cabelas.com

NAIC Code: 451110

TYPES OF BUSINESS:
Sporting Goods Stores
Hunting & Fishing Supplies
Camping Equipment
Outdoor Apparel
Catalog & Online Sales
Credit Card Programs

BRANDS/DIVISIONS/AFFILIATES:
BPS Direct LLC (Bass Pro Shops)
Cabelas.com
Cabelas.ca
World's Foremeost Bank
Cabela's CLUB VISA

CONTACTS:
Note: Officers with more than one job title may be intentionally listed here more than once.

Scott K. Williams, Pres.
Thomas Millner, CEO
Ralph W. Castner, CFO
Douglas R. Means, CIO
Douglas Means, Executive VP
Scott Williams, President
Brent LaSure, Secretary

GROWTH PLANS/SPECIAL FEATURES:

Cabela's, Inc., a subsidiary of BPS Direct, LLC (dba Bass Pro Shops), is a leading retailer of outdoor and hunting supply merchandise. The company's products include merchandise and equipment for hunting, fishing, marine use, camping and recreational sport shooting, as well as casual and outdoor apparel, footwear, optics, vehicle accessories and gifts and home furnishings comprising an outdoor theme. Retail stores range in size from 40,000 to 246,000 square feet, which either comprise the company's standard format or its large/tourist format. Cabela's also offers its products via e-commerce websites (Cabelas.com and Cabelas.ca), mobile apps, in-bound telemarketing and print catalog distributions. Wholly-owned bank subsidiary, World's Foremost Bank (WFB), issues and manages the Cabela's CLUB VISA credit card, a rewards-based program. WFB is a Nebraska state-chartered bank insured by the Federal Deposit Insurance Corporation and manages more than 2 million active credit card accounts.

FINANCIAL DATA:
Note: Data for latest year may not have been available at press time.

In U.S. $	2018	2017	2016	2015	2014	2013
Revenue	4,410,000,000	4,200,000,000	4,129,359,104	3,997,701,888	3,647,650,048	3,599,577,088
R&D Expense						
Operating Income						
Operating Margin %						
SGA Expense						
Net Income			146,947,008	189,330,000	201,715,008	224,390,000
Operating Cash Flow						
Capital Expenditure						
EBITDA						
Return on Assets %						
Return on Equity %						
Debt to Equity						

CONTACT INFORMATION:
Phone: 308 254-5505   Fax: 308 254-4800
Toll-Free: 800-237-4444
Address: One Cabela Dr., Sidney, NE 69160 United States

STOCK TICKER/OTHER:
Stock Ticker: Private   Exchange:
Employees: 19,100   Fiscal Year Ends: 12/31
Parent Company: BPS Direct LLC (Bass Pro Shops)

SALARIES/BONUSES:
Top Exec. Salary: $ Bonus: $
Second Exec. Salary: $ Bonus: $

OTHER THOUGHTS:
Estimated Female Officers or Directors: 2
Hot Spot for Advancement for Women/Minorities:

Sales, profits and employees may be estimates. Financial information, benefits and other data can change quickly and may vary from those stated here.

CACI International Inc

www.caci.com

NAIC Code: 541512

TYPES OF BUSINESS:
Consulting-InfoTech Related
Engineering Simulation Software
Custom Software Engineering
Managed Network Services
Information Management Tools
Knowledge Management
Systems Integration
Radio Frequency Identification (RFID)

BRANDS/DIVISIONS/AFFILIATES:
CACI Limited
CACI BV

CONTACTS:
Note: Officers with more than one job title may be intentionally listed here more than once.

Gregory Bradford, CEO, Subsidiary
Kenneth Asbury, CEO
Thomas Mutryn, CFO
J. London, Chairman of the Board
Christopher Voci, Chief Accounting Officer
John Mengucci, COO
J. Koegel, Executive VP
DeEtte Gray, President, Divisional

GROWTH PLANS/SPECIAL FEATURES:

CACI International, Inc. is a technology development company that provides IT and network services to defense, intelligence and other government departments. Contracts with the U.S. government make up approximately 93.5% of the company's annual revenue. CACI's domestic operations provide business solutions that combine federal domain expertise with technology solutions; command and control (C2) solutions, consisting of hardware, software and interfaces for seamless C2 capabilities; communications solutions for soldier systems, mobile platforms, fixed facilities and the enterprise; cyber security solutions; enterprise IT solutions; health delivery systems, integrating electronic health records, sharpening emergency responsiveness and improving costs; intelligence services that converts data collected into knowledge for decision-making; investigation and litigation support; logistics and material readiness solutions for the secure global flow and storage of goods, services and information in support of U.S. government agencies; space operations and resiliency services in support of the U.S. critical space ground and launch systems; and the integration of surveillance and reconnaissance technologies into platforms that enhance soldier and unit situational awareness, mobility, lethality, interoperability and survivability. International operations are conducted primarily through the firm's European subsidiaries, CACI Limited and CACI BV, which provide a diverse mix of IT services and proprietary data and software products. This division serves commercial and government customers throughout the U.K., continental Europe and around the world. In August 2018, CACI completed its acquisition of the Systems Engineering and Acquisition Support Services Business Unit of CSRA LLC, a managed affiliate of General Dynamics Information Technology, Inc.

The company offers employees medical, dental and vision insurance; life and AD&D insurance; short- and long-term disability coverage; flexible spending accounts; health club discounts; a 401(k); a discount stock purchase plan; credit union membership; tuition reimbursement; a group legal plan; an employee assistance program; a commuter benefit program; pet care discounts; and merchandise discounts.

FINANCIAL DATA:
Note: Data for latest year may not have been available at press time.

In U.S. $	2018	2017	2016	2015	2014	2013
Revenue	4,467,860,000	4,354,617,000	3,744,053,000	3,313,452,000	3,564,562,000	3,681,990,000
R&D Expense						
Operating Income	340,700,000	297,261,000	264,750,000	236,381,000	257,403,000	270,841,000
Operating Margin %		.07%	.07%	.07%	.07%	.07%
SGA Expense						
Net Income	301,171,000	163,671,000	142,799,000	126,195,000	135,316,000	151,689,000
Operating Cash Flow	325,127,000	281,250,000	242,577,000	223,215,000	198,643,000	249,331,000
Capital Expenditure	41,594,000	43,268,000	20,835,000	17,444,000	15,279,000	15,439,000
EBITDA	412,896,000	369,021,000	329,502,000	302,464,000	322,584,000	324,919,000
Return on Assets %		.04%	.04%	.04%	.05%	.06%
Return on Equity %		.10%	.09%	.09%	.11%	.13%
Debt to Equity		0.657	0.872	0.695	0.913	0.25

CONTACT INFORMATION:
Phone: 703 841-7800 Fax: 703 841-7882
Toll-Free:
Address: 1100 N. Glebe Rd., Arlington, VA 22201 United States

STOCK TICKER/OTHER:
Stock Ticker: CACI
Employees: 18,600
Parent Company:

Exchange: NYS
Fiscal Year Ends: 06/30

SALARIES/BONUSES:
Top Exec. Salary: $921,883 Bonus: $
Second Exec. Salary: $650,658 Bonus: $

OTHER THOUGHTS:
Estimated Female Officers or Directors: 5
Hot Spot for Advancement for Women/Minorities: Y

Sales, profits and employees may be estimates. Financial information, benefits and other data can change quickly and may vary from those stated here.

Cadence Design Systems Inc

www.cadence.com

NAIC Code: 0

TYPES OF BUSINESS:
Software-Electronic Design Automation
Training & Support Services
Design & Methodology Services

BRANDS/DIVISIONS/AFFILIATES:

CONTACTS:
Note: Officers with more than one job title may be intentionally listed here more than once.

Lip-Bu Tan, CEO
John Wall, CFO
John Shoven, Chairman of the Board
James Cowie, General Counsel
Anirudh Devgan, President
Chin-Chi Teng, Senior Executive VP, Divisional
Neil Zaman, Senior VP, Divisional
Surendra Babu Mandava, Senior VP, Divisional
Thomas Beckley, Senior VP, Divisional

GROWTH PLANS/SPECIAL FEATURES:

Cadence Design Systems, Inc. is a leading provider of system design enablement solutions and electronic design automation software/hardware used by semiconductor and electronic system customers to develop and design integrated circuits (ICs) and electronic devices. It licenses, sells and leases its hardware technology and provides design and methodology services throughout the world to help manage and accelerate electronic product development processes. Cadence combines its design technologies into platforms for five major design activities: functional verification, digital IC and signoff, custom IC, system interconnect and analysis and IP. Functional verification products are used to verify that the circuitry designed by customers will perform as intended. Digital IC design offerings are used by customers to create logical representations of a digital circuit or an IC that can be verified for correctness prior to implementation. Once the logic is verified, the design is converted to a format ready for silicon manufacturing. This division's signoff offering is comprised of tools used to signoff the design as ready for manufacture by a silicon foundry, which provides certification for this step. Custom IC design and verification offerings are used to create schematic and physical representations of circuits down to the transistor level for analog, mixed-signal, custom digital, memory and radio frequency designs. System interconnect and analysis offerings are used to develop PCBs and IC packages. IP offerings consist of pre-verified, customizable functional blocks which customers integrate into their system-on-a-chips to accelerate the development process and to reduce the risk of errors in the design process

Cadence employees receive medical, dental, vision, short/long-term and life insurance; retiree health access; a 401(k); an employee stock purchase plan; and tuition reimbursement.

FINANCIAL DATA:
Note: Data for latest year may not have been available at press time.

In U.S. $	2018	2017	2016	2015	2014	2013
Revenue	2,138,022,000	1,943,032,000	1,816,083,000	1,702,091,000	1,580,932,000	1,460,116,000
R&D Expense	884,816,000	804,223,000	735,340,000	637,567,000	603,006,000	534,022,000
Operating Income	407,298,000	333,361,000	285,856,000	289,941,000	216,896,000	207,006,000
Operating Margin %		.17%	.16%	.17%	.14%	.14%
SGA Expense	573,075,000	553,342,000	520,300,000	512,414,000	513,307,000	499,471,000
Net Income	345,777,000	204,101,000	203,086,000	252,417,000	158,898,000	164,243,000
Operating Cash Flow	604,751,000	470,740,000	444,879,000	378,200,000	316,722,000	367,605,000
Capital Expenditure	61,503,000	57,901,000	53,712,000	44,808,000	39,810,000	44,929,000
EBITDA	518,250,000	456,234,000	380,411,000	414,072,000	330,757,000	294,885,000
Return on Assets %		.09%	.09%	.09%	.06%	.07%
Return on Equity %		.24%	.19%	.19%	.13%	.16%
Debt to Equity		0.651	0.868	0.253	0.261	

CONTACT INFORMATION:
Phone: 408 943-1234   Fax: 408 428-5001
Toll-Free: 800-746-6223
Address: 2655 Seely Ave., Bldg. 5, San Jose, CA 95134 United States

SALARIES/BONUSES:
Top Exec. Salary: $725,000   Bonus: $
Second Exec. Salary: $500,000   Bonus: $

STOCK TICKER/OTHER:
Stock Ticker: CDNS   Exchange: NAS
Employees: 7,100   Fiscal Year Ends: 12/31
Parent Company:

OTHER THOUGHTS:
Estimated Female Officers or Directors: 2
Hot Spot for Advancement for Women/Minorities:

Capital One Financial Corporation

www.capitalone.com

NAIC Code: 522110

TYPES OF BUSINESS:
Credit Card Issuing
Credit Card Products & Services
Mortgage Services
Consumer Lending
Health Care Financing
Small Business Loans
Mortgages
Commercial Banking

BRANDS/DIVISIONS/AFFILIATES:
Capital One Bank (USA) National Association
Capital One National Association

CONTACTS: Note: Officers with more than one job title may be intentionally listed here more than once.
Richard Fairbank, CEO
Michael Slocum, Pres., Divisional
R. Blackley, CFO
Timothy Golden, Chief Accounting Officer
Robert Alexander, Chief Information Officer
Sheldon Hall, Chief Risk Officer
Matthew Cooper, General Counsel
Lia Dean, Other Corporate Officer
Kevin Borgmann, Other Corporate Officer
Frank LaPrade, Other Corporate Officer
John Finneran, Other Corporate Officer
Jory Berson, Other Executive Officer
Celia Karam, Other Executive Officer
Sanjiv Yajnik, President, Divisional
Michael Wassmer, President, Divisional
Christopher Newkirk, President, Divisional
Kleber Santos, President, Divisional

GROWTH PLANS/SPECIAL FEATURES:

Capital One Financial Corporation is a financial holding company whose banking and non-banking subsidiaries market a variety of financial products and services. The business operates in three segments: credit card, commercial banking and consumer banking. The credit card segment includes domestic consumer and small business card lending, domestic small business lending, closed end installment lending and the international card lending businesses in Canada and the U.K. Commercial banking is comprised of lending, deposit gathering and treasury management services provided to commercial real estate and middle market customers. This segment also includes a portfolio of small commercial real estate loans that are in run-off mode. Consumer banking includes branch-based lending and deposit gathering activities for small business customers as well as consumer deposit gathering and lending activities, auto financing and mortgage loan servicing. The company's principle subsidiaries are Capital One Bank (USA), National Association (COBNA) and Capital One, National Association (CONA). COBNA offers consumers credit and debit card services, as well as lending and deposit products. CONA offers banking products and financial services to consumers, small businesses and commercial clients. In May 2018, Capital One Financial sold approximately $17 billion of first and second lien mortgages to DLJ Mortgage Capital, Inc., a subsidiary of Credit Suisse AG. The transaction is the result of the company ending its new originations of residential mortgages and home equity loan products.

Employees of Capital One receive flex spending accounts; medical, dental, vision, prescription drug and employee assistance programs; a 401(k); life, long-term care and disability insurance; military and parental leave; adoption assistance; and an employee discount stock purchase program.

FINANCIAL DATA: Note: Data for latest year may not have been available at press time.

In U.S. $	2018	2017	2016	2015	2014	2013
Revenue	27,173,000,000	26,247,000,000	24,648,000,000	22,647,000,000	21,453,000,000	21,352,000,000
R&D Expense						
Operating Income						
Operating Margin %						
SGA Expense	9,161,000,000	8,746,000,000	8,182,000,000	7,602,000,000	6,952,000,000	6,690,000,000
Net Income	6,015,000,000	1,982,000,000	3,751,000,000	4,050,000,000	4,428,000,000	4,159,000,000
Operating Cash Flow	12,978,000,000	14,182,000,000	11,856,000,000	10,127,000,000	9,304,001,000	9,984,000,000
Capital Expenditure	874,000,000	1,018,000,000	779,000,000	532,000,000	502,000,000	818,000,000
EBITDA						
Return on Assets %		.00%	.01%	.01%	.01%	.01%
Return on Equity %		.04%	.07%	.08%	.10%	.10%
Debt to Equity		1.225	1.252	1.229	1.056	0.952

CONTACT INFORMATION:
Phone: 703 720-1000 Fax:
Toll-Free: 800-801-1164
Address: 1680 Capital One Dr., McLean, VA 22102 United States

SALARIES/BONUSES:
Top Exec. Salary: $ Bonus: $4,200,000
Second Exec. Salary: $1,078,423 Bonus: $1,623,600

STOCK TICKER/OTHER:
Stock Ticker: COF
Employees: 47,300
Parent Company:

Exchange: NYS
Fiscal Year Ends: 12/31

OTHER THOUGHTS:
Estimated Female Officers or Directors: 3
Hot Spot for Advancement for Women/Minorities: Y

Cardinal Health Inc

NAIC Code: 424210

www.cardinalhealth.com

TYPES OF BUSINESS:
Healthcare Products & Services
Supply Chain Services
Medical Products

BRANDS/DIVISIONS/AFFILIATES:
Cardinal.com
Cardinal Health at-Home Solutions
mscripts

CONTACTS:
Note: Officers with more than one job title may be intentionally listed here more than once.

Jon Giacomin, CEO, Divisional
Michael Kaufmann, CEO
Jorge Gomez, CFO
Gregory Kenny, Chairman of the Board
Stuart Laws, Chief Accounting Officer
Michele Holcomb, Executive VP, Divisional
Pamela Kimmet, Other Executive Officer

GROWTH PLANS/SPECIAL FEATURES:

Cardinal Health, Inc. is a provider of products and services that improve the safety and productivity of health care. The company operates in two segments: pharmaceuticals and medical products. The pharmaceutical segment distributes a broad line of branded and generic pharmaceutical products, specialty pharmaceutical, over-the-counter health care products and consumer products. It is also a full-service wholesale distributor to retail customers, hospitals and alternate care providers located throughout the U.S. In addition, this segment operates nuclear pharmacies and cyclotron facilities, provides pharmacy operations, medication therapy management and patient outcomes services to hospitals and other healthcare providers. The segment offers a broad range of support services including computerized order entry provided through Cardinal.com; generic sourcing programs; product movement, inventory and management reports; and consultation on store operations and merchandising. Through its medical products segment, the company distributes a broad range of medical, surgical and laboratory products to hospitals, ambulatory surgery centers, clinical laboratories, physician offices and other health care providers in the U.S. and Canada, and to patients in the home in the U.S. through its Cardinal Health at-Home Solutions division. This segment also manufactures, sources and develops its own line of private brand medical and surgical products which include: single-use surgical drapes, gowns and apparel, exam and surgical gloves and fluid suction and collection systems; and manufactures extravascular closure devices. In April 2019, Cardinal Health acquired mscripts, a company that provides a digital communication platform to help patients stay on track with their healthcare by delivering targeted messages via mobile and web applications connected directly to the pharmacy dispensing system.

Employee benefits include medical, dental, vision short/long-term disability and life insurance; a 401(k); and various employee assistance programs.

FINANCIAL DATA:
Note: Data for latest year may not have been available at press time.

In U.S. $	2018	2017	2016	2015	2014	2013
Revenue	136,809,000,000	129,976,000,000	121,546,000,000	102,531,000,000	91,084,000,000	101,093,000,000
R&D Expense						
Operating Income	1,878,000,000	2,242,000,000	2,436,000,000	2,191,000,000	1,910,000,000	1,888,000,000
Operating Margin %		.02%	.02%	.02%	.02%	.02%
SGA Expense	4,596,000,000	3,775,000,000	3,648,000,000	3,240,000,000	3,028,000,000	2,875,000,000
Net Income	256,000,000	1,288,000,000	1,427,000,000	1,215,000,000	1,166,000,000	334,000,000
Operating Cash Flow	2,768,000,000	1,184,000,000	2,971,000,000	2,540,000,000	2,524,000,000	1,727,000,000
Capital Expenditure	384,000,000	387,000,000	465,000,000	300,000,000	249,000,000	195,000,000
EBITDA	2,910,000,000	2,959,000,000	3,077,000,000	2,642,000,000	2,369,000,000	2,285,000,000
Return on Assets %		.03%	.04%	.04%	.04%	.01%
Return on Equity %		.19%	.22%	.19%	.19%	.05%
Debt to Equity		1.332	0.756	0.833	0.495	0.617

CONTACT INFORMATION:
Phone: 614 757-5000 Fax:
Toll-Free: 800-234-8701
Address: 7000 Cardinal Pl., Dublin, OH 43017 United States

SALARIES/BONUSES:
Top Exec. Salary: $1,354,374 Bonus: $
Second Exec. Salary: $955,699 Bonus: $

STOCK TICKER/OTHER:
Stock Ticker: CAH
Employees: 49,800
Parent Company:

Exchange: NYS
Fiscal Year Ends: 06/30

OTHER THOUGHTS:
Estimated Female Officers or Directors: 8
Hot Spot for Advancement for Women/Minorities: Y

Sales, profits and employees may be estimates. Financial information, benefits and other data can change quickly and may vary from those stated here.

Cargill Incorporated

www.cargill.com

NAIC Code: 311200

TYPES OF BUSINESS:
Crop Production, Milling & Distribution
Meat Processing
Food Ingredients
Fertilizers
Steel
Money Markets & Commodity Trading
Supply Chain Solutions
Risk Management & Financial Services

BRANDS/DIVISIONS/AFFILIATES:

CONTACTS:
Note: Officers with more than one job title may be intentionally listed here more than once.

David W. MacLennan, CEO
Ruth Kimmelshue, Head-Bus. Oper. & Supply Chain
David W. MacLennan, Pres.
David Dines, CFO
LeighAnne Baker, Corp. VP-Human Resources
Christopher P. Mallett, Corp. VP-R&D
Laura Witte, General Counsel
Thomas M. Hayes, Corp. VP-Oper.
Sarena Lin, Corp. VP-Strategy & Bus. Dev.
Michael A. Fernandez, Corp. VP-Corp. Affairs
Kimberly A. Lattu, Controller
Emery N. Koenig, Chief Risk Officer
Jayme D. Olson, Treas.

GROWTH PLANS/SPECIAL FEATURES:

Cargill, Incorporated, established in 1865, is a leading provider and marketer of food, agricultural, financial and industrial products and services operating in 70 countries worldwide. The company operates through five business segments: food ingredients & bio-industrial, animal nutrition, protein & salt, agricultural supply chain and metals & shipping. The food ingredients & bio-industrial segment serves food and beverage manufacturers, foodservice companies and retailers with food ingredients, as well as food and non-food applications. Non-food applications encompass specialty ingredients for personal care as well as for pharmaceutical applications. Among these products are sustainable, nature-derived ingredients for a range of bio-industrial applications. The animal nutrition segment helps livestock and aquaculture farmers, feed manufacturers and distributors of all sizes to deliver better animal nutrition via innovative feed and pre-mix products and services, as well as digital modeling and formulation solutions. The protein & salt segment processes beef, poultry, value-added meats and egg products to food makers, food service companies and food retailers. This division's salt is used in food, agriculture, water softening and for deicing winter roads. The agricultural supply chain segment connects producers and users of grains and oilseeds worldwide through origination, trading, processing and distribution. This division also offers a range of farmer services and risk management solutions. Last, the metals & shipping segment offers Cargill customers physical supply and risk management solutions in global ferrous markets, including iron ore and steel. This division also provides ocean freight shipping services through its own sizable fleet, enabling customers to ship their products to global ports via Cargill.

FINANCIAL DATA:
Note: Data for latest year may not have been available at press time.

In U.S. $	2018	2017	2016	2015	2014	2013
Revenue	114,695,000,000	109,700,000,000	109,699,000,000	107,164,000,000	120,393,000,000	134,872,000,000
R&D Expense						
Operating Income						
Operating Margin %						
SGA Expense						
Net Income	3,103,000,000	2,800,000,000	2,835,000,000	2,377,000,000	1,926,000,000	1,822,000,000
Operating Cash Flow						
Capital Expenditure						
EBITDA						
Return on Assets %						
Return on Equity %						
Debt to Equity						

CONTACT INFORMATION:
Phone: 952-742-7575 Fax: 952-742-7393
Toll-Free: 800-227-4455
Address: P.O. Box 9300, Minneapolis, MN 55440-9300 United States

STOCK TICKER/OTHER:
Stock Ticker: Private
Employees: 155,000
Parent Company:

Exchange:
Fiscal Year Ends: 05/31

SALARIES/BONUSES:
Top Exec. Salary: $ Bonus: $
Second Exec. Salary: $ Bonus: $

OTHER THOUGHTS:
Estimated Female Officers or Directors: 4
Hot Spot for Advancement for Women/Minorities: Y

Sales, profits and employees may be estimates. Financial information, benefits and other data can change quickly and may vary from those stated here.

CarMax Inc

NAIC Code: 441120

www.carmax.com

TYPES OF BUSINESS:
Used Auto Dealers
New Auto Dealers
Online Sales
Vehicle Repair Services
Financial Services

BRANDS/DIVISIONS/AFFILIATES:
CarMax Auto Finance

CONTACTS: *Note: Officers with more than one job title may be intentionally listed here more than once.*
William Nash, CEO
Thomas Reedy, CFO
Thomas Folliard, Chairman of the Board
Jill Livesay, Chief Accounting Officer
Shamim Mohammad, Chief Information Officer
James Lyski, Chief Marketing Officer
Edwin Hill, COO
Eric Margolin, Executive VP
Diane Cafritz, Other Executive Officer
Jon Daniels, Senior VP, Divisional
Darren Newberry, Senior VP, Divisional
Joe Wilson, Senior VP, Divisional

GROWTH PLANS/SPECIAL FEATURES:
CarMax, Inc. is a leading retailer of used cars in the U.S. The firm purchases, reconditions and sells used vehicles through more than 200 used car superstores across the U.S. CarMax vehicles are typically 0 to 10 years old and range in price from $11,000 to $35,000. The firm also sells new vehicles at two of its locations under franchise agreements with car manufacturers. The company offers a wide selection of makes and models of both domestic and imported vehicles to appeal to diverse consumer preferences and budgets, including popular brands from manufacturers such as Chrysler, Ford, General Motors, Honda, Hyundai, Kia, Mazda, Nissan, Toyota and Volkswagen, and luxury brands such as Acura, BMW, Infiniti, Lexus and Mercedes-Benz. The company will also transfer any used vehicle in its nationwide inventory to a local superstore. Vehicles purchased through the company's in-store appraisal process that fall short of retail standards are sold at onsite wholesale auctions restricted to licensed automobile dealers. All store locations provide vehicle repair service and used-car warranty service. In addition, through the company's web site, customers can search new and used cars as well as find information on Kelley Blue Book figures, car buying tips, rebates and incentives. CarMax offers financing options through CarMax Auto Finance, including revolving credit and automobile installment loans. The firm retailed approximately 748,961 used vehicles in fiscal 2019. Vehicles purchased through CarMax's appraisal process that do not meet its retail standards (average age, mileage or vehicle condition) are sold to licensed dealers through onsite wholesale auctions. In mid-2019, CarMax launched a new car-buying experience to customers in Florida, where they can choose to complete the entire purchase process from home and have the car delivered, including the ability to test drive prior to purchase.

CarMax offers comprehensive benefits.

FINANCIAL DATA: *Note: Data for latest year may not have been available at press time.*

In U.S. $	2018	2017	2016	2015	2014	2013
Revenue	17,120,210,000	15,875,120,000	15,149,670,000	14,268,720,000	12,574,300,000	
R&D Expense						
Operating Income	711,808,000	694,790,000	666,825,000	629,802,000	493,486,000	
Operating Margin %	.04%	.04%	.04%	.04%	.04%	
SGA Expense	1,617,051,000	1,488,504,000	1,351,935,000	1,257,725,000	1,155,215,000	
Net Income	664,112,000	626,970,000	623,428,000	597,358,000	492,586,000	
Operating Cash Flow	-80,550,000	-468,138,000	-148,893,000	-968,130,000	-613,163,000	
Capital Expenditure	296,816,000	418,144,000	315,584,000	309,817,000	310,317,000	
EBITDA	1,314,295,000	1,231,696,000	1,183,662,000	1,108,977,000	930,067,000	
Return on Assets %	.04%	.04%	.05%	.05%	.05%	
Return on Equity %	.21%	.21%	.21%	.18%	.16%	
Debt to Equity	3.845	3.804	3.56	2.794	2.213	

CONTACT INFORMATION:
Phone: 804 747-0422   Fax: 804 747-5848
Toll-Free: 800-519-1511
Address: 12800 Tuckahoe Creek Pkwy., Richmond, VA 23238 United States

STOCK TICKER/OTHER:
Stock Ticker: KMX
Employees: 24,344
Parent Company:

Exchange: NYS
Fiscal Year Ends: 02/28

SALARIES/BONUSES:
Top Exec. Salary: $1,063,157   Bonus: $
Second Exec. Salary: $744,210   Bonus: $

OTHER THOUGHTS:
Estimated Female Officers or Directors: 9
Hot Spot for Advancement for Women/Minorities: Y

Sales, profits and employees may be estimates. Financial information, benefits and other data can change quickly and may vary from those stated here.

Carnival Corporation

NAIC Code: 483112

www.carnival.com

TYPES OF BUSINESS:
Cruise Line
On-Board Casinos
Tours
Resort Hotels

BRANDS/DIVISIONS/AFFILIATES:
Carnival Cruise plc
Carnival Cruise Lines
Princess Cruises
Holland America Line
Seabourn Cruise Line
Costa Cruises
P&O Cruises
Cunard

CONTACTS:
Note: Officers with more than one job title may be intentionally listed here more than once.

Stein Kruse, CEO, Subsidiary
Michael Thamm, CEO, Subsidiary
Arnold Donald, CEO
David Bernstein, CFO
Micky Arison, Chairman of the Board
Arnaldo Perez, Secretary

GROWTH PLANS/SPECIAL FEATURES:

Carnival Corporation is a leading provider of cruises and vacation packages to destinations worldwide. The firm operates as a dual listed company with its sister company Carnival plc. The firm divides its cruise brands into two segments: North America, which includes Carnival Cruise Lines, Princess Cruises, Holland America Line, P&O Cruises (Australia) and Seabourn Cruise Line; and Europe, Australia & Asia (EAA), comprised of Costa Cruises, P&O Cruises (U.K.), Cunard and AIDA Cruises. In total, the company operates over 100 ships and hosted 12.4 million guests in 2018. Carnival Cruise Lines operates 26 ships and is based in North America. Princess is a global cruise and tour company operating 17 ships. Holland America Line serves the industry's premium segment, with 15 ships sailing to all seven continents. P&O Cruises, operates in Australia, with five ships cruising Australia, New Zealand, Asia and the South Pacific. Seabourn offers single class luxury cruises on its five ships. Costa Cruises is a leading cruise company in Europe, Spain and South America, operating a modern fleet of 14 ships. P&O Cruises, operating from the U.K., sails to destinations in the Caribbean, South America, Scandinavia, the Mediterranean and Atlantic Islands as well as Round the World cruises. Cunard operates the Queen Mary 2, Queen Elizabeth and Queen Victoria ships. AIDA operates in the German-speaking cruise market via a fleet of 12 ships. The company also owns Holland America Princess Alaska Tours, a leading tour operator in Alaska and the Canadian Yukon, offering lodging, chartered motorcoaches, glass-domed railcars, luxury day boats and sightseeing packages.

FINANCIAL DATA:
Note: Data for latest year may not have been available at press time.

In U.S. $	2018	2017	2016	2015	2014	2013
Revenue	18,881,000,000	17,510,000,000	16,389,000,000	15,714,000,000	15,884,000,000	15,456,000,000
R&D Expense						
Operating Income	3,325,000,000	2,898,000,000	3,071,000,000	2,574,000,000	1,792,000,000	1,365,000,000
Operating Margin %		.17%	.19%	.16%	.11%	.09%
SGA Expense	2,450,000,000	2,265,000,000	2,197,000,000	2,067,000,000	2,054,000,000	1,879,000,000
Net Income	3,152,000,000	2,606,000,000	2,779,000,000	1,757,000,000	1,236,000,000	1,078,000,000
Operating Cash Flow	5,549,000,000	5,322,000,000	5,134,000,000	4,545,000,000	3,430,000,000	2,834,000,000
Capital Expenditure	3,749,000,000	2,944,000,000	3,062,000,000	2,294,000,000	2,583,000,000	2,149,000,000
EBITDA	5,418,000,000	4,710,000,000	4,789,000,000	3,642,000,000	3,168,000,000	2,979,000,000
Return on Assets %		.07%	.07%	.04%	.03%	.03%
Return on Equity %		.11%	.12%	.07%	.05%	.04%
Debt to Equity		0.289	0.37	0.312	0.303	0.33

CONTACT INFORMATION:
Phone: 305 599-2600 Fax: 305 471-4700
Toll-Free:
Address: 3655 NW 87th Ave., Miami, FL 33178 United States

STOCK TICKER/OTHER:
Stock Ticker: CCL
Employees: 120,000
Parent Company:

Exchange: NYS
Fiscal Year Ends: 11/30

SALARIES/BONUSES:
Top Exec. Salary: $1,500,000 Bonus: $
Second Exec. Salary: $1,023,698 Bonus: $

OTHER THOUGHTS:
Estimated Female Officers or Directors: 1
Hot Spot for Advancement for Women/Minorities: Y

CBRE Group Inc

NAIC Code: 531210

www.cbre.com

TYPES OF BUSINESS:
Real Estate Brokerage
Real Estate Management Services
Mortgage Banking
Investment Management
Consulting Services

BRANDS/DIVISIONS/AFFILIATES:
CBRE
CBRE Global Investors
Trammell Crow Company

CONTACTS:
Note: Officers with more than one job title may be intentionally listed here more than once.

Michael Lafitte, CEO, Divisional
William Concannon, CEO, Divisional
Daniel Queenan, CEO, Divisional
Robert Sulentic, CEO
Leah Stearns, CFO
Arlin Gaffner, CFO, Divisional
Brandon Boze, Chairman of the Board
Dara Bazzano, Chief Accounting Officer
J. Kirk, Chief Administrative Officer
James Groch, Chief Investment Officer
Laurence Midler, Chief Risk Officer
Chandra Dhandapani, Chief Technology Officer
John Durburg, COO

GROWTH PLANS/SPECIAL FEATURES:

CBRE Group, Inc. is one of the world's largest commercial real estate services and investment companies, with approximately 480 offices, serving clients in more than 100 countries. The firm's business is focused on providing services to both occupiers and investors of real estate. For occupiers, CBRE provides facilities management, project management, transaction (sales and leasing) and consulting services. For investors, the company provides: capital markets, including property sales, commercial mortgage brokerage, loan origination and services; leasing; investment management; property management; valuation; and development services. The firm provides: commercial real estate services under the CBRE brand name; investment management services under the CBRE Global Investors brand name; and development services under the Trammell Crow Company brand name. CBRE Group operates geographically throughout the Americas, Europe, the Middle East, Africa and Asia-Pacific, with the Americas being its largest reporting segment, with operations throughout the U.S., Canada and Latin America. In March 2019, CBRE acquired Florida Valuation Group, Inc., a commercial real estate appraisal firm specializing in right-of-way appraisal and litigation support related to eminent domain proceedings across Florida and the Southeast.

The company offers its employees medical, dental and vision insurance; a 401(k); flexible spending accounts; an employee assistance program; and paid vacation and holidays.

FINANCIAL DATA:
Note: Data for latest year may not have been available at press time.

In U.S. $	2018	2017	2016	2015	2014	2013
Revenue	21,340,090,000	14,209,610,000	13,071,590,000	10,855,810,000	9,049,918,000	7,184,794,000
R&D Expense						
Operating Income	1,073,115,000	1,051,614,000	799,625,000	825,173,000	734,595,000	700,705,000
Operating Margin %		.07%	.06%	.08%	.08%	.10%
SGA Expense	3,365,773,000	2,858,654,000	2,781,310,000	2,633,609,000	2,438,960,000	2,104,310,000
Net Income	1,063,219,000	691,479,000	571,973,000	547,132,000	484,503,000	316,538,000
Operating Cash Flow	1,131,249,000	710,505,000	450,315,000	651,897,000	661,780,000	745,108,000
Capital Expenditure	227,803,000	178,042,000	191,205,000	139,464,000	171,242,000	156,358,000
EBITDA	1,938,264,000	1,707,021,000	1,392,504,000	1,312,706,000	1,154,398,000	835,337,000
Return on Assets %		.06%	.05%	.06%	.07%	.04%
Return on Equity %		.20%	.20%	.22%	.23%	.18%
Debt to Equity		0.497	0.845	0.975	0.82	0.985

CONTACT INFORMATION:
Phone: 213-613-3333 Fax: 213 438-4820
Toll-Free:
Address: 400 S. Hope St., 25/Fl, Los Angeles, CA 90071 United States

STOCK TICKER/OTHER:
Stock Ticker: CBRE
Employees: 75,000
Parent Company:

Exchange: NYS
Fiscal Year Ends: 12/31

SALARIES/BONUSES:
Top Exec. Salary: $997,500   Bonus: $
Second Exec. Salary: $770,000   Bonus: $

OTHER THOUGHTS:
Estimated Female Officers or Directors: 2
Hot Spot for Advancement for Women/Minorities:

CBS Corporation

www.cbscorporation.com

NAIC Code: 515120

TYPES OF BUSINESS:
Television Broadcasting
News Organization
Outdoor Advertising
Radio Networks & Programming
Television Production
Cable TV Networks
Book Publishing

BRANDS/DIVISIONS/AFFILIATES:
National Amusements Inc
CBS Television Network
CBS Films
CBS All Access
Showtime Networks
CBS Television Stations
CBS Local Digital Media
Simon & Schuster

CONTACTS: Note: Officers with more than one job title may be intentionally listed here more than once.
Joseph Ianniello, CEO
Christina Spade, CFO
Strauss Zelnick, Chairman of the Board
David Byrnes, Chief Accounting Officer
Jonathan Anschell, Deputy General Counsel
Shari Redstone, Director
Richard Jones, Executive VP
Lawrence Liding, Other Corporate Officer
David Nevins, Other Executive Officer

GROWTH PLANS/SPECIAL FEATURES:

CBS Corporation is a leading mass media company in the U.S. National Amusements, Inc. owns approximately 80% of the voting stock of CBS. The firm operates through four segments: entertainment, accounting for 67% of annual revenues; cable networks, 18%; local media, 12%; and publishing 6%. The entertainment division is composed of the following: CBS Television Network, CBS Television Studios, CBS Studios International, CBS Television Distribution, CBS Interactive and CBS Films; and the digital streaming services of CBS All Access and CBSN. The cable networks segment is composed of Showtime Networks, which operates the firm's premium subscription program services: Showtime, The Movie Channel and Flix; CBS Sports Network, the company's cable network which focuses on college athletics and other sports; and Smithsonian Networks, a venture between Showtime Networks and Smithsonian Institution, which operates Smithsonian Channel, a basic cable program service. The local media segment is composed of CBS Television Stations, the company's 29 owned broadcast television stations; and CBS Local Digital Media, which operates local websites, including content from the company's television stations. The publishing segment is composed of Simon & Schuster, which publishes and distributes consumer books under imprints such as Simon & Schuster, Pocket Books, Scribner, Gallery Books, Touchstone and Atria Books. In late-2017, the firm disposed of its radio business, CBS Radio, Inc., along with radio-related subsidiaries, in a transaction that involved the split-off of CBS Radio through an exchange offer followed by the merger of CBS Radio with a subsidiary of Entercom Communications Corporation. In August 2019, in order to compete with larger rivals, CBS and Viacom agreed to reunite into a company to be named ViacomCBS. Details of the transaction were not released.

CBS offers employees health, vision, dental & life insurance; a 401(k) plan; short & long term disability; flexible spending accounts; and paid leave.

FINANCIAL DATA: Note: Data for latest year may not have been available at press time.

In U.S. $	2018	2017	2016	2015	2014	2013
Revenue	14,514,000,000	13,692,000,000	13,166,000,000	13,886,000,000	13,806,000,000	15,284,000,000
R&D Expense						
Operating Income	2,963,000,000	2,486,000,000	2,659,000,000	2,843,000,000	2,974,000,000	3,279,000,000
Operating Margin %		.18%	.20%	.20%	.22%	.21%
SGA Expense	2,217,000,000	2,564,000,000	2,335,000,000	2,455,000,000	2,462,000,000	2,735,000,000
Net Income	1,960,000,000	357,000,000	1,261,000,000	1,413,000,000	2,959,000,000	1,879,000,000
Operating Cash Flow	1,426,000,000	887,000,000	1,685,000,000	1,394,000,000	1,275,000,000	1,873,000,000
Capital Expenditure	165,000,000	185,000,000	196,000,000	193,000,000	206,000,000	270,000,000
EBITDA	2,979,000,000	2,659,000,000	2,866,000,000	2,679,000,000	2,808,000,000	3,730,000,000
Return on Assets %		.02%	.05%	.06%	.12%	.07%
Return on Equity %		.13%	.27%	.23%	.35%	.19%
Debt to Equity		4.785	2.413	1.479	0.934	0.596

CONTACT INFORMATION:
Phone: 212 975-4321   Fax: 212 975-4516
Toll-Free:
Address: 51 W. 52nd St., New York, NY 10019 United States

SALARIES/BONUSES:
Top Exec. Salary: $2,500,000   Bonus: $12,250,000
Second Exec. Salary: $1,350,000   Bonus: $3,500,000

STOCK TICKER/OTHER:
Stock Ticker: CBS
Employees: 21,270
Parent Company: National Amusements Inc

Exchange: NYS
Fiscal Year Ends: 12/31

OTHER THOUGHTS:
Estimated Female Officers or Directors: 3
Hot Spot for Advancement for Women/Minorities: Y

Sales, profits and employees may be estimates. Financial information, benefits and other data can change quickly and may vary from those stated here.

CDW Corporation

www.cdw.com

NAIC Code: 423430

TYPES OF BUSINESS:
Direct Selling-Computer Products
Online Sales
Custom Installation & Repair-Computers

BRANDS/DIVISIONS/AFFILIATES:
CDW Government LLC
CDW Canada Inc
CDW Ltd
CDW UK

CONTACTS:
Note: Officers with more than one job title may be intentionally listed here more than once.

Christine Leahy, CEO
Mark Chong, Senior VP, Divisional
Collin Kebo, CFO
Thomas Richards, Chairman of the Board
Neil Fairfield, Chief Accounting Officer
Jonathan Stevens, Chief Information Officer
Christina Corley, COO
Elizabeth Connelly, Other Executive Officer
Frederick Kulevich, Secretary
Robert Kirby, Senior VP, Divisional
Jill Billhorn, Senior VP, Divisional
Christina Rother, Senior VP, Divisional
Matthew Troka, Senior VP, Divisional
Douglas Eckrote, Senior VP, Divisional

GROWTH PLANS/SPECIAL FEATURES:

CDW Corporation is one of the leading providers of multi-branded information technology products and services to business, government, education and healthcare customers in the U.S., Canada and the U.K. The firm offers over 100,000 products from over 1,000 leading technology brands, in addition to customized solution design and management with focus areas including notebooks, desktops, printers, servers and storage, unified communications, security, wireless, power and cooling, networking, software licensing, cloud computing, data center optimization and mobility solutions. The company manages its inventory through a 442,000-square-foot distribution center in Vernon Hills, Illinois; a 513,000-square-foot distribution center in Las Vegas, Nevada; and a 120,000-square foot distribution center in Rugby, Warwickshire, U.K. CDW offers customers free access to certified technicians for telephone support and complete custom installation and repair services via the company's configuration center, in addition to access to a database of frequently asked technical questions and direct links to manufacturers' tech support websites. Its CDW Government, LLC subsidiary provides specialized product offerings and services to federal, state and local governments as well as the educational sector. Subsidiaries CDW Canada, Inc. and CDW Ltd. (doing business as CDW UK) provide IT solutions, serving commercial and public sector customers.

The company offers its employees medical, dental and vision insurance; a 401(k) plan; a profit sharing plan; life and AD&D insurance; flexible spending accounts; tuition reimbursement; short- and long-term disability insurance; and an employee assistance program.

FINANCIAL DATA:
Note: Data for latest year may not have been available at press time.

In U.S. $	2018	2017	2016	2015	2014	2013
Revenue	16,240,500,000	15,191,500,000	13,981,900,000	12,988,700,000	12,074,500,000	10,768,600,000
R&D Expense						
Operating Income	987,300,000	866,100,000	819,200,000	742,000,000	673,000,000	508,600,000
Operating Margin %		.06%	.06%	.06%	.06%	.05%
SGA Expense	1,719,600,000	1,583,800,000	1,508,000,000	1,373,800,000	1,248,300,000	1,251,700,000
Net Income	643,000,000	523,000,000	424,400,000	403,100,000	244,900,000	132,800,000
Operating Cash Flow	905,900,000	777,700,000	604,000,000	277,500,000	435,000,000	366,300,000
Capital Expenditure	86,100,000	81,100,000	63,500,000	90,100,000	55,000,000	47,100,000
EBITDA	1,252,900,000	1,127,000,000	1,073,700,000	969,400,000	880,900,000	716,800,000
Return on Assets %		.08%	.06%	.06%	.04%	.02%
Return on Equity %		.52%	.40%	.40%	.30%	.31%
Debt to Equity		3.266	3.076	2.95	3.39	4.504

CONTACT INFORMATION:
Phone: 847-465-6000   Fax: 847-465-6800
Toll-Free: 800-750-4239
Address: 75 Tri-State International, Lincolnshire, IL 60069 United States

STOCK TICKER/OTHER:
Stock Ticker: CDW
Employees: 8,516
Parent Company:

Exchange: NAS
Fiscal Year Ends: 12/31

SALARIES/BONUSES:
Top Exec. Salary: $990,769   Bonus: $
Second Exec. Salary: $506,188   Bonus: $

OTHER THOUGHTS:
Estimated Female Officers or Directors: 10
Hot Spot for Advancement for Women/Minorities: Y

Sales, profits and employees may be estimates. Financial information, benefits and other data can change quickly and may vary from those stated here.

Celanese Corporation

www.celanese.com

NAIC Code: 325211

TYPES OF BUSINESS:
Manufacturing-Acetyl Intermediate Chemicals
Industrial Products
Technical & High-Performance Polymers
Sweeteners & Sorbates
Ethanol Production
Food Ingredients
Cellulose Derivative Fibers

BRANDS/DIVISIONS/AFFILIATES:
Celanex
Cestran
Riteflex
Vandar
Sunett
CelFX
Celaire
Ateva

CONTACTS: Note: Officers with more than one job title may be intentionally listed here more than once.
Mark Rohr, CEO
Lori Ryerkerk, CEO
Scott Richardson, CFO
Benita Casey, Chief Accounting Officer
Shannon Jurecka, Other Executive Officer

GROWTH PLANS/SPECIAL FEATURES:

Celanese Corporation is a producer of industrial chemicals and advanced materials. The firm manufactures acetyl products, which are intermediate chemicals for nearly all major industries, and produces high-performance engineered polymers. The company operates through six business segments: engineered materials, food ingredients, cellulose derivatives, intermediate chemistry, EVA polymers and emulsion polymers. The engineered materials segment engineers high-performance polymers for a variety of industries. Products include Celanex thermoplastic polyester, Cestran long fiber reinforced thermoplastic, GUR ultra-high molecular wright polyethylene, Riteflex thermoplastic polyester elastomer, Vandar thermoplastic polyester alloy and more. The food ingredients segment produces Sunett acesulfame potassium and sorbates. The cellulose derivatives segment manufactures cellulose acetate products for use in filtration, luxury packaging, insulation, acetate granules, the medical industry and nonwovens. Products for this segment include acetate flake, acetate tow, Celaire acetate nonwoven and CelFX matrix technology. The intermediate chemistry segment manufactures intermediate chemistry products. Products include acetic acid, vinyl acetate monomer, acetic anhydride and other specialty derivative products. The EVA polymers segment produces a full range ethylene vinyl acetate (EVA) polymers. Products include Ateva EVA polymers, Ateva G Medical EVA grades, LDPE polymers and VitalDose Pharmaceutical EVA-based excipients. Headquartered in Irving, Texas, the company's operations are primarily located in North America, Europe and Asia, consisting of 27 global production facilities and strategic affiliate production facilities. In February 2018, Celanese acquired Omni Plastics LLC, a specializer in custom compounding of various thermoplastic materials. In January 2019, Celanese signed a definitive agreement to acquired a synthesis gas production unit from Linde PLC.

FINANCIAL DATA: Note: Data for latest year may not have been available at press time.

In U.S. $	2018	2017	2016	2015	2014	2013
Revenue	7,155,000,000	6,140,000,000	5,389,000,000	5,674,000,000	6,802,000,000	6,510,000,000
R&D Expense	72,000,000	72,000,000	78,000,000	119,000,000	86,000,000	85,000,000
Operating Income	1,330,000,000	967,000,000	902,000,000	682,000,000	752,000,000	937,000,000
Operating Margin %		.16%	.17%	.12%	.11%	.14%
SGA Expense	546,000,000	456,000,000	416,000,000	506,000,000	758,000,000	311,000,000
Net Income	1,207,000,000	843,000,000	900,000,000	304,000,000	624,000,000	1,101,000,000
Operating Cash Flow	1,558,000,000	803,000,000	893,000,000	862,000,000	962,000,000	762,000,000
Capital Expenditure	337,000,000	267,000,000	246,000,000	520,000,000	678,000,000	377,000,000
EBITDA	1,984,000,000	1,507,000,000	1,445,000,000	970,000,000	1,386,000,000	2,100,000,000
Return on Assets %		.09%	.11%	.03%	.07%	.12%
Return on Equity %		.31%	.36%	.12%	.23%	.50%
Debt to Equity		1.148	1.117	1.038	0.925	1.07

CONTACT INFORMATION:
Phone: 972 443-4000 Fax: 972 332-9373
Toll-Free:
Address: 222 West Las Colinas Blvd, Ste 900N, Irving, TX 75039-5421 United States

SALARIES/BONUSES:
Top Exec. Salary: $1,155,000 Bonus: $
Second Exec. Salary: $750,000 Bonus: $

STOCK TICKER/OTHER:
Stock Ticker: CE
Employees: 7,293
Parent Company:

Exchange: NYS
Fiscal Year Ends: 12/31

OTHER THOUGHTS:
Estimated Female Officers or Directors: 1
Hot Spot for Advancement for Women/Minorities: Y

Celgene Corporation

www.celgene.com

NAIC Code: 325412

TYPES OF BUSINESS:
Cancer & Immune-Inflammatory Related Diseases Drugs

BRANDS/DIVISIONS/AFFILIATES:
Revlimid
Abraxane
Pomalyst/Imnovid
Vidaza
Otezla
Impact Biomedicines
Juno Therapeutics Inc

CONTACTS:
Note: Officers with more than one job title may be intentionally listed here more than once.

Mark Alles, CEO
David Elkins, CFO
Gerald Masoudi, Executive VP
Peter Kellogg, Executive VP
Rupert Vessey, President, Divisional
Terrie Curran, President, Divisional
Nadim Ahmed, President, Divisional
Alise Reicin, President, Divisional

GROWTH PLANS/SPECIAL FEATURES:

Celgene Corporation is a global biopharmaceutical company involved in discovering, developing and commercializing cancer and immune-inflammatory related disease treatment therapies. Celgene's current preclinical and clinical-stage pipeline of new drug candidates and cell therapies include both small molecule and biologic therapeutic agents designed to selectively regulate disease-associated genes and proteins. Celgene's commercial stage products include Revlimid, Abraxane, Pomalyst/Imnovid, Vidaza and Otezla. Revlimid (lenalidomide) is an oral immunomodulatory drug approved in the U.S. and many international markets for uses such as multiple myeloma (MM), myelodysplastic syndromes (MDS), mantle cell lymphoma (MCL) and relapsed or refractory (RR) adult T-cell leukemia/lymphoma (ATLL). Abraxane (paclitaxel albumin-bound particles for injectable suspension) is a solvent-free chemotherapy product developed using Celgene's proprietary nab technology platform. This protein-bound chemotherapy agent combines paclitaxel with albumin, and is approved for uses such as breast cancer, non-small cell lung cancer, pancreatic cancer and gastric cancer. Pomalyst/Imnovid (pomalidomide) is a proprietary, distinct, small molecule that is administered orally and modulates the immune system and other biologically-important targets, and is used for MM and RRMM. Vidaza (azacitidine for injection) is a pyrimidine nucleoside analog shown to reverse the effects of DNA hypermethylation and promote subsequent gene re-expression, and is used for MDS and AML. Last, Otezla (apremilast) is an oral small-molecule inhibitor of phosphodiesterase 4 specific for cyclic adenosine monophosphate, approved for psoriatic arthritis and psoriasis. During 2018, Celgene completed the acquisitions of Impact Biomedicines and of Juno Therapeutics, Inc. In January 2019, Celgene agreed to be acquired by Bristol-Myers Squibb Company, with the stockholders of each firm approving the merger. The transaction was expected to be complete by year's end, with Bristol-Meyers Squibb stockholders owning approximately 70% of the company and Celgene stockholders owning the remainder.

FINANCIAL DATA:
Note: Data for latest year may not have been available at press time.

In U.S. $	2018	2017	2016	2015	2014	2013
Revenue	15,281,000,000	13,003,000,000	11,229,200,000	9,255,999,000	7,670,400,000	6,493,900,000
R&D Expense	5,673,000,000	5,915,000,000	4,470,100,000	3,697,300,000	2,430,600,000	2,226,200,000
Operating Income	5,303,000,000	3,357,000,000	3,204,400,000	2,554,200,000	2,567,700,000	1,980,000,000
Operating Margin %		.26%	.29%	.28%	.33%	.30%
SGA Expense	3,250,000,000	2,941,000,000	2,657,700,000	2,305,400,000	2,027,900,000	1,684,500,000
Net Income	4,046,000,000	2,940,000,000	1,999,200,000	1,602,000,000	1,999,900,000	1,449,900,000
Operating Cash Flow	5,171,000,000	5,246,000,000	3,976,300,000	2,483,900,000	2,806,300,000	2,225,900,000
Capital Expenditure	330,000,000	279,000,000	236,200,000	286,300,000	175,100,000	139,100,000
EBITDA	6,208,000,000	5,307,000,000	3,377,300,000	2,743,000,000	2,877,100,000	2,131,100,000
Return on Assets %		.10%	.07%	.07%	.13%	.12%
Return on Equity %		.43%	.32%	.26%	.33%	.26%
Debt to Equity		2.288	2.089	2.408	0.96	0.751

CONTACT INFORMATION:
Phone: 908 673-9000 Fax: 908 673-9001
Toll-Free:
Address: 86 Morris Ave., Summit, NJ 07901 United States

SALARIES/BONUSES:
Top Exec. Salary: $1,500,000 Bonus: $
Second Exec. Salary: $1,266,667 Bonus: $

STOCK TICKER/OTHER:
Stock Ticker: CELG Exchange: NAS
Employees: 7,132 Fiscal Year Ends: 12/31
Parent Company:

OTHER THOUGHTS:
Estimated Female Officers or Directors: 3
Hot Spot for Advancement for Women/Minorities: Y

Sales, profits and employees may be estimates. Financial information, benefits and other data can change quickly and may vary from those stated here.

Centene Corporation

NAIC Code: 524114

www.centene.com

TYPES OF BUSINESS:
Insurance-Medical & Health, HMOs & PPOs
Medicaid Managed Care
Specialty Services
Behavioral Health
Disease Management
Managed Vision
Nurse Triage
Pharmacy Benefit Management

BRANDS/DIVISIONS/AFFILIATES:
CentAccount
MemberConnections
Smart For Your Baby
Ribera Salud

CONTACTS:
Note: Officers with more than one job title may be intentionally listed here more than once.

Michael Neidorff, CEO
Jeffrey Schwaneke, CFO
Mark Brooks, Chief Information Officer
Jesse Hunter, Chief Strategy Officer
Christopher Bowers, Executive VP, Divisional
Brandy Burkhalter, Executive VP, Divisional
Keith Williamson, Executive VP
Christopher Isaak, Senior VP

GROWTH PLANS/SPECIAL FEATURES:

Centene Corporation is a multi-line healthcare plan firm operating in two segments: managed care and specialty services. In the managed care segment, the company provides programs and services to people receiving benefits from foster care, Medicaid, the State Children's Health Insurance Program (CHIP), Medicare special needs plans, supplemental security income (SSI), dual eligible individuals (Duals), long term care (LTC) and federally-facilitated and state-based Marketplaces. This segment accounted for 95% of total revenue in 2018. Centene's specialty services segment provides healthcare services to state programs, correctional facilities, healthcare organizations, and to the firm's own subsidiaries. Specialty Services accounted for 5% of total revenue in 2018. The firm's CentAccount program offers financial incentives to members for achieving healthy behavior. Additionally, the company offers a number of education and outreach programs, including MemberConnections, which is designed to create face-to-face links between members and care providers; Start Smart For Your Baby, a prenatal and infant health program; EPSDT (early and periodic screening, diagnostic and treatment) case management, which encourages early and periodic screening, diagnosis and treatment services; and life and health management programs, designed to educate patients on the best and most cost effective treatment options for specific diseases. In March 2019, the firm agreed to acquire WellCare Health Plans, Inc., a manager of government-sponsored healthcare programs, for $15.3 billion. The following July, Centene acquired an additional 40%, bringing its stake to 90%, of the Spanish health care company Ribera Salud from Banco Sabadell.

The company offers employees health, vision and dental coverage; flexible spending accounts; short- and long-term disability; life and supplemental life insurance; 401(k); an employee stock purchase plan; an employee assistance program; tuition reimbursement; a wellness program; an onsite fitness center; and employee discounts.

FINANCIAL DATA:
Note: Data for latest year may not have been available at press time.

In U.S. $	2018	2017	2016	2015	2014	2013
Revenue	60,116,000,000	48,382,000,000	40,607,000,000	22,760,000,000	16,560,000,000	10,863,330,000
R&D Expense						
Operating Income	1,458,000,000	1,199,000,000	1,260,000,000	705,000,000	464,000,000	277,417,000
Operating Margin %		.02%	.03%	.03%	.03%	.03%
SGA Expense	6,043,000,000	4,446,000,000	3,676,000,000	1,826,000,000	1,314,000,000	931,137,000
Net Income	900,000,000	828,000,000	562,000,000	355,000,000	271,000,000	165,099,000
Operating Cash Flow	1,234,000,000	1,489,000,000	1,851,000,000	658,000,000	1,223,000,000	382,526,000
Capital Expenditure	675,000,000	422,000,000	306,000,000	150,000,000	103,000,000	67,835,000
EBITDA	2,206,000,000	1,750,000,000	1,652,000,000	851,000,000	581,000,000	363,294,000
Return on Assets %		.04%	.04%	.05%	.06%	.05%
Return on Equity %		.13%	.14%	.18%	.18%	.15%
Debt to Equity		0.685	0.789	0.564	0.509	0.539

CONTACT INFORMATION:
Phone: 314 725-4477 Fax: 314 725-5180
Toll-Free:
Address: 7700 Forsyth Blvd., Centene Plz., St. Louis, MO 63105 United States

SALARIES/BONUSES:
Top Exec. Salary: $1,500,000 Bonus: $
Second Exec. Salary: $800,000 Bonus: $

STOCK TICKER/OTHER:
Stock Ticker: CNC
Employees: 30,500
Parent Company:

Exchange: NYS
Fiscal Year Ends: 12/31

OTHER THOUGHTS:
Estimated Female Officers or Directors: 4
Hot Spot for Advancement for Women/Minorities: Y

Sales, profits and employees may be estimates. Financial information, benefits and other data can change quickly and may vary from those stated here.

CenturyLink Inc

NAIC Code: 517110

www.centurylink.com

TYPES OF BUSINESS:
Local Telephone Service
Long-Distance Services
Internet Service Provider
Business Information Services
Fiber Network Services
Satellite TV
IPTV

BRANDS/DIVISIONS/AFFILIATES:

CONTACTS:
Note: Officers with more than one job title may be intentionally listed here more than once.

Jeffrey Storey, CEO
Indraneel Dev, CFO
Harvey Perry, Chairman of the Board
Eric Mortensen, Chief Accounting Officer
W. Hanks, Director
Scott Trezise, Executive VP, Divisional
Stacey Goff, Executive VP

GROWTH PLANS/SPECIAL FEATURES:

CenturyLink, Inc. is an international facilities-based communications company primarily engaged in providing an integrated array of services to business and residential customers. The firm's communications services include local and long-distance voice, virtual private network (VPN) data network, private line, Ethernet, information technology, wavelength, broadband, managed services, professional and other services. These services are provided in connection with selling equipment, network security and various other ancillary services. CenturyLink comprises approximately 450,000 route miles of fiber optic cable globally, and its terrestrial and subsea fiber optic long-haul network spans North America, Europe and Latin America, connecting to metropolitan fiber network that it operates. The company operates in more than 60 countries, with the majority being in the U.S. For businesses, CenturyLink provides products and services to small, medium and enterprise firms, as well as wholesale and government customers. For residential consumers, CenturyLink primarily provides broadband, local and long-distance voice, video and other ancillary services. More than 60% of the firm's annual revenue is derived from business customers, approximately 30% from residential consumers and the remainder from non-segment services. During 2018, CenturyLink sold certain former Level 3 metro network assets in the Albuquerque, New Mexico area to Unite Private Networks.

Employee benefits include medical, dental, prescription and vision coverage; an employee assistance program; retirement plans and a 401(k); flexible spending accounts; life and AD&D insurance; short-and long-term disability; and career development programs.

FINANCIAL DATA:
Note: Data for latest year may not have been available at press time.

In U.S. $	2018	2017	2016	2015	2014	2013
Revenue	23,443,000,000	17,656,000,000	17,470,000,000	17,900,000,000	18,031,000,000	18,095,000,000
R&D Expense						
Operating Income	3,296,000,000	2,009,000,000	2,331,000,000	2,605,000,000	2,410,000,000	2,545,000,000
Operating Margin %		.11%	.13%	.15%	.13%	.14%
SGA Expense	4,165,000,000	3,508,000,000	3,449,000,000	3,328,000,000	3,347,000,000	3,502,000,000
Net Income	-1,733,000,000	1,389,000,000	626,000,000	878,000,000	772,000,000	-239,000,000
Operating Cash Flow	7,032,000,000	3,878,000,000	4,608,000,000	5,152,000,000	5,188,000,000	5,559,000,000
Capital Expenditure	3,175,000,000	3,106,000,000	2,981,000,000	2,872,000,000	3,047,000,000	3,048,000,000
EBITDA	5,734,000,000	5,957,000,000	6,254,000,000	6,817,000,000	6,849,000,000	6,063,000,000
Return on Assets %		.02%	.01%	.02%	.02%	.00%
Return on Equity %		.08%	.05%	.06%	.05%	-.01%
Debt to Equity		1.587	1.357	1.332	1.339	1.174

CONTACT INFORMATION:
Phone: 318 388-9000
Fax: 318 789-8656
Toll-Free:
Address: 100 CenturyLink Dr., Monroe, LA 71203 United States

STOCK TICKER/OTHER:
Stock Ticker: CTL
Employees: 40,000
Parent Company:
Exchange: NYS
Fiscal Year Ends: 12/31

SALARIES/BONUSES:
Top Exec. Salary: $1,683,299
Bonus: $5,842,000
Second Exec. Salary: $556,854
Bonus: $1,214,500

OTHER THOUGHTS:
Estimated Female Officers or Directors: 5
Hot Spot for Advancement for Women/Minorities: Y

Cerner Corporation

www.cerner.com

NAIC Code: 0

TYPES OF BUSINESS:
Computer Software, Healthcare & Biotechnology
Medical Information Systems
Application Hosting
Integrated Delivery Networks
Access Management
Consulting Services
Safety & Risk Management

BRANDS/DIVISIONS/AFFILIATES:
Cerner Millennium
HealtheIntent
Cerner Health Services
CernerWorks

CONTACTS: Note: Officers with more than one job title may be intentionally listed here more than once.
Marc Naughton, CFO
David Shafer, Chairman of the Board
Michael Battaglioli, Chief Accounting Officer
Michael Nill, COO
Donald Trigg, Executive VP, Divisional
Jeffrey Townsend, Executive VP
John Peterzalek, Executive VP
Randy Sims, Executive VP
Julia Wilson, Other Executive Officer

GROWTH PLANS/SPECIAL FEATURES:
Cerner Corporation designs, develops, installs and supports information technology and content applications for health care organizations, consumers and physicians. Cerner's applications are designed to help eliminate error, variance and waste in the care process as well as provide appropriate health information and knowledge to care givers, clinicians and consumers, and appropriate management information to healthcare administrations. Cerner solutions are offered on the unified Cerner Millennium architecture and on the HealtheIntent cloud-based platform. The Millennium framework combines clinical, financial and management information systems and provides secure access to an individual's electronic medical record at the point of care and organizes and proactively delivers information to meet the specific needs of the physician, nurse, laboratory technician, pharmacist or other care provider, front- and back-office professionals as well as consumers. The HealtheIntent platform offers EHR-agnostic (electronic health record) solutions based on sophisticated, statistical algorithms to help providers predict and improve outcomes, control costs, improve quality and manage the health of their patients. Cerner also offers a broad range of services including implementation and training, remote hosting, operational management services, revenue cycle services, support and maintenance, healthcare data analysis, clinical process optimization, transaction processing, employer health centers, employee wellness programs and third-party administrator (TPA) services for employer-based health plans. Cerner Health Services offers a portfolio of enterprise-level clinical and financial healthcare information technology solutions, as well as departmental, connectivity, population health and care coordination solutions globally. CernerWorks is the company's remote-hosting business. Roughly more than 27,500 facilities around the world license Cerner's products. These facilities include hospitals; physician practices; ambulatory facilities such as laboratories, ambulatory centers, cardiac facilities, radiology clinics and surgery centers; home health facilities; and retail pharmacies.

FINANCIAL DATA: Note: Data for latest year may not have been available at press time.

In U.S. $	2018	2017	2016	2015	2014	2013
Revenue	5,366,325,000	5,142,272,000	4,796,473,000	4,425,267,000	3,402,703,000	2,910,748,000
R&D Expense	683,663,000	605,046,000	551,418,000	539,799,000	392,805,000	338,786,000
Operating Income	774,785,000	960,471,000	911,013,000	781,136,000	763,084,000	576,012,000
Operating Margin %		.19%	.19%	.18%	.22%	.20%
SGA Expense	2,883,165,000	2,632,088,000	2,464,380,000	2,262,024,000	1,642,437,000	1,481,228,000
Net Income	630,059,000	866,978,000	636,484,000	539,362,000	525,433,000	398,354,000
Operating Cash Flow	1,454,009,000	1,307,675,000	1,155,612,000	947,526,000	847,027,000	695,865,000
Capital Expenditure	757,440,000	665,877,000	771,595,000	648,220,000	467,901,000	584,331,000
EBITDA	1,451,429,000	1,555,864,000	1,427,149,000	1,245,425,000	1,080,520,000	855,818,000
Return on Assets %		.14%	.11%	.11%	.12%	.10%
Return on Equity %		.20%	.16%	.15%	.16%	.13%
Debt to Equity		0.108	0.137	0.146	0.018	0.035

CONTACT INFORMATION:
Phone: 816 221-1024 Fax:
Toll-Free:
Address: 2800 Rockcreek Pkwy., North Kansas City, MO 64117 United States

STOCK TICKER/OTHER:
Stock Ticker: CERN
Employees: 24,400
Parent Company:

Exchange: NAS
Fiscal Year Ends: 12/31

SALARIES/BONUSES:
Top Exec. Salary: $729,231 Bonus: $
Second Exec. Salary: $683,750 Bonus: $

OTHER THOUGHTS:
Estimated Female Officers or Directors: 13
Hot Spot for Advancement for Women/Minorities: Y

Sales, profits and employees may be estimates. Financial information, benefits and other data can change quickly and may vary from those stated here.

CH Robinson Worldwide Inc

www.chrobinson.com

NAIC Code: 488510

TYPES OF BUSINESS:
3PL Third Party Logistics
Produce Sourcing
Expedited Services
Fuel Purchasing Management Services
Warehousing
Customs Brokerage
Freight Transportation Arrangements

BRANDS/DIVISIONS/AFFILIATES:
Robinson Fresh

CONTACTS: *Note: Officers with more than one job title may be intentionally listed here more than once.*
Robert Biesterfeld, CEO
Scott Hagen, CFO
John Wiehoff, Chairman of the Board
Michael Neill, Chief Technology Officer
Christopher OBrien, Other Executive Officer
Angela Freeman, Other Executive Officer
Ben Campbell, Other Executive Officer
Jereon Eijsink, President, Divisional
Jordan Kass, President, Divisional
Michael Short, President, Divisional
Mac Pinkerton, President, Divisional

GROWTH PLANS/SPECIAL FEATURES:
C.H. Robinson Worldwide, Inc. (CHRW) is one of the world's largest third-party logistics (3PL) providers and a global provider of multimodal transportation services. CHRW operates through four segments: North America surface transportation, global forwarding, Robinson Fresh and other/corporate. The North America surface transportation segment provides freight transportation services across North America through a network of offices located in the U.S., Canada and Mexico. This division's primary services include truckload, less-than-truckload and intermodal. The global forwarding segment provides logistics services through an international network of offices in North America, Europe, Asia, Australia, New Zealand and South America. It also contracts with independent agents worldwide. This division's primary services include ocean freight services, air freight services and customs brokerage. The Robinson Fresh segment provides sourcing under the Robinson Fresh trade name. Sourcing services include the buying, selling and marketing of fresh fruits, vegetables and other perishable items. It sources products from around the world and has a physical presence in North America, Europe, Asia and South America; and it provides the logistics and transportation of the products they sell, in addition to temperature-controlled transportation services for customers. Last, the other/corporate segment consists of managed services and surface transportation outside of North America, primarily Europe. This division's customers can access cloud-based technology, logistics experts and supply chain engineers to manage their day-to-day operations and optimize supply chain performance.

The firm offers employees medical, dental and vision insurance; a 401(k); an employee stock purchase plan; flexible spending accounts; an employee assistance plan; and employee discounts.

FINANCIAL DATA: *Note: Data for latest year may not have been available at press time.*

In U.S. $	2018	2017	2016	2015	2014	2013
Revenue	16,631,170,000	14,869,380,000	13,144,410,000	13,476,080,000	13,470,070,000	12,752,080,000
R&D Expense						
Operating Income	912,083,000	775,119,000	837,531,000	858,310,000	748,418,000	682,650,000
Operating Margin %		.05%	.06%	.06%	.06%	.05%
SGA Expense	449,610,000	413,404,000	375,061,000	358,760,000	320,213,000	326,784,000
Net Income	664,505,000	504,893,000	513,384,000	509,699,000	449,711,000	415,904,000
Operating Cash Flow	792,896,000	384,001,000	529,408,000	718,336,000	513,426,000	347,777,000
Capital Expenditure	63,871,000	57,945,000	91,437,000	44,642,000	29,502,000	48,206,000
EBITDA	1,008,812,000	868,096,000	912,200,000	924,719,000	805,427,000	739,532,000
Return on Assets %		.13%	.15%	.16%	.15%	.15%
Return on Equity %		.38%	.43%	.46%	.45%	.34%
Debt to Equity		0.526	0.398	0.435	0.478	0.532

CONTACT INFORMATION:
Phone: 952 937-8500   Fax: 952 937-6714
Toll-Free:
Address: 14701 Charlson Rd., Eden Prairie, MN 55347 United States

SALARIES/BONUSES:
Top Exec. Salary: $1,167,000   Bonus: $
Second Exec. Salary: $600,000   Bonus: $

STOCK TICKER/OTHER:
Stock Ticker: CHRW
Employees: 14,125
Parent Company:

Exchange: NAS
Fiscal Year Ends: 12/31

OTHER THOUGHTS:
Estimated Female Officers or Directors: 4
Hot Spot for Advancement for Women/Minorities: Y

Charles River Laboratories International Inc

www.criver.com

NAIC Code: 541711

TYPES OF BUSINESS:
Medical and Drug Research Models
Consulting
Bioactivity Software
Biosafety Testing
Contract Staffing
Laboratory Diagnostics
Intellectual Property Consulting
Analytical Testing

BRANDS/DIVISIONS/AFFILIATES:
Citoxlab

CONTACTS: Note: Officers with more than one job title may be intentionally listed here more than once.
James Foster, CEO
David Smith, CFO
Michael Knell, Chief Accounting Officer
David Johst, Chief Administrative Officer
Birgit Girshick, Executive VP, Divisional
Joseph LaPlume, Executive VP, Divisional
William Barbo, Executive VP

GROWTH PLANS/SPECIAL FEATURES:
Charles River Laboratories International, Inc. (CRL) is a global provider of solutions that accelerate the drug discovery and development process, including research models and outsourced preclinical services. CRL operates 80 facilities in approximately 20 countries. The firm's customer base includes global pharmaceutical companies, biotechnology companies, government agencies, hospitals and academic institutions. CRL operates in three segments: research models and services (RMS), discovery and safety assessment (DSA) and manufacturing. RMS supplies research models to the drug development industry, and is a global leader in the production and sale of rodent research model strains, principally genetically and microbiologically defined purpose-bred rats and mice. RMS accounted for 22.9% of 2018 total revenue. DSA (accounting for 58.1% of revenues) provides services that enable clients to outsource their drug discovery research; their critical, regulatory-required safety assessment testing; and related drug discovery and development activities to CRL. Manufacturing (19%) helps ensure the safe production and release of products manufactured by the firm's clients. This division's endotoxin and microbial detection business provides non-animal, or in vitro, methods for lot release testing of medical devices and injectable drugs for endotoxin contamination. Its avian vaccine services business provides specific pathogen free (SPF) fertile chicken eggs and chickens for the manufacture of live viruses. Its Biologics Testing Services business provides specialized testing of biologics and devices frequently outsourced by global pharmaceutical and biotechnology companies. In April 2019, CRL acquired Citoxlab, a premier, non-clinical contract research organization specializing in regulated safety assessment services, non-regulated discovery services and medical device testing.

The firm offers employees medical, dental, vision and life insurance; flexible spending accounts; short- and long-term disability; a 401(k); an employee stock purchase plan; an employee assistance plan; and more.

FINANCIAL DATA: Note: Data for latest year may not have been available at press time.

In U.S. $	2018	2017	2016	2015	2014	2013
Revenue	2,266,096,000	1,857,601,000	1,681,432,000	1,363,302,000	1,297,662,000	1,165,528,000
R&D Expense						
Operating Income	331,383,000	287,498,000	237,419,000	206,449,000	177,670,000	155,603,000
Operating Margin %		.15%	.14%	.15%	.14%	.13%
SGA Expense	443,854,000	373,446,000	367,548,000	300,414,000	269,033,000	225,695,000
Net Income	226,373,000	123,355,000	154,765,000	149,313,000	126,698,000	102,828,000
Operating Cash Flow	441,140,000	316,265,000	298,319,000	286,358,000	251,051,000	207,139,000
Capital Expenditure	140,054,000	82,431,000	55,288,000	63,252,000	56,925,000	39,154,000
EBITDA	507,232,000	457,891,000	377,288,000	305,381,000	285,990,000	255,932,000
Return on Assets %		.04%	.06%	.08%	.07%	.06%
Return on Equity %		.13%	.20%	.21%	.19%	.17%
Debt to Equity		1.066	1.443	1.154	1.11	1.002

CONTACT INFORMATION:
Phone: 781 222-6000   Fax: 978 658-7841
Toll-Free:
Address: 251 Ballardvale St., Wilmington, MA 01887 United States

SALARIES/BONUSES:
Top Exec. Salary: $1,225,473   Bonus: $
Second Exec. Salary: $650,509   Bonus: $

STOCK TICKER/OTHER:
Stock Ticker: CRL   Exchange: NYS
Employees: 11,000   Fiscal Year Ends: 12/31
Parent Company:

OTHER THOUGHTS:
Estimated Female Officers or Directors: 3
Hot Spot for Advancement for Women/Minorities: Y

Charles Schwab Corporation (The)

NAIC Code: 523120

www.schwab.com

TYPES OF BUSINESS:
Stock Brokerage-Retail, Online & Discount
Investment Services
Physical Branch Investment Offices
Mutual Funds
Wealth Management
Financial Information
Retail Banking
Online Trading Platform

BRANDS/DIVISIONS/AFFILIATES:
Charles Schwab & Co Inc
Charles Schwab Bank
Charles Schwab Investment Management Inc

CONTACTS: Note: Officers with more than one job title may be intentionally listed here more than once.
Walter Bettinger, CEO
Peter Crawford, CFO
Charles Schwab, Chairman of the Board
Joseph Martinetto, COO
Nigel Murtagh, Executive VP, Divisional
Terri Kallsen, Executive VP, Divisional
Bernard Clark, Executive VP, Divisional
David Garfield, Executive VP
Jonathan Craig, Senior Executive VP

GROWTH PLANS/SPECIAL FEATURES:
The Charles Schwab Corporation (CSC) engages in securities brokerage, banking, money management and related financial advisory services. The company manages $3.36 trillion in client brokerage accounts, 10.8 million active brokerage accounts, 1.6 million corporate retirement plan participants and 1.2 million banking accounts through its primary subsidiary, Charles Schwab & Co., Inc. (Schwab). Schwab is a securities broker-dealer with more than 345 domestic branch offices in 46 states, as well as a branch in each of the Commonwealth of Puerto Rico and London, England. It serves clients in Hong Kong through CSC subsidiaries Charles Schwab Bank, a federal savings bank located in Reno, Nevada; and Charles Schwab Investment Management, Inc., an investment advisor for the company's proprietary mutual and exchange-traded funds. CSC provides its financial services and products such as brokerage, banking, trust, advice and mutual/exchange trade funds to individuals and institutional clients through two segments: investor services and advisor services. Investor services provides retail brokerage and banking services to individual investors, retirement plan services and corporate brokerage services. Advisor services provides custodial, trading and support services to independent investment advisors (IAs), and retirement business services to independent retirement plan advisors and record keepers whose plan assets are held at Schwab Bank. In May 2018, Charles Schwab announced it was opening two Digital Accelerator hubs in Austin and San Francisco. Digital Accelerator hubs are designed to house hundreds of current and new employees focused on digital solutions.

The firm offers employees medical, dental, life, AD&D and vision insurance; health and dependent care flexible spending accounts; disability coverage; a 401(k) plan; a legal services plan; an employee discount program; an employee stock purchase plan; discounts on company products; and an employee assistance program.

FINANCIAL DATA: Note: Data for latest year may not have been available at press time.

In U.S. $	2018	2017	2016	2015	2014	2013
Revenue	9,943,000,000	8,439,000,000	7,473,000,000	6,369,000,000	6,054,000,000	5,434,000,000
R&D Expense						
Operating Income						
Operating Margin %						
SGA Expense	3,612,000,000	3,236,000,000	2,968,000,000	2,723,000,000	2,652,000,000	2,504,000,000
Net Income	3,507,000,000	2,354,000,000	1,889,000,000	1,447,000,000	1,321,000,000	1,071,000,000
Operating Cash Flow	12,456,000,000	1,263,000,000	2,662,000,000	1,246,000,000	2,348,000,000	1,656,000,000
Capital Expenditure	570,000,000	400,000,000	346,000,000	266,000,000	400,000,000	249,000,000
EBITDA						
Return on Assets %		.01%	.01%	.01%	.01%	.01%
Return on Equity %		.15%	.14%	.12%	.12%	.11%
Debt to Equity		0.302	0.211	0.242	0.174	0.20

CONTACT INFORMATION:
Phone: 415 667-7000 Fax: 415 627-8894
Toll-Free: 800-648-5300
Address: 211 Main St., San Francisco, CA 94105 United States

SALARIES/BONUSES:
Top Exec. Salary: $1,275,000 Bonus: $
Second Exec. Salary: $687,500 Bonus: $

STOCK TICKER/OTHER:
Stock Ticker: SCHW
Employees: 16,200
Parent Company:

Exchange: NYS
Fiscal Year Ends: 12/31

OTHER THOUGHTS:
Estimated Female Officers or Directors: 6
Hot Spot for Advancement for Women/Minorities: Y

Sales, profits and employees may be estimates. Financial information, benefits and other data can change quickly and may vary from those stated here.

Charter Communications Inc

NAIC Code: 517110

www.charter.com

TYPES OF BUSINESS:
Cable TV Service
Internet Access
Advanced Broadband Cable Services
Telephony Services
Voice Over Internet Protocol

BRANDS/DIVISIONS/AFFILIATES:
Spectrum
Spectrum TV
Spectrum Internet
Spectrum Voice
Spectrum Business
Spectrum Enterprise Solutions
Spectrum Community Solutions
Spectrum Reach

CONTACTS:
Note: Officers with more than one job title may be intentionally listed here more than once.

Thomas Rutledge, CEO
James Blackley, Executive VP, Divisional
Christopher Winfrey, CFO
Kevin Howard, Chief Accounting Officer
Jonathan Hargis, Chief Marketing Officer
John Bickham, COO
John Malone, Director Emeritus
Tom Montemagno, Executive VP, Divisional
Paul Marchand, Executive VP, Divisional
Kathleen Mayo, Executive VP, Divisional
Thomas Adams, Executive VP, Divisional
Scott Weber, Executive VP, Divisional
Catherine Bohigian, Executive VP, Divisional
James Nuzzo, Executive VP, Divisional

GROWTH PLANS/SPECIAL FEATURES:
Charter Communications, Inc. operates broadband communications businesses in the U.S., offering traditional cable video programming, high-speed internet access and voice service as well as advanced broadband services. The company serves more than 27 million residential and business customers. In addition, Charter sells video and online advertising inventory to local, regional and national advertising customers, as well as fiber-delivered communications and managed information technology (IT) solutions to larger enterprise customers. The firm owns and operates regional sports networks and local sports, news and lifestyle channels; and sells security and home management services to the residential marketplace. Charter's products and services include subscription-based video services, including video on demand (VOD), high definition (HD) television, and digital video recorder (DVR), internet services and voice services. Video, internet and voice services are offered to residential and commercial customers on a subscription basis, sold as bundled or individually. The firm sells its products and services under the Spectrum brand name, including Spectrum TV, Spectrum Internet, Spectrum Voice, Spectrum Business, Spectrum Enterprise Solutions, Spectrum Community Solutions, Spectrum Reach and Spectrum Guide.

Employee benefits include medical, dental and vision coverage; a 401(k); flexible spending accounts; health savings accounts; life and AD&D insurance; short- and long-term disability; adoption reimbursement; tuition reimbursement; and employee discounts.

FINANCIAL DATA:
Note: Data for latest year may not have been available at press time.

In U.S. $	2018	2017	2016	2015	2014	2013
Revenue	43,634,000,000	41,581,000,000	29,003,000,000	9,754,000,000	9,108,000,000	8,155,000,000
R&D Expense						
Operating Income	5,648,000,000	4,453,000,000	4,340,000,000	1,203,000,000	1,033,000,000	956,000,000
Operating Margin %		.11%	.23%	.22%	.21%	.12%
SGA Expense	192,000,000	1,000,000	899,000,000			
Net Income	1,230,000,000	9,895,000,000	3,522,000,000	-271,000,000	-183,000,000	-169,000,000
Operating Cash Flow	11,767,000,000	11,954,000,000	8,041,000,000	2,359,000,000	2,359,000,000	2,158,000,000
Capital Expenditure	9,595,000,000	7,870,000,000	33,532,000,000	1,812,000,000	2,177,000,000	2,425,000,000
EBITDA	15,966,000,000	15,041,000,000	11,247,000,000	3,328,000,000	3,135,000,000	2,810,000,000
Return on Assets %		.07%	.04%	-.01%	-.01%	-.01%
Return on Equity %		.25%	.18%	-5.42%	-1.23%	-1.13%
Debt to Equity		1.745	1.488		143.993	93.914

CONTACT INFORMATION:
Phone: 203-905-7801 Fax:
Toll-Free:
Address: 400 Atlantic St., Stamford, CT 06901 United States

STOCK TICKER/OTHER:
Stock Ticker: CHTR
Employees: 98,000
Parent Company:

Exchange: NAS
Fiscal Year Ends: 12/31

SALARIES/BONUSES:
Top Exec. Salary: $2,000,000 Bonus: $
Second Exec. Salary: $1,500,000 Bonus: $

OTHER THOUGHTS:
Estimated Female Officers or Directors: 1
Hot Spot for Advancement for Women/Minorities:

Sales, profits and employees may be estimates. Financial information, benefits and other data can change quickly and may vary from those stated here.

Chemed Corporation

NAIC Code: 621610

www.chemed.com

TYPES OF BUSINESS:
Home Health Care Services
Plumbing Services

BRANDS/DIVISIONS/AFFILIATES:
VITAS Healthcare Corporation
Roto-Rooter Corporation

CONTACTS:
Note: Officers with more than one job title may be intentionally listed here more than once.

Nicholas Westfall, CEO, Subsidiary
Kevin Mcnamara, CEO
David Williams, CFO
George Walsh, Chairman of the Board
Michael Witzeman, Chief Accounting Officer
Thomas Hutton, Director
Spencer Lee, Executive VP
Naomi Dallob, Secretary

GROWTH PLANS/SPECIAL FEATURES:
Chemed Corporation, through its wholly-owned subsidiaries VITAS Healthcare Corporation and Roto-Rooter Corporation, offers hospice care and plumbing services, respectively. VITAS is one of the largest national providers of hospice care and end-of-life services. Its team members include registered nurses, licensed practical nurses, home health aides, physicians, social workers, chaplains and other caregiving professionals. VITAS provides hospice care services in the patient's home, including music therapy and pet visits. Additionally, the firm manages inpatient hospice units, providing service in hospitals, nursing homes and assisted living communities/residential care facilities. Approximately 95% of VITAS' service revenues consist of payments from Medicare and Medicaid. Roto-Rooter supports the maintenance needs of residential and commercial markets by providing services such as plumbing, drain cleaning, high-pressure water jetting, underground leak and line detection, video camera pipe inspections, grease trap and liquid waste pumping, backflow protection, emergency services, automated drain care programs and pipe repair and replacement. One of the largest businesses of its type in North America, Roto-Rooter operates hundreds of company-owned and franchises throughout the U.S. Concerning revenues, Roto-Rooter's largest share is generated by plumbing repair and maintenance, followed by sewer and drain cleaning, HVAC (heating, ventilation and air conditioning) repair and other products and services.

Employee benefits include medical, prescription and dental coverage; life insurance; short- and long-term disability; a 401(k); profit sharing; flexible spending accounts; and tuition reimbursement.

FINANCIAL DATA:
Note: Data for latest year may not have been available at press time.

In U.S. $	2018	2017	2016	2015	2014	2013
Revenue	1,782,648,000	1,666,724,000	1,576,881,000	1,543,388,000	1,456,282,000	1,413,329,000
R&D Expense						
Operating Income	245,219,000	212,345,000	180,810,000	184,606,000	171,537,000	164,597,000
Operating Margin %		.13%	.11%	.12%	.12%	.12%
SGA Expense	269,922,000	268,222,000	241,511,000	237,673,000	217,000,000	207,536,000
Net Income	205,544,000	98,177,000	108,743,000	110,274,000	99,317,000	77,227,000
Operating Cash Flow	287,138,000	162,495,000	135,393,000	171,500,000	110,279,000	150,847,000
Capital Expenditure	52,872,000	64,300,000	39,772,000	44,135,000	43,571,000	29,324,000
EBITDA	283,453,000	156,814,000	215,407,000	217,270,000	204,012,000	171,252,000
Return on Assets %		.11%	.13%	.13%	.11%	.09%
Return on Equity %		.18%	.21%	.23%	.22%	.17%
Debt to Equity		0.169	0.191	0.163	0.313	

CONTACT INFORMATION:
Phone: 513 762-6900   Fax: 513 762-6919
Toll-Free:
Address: 255 E. 5th St., Ste. 2600, Cincinnati, OH 45202 United States

STOCK TICKER/OTHER:
Stock Ticker: CHE
Employees: 14,613
Parent Company:

Exchange: NYS
Fiscal Year Ends: 12/31

SALARIES/BONUSES:
Top Exec. Salary: $1,149,908   Bonus: $
Second Exec. Salary: $637,667   Bonus: $

OTHER THOUGHTS:
Estimated Female Officers or Directors: 3
Hot Spot for Advancement for Women/Minorities: Y

Sales, profits and employees may be estimates. Financial information, benefits and other data can change quickly and may vary from those stated here.

Chevron Corporation

www.chevron.com

NAIC Code: 211111

TYPES OF BUSINESS:
Oil & Gas Exploration & Production
Power Generation
Petrochemicals
Gasoline Retailing
Coal Mining
Fuel & Oil Additives
Convenience Stores
Pipelines

BRANDS/DIVISIONS/AFFILIATES:
Texaco
Chevron
Chevron Phillips Chemical Company LLC

CONTACTS:
Note: Officers with more than one job title may be intentionally listed here more than once.

Pierre Breber, CFO
Michael Wirth, Chairman of the Board
Jeanette Ourada, Controller
Joseph Geagea, Executive VP, Divisional
James Johnson, Executive VP, Divisional
Mark Nelson, Executive VP, Divisional
R Pate, General Counsel
David Inchausti, Other Corporate Officer
Rhonda Morris, Other Executive Officer

GROWTH PLANS/SPECIAL FEATURES:
Chevron Corporation is an integrated energy company that conducts petroleum, mining and chemical operations as well as power generation and energy services. The firm is divided into two operations: upstream operations, consisting of exploring, developing and producing crude oil and natural gas; and downstream operations, consisting of refining, marketing and transportation of crude oil and refined products as well as the manufacturing and marketing of commodity petrochemicals, fuel and plastics. The company maintains a refining network capable of processing more than 1.7 million barrels of crude oil per day. Its marketing operations in the USA consist of 7,700 Chevron and Texaco branded motor vehicle fuel retail outlets. Outside the USA, the firm supplies approximately 5,800 branded service stations, including affiliates. Chevron's transportation infrastructure includes an owned and operated system of crude oil, refined products, chemicals, natural gas liquids and natural gas pipelines in the USA. The company also has direct or indirect interests in other USA and international pipelines. Its chemical operations include the manufacturing and marketing of fuel and lubricating oil additives and commodity petrochemicals through joint venture Chevron Phillips Chemical Company, LLC. The power generation business develops and operates commercial power projects.

Employee benefits include health and dental coverage, retirement and savings plans, disability and life insurance, adoption benefits, domestic partner benefits, counseling services, dependent care reimbursements and fitness memberships.

FINANCIAL DATA:
Note: Data for latest year may not have been available at press time.

In U.S. $	2018	2017	2016	2015	2014	2013
Revenue	158,902,000,000	134,674,000,000	110,215,000,000	129,925,000,000	200,494,000,000	220,156,000,000
R&D Expense						
Operating Income	14,446,000,000	2,480,000,000	-6,216,000,000	-3,710,000,000	19,726,000,000	27,213,000,000
Operating Margin %		.02%	-.06%	-.03%	.10%	.12%
SGA Expense	3,838,000,000	4,448,000,000	4,684,000,000	4,443,000,000	4,494,000,000	4,510,000,000
Net Income	14,824,000,000	9,195,000,000	-497,000,000	4,587,000,000	19,241,000,000	21,423,000,000
Operating Cash Flow	30,618,000,000	20,515,000,000	12,846,000,000	19,456,000,000	31,475,000,000	35,002,000,000
Capital Expenditure	13,792,000,000	13,404,000,000	18,109,000,000	29,504,000,000	35,407,000,000	37,985,000,000
EBITDA	40,742,000,000	28,877,000,000	17,498,000,000	17,327,000,000	36,519,000,000	41,399,000,000
Return on Assets %		.04%	.00%	.02%	.07%	.09%
Return on Equity %		.06%	.00%	.03%	.13%	.15%
Debt to Equity		0.227	0.242	0.22	0.155	0.135

CONTACT INFORMATION:
Phone: 925 842-1000 Fax:
Toll-Free:
Address: 6001 Bollinger Canyon Rd., San Ramon, CA 94583 United States

STOCK TICKER/OTHER:
Stock Ticker: CVX
Employees: 55,200
Parent Company:

Exchange: NYS
Fiscal Year Ends: 12/31

SALARIES/BONUSES:
Top Exec. Salary: $1,468,750   Bonus: $
Second Exec. Salary: $1,133,458   Bonus: $

OTHER THOUGHTS:
Estimated Female Officers or Directors: 5
Hot Spot for Advancement for Women/Minorities: Y

Sales, profits and employees may be estimates. Financial information, benefits and other data can change quickly and may vary from those stated here.

Chevron Phillips Chemical Company LLC

www.cpchem.com

NAIC Code: 325110

TYPES OF BUSINESS:
Petrochemical & Plastics Manufacturing
Olefins & Polyolefins
Aromatics & Styrenics
Specialty Chemicals

BRANDS/DIVISIONS/AFFILIATES:
Chevron Corporation
Phillips 66
Marlex
Aromax
Scentinel
Soltex

CONTACTS: Note: Officers with more than one job title may be intentionally listed here more than once.
Mark Lashier, CEO
Carolyn J. Burke, Sr. VP
Maricela Caballero, VP-Human Resources
Dennis Holtermann, VP-Research & Tech.
Peggy Colsman, CIO
Rick Roberts, Sr. VP-Mfg.
Tim Hill, General Counsel
Ron Corn, VP-Corp. Planning & Dev.
Brian Cain, Head-Corp. Comm.
Tim D. Leveille, Controller
Dan Coombs, Sr. VP-Specialties, Aromatics & Styrenics
Mark Lashier, Exec. VP-Olefins & Polyolefins
Trevor Roberts, Treas.
David Morgan, VP-Polyethylene

GROWTH PLANS/SPECIAL FEATURES:

Chevron Phillips Chemical Company, LLC (CPChem) is the combined petrochemical businesses of Chevron Corporation and Phillips 66, both 50% owners. With 31 global production facilities, CPChem is an international producer of olefins and polyalphaolefins. It is also a supplier of aromatics, alpha olefins, specialty chemicals, polyethylene pipe and proprietary plastics. The company manufactures chemical products that are vital in the various production processes of over 70,000 consumer and industrial products. Its business is separated into three divisions: petrochemicals, which derives 56% of annual revenues; polymers (32%) and specialty chemicals (12%). Products from these divisions encompass ethylene, polyethylene, normal alpha olefins, polyalphaolefins, propylene, high-density polyethylene pipe, conduit, pipe fittings, cyclohexane, styrene, polystyrene, benzene, mining chemicals, drilling mud additives, mercaptans, specialty organosulfur compounds, racing fuels and acetylene hydrogenation catalysts. Primary brands of CPChem include Marlex (polyethylene), Aromax (benzene), Scentinel (gas odorant additives) and Soltex (drilling mud additive). Markets served by CPChem span adhesives, sealants, agricultural, appliances, automotive, building/construction, chemical manufacturing, dry cleaning, electronics, healthcare, medical, imaging, photography, industrial, oil/gas, mining, packaging, paint/coatings, personal care, cosmetics, pharmaceuticals, pipe, plastics, rubber and textiles. Production facilities are located in the U.S., Singapore, Saudi Arabia, Qatar and Belgium.

CPChem offers employees medical, dental and vision benefits; educational assistance; an employee assistance program; discounts on personal items; and relocation assistance.

FINANCIAL DATA: Note: Data for latest year may not have been available at press time.

In U.S. $	2018	2017	2016	2015	2014	2013
Revenue	11,310,000,000	9,063,000,000	8,455,000,000	9,248,000,000	13,416,000,000	13,147,000,000
R&D Expense						
Operating Income						
Operating Margin %						
SGA Expense						
Net Income	2,069,000,000	1,446,000,000	1,687,000,000	2,651,000,000	3,288,000,000	2,743,000,000
Operating Cash Flow						
Capital Expenditure						
EBITDA						
Return on Assets %						
Return on Equity %						
Debt to Equity						

CONTACT INFORMATION:
Phone: 832-813-4100   Fax:
Toll-Free: 800-231-1212
Address: 10001 Six Pines Dr., The Woodlands, TX 77380 United States

STOCK TICKER/OTHER:
Stock Ticker: Joint Venture   Exchange:
Employees: 5,000   Fiscal Year Ends: 12/31
Parent Company: Chevron Corporation

SALARIES/BONUSES:
Top Exec. Salary: $ Bonus: $
Second Exec. Salary: $ Bonus: $

OTHER THOUGHTS:
Estimated Female Officers or Directors: 1
Hot Spot for Advancement for Women/Minorities: Y

Sales, profits and employees may be estimates. Financial information, benefits and other data can change quickly and may vary from those stated here.

Chewy Inc (Chewy.com)

NAIC Code: 454111

www.chewy.com

TYPES OF BUSINESS:
Electronic Shopping
Pet and Pet Supplies Stores

BRANDS/DIVISIONS/AFFILIATES:
PetSmart Inc
Chewy.com
Chewy.com Rescue and Shelter Network

CONTACTS:
Note: Officers with more than one job title may be intentionally listed here more than once.
Sumit Singh, CEO
Mario Marte, CFO
Raymond Svider, Chairman of the Board
Satish Mehta, Chief Technology Officer
Susan Helfrick, General Counsel

GROWTH PLANS/SPECIAL FEATURES:
Chewy, Inc., commonly referred to as Chewy.com, is an online retailer of pet food and other pet related products. The firm is a subsidiary of PetSmart, Inc. With items from over 1,000 brands in stock and ready to ship, Chewy offers pet foods and pet products for dogs; cats; fish; birds; small pets such as rabbits, hamsters, gerbils, guinea pigs and chinchillas; reptiles; and horses. Headquartered in Dania Beach, Florida, with fulfillment centers in Nevada, Pennsylvania and Indiana, the firm offers same day shipping on all orders placed before 4 pm and a freshness guarantee combined with a 365-day hassle-free return policy. Customer service agents make up approximately one sixth of the firm's total employees, teams of which are available 24/7/365, and are trained in pet care in order to be better able to address customer questions, concerns and needs. In addition to its online pet food and pet products business, Chewy also operates the Chewy.com Rescue and Shelter Network. This network is free to all registered nonprofit organizations specializing in assisting the needs of pets and grants these organizations access to programs providing donations and fundraising opportunities. A portion of each purchase made on Chewy.com is donated to the organizations within the network.

FINANCIAL DATA:
Note: Data for latest year may not have been available at press time.

In U.S. $	2018	2017	2016	2015	2014	2013
Revenue	2,104,287,000		900,566,000			
R&D Expense						
Operating Income	-337,851,000		-107,427,000			
Operating Margin %						
SGA Expense	705,401,000		257,258,000			
Net Income	-338,057,000		-107,164,000			
Operating Cash Flow	-79,747,000		7,252,000			
Capital Expenditure	40,282,000		22,272,000			
EBITDA	-324,965,000		-101,825,000			
Return on Assets %						
Return on Equity %						
Debt to Equity						

CONTACT INFORMATION:
Phone: 954-793-4144 Fax:
Toll-Free: 800-672-4399
Address: 1855 Griffin Rd., Dania Beach, FL 33004 United States

STOCK TICKER/OTHER:
Stock Ticker: CHWY
Employees: 9,833
Parent Company: PetSmart Inc

Exchange: NYS
Fiscal Year Ends:

SALARIES/BONUSES:
Top Exec. Salary: $1,161,154 Bonus: $
Second Exec. Salary: $412,692 Bonus: $74,674

OTHER THOUGHTS:
Estimated Female Officers or Directors:
Hot Spot for Advancement for Women/Minorities:

Chick-fil-A Inc

www.chick-fil-a.com

NAIC Code: 722513

TYPES OF BUSINESS:
Fast Food Restaurants

BRANDS/DIVISIONS/AFFILIATES:
Chick-fil-A Chicken Sandwich
Chick-fil-A Kid's Meal Program
Truett's Grill
Truett's Luau
Dwarf House
Chick-fil-A One

CONTACTS:
Note: Officers with more than one job title may be intentionally listed here more than once.

Dan T. Cathy, CEO
Tim Tassopoulos, Pres.
Brent Ragsdale, CFO
Jon Bridges, CMO
Andrew Cathy, Chief People Officer
William (Woody) F. Faulk, VP-Innovation & Design
Cliff Robinson, Sr. VP-Operations
Roger H. Shealy, Dir.-Production Design
Tim Boggs, Sr. Dir.-Admin.
Kelly D. Ludwick, Sr. Dir.-Corp. Legal
Timothy Tassopoulos, Exec. VP-Oper.
Roger E. Blythe, Jr., VP-Bus. Analysis
Greg Thompson, Dir.-Corp. Comm.
James (Buck) McCabe, Exec. VP-Finance
Donald M. (Bubba) Cathy, Pres., Dwarf House
Perry Ragsdale, Sr. VP-Real Estate, Design & Construction
Thomas E. Childers, Sr. Dir.-Menu Innovation & Quality
Brent Ragsdale, VP
Dan T. Cathy, Chmn.
Onome Okuma, Sr. Dir.-Supply Chain & Business Growth Solutions

GROWTH PLANS/SPECIAL FEATURES:

Chick-fil-A, Inc., headquartered in Atlanta, Georgia, is a fast food chain with a focus on chicken sandwiches and chicken products. The company has more than 2,400 restaurants throughout the U.S. and in Canada, including both freestanding buildings with drive-through lanes and mall-based locations. Stores are also licensed to college campuses, hospitals, airports and other similar institutions. Offerings include chicken entrees, sandwiches, salads, waffle fries and fresh-squeezed lemonade and desserts served separately and in combo meals. The company's proprietary menu item is the Chick-fil-A Chicken Sandwich. The firm boasts a trans-fat free menu, cooking all foods in 100% refined peanut oil. The Chick-fil-A Kid's Meal Program includes activities to educate children in math and language arts skills and provides healthy alternatives to fries and soda. Sister restaurants include Truett's Grill, a full-service 50's diner themed restaurant; Truett's Luau, which serves fresh sea food items and Hawaii-inspired dishes; and Dwarf House, a full-service restaurant. The company also offers catering services with large trays of menu items. Chick-fil-A One is a rewards program in which members earn points with every purchase, and can be redeemed in various ways. Chick-fil-A attributes its growth over the past 50 years to dedicated franchisee owners and the company's emphasis on product quality. The company advertises through its signature Eat Mor Chikin campaign, featuring ads with cows trying to convince consumers to eat more chicken.

Corporate employee benefits include health, dental and vision coverage; short- and long-term disability insurance; life insurance; a 401(k) plan with a 5% company match; a pension plan; tuition reimbursement; and an onsite fitness center, childcare center and cafeteria.

FINANCIAL DATA:
Note: Data for latest year may not have been available at press time.

In U.S. $	2018	2017	2016	2015	2014	2013
Revenue	10,200,000,000	7,915,000,000	7,154,000,000	6,600,000,000	5,890,000,000	5,052,600,000
R&D Expense						
Operating Income						
Operating Margin %						
SGA Expense						
Net Income						
Operating Cash Flow						
Capital Expenditure						
EBITDA						
Return on Assets %						
Return on Equity %						
Debt to Equity						

CONTACT INFORMATION:
Phone: 404-765-8038　Fax:
Toll-Free: 800-232-2677
Address: 5200 Buffington Rd., Atlanta, GA 30349 United States

SALARIES/BONUSES:
Top Exec. Salary: $　Bonus: $
Second Exec. Salary: $　Bonus: $

STOCK TICKER/OTHER:
Stock Ticker: Private
Employees: 15,000
Parent Company:

Exchange:
Fiscal Year Ends: 12/31

OTHER THOUGHTS:
Estimated Female Officers or Directors: 14
Hot Spot for Advancement for Women/Minorities: Y

Sales, profits and employees may be estimates. Financial information, benefits and other data can change quickly and may vary from those stated here.

Cigna Corporation

NAIC Code: 524114

www.cigna.com

TYPES OF BUSINESS:
Insurance-Medical & Health, HMOs & PPOs
Indemnity Insurance
Investment Management Services
Group Life, Accident & Disability

BRANDS/DIVISIONS/AFFILIATES:
Express Scripts PBM

CONTACTS: Note: Officers with more than one job title may be intentionally listed here more than once.
David Cordani, CEO
Michael Triplett, Pres., Divisional
Eric Palmer, CFO
Isaiah Harris, Chairman of the Board
Mary Agoglia Hoeltzel, Chief Accounting Officer
Mark Boxer, Chief Information Officer
Lisa Bacus, Chief Marketing Officer
John Murabito, Executive VP, Divisional
Alan Muney, Executive VP
Nicole Jones, Executive VP
Steven Miller, Executive VP
Jason Sadler, President, Divisional
Brian Evanko, President, Divisional
Timothy Wentworth, President, Divisional
Matthew Manders, President, Divisional

GROWTH PLANS/SPECIAL FEATURES:
Cigna Corporation is a global health services organization. Along with its insurance subsidiaries, the company is a major provider of medical, dental, disability, life and accident insurance and related products and services, the majority of which are offered through employers and other groups. Cigna operates in three main segments: integrated medical, health services and international markets. The integrated medical segment accounts for approximately 67% of annual revenue and is comprised of two divisions: commercial and government. The commercial division consists of managed care plans, PPO plans and consumer-driven products such as health savings accounts and flexible spending accounts. The government division offers Medicare Advantage and Medicare Part D plans to seniors, as well as Medicaid plans. The health services segment accounts for approximately 13% of annual revenue and consists of the Express Scripts PBM business as well as the legacy home delivery operations that offer mail order, telephone and on-line pharmaceutical fulfillment services. The international markets segment accounts for approximately 10% of annual revenue. This segment has operations in over 30 countries or jurisdictions providing a full range of comprehensive medical and supplemental health, life and accident benefits to individuals and employers. Products and services include comprehensive health coverage, hospitalization, dental, critical illness, personal accident, term life and variable universal life. The remainder of Cigna's business is reported in group disability and other segment, accounting for 10% of annual revenue, which consists of the firm's group disability and life operations, corporate-owned life insurance business and the run-off businesses of reinsurance, settlement annuity and individual life insurance and annuity and retirement benefits businesses, as well as certain international run-off businesses. In December 2018, Cigna completed its $54 billion acquisition of Express Scripts Holding Company, one of the largest pharmacy benefit managers in the U.S.

FINANCIAL DATA: Note: Data for latest year may not have been available at press time.

In U.S. $	2018	2017	2016	2015	2014	2013
Revenue	48,569,000,000	41,616,000,000	39,668,000,000	37,876,000,000	34,914,000,000	32,380,000,000
R&D Expense						
Operating Income						
Operating Margin %						
SGA Expense	11,934,000,000					
Net Income	2,637,000,000	2,237,000,000	1,867,000,000	2,094,000,000	2,102,000,000	1,476,000,000
Operating Cash Flow	3,770,000,000	4,086,000,000	4,026,000,000	2,717,000,000	1,994,000,000	719,000,000
Capital Expenditure	528,000,000	471,000,000	461,000,000	510,000,000	473,000,000	527,000,000
EBITDA						
Return on Assets %		.04%	.03%	.04%	.04%	.03%
Return on Equity %		.16%	.14%	.18%	.20%	.15%
Debt to Equity		0.379	0.347	0.417	0.465	0.474

CONTACT INFORMATION:
Phone: 860 226-6000 Fax: 215 761-3596
Toll-Free: 800-997-1654
Address: 900 Cottage Grove Rd., Bloomfield, CT 06002 United States

SALARIES/BONUSES:
Top Exec. Salary: $1,284,615 Bonus: $
Second Exec. Salary: $634,615 Bonus: $

STOCK TICKER/OTHER:
Stock Ticker: CI
Employees: 41,000
Parent Company:

Exchange: NYS
Fiscal Year Ends: 12/31

OTHER THOUGHTS:
Estimated Female Officers or Directors: 4
Hot Spot for Advancement for Women/Minorities: Y

Cintas Corporation

NAIC Code: 812331

www.cintas.com

TYPES OF BUSINESS:
Linen & Uniform Supply
Uniform Rental, Sales & Cleaning
Uniform Design & Manufacturing
Outsourcing Services
Dust Control Services
Restroom Cleaning Services
First Aid & Safety Products

BRANDS/DIVISIONS/AFFILIATES:

CONTACTS:
Note: Officers with more than one job title may be intentionally listed here more than once.

Scott Farmer, CEO
J. Hansen, CFO
Richard Farmer, Chairman Emeritus
Michael Thompson, Chief Administrative Officer
Todd Schneider, COO
Thomas Frooman, General Counsel
Paul Adler, Vice President

GROWTH PLANS/SPECIAL FEATURES:

Cintas Corporation provides highly specialized products and services to corporate customers in North America. The company is a leading corporate identity uniform supplier, as well as a supplier of entrance and logo mats, restroom supplies, promotional products, first aid, safety, fire protection products and industrial carpet/tile cleaning services. Cintas operates through two business primary segments: uniform rental & facilities services and first aid & safety services. The uniform rental & facility services segment consists of the rental and servicing of uniforms and other garments, including flame-resistant clothing, mats, mops, shop towels and other ancillary items. This segment also provides restroom cleaning supplies and services; carpet and tile cleaning services; and the sale of items from Cintas' catalogs. The first aid & safety services segment consists of first aid and safety products and services, as well as fire protection products and services. The company provides these products and services to over one million businesses of all types, from small service and manufacturing companies to major corporations that employ thousands of people.

Employee benefits include flexible spending accounts; medical, prescription drug, dental and vision coverage; disability; and wellness programs.

FINANCIAL DATA:
Note: Data for latest year may not have been available at press time.

In U.S. $	2018	2017	2016	2015	2014	2013
Revenue	6,476,632,000	5,323,381,000	4,905,458,000	4,476,886,000	4,551,812,000	
R&D Expense						
Operating Income	991,731,000	852,915,000	781,748,000	696,407,000	611,634,000	
Operating Margin %		.16%	.16%	.16%	.13%	
SGA Expense	1,916,792,000	1,527,380,000	1,348,122,000	1,224,930,000	1,302,752,000	
Net Income	842,586,000	480,708,000	693,520,000	430,618,000	374,442,000	
Operating Cash Flow	964,160,000	763,887,000	465,845,000	580,276,000	607,969,000	
Capital Expenditure	271,699,000	273,317,000	275,385,000	217,720,000	145,580,000	
EBITDA	1,230,592,000	970,523,000	947,923,000	878,519,000	864,542,000	
Return on Assets %		.09%	.17%	.10%	.09%	
Return on Equity %		.23%	.37%	.21%	.17%	
Debt to Equity		1.203	0.57	0.673	0.593	

CONTACT INFORMATION:
Phone: 513 459-1200   Fax: 513 573-4030
Toll-Free:
Address: 6800 Cintas Blvd., Cincinnati, OH 45262 United States

SALARIES/BONUSES:
Top Exec. Salary: $1,200,000   Bonus: $
Second Exec. Salary: $683,184   Bonus: $

STOCK TICKER/OTHER:
Stock Ticker: CTAS   Exchange: NAS
Employees: 42,000   Fiscal Year Ends: 05/31
Parent Company:

OTHER THOUGHTS:
Estimated Female Officers or Directors: 1
Hot Spot for Advancement for Women/Minorities:

Cisco Systems Inc

www.cisco.com

NAIC Code: 0

TYPES OF BUSINESS:
Computer Networking Equipment
Routers & Switches
Real-Time Conferencing Technology
Server Virtualization Software
Data Storage Products
Security Products
Teleconference Systems and Technology
Unified Communications Systems

BRANDS/DIVISIONS/AFFILIATES:
Jasper
AppDynamics Inc
MindMeld
Stealthwatch Cloud
BroadSoft
Accompany
Duo Security

CONTACTS:
Note: Officers with more than one job title may be intentionally listed here more than once.

Charles Robbins, CEO
Prat Bhatt, Chief Accounting Officer
Geraldine Elliott, Chief Marketing Officer
Kelly Kramer, Executive VP
David Goeckeler, Executive VP
Maria Martinez, Executive VP
Mark Chandler, Executive VP
Irving Tan, Senior VP, Divisional

GROWTH PLANS/SPECIAL FEATURES:

Cisco Systems, Inc. designs and sells a broad range of technologies that power the internet. The company's products and services are grouped into the categories of infrastructure platforms, applications and security. Infrastructure platforms consist of Cisco's core networking technologies of switching, routing, data center products, and wireless that are designed to work together to deliver networking capabilities and transport and/or store data. These technologies consist of both hardware and software that help customers build networks, automate, orchestrate, integrate and digitize data. The applications category primarily consists of software-related offerings that utilize the core networking and data center platforms to provide their function. These offerings encompass hardware- and software-based solutions, including licenses and software-as-a-service (SaaS). Applications include collaboration products/solutions such as unified communications, telepresence and conferencing; and the Internet of Things (IoT) and analytics software from Jasper and AppDynamics. Cisco's Jasper control center platform enables enterprises to automate the lifecycle of connected devices, including tools designed to automatically and remotely onboard, manage and monetize their IoT devices. Subsidiary AppDynamics, Inc. is an application intelligence software company, whose products enable companies to improve application and business performance. Subsidiary MindMeld is an AI company with a platform that enables customers to build intelligent and human-like conversational interfaces for any application or device. Last, the security category includes Cisco's unified threat management products, advanced threat security products and web security products, all of which are designed to provide a highly secure environment for customers. Its Stealthwatch Cloud offering offers behavioral threat detection for infrastructure-as-a-service and platform-as-a-service environments. During 2018, Cisco acquired BroadSoft, Accompany and Duo Security; sold its service provider video software solutions business to Permira Funds; and announced its intent to purchase silicon photonics leader, Luxtera, Inc.

FINANCIAL DATA:
Note: Data for latest year may not have been available at press time.

In U.S. $	2018	2017	2016	2015	2014	2013
Revenue	49,330,000,000	48,005,000,000	49,247,000,000	49,161,000,000	47,142,000,000	48,607,000,000
R&D Expense	6,332,000,000	6,059,000,000	6,296,000,000	6,207,000,000	6,294,000,000	5,942,000,000
Operating Income	12,667,000,000	12,729,000,000	12,928,000,000	11,254,000,000	9,763,000,000	11,301,000,000
Operating Margin %		.27%	.26%	.23%	.21%	.23%
SGA Expense	11,386,000,000	11,177,000,000	11,433,000,000	11,861,000,000	11,437,000,000	11,802,000,000
Net Income	110,000,000	9,609,000,000	10,739,000,000	8,981,000,000	7,853,000,000	9,983,000,000
Operating Cash Flow	13,666,000,000	13,876,000,000	13,570,000,000	12,552,000,000	12,332,000,000	12,894,000,000
Capital Expenditure	834,000,000	964,000,000	1,146,000,000	1,227,000,000	1,275,000,000	1,160,000,000
EBITDA	16,174,000,000	15,434,000,000	15,746,000,000	14,209,000,000	12,711,000,000	14,161,000,000
Return on Assets %		.08%	.09%	.08%	.08%	.10%
Return on Equity %		.15%	.17%	.15%	.14%	.18%
Debt to Equity		0.389	0.385	0.359	0.36	0.219

CONTACT INFORMATION:
Phone: 408 526-4000 Fax: 408 526-4100
Toll-Free: 800-553-6387
Address: 170 W. Tasman Dr., San Jose, CA 95134 United States

SALARIES/BONUSES:
Top Exec. Salary: $194,712 Bonus: $6,500,000
Second Exec. Salary: $187,500 Bonus: $6,000,000

STOCK TICKER/OTHER:
Stock Ticker: CSCO
Employees: 74,200
Parent Company:

Exchange: NAS
Fiscal Year Ends: 07/31

OTHER THOUGHTS:
Estimated Female Officers or Directors: 10
Hot Spot for Advancement for Women/Minorities: Y

Citigroup Inc

NAIC Code: 522110

www.citigroup.com

TYPES OF BUSINESS:
Banking
Commercial, Residential & Consumer Lending
Credit Cards
Investment Banking
Insurance
Brokerage Services
Equity
Cash Management

BRANDS/DIVISIONS/AFFILIATES:
Citicorp
Citi Holdings
Citi
Citibank
CitiMortgage
Citibanamex

CONTACTS: Note: Officers with more than one job title may be intentionally listed here more than once.
Stephen Bird, CEO, Divisional
James Forese, CEO, Divisional
William Mills, CEO, Geographical
Jim Cowles, CEO, Geographical
Francisco Aristeguieta, CEO, Geographical
Jane Fraser, CEO, Geographical
Barbara Desoer, CEO, Subsidiary
Michael Corbat, CEO
John Gerspach, CFO
Michael ONeill, Chairman of the Board
Jeffrey Walsh, Chief Accounting Officer
Bradford Hu, Chief Risk Officer
Rohan Weerasinghe, General Counsel

GROWTH PLANS/SPECIAL FEATURES:
Citigroup, Inc. is a diversified financial services holding company and one of the largest banking organizations in the world. The firm is organized into two segments: Citicorp and Citi Holdings. Citicorp consists of the company's global consumer banking business, which provides retail banking, local commercial banking, investment services and Citi-branded credit cards; and the institutional clients group, which provides investment banking, debt and equity, lending, real estate, cash management, clearing and trade services. This segment also includes corporate/other, which overssees the firm's treasury operations, its technology and global staff functions, as well as other corporate expenses. Citicorp has operations in North America, Europe, Latin America, Middle East, Africa and Asia. Half of its loans, deposits, revenues and net income are generated from outside the U.S. Citi Holdings operates the company's brokerage and asset management and local consumer lending businesses as well as managing a special asset pool. Citigroup has several brands including Citibank, which offers banking services from more than 2,649 branches in 19 countries worldwide; CitiMortgage, which offers a variety of mortgage products; and Citibanamex, a major commercial bank in Mexico. In November 2017, BlackRock and Citibanamex, a subsidiary of Citigroup, announced a definitive agreement for BlackRock to acquire the asset management business of Citibanamex, subject to regulatory approvals and customary closing conditions.

FINANCIAL DATA: Note: Data for latest year may not have been available at press time.

In U.S. $	2018	2017	2016	2015	2014	2013
Revenue	72,854,000,000	71,449,000,000	69,875,000,000	76,354,000,000	76,882,000,000	76,366,000,000
R&D Expense						
Operating Income						
Operating Margin %						
SGA Expense	29,892,000,000	29,680,000,000	29,287,000,000	29,897,000,000	32,239,000,000	31,991,000,000
Net Income	18,045,000,000	-6,798,000,000	14,912,000,000	17,242,000,000	7,313,000,000	13,673,000,000
Operating Cash Flow	36,952,000,000	-8,587,000,000	53,932,000,000	39,737,000,000	45,434,000,000	57,410,000,000
Capital Expenditure	3,774,000,000	3,361,000,000	2,756,000,000	3,198,000,000	3,386,000,000	3,490,000,000
EBITDA						
Return on Assets %		.00%	.01%	.01%	.00%	.01%
Return on Equity %		-.04%	.07%	.08%	.03%	.07%
Debt to Equity		1.304	1.002	0.981	1.115	1.119

CONTACT INFORMATION:
Phone: 212 559-1000   Fax: 212 816-8913
Toll-Free: 800-285-3000
Address: 388 Greenwich St., New York, NY 10013 United States

SALARIES/BONUSES:
Top Exec. Salary: $500,000   Bonus: $7,800,000
Second Exec. Salary: $1,500,000   Bonus: $6,450,000

STOCK TICKER/OTHER:
Stock Ticker: C
Employees: 204,000
Parent Company:

Exchange: NYS
Fiscal Year Ends: 12/31

OTHER THOUGHTS:
Estimated Female Officers or Directors: 5
Hot Spot for Advancement for Women/Minorities: Y

Citrix Systems Inc

www.citrix.com

NAIC Code: 0

TYPES OF BUSINESS:
Computer Software: Network Management (IT), System Testing & Storage
Consulting Services
Training & Technical Support
Online Services

BRANDS/DIVISIONS/AFFILIATES:
XenApp
XenDesktop
Citrix Workspace Suite
Citrix Receiver
NetScaler ADC
ShareFile
Citrix HDX Technologies
XenMobile

CONTACTS: Note: Officers with more than one job title may be intentionally listed here more than once.
David Henshall, CEO
Jessica Soisson, CFO
Robert Calderoni, Chairman of the Board
Timothy Minahan, Chief Marketing Officer
Jeroen van Rotterdam, Executive VP, Divisional
Antonio Gomes, Executive VP
Donna Kimmel, Executive VP
Mark Ferrer, Executive VP
Paul Hough, Executive VP

GROWTH PLANS/SPECIAL FEATURES:

Citrix Systems, Inc. designs, develops and markets products that allow applications to be delivered, supported and shared on demand. The firm's desktop virtualization solutions, XenApp and XenDesktop, reduce the complexity and cost of desktop management by virtualizing the desktop and applications in the datacenter. XenApp runs the business logic of applications on a central server, transmitting only screen pixels, keystrokes and mouse movements through an encrypted channel to users' computers. XenDesktop streams desktop images through multiple virtual machines. Citrix Workspace Suite delivers user experience solutions for any app or desktop using a universal client, Citrix Receiver, which is available on tablets, smartphones, PCs, Macs or thin clients. NetScaler ADC is a software-defined application delivery controller (ADC) and load balancer designed to improve application performance and reliability for mobile, remote and branch users. NetScaler SD-WAN increased the security, performance and reliability of traditional enterprise applications, software-as-a-service (SaaS) applications and virtual desktops for remote users. For content collaboration, ShareFile is a secure, cloud-based file sharing and storage solutions built for mobile business, giving users enterprise-class data services across all corporate and personal mobile devices, while maintaining total IT control. Professional services include consulting for the implementation of Citrix technologies and solutions, as well as product training and certification services. Technology products include: Citrix HDX Technologies, a family of innovations that optimize the end-to-end user experience in virtual desktop and virtual application environments; NetScaler nCore Technology, an architecture that enables execution of multiple packet engines in parallel; and XenMobile, a foundational technology that delivers a holistic mobile computing platform for enterprises, with its main components including MDM, MAM, MCM and UEM, end-to-end security and mobile productivity apps.

Citrix offers employees medical, dental, prescription and vision benefits; on-site fitness centers; 401(k); and paid time off.

FINANCIAL DATA: Note: Data for latest year may not have been available at press time.

In U.S. $	2018	2017	2016	2015	2014	2013
Revenue	2,973,903,000	2,824,686,000	3,418,265,000	3,275,594,000	3,142,856,000	2,918,434,000
R&D Expense	439,984,000	415,801,000	489,265,000	563,975,000	553,817,000	516,338,000
Operating Income	694,685,000	645,910,000	776,904,000	450,496,000	322,735,000	380,717,000
Operating Margin %		.23%	.23%	.14%	.10%	.13%
SGA Expense	1,389,577,000	1,308,677,000	1,563,382,000	1,538,027,000	1,600,187,000	1,476,916,000
Net Income	575,667,000	-20,719,000	536,112,000	319,361,000	251,723,000	339,523,000
Operating Cash Flow	1,035,345,000	908,276,000	1,115,830,000	1,034,548,000	845,981,000	928,343,000
Capital Expenditure	72,564,000	88,280,000	160,512,000	172,228,000	179,093,000	175,042,000
EBITDA	851,513,000	771,970,000	910,751,000	748,909,000	634,308,000	648,217,000
Return on Assets %		.00%	.09%	.06%	.05%	.07%
Return on Equity %		-.01%	.23%	.15%	.09%	.11%
Debt to Equity		2.144		0.671	0.595	

CONTACT INFORMATION:
Phone: 954 267-3000   Fax: 954 267-9319
Toll-Free: 800-424-8749
Address: 851 W. Cypress Creek Rd., Fort Lauderdale, FL 33309 United States

SALARIES/BONUSES:
Top Exec. Salary: $1,000,000   Bonus: $
Second Exec. Salary: $492,500   Bonus: $

STOCK TICKER/OTHER:
Stock Ticker: CTXS
Employees: 9,600
Parent Company:

Exchange: NAS
Fiscal Year Ends: 12/31

OTHER THOUGHTS:
Estimated Female Officers or Directors: 2
Hot Spot for Advancement for Women/Minorities:

Sales, profits and employees may be estimates. Financial information, benefits and other data can change quickly and may vary from those stated here.

Clayton Homes Inc

NAIC Code: 321992

www.claytonhomes.com

TYPES OF BUSINESS:
Construction Services
Manufactured Housing
Insurance & Financing

BRANDS/DIVISIONS/AFFILIATES:
Berkshire Hathaway Inc
Vanderbilt Mortgage and Finance Inc
Mungo Homes

CONTACTS: Note: Officers with more than one job title may be intentionally listed here more than once.
Kevin T. Clayton, CEO
Kevin T. Clayton, Pres.
Richard D. Strachan, Pres., Mfg.
Leon Van Tonder, Dir.-Oper.

GROWTH PLANS/SPECIAL FEATURES:

Clayton Homes, Inc., a subsidiary of Berkshire Hathaway, Inc., produces, sells, finances and insures modular and manufactured homes, in addition to commercial and educational relocatable buildings. The company's manufacturing plants produce homes that are marketed in 49 states through independent retailers and company-owned sales centers. Clayton's factory-built manufactured homes are completely-finished dwellings that are constructed under federal code in factories and then transported by truck to its targeted location. The homes are designed to be permanent, owner-occupied residential sites with attached utilities. The firm manufactures a variety of single- and multi-sectional homes from 1,000 to 2,000 square feet and larger. Standard features offered in Clayton homes include central heating, flooring systems and wall and floor treatments. Customers can choose predesigned homes or custom-design a home by size, number of bedrooms and other features. Through financial subsidiary Vanderbilt Mortgage and Finance, Inc. (VMF), the firm offers financing to manufactured home customers as well as customers purchasing homes from certain third parties. VMF's financing products include manufactured home loans, Federal Housing Authority (FHA) loans, Land Home financing and more. Clayton also offers home insurance products. In addition, Clayton acts as a reinsurance agent for physical damage, family protection and homebuyer protection insurance and other policies issued by insurance companies in connection with the firm's homes. Affiliates and brands include Schult, Crest, Karsten, Marlette, Golden West, SEhomes, Clayton Norris, Cavalier, Giles and Buccaneer. In December 2018, Clayton acquired Mungo Homes, a new-home builder since 1954. In April 2019, the firm announced plans to establish a truss and wall panel manufacturing facility in Westmoreland, Tennessee, creating approximately 110 jobs in Sumner County, with operations expected to commence in early 2020.

Clayton offers employees medical, dental, vision and life insurance; 401(k); and various employee assistance programs.

FINANCIAL DATA: Note: Data for latest year may not have been available at press time.

In U.S. $	2018	2017	2016	2015	2014	2013
Revenue	6,046,000,000	5,010,000,000	4,230,000,000	3,580,000,000	3,310,000,000	3,199,000,000
R&D Expense						
Operating Income						
Operating Margin %						
SGA Expense						
Net Income	911,000,000	765,000,000	744,000,000	706,000,000	558,000,000	416,000,000
Operating Cash Flow						
Capital Expenditure						
EBITDA						
Return on Assets %						
Return on Equity %						
Debt to Equity						

CONTACT INFORMATION:
Phone: 865-380-3000 Fax: 865-380-3742
Toll-Free: 800-822-0633
Address: 500 Clayton Rd., Maryville, TN 37804 United States

STOCK TICKER/OTHER:
Stock Ticker: Subsidiary
Employees: 17,000
Parent Company: Berkshire Hathaway Inc

Exchange:
Fiscal Year Ends: 06/30

SALARIES/BONUSES:
Top Exec. Salary: $ Bonus: $
Second Exec. Salary: $ Bonus: $

OTHER THOUGHTS:
Estimated Female Officers or Directors:
Hot Spot for Advancement for Women/Minorities:

Sales, profits and employees may be estimates. Financial information, benefits and other data can change quickly and may vary from those stated here.

Cleveland Clinic Foundation (The)

www.clevelandclinic.org

NAIC Code: 622110

TYPES OF BUSINESS:
General Medical and Surgical Hospitals

BRANDS/DIVISIONS/AFFILIATES:
Health Education Campus
Cleveland Clinic Lerner College of Medicine

CONTACTS:
Note: Officers with more than one job title may be intentionally listed here more than once.

Delos M. Cosgrove, CEO
William M. Peacock, III, Chief of Oper.
Steven C. Glass, CFO
Paul Matsen, CMO
Linda McHugh, Chief Human Resources Officer
Robert Wyllie, Chief Medical Oper. Officer
Doug Smith, Interim CIO
Cindy Hundorfean, Chief Admin. Officer-Clinical Svcs.
David W. Rowan, Chief Legal Officer
Michael Harrington, Chief Acct. Officer
Kristen D.W. Morris, Chief Gov't. & Community Rel. Officer
Linda McHugh, Exec. Admin.-CEO & Board of Governors
K. Kelly Hancock, Interim Exec. Chief Nursing Officer
Ann Huston, Chief Strategy Officer
Robert E. Rich, Jr., Chmn.

GROWTH PLANS/SPECIAL FEATURES:

The Cleveland Clinic Foundation is a nonprofit clinic in Ohio that combines medical care with education and research. It is noted for very advanced surgical techniques and advanced care. Founded in 1921, Cleveland Clinic cares for 2 million patients annually, with nearly 8 million outpatient visits in locations throughout the world. They firm's health system includes 18 hospitals, more than 210 outpatient locations and nearly 6,000 beds. These locations include a main campus in Cleveland, 11 regional hospitals in northeast Ohio, five hospitals in southeast Florida, a brain center in Las Vegas, and outpatient center in Toronto and a quaternary care hospital in Abu Dhabi. Clinical institutes specialize in anesthesiology, eye care, medicine, wellness, dermatology, plastic surgery, digestive disease, surgery, emergency services, endocrinology, metabolism, urological, kidney, head/neck, imaging, Ob/Gyn, orthopedic, rheumatologic, pediatric, respiratory, heart/vascular, pathology, cancer and more. In addition, The Cleveland Clinic Foundation constructed a 475,115-square-foot Health Education Campus in collaboration with Case Western Reserve University, which welcomes more than 2,200 students from the university's dental, nursing and medical schools, including the Cleveland Clinic Lerner College of Medicine.

Employee benefits include pension and savings plans; health, dental and vision insurance; life insurance; short- and long-term disability; adoption assistance; and an employee wellness program.

FINANCIAL DATA:
Note: Data for latest year may not have been available at press time.

In U.S. $	2018	2017	2016	2015	2014	2013
Revenue	8,900,000,000	8,400,000,000	8,037,207,000	7,156,972,000	6,687,379,000	6,450,159,000
R&D Expense						
Operating Income						
Operating Margin %						
SGA Expense						
Net Income	266,000,000	328,000,000	139,352,000	480,224,000	467,543,000	293,995,000
Operating Cash Flow						
Capital Expenditure						
EBITDA						
Return on Assets %						
Return on Equity %						
Debt to Equity						

CONTACT INFORMATION:
Phone: 216-444-2200 Fax:
Toll-Free: 800-223-2273
Address: 9500 Euclid Ave., Cleveland, OH 44195 United States

SALARIES/BONUSES:
Top Exec. Salary: $ Bonus: $
Second Exec. Salary: $ Bonus: $

STOCK TICKER/OTHER:
Stock Ticker: Nonprofit
Employees: 60,000
Parent Company:

Exchange:
Fiscal Year Ends: 12/31

OTHER THOUGHTS:
Estimated Female Officers or Directors: 22
Hot Spot for Advancement for Women/Minorities: Y

Clorox Company (The)

NAIC Code: 325611

www.thecloroxcompany.com

TYPES OF BUSINESS:
Cleaning/Laundry Products-Manufacturing
Automotive Care Products
Pesticides
Cat Litter
Water Filtration Products
Charcoal
Domestic Plastics
Dressings & Sauces

BRANDS/DIVISIONS/AFFILIATES:
Clorox
Clorox 2
Tilex
Liquid-Plumr
Formula 409
Hidden Valley
Ayudin
Brita

CONTACTS:
Note: Officers with more than one job title may be intentionally listed here more than once.

Benno Dorer, CEO
Andrew Mowery, Other Executive Officer
Kevin Jacobsen, CFO
Jeff Baker, Chief Accounting Officer
John McNulty, Chief Information Officer
Stacey Grier, Chief Marketing Officer
Linda Rendle, Executive VP, Divisional
Eric Reynolds, Executive VP, Divisional
Jon Balousek, Executive VP, Divisional
Laura Stein, Executive VP, Divisional
Kirsten Marriner, Executive VP
Michael Costello, General Manager, Divisional
Diego Barral, General Manager, Divisional
Matthew Laszlo, Other Executive Officer
Denise Garner, Other Executive Officer
William Bailey, Senior VP, Divisional

GROWTH PLANS/SPECIAL FEATURES:
The Clorox Company is a leading producer of consumer and institutional products. Its operations consist of four business segments: cleaning, lifestyle, household and international. Cleaning consists of laundry, home-care and professional products that are sold in the U.S. These products include Clorox branded bleaches; Clorox 2 branded color boosters and stain fighters; home-care products sold under the Pine-Sol, S.O.S., Tilex, Liquid-Plumr and Formula 409 brands; and natural cleaning products sold under the Green Works brand name. The lifestyle segment consists of food products, water-filtration systems, filters and all-natural personal care products. These products include sauces and dressing marketed under the KC Masterpiece and Hidden Valley brands, Brita water-filtration systems and filters and Burt's Bees natural personal care products. The household segment consists of charcoal, cat litter, plastic bags, wraps and container products. Brands in this division include Glad, Kingsford, Match Light, Ever Clean, Scoop Away, RenewLife and Fresh Step. The international segment includes brands and products marketed outside the U.S. Clorox sells its products internationally under such brand names as Ayudin, PinoLuz, Bon Bril and Lestoil. Clorox's products are manufactured internationally and are sold through grocery stores, retail outlets and mass merchandisers to consumers in more than 100 countries. Within the U.S., the company also sells institutional, janitorial, healthcare and food-service versions of many of its products through distributors as well as natural personal care products through the Internet. In March 2018, Clorox agreed to acquire Nutranext, a health and wellness company.

FINANCIAL DATA:
Note: Data for latest year may not have been available at press time.

In U.S. $	2018	2017	2016	2015	2014	2013
Revenue	6,124,000,000	5,973,000,000	5,761,000,000	5,655,000,000	5,591,000,000	5,623,000,000
R&D Expense	132,000,000	135,000,000	141,000,000	136,000,000	125,000,000	130,000,000
Operating Income	1,125,000,000	1,117,000,000	1,056,000,000	1,001,000,000	959,000,000	969,000,000
Operating Margin %		.19%	.18%	.18%	.17%	.17%
SGA Expense	1,407,000,000	1,409,000,000	1,393,000,000	1,321,000,000	1,269,000,000	1,307,000,000
Net Income	823,000,000	701,000,000	648,000,000	580,000,000	558,000,000	572,000,000
Operating Cash Flow	974,000,000	868,000,000	778,000,000	874,000,000	767,000,000	775,000,000
Capital Expenditure	194,000,000	231,000,000	172,000,000	125,000,000	138,000,000	194,000,000
EBITDA	1,305,000,000	1,284,000,000	1,236,000,000	1,190,000,000	1,144,000,000	1,157,000,000
Return on Assets %		.15%	.15%	.14%	.13%	.13%
Return on Equity %		1.67%	3.12%	4.26%	3.72%	104.00%
Debt to Equity		2.566	6.051	15.22	10.357	14.863

CONTACT INFORMATION:
Phone: 510 271-7000   Fax: 510 832-1463
Toll-Free:
Address: 1221 Broadway, Oakland, CA 94612-1888 United States

STOCK TICKER/OTHER:
Stock Ticker: CLX
Employees: 8,100
Parent Company:

Exchange: NYS
Fiscal Year Ends: 06/30

SALARIES/BONUSES:
Top Exec. Salary: $1,061,538   Bonus: $
Second Exec. Salary: $607,288   Bonus: $

OTHER THOUGHTS:
Estimated Female Officers or Directors: 3
Hot Spot for Advancement for Women/Minorities: Y

Coca-Cola Bottling Co Consolidated

www.cokeconsolidated.com

NAIC Code: 312111

TYPES OF BUSINESS:
Beverages-Soft Drink Manufacturing
Bottling Services

BRANDS/DIVISIONS/AFFILIATES:
Coca-Cola Company (The)
POWERade
Dasani
glaceau vitaminwater
Minute Maide
Dr Pepper
Monster Energy
Tum-E Yummies

CONTACTS:
Note: Officers with more than one job title may be intentionally listed here more than once.

J. Harrison, CEO
F. Anthony, CFO
William Billiard, Chief Accounting Officer
David Katz, COO
Umesh Kasbekar, Co-Vice Chairman of the Board
Henry Flint, Co-Vice Chairman of the Board
Morgan Everett, Director
Robert Chambless, Executive VP, Divisional
E. Fisher, Executive VP
Kimberly Kuo, Senior VP, Divisional
James Matte, Senior VP, Divisional

GROWTH PLANS/SPECIAL FEATURES:

Coca-Cola Bottling Co. Consolidated (CCB), founded in 1902, is a nonalcoholic beverage manufacturer and distributor. The firm primarily produces, markets and distributes products of The Coca-Cola Company, which owns approximately 35% of CCB. The company manufactures products in two categories: sparkling beverages, which consist of beverages with carbonation, including energy drinks; and still beverages, including bottled water, tea, ready-to-drink coffee, enhanced water, juices and sports drinks. CCB distributes and markets still beverages of The Coca-Cola Company such as POWERade, Dasani water, glaceau vitaminwater, ZICO coconut water and Minute Maid Juices To Go in certain regions. It also produces and markets Dr. Pepper, Monster Energy and Sundrop in some of its regions. In addition, the company markets and distributes certain products which it owns, including Gold Peak Tea; coffee beverages; and Tum-E Yummies, a vitamin C enhanced flavored drink. The company's principal soft drink is Coca-Cola classic, and products of The Coca-Cola Company generate more than half of CCB's bottle/can volume to retail customers. CCB holds bottling rights from The Coca-Cola Company covering the majority of North Carolina, South Carolina, and West Virginia, as well as portions of Alabama, Mississippi, Tennessee, Kentucky, Illinois, Indiana, Ohio, Virginia, Pennsylvania, Maryland, Georgia and Florida. The main packaging materials for the firm's beverages are plastic bottles and aluminum cans. In addition, the company provides restaurants and other immediate consumption outlets with fountain products. CCB has 13 manufacturing facilities, and 76 distribution and sales centers.

The firm offers employees medical, dental and vision insurance as well as a 401(k) plan.

FINANCIAL DATA:
Note: Data for latest year may not have been available at press time.

In U.S. $	2018	2017	2016	2015	2014	2013
Revenue	4,625,364,000	4,323,668,000	3,156,428,000	2,306,458,000	1,746,369,000	1,641,331,000
R&D Expense						
Operating Income	57,902,000	96,179,000	127,859,000	98,144,000	85,967,000	73,647,000
Operating Margin %		.02%	.04%	.04%	.05%	.04%
SGA Expense	1,497,810,000	1,444,768,000	1,087,863,000	802,888,000	619,272,000	584,993,000
Net Income	-19,930,000	96,535,000	50,146,000	59,002,000	31,354,000	27,675,000
Operating Cash Flow	168,879,000	307,816,000	161,995,000	108,290,000	91,903,000	96,374,000
Capital Expenditure	138,235,000	192,199,000	172,586,000	163,887,000	84,364,000	61,432,000
EBITDA	245,158,000	265,020,000	244,482,000	179,040,000	147,097,000	132,318,000
Return on Assets %		.03%	.02%	.04%	.02%	.02%
Return on Equity %		.30%	.19%	.28%	.17%	.17%
Debt to Equity		3.063	3.422	2.767	2.709	2.287

CONTACT INFORMATION:
Phone: 704 557-4400 Fax: 704 551-4451
Toll-Free: 800-777-2653
Address: 4100 Coca-Cola Plaza, Charlotte, NC 28211 United States

STOCK TICKER/OTHER:
Stock Ticker: COKE
Employees: 13,200
Parent Company:

Exchange: NAS
Fiscal Year Ends: 12/31

SALARIES/BONUSES:
Top Exec. Salary: $1,123,859 Bonus: $
Second Exec. Salary: $862,496 Bonus: $

OTHER THOUGHTS:
Estimated Female Officers or Directors: 3
Hot Spot for Advancement for Women/Minorities: Y

Sales, profits and employees may be estimates. Financial information, benefits and other data can change quickly and may vary from those stated here.

Cognizant Technology Solutions Corporation www.cognizant.com

NAIC Code: 541512

TYPES OF BUSINESS:
Computer Systems Design Services
Outsourced Services
Software Engineering

BRANDS/DIVISIONS/AFFILIATES:
The Collaboratory
LaunchPad
Cognizant Digital Business
Cognizant Digital Operations
Cognizant Digital Systems and Technology
Cognizant Consulting
Softvision

CONTACTS: Note: Officers with more than one job title may be intentionally listed here more than once.
Brian Humphries, CEO
Sean Middleton, Senior VP
Karen McLoughlin, CFO
Michael Patsalos-Fox, Chairman of the Board
Srinivasan Veeraraghavachary, COO
Allen Shaheen, Executive VP, Divisional
Malcolm Frank, Executive VP, Divisional
Matthew Friedrich, Executive VP
Gajakarnan Kandiah, Executive VP
Debashis Chatterjee, Executive VP
Ramakrishna Chintamaneni, Executive VP
Dharmendra Sinha, Executive VP
Santosh Thomas, Executive VP
Sumithra Gomatam, Executive VP
James Lennox, Other Executive Officer
Robert Telesmanic, Senior VP
Venkat Krishnaswamy, Vice Chairman, Divisional
Ramakrishnan Chandrasekaran, Vice Chairman, Subsidiary
Ramakrishnan Chandrasekaran, Vice Chairman, Subsidiary

GROWTH PLANS/SPECIAL FEATURES:
Cognizant Technology Solutions Corporation specializes in custom IT design, development, integration and maintenance services. The firm provides these services primarily to Global 2000 companies located in the U.S., Europe and Asia. Cognizant operates in three segments: Digital Business, Digital Operations and Digital Systems and Technology. Cognizant Digital Business works with clients to build products and experiences by using data science and industry-specific knowledge to create the best solution. This segment serves AI and analytics, connect products, digital engineering and digital strategy. Cognizant Digital Operations works with clients to update operating models to ensure that clients can keep with the modern marketplace demands by reimagining and creating specific digital processes that drive performance but brings customer, suppliers and automation closer together. This segment offers enterprise services, industry and platform solutions and intelligent process automation. Cognizant Digital Systems and Technology helps clients evolve applications, platforms and infrastructure to create a modern and efficient digital enterprise. This segment offers services ranging from application services to security to quality engineering and assurance. The firm also offers consulting, Cognizant Consulting, to clients in all areas of digital operations, business and technology. This business model combines technical and account management teams located onsite at the customer location and offshore at dedicated development centers located primarily in India, Argentina, the U.S., the Philippines, China, France, Canada and Hungary. Cognizant also operates The Collaboratory, a space where the company can come up with an initial assessment of a project, split the project into teams, enables testing, allows creation of the product whether physical or digital and allows for up-to-date client feedback. The Collaboratory locations include Amsterdam, New York City, London and Melbourne. The firm also runs LaunchPad, a six-month, twice-yearly program for to create internal startups and products through a structured process. In October 2018, Cognizant acquired Softvision.

FINANCIAL DATA: Note: Data for latest year may not have been available at press time.

In U.S. $	2018	2017	2016	2015	2014	2013
Revenue	16,125,000,000	14,810,000,000	13,487,000,000	12,416,000,000	10,262,680,000	8,843,189,000
R&D Expense						
Operating Income	2,801,000,000	2,481,000,000	2,289,000,000	2,142,000,000	1,884,878,000	1,677,910,000
Operating Margin %		.17%	.17%	.17%	.18%	.19%
SGA Expense	3,026,000,000	2,769,000,000	2,731,000,000	2,508,600,000	2,037,021,000	1,727,609,000
Net Income	2,101,000,000	1,504,000,000	1,553,000,000	1,623,600,000	1,439,267,000	1,228,578,000
Operating Cash Flow	2,592,000,000	2,407,000,000	1,621,000,000	2,153,300,000	1,473,010,000	1,423,776,000
Capital Expenditure	377,000,000	284,000,000	300,000,000	272,800,000	212,203,000	261,626,000
EBITDA	3,322,000,000	3,121,000,000	2,755,000,000	2,511,300,000	2,134,566,000	1,857,840,000
Return on Assets %		.10%	.11%	.13%	.14%	.17%
Return on Equity %		.14%	.16%	.19%	.21%	.22%
Debt to Equity		0.065	0.074	0.095	0.121	

CONTACT INFORMATION:
Phone: 201 801-0233   Fax: 201 801-0243
Toll-Free: 888-937-3277
Address: 500 Frank W. Burr Blvd., Teaneck, NJ 07666 United States

SALARIES/BONUSES:
Top Exec. Salary: $750,000   Bonus: $
Second Exec. Salary: $700,000   Bonus: $

STOCK TICKER/OTHER:
Stock Ticker: CTSH   Exchange: NAS
Employees: 260,200   Fiscal Year Ends: 12/31
Parent Company:

OTHER THOUGHTS:
Estimated Female Officers or Directors: 1
Hot Spot for Advancement for Women/Minorities:

Sales, profits and employees may be estimates. Financial information, benefits and other data can change quickly and may vary from those stated here.

Collins Aerospace

www.collinsaerospace.com

NAIC Code: 334511

TYPES OF BUSINESS:
Aerospace Electronics
Defense Systems
Avionics
Aviation Technologies

BRANDS/DIVISIONS/AFFILIATES:
United Technologies Corporation
Rockwell Collins Inc
UTC Aerospace Systems

CONTACTS:
Note: Officers with more than one job title may be intentionally listed here more than once.

Kelly Ortberg, CEO
David L. Gitlin, Pres.
Patrick Allen, CFO
Doug Balsbough, Dir.-Human Resources
Kent Statler, COO, Divisional
Robert Perna, General Counsel
Robert Sturgell, Senior VP, Divisional
Colin Mahoney, Senior VP, Divisional
Jeffrey MacLauchlan, Senior VP, Divisional
Bruce King, Senior VP, Divisional
Nan Mattai, Senior VP, Divisional
Jeffrey Standerski, Senior VP, Divisional
David Nieuwsma, Senior VP, Divisional

GROWTH PLANS/SPECIAL FEATURES:
Collins Aerospace, a subsidiary of United Technologies Corporation (UTC), is a world-leading supplier of aerospace and defense products. The company was formed after UTC acquired Rockwell Collins, Inc. in November 2018, which subsequently merged it with UTC Aerospace Systems to form Collins Aerospace. The firm focuses on providing technologically-advanced and intelligent solutions for the global aerospace and defense industry. These solutions include aerospace systems, avionics, interior systems and information management services, for the purpose of delivering enhanced passenger safety and comfort, maximized operational efficiency, secure and reliable connectivity, improved availability, maintainability and sustainability, and to complete military/defense missions safely and effectively. Collins Aerospace is a world-leading provider of advanced systems for commercial and military helicopters. It equips rotocraft from all major manufacturers. For airports, the firm offers integrated and intelligent solutions for passenger processing and facilitation, airport operations and baggage management. Beyond these sectors, Collins Aerospace provides network communications capabilities for the train/rail industry, life rafts and life support systems for the marine industry, and security and monitoring systems for the public sector and critical infrastructure industries. Based in Florida, USA, Collins Aerospace has a worldwide presence across 30 countries.

FINANCIAL DATA:
Note: Data for latest year may not have been available at press time.

In U.S. $	2018	2017	2016	2015	2014	2013
Revenue	16,634,000,000	14,691,000,000	14,465,000,000			
R&D Expense						
Operating Income						
Operating Margin %						
SGA Expense						
Net Income	2,303,000,000	2,191,000,000	2,167,000,000			
Operating Cash Flow						
Capital Expenditure						
EBITDA						
Return on Assets %						
Return on Equity %						
Debt to Equity						

CONTACT INFORMATION:
Phone: 619-691-4111 Fax: 619-691-3030
Toll-Free:
Address: 777 S. Flagler Dr., West Tower, Ste. 1800, West Palm Beach, FL 33401 United States

STOCK TICKER/OTHER:
Stock Ticker: Subsidiary
Employees: 73,300
Parent Company: United Technologies Corporation

Exchange:
Fiscal Year Ends: 09/30

SALARIES/BONUSES:
Top Exec. Salary: $ Bonus: $
Second Exec. Salary: $ Bonus: $

OTHER THOUGHTS:
Estimated Female Officers or Directors:
Hot Spot for Advancement for Women/Minorities:

Comcast Corporation

corporate.comcast.com

NAIC Code: 517110

TYPES OF BUSINESS:
Cable Television
VoIP Service
Cable Network Programming
High-Speed Internet Service
Video-on-Demand
Advertising Services
Interactive Program Schedules
Wireless Services

BRANDS/DIVISIONS/AFFILIATES:
XFINITY
NBC Universal
Telemundo
Sky plc
Comcast Spectator
Philadelphia Flyers
Wells Fargo Center
Amblin Partners

CONTACTS:
Note: Officers with more than one job title may be intentionally listed here more than once.

Stephen Burke, CEO, Subsidiary
Dave Watson, CEO, Subsidiary
Brian Roberts, CEO
Michael Cavanagh, CFO
Daniel Murdock, Chief Accounting Officer
Joseph Collins, Director Emeritus
Judith Rodin, Director Emeritus
Arthur Block, Executive VP
David Cohen, Senior Executive VP

GROWTH PLANS/SPECIAL FEATURES:
Comcast Corporation provides information, entertainment and communications products and services. Comcast operates through five segments: cable communications, cable networks, broadcast television, filmed entertainment and theme parks. The cable communications segment maintains the firm's video, high-speed internet and voice servicing operations, serving residential customers under the XFINITY brand. This division also sells advertising, as well as video, high-speed internet, voice and other services to small- and medium-sized businesses. The cable networks segment includes the firm's national cable networks, its regional sports and news networks, its international cable networks and its cable television production operations. The broadcast television segment consists primarily of the company's NBC and Telemundo broadcast networks, its 11 NBC- and 17 Telemundo-owned local broadcast television stations and its broadcast television production operations. Filmed entertainment is comprised of the studio operations of Universal Pictures, which produces, acquires, markets and distributes filmed entertainment worldwide. Theme parks is comprised of the Universal theme parks in Orlando, Florida; Hollywood, California; and Osaka, Japan. Additionally, subsidiary Comcast Spectator owns the Philadelphia Flyers and the Wells Fargo Center in Philadelphia, Pennsylvania, and operates arena management-related businesses. In October 2018, Comcast acquired control of UK/EU media and telecommunications giant Sky plc at a value of $38.8 billion. In December 2018, Comcast announced that, in conjunction with Amazon, its customers will be able to watch Amazon Prime Video on Comcast's Xfinity X1 at no additional cost.

FINANCIAL DATA:
Note: Data for latest year may not have been available at press time.

In U.S. $	2018	2017	2016	2015	2014	2013
Revenue	94,507,000,000	84,526,000,000	80,403,000,000	74,510,000,000	68,775,000,000	64,657,000,000
R&D Expense						
Operating Income	19,009,000,000	17,987,000,000	16,859,000,000	15,998,000,000	14,904,000,000	13,563,000,000
Operating Margin %		.21%	.21%	.21%	.22%	.21%
SGA Expense	35,130,000,000	31,330,000,000	29,523,000,000	27,282,000,000	24,940,000,000	23,553,000,000
Net Income	11,731,000,000	22,714,000,000	8,695,000,000	8,163,000,000	8,380,000,000	6,816,000,000
Operating Cash Flow	24,297,000,000	21,403,000,000	19,240,000,000	18,778,000,000	16,945,000,000	14,160,000,000
Capital Expenditure	11,709,000,000	11,297,000,000	10,821,000,000	9,869,000,000	8,542,000,000	7,605,000,000
EBITDA	29,801,000,000	28,675,000,000	26,853,000,000	24,754,000,000	23,101,000,000	29,809,000,000
Return on Assets %		.12%	.05%	.05%	.05%	.04%
Return on Equity %		.37%	.16%	.16%	.16%	.14%
Debt to Equity		0.866	1.03	0.937	0.835	0.879

CONTACT INFORMATION:
Phone: 215 286-1700 Fax:
Toll-Free: 800-266-2278
Address: One Comcast Center, Philadelphia, PA 19103 United States

STOCK TICKER/OTHER:
Stock Ticker: CMCSA Exchange: NAS
Employees: 159,000 Fiscal Year Ends: 12/31
Parent Company:

SALARIES/BONUSES:
Top Exec. Salary: $3,103,566 Bonus: $
Second Exec. Salary: $2,881,100 Bonus: $

OTHER THOUGHTS:
Estimated Female Officers or Directors: 16
Hot Spot for Advancement for Women/Minorities: Y

Sales, profits and employees may be estimates. Financial information, benefits and other data can change quickly and may vary from those stated here.

CommScope Holding Company Inc

www.commscope.com

NAIC Code: 335921

TYPES OF BUSINESS:
Cable-Coaxial & Fiber Optic
Local Area Network Products
Wireless Products

BRANDS/DIVISIONS/AFFILIATES:
CommScope Inc
CommScope Connectivity Solutions
CommScope Mobility Solutions
SYSTIMAX
NETCONNECT
Uniprise
Arris International plc

CONTACTS: Note: Officers with more than one job title may be intentionally listed here more than once.
Alexander Pease, CFO
Frank Drendel, Chairman of the Board
Brooke Clark, Chief Accounting Officer
Bruce McClelland, COO
Morgan Kurk, Executive VP
Frank Wyatt, General Counsel
Robyn Mingle, Other Executive Officer
Marvin Edwards, President
Peter Karlsson, Senior VP, Divisional

GROWTH PLANS/SPECIAL FEATURES:
CommScope Holding Company, Inc., operating primarily through CommScope, Inc., is a global leader in connectivity solutions for communications networks. It provides infrastructure solutions for wireless, residential broadband, business enterprise and carrier wireline networks. CommScope's operations are divided into two segments: CommScope Connectivity Solutions (CCS) and CommScope Mobility Solutions (CMS). The CCS segment provides connectivity and network intelligence for indoor and outdoor network applications. Indoor network solutions are found in commercial buildings and in the network core, which includes data centers, central offices and cable television head-ends. Indoor network solution products are marketed under the SYSTIMAX, NETCONNECT and Uniprise brand names. Outdoor network solutions are found in access and edge networks and include coaxial cabling, fiber optic cable and connectivity solutions, including a robust portfolio of fiber optic connectors and fiber management systems. The CMS segment provides merchant RF wireless network solutions, as well as metro cell, DAS and small cell solutions. Metro cell solutions can be found on street poles and on other urban structures. DAS and small cell solutions allow wireless operators to increase spectral efficiency and enhance cellular coverage and capacity in challenging network conditions such as commercial buildings, urban areas, stadiums and transportation systems. CMS solutions are marketed primarily under the Andrew brand. CommScope's focus on research and innovation has led to approximately 9,500 patents and patent applications, and approximately 2,300 registered trademarks. In April 2019, CommScope acquired Arris International plc, a U.S.-based telecommunications equipment manufacturing company.

The firm offers employees a 401(k) plan; educational assistance; medical, dental and vision insurance; life and AD&D insurance; short- and long-term disability; and an employee assistance program.

FINANCIAL DATA: Note: Data for latest year may not have been available at press time.

In U.S. $	2018	2017	2016	2015	2014	2013
Revenue	4,568,507,000	4,560,582,000	4,923,621,000	3,807,828,000	3,829,614,000	3,480,117,000
R&D Expense	185,696,000	185,222,000	200,715,000	135,964,000	125,301,000	126,431,000
Operating Income	508,993,000	521,392,000	656,177,000	301,865,000	608,812,000	397,347,000
Operating Margin %		.11%	.13%	.08%	.16%	.11%
SGA Expense	729,032,000	794,291,000	879,495,000	687,389,000	484,891,000	502,275,000
Net Income	140,217,000	193,764,000	222,838,000	-70,875,000	236,772,000	19,396,000
Operating Cash Flow	494,144,000	586,286,000	606,225,000	302,060,000	289,418,000	237,701,000
Capital Expenditure	82,347,000	68,721,000	68,314,000	56,501,000	36,935,000	36,780,000
EBITDA	770,187,000	844,803,000	949,156,000	476,160,000	755,502,000	541,400,000
Return on Assets %		.03%	.03%	-.01%	.05%	.00%
Return on Equity %		.13%	.17%	-.06%	.20%	.02%
Debt to Equity		2.652	3.263	4.278	2.064	2.302

CONTACT INFORMATION:
Phone: 828-324-2200 Fax:
Toll-Free: 800-982-1708
Address: 1100 CommScope Place SE, Hickory, NC 28602 United States

SALARIES/BONUSES:
Top Exec. Salary: $1,091,250 Bonus: $
Second Exec. Salary: $610,000 Bonus: $1,100

STOCK TICKER/OTHER:
Stock Ticker: COMM
Employees: 25,000
Parent Company:

Exchange: NAS
Fiscal Year Ends: 12/31

OTHER THOUGHTS:
Estimated Female Officers or Directors: 2
Hot Spot for Advancement for Women/Minorities:

Community Health Systems Inc

NAIC Code: 622110

www.chs.net

TYPES OF BUSINESS:
General Medical and Surgical Hospitals
Surgical & Emergency Services
Acute Care Services
Internal Medicine
Obstetrics
Emergency Room Services
Diagnostic Services
Ambulatory Surgery Centers

BRANDS/DIVISIONS/AFFILIATES:

GROWTH PLANS/SPECIAL FEATURES:
Community Health Systems, Inc. operates general acute care hospitals and outpatient facilities throughout the U.S. As of September 2019, the company owned, leased or operated 103 hospitals in 18 states, with an aggregate of approximately 17,000 licensed beds. Community Health Systems provides healthcare for local residents, offering a wide range of diagnostic, medical and surgical services in inpatient and outpatient settings. During the first half of 2019, Community Health divested hospitals located in Davenport and Lake Wales, Florida, and Lebanon, Tennessee.

The company offers employees medical, dental and vision insurance; flexible spending accounts; life and disability insurance; and a 401(k) savings plan.

CONTACTS:
Note: Officers with more than one job title may be intentionally listed here more than once.

Benjamin Fordham, Assistant Secretary
Wayne Smith, CEO
Kevin Hammons, Chief Accounting Officer
Lynn Simon, Chief Medical Officer
Tim Hingtgen, COO
Thomas Aaron, Executive VP
Beryl Ramsey, President, Divisional
P. Smith, President, Divisional

FINANCIAL DATA:
Note: Data for latest year may not have been available at press time.

In U.S. $	2018	2017	2016	2015	2014	2013
Revenue	14,155,000,000	15,353,000,000	18,438,000,000	19,437,000,000	18,639,000,000	12,997,690,000
R&D Expense				68,000,000		
Operating Income	872,000,000	217,000,000	1,005,000,000	1,181,000,000	1,222,000,000	835,386,000
Operating Margin %		.01%	.05%	.06%	.07%	.06%
SGA Expense	6,732,000,000	7,739,000,000	9,074,000,000	9,447,999,000	9,052,000,000	6,505,159,000
Net Income	-788,000,000	-2,459,000,000	-1,721,000,000	158,000,000	92,000,000	141,203,000
Operating Cash Flow	274,000,000	773,000,000	1,137,000,000	921,000,000	1,615,000,000	1,088,719,000
Capital Expenditure	527,000,000	564,000,000	867,000,000	1,010,000,000	3,944,000,000	613,992,000
EBITDA	1,572,000,000	-1,030,000,000	361,000,000	2,355,000,000	2,501,000,000	1,703,684,000
Return on Assets %		-.12%	-.07%	.01%	.00%	.01%
Return on Equity %		-5.80%	-.61%	.04%	.03%	.05%
Debt to Equity			9.157	4.186	4.167	3.027

CONTACT INFORMATION:
Phone: 615 465-7000 Fax: 615 645-7001
Toll-Free:
Address: 4000 Meridian Blvd., Franklin, TN 37067 United States

STOCK TICKER/OTHER:
Stock Ticker: CYH
Employees: 120,000
Parent Company:

Exchange: NYS
Fiscal Year Ends: 12/31

SALARIES/BONUSES:
Top Exec. Salary: $1,600,000 Bonus: $
Second Exec. Salary: $900,000 Bonus: $

OTHER THOUGHTS:
Estimated Female Officers or Directors: 18
Hot Spot for Advancement for Women/Minorities: Y

Sales, profits and employees may be estimates. Financial information, benefits and other data can change quickly and may vary from those stated here.

Concentrix Corporation

NAIC Code: 541512

www.concentrix.com

TYPES OF BUSINESS:
Information Technology Outsourcing
Technical Support
Sales & Marketing Support
Customer Support
Back Office Solutions

BRANDS/DIVISIONS/AFFILIATES:
SYNNEX Corporation
Convergys

GROWTH PLANS/SPECIAL FEATURES:
Concentrix Corporation, a subsidiary of SYNNEX Corporation, is a provider of global business services. The company aims to transform customer experience and streamline front and back office and industry-specific processes for high-value business-to-consumer interaction. The firm provides industry expertise in the fields of automotive, banking/financial services, consumer electronics, energy, public sector, healthcare services, insurance, media/communications, retail, eCommerce, technology, transportation and travel/tourism. Concentrix's solutions include customer lifecycle management, marketing, analytics/insights, automation, process optimization, finance/accounting, consulting, IT services and technology assets. The company has operations in 40 countries across six continents. In October 2018, Concentrix acquired Convergys, a global leader in customer experience outsourcing. Convergys was merged with/into Concentrix.

CONTACTS:
Note: Officers with more than one job title may be intentionally listed here more than once.

Christopher Caldwell, Pres.
Dick Rapach, VP-Oper

FINANCIAL DATA:
Note: Data for latest year may not have been available at press time.

In U.S. $	2018	2017	2016	2015	2014	2013
Revenue	2,463,151,000	1,990,180,000	1,587,736,000	1,416,670,000	1,096,214,000	189,463,000
R&D Expense						
Operating Income						
Operating Margin %						
SGA Expense						
Net Income						
Operating Cash Flow						
Capital Expenditure						
EBITDA						
Return on Assets %						
Return on Equity %						
Debt to Equity						

CONTACT INFORMATION:
Phone: 510-656-3333 Fax:
Toll-Free: 800-747-0583
Address: 44201 Nobel Dr., Freemont, CA 94538 United States

STOCK TICKER/OTHER:
Stock Ticker: Subsidiary
Employees: 225,000
Parent Company: SYNNEX Corporation

Exchange:
Fiscal Year Ends: 11/30

SALARIES/BONUSES:
Top Exec. Salary: $ Bonus: $
Second Exec. Salary: $ Bonus: $

OTHER THOUGHTS:
Estimated Female Officers or Directors:
Hot Spot for Advancement for Women/Minorities:

Concur Technologies Inc

www.concur.com

NAIC Code: 0

TYPES OF BUSINESS:
Software Manufacturer-Expense Reporting
Corporate Expense Management Solutions
Professional Services
Travel and Entertainment Expense Reporting Software
Meeting Expense Reporting Software

BRANDS/DIVISIONS/AFFILIATES:
SAP SE
SAP Concur

CONTACTS:
Note: Officers with more than one job title may be intentionally listed here more than once.

Jim Lucier, Pres.
Chris Arendale, CFO
Kim Albrecht, CMO
Seema Kumar, VP-Human Resources
Michael Weingartner, CTO
John Torrey, Executive VP, Divisional
Robert Cavanaugh, Executive VP
Elena Donio, Executive VP

GROWTH PLANS/SPECIAL FEATURES:
Concur Technologies, Inc. does business as SAP Concur, and provides automated software products that simplify the employee travel expense management process. The firm's solutions cover three primary aspects of corporate travel management: travel procurement, expense management and itinerary management. Travel procurement software automates corporate travel booking and processing functions and can be tailored to a company's specific travel policies and preferred vendors. Employees using SAP Concur travel procurement solutions are able to set their own travel preferences while organizations set policy through technology filters to retain control. Expense management solutions simplify the expense reporting process, while reducing costs and improving internal controls. Its software automatically imports corporate or personal credit card charges to create expense reports and reconciles transaction data from itinerary data captured at the time of booking. Corporate card charges incurred during travel are also imported, along with electronic receipts captured directly from the supplier. SAP Concur's itinerary management solutions enable individual business travelers and their organizations to manage and share travel itinerary information and can be imported into other SAP Concur solutions to provide greater insight and control over travel and expense spend for organizations. The firm also offers value-added services and software that integrate with the company's primary products. In addition, SAP Concur offers professional services including consulting, customer support and training. Concur Technologies is owned by German software giant SAP SE.

The firm offers employees life, disability, medical, dental and vision insurance; flexible spending accounts; and a 401(k).

FINANCIAL DATA:
Note: Data for latest year may not have been available at press time.

In U.S. $	2018	2017	2016	2015	2014	2013
Revenue	1,767,980,000	1,743,120,000	1,381,972,534	724,603,419	702,588,032	545,800,000
R&D Expense						
Operating Income						
Operating Margin %						
SGA Expense						
Net Income	2,043,960	155,798,000	1,291,875,652	-20,571,530	-118,295,000	-24,394,000
Operating Cash Flow						
Capital Expenditure						
EBITDA						
Return on Assets %						
Return on Equity %						
Debt to Equity						

CONTACT INFORMATION:
Phone: 425 590-5000 Fax: 425 702-8828
Toll-Free: 800-401-8412
Address: 601 108th Avenue NE, Suite 1000, Bellevue, WA 98004 United States

STOCK TICKER/OTHER:
Stock Ticker: Subsidiary
Employees: 3,569
Parent Company: SAP SE

Exchange:
Fiscal Year Ends: 12/31

SALARIES/BONUSES:
Top Exec. Salary: $ Bonus: $
Second Exec. Salary: $ Bonus: $

OTHER THOUGHTS:
Estimated Female Officers or Directors: 2
Hot Spot for Advancement for Women/Minorities:

ConocoPhillips Company

www.conocophillips.com

NAIC Code: 211111

TYPES OF BUSINESS:
Oil & Gas Exploration & Production
Natural Gas Distribution
Oil Sands
Pipelines

BRANDS/DIVISIONS/AFFILIATES:

CONTACTS: Note: Officers with more than one job title may be intentionally listed here more than once.
Ryan Lance, CEO
Don Wallette, CFO
Catherine Brooks, Chief Accounting Officer
Matthew Fox, COO
Kelly Rose, General Counsel
Dominic Macklon, President, Divisional
Michael Hatfield, President, Geographical
William Bullock, President, Geographical
Andrew Lundquist, Senior VP, Divisional
Ellen DeSanctis, Senior VP, Divisional

GROWTH PLANS/SPECIAL FEATURES:
ConocoPhillips Company explores for, produces, transports and markets crude oil bitumen, natural gas, liquefied natural gas (LNG) and natural gas liquids. Its net proved reserves total more than 5 million barrels of oil equivalent (MBOE). In all, ConocoPhillips produces about 1,377 MBOE per day. The firm reports under six geographic segments, dividing operations in over 17 countries: Alaska, lower 48, Canada, Europe and North Africa, Asia Pacific and Middle East and other international. The Alaska segment primarily explores for, produces, transports and markets crude oil, natural gas and LNG. Alaska contributes approximately 22% of the firm's worldwide liquids productions and less than 1% of its natural gas production. The lower 48 segment (covering Gulf Coast, mid-continent and Rockies) holds onshore and offshore acreage utilized for liquids and natural gas production. Canadian operations mainly consist of natural gas fields and oil sands developments. Europe and North Africa consists of Norway, the U.K. and Libya, contributing to liquids and natural gas production. The Asia Pacific and Middle East segment accounts for about 14% of the company's liquids production and 52% of its natural gas. Finally, other international includes exploration activities in Colombia and Chile. In addition, ConocoPhillips owns and licenses the Optimized Cascade technology for liquefying natural gas, which provides cost-effective, high-value natural gas liquefaction solutions. During 2018, ConocoPhillips: agreed to sell its 30% interest in the Greater Sunrise Fields to the government of Timor-Leste; sold its Barnett assets to Lime Rock Resources for approximately $239 million; sold a subsidiary that holds a 16.5% interest in Clair Field in the U.K., to BP, with ConocoPhillips retaining a 7.5% interest in the field; and acquired a 39.2% interest in BP's Greater Kuparuk Area in Alaska, as well as a 38% interest in the Kuparuk Transportation Company.

FINANCIAL DATA: Note: Data for latest year may not have been available at press time.

In U.S. $	2018	2017	2016	2015	2014	2013
Revenue	36,417,000,000	29,106,000,000	23,693,000,000	29,564,000,000	52,524,000,000	54,413,000,000
R&D Expense						
Operating Income	8,859,000,000	2,360,000,000	-4,634,000,000	-5,440,000,000	8,118,000,000	11,955,000,000
Operating Margin %		.08%	-.17%	-.16%	.16%	.24%
SGA Expense	401,000,000	561,000,000	723,000,000	953,000,000	735,000,000	854,000,000
Net Income	6,257,000,000	-855,000,000	-3,615,000,000	-4,428,000,000	6,869,000,000	9,156,000,000
Operating Cash Flow	12,934,000,000	7,077,000,000	4,403,000,000	7,572,000,000	16,735,000,000	16,087,000,000
Capital Expenditure	6,750,000,000	4,591,000,000	4,869,000,000	10,050,000,000	17,085,000,000	15,537,000,000
EBITDA	16,664,000,000	5,328,000,000	4,777,000,000	2,794,000,000	18,367,000,000	22,492,000,000
Return on Assets %		-.01%	-.04%	-.04%	.06%	.08%
Return on Equity %		-.03%	-.10%	-.10%	.13%	.18%
Debt to Equity		0.56	0.749	0.59	0.431	0.405

CONTACT INFORMATION:
Phone: 281 293-1000 Fax:
Toll-Free:
Address: 925 N. Eldridge Pkwy., Houston, TX 77079-2703 United States

SALARIES/BONUSES:
Top Exec. Salary: $1,700,000 Bonus: $
Second Exec. Salary: $1,241,000 Bonus: $

STOCK TICKER/OTHER:
Stock Ticker: COP
Employees: 18,400
Parent Company:

Exchange: NYS
Fiscal Year Ends: 12/31

OTHER THOUGHTS:
Estimated Female Officers or Directors: 5
Hot Spot for Advancement for Women/Minorities: Y

Sales, profits and employees may be estimates. Financial information, benefits and other data can change quickly and may vary from those stated here.

Constellation Brands Inc

www.cbrands.com

NAIC Code: 312130

TYPES OF BUSINESS:
Beverages-Wineries
Beer & Distilled Spirits
Wine Distribution
Bottled Water
Import/Export

BRANDS/DIVISIONS/AFFILIATES:
Corona
Modelo
Pacifico
Victoria
Black Box
Nobilo
Casa Noble
SVEDKA

CONTACTS:
Note: Officers with more than one job title may be intentionally listed here more than once.

William Newlands, CEO
David Klein, CFO
Robert Sands, Chairman of the Board
James Sabia, Chief Marketing Officer
Richard Sands, Director
James Bourdeau, Executive VP
Thomas Kane, Executive VP
F. Hetterich, Executive VP
Robert Hanson, Executive VP

GROWTH PLANS/SPECIAL FEATURES:
Constellation Brands, Inc. is one of the largest wine companies in the world as well as a leading alcoholic beverage supplier in the U.S. and Canada, and a major producer and exporter of wine from New Zealand. The firm has more than 100 brands in its portfolio and operates through three business segments: beer, wine and spirits, and corporate operations and other. The beer segment markets and sells popular imported brands, such as Corona, Modelo, Pacifico and Victoria. The wine and spirits segment produces and markets premium wines in all major categories, including dessert wine, table wine and sparkling wine in the U.S. and Canada, as well as other countries. Wine brands include 7 Moons, Black Box, Clos du Bois, Estancia, Franciscan Estate, Kim Crawford, Kung Fu Girl, Mark West, Meiomi, Mount Veeder, Nobilo, Ravage, Robert Mondavi, Ruffino, Simi, The Dreaming Tree, The Prisoner and The Velvet Devil. Spirit products include Casa Noble (tequila), High West (whiskey) and SVEDKA (vodka). The corporate and other segment oversees traditional corporate-related activities, such as corporate development, corporate finance, human resources, internal audit, investor relations, legal, public relations and global information technology. In April 2019, Constellation Brands reached a deal to sell wine brands including Clos du Bois and Mark West to E & J Gallo Winery for $1.7 billion.

FINANCIAL DATA:
Note: Data for latest year may not have been available at press time.

In U.S. $	2018	2017	2016	2015	2014	2013
Revenue	7,585,000,000	7,331,500,000	6,548,400,000	6,028,000,000	4,867,700,000	
R&D Expense						
Operating Income	2,284,500,000	2,137,000,000	1,765,100,000	1,500,200,000	1,096,600,000	
Operating Margin %	.30%	.29%	.27%	.25%	.23%	
SGA Expense	1,532,700,000	1,392,400,000	1,177,200,000	1,078,400,000	895,100,000	
Net Income	2,318,900,000	1,535,100,000	1,054,900,000	839,300,000	1,943,100,000	
Operating Cash Flow	1,931,400,000	1,696,000,000	1,413,700,000	1,081,000,000	826,200,000	
Capital Expenditure	1,057,600,000	907,400,000	891,300,000	719,400,000	223,500,000	
EBITDA	2,968,500,000	2,720,600,000	2,036,100,000	1,719,300,000	2,680,800,000	
Return on Assets %	.12%	.09%	.07%	.06%	.18%	
Return on Equity %	.31%	.23%	.17%	.16%	.50%	
Debt to Equity	1.17	1.12	1.039	1.237	1.279	

CONTACT INFORMATION:
Phone: 585 678-7100   Fax: 585 678-7103
Toll-Free: 888-724-2169
Address: 207 High Point Dr., Bldg. 100, Victor, NY 14564 United States

STOCK TICKER/OTHER:
Stock Ticker: STZ
Employees: 8,700
Parent Company:

Exchange: NYS
Fiscal Year Ends: 02/28

SALARIES/BONUSES:
Top Exec. Salary: $1,388,715   Bonus: $
Second Exec. Salary: $1,361,731   Bonus: $

OTHER THOUGHTS:
Estimated Female Officers or Directors: 2
Hot Spot for Advancement for Women/Minorities:

Sales, profits and employees may be estimates. Financial information, benefits and other data can change quickly and may vary from those stated here.

Container Store Inc (The)

NAIC Code: 442299

www.containerstore.com

TYPES OF BUSINESS:
Household Goods
Luggage
Packing Materials
Specialty Boxes
Online Sales

BRANDS/DIVISIONS/AFFILIATES:
Leonard Green & Partners LP
Container Store (The)
Elfa International AB
Elfa
Contained Home
Custom Closets

CONTACTS:
Note: Officers with more than one job title may be intentionally listed here more than once.

Melissa Reiff, CEO
Jodi Taylor, CFO
William Tindell, Chairman of the Board
Melissa Collins, Chief Marketing Officer
Sharon Tindell, Director
John Gehre, Executive VP, Divisional
Jeffrey Miller, Vice President

GROWTH PLANS/SPECIAL FEATURES:

The Container Store, Inc., controlled by private equity firm Leonard Green & Partners LP, is a national retailer selling organizational and storage products. Products include drawer and cabinet organizers, luggage, tool racks, packing materials, specialty and shipping boxes and locker organizers, among many other household objects designed to manage space efficiently. Store interiors have an open layout which is divided into sections with brightly colored banners such as Closet, Kitchen and Laundry. The company's operations are divided into two segments: The Container Store, made up of retail stores, web site and call center; and Elfa, a design and manufacturing business. The firm's stores average 25,000 square feet and carry more than 10,000 items. Most the company's 90+ stores are located in 33 states and Washington, D.C. The Container Store processes and ships its entire product line from its 1 million-square-foot warehouse/distribution facility in Coppell, Texas. The company's website allows customers to view and order store products, plan organizational and storage projects and receive free customized assistance from in-store space planning experts. The container segment represents approximately 92% of total annual net sales. The firm is the exclusive distributor of Elfa International AB, a wholly-owned Swedish subsidiary, which designs and manufactures component-based shelving and drawer systems, as well as made-to-measure sliding doors. Elfa represents 7% of net sales and has manufacturing facilities located in Sweden and Poland. Contained Home is the firm's in-home, customized design and organization service, where expert organizers go directly to customer homes. In mid-2019, The Container Stores opened its first Custom Closets store, which is located in Los Angeles, California. The new store concept features more than 65 closet and lifestyle displays and a personalized design experience.

The company offers employees medical, dental and vision plans; 401(k); paid time off; discounts; and various employee assistance programs.

FINANCIAL DATA:
Note: Data for latest year may not have been available at press time.

In U.S. $	2018	2017	2016	2015	2014	2013
Revenue	857,228,000	819,930,000	794,630,000	781,866,000	748,538,000	
R&D Expense						
Operating Income	34,365,000	41,099,000	24,922,000	43,484,000	31,765,000	
Operating Margin %	.04%	.05%	.03%	.06%	.04%	
SGA Expense	413,747,000	389,937,000	395,366,000	374,156,000	369,408,000	
Net Income	19,428,000	14,953,000	5,142,000	22,673,000	8,166,000	
Operating Cash Flow	62,176,000	44,639,000	42,307,000	64,625,000	50,762,000	
Capital Expenditure	27,646,000	28,515,000	46,431,000	48,740,000	48,565,000	
EBITDA	69,640,000	78,166,000	59,091,000	77,982,000	60,151,000	
Return on Assets %	.03%	.02%	.01%	.03%	-.07%	
Return on Equity %	.08%	.07%	.03%	.11%	-.24%	
Debt to Equity	1.115	1.407	1.554	1.619	1.662	

CONTACT INFORMATION:
Phone: 972-538-6900 Fax: 972-538-7623
Toll-Free: 800-733-3532
Address: 500 Freeport Pkwy., Coppell, TX 75019 United States

SALARIES/BONUSES:
Top Exec. Salary: $812,692 Bonus: $
Second Exec. Salary: $650,000 Bonus: $

STOCK TICKER/OTHER:
Stock Ticker: TCS
Employees: 5,100
Parent Company: Leonard Green & Partners LP

Exchange: NYS
Fiscal Year Ends: 03/31

OTHER THOUGHTS:
Estimated Female Officers or Directors: 5
Hot Spot for Advancement for Women/Minorities: Y

Cooper Companies Inc (The)

NAIC Code: 339100

www.coopercos.com

TYPES OF BUSINESS:
Medical Devices
Contact Lenses
Gynecological Instruments
Diagnostic Products

BRANDS/DIVISIONS/AFFILIATES:
CooperVision
CooperSurgical
Proclear
Phosphorylcholine (PC) Technology

CONTACTS:
Note: Officers with more than one job title may be intentionally listed here more than once.

Albert White, CEO
A. Bender, Chairman of the Board
Agostino Ricupati, Chief Accounting Officer
Holly Sheffield, Chief Strategy Officer
Daniel McBride, COO
Allan Rubenstein, Director
Randal Golden, General Counsel
Robert Auerbach, President, Subsidiary
Brian Andrews, Senior VP

GROWTH PLANS/SPECIAL FEATURES:
The Cooper Companies, Inc. develops, manufactures and markets healthcare products, primarily medical devices. The company operates through two business units: CooperVision and CooperSurgical. CooperVision develops, manufactures and markets a broad range of contact lenses, including disposable spherical and specialty contact lenses. It is a leading manufacturer of toric and multifocal lenses, which correct astigmatism; multifocal lenses for presbyopia, the blurring of vision due to advancing age; and spherical lenses, including hydrogel lenses, which correct the most common near- and far-sighted visual defects. CooperVision offers single-use, two-week, monthly and quarterly disposable sphere and toric lenses as well as custom toric lenses to correct a high degree of astigmatism. CooperVision's Proclear line of spherical, toric and multifocal lenses are manufactured with omafilcon, a material that incorporates its proprietary Phosphorylcholine (PC) Technology to enhance tissue-device compatibility. CooperVision's products are primarily manufactured at its facilities in the U.S., the U.K., Hungary, Costa Rico and Puerto Rico. It distributes its products out of its facilities in the U.S., the U.K., Belgium and various smaller international distribution facilities. CooperSurgical develops, manufactures and markets medical devices, diagnostic products and surgical instruments and accessories used primarily by gynecologists and obstetricians. This unit manufactures and distributes its products at its facilities in Connecticut, Texas and New York, USA, as well as in Denmark, Costa Rica and the U.K.

FINANCIAL DATA:
Note: Data for latest year may not have been available at press time.

In U.S. $	2018	2017	2016	2015	2014	2013
Revenue	2,532,800,000	2,139,000,000	1,966,814,000	1,797,060,000	1,717,776,000	1,587,725,000
R&D Expense	84,800,000	69,200,000	65,411,000	69,589,000	66,259,000	58,827,000
Operating Income	427,500,000	429,100,000	324,080,000	236,671,000	306,486,000	341,091,000
Operating Margin %		.20%	.16%	.13%	.18%	.21%
SGA Expense	973,300,000	799,100,000	722,798,000	712,543,000	683,115,000	596,651,000
Net Income	139,900,000	372,900,000	273,917,000	203,523,000	269,856,000	296,151,000
Operating Cash Flow	668,900,000	593,600,000	509,637,000	390,970,000	454,823,000	415,925,000
Capital Expenditure	193,600,000	127,200,000	152,640,000	243,023,000	238,065,000	178,127,000
EBITDA	689,700,000	615,800,000	520,097,000	424,991,000	442,700,000	446,788,000
Return on Assets %		.08%	.06%	.05%	.07%	.10%
Return on Equity %		.13%	.10%	.08%	.11%	.13%
Debt to Equity		0.362	0.41	0.415	0.498	0.125

CONTACT INFORMATION:
Phone: 925 460-3600   Fax: 949 597-0662
Toll-Free:
Address: 6140 Stoneridge Mall Rd., Ste. 590, Pleasanton, CA 94588 United States

STOCK TICKER/OTHER:
Stock Ticker: COO
Employees: 10,600
Parent Company:

Exchange: NYS
Fiscal Year Ends: 10/31

SALARIES/BONUSES:
Top Exec. Salary: $925,000   Bonus: $234,950
Second Exec. Salary: $683,500   Bonus: $165,427

OTHER THOUGHTS:
Estimated Female Officers or Directors: 2
Hot Spot for Advancement for Women/Minorities: Y

Sales, profits and employees may be estimates. Financial information, benefits and other data can change quickly and may vary from those stated here.

Plunkett Research, Ltd. 237

Corning Incorporated

NAIC Code: 327212

www.corning.com

TYPES OF BUSINESS:
Glass & Optical Fiber Manufacturing
Glass Substrates for LCDs
Optical Switching Products
Photonic Modules & Components
Networking Devices
Semiconductor Materials
Laboratory Supplies
Emissions Control Products

BRANDS/DIVISIONS/AFFILIATES:
Eagle XG
Iris
Vascade
LEAF
ClearCurve
InfiniCor
Gorilla

CONTACTS: Note: Officers with more than one job title may be intentionally listed here more than once.

Wendell Weeks, CEO
Martin Curran, Executive VP
R. Tripeny, CFO
Edward Schlesinger, Chief Accounting Officer
Jeffrey Evenson, Chief Strategy Officer
David Morse, Chief Technology Officer
Clark Kinlin, Executive VP
Christine Pambianchi, Executive VP, Divisional
James Clappin, Executive VP, Divisional
Eric Musser, Executive VP, Divisional
Lewis Steverson, Executive VP
Lawrence McRae, Other Corporate Officer

GROWTH PLANS/SPECIAL FEATURES:

Corning Incorporated is an international technology-based corporation. The firm operates in five business segments: display technologies, optical communications, specialty materials, environmental technologies and life sciences. The display technologies segment manufactures glass substrates for active matrix liquid crystal displays (LCDs), used in notebook computers, flat panel desktop monitor and LCD televisions. Its Eagle XG glass is an LCD glass substrate free of heavy metals; and its Eagle XG slim glass and Iris glass products enables lighter-weight portable devices and thinner televisions and monitors. The optical communications segment is divided into carrier network and enterprise network. The carrier network products include: Vascade submarine optical fibers for use in submarine networks; LEAF optical fiber for long-haul, regional and metropolitan networks; SMF-28e single mode optical fiber for additional transmission wavelengths in metropolitan and access networks; and ClearCurve fiber for use in multiple dwelling units. Enterprise network products include ClearCurve ultra-bendable multimode fiber for data centers and other enterprise network applications; InfiniCor fibers for local area networks; and ClearCurve VSDN ultra-bendable optical fiber designed to support emerging high-speed interconnects between computers and other consumer electronics devices. The specialty materials segment offers products such as glass windows for space shuttles and optical components for high-tech industries and includes the firm's Gorilla glass product line of protective cover glass for portable display devices. The environmental technologies segment produces ceramic products for emissions and pollution control, such as gasoline/diesel substrate and filter products. The life sciences segment manufactures laboratory products such as consumables (plastic vessels, specialty surfaces and media), as well as general labware and equipment used for cell culture research, bioprocessing, genomics, drug discovery, microbiology and chemistry. During 2018, Corning acquired substantially all of 3M's communication markets division for $841 million. In March 2019, it opened a software innovation center in Montreal, Canada.

FINANCIAL DATA: Note: Data for latest year may not have been available at press time.

In U.S. $	2018	2017	2016	2015	2014	2013
Revenue	11,290,000,000	10,116,000,000	9,390,000,000	9,111,000,000	9,715,000,000	7,819,000,000
R&D Expense	993,000,000	860,000,000	742,000,000	769,000,000	815,000,000	710,000,000
Operating Income	1,575,000,000	1,630,000,000	1,468,000,000	1,307,000,000	1,993,000,000	1,513,000,000
Operating Margin %		.16%	.16%	.14%	.21%	.19%
SGA Expense	1,799,000,000	1,467,000,000	1,472,000,000	1,523,000,000	1,211,000,000	1,126,000,000
Net Income	1,066,000,000	-497,000,000	3,695,000,000	1,339,000,000	2,472,000,000	1,961,000,000
Operating Cash Flow	2,919,000,000	2,004,000,000	2,521,000,000	2,809,000,000	4,709,000,000	2,787,000,000
Capital Expenditure	2,310,000,000	1,804,000,000	1,130,000,000	1,250,000,000	1,076,000,000	1,019,000,000
EBITDA	2,987,000,000	2,970,000,000	5,046,000,000	2,810,000,000	4,891,000,000	3,595,000,000
Return on Assets %		-.02%	.13%	.04%	.08%	.07%
Return on Equity %		-.04%	.22%	.07%	.12%	.09%
Debt to Equity		0.354	0.234	0.237	0.167	0.155

CONTACT INFORMATION:
Phone: 607 974-9000   Fax: 607 974-8688
Toll-Free:
Address: 1 Riverfront Plaza, Corning, NY 14831 United States

SALARIES/BONUSES:
Top Exec. Salary: $1,412,769   Bonus: $
Second Exec. Salary: $780,113   Bonus: $

STOCK TICKER/OTHER:
Stock Ticker: GLW
Employees: 40,700
Parent Company:

Exchange: NYS
Fiscal Year Ends: 12/31

OTHER THOUGHTS:
Estimated Female Officers or Directors: 1
Hot Spot for Advancement for Women/Minorities: Y

Sales, profits and employees may be estimates. Financial information, benefits and other data can change quickly and may vary from those stated here.

CoStar Group Inc

www.costar.com

NAIC Code: 519130

TYPES OF BUSINESS:
Online Commercial Real Estate Information

BRANDS/DIVISIONS/AFFILIATES:
CoStar
LoopNet
Apartments.com
BizBuySell
LandsofAmerica
CoStar Property
Cozy Services Ltd
Realla

CONTACTS: Note: Officers with more than one job title may be intentionally listed here more than once.
Andrew Florance, CEO
Scott Wheeler, CFO
Michael Klein, Chairman of the Board
Frank Simuro, Chief Technology Officer
Matthew Linnington, Executive VP, Divisional
Giles Newman, Managing Director, Geographical
Charles Brodnax, President, Divisional
Frederick Saint, President, Subsidiary
Jonathan Coleman, Secretary
Lisa Ruggles, Senior VP, Divisional

GROWTH PLANS/SPECIAL FEATURES:
CoStar Group, Inc. provides information, analytics and online marketplaces to the commercial real estate industry in the U.S. and the U.K. The firm provides industry professionals and consumers of commercial real estate and apartments ways to explore and complete transactions. The company's five flagship brands include CoStar, LoopNet, Apartments.com, BizBuySell and LandsofAmerica. Subscription-based information services comprise the CoStar suite, which is sold as a platform consisting of CoStar Property, CoStar COMPS, CoStar Tenant, CoStar Investment Analysis, CoStar Real Estate Manager, CoStar Private Sale Network, CoStar Portfolio Strategy, CoStar Brokerage Applications, CoStar Mobile, CoStar Lease, CoStar Risk and CoStar Advertising. LoopNet is an online marketplace that enables commercial property owners, landlords and real estate agents working on their behalf to list properties for sale or for lease, and to submit detailed information about property listings. Apartments.com comprises a network of apartment marketing sites, including ApartmentFinder.com and ApartmentHomeLiving.com. This network of subscription-based services offers renters a searchable database of apartment listings and provides professional property management companies and landlords with an advertising destination. BizBuySell and BizQuest.com are leading online marketplaces for operating businesses for sale. Business sellers pay a fee to list their operating businesses for sale, and interested buyers can search the respective sites' listings for free. These sites also allow interested business buyers to search hundreds of franchise opportunities, and franchisors can list their availabilities in the directory on a cost-per-lead basis. LandsofAmerica and LandAndFarm are online marketplaces for rural land for sale. Sellers pay a fee to list their land for sale, and interested buyers can search the listings for free. During 2018, CoStar Group acquired Cozy Services Ltd., a provider of online rental solutions; and U.K. commercial property marketplace, Realla.

The firm offers employees medical, dental, vision, life and disability insurance; 401(k); and various employee assistance programs.

FINANCIAL DATA: Note: Data for latest year may not have been available at press time.

In U.S. $	2018	2017	2016	2015	2014	2013
Revenue	1,191,832,000	965,230,000	837,630,000	711,764,000	575,936,000	440,943,000
R&D Expense	100,937,000	88,850,000	76,400,000	65,760,000	55,426,000	46,757,000
Operating Income	273,564,000	173,816,000	144,905,000	39,386,000	109,310,000	69,337,000
Operating Margin %		.18%	.17%	.02%	.14%	.12%
SGA Expense	516,517,000	464,490,000	419,780,000	417,733,000	254,221,000	195,664,000
Net Income	238,334,000	122,695,000	85,071,000	-3,465,000	44,869,000	29,734,000
Operating Cash Flow	335,458,000	234,703,000	195,944,000	131,245,000	143,909,000	108,298,000
Capital Expenditure	29,632,000	24,499,000	18,766,000	35,061,000	27,444,000	19,042,000
EBITDA	364,588,000	237,715,000	216,843,000	90,524,000	151,766,000	94,538,000
Return on Assets %		.05%	.04%	.00%	.03%	.02%
Return on Equity %		.06%	.05%	.00%	.04%	.03%
Debt to Equity			0.185	0.219	0.241	0.139

CONTACT INFORMATION:
Phone: 202-346-6500 Fax: 202 346-6370
Toll-Free: 800-204-5960
Address: 1331 L Street NW, Northwest, WA 20005 United States

STOCK TICKER/OTHER:
Stock Ticker: CSGP Exchange: NAS
Employees: 3,064 Fiscal Year Ends: 12/31
Parent Company:

SALARIES/BONUSES:
Top Exec. Salary: $750,000 Bonus: $
Second Exec. Salary: $469,231 Bonus: $

OTHER THOUGHTS:
Estimated Female Officers or Directors:
Hot Spot for Advancement for Women/Minorities: Y

Costco Wholesale Corporation

NAIC Code: 452910

www.costco.com

TYPES OF BUSINESS:
Warehouse Clubs, Retail
Food
Health & Beauty Products
Electronics
Furniture
Apparel
Automotive Supplies
Gasoline Sales

BRANDS/DIVISIONS/AFFILIATES:
Costco Wholesale Industries
Kirkland Signature

CONTACTS: Note: Officers with more than one job title may be intentionally listed here more than once.
Hamilton James, Chairman of the Board
James Murphy, COO, Divisional
Roland Vachris, COO, Divisional
Russell Miller, COO, Geographical
James Klauer, COO, Geographical
Joseph Portera, COO, Geographical
W. Jelinek, Director
Franz Lazarus, Executive VP, Divisional
Timothy Rose, Executive VP, Divisional
Richard Galanti, Executive VP
Paul Moulton, Executive VP
Daniel Hines, Senior VP

GROWTH PLANS/SPECIAL FEATURES:

Costco Wholesale Corporation operates membership warehouses based on the concept that offering members very low prices on a limited selection of branded and private-label products will produce high sales volumes and rapid inventory turnover. This rapid turnover, combined with volume purchasing, efficient distribution and reduced handling of merchandise in self-service warehouse facilities, allows the firm to operate at significantly lower margins than traditional discount retailers. Costco buys the majority of its merchandise directly from manufacturers for shipment to warehouses or to consolidation points, minimizing freight and handling costs. Products include health and beauty aids, cleaning supplies, foods, alcohol, appliances, electronics, tools, office supplies, furniture, automotive supplies, apparel, cameras, house wares and books. Stores contain other features, including pharmacies, print shops, photo labs and gas stations. Costco's private products are marketed under the Kirkland Signature label brand. It has three types of memberships: executive, business and gold star. Memberships are designed to build customer loyalty and start at $60 per year (for U.S. and Canadian operations). The firm operates 759 warehouses, including 527 in the U.S.; 100 in Canada; 38 in Mexico; 28 in the U.K.; 26 in Japan; 15 in South Korea; 14 in Taiwan; nine in Australia; two in Spain; and one each in Iceland and France (as of August 2018). The stores average approximately 144,000 square feet and stock distinct products including upscale items such as jewelry and wines. Costco Wholesale Industries, a division of the company, operates manufacturing businesses, including special food packaging, optical laboratories, meat processing and jewelry distribution. The company also operates eCommerce websites in the U.S., Canada, the U.K. and Mexico

Costco offers employees health, dental, vision, life insurance, short- and long-term disability and prescription coverage; 401(k); and employee assistance plans.

FINANCIAL DATA: Note: Data for latest year may not have been available at press time.

In U.S. $	2018	2017	2016	2015	2014	2013
Revenue	141,576,000,000	129,025,000,000	118,719,000,000	116,199,000,000	112,640,000,000	105,156,000,000
R&D Expense						
Operating Income	4,480,000,000	4,111,000,000	3,672,000,000	3,624,000,000	3,220,000,000	3,053,000,000
Operating Margin %		.03%	.03%	.03%	.03%	.03%
SGA Expense	13,876,000,000	12,950,000,000	12,068,000,000	11,445,000,000	10,899,000,000	10,104,000,000
Net Income	3,134,000,000	2,679,000,000	2,350,000,000	2,377,000,000	2,058,000,000	2,039,000,000
Operating Cash Flow	5,774,000,000	6,726,000,000	3,292,000,000	4,285,000,000	3,984,000,000	3,437,000,000
Capital Expenditure	2,969,000,000	2,502,000,000	2,649,000,000	2,393,000,000	1,993,000,000	2,083,000,000
EBITDA	6,038,000,000	5,543,000,000	5,007,000,000	4,855,000,000	4,339,000,000	4,096,000,000
Return on Assets %		.08%	.07%	.07%	.07%	.07%
Return on Equity %		.23%	.21%	.21%	.18%	.18%
Debt to Equity		0.61	0.336	0.458	0.414	0.461

CONTACT INFORMATION:
Phone: 425 313-8100 Fax: 425 313-8103
Toll-Free: 800-774-2678
Address: 999 Lake Dr., Issaquah, WA 98027 United States

SALARIES/BONUSES:
Top Exec. Salary: $800,000 Bonus: $97,000
Second Exec. Salary: $740,000 Bonus: $59,040

STOCK TICKER/OTHER:
Stock Ticker: COST
Employees: 245,000
Parent Company:

Exchange: NAS
Fiscal Year Ends: 08/31

OTHER THOUGHTS:
Estimated Female Officers or Directors: 4
Hot Spot for Advancement for Women/Minorities: Y

Cox Automotive Inc

www.coxautoinc.com

NAIC Code: 519130

TYPES OF BUSINESS:
Internet Search Portals

BRANDS/DIVISIONS/AFFILIATES:
Cox Enterprises Inc
VinSolutions
Dealertrack
Manheim
vAuto
Autotrader
Kelly Blue Book
Clutch Technologies

CONTACTS:
Note: Officers with more than one job title may be intentionally listed here more than once.

Sandy Schwartz, Pres.
Janet Barnard, Chief People Officer
David Brooks, CTO

GROWTH PLANS/SPECIAL FEATURES:
Cox Automotive, Inc. provides automotive resources and tools for consumers, dealers and manufacturers to maximize value at every step of the car buying and selling processes. These sources and tools consist of several brands, some of which provide multiple solutions. For example, VinSolutions provides a cloud-based internal management, sales, service and consumer engagement management platform that can be used from any PC, laptop or mobile device. Dealertrack is a dealer operations solution and brand. Inventory management brands include Manheim, NextGear Capital and vAuto. Inventory solutions address the acquisition and disposal of cars, vehicle floor plans, reconditioning of cars and transport of cars. Marketing brands include Autotrader, Dealer.com, HomeNet, Kelly Blue Book, vAuto and VinSolutions. Marketing solutions include advertising vehicles, attracting trade-in customers, creating a vehicle website, managing customer price expectations, managing the social community, measuring marketing performance and obtaining search results. Sales brands include Dealertrack, F&I Express, Kelley Blue Book, Manheim, vAuto and VinSolutions. Sales solutions include access to credit application information, connecting sales with the finance and insurance (F&I) processes, making deals online, managing rebates and incentives, and speeding up the registration and titling processes. Service solutions include the Dealertrack, VinSolutions and Xtime brands. Service solutions are for attracting and retaining business. And mobility solutions include the Clutch Technologies, Pivet and RideKleen brands. Mobility solutions provide end-to-end services for fleets, including in-fleeting, de-fleeting, reconditioning, maintenance and cleaning. Cox Automotive operates as a subsidiary of Cox Enterprises, Inc.

FINANCIAL DATA:
Note: Data for latest year may not have been available at press time.

In U.S. $	2018	2017	2016	2015	2014	2013
Revenue	7,780,500,000	7,410,000,000	7,300,000,000	7,100,000,000	6,600,000,000	6,200,000,000
R&D Expense						
Operating Income						
Operating Margin %						
SGA Expense						
Net Income						
Operating Cash Flow						
Capital Expenditure						
EBITDA						
Return on Assets %						
Return on Equity %						
Debt to Equity						

CONTACT INFORMATION:
Phone: Fax:
Toll-Free: 855-449-0010
Address: 3003 Summit Blvd., Ste. 200, Atlanta, GA 30319 United States

STOCK TICKER/OTHER:
Stock Ticker: Subsidiary   Exchange:
Employees: 33,000   Fiscal Year Ends: 12/31
Parent Company: Cox Enterprises Inc

SALARIES/BONUSES:
Top Exec. Salary: $ Bonus: $
Second Exec. Salary: $ Bonus: $

OTHER THOUGHTS:
Estimated Female Officers or Directors:
Hot Spot for Advancement for Women/Minorities:

Sales, profits and employees may be estimates. Financial information, benefits and other data can change quickly and may vary from those stated here.

Cox Communications Inc

NAIC Code: 517110

www.cox.com/residential/home.cox

TYPES OF BUSINESS:
Cable TV Service and Internet Access
Digital Cable TV Service
Cable-Based Internet Access
Local & Long-Distance Phone Service
Commercial Telecommunications Services
Data & Video Transport Services

BRANDS/DIVISIONS/AFFILIATES:
Cox Enterprises Inc
Cox Business Services
Managed IP PBX
Cox Media
Kudzu.com

CONTACTS:
Note: Officers with more than one job title may be intentionally listed here more than once.

Patrick J. Esser, Pres.
Len Barlik, Exec. VP-Prod. Mgmt. & Dev.
Asheesh Saksena, Chief Strategy Officer
Joseph J. Rooney, Sr. VP-Social Media, Advertising & Brand Mktg.
William (Bill) J. Fitzsimmons, Chief Acct. Officer
Philip G. Meeks, Sr. VP-Cox Bus.
Jennifer W. Hightower, Sr. VP-Law & Policy
David Pugliese, Sr. VP-Product Mktg.
Mark A. Kaish, Sr. VP-Tech. Oper.
George Richter, VP-Supply Chain Mgmt.

GROWTH PLANS/SPECIAL FEATURES:

Cox Communications, Inc., owned by Cox Enterprises, Inc., is a broadband communications and entertainment company, serving millions of customers throughout the U.S. Cox offers advanced digital video, high speed internet, and local and long-distance telephone services over its own nationwide IP network in 18 states. Cox Business Services provides data, video and voice solutions to small and regional businesses such as schools and universities, government organizations and financial institutions. The firm's Managed IP PBX service provides small business customers that have limited internal information technology departments with telecommunication systems that are monitored and managed around the clock by Cox Business. Cox Media offers national and local cable advertising in traditional spot and new media formats, along with promotional opportunities and production services. The company also maintains Kudzu.com, an online directory that aggregates user reviews and ratings on local businesses, merchants and service providers.

FINANCIAL DATA:
Note: Data for latest year may not have been available at press time.

In U.S. $	2018	2017	2016	2015	2014	2013
Revenue	12,000,000,000	11,550,000,000	11,000,000,000	10,650,000,000	10,400,000,000	9,900,000,000
R&D Expense						
Operating Income						
Operating Margin %						
SGA Expense						
Net Income						
Operating Cash Flow						
Capital Expenditure						
EBITDA						
Return on Assets %						
Return on Equity %						
Debt to Equity						

CONTACT INFORMATION:
Phone: 404-843-5000 Fax: 404-843-5939
Toll-Free: 888-566-7751
Address: 1400 Lake Hearn Dr., Atlanta, GA 30319 United States

STOCK TICKER/OTHER:
Stock Ticker: Subsidiary
Employees: 23,000
Parent Company: Cox Enterprises Inc

Exchange:
Fiscal Year Ends: 12/31

SALARIES/BONUSES:
Top Exec. Salary: $ Bonus: $
Second Exec. Salary: $ Bonus: $

OTHER THOUGHTS:
Estimated Female Officers or Directors: 3
Hot Spot for Advancement for Women/Minorities: Y

Sales, profits and employees may be estimates. Financial information, benefits and other data can change quickly and may vary from those stated here.

Cox Enterprises Inc

NAIC Code: 515120

www.coxenterprises.com

TYPES OF BUSINESS:
Cable Television and Internet Services
Television Broadcasting
Newspaper Publishing
Radio Stations
Online News, Information and Services Sites
Auctions
Automotive E-Commerce
Technology Products

BRANDS/DIVISIONS/AFFILIATES:
Cox Communications Inc
Cox Business Services
Cox Media Group
Cox Automotive
autotrader.com
Kelley Blue Book
Clutch
Flexdrive

CONTACTS: Note: Officers with more than one job title may be intentionally listed here more than once.
Alex Taylor, CEO
Jill Campbell, Exec. VP
Jimmy W. Hayes, Pres.
Dallas S. Clement, CFO
Marybeth N. Leamer, Exec. VP-Admin.
Shauna Sullivan Muhl, VP-Legal
Roberto I. Jimenez, VP-Corp. Comm. & Public Affairs
J. Lacey Lewis, Sr. VP-Finance
Patrick J. Esser, Pres., Cox Comm.
Sanford Schwartz, Pres., Manheim
Bill Hoffman, Pres., Cox Media Group
Kathy Decker, Treas.
James Cox Kennedy, Chmn.

GROWTH PLANS/SPECIAL FEATURES:
Cox Enterprises, Inc., through subsidiary Cox Communications, Inc., is a broadband communications and entertainment company, serving millions of customers across the U.S. Cox offers advanced digital video, high-speed internet and local and long-distance telephone services over its own nationwide IP network. Cox Business Services provides data, video and voice solutions to small and regional businesses such as schools and universities, government organizations and financial institutions. The firm provides small business customers that have limited internal information technology departments with telecommunication systems that are monitored and managed around the clock by Cox Business. Cox Media Group offers national and local cable advertising in traditional spot and new media formats, along with promotional opportunities and production services. Cox Automotive owns significant automobile industry websites and marketing platforms, including autotrader.com, Kelley Blue Book and motors.co.uk. In late-2018, this division announced it was expanding its business model to include vehicle subscription services, namely Clutch and Flexdrive, in which customers pay a recurring fee for the right to use one or more automotive vehicles. This form of automobile ownership enables subscribers to use the kind of vehicles they need at the times they need them.

Cox offers employees medical, dental, vision, life and disability insurance coverage; and a 401(k) plan.

FINANCIAL DATA: Note: Data for latest year may not have been available at press time.

In U.S. $	2018	2017	2016	2015	2014	2013
Revenue	20,750,000,000	20,500,000,000	20,250,000,000	18,885,000,000	17,450,000,000	15,920,000,000
R&D Expense						
Operating Income						
Operating Margin %						
SGA Expense						
Net Income						
Operating Cash Flow						
Capital Expenditure						
EBITDA						
Return on Assets %						
Return on Equity %						
Debt to Equity						

CONTACT INFORMATION:
Phone: 678-645-0000 Fax:
Toll-Free:
Address: 6205 Peachtree Dunwoody Rd. 1400 Lake Hearn Dr., Atlanta, GA 30328 United States

STOCK TICKER/OTHER:
Stock Ticker: Private
Employees: 60,000
Parent Company:

Exchange:
Fiscal Year Ends: 12/31

SALARIES/BONUSES:
Top Exec. Salary: $ Bonus: $
Second Exec. Salary: $ Bonus: $

OTHER THOUGHTS:
Estimated Female Officers or Directors: 7
Hot Spot for Advancement for Women/Minorities: Y

Sales, profits and employees may be estimates. Financial information, benefits and other data can change quickly and may vary from those stated here.

Crown Castle International Corp

www.crowncastle.com

NAIC Code: 237130

TYPES OF BUSINESS:
Cellular Service Antenna Towers
Antenna Site Leasing
Site Management Services
Construction & Engineering Services
Radio & Television Broadcast Towers

BRANDS/DIVISIONS/AFFILIATES:
Crown Castle USA Inc

CONTACTS:
Note: Officers with more than one job title may be intentionally listed here more than once.

Daniel Schlanger, CFO
J. Martin, Chairman of the Board
Robert Collins, Chief Accounting Officer
Robert Ackerman, COO, Divisional
James Young, COO, Divisional
Michael Kavanagh, Other Executive Officer
Jay Brown, President
Philip Kelley, Senior VP, Divisional
Kenneth Simon, Senior VP

GROWTH PLANS/SPECIAL FEATURES:

Crown Castle International Corp. owns, operates and leases towers and other communications structures for wireless communication purposes. Approximately 40,000 towers are dispersed throughout the U.S., and approximately 65,000 route miles of fiber optics primarily supports outdoor/indoor small cell networks and related solutions. Crown Castle's core business is the provision of access, including space or capacity, to its shared communications infrastructure via long-term contracts in various forms, including lease, license, sublease and service agreements. The firm partners with wireless carriers, technology companies, broadband providers and municipalities to design and delivery end-to-end infrastructure solutions to consumers and businesses. Crown Castle's largest tenants include AT&T, T-Mobile, Verizon Wireless and Sprint, which collectively accounted for 73% of 2018 site rental revenues. Site rental revenues represent nearly 90% of consolidated net revenues, of which approximately 66% and 34% were from the towers segment and the fiber segment, respectively.

Employee benefits include medical, dental, vision and prescription drug coverage; a 401(k); short- and long-term disability; life insurance; tuition reimbursement; an employee assistance program; and flexible spending accounts.

FINANCIAL DATA:
Note: Data for latest year may not have been available at press time.

In U.S. $	2018	2017	2016	2015	2014	2013
Revenue	5,423,000,000	4,355,605,000	3,921,225,000	3,663,851,000	3,689,884,000	3,022,384,000
R&D Expense						
Operating Income	1,485,000,000	1,122,798,000	1,001,122,000	995,326,000	1,043,658,000	962,671,000
Operating Margin %		.26%	.26%	.27%	.28%	.32%
SGA Expense	563,000,000	426,698,000	371,031,000	310,921,000	282,696,000	238,702,000
Net Income	671,000,000	444,550,000	356,973,000	1,520,992,000	390,513,000	90,111,000
Operating Cash Flow	2,502,000,000	2,044,186,000	1,782,264,000	1,796,725,000	1,666,130,000	1,237,656,000
Capital Expenditure	1,741,000,000	1,228,071,000	873,883,000	908,892,000	780,077,000	567,810,000
EBITDA	2,838,000,000	2,282,770,000	1,976,094,000	1,994,175,000	1,890,007,000	1,565,670,000
Return on Assets %		.01%	.01%	.07%	.02%	.00%
Return on Equity %		.04%	.04%	.21%	.05%	.02%
Debt to Equity		1.30	1.597	1.713	1.758	1.659

CONTACT INFORMATION:
Phone: 713 570-3050 Fax:
Toll-Free: 877-486-9377
Address: 1220 Augusta Dr., Ste. 600, Houston, TX 77057 United States

STOCK TICKER/OTHER:
Stock Ticker: CCI
Employees: 3,200
Parent Company:

Exchange: NYS
Fiscal Year Ends: 12/31

SALARIES/BONUSES:
Top Exec. Salary: $905,769   Bonus: $
Second Exec. Salary: $591,263   Bonus: $

OTHER THOUGHTS:
Estimated Female Officers or Directors:
Hot Spot for Advancement for Women/Minorities:

Crown Holdings Inc

NAIC Code: 332431

www.crowncork.com

TYPES OF BUSINESS:
Metal Can Manufacturing
Food and Beverage Cans
Plastic Containers

BRANDS/DIVISIONS/AFFILIATES:

CONTACTS:
Note: Officers with more than one job title may be intentionally listed here more than once.

Timothy Donahue, CEO
Thomas Kelly, CFO
John Conway, Chairman of the Board
David Beaver, Controller
Gerard Gifford, COO
Caesar Sweitzer, Independent Director
Djalma Novaes, President, Divisional
Robert Bourque, President, Divisional
Hok Goh, President, Divisional
Didier Sourisseau, President, Divisional

GROWTH PLANS/SPECIAL FEATURES:

Crown Holdings, Inc. is a worldwide leader in the design, manufacture and sale of packaging products and equipment for consumer goods and industrial products. Crown is organized by product line and geography within four divisions: Americas, Europe, Asia Pacific and transit packaging. The Americas division includes operations in the U.S., Brazil, Canada, the Caribbean, Colombia and Mexico. These operations manufacture beverage, food and aerosol cans and ends, glass bottles, specialty packaging, metal vacuum closures, steel crowns and caps. This division operated 48 plants in seven countries at December 31, 2018. The European division includes operations in Europe, the Middle East and Africa, manufacturing beverage, food and aerosol cans and ends, promotional packaging and metal vacuum closures and caps. This division operated 61 plants in 22 countries. The Asia Pacific division primarily consists of beverage can operations in Cambodia, China, Indonesia, Malaysia, Myanmar, Singapore, Thailand and Vietnam, and also includes Crown Holdings' non-beverage can operations, primarily food cans and specialty packaging. This division operated 30 plants in eight countries. Last, the transit packaging division encompasses the company's industrial and protective solutions and equipment and tools businesses. Industrial solutions include steel strap, plastic strap, industrial film and other related products used in a wide range of industries, including steel lumber, brick/block, corrugated boxes, food and beverage goods, agriculture products and a variety of other goods. Protective solutions include transit protection products such as airbags, edge protectors and honeycomb products that help prevent movement of, and/or damage to industrial and consumer goods during transport. Equipment and tools includes manual, semi-automatic equipment and tools, which are primarily used in end of line manufacturing applications to apply consumables such as strap and film. This division operated 99 plants in 23 countries.

FINANCIAL DATA:
Note: Data for latest year may not have been available at press time.

In U.S. $	2018	2017	2016	2015	2014	2013
Revenue	11,151,000,000	8,698,000,000	8,284,000,000	8,762,000,000	9,097,000,000	8,656,000,000
R&D Expense						
Operating Income	1,140,000,000	1,125,000,000	1,065,000,000	993,000,000	939,000,000	885,000,000
Operating Margin %		.13%	.13%	.11%	.10%	.10%
SGA Expense	558,000,000	371,000,000	368,000,000	390,000,000	398,000,000	425,000,000
Net Income	439,000,000	323,000,000	496,000,000	393,000,000	387,000,000	324,000,000
Operating Cash Flow	571,000,000	760,000,000	930,000,000	956,000,000	912,000,000	885,000,000
Capital Expenditure	462,000,000	498,000,000	473,000,000	354,000,000	328,000,000	275,000,000
EBITDA	1,549,000,000	1,328,000,000	1,259,000,000	1,146,000,000	959,000,000	946,000,000
Return on Assets %		.03%	.05%	.04%	.04%	.04%
Return on Equity %		.67%	1.95%	2.99%	6.29%	
Debt to Equity		8.681	12.888	36.493	42.076	867.25

CONTACT INFORMATION:
Phone: 215 698-5100 Fax:
Toll-Free:
Address: 770 Township Line Rd., Yardley, PA 19067-4232 United States

STOCK TICKER/OTHER:
Stock Ticker: CCK
Employees: 24,000
Parent Company:

Exchange: NYS
Fiscal Year Ends: 12/31

SALARIES/BONUSES:
Top Exec. Salary: $1,100,000 Bonus: $
Second Exec. Salary: $680,000 Bonus: $

OTHER THOUGHTS:
Estimated Female Officers or Directors: 3
Hot Spot for Advancement for Women/Minorities: Y

Cullen-Frost Bankers Inc

NAIC Code: 522110

www.frostbank.com

TYPES OF BUSINESS:
Banking
Insurance
Loans
Discount Brokerage
Trust Services
Cash Management
Investment Services

BRANDS/DIVISIONS/AFFILIATES:
Frost Bank
Frost Insurance Agency Inc
Frost Brokerage Services Inc
Frost Investment Advisors LLC
Tri-Frost Corporation
Main Plaza Corporation
Cullen-Frost Capital Trust
WNB Capital Trust

CONTACTS:
Note: Officers with more than one job title may be intentionally listed here more than once.

Phillip Green, CEO
Annette Alonzo, Executive VP, Subsidiary
Jerry Salinas, CFO
William Perotti, Chief Credit Officer
Michael Russell, COO, Subsidiary
Mike Russell, COO
Patrick Frost, Director
Robert Berman, Executive VP, Subsidiary
Candace Wolfshohl, Executive VP, Subsidiary
Carol Severyn, Executive VP, Subsidiary
Jimmy Stead, Executive VP, Subsidiary
Paul Bracher, Executive VP, Subsidiary
James Waters, Executive VP

GROWTH PLANS/SPECIAL FEATURES:

Cullen-Frost Bankers, Inc., with $31.7 billion in assets in 2017, is a financial holding company and a bank holding company headquartered in San Antonio, Texas. Through its subsidiaries, Cullen/Frost provides an array of products and services throughout numerous Texas markets, offering commercial and consumer banking services, as well as trust and investment management, insurance, brokerage, mutual funds, leasing, treasury management, capital markets advisory and item processing services. Cullen-Frost serves a variety of industries, including energy, manufacturing, services, construction, retail, telecommunications, healthcare, military and transportation. The company's loan portfolio has a significant concentration of energy-related loans totaling approximately 11.4% of total loans, but is not dependent upon any single industry or customer. Subsidiaries of the firm include Frost Bank, the principal operating subsidiary and sole banking subsidiary of Cullen-Frost; Frost Insurance Agency, Inc.; Frost Brokerage Services, Inc.; Frost Investment Advisors, LLC; Frost Investment Services, LLC; Tri-Frost Corporation, which holds securities for investment purposes; Main Plaza Corporation, a loan provider; Cullen-Frost Capital Trust I, II; and WNB Capital Trust I.

Cullen/Frost offers its employees life, medical, dental and vision insurance; long-term disability insurance; a 401(k) plan; a flexible spending account; banking benefits; an employee assistance program; tuition reimbursement; the Tom Frost Scholarship ($5,000 to qualifying child of employee); and a profit sharing plan.

FINANCIAL DATA:
Note: Data for latest year may not have been available at press time.

In U.S. $	2018	2017	2016	2015	2014	2013
Revenue	1,309,178,000	1,202,892,000	1,126,044,000	1,065,362,000	1,007,078,000	923,373,000
R&D Expense						
Operating Income						
Operating Margin %						
SGA Expense	491,576,000	476,174,000	451,957,000	438,973,000	409,543,000	387,584,000
Net Income	454,918,000	364,149,000	304,261,000	279,328,000	277,977,000	237,866,000
Operating Cash Flow	562,388,000	538,079,000	437,842,000	393,471,000	286,670,000	173,606,000
Capital Expenditure	79,270,000	34,089,000	53,648,000	147,129,000	131,970,000	39,599,000
EBITDA						
Return on Assets %		.01%	.01%	.01%	.01%	.01%
Return on Equity %		.12%	.11%	.10%	.11%	.10%
Debt to Equity		0.074	0.083	0.086	0.088	0.094

CONTACT INFORMATION:
Phone: 210 220-4011 Fax: 210 220-5578
Toll-Free: 877-513-7678
Address: 100 W. Houston St., San Antonio, TX 78205 United States

STOCK TICKER/OTHER:
Stock Ticker: CFR
Employees: 4,217
Parent Company:

Exchange: NYS
Fiscal Year Ends: 12/31

SALARIES/BONUSES:
Top Exec. Salary: $990,000 Bonus: $
Second Exec. Salary: $565,000 Bonus: $

OTHER THOUGHTS:
Estimated Female Officers or Directors: 3
Hot Spot for Advancement for Women/Minorities: Y

Sales, profits and employees may be estimates. Financial information, benefits and other data can change quickly and may vary from those stated here.

Cummins Inc

www.cummins.com

NAIC Code: 336300

TYPES OF BUSINESS:
Automotive Products, Motors & Parts Manufacturing
Engines
Filtration Systems
Power Generation Systems
Alternators
Air Handling Systems
Filtration & Emissions Solutions
Fuel Systems

BRANDS/DIVISIONS/AFFILIATES:

CONTACTS: Note: Officers with more than one job title may be intentionally listed here more than once.
N. Linebarger, CEO
Peter Anderson, VP, Divisional
Mark Smith, CFO
Christopher Clulow, Chief Accounting Officer
Marya Rose, Chief Administrative Officer
Sherry Aaholm, Chief Information Officer
Jennifer Rumsey, Chief Technology Officer
Richard Freeland, Director
Sharon Barner, General Counsel
Jill Cook, Other Executive Officer
Livingston Satterthwaite, President, Divisional
Tracy Embree, President, Divisional
Norbert Nusterer, President, Divisional
Donald Jackson, Treasurer
Thaddeaus Ewald, Vice President, Divisional
Mark Osowick, Vice President, Divisional
Steven Chapman, Vice President, Geographical

GROWTH PLANS/SPECIAL FEATURES:
Cummins, Inc. designs, manufactures, distributes and services diesel and natural gas engines and powertrain-related component products. Cummins' products are sold to original equipment manufacturers (OEMs), distributors, dealers and other customers worldwide. These customers are served through a network of approximately 600 wholly-owned and independent distributor locations and over 7,600 dealer locations in more than 190 countries and territories. Cummins operates its business through five segments: engine, distribution, components, power systems and electrified power. The engine segment manufactures and markets a broad range of diesel and natural gas-powered engines under the Cummins brand name, as well as certain customer brand names, for the heavy- and medium-duty truck, bus recreational vehicle (RV), light-duty automotive, construction, mining, marine, rail, oil/gas, defense and agricultural markets. The distribution segment service and distribute the full range of Cummins' products to end-users at approximately 450 locations in more than 90 distribution territories. The components segment supplies products which complement Cummins' engine and power systems segments, including aftertreatment systems, turbochargers, transmissions, filtration products, electronics and fuel systems for commercial diesel and natural gas applications. The power systems segment offers three product lines: power generation, consisting of backup and prime power generators ranging from 2 kilowatts to 3.5 megawatts, as well as controls, paralleling systems and transfer switches for an array of applications; industrial, consisting of diesel and natural gas high-horsepower engines up to 5,500hp for a variety of equipment in the mining, rail, defense, oil/gas and commercial marine applications worldwide; and generator technologies, consisting of A/C generator/alternator products for internal consumption and for external generator set assemblers. Last, the electrified power segment offers electrified power systems, ranging from fully-electric to hybrid.

Cummins offers employees life, medical and dental insurance; and various employee assistance programs.

FINANCIAL DATA: Note: Data for latest year may not have been available at press time.

In U.S. $	2018	2017	2016	2015	2014	2013
Revenue	23,771,000,000	20,428,000,000	17,509,000,000	19,110,000,000	19,221,000,000	17,301,000,000
R&D Expense	902,000,000	752,000,000	636,000,000	735,000,000	754,000,000	713,000,000
Operating Income	2,467,000,000	2,046,000,000	1,822,000,000	2,100,000,000	2,061,000,000	1,791,000,000
Operating Margin %		.10%	.10%	.11%	.10%	.10%
SGA Expense	2,437,000,000	2,390,000,000	2,046,000,000	2,092,000,000	2,095,000,000	1,920,000,000
Net Income	2,141,000,000	999,000,000	1,394,000,000	1,399,000,000	1,651,000,000	1,483,000,000
Operating Cash Flow	2,378,000,000	2,277,000,000	1,935,000,000	2,059,000,000	2,266,000,000	2,089,000,000
Capital Expenditure	784,000,000	587,000,000	594,000,000	799,000,000	798,000,000	740,000,000
EBITDA	3,478,000,000	3,029,000,000	2,529,000,000	2,604,000,000	2,953,000,000	2,567,000,000
Return on Assets %		.06%	.09%	.09%	.11%	.11%
Return on Equity %		.14%	.20%	.18%	.22%	.21%
Debt to Equity		0.219	0.228	0.213	0.205	0.223

CONTACT INFORMATION:
Phone: 812 377-5000   Fax:
Toll-Free:
Address: 500 Jackson St., Columbus, IN 47202 United States

STOCK TICKER/OTHER:
Stock Ticker: CMI
Employees: 55,400
Parent Company:

Exchange: NYS
Fiscal Year Ends: 12/31

SALARIES/BONUSES:
Top Exec. Salary: $1,442,500   Bonus: $
Second Exec. Salary: $874,000   Bonus: $

OTHER THOUGHTS:
Estimated Female Officers or Directors: 2
Hot Spot for Advancement for Women/Minorities: Y

Sales, profits and employees may be estimates. Financial information, benefits and other data can change quickly and may vary from those stated here.

Plunkett Research, Ltd.

CVS Health Corporation
NAIC Code: 446110

cvshealth.com

TYPES OF BUSINESS:
Drug Stores
Pharmacy Benefits Management
Online Pharmacy Services

BRANDS/DIVISIONS/AFFILIATES:
MinuteClinic
Omnicare
SilverScript Insurance Company
CVS Pharmacy
Aetna Inc

CONTACTS: Note: Officers with more than one job title may be intentionally listed here more than once.
Larry Merlo, CEO
Thomas Moriarty, Executive VP
Eva Boratto, CFO
David Dorman, Chairman of the Board
James Clark, Chief Accounting Officer
Troyen Brennan, Chief Medical Officer
Joshua Flum, Executive VP, Divisional
Alan Lotvin, Executive VP, Divisional
Karen Lynch, Executive VP, Divisional
Jonathan Roberts, Executive VP
Derica Rice, Executive VP
Kevin Hourican, Executive VP
Lisa Bisaccia, Other Executive Officer

GROWTH PLANS/SPECIAL FEATURES:
CVS Health Corporation is a leading provider of prescription and related healthcare services in the U.S. It operates in four segments: corporate, retail/LTC, pharmacy services and health care benefits. The corporate segment provides management and administrative services to support the company's overall operations. The retail/LTC (long-term care) segment operated more than 9,900 retail locations, over 1,100 MinuteClinic locations as well as online retail pharmacy websites, LTC pharmacies and onsite pharmacies. LTC pharmacy services are through the Omnicare business. Omnicare provides pharmacy consulting, including monthly patient drug therapy evaluations, to assist in compliance with state and federal regulations and provide proprietary clinical and health management programs. It also provides pharmaceutical case management services for retirees, employees and dependents who have drug benefits under corporate-sponsored health care programs. The pharmacy services segment provides a full range of pharmacy benefit management services, including mail order pharmacy services, plan design and administration, formulary management, claims processing and health management programs. Through subsidiary SilverScript Insurance Company, the division is a national provider of drug benefits to eligible beneficiaries under Medicare Part D. The segment operates a national network of more than 68,000 retail pharmacies, consisting of approximately 41,000 chain pharmacies (which includes CVS Pharmacy locations) and 27,000 independent pharmacies, in the U.S., including Puerto Rico, the District of Columbia, Guam and the U.S. Virgin Islands. The health care benefits segment is one of the nation's leading diversified health care benefits providers, serving an estimated 38 million people. The segment offers a range of traditional, voluntary and consumer-directed health insurance products and related services. In November 2018, CVS completed its $70 billion acquisition of Aetna Inc. Aetna will continue to operate as a standalone unit.

Employee benefits include medical, dental, vision and prescription coverage; free health screenings at MinuteClinic; a 401(k); employee stock purchase plan; short- and long-term disability; employee discounts; education reimbursement; an employee assistance program; and flexible spending accounts.

FINANCIAL DATA: Note: Data for latest year may not have been available at press time.

In U.S. $	2018	2017	2016	2015	2014	2013
Revenue	194,579,000,000	184,765,000,000	177,526,000,000	153,290,000,000	139,367,000,000	126,761,000,000
R&D Expense						
Operating Income	10,170,000,000	9,517,000,000	10,338,000,000	9,454,000,000	8,799,000,000	8,037,000,000
Operating Margin %		.05%	.06%	.06%	.06%	.06%
SGA Expense						
Net Income	-594,000,000	6,622,000,000	5,317,000,000	5,237,000,000	4,644,000,000	4,592,000,000
Operating Cash Flow	8,865,000,000	8,007,000,000	10,069,000,000	8,412,000,000	8,137,000,000	5,783,000,000
Capital Expenditure	2,037,000,000	1,918,000,000	2,224,000,000	2,367,000,000	2,136,000,000	1,984,000,000
EBITDA	6,743,000,000	11,809,000,000	12,190,000,000	11,567,000,000	10,224,000,000	9,915,000,000
Return on Assets %		.07%	.06%	.06%	.06%	.07%
Return on Equity %		.18%	.14%	.14%	.12%	.12%
Debt to Equity		0.588	0.695	0.706	0.308	0.338

CONTACT INFORMATION:
Phone: 401 765-1500 Fax: 401 762-2137
Toll-Free: 888-746-7287
Address: 1 CVS Dr., Woonsocket, RI 02895 United States

STOCK TICKER/OTHER:
Stock Ticker: CVS
Employees: 295,000
Parent Company:

Exchange: NYS
Fiscal Year Ends: 12/31

SALARIES/BONUSES:
Top Exec. Salary: $791,477 Bonus: $950,000
Second Exec. Salary: $1,630,000 Bonus: $

OTHER THOUGHTS:
Estimated Female Officers or Directors: 4
Hot Spot for Advancement for Women/Minorities: Y

Sales, profits and employees may be estimates. Financial information, benefits and other data can change quickly and may vary from those stated here.

Dana Incorporated

www.dana.com

NAIC Code: 336300

TYPES OF BUSINESS:
Automotive Products, Motors & Parts Manufacturing
Engine Systems
Fluid Systems
Heavy Vehicle Technologies
Brake Components
Chassis & Drive Train Components
Filtration Products
Financial Services

BRANDS/DIVISIONS/AFFILIATES:
TM4 Inc

CONTACTS: Note: Officers with more than one job title may be intentionally listed here more than once.
Jonathan Collins, CFO
Keith Wandell, Chairman of the Board
James Kellett, Chief Accounting Officer
James Kamsickas, Director
Mark Wallace, Executive VP
Aziz Aghili, Executive VP
Douglas Liedberg, General Counsel
Robert Pyle, President, Divisional
Dwayne Matthews, President, Divisional

GROWTH PLANS/SPECIAL FEATURES:
Dana Incorporated supplies high technology driveline, sealing, thermal management and fluid-power products for global vehicle manufacturers. The company operates 135 facilities in 33 countries. Dana divides its operations into four segments: light vehicle, commercial vehicle, off-highway and power technologies. The light vehicle segment manufactures axles, driveshafts differentials, torque couplings, modular assemblies, drive units, power transfer units and electric vehicle (EV) gearboxes for the light vehicle market. The commercial vehicle segment manufactures parts for the medium/heavy duty vehicle market, including medium duty trucks, heavy duty trucks, buses and specialty vehicles. Products include axles, driveshafts and tire inflation systems. The off-highway segment manufactures axels, driveshafts, transmissions, torque converters, industrial gear boxes, tire inflation systems, hydraulic valves/pumps/motors and electronic controls for off-highway use such as construction, earth moving, agriculture, mining, forestry, rail and material handling. Last, the power technologies segment manufactures parts for the light vehicle, medium/heavy vehicle and off-highway markets. Products include gaskets, cover modules, heat shields, engine sealing systems, cooling and heat transfer products. Major customers of the company include: Ford Motor Company; Toyota Motor Company; General Motors Company; PACCAR, Inc.; Daimler AG; Deere & Company, Manitou Group; Cummins, Inc.; and Volkswagen AG, among others. During 2018, Dana acquired a 55% ownership interest TM4, Inc., which designs and manufactures motors, power inverters and control systems for electric vehicles. In March 2019, it acquired Oerlikon Group's drive systems segment.

FINANCIAL DATA: Note: Data for latest year may not have been available at press time.

In U.S. $	2018	2017	2016	2015	2014	2013
Revenue	8,143,000,000	7,209,000,000	5,826,000,000	6,060,000,000	6,617,000,000	6,769,000,000
R&D Expense						
Operating Income	662,000,000	547,000,000	448,000,000	451,000,000	456,000,000	452,000,000
Operating Margin %		.08%	.08%	.07%	.07%	.07%
SGA Expense	499,000,000	511,000,000	396,000,000	387,000,000	451,000,000	397,000,000
Net Income	427,000,000	111,000,000	640,000,000	159,000,000	319,000,000	244,000,000
Operating Cash Flow	568,000,000	554,000,000	384,000,000	406,000,000	510,000,000	577,000,000
Capital Expenditure	325,000,000	393,000,000	322,000,000	260,000,000	234,000,000	209,000,000
EBITDA	860,000,000	715,000,000	510,000,000	579,000,000	591,000,000	729,000,000
Return on Assets %		.02%	.14%	.03%	.06%	.00%
Return on Equity %		.10%	.68%	.18%	.31%	-.01%
Debt to Equity		1.736	1.379	2.133	1.494	1.672

CONTACT INFORMATION:
Phone: 419 887-3000 Fax: 419 535-4643
Toll-Free: 800-537-8823
Address: 3939 Technology Dr., Maumee, OH 43537 United States

STOCK TICKER/OTHER:
Stock Ticker: DAN Exchange: NYS
Employees: 24,900 Fiscal Year Ends: 12/31
Parent Company:

SALARIES/BONUSES:
Top Exec. Salary: $1,146,950 Bonus: $
Second Exec. Salary: $605,000 Bonus: $

OTHER THOUGHTS:
Estimated Female Officers or Directors:
Hot Spot for Advancement for Women/Minorities: Y

Sales, profits and employees may be estimates. Financial information, benefits and other data can change quickly and may vary from those stated here.

Darden Restaurants Inc

www.darden.com

NAIC Code: 722513

TYPES OF BUSINESS:
Limited-Service Restaurants

BRANDS/DIVISIONS/AFFILIATES:
Olive Garden
LongHorn Steakhouse
Cheddar's Scratch Kitchen
Capital Grille (The)
Bahama Breeze
Eddie V's
Yard House
Seasons 52

CONTACTS:
Note: Officers with more than one job title may be intentionally listed here more than once.

Eugene Lee, CEO
Ricardo Cardenas, CFO
Charles Sonsteby, Chairman of the Board
John Madonna, Chief Accounting Officer
David George, Executive VP
Matthew Broad, General Counsel
Sarah King, Other Executive Officer
Richard Renninger, Other Executive Officer
Douglas Milanes, Other Executive Officer
Todd Burrowes, President, Divisional
Daniel Kiernan, President, Subsidiary

GROWTH PLANS/SPECIAL FEATURES:

Darden Restaurants, Inc. is a leading publicly-held casual dining company in the U.S. It owns and operates more than 1,700 restaurants throughout the U.S. and Canada. Darden operates eight restaurant chains: Olive Garden, LongHorn Steakhouse, Cheddar's Scratch Kitchen, The Capital Grille, Bahama Breeze, Eddie V's, Yard House and Seasons 52 (as of November 2018). The company served nearly 390 million meals in 2018. Olive Garden, with 858 restaurants, is a casual dining Italian restaurant in the U.S. and Canada. Its menu includes a variety of Italian foods, including antipasti; soups, salad and garlic breadsticks; baked pastas; sauteed chicken, seafood and vegetables; grilled meats; and a variety of desserts. It also offers imported Italian wines, coffee and espresso. LongHorn Steakhouse restaurants, with 510 locations, are full-service establishments serving both lunch and dinner with American West-themed decor. Cheddar's Scratch Kitchen, with 158 locations, is a casual dining restaurant located primarily in Texas. The Capital Grille is a chain of upscale full-service restaurants that dry-ages its steaks on the premises and flies in fresh seafood daily to its 58 locations as well as featuring a 350-selection wine list. The firm's 41 Bahama Breeze locations offer guests an island dining experience with a menu featuring Caribbean-style beef, chicken and seafood. Eddie V's is a steak and seafood restaurant with 20 locations. Yard House is a casual American-style restaurant with more than 100 taps of draft beers with 75 locations. Seasons 52, with 42 restaurants, is a fresh grill and wine bar with seasonally inspired menus, offering nutritionally balanced meals lower in calories than comparable restaurant meals. Additionally, the firm has restaurants operated by independent third parties.

FINANCIAL DATA:
Note: Data for latest year may not have been available at press time.

In U.S. $	2018	2017	2016	2015	2014	2013
Revenue	8,080,100,000	7,170,200,000	6,933,500,000	6,764,000,000	6,285,600,000	
R&D Expense						
Operating Income	770,200,000	669,100,000	628,000,000	429,700,000	327,200,000	
Operating Margin %		.09%	.09%	.06%	.05%	
SGA Expense	662,100,000	627,400,000	622,900,000	673,500,000	663,500,000	
Net Income	596,000,000	479,100,000	375,000,000	709,500,000	286,200,000	
Operating Cash Flow	1,001,300,000	899,900,000	778,000,000	471,000,000	410,900,000	
Capital Expenditure	418,800,000	318,300,000	251,600,000	296,500,000	414,800,000	
EBITDA	1,080,700,000	951,700,000	913,500,000	687,500,000	613,900,000	
Return on Assets %		.09%	.07%	.11%	.04%	
Return on Equity %		.24%	.18%	.32%	.14%	
Debt to Equity		0.446	0.225	0.622	1.175	

CONTACT INFORMATION:
Phone: 407 245-4000
Fax: 407 245-4989
Toll-Free:
Address: 1000 Darden Ctr. Dr., Orlando, FL 32837 United States

STOCK TICKER/OTHER:
Stock Ticker: DRI
Employees: 180,000
Parent Company:

Exchange: NYS
Fiscal Year Ends: 05/31

SALARIES/BONUSES:
Top Exec. Salary: $1,000,000   Bonus: $
Second Exec. Salary: $695,673   Bonus: $

OTHER THOUGHTS:
Estimated Female Officers or Directors: 7
Hot Spot for Advancement for Women/Minorities: Y

Sales, profits and employees may be estimates. Financial information, benefits and other data can change quickly and may vary from those stated here.

DaVita Healthcare Partners Inc

NAIC Code: 621492

www.davita.com

TYPES OF BUSINESS:
Renal Care Services
Clinical Research

BRANDS/DIVISIONS/AFFILIATES:

CONTACTS: *Note: Officers with more than one job title may be intentionally listed here more than once.*
Javier Rodriguez, CEO
Joel Ackerman, CFO
Kent Thiry, Chairman of the Board
James Hilger, Chief Accounting Officer
James Hearty, Chief Compliance Officer
Kathleen Waters, Chief Legal Officer
Leanne Zumwalt, Vice President, Divisional

GROWTH PLANS/SPECIAL FEATURES:
DaVita, Inc. is a leading provider of dialysis services in the U.S. for patients suffering from chronic kidney failure, also known as end stage renal disease (ESRD). The company operates through a network of 2,664 outpatient dialysis centers located in 46 states and Washington, D.C., serving approximately 202,700 patients. The firm also provides acute inpatient dialysis services in approximately 900 hospitals and related laboratory services. The loss of kidney function is normally irreversible, and kidney failure is typically caused by Type 1 and 2 diabetes, high blood pressure, polycystic kidney disease, long-term autoimmune attack on the kidney and prolonged urinary tract obstruction. ESRD is the stage of advanced kidney impairment that requires continued dialysis treatment or a kidney transplant to sustain life. Dialysis removes toxins, fluids and salt from the blood of patients via artificial means, and patients generally require dialysis at least three times a week for the rest of their lives. In June 2019, DaVita sold its medical group division (DMG) to Collaborative Care Holdings, LLC (Optum). DMG is a patient- and physician-focused integrated healthcare delivery and management company that provides coordinated, outcomes-based medical care in a cost-effective manner.

The firm offers employees medical, dental and vision insurance; short- and long-term disability insurance; life insurance; a 401(k) plan; tuition reimbursement; flexible spending accounts; and an employee assistance program.

FINANCIAL DATA: *Note: Data for latest year may not have been available at press time.*

In U.S. $	2018	2017	2016	2015	2014	2013
Revenue	11,404,850,000	10,876,630,000	14,745,110,000	13,781,840,000	12,795,110,000	11,764,050,000
R&D Expense						
Operating Income	1,490,149,000	1,619,725,000	1,773,742,000	1,362,604,000	1,791,907,000	1,458,599,000
Operating Margin %		.15%	.12%	.10%	.14%	.13%
SGA Expense	1,135,454,000	1,064,026,000	1,592,698,000	1,452,135,000	1,261,506,000	1,176,485,000
Net Income	159,394,000	663,618,000	879,874,000	269,732,000	723,114,000	633,446,000
Operating Cash Flow	1,771,640,000	1,907,449,000	1,963,444,000	1,557,200,000	1,459,407,000	1,773,341,000
Capital Expenditure	987,138,000	905,250,000	829,095,000	707,998,000	642,348,000	617,597,000
EBITDA	2,126,948,000	2,607,905,000	2,623,529,000	1,769,540,000	2,310,902,000	2,083,658,000
Return on Assets %		.04%	.05%	.01%	.04%	.04%
Return on Equity %		.14%	.18%	.05%	.15%	.15%
Debt to Equity		1.953	1.925	1.848	1.621	1.837

CONTACT INFORMATION:
Phone: 303 405-2100   Fax: 310 792-8928
Toll-Free:
Address: 2000 16th St., Denver, CO 80202 United States

SALARIES/BONUSES:
Top Exec. Salary: $1,300,000   Bonus: $
Second Exec. Salary: $900,000   Bonus: $

STOCK TICKER/OTHER:
Stock Ticker: DVA   Exchange: NYS
Employees: 41,000   Fiscal Year Ends: 12/31
Parent Company:

OTHER THOUGHTS:
Estimated Female Officers or Directors: 3
Hot Spot for Advancement for Women/Minorities: Y

Deere & Company (John Deere)

NAIC Code: 333111

www.deere.com

TYPES OF BUSINESS:
Construction & Agricultural Equipment
Commercial & Consumer Equipment
Forestry Equipment
Financing

BRANDS/DIVISIONS/AFFILIATES:
John Deere

CONTACTS:
Note: Officers with more than one job title may be intentionally listed here more than once.

Samuel Allen, CEO
Ryan Campbell, CFO
Marc Howze, Chief Administrative Officer
Rajesh Kalathur, Chief Information Officer
John May, COO
James Field, President, Divisional
Markwart Pentz, President, Divisional
Cory Reed, President, Divisional
Mary Jones, Senior VP

GROWTH PLANS/SPECIAL FEATURES:
Deere & Company is known for its John Deere brand name. The firm conducts business in three divisions: agriculture and turf; construction and forestry; and financial services. The agriculture and turf segment manufactures and distributes farm, lawn and garden equipment including tractors; combines; harvesters; tillage, seeding and soil preparation machinery; sprayers; hay and forage equipment; material handling equipment; integrated agricultural management systems technology; mowers; golf course equipment; utility tractors; landscape and irrigation equipment; and other outdoor power products. The construction and forestry division offers equipment and service parts used in construction, earthmoving, material handling and timber harvesting, including backhoe loaders, crawler dozers and loaders, four-wheel-drive loaders, excavators and more. The financial services segment primarily finances sales and leases by John Deere dealers of new and used agriculture and turf equipment and construction and forestry equipment. In addition, the segment provides wholesale financing to dealers of the foregoing equipment, finances retail revolving charge accounts and operating loans, and offers crop risk mitigation products and extended equipment warranties. Sales are generally conducted through nearly 2,000 dealer locations (largely independently-owned and operated), 1,539 of which sell agricultural equipment and about 430 of which sell construction, earthmoving, material handling and/or forestry equipment.

FINANCIAL DATA:
Note: Data for latest year may not have been available at press time.

In U.S. $	2018	2017	2016	2015	2014	2013
Revenue	37,021,300,000	29,115,600,000	26,363,500,000	28,609,300,000	35,815,700,000	37,621,000,000
R&D Expense	1,657,600,000	1,367,700,000	1,389,100,000	1,425,100,000	1,452,000,000	1,477,300,000
Operating Income	4,056,400,000	2,761,300,000	2,208,100,000	2,754,700,000	4,780,500,000	5,467,600,000
Operating Margin %		.13%	.11%	.12%	.15%	.17%
SGA Expense	3,630,500,000	3,253,600,000	2,951,700,000	3,056,500,000	3,608,400,000	3,809,500,000
Net Income	2,368,400,000	2,159,100,000	1,523,900,000	1,940,000,000	3,161,700,000	3,537,300,000
Operating Cash Flow	1,820,300,000	2,199,800,000	3,764,300,000	3,740,300,000	3,525,900,000	3,254,300,000
Capital Expenditure	2,950,100,000	2,592,300,000	2,955,100,000	2,826,100,000	2,659,300,000	2,375,300,000
EBITDA	5,983,500,000	4,476,800,000	3,767,900,000	4,137,100,000	6,087,000,000	6,607,900,000
Return on Assets %		.03%	.03%	.03%	.05%	.06%
Return on Equity %		.27%	.23%	.25%	.33%	.41%
Debt to Equity		2.709	3.644	3.534	2.69	2.102

CONTACT INFORMATION:
Phone: 309 765-8000   Fax: 309 765-9929
Toll-Free:
Address: 1 John Deere Plaza, Moline, IL 61265 United States

SALARIES/BONUSES:
Top Exec. Salary: $1,500,000   Bonus: $
Second Exec. Salary: $724,217   Bonus: $

STOCK TICKER/OTHER:
Stock Ticker: DE
Employees: 56,800
Parent Company:

Exchange: NYS
Fiscal Year Ends: 10/31

OTHER THOUGHTS:
Estimated Female Officers or Directors: 7
Hot Spot for Advancement for Women/Minorities: Y

Dell EMC

NAIC Code: 334112

www.dellemc.com/en-us/index.htm

TYPES OF BUSINESS:
Networked Computer Storage Systems
Virtual Server Software
Management Protection Software
Consulting Services
Storage Management Services

BRANDS/DIVISIONS/AFFILIATES:
Dell Technologies Inc

GROWTH PLANS/SPECIAL FEATURES:
Dell EMC provides the essential infrastructure for organizations to build their digital future, transform information technology (IT) and protect information assets. The company enables enterprise customers' digital and IT transformation through the hybrid cloud and big data solutions built on a data center infrastructure that incorporates industry-leading converged infrastructure, servers, storage and cybersecurity technologies. Dell EMC works with organizations around the globe, in every industry, in both the public and private sectors, and of every size, including startups and Fortune Global 500 entities. The company services customers across 180 countries. Dell EMC operates as a subsidiary of Dell Technologies, Inc.

CONTACTS: Note: Officers with more than one job title may be intentionally listed here more than once.

Michael Dell, CEO
Bill Scannell, Pres., Global Enterprise Sales & Customer Oper.
Robert Mee, CEO, Divisional
Howard Elias, COO, Divisional
Erin McSweeney, Executive VP, Divisional
Paul Dacier, Executive VP
Harry You, Executive VP
Jeremy Burton, President, Divisional
Amit Yoran, President, Divisional
William Scannell, President, Divisional
William Teuber, Vice Chairman
Michael Dell, Chmn.

FINANCIAL DATA: Note: Data for latest year may not have been available at press time.

In U.S. $	2018	2017	2016	2015	2014	2013
Revenue	28,000,000,000	27,500,000,000	25,000,000,000	24,704,000,000	24,440,000,512	23,221,999,616
R&D Expense						
Operating Income						
Operating Margin %						
SGA Expense						
Net Income			-2,100,000,000	1,990,000,000	2,713,999,872	2,888,999,936
Operating Cash Flow						
Capital Expenditure						
EBITDA						
Return on Assets %						
Return on Equity %						
Debt to Equity						

CONTACT INFORMATION:
Phone: 508 435-1000 Fax: 508 435-5222
Toll-Free:
Address: 176 South St., Hopkinton, MA 01748 United States

SALARIES/BONUSES:
Top Exec. Salary: $ Bonus: $
Second Exec. Salary: $ Bonus: $

STOCK TICKER/OTHER:
Stock Ticker: Subsidiary Exchange:
Employees: 72,000 Fiscal Year Ends: 02/28
Parent Company: Dell Technologies Inc

OTHER THOUGHTS:
Estimated Female Officers or Directors: 2
Hot Spot for Advancement for Women/Minorities: Y

Dell Technologies Inc

NAIC Code: 334111

www.delltechnologies.com/en-us/index.htm

TYPES OF BUSINESS:
Computer Manufacturing
Direct Sales
Technical & Support Services
Online Music Service
Web Hosting Services
Printers & Accessories
Personal Music Players
Storage Devices

BRANDS/DIVISIONS/AFFILIATES:
Dell
Dell EMC
Pivotal
RSA
Secureworks
VirtuStream
Vmware

CONTACTS:
Note: Officers with more than one job title may be intentionally listed here more than once.

Michael Dell, CEO
Thomas Sweet, CFO
Maya McReynolds, Chief Accounting Officer
Allison Dew, Chief Marketing Officer
Allison Dew, Chief Marketing Officer
Rory Read, COO, Subsidiary
Richard Rothberg, General Counsel
Karen Quintos, Other Executive Officer
Steven Price, Other Executive Officer
Marius Haas, Other Executive Officer
Howard Elias, President, Divisional
William Scannell, President, Subsidiary
Jeffrey Clarke, Vice President, Divisional

GROWTH PLANS/SPECIAL FEATURES:

Dell Technologies, Inc. is a multinational information technology corporation. The firm provides transformational devices, processes and services in order to modernize data centers, drive progress and help clients thrive within the digital era. Dell organizes its products and services into the following business units: Client Solutions Group (CSG), Infrastructure Solutions Group (ISG) and VMware. Offerings by CSG include branded hardware, such as personal computers (PCs), notebooks, and branded peripherals, such as monitors and projectors, as well as third-party software and peripherals. CSG hardware and services also provide the architecture to enable the Internet of Things and connected ecosystems to securely and efficiently capture massive amounts of data for analytics and actionable insights for commercial customers. CSG also offers attached software, peripherals, and services, including support and deployment, configuration, and extended warranty services. Services and products offered by the ISG includes traditional storage solutions as well as next-generation storage solutions of Dell EMC; high-performance rack, blade, tower, and hyperscale servers; and networking products that help business customers transform and modernize their infrastructure, mobilize and enrich end-user experiences, and accelerate business applications and processes. ISG also includes the cloud software and infrastructure-as-a-service solutions of Virtustream. The VMware reportable segment reflects the operations of VMware, Inc. within Dell Technologies. VMware provides compute, cloud, mobility, networking and security infrastructure software to businesses that provides a flexible digital foundation for the applications that empower businesses to serve their customers globally. Brands by Dell Technologies include Dell, Dell EMC, Pivotal, RSA, Secureworks, VirtuStream and VMware.

Dell offers employees medical, dental, vision, life, disability, auto and home insurance; 401(k); and discounts and various assistance programs.

FINANCIAL DATA:
Note: Data for latest year may not have been available at press time.

In U.S. $	2018	2017	2016	2015	2014	2013
Revenue	78,660,000,000	61,642,000,000	50,911,000,000	54,142,000,000		
R&D Expense	4,384,000,000	2,636,000,000	1,051,000,000	920,000,000		
Operating Income	-3,333,000,000	-3,252,000,000	-514,000,000	-316,000,000		
Operating Margin %						
SGA Expense	19,003,000,000	13,575,000,000	7,850,000,000	8,292,000,000		
Net Income	-3,728,000,000	-1,672,000,000	-1,104,000,000	-1,221,000,000		
Operating Cash Flow	6,810,000,000	2,222,000,000	2,162,000,000	2,551,000,000		
Capital Expenditure	1,581,000,000	906,000,000	482,000,000	478,000,000		
EBITDA	5,352,000,000	1,333,000,000	2,266,000,000	2,569,000,000		
Return on Assets %						
Return on Equity %						
Debt to Equity						

CONTACT INFORMATION:
Phone: 512 338-4400 Fax: 512 283-6161
Toll-Free: 800-289-3355
Address: One Dell Way, Round Rock, TX 78682 United States

STOCK TICKER/OTHER:
Stock Ticker: DELL
Employees: 145,000
Parent Company:

Exchange: NYS
Fiscal Year Ends: 01/31

SALARIES/BONUSES:
Top Exec. Salary: $725,000 Bonus: $4,666,667
Second Exec. Salary: $851,160 Bonus: $4,000,000

OTHER THOUGHTS:
Estimated Female Officers or Directors: 1
Hot Spot for Advancement for Women/Minorities: Y

Deloitte LLP

NAIC Code: 541211

www2.deloitte.com/us/en.html

TYPES OF BUSINESS:
Accounting Services
Management Consulting
Risk Management Services
Financial Advisory Services
Outsourcing Services
Legal & Compliance Advisory Services
Consulting Services

BRANDS/DIVISIONS/AFFILIATES:
Deloitte Touche Tohmatsu Lmited
Deloitte Consulting

CONTACTS:
Note: Officers with more than one job title may be intentionally listed here more than once.
Cathy Engelbert, CEO
Mike Fucci, Chmn.

GROWTH PLANS/SPECIAL FEATURES:

Deloitte, LLP, the U.S. division of global accounting firm Deloitte Touche Tohmatsu Limited, offers a variety of financial and consulting services. The company divides its services into eight groups: tax, consulting, audit & assurance, private company services, mergers & acquisitions, risk and financial advisory, analytics and cloud. The tax division offers global business tax, global employer tax and multi-state tax services, as well as tax-related operations transformation. The consulting division helps address its client's most challenging issues by providing strategic, financial, operational, human capital and IT services. The audit & assurance division provides independent financial statement and internal control audits, in accordance with the latest professional standards. This division's accounting and reporting advisory services can help organizations navigate financial and non-financial reporting challenges. Services for private companies provide consulting services in relation to investing in emerging technologies, expanding global markets, navigating tax reform and restyling the workforce. The mergers & acquisitions division provides value-added services ranging from strategy and execution through integration and divestiture. The risk and financial advisory division helps organizations navigate a variety of risks and opportunities, including assurance, internal audit, cyber risk, financial risk, transactions, restructuring, forensic, regulatory risk, operations risk and risk intelligence. The analytics division translates the science of analytics and artificial intelligence (AI) into reality for its business customers, helping them to harness the power of analytics and AI for identifying advantages to move faster, improve decision making and creating beneficial connections with customers. Last, the cloud division offers cloud strategy and readiness, software-as-a-service (SaaS) implementation, custom implementation, cloud migration, cloud enablement and managed services. Deloitte serves many industries within segments such as consumer, energy, resources, industrial, financial services, government, public services, life sciences, healthcare, technology, media and telecommunications.

Deloitte offers comprehensive health benefits and various employee assistance programs.

FINANCIAL DATA:
Note: Data for latest year may not have been available at press time.

In U.S. $	2018	2017	2016	2015	2014	2013
Revenue	19,897,000,000	18,551,000,000	17,518,000,000	16,147,000,000	14,910,000,000	13,894,000,000
R&D Expense						
Operating Income						
Operating Margin %						
SGA Expense						
Net Income						
Operating Cash Flow						
Capital Expenditure						
EBITDA						
Return on Assets %						
Return on Equity %						
Debt to Equity						

CONTACT INFORMATION:
Phone: 212-492-4000　　Fax: 212-489-1687
Toll-Free:
Address: 30 Rockefeller Plz., Fl. 41, New York, NY 10112-0015 United States

STOCK TICKER/OTHER:
Stock Ticker: Subsidiary　　Exchange:
Employees: 94,637　　Fiscal Year Ends: 05/31
Parent Company: Deloitte Touche Tohmatsu Limited

SALARIES/BONUSES:
Top Exec. Salary: $　　Bonus: $
Second Exec. Salary: $　　Bonus: $

OTHER THOUGHTS:
Estimated Female Officers or Directors: 18
Hot Spot for Advancement for Women/Minorities: Y

Sales, profits and employees may be estimates. Financial information, benefits and other data can change quickly and may vary from those stated here.

Delta Air Lines Inc

www.delta.com

NAIC Code: 481111

TYPES OF BUSINESS:
Airline
Air Freight

BRANDS/DIVISIONS/AFFILIATES:

GROWTH PLANS/SPECIAL FEATURES:
Delta Air Lines, Inc. is a major air carrier that provides scheduled air passenger and freight transportation both domestically and internationally. From its primary hubs (Atlanta, Boston, Detroit, Los Angeles, Minneapolis/St. Paul, New York-JFK, New York-LaGuardia, Salt Lake City and Seattle/Tacoma), the company serves 325 destinations in 52 countries on six continents. Delta has a total 918 aircraft (as of July 2019) manufactured by Airbus, Boeing and McDonnell Douglas. The airline is a founding member of the SkyTeam international alliance, a global airline alliance that provides customers with 1,075 worldwide destinations, flights and services. Delta and its alliance partners operate more than 15,000 flights per day, as of June 2019. Delta also has joint ventures with the following airlines: Air France-KLM/Alitalia, Virgin Atlantic, Aeromexico, WestJet, Virgin Australia and Korean Air.

Delta offers its employees medical, dental, vision and life insurance; flexible spending accounts; a 401(k) plan; profit sharing; credit union membership; employee assistance programs; adoption assistance, paid holiday and vacation; and free and reduced rate travel benefits for employees and their close family members.

CONTACTS: Note: Officers with more than one job title may be intentionally listed here more than once.
Paul Jacobson, CFO
Rahul Samant, Chief Information Officer
Peter Carter, Chief Legal Officer
William Carroll, Controller
Edward Bastian, Director
Francis Blake, Director
David Dewalt, Director
William Lentsch, Executive VP, Divisional
Steven Sear, Executive VP, Divisional
Joanne Smith, Executive VP
Glen Hauenstein, President
Wayne West, Senior Executive VP
Craig Meynard, Vice President

FINANCIAL DATA: Note: Data for latest year may not have been available at press time.

In U.S. $	2018	2017	2016	2015	2014	2013
Revenue	44,438,000,000	41,244,000,000	39,639,000,000	40,704,000,000	40,362,000,000	37,773,000,000
R&D Expense						
Operating Income	5,264,000,000	6,114,000,000	6,952,000,000	7,837,000,000	2,922,000,000	3,802,000,000
Operating Margin %		.15%	.18%	.19%	.07%	.10%
SGA Expense	1,941,000,000	1,787,000,000	1,710,000,000	1,672,000,000	1,700,000,000	1,603,000,000
Net Income	3,935,000,000	3,577,000,000	4,373,000,000	4,526,000,000	659,000,000	10,540,000,000
Operating Cash Flow	7,014,000,000	5,148,000,000	7,205,000,000	7,927,000,000	4,947,000,000	4,504,000,000
Capital Expenditure	5,168,000,000	3,891,000,000	3,391,000,000	2,945,000,000	2,249,000,000	2,568,000,000
EBITDA	7,791,000,000	8,332,000,000	8,926,000,000	9,473,000,000	3,493,000,000	5,037,000,000
Return on Assets %		.07%	.08%	.08%	.01%	.22%
Return on Equity %		.27%	.38%	.46%	.06%	2.22%
Debt to Equity		0.474	0.505	0.624	0.971	0.841

CONTACT INFORMATION:
Phone: 404 715-2600
Fax: 404 715-1400
Toll-Free: 866-715-2170
Address: PO Box 20706, Atlanta, GA 30320-6001 United States

SALARIES/BONUSES:
Top Exec. Salary: $891,667   Bonus: $
Second Exec. Salary: $693,750   Bonus: $

STOCK TICKER/OTHER:
Stock Ticker: DAL
Employees: 89,000
Parent Company:
Exchange: NYS
Fiscal Year Ends: 12/31

OTHER THOUGHTS:
Estimated Female Officers or Directors: 2
Hot Spot for Advancement for Women/Minorities: Y

Dentsply Sirona Inc

NAIC Code: 339100

www.dentsplysirona.com/en-us

TYPES OF BUSINESS:
Dental Device Manufacturing

BRANDS/DIVISIONS/AFFILIATES:
Dentsply Sirona Charlotte Academy

CONTACTS:
Note: Officers with more than one job title may be intentionally listed here more than once.

Nick Alexos, CFO
Donald Casey, Director
Eric Brandt, Director
Keith Ebling, Executive VP
Walter Petersohn, Other Executive Officer
Daniel Key, Other Executive Officer
Maureen MacInnis, Other Executive Officer
Markus Boehringer, Senior VP, Divisional
William Newell, Senior VP, Divisional
Henning Mueller, Vice President, Divisional

GROWTH PLANS/SPECIAL FEATURES:

Dentsply Sirona, Inc. is a world-leading manufacturer of professional dental products and technologies. With a 134-year history (from 1886 through 2020) of innovation and service to the dental industry and to patients worldwide, the firm's products and solutions include dental and oral health products as well as other consumable medical devices under a strong portfolio of renowned brands. Dentsply's products provide innovative, high-quality and effective solutions for the purpose of advancing patient care and for delivering better, safer and faster dentistry. The company's primary products consist of: dental technology and equipment, including imaging equipment, computer aided design and machining (CAD/CAM) systems, dental implants, scanning equipment, treatment software, orthodontic appliances and a variety of dental restoration products; dental consumables, including endodontic (root canal) instruments and materials, dental anesthetics, prophylaxis paste, dental sealants, impression materials, restorative materials, tooth whiteners, topical fluoride, dental handpieces, intraoral curing light systems, dental diagnostic systems and ultrasonic scalers and polishers; and healthcare consumables, including urology catheters, surgical products, medical drills and other non-medical products. Dentsply Sirona's global headquarters are based in Charlotte, North Carolina. Approximately two-thirds of the company's sales are derived from regions outside the U.S. During 2019, the firm relocated its global headquarters from Pennsylvania to North Carolina to build on Dentsply Sirona's reorganization plan to centralize its sales and service infrastructure in Charlotte, and to enhance its clinical education capabilities and functionality at the Dentsply Sirona Charlotte Academy.

FINANCIAL DATA:
Note: Data for latest year may not have been available at press time.

In U.S. $	2018	2017	2016	2015	2014	2013
Revenue	3,986,300,000	3,993,400,000	3,745,300,000	2,674,300,000	2,922,620,000	2,950,770,000
R&D Expense						
Operating Income	348,700,000	513,800,000	477,900,000	439,900,000	456,683,000	432,522,000
Operating Margin %		.13%	.13%	.16%	.16%	.15%
SGA Expense	1,719,100,000	1,674,700,000	1,523,000,000	1,077,300,000	1,143,106,000	1,144,890,000
Net Income	-1,011,000,000	-1,550,000,000	429,900,000	251,200,000	322,854,000	313,192,000
Operating Cash Flow	499,800,000	601,900,000	563,400,000	497,400,000	560,401,000	417,846,000
Capital Expenditure	188,000,000	151,000,000	126,100,000	72,000,000	105,767,000	101,421,000
EBITDA	-590,300,000	-1,248,800,000	748,500,000	508,500,000	580,360,000	546,863,000
Return on Assets %		-.14%	.05%	.06%	.07%	.06%
Return on Equity %		-.21%	.08%	.11%	.13%	.13%
Debt to Equity		0.244	0.186	0.488	0.497	0.46

CONTACT INFORMATION:
Phone: 844-546-3722 Fax:
Toll-Free: 800-877-0020
Address: 13320 Ballantyne Corporate Pl., Charlotte, NC 28277-3607 United States

STOCK TICKER/OTHER:
Stock Ticker: XRAY
Employees: 15,700
Parent Company:

Exchange: NAS
Fiscal Year Ends: 09/30

SALARIES/BONUSES:
Top Exec. Salary: $818,562 Bonus: $500,000
Second Exec. Salary: $512,618 Bonus: $237,563

OTHER THOUGHTS:
Estimated Female Officers or Directors: 1
Hot Spot for Advancement for Women/Minorities:

Sales, profits and employees may be estimates. Financial information, benefits and other data can change quickly and may vary from those stated here.

Diodes Inc

NAIC Code: 334413

www.diodes.com

TYPES OF BUSINESS:
Semiconductor Manufacturing
Semiconductor Design
Semiconductor Marketing

BRANDS/DIVISIONS/AFFILIATES:
Diodes FabTech Inc
Shanghai Kaihong Technology Electronic Co Ltd
Diodes Hong Kong Holding Company Limited

CONTACTS: Note: Officers with more than one job title may be intentionally listed here more than once.
Keh-Shew Lu, CEO
Brett Whitmire, CFO
Raymond Soong, Chairman of the Board
Richard White, Secretary
C.H. Chen, Vice Chairman of the Board
Francis Tang, Vice President, Divisional
Emily Yang, Vice President, Divisional
Evan Yu, Vice President, Divisional
Julie Holland, Vice President, Divisional

GROWTH PLANS/SPECIAL FEATURES:
Diodes, Inc. designs, manufactures and markets discrete and analogue semiconductor products. The semiconductors are found in a variety of end-user products in the consumer electronics, computing, industrial, communications and automotive sectors. Diodes' product line includes more than 25,000 offerings such as diodes, rectifiers, transistors, metal oxide semiconductor field-effect transistors (MOSFETs), protection devices and functional specific arrays. The company also produces amplifiers and comparators, Hall effect and temperature sensors, power management devices (including light emitting diode drivers), DC-DC switching and linear voltage regulators, voltage references, special function devices (including USB power switch, load switch, voltage supervisor and motor controllers) and silicon wafers used to manufacture these products. Corporate headquarters are located in Plano, Texas; Americas sales offices are located in Texas and California; design, marketing and engineering centers are located in the U.S., Taiwan, England and Germany; wafer fabrication facilities are located in England and China; and assembly and test facilities are located in Taiwan, China and Germany. The firm conducts a number of operations through its subsidiaries, including Diodes FabTech, Inc., which is responsible for wafer fabrication, research and development, engineering and sales; Shanghai Kaihong Technology Electronic Co. Ltd., which also handles packaging, assembly, testing, research and development and engineering; and Diodes Hong Kong Holding Company Limited, which contains a logistical center and handles sales and marketing. Diodes serves more than 375 direct customers worldwide, including original equipment manufacturers and electronic manufacturing services providers. The firm also has roughly 122 distributor customers around the world, through which it indirectly serves tens of thousands customers.

FINANCIAL DATA: Note: Data for latest year may not have been available at press time.

In U.S. $	2018	2017	2016	2015	2014	2013
Revenue	1,213,989,000	1,054,204,000	942,162,000	848,904,000	890,651,000	826,846,000
R&D Expense	86,286,000	77,877,000	69,937,000	57,027,000	52,136,000	48,302,000
Operating Income	155,078,000	92,708,000	38,056,000	43,715,000	83,528,000	49,350,000
Operating Margin %		.09%	.04%	.05%	.09%	.06%
SGA Expense	176,197,000	167,639,000	158,256,000	139,245,000	133,701,000	132,106,000
Net Income	104,021,000	-1,805,000	15,935,000	24,274,000	63,678,000	26,532,000
Operating Cash Flow	185,566,000	181,123,000	124,742,000	118,111,000	134,272,000	109,891,000
Capital Expenditure	87,507,000	111,161,000	58,549,000	133,244,000	57,766,000	47,054,000
EBITDA	264,507,000	171,720,000	137,257,000	124,927,000	167,095,000	117,772,000
Return on Assets %		.00%	.01%	.02%	.05%	.03%
Return on Equity %		.00%	.02%	.03%	.09%	.04%
Debt to Equity		0.298	0.532	0.573	0.183	0.26

CONTACT INFORMATION:
Phone: 972 987-3900 Fax: 972 731-3510
Toll-Free:
Address: 4949 Hedgcoxe Rd., Ste. 200, Plano, TX 75024 United States

STOCK TICKER/OTHER:
Stock Ticker: DIOD
Employees: 7,693
Parent Company:

Exchange: NAS
Fiscal Year Ends: 12/31

SALARIES/BONUSES:
Top Exec. Salary: $689,320 Bonus: $26,683
Second Exec. Salary: $418,515 Bonus: $16,200

OTHER THOUGHTS:
Estimated Female Officers or Directors: 1
Hot Spot for Advancement for Women/Minorities:

Sales, profits and employees may be estimates. Financial information, benefits and other data can change quickly and may vary from those stated here.

Discount Tire Company

NAIC Code: 441320

www.discounttire.com

TYPES OF BUSINESS:
Tire Stores
Mail-Order & Online Tire Sales
Roadside Assistance

BRANDS/DIVISIONS/AFFILIATES:
Discount Tire
America's Tire Co
Discount Tire Credit Card

CONTACTS: Note: Officers with more than one job title may be intentionally listed here more than once.
Michael Zuieback, CEO
Ed Kaminski, COO
Christian Roe, CFO

GROWTH PLANS/SPECIAL FEATURES:

Discount Tire Company, based in Arizona, is one of the largest independent tire dealers in the U.S. The firm operates over 1,035 stores in 35 states (as of July 2019). These stores primarily operate under the Discount Tire name, but also as America's Tire Co. in certain parts of California. Discount Tire carries leading tire brands such as BF Goodrich, Michelin, Goodyear, Pirelli and GT Radial as well as in-house exclusive brands Road Hugger, Arizonian, MB Wheels and Maxxim tires and wheels. Types of tires offered by the company are lawn/garden, ATV/UTV, trailer, temporary spares, winter, performance truck, ribbed, highway all-season, mud-terrain, all-terrain, all-purpose, track and competition, summer performance, all-season performance, grand touring and the standard all-season touring. The company also repairs tires, offers tire rotations and balancing and provides free air pressure checking to its customers. In addition, the firm sells and delivers tires through its mail-order/online division (Discount Tire direct), which provides fast free shipping to a customer's door as well as through its website. This website also provides extensive information for its customers on all aspects of wheel and tire care. The company offers a Discount Tire Credit Card, which can be applied for online and is underwritten by Synchrony Bank.

Discount Tires offers its employees benefits including flexible spending accounts; an employee assistance program; medical, vision, life and dental insurance; paid vacation; a 401(k) plan; and profit sharing plans. Part-time employees are eligible for medical insurance and a 401(k).

FINANCIAL DATA: Note: Data for latest year may not have been available at press time.

In U.S. $	2018	2017	2016	2015	2014	2013
Revenue	4,784,850,000	4,557,000,000	4,340,000,000	4,200,000,000	3,900,000,000	3,500,000,000
R&D Expense						
Operating Income						
Operating Margin %						
SGA Expense						
Net Income						
Operating Cash Flow						
Capital Expenditure						
EBITDA						
Return on Assets %						
Return on Equity %						
Debt to Equity						

CONTACT INFORMATION:
Phone: 480-606-6000 Fax: 480-951-8619
Toll-Free:
Address: 20225 N. Scottsdale Rd., Scottsdale, AZ 85254 United States

SALARIES/BONUSES:
Top Exec. Salary: $ Bonus: $
Second Exec. Salary: $ Bonus: $

STOCK TICKER/OTHER:
Stock Ticker: Private Exchange:
Employees: 18,635 Fiscal Year Ends: 12/31
Parent Company:

OTHER THOUGHTS:
Estimated Female Officers or Directors:
Hot Spot for Advancement for Women/Minorities:

Sales, profits and employees may be estimates. Financial information, benefits and other data can change quickly and may vary from those stated here.

Discovery Inc

NAIC Code: 515210

corporate.discovery.com

TYPES OF BUSINESS:
Cable TV Networks
Digital Media
Catalog & Online Sales
Educational Products
E-commerce
Merchandising

BRANDS/DIVISIONS/AFFILIATES:
Discovery Channel
TLC
Eurosport
Oprah Winfrey Network (OWN, The)
DMAX
Investigation Discovery
Velocity

CONTACTS: Note: Officers with more than one job title may be intentionally listed here more than once.
Peter Faricy, CEO, Divisional
Jean-Briac Perrette, CEO, Divisional
David Zaslav, CEO
Gunnar Wiedenfels, CFO
Robert Miron, Chairman of the Board
Lori Locke, Chief Accounting Officer
Kurt Wehner, Chief Accounting Officer
Bruce Campbell, Chief Legal Officer
Savalle Sims, Executive VP
Adria Romm, Other Corporate Officer
David Leavy, Other Executive Officer

GROWTH PLANS/SPECIAL FEATURES:

Discovery, Inc, formerly Discovery Communications, is a global media and entertainment company that produces and distributes original and purchased programming across multiple platforms to 3 billion cumulative subscribers. Discovery spans a variety of diverse genres, including exploration, survival, natural history, environment, technology, docu-series, health and wellness and space. The firm operates in four segments: U.S. networks, international networks, education and other. The U.S. networks segment operates and owns ten national TV networks: Discovery Channel, TLC, Animal Planet, Investigation Discovery, Science and Velocity. The division also includes the firm's interests in The Oprah Winfrey Network (OWN) and Discovery Family. The firm's international networks reach more than 220 countries and territories around the world and are distributed in over 50 languages. Networks include Discovery Channel, Animal Planet, Eurosport, Turbo, Real Time, DMAX and Discovery Kids. Education offers a suite of curriculum-based tools and educator enhancement resources that promote the integration of media and technology in the classroom. Other is largely comprised of production studios that develop television content for our networks and television service providers throughout the world. The company's portfolio also includes websites, retail, merchandising and various digital media products and services. In March 2018, Discovery announced it had acquired Scripps Networks Interactive, a lifestyle programming firm that specializes in comfort-food television.

FINANCIAL DATA: Note: Data for latest year may not have been available at press time.

In U.S. $	2018	2017	2016	2015	2014	2013
Revenue	10,553,000,000	6,873,000,000	6,497,000,000	6,394,000,000	6,265,000,000	5,535,000,000
R&D Expense						
Operating Income	2,600,000,000	2,119,000,000	2,053,000,000	2,052,000,000	2,120,000,000	1,995,000,000
Operating Margin %		.31%	.32%	.32%	.34%	.36%
SGA Expense	2,620,000,000	1,768,000,000	1,690,000,000	1,669,000,000	1,692,000,000	1,575,000,000
Net Income	614,000,000	-313,000,000	1,217,000,000	1,047,000,000	1,135,000,000	1,076,000,000
Operating Cash Flow	2,576,000,000	1,629,000,000	1,373,000,000	1,277,000,000	1,318,000,000	1,285,000,000
Capital Expenditure	147,000,000	135,000,000	88,000,000	103,000,000	120,000,000	115,000,000
EBITDA	6,437,000,000	2,578,000,000	4,119,000,000	3,928,000,000	3,961,000,000	3,508,000,000
Return on Assets %		-.02%	.08%	.06%	.07%	.08%
Return on Equity %		-.07%	.22%	.19%	.19%	.17%
Debt to Equity		3.201	1.518	1.398	1.08	1.046

CONTACT INFORMATION:
Phone: 240 662-2000　　Fax: 240 662-1868
Toll-Free:
Address: 1 Discovery Pl., Silver Spring, MD 20910 United States

STOCK TICKER/OTHER:
Stock Ticker: DISCA
Employees: 7,000
Parent Company:

Exchange: NAS
Fiscal Year Ends: 12/31

SALARIES/BONUSES:
Top Exec. Salary: $3,000,000　　Bonus: $
Second Exec. Salary: $1,769,088　　Bonus: $

OTHER THOUGHTS:
Estimated Female Officers or Directors: 1
Hot Spot for Advancement for Women/Minorities: Y

Disney Media Networks

thewaltdisneycompany.com/disney-companies/media-networks

NAIC Code: 515120

TYPES OF BUSINESS:
Broadcast TV
Cable Networks
Television Production
Online Television
Radio Broadcasting

BRANDS/DIVISIONS/AFFILIATES:
Walt Disney Company (The)
ABC Television Network
ABC Family Worldwide
ABC Owned Television Stations Group
A+E Networks
Disney XD
Hulu
ESPN Inc

CONTACTS:
Note: Officers with more than one job title may be intentionally listed here more than once.

Bob Iger, CEO
James Pitar, Pres.-ESPN
Vince Roberts, CTO
Peter DiCecco, Sr. VP-Bus. & Legal Affairs, Music
Vince Roberts, Exec. VP-Global Oper.
Albert Cheng, Exec. VP
Kevin Brockman, Exec. VP-Global Comm.
Ben Sherwood, Co-Pres., Disney
James Goldston, Pres., ABC News
Paul Lee, Pres., ABC Entertainment Group
Gary Marsh, Pres.

GROWTH PLANS/SPECIAL FEATURES:

The Disney Media Networks is a diverse media holding company that contains the company's various television networks, cable channels, associated production and distribution companies and owned/operated television stations. Disney Media is organized into two divisions: Disney-ABC Television Group and ESPN, Inc. The Disney-ABC Television Group division is comprised of the ABC Television Network, an American commercial broadcast television network which owns and operates eight television stations, as well as more than 244 affiliated television stations throughout the U.S. and Canada; ABC Family Worldwide, which is responsible for the operations of the U.S. cable network Freeform; ABC Owned Television Stations Group, which oversees the owned and operated stations of ABC; A+E Networks (a 50/50 joint venture), an American media company that owns a group of television channels available via cable and satellite in the U.S. and abroad; Disney Channels Worldwide, which operates various children and family television channels worldwide, including Disney Channel, Disney Junior, Disney XD and Radio Disney; and Hulu (30% owned), an American online company and partially ad-supported streaming service offering a variety of television shows, clips, movies and other media. ESPN is an American sports media conglomerate which owns various sports broadcasting operations, including cable channels, a sports radio network, an accompanying website and other assets. ESPN operates eight domestic channels and 19 international channels in 64 countries. Disney Media Networks is a subsidiary of The Walt Disney Company. In December 2018, Disney announced that it planned to launch the ACC Network, a sports channel dedicated to the Atlantic Coast Conference, under ESPN, Inc. in 2019.

FINANCIAL DATA:
Note: Data for latest year may not have been available at press time.

In U.S. $	2018	2017	2016	2015	2014	2013
Revenue	23,800,000,000	23,510,000,000	23,689,000,000	23,264,000,000	21,152,000,000	20,356,000,000
R&D Expense						
Operating Income						
Operating Margin %						
SGA Expense						
Net Income		6,902,000,000	7,755,000,000	7,793,000,000	7,321,000,000	6,818,000,000
Operating Cash Flow						
Capital Expenditure						
EBITDA						
Return on Assets %						
Return on Equity %						
Debt to Equity						

CONTACT INFORMATION:
Phone: 818-560-1000 Fax:
Toll-Free:
Address: 500 S. Buena Vista St., Burbank, CA 91521 United States

SALARIES/BONUSES:
Top Exec. Salary: $ Bonus: $
Second Exec. Salary: $ Bonus: $

STOCK TICKER/OTHER:
Stock Ticker: Subsidiary   Exchange:
Employees: 21,000   Fiscal Year Ends: 09/30
Parent Company: Walt Disney Company (The)

OTHER THOUGHTS:
Estimated Female Officers or Directors: 3
Hot Spot for Advancement for Women/Minorities: Y

Sales, profits and employees may be estimates. Financial information, benefits and other data can change quickly and may vary from those stated here.

Disney Parks, Experiences and Products (DPEP) dpep.disney.com

NAIC Code: 0

TYPES OF BUSINESS:
Computer Software, Electronic Games, Apps & Entertainment
Digital Content
Apps

BRANDS/DIVISIONS/AFFILIATES:
Walt Disney Company (The)
Disney Direct-to-consumer and International
Disney Consumer Products and Interactive Media

CONTACTS: Note: Officers with more than one job title may be intentionally listed here more than once.
Robert A. Chapek, Pres., Disney Consumer Products
Bob Chapek, Chmn.

GROWTH PLANS/SPECIAL FEATURES:

Disney Parks, Experiences and Products (DPEP) is a business segment and subsidiary of The Walt Disney Company, with operations comprising licensing operations, children's print publishing, games licensing and Disney retail and eCommerce platforms. DPEP's parks and resorts division encompasses Disneyland Resort, Walt Disney World Resort, Tokyo Disney Resort, Disneyland Paris, Hong Kong Disneyland, Shanghai Disney Resort, Disney Cruise Line, Disney Vacation Club, Aulani-A Disney Resort & Spa, Adventures by Disney and Walt Disney Engineering. DPEP's consumer products division creates innovative and engaging physical products and digital experiences across more than 100 categories, from toys and t-shirts to apps, books and console games. it is engaged in licensing Disney and related partnership products; publishing children's books and magazines through a licensing structure in 68 countries in more than 45 languages; creating and licensing interactive and gaming experiences across mobile and console platforms; and establishing retail and eCommerce Disney stores, operating more than 200 stores in North America, Europe and Asia. During 2018, Disney Consumer Products and Interactive Media was merged with Walt Disney Parks and Resorts to form Disney Parks, Experiences and Products; the medial network was transferred to Disney Direct-to-Consumer and International, another business segment and subsidiary of The Walt Disney Company.

DPEP offers medical, dental, vision, long-term care, auto, home and life insurance;401(k) and pension plans; and various employe assistance programs.

FINANCIAL DATA: Note: Data for latest year may not have been available at press time.

In U.S. $	2018	2017	2016	2015	2014	2013
Revenue	24,947,000,000	23,248,000,000	22,502,000,000	20,661,000,000	19,084,000,000	17,642,000,000
R&D Expense						
Operating Income						
Operating Margin %						
SGA Expense						
Net Income	6,001,000,000	5,548,000,000	5,263,000,000	4,783,000,000	4,019,000,000	3,332,000,000
Operating Cash Flow						
Capital Expenditure						
EBITDA						
Return on Assets %						
Return on Equity %						
Debt to Equity						

CONTACT INFORMATION:
Phone: 818-553-5000   Fax: 818-567-0284
Toll-Free:
Address: 500 S. Buena Vista St., Burbank, CA 91521 United States

STOCK TICKER/OTHER:
Stock Ticker: Subsidiary
Employees: 152,000
Parent Company: Walt Disney Company (The)

Exchange:
Fiscal Year Ends: 12/31

SALARIES/BONUSES:
Top Exec. Salary: $ Bonus: $
Second Exec. Salary: $ Bonus: $

OTHER THOUGHTS:
Estimated Female Officers or Directors:
Hot Spot for Advancement for Women/Minorities:

Sales, profits and employees may be estimates. Financial information, benefits and other data can change quickly and may vary from those stated here.

Dollar Thrifty Automotive Group Inc

www.thrifty.com/AboutUs/content.aspx
NAIC Code: 532111

TYPES OF BUSINESS:
Automobile Rental
Used Car Sales
Financial Services

BRANDS/DIVISIONS/AFFILIATES:
Hertz Global Holdings Inc
Dollar
Thrifty

CONTACTS: Note: Officers with more than one job title may be intentionally listed here more than once.
H. Clofford Buster, CFO

GROWTH PLANS/SPECIAL FEATURES:
Dollar Thrifty Automotive Group, Inc. (DTG) operates vehicle rental agencies under the brand names Dollar and Thrifty. These agencies comprise one of the largest car rental networks in the world. DTG itself is a wholly-owned subsidiary of Hertz Global Holdings, Inc. There are more than 4,000 corporately-owned and franchised Dollar and Thrifty stores, in conjunction with Hertz, strategically located in 77 countries throughout North, Central and South America, Africa, the Middle East, the Caribbean, Asia and the Pacific. DTG also sells vehicle rental franchises worldwide, and provides sales and marketing, reservations, data processing systems, insurance and other services to franchisees. DTG offers customers supplemental equipment and optional products, including global positioning system equipment, ski racks, infant/child seats, as well as rent-a-toll products for electronic toll payments.

The company offers employees medical, dental and vision coverage; domestic partner benefits; flexible spending accounts; a wellness program; short- and long-term disability; life and AD&D insurance; an employee assistance program; a 401(k); tuition reimbursement; and employee discounts.

FINANCIAL DATA: Note: Data for latest year may not have been available at press time.

In U.S. $	2018	2017	2016	2015	2014	2013
Revenue	1,620,000,000	1,600,000,000	1,528,500,000	1,800,000,000	1,910,000,000	1,875,000,000
R&D Expense						
Operating Income						
Operating Margin %						
SGA Expense						
Net Income						
Operating Cash Flow						
Capital Expenditure						
EBITDA						
Return on Assets %						
Return on Equity %						
Debt to Equity						

CONTACT INFORMATION:
Phone: 918-660-7700   Fax: 918-669-2934
Toll-Free: 888-700-9803
Address: 5330 E. 31st St., Tulsa, OK 74135 United States

SALARIES/BONUSES:
Top Exec. Salary: $ Bonus: $
Second Exec. Salary: $ Bonus: $

STOCK TICKER/OTHER:
Stock Ticker: Subsidiary   Exchange:
Employees: 6,000   Fiscal Year Ends: 12/31
Parent Company: Hertz Global Holdings Inc

OTHER THOUGHTS:
Estimated Female Officers or Directors: 2
Hot Spot for Advancement for Women/Minorities:

Sales, profits and employees may be estimates. Financial information, benefits and other data can change quickly and may vary from those stated here.

DowDupont Inc

NAIC Code: 325199

www.dow-dupont.com/home/default.aspx

TYPES OF BUSINESS:
Specialty Chemicals Manufacturer
Electronic & Functional Materials
Coatings & Infrastructure
Agricultural Sciences
Performance Materials
Performance Plastics
Feedstocks & Energy

BRANDS/DIVISIONS/AFFILIATES:

CONTACTS:
Note: Officers with more than one job title may be intentionally listed here more than once.

Edward Breen, CEO
Amy Wilson, General Counsel, Subsidiary
Howard Ungerleider, CFO
Jeff Fettig, Chairman of the Board
Ronald Edmonds, Co-Controller
Jeanmarie Desmond, Co-Controller
James Collins, COO, Divisional
Christopher Doyle, COO, Divisional
James Fitterling, COO, Divisional
Charles Kalil, Executive VP, Subsidiary
Stacy Fox, General Counsel

GROWTH PLANS/SPECIAL FEATURES:

DowDuPont, Inc., formed by the 2017 merger between Dow and DuPont, operates through three divisions covering agriculture, materials science and specialty products. The agriculture division offers a complete portfolio of products and technologies, as well as a pipeline of germplasm, traits and crop protection. Its solutions include various herbicides, fungicides, insecticides, pasture and land management, seed-applied technologies, structural pest management and turf and ornamental pest management. Its seeds solutions apply to alfalfa, canola, cereals, corn, cotton, rice, silage inoculants, sorghum, soybeans, sunflowers and wheat. The materials science division is further divided into three categories: performance materials and coatings, offering technology platforms that empower DowDuPont customers to create ingredients and solutions with performance and process enhancements for home and beauty care applications; industrial intermediates and infrastructure, which enable unique properties in manufacturing processes, infrastructure markets and downstream finished goods; and packaging and specialty plastics, comprising plastic portfolios that offer solutions and technologies for addressing consumer and brand owner demand for increased packaging convenience, food waste reduction and the global development of telecommunications and electric transmission and distribution infrastructure. Last, the specialty products division is divided into six categories: electronics and imaging, serving the semiconductor, advanced chip packaging, circuit board, electronic and other industries; industrial biosciences, offering solutions that improve the performance, productivity and sustainability of customer products; nutrition and health, offering sustainable, bio-based ingredients; safety and construction, offering high-performance fibers and foams, aramid papers, non-woven structures, membranes and filtration technologies and more; sustainable solutions, offering operations management consulting, services and technologies; and transportation and advanced polymers, providing high-performance engineering resins, adhesives, lubricants and parts to engineers and designers in the transportation, electronics and medical markets.

FINANCIAL DATA:
Note: Data for latest year may not have been available at press time.

In U.S. $	2018	2017	2016	2015	2014	2013
Revenue	85,976,997,888	62,484,000,768	48,157,999,104	48,777,998,336	58,167,001,088	57,080,000,512
R&D Expense						
Operating Income						
Operating Margin %						
SGA Expense						
Net Income	3,844,000,000	1,460,000,000	4,318,000,128	7,685,000,192	3,772,000,000	4,786,999,808
Operating Cash Flow						
Capital Expenditure						
EBITDA						
Return on Assets %						
Return on Equity %						
Debt to Equity						

CONTACT INFORMATION:
Phone: 989 636-1000   Fax: 989 636-3518
Toll-Free: 800-422-8193
Address: 2030 Dow Ctr., Midland, MI 48674 United States

STOCK TICKER/OTHER:
Stock Ticker: DWDP
Employees: 56,000
Parent Company:

Exchange: NYS
Fiscal Year Ends: 12/31

SALARIES/BONUSES:
Top Exec. Salary: $ Bonus: $
Second Exec. Salary: $ Bonus: $

OTHER THOUGHTS:
Estimated Female Officers or Directors: 3
Hot Spot for Advancement for Women/Minorities: Y

Sales, profits and employees may be estimates. Financial information, benefits and other data can change quickly and may vary from those stated here.

DR Horton Inc

www.drhorton.com

NAIC Code: 236117

TYPES OF BUSINESS:
Construction, Home Building and Residential Mortgages
Title Insurance

BRANDS/DIVISIONS/AFFILIATES:
DHI Mortgage
Westport Homes
Classic Builders

CONTACTS:
Note: Officers with more than one job title may be intentionally listed here more than once.

David Auld, CEO
Bill Wheat, CFO
Donald Horton, Chairman of the Board
Michael Murray, COO
Thomas Montano, Secretary

GROWTH PLANS/SPECIAL FEATURES:

D.R. Horton, Inc. is a leading national builder of single-family homes with a diversified set of holdings and operating divisions in 27 states and 81 metropolitan markets. The firm generally builds homes between 1,000 to more than 4,000 square feet, ranging in price from $100,000 to over 1 million. In fiscal (September) 2018, the company closed approximately 51,857 homes, with an average closing sales price approximating $298,900. D.R. Horton divides its business into six regional homebuilding segments and one financial services segment. The homebuilding segments are: East, operating in eight states; Midwest, four states; Southeast, five states; South Central, three states; Southwest, two states; and West, six states. This segment constructs residences, tailored to the particular community where they are being built, including single-family residential homes, townhouses, condominiums, duplexes and triplexes. Detached homes sales accounted for 89% of the firm's 2018 revenues. Subcontractors under the supervision of D. R. Horton do substantially all the actual building. The financial services segment of the company provides mortgage financing and title insurance through its wholly-owned subsidiary, DHI Mortgage. D.R. Horton's current business strategy is to enter new lot option contracts to purchase finished lots in selected communities to potentially increase sales volumes and profitability. The firm plans to renegotiate existing lot option contracts as necessary to reduce lot costs and better match the scheduled lot purchases with new home demand in each community. The company also manages inventory of homes under construction by selectively starting construction on unsold homes to capture new home demand while monitoring the number and aging of unsold homes and aggressively marketing its unsold, completed homes in inventory. In late-2018, D.R. Horton acquired the homebuilding operations of Westport Homes, Classic Builders and Terramor Homes (Raleigh, North Carolina).

FINANCIAL DATA:
Note: Data for latest year may not have been available at press time.

In U.S. $	2018	2017	2016	2015	2014	2013
Revenue	16,068,000,000	14,091,000,000	12,157,400,000	10,824,000,000	8,024,900,000	6,259,300,000
R&D Expense						
Operating Income	2,038,400,000	1,587,600,000	1,347,200,000	1,120,700,000	804,000,000	654,400,000
Operating Margin %		.11%	.11%	.10%	.10%	.10%
SGA Expense	1,676,800,000	1,471,600,000	1,320,300,000	1,186,000,000	965,400,000	766,300,000
Net Income	1,460,300,000	1,038,400,000	886,300,000	750,700,000	533,500,000	462,700,000
Operating Cash Flow	545,200,000	435,100,000	618,000,000	700,400,000	-661,400,000	-1,231,100,000
Capital Expenditure	138,300,000	157,300,000	86,100,000	56,100,000	100,200,000	58,000,000
EBITDA	2,100,800,000	1,642,300,000	1,408,200,000	1,177,500,000	852,600,000	685,600,000
Return on Assets %		.09%	.08%	.07%	.06%	.06%
Return on Equity %		.14%	.14%	.14%	.12%	.12%
Debt to Equity		0.316	0.412	0.566	0.65	0.806

CONTACT INFORMATION:
Phone: 817-390-8200 Fax: 817 856-8429
Toll-Free:
Address: 1341 Horton Cir., Arlington, TX 76011 United States

SALARIES/BONUSES:
Top Exec. Salary: $500,000 Bonus: $1,500,000
Second Exec. Salary: $1,000,000 Bonus: $

STOCK TICKER/OTHER:
Stock Ticker: DHI Exchange: NYS
Employees: 6,976 Fiscal Year Ends: 09/30
Parent Company:

OTHER THOUGHTS:
Estimated Female Officers or Directors: 1
Hot Spot for Advancement for Women/Minorities:

Sales, profits and employees may be estimates. Financial information, benefits and other data can change quickly and may vary from those stated here.

DriveTime Automotive Group Inc

www.drivetime.com

NAIC Code: 441120

TYPES OF BUSINESS:
Used Auto Dealers
Auto Financing
Auto Leasing

BRANDS/DIVISIONS/AFFILIATES:
DriveCare Powertrain Protection Plan
Bridgecrest Acceptance Company

CONTACTS:
Note: Officers with more than one job title may be intentionally listed here more than once.

Don Reese, CEO
Mary L. N. Phillips, CFO
Jon Ehlinger, General Counsel
Jon Ehlinger, VP-Public Rel.
Al Appelman, VP-Risk & Customer Analytics

GROWTH PLANS/SPECIAL FEATURES:

DriveTime Automotive Group, Inc. is a leading chain of buy-here-pay-here used car dealerships. The company targets its products and services to the sub-prime segment of the automobile financing industry. This segment serves customers with limited credit histories, low income or past credit problems who cannot access traditional financing. Advantages of buy-here-pay-here dealerships include the ability to offer customers expanded credit opportunities and flexible payment terms as well as the ability to make payments at the dealership. For each used vehicle sold, DriveTime offers a 30-day limited warranty, 5-day return guarantee, autocheck history report and a certified multi-point inspection. The firm finances all the used cars through retail installment contracts. DriveTime currently operates 145 dealerships nationwide. The dealerships are located in high-visibility, high-traffic commercial areas and comprise more than 11,300 available vehicles (all DriveTime dealerships combined), featuring a wide selection of makes and models. The ages of the cars typically range from three to seven years. DriveTime acquires its inventory primarily from used vehicle auctions. After purchase, the cars are delivered to one of the company's centers, where they are inspected thoroughly and reconditioned for sale. The company offers its DriveCare Powertrain Protection Plan to customers interested in extended protection coverage. Besides flexible auto loan financing, no-commitment lease options are also offered. Subsidiary Bridgecrest Acceptance Company is a licensed third-party servicer that services loans for DriveTime and other affiliated finance companies. All credit scoring, risk decision analytics and verifications remain the responsibility of DriveTime. In May 2018, DriveTime opened a new 110,000-square-foot inspection center in Morrisville, Pennsylvania.

DriveTime offers employees a choice of medical plans, tuition reimbursement plans, vacation pay, paid time off and fitness room.

FINANCIAL DATA:
Note: Data for latest year may not have been available at press time.

In U.S. $	2018	2017	2016	2015	2014	2013
Revenue	1,764,000,000	1,680,000,000	1,600,000,000	1,525,000,000	1,475,000,000	1,400,896,000
R&D Expense						
Operating Income						
Operating Margin %						
SGA Expense						
Net Income						
Operating Cash Flow						
Capital Expenditure						
EBITDA						
Return on Assets %						
Return on Equity %						
Debt to Equity						

CONTACT INFORMATION:
Phone: 314-824-1170 Fax: 866-271-6010
Toll-Free: 888-418-1212
Address: 1720 W. Rio Salado Pkwy, Tempe, AZ 85281 United States

SALARIES/BONUSES:
Top Exec. Salary: $ Bonus: $
Second Exec. Salary: $ Bonus: $

STOCK TICKER/OTHER:
Stock Ticker: Private
Employees: 5,000
Parent Company:

Exchange:
Fiscal Year Ends: 12/31

OTHER THOUGHTS:
Estimated Female Officers or Directors:
Hot Spot for Advancement for Women/Minorities:

DTE Energy Company

NAIC Code: 221112

www.dteenergy.com

TYPES OF BUSINESS:
Utilities-Electricity & Natural Gas
Energy Management
Wholesale Energy Trading
Fuel Supply Services
Hydroelectric Power
Nuclear Power
Coal Shipping-Rail & Boat
Consulting Services

BRANDS/DIVISIONS/AFFILIATES:
DTE Electric
DTE Gas

CONTACTS:
Note: Officers with more than one job title may be intentionally listed here more than once.

Gerard Anderson, CEO
Peter Oleksiak, CFO
Mark Rolling, Chief Accounting Officer
David Meador, Chief Administrative Officer
Mark Stiers, COO, Subsidiary
Trevor Lauer, COO, Subsidiary
Gerardo Norcia, COO
Bruce Peterson, General Counsel
Lisa Muschong, Other Executive Officer
David Ruud, President, Divisional
David Slater, President, Subsidiary

GROWTH PLANS/SPECIAL FEATURES:

DTE Energy Company is a diversified energy and energy technology company that develops merchant power and industrial energy projects and works in energy trading, selling electricity, natural gas, coal, chilled water, landfill gas and steam. DTE is also one of the nation's largest purchasers, transporters and marketers of coal. The company's operations are divided into four segments: electric, gas, non-utility operations and corporate & other. The electric segment consists of DTE Electric, which is engaged in the generation, purchase, distribution and sale of electricity to approximately 2.2 million residential, commercial and industrial customers in southeastern Michigan. The gas segment is represented by DTE Gas, which buys, stores, transports and distributes natural gas to 1.3 million residential, commercial and industrial customers. The firm's non-utility operations segment include gas storage & pipelines, encompassing DTE's interstate gas transmission pipelines and storage facilities; power and industrial projects, primarily consisting of energy product delivery, coal transportation, as well as marketing and electricity provided by biomass-fueled energy projects; and energy trading, which buys, sells and trades electricity, coal and natural gas, and provides risk management services such as energy marketing and trading operations. The corporate & other segment consists of various holding company activities, certain non-utility debt and energy-related investments.

DTE offers its employees medical, dental and vision coverage; comprehensive wellness programs; a 401(k) plan; flexible spending accounts; an employee assistance program; long-term care insurance; life, disability and AD&D insurance; and flex time.

FINANCIAL DATA:
Note: Data for latest year may not have been available at press time.

In U.S. $	2018	2017	2016	2015	2014	2013
Revenue	14,212,000,000	12,607,000,000	10,630,000,000	10,337,000,000	12,301,000,000	9,661,000,000
R&D Expense						
Operating Income	1,621,000,000	1,687,000,000	1,452,000,000	1,345,000,000	1,578,000,000	1,203,000,000
Operating Margin %		.13%	.14%	.13%	.13%	.12%
SGA Expense						
Net Income	1,120,000,000	1,134,000,000	868,000,000	727,000,000	905,000,000	661,000,000
Operating Cash Flow	2,680,000,000	2,117,000,000	2,084,000,000	1,911,000,000	1,839,000,000	2,154,000,000
Capital Expenditure	2,713,000,000	2,250,000,000	2,045,000,000	2,020,000,000	2,049,000,000	1,876,000,000
EBITDA	2,899,000,000	2,853,000,000	2,553,000,000	2,252,000,000	2,849,000,000	2,452,000,000
Return on Assets %		.03%	.03%	.03%	.03%	.03%
Return on Equity %		.12%	.10%	.09%	.11%	.09%
Debt to Equity		1.281	1.251	1.007	1.002	0.911

CONTACT INFORMATION:
Phone: 313 235-4000   Fax: 313 235-6743
Toll-Free: 866-966-5555
Address: 1 Energy Plaza, Detroit, MI 48226 United States

SALARIES/BONUSES:
Top Exec. Salary: $1,344,231   Bonus: $
Second Exec. Salary: $826,923   Bonus: $

STOCK TICKER/OTHER:
Stock Ticker: DTE   Exchange: NYS
Employees: 10,000   Fiscal Year Ends: 12/31
Parent Company:

OTHER THOUGHTS:
Estimated Female Officers or Directors: 8
Hot Spot for Advancement for Women/Minorities: Y

Duke Energy Corporation

NAIC Code: 221112

www.duke-energy.com

TYPES OF BUSINESS:
Utilities-Electricity & Natural Gas
Merchant Power Generation
Natural Gas Transportation & Storage
Electricity Transmission
Energy Marketing
Real Estate
Telecommunications
Facility & Plant Services

BRANDS/DIVISIONS/AFFILIATES:
Duke Energy Carolinas
Duke Energy Progress
Duke Energy Florida
Duke Energy Indiana
Duke Energy Ohio
Duke-American Transmission Co
REC Solar
Piedmont Natural Gas Company Inc

CONTACTS:
Note: Officers with more than one job title may be intentionally listed here more than once.

Lynn Good, CEO
Steven Young, CFO
Dwight Jacobs, Chief Accounting Officer
Julie Janson, Chief Legal Officer
Melissa Anderson, Executive VP, Divisional
Douglas Esamann, Executive VP, Divisional
Lloyd Yates, Executive VP, Divisional
Dhiaa Jamil, Executive VP
Franklin Yoho, Executive VP
William Currens, Senior VP, Divisional

GROWTH PLANS/SPECIAL FEATURES:

Duke Energy Corporation is an energy services provider that offers delivery and management of electricity and natural gas throughout the U.S. The company operates in three segments: Electric Utilities and Infrastructure (EUI), Gas Utilities and Infrastructure (GUI) and Commercial Renewables. EUI conducts operations primarily through the regulated public utilities of Duke Energy Carolinas, Duke Energy Progress, Duke Energy Florida, Duke Energy Indiana and Duke Energy Ohio. This segment provides retail electric service through the generation, transmission, distribution and sale of electricity to approximately 7.6 million customers within the Southeast and Midwest regions of the U.S. EUI also has a 50% stake in Duke-American Transmission Co., a partnership with American Transmission Company, formed to design, build and operate transmission infrastructure. GUI conducts natural gas operations primarily through the regulated public utilities of Piedmont and Duke Energy Ohio. This segment serves 1.5 million residential, commercial, industrial and power generation natural gas customers. GUI also owns, operates and has investments in various pipeline transmission and natural gas storage facilities. The Commercial Renewables segment primarily acquires, builds, develops and operates wind and solar renewable generation throughout the continental U.S. The portfolio includes nonregulated renewable energy and energy storage businesses. Included within the segment is utility-scale wind and solar generation assets which total 2,907 megawatts across 14 states from 21 wind farms and 63 commercial solar farms. In December 2017, Duke Energy acquired the remaining interest in California-based REC Solar, a provider of renewable energy solutions for commercial customers throughout the U.S. In February 2018, the firm, along with other joint owners, finalized the sales transaction of their retired Walter C. Beckjord coal-fired power plant in Clermont County, Ohio, to Commercial Liability Partners. The following May, Duke Energy announced it will sell five small hydroelectric plants in the Western Carolinas region to Northbrook Energy.

The firm offers employees life, disability, medical, dental and vision insurance; retirement benefits; and wellness programs.

FINANCIAL DATA:
Note: Data for latest year may not have been available at press time.

In U.S. $	2018	2017	2016	2015	2014	2013
Revenue	24,521,000,000	23,565,000,000	22,743,000,000	23,459,000,000	23,925,000,000	24,598,000,000
R&D Expense						
Operating Income	5,176,000,000	6,035,000,000	5,332,000,000	5,452,000,000	5,323,000,000	5,397,000,000
Operating Margin %		.26%	.23%	.23%	.22%	.22%
SGA Expense						
Net Income	2,666,000,000	3,059,000,000	2,152,000,000	2,816,000,000	1,883,000,000	2,665,000,000
Operating Cash Flow	7,186,000,000	6,634,000,000	6,798,000,000	6,676,000,000	6,586,000,000	6,382,000,000
Capital Expenditure	9,389,000,000	8,052,000,000	7,901,000,000	6,766,000,000	5,384,000,000	5,526,000,000
EBITDA	9,863,000,000	10,298,000,000	9,530,000,000	9,363,000,000	9,263,000,000	8,695,000,000
Return on Assets %		.02%	.02%	.02%	.02%	.02%
Return on Equity %		.07%	.05%	.07%	.05%	.06%
Debt to Equity		1.175	1.111	0.944	0.91	0.923

CONTACT INFORMATION:
Phone: 704-382-3853 Fax: 704-382-3814
Toll-Free: 800-873-3853
Address: 550 S. Tryon St., Charlotte, NC 28202 United States

SALARIES/BONUSES:
Top Exec. Salary: $1,350,000 Bonus: $
Second Exec. Salary: $803,907 Bonus: $

STOCK TICKER/OTHER:
Stock Ticker: DUK
Employees: 28,798
Parent Company:

Exchange: NYS
Fiscal Year Ends: 12/31

OTHER THOUGHTS:
Estimated Female Officers or Directors: 8
Hot Spot for Advancement for Women/Minorities: Y

Sales, profits and employees may be estimates. Financial information, benefits and other data can change quickly and may vary from those stated here.

Dycom Industries Inc

NAIC Code: 237130

www.dycomind.com

TYPES OF BUSINESS:
Construction, Maintenance & Installation Services
Engineering Services
Utility Maintenance Services

BRANDS/DIVISIONS/AFFILIATES:

CONTACTS: Note: Officers with more than one job title may be intentionally listed here more than once.
Steven Nielsen, CEO
H. Deferrari, CFO
Sharon Villaverde, Chief Accounting Officer
Timothy Estes, Executive VP
Scott Horton, Other Executive Officer

GROWTH PLANS/SPECIAL FEATURES:

Dycom Industries, Inc. is a leading provider of specialty contracting services. The firm provides services throughout the U.S., and on a limited basis, in Canada. Services include engineering, construction, maintenance and installation services to telecommunications providers; underground locating services to various utilities including telecommunications providers; and other construction and maintenance services to electric utilities. Dycom's top five customers accounted for approximately 78.4% of its 2018 revenue, and received 21.2% of its revenue from AT&T, 20.8% from Comcast Corporation, 19.2% from Verizon Communications, 13.6% from CenturyLink, and 3.6% from Windstream Corporation. Dycom provides outside plant engineers and drafters to telecommunication providers who design aerial, underground and buried fiber optic, copper and coaxial cable systems that extend from the telephone company's central office, or cable operator headend, to the consumer's home or business. Engineering services the firm provides to telephone companies include fiber cable routing and design; the design of service area concept boxes, terminals, drops and transmission and central office equipment; and the proper administration of feeder and distribution cable pairs. For cable television multiple system operators, Dycom performs make-ready studies, strand mapping, field walk-out, computer-aided radio frequency design and fiber cable routing and design. The firm's construction, maintenance and installation services include placing and splicing fiber, copper and coaxial cables; excavating trenches in which to place cables; placing related structures such as poles, anchors, conduits, manholes, cabinets and closures; placing drop lines from main distribution lines to the consumer's home or business; and maintaining and removing these facilities. It also provides premise wiring services to various corporations and state and local governments, predominantly limited to the installation, repair and maintenance of telecommunications infrastructure within improved structures.

FINANCIAL DATA: Note: Data for latest year may not have been available at press time.

In U.S. $	2018	2017	2016	2015	2014	2013
Revenue	1,411,348,000	3,066,880,000	2,672,542,000	2,022,312,000	1,811,593,000	
R&D Expense						
Operating Income	59,885,000	275,009,000	246,874,000	154,318,000	81,918,000	
Operating Margin %		.09%	.09%	.08%	.05%	
SGA Expense	124,930,000	239,231,000	217,149,000	178,700,000	161,858,000	
Net Income	68,835,000	157,217,000	128,740,000	84,324,000	39,978,000	
Operating Cash Flow	160,533,000	256,443,000	261,488,000	141,900,000	84,185,000	
Capital Expenditure	87,839,000	201,197,000	186,011,000	102,997,000	89,136,000	
EBITDA	144,938,000	422,915,000	371,814,000	250,362,000	174,690,000	
Return on Assets %		.09%	.08%	.07%	.03%	
Return on Equity %		.26%	.24%	.17%	.09%	
Debt to Equity		1.099	1.267	1.029	0.921	

CONTACT INFORMATION:
Phone: 561 627-7171   Fax: 561 627-7709
Toll-Free:
Address: 11780 U.S. Highway 1, Ste. 600, Palm Beach Gardens, FL 33408 United States

STOCK TICKER/OTHER:
Stock Ticker: DY   Exchange: NYS
Employees: 14,225   Fiscal Year Ends: 01/27
Parent Company:

SALARIES/BONUSES:
Top Exec. Salary: $1,000,000   Bonus: $
Second Exec. Salary: $495,000   Bonus: $222,750

OTHER THOUGHTS:
Estimated Female Officers or Directors:
Hot Spot for Advancement for Women/Minorities:

Sales, profits and employees may be estimates. Financial information, benefits and other data can change quickly and may vary from those stated here.

EchoStar Corporation

www.echostar.com

NAIC Code: 517110

TYPES OF BUSINESS:
Digital Set-Top Boxes & Related Products
Fixed Satellite Services

BRANDS/DIVISIONS/AFFILIATES:
Hughes Communications Inc
Echostar Satellite Services
EchoStar Mobile Limited

CONTACTS:
Note: Officers with more than one job title may be intentionally listed here more than once.

Michael Dugan, CEO
David Rayner, CFO
Charles Ergen, Chairman of the Board
Anders Johnson, Chief Strategy Officer
Pradman Kaul, Director
Dean Manson, Executive VP

GROWTH PLANS/SPECIAL FEATURES:
EchoStar Corporation is a global provider of satellite operations, video delivery solutions and broadband satellite technologies and services for home and office, delivering innovative network technologies, managed services and solutions for enterprises and governments. The company operates in two business segments: Hughes Communications, Inc. and EchoStar Satellite Services. Hughes Communications provides satellite broadband internet to North American consumers and broadband network services and equipment to domestic and international enterprise markets. The Hughes segment also offers managed services to large enterprises, as well as solutions to customers for mobile satellite systems. EchoStar Satellite Services provides satellite services on a full-time and occasional-use basis primarily to DISH Network Corporation, Dish Mexico S de RI de CV, U.S. government service providers, internet service providers, broadcast news organizations, programmers and private enterprise customers. Subsidiary EchoStar Mobile Limited is based in Ireland and licensed by the European Union (EU) to provide mobile satellite service/complementary ground component (MSS/CGC) services covering the entire EU using S-band spectrum. In May 2019, EchoStar agreed to transfer to DISH Network Corporation the portion of its EchoStar Satellite Services business (including Dish Mexico) that manages and provides broadcast satellite services primarily to DISH and its subsidiaries. The transaction enables EchoStar to focus on its high-growth business of broadband services and other initiatives.

EchoStar offers employees medical, dental, vision, life, AD&D and disability insurance; various assistance programs; 401(k) and other retirement/savings plans; paid vacation/holidays; tuition reimbursement and more.

FINANCIAL DATA:
Note: Data for latest year may not have been available at press time.

In U.S. $	2018	2017	2016	2015	2014	2013
Revenue	2,091,363,000	1,885,508,000	3,056,730,000	3,143,714,000	3,445,578,000	3,282,452,000
R&D Expense	27,570,000	31,745,000	76,024,000	78,287,000	60,886,000	67,942,000
Operating Income	248,463,000	207,069,000	364,398,000	358,433,000	328,090,000	142,002,000
Operating Margin %		.11%	.12%	.11%	.10%	.04%
SGA Expense	436,247,000	366,007,000	385,634,000	374,116,000	372,010,000	358,499,000
Net Income	-40,475,000	392,561,000	179,930,000	153,357,000	152,874,000	2,525,000
Operating Cash Flow	734,522,000	726,892,000	803,343,000	776,451,000	840,131,000	450,507,000
Capital Expenditure	586,780,000	610,231,000	721,506,000	729,275,000	680,026,000	433,621,000
EBITDA	838,786,000	851,783,000	905,542,000	871,796,000	906,358,000	665,629,000
Return on Assets %		.04%	.02%	.02%	.02%	.00%
Return on Equity %		.10%	.05%	.05%	.05%	.00%
Debt to Equity		0.863	0.924	0.592	0.658	0.731

CONTACT INFORMATION:
Phone: 303 706-4000 Fax:
Toll-Free:
Address: 100 Inverness Terrace E., Englewood, CO 80112 United States

STOCK TICKER/OTHER:
Stock Ticker: SATS
Employees: 4,000
Parent Company:

Exchange: NAS
Fiscal Year Ends: 12/31

SALARIES/BONUSES:
Top Exec. Salary: $1,000,002 Bonus: $
Second Exec. Salary: $800,010 Bonus: $

OTHER THOUGHTS:
Estimated Female Officers or Directors: 1
Hot Spot for Advancement for Women/Minorities:

Edward D Jones & Co LP

NAIC Code: 523120

www.edwardjones.com

TYPES OF BUSINESS:
Stock Brokerage
Financial Planning
Retirement & Estate Planning
Life Insurance
Banking Services
Annuities

BRANDS/DIVISIONS/AFFILIATES:
Jones Financial Companies LLLP (The)
Edward Jones

CONTACTS: *Note: Officers with more than one job title may be intentionally listed here more than once.*
James D. Weddle, Managing Partner
Norman Eaker, Principal-Firm Admin.
James A. Tricarico, General Counsel

GROWTH PLANS/SPECIAL FEATURES:

Edward D. Jones & Co. LP, which trades under the name Edward Jones, is an investment brokerage network. The company specifically focuses on individual investors, most of whom are retired, as well as small-business owners in rural communities and suburbs. Edward Jones serves nearly 7 million clients and has a network of more than 12,700 offices in the U.S. and Canada. The firm keeps its offices continuously connected through satellite uplinks. Edward Jones brokers target conservative long-term investors with the intention of buying and holding stocks in relatively low-risk investment portfolios in government bonds, blue-chip stocks and high-quality mutual funds. Other products from the company include annuities, college saving programs, estate planning, life insurance, retirement plans and traditional banking services, such as savings and checking accounts. The firm also maintains a research department to provide specific investment recommendations and market information for retail customers. Edward Jones' website offers financial planning for life events, including buying a home, expecting a child, changing jobs and the loss of a loved one. Edward D. Jones & Co. is a wholly-owned subsidiary of Jones Financial Companies LLLP.

The company offers employees medical and dental benefits, 401(k) plans, life and disability insurance, a profit sharing plan and tuition reimbursement.

FINANCIAL DATA: *Note: Data for latest year may not have been available at press time.*

In U.S. $	2018	2017	2016	2015	2014	2013
Revenue	7,500,000,000	7,000,000,000	6,557,000,000	6,619,000,000	6,278,000,000	5,657,000,000
R&D Expense						
Operating Income						
Operating Margin %						
SGA Expense						
Net Income			746,000,000	838,000,000	770,000,000	674,338,000
Operating Cash Flow						
Capital Expenditure						
EBITDA						
Return on Assets %						
Return on Equity %						
Debt to Equity						

CONTACT INFORMATION:
Phone: 314-515-2000 Fax: 314-515-2622
Toll-Free:
Address: 12555 Manchester Rd., Des Peres, MO 63131 United States

SALARIES/BONUSES:
Top Exec. Salary: $ Bonus: $
Second Exec. Salary: $ Bonus: $

STOCK TICKER/OTHER:
Stock Ticker: Subsidiary   Exchange:
Employees: 45,000   Fiscal Year Ends: 12/31
Parent Company: Jones Financial Companies LLLP (The)

OTHER THOUGHTS:
Estimated Female Officers or Directors: 3
Hot Spot for Advancement for Women/Minorities: Y

Sales, profits and employees may be estimates. Financial information, benefits and other data can change quickly and may vary from those stated here.

Edwards Lifesciences Corporation

www.edwards.com

NAIC Code: 339100

TYPES OF BUSINESS:
Supplies-Cardiovascular Disease Related
Cardiac Surgery Products
Critical Care Products
Vascular Products
Heart Valve Implants

BRANDS/DIVISIONS/AFFILIATES:
Carpentier-Edwards PERIMOUNT
Edwards Intuity
Edwards SAPIEN
Swan-Ganz
FloTrac
ClearSight
EV1000
Acumen Hypotension Prediction Index

CONTACTS:
Note: Officers with more than one job title may be intentionally listed here more than once.

Michael Mussallem, CEO
Scott Ullem, CFO
Donald Bobo, Vice President
Larry Wood, Vice President, Divisional
Catherine Szyman, Vice President, Divisional
Daveen Chopra, Vice President, Divisional
Jean-Luc Lemercier, Vice President, Geographical
Huimin Wang, Vice President, Geographical

GROWTH PLANS/SPECIAL FEATURES:

Edwards Lifesciences Corporation designs products for cardiovascular diseases, such as heart valve disease, coronary artery disease, peripheral vascular disease (PVD) and congestive heart failure. The firm operates in three main areas: surgical structural heart (18% of 2018 net sales), transcatheter aortic valve replacement (61%) and core hemodynamic products (10%). Surgical structural heart products include the Carpentier-Edwards PERIMOUNT line of pericardial heart valves made from biologically inert porcine tissue, often on a wire-form stent; and valve repair therapies, such as the Edwards Intuity valve system, a minimally-invasive aortic system designed to enable a faster procedure and a smaller incision. Transcatheter aortic valve replacement technologies are designed for the non-surgical replacement of heart valves. Its main products are the Edwards SAPIEN, Edwards Sapien XT, Edwards Sapien 3 and Edwards Sapien 3 Ultra transcatheter aortic heart valves and delivery systems used to treat heart valve disease using catheter-based approaches for patients deemed at high risk for traditional open-heart surgery. The company's core hemodynamic products include the Swan-Ganz brand hemodynamic monitoring devices used during surgery; FloTrac, a minimally invasive continuous cardiac output monitoring system; ClearSight hemodynamic monitor that provides real-time, beat-to-beat information; EV1000 and HemoSphere clinical monitoring platforms which displays a patient's physiological status and integrates many of the firm's sensors and catheters into one platform; and Acumen Hypotension Prediction Index, an advanced algorithm that indicates the likelihood of a patient developing hypotension. This division also produces disposable pressure monitoring devices and innovative closed blood sampling systems to help protect patients and clinicians from risk of infection. Internationally, the firm sells its products in approximately 100 countries, including Canada, China, France, Germany, Italy, Japan, Spain and the U.K. In August 2019, Edwards SAPIEN 3 received U.S. Food and Drug Administration (FDA) approval for low-risk patients.

Edwards offers comprehensive benefits and retirement plans.

FINANCIAL DATA:
Note: Data for latest year may not have been available at press time.

In U.S. $	2018	2017	2016	2015	2014	2013
Revenue	3,722,800,000	3,435,300,000	2,963,700,000	2,493,700,000	2,322,900,000	2,045,500,000
R&D Expense	622,200,000	552,600,000	477,800,000	383,100,000	356,700,000	323,000,000
Operating Income	1,072,700,000	1,022,700,000	783,800,000	642,700,000	482,600,000	454,500,000
Operating Margin %		.30%	.26%	.26%	.21%	.22%
SGA Expense	1,088,500,000	984,700,000	904,700,000	850,700,000	858,000,000	745,600,000
Net Income	722,200,000	583,600,000	569,500,000	494,900,000	811,100,000	391,700,000
Operating Cash Flow	926,800,000	1,000,700,000	704,400,000	549,700,000	1,022,300,000	472,700,000
Capital Expenditure	241,700,000	175,500,000	217,400,000	106,500,000	93,700,000	110,100,000
EBITDA	868,700,000	1,140,000,000	828,300,000	705,400,000	1,229,800,000	593,800,000
Return on Assets %		.11%	.13%	.13%	.26%	.16%
Return on Equity %		.21%	.22%	.21%	.43%	.26%
Debt to Equity		0.148	0.314	0.24	0.273	0.38

CONTACT INFORMATION:
Phone: 949 250-2500 Fax: 949 250-2525
Toll-Free: 800-424-3278
Address: 1 Edwards Way, Irvine, CA 92614 United States

SALARIES/BONUSES:
Top Exec. Salary: $1,034,769   Bonus: $
Second Exec. Salary: $592,999   Bonus: $4,000

STOCK TICKER/OTHER:
Stock Ticker: EW
Employees: 11,100
Parent Company:

Exchange: NYS
Fiscal Year Ends: 12/31

OTHER THOUGHTS:
Estimated Female Officers or Directors: 3
Hot Spot for Advancement for Women/Minorities: Y

Sales, profits and employees may be estimates. Financial information, benefits and other data can change quickly and may vary from those stated here.

Eli Lilly and Company

NAIC Code: 325412

www.lilly.com

TYPES OF BUSINESS:
Pharmaceuticals Discovery & Development

BRANDS/DIVISIONS/AFFILIATES:
Humulin
Trajenta
Alimta
Cyramza
Portrazza
Verzenio
Taltz
Effient

CONTACTS:
Note: Officers with more than one job title may be intentionally listed here more than once.

Jeffrey Simmons, CEO, Subsidiary
Anne White, Pres., Divisional
Davic Ricks, CEO
Joshua Smiley, CFO
Donald Zakrowski, Chief Accounting Officer
Melissa Barnes, Chief Compliance Officer
Aarti Shah, Chief Information Officer
Daniel Skovronsky, Chief Scientific Officer
Michael Harrington, General Counsel
Alfonso Zulueta, President, Divisional
Enrique Conterno, President, Divisional
Myles ONeill, President, Divisional
Leigh Pusey, Senior VP, Divisional
Johna Norton, Senior VP, Divisional
Stephen Fry, Senior VP, Divisional

GROWTH PLANS/SPECIAL FEATURES:

Eli Lilly and Company discovers, develops, manufactures and markets human pharmaceutical products. Human pharmaceutical products are grouped into five divisions: endocrinology, neuroscience, oncology, immunology and cardiovascular. Endocrinology products include: Humalog, Humulin, Basaglar, Trajenta, Jentadueto, Jardiance, Synjardy, Trulicity and Glyxambi, for the treatment of diabetes; Forteo and Evista, for osteoporosis in women; and Humatrope, for human growth hormone deficiency. Neuroscience products include: Cymbalta and Prozac, for major depressive disorder; Zyprexa, for schizophrenia; Strattera, for attention-deficit hyperactivity disorder; Emgality, for migraine prevention; and Amyvid, a radioactive diagnostic agent for brain imaging of people with cognitive decline. Oncology products include: Alimta, for non-small cell lung cancer; Erbitux, for colorectal cancers; Gemzar, for pancreatic cancer/metastatic breast cancer/ovarian cancer/bladder cancer; Cyramza, for advanced or metastatic gastric cancer; Portrazza, to treat epidermal growth factor receptor expressing squamous non-small cell lung cancer; Lartruvo, for soft tissue carcinoma; and Verzenio, for advanced/metastatic breast cancer. Immunology products include: Olumiant, for adults with moderately-to-severe active rheumatoid arthritis; and Taltz, for moderate-to-severe plaque psoriasis and active psoriatic arthritis. Cardiovascular products include: Cialis, for erectile dysfunction; and Effient, for reduction of thrombotic cardiovascular events. In September 2018, the firm completed the IPO of its spun off animal health products business, Elanco Animal Health, Inc., on the New York Stock Exchange under the ticker symbol ELAN. In January 2019, Eli Lilly agreed to acquire Loxo Oncology, Inc. for approximately $8 billion, expanding its oncology-treatment portfolio.

Eli Lilly offers employees life and health insurance, an employee assistance program, a 401(k), flexible spending accounts, adoption assistance; and tuition reimbursement.

FINANCIAL DATA:
Note: Data for latest year may not have been available at press time.

In U.S. $	2018	2017	2016	2015	2014	2013
Revenue	24,555,700,000	22,871,300,000	21,222,100,000	19,958,700,000	19,615,600,000	23,113,100,000
R&D Expense	5,307,100,000	5,281,800,000	5,243,900,000	4,796,400,000	4,733,600,000	5,531,300,000
Operating Income	6,428,900,000	4,931,200,000	3,871,300,000	3,592,100,000	3,328,700,000	5,548,100,000
Operating Margin %		.14%	.18%	.15%	.15%	.23%
SGA Expense	6,389,700,000	6,588,100,000	6,452,000,000	6,533,000,000	6,620,800,000	7,125,600,000
Net Income	3,232,000,000	-204,100,000	2,737,600,000	2,408,400,000	2,390,500,000	4,684,800,000
Operating Cash Flow	5,524,500,000	5,615,600,000	4,851,000,000	2,772,800,000	4,367,100,000	5,735,000,000
Capital Expenditure	3,018,200,000	2,163,600,000	1,092,000,000	1,626,200,000	1,565,900,000	1,093,300,000
EBITDA	5,676,800,000	3,989,700,000	5,055,800,000	4,378,900,000	4,528,100,000	7,495,000,000
Return on Assets %		.00%	.07%	.07%	.07%	.13%
Return on Equity %		-.02%	.19%	.16%	.14%	.29%
Debt to Equity		0.858	0.597	0.547	0.349	0.238

CONTACT INFORMATION:
Phone: 317 276-2000 Fax:
Toll-Free:
Address: Lilly Corporate Center, Indianapolis, IN 46285 United States

STOCK TICKER/OTHER:
Stock Ticker: LLY
Employees: 41,975
Parent Company:

Exchange: NYS
Fiscal Year Ends: 12/31

SALARIES/BONUSES:
Top Exec. Salary: $1,400,000 Bonus: $
Second Exec. Salary: $875,000 Bonus: $

OTHER THOUGHTS:
Estimated Female Officers or Directors: 8
Hot Spot for Advancement for Women/Minorities: Y

EMCOR Group Inc

www.emcorgroup.com

NAIC Code: 238210

TYPES OF BUSINESS:
Electric, Heating and AC Contractors
Mechanical Contracting
Technical Consulting Services
Facilities Management

BRANDS/DIVISIONS/AFFILIATES:

CONTACTS: Note: Officers with more than one job title may be intentionally listed here more than once.
Anthony Guzzi, CEO
Mark Pompa, CFO
R. Matz, Executive VP, Divisional
Maxine Mauricio, Executive VP

GROWTH PLANS/SPECIAL FEATURES:

EMCOR Group, Inc. is a global leader in mechanical and electrical contracting and facilities services. The company offers its services through approximately 80 operating subsidiaries and joint ventures in 170 offices located throughout the U.S., as well as in Canada, the U.K. and the Middle East. Services provided to customers include the design, integration, installation, start up, operation and maintenance of systems for generation and distribution of electrical power; lighting systems; low-voltage systems, such as fire alarm, security, communications and process control systems; voice and data communication systems; heating, ventilation, air conditioning, refrigeration and clean-room process ventilation systems; plumbing, process and high-purity piping systems; water and wastewater treatment systems; and central plant heating and cooling systems. In addition to its construction services, EMCOR offers facilities services, such as site-based operations and maintenance, mobile maintenance and service, facilities management, installation and support for building systems, technical consulting and diagnostic services, small modification and retrofit projects and program development and management for energy systems. Most of the firm's business is done with corporations, municipalities and other government agencies, owner/developers and building tenants. Additional services are provided to a range of general and specialty contractors, with EMCOR operating as a subcontractor.

EMCOR offers its employees benefits including medical, vision and dental coverage; life insurance; flexible spending accounts; disability income; employee wellness and assistance programs; and a 401(k) and stock purchase options.

FINANCIAL DATA: Note: Data for latest year may not have been available at press time.

In U.S. $	2018	2017	2016	2015	2014	2013
Revenue	8,130,631,000	7,686,999,000	7,551,524,000	6,718,726,000	6,424,965,000	6,417,158,000
R&D Expense						
Operating Income	406,296,000	389,950,000	312,324,000	287,906,000	280,768,000	221,995,000
Operating Margin %		.05%	.04%	.04%	.04%	.03%
SGA Expense	799,157,000	757,062,000	725,538,000	656,573,000	626,478,000	591,063,000
Net Income	283,531,000	227,196,000	181,935,000	172,286,000	168,664,000	123,792,000
Operating Cash Flow	271,011,000	366,134,000	264,561,000	266,666,000	246,657,000	150,069,000
Capital Expenditure	43,479,000	34,684,000	39,648,000	35,460,000	38,035,000	35,497,000
EBITDA	489,487,000	420,028,000	388,910,000	361,944,000	365,210,000	278,758,000
Return on Assets %		.06%	.05%	.05%	.05%	.04%
Return on Equity %		.14%	.12%	.12%	.12%	.09%
Debt to Equity		0.176	0.266	0.203	0.223	0.229

CONTACT INFORMATION:
Phone: 203 849-7800   Fax: 203 849-7900
Toll-Free: 866-890-7794
Address: 301 Merritt Seven, Norwalk, CT 06851 United States

STOCK TICKER/OTHER:
Stock Ticker: EME
Employees: 31,000
Parent Company:

Exchange: NYS
Fiscal Year Ends: 12/31

SALARIES/BONUSES:
Top Exec. Salary: $1,125,000   Bonus: $
Second Exec. Salary: $703,800   Bonus: $

OTHER THOUGHTS:
Estimated Female Officers or Directors: 3
Hot Spot for Advancement for Women/Minorities: Y

Emerson Electric Co

NAIC Code: 334513

www.emerson.com

TYPES OF BUSINESS:
Engineering & Technology Products & Services
Industrial Automation Products
Power Products
Air Conditioning & Refrigeration Products
Appliances & Tools

BRANDS/DIVISIONS/AFFILIATES:
Paradigm
ProSys Inc
Cooper-Atkins
Textron
Intelligent Platforms
Advanced Engineering Valves

CONTACTS:
Note: Officers with more than one job title may be intentionally listed here more than once.

David Farr, CEO
Frank Dellaquila, CFO
Michael Baughman, Chief Accounting Officer
K Bell, Chief Marketing Officer
Steven Pelch, COO
Lal Karsanbhai, Executive VP, Divisional
Robert Sharp, Executive VP, Divisional
Sara Bosco, General Counsel
Michael Train, President
Mark Bulanda, Senior VP, Divisional

GROWTH PLANS/SPECIAL FEATURES:
Emerson Electric Co. designs and supplies technology products and engineering services to a wide range of industrial, commercial and consumer markets worldwide. The company is organized into two business segments: automation solutions and commercial and residential solutions. The automation solutions segment enables process, hybrid and discrete manufacturers to maximize production, protect personnel and the environment, and optimize their energy efficiency and operating costs through a broad offering of integrated solutions and products. These include measurement and analytical instrumentation, industrial valves and equipment, and process control systems. The commercial & residential solutions segment provides products that promote energy efficiency, enhance household and commercial comfort, and protect food quality and sustainability through heating, air conditioning and refrigeration technology, as well as a broad range of tools and appliance solutions. In 2018, the firm acquired ProSys, Inc., a global supplier of software and services that increase production and safety for the chemical, oil/gas, pulp/paper and refining industries; acquired Cooper-Atkins, which manufactures temperature management and environmental measurement devices, as well as wireless monitoring solutions for foodservice, healthcare and industrial markets; agreed to acquire Textron, Inc.'s tools and test equipment business for approximately $810 million; acquired Intelligent Platforms from General Electric; and acquired Advanced Engineering Valves, a valve technology manufacturer.

FINANCIAL DATA:
Note: Data for latest year may not have been available at press time.

In U.S. $	2018	2017	2016	2015	2014	2013
Revenue	17,408,000,000	15,264,000,000	14,522,000,000	22,304,000,000	24,537,000,000	24,669,000,000
R&D Expense						
Operating Income	2,891,000,000	2,578,000,000	2,600,000,000	3,293,000,000	4,050,000,000	3,941,000,000
Operating Margin %		.17%	.18%	.15%	.17%	.16%
SGA Expense	4,258,000,000	3,618,000,000	3,464,000,000	5,184,000,000	5,715,000,000	5,648,000,000
Net Income	2,203,000,000	1,518,000,000	1,635,000,000	2,710,000,000	2,147,000,000	2,004,000,000
Operating Cash Flow	2,892,000,000	1,912,000,000	2,881,000,000	2,529,000,000	3,692,000,000	3,649,000,000
Capital Expenditure	617,000,000	476,000,000	447,000,000	685,000,000	767,000,000	678,000,000
EBITDA	3,627,000,000	3,172,000,000	3,099,000,000	5,176,000,000	4,397,000,000	4,249,000,000
Return on Assets %		.07%	.07%	.12%	.09%	.08%
Return on Equity %		.19%	.21%	.30%	.21%	.19%
Debt to Equity		0.435	0.537	0.531	0.352	0.383

CONTACT INFORMATION:
Phone: 314 553-2000 Fax: 314 553-3527
Toll-Free:
Address: 8000 W. Florissant Ave., St. Louis, MO 63136 United States

STOCK TICKER/OTHER:
Stock Ticker: EMR
Employees: 103,500
Parent Company:

Exchange: NYS
Fiscal Year Ends: 09/30

SALARIES/BONUSES:
Top Exec. Salary: $1,350,000 Bonus: $2,700,000
Second Exec. Salary: $775,000 Bonus: $1,250,000

OTHER THOUGHTS:
Estimated Female Officers or Directors: 2
Hot Spot for Advancement for Women/Minorities: Y

Plunkett Research, Ltd.

Endeavor LLC
NAIC Code: 711410

www.endeavorco.com

TYPES OF BUSINESS:
Talent Agency
Literary Agency
Sports Marketing & Agents
Media Consulting

BRANDS/DIVISIONS/AFFILIATES:
160over90
art+commerce
Clifford/French
dixon talent Inc
Endeavor
Endeavor Streaming
Turkish Airlines EuroLeague
Fusion Marketing

CONTACTS: *Note: Officers with more than one job title may be intentionally listed here more than once.*
Ariel Emanuel, Co-CEO
Patrick Whitesell, Co-CEO
David Wirtschafter, Pres.
David Wirtschafter, Co-CEO

GROWTH PLANS/SPECIAL FEATURES:
Endeavor LLC, formed by the 2009 merger of the William Morris Agency and the Endeavor Talent Agency, is one of the largest talent and literary agencies in the world. The firm offers its clients and partners with global access and insights into every facet of entertainment, sports and fashion. Endeavor represents artists across all media platforms, specifically movies, television, music, theater, comedy, culinary, sports, public speaking, voiceover, digital and book publishing. Some of the companies in Endeavor's network, including those it owns, has joint venture partnerships with or has helped to create, encompass the following: 160over90, a full-service branding agency and marketing consultancy, specializing in data-led solutions and storytelling; art+commerce, an agency representing image makers working in photography, film, set design, illustration, styling and more; Clifford/French, a sport and entertainment communications agency; dixon talent, Inc., which represents comedic artists and personalities; Endeavor, a subsidiary formed to expand Endeavor's presence in China; Endeavor Streaming, a global leader in premium video distribution across the entertainment and sports industries; Turkish Airlines EuroLeague, a JV partner that is creating a platform for the development of European basketball; Fusion Marketing, an agency offering large-scale production capabilities that leverage experiential events, social and digital activations; frieze, an arts media and events company; IMG, representing global sports, events, media and fashion, with operations in more than 30 countries; and Kovert Creative, an agency engaged in the core areas of digital services, personal representation, brand marketing and communications. Headquartered in Beverly Hills, California, the firm has additional offices in the U.S., the U.K., Singapore and Australia. During 2018, the firm acquired over-the-top leader, NeuLion (now Endeavor Streaming); and sold advertising agency Droga5 to Accenture plc during 2019. Also in 2019, Endeavor planned to file for an initial public offering.

FINANCIAL DATA: *Note: Data for latest year may not have been available at press time.*

In U.S. $	2018	2017	2016	2015	2014	2013
Revenue	3,613,478,000	3,020,116,000	2,366,960,000	1,761,850,000	1,310,364,000	
R&D Expense						
Operating Income						
Operating Margin %						
SGA Expense						
Net Income	231,304,000	-173,168,000	-98,316,000	-78,292,000	-508,909,000	
Operating Cash Flow						
Capital Expenditure						
EBITDA						
Return on Assets %						
Return on Equity %						
Debt to Equity						

CONTACT INFORMATION:
Phone: 310-859-4000 Fax: 310-859-4440
Toll-Free:
Address: 9601 Wilshire Blvd., Beverly Hills, CA 90210 United States

SALARIES/BONUSES:
Top Exec. Salary: $ Bonus: $
Second Exec. Salary: $ Bonus: $

STOCK TICKER/OTHER:
Stock Ticker: Private
Employees: 7,000
Parent Company:

Exchange:
Fiscal Year Ends: 12/31

OTHER THOUGHTS:
Estimated Female Officers or Directors:
Hot Spot for Advancement for Women/Minorities:

Sales, profits and employees may be estimates. Financial information, benefits and other data can change quickly and may vary from those stated here.

Enterprise Holdings Inc

NAIC Code: 532111

www.enterpriseholdings.com

TYPES OF BUSINESS:
Car & Truck Rental
Vanpool Services

BRANDS/DIVISIONS/AFFILIATES:
Alamo Rent A Car
National Car Rental
Enterprise Rent-A-Car
Enterprise Car Sales
Enterprise Truck Rental
Exotic Car Collection by Enterprise
Enterprise CarShare
Zimride

CONTACTS:
Note: Officers with more than one job title may be intentionally listed here more than once.

Pamela Nicholson, CEO
Christine Taylor, Exec. VP
Rick Short, CFO
Frank Thurman, VP-Mktg.
Shelley Roither, VP-Human Resources
Michael Nolfo, CIO
Lee Kaplan, Chief Admin. Officer
Matthew G. Darrah, Exec. VP-North American Oper.
Greg Stubblefield, Chief Strategy Officer
Patrick T. Farrell, Chief Comm. Officer
Rose Langhorst, Treas.
Steve Bloom, Pres., Enterprise Fleet Mgmt.
Jo Ann Taylor Kindle, Pres., Enterprise Holdings Foundation
Andrew C. Taylor, Chmn.
Greg Stubblefield, Exec. VP-Global Sales & Mktg.

GROWTH PLANS/SPECIAL FEATURES:

Enterprise Holdings, Inc. is the parent company of Alamo Rent A Car, National Car Rental and Enterprise Rent-A-Car car rental agencies. The company also owns Enterprise Car Sales, Enterprise Truck Rental and Exotic Car Collection by Enterprise, as well as car/ride sharing programs Enterprise CarShare, Enterprise Rideshare and Zimride by Enterprise. The firm's combined rental fleet is the largest in the world, at nearly 2 million vehicles. It serves 10,000 fully-staffed neighborhood and airport locations in more than 90 countries worldwide. Alamo Rent A Car is a budget rental car company catering to leisure and vacation customers, particularly international travelers visiting North America. Enterprise Holdings operates self-service kiosks throughout the U.S. National Car Rental is a premium rental brand that serves frequent business travelers and offers the Emerald Club frequent-renter benefits program. Enterprise Rent-A-Car boasts over 7,600 retail and airport offices in the U.S. Enterprise Car Sales is a used-car reseller that provides non-negotiable pricing and after-market warranties on used cars acquired through trade-in or extracted from the rental fleet. Enterprise Truck Rental provides commercial-grade trucks such as ¾- to 1-ton pickups, cargo vans, straight trucks, as well as stakebed trucks (from 16 to 26 feet long), all equipped for commercial use. Exotic Car Collection enables customers to rent vehicles such as exotic sports cars and luxury sedans, including Ferrari, Maserati, Porsche, Bentley, Range Rover and more. Enterprise CarShare is a car sharing program that allows customers to rent a car for flexible periods of time through an online membership portal. Enterprise Rideshare specializes in customized vanpool programs and commuter services for individuals and/or companies. Zimride is a ride-sharing platform for companies and universities.

Enterprise Holdings offers its employees medical, dental and vision insurance; prescription drug coverage; flexible spending accounts; life insurance; and long-term disability plans.

FINANCIAL DATA:
Note: Data for latest year may not have been available at press time.

In U.S. $	2018	2017	2016	2015	2014	2013
Revenue	24,100,000,000	22,300,000,000	20,900,000,000	19,400,000,000	17,800,000,000	16,400,000,000
R&D Expense						
Operating Income						
Operating Margin %						
SGA Expense						
Net Income						
Operating Cash Flow						
Capital Expenditure						
EBITDA						
Return on Assets %						
Return on Equity %						
Debt to Equity						

CONTACT INFORMATION:
Phone: 314-512-2880 Fax: 314-512-4706
Toll-Free:
Address: 600 Corporate Park Dr., St. Louis, MO 63105 United States

SALARIES/BONUSES:
Top Exec. Salary: $ Bonus: $
Second Exec. Salary: $ Bonus: $

STOCK TICKER/OTHER:
Stock Ticker: Private Exchange:
Employees: 100,000 Fiscal Year Ends: 03/31
Parent Company:

OTHER THOUGHTS:
Estimated Female Officers or Directors: 5
Hot Spot for Advancement for Women/Minorities: Y

Sales, profits and employees may be estimates. Financial information, benefits and other data can change quickly and may vary from those stated here.

Enterprise Products Partners LP

NAIC Code: 486210

www.enterpriseproducts.com/

TYPES OF BUSINESS:
Pipelines-Natural Gas
Natural Gas Transportation, Processing & Storage
Natural Gas Liquid Fractionation & Processing
Import/Export Terminals

BRANDS/DIVISIONS/AFFILIATES:
Dan Duncan LLC
Enterprise Products Holdings LLC
Enterprise Products Operating LLC

CONTACTS:
Note: Officers with more than one job title may be intentionally listed here more than once.
W. Fowler, CFO
Randa Williams, Chairman of the Board
A. Teague, Director
Harry Weitzel, Director
William Ordemann, Executive VP, Divisional
Graham Bacon, Executive VP, Divisional
R. Boss, Senior VP, Divisional
Brent Secrest, Senior VP, Divisional
Richard Bachmann, Vice Chairman of the Board
Michael Hanson, Vice President

GROWTH PLANS/SPECIAL FEATURES:
Enterprise Products Partners LP provides midstream energy services to producers and consumers of natural gas, natural gas liquids (NGLs) crude oil, petrochemicals and refined products. The company's midstream operations include natural gas gathering, treating, processing, transportation and storage; NGL transportation, fractionation, storage and import/export terminals; crude oil gathering, transportation, storage and terminals; and petrochemical and refined products transportation, storage and terminals, as well as other related services. Enterprise Products also has a marine transportation business that operates primarily on the U.S. inland and intra-coastal waterway systems in the Gulf of Mexico. Assets of the firm include 50,000 miles of pipelines; 260 million barrels (MMBbls) of storage capacity for NGLs, crude oil, petrochemicals and refined products; and 14 billion cubic feet (Bcf) of natural gas storage capacity. Enterprise conducts primarily all of its business through wholly-owned subsidiary, Enterprise Products Operating, LLC, and its subsidiaries. Enterprise is managed by its general partners, Enterprise Products Holdings, LLC, which itself is a wholly-owned subsidiary of Dan Duncan, LLC. During 2018, Enterprise Products Partners announced plans to develop an offshore crude oil export terminal off the Texas Gulf Coast, capable of fully loading very large crude carriers; began construction on its tenth NGL fractionator, adjacent to its Mont Belvieu, Texas complex, which will have a capacity of 150,000 barrels per day, and is scheduled for service in 2020; and is currently (as of September 2018) expanding its Enterprise Hydrocarbon Terminal to increase loading capacity for liquefied petroleum gas (LPG), primarily propane and butane, by 175,000 barrels per day, and expects the terminal to be available in mid-2019.

FINANCIAL DATA:
Note: Data for latest year may not have been available at press time.

In U.S. $	2018	2017	2016	2015	2014	2013
Revenue	36,534,200,000	29,241,500,000	23,022,300,000	27,027,900,000	47,951,200,000	47,727,000,000
R&D Expense						
Operating Income	4,928,600,000	3,502,900,000	3,218,700,000	3,166,600,000	3,516,200,000	3,300,000,000
Operating Margin %		.12%	.14%	.12%	.07%	.07%
SGA Expense	208,300,000	181,100,000	160,100,000	192,600,000	214,500,000	188,300,000
Net Income	4,172,400,000	2,799,300,000	2,513,100,000	2,521,200,000	2,787,400,000	2,596,900,000
Operating Cash Flow	6,126,300,000	4,666,300,000	4,066,800,000	4,002,400,000	4,162,200,000	3,865,500,000
Capital Expenditure	4,223,200,000	3,147,900,000	3,025,100,000	3,830,700,000	2,892,900,000	3,408,200,000
EBITDA	7,146,000,000	5,481,800,000	5,111,000,000	5,001,600,000	5,138,100,000	4,684,700,000
Return on Assets %		.05%	.05%	.05%	.06%	.07%
Return on Equity %		.13%	.12%	.13%	.17%	.18%
Debt to Equity		0.963	0.958	1.026	1.061	1.066

CONTACT INFORMATION:
Phone: 713 381-6500 Fax: 713 880-6668
Toll-Free:
Address: 1100 Louisiana St., 10/Fl, Houston, TX 77002 United States

STOCK TICKER/OTHER:
Stock Ticker: EPD Exchange: NYS
Employees: 6,600 Fiscal Year Ends: 12/31
Parent Company:

SALARIES/BONUSES:
Top Exec. Salary: $837,500 Bonus: $2,716,250
Second Exec. Salary: $567,188 Bonus: $1,845,000

OTHER THOUGHTS:
Estimated Female Officers or Directors: 2
Hot Spot for Advancement for Women/Minorities:

Sales, profits and employees may be estimates. Financial information, benefits and other data can change quickly and may vary from those stated here.

Envision Healthcare Corporation

www.evhc.net

NAIC Code: 621610

TYPES OF BUSINESS:
Home Health Care Services
Other Human Health Activities

BRANDS/DIVISIONS/AFFILIATES:
KKR & Co Inc
Envision Physician Services
Evolution Health
AMSURG

CONTACTS: Note: Officers with more than one job title may be intentionally listed here more than once.
Christopher A. Holden, CEO
Karey Witty, COO
William Sanger, Chairman of the Board
Teresa Sparks, CFO
Bob Kneeley, Sr. VP-Mktg. & Communications
Kristin Darby, CIO
Karey Witty, Executive VP
Phillip Clendenin, Executive VP
Brian Jackson, Executive VP
Craig Wilson, General Counsel
Patrick Solomon, Other Executive Officer
Christopher Holden, President
Kenneth Zongor, Senior VP

GROWTH PLANS/SPECIAL FEATURES:

Envision Healthcare Corporation is a clinician-led organization operating through three primary business units: Envision Physician Services, Evolution Health and AMSURG. The company delivers its services to more than 1,800 clinical departments in healthcare facilities in 45 U.S. states and the District of Columbia. The Envision Physician Services business unit provides tailored physician services to hospital and health systems, including anesthesia, emergency medicine, hospital medicine, radiology and surgical services, as well as women's and children's services. The Evolution Health business unit provides home health, hospice and home infusion services, which are patient-centered solutions. Evolution Health focuses on hiring compassionate, highly-experienced clinicians to deliver outcomes that will reduce re-hospitalizations and increase patient satisfaction. This division provides comprehensive traditional home health services reimbursed by Medicare, Medicaid and commercial payers or can provide custom solutions to health plans, hospital partners and other care models. Last, AMSURG owns and operates more than 260 surgery centers and one surgical hospital across 35 U.S. states and the District of Columbia. The company's medical specialties range from gastroenterology to ophthalmology and orthopedics. AMSURG is a leader in the ambulatory surgery center quality movement, and therefore provides an approach that combines technology, data analytics, patient engagement and quality reporting for optimal outcomes for patients. In October 2018, the firm was wholly-acquired by private equity firm KKR & Co., Inc. for approximately $5.5 billion, and ceased from public trading.

FINANCIAL DATA: Note: Data for latest year may not have been available at press time.

In U.S. $	2018	2017	2016	2015	2014	2013
Revenue	8,500,000,000	7,819,299,840	3,696,000,000	2,566,884,096	1,621,949,056	1,079,342,976
R&D Expense						
Operating Income						
Operating Margin %						
SGA Expense						
Net Income		-228,000,000	-18,600,000	162,947,008	53,701,000	72,703,000
Operating Cash Flow						
Capital Expenditure						
EBITDA						
Return on Assets %						
Return on Equity %						
Debt to Equity						

CONTACT INFORMATION:
Phone: 615-665-1283 Fax:
Toll-Free:
Address: 1A Burton Hills Blvd., Nashville, TN 37215 United States

STOCK TICKER/OTHER:
Stock Ticker: Subsidiary Exchange: NYS
Employees: 65,200 Fiscal Year Ends: 12/31
Parent Company: KKR & Co Inc

SALARIES/BONUSES:
Top Exec. Salary: $ Bonus: $
Second Exec. Salary: $ Bonus: $

OTHER THOUGHTS:
Estimated Female Officers or Directors:
Hot Spot for Advancement for Women/Minorities:

Sales, profits and employees may be estimates. Financial information, benefits and other data can change quickly and may vary from those stated here.

Epic Systems Corporation

www.epic.com

NAIC Code: 0

TYPES OF BUSINESS:
Computer Software, Healthcare & Biotechnology
Information Networks
Support Services

BRANDS/DIVISIONS/AFFILIATES:
Epicenter
EpicCare
Lucy
Community Library Exchange

CONTACTS:
Note: Officers with more than one job title may be intentionally listed here more than once.

Judy Faulkner, CEO
Carl Dvorak, Exec. VP

GROWTH PLANS/SPECIAL FEATURES:

Epic Systems Corporation is a developer of health industry clinical, access and revenue software for mid-and large-sized medical groups, hospitals, academic facilities, children's organizations, multi-hospital systems and integrated health care organizations. All Epic software applications are designed to share a single database, called Epicenter, so that each viewer can access available patient data through a single interface from anywhere in the organization. The firm's clinical software products include integrated inpatient and ambulatory systems under the EpicCare brand as well as health information management tools and specialty information systems. The firm's interoperability service, Lucy, personal health record that allows patients to organize and access their medical history independently of any one facility. Other products offer access services, including scheduling, inpatient and ambulatory registration, call management and nurse triage; revenue cycle services, such as hospital and professional billing; health plan and managed care administration systems; clinical and financial data repositories; enterprise reporting; patient medical record access systems; and connectivity tools, including voice recognition, interfacing and patient monitoring devices. In conjunction with its software applications, the company provides extensive client services, including training, process engineering, tailoring of applications to the client's situation and access to network specialists who plan and implement client systems. In addition, Epic hosts Community Library Exchange, an online collection of application tools and pre-made content that allows clients to share report and registration templates, custom forms, enterprise report formats and documentation shortcuts. Epic is headquartered in Wisconsin, USA, with international offices in the Netherlands, Austria, Denmark, United Arab Emirates, the U.K., Saudi Arabia, Finland and Singapore.

Employees of the firm are offered medical, dental, vision, life and disability insurance; a 401(k) plan; and flexible spending accounts.

FINANCIAL DATA: Note: Data for latest year may not have been available at press time.

In U.S. $	2018	2017	2016	2015	2014	2013
Revenue	2,890,000,000	2,740,000,000	2,550,000,000	2,015,000,000	1,856,000,000	1,750,000,000
R&D Expense						
Operating Income						
Operating Margin %						
SGA Expense						
Net Income						
Operating Cash Flow						
Capital Expenditure						
EBITDA						
Return on Assets %						
Return on Equity %						
Debt to Equity						

CONTACT INFORMATION:
Phone: 608-271-9000 Fax: 608-271-7237
Toll-Free:
Address: 1979 Milky Way, Verona, WI 53593 United States

SALARIES/BONUSES:
Top Exec. Salary: $ Bonus: $
Second Exec. Salary: $ Bonus: $

STOCK TICKER/OTHER:
Stock Ticker: Private
Employees: 9,700
Parent Company:

Exchange:
Fiscal Year Ends: 12/31

OTHER THOUGHTS:
Estimated Female Officers or Directors: 1
Hot Spot for Advancement for Women/Minorities:

Estee Lauder Companies Inc (The)

NAIC Code: 325620

www.elcompanies.com

TYPES OF BUSINESS:
Cosmetics
Cosmetic & Fragrance Sales
Retail Cosmetics Stores
Hair Care Products

BRANDS/DIVISIONS/AFFILIATES:

CONTACTS:
Note: Officers with more than one job title may be intentionally listed here more than once.

Fabrizio Freda, CEO
John Demsey, Pres., Divisional
Tracey Travis, CFO
Leonard Lauder, Chairman Emeritus
William Lauder, Chairman of the Board
Ronald Lauder, Chairman, Divisional
Michael OHare, Executive VP, Divisional
Carl Haney, Executive VP, Divisional
Gregory Polcer, Executive VP, Divisional
Alexandra Trower, Executive VP, Divisional
Sara Moss, Executive VP
Cedric Prouve, President, Divisional
Jane Hudis, President, Divisional

GROWTH PLANS/SPECIAL FEATURES:

The Estee Lauder Companies, Inc. is a global manufacturer and marketer of skin care, cosmetic, fragrance and hair care products. Skin care products include moisturizers, serums, cleansers, toners, body care, exfoliators, acne care, facial masks, cleansing devices and sun care. Makeup products consist of lipsticks, lip glosses, mascaras, foundations, eyeshadows, nail polishes and powders. Fragrances are sold in various forms, including eau de parfum sprays and colognes, as well as lotions, powders, creams, candles and soaps that are infused with a particular fragrance. Hair care products include shampoos, conditioners, styling products, treatments, finishing sprays and hair color. Estee Lauder's products are sold in over 150 countries and territories under brand names such as Estee Lauder, Aramis, Clinique, Origins, M.A.C., Bobbi Brown, La Mer, Jo Malone London, Too Faced and Aveda. The firm is also the global licensee for fragrances and cosmetics sold under the Tommy Hilfiger, Donna Karan New York, DKNY, Michael Kors, Ermenegildo Zegna and Tory Burch brand names. Estee Lauder sells its products principally through 46,000 points of sale, including upscale department stores, specialty retailers, upscale perfumeries and pharmacies and prestige salons and spas as well as freestanding company-owned stores and spas, authorized retailer web sites, stores on cruise ships, television direct marketing, in-flight and duty-free shops and self-select outlets. The founding Lauder family still controls approximately 87% of the company's voting shares. The firm operates on a global basis, with over half of its sales generated outside the U.S. Makeup brings in the majority of Estee Lauder's net sales (more than 40%), with skin care coming in second (nearly 40%), fragrance third (more than 10%), hair care fourth (approximately 5%) and other products last (about 1%). The firm's manufacturing operations are located in the Americas, EMEA (Europe, Middle East, Africa) and Asia-Pacific.

FINANCIAL DATA:
Note: Data for latest year may not have been available at press time.

In U.S. $	2018	2017	2016	2015	2014	2013
Revenue	13,683,000,000	11,824,000,000	11,262,300,000	10,780,400,000	10,968,800,000	10,181,700,000
R&D Expense						
Operating Income	2,283,000,000	1,918,000,000	1,743,400,000	1,606,300,000	1,824,700,000	1,558,800,000
Operating Margin %		.16%	.15%	.15%	.17%	.15%
SGA Expense	8,556,000,000	7,469,000,000	7,337,800,000	7,073,500,000	6,985,900,000	6,597,000,000
Net Income	1,108,000,000	1,249,000,000	1,114,600,000	1,088,900,000	1,204,100,000	1,019,800,000
Operating Cash Flow	2,573,000,000	1,800,000,000	1,788,700,000	1,943,300,000	1,535,200,000	1,226,300,000
Capital Expenditure	629,000,000	504,000,000	525,300,000	473,000,000	510,200,000	461,000,000
EBITDA	2,639,000,000	2,184,000,000	2,040,600,000	2,029,900,000	2,212,200,000	1,866,900,000
Return on Assets %		.12%	.13%	.14%	.16%	.15%
Return on Equity %		.31%	.31%	.29%	.34%	.34%
Debt to Equity		0.772	0.535	0.441	0.344	0.403

CONTACT INFORMATION:
Phone: 212 572-4200 Fax: 212 572-3941
Toll-Free:
Address: 767 5th Ave., New York, NY 10153 United States

SALARIES/BONUSES:
Top Exec. Salary: $1,900,000 Bonus: $
Second Exec. Salary: $1,500,000 Bonus: $

STOCK TICKER/OTHER:
Stock Ticker: EL
Employees: 46,000
Parent Company:

Exchange: NYS
Fiscal Year Ends: 06/30

OTHER THOUGHTS:
Estimated Female Officers or Directors: 10
Hot Spot for Advancement for Women/Minorities: Y

Exelon Corporation

www.exeloncorp.com

NAIC Code: 221113

TYPES OF BUSINESS:
Electric Power Generation-Nuclear
Energy Marketing

BRANDS/DIVISIONS/AFFILIATES:
Exelon Generation Company LLC
Pepco Holdings LLC
Commonwealth Edison Company
PECO Energy Company
Baltimore Gas and Electric Company
Potomac Electric Power Company
Delmarva Power & Light Company
Atlantic City Electric Company

CONTACTS:
Note: Officers with more than one job title may be intentionally listed here more than once.
Denis OBrien, CEO, Divisional
Michael Innocenzo, COO, Subsidiary
Christopher Crane, CEO

GROWTH PLANS/SPECIAL FEATURES:
Exelon Corporation is a Fortune 100 utility services holding company, delivering electricity and natural gas to customers in 48 U.S. states, the District of Columbia and Canada. The firm's primary subsidiaries include Exelon Generation Company, LLC (ExGen); Pepco Holdings, LLC (PH); Commonwealth Edison Company (ComEd); PECO Energy Company; Baltimore Gas and Electric Company (BGE); Potomac Electric Power Company (PepCo); Delmarva Power & Light Company; and Atlantic City Electric Company (Atlanta Electric). ExGen's business consists of the generation, delivery and marketing of power across multiple geographical regions through 50.01%-owned Constellation Energy Nuclear Group, Inc., which sells electricity to both wholesale and retail customers. ExGen also sells natural gas and other energy-related products and services. PH is a utility services holding company engaged in the energy delivery business, and is based in Washington, D.C. ComEd purchases and sells regulated retail electricity, and also provides electric transmission and distribution services to retail customers in northern Illinois. PECO, BGE, PepCo, Delmarva and Atlanta Electric operate the same as ComEd: PECO serves retail customers in southeastern Pennsylvania; BGE serves central Maryland; PepCo serves the District of Columbia and major portions of Montgomery County and Prince George's County; Delmarva serves portions of Delaware and Maryland; and Atlantic Electric serves portions of southern New Jersey. In November 2017, ExGen Texas Power, LLC and all of its wholly-owned subsidiaries filed bankruptcy and its assets and liabilities were deconsolidated from Exelon Corporation. In October 2018, Exelon Corporation acquired the Everett LNG Facility in Massachusetts, assuming both facility ownership and management of operations.

Exelon offers employees health and life insurance, disability coverage, a 401(k) and an employee stock purchase plan.

FINANCIAL DATA:
Note: Data for latest year may not have been available at press time.

In U.S. $	2018	2017	2016	2015	2014	2013
Revenue	35,985,000,000	33,531,000,000	31,360,000,000	29,447,000,000	27,429,000,000	24,888,000,000
R&D Expense						
Operating Income	3,842,000,000	3,811,000,000	3,160,000,000	4,391,000,000	2,390,000,000	3,646,000,000
Operating Margin %		.11%	.10%	.15%	.09%	.15%
SGA Expense						
Net Income	2,010,000,000	3,770,000,000	1,134,000,000	2,269,000,000	1,623,000,000	1,719,000,000
Operating Cash Flow	8,644,000,000	7,480,000,000	8,445,000,000	7,616,000,000	4,457,000,000	6,343,000,000
Capital Expenditure	7,594,000,000	7,584,000,000	8,553,000,000	7,624,000,000	6,077,000,000	5,395,000,000
EBITDA	9,757,000,000	10,743,000,000	9,101,000,000	8,350,000,000	7,419,000,000	7,908,000,000
Return on Assets %		.03%	.01%	.02%	.02%	.02%
Return on Equity %		.14%	.04%	.09%	.07%	.08%
Debt to Equity		1.091	1.247	0.942	0.885	0.804

CONTACT INFORMATION:
Phone: 312 394-7398 Fax: 312 394-7945
Toll-Free: 800-483-3220
Address: 10 S. Dearborn St., 48/Fl., Chicago, IL 60680-5379 United States

STOCK TICKER/OTHER:
Stock Ticker: EXC
Employees: 34,396
Parent Company:

Exchange: NYS
Fiscal Year Ends: 12/31

SALARIES/BONUSES:
Top Exec. Salary: $1,255,515 Bonus: $
Second Exec. Salary: $857,477 Bonus: $

OTHER THOUGHTS:
Estimated Female Officers or Directors: 6
Hot Spot for Advancement for Women/Minorities: Y

Sales, profits and employees may be estimates. Financial information, benefits and other data can change quickly and may vary from those stated here.

Expedia Group Inc

NAIC Code: 561510

www.expedia.com

TYPES OF BUSINESS:
Online Travel Services
Online Reservations
Corporate Travel Services
Vacation Packages
Retail Travel Services Kiosks
Destination Activities & Tours
Online Travel Information
Inventory-Based Hotel Room Offerings

BRANDS/DIVISIONS/AFFILIATES:
Expedia.com
Hotels.com
Expedia Partner Solutions
trivago
HomeAway
Travelocity
CarRentals.com
SilverRail Technologies Inc

CONTACTS:
Note: Officers with more than one job title may be intentionally listed here more than once.

Mark Okerstrom, CEO
Alan Pickerill, CFO
Barry Diller, Chairman of the Board
Lance Soliday, Chief Accounting Officer
Jonathan Dolgen, Director Emeritus
Peter Kern, Director
Robert Dzielak, Other Executive Officer

GROWTH PLANS/SPECIAL FEATURES:

Expedia Group, Inc. is an online travel company that offers business and leisure travelers the ability to research, plan, book and experience travel via technology tools and related information. The group seeks to grow its business through a portfolio of travel brands, including majority-owned subsidiaries that feature various types of travel-related bookings, including properties, flights, rental cars, cruises, activities as well as insurance. Travel suppliers within Expedia's portfolio distribute and market products through its desktop and mobile offerings, as well as through alternative distribution channels, its private label business and its call centers. Expedia's advertising and media businesses help other businesses reach a large audience of travelers across the globe. The company's portfolio of brands include: Expedia.com, Hotels.com, Expedia Partner Solutions, trivago, HomeAway, Egencia, Orbitz, CheapTickets, Travelocity, Hotwire, Wotif Group, Expedia Group Media Solutions, CarRentals.com, Classic Vacations, Expedia Local Expert, Expedia CruiseShipCenters, and SilverRail Technologies, Inc. In April 2019, Expedia Group agreed to acquire Liberty Expedia Holdings, Inc., which holds an approximate 23.9 million shares of Expedia Group. This will result with about 5.7 million shares of Expedia Group to be outstanding at the closing of the transaction.

Expedia Group offers employees medical, life, AD&D, disability, dental and vision insurance; 401(k); and various employee assistance programs.

FINANCIAL DATA:
Note: Data for latest year may not have been available at press time.

In U.S. $	2018	2017	2016	2015	2014	2013
Revenue	11,223,000,000	10,059,840,000	8,773,564,000	6,672,317,000	5,763,485,000	4,771,259,000
R&D Expense	1,617,000,000	1,386,787,000	1,235,019,000	830,244,000	686,154,000	577,820,000
Operating Income	842,000,000	641,876,000	552,499,000	518,437,000	543,394,000	432,532,000
Operating Margin %		.06%	.06%	.08%	.09%	.09%
SGA Expense	6,516,000,000	5,999,205,000	5,072,207,000	3,850,412,000	3,275,241,000	2,651,142,000
Net Income	406,000,000	377,964,000	281,848,000	764,465,000	398,097,000	232,850,000
Operating Cash Flow	1,975,000,000	1,799,154,000	1,564,334,000	1,368,045,000	1,366,959,000	763,200,000
Capital Expenditure	878,000,000	710,330,000	749,348,000	787,041,000	328,387,000	308,581,000
EBITDA	1,676,000,000	1,488,020,000	1,243,950,000	1,552,502,000	908,162,000	671,526,000
Return on Assets %		.02%	.02%	.06%	.05%	.03%
Return on Equity %		.09%	.06%	.23%	.20%	.11%
Debt to Equity		0.829	0.765	0.658	0.979	0.582

CONTACT INFORMATION:
Phone: 425 679-7200 Fax: 425 564-7240
Toll-Free: 800-397-3342
Address: 333 108th Ave. NE, Bellevue, WA 98004 United States

SALARIES/BONUSES:
Top Exec. Salary: $824,039 Bonus: $1,250,000
Second Exec. Salary: $465,000 Bonus: $1,000,000

STOCK TICKER/OTHER:
Stock Ticker: EXPE
Employees: 20,075
Parent Company:

Exchange: NAS
Fiscal Year Ends: 12/31

OTHER THOUGHTS:
Estimated Female Officers or Directors: 1
Hot Spot for Advancement for Women/Minorities:

Sales, profits and employees may be estimates. Financial information, benefits and other data can change quickly and may vary from those stated here.

Expeditors International of Washington Inc   www.expeditors.com

NAIC Code: 488510

TYPES OF BUSINESS:
Freight Transportation Arrangement
Online Services
Logistics Software
Freight Consolidation
Customs Brokerage

BRANDS/DIVISIONS/AFFILIATES:
exp.o
exp.o Booking
exp.o ISF
TradeFlow
Expeditors Tradewin LLC
Cargo Signal Solutions LLC
Expeditors Cargo Insurance Brokers

CONTACTS:
Note: Officers with more than one job title may be intentionally listed here more than once.

Jeffrey Musser, CEO
Bradley Powell, CFO
Christopher McClincy, Chief Information Officer
Philip Coughlin, Chief Strategy Officer
Robert Wright, Director
Benjamin Clark, General Counsel
Richard Rostan, President, Divisional
Daniel Wall, President, Divisional
Eugene Alger, President, Divisional

GROWTH PLANS/SPECIAL FEATURES:

Expeditors International of Washington, Inc. provides global logistics services through an international network spanning 322 locations in 103 countries, which includes four regional headquarters in London, Dubai, Shanghai and Singapore. The company's services include consolidation or forwarding of air and ocean freight, customs brokerage, distribution management, vendor consolidation, cargo insurance, real-time monitoring, purchase order management and customized logistics information. Ocean freight services account for 30% of the firm's revenue, airfreight accounts for 42%, and customs brokerage and other services account for 28%. Expeditors International does not compete for domestic freight, overnight courier or small parcel business and does not own aircraft or steamships. The company provides many services over the internet. Expeditors International's web-based tracking system, exp.o, offers query capabilities to find the status of inbound shipments or orders and to view customs details. Linked to exp.o, exp.o Booking is the company's web-based electronic booking tool that provides notifications, pick-up arrangements, shipment tracking and document generation. Exp.o ISF (importer security filing) assists importers in fulfilling U.S. Customs Importer Security Filing requirements. Through web access to international tariff data and rules, TradeFlow helps international companies reduce the risks and manage the costs associated with importing and exporting. Subsidiary Expeditors Tradewin, LLC provides customs consulting services. Other subsidiaries include Cargo Signal Solutions LLC and Expeditors Cargo Insurance Brokers. Expeditors International primarily serves the aerospace, automotive, fashion, healthcare, manufacturing, oil/energy, retail and technology industries.

Expeditors International offers its employees a comprehensive benefits package, a 401(k) plan and a stock purchase plan.

FINANCIAL DATA:
Note: Data for latest year may not have been available at press time.

In U.S. $	2018	2017	2016	2015	2014	2013
Revenue	8,138,365,000	6,920,948,000	6,098,037,000	6,616,632,000	6,564,721,000	6,080,257,000
R&D Expense						
Operating Income	796,563,000	700,260,000	670,163,000	721,484,000	594,648,000	552,073,000
Operating Margin %		.10%	.11%	.11%	.09%	.09%
SGA Expense	45,346,000	44,290,000	41,763,000	41,990,000	38,125,000	33,243,000
Net Income	618,199,000	489,345,000	430,807,000	457,223,000	376,888,000	348,526,000
Operating Cash Flow	572,804,000	488,639,000	529,099,000	564,712,000	394,966,000	407,536,000
Capital Expenditure	47,474,000	95,016,000	59,316,000	44,383,000	64,573,000	53,411,000
EBITDA	850,582,000	749,570,000	716,959,000	767,496,000	643,940,000	600,144,000
Return on Assets %		.17%	.16%	.17%	.13%	.12%
Return on Equity %		.26%	.24%	.26%	.19%	.17%
Debt to Equity						

CONTACT INFORMATION:
Phone: 206 674-3400   Fax: 206 674-3459
Toll-Free:
Address: 1015 3rd Ave., 12/Fl, Seattle, WA 98104 United States

STOCK TICKER/OTHER:
Stock Ticker: EXPD
Employees: 16,000
Parent Company:

Exchange: NAS
Fiscal Year Ends: 12/31

SALARIES/BONUSES:
Top Exec. Salary: $120,000   Bonus: $
Second Exec. Salary: $100,000   Bonus: $

OTHER THOUGHTS:
Estimated Female Officers or Directors: 2
Hot Spot for Advancement for Women/Minorities:

Exxon Mobil Corporation (ExxonMobil)

NAIC Code: 211111

www.exxonmobil.com

TYPES OF BUSINESS:
Oil & Gas Exploration & Production
Gas Refining & Supply
Fuel Marketing
Power Generation
Chemicals
Petroleum Products
Convenience Stores

BRANDS/DIVISIONS/AFFILIATES:
ExxonMobil
Esso
Exxon
XTO
Mobil

CONTACTS:
Note: Officers with more than one job title may be intentionally listed here more than once.

Darren Woods, CEO
Peter Clarke, VP
Andrew Swiger, CFO
David Rosenthal, Chief Accounting Officer
James Spellings, Other Corporate Officer
Bryan Milton, President, Divisional
Sara Ortwein, President, Subsidiary
Liam Mallon, President, Subsidiary
John Verity, President, Subsidiary
Bradley Corson, President, Subsidiary
Neil Duffin, President, Subsidiary
Stephen Greenlee, President, Subsidiary
Neil Hansen, Secretary
Neil Chapman, Senior VP
Jack Williams, Senior VP
Theodore Wojnar, Vice President, Divisional
Randall Ebner, Vice President
Robert Schleckser, Vice President

GROWTH PLANS/SPECIAL FEATURES:

Exxon Mobil Corporation (ExxonMobil) is one of the largest international petroleum and natural gas exploration and production companies in the world. Its principal business is energy, involving exploration for and production of crude oil and natural gas; the manufacture of petroleum products; and the transportation and sale of crude oil, natural gas and petroleum products. The company has hundreds of affiliates, many with names that include ExxonMobil, Esso, Exxon, XTO or Mobil. Overall, the firm divides its business units into three areas: upstream, downstream and chemical. The upstream business focuses on conventional oil, heavy oil, shale gas, deepwater, liquefied natural gas (LNG), Arctic and sour gas projects. The downstream business is concerned with refining crude oil and other feedstocks into fuels, lubricants and other chemicals and delivering it to customers through a global distributor network. The chemical business is focused on the production of olefins, such as ethylene and propylene, and polyolefins, such as polyethylene and polypropylene. In addition, it manufactures specialty chemicals for use in water treatment, coatings, lubricants and oil drilling fluids. In January 2019, ExxonMobil announced that it had begun drilling the Haimara-1 exploration well offshore Guyana, the first of two planned wells in South America; and signed a partnership agreement with IBM to advance the potential use of quantum computing in developing next-generation energy and manufacturing technologies.

U.S. employee benefits include health, dental and vision coverage; life insurance; education assistance; childcare, elder care and adoption assistance; and spousal relocation assistance.

FINANCIAL DATA:
Note: Data for latest year may not have been available at press time.

In U.S. $	2018	2017	2016	2015	2014	2013
Revenue	279,332,000,000	237,162,000,000	218,608,000,000	259,488,000,000	394,105,000,000	420,836,000,000
R&D Expense						
Operating Income	22,124,000,000	12,074,000,000	936,000,000	12,883,000,000	34,082,000,000	40,301,000,000
Operating Margin %		.05%	.00%	.05%	.09%	.10%
SGA Expense	11,480,000,000	10,956,000,000	10,799,000,000	11,501,000,000	12,598,000,000	12,877,000,000
Net Income	20,840,000,000	19,710,000,000	7,840,000,000	16,150,000,000	32,520,000,000	32,580,000,000
Operating Cash Flow	36,014,000,000	30,066,000,000	22,082,000,000	30,344,000,000	45,116,000,000	44,914,000,000
Capital Expenditure	19,574,000,000	15,402,000,000	16,163,000,000	26,490,000,000	32,952,000,000	33,669,000,000
EBITDA	50,464,000,000	39,168,000,000	30,730,000,000	40,325,000,000	69,213,000,000	74,902,000,000
Return on Assets %		.06%	.02%	.05%	.09%	.10%
Return on Equity %		.11%	.05%	.09%	.19%	.19%
Debt to Equity		0.13	0.173	0.117	0.067	0.04

CONTACT INFORMATION:
Phone: 972 444-1000   Fax: 972 444-1348
Toll-Free:
Address: 5959 Las Colinas Blvd., Irving, TX 75039 United States

SALARIES/BONUSES:
Top Exec. Salary: $1,400,000   Bonus: $2,464,000
Second Exec. Salary: $1,395,750   Bonus: $1,848,000

STOCK TICKER/OTHER:
Stock Ticker: XOM
Employees: 71,100
Parent Company:
Exchange: NYS
Fiscal Year Ends: 12/31

OTHER THOUGHTS:
Estimated Female Officers or Directors: 2
Hot Spot for Advancement for Women/Minorities: Y

Sales, profits and employees may be estimates. Financial information, benefits and other data can change quickly and may vary from those stated here.

ExxonMobil Chemical Company Inc

www.exxonmobilchemical.com

NAIC Code: 325110

TYPES OF BUSINESS:
Plastics & Rubber Manufacturing
Petrochemicals
Catalyst Technology
Polypropylene

BRANDS/DIVISIONS/AFFILIATES:
Exxon Mobil Corporation
ExxonMobil Chemical Technology Licensing LLC
Exxcore
Enable

CONTACTS:
Note: Officers with more than one job title may be intentionally listed here more than once.
Karen McKee, Pres.
Sherman J. Glass Jr., Pres., ExxonMobil Refining & Amp
Donald D. Humphreys, Sr. VP

GROWTH PLANS/SPECIAL FEATURES:
ExxonMobil Chemical Company, Inc., a subsidiary of Exxon Mobil Corporation, is a global leader in the petrochemicals industry. The firm applies proprietary technology to create products that improve the quality of life for people worldwide. Its products and services are divided into three units: polymers, chemicals and fluids, and technology licensing and catalysts. These units produce sustainable solutions in relation to olefins, aromatics, fluids, synthetic rubber, polyethylene, polypropylene, plasticizers, synthetic lubricant base-stocks, additives for fuels and lubricants, and zeolite catalysts. The company's products span a variety of markets, but most can be grouped into the following areas: automotive, packaging, construction/industrial and personal care. ExxonMobile Chemical's technology division focuses on developing new products with environmentally-preferred characteristics, including tire innerliners made with Exxcore, a vulcanized allow resin that holds air longer; and Enable metallocene polyethylene chemicals, which significantly reduces waste and energy consumption across a wide range of film applications. Technologies are available for licensing through ExxonMobile Chemical Technology Licensing, LLC. These cutting-edge proprietary catalysts and license advantaged process technologies are designed to serve refining, gas and chemical needs. This division's services typically include: planning and process studies, development of design specifications, operations support during startup and commissioning, ongoing technical services for optimization or troubleshooting, and catalyst performance monitoring. Based in Texas, USA, the firm has regional offices in Singapore and Belgium. During 2018, ExxonMobil Chemical announced that it had started detailed engineering work on a potential U.S. Gulf Coast project to expand polypropylene manufacturing capacity by up to 450,000 tons a year. Facility startup could come as early as 2021.

The firm employs 19,000 scientists and engineers and invests very heavily in research and development.

FINANCIAL DATA:
Note: Data for latest year may not have been available at press time.

In U.S. $	2018	2017	2016	2015	2014	2013
Revenue	35,500,000,000	33,000,000,000	31,000,000,000	28,134,000,000	38,179,000,000	
R&D Expense						
Operating Income						
Operating Margin %						
SGA Expense						
Net Income	3,351,000,000	4,518,000,000	4,615,000,000	4,418,000,000	4,315,000,000	3,828,000,000
Operating Cash Flow						
Capital Expenditure						
EBITDA						
Return on Assets %						
Return on Equity %						
Debt to Equity						

CONTACT INFORMATION:
Phone: 281-870-6000   Fax: 281-870-6661
Toll-Free:
Address: 22777 Springwoods Village Pkwy., Spring, TX 77389-1425 United States

STOCK TICKER/OTHER:
Stock Ticker: Subsidiary   Exchange:
Employees: 28,000   Fiscal Year Ends: 12/31
Parent Company: Exxon Mobil Corporation

SALARIES/BONUSES:
Top Exec. Salary: $ Bonus: $
Second Exec. Salary: $ Bonus: $

OTHER THOUGHTS:
Estimated Female Officers or Directors: 1
Hot Spot for Advancement for Women/Minorities: Y

Sales, profits and employees may be estimates. Financial information, benefits and other data can change quickly and may vary from those stated here.

EY LLP

www.ey.com/us/en/home

NAIC Code: 541211

TYPES OF BUSINESS:
Accounting
Risk Management
Tax Preparation Services
Human Resources Management
IT Services
Transaction Support Services
Industry Publications

BRANDS/DIVISIONS/AFFILIATES:
EY

CONTACTS: Note: Officers with more than one job title may be intentionally listed here more than once.
Mark Weinberger, Global CEO
Michael Inserra, Regional Managing Partner-Financial Svcs.
Tom Hough, Vice Chair-Assurance Svcs.
Richard Jeanneret, Vice Chair-Transaction Advisory Svcs.
Jean-Yves, Vice Chair-Quality & Risk Mgmt.
Tom McGrath, Sr. Vice Chair-Accounts
Ronen Barel, Chmn.

GROWTH PLANS/SPECIAL FEATURES:
EY, LLP, the U.S. branch of the global accounting firm EY, is a professional services company. EY, LLP provides advisory, tax, assurance and transaction services. Advisory services include actuarial, customer, cyber security, finance, risk management, internal audit, people advisory, program management, risk assurance, risk transformation, strategy, supply chain, operations and technology. Tax services include global tax, country tax, cross border tax, global trade, global compliance and reporting, human capital, private client, law, tax accounting, tax performance, tax policy and controversy, transaction tax, sales tax, transfer pricing and operating model effectiveness. Assurance services include accounting compliance, reporting, climate change, sustainability, financial accounting, financial statement audit, fraud investigation and dispute services. Transactions service include corporate development, divesture, lead advisory, operational transaction, restructuring, strategy, transaction support, transaction tax, valuation and business modeling. Industries served by EY, LLP include automotive, transportation, health, oil and gas, technology, consumer products, retail, life sciences, power/utilities, telecommunications, financial services, media/entertainment, private equity, government, public sector, mining/metals, real estate, hospitality and construction.

FINANCIAL DATA: Note: Data for latest year may not have been available at press time.

In U.S. $	2018	2017	2016	2015	2014	2013
Revenue	15,600,000,000	13,000,000,000	12,200,000,000	11,200,000,000	9,900,000,000	9,100,000,000
R&D Expense						
Operating Income						
Operating Margin %						
SGA Expense						
Net Income						
Operating Cash Flow						
Capital Expenditure						
EBITDA						
Return on Assets %						
Return on Equity %						
Debt to Equity						

CONTACT INFORMATION:
Phone: 212-773-3000 Fax: 212-773-6350
Toll-Free:
Address: 5 Times Sq., New York, NY 10036-6530 United States

STOCK TICKER/OTHER:
Stock Ticker: Subsidiary   Exchange:
Employees: 70,341   Fiscal Year Ends: 06/30
Parent Company: EY

SALARIES/BONUSES:
Top Exec. Salary: $ Bonus: $
Second Exec. Salary: $ Bonus: $

OTHER THOUGHTS:
Estimated Female Officers or Directors: 5
Hot Spot for Advancement for Women/Minorities: Y

F5 Networks Inc

www.f5.com

NAIC Code: 0

TYPES OF BUSINESS:
Computer Software: Network Management (IT), System Testing & Storage
Internet Traffic Management Solutions
Firewall Software
File Virtualization

BRANDS/DIVISIONS/AFFILIATES:
BIG-IP
VIPRION
Silverline
iRules
iRules LX
iControl
iApps
iCall

CONTACTS: Note: Officers with more than one job title may be intentionally listed here more than once.
Francis Pelzer, CFO
Ryan Kearny, Chief Technology Officer
Alan Higginson, Director
Francois Locoh-Donou, Director
Steve McMillan, Executive VP, Divisional
Chad Whalen, Executive VP, Divisional
Scot Rogers, Executive VP
Ana White, Executive VP
Tom Fountain, Executive VP
Kara Sprague, General Manager, Divisional

GROWTH PLANS/SPECIAL FEATURES:
F5 Networks, Inc. provides application delivery networking products that improve the security, availability and performance of network applications. The core technology of the firm is the full-proxy, programmable, massively-scalable software platform called TMOS (Traffic Management Operating System). The TMOS platform supports a broadest array of application services, including local and global traffic management, network and application security, access management, web acceleration and several other network and application services. These services are available as software modules that can run individually or as part of an integrated solution on the high-performance, scalable, purpose-built BIG-IP appliances and chassis-based VIPRION systems; or as software-only Virtual Editions that run on major hypervisors in public and private clouds, with network virtualization software comprising built-in capabilities to enable 5G and automation requirements. The cloud-based Silverline software-as-a-service (SaaS) offerings allow customers to subscribe to online denial-of-service protection and application security services. The core features and functions of TMOS enable the firm's products to inspect and modify the content of IP traffic flows at network speeds and sessions between users and applications and support a broad and growing array of services. The built-in scripting language, iRules and iRules LX, enables customers and third parties to write customized rules to inspect and modify traffic. TMOS also has an open software interface called iControl, which allows the firm's products to communicate with one another and with third-party products; a set of features called iApps that speed deployment of services and give users an application-centric view of how applications are managed and delivered; and a scripting framework called iCall that lets users configure their F5 devices inline.

Employee benefits include medical, dental and vision coverage; flexible spending accounts; life and disability insurance; employee stock and employee assistance programs; 401(k); and tuition assistance.

FINANCIAL DATA: Note: Data for latest year may not have been available at press time.

In U.S. $	2018	2017	2016	2015	2014	2013
Revenue	2,161,407,000	2,090,041,000	1,995,034,000	1,919,823,000	1,732,046,000	1,481,314,000
R&D Expense	366,084,000	350,365,000	334,227,000	296,583,000	263,792,000	209,614,000
Operating Income	609,325,000	577,065,000	556,428,000	552,899,000	493,557,000	430,818,000
Operating Margin %		.28%	.28%	.29%	.28%	.29%
SGA Expense	824,517,000	809,126,000	767,174,000	738,080,000	664,738,000	585,442,000
Net Income	453,689,000	420,761,000	365,855,000	365,014,000	311,183,000	277,314,000
Operating Cash Flow	761,068,000	740,281,000	711,535,000	684,541,000	548,992,000	499,693,000
Capital Expenditure	53,465,000	42,681,000	68,238,000	67,086,000	22,718,000	26,583,000
EBITDA	668,816,000	638,213,000	613,204,000	605,482,000	539,678,000	470,823,000
Return on Assets %		.18%	.16%	.16%	.14%	.13%
Return on Equity %		.35%	.29%	.27%	.21%	.19%
Debt to Equity						

CONTACT INFORMATION:
Phone: 206 272-5555 Fax: 206 272-5556
Toll-Free: 888-882-4447
Address: 401 Elliott Ave. W., Seattle, WA 98119 United States

SALARIES/BONUSES:
Top Exec. Salary: $348,968 Bonus: $500,000
Second Exec. Salary: $810,000 Bonus: $

STOCK TICKER/OTHER:
Stock Ticker: FFIV
Employees: 4,395
Parent Company:

Exchange: NAS
Fiscal Year Ends: 09/30

OTHER THOUGHTS:
Estimated Female Officers or Directors: 3
Hot Spot for Advancement for Women/Minorities: Y

Facebook Inc

NAIC Code: 519130

investor.fb.com/

TYPES OF BUSINESS:
Social Networking
Advertising Services
Developer Tools
Online Video
3-D Headset Manufacturing
Apps

BRANDS/DIVISIONS/AFFILIATES:
Facebook Platform
Instagram
Messenger
WhatsApp Messenger
Oculus
Portal
Portal+

CONTACTS:
Note: Officers with more than one job title may be intentionally listed here more than once.

Mark Zuckerberg, CEO
David Wehner, CFO
Susan Taylor, Chief Accounting Officer
Michael Schroepfer, Chief Technology Officer
Sheryl Sandberg, COO
Christopher Cox, Other Executive Officer
David Fischer, Other Executive Officer
Colin Stretch, Vice President

GROWTH PLANS/SPECIAL FEATURES:

Facebook, Inc. owns and operates a free social networking utility for communicating online with family, friends and acquaintances. As of September 2018, the company had 2.27 billion monthly active users in general, and 1.49 billion daily active users who specifically used the company's mobile products. Some of the site's core functions and applications include individual profiles and home pages; friend lists; group pages; and photos, videos, events and other shared items. Communication is enabled through means such as in-site instant messaging, personal messages, public posts and status updates. Third-party applications (such as games, quizzes and personality tests) can also be added to users' pages to further personalize the site. For privacy, the firm gives users the ability to limit, to some extent, who can view their profile, postings and other personal information. The company's Facebook Platform is a set of development tools and application programming interfaces that enable developers to integrate with Facebook to create social apps and websites. Millions of apps and websites have been integrated as part of the platform. Facebook generates the majority of its revenues from advertising, which can be customized to reach specifically targeted audiences by accessing information users provide the company on their individual profiles. Subsidiary Instagram is a mobile phone-based photo-sharing service that makes it simple for users to upload photos to their profiles; Messenger is a mobile-to-mobile messaging application; WhatsApp Messenger is a cross-platform mobile messaging app that allows people to exchange messages on mobile devices; and Oculus, a virtual reality technology and content platform that power products and enable users to immerse and interact in connected environments. In late-2018, Facebook launched a brand of smart displays called Portal and Portal+, comprising enhanced smart speakers for Amazon's Alexa and Facebook Messenger.

Facebook offers its employees comprehensive benefits.

FINANCIAL DATA: Note: Data for latest year may not have been available at press time.

In U.S. $	2018	2017	2016	2015	2014	2013
Revenue	55,838,000,000	40,653,000,000	27,638,000,000	17,928,000,000	12,466,000,000	7,872,000,000
R&D Expense	10,273,000,000	7,754,000,000	5,919,000,000	4,816,000,000	2,666,000,000	1,415,000,000
Operating Income	24,913,000,000	20,203,000,000	12,427,000,000	6,225,000,000	4,994,000,000	2,804,000,000
Operating Margin %		.50%	.45%	.35%	.40%	.36%
SGA Expense	11,297,000,000	7,242,000,000	5,503,000,000	4,020,000,000	2,653,000,000	1,778,000,000
Net Income	22,112,000,000	15,934,000,000	10,217,000,000	3,688,000,000	2,940,000,000	1,500,000,000
Operating Cash Flow	29,274,000,000	24,216,000,000	16,108,000,000	8,599,000,000	5,457,000,000	4,222,000,000
Capital Expenditure	13,915,000,000	6,733,000,000	4,491,000,000	2,523,000,000	1,831,000,000	1,362,000,000
EBITDA	29,685,000,000	23,625,000,000	14,870,000,000	8,162,000,000	6,176,000,000	3,821,000,000
Return on Assets %		.21%	.18%	.08%	.10%	.09%
Return on Equity %		.24%	.20%	.09%	.11%	.11%
Debt to Equity				0.002	0.003	0.015

CONTACT INFORMATION:
Phone: 650 543-4800 Fax:
Toll-Free:
Address: 1601 Willow Rd., Menlo Park, CA 94025 United States

SALARIES/BONUSES:
Top Exec. Salary: $843,077 Bonus: $638,310
Second Exec. Salary: $753,846 Bonus: $570,744

STOCK TICKER/OTHER:
Stock Ticker: FB
Employees: 17,048
Parent Company:

Exchange: NAS
Fiscal Year Ends: 12/31

OTHER THOUGHTS:
Estimated Female Officers or Directors: 2
Hot Spot for Advancement for Women/Minorities: Y

Sales, profits and employees may be estimates. Financial information, benefits and other data can change quickly and may vary from those stated here.

FactSet Research Systems Inc

www.factset.com

NAIC Code: 0

TYPES OF BUSINESS:
Online Financial & Economic Data
Financial Software
Consulting Services

BRANDS/DIVISIONS/AFFILIATES:
BISAM Technologies SA
Interactive Data Managed Solutions

CONTACTS: Note: Officers with more than one job title may be intentionally listed here more than once.
F. Snow, CEO
Helen Shan, CFO
Philip Hadley, Chairman of the Board
Brian Daly, Chief Accounting Officer
Gene Fernandez, Chief Technology Officer
John Wiseman, Executive VP, Divisional
Rachel Stern, Executive VP
Robert Robie, Executive VP

GROWTH PLANS/SPECIAL FEATURES:
FactSet Research Systems, Inc. supplies financial information and analytical applications to global investors, including portfolio managers, performance analysts, risk managers, sell-side equity researchers, investment bankers and fixed income professionals. Headquartered in Norwalk, Connecticut, the company operates 63 locations in 23 countries. FactSet has more than 89,000 users and 3,500 clients in over 50 countries worldwide, with access to data from more than 220 data suppliers, 115 news sources and 85 exchanges. It combines the content of tens of thousands of companies from multiple sources (stock markets, research firms, governments and others) into a single online platform of information and analytics. The firm integrates content from premier providers such as Thomson Reuters, Standard & Poor's, Axioma, Interactive Data Corporation, Dow Jones & Company, Northfield Information Services, Barclays Capital, Intex Solutions and many more. FactSet's operations are organized into three reportable segments based on geographic operations: the U.S., Europe and Asia Pacific. The majority of fiscal revenue is derived from its U.S. clients, with Europe being next and Asia Pacific the remainder. The U.S. segment services finance professionals including financial institutions throughout the Americas, while the European and Asia Pacific segments service investment professionals located throughout Europe and Asia, respectively. The European segment is headquartered in London, England and maintains offices in France, Germany, the Netherlands, Latvia, Dubai, Bulgaria, Switzerland, Spain and Italy. The Asia Pacific segment is headquartered in Tokyo, Japan with offices in Hong Kong, Australia, the Philippines, China and India. FactSet's client retention rate is over 95%.

FactSet offers U.S. employees medical, dental, life, disability, vision, AD&D and business travel insurance; wellness programs; disability and maternity leave; counseling services; flexible spending accounts; 401(k) and employee stock purchase plans; and tuition reimbursement.

FINANCIAL DATA: Note: Data for latest year may not have been available at press time.

In U.S. $	2018	2017	2016	2015	2014	2013
Revenue	1,350,145,000	1,221,179,000	1,127,092,000	1,006,768,000	920,335,000	858,112,000
R&D Expense						
Operating Income	366,204,000	352,135,000	349,676,000	331,918,000	302,219,000	269,419,000
Operating Margin %		.29%	.31%	.33%	.33%	.31%
SGA Expense	324,645,000	302,464,000	290,007,000	269,511,000	264,430,000	282,314,000
Net Income	267,085,000	258,259,000	338,815,000	241,051,000	211,543,000	198,637,000
Operating Cash Flow	385,668,000	320,527,000	331,140,000	306,442,000	265,023,000	269,809,000
Capital Expenditure	33,520,000	36,862,000	47,740,000	25,682,000	17,743,000	18,517,000
EBITDA	423,489,000	400,429,000	387,728,000	363,267,000	336,654,000	305,198,000
Return on Assets %		.21%	.39%	.34%	.31%	.29%
Return on Equity %		.48%	.65%	.46%	.40%	.36%
Debt to Equity		1.027	0.58	0.066		

CONTACT INFORMATION:
Phone: 203 810-1000 Fax: 203 810-1001
Toll-Free:
Address: 601 Merritt 7, Fl. 3, Norwalk, CT 06851 United States

STOCK TICKER/OTHER:
Stock Ticker: FDS
Employees: 8,375
Parent Company:

Exchange: NYS
Fiscal Year Ends: 08/31

SALARIES/BONUSES:
Top Exec. Salary: $445,833 Bonus: $1,150,000
Second Exec. Salary: $300,000 Bonus: $725,000

OTHER THOUGHTS:
Estimated Female Officers or Directors: 3
Hot Spot for Advancement for Women/Minorities: Y

Fairview Health Services

NAIC Code: 622110

www.fairview.org

TYPES OF BUSINESS:
General Medical and Surgical Hospitals
Specialty Clinics
Home Care
Hospice Services
Children's Services
Cancer Care
Senior Care
Academic Teaching Hospital

BRANDS/DIVISIONS/AFFILIATES:
www.fairview.org

CONTACTS: Note: Officers with more than one job title may be intentionally listed here more than once.
James Hereford, CEO
Laura Reed, COO
Hayes Batson, CFO
Scott Weber, CMO
Carolyn Jacobson, Chief Human Resources Officer
Brent Asplin, Chief Clinical Officer
Sameer Badlani, CIO
Mark Hansberry, VP-Strategic Planning
Mark Hansberry, VP-Comm.
Brent Asplin, Pres., Fairview Medical Group
Daniel K. Anderson, Pres., Fairview Community Hospitals
Bob Beacher, Pres., Fairview Pharmacy Services
Richard Howard, Pres., Fairview Foundation
Rich Ostlund, Chmn.
Mark Thomas, Pres., Senior Services

GROWTH PLANS/SPECIAL FEATURES:
Fairview Health Services is a nonprofit health care system with numerous primary care and specialty clinics in 30 cities across Minnesota. The company's network is comprised of more than 5,000 doctors and providers, 12 hospitals and medical centers, 56 primary-care clinics and 36 pharmacy locations. Fairview's services and specialties include family medicine, obstetrics, gynecology, urgent care, pharmacy, pediatrics, orthopedics, sports medicine, weight loss, caregiver assurance, acupuncture, aquatic therapy, audiology, bone marrow transplant, cancer care, counseling, dermatology, ear/nose/throat, home infusion, imaging, kidney care, laboratory/diagnostic, neonatal intensive care, pain management and many more. For employers, Fairview offers a portfolio of services that include: an employee assistance program; a single-day, comprehensive annual physical and wellness consultation performed at the University of Minnesota Health Clinics and Surgery Center; an online clinic available 24/7 for the treatment of routine health conditions such as cold, flu, allergies, ear infections, pink eye and more; a customized onsite clinic solution that offers convenient access to high-quality care for employees and dependents; and sleep health. Fairview's website, www.fairview.org, offers patients the capability to pay their related health bills, obtain a prescription refill, pre-register for a hospital visit, obtain personal medical records and request for an appointment. Ebenezer is a part of Fairview's health services and is focused on serving senior adults. For medical professionals, Fairview offers continuing medical education and credentialing services.

Fairview offers employees life, disability, health and dental insurance; various employee assistance programs; and 403(b) and other retirement options.

FINANCIAL DATA: Note: Data for latest year may not have been available at press time.

In U.S. $	2018	2017	2016	2015	2014	2013
Revenue	5,600,000,000	5,300,000,000	4,363,540,000	3,867,550,000	3,560,832,000	3,318,513,000
R&D Expense						
Operating Income						
Operating Margin %						
SGA Expense						
Net Income	96,700,000	456,900,000	213,786,000	64,908,000	166,695,000	244,300,000
Operating Cash Flow						
Capital Expenditure						
EBITDA						
Return on Assets %						
Return on Equity %						
Debt to Equity						

CONTACT INFORMATION:
Phone: 612-672-7272   Fax: 612-672-7186
Toll-Free: 800-824-1953
Address: 2450 Riverside Ave., Minneapolis, MN 55454 United States

SALARIES/BONUSES:
Top Exec. Salary: $ Bonus: $
Second Exec. Salary: $ Bonus: $

STOCK TICKER/OTHER:
Stock Ticker: Nonprofit   Exchange:
Employees: 34,000   Fiscal Year Ends: 12/31
Parent Company:

OTHER THOUGHTS:
Estimated Female Officers or Directors: 9
Hot Spot for Advancement for Women/Minorities: Y

Sales, profits and employees may be estimates. Financial information, benefits and other data can change quickly and may vary from those stated here.

Fastenal Company

NAIC Code: 423810

www.fastenal.com

TYPES OF BUSINESS:
Construction and Mining Equipment Wholesalers
Office Equipment Merchant Wholesalers

BRANDS/DIVISIONS/AFFILIATES:
Fastenal

CONTACTS:
Note: Officers with more than one job title may be intentionally listed here more than once.

Daniel Florness, CEO
Nicholas Lundquist, Sr. Exec. VP - Operations
Willard Oberton, Chairman of the Board
Holden Lewis, Exec. VP
Leland Hein, Sr. Exec. VP - Sales
Reyne Wisecup, Sr. Exec. VP - HR
John Soderberg, Exec. VP-IT
Reyne Wisecup, Director
James Jansen, Executive VP, Divisional
William Drazkowski, Executive VP, Divisional
Jeffery Watts, Executive VP, Divisional
John Soderberg, Executive VP, Divisional
Charles Miller, Executive VP, Divisional
Holden Lewis, Executive VP
Terry Owen, Senior Executive VP, Divisional
Leland Hein, Senior Executive VP, Divisional
Nicholas Lundquist, Senior Executive VP, Divisional
William Oberton, Chmn.

GROWTH PLANS/SPECIAL FEATURES:

Fastenal Company is a retailer and wholesaler of industrial and construction supplies, many of which are sold under the Fastenal name. The firm sells fasteners, tools and supplies needed by companies to manufacture, build and maintain. The firm's fastener product line consists of two broad categories: threaded fasteners, such as bolts, nuts, screws, studs which makes up 84% of total fastener sales, and related washers; and miscellaneous supplies and hardware, such as pins and machinery keys, concrete anchors, metal framing systems, wire rope, strut, rivets and related accessories which makes up the rest of fastener sales. Fastener sales make up 34.9% of Fastenal's business. Fastenal operates roughly 2,227 store locations in 26 countries, supported by 14 distribution centers in North America (11 in the U.S., two in Canada and one in Mexico).

Fastenal offers its employees medical, dental, life, disability and AD&D insurance; a retirement savings plan; company profit sharing; and employee discount programs.

FINANCIAL DATA:
Note: Data for latest year may not have been available at press time.

In U.S. $	2018	2017	2016	2015	2014	2013
Revenue	4,965,100,000	4,390,500,000	3,962,036,000	3,869,187,000	3,733,507,000	3,326,106,000
R&D Expense						
Operating Income	998,700,000	880,800,000	795,307,000	827,344,000	786,626,000	712,014,000
Operating Margin %		.20%	.20%	.21%	.21%	.21%
SGA Expense	1,400,200,000	1,282,800,000	1,169,470,000	1,121,590,000	1,110,776,000	1,007,431,000
Net Income	751,900,000	578,600,000	499,478,000	516,361,000	494,150,000	448,636,000
Operating Cash Flow	674,200,000	585,200,000	513,999,000	546,940,000	499,392,000	416,120,000
Capital Expenditure	176,300,000	119,900,000	189,451,000	155,168,000	189,474,000	206,540,000
EBITDA	1,137,800,000	1,009,600,000	900,285,000	915,726,000	861,021,000	777,772,000
Return on Assets %		.21%	.19%	.21%	.22%	.23%
Return on Equity %		.29%	.27%	.28%	.27%	.27%
Debt to Equity		0.196	0.196	0.168		

CONTACT INFORMATION:
Phone: 507 453-8875 Fax:
Toll-Free:
Address: 2001 Theurer Blvd., Winona, MN 55987-0978 United States

SALARIES/BONUSES:
Top Exec. Salary: $592,500 Bonus: $
Second Exec. Salary: $442,508 Bonus: $

STOCK TICKER/OTHER:
Stock Ticker: FAST
Employees: 19,624
Parent Company:

Exchange: NAS
Fiscal Year Ends: 12/31

OTHER THOUGHTS:
Estimated Female Officers or Directors: 2
Hot Spot for Advancement for Women/Minorities:

Federal-Mogul LLC

NAIC Code: 336300

www.federalmogul.com

TYPES OF BUSINESS:
Aftermarket Products & Services
Powertrain Products
Sealing Systems
Vehicle Safety & Performance Products

BRANDS/DIVISIONS/AFFILIATES:
Tenneco Inc

CONTACTS:
Note: Officers with more than one job title may be intentionally listed here more than once.

Brian Kesseler, Co-CEO
Roger Wood, Co-CEO
Jason Hollar, CFO
Mark Bradbury, VP-IT
Kaled Awada, Sr. VP-Human Resources
Rusty Patel, CIO
Martin Hendricks, President, Divisional
Scott Pepin, Senior VP, Divisional
Jerome Rouquet, Senior VP
John Patouhas, Vice President

GROWTH PLANS/SPECIAL FEATURES:
Federal-Mogul, LLC is a global supplier of vehicle and industrial products for fuel economy, alternative energies and safety systems. The company operates two divisions: powertrain and motor parts. Powertrain focuses on original equipment (OE) products for automotive, heavy duty and industrial applications. This segment offers its customers a diverse array of market-leading products for OE applications, including pistons, piston rings, piston pins, cylinder liners, valve seats and guides, ignition products, dynamic seals, bonded piston seals, combustion & exhaust gaskets, static gaskets/seals, rigid heat shields, engine bearings, industrial bearings, brushings, washers, plus element resistant systems protection sleeving products, acoustic shielding and flexible heat shields. The motor parts segment sells and distributes a broad portfolio of products manufactured by Powertrain. Motor parts' products include brake disc pads, brake linings, brake linings, brake blocks, brake system components, chassis products, wipers and other product lines to OE and aftermarket customers. Federal-Mogul maintains manufacturing facilities and distribution centers in 24 countries. In late-2018, parent company Icahn Enterprises LP sold the firm to Tenneco, Inc. for $2.5 billion. Tenneco announced plans to separate its business to form two new independent companies by the end of 2019: an aftermarket and ride performance company as well as a powertrain technology company.

FINANCIAL DATA:
Note: Data for latest year may not have been available at press time.

In U.S. $	2018	2017	2016	2015	2014	2013
Revenue	8,190,000,000	7,800,000,000	7,434,000,000	7,418,999,808	7,317,000,192	6,785,999,872
R&D Expense						
Operating Income						
Operating Margin %						
SGA Expense						
Net Income			90,000,000	-110,000,000	-168,000,000	41,000,000
Operating Cash Flow						
Capital Expenditure						
EBITDA						
Return on Assets %						
Return on Equity %						
Debt to Equity						

CONTACT INFORMATION:
Phone: 248 354-7700 Fax: 248 354-8950
Toll-Free:
Address: 27300 West 11 Mile Rd., Southfield, MI 48034 United States

STOCK TICKER/OTHER:
Stock Ticker: Subsidiary
Employees: 53,000
Parent Company: Tenneco Inc
Exchange:
Fiscal Year Ends: 12/31

SALARIES/BONUSES:
Top Exec. Salary: $ Bonus: $
Second Exec. Salary: $ Bonus: $

OTHER THOUGHTS:
Estimated Female Officers or Directors: 1
Hot Spot for Advancement for Women/Minorities:

FedEx Corporation

NAIC Code: 492110

www.fedex.com

TYPES OF BUSINESS:
Couriers and Express Delivery Services
Ground Delivery Services
Freight Services
Document Solutions & Business Services
International Trade Services

BRANDS/DIVISIONS/AFFILIATES:
Federal Express Corporation
FedEx Ground Package System Inc
FedEx Freight Corporation
FedEx Corporate Services Inc
FedEx SmartPost
FedEx Freight Priority
FedEx Freight Economy
FedEx Office and Print Services Inc

CONTACTS: Note: Officers with more than one job title may be intentionally listed here more than once.
Rajesh Subramaniam, CEO, Subsidiary
Henry Maier, CEO, Subsidiary
John Smith, CEO, Subsidiary
Frederick Smith, CEO
Robert Carter, Chief Information Officer
Alan Graf, Executive VP
Mark Allen, Executive VP
Donald Colleran, Executive VP
John Merino, Vice President

GROWTH PLANS/SPECIAL FEATURES:
FedEx Corporation is a holding company that offers transportation, eCommerce and business services through four subsidiary segments. The FedEx Express Corporation segment provides time-definitive delivery to more than 220 countries and territories, connecting markets that comprise more than 99% of the world's gross domestic product. The FedEx Ground Package System, Inc. segment is a North American provider of small-package ground delivery services. It provides day-certain service to any business address in the U.S. and Canada, as well as residential delivery to 100% of U.S. residences through its FedEx Home Delivery service. This division's FedEx SmartPost ground service specializes in the consolidation and delivery of high volumes of low-weight, less time-sensitive business-to-consumer packages primarily using the U.S. Postal Service for final delivery to residences. The FedEx Freight Corporation segment is a leading U.S. provider of less-than-truckload freight services across all lengths of haul. This division includes: FedEx Freight Priority, when speed is critical for supply chain needs; and FedEx Freight Economy, for when a customer can trade time for cost savings. This segment also offers freight delivery service to most points in Canada, Mexico, Puerto Rico and the U.S. Virgin Islands. Last, the FedEx Corporate Services, Inc. segment provides sales, marketing, IT, communications, customer service, technical support, billing and collections services, as well as certain back-office functions that support FedEx Corporation's transportation segments. This division includes FedEx Office and Print Services, Inc., which provides of document and business services, as well as retail access to FedEx's package transportation businesses. FedEx Corporation agreed to acquire Manton Air-Sea Pty Ltd. in October 2018; and agreed to acquire Flying Cargo Group in early 2019.

FedEx Corporation offers comprehensive health benefits and retirement/pension plans.

FINANCIAL DATA: Note: Data for latest year may not have been available at press time.

In U.S. $	2018	2017	2016	2015	2014	2013
Revenue	65,450,000,000	60,319,000,000	50,365,000,000	47,453,000,000	45,567,000,000	
R&D Expense						
Operating Income	5,250,000,000	5,037,000,000	3,077,000,000	2,143,000,000	3,446,000,000	
Operating Margin %		.08%	.06%	.05%	.08%	
SGA Expense	10,000,000	24,000,000	1,498,000,000	2,190,000,000		
Net Income	4,572,000,000	2,997,000,000	1,820,000,000	1,050,000,000	2,097,000,000	
Operating Cash Flow	4,674,000,000	4,930,000,000	5,708,000,000	5,366,000,000	4,264,000,000	
Capital Expenditure	5,663,000,000	5,116,000,000	4,818,000,000	4,347,000,000	3,533,000,000	
EBITDA	8,006,000,000	8,086,000,000	5,707,000,000	4,473,000,000	6,036,000,000	
Return on Assets %		.06%	.04%	.03%	.06%	
Return on Equity %		.20%	.13%	.07%	.13%	
Debt to Equity		0.928	1.004	0.483	0.31	

CONTACT INFORMATION:
Phone: 901 818-7500　　Fax: 901 346-1013
Toll-Free:
Address: 942 S. Shady Grove Rd., Memphis, TN 38120 United States

STOCK TICKER/OTHER:
Stock Ticker: FDX
Employees: 235,000
Parent Company:

Exchange: NYS
Fiscal Year Ends: 05/31

SALARIES/BONUSES:
Top Exec. Salary: $1,342,212　　Bonus: $
Second Exec. Salary: $1,122,016　　Bonus: $75,000

OTHER THOUGHTS:
Estimated Female Officers or Directors: 3
Hot Spot for Advancement for Women/Minorities: Y

Fidelity Investments Financial Services

www.fidelity.com

NAIC Code: 523920

TYPES OF BUSINESS:
Mutual Funds
Human Resources Administration Services
Employee Benefits Services
Online Brokerage
Physical Branch Investment Offices
Clearing and Execution Products and Services
Real Estate Investments
Institutional Account Management and Services

BRANDS/DIVISIONS/AFFILIATES:
Fidelity Insitutional Asset Management
Fidelity Charitable

CONTACTS:
Note: Officers with more than one job title may be intentionally listed here more than once.

Abigail Johnson, CEO
Kathleen Murphy, Pres.
Bart Grenier, Head, Asset Mgt-International
Jim Speros, Chief Creative Officer
Brian Hogan, Head, Investment Solutions
Steve A. Scullen, III, Pres., Corp. Oper.
Lori Kalahar Johnson, VP-Online Strategy
Jacques Perold, Pres., Fidelity Management & Research Company
Charles Morrison, Pres., Asset Mgmt.
Nancy D. Prior, Pres., Fixed Income Div.

GROWTH PLANS/SPECIAL FEATURES:

Fidelity Investments Financial Services (FIFS) is one of the world's largest providers of financial services. With approximately $2.5 trillion in assets under management (as of March 2018), the company offers personal investment services, workplace investment services, institutional solutions and asset management. The personal investment division offers financial planning and retirement options such as independent retirement accounts (IRAs), annuities and managed accounts; brokerage and cash management products; college savings accounts; and other financial services for individual investors. The workplace investment division works with employers to build benefit programs for their employees. This segment provides recordkeeping, investments and servicing in relation to contributions, benefits, health and welfare and stock plans. For financial institutions, FIFS provides technology and personalized service such as clearing, custody, investment products, brokerage and trading services to a wide range of financial firms. Fidelity Institutional Asset Management is a distribution organization dedicated to the institutional marketplace. It serves as a gateway to Fidelity's broad and deep institutional investment management capabilities, including U.S. equity, international equity, fixed income and asset allocation. In addition, Fidelity Charitable is an independent public charity that allows donors to establish a dedicated donor-advised fund to support their favorite charities in the short-term, and create a systematic plan for longer-term philanthropic goals. Headquartered in Boston, Massachusetts, FIS serves customers through 10 regional offices and more than 190 investor centers in the U.S. Globally, the company spans eight other countries outside the U.S.

The company is owned approximately 50% by the founding family and 50% by employees.

FINANCIAL DATA:
Note: Data for latest year may not have been available at press time.

In U.S. $	2018	2017	2016	2015	2014	2013
Revenue	20,400,000,000	18,200,000,000	15,900,000,000	15,350,000,000	14,900,000,000	13,600,000,000
R&D Expense						
Operating Income						
Operating Margin %						
SGA Expense						
Net Income	6,300,000,000	5,300,000,000	3,450,000,000	3,000,000,000	3,400,000,000	2,600,000,000
Operating Cash Flow						
Capital Expenditure						
EBITDA						
Return on Assets %						
Return on Equity %						
Debt to Equity						

CONTACT INFORMATION:
Phone: 617-563-7000   Fax:
Toll-Free: 800-343-3548
Address: 82 Devonshire St., Boston, MA 02109 United States

STOCK TICKER/OTHER:
Stock Ticker: Private
Employees: 45,000
Parent Company:

Exchange:
Fiscal Year Ends: 12/31

SALARIES/BONUSES:
Top Exec. Salary: $ Bonus: $
Second Exec. Salary: $ Bonus: $

OTHER THOUGHTS:
Estimated Female Officers or Directors: 2
Hot Spot for Advancement for Women/Minorities:

Fidelity National Financial Inc

NAIC Code: 524127

www.fnf.com

TYPES OF BUSINESS:
Title Insurance
Title Insurance
Escrow
Real Estate Mortgage

BRANDS/DIVISIONS/AFFILIATES:
Fidelity National Title Insurance Company
Chicago Title Insurance Company
Commonwealth Land Title Insurance Company
Alamo Title Insurance
National Title Insurance of New York Inc
ServiceLink Holdings LLC

CONTACTS:
Note: Officers with more than one job title may be intentionally listed here more than once.
Raymond Quirk, CEO
Anthony Park, CFO
William Foley, Chairman of the Board
Roger Jewkes, COO
Brent Bickett, Executive VP, Divisional
Michael Gravelle, Executive VP
Peter Sadowski, Executive VP
Michael Nolan, President

GROWTH PLANS/SPECIAL FEATURES:
Fidelity National Financial, Inc. (FNF) is a holding company that provides title insurance, escrow and other related services to the real estate and mortgage industries. FNF is a leading title insurance company operating through its title insurance underwriters: Fidelity National Title Insurance Company, Chicago Title Insurance Company, Commonwealth Land Title Insurance Company, Alamo Title Insurance and National Title Insurance of New York, Inc. Subsidiary ServiceLink Holdings, LLC provides mortgage transaction services, including title-related services and facilitation of production and management of mortgage loans. Therefore, FNF operates through two business segments: title and corporate and other. The title segment consists of the title insurance underwriters and related businesses, providing core title insurance and escrow and other title-related services such as trust activities, trustee sales guarantees, recordings, reconveyances and home warranty products. This division also includes FNF's transactions services business in relation to mortgage loans. The corporate and other segment consists of various real estate brokerage and real estate technology businesses and subsidiaries. During 2018, FNF agreed to acquire Stewart Information Services Corporation, a real estate information, title insurance and transaction management company. As of early-2019, the FNF-Stewart transaction continued to be subject to certain closing conditions, including federal and state regulatory approvals and the satisfaction of other customer closing conditions.

FINANCIAL DATA: Note: Data for latest year may not have been available at press time.

In U.S. $	2018	2017	2016	2015	2014	2013
Revenue	7,594,000,000	7,663,000,000	9,554,000,000	9,132,000,000	8,024,000,000	8,565,000,000
R&D Expense						
Operating Income						
Operating Margin %						
SGA Expense	2,538,000,000	2,460,000,000	2,832,000,000	2,671,000,000	2,540,000,000	2,134,000,000
Net Income	628,000,000	771,000,000	650,000,000	527,000,000	583,000,000	402,000,000
Operating Cash Flow	943,000,000	737,000,000	1,162,000,000	917,000,000	567,000,000	484,000,000
Capital Expenditure	83,000,000	149,000,000	290,000,000	241,000,000	210,000,000	145,000,000
EBITDA						
Return on Assets %		.07%	.05%	.04%	.05%	.04%
Return on Equity %		.15%	.11%	.09%	.11%	.09%
Debt to Equity		0.171	0.458	0.485	0.471	0.261

CONTACT INFORMATION:
Phone: 904 854-8100   Fax: 904 357-1007
Toll-Free: 888-934-3354
Address: 601 Riverside Ave., Jacksonville, FL 32204 United States

STOCK TICKER/OTHER:
Stock Ticker: FNF
Employees: 55,219
Parent Company:

Exchange: NYS
Fiscal Year Ends: 12/31

SALARIES/BONUSES:
Top Exec. Salary: $831,692   Bonus: $
Second Exec. Salary: $630,000   Bonus: $

OTHER THOUGHTS:
Estimated Female Officers or Directors: 1
Hot Spot for Advancement for Women/Minorities:

Sales, profits and employees may be estimates. Financial information, benefits and other data can change quickly and may vary from those stated here.

FirstEnergy Corporation

NAIC Code: 221112

www.firstenergycorp.com

TYPES OF BUSINESS:
Electric Utility
Power Generation
Energy Management
Telecommunications

BRANDS/DIVISIONS/AFFILIATES:
FirstEnergy Solutions Corporation

CONTACTS:
Note: Officers with more than one job title may be intentionally listed here more than once.

Charles Jones, CEO
Eileen Mikkelsen, VP, Subsidiary
Donald Misheff, Director
Leila Vespoli, Executive VP, Divisional
Robert Reffner, General Counsel, Subsidiary
Charles Lasky, Other Corporate Officer
Ebony Yeboah-Amankwah, Other Executive Officer
Bennett Gaines, Other Executive Officer
Samuel Belcher, President, Subsidiary
Steven Strah, President, Subsidiary
Gary Benz, Senior VP, Subsidiary
M. Dowling, Senior VP, Subsidiary
Dennis Chack, Senior VP, Subsidiary
Christine Walker, Vice President, Subsidiary
Irena Prezelj, Vice President, Subsidiary
Jason Lisowski, Vice President

GROWTH PLANS/SPECIAL FEATURES:

FirstEnergy Corporation and its subsidiaries are principally involved in the generation, transmission and distribution of electricity. Its 10 utility operating companies serve more than 6 million customers in the Midwest and Mid-Atlantic regions. FirstEnergy's regulated and unregulated generation subsidiaries control over 16,000 megawatts (MWs) of capacity from a diverse mix of non-emitting nuclear, scrubbed coal, natural gas, hydroelectric and other renewables. The firm's transmission operations include approximately 24,500 miles of lines and two regional transmission operation centers. FirstEnergy's revenues are primarily derived from: the sale of energy and related products and services by its unregulated competitive subsidiaries; the electric service provided by its utility operating subsidiaries; and its transmission subsidiaries. In April 2018, FirstEnergy Solutions Corporation filed for chapter 11 bankruptcy; the bankruptcy court approved the company's definitive settlement agreement that September. FirstEnergy Corporation and its distribution, transmission, regulated generation and Allegheny Energy Supply subsidiaries were not part of the filing.

Employee benefits include medical, prescription, dental and vision coverage; flexible spending accounts; life insurance; long-term care insurance; long-term disability; a 401(k) savings plan; pension plan; education assistance; adoption assistance; an employee assistance program; and employee discounts.

FINANCIAL DATA:
Note: Data for latest year may not have been available at press time.

In U.S. $	2018	2017	2016	2015	2014	2013
Revenue	11,261,000,000	14,017,000,000	14,562,000,000	15,026,000,000	15,049,000,000	14,917,000,000
R&D Expense						
Operating Income	2,358,000,000	2,578,000,000	2,403,000,000	2,334,000,000	1,062,000,000	2,402,000,000
Operating Margin %		.18%	.17%	.16%	.07%	.16%
SGA Expense	144,000,000	141,000,000	147,000,000	242,000,000	835,000,000	256,000,000
Net Income	1,348,000,000	-1,724,000,000	-6,177,000,000	578,000,000	299,000,000	392,000,000
Operating Cash Flow	1,410,000,000	3,808,000,000	3,371,000,000	3,447,000,000	2,713,000,000	2,662,000,000
Capital Expenditure	2,675,000,000	2,841,000,000	3,067,000,000	2,894,000,000	3,545,000,000	2,888,000,000
EBITDA	3,947,000,000	1,970,000,000	-6,181,000,000	3,744,000,000	2,626,000,000	2,922,000,000
Return on Assets %		-.04%	-.13%	.01%	.01%	.01%
Return on Equity %		-.34%	-.66%	.05%	.02%	.03%
Debt to Equity		5.38	2.915	1.545	1.544	1.247

CONTACT INFORMATION:
Phone: 800 736-3402 Fax:
Toll-Free: 800-633-4766
Address: 76 S. Main St., Akron, OH 44308 United States

SALARIES/BONUSES:
Top Exec. Salary: $1,136,113 Bonus: $
Second Exec. Salary: $548,060 Bonus: $434,700

STOCK TICKER/OTHER:
Stock Ticker: FE Exchange: NYS
Employees: 15,707 Fiscal Year Ends: 12/31
Parent Company:

OTHER THOUGHTS:
Estimated Female Officers or Directors: 6
Hot Spot for Advancement for Women/Minorities: Y

Fiserv Inc

NAIC Code: 522320

www.fiserv.com

TYPES OF BUSINESS:
Financial Services
Investment Services
Online Banking
Electronic Billing & Payment
Software Applications & Investment Management Solutions

BRANDS/DIVISIONS/AFFILIATES:
First Data Corp

CONTACTS:
Note: Officers with more than one job title may be intentionally listed here more than once.

Jeffery Yabuki, CEO
Frank Bisignano, Pres.
Glenn Renwick, Chairman of the Board
Robert Hua, CFO
Byron Vielehr, Chief Administrative Officer
Lynn McCreary, Chief Legal Officer
Kevin Schultz, Executive VP
Devin McGranahan, President, Divisional
Jeffery Yabuki, Chmn.

GROWTH PLANS/SPECIAL FEATURES:
Fiserv, Inc. provides integrated data processing and information management systems to more than 12,000 financial services providers, including banks, thrifts, credit unions, investment management firms, leasing and finance companies, retailers, merchants and government agencies. It operates in two primary segments: financial institution services (financial) and payments and industry products (payments). The financial segment provides banks, thrifts and credit unions with account processing services, item processing services, loan origination and servicing products, cash management and consulting services as well as other products and services that support a variety of financial transactions. The payments segment provides products and services that address a range of technology needs for the financial services industry, including internet banking, electronic bill payment, electronic funds transfer and debit processing, fraud and risk management capabilities, card and print personalization services, check imaging and investment account processing services for separately managed accounts. The company operates centers nationwide for full-service data processing, software development, item processing and check imaging, technology support and related product businesses. It operates data, development, item processing and support centers in approximately 95 cities worldwide. In July 2019, the firm acquired First Data Corp., an electronic payment processing firm, for $22 billion.

FINANCIAL DATA:
Note: Data for latest year may not have been available at press time.

In U.S. $	2018	2017	2016	2015	2014	2013
Revenue	5,823,000,000	5,696,000,000	5,505,000,000	5,254,000,000	5,066,000,000	4,814,000,000
R&D Expense						
Operating Income	1,526,000,000	1,522,000,000	1,445,000,000	1,311,000,000	1,210,000,000	1,061,000,000
Operating Margin %		.27%	.26%	.25%	.24%	.22%
SGA Expense	1,228,000,000	1,150,000,000	1,101,000,000	1,034,000,000	975,000,000	977,000,000
Net Income	1,187,000,000	1,246,000,000	930,000,000	712,000,000	754,000,000	648,000,000
Operating Cash Flow	1,552,000,000	1,483,000,000	1,431,000,000	1,346,000,000	1,307,000,000	1,039,000,000
Capital Expenditure	360,000,000	287,000,000	290,000,000	359,000,000	292,000,000	236,000,000
EBITDA	2,304,000,000	1,967,000,000	1,849,000,000	1,643,000,000	1,615,000,000	1,465,000,000
Return on Assets %		.12%	.10%	.08%	.08%	.07%
Return on Equity %		.47%	.36%	.24%	.22%	.19%
Debt to Equity		1.793	1.758	1.612	1.126	1.048

CONTACT INFORMATION:
Phone: 262 879-5000   Fax: 262 879-5275
Toll-Free: 800-872-7882
Address: 255 Fiserv Dr., Brookfield, WI 53045 United States

STOCK TICKER/OTHER:
Stock Ticker: FISV
Employees: 23,000
Parent Company:

Exchange: NAS
Fiscal Year Ends: 12/31

SALARIES/BONUSES:
Top Exec. Salary: $840,000   Bonus: $
Second Exec. Salary: $625,000   Bonus: $

OTHER THOUGHTS:
Estimated Female Officers or Directors: 1
Hot Spot for Advancement for Women/Minorities:

FleetCor Technologies Inc

www.fleetcor.com

NAIC Code: 522320

TYPES OF BUSINESS:
Payment & Transaction Processing Services

BRANDS/DIVISIONS/AFFILIATES:
Cambridge Global Payments
Creative Lodging Solutions

CONTACTS:
Note: Officers with more than one job title may be intentionally listed here more than once.

Ronald Clarke, CEO
Eric Dey, CFO
John Coughlin, Executive VP, Divisional
Scott Dufour, Other Executive Officer
Kurt Adams, President, Divisional
David Krantz, President, Geographical
Armando Netto, President, Geographical

GROWTH PLANS/SPECIAL FEATURES:

FleetCor Technologies, Inc. is a leading independent global provider of fuel cards, workforce payment products and services to businesses, commercial fleets, major oil companies, petroleum marketers and government entities in countries throughout North America, Latin America and Europe. The company's payment programs enable customers to better manage and control employee spending and provide card-accepting merchants with a high-volume customer base that can increase their sales. In 2017, FleetCor processed approximately 3 billion transactions on its proprietary networks and third-party networks. The company sells a range of customized fleet and lodging payment programs directly and indirectly through partners such as major oil companies and petroleum marketers. It provides customers with various card products that typically function like a charge card to purchase fuel, lodging and related products and services at participating locations. Depending on the customer's and partner's needs, the firm provides these services in a variety of outsourced solutions ranging from end-to-end solutions (encompassing issuing, processing and network services) to limited back office processing services. Other services include the company's proprietary equipment which, when installed at the fueling site and on the vehicle, reduces the chances of unauthorized or fraudulent transactions; a telematics solution in Europe that combines GPS, satellite tracking and other wireless technology to allow fleet operators to monitor their vehicles; and prepaid fuel and food vouchers in Mexico. In order to deliver its payment programs and services, FleetCor owns and operates proprietary closed-loop networks in North America and internationally. During 2017, FleetCor acquired Cambridge Global Payments; acquired Creative Lodging Solutions, a small lodging tuck-in business in the U.S.; and sold subsidiary and telematics provider, NexTraq to Michelin Group.

FINANCIAL DATA:
Note: Data for latest year may not have been available at press time.

In U.S. $	2018	2017	2016	2015	2014	2013
Revenue	2,433,492,000	2,249,538,000	1,831,546,000	1,702,865,000	1,199,390,000	895,171,000
R&D Expense						
Operating Income	1,242,864,000	1,057,196,000	751,171,000	665,011,000	566,149,000	420,030,000
Operating Margin %		.39%	.41%	.39%	.45%	.47%
SGA Expense	571,765,000	671,544,000	519,413,000	515,047,000	377,744,000	267,772,000
Net Income	811,483,000	740,200,000	452,385,000	362,431,000	368,707,000	284,501,000
Operating Cash Flow	903,382,000	675,723,000	705,912,000	754,584,000	608,334,000	375,685,000
Capital Expenditure	81,387,000	70,093,000	59,011,000	41,875,000	27,070,000	20,785,000
EBITDA	1,508,228,000	1,265,296,000	918,071,000	800,796,000	654,160,000	492,767,000
Return on Assets %		.07%	.05%	.04%	.06%	.09%
Return on Equity %		.22%	.15%	.13%	.18%	.26%
Debt to Equity		0.789	0.818	0.728	0.788	0.382

CONTACT INFORMATION:
Phone: 770 449-0479   Fax: 770 449-3471
Toll-Free: 800-877-9019
Address: 5445 Triangle Pkwy, Ste. 400, Norcross, GA 30092 United States

STOCK TICKER/OTHER:
Stock Ticker: FLT
Employees: 7,100
Parent Company:

Exchange: NYS
Fiscal Year Ends: 12/31

SALARIES/BONUSES:
Top Exec. Salary: $1,000,000   Bonus: $
Second Exec. Salary: $500,000   Bonus: $

OTHER THOUGHTS:
Estimated Female Officers or Directors:
Hot Spot for Advancement for Women/Minorities:

Fluor Corporation

NAIC Code: 237000

www.fluor.com

TYPES OF BUSINESS:
Heavy Construction and Engineering
Power Plant Construction and Management
Facilities Management
Procurement Services
Consulting Services
Project Management
Asset Management
Staffing Services

BRANDS/DIVISIONS/AFFILIATES:
Stork Holding BV
Fluor Constructors International Inc

CONTACTS:
Note: Officers with more than one job title may be intentionally listed here more than once.

Carlos Hernandez, CEO
Bruce Stanski, CFO
Alan Boeckmann, Chairman of the Board
Robin Chopra, Controller
Ray Barnard, Executive VP, Divisional
Jose Luis Bustamante, Executive VP, Divisional
Mark Landry, Executive VP, Divisional
Matthew McSorley, Executive VP, Divisional
James Brittain, President, Divisional
Taco de Haan, President, Divisional
Nestoras Koumouris, President, Divisional
Thomas DAgostino, President, Divisional

GROWTH PLANS/SPECIAL FEATURES:

Fluor Corporation is a holding company with businesses engaged in professional services, providing engineering, procurement, construction, fabrication/modularization, operations, maintenance and asset integrity on a global basis. The firm operates in four business segments: energy and chemicals (E&C); mining, industrial, infrastructure and power (MIIP); government; and diversified services. E&C focuses on opportunities in the upstream, midstream, downstream, chemical, petrochemical, offshore and onshore oil and gas production, liquefied natural gas (LNG) and pipeline markets. MIIP provides design, engineering, procurement, construction and project management services to the mining and metals, transportation, life sciences, advanced manufacturing and power sectors. The government segment provides engineering, construction, logistics, base and facilities, operations and maintenance, contingency response and environmental and nuclear services to the U.S. government and governments abroad. This division provides site management, environmental remediation, decommissioning, engineering and construction services. The diversified services segment provides an array of asset services, asset integrity services, equipment solutions and staffing services. These services are provided worldwide during both the project delivery phase as well as to new or existing production assets. This division's Stork Holding BV subsidiary provides asset services and asset integrity services such as management solutions, electrical and instrumentation, fabric maintenance, mechanical and piping. In addition to these segments, subsidiary Fluor Constructors International, Inc. provides unionized management and construction services in the U.S. and Canada, both independently and as a subcontractor on projects in each of Fluor's segments.

Fluor offers its employees health, dental, vision, life and accident insurance; disability coverage; savings and retirement plans; a tax savings account; and educational assistance.

FINANCIAL DATA:
Note: Data for latest year may not have been available at press time.

In U.S. $	2018	2017	2016	2015	2014	2013
Revenue	19,166,600,000	19,520,970,000	19,036,520,000	18,114,050,000	21,531,580,000	27,351,570,000
R&D Expense						
Operating Income	521,966,000	426,303,000	599,243,000	926,367,000	1,216,322,000	1,190,043,000
Operating Margin %		.02%	.03%	.05%	.06%	.04%
SGA Expense	147,958,000	192,187,000	191,073,000	168,329,000	182,711,000	175,148,000
Net Income	224,833,000	191,377,000	281,401,000	412,512,000	510,909,000	667,711,000
Operating Cash Flow	162,164,000	601,971,000	705,919,000	849,132,000	642,574,000	788,906,000
Capital Expenditure	210,998,000	283,107,000	235,904,000	240,220,000	324,704,000	288,487,000
EBITDA	775,587,000	679,348,000	842,202,000	961,060,000	1,427,184,000	1,411,584,000
Return on Assets %		.02%	.03%	.05%	.06%	.08%
Return on Equity %		.06%	.09%	.14%	.15%	.19%
Debt to Equity		0.476	0.486	0.331	0.319	0.132

CONTACT INFORMATION:
Phone: 469 398-7000   Fax: 469 398-7255
Toll-Free:
Address: 6700 Las Colinas Blvd., Irving, TX 75039 United States

STOCK TICKER/OTHER:
Stock Ticker: FLR
Employees: 61,551
Parent Company:

Exchange: NYS
Fiscal Year Ends: 12/31

SALARIES/BONUSES:
Top Exec. Salary: $1,328,029   Bonus: $
Second Exec. Salary: $714,861   Bonus: $

OTHER THOUGHTS:
Estimated Female Officers or Directors: 3
Hot Spot for Advancement for Women/Minorities: Y

Ford Motor Company

NAIC Code: 336111

www.ford.com

TYPES OF BUSINESS:
Automobile Manufacturing
Automobile Financing
Fuel-Cell & Hybrid Research

BRANDS/DIVISIONS/AFFILIATES:
Ford
Lincoln
Ford Motor Credit Co
Ford Mustang
Ford F150
Ford Focus
Lincoln Navigator SUV
Ford Escape Hybrid SUV

CONTACTS:
Note: Officers with more than one job title may be intentionally listed here more than once.

David McClelland, CEO, Subsidiary
James Hackett, CEO
Cathy O'Callaghan, CFO, Divisional
Tim Stone, CFO
William Ford, Chairman of the Board
Bradley Gayton, Chief Administrative Officer
Hau Thai-Tang, Other Corporate Officer
Kiersten Robinson, Other Executive Officer
Marcy Klevorn, President, Divisional
James Farley, President, Divisional
Joseph Hinrichs, President, Divisional

GROWTH PLANS/SPECIAL FEATURES:
Ford Motor Company is a designer and manufacturer of automobiles and automotive systems. The firm operates in two primary segments: automotive and financial services. The automotive segment designs, manufactures, sells and services cars, trucks, sport utility vehicles (SUVs), electrified vehicles and luxury vehicles under the Ford and Lincoln brand names. Ford is engaged in researching and developing human machine interaction (HMI) digital technology for the Ford brand, currently its F-150 truck (as of early-2019), and has developed My View, an innovative feature that lets owners customize the content and order of the truck's driver cockpit screens, and access them via touch. The company sells its vehicles to the public via independently owned dealerships, including more than 10,345 Ford; more than 260 Lincoln; and approximately 820 Ford/Lincoln dealerships. These dealerships are in North America, South America, Europe, Asia Pacific and Africa. In addition to new car sales, the firm also sells vehicles to its dealerships for sale to fleet customers, including commercial fleet customers, daily rental car companies and governments, and sells parts and accessories to authorized parts distributors. The firm's financial services segment, operating through Ford Motor Credit Company, LLC, offers vehicle-related financing, leasing and insurance. Some of Ford's most popular vehicles include the Ford Mustang sports car, the Ford F150 truck, the compact Ford Focus, the Lincoln Navigator SUV and the Ford Escape Hybrid SUV. In February 2019, Ford announced that it will exit the commercial heavy truck business in South America, ceasing production at the Sao Bernardo do Campo plant in Brazil that year, which will end sales of the F-4000, F-350 and Fiesta small car.

FINANCIAL DATA:
Note: Data for latest year may not have been available at press time.

In U.S. $	2018	2017	2016	2015	2014	2013
Revenue	160,338,000,000	156,776,000,000	151,800,000,000	149,558,000,000	144,077,000,000	146,917,000,000
R&D Expense						
Operating Income	3,203,000,000	4,813,000,000	4,272,000,000	7,780,000,000	3,565,000,000	5,558,000,000
Operating Margin %		.05%	.03%	.06%	.03%	.04%
SGA Expense	11,403,000,000	11,527,000,000	12,196,000,000	14,999,000,000	14,117,000,000	13,176,000,000
Net Income	3,677,000,000	7,602,000,000	4,596,000,000	7,373,000,000	3,187,000,000	7,155,000,000
Operating Cash Flow	15,022,000,000	18,096,000,000	19,792,000,000	16,170,000,000	14,507,000,000	10,444,000,000
Capital Expenditure	7,785,000,000	7,049,000,000	6,992,000,000	7,196,000,000	7,463,000,000	6,597,000,000
EBITDA	13,881,000,000	17,734,000,000	16,407,000,000	18,991,000,000	12,562,000,000	14,286,000,000
Return on Assets %		.03%	.02%	.03%	.02%	.04%
Return on Equity %		.24%	.16%	.28%	.12%	.34%
Debt to Equity		2.943	3.199	3.137	3.225	2.904

CONTACT INFORMATION:
Phone: 313 322-3000 Fax: 313 222-4177
Toll-Free: 800-392-3673
Address: 1 American Rd., Dearborn, MI 48126 United States

STOCK TICKER/OTHER:
Stock Ticker: F
Employees: 201,000
Parent Company:

Exchange: NYS
Fiscal Year Ends: 12/31

SALARIES/BONUSES:
Top Exec. Salary: $1,800,000 Bonus: $
Second Exec. Salary: $1,700,000 Bonus: $

OTHER THOUGHTS:
Estimated Female Officers or Directors: 4
Hot Spot for Advancement for Women/Minorities: Y

Sales, profits and employees may be estimates. Financial information, benefits and other data can change quickly and may vary from those stated here.

Frito-Lay North America Inc

NAIC Code: 311919

www.fritolay.com

TYPES OF BUSINESS:
Snack Products
Salsas/Dips
Chips
Cookies

BRANDS/DIVISIONS/AFFILIATES:
PepsiCo Inc
Lay's
Doritos
Cheetos
SunChips
Rold Gold
Grandma's
Smartfood

CONTACTS: Note: Officers with more than one job title may be intentionally listed here more than once.
Vivek Sankaran, CEO
Stefano Sartoretti, Sr. VP
Jennifer Saenz, Sr. VP
Patrick McLaughlin, -Human Resources
Mike Zbuchalski, Sr. VP-R&D
Marc Kesselman, General Counsel
Christopher Wyse, VP-Public Affairs
Randy Melville, Gen. Mgr.-Central Bus. Unit
Vivek Sankaran, Chief Customer Officer
Dave Scalera, Sr. VP-Go-to-Market Capability & Productivity
Ted Herrod, Gen. Mgr.-West Bus. Unit
Marc Guay, Pres., PepsiCo Foods Canada
Leslie Starr Keating, Sr. VP-Supply Chain

GROWTH PLANS/SPECIAL FEATURES:

Frito-Lay North America, Inc., a subsidiary of PepsiCo, Inc., manufactures, markets, sells and distributes branded snacks. The firm's proprietary products include: Lay's potato chips, Doritos tortilla chips, Tostitos tortilla chips and salsas, Cheetos cheese-flavored snacks, Fritos corn chips, Ruffles potato chips, SunChips and multigrain snacks. Additionally, the company's brand portfolio includes: Rold Gold pretzels, Baked! Cheetos, Grandma's cookies, Cracker Jack candy-coated popcorn, Matador beef jerky, Funyuns fried onion rings, Sabritones puffed wheat snacks, El Isleno plantain chips, Smartfood popcorn, Stacy's pita chips, 100-calorie mini bite portion control snack packs and more. The firm's joint venture with Strauss Group markets refrigerated spreads and dips under the Sabra brand name, including hummus, salsas and guacamole. Over time, the firm updated its Lay's Classic Potato Chips recipe to feature only potatoes, healthier oils such as corn and sunflower oil and a dash of salt; and updated the Tostitos and SunChips brands to feature healthier recipes with no MSG (monosodium glutamate), artificial preservatives or artificial flavorings. The company offers a gluten-free recipe section on its website for customers with Celiac Disease or gluten sensitivities.

Employee benefits include medical, dental and vision coverage; life insurance; disability coverage; a flexible spending account; wellness programs; an employee assistance program; tuition reimbursement; a pension plan; a retirement plan; a discount stock purchase plan; discounts on electronics, entertainment and automobiles; childcare and elderly care; and commuter reimbursement.

FINANCIAL DATA: Note: Data for latest year may not have been available at press time.

In U.S. $	2018	2017	2016	2015	2014	2013
Revenue	16,578,450,000	15,798,000,000	15,549,000,000	14,782,000,000	14,502,000,000	14,126,000,000
R&D Expense						
Operating Income						
Operating Margin %						
SGA Expense						
Net Income	4,566,600,000	4,823,000,000	4,659,000,000	4,304,000,000	4,054,000,000	3,877,000,000
Operating Cash Flow						
Capital Expenditure						
EBITDA						
Return on Assets %						
Return on Equity %						
Debt to Equity						

CONTACT INFORMATION:
Phone: 972-334-7000 Fax: 972-334-2019
Toll-Free: 800-352-4477
Address: 7701 Legacy Dr., Plano, TX 75024 United States

SALARIES/BONUSES:
Top Exec. Salary: $ Bonus: $
Second Exec. Salary: $ Bonus: $

STOCK TICKER/OTHER:
Stock Ticker: Subsidiary Exchange:
Employees: 49,120 Fiscal Year Ends: 12/31
Parent Company: PepsiCo Inc

OTHER THOUGHTS:
Estimated Female Officers or Directors: 3
Hot Spot for Advancement for Women/Minorities: Y

Sales, profits and employees may be estimates. Financial information, benefits and other data can change quickly and may vary from those stated here.

FTI Consulting Inc

NAIC Code: 541610

www.fticonsulting.com

TYPES OF BUSINESS:
Bankruptcy & Restructuring Consulting
Interim Management Staffing
Performance, Change and Operational Consulting
Legal & Compliance Consulting
Accounting & Advisory Services
Reputational Consulting
Technology Consulting
Software Development

BRANDS/DIVISIONS/AFFILIATES:

CONTACTS: Note: Officers with more than one job title may be intentionally listed here more than once.
Steven Gunby, CEO
Ajay Sabherwal, CFO
Gerard Holthaus, Chairman of the Board
Brendan Keating, Chief Accounting Officer
Matthew Pachman, Chief Risk Officer
Curtis Lu, General Counsel
Paul Linton, Other Executive Officer
Holly Paul, Other Executive Officer

GROWTH PLANS/SPECIAL FEATURES:

FTI Consulting, Inc. is a global consulting firm that provides turnaround, technology, change management and many other high-level consulting services. The firm works across a myriad of industries, including aerospace, defense, agriculture, automotive, construction, energy/power, environmental, financial institutions, healthcare, life sciences, hospitality, gaming, leisure, insurance, mining, public sector, government contracts, real estate, retail, consumer products, transportation, telecommunications, media and technology. FTI Consulting operates through five segments: corporate finance & restructuring (including bankruptcy), forensic and litigation consulting, economic consulting, technology, and strategic communications. Collectively, these business segments offer a comprehensive suite of services designed to assist FTI's clients across the business cycle, from proactive risk management to rapid response to unexpected events and dynamic environments. FTI works closely with its clients to help them anticipate, illuminate and overcome complex business challenges and make the most of opportunities arising from factors such as the economy, financial and credit markets, governmental legislation and regulation, and litigation. FTI operates offices in 27 major nations on six continents.

The firm offers employees life, disability, AD&D, medical, dental and vision insurance; health and dependent care flexible spending accounts; a 401(k); and an employee assistance program.

FINANCIAL DATA: Note: Data for latest year may not have been available at press time.

In U.S. $	2018	2017	2016	2015	2014	2013
Revenue	2,027,877,000	1,807,732,000	1,810,394,000	1,779,149,000	1,756,212,000	1,652,432,000
R&D Expense						
Operating Income	226,005,000	151,887,000	154,765,000	163,311,000	162,089,000	192,736,000
Operating Margin %		.06%	.08%	.09%	.08%	.09%
SGA Expense	465,636,000	429,722,000	434,552,000	432,668,000	433,845,000	394,681,000
Net Income	150,611,000	107,962,000	85,520,000	66,053,000	58,807,000	-10,594,000
Operating Cash Flow	230,672,000	147,625,000	233,488,000	139,920,000	135,401,000	193,271,000
Capital Expenditure	32,270,000	32,004,000	28,935,000	31,399,000	39,256,000	42,544,000
EBITDA	274,639,000	154,203,000	201,628,000	191,272,000	202,743,000	138,779,000
Return on Assets %		.05%	.04%	.03%	.02%	.00%
Return on Equity %		.09%	.07%	.06%	.05%	-.01%
Debt to Equity		0.332	0.303	0.431	0.635	0.682

CONTACT INFORMATION:
Phone: 202-312-9100 Fax: 202-312-9101
Toll-Free: 800-334-5701
Address: 555 12th St. NW, Washington, DC 20004 United States

SALARIES/BONUSES:
Top Exec. Salary: $1,000,000 Bonus: $
Second Exec. Salary: $536,539 Bonus: $

STOCK TICKER/OTHER:
Stock Ticker: FCN Exchange: NYS
Employees: 4,718 Fiscal Year Ends: 12/31
Parent Company:

OTHER THOUGHTS:
Estimated Female Officers or Directors: 3
Hot Spot for Advancement for Women/Minorities: Y

Sales, profits and employees may be estimates. Financial information, benefits and other data can change quickly and may vary from those stated here.

Gartner Inc

NAIC Code: 541910

www.gartner.com

TYPES OF BUSINESS:
Research-Computer Hardware & Software
Industry Research
IT Symposia & Conferences
Measurement & Advisory Services

BRANDS/DIVISIONS/AFFILIATES:
Symposium/Itxpo

CONTACTS: Note: Officers with more than one job title may be intentionally listed here more than once.
Eugene Hall, CEO
Craig Safian, CFO
Michael Diliberto, Chief Information Officer
Robin Kranich, Exec. VP-Human Resources
Alwyn Dawkins, Senior VP, Divisional
Per Waern, Senior VP, Divisional
Robin Kranich, Senior VP, Divisional
Peter Sondergaard, Senior VP, Divisional
David McVeigh, Senior VP, Divisional
David Godfrey, Senior VP, Divisional
Thomas Christopher, Senior VP, Divisional
Kendall Davis, Senior VP, Divisional
Daniel Peale, Senior VP
James Smith, Chairman of the Board

GROWTH PLANS/SPECIAL FEATURES:
Gartner, Inc. is a research and advisory firm that offers independent research and analysis on IT, computer hardware, software, communications and related technology industries. With consultants in 100 countries, the firm serves more than 15,000 organizations worldwide. The company operates in four segments: research and advisory, consulting, conferences and digital markets. The research and advisory segment, the main service of the company, provides research content and advice for IT professionals, technology companies and the investment community in the form of reports and briefings, as well as peer networking services and membership programs designed specifically for Chief Information Officers (CIOs) and other senior executives. The consulting division provides customized solutions to unique client needs through on-site, day-to-day support, as well as proprietary tools for measuring and improving IT performance with a focus on coast, performance, efficiency and quality. The conferences group provides IT, supply chain, digital marketing and other business professionals the opportunity to attend various symposia, conferences and exhibitions to learn, contribute and network with their peers. Its flagship event, Symposium/ITxpo, as well as summits, focus on specific technologies and industries and offer experimental workshop-style seminars. This division also provides the latest Gartner research into applicable insight and advice at its events. Last, the company's digital markets segment gives software buyers with information to make purchasing decisions. This segment also helps software companies attract customers.

FINANCIAL DATA: Note: Data for latest year may not have been available at press time.

In U.S. $	2018	2017	2016	2015	2014	2013
Revenue	3,975,454,000	3,311,494,000	2,444,540,000	2,163,056,000	2,021,441,000	1,784,213,000
R&D Expense						
Operating Income	366,912,000	152,121,000	347,739,000	314,172,000	308,029,000	275,829,000
Operating Margin %		.05%	.14%	.15%	.15%	.15%
SGA Expense	1,884,141,000	1,599,004,000	1,089,184,000	962,677,000	876,067,000	760,458,000
Net Income	122,456,000	3,279,000	193,582,000	175,635,000	183,766,000	182,801,000
Operating Cash Flow	471,158,000	254,517,000	365,632,000	345,561,000	346,779,000	315,654,000
Capital Expenditure	126,873,000	110,765,000	49,863,000	46,128,000	38,486,000	36,498,000
EBITDA	563,496,000	240,301,000	377,965,000	341,890,000	326,395,000	311,269,000
Return on Assets %		.00%	.09%	.09%	.10%	.11%
Return on Equity %		.01%		12.21%	.70%	.55%
Debt to Equity		2.948	10.913		2.389	0.377

CONTACT INFORMATION:
Phone: 203 316-1111   Fax:
Toll-Free:
Address: 56 Top Gallant Rd., Stamford, CT 06902-7700 United States

SALARIES/BONUSES:
Top Exec. Salary: $901,584   Bonus: $
Second Exec. Salary: $503,260   Bonus: $

STOCK TICKER/OTHER:
Stock Ticker: IT
Employees: 8,813
Parent Company:

Exchange: NYS
Fiscal Year Ends: 12/31

OTHER THOUGHTS:
Estimated Female Officers or Directors: 3
Hot Spot for Advancement for Women/Minorities: Y

GEICO Corporation

www.geico.com

NAIC Code: 524126

TYPES OF BUSINESS:
Insurance-Direct Property & Casualty
Automobile Insurance
Homeowners' Insurance

BRANDS/DIVISIONS/AFFILIATES:
Berkshire Hathaway Inc
National Indemnity Company
GEICO General Insurance Company
GEICO Indemnity Company
GEICO Casualty Company
GEICO Advantage Insurance Company
GEICO Choice Insurance Company
GEICO County Mutual

CONTACTS:
Note: Officers with more than one job title may be intentionally listed here more than once.

Bill Roberts, CEO
Nancy Pierce, VP-Mid-Atlantic Oper.
Seth Ingall, Sr. VP-Comm.
Seth Ingall, Sr. VP-Claims
John Pham, VP-New York
Rick Hoagland, VP-Buffalo
Tony Nicely, Chmn.

GROWTH PLANS/SPECIAL FEATURES:

GEICO Corporation and its subsidiaries provide automobile, homeowner and other types of insurance under the GEICO and GEICO Direct brand names. GEICO stands for Government Employees Insurance Company, relating to when the firm's founder first targeted a customer base of U.S. government employees and military personnel. Today, the firm serves a wide range of customers. The group insures approximately 16 million automobile owners, representing more than 27 million vehicles. Vehicle insurance products include coverage for automobiles, motorcycles, all-terrain vehicles (ATVs), recreational vehicles (RVs), boats, collector autos and ridesharing vehicles. GEICO also offers emergency road service. Property insurance products include coverage for homeowners, renters, condos, co-op housing, mobile homes, landlords and flood protection. For businesses, GEICO offers coverage options for business owners, general liability, professional liability, workers' compensation, commercial auto and ridesharing. Additional insurance products include umbrella, life, travel, overseas, identity protection, pet and jewelry coverage. From its regional offices and service centers throughout the U.S., the company provides 24-hour-a-day service, seven-days-a-week. Its online eBilling service sends email notifications to members of when bills will be due, as well as the ability to view, pay and maintain a billing history online. The company offers discount programs and service options to the U.S. military. GEICO operates as a subsidiary of National Indemnity Company, which itself is owned by global investment and holding conglomerate, Berkshire Hathaway, Inc. Affiliates include GEICO General Insurance Company, GEICO Indemnity Company, GEICO Casualty Company, GEICO Advantage Insurance Company, GEICO Choice Insurance Company, GEICO County Mutual and GEICO Secure Insurance Company.

The company offers its employees medical and dental coverage, life insurance, disability plans, scholarships programs for associates' children, a savings plan and paid college tuition for associates.

FINANCIAL DATA:
Note: Data for latest year may not have been available at press time.

In U.S. $	2018	2017	2016	2015	2014	2013
Revenue	33,363,000,000	29,441,000,000	25,483,000,000	22,718,000,000	20,496,000,000	18,572,000,000
R&D Expense						
Operating Income						
Operating Margin %						
SGA Expense						
Net Income	2,449,000,000	-310,000,000	462,000,000	460,000,000	1,159,000,000	1,127,000,000
Operating Cash Flow						
Capital Expenditure						
EBITDA						
Return on Assets %						
Return on Equity %						
Debt to Equity						

CONTACT INFORMATION:
Phone: 301-986-2500 Fax:
Toll-Free: 800-841-3000
Address: 5260 Western Ave., Chevy Chase, MD 20815 United States

SALARIES/BONUSES:
Top Exec. Salary: $ Bonus: $
Second Exec. Salary: $ Bonus: $

STOCK TICKER/OTHER:
Stock Ticker: Subsidiary
Employees: 39,982
Parent Company: Berkshire Hathaway Inc

Exchange:
Fiscal Year Ends: 12/31

OTHER THOUGHTS:
Estimated Female Officers or Directors: 1
Hot Spot for Advancement for Women/Minorities:

Sales, profits and employees may be estimates. Financial information, benefits and other data can change quickly and may vary from those stated here.

Genentech Inc

NAIC Code: 325412

www.gene.com

TYPES OF BUSINESS:
Drug Development & Manufacturing
Genetically Engineered Drugs

BRANDS/DIVISIONS/AFFILIATES:
Roche Holding AG
www.gene.com
Tecentriq

CONTACTS:
Note: Officers with more than one job title may be intentionally listed here more than once.

Alexander Hardy, CEO
Ed Harrington, CFO
Nancy Vitale, Sr. VP-Human Resources
Richard H. Scheller, Exec. VP-Research
Frederick C. Kentz, Sec.
Timothy Moore, Head-Pharmaceutical Technical Operation Biologics
Severin Schwan, Chmn.

GROWTH PLANS/SPECIAL FEATURES:

Genentech, Inc., a wholly-owned subsidiary of Roche Holding AG, is a biotechnology company that discovers, develops, manufactures and commercializes medicines to treat patients with serious or life-threatening medical conditions. The firm makes medicines by splicing genes into fast-growing bacteria that then produce therapeutic proteins and combat diseases on a molecular level. Genentech uses cutting-edge technologies such as computer visualization of molecules, micro arrays and sensitive assaying techniques to develop, manufacture and market pharmaceuticals for unmet medical needs. For patients, the company's website (www.gene.com) provides access for viewing medicine information, investigational medicines, finding open clinical trials and information on diseases in general. Genentech's range of programs and services help make sure that price is not a barrier for patients. For medical professionals, the website offers information on the medicines that are on the market by Genentech, as well as what is on the current pipeline, compliance, product security and various types of medical resources. As of April 2019, there were 40 medicines on the market by the company, and 48 molecules in the pipeline. These medicines and molecules are in various phases in relation to oncology, metabolism, immunology, infectious disease, neuroscience, ophthalmology or other conditions. Approximately half of Genentech's marketed and pipeline products are derived from collaborations with companies and institutions worldwide; therefore, the firm is open to having partners. In March 2019, the U.S. FDA approved Genentech's Tecentriq (atezolizumab), in combination with carboplatin and etoposide (chemotherapy), for the initial treatment of adults with extensive-stage small cell lung cancer.

Genentech provides employees benefits including a 401(k); disability, life, AD&D, medical, dental and vision coverage; flexible spending accounts; and paid vacations.

FINANCIAL DATA:
Note: Data for latest year may not have been available at press time.

In U.S. $	2018	2017	2016	2015	2014	2013
Revenue	20,000,000,000	19,000,000,000	18,000,000,000	17,000,000,000	16,300,000,000	
R&D Expense						
Operating Income						
Operating Margin %						
SGA Expense						
Net Income						
Operating Cash Flow						
Capital Expenditure						
EBITDA						
Return on Assets %						
Return on Equity %						
Debt to Equity						

CONTACT INFORMATION:
Phone: 650-225-1000 Fax: 650-225-6000
Toll-Free: 800-626-3553
Address: 1 DNA Way, South San Francisco, CA 94080-4990 United States

STOCK TICKER/OTHER:
Stock Ticker: Subsidiary
Employees: 13,697
Parent Company: Roche Holding AG
Exchange:
Fiscal Year Ends: 12/31

SALARIES/BONUSES:
Top Exec. Salary: $ Bonus: $
Second Exec. Salary: $ Bonus: $

OTHER THOUGHTS:
Estimated Female Officers or Directors: 1
Hot Spot for Advancement for Women/Minorities: Y

General Dynamics Corporation

www.generaldynamics.com

NAIC Code: 336411

TYPES OF BUSINESS:
Aircraft Manufacturing
Combat Vehicles & Systems
Telecommunications Systems
Naval Vessels & Submarines
Ship Management Services
Information Systems & Technology
Defense Systems & Services
Business Jets

BRANDS/DIVISIONS/AFFILIATES:
Gulfstream Aerospace Corporation
CSRA Inc
G500
G600
Hawker Pacific

CONTACTS:
Note: Officers with more than one job title may be intentionally listed here more than once.

Phebe Novakovic, CEO
Robert Helm, Sr. VP, Divisional
Jason Aiken, CFO
William Moss, Chief Accounting Officer
Mark Roualet, Executive VP, Divisional
Christopher Marzilli, Executive VP, Divisional
John Casey, Executive VP, Divisional
Gregory Gallopoulos, General Counsel
Marguerite Gilliland, President, Subsidiary
Mark Burns, President, Subsidiary
Gary Whited, President, Subsidiary
Jeffrey Geiger, President, Subsidiary
Christopher Brady, President, Subsidiary
Kimberly Kuryea, Senior VP, Divisional

GROWTH PLANS/SPECIAL FEATURES:

General Dynamics Corporation is one of the world's largest aerospace and defense contractors, with a portfolio of over 60 businesses. Its customers include the U.S. military, other government organizations, armed forces of allied nations and a diverse base of corporate and industrial buyers. The firm's operations are divided into five segments: information technology (IT), marine systems, combat system, aerospace, and mission systems. The IT group designs, manufactures and delivers tactical and strategic mission systems, information technology and mission services as well as intelligence mission systems to the U.S. Department of Defense and other customers. The marine systems division provides the U.S. Navy with combat vessels, including nuclear submarines, surface combatants and auxiliary ships. The segment also provides ship management services, such as overhaul, repair and lifecycle support services, and builds commercial ships. The combat systems group provides design, development, production, support and enhancement for tracked and wheeled military vehicles, weapons systems and munitions, with product lines including medium armored vehicles, main battle tanks, munitions, rockets and missile components and armament and detection systems. It is the leading builder of armored vehicles. The aerospace group designs, manufactures and provides services for technologically advanced business jet aircraft under the Gulfstream name. Wholly-owned Gulfstream Aerospace Corporation's new family of business jets, the G500 and G600, can fly 5,000 and 6,200 nautical miles at Mach 0.85, and carry approximately 19 passengers. The mission systems segment provides and manufactures communications systems, command and control systems, cyber security solutions and products and imagery, signals intelligence and multi-intelligence solutions to multiple defense agencies. In April 2018, General Dynamics, as part of its expansion in government information-technology services, acquired CSRA, Inc. In May of that year, the firm acquired Hawker Pacific, a provider of integrated aviation solutions across the Asia Pacific and the Middle East.

FINANCIAL DATA:
Note: Data for latest year may not have been available at press time.

In U.S. $	2018	2017	2016	2015	2014	2013
Revenue	36,193,000,000	30,973,000,000	31,353,000,000	31,469,000,000	30,852,000,000	31,218,000,000
R&D Expense						
Operating Income	4,457,000,000	4,177,000,000	4,309,000,000	4,178,000,000	3,889,000,000	3,685,000,000
Operating Margin %		.13%	.14%	.13%	.13%	.12%
SGA Expense	2,258,000,000	2,010,000,000	1,940,000,000	1,952,000,000	1,984,000,000	2,079,000,000
Net Income	3,345,000,000	2,912,000,000	2,955,000,000	2,965,000,000	2,533,000,000	2,357,000,000
Operating Cash Flow	3,148,000,000	3,879,000,000	2,198,000,000	2,499,000,000	3,728,000,000	3,106,000,000
Capital Expenditure	690,000,000	428,000,000	392,000,000	569,000,000	521,000,000	440,000,000
EBITDA	5,222,000,000	4,635,000,000	4,784,000,000	4,682,000,000	4,401,000,000	4,266,000,000
Return on Assets %		.09%	.09%	.09%	.07%	.07%
Return on Equity %		.26%	.27%	.26%	.19%	.18%
Debt to Equity		0.348	0.272	0.27	0.288	0.269

CONTACT INFORMATION:
Phone: 703 876-3000 Fax: 703 876-3125
Toll-Free:
Address: 2941 Fairview Park Dr., Ste. 100, Falls Church, VA 22042 United States

STOCK TICKER/OTHER:
Stock Ticker: GD
Employees: 98,800
Parent Company:

Exchange: NYS
Fiscal Year Ends: 12/31

SALARIES/BONUSES:
Top Exec. Salary: $1,585,000 Bonus: $
Second Exec. Salary: $830,000 Bonus: $

OTHER THOUGHTS:
Estimated Female Officers or Directors: 3
Hot Spot for Advancement for Women/Minorities: Y

Sales, profits and employees may be estimates. Financial information, benefits and other data can change quickly and may vary from those stated here.

General Motors Company (GM)

NAIC Code: 336111

www.gm.com

TYPES OF BUSINESS:
Automobile Manufacturing
Security & Information Services
Automotive Electronics
Financing & Insurance
Parts & Service
Transmissions
Engines
Locomotives

BRANDS/DIVISIONS/AFFILIATES:
General Motors Financial Company Inc
OnStar LLC
Maven
GM Cruise
Buick
Cadillac
Chevrolet
GMC

CONTACTS:
Note: Officers with more than one job title may be intentionally listed here more than once.

Daniel Ammann, CEO, Subsidiary
Mary Barra, CEO
Dhivya Suryadevara, CFO
Christopher Hatto, Chief Accounting Officer
Alicia Boler-Davis, Executive VP, Divisional
Craig Glidden, Executive VP
Barry Engle, Executive VP
Alan Batey, Executive VP
Matthew Tsien, Executive VP
Mark Reuss, President

GROWTH PLANS/SPECIAL FEATURES:

General Motors Company (GM) is engaged in the worldwide design, production and marketing of cars, crossovers, trucks and automotive parts. GM's automotive operations are grouped into two segments: GM North America, which derived 75.5% of vehicle sales in 2018; and GM International, 24.5%. GM North America serves customers in the U.S., Mexico and Canada, and develops, manufactures and/or markets vehicles under the Buick, Cadillac, Chevrolet and GMC brands. GM International develops, manufactures and/or markets vehicles under the Buick, Cadillac, Chevrolet, GMC and Holden brands. This division also has equity ownership stakes in entities located in China, which develop, manufacture and/or market vehicles under the Baojun, Buick, Cadillac, Chevrolet, Jiefang and Wuling brands. Subsidiary General Motors Financial Company, Inc. provides automotive financing services. OnStar, LLC provides subscription-based and complementary services to more than 20 million connected vehicles globally. OnStar products include connected safety, security and mobility solutions for retail and fleet customers, including automatic crash response, stolen vehicle assistance, roadside assistance, dealer maintenance notifications, remote door unlock, turn-by-turn navigation, vehicle location services, hands-free calling, smart driver and more. Maven is GM's shared vehicle marketplace that provides members with on-demand access to ride- and car-sharing vehicles through: Maven Gig and Maven Car Sharing. Last, GM Cruise is responsible for the development and commercialization of autonomous vehicle technology, as well as an autonomous vehicle (in partnership with Honda Motor Co., Ltd.).

FINANCIAL DATA:
Note: Data for latest year may not have been available at press time.

In U.S. $	2018	2017	2016	2015	2014	2013
Revenue	147,049,000,000	145,588,000,000	166,380,000,000	152,356,000,000	155,929,000,000	155,427,000,000
R&D Expense						
Operating Income	4,445,000,000	10,016,000,000	9,545,000,000	4,897,000,000	1,650,000,000	5,672,000,000
Operating Margin %		.07%	.06%	.03%	.01%	.04%
SGA Expense	9,650,000,000	9,575,000,000	11,710,000,000	13,405,000,000	12,158,000,000	12,382,000,000
Net Income	8,014,000,000	-3,864,000,000	9,427,000,000	9,687,000,000	3,949,000,000	5,346,000,000
Operating Cash Flow	15,256,000,000	17,328,000,000	16,545,000,000	11,978,000,000	10,058,000,000	12,630,000,000
Capital Expenditure	25,497,000,000	27,633,000,000	29,166,000,000	23,032,000,000	11,867,000,000	9,819,000,000
EBITDA	22,873,000,000	24,699,000,000	22,664,000,000	16,178,000,000	11,887,000,000	15,833,000,000
Return on Assets %		-.02%	.05%	.05%	.02%	.02%
Return on Equity %		-.10%	.23%	.26%	.07%	.12%
Debt to Equity		1.921	1.268	1.092	0.898	0.558

CONTACT INFORMATION:
Phone: 313 556-5000   Fax:
Toll-Free:
Address: 300 Renaissance Ctr., Detroit, MI 48265-3000 United States

STOCK TICKER/OTHER:
Stock Ticker: GM
Employees: 135,000
Parent Company:

Exchange: NYS
Fiscal Year Ends: 12/31

SALARIES/BONUSES:
Top Exec. Salary: $2,100,000   Bonus: $
Second Exec. Salary: $1,450,000   Bonus: $

OTHER THOUGHTS:
Estimated Female Officers or Directors: 8
Hot Spot for Advancement for Women/Minorities: Y

Sales, profits and employees may be estimates. Financial information, benefits and other data can change quickly and may vary from those stated here.

Gentex Corporation

www.gentex.com

NAIC Code: 336300

TYPES OF BUSINESS:
Specialty Automobile Parts Manufacturer
Electro-Optic Technology
Rearview Mirrors & Mirror Sub-Assemblies
Headlight Systems
Smoke Alarms & Smoke Detectors
Electrochromic Window Shades

BRANDS/DIVISIONS/AFFILIATES:
HomeLink
HomeLink Connect
ActiveIRIS

CONTACTS: Note: Officers with more than one job title may be intentionally listed here more than once.
Steve Downing, CEO
Kevin Nash, CFO
Neil Boehm, Chief Technology Officer
James Wallace, Director
Scott Ryan, General Counsel
James Hollars, Independent Director
Matthew Chiodo, Vice President, Divisional

GROWTH PLANS/SPECIAL FEATURES:

Gentex Corporation is a global high-tech electronics company, specializing in a broad spectrum of technologies and processes that deliver products to the automotive, aerospace and fire protection industries. For the automotive industry, Gentex designs and manufactures automatic-dimming rearview and non-dimming mirrors and electronics. The electrochromic automatic-dimming rearview mirrors darken to reduce glare and improve visibility for the driver. These interior mirrors can also include additional electronic features such as compass, microphones, HomeLink applications (see below), lighting assist and driver assist forward safety camera systems, various lighting systems, telematic systems and a variety of displays. This division also ships interior non-automatic-dimming rearview mirrors with and without features. HomeLink is a wireless vehicle/home communications product that enables users to remotely activate doors, lighting, security systems and other connected things. HomeLink Connect is a home automation app that pairs with the vehicle and allows drivers to operate home automation devices from the vehicle's center console display. Gentex has a license agreement with Fingerprint Cards AB to deploy its ActiveIRIS iris-scanning biometric technology in automotive applications. For the aerospace industry, Gentex manufactures and sells variable dimmable windows for the passenger compartment on the Boeing 787 Dreamliner and 777X aircraft. For the fire protection industry, the firm manufactures photoelectric smoke detectors and alarms, visual signaling alarms, photoelectric smoke detectors and electrochemical carbon monoxide alarms, electrochemical carbon monoxide detectors and alarms, audible and visual signaling alarms, and bells and speakers for use in fire detection systems in office buildings, hotels and other commercial and residential establishments. Gentex owns 38 U.S. registered trademarks and 635 U.S. patents, and 309 foreign registered trademarks and 787 foreign patents. Genetex's manufacturing facilities are located in Zeeland and Holland, Michigan.

Gentex offers comprehensive health benefits, 401(k) and retirement plans, and a variety of employee assistance programs.

FINANCIAL DATA: Note: Data for latest year may not have been available at press time.

In U.S. $	2018	2017	2016	2015	2014	2013
Revenue	1,834,064,000	1,794,873,000	1,678,925,000	1,543,618,000	1,375,501,000	1,171,864,000
R&D Expense	107,134,900	99,726,440	94,238,030	88,392,920	84,175,740	76,495,050
Operating Income	508,125,500	523,358,300	511,742,900	458,766,400	398,834,200	304,741,800
Operating Margin %		.29%	.30%	.30%	.29%	.26%
SGA Expense	75,206,280	71,443,470	62,471,280	56,616,700	55,879,780	49,496,040
Net Income	437,883,100	406,791,900	347,591,300	318,469,900	288,604,600	222,930,000
Operating Cash Flow	552,418,600	501,002,800	471,464,800	351,578,400	327,223,100	317,338,800
Capital Expenditure	85,990,570	104,040,900	120,955,600	97,941,760	72,518,980	55,380,460
EBITDA	610,312,400	622,929,300	600,330,400	539,365,600	476,210,500	367,596,000
Return on Assets %		.17%	.16%	.15%	.15%	.15%
Return on Equity %		.21%	.19%	.19%	.20%	.18%
Debt to Equity			0.093	0.131	0.164	0.20

CONTACT INFORMATION:
Phone: 616 772-1800 Fax: 616 772-7348
Toll-Free:
Address: 600 N. Centennial St., Zeeland, MI 49464 United States

STOCK TICKER/OTHER:
Stock Ticker: GNTX
Employees: 5,315
Parent Company:

Exchange: NAS
Fiscal Year Ends: 12/31

SALARIES/BONUSES:
Top Exec. Salary: $618,173 Bonus: $180,000
Second Exec. Salary: $327,075 Bonus: $90,000

OTHER THOUGHTS:
Estimated Female Officers or Directors: 1
Hot Spot for Advancement for Women/Minorities:

Sales, profits and employees may be estimates. Financial information, benefits and other data can change quickly and may vary from those stated here.

GoDaddy Inc

www.godaddy.com

NAIC Code: 518210

TYPES OF BUSINESS:
Domain Name Registration
Domain Name Reselling
Research & Development, Internet Services

BRANDS/DIVISIONS/AFFILIATES:

CONTACTS: Note: Officers with more than one job title may be intentionally listed here more than once.
Scott Wagner, CEO
Ray Winborne, CFO
Charles Robel, Chairman of the Board
Rebecca Morrow, Chief Accounting Officer
Arne Josefsberg, Chief Information Officer
Nima Kelly, Chief Legal Officer
Ah Kee Low, COO
James Carroll, Executive VP, Divisional

GROWTH PLANS/SPECIAL FEATURES:

GoDaddy, Inc. provides domain name registration and related services. The company has 18.5 million customers made up of individuals and organizations. GoDaddy operates the world's largest domain marketplace where customers can find a domain name to match their concept, with more than 77 million domains under management. The firm is a leading technology provider to small businesses, web design professionals and individuals, offering easy-to-use cloud-based products. GoDaddy provides website building, hosting and security tools to construct and protect each customer's online presence. Products are developed internally, and include shared website hosting, website hosting on virtual dedicated servers and dedicated services, managed hosting services, cloud services, cloud applications, website builder, eCommerce solutions, search engine visibility, email accounts, office solutions, email marketing solutions and payment solutions. GoDaddy provides localized solutions in over 50 markets, with 35% of its total bookings attributable to customers outside the U.S.

The firm offers employees 100% paid medical and dental premiums, employee appreciation outings, a 401(k) plan, life and disability insurance, maternity and paternity leave, adoption assistance, subsidized lunches and employee discounts.

FINANCIAL DATA: Note: Data for latest year may not have been available at press time.

In U.S. $	2018	2017	2016	2015	2014	2013
Revenue	2,660,100,000	2,231,900,000	1,847,900,000	1,607,300,000	1,387,262,000	1,130,845,000
R&D Expense	434,000,000	355,800,000	287,800,000	270,200,000	254,440,000	207,941,000
Operating Income	149,600,000	66,900,000	50,100,000	-31,000,000	-61,876,000	-131,925,000
Operating Margin %		.03%	.03%	-.02%	-.04%	-.12%
SGA Expense	948,500,000	827,900,000	692,100,000	643,400,000	523,557,000	440,394,000
Net Income	77,100,000	136,400,000	-16,500,000	-75,600,000	-143,305,000	-199,884,000
Operating Cash Flow	559,800,000	475,600,000	386,500,000	259,400,000	180,568,000	153,313,000
Capital Expenditure	97,000,000	135,200,000	62,800,000	79,300,000	67,901,000	52,089,000
EBITDA	405,500,000	395,600,000	195,800,000	107,400,000	91,627,000	10,519,000
Return on Assets %		.03%	.00%	-.01%	-.04%	-.06%
Return on Equity %		.26%	-.03%	-.11%	-.23%	-.22%
Debt to Equity		4.955	1.841	2.442	3.445	1.334

CONTACT INFORMATION:
Phone: 480-505-8800 Fax: 480-505-8844
Toll-Free:
Address: 14455 N. Hayden Rd., Ste. 219, Scottsdale, AZ 85260 United States

STOCK TICKER/OTHER:
Stock Ticker: GDDY
Employees: 4,749
Parent Company:

Exchange: NYS
Fiscal Year Ends: 12/31

SALARIES/BONUSES:
Top Exec. Salary: $750,000   Bonus: $
Second Exec. Salary: $515,000   Bonus: $

OTHER THOUGHTS:
Estimated Female Officers or Directors: 3
Hot Spot for Advancement for Women/Minorities: Y

Sales, profits and employees may be estimates. Financial information, benefits and other data can change quickly and may vary from those stated here.

Goldman Sachs Group Inc (The)

NAIC Code: 523110

www.goldmansachs.com

TYPES OF BUSINESS:
Investment Banking
Securities & Investment Management
Financial Services
Asset Management
Bank Holding Company
Retail Banking
Online Banking

BRANDS/DIVISIONS/AFFILIATES:
Marcus

CONTACTS:
Note: Officers with more than one job title may be intentionally listed here more than once.

David Solomon, CEO
Stephen Scherr, CFO
Brian Lee, Controller
John Waldron, COO
Karen Seymour, Executive VP
Dane Holmes, Executive VP
Sarah Smith, Executive VP
John Rogers, Executive VP

GROWTH PLANS/SPECIAL FEATURES:

The Goldman Sachs Group, Inc. is a financial holding company regulated by the Board of Governors of the Federal Reserve System, operating in over 30 countries. The firm has four main business segments: institutional client services, investment management, investment banking and investing & lending. The institutional client services segment accounts for the majority of the company's annual profits (more than 45%). It provides clients with services regarding fixed income currency and commodities execution on a variety of products such as interest rate and credit products, mortgages, currencies and commodities. The investment management segment provides investment and wealth advisory services on a range of asset classes and investment plans, including equity, fixed income, hedge funds, private equity, real estate, currencies, commodities and asset allocation of strategies to institutions and high-net-worth individuals who access the companies' products through third-party distributors. The investment banking segment provides financial advisory services including strategic advisory assignments with respect to mergers and acquisitions, divestitures, corporate defense activities, risk management, debt and equity underwriting, restructurings and spin-offs to corporate and government clients around the world. The investing & lending segment manages a portfolio of investments consisting of equity and debt securities in addition to other investments in privately-negotiated transactions, leveraged buyouts, acquisitions and investment funds managed by external parties. This division's Marcus platform is a digital retail banking unit that provides banking and lending services to middle-income U.S. households. Moreover, Goldman Sachs' prime brokerage program in Europe and the U.S. delivers investment research, products and execution services to brokerage firms. In June 2019, the firm acquired Capital Vision Services L.P., the manager of MrEyeDr. optometry practices, in a deal valued at $2.7 billion.

Goldman Sachs offers employees medical, prescription, life, disability, accident, travel, dental and vision insurance; a 401(k); adoption assistance; and investing services.

FINANCIAL DATA:
Note: Data for latest year may not have been available at press time.

In U.S. $	2018	2017	2016	2015	2014	2013
Revenue	33,416,000,000	29,533,000,000	28,053,000,000	31,244,000,000	32,027,000,000	31,865,000,000
R&D Expense						
Operating Income						
Operating Margin %						
SGA Expense	14,091,000,000	13,338,000,000	12,913,000,000	14,041,000,000	14,019,000,000	14,106,000,000
Net Income	10,459,000,000	4,286,000,000	7,398,000,000	6,083,000,000	8,477,000,000	8,040,000,000
Operating Cash Flow	20,421,000,000	-17,742,000,000	5,570,000,000	6,961,000,000	-7,623,000,000	4,543,000,000
Capital Expenditure	7,982,000,000	3,185,000,000	2,876,000,000	1,833,000,000	678,000,000	706,000,000
EBITDA						
Return on Assets %		.00%	.01%	.01%	.01%	.01%
Return on Equity %		.05%	.09%	.07%	.11%	.11%
Debt to Equity		3.445	2.783	2.65	2.587	2.607

CONTACT INFORMATION:
Phone: 212 902-1000 Fax: 212 902-3000
Toll-Free:
Address: 200 West St., New York, NY 10282 United States

STOCK TICKER/OTHER:
Stock Ticker: GS
Employees: 34,400
Parent Company:

Exchange: NYS
Fiscal Year Ends: 12/31

SALARIES/BONUSES:
Top Exec. Salary: $1,587,500 Bonus: $6,812,625
Second Exec. Salary: $1,587,500 Bonus: $6,442,625

OTHER THOUGHTS:
Estimated Female Officers or Directors: 5
Hot Spot for Advancement for Women/Minorities: Y

Graco Inc

NAIC Code: 333911

www.graco.com

TYPES OF BUSINESS:
Pump and Pumping Equipment Manufacturing

BRANDS/DIVISIONS/AFFILIATES:

CONTACTS:
Note: Officers with more than one job title may be intentionally listed here more than once.

Patrick McHale, CEO
Angela Wordell, Exec. VP-Operations
Mark Sheahan, CFO
Mark Sheahan, CFO
David Ahlers, Exec. VP-HR and Corporate Comms
Caroline Chambers, Exec. VP-Corporate Controller and IS
David Lowe, Executive VP, Divisional
Karen Gallivan, Executive VP
Mark Eberlein, General Manager, Divisional
Peter OShea, General Manager, Divisional
Bernard Moreau, General Manager, Geographical
Jeffrey Johnson, General Manager, Geographical
Brian Zumbolo, General Manager, Geographical
Dale Johnson, President, Divisional
Christian Rothe, President, Divisional
David Ahlers, Vice President, Divisional
Lee Mitau, Chairman of the Board

GROWTH PLANS/SPECIAL FEATURES:

Graco, Inc. provides fluid handling solutions to customers in the manufacturing, processing, construction and maintenance industries throughout the world. The company operates in three segments: industrial, contractor and process. The industrial segment (47% of sales in 2018) includes the industrial products and the applied fluid technologies divisions. The industrial products division markets equipment and services to customers who manufacture, assemble, maintain, repair and refinish products such as appliances, vehicles, airplanes, electronics, cabinets and furniture. The applied fluid technologies division designs and sells equipment for use by industrial customers, including systems used to spray polyurethane foam and polyuria coatings. The contractor segment (32% of sales in 2018) markets a complete line of airless paint and texture sprayers; accessories such as spray guns, hoses and filters; and spare parts such as tips and seals. The process segment includes process, oil and natural gas and lubrication divisions. Process (21% of sales in 2018) markets pumps, valves, meters and accessories to move and dispense chemicals, oil and natural gas, water, wastewater, petroleum, food lubricants and other fluids. Markets served include food, beverage, dairy, oil and natural gas, pharmaceutical, cosmetics, semi-conductor, electronics, wastewater, mining, fast oil change facilities, service garages, fleet service centers, automobile dealerships and industrial lubrication applications. Oil and natural gas markets chemical injection pumping solutions, high pressure and ultra-high-pressure valves. The lubrication division designs and sells equipment for use in vehicle servicing, supplying pumps, hose reels, meters, valves and accessories. It also offers systems, components and accessories for the automatic lubrication of bearings, gears and generators in industrial and commercial equipment, compressors, turbines and on- and off-road vehicles.

FINANCIAL DATA:
Note: Data for latest year may not have been available at press time.

In U.S. $	2018	2017	2016	2015	2014	2013
Revenue	1,653,292,000	1,474,744,000	1,329,293,000	1,286,485,000	1,221,130,000	1,104,024,000
R&D Expense	63,124,000	60,106,000	60,606,000	58,559,000	54,246,000	51,428,000
Operating Income	436,427,000	360,447,000	305,899,000	302,125,000	308,925,000	279,769,000
Operating Margin %		.24%	.23%	.23%	.25%	.25%
SGA Expense	382,988,000	372,496,000	341,734,000	324,016,000	303,565,000	276,258,000
Net Income	341,054,000	252,412,000	40,674,000	345,713,000	225,573,000	210,822,000
Operating Cash Flow	367,985,000	337,864,000	269,093,000	189,639,000	241,255,000	243,055,000
Capital Expenditure	53,854,000	40,194,000	42,113,000	41,749,000	30,636,000	23,319,000
EBITDA	472,905,000	408,879,000	162,535,000	536,963,000	369,321,000	344,285,000
Return on Assets %		.19%	.03%	.24%	.16%	.16%
Return on Equity %		.39%	.07%	.56%	.37%	.39%
Debt to Equity		0.313	0.533	0.618	1.032	0.644

CONTACT INFORMATION:
Phone: 612 623-6000   Fax: 612 623-6777
Toll-Free:
Address: 88 11th Ave. NE, Minneapolis, MN 55413 United States

STOCK TICKER/OTHER:
Stock Ticker: GGG
Employees: 3,300
Parent Company:

Exchange: NYS
Fiscal Year Ends: 12/31

SALARIES/BONUSES:
Top Exec. Salary: $816,000   Bonus: $
Second Exec. Salary: $457,400   Bonus: $

OTHER THOUGHTS:
Estimated Female Officers or Directors:
Hot Spot for Advancement for Women/Minorities:

Sales, profits and employees may be estimates. Financial information, benefits and other data can change quickly and may vary from those stated here.

Grant Thornton LLP

NAIC Code: 541211

www.grantthornton.com

TYPES OF BUSINESS:
Accounting & Auditing Services
Financial Services
Administration Consulting

BRANDS/DIVISIONS/AFFILIATES:
Grant Thornton International Ltd

CONTACTS:
Note: Officers with more than one job title may be intentionally listed here more than once.

Mike McGuire, CEO
J. Michael McGuire, Nat'l Managing Partner-Oper.
Trent Gazzaway, Managing Partner-Audit Svcs.
Doreen Griffith, Managing Partner-Tax Svcs.
Steve Lukens, Managing Partner-Advisory Svcs.

GROWTH PLANS/SPECIAL FEATURES:

Grant Thornton, LLP is the U.S. arm of Grant Thornton International Ltd., and provides advisory, audit and tax services to both public and private corporations. The company's advisory services include business consulting; forensic, investigative and dispute services; governance, risk and compliance; restructuring and turnaround; technology solutions; transaction advisory; and valuation. Its audit solutions include employee benefit plan audit, financial statement audit, fresh start accounting, international financial reporting standards reporting and resources and public finance. Tax services include tax, human capital, international tax, private wealth, SALT alerts, state and local tax, strategic federal tax, tax reporting, advisory, tax hot topics, tax innovation and more. Industries served by the firm include construction, distribution, energy, financial services, food and beverage, healthcare, life sciences, hospitality, restaurants, manufacturing, not-for-profit organizations, private equity, public policy, public sector, real estate, retail, technology and transportation. Grant Thornton, LLP has 59 offices across the U.S.

Grant Thornton's employee benefits include medical and dental plans, reimbursement accounts and a 401(k) plan.

FINANCIAL DATA:
Note: Data for latest year may not have been available at press time.

In U.S. $	2018	2017	2016	2015	2014	2013
Revenue	1,790,000,000	1,740,000,000	1,650,000,000	1,450,000,000	1,354,000,000	1,300,000,000
R&D Expense						
Operating Income						
Operating Margin %						
SGA Expense						
Net Income						
Operating Cash Flow						
Capital Expenditure						
EBITDA						
Return on Assets %						
Return on Equity %						
Debt to Equity						

CONTACT INFORMATION:
Phone: 312-856-0200   Fax: 312-602-8099
Toll-Free:
Address: 171 N. Clark St., Ste. 200, Chicago, IL 60601 United States

STOCK TICKER/OTHER:
Stock Ticker: Private   Exchange:
Employees: 8,122   Fiscal Year Ends: 07/31
Parent Company: Grant Thornton International Ltd

SALARIES/BONUSES:
Top Exec. Salary: $ Bonus: $
Second Exec. Salary: $ Bonus: $

OTHER THOUGHTS:
Estimated Female Officers or Directors: 2
Hot Spot for Advancement for Women/Minorities:

Group 1 Automotive Inc

www.group1auto.com

NAIC Code: 441110

TYPES OF BUSINESS:
Auto Dealers
Auto Repair Services
Insurance Services
Automotive Replacement Parts
Financing Services
Collision Service Centers

BRANDS/DIVISIONS/AFFILIATES:

CONTACTS:
Note: Officers with more than one job title may be intentionally listed here more than once.

Earl Hesterberg, CEO
John Rickel, CFO
Stephen Quinn, Chairman of the Board
Lincoln Pereira, Director
Daryl Kenningham, President, Divisional
Peter DeLongchamps, Senior VP, Divisional
Frank Grese, Senior VP, Divisional

GROWTH PLANS/SPECIAL FEATURES:

Group 1 Automotive, Inc. is a leading operator in the automotive retail industries, with locations throughout the U.S., the U.K. and Brazil. The company, through its subsidiaries, sells new and used cars and light trucks, provides maintenance and repair services, sells replacement parts and arranges vehicle financing and insurance through its dealerships and franchises. In total, Group 1 owns and operates 184 dealerships, 238 franchises and 48 collision centers (as of July 2019). The dealerships offer approximately 30 brands of automobiles, which may include Toyota, BMW, Ford, Audi, Mercedes-Benz, Honda, Nissan, Lexus, Chevrolet, MINI, Volkswagen, GMC, Hyundai, Jeep, Acura, RAM, Land Rover, Kia, Cadillac, Dodge, Subaru, Jaguar, Buick, Sprinter, Chrysler, SEAT, Lincoln, Mazda, Skoda, Vauxhall, Volvo and Smart. Group 1's dealerships have taken several steps toward building customer confidence in their used vehicle inventory, including participation in manufacturer certification processes. These processes make used vehicles eligible for new vehicle benefits such as new vehicle finance rates and extended manufacturer warranties. In July 2019, Group 1 acquired five Volkswagen franchises in the U.K., which includes one commercial vehicle franchise.

FINANCIAL DATA:
Note: Data for latest year may not have been available at press time.

In U.S. $	2018	2017	2016	2015	2014	2013
Revenue	11,601,360,000	11,123,720,000	10,887,610,000	10,632,510,000	9,937,889,000	8,918,581,000
R&D Expense						
Operating Income	384,966,000	361,378,000	373,072,000	365,900,000	343,630,000	279,864,000
Operating Margin %		.03%	.03%	.03%	.03%	.03%
SGA Expense	1,273,057,000	1,226,195,000	1,170,763,000	1,120,833,000	1,061,964,000	976,856,000
Net Income	157,772,000	213,442,000	147,065,000	93,999,000	93,004,000	113,992,000
Operating Cash Flow	269,978,000	198,925,000	384,857,000	141,047,000	198,288,000	52,372,000
Capital Expenditure	141,033,000	215,832,000	156,521,000	120,252,000	150,392,000	102,858,000
EBITDA	408,153,000	399,808,000	391,468,000	325,577,000	298,051,000	308,359,000
Return on Assets %		.04%	.03%	.02%	.02%	.03%
Return on Equity %		.20%	.15%	.10%	.09%	.11%
Debt to Equity		1.172	1.304	1.311	1.032	0.624

CONTACT INFORMATION:
Phone: 713 647-5700 Fax: 713 647-5858
Toll-Free:
Address: 800 Gessner, Ste. 500, Houston, TX 77024 United States

STOCK TICKER/OTHER:
Stock Ticker: GPI
Employees: 13,500
Parent Company:

Exchange: NYS
Fiscal Year Ends: 12/31

SALARIES/BONUSES:
Top Exec. Salary: $1,150,000 Bonus: $
Second Exec. Salary: $624,000 Bonus: $

OTHER THOUGHTS:
Estimated Female Officers or Directors:
Hot Spot for Advancement for Women/Minorities: Y

Sales, profits and employees may be estimates. Financial information, benefits and other data can change quickly and may vary from those stated here.

Gulfstream Aerospace Corporation

www.gulfstream.com

NAIC Code: 336411

TYPES OF BUSINESS:
Aircraft Manufacturing
Business Jets
Support Services
Leasing & Financing

BRANDS/DIVISIONS/AFFILIATES:
General Dynamics Corporation
G280
G500
G550
G600
G650
G650ER

CONTACTS: Note: Officers with more than one job title may be intentionally listed here more than once.
Mark Burns, Pres.
Daniel G. Clare, CFO
Dan Nale, Sr. VP-Programs, Eng. & Test
Ira Berman, Sr. VP-Admin.
Ira Berman, General Counsel
Dennis Stuligross, Sr. VP-Oper.
Joe Lombardo, Exec. VP-Aerospace Group, General Dynamics
Mark Burns, Pres., Product Support
Scott Neal, Sr. VP-Worldwide Sales & Mktg.
Buddy Sams, Sr. VP-Gov't Programs & Sales

GROWTH PLANS/SPECIAL FEATURES:

Gulfstream Aerospace Corporation, a subsidiary of General Dynamics Corporation, designs, develops, manufactures, markets and provides maintenance and support services for technologically-advanced business jet aircraft. Established in 1958, Gulfstream operates facilities on four continents and employs more than 15,000 people worldwide. The company is also a leading provider of land and expeditionary combat systems, armaments and munitions; shipbuilding and marine systems; and information systems and technologies. Gulfstream's current aircraft includes six product lines: the mid-size G280; the ultra-long-range G500, G550, G600 and G650; and the extended reach G650ER, extending the nonstop reach of the industry's highest performance long-range business aircraft to 7,500 nautical miles at Mach 0.85. The maximum operating speed for G650ER is 0.925. Gulfstream also routinely accepts aircraft trade-ins for the sale of new Gulfstream models and resells the used planes on the pre-owned market. The group offers several product enhancements for its planes, including the ultra-high-speed broadband multi-link (BBML) system, which allows customers to access the internet at altitudes up to 51,000 feet; and the enhanced vision system (EVS), a forward-looking infrared (FLIR) camera that projects an infrared real-world image on the pilot's heads-up display, which allows the flight crew to see in conditions of low light and reduced visibility. In October 2018, the firm acquired a manufacturing line that produces nacelles for the G500 and G600 from The NORDAM Group Inc.

Employees of the firm receive tuition reimbursement; relocation assistance; a performance-based incentive plan; a wellness program; flexible spending accounts; and medical, dental, vision, disability and life insurance.

FINANCIAL DATA: Note: Data for latest year may not have been available at press time.

In U.S. $	2018	2017	2016	2015	2014	2013
Revenue	8,977,500,000	8,550,000,000	8,500,000,000	8,851,000,000	8,649,000,000	8,118,000,000
R&D Expense						
Operating Income						
Operating Margin %						
SGA Expense						
Net Income		1,600,000,000	1,500,000,000	1,706,000,000	1,611,000,000	1,416,000,000
Operating Cash Flow						
Capital Expenditure						
EBITDA						
Return on Assets %						
Return on Equity %						
Debt to Equity						

CONTACT INFORMATION:
Phone: 912-965-3000 Fax: 912-965-3084
Toll-Free:
Address: 500 Gulfstream Rd., Savannah, GA 31407 United States

STOCK TICKER/OTHER:
Stock Ticker: Subsidiary Exchange:
Employees: 15,000 Fiscal Year Ends: 12/31
Parent Company: General Dynamics Corporation

SALARIES/BONUSES:
Top Exec. Salary: $ Bonus: $
Second Exec. Salary: $ Bonus: $

OTHER THOUGHTS:
Estimated Female Officers or Directors:
Hot Spot for Advancement for Women/Minorities:

Sales, profits and employees may be estimates. Financial information, benefits and other data can change quickly and may vary from those stated here.

HanesBrands Inc

www.hanesbrands.com

NAIC Code: 424300

TYPES OF BUSINESS:
Apparel and Clothing Brands, Designers, Importers and Distributors
Outerwear
Hosiery
Internet Sales
Catalogs

BRANDS/DIVISIONS/AFFILIATES:
Hanes
Playtex
JMS|Just My Size
Maidenform
Champion
Hanes Beefy-T
Bali
Knights Apparel

CONTACTS:
Note: Officers with more than one job title may be intentionally listed here more than once.

Gerald Evans, CEO
Barry Hytinen, CFO
Ronald Nelson, Chairman of the Board
M. Scott Lewis, Chief Accounting Officer
Joia Johnson, General Counsel
David Bortolussi, Managing Director, Divisional
Jonathan Ram, President, Divisional
W. Upchurch, President, Divisional
Michael Faircloth, President, Divisional

GROWTH PLANS/SPECIAL FEATURES:
Hanesbrands, Inc. designs, manufactures, sources and sells apparel including t-shirts, bras, panties, men's underwear, kids' underwear, socks, hosiery, casual wear and active wear. The company is organized into three operating segments: innerwear, which accounted for 35% of its 2018 revenue; activewear, 26%; and international, 34%. HanesBrands' innerwear segment produces bras, panties, men's underwear, kids' underwear and socks marketed under the Hanes, Playtex, Bali, JMS|Just My Size, Maidenform, Donna Karan, Champion and DKNY brands. HanesBrands also maintains a licensing agreement with Polo Ralph Lauren to produce underwear. The activewearwear segment produces t-shirts, fleece, athletic uniforms, thermals sleepwear and casual wear marketed under the Hanes, JMS|Just My Size, Champion, Hanes Beefy-T and Knights Apparel. The international segment includes sales in Europe, Asia, Latin America, Canada, Australia, the Middle East, and Africa, with the company's largest international markets comprising Europe, Canada, Japan, Mexico, Brazil and Australia. Its largest customers are Wal-Mart and Target, which accounted for 16% and 12%, respectively, of total revenue. HanesBrands engages in manufacturing through both company-owned and operated facilities and third-party contractors. The firm's design, research and product development activities are primarily located in a North Carolina facility, with some activities in New York City and Lenexa, Kansas.

FINANCIAL DATA:
Note: Data for latest year may not have been available at press time.

In U.S. $	2018	2017	2016	2015	2014	2013
Revenue	6,803,955,000	6,471,410,000	6,028,199,000	5,731,549,000	5,324,746,000	4,627,802,000
R&D Expense						
Operating Income	867,951,000	750,920,000	775,649,000	595,118,000	563,954,000	515,186,000
Operating Margin %		.12%	.13%	.10%	.11%	.11%
SGA Expense	1,788,568,000	1,739,631,000	1,500,399,000	1,541,214,000	1,340,453,000	1,096,507,000
Net Income	553,084,000	61,894,000	539,382,000	428,855,000	404,519,000	330,494,000
Operating Cash Flow	643,402,000	655,718,000	605,607,000	227,007,000	508,090,000	591,281,000
Capital Expenditure	86,293,000	87,008,000	83,399,000	99,375,000	64,311,000	43,627,000
EBITDA	999,747,000	873,407,000	878,824,000	699,021,000	662,156,000	606,076,000
Return on Assets %		.01%	.09%	.08%	.09%	.09%
Return on Equity %		.06%	.43%	.32%	.31%	.31%
Debt to Equity		5.395	2.866	1.767	1.164	1.192

CONTACT INFORMATION:
Phone: 336 519-8080   Fax: 312 726-3712
Toll-Free:
Address: 1000 E. Hanes Mill Rd., Winston-Salem, NC 27105 United States

STOCK TICKER/OTHER:
Stock Ticker: HBI
Employees: 67,800
Parent Company:

Exchange: NYS
Fiscal Year Ends: 12/30

SALARIES/BONUSES:
Top Exec. Salary: $1,100,000   Bonus: $
Second Exec. Salary: $600,000   Bonus: $

OTHER THOUGHTS:
Estimated Female Officers or Directors: 4
Hot Spot for Advancement for Women/Minorities: Y

Sales, profits and employees may be estimates. Financial information, benefits and other data can change quickly and may vary from those stated here.

Harris Corporation

NAIC Code: 334220

www.harris.com

TYPES OF BUSINESS:
Communications Equipment Manufacturing
Wireless Communications Equipment
Healthcare IT Systems
Managed Satellite Communications
Integrated IT Systems

BRANDS/DIVISIONS/AFFILIATES:
Harris Satellite (HSAT)

CONTACTS:
Note: Officers with more than one job title may be intentionally listed here more than once.

William Brown, CEO
Rahul Ghai, CFO
Todd Taylor, Chief Accounting Officer
Scott Mikuen, General Counsel
Dana Mehnert, Other Executive Officer
Christopher Young, President, Divisional
Edward Zoiss, President, Divisional
William Gattle, President, Divisional
Robert Duffy, Senior VP, Divisional
Sheldon Fox, Senior VP, Divisional

GROWTH PLANS/SPECIAL FEATURES:

Harris Corporation is an international communications and information technology company. The firm, along with its subsidiaries, serves government and commercial markets in over 100 countries. Harris operates through three divisions: communication systems, space and intelligence systems and electronic systems. The communication systems division serves tactical communication, defense and public safety network markets with products that include tactical ground and airborne radio communications solutions, as well as night vision technology. The space and intelligence systems division provides intelligence, space protection, geospatial, complete Earth observation, universe exploration, positioning/navigation/timing (PNT), and environmental solutions for national security, defense, civil and commercial customers. This division offers advanced sensors, antennas and payloads, as well as ground processing and information analytics. The electronic systems division provides electronic warfare, avionics and C4ISR (command, control, communications, computers, intelligence, surveillance and reconnaissance) solutions for the defense industry; and air traffic management solutions for the civil aviation industry. In December 2018, Harris successfully launched and communicated with its first small satellite from India's Polar Satellite Launch Vehicle, showcasing the firm's ability to provide complete end-to-end mission solutions for the smallsat market. Harris Satellite (HSAT) is a briefcase-size cubesat that provides and affordable solution for defense and commercial customers with very high-speed satellite communications requirements. It is designed to fly in low Earth orbit and features a resilient mission architecture that can be reconfigured after launch. In October 2018, Harris Corporation agreed to combine with L3 Technologies, Inc. in an all-stock merger of equals, subject to regulatory approval.

The firm offers employees benefits including medical, dental and vision insurance; a 401(k); paid time off; tuition reimbursement; and health and dependent care spending accounts.

FINANCIAL DATA:
Note: Data for latest year may not have been available at press time.

In U.S. $	2018	2017	2016	2015	2014	2013
Revenue	6,182,000,128	5,900,000,256	7,466,999,808	5,082,999,808	5,011,999,744	5,111,699,968
R&D Expense						
Operating Income						
Operating Margin %						
SGA Expense						
Net Income	718,000,000	553,000,000	324,000,000	334,000,000	534,800,000	113,000,000
Operating Cash Flow						
Capital Expenditure						
EBITDA						
Return on Assets %						
Return on Equity %						
Debt to Equity						

CONTACT INFORMATION:
Phone: 321 727-9100 Fax: 321 724-3973
Toll-Free: 800-442-7747
Address: 1025 W. NASA Blvd., Melbourne, FL 32919 United States

STOCK TICKER/OTHER:
Stock Ticker: HRS
Employees: 17,000
Parent Company:

Exchange: NYS
Fiscal Year Ends: 06/30

SALARIES/BONUSES:
Top Exec. Salary: $ Bonus: $
Second Exec. Salary: $ Bonus: $

OTHER THOUGHTS:
Estimated Female Officers or Directors: 2
Hot Spot for Advancement for Women/Minorities: Y

Hartford Financial Services Group Inc (The) www.thehartford.com

NAIC Code: 524113

TYPES OF BUSINESS:
Life Insurance
Mutual Funds
Property & Casualty Insurance
Group Life & Accident Insurance
Reinsurance
Employee Benefits Administration
Asset Management
Bank Holding Company

BRANDS/DIVISIONS/AFFILIATES:
Hartford Life Insurance Company
Navigators Group Inc

CONTACTS:
Note: Officers with more than one job title may be intentionally listed here more than once.

Christopher Swift, CEO
Beth Costello, CFO
Scott Lewis, Chief Accounting Officer
Kathleen Bromage, Chief Marketing Officer
Robert Paiano, Chief Risk Officer
William Bloom, Executive VP, Divisional
Martha Gervasi, Executive VP, Divisional
David Robinson, Executive VP
Brion Johnson, Executive VP
Douglas Elliot, President

GROWTH PLANS/SPECIAL FEATURES:

The Hartford Financial Services Group, Inc. is a diversified insurance and financial services company that offers insurance and investment products. Through Hartford Life Insurance Company and its many subsidiaries, it is a leading provider of investment products, individual life, group life and group disability insurance products and property and casualty insurance products in the U.S., Canada and select overseas markets. The Hartford is organized into five major divisions: commercial lines, personal lines, property and casualty (P&C) other operations, group benefits, Hartford funds and corporate. The Commercial lines division provides standard workers' compensation, property, automobile, liability, marine, livestock and umbrella coverages as well as a variety of customized insurance products and risk management services. Personal lines provide standard automobile, homeowners and home-based business coverages, including a special program designed for members of AARP. P&C other operations includes certain property and casualty operations that have discontinued writing new business and includes substantially all the firm's asbestos and environmental exposures. Group benefits offers group life, accident and disability coverage as well as group retiree health and voluntary benefits to individual members of employer groups. Mutual funds offer investment management, administration, distribution and related services to investors through financial products in both domestic and international markets. The corporate division includes Hartford's capital raising activities, including debt financing and interest expense; purchase accounting adjustments; and other expenses. In May 2019, Hartford completed its $2.1 billion acquisition of Navigators Group, Inc., an international insurance company specializing in marine insurance.

The firm offers employees medical, dental and vision insurance; a wellness program; investment, savings, stock and bond purchase plans; and short- and long-term disability.

FINANCIAL DATA:
Note: Data for latest year may not have been available at press time.

In U.S. $	2018	2017	2016	2015	2014	2013
Revenue	18,955,000,000	16,974,000,000	18,300,000,000	18,377,000,000	18,614,000,000	24,661,000,000
R&D Expense						
Operating Income						
Operating Margin %						
SGA Expense						
Net Income	1,807,000,000	-3,131,000,000	896,000,000	1,682,000,000	798,000,000	176,000,000
Operating Cash Flow	2,843,000,000	2,186,000,000	2,066,000,000	2,756,000,000	1,886,000,000	1,237,000,000
Capital Expenditure	122,000,000	250,000,000	224,000,000	307,000,000	121,000,000	
EBITDA						
Return on Assets %		-.01%	.00%	.01%	.00%	.00%
Return on Equity %		-.21%	.05%	.09%	.04%	.01%
Debt to Equity		0.347	0.274	0.288	0.302	0.327

CONTACT INFORMATION:
Phone: 860 547-5000   Fax: 860 720-6097
Toll-Free:
Address: 690 Asylum Ave., 1 Hartford Plaza, Hartford, CT 06115 United States

SALARIES/BONUSES:
Top Exec. Salary: $1,137,500   Bonus: $
Second Exec. Salary: $943,750   Bonus: $

STOCK TICKER/OTHER:
Stock Ticker: HIG
Employees: 16,900
Parent Company:

Exchange: NYS
Fiscal Year Ends: 12/31

OTHER THOUGHTS:
Estimated Female Officers or Directors: 1
Hot Spot for Advancement for Women/Minorities: Y

Sales, profits and employees may be estimates. Financial information, benefits and other data can change quickly and may vary from those stated here.

HCA Healthcare Inc

www.hcahealthcare.com

NAIC Code: 622110

TYPES OF BUSINESS:
General Medical and Surgical Hospitals
Outpatient Surgery Centers
Sub-Acute Care
Psychiatric Hospitals
Rehabilitation Services
Hospital Management Services

BRANDS/DIVISIONS/AFFILIATES:
HCA Holdings Inc
Civica Rx

CONTACTS:
Note: Officers with more than one job title may be intentionally listed here more than once.

Samuel Hazen, CEO
Victor Campbell, Senior VP, Divisional
William Rutherford, CFO
Thomas Frist, Chairman of the Board
Kathleen Whalen, Chief Compliance Officer
Martin Paslick, Chief Information Officer
Jonathan Perlin, Chief Medical Officer
Robert Waterman, General Counsel
John Steele, Other Executive Officer
Joseph Sowell, Other Executive Officer
Jane Englebright, Other Executive Officer
Michael Cuffe, President, Divisional
A. Moore, President, Divisional
Jon Foster, President, Geographical
Charles Hall, President, Geographical
Kathryn Torres, Senior VP, Divisional
Sandra Morgan, Senior VP, Divisional
Phillip Billington, Senior VP, Divisional

GROWTH PLANS/SPECIAL FEATURES:

HCA Healthcare, Inc., formerly HCA Holdings, Inc., owns and operates 175 general, acute care hospitals; three psychiatric hospitals; one rehabilitation hospital; and 123 freestanding surgery centers in 20 U.S. states and in London, England. The company's acute care hospitals provide a full range of services, including internal medicine, general surgery, neurosurgery, orthopedics, obstetrics, cardiac care, diagnostic services, emergency services, radiology, respiratory therapy, cardiology and physical therapy. The psychiatric hospitals provide therapeutic programs including child, adolescent and adult psychiatric care and adult and adolescent alcohol and drug abuse treatment and counseling. The outpatient healthcare facilities operated by HCA include surgery centers, diagnostic and imaging centers, comprehensive outpatient rehabilitation and physical therapy centers. The company's hospitals do not engage in extensive medical research and education programs; however, some facilities are affiliated with medical schools and may participate in the clinical rotation of medical interns and residents. In addition, HCA provides a variety of management services to healthcare facilities such as patient safety programs; ethics and compliance programs; national supply contracts; equipment purchasing and leasing contracts; and accounting, financial and clinical systems. Other services include governmental reimbursement assistance, construction planning and coordination, information technology systems, legal counsel, human resource services and internal audit. In September 2018, HCA partnered with six other health organizations to create Civica Rx, a new not-for-profit generic drug company that will help patients by addressing shortages and high prices of lifesaving medications.

Employee benefits include medical, vision and dental coverage; a 401(k); life insurance; disability; and financial education resources.

FINANCIAL DATA:
Note: Data for latest year may not have been available at press time.

In U.S. $	2018	2017	2016	2015	2014	2013
Revenue	46,677,000,000	43,614,000,000	41,490,000,000	39,678,000,000	36,918,000,000	34,182,000,000
R&D Expense						
Operating Income	6,642,000,000	6,057,000,000	6,198,000,000	5,965,000,000	5,565,000,000	4,792,000,000
Operating Margin %		.14%	.15%	.15%	.15%	.13%
SGA Expense						
Net Income	3,787,000,000	2,216,000,000	2,890,000,000	2,129,000,000	1,875,000,000	1,556,000,000
Operating Cash Flow	6,761,000,000	5,426,000,000	5,653,000,000	4,734,000,000	4,448,000,000	3,680,000,000
Capital Expenditure	3,573,000,000	3,015,000,000	2,760,000,000	2,375,000,000	2,176,000,000	1,943,000,000
EBITDA	9,368,001,000	8,202,000,000	8,483,000,000	7,526,000,000	7,044,000,000	6,547,000,000
Return on Assets %		.06%	.09%	.07%	.06%	.05%
Return on Equity %						
Debt to Equity						

CONTACT INFORMATION:
Phone: 615 344-9551 Fax: 615 320-2266
Toll-Free:
Address: 1 Park Plaza, Nashville, TN 37203 United States

SALARIES/BONUSES:
Top Exec. Salary: $1,494,167 Bonus: $
Second Exec. Salary: $1,120,167 Bonus: $

STOCK TICKER/OTHER:
Stock Ticker: HCA Exchange: NYS
Employees: 249,000 Fiscal Year Ends: 12/31
Parent Company:

OTHER THOUGHTS:
Estimated Female Officers or Directors: 2
Hot Spot for Advancement for Women/Minorities:

Sales, profits and employees may be estimates. Financial information, benefits and other data can change quickly and may vary from those stated here.

Health Care Service Corporation (HCSC)

www.hcsc.com

NAIC Code: 524114

TYPES OF BUSINESS:
Insurance-Medical & Health, HMOs & PPOs
Traditional Indemnity Plans
Medicare Supplemental Health
Life Insurance
Dental & Vision Insurance
Electronic Claims & Information Network
Workers' Compensation
Retirement Services

BRANDS/DIVISIONS/AFFILIATES:
Blue Cross and Blue Shield
Dental Network of America Inc
Availity LLC
Dearborn National
Medecision Inc
HCSC Insurance Service Company
Prime Therapeutics LLC
TriWest Healthcare Alliance

CONTACTS:
Note: Officers with more than one job title may be intentionally listed here more than once.

David J. Lesar, Interim CEO
Maurice Smith, Pres.
Opella Ernest, Sr. VP-Operations
Stephen Ondra, Chief Medical Officer
John Cannon, Chief Admin. Officer
Deborah Dorman-Rodriguez, Corp. Sec.
Martin G. Foster, Pres., Plan Oper.
Paula A. Steiner, Chief Strategy Officer
Ross Blackstone, Contact-Media
Ted Haynes, Pres., Oklahoma Div.
Kurt Shipley, Pres., New Mexico Div.
Karen M. Atwood, Pres., Illinois Div.
Bert E. Marshall, Pres., Texas Div.

GROWTH PLANS/SPECIAL FEATURES:

Health Care Service Corporation (HCSC) is a customer-owned health insurer which operates through its Blue Cross and Blue Shield divisions in Illinois, Montana, Texas, New Mexico, Oklahoma and Texas. HCSC is a legal reserve company, meaning that it maintains policy reserves according to the standards established by the insurance laws of the various states it serves. The firm provides preferred provider organizations (PPOs), health maintenance organizations (HMOs), point of service (POS), traditional indemnity and Medicare supplemental health plans to over 15 million members. The company also has several subsidiaries that offer a variety of health and life insurance products and related services to employers and individuals. Through its non-Blue Cross and Blue Shield subsidiaries, HCSC offers prescription drug plans, Medicare supplemental insurance, dental and vision coverage, life and disability insurance, workers' compensation, retirement services and medical financial services. One such subsidiary, Dental Network of America, Inc., functions as a third-party administrator for all company dental programs and is registered in every state except Florida. It also offers a dental discount card program. Availity, LLC, a partially-owned subsidiary, operates a health care clearinghouse and provides internet-based health information services. Dearborn National operates as the brand name for HCSC's ancillary benefits subsidiaries, offering group life, disability, dental, worksite and voluntary products. Other subsidiaries include: Medecision, Inc.; HCSC Insurance Service Company; Prime Therapeutics, LLC; and TriWest Healthcare Alliance. During 2019, HCSC announced an in-house educational program aimed at developing the skills of its employees, named Blue University.

Employee benefits include: medical, short/long-term disability, AD&D and life insurance; 401(k) and pension plans; and various employee assistance programs.

FINANCIAL DATA:
Note: Data for latest year may not have been available at press time.

In U.S. $	2018	2017	2016	2015	2014	2013
Revenue	35,900,000,000	36,800,000,000	33,000,000,000	35,000,000,000	31,200,000,000	22,690,000,000
R&D Expense						
Operating Income						
Operating Margin %						
SGA Expense						
Net Income			106,300,000	-65,800,000	-281,000,000	684,300,000
Operating Cash Flow						
Capital Expenditure						
EBITDA						
Return on Assets %						
Return on Equity %						
Debt to Equity						

CONTACT INFORMATION:
Phone: 312-653-6000   Fax: 312-819-1220
Toll-Free: 800-654-7385
Address: 300 E. Randolph St., Chicago, IL 60601 United States

STOCK TICKER/OTHER:
Stock Ticker: Mutual Company
Employees: 23,000
Parent Company:

Exchange:
Fiscal Year Ends: 12/31

SALARIES/BONUSES:
Top Exec. Salary: $ Bonus: $
Second Exec. Salary: $ Bonus: $

OTHER THOUGHTS:
Estimated Female Officers or Directors: 6
Hot Spot for Advancement for Women/Minorities: Y

Heartland Payment Systems Inc   www.heartlandpaymentsystems.com

NAIC Code: 522320

TYPES OF BUSINESS:
Financial Processing Services
Credit/Debit Processing
Payroll Processing Services
Processing Equipment Provider
Micropayments

BRANDS/DIVISIONS/AFFILIATES:
Global Payments Inc

GROWTH PLANS/SPECIAL FEATURES:
Heartland Payment Systems, Inc. (HPS), a wholly-owned subsidiary of Global Payments, Inc., is a provider of credit/debit/prepaid card, payroll and other associated processing and customer/client engagement services to more than 300,000 businesses and educational institutions throughout the U.S. HPS serves restaurant, retail, entertainment, automotive, medical, home services, lodging, pharmacy, education (K-12), grocery, laundry, municipalities, nonprofit, parking and petroleum industries throughout the U.S. Products by HPS span customer engagement, capital, payment, payroll, point of sale, online payments, billing solutions, Internet of Things (IoT), mobile ordering, mobile payments, payment solutions and school nutrition.

CONTACTS:
Note: Officers with more than one job title may be intentionally listed here more than once.

Jeffrey S. Sloan, CEO-Global Payments
Charles Kallenbach, General Counsel
David Gilbert, President, Divisional
Michael Lawler, President, Divisional
Robert Baldwin, Vice Chairman

FINANCIAL DATA:
Note: Data for latest year may not have been available at press time.

In U.S. $	2018	2017	2016	2015	2014	2013
Revenue	2,717,400,000	2,588,000,000	2,550,500,000	2,682,395,904	2,311,380,992	2,135,372,032
R&D Expense						
Operating Income						
Operating Margin %						
SGA Expense						
Net Income				84,732,000	33,879,000	78,626,000
Operating Cash Flow						
Capital Expenditure						
EBITDA						
Return on Assets %						
Return on Equity %						
Debt to Equity						

CONTACT INFORMATION:
Phone: 609 683-3831   Fax: 609 683-3815
Toll-Free: 888-963-3600
Address: 10 Glenlake Pkwy. North Tower, Atlanta, GA 30328-3495 United States

STOCK TICKER/OTHER:
Stock Ticker: Subsidiary
Employees: 3,734
Parent Company: Global Payments Inc
Exchange:
Fiscal Year Ends: 12/31

SALARIES/BONUSES:
Top Exec. Salary: $ Bonus: $
Second Exec. Salary: $ Bonus: $

OTHER THOUGHTS:
Estimated Female Officers or Directors: 2
Hot Spot for Advancement for Women/Minorities:

Sales, profits and employees may be estimates. Financial information, benefits and other data can change quickly and may vary from those stated here.

HEB Grocery Company LP

www.heb.com

NAIC Code: 445110

TYPES OF BUSINESS:
Supermarkets
Grocery Stores
Gourmet Food Stores
Dairy Processing
Bakery
Pharmacy Services

BRANDS/DIVISIONS/AFFILIATES:
H-E-B
H-E-B plus!
Mi Tienda
Central Market
Joe V's Smart Shop
H-E-B Blooms
Temple Retail Support Center

CONTACTS: Note: Officers with more than one job title may be intentionally listed here more than once.
Craig Boyan, CEO
Craig Boyan, COO
Martin Otto, CFO
Judy Lindquist, General Counsel
Lynette Padalecki, VP-Corp. Planning & Analysis
Winell Herron, VP-Public Affairs & Diversity
Scott McClelland, Pres., Houston Food & Drug Stores Div.
Suzanne Wade, Pres., San Antonio Food & Drug Stores Div.
William Fry, VP-Quality Assurance & Environmental Affairs
Roxanne Orsak, Exec. VP-Drug
Mike Graham, Sr. VP-Logistics & Supply Chain

GROWTH PLANS/SPECIAL FEATURES:

HEB Grocery Company, LP is one of the largest regional food retailers in the southwestern U.S. and Mexico. It operates over 355 grocery stores in 150 communities in Texas and Mexico under the H-E-B, H-E-B Plus! and Mi Tienda brand names. The firm owns one of the largest milk plants in Texas as well as a large bread bakery, a meat plant, a pastry bakery, an ice cream plant, a chip plant and a photo processing lab. H-E-B stores carry a wide variety of merchandise, including a line of products under the H-E-B brand. H-E-B Plus! Stores offer merchandise beyond normal groceries, including toys, housewares, outdoor entertaining products, apparel and baby items (strollers, high chairs, bounces, etc.). Mi Tienda stores offer fresh produce, authentic Mexican grocery products, fish and meats, a bakery, a tortilleria and more. HEB also operates 10 Central Market stores, with locations in Houston, Dallas, Fort Worth, Plano, San Antonio, Southlake and Austin. Central Markets are gourmet specialty stores featuring large prepared foods-to-go areas, eat-in areas, comprehensive wine departments, specialty butcher and fish counters, a European bakery, a deli with meats, a large selection of cheeses from around the globe and a juice and ice cream bar. The firm also owns a series of eight discount stores in the Houston and Baytown, Texas area known as Joe V's Smart Shop; and H-E-B Blooms, a premier flower delivery and floral design center in Houston, which also provides consultation services in regards to weddings and special events. HEB Grocery Company owns and operates a retail support center in Monterrey, Mexico, as well as the Temple Retail Support Center, a 450,000-square-foot warehouse and transportation facility in central Texas.

Employees of the firm are offered a variety of benefits, including discounts on groceries and a prescription plan. In 2015, the company launched a benefit whereby qualified employees receive an annual grant of shares of nonvoting stock equal to 3% of wages.

FINANCIAL DATA: Note: Data for latest year may not have been available at press time.

In U.S. $	2018	2017	2016	2015	2014	2013
Revenue	25,000,000,000	24,650,000,000	24,000,000,000	23,000,000,000	22,000,000,000	20,400,000,000
R&D Expense						
Operating Income						
Operating Margin %						
SGA Expense						
Net Income						
Operating Cash Flow						
Capital Expenditure						
EBITDA						
Return on Assets %						
Return on Equity %						
Debt to Equity						

CONTACT INFORMATION:
Phone: 210-938-8000 Fax: 210-938-8169
Toll-Free: 800-432-3113
Address: 646 S. Main Ave, San Antonio, TX 78204 United States

SALARIES/BONUSES:
Top Exec. Salary: $ Bonus: $
Second Exec. Salary: $ Bonus: $

STOCK TICKER/OTHER:
Stock Ticker: Private
Employees: 116,000
Parent Company:

Exchange:
Fiscal Year Ends: 10/31

OTHER THOUGHTS:
Estimated Female Officers or Directors: 5
Hot Spot for Advancement for Women/Minorities: Y

Sales, profits and employees may be estimates. Financial information, benefits and other data can change quickly and may vary from those stated here.

Hendrick Automotive Group

NAIC Code: 441110

www.hendrickauto.com

TYPES OF BUSINESS:
Auto Dealers
Parts & Service
Accessories
Racing & Motorsports

BRANDS/DIVISIONS/AFFILIATES:
Hendrick Motorsports

GROWTH PLANS/SPECIAL FEATURES:
Hendrick Automotive Group sells new and used automobiles from 27 automakers. These automakers include Acura, Audi, BMW, Buick, Cadillac, Chevrolet, Chrysler, Dodge, Fiat, GMA, Harley-Davidson, Honda, Jaguar, Jeep, Kia, Land Rover, Lexus, MINI, Mazda, Mercedes-Benz, Nissan, Porsche, RAM, Subaru, Toyota, Volkswagen and Volvo. The firm boasts a network of 96 dealerships in 14 U.S. states as well as 130 franchise locations. Hendrick's automobile offerings include cars as well as light trucks. The company offers other services, including financing, maintenance, body repair and parts and accessories. The group has 29 collision centers and four accessories distributor installers located across the U.S. Customers can access a database of pre-owned and new cars on the company website. Hendrick offers financing, warranties, automobile parts, accessories and autobody repair services. In addition, Hendrick Automotive operates Hendrick Motorsports, which sponsors a number of NASCAR teams.

CONTACTS:
Note: Officers with more than one job title may be intentionally listed here more than once.

Edward J. Brown, III, CEO
Edward J. Brown, III, Pres.
Brian Williams, VP-Mktg. & Advertising
Veronica Zayatz, VP-Acct., Audits & Taxes
Rick Hendrick, Chmn.

FINANCIAL DATA:
Note: Data for latest year may not have been available at press time.

In U.S. $	2018	2017	2016	2015	2014	2013
Revenue	9,427,756,576	8,978,815,787	8,551,253,132	8,400,000,000	7,500,000,000	7,000,000,000
R&D Expense						
Operating Income						
Operating Margin %						
SGA Expense						
Net Income						
Operating Cash Flow						
Capital Expenditure						
EBITDA						
Return on Assets %						
Return on Equity %						
Debt to Equity						

CONTACT INFORMATION:
Phone: 704-568-5550   Fax: 704-566-3295
Toll-Free:
Address: 6000 Monroe Rd., Ste. 100, Charlotte, NC 28212 United States

STOCK TICKER/OTHER:
Stock Ticker: Private
Employees: 10,000
Parent Company:

Exchange:
Fiscal Year Ends: 12/31

SALARIES/BONUSES:
Top Exec. Salary: $ Bonus: $
Second Exec. Salary: $ Bonus: $

OTHER THOUGHTS:
Estimated Female Officers or Directors: 1
Hot Spot for Advancement for Women/Minorities:

Henry Schein Inc

www.henryschein.com

NAIC Code: 423450

TYPES OF BUSINESS:
Health Care Products Distribution
Dental Supplies Distribution
Veterinary Products Distribution
Electronic Catalogs

BRANDS/DIVISIONS/AFFILIATES:
Oasis
Dentix
EXACT
Easy Dental
MicroMD
Direct Vet Marketing Inc
Vets First Choice
Cliniclands

CONTACTS:
Note: Officers with more than one job title may be intentionally listed here more than once.

Jonathan Koch, CEO, Divisional
Brad Connett, Pres., Divisional
James Harding, CEO, Subsidiary
Stanley Bergman, CEO
Steven Paladino, CFO
Gerald Benjamin, Chief Administrative Officer
Mark Mlotek, Chief Strategy Officer
Christopher Pendergast, Chief Technology Officer
James Breslawski, Director
Walter Siegel, General Counsel
Michael Ettinger, Other Executive Officer
Lorelei McGlynn, Other Executive Officer
Michael Racioppi, Other Executive Officer
David Brous, President, Divisional
James Mullins, Senior VP, Divisional

GROWTH PLANS/SPECIAL FEATURES:

Henry Schein, Inc. distributes products and services to office-based health care practitioners in North America and Europe. The firm serves more than 1 million customers worldwide and distributes more than 120,000 national and Henry Schein private-brand products and 180,000 special order items. The company operates in two segments: health care distribution and technology. The health care distribution segment, which accounts for roughly 96.5% of annual revenue, aggregates the dental and medical divisions. This segment distributes branded and generic pharmaceuticals, small equipment, laboratory products, large dental equipment, consumable products, infection-control products, vaccines, diagnostic tests, surgical products and vitamins. The global dental unit serves office-based dental practitioners, dental laboratories, schools and other institutions; and the global medical unit serves office-based medical practitioners, ambulatory surgery centers, alternate-care settings and other institutions. The technology segment provides software, technology and other value-added services to health care practitioners, primarily in the U.S. and Canada. Value-added solutions include practice-management software systems for dental and medical practitioners. Practice-management software solutions include Oasis, Dentrix, EXACT and Easy Dental for dental practices; and MicroMD for physician usage. The technology group also provides financial services and continuing education for practitioners. In early-2019, Henry Schein spun off its animal health business and merged it with wholly-owned subsidiary Direct Vet Marketing, Inc. (dba Vets First Choice). That August, Henry Schein acquired a majority equity stake in Cliniclands, an innovative distributor serving dental practices throughout Sweden, Denmark and Norway.

The company offers employees medical, dental, vision, life, AD&D and disability insurance; flexible spending accounts; 401(k); college savings plan; tuition assistance; and paid time off.

FINANCIAL DATA:
Note: Data for latest year may not have been available at press time.

In U.S. $	2018	2017	2016	2015	2014	2013
Revenue	13,201,990,000	12,461,540,000	11,571,670,000	10,629,720,000	10,371,390,000	9,560,647,000
R&D Expense						
Operating Income	854,452,000	859,369,000	817,465,000	768,903,000	715,142,000	677,054,000
Operating Margin %		.07%	.07%	.07%	.07%	.07%
SGA Expense	2,701,376,000	2,539,734,000	2,416,504,000	2,243,356,000	2,196,173,000	1,978,960,000
Net Income	535,381,000	406,299,000	506,778,000	479,058,000	466,077,000	431,554,000
Operating Cash Flow	684,706,000	545,515,000	615,461,000	586,841,000	592,504,000	664,175,000
Capital Expenditure	90,637,000	81,501,000	70,179,000	71,684,000	82,116,000	60,215,000
EBITDA	981,694,000	1,069,574,000	957,508,000	905,893,000	885,607,000	820,267,000
Return on Assets %		.06%	.08%	.08%	.08%	.08%
Return on Equity %		.14%	.18%	.17%	.17%	.16%
Debt to Equity		0.323	0.256	0.161	0.193	0.162

CONTACT INFORMATION:
Phone: 631 843-5500   Fax: 631 843-5665
Toll-Free:
Address: 135 Duryea Rd., Melville, NY 11747 United States

SALARIES/BONUSES:
Top Exec. Salary: $1,417,577   Bonus: $
Second Exec. Salary: $737,654   Bonus: $50,000

STOCK TICKER/OTHER:
Stock Ticker: HSIC
Employees: 21,000
Parent Company:

Exchange: NAS
Fiscal Year Ends: 12/31

OTHER THOUGHTS:
Estimated Female Officers or Directors: 6
Hot Spot for Advancement for Women/Minorities: Y

Hershey Company (The)

www.hersheys.com

NAIC Code: 311351

TYPES OF BUSINESS:
Candy Manufacturing
Baking Supplies
Chocolate Products
Confectionaries & Snacks
Amusement Parks
Resorts/Hotels

BRANDS/DIVISIONS/AFFILIATES:
Reese's
Kit Kat
Hershey Bars
Hershey Kisses
Hershey's Chocolate World
Amplify Snack Brands Inc
SkinnyPop
Pirate Brands

CONTACTS: Note: Officers with more than one job title may be intentionally listed here more than once.
Michele Buck, CEO
Steven Voskuil, CFO
Charles Davis, Chairman of the Board
Javier Idrovo, Chief Accounting Officer
Terence ODay, Chief Technology Officer
Damien Atkins, General Counsel
Mary Stone West, Other Executive Officer
Kevin Walling, Other Executive Officer
Todd Tillemans, President, Divisional

GROWTH PLANS/SPECIAL FEATURES:

The Hershey Company is an industry-leading snacks company known for its iconic brands. The company's more than 80 branded products are marketed in approximately 70 countries worldwide. Hershey's principal product groups include confectionery products such as Reese's, Kit Kat, Hershey Bars and Hershey Kisses; packaged items; and grocery products, such as baking ingredients, chocolate drink mixes, peanut butter, dessert toppings and beverages. Its products are sold primarily to wholesale distributors, chain grocery stores, mass merchandisers, chain drug stores, vending companies, wholesale clubs, convenience stores, dollar stores, concessionaires, department stores and natural food stores. Its direct retail operations include Hershey's Chocolate World in Hershey, Pennsylvania, and Hershey's retail stores in New York City, Las Vegas, Shanghai, Niagara Falls (Ontario), Dubai and Singapore. The firm's operations are therefore divided into geographical segments: North America and international and other. The North America segment is responsible for Hershey's traditional chocolate and non-chocolate confectionery market position, as well as its grocery and snacks market positions in the U.S. and Canada. The international and other segment is a combination of all other Hershey business. This includes operations and product manufacturing facilities in China, Mexico, Brazil, India and Malaysia, which also distribute and sell confectionery products in the export markets of Asia, Latin America, the Middle East, Europe, Africa and other regions. This segment also includes the Hershey's Chocolate World stores (even the ones in the U.S.); and is responsible for licensing the use of certain of the company's trademarks and products to third parties worldwide. During 2018, the firm acquired Amplify Snack Brands, Inc., which owns better-for-you snack brands such as SkinnyPop, Oatmega, Pagui and Tyrrells; and acquired Pirate Brands from B&G Foods, Inc., including the Pirate's Booty, Smart Puffs and Original Tings brands.

The firm offers employees comprehensive health benefits and retirement plans.

FINANCIAL DATA: Note: Data for latest year may not have been available at press time.

In U.S. $	2018	2017	2016	2015	2014	2013
Revenue	7,791,069,000	7,515,426,000	7,440,181,000	7,386,626,000	7,421,768,000	7,146,079,000
R&D Expense						
Operating Income	1,700,496,000	1,531,116,000	1,242,513,000	1,413,367,000	1,435,196,000	1,358,340,000
Operating Margin %		.20%	.17%	.19%	.19%	.19%
SGA Expense	1,874,829,000	1,913,403,000	1,915,378,000	1,969,308,000	1,900,970,000	1,922,508,000
Net Income	1,177,562,000	782,981,000	720,044,000	512,951,000	846,912,000	820,470,000
Operating Cash Flow	1,599,993,000	1,249,515,000	983,475,000	1,214,456,000	838,221,000	1,188,405,000
Capital Expenditure	328,601,000	257,675,000	269,476,000	356,810,000	370,789,000	350,911,000
EBITDA	1,852,063,000	1,472,587,000	1,493,266,000	1,227,758,000	1,605,173,000	1,543,866,000
Return on Assets %		.14%	.13%	.09%	.15%	.16%
Return on Equity %		.92%	.81%	.42%	.55%	.62%
Debt to Equity		2.252	2.987	1.56	1.065	1.119

CONTACT INFORMATION:
Phone: 717 534-4200 Fax: 717 531-6161
Toll-Free: 800-468-1714
Address: 100 Crystal A Dr., Hershey, PA 17033 United States

STOCK TICKER/OTHER:
Stock Ticker: HSY
Employees: 17,980
Parent Company:

Exchange: NYS
Fiscal Year Ends: 12/31

SALARIES/BONUSES:
Top Exec. Salary: $1,137,357 Bonus: $
Second Exec. Salary: $681,863 Bonus: $

OTHER THOUGHTS:
Estimated Female Officers or Directors: 4
Hot Spot for Advancement for Women/Minorities: Y

Sales, profits and employees may be estimates. Financial information, benefits and other data can change quickly and may vary from those stated here.

Hillenbrand Inc

www.hillenbrandinc.com

NAIC Code: 333120

TYPES OF BUSINESS:
Materials Handling Equipment
Burial Caskets and Cases Manufacturing
Conveying Equipment
Size Reduction Equipment

BRANDS/DIVISIONS/AFFILIATES:
Batesville Casket Company
ABEL GmbH
Coperion Capital GmbH
Red Valve Company Inc
Rotex Global LLC
TerraSource Global
Pennsylvania Crusher
Gundlach

CONTACTS: Note: Officers with more than one job title may be intentionally listed here more than once.
Joe Raver, CEO
F. Loughrey, Chairman of the Board
Timothy Ryan, Chief Accounting Officer
Nicholas Farrell, Chief Compliance Officer
Glennis Williams, Other Executive Officer
Christopher Trainor, President, Subsidiary
Michael Whitted, Senior VP, Divisional
Kristina Cerniglia, Senior VP
Kimberly Ryan, Senior VP
James Hooven, Vice President, Divisional

GROWTH PLANS/SPECIAL FEATURES:
Hillenbrand, Inc. is a holding company involved in funeral products and bulk solid material handling equipment. The firm operates through two primary business platforms: Batesville and process equipment group. Batesville, which includes subsidiary Batesville Casket Company, manufactures and sells non-gasketed steel, hardwood and veneer hardwood caskets as well as cloth-covered and all-wood caskets. Additional products include urns, containers and other similar products. The company's hardwood caskets are made from mahogany, cherry, walnut, maple, pile, oak, pecan, poplar and sycamore woods, and are manufactured to resist the entrance of outside elements as well as rust and corrosion. Urns and containers are primarily made of hardwoods, fiberboard, bronze, acrylic and marble. The process equipment group segment designs, produces, markets, sells and services feeders and pneumatic conveying equipment as well as equipment that is used to reduce materials in size, such as coal-crushing tools. The segment consists of five companies: ABEL GmbH, which develops and manufactures highly-engineered, energy efficient positive displacement pumps; Coperion Capital GmbH, which is involved in compounding and extruding equipment, bulk materials handling systems and related engineering services, as well as in feeding and pneumatic conveying equipment; Red Valve Company, Inc., which produces highly-engineered, mission-critical flow control solutions; Rotex Global, LLC, which manufactures separation equipment such as gyratory and vibratory screeners and sifters; and TerraSource Global, a creator of size reduction equipment, conveying systems and screening equipment, operating under the Pennsylvania Crusher, Gundlach and Jeffrey Rader brands. In mid-2019, Hillenbrand agreed to acquire Milacron Holdings Corp. for approximately $2 billion. Milacron manufactures, distributes and services engineered and customized systems in the plastics technology and processing industry, as well as fluid technologies and processing systems.

FINANCIAL DATA: Note: Data for latest year may not have been available at press time.

In U.S. $	2018	2017	2016	2015	2014	2013
Revenue	1,770,100,000	1,590,200,000	1,538,400,000	1,596,800,000	1,667,200,000	1,553,400,000
R&D Expense						
Operating Income	233,800,000	217,700,000	191,100,000	194,000,000	174,500,000	118,100,000
Operating Margin %		.14%	.12%	.12%	.10%	.08%
SGA Expense				17,700,000		
Net Income	76,600,000	126,200,000	112,800,000	111,400,000	109,700,000	63,400,000
Operating Cash Flow	248,300,000	246,200,000	238,600,000	105,000,000	179,600,000	127,200,000
Capital Expenditure	27,000,000	22,000,000	21,200,000	31,000,000	23,600,000	29,900,000
EBITDA	226,300,000	270,100,000	249,800,000	240,400,000	241,600,000	207,100,000
Return on Assets %		.06%	.06%	.06%	.06%	.04%
Return on Equity %		.18%	.18%	.19%	.19%	.12%
Debt to Equity		0.595	0.943	0.873	0.932	1.151

CONTACT INFORMATION:
Phone: 812 934-7500   Fax: 812 934-7613
Toll-Free:
Address: 1 Batesville Blvd., Batesville, IN 47006 United States

SALARIES/BONUSES:
Top Exec. Salary: $809,685   Bonus: $
Second Exec. Salary: $521,695   Bonus: $

STOCK TICKER/OTHER:
Stock Ticker: HI
Employees: 6,100
Parent Company:

Exchange: NYS
Fiscal Year Ends: 09/30

OTHER THOUGHTS:
Estimated Female Officers or Directors: 3
Hot Spot for Advancement for Women/Minorities: Y

Hill-Rom Holdings Inc

NAIC Code: 339100

www.hillrom.com/

TYPES OF BUSINESS:
Equipment-Hospital Beds & Related Products
Specialized Therapy Products
Rentals

BRANDS/DIVISIONS/AFFILIATES:
Hillrom
Breathe Technologies inc

CONTACTS:
Note: Officers with more than one job title may be intentionally listed here more than once.

John Groetelaars, CEO
Barbara Bodem, CFO
William Dempsey, Chairman of the Board
Richard Wagner, Chief Accounting Officer
Deborah Rasin, Chief Legal Officer
Kenneth Meyers, Other Executive Officer
Francisco Vega, President, Divisional
Paul Johnson, President, Divisional
Andreas Frank, President, Divisional
Carlos Alonso-Marum, President, Subsidiary
Mary Ladone, Senior VP, Divisional
Jason Richardson, Treasurer

GROWTH PLANS/SPECIAL FEATURES:

Hill-Rom Holdings, Inc. (branded as Hillrom) is a global medical technology company. Hillrom partners with healthcare providers in more than 100 countries, with a focus on patient care solutions that improve clinical and economic outcomes. The firm operates through three segments: patient support systems, front line care and surgical solutions. The patient support systems segment globally provides the following products: surgical beds, intensive care unit beds and bariatric patient beds; mobility lifts and other devices to safely move patients; non-invasive therapeutic products and surfaces; and clinical workflow solutions such as software and information technologies to improve care and deliver actionable insight to caregivers and patients. The front line care segment globally provides respiratory care products, sells medical diagnostic monitoring equipment, and sells a diversified portfolio of physical assessment tolls that asses, diagnose, treat and manage a wide variety of illnesses and diseases. Products include patient monitoring and diagnostics products from Welch Allyn, Inc. and Mortara Instruments, Inc., and Hillrom's respiratory health products. Patient monitoring and diagnostics products include blood pressure, physical assessment, vital signs monitoring, diagnostic cardiopulmonary, diabetic retinopathy screening and thermometry products. Respiratory health products are designed to assist patients in the mobilization of retained blockages that, if not removed, may lead to increased rates of respiratory infection, hospitalization and reduced lung function. Last, the surgical solutions segment provides products that improve surgical safety and efficiency in the operating room, including tables, lights, pendants, positioning devices and various other surgical products and accessories. This division also offers operating room surgical safety and accessory products such as scalpels, blades, light handle systems, skin markers and disposable products. In August 2019, Hill-Rom acquired Breathe Technologies, Inc., a developer and manufacturer of a patented wearable, non-invasive ventilation technology that supports improved patient mobility.

FINANCIAL DATA:
Note: Data for latest year may not have been available at press time.

In U.S. $	2018	2017	2016	2015	2014	2013
Revenue	2,848,000,000	2,743,700,000	2,655,200,000	1,988,200,000	1,686,100,000	1,716,200,000
R&D Expense	135,600,000	133,700,000	133,500,000	91,800,000	71,900,000	70,200,000
Operating Income	367,100,000	310,800,000	270,200,000	124,300,000	159,700,000	160,600,000
Operating Margin %		.11%	.10%	.06%	.09%	.09%
SGA Expense	891,500,000	876,100,000	853,300,000	664,200,000	548,300,000	549,500,000
Net Income	252,400,000	133,600,000	124,100,000	47,700,000	60,600,000	105,000,000
Operating Cash Flow	395,200,000	311,100,000	281,200,000	213,800,000	210,300,000	263,200,000
Capital Expenditure	89,500,000	97,500,000	83,300,000	121,300,000	62,700,000	65,300,000
EEITDA	488,700,000	482,700,000	437,700,000	201,700,000	231,400,000	270,300,000
Return on Assets %		.03%	.03%	.02%	.04%	.07%
Return on Equity %		.10%	.10%	.05%	.07%	.13%
Debt to Equity		1.561	1.58	1.897	0.452	0.263

CONTACT INFORMATION:
Phone: 3120819-7200   Fax:
Toll-Free:
Address: 130 E. Randolph St., Ste. 1000, Chicago, IL 60601 United States

STOCK TICKER/OTHER:
Stock Ticker: HRC
Employees: 10,000
Parent Company:

Exchange: NYS
Fiscal Year Ends: 09/30

SALARIES/BONUSES:
Top Exec. Salary: $668,500   Bonus: $
Second Exec. Salary: $517,558   Bonus: $

OTHER THOUGHTS:
Estimated Female Officers or Directors: 1
Hot Spot for Advancement for Women/Minorities: Y

Hilton Worldwide Holdings Inc

www.hiltonworldwide.com

NAIC Code: 721110

TYPES OF BUSINESS:
Hotels & Resorts
Management Services
Conference Centers
Franchising

BRANDS/DIVISIONS/AFFILIATES:
Waldorf Astoria Hotels & Resorts
LXR Hotel & Resorts
Conrad Hotels & Resorts
Canopy by Hilton
Hilton Hotels & Resorts
Curio Collection by Hilton
DoubleTree by Hilton
Motto by Hilton

CONTACTS: Note: Officers with more than one job title may be intentionally listed here more than once.
Christopher Nassetta, CEO
Kevin Jacobs, CFO
Jonathan Gray, Chairman of the Board
Michael Duffy, Chief Accounting Officer
Kristin Campbell, Executive VP
Matthew Schuyler, Executive VP
Jonathan Witter, Executive VP
Christopher Silcock, Executive VP
Ian Carter, Executive VP

GROWTH PLANS/SPECIAL FEATURES:
Hilton Worldwide Holdings, Inc. is one of the largest hospitality companies in the world. Hilton consists of more than 13 hotel brands with 5,685 hotels in 113 countries, ranging from affordable focus-service hotels to luxury extended stay suites. The firm's brands are categorized by type of hotel, including: luxury and lifestyle brands such as Waldorf Astoria Hotels & Resorts, LXR Hotels & Resorts, Conrad Hotels & Resorts and Canopy by Hilton; full-service hotel brands such as Hilton Hotels & Resorts, Curio Collection by Hilton, DoubleTree by Hilton, Tapestry Collection by Hilton and Embassy Suites by Hilton; service-focused hotel brands such as Motto by Hilton, Hilton Garden Inn, Hampton by Hilton, Tru by Hilton, Homewood Suites by Hilton and Home2 Suites by Hilton; and timeshare brand, Hilton Grand Vacations. Hhonors, the firm's loyalty enrollment program for returning customers, has over 85 million members worldwide and includes partner benefits with several airlines. In addition, Hilton offers architecture and construction and management services to individuals interested in developing their own Hilton-branded properties.

Hilton has been recognized with awards for 100 Best Workplaces, World's 25 Best Multinational Workplaces, Best Workplaces for Women and Best Workplaces for Millennials.

FINANCIAL DATA: Note: Data for latest year may not have been available at press time.

In U.S. $	2018	2017	2016	2015	2014	2013
Revenue	8,906,000,000	9,140,000,000	11,663,000,000	11,272,000,000	10,502,000,000	9,735,000,000
R&D Expense						
Operating Income	1,432,000,000	1,372,000,000	1,841,000,000	1,773,000,000	1,710,000,000	1,109,000,000
Operating Margin %		.15%	.54%	.53%	.51%	.46%
SGA Expense	443,000,000	434,000,000	616,000,000	611,000,000	491,000,000	748,000,000
Net Income	764,000,000	1,259,000,000	348,000,000	1,404,000,000	673,000,000	415,000,000
Operating Cash Flow	1,255,000,000	924,000,000	1,350,000,000	1,394,000,000	1,366,000,000	2,101,000,000
Capital Expenditure	159,000,000	133,000,000	398,000,000	372,000,000	337,000,000	332,000,000
EBITDA	1,801,000,000	1,685,000,000	2,528,000,000	2,763,000,000	2,393,000,000	1,921,000,000
Return on Assets %		.06%	.01%	.05%	.03%	.02%
Return on Equity %		.32%	.06%	.26%	.15%	.12%
Debt to Equity		3.164	1.804	1.724	2.432	2.904

CONTACT INFORMATION:
Phone: 703-883-1000 Fax:
Toll-Free: 800-445-8667
Address: 7930 Jones Branch Dr., Ste. 1100, McLean, VA 22102 United States

STOCK TICKER/OTHER:
Stock Ticker: HLT
Employees: 169,000
Parent Company:

Exchange: NYS
Fiscal Year Ends: 12/31

SALARIES/BONUSES:
Top Exec. Salary: $1,250,000 Bonus: $
Second Exec. Salary: $820,308 Bonus: $

OTHER THOUGHTS:
Estimated Female Officers or Directors: 2
Hot Spot for Advancement for Women/Minorities: Y

HMSHost Corporation

NAIC Code: 722310

www.hmshost.com

TYPES OF BUSINESS:
Food Service Contractors
Food, Beverage & Retail Concessions
Travel Plazas
Food Courts

BRANDS/DIVISIONS/AFFILIATES:
Autogrill SpA

CONTACTS: Note: Officers with more than one job title may be intentionally listed here more than once.
Steve Johnson, CEO
Jeff Yablun, Exec. VP
Mark Ratych, Exec. VP
Laura E. FitzRandolph, Exec. VP
Sarah Naqvi, Exec. VP-CIO

GROWTH PLANS/SPECIAL FEATURES:
HMSHost Corporation, a wholly-owned subsidiary of Italy-based Autogrill SpA, is a leading provider of food and beverage concessions for travelers. The firm operates facilities in over 120 airports worldwide as well as 100+ roadside travel plazas along major U.S. and Canada toll roads and turnpikes in the Northeast and Midwest. HMSHost also serves tourist destinations such as Space Center Houston and the Empire State Building. The company's international airport operations include food service outlets at major and regional airports in Canada, Australia, Singapore, Ireland, India, Denmark, Sweden, the Netherlands, the U.K., Malaysia, France, Finland, Russia, the Middle East, Vietnam, Indonesia and New Zealand. HMSHost has a team of internal executive chefs and celebrity chef/restaurant partners that personally develop its menus. Featured chefs include Rick Bayless, Hugo Ortega, Lorena Garcia, Jeff Steelman, Todd English, Bryan Caswell and Silvana Salcido Esparaza, among others. Exclusive brands of HMSHost include 1897 Market, La Familia Tacos & Tequila, Book & Bourbon Southern Kitchen, Wicker Park Seafood & Sushi and The Local, among others. Local brands include Tortas Frontera, Hugo's Cocina, Publican Tavern, Flying Dog and The Hearth. The firm also partners with well-known national brands, including Starbucks, California Pizza Kitchen, SmashBurger, Carrabba's Italian Grill, P.F. Chang's, Pei Wei Asian Diner, Outback Steakhouse, Burger King, La Madeleine Country French Cafe, Chick-fil-A, Longhorn Steakhouse and Blaze Pizza.

FINANCIAL DATA: Note: Data for latest year may not have been available at press time.

In U.S. $	2018	2017	2016	2015	2014	2013
Revenue	3,500,000,000	3,200,000,000	3,100,000,000	2,800,000,000	2,704,700,000	2,759,400,000
R&D Expense						
Operating Income						
Operating Margin %						
SGA Expense						
Net Income						
Operating Cash Flow						
Capital Expenditure						
EBITDA						
Return on Assets %						
Return on Equity %						
Debt to Equity						

CONTACT INFORMATION:
Phone: 240-694-4100   Fax: 240-694-4790
Toll-Free:
Address: 6905 Rockledge Dr., Bethesda, MD 20817 United States

STOCK TICKER/OTHER:
Stock Ticker: Subsidiary   Exchange:
Employees: 43,000   Fiscal Year Ends: 12/31
Parent Company: Autogrill SpA

SALARIES/BONUSES:
Top Exec. Salary: $ Bonus: $
Second Exec. Salary: $ Bonus: $

OTHER THOUGHTS:
Estimated Female Officers or Directors: 1
Hot Spot for Advancement for Women/Minorities:

Sales, profits and employees may be estimates. Financial information, benefits and other data can change quickly and may vary from those stated here.

Plunkett Research, Ltd.

Home Depot Inc (The)

NAIC Code: 444110

www.homedepot.com

TYPES OF BUSINESS:
Home Centers, Retail
Home Improvement Products
Building Materials
Lawn & Garden Products
Online & Catalog Sales
Tool & Truck Rental
Installation & Design Services

BRANDS/DIVISIONS/AFFILIATES:
Hampton Bay
Husky
Vigoro
RIDGID
Ryobi
Glacier Bay
HDX
Home Depot Backyard (The)

CONTACTS: Note: Officers with more than one job title may be intentionally listed here more than once.

Carol Tome, CFO
Matthew Carey, Chief Information Officer
Mark Holifield, Executive VP, Divisional
Ann-Marie Campbell, Executive VP, Divisional
Edward Decker, Executive VP, Divisional
William Lennie, Executive VP, Divisional
Timothy Hourigan, Executive VP, Divisional
Teresa Roseborough, Executive VP
Craig Menear, President
Richard McPhail, Senior VP, Divisional

GROWTH PLANS/SPECIAL FEATURES:

The Home Depot, Inc. is one of the world's largest home improvement retailers. The company operates more than 2,285 Home Depot stores throughout the U.S., Canada, Guam, Puerto Rico, the Virgin Islands and Mexico. A typical store encompasses 104,000-square-feet of enclosed space with a 24,000-square-foot outdoor garden center; these locations usually stock between 30,000 and 40,000 items. Approximately 1 million products can be accessed through the homedepot.com website. These stores sell an assortment of building materials, plumbing materials, electrical materials, kitchen products, hardware, seasonal items, paint, flooring and wall coverings. The firm's proprietary brands include Hampton Bay lighting, Husky hand tools, Vigoro lawn care products, RIDGID and Ryobi power tools, Glacier Bay bath fixtures and HDX storage and cleaning products. Home Depot markets its products primarily to three types of customers: professional customers, such as remodelers, contractors, repairmen and small business owners; do-it-for-me shoppers, who are homeowners that personally purchase Home Depot products but hire third-party individuals for installation and/or project completion; and do-it-yourself (DIY) customers, who are homeowners that both shop for and personally install and/or utilize the firm's materials. During 2017, The Home Depot acquired the naming rights to an 11-acre park adjacent to the Atlanta Falcon's (national football league) and Atlanta United FC (major league soccer) stadium, and built a parking and tailgating space to utilize during the teams' home games and to utilize as a greenspace for public use during non-event days. The park is called The Home Depot Backyard, and opened in September 2018.

The company offers its employees medical, dental, vision, life, AD&D and disability insurance; a 401(k) plan; a stock purchase plan; adoption, education and relocation assistance; flexible spending accounts; a legal services plan; auto and homeowners insurance; and veterinary coverage.

FINANCIAL DATA: Note: Data for latest year may not have been available at press time.

In U.S. $	2018	2017	2016	2015	2014	2013
Revenue	100,904,000,000	94,595,000,000	88,519,000,000	83,176,000,000	78,812,000,000	
R&D Expense						
Operating Income	14,681,000,000	13,427,000,000	11,774,000,000	10,469,000,000	9,166,000,000	
Operating Margin %	.15%	.14%	.13%	.13%	.12%	
SGA Expense	17,864,000,000	17,132,000,000	16,801,000,000	16,834,000,000	16,597,000,000	
Net Income	8,630,000,000	7,957,000,000	7,009,000,000	6,345,000,000	5,385,000,000	
Operating Cash Flow	12,031,000,000	9,783,000,000	9,373,000,000	8,242,000,000	7,628,000,000	
Capital Expenditure	1,897,000,000	1,621,000,000	1,503,000,000	1,442,000,000	1,389,000,000	
EBITDA	16,817,000,000	15,436,000,000	13,803,000,000	12,592,000,000	10,935,000,000	
Return on Assets %	.20%	.19%	.17%	.16%	.13%	
Return on Equity %	2.98%	1.49%	.90%	.58%	.36%	
Debt to Equity	16.69	5.158	3.307	1.81	1.173	

CONTACT INFORMATION:
Phone: 770 433-8211 Fax: 770 431-2707
Toll-Free: 800-553-3199
Address: 2455 Paces Ferry Rd. N.W., Atlanta, GA 30339 United States

SALARIES/BONUSES:
Top Exec. Salary: $1,325,000 Bonus: $
Second Exec. Salary: $1,154,423 Bonus: $

STOCK TICKER/OTHER:
Stock Ticker: HD
Employees: 406,000
Parent Company:

Exchange: NYS
Fiscal Year Ends: 01/31

OTHER THOUGHTS:
Estimated Female Officers or Directors: 7
Hot Spot for Advancement for Women/Minorities: Y

Sales, profits and employees may be estimates. Financial information, benefits and other data can change quickly and may vary from those stated here.

Houston Methodist

NAIC Code: 622110

www.houstonmethodist.org

TYPES OF BUSINESS:
General Medical and Surgical Hospitals

BRANDS/DIVISIONS/AFFILIATES:
Houston Methodist Hospital-Central
Houston Methodist Baytown Hospital
Houston Methodist Clear Lake Hospital
Houston Methodist Sugar Land Hospital
Houston Methodist West Hospital
Houston Methodist Willowbrook Hospital
Houston Methodist The Woodlands Hospital
Houston Methodist Continuing Care Hospital

CONTACTS:
Note: Officers with more than one job title may be intentionally listed here more than once.

Marc L. Boom, CEO
Marc L. Boom, Pres.
Gregory Nelson, Sec.
Carlton Caucum, Treas.
Joseph Walter III, Assistant Treas.
Robert K. Moses, Jr., Assistant Sec.
Ewing Werlein, Jr., Chmn.

GROWTH PLANS/SPECIAL FEATURES:

Houston Methodist is a nonprofit healthcare organization that owns and operates several hospitals and facilities located in Houston. Its hospitals include Houston Methodist Hospital-Central, Houston Methodist Baytown Hospital, Houston Methodist Clear Lake Hospital, Houston Methodist Sugar Land Hospital, Houston Methodist West Hospital, Houston Methodist Willowbrook Hospital, Houston Methodist The Woodlands Hospital and Houston Methodist Continuing Care Hospital. Each campus is staffed by highly-trained specialists who provide advanced treatment as well as follow-up care. Other centers include Houston Methodist Emergency Care, Houston Methodist Imaging Center, Houston Methodist Breast Care Center and Houston Methodist Outpatient Center. Houston Methodist Research Institute is home to physicians that collaborate on clinical trials. The Houston Methodist Institute for Technology, Innovation and Education is a 35,000-square-foot surgical training center and virtual hospital which provides ongoing education. Houston Methodist Hospital Foundation accepts all gifts on Houston Methodist's behalf and views donor contribution as essential to its growth and success. Houston Methodist Community Benefits support individuals and organizations that provide financial and medical assistance to patients on an annual basis. Houston Methodist Specialty Physician Group are physicians employed by Houston Methodist that are rooted in an academic and research environment where teaching and continued education are encouraged. Houston Methodist Primary Care Group is dedicated to providing patient care for the entire family. In 2019, in partnership with Texas A&M University, Houston Methodist Hospital launched the EnMed program, an innovative engineering medicine program designed to educate physicians to create transformational technology for health care.

FINANCIAL DATA:
Note: Data for latest year may not have been available at press time.

In U.S. $	2018	2017	2016	2015	2014	2013
Revenue	4,000,000,000	3,045,000,000	2,900,000,000	2,800,000,000	2,616,170,000	2,616,169,000
R&D Expense						
Operating Income						
Operating Margin %						
SGA Expense						
Net Income						
Operating Cash Flow						
Capital Expenditure						
EBITDA						
Return on Assets %						
Return on Equity %						
Debt to Equity						

CONTACT INFORMATION:
Phone: 713-790-3311 Fax:
Toll-Free:
Address: 6565 Fannin St., Houston, TX 77030 United States

SALARIES/BONUSES:
Top Exec. Salary: $ Bonus: $
Second Exec. Salary: $ Bonus: $

STOCK TICKER/OTHER:
Stock Ticker: Nonprofit Exchange:
Employees: 23,669 Fiscal Year Ends: 12/31
Parent Company:

OTHER THOUGHTS:
Estimated Female Officers or Directors: 5
Hot Spot for Advancement for Women/Minorities: Y

Sales, profits and employees may be estimates. Financial information, benefits and other data can change quickly and may vary from those stated here.

Hub International Limited

NAIC Code: 524210

www.hubinternational.com

TYPES OF BUSINESS:
Insurance Brokerage & Management
Risk Management
Property & Casualty Insurance
Employee Benefit Services
Investments & Financial Planning
Life Insurance
Health & Disability Insurance

BRANDS/DIVISIONS/AFFILIATES:
Hellman & Friedman LLC

CONTACTS:
Note: Officers with more than one job title may be intentionally listed here more than once.

Marc I. Coehn, CEO
Joseph C. Hyde, CFO
Trey Biggs, Chief Sales Officer
Amber Kennelly, Chief Human Resources Officer
Carla Moradi, Exec. VP-IT & Operations
Scott Goodreau, Chief Legal Officer
Roy H. Taylor, Pres., West Region
Lawrence J. Lineker, Pres., Canadian Region
Scott Goodreau, Pres., Central Region
Deborah Deters, Sr. VP
Martin P. Hughes, Chmn.
James Barton, Pres., Canada & Midwest Regions

GROWTH PLANS/SPECIAL FEATURES:
Hub International Limited is an insurance brokerage providing an array of property, casualty, life and health insurance as well as employee benefits, investment and risk management products and consultancy services. The company focuses primarily on middle-market commercial accounts in the U.S. and Canada, and operates through approximately 450 integrated broker offices using a variety of retail and wholesale distribution channels. Hub operates through five divisions: personal insurance, business insurance, employee benefits, risk services and human resources consulting. Personal insurance includes homeowner's, condominiums, co-op housing, health and renter's insurance; auto, boat, collector car, recreational vehicle and travel insurance; and specialty insurance such as personal excess liability and aviation. Business insurance includes aviation, business owners, commercial auto, employment practices, marine, professional liability, boiler and machinery, business property, cyber liability, director/officer liability, executive liability, environmental protection, financial services, workers' compensation, business travel, trade credit and political risk, surety bonds, mergers & acquisitions, general liability and contest and prize insurance. Employee benefits comprises group medical plans, disability, group life insurance, voluntary benefits, dental plans, individual health, employee benefits consulting, absence management, wellness programs, health advocacy and benefits administration. Risk services include regulatory compliance assistance, safety management, emergency response planning, business continuity, fleet safety management, property protection, claim data analysis, disability management, claim reporting guidance, return-to-work planning, crisis management and webinars. Last, human resources (HR) consulting spans employee engagement strategies, employee value proposition, HR analysis and selection, HR audits, HR staffing alternatives and Total Compensation Statements. Hub International is privately-owned by Hellman & Friedman, LLC.

FINANCIAL DATA:
Note: Data for latest year may not have been available at press time.

In U.S. $	2018	2017	2016	2015	2014	2013
Revenue	2,000,000,000	1,500,000,000	1,470,000,000	1,260,000,000	1,230,000,000	1,147,560,000
R&D Expense						
Operating Income						
Operating Margin %						
SGA Expense						
Net Income						
Operating Cash Flow						
Capital Expenditure						
EBITDA						
Return on Assets %						
Return on Equity %						
Debt to Equity						

CONTACT INFORMATION:
Phone: 312-922-5000   Fax: 877-402-6606
Toll-Free: 877-402-4187
Address: 300 N. LaSalle St., 17/F, Chicago, IL 60654 United States

SALARIES/BONUSES:
Top Exec. Salary: $ Bonus: $
Second Exec. Salary: $ Bonus: $

STOCK TICKER/OTHER:
Stock Ticker: Private
Employees: 10,000
Parent Company: Hellman & Friedman LLC

Exchange:
Fiscal Year Ends: 12/31

OTHER THOUGHTS:
Estimated Female Officers or Directors: 1
Hot Spot for Advancement for Women/Minorities: Y

Hubbell Incorporated

www.hubbell.com

NAIC Code: 335931

TYPES OF BUSINESS:
Current-Carrying Wiring Device Manufacturing

BRANDS/DIVISIONS/AFFILIATES:
Hubbell
Raco
Wiegmann
Kim Lighting
Alera Lighting
Hubbell Outdoor Lighting
Ohio Brass
Quazite

CONTACTS: Note: Officers with more than one job title may be intentionally listed here more than once.
David Nord, CEO
William Sperry, CFO
Joseph Capozzoli, Chief Accounting Officer
Gerben Bakker, COO
Darrin Wegman, President, Divisional
Kevin Poyck, President, Divisional
Rodd Ruland, President, Divisional
Stephen Mais, Senior VP, Divisional
Maria Lee, Treasurer

GROWTH PLANS/SPECIAL FEATURES:
Hubbell Incorporated designs, manufactures and distributes electrical and electronic products for a range of non-residential and residential construction, industrial and utility applications. The company operates in two segments: electrical and power. The electrical segment is comprised of businesses that sell stock and custom products including standard and special application wiring device products, rough-in electrical products, connector and grounding products, lighting fixtures and controls, as well as other electrical equipment. The products are typically used in and around industrial, commercial and institutional facilities by electrical contractors, maintenance personnel, electricians and telecommunications companies. Hubbell's products are supplied principally to industrial, non-residential and residential customers. These products are sold under brand and trademarks including, such as Hubbell, Raco, Kellems, Bell, Wiegmann, Hawke, Hipotronics, Chalmit and Austdac. Hubbell manufactures and sells lighting fixtures and controls for indoor and outdoor applications within residential, commercial, institutional and industrial markets. These products are sold under a number of brand and trademarks, such as Kim Lighting, Sportsliter Solutions, Kurt Versen, Beacon Products, Spaulding Lighting, Alera Lighting, Dual-Lite, Litecontrol and Hubbell Outdoor Lighting. The power segment consists of operations that design and manufacture various transmission, distribution, substation and telecommunications products mainly used by the electrical utility industry. Hubbell manufactures and sells a number of electrical distribution, transmission, and substation products. These products are sold under a number of brand and trademarks, such as Ohio Brass, Chance, Anderson, Fargo, Hubbell, Quazite, Electro Composites, Hot Box, PCORE and Delmar.

FINANCIAL DATA: Note: Data for latest year may not have been available at press time.

In U.S. $	2018	2017	2016	2015	2014	2013
Revenue	4,481,700,000	3,668,800,000	3,505,200,000	3,390,400,000	3,359,400,000	3,183,900,000
R&D Expense						
Operating Income	556,900,000	503,700,000	477,800,000	474,600,000	517,400,000	507,600,000
Operating Margin %		.14%	.14%	.14%	.15%	.16%
SGA Expense	743,500,000	648,200,000	622,900,000	617,200,000	591,600,000	562,900,000
Net Income	360,200,000	243,100,000	293,000,000	277,300,000	325,300,000	326,500,000
Operating Cash Flow	517,100,000	379,000,000	398,200,000	331,100,000	391,500,000	381,800,000
Capital Expenditure	96,200,000	79,700,000	67,200,000	77,100,000	60,300,000	58,800,000
EBITDA	687,800,000	587,800,000	566,100,000	534,800,000	595,900,000	575,200,000
Return on Assets %		.07%	.09%	.08%	.10%	.11%
Return on Equity %		.15%	.18%	.15%	.17%	.18%
Debt to Equity		0.604	0.622	0.342	0.31	0.313

CONTACT INFORMATION:
Phone: 475 882-4000   Fax: 203 799-4333
Toll-Free:
Address: 40 Waterview Dr., Shelton, CT 06484 United States

STOCK TICKER/OTHER:
Stock Ticker: HUBB
Employees: 17,400
Parent Company:

Exchange: NYS
Fiscal Year Ends: 12/31

SALARIES/BONUSES:
Top Exec. Salary: $1,000,000   Bonus: $
Second Exec. Salary: $525,000   Bonus: $

OTHER THOUGHTS:
Estimated Female Officers or Directors:
Hot Spot for Advancement for Women/Minorities:

Humana Inc

www.humana.com

NAIC Code: 524114

TYPES OF BUSINESS:
Insurance-Medical & Health, HMOs & PPOs
Insurance-Dental
Employee Benefit Plans
Insurance-Group Life
Wellness Programs

BRANDS/DIVISIONS/AFFILIATES:

CONTACTS:
Note: Officers with more than one job title may be intentionally listed here more than once.

Bruce Broussard, CEO
Alan Wheatley, Pres., Divisional
Brian Kane, CFO
Kurt Hilzinger, Chairman of the Board
Cynthia Zipperle, Chief Accounting Officer
Brian LeClaire, Chief Information Officer
Joseph Ventura, Chief Legal Officer
Roy Beveridge, Chief Medical Officer
Samir Deshpande, Chief Risk Officer
Vishal Agrawal, Chief Strategy Officer
Christopher Hunter, Other Corporate Officer
Jody Bilney, Other Executive Officer
Timothy Huval, Other Executive Officer
Elizabeth Bierbower, President, Divisional
William Fleming, President, Divisional

GROWTH PLANS/SPECIAL FEATURES:

Humana, Inc. is a leading health benefits company in the U.S., serving approximately 17 million medical benefit plan members and 6 million specialty products members in the U.S. and Puerto Rico. It operates in three segments: retail, group and specialty and healthcare services. The retail segment consists of Medicare and commercial fully-insured medical and specialty health insurance benefits, including dental, vision and other supplemental health and financial protection products, marketed directly to individuals. The group and specialty segment consist of employer group commercial fully-insured medical and specialty health insurance benefits marketed to individuals and employer groups, including dental, vision, and other supplemental health and voluntary insurance benefits, as well as administrative services only (ASO) products marketed to employer groups. Humana provides health benefits and related services to companies ranging from fewer than 10 to over 10,000 employees. The healthcare services segment includes services offered to health plan members as well as to third parties that promote health and wellness, including provider services, pharmacies, integrated wellness and home care services. Other businesses consist of military services, primarily the TRICARE South Region, Medicaid and closed-block long-term care businesses as well as the firm's contract with the Centers for Medicare and Medicaid Services to administer the Limited Income Newly Eligible Transition program, known as LI-NET. Many of its products are offered through HMOs (health maintenance organizations), private fee-for-service (PFFS) and preferred provider organizations (PPOs).

The firm offers employees an array of comprehensive benefits.

FINANCIAL DATA:
Note: Data for latest year may not have been available at press time.

In U.S. $	2018	2017	2016	2015	2014	2013
Revenue	56,912,000,000	53,767,000,000	54,379,000,000	54,289,000,000	48,500,000,000	41,313,000,000
R&D Expense						
Operating Income						
Operating Margin %						
SGA Expense	7,525,000,000	6,567,000,000	7,277,000,000	7,318,000,000	7,639,000,000	6,355,000,000
Net Income	1,683,000,000	2,448,000,000	614,000,000	1,276,000,000	1,147,000,000	1,231,000,000
Operating Cash Flow	2,173,000,000	4,051,000,000	1,936,000,000	868,000,000	1,618,000,000	1,716,000,000
Capital Expenditure	612,000,000	526,000,000	527,000,000	523,000,000	528,000,000	441,000,000
EBITDA						
Return on Assets %		.09%	.02%	.05%	.05%	.06%
Return on Equity %		.24%	.06%	.13%	.12%	.14%
Debt to Equity		0.485	0.355	0.369	0.397	0.279

CONTACT INFORMATION:
Phone: 502 580-1000 Fax: 502 580-1441
Toll-Free:
Address: 500 W. Main St., Louisville, KY 40202 United States

STOCK TICKER/OTHER:
Stock Ticker: HUM
Employees: 54,200
Parent Company:

Exchange: NYS
Fiscal Year Ends: 12/31

SALARIES/BONUSES:
Top Exec. Salary: $1,273,080 Bonus: $
Second Exec. Salary: $700,000 Bonus: $

OTHER THOUGHTS:
Estimated Female Officers or Directors: 3
Hot Spot for Advancement for Women/Minorities: Y

Sales, profits and employees may be estimates. Financial information, benefits and other data can change quickly and may vary from those stated here.

Huntsman Corporation

NAIC Code: 325211

www.huntsman.com

TYPES OF BUSINESS:
Chemicals Manufacturing
Polyurethane Manufacturing
Advanced Materials & Surface Technologies
Performance Chemicals
Pigments

BRANDS/DIVISIONS/AFFILIATES:
Huntsman International LLC
Demilec

CONTACTS: Note: Officers with more than one job title may be intentionally listed here more than once.
Anthony Hankins, CEO, Geographical
Pierre Poukens, VP, Divisional
Sean Douglas, CFO
Peter Huntsman, Chairman of the Board
Randy Wright, Chief Accounting Officer
Twila Day, Chief Information Officer
Nolan Archibald, Director
David Stryker, Executive VP
Monte Edlund, President, Divisional
Scott Wright, President, Divisional
Ronit Aggarwal, President, Divisional
R. Rogers, Senior VP, Divisional
Ronald Gerrard, Senior VP, Divisional
Claire Mei, Treasurer
Nooshin Vaughn, Vice President, Divisional
Ivan Marcuse, Vice President, Divisional
Luciano Reyes, Vice President, Divisional
Kevin Hardman, Vice President, Divisional

GROWTH PLANS/SPECIAL FEATURES:

Huntsman Corporation is a global manufacturer of differentiated organic chemical products and inorganic chemical products. The company operates all its businesses through wholly-owned subsidiary Huntsman International, LLC. The firm operates in four business segments: polyurethanes, advanced materials, textile effects and performance products. The polyurethanes segment produces MDI (Methylene diphenyl diisocyanate) products, propylene oxide, polyols, propylene glycol, thermoplastic urethane, aniline and methyl tert-butyl ether products. The advanced materials segment manufactures epoxy resin compounds and formulations; cross-linking, matting and curing agents; and epoxy, acrylic and polyurethane-based adhesives. The textile effects division produces textile chemicals and dyes. Last, the performance products segment is organized around three market groups: performance specialties, performance intermediates and maleic anhydride and licensing. It produces amines, carbonates and certain specialty surfactants; consumes internally produced and third-party-sourced base petrochemicals in the manufacture of its surfactants and ethanolamines products; licenses maleic anhydride manufacturing technology (mainly used in the production of fiberglass reinforced resins); and supplies butane fixed bed catalyst used in the manufacture of maleic anhydrides. During 2018, Huntsman acquired Demilec, a North American spray polyurethane foam insulation manufacturer; opened a formulations manufacturing facility in Vietnam; and announced plans to build a new polyurethane systems house in Dubai.

FINANCIAL DATA: Note: Data for latest year may not have been available at press time.

In U.S. $	2018	2017	2016	2015	2014	2013
Revenue	9,379,000,000	8,358,000,000	9,657,000,000	10,299,000,000	11,578,000,000	11,079,000,000
R&D Expense	152,000,000	138,000,000	152,000,000	160,000,000	158,000,000	140,000,000
Operating Income	1,035,000,000	899,000,000	746,000,000	707,000,000	791,000,000	661,000,000
Operating Margin %		.11%	.08%	.07%	.07%	.06%
SGA Expense	830,000,000	798,000,000	920,000,000	982,000,000	974,000,000	942,000,000
Net Income	337,000,000	636,000,000	326,000,000	93,000,000	323,000,000	128,000,000
Operating Cash Flow	1,207,000,000	1,219,000,000	1,088,000,000	575,000,000	760,000,000	708,000,000
Capital Expenditure	313,000,000	282,000,000	421,000,000	663,000,000	601,000,000	471,000,000
EBITDA	1,400,000,000	1,131,000,000	1,082,000,000	780,000,000	1,054,000,000	917,000,000
Return on Assets %		.07%	.03%	.01%	.03%	.01%
Return on Equity %		.33%	.24%	.06%	.17%	.07%
Debt to Equity		0.862	3.214	3.208	2.778	1.838

CONTACT INFORMATION:
Phone: 281-719-6000 Fax:
Toll-Free:
Address: 10003 Woodloch Forest Dr., The Woodlands, TX 77380 United States

STOCK TICKER/OTHER:
Stock Ticker: HUN
Employees: 15,000
Parent Company:

Exchange: NYS
Fiscal Year Ends: 12/31

SALARIES/BONUSES:
Top Exec. Salary: $1,700,000 Bonus: $
Second Exec. Salary: $918,410 Bonus: $

OTHER THOUGHTS:
Estimated Female Officers or Directors: 2
Hot Spot for Advancement for Women/Minorities:

Sales, profits and employees may be estimates. Financial information, benefits and other data can change quickly and may vary from those stated here.

Hyatt Hotels Corporation

www.hyatt.com

NAIC Code: 721110

TYPES OF BUSINESS:
Hotel Ownership & Management
Timeshares
Golf Courses
Gaming
Retirement Communities
Motels & Inns
Hotel Franchising

BRANDS/DIVISIONS/AFFILIATES:
Hyatt Regency
Grand Hyatt
Park Hyatt
Andaz
Hyatt House
Hyatt Ziva
Exhale
World of Hyatt

CONTACTS:
Note: Officers with more than one job title may be intentionally listed here more than once.

Mark Hoplamazian, CEO
Joan Bottarini, CFO
Thomas Pritzker, Chairman of the Board
Elizabeth Bauer, Chief Accounting Officer
Margaret Egan, Executive VP
Malaika Myers, Executive VP
Mark Vondrasek, Executive VP
David Udell, Executive VP
H. Floyd, Executive VP
Peter Fulton, Executive VP
Peter Sears, Executive VP
Bradley O'Bryan, Senior VP, Divisional

GROWTH PLANS/SPECIAL FEATURES:

Hyatt Hotels Corporation owns, operates, manages and franchises full-service luxury hotels in 60 countries across the globe. The company owns, manages or franchises 843 hotels with approximately 208,207 rooms (as of December 2018). Hyatt's operations consist of several brands. Hyatt and Hyatt Regency host business and leisure travelers, although Hyatt Regency caters mainly to larger groups. Grand Hyatt hotels cater to leisure and business travelers and include accommodations for banquets and conferences. Park Hyatt hotels are smaller, full-service luxury hotels featuring world class art and restaurants in a few of the world's most visited cities. The Andaz branded hotels are boutique-style hotels that feature restaurants and bars aimed at local clientele as well as single travelers. The two select service brands, Hyatt House and Hyatt Place, are extended-stay brands designed to feel more like home. Hyatt Residence Club provides vacation ownership and vacation rental opportunities, offering members timeshare or points-based resort vacation opportunities. Hyatt Ziva and Hyatt Zilara are the company's all-inclusive resort brands which are developed, sold and managed as part of the Hyatt Residence club. Exhale is a wellness brand, offering dozens of proprietary boutique fitness class programs and spa therapies. Hyatt's guest loyalty program, World of Hyatt, has over 16 million active members.

The firm offers employees complementary hotel rooms; medical, dental, vision and prescription drug coverage; and tuition assistance.

FINANCIAL DATA:
Note: Data for latest year may not have been available at press time.

In U.S. $	2018	2017	2016	2015	2014	2013
Revenue	4,474,000,000	4,685,000,000	4,429,000,000	4,328,000,000	4,415,000,000	4,184,000,000
R&D Expense						
Operating Income	332,000,000	302,000,000	299,000,000	323,000,000	279,000,000	233,000,000
Operating Margin %		.06%	.07%	.07%	.06%	.06%
SGA Expense	320,000,000	379,000,000	315,000,000	308,000,000	349,000,000	323,000,000
Net Income	769,000,000	249,000,000	204,000,000	124,000,000	344,000,000	207,000,000
Operating Cash Flow	341,000,000	620,000,000	489,000,000	538,000,000	473,000,000	456,000,000
Capital Expenditure	297,000,000	298,000,000	211,000,000	269,000,000	253,000,000	232,000,000
EBITDA	1,354,000,000	1,019,000,000	707,000,000	582,000,000	950,000,000	731,000,000
Return on Assets %		.03%	.03%	.02%	.04%	.03%
Return on Equity %		.07%	.05%	.03%	.07%	.04%
Debt to Equity		0.409	0.37	0.262	0.298	0.27

CONTACT INFORMATION:
Phone: 312 750-1234   Fax:
Toll-Free: 800-323-7249
Address: 150 N. Riverside Plz., 8/Fl, Chicago, IL 60606 United States

SALARIES/BONUSES:
Top Exec. Salary: $1,203,167   Bonus: $
Second Exec. Salary: $784,833   Bonus: $

STOCK TICKER/OTHER:
Stock Ticker: H
Employees: 45,000
Parent Company:

Exchange: NYS
Fiscal Year Ends: 12/31

OTHER THOUGHTS:
Estimated Female Officers or Directors: 3
Hot Spot for Advancement for Women/Minorities: Y

Hyundai Motor America

NAIC Code: 336111

www.hyundaiusa.com

TYPES OF BUSINESS:
Automobile Manufacturing
Automobile Manufacturing

BRANDS/DIVISIONS/AFFILIATES:
Hyundai Motor Company
Elantra
Sonata
Tucson
Kona
Veloster
Genesis
Ioniq

CONTACTS:
Note: Officers with more than one job title may be intentionally listed here more than once.

Kenny Lee, CEO
Dean Evans, CMO
Michael J. O'Brien, VP-Prod. Planning
Michael J. O'Brien, VP-Corp. Planning
Christopher Hosford, Exec. Dir.-Comm.
Frank Ferrara, Exec. VP-Customer Satisfaction
Christopher Chapman, Chief Designer

GROWTH PLANS/SPECIAL FEATURES:

Hyundai Motor America is the U.S. subsidiary of Hyundai Motor Company, which is based in Korea. It is responsible for the distribution of Hyundai vehicles nationwide and for manufacturing Hyundai vehicles. The company sells Hyundai models such as the Elantra and Sonata sedans; Tucson, Kona and Santa Fe SUVs and crossovers; Accent, Veloster and Elantra compact hatchbacks; Genesis luxury vehicles; and Ioniq and Sonata hybrid/fuel cell vehicles. Hyundai Motor America supports over 800 U.S. Hyundai dealers through its manufacturing facilities in Michigan, Alabama and California. The firm operates one of the most technologically advanced manufacturing facilities in the world in Alabama, comprised of over 2 million square-feet, with nearly 300 welding robots and the capability to produce approximately 300,000 vehicles annually. The company's website possesses shopping tools that allow customers to build their own cars, receive quotes, schedule test drives, locate dealers and obtain trade-in appraisals.

Hyundai Motor America offers its employees medical, dental and vision coverage; life, disability, business travel and AD&D insurance; flexible spending accounts; a 401(k); dependent and long-term care programs; an employee assistance program; employee discounts; corporate onsite fitness centers and convenience stores with laundry and tailoring services; education reimbursement; training and mentoring; and relocation assistance.

FINANCIAL DATA:
Note: Data for latest year may not have been available at press time.

In U.S. $	2018	2017	2016	2015	2014	2013
Revenue	13,689,800,000	15,060,100,000	16,144,000,000	15,397,949,697	15,052,444,331	16,359,450,809
R&D Expense						
Operating Income						
Operating Margin %						
SGA Expense						
Net Income	-295,529,000	-812,911,000	-55,295,882	-146,794,703	338,785,997	483,362,165
Operating Cash Flow						
Capital Expenditure						
EBITDA						
Return on Assets %						
Return on Equity %						
Debt to Equity						

CONTACT INFORMATION:
Phone: 714-965-3000 Fax: 714-965-3149
Toll-Free: 800-633-5151
Address: 10550 Talbert Ave., Fountain Valley, CA 92708 United States

STOCK TICKER/OTHER:
Stock Ticker: Subsidiary
Employees: 31,100
Parent Company: Hyundai Motor Company

Exchange:
Fiscal Year Ends: 12/31

SALARIES/BONUSES:
Top Exec. Salary: $ Bonus: $
Second Exec. Salary: $ Bonus: $

OTHER THOUGHTS:
Estimated Female Officers or Directors:
Hot Spot for Advancement for Women/Minorities:

Sales, profits and employees may be estimates. Financial information, benefits and other data can change quickly and may vary from those stated here.

IAC/InterActiveCorp

www.iac.com

NAIC Code: 519130

TYPES OF BUSINESS:
E-Commerce, Online Advertising & Search Engines
Online Personals & Dating Services
Online Entertainment & Shopping Directories
Service Provider Listings Online

BRANDS/DIVISIONS/AFFILIATES:
Match Group Inc
ANGI Homeservices Inc
Angie's List
Vimeo
IAC Films
Apalon
SlimWare
Dotdash

CONTACTS:
Note: Officers with more than one job title may be intentionally listed here more than once.

Barry Diller, Chairman of the Board
Mark Stein, Chief Strategy Officer
Joseph Levin, Director
Victor Kaufman, Director
Glenn Schiffman, Executive VP
Gregg Winiarski, General Counsel
Michael Schwerdtman, Senior VP

GROWTH PLANS/SPECIAL FEATURES:
IAC/InterActiveCorp is a leading media and internet company organized into five segments: Match Group, ANGI Homeservices, video, applications and publishing. The Match Group consists of Match Group, Inc., which operates a dating business available in 42 languages across more than 190 countries. It offers subscription dating products via websites and mobile applications, which enable users to establish a profile and review the profiles of other users without charge. Additional features are either free or obtained by purchase. Access to premium features require a subscription. The ANGI Homeservices segment consists of ANGI Homeservices, Inc., which owns and operates HomeAdvisor, Angie's List, mHelpDesk, CraftJack and Felix, which are digital marketplaces for home services. The video segment consists of Vimeo, Electus, IAC Films and Daily Burn. Vimeo operates a global video sharing platform for creators and their audiences; Electus provides production and producer services for both unscripted and scripted television and digital content, primarily for initial sale and distribution in the U.S.; IAC Films provides production and producer services for feature films, primarily for initial sale and distribution in the U.S. and internationally; and Daily Burn is a health and fitness property that provides streaming fitness and workout videos across a variety of platforms. The applications segment consists of two divisions: consumer and partnerships. The consumers division develops and distributes downloadable desktop and mobile apps, and includes: Apalon, which houses the firm's mobile apps; and SlimWare, a community-powered software that cleans, repairs, updates, secures and optimizes computers, mobile phones and digital devices. The partnership division designs and develops browser-based search applications to be bundled and distributed with the partners' products and services. Last, the publishing segment consists of: Dotdash, Dictionary.com, The Daily Beast, Ask.com and CityGrid, which publish digital content and/or provide search services to users.

FINANCIAL DATA:
Note: Data for latest year may not have been available at press time.

In U.S. $	2018	2017	2016	2015	2014	2013
Revenue	4,262,892,000	3,307,239,000	3,139,882,000	3,230,933,000	3,109,547,000	3,022,987,000
R&D Expense	309,329,000	250,879,000	197,885,000	185,766,000	160,515,000	141,330,000
Operating Income	565,139,000	188,466,000	242,742,000	193,644,000	378,727,000	426,203,000
Operating Margin %		.06%	.08%	.06%	.12%	.14%
SGA Expense	2,293,519,000	2,100,478,000	1,792,423,000	1,871,205,000	1,568,047,000	1,336,601,000
Net Income	626,961,000	304,924,000	-41,280,000	119,472,000	414,873,000	285,784,000
Operating Cash Flow	988,128,000	416,690,000	292,377,000	349,405,000	424,048,000	410,961,000
Capital Expenditure	85,634,000	75,523,000	78,039,000	62,049,000	57,233,000	80,311,000
EBITDA	1,054,644,000	288,661,000	178,938,000	418,666,000	445,325,000	568,649,000
Return on Assets %		.06%	-.01%	.03%	.10%	.07%
Return on Equity %		.14%	-.02%	.06%	.23%	.17%
Debt to Equity		0.815	0.847	0.969	0.542	0.64

CONTACT INFORMATION:
Phone: 212 314-7300   Fax: 212 314-7399
Toll-Free:
Address: 555 W. 18th St., New York, NY 10011 United States

SALARIES/BONUSES:
Top Exec. Salary: $1,000,000   Bonus: $5,000,000
Second Exec. Salary: $600,000   Bonus: $3,500,000

STOCK TICKER/OTHER:
Stock Ticker: IAC
Employees: 9,100
Parent Company:

Exchange: NAS
Fiscal Year Ends: 12/31

OTHER THOUGHTS:
Estimated Female Officers or Directors: 6
Hot Spot for Advancement for Women/Minorities: Y

IDEXX Laboratories Inc

www.idexx.com

NAIC Code: 334510

TYPES OF BUSINESS:
Veterinary Laboratory Testing Equipment
Point-of-Care Diagnostic Products
Veterinary Pharmaceuticals
Information Management Software
Food & Water Testing Products
Laboratory Testing Services
Consulting

BRANDS/DIVISIONS/AFFILIATES:
IDEXX VetLab
VetLyte
VetStat
Catalyst Dx
SNAPshot DX
SNAP Beta-Lactam
Colilert
SNAP Lepto

CONTACTS:
Note: Officers with more than one job title may be intentionally listed here more than once.

Jonathan Ayers, CEO
Brian Mckeon, CFO
Jay Mazelsky, Executive VP
Sharon Underberg, General Counsel
Giovani Twigge, Other Executive Officer
Kathy Turner, Vice President
Michael Lane, Vice President

GROWTH PLANS/SPECIAL FEATURES:

IDEXX Laboratories, Inc. develops, manufactures and distributes products and provides services for the veterinary and the food and water testing markets. The company operates in three business segments: companion animal group, which provides diagnostic and information technology-based products and services for the veterinary markets; livestock, poultry and dairy, which provides diagnostic products and services for animal health, and to ensure the quality and safety of milk and food; and water quality products. IDEXX markets an integrated and flexible suite of in-house laboratory analyzers for use in veterinary practices, which is referred to as the IDEXX VetLab suite. The suite includes in-clinic chemistry, hematology, immunoassay, urinalysis and coagulation analyzers such as the VetTest, VetLyte, VetStat, LaserCyte Dx, Catalyst One, Catalyst Dx, Coag Dx and ProCyte Dx; and the hand-held IDEXX SNAPshot Dx rapid assay test kits which provide quick, accurate and convenient point-of-care diagnostic test results. Catalyst SDMA allows customers to use the Catalyst One and Catalyst Dx to screen for symmetrical dimethyl arginine (SDMA), a biomarker that detects kidney disease. In addition, the company provides assay kits, software and instrumentation for accurate assessment of infectious disease in production animals, such as cattle, swine and poultry. IDEXX's principal product for use in testing for antibiotic residue in milk is the SNAP Beta-Lactam test, which detects penicillin, amoxicillin, ampicillin, ceftiofur and cephapirin residues. SNAPduo Beta-Tetra ST detects certain tetracycline antibiotic residues in addition to those detected by the Beta-Lactam test kits. Last, water quality products include Colilert, Colilert-18 and Colisure tests, which simultaneously detect total coliforms and E. coli in water. SNAP Giardia is a fecal test for soluble Giardia antigens, a common cause of water-born infection; and SNAP Lepto tests for leptospirosis, a bacterial infection spread through contact with water or soil contaminated by the urine of infected animals.

FINANCIAL DATA:
Note: Data for latest year may not have been available at press time.

In U.S. $	2018	2017	2016	2015	2014	2013
Revenue	2,213,242,000	1,969,058,000	1,775,423,000	1,601,892,000	1,485,807,000	1,377,058,000
R&D Expense	117,863,000	109,182,000	101,122,000	99,681,000	98,263,000	88,003,000
Operating Income	491,335,000	413,028,000	350,239,000	308,124,000	260,255,000	266,762,000
Operating Margin %		.21%	.20%	.19%	.18%	.19%
SGA Expense	632,344,000	575,172,000	524,075,000	482,465,000	457,598,000	401,353,000
Net Income	377,031,000	263,144,000	222,045,000	192,078,000	181,906,000	187,800,000
Operating Cash Flow	400,084,000	373,276,000	334,571,000	216,364,000	235,846,000	245,996,000
Capital Expenditure	122,936,000	76,704,000	64,787,000	82,921,000	60,698,000	78,636,000
EBITDA	575,664,000	501,422,000	432,113,000	371,336,000	320,872,000	323,243,000
Return on Assets %		.16%	.15%	.13%	.14%	.16%
Return on Equity %				11.50%	.57%	.33%
Debt to Equity					2.978	0.29

CONTACT INFORMATION:
Phone: 207 556-0300   Fax: 207 856-0346
Toll-Free: 800-548-6733
Address: 1 Idexx Dr., Westbrook, ME 04092 United States

SALARIES/BONUSES:
Top Exec. Salary: $800,000   Bonus: $
Second Exec. Salary: $570,577   Bonus: $

STOCK TICKER/OTHER:
Stock Ticker: IDXX   Exchange: NAS
Employees: 7,365   Fiscal Year Ends: 12/31
Parent Company:

OTHER THOUGHTS:
Estimated Female Officers or Directors: 2
Hot Spot for Advancement for Women/Minorities: Y

Illinois Tool Works Inc

www.itw.com

NAIC Code: 333249

TYPES OF BUSINESS:
Industrial Products & Equipment
Steel, Plastic & Paper Products
Power Systems & Electronics
Transportation-Related Components, Fasteners, Fluids & Polymers
Construction-Related Fasteners & Tools
Food Equipment & Adhesives
Decorative Surfacing Materials
Adhesives, Sealants & Lubrication

BRANDS/DIVISIONS/AFFILIATES:

GROWTH PLANS/SPECIAL FEATURES:

Illinois Tool Works, Inc. is a multinational manufacturer of a diversified range of industrial products and equipment, with operations in 55 countries. It operates in seven primary segments: automotive OEM, test & measurement and electronics, food equipment, polymers and fluids, welding, construction products and specialty products. The automotive OEM segment produces components and fasteners for automotive-related applications. Products include plastic and metal components, fasteners and assemblies for automobiles, light trucks and other industrial uses. The test & measurement and electronics segment produces equipment, consumables and related software for testing and measuring of materials and structures as well as equipment and consumables used in the production of electronic subassemblies and microelectronics. The food equipment division provides commercial food equipment and related services. Products include warewashing equipment; cooking and refrigeration equipment; food processing equipment; and kitchen exhaust, ventilation and pollution control systems. The polymer and fluids segment offers adhesives, sealants, lubrication and cutting fluids, janitorial and hygiene products and fluids and polymers for auto aftermarket maintenance and appearance. The welding segment produces arc welding equipment, consumables and accessories for a wide array of industrial and commercial applications. The construction products segment produces tools, fasteners and other products for construction applications. Products include packaged hardware, fasteners, anchors and other products for retail. Finally, the specialty products segment produces beverage packaging equipment and consumables; product coding and marking equipment and consumables; and appliance components and fasteners.

CONTACTS:
Note: Officers with more than one job title may be intentionally listed here more than once.

E. Santi, CEO
Michael Larsen, CFO
Randall Scheuneman, Chief Accounting Officer
Andrew Mines, Executive VP
Steven Martindale, Executive VP
John Hartnett, Executive VP
Michael Zimmerman, Executive VP
Lei Zhang Schlitz, Executive VP
Juan Valls, Executive VP
Sundaram Nagarajan, Executive VP
Norman Finch, General Counsel
Mary Lawler, Other Executive Officer
Christopher OHerlihy, Vice Chairman

FINANCIAL DATA:
Note: Data for latest year may not have been available at press time.

In U.S. $	2018	2017	2016	2015	2014	2013
Revenue	14,768,000,000	14,314,000,000	13,599,000,000	13,405,000,000	14,484,000,000	14,135,000,000
R&D Expense						
Operating Income	3,584,000,000	3,399,000,000	3,064,000,000	2,869,000,000	2,891,000,000	2,516,000,000
Operating Margin %		.24%	.23%	.21%	.20%	.18%
SGA Expense	2,391,000,000	2,400,000,000	2,415,000,000	2,417,000,000	2,678,000,000	2,815,000,000
Net Income	2,563,000,000	1,687,000,000	2,035,000,000	1,899,000,000	2,946,000,000	1,679,000,000
Operating Cash Flow	2,811,000,000	2,402,000,000	2,302,000,000	2,299,000,000	1,616,000,000	2,528,000,000
Capital Expenditure	364,000,000	297,000,000	273,000,000	284,000,000	361,000,000	368,000,000
EBITDA	4,112,000,000	3,992,000,000	3,615,000,000	3,422,000,000	3,456,000,000	3,199,000,000
Return on Assets %		.11%	.13%	.11%	.16%	.09%
Return on Equity %		.38%	.43%	.32%	.36%	.17%
Debt to Equity		1.631	1.687	1.32	0.877	0.288

CONTACT INFORMATION:
Phone: 847 724-7500   Fax: 847 657-4261
Toll-Free:
Address: 155 Harlem Ave., Glenview, IL 60025 United States

STOCK TICKER/OTHER:
Stock Ticker: ITW
Employees: 50,000
Parent Company:

Exchange: NYS
Fiscal Year Ends: 12/31

SALARIES/BONUSES:
Top Exec. Salary: $1,306,747   Bonus: $
Second Exec. Salary: $754,671   Bonus: $

OTHER THOUGHTS:
Estimated Female Officers or Directors: 4
Hot Spot for Advancement for Women/Minorities: Y

Illumina Inc

NAIC Code: 325413

www.illumina.com

TYPES OF BUSINESS:
DNA Analysis Technology
Array Technology
Genotyping Services

BRANDS/DIVISIONS/AFFILIATES:
BeadArray

CONTACTS:
Note: Officers with more than one job title may be intentionally listed here more than once.

Francis DeSouza, CEO
Sam Samad, CFO
Mostafa Ronaghi, Chief Technology Officer
Jay Flatley, Director
Charles Dadswell, General Counsel
Oene Van, Other Executive Officer
Aimee Hoyt, Other Executive Officer
Malcolm Hampton, Senior VP, Divisional
Omead Ostadan, Senior VP, Divisional
Robert Ragusa, Senior VP, Divisional
Karen McGinnis, Vice President

GROWTH PLANS/SPECIAL FEATURES:

Illumina, Inc. provides sequencing- and array-based solutions for genetic analysis. The firm's products and services enable the adoption of genomics solutions in research and clinical settings. Customers include genomic research centers, academic institutions, government laboratories and hospitals, as well as pharmaceutical, biotechnology, commercial molecular diagnostic and consumer genomics companies. Most of the company's product sales consist of instruments and consumables based on proprietary technology, including reagents, flow cells and microarrays. Illumina's genome discovery platform involves sequencing, arrays and consumables. Sequencing is the process of determining the order of nucleotide bases (A, C, G or T) in a DNA sample. Customers use the platforms to perform whole-genome and exome sequencing, as well as targeted sequencing of specific gene regions and genes. Arrays are used for a broad range of DNA (deoxyribonucleic acid) and RNA (ribonucleic acid) analysis applications, including single nucleotide polymorphism (SNP) genotyping, copy number variations (CNV) analysis, gene expression analysis and methylation analysis. The technology allows for the detection of millions of known genetic markers on a single array. The firm's BeadArray technology combines microscopic beads and a substrate in a proprietary manufacturing process to produce arrays that can perform many assays simultaneously. Consumables involve the array-based genotyping consumables that customers use for analyses, including diverse species, disease-related mutations and genetic characteristics associated with cancer. Customers can select from a range of human, animal and agriculturally-relevant genome panels or create their own. Illumina owns or has exclusive licenses to 709 U.S. patents and 529 pending U.S. patent applications, which cover various aspects of its arrays, assays, oligo synthesis, sequencing technology, instruments, digital microfluidics, software, bioinformatics and chemical-detection technologies.

Illumina offers its employees medical, disability, dental, vision and prescription insurance; flexible spending accounts; and a stock purchase plan.

FINANCIAL DATA:
Note: Data for latest year may not have been available at press time.

In U.S. $	2018	2017	2016	2015	2014	2013
Revenue	3,333,000,000	2,752,000,000	2,398,373,000	2,219,762,000	1,861,358,000	1,421,178,000
R&D Expense	623,000,000	546,000,000	504,415,000	401,527,000	388,055,000	276,743,000
Operating Income	883,000,000	606,000,000	579,028,000	623,106,000	443,372,000	254,104,000
Operating Margin %		.22%	.24%	.28%	.24%	.18%
SGA Expense	794,000,000	674,000,000	583,005,000	524,657,000	466,283,000	381,040,000
Net Income	826,000,000	726,000,000	462,649,000	461,559,000	353,351,000	125,308,000
Operating Cash Flow	1,142,000,000	875,000,000	687,238,000	659,596,000	501,271,000	386,421,000
Capital Expenditure	296,000,000	312,000,000	271,381,000	143,247,000	142,216,000	90,559,000
EBITDA	1,130,000,000	1,236,000,000	735,274,000	751,682,000	603,060,000	296,929,000
Return on Assets %		.15%	.11%	.13%	.11%	.04%
Return on Equity %		.29%	.22%	.28%	.24%	.09%
Debt to Equity		0.43	0.477	0.549	0.675	0.547

CONTACT INFORMATION:
Phone: 858 202-4500 Fax: 858 587-4297
Toll-Free: 800-809-4566
Address: 5200 Illumina Way, San Diego, CA 92122 United States

STOCK TICKER/OTHER:
Stock Ticker: ILMN   Exchange: NAS
Employees: 7,300   Fiscal Year Ends: 12/31
Parent Company:

SALARIES/BONUSES:
Top Exec. Salary: $937,692   Bonus: $
Second Exec. Salary: $569,938   Bonus: $

OTHER THOUGHTS:
Estimated Female Officers or Directors:
Hot Spot for Advancement for Women/Minorities:

Ingram Micro Inc

www.ingrammicro.com

NAIC Code: 423430

TYPES OF BUSINESS:
Microcomputers, Distribution
Networking Equipment
Software & Accessories Distribution
Supply Chain Management Services
Online Marketing Services

BRANDS/DIVISIONS/AFFILIATES:
HGN Group Co Ltd
Tianjin Tianhai Investment Co Ltd
CloudBlue

CONTACTS: Note: Officers with more than one job title may be intentionally listed here more than once.
Alain Monie, CEO
William Humes, CFO
Gina Mastantuono, CFO
Larry Boyd, Executive VP
Shailendra Gupta, President, Divisional
Scott Sherman, Vice President, Divisional

GROWTH PLANS/SPECIAL FEATURES:

Ingram Micro, Inc. is a global distributor of IT products. The company markets microcomputer hardware, networking equipment and software products to over 200,000 resellers in approximately 160 countries. Ingram provides a comprehensive inventory of hundreds of thousands of distinct items from approximately 1,700 vendors. Its products are sold in five primary segments: IT peripherals, systems, software, networking and mobility. IT peripherals include printers, scanners, displays, projectors, monitors, panels, mass storage, tape, digital signage products, digital cameras, digital video disc players, game consoles, TVs, audio products, small appliances, media management, home control systems, barcode/card printers, AIDC scanners and software, wireless infrastructure products, physical security products, processors, motherboards, hard drives, memory, as well as ink and toner supplies, paper, carrying cases and anti-glare screens. Systems products include rack, tower and blade servers; desktops; and portable personal computers and tablets. Software products include business application software, operating system software, entertainment software, middleware, developer software tools, security software, storage software and virtualization software. Networking products include networking hardware, communication products and network security hardware such as switches, hubs, routers, wireless local area networks, wireless wide area networks, network interface cards, cellular data cards, network-attached storage and storage area networks. Mobility products include mobile handsets, tablets, navigation devices, aircards, SIM cards, flash memory and other mobile companion products, including health and fitness bands, wearables, app-cessories and services. Ingram also offers supply chain management services such as sales and marketing, customer care, financial services and logistics to suppliers and resellers. Ingram Micro operates as a private subsidiary of Tianjin Tianhai Investment Co. Ltd., which itself is a subsidiary of HGN Group Co. Ltd. During 2018, Ingram Micro formed CloudBlue, a software division that sells the CloudBlue commerce platform directly to service providers.

FINANCIAL DATA: Note: Data for latest year may not have been available at press time.

In U.S. $	2018	2017	2016	2015	2014	2013
Revenue	50,436,670,000	46,674,792,000	41,928,799,000	43,025,850,368	46,487,425,024	42,553,917,440
R&D Expense						
Operating Income						
Operating Margin %						
SGA Expense						
Net Income	352,186,000	198,958,000	100,426,000	215,104,992	266,691,008	310,583,008
Operating Cash Flow						
Capital Expenditure						
EBITDA						
Return on Assets %						
Return on Equity %						
Debt to Equity						

CONTACT INFORMATION:
Phone: 714 566-1000　　Fax: 714 566-7604
Toll-Free:
Address: 3351 Michelson Dr., Ste. 100, Irvine, CA 92612-0697 United States

STOCK TICKER/OTHER:
Stock Ticker: Subsidiary
Employees: 33,000
Parent Company: HNA Group Co Ltd

Exchange:
Fiscal Year Ends: 12/31

SALARIES/BONUSES:
Top Exec. Salary: $　　Bonus: $
Second Exec. Salary: $　　Bonus: $

OTHER THOUGHTS:
Estimated Female Officers or Directors: 2
Hot Spot for Advancement for Women/Minorities: Y

Sales, profits and employees may be estimates. Financial information, benefits and other data can change quickly and may vary from those stated here.

Ingredion Incorporated

NAIC Code: 311221

www.ingredion.us

TYPES OF BUSINESS:
Food Products, Manufacturing
Wet Milling
Food Ingredients
Starch-Based Products
Cornstarch
Liquid Sweeteners

BRANDS/DIVISIONS/AFFILIATES:

CONTACTS: Note: Officers with more than one job title may be intentionally listed here more than once.
James Zallie, CEO
Gregory Kenny, Director
Jorgen Kokke, Executive VP, Divisional
James Gray, Executive VP
Elizabeth Adefioye, Other Executive Officer
Larry Fernandes, Other Executive Officer
Robert Stefansic, Other Executive Officer
Anthony Delio, Other Executive Officer
Pierre Perez Landazuri, President, Divisional
Valdirene Bastos-Licht, President, Geographical
Ernesto Peres Pousada, President, Geographical
Stephen Latreille, Vice President

GROWTH PLANS/SPECIAL FEATURES:

Ingredion Inc. is one of the world's largest corn refiners and a major supplier of food ingredients and industrial products derived from wet milling and processing of corn and other starch-based materials such as tapioca, potatoes and rice. Corn processing is a two-step process. During the front-end process, corn is steeped in a water-based solution and separated into starch and other co-products such as animal feed and germ. The starch is then dried for sale or further processed to make sweeteners and other ingredients that serve the particular needs of various industries. The company's sweetener products include high fructose corn syrup, glucose corn syrups, high maltose corn syrups, caramel color, dextrose, polyols, maltodextrins and glucose and corn syrup solids. Starch-based products include both industrial and food-grade starches. Ingredion's specialty ingredients comprise select starch and sweetener ingredients that provide clean-label solutions that enable front-of-pack claims for customers. The firm serves customers in many diverse industries, including the food and beverage, pharmaceutical, paper products, laminated paper, textile and brewing industries as well as the global animal feed and corn oil markets. Ingredion supplies a broad range of customers, including food, beverage, brewing, pharmaceutical, paper/corrugated products, textile, personal care, animal feed and corn oil markets. Ingredion owns and operates 44 manufacturing facilities worldwide.

FINANCIAL DATA: Note: Data for latest year may not have been available at press time.

In U.S. $	2018	2017	2016	2015	2014	2013
Revenue	6,289,000,000	6,180,000,000	6,022,000,000	5,958,000,000	5,998,000,000	6,653,000,000
R&D Expense						
Operating Income	767,000,000	880,000,000	827,000,000	685,000,000	606,000,000	613,000,000
Operating Margin %		.14%	.14%	.11%	.10%	.09%
SGA Expense			579,000,000	555,000,000	525,000,000	534,000,000
Net Income	443,000,000	519,000,000	485,000,000	402,000,000	355,000,000	396,000,000
Operating Cash Flow	703,000,000	769,000,000	771,000,000	686,000,000	731,000,000	619,000,000
Capital Expenditure	350,000,000	314,000,000	284,000,000	280,000,000	276,000,000	298,000,000
EBITDA	949,000,000	1,057,000,000	1,011,000,000	862,000,000	788,000,000	815,000,000
Return on Assets %		.09%	.09%	.08%	.07%	.07%
Return on Equity %		.19%	.21%	.19%	.15%	.16%
Debt to Equity		0.603	0.721	0.848	0.829	0.714

CONTACT INFORMATION:
Phone: 708-551-2600 Fax: 708-551-2700
Toll-Free: 800-443-2746
Address: 5 Westbrook Corporate Ctr., Westchester, IL 60154 United States

STOCK TICKER/OTHER:
Stock Ticker: INGR
Employees: 11,000
Parent Company:

Exchange: NYS
Fiscal Year Ends: 12/31

SALARIES/BONUSES:
Top Exec. Salary: $950,000 Bonus: $
Second Exec. Salary: $716,931 Bonus: $

OTHER THOUGHTS:
Estimated Female Officers or Directors: 7
Hot Spot for Advancement for Women/Minorities: Y

Sales, profits and employees may be estimates. Financial information, benefits and other data can change quickly and may vary from those stated here.

In-N-Out Burgers Inc

in-n-out.com

NAIC Code: 722513

TYPES OF BUSINESS:
Fast-Food Restaurants
Hamburger Restaurants

BRANDS/DIVISIONS/AFFILIATES:
In-N-Out Burger
Animal Style

CONTACTS:
Note: Officers with more than one job title may be intentionally listed here more than once.

Lynsi Snyder, Pres.
Mark Taylor, COO
Roger Kotch, CFO

GROWTH PLANS/SPECIAL FEATURES:

In-N-Out Burgers, Inc. is a chain of fast food restaurants that began in 1948 and primarily serve hamburgers, French fries, ice cream shakes and beverages. Founded in Baldwin Park, California, it has slowly expanded outside of the state and into Arizona, Nevada, Colorado, Utah, Oregon and Texas with over 333 locations. Hamburgers and cheeseburgers consist of 100% pure beef, American cheese, leaf lettuce, tomato, a special spread, with or without onions and stacked high on a freshly-baked bun. The restaurants have an extras menu where hamburger choices include double meat; 3x3, containing three patties and three slices of cheese; 4x4, four patties and four slices of cheese; protein style, the burger wrapped in lettuce instead of a bun; and Animal Style, which is any size burger choice with the patties cooked with mustard and all the fixings. All hamburger patties are free of additives, fillers and preservatives of any kind. The firm pays a premium to purchase fresh, high quality beef chuck, and has in-house butchers that remove the bones, grind the meat and make every patty ready for cooking. Potatoes are shipped directly from farms, individually cut in the firm's stores, then cooked in 100% pure vegetable oil. Shakes are made with milk and real ice cream. In-N-Out's website offers products to purchase such as apparel, gift cards and other items, as well as limited time offers.

Typical fast food equipment such as heat lamps, microwaves and freezers are never found in their kitchens. The firm offers full-time employees a comprehensive health plan; paid holidays and vacations; and a 401(k) plan. Pay levels are far above the industry average. It receives high ranks in many surveys of top employers. Employees also enjoy flexible work schedules, ongoing training programs (In-N-Out University) and promote-from-within opportunities.

FINANCIAL DATA:
Note: Data for latest year may not have been available at press time.

In U.S. $	2018	2017	2016	2015	2014	2013
Revenue	984,900,000	938,000,000	870,000,000	740,000,000	630,000,000	558,200,000
R&D Expense						
Operating Income						
Operating Margin %						
SGA Expense						
Net Income		95,000,000	88,000,000	75,000,000	64,000,000	57,000,000
Operating Cash Flow						
Capital Expenditure						
EBITDA						
Return on Assets %						
Return on Equity %						
Debt to Equity						

CONTACT INFORMATION:
Phone: 949-509-6200   Fax: 949-509-6389
Toll-Free: 800-786-1000
Address: 4199 Campus Dr., Fl. 9, Irvine, CA 92612 United States

STOCK TICKER/OTHER:
Stock Ticker: Private
Employees: 26,000
Parent Company:

Exchange:
Fiscal Year Ends: 12/31

SALARIES/BONUSES:
Top Exec. Salary: $ Bonus: $
Second Exec. Salary: $ Bonus: $

OTHER THOUGHTS:
Estimated Female Officers or Directors:
Hot Spot for Advancement for Women/Minorities: Y

Intel Corporation

NAIC Code: 334413

www.intel.com

TYPES OF BUSINESS:
Microprocessors
Semiconductors
Circuit Boards
Flash Memory Products
Software Development
Home Network Equipment
Digital Imaging Products
Healthcare Products

BRANDS/DIVISIONS/AFFILIATES:
Intel Neural Compute Stick 2

CONTACTS:
Note: Officers with more than one job title may be intentionally listed here more than once.
Robert Swan, CEO
George Davis, CFO
Andy Bryant, Chairman of the Board
Kevin McBride, Chief Accounting Officer
Steven Rodgers, Executive VP
Navin Shenoy, Executive VP
Venkata Renduchintala, Executive VP
Todd Underwood, Other Corporate Officer

GROWTH PLANS/SPECIAL FEATURES:
Intel Corporation designs and manufactures products and technologies that power the cloud and smart connectivity. The company produces computer, networking and communications platforms to a broad set of customers, including original equipment manufacturers (OEMs), original design manufacturers (ODMs), cloud and communications service providers, as well as industrial, communications and automotive equipment manufacturers. Intel's business across the cloud and data center are focused on memory and field-programmable gate array technologies. Its devices include everything smart: personal computers (PCs), sensors, consoles and other edge devices that are connected to the cloud. Memory and programmable solutions make possible new classes of products for the data center and Internet of Things. Intel is a leader in silicon manufacturing process technology, of which its products are manufactured in the company's own facilities. Its intellectual property can be shared across its platforms and operating segments, providing cost reduction and seamless production capabilities. Intel also offers software and services for consumer and corporate environments, as well as for assisting software developers in creating software applications via Intel platforms. Its client computing product group includes platforms for notebooks, 2-in-1 systems, desktops, tablets, phones, wired/wireless connectivity products and mobile communications components. The firm's non-volatile memory solutions (NAND) flash memory products are primarily used in solid-state drives. In November 2018, Intel introduced the Intel Neural Compute Stick 2 (Intel NCS 2), which is designed to build smarter artificial intelligence (AI) algorithms and for prototyping computer vision at the network edge.

FINANCIAL DATA:
Note: Data for latest year may not have been available at press time.

In U.S. $	2018	2017	2016	2015	2014	2013
Revenue	70,848,000,000	62,761,000,000	59,387,000,000	55,355,000,000	55,870,000,000	52,708,000,000
R&D Expense	13,543,000,000	13,098,000,000	12,740,000,000	12,128,000,000	11,537,000,000	10,611,000,000
Operating Income	23,244,000,000	18,320,000,000	14,760,000,000	14,356,000,000	15,642,000,000	12,531,000,000
Operating Margin %		.29%	.25%	.26%	.28%	.24%
SGA Expense	6,750,000,000	7,474,000,000	8,397,000,000	7,930,000,000	8,136,000,000	8,088,000,000
Net Income	21,053,000,000	9,601,000,000	10,316,000,000	11,420,000,000	11,704,000,000	9,620,000,000
Operating Cash Flow	29,432,000,000	22,110,000,000	21,808,000,000	19,017,000,000	20,418,000,000	20,776,000,000
Capital Expenditure	15,181,000,000	11,778,000,000	9,625,000,000	7,446,000,000	10,197,000,000	10,747,000,000
EBITDA	32,870,000,000	29,127,000,000	21,459,000,000	23,260,000,000	24,542,000,000	20,887,000,000
Return on Assets %		.08%	.10%	.12%	.13%	.11%
Return on Equity %		.14%	.16%	.20%	.21%	.18%
Debt to Equity		0.363	0.312	0.328	0.217	0.226

CONTACT INFORMATION:
Phone: 408 765-8080 Fax: 408 765-2633
Toll-Free: 800-628-8686
Address: 2200 Mission College Blvd., Santa Clara, CA 95054 United States

STOCK TICKER/OTHER:
Stock Ticker: INTC
Employees: 106,000
Parent Company:

Exchange: NAS
Fiscal Year Ends: 12/31

SALARIES/BONUSES:
Top Exec. Salary: $898,000 Bonus: $2,500,000
Second Exec. Salary: $1,008,000 Bonus: $

OTHER THOUGHTS:
Estimated Female Officers or Directors: 10
Hot Spot for Advancement for Women/Minorities: Y

Interpublic Group of Companies Inc

www.interpublic.com

NAIC Code: 541810

TYPES OF BUSINESS:
Advertising Services
Marketing & Branding
Market Research
Public Relations
Online Marketing
Direct Marketing
Promotions & Events
Sports & Entertainment Marketing

BRANDS/DIVISIONS/AFFILIATES:
McCann Worldgroup
Foot Con & Belding
MullenLowe Group
Weber Shandwick
Golin
FutureBrand
Jack Morton
Octagon Worldwide

CONTACTS:
Note: Officers with more than one job title may be intentionally listed here more than once.

Michael Roth, CEO
Ellen Johnson, CFO, Subsidiary
Frank Mergenthaler, CFO
Christopher Carroll, Chief Accounting Officer
Julie Connors, Chief Risk Officer
Andrew Bonzani, Executive VP
Philippe Krakowsky, Executive VP

GROWTH PLANS/SPECIAL FEATURES:

Interpublic Group of Companies, Inc. (IPG) is a group comprising hundreds of advertising and specialized marketing and communications services companies that combined represent one of the largest resources of advertising and marketing expertise in the world, with offices and affiliations in over 100 countries. The firm has three global networks: McCann Worldgroup; Foot, Cone & Belding; and MullenLowe Group. IPG operates through two divisions: integrated agency networks (IAN) and constituency management group (CMG). IAN is comprised of its three global networks and IPG Mediabrands. IAN agencies provide an array of global communications and marketing services, each offering a distinctive range of solutions. Its digital specialist agencies provide digital capabilities, and its domestic integrated agencies provide advertising, marketing, communications services and/or marketing services and partner with the firm's global operating divisions as needed. CMG has a number of specialist marketing service offerings which include Weber Shandwick, Golin, FutureBrand, Jack Morton and Octagon Worldwide. These marketing service subsidiaries provide clients with public relations, meeting and event production, sports and entertainment marketing, corporate and brand identity and marketing consulting. IPG's largest client sectors include the auto, transportation, healthcare, technology and telecom. In October 2018, the firm completed the acquisition Acxiom LLC, formerly Acxiom Marketing Solutions, from Acxiom corporation for $2.3 billion.

FINANCIAL DATA:
Note: Data for latest year may not have been available at press time.

In U.S. $	2018	2017	2016	2015	2014	2013
Revenue	9,714,400,000	7,882,400,000	7,846,600,000	7,613,800,000	7,537,100,000	7,122,300,000
R&D Expense						
Operating Income	1,008,800,000	973,600,000	938,000,000	871,100,000	788,600,000	658,900,000
Operating Margin %		.12%	.12%	.11%	.10%	.09%
SGA Expense	166,500,000	1,840,700,000	1,870,500,000	1,885,000,000	1,928,100,000	1,917,900,000
Net Income	618,900,000	579,000,000	608,500,000	454,600,000	477,100,000	267,900,000
Operating Cash Flow	565,100,000	881,800,000	513,400,000	674,000,000	669,500,000	592,900,000
Capital Expenditure	177,100,000	155,900,000	200,700,000	161,100,000	148,700,000	173,000,000
EBITDA	1,163,900,000	1,123,900,000	1,081,000,000	1,005,000,000	968,600,000	748,100,000
Return on Assets %		.05%	.05%	.04%	.04%	.02%
Return on Equity %		.27%	.31%	.22%	.22%	.12%
Debt to Equity		0.584	0.635	0.819	0.767	0.51

CONTACT INFORMATION:
Phone: 212 704-1200 Fax: 212 399-8130
Toll-Free:
Address: 909 Third Ave., New York, NY 10022 United States

STOCK TICKER/OTHER:
Stock Ticker: IPG
Employees: 49,800
Parent Company:

Exchange: NYS
Fiscal Year Ends: 12/31

SALARIES/BONUSES:
Top Exec. Salary: $1,500,000 Bonus: $
Second Exec. Salary: $1,250,000 Bonus: $

OTHER THOUGHTS:
Estimated Female Officers or Directors: 9
Hot Spot for Advancement for Women/Minorities: Y

Sales, profits and employees may be estimates. Financial information, benefits and other data can change quickly and may vary from those stated here.

Intuit Inc

www.intuit.com

NAIC Code: 0

TYPES OF BUSINESS:
Computer Software-Financial Management
Business Accounting Software
Consumer Finance Software
Tax Preparation Software
Online Financial Services

BRANDS/DIVISIONS/AFFILIATES:
QuickBooks Online
Mint
Turbo
Turbo Tax
Intuit Tax Freedom Project
Lacerte
ProSeries
ProConnect Tax Online

CONTACTS:
Note: Officers with more than one job title may be intentionally listed here more than once.

Sasan Goodarzi, CEO
Michelle Clatterbuck, CFO
Brad Smith, Chairman of the Board
Mark Flournoy, Chief Accounting Officer
Marianna Tessel, Chief Technology Officer
Alex Chriss, Executive VP, Divisional
Gregory Johnson, Executive VP
Laura Fennell, Executive VP
Scott Cook, Founder
Kerry McLean, General Counsel

GROWTH PLANS/SPECIAL FEATURES:

Intuit, Inc. is a provider of software and web-based services, specializing in financial management and tax solutions. The company has three business segments: small business, consumer and strategic partner. The small business segment targets small businesses, as well as the accounting professionals who serve them. This division's products include QuickBooks Online, which offers financial management tools; online payroll solutions; online payment solutions; an Intuit developer group, which provides tools that third-party developers need to create online and mobile applications that personalize and add value to QuickBooks; desktop payments solutions; technical support; and financial supplies. The consumer segment offers the Mint and Turbo brands of financial improvement products. Mint and Turbo help consumers understand and improve their financial lives by offering a view of their financial health. Turbo Tax solutions are designed to enable individuals to prepare and file their own federal and state personal income tax returns quickly and accurately. This division's Intuit Tax Freedom Project offers online federal and state income tax return preparation and electronic filing services at no charge to eligible taxpayers. The strategic partner segment targets professional accountants in the U.S. and Canada, who are essential to both small business success and tax preparation and filing. This division's tax offerings include Lacerte, ProSeries, ProFile and ProConnect Tax Online. During 2018, the firm acquired Exactor, Inc.; TSheets.com, LLC; and Applatix, Inc.

Intuit employees receive health, dental and life insurance; and 401(k) and employee stock purchase plans.

FINANCIAL DATA:
Note: Data for latest year may not have been available at press time.

In U.S. $	2018	2017	2016	2015	2014	2013
Revenue	5,964,000,000	5,177,000,000	4,694,000,000	4,192,000,000	4,506,000,000	4,171,000,000
R&D Expense	1,186,000,000	998,000,000	881,000,000	798,000,000	758,000,000	685,000,000
Operating Income	1,497,000,000	1,395,000,000	1,242,000,000	886,000,000	1,314,000,000	1,233,000,000
Operating Margin %		.27%	.26%	.21%	.29%	.30%
SGA Expense	2,298,000,000	1,973,000,000	1,807,000,000	1,771,000,000	1,746,000,000	1,641,000,000
Net Income	1,211,000,000	971,000,000	979,000,000	365,000,000	907,000,000	858,000,000
Operating Cash Flow	2,112,000,000	1,599,000,000	1,401,000,000	1,504,000,000	1,446,000,000	1,366,000,000
Capital Expenditure	124,000,000	230,000,000	522,000,000	261,000,000	201,000,000	209,000,000
EBITDA	1,776,000,000	1,634,000,000	1,476,000,000	970,000,000	1,542,000,000	1,472,000,000
Return on Assets %		.23%	.21%	.07%	.17%	.17%
Return on Equity %		.77%	.56%	.13%	.27%	.27%
Debt to Equity		0.323	0.42	0.214	0.162	0.141

CONTACT INFORMATION:
Phone: 650 944-6000 Fax: 650 944-3060
Toll-Free: 800-446-8848
Address: 2700 Coast Ave., Mountain View, CA 94043 United States

SALARIES/BONUSES:
Top Exec. Salary: $1,000,000 Bonus: $
Second Exec. Salary: $750,000 Bonus: $

STOCK TICKER/OTHER:
Stock Ticker: INTU
Employees: 8,200
Parent Company:

Exchange: NAS
Fiscal Year Ends: 07/31

OTHER THOUGHTS:
Estimated Female Officers or Directors: 5
Hot Spot for Advancement for Women/Minorities: Y

IQVIA Holdings Inc

NAIC Code: 541711

www.iqvia.com

TYPES OF BUSINESS:
Contract Research
Pharmaceutical, Biotech & Medical Device Research
Consulting & Training Services
Sales & Marketing Services

BRANDS/DIVISIONS/AFFILIATES:
IQVIA CORE

CONTACTS:
Note: Officers with more than one job title may be intentionally listed here more than once.
Michael Mcdonnell, CFO
Ari Bousbib, Chairman of the Board
Emmanuel Korakis, Chief Accounting Officer
Eric Sherbet, Executive VP
W. Staub, President, Divisional
Kevin Knightly, President, Divisional

GROWTH PLANS/SPECIAL FEATURES:
IQVIA Holdings, Inc. provides advanced analytics, technology solutions and contract research services to the life sciences industry. The firm applies human data science, leveraging analytics and data science to the scope of human science, to enable companies to reimagine and develop new approaches to clinical development and commercialization, speed innovation and accelerate improvements in healthcare outcomes. Its IQVIA CORE platform delivers actionable insights at the intersection of large-scale analytics, transformative technology and extensive domain expertise as well as execution capabilities to help biotech, medical device and pharmaceutical companies, medical researchers, government agencies, payers and other healthcare stakeholders better understand diseases, human behaviors and scientific advances, for the purpose of finding cures. Capabilities of the company include healthcare-specific global IT infrastructure, analytics-driven clinical development, real-world insights ecosystem, proprietary clinical and commercial applications and more. IQVIA'a product portfolio spans research and development, pre-launch, launch and in-market. The company conducts operations in more than 100 countries worldwide.

FINANCIAL DATA:
Note: Data for latest year may not have been available at press time.

In U.S. $	2018	2017	2016	2015	2014	2013
Revenue	10,412,000,000	9,739,000,000	6,878,000,000	5,737,619,000	5,459,998,000	5,099,545,000
R&D Expense						
Operating Income	809,000,000	822,000,000	828,000,000	679,848,000	599,378,000	476,404,000
Operating Margin %		.08%	.12%	.12%	.11%	.09%
SGA Expense	1,716,000,000	1,605,000,000	1,011,000,000	920,985,000	882,338,000	860,510,000
Net Income	259,000,000	1,309,000,000	115,000,000	387,205,000	356,383,000	226,591,000
Operating Cash Flow	1,254,000,000	970,000,000	860,000,000	475,691,000	431,754,000	397,370,000
Capital Expenditure	459,000,000	369,000,000	164,000,000	78,391,000	82,650,000	92,346,000
EBITDA	1,883,000,000	1,688,000,000	912,000,000	768,529,000	723,791,000	554,128,000
Return on Assets %		.06%	.01%	.11%	.11%	.08%
Return on Equity %		.16%	.03%			
Debt to Equity		1.248	0.823			

CONTACT INFORMATION:
Phone: 919-998-2000 Fax:
Toll-Free: 866-267-4479
Address: 4820 Emperor Blvd., Durham, NC 27703 United States

SALARIES/BONUSES:
Top Exec. Salary: $1,600,000   Bonus: $
Second Exec. Salary: $650,000   Bonus: $

STOCK TICKER/OTHER:
Stock Ticker: IQV   Exchange: NYS
Employees: 50,000   Fiscal Year Ends: 12/31
Parent Company:

OTHER THOUGHTS:
Estimated Female Officers or Directors: 3
Hot Spot for Advancement for Women/Minorities: Y

Jabil Inc

NAIC Code: 334418

www.jabil.com

TYPES OF BUSINESS:
Contract Electronics Manufacturing
Maintenance & Support Services
Custom Design Services

BRANDS/DIVISIONS/AFFILIATES:

CONTACTS:
Note: Officers with more than one job title may be intentionally listed here more than once.

Michael Loparco, CEO, Divisional
Alessandro Parimbelli, CEO, Divisional
Steven Borges, CEO, Divisional
Kenneth Wilson, CEO, Divisional
Brenda Chamulak, CEO, Divisional
Mark Mondello, CEO
Meheryar Dastoor, CFO
Timothy Main, Chairman of the Board
Thomas Sansone, Director
Courtney Ryan, Executive VP, Divisional
Robert Katz, Executive VP
Bruce Johnson, Other Executive Officer
Daryn Smith, Senior VP, Divisional
Sergio Cadavid, Senior VP

GROWTH PLANS/SPECIAL FEATURES:

Jabil, Inc. is a provider of worldwide electronic manufacturing services and solutions. Through its more than 100 plants in 29 countries, the firm develops and manufactures products that help to connect people, advance technology and more. Jabil divides its operations into two segments: diversified manufacturing services (DMS) and electronics manufacturing services (EMS). DMS is focused on providing engineering solutions and on material sciences and technologies. This segment includes customers primarily in the consumer lifestyles and wearable technologies, defense & aerospace, emerging growth, healthcare, mobility and packaging industries. EMS is focused around leveraging information technology, supply chain design and engineering, technologies largely centered on core electronics, sharing of Jabil's large-scale manufacturing infrastructure and the ability to serve a broad range of end markets. This segment includes customers primarily in the automotive, digital home, industrial and energy, networking and telecommunications, point of sale, printing and storage industries. As of fiscal 2018, Jabil's largest customers include Apple, Inc.; Cisco Systems, Inc.; Hewlett-Packard Company; Keysight Technologies; LM Ericsson Telephone Company; NetApp, Inc.; Nokia Networks; SolarEdge Technologies, Inc.; Valeo SA; and Zebra Technologies Corporation.

FINANCIAL DATA:
Note: Data for latest year may not have been available at press time.

In U.S. $	2018	2017	2016	2015	2014	2013
Revenue	22,095,420,000	19,063,120,000	18,353,090,000	17,899,200,000	15,762,150,000	18,336,890,000
R&D Expense	38,531,000	29,680,000	31,954,000	27,645,000	28,611,000	28,468,000
Operating Income	579,055,000	572,737,000	534,202,000	588,477,000	297,405,000	626,488,000
Operating Margin %		.03%	.03%	.03%	.02%	.03%
SGA Expense	1,050,716,000	907,702,000	924,427,000	862,647,000	675,730,000	688,752,000
Net Income	86,330,000	129,090,000	254,095,000	284,019,000	241,313,000	371,482,000
Operating Cash Flow	933,850,000	1,256,643,000	916,207,000	1,240,282,000	498,857,000	1,213,889,000
Capital Expenditure	1,036,651,000	716,485,000	924,239,000	963,145,000	624,060,000	736,858,000
EBITDA	1,296,107,000	1,154,712,000	1,220,333,000	1,088,913,000	687,456,000	925,243,000
Return on Assets %		.01%	.03%	.03%	.03%	.04%
Return on Equity %		.05%	.11%	.12%	.11%	.17%
Debt to Equity		0.694	0.851	0.582	0.745	0.724

CONTACT INFORMATION:
Phone: 727 577-9749 Fax: 727 579-8529
Toll-Free:
Address: 10560 Dr. Martin Luther King Jr. St. N., St. Petersburg, FL 33716 United States

STOCK TICKER/OTHER:
Stock Ticker: JBL
Employees: 179,333
Parent Company:

Exchange: NYS
Fiscal Year Ends: 08/31

SALARIES/BONUSES:
Top Exec. Salary: $1,150,000 Bonus: $
Second Exec. Salary: $720,000 Bonus: $

OTHER THOUGHTS:
Estimated Female Officers or Directors:
Hot Spot for Advancement for Women/Minorities: Y

Sales, profits and employees may be estimates. Financial information, benefits and other data can change quickly and may vary from those stated here.

Jack Henry & Associates Inc

www.jackhenry.com

NAIC Code: 0

TYPES OF BUSINESS:
Software-Data Processing
Financial Services Software
Consulting Services
Hardware Sales

BRANDS/DIVISIONS/AFFILIATES:
Jack Henry Banking
Symitar
ProfitStars
SilverLake
CIF 20/20
Core Director
Episys
Ensenta Corporation

CONTACTS:
Note: Officers with more than one job title may be intentionally listed here more than once.

David Foss, CEO
Kevin Williams, CFO
John Prim, Chairman of the Board
Mark Forbis, Chief Technology Officer
Matthew Flanigan, Director
Craig Morgan, General Counsel
Gregory Adelson, General Manager, Divisional
Ronald Moses, General Manager, Divisional
Russell Bernthal, President, Divisional
Teddy Bilke, President, Divisional
Stacey Zengel, President, Divisional

GROWTH PLANS/SPECIAL FEATURES:

Jack Henry & Associates, Inc. is a provider of integrated computer systems relating to data processing and management information for banks, credit unions and other financial institutions in the U.S. The company serves more than 9,000 financial institutions and corporate entities. It provides products and services through three marketed brands: Jack Henry Banking, Symitar and ProfitStars. Jack Henry Banking currently supports more than 1,100 commercial banks ranging from community banks to multi-billion-dollar banks, with information and transaction processing platforms that provide enterprise-wide automation. Its core banking software platforms include SilverLake, an IBM System i-based product designed for commercial-focused banks with assets ranging from $1 billion to $30 billion, as well as some progressive smaller banks and startup banks; CIF 20/20, an IBM-System i-based system that supports more than 700 banks; and Core Director, a Windows-based client/server system that serves more than 200 banks ranging from new institutions to banks with assets over $2 billion. The Symitar brand supports credit unions through its two core platforms: Episys, an IBM power system-based program designed for credit unions with more than $1 billion in assets; and CruiseNet, designed for credit unions with $1 million to $50 million in assets. ProfitStars provides specialized products and services to over 8,000 financial services organizations. Products include business intelligence and management applications, retail delivery products, business banking systems, electronic funds transfer products, internet banking products, risk management and protection programs, document imaging products and professional services and education products.

The firm offers employees medical, dental and vision insurance; flexible spending accounts; and education assistance.

FINANCIAL DATA:
Note: Data for latest year may not have been available at press time.

In U.S. $	2018	2017	2016	2015	2014	2013
Revenue	1,536,603,000	1,431,117,000	1,354,646,000	1,256,190,000	1,210,053,000	1,129,386,000
R&D Expense	90,340,000	84,753,000	81,234,000	71,495,000	66,748,000	63,202,000
Operating Income	390,475,000	364,432,000	342,168,000	317,865,000	311,999,000	265,547,000
Operating Margin %		.25%	.25%	.25%	.26%	.24%
SGA Expense	182,146,000	162,898,000	157,593,000	146,494,000	139,882,000	148,243,000
Net Income	376,660,000	245,793,000	248,867,000	211,221,000	201,136,000	176,645,000
Operating Cash Flow	412,142,000	357,322,000	365,116,000	373,790,000	341,659,000	309,174,000
Capital Expenditure	149,920,000	148,186,000	164,562,000	145,301,000	111,667,000	97,774,000
EBITDA	544,930,000	507,736,000	491,614,000	437,030,000	420,147,000	366,528,000
Return on Assets %		.13%	.14%	.12%	.12%	.11%
Return on Equity %		.24%	.25%	.21%	.19%	.17%
Debt to Equity		0.048		0.051	0.004	0.007

CONTACT INFORMATION:
Phone: 417 235-6652 Fax:
Toll-Free: 800-299-4222
Address: 663 W. Highway 60, Monett, MO 65708 United States

SALARIES/BONUSES:
Top Exec. Salary: $675,000 Bonus: $
Second Exec. Salary: $461,250 Bonus: $

STOCK TICKER/OTHER:
Stock Ticker: JKHY
Employees: 5,972
Parent Company:

Exchange: NAS
Fiscal Year Ends: 06/30

OTHER THOUGHTS:
Estimated Female Officers or Directors: 3
Hot Spot for Advancement for Women/Minorities: Y

Sales, profits and employees may be estimates. Financial information, benefits and other data can change quickly and may vary from those stated here.

Jacobs Engineering Group Inc

www.jacobs.com

NAIC Code: 237000

TYPES OF BUSINESS:
Engineering & Design Services
Facility Management
Construction & Field Services
Technical Consulting Services
Environmental Services

BRANDS/DIVISIONS/AFFILIATES:

CONTACTS:
Note: Officers with more than one job title may be intentionally listed here more than once.

Steven Demetriou, CEO
Kevin Berryman, CFO
Joanne Caruso, Chief Administrative Officer
Michael Tyler, Chief Compliance Officer
Robert Pragada, COO
Dawne Hickton, Executive VP
Vinayak Pai, President, Divisional
William Allen, Senior VP

GROWTH PLANS/SPECIAL FEATURES:

Jacobs Engineering Group, Inc. offers technical, professional and construction services to industrial, commercial and governmental clients throughout the Americas, Europe, Asia, India, the Middle East, Africa, the U.K. and Australia. Jacobs provides project services, which include engineering, design and architecture; process, scientific and systems consulting services; operations and maintenance services; and construction services, which include direct-hire construction and management services. Services are offered to industry groups such as oil and gas exploration, production and refining; pharmaceuticals and biotechnology; chemicals and polymers; buildings, which includes projects in the fields of health care and education as well as civic, governmental and other buildings; infrastructure; technology; energy; consumer and forest products; automotive and industrial; and environmental programs. Jacobs also provides pricing studies, project feasibility reports and automation and control system analysis for U.S. government agencies involved in defense and aerospace programs. In addition, the company is one of the leading providers of environmental engineering and consulting services in the U.S. and abroad, providing support in such areas as underground storage tank removal, contaminated soil and water remediation and long-term groundwater monitoring. Jacobs also designs, builds, installs, operates and maintains various types of soil and groundwater cleanup systems. In October 2018, Jacobs agreed to sell its energy, chemicals and resource operations to Worley Parsons Limited for approximately $3.3 billion; the transaction was expected to close by mid-2019. Afterward, the firm will focus on two lines of business: aerospace, technology, environmental and nuclear (ATEN); and buildings, infrastructure and advanced facilities (BIAF).

Jacobs offers its employees medical, disability, life and AD&D insurance; an employee stock purchase plan; and tuition reimbursement.

FINANCIAL DATA:
Note: Data for latest year may not have been available at press time.

In U.S. $	2018	2017	2016	2015	2014	2013
Revenue	14,984,650,000	10,022,790,000	10,964,160,000	12,114,830,000	12,695,160,000	11,818,380,000
R&D Expense						
Operating Income	647,971,000	392,269,000	338,598,000	445,527,000	528,068,000	668,979,000
Operating Margin %		.04%	.03%	.04%	.04%	.06%
SGA Expense	2,180,399,000	1,379,983,000	1,429,233,000	1,522,811,000	1,545,716,000	1,173,340,000
Net Income	163,431,000	293,727,000	210,463,000	302,971,000	328,108,000	423,093,000
Operating Cash Flow	481,152,000	574,881,000	680,173,000	484,572,000	721,716,000	448,516,000
Capital Expenditure	94,884,000	118,060,000	77,715,000	88,404,000	132,146,000	127,270,000
EBITDA	830,052,000	527,765,000	431,954,000	598,932,000	699,015,000	773,328,000
Return on Assets %		.04%	.03%	.04%	.04%	.06%
Return on Equity %		.07%	.05%	.07%	.08%	.11%
Debt to Equity		0.053	0.09	0.136	0.171	0.099

CONTACT INFORMATION:
Phone: 214-583-8500 Fax:
Toll-Free:
Address: 1999 Bryan St., Ste. 1200, Dallas, CA 75201 United States

SALARIES/BONUSES:
Top Exec. Salary: $1,300,000 Bonus: $
Second Exec. Salary: $713,269 Bonus: $300,000

STOCK TICKER/OTHER:
Stock Ticker: JEC
Employees: 43,800
Parent Company:

Exchange: NYS
Fiscal Year Ends: 09/30

OTHER THOUGHTS:
Estimated Female Officers or Directors: 1
Hot Spot for Advancement for Women/Minorities: Y

JB Hunt Transport Services Inc

www.jbhunt.com

NAIC Code: 484121

TYPES OF BUSINESS:
General Freight Trucking
Logistics Services
Intermodal Services
Dedicated Fleet Services
Local Delivery
Oversize Consumer Deliveries
Warehousing

BRANDS/DIVISIONS/AFFILIATES:

CONTACTS:
Note: Officers with more than one job title may be intentionally listed here more than once.

Kevin Bracy, Assistant Secretary
John Roberts, CEO
David Mee, CFO
Kirk Thompson, Chairman of the Board
John Kuhlow, Chief Accounting Officer
Stuart Scott, Chief Information Officer
Shelley Simpson, Chief Medical Officer
Craig Harper, Executive VP
Darren Field, Executive VP, Divisional
Bradley Hicks, Executive VP, Divisional
Eric McGee, Executive VP, Divisional
Nicholas Hobbs, Executive VP
Terrence Matthews, Executive VP
Jennifer Boattini, General Counsel

GROWTH PLANS/SPECIAL FEATURES:

J.B. Hunt Transport Services, Inc. is a North American truckload transportation and logistics company serving the U.S., Canada and Mexico. The firm's operations are organized into four business segments: intermodal (JBI), dedicated contract services (DCS), truckload (JBT) and integrated capacity solutions (ICS). The JBI segment utilizes agreements with rail carriers under which those carriers provide for railway movement of goods, while J.B. Hunt provides for the drayage (i.e. transport of goods by truck to and from rail terminals). The segment operates 77,946 company-controlled containers system wide. It also manages a fleet of 4,776 company-owned tractors. The DCS segment involves the provision of customized services governed by long-term contracts and currently includes dry-van, flatbed, temperature-controlled, dump trailers and local inner-city operations. This segment specializes in the design, development and execution of customer-specific fleet services, including private fleet conversion, dedicated fleet creation and transportation system augmentation. It operates 8,124 company-owned trucks, 544 customer-owned trucks and 59 independent contractor trucks. The JBT segment offers full-load, dry-van freight, utilizing tractors operating over roads and highways. This segment operates 1,291 company-owned tractors. The ICS segment provides traditional freight brokerage and transportation logistics solutions to customers. These solutions include flatbed, refrigerated, expedited and less-than-truckload services, as well as a variety of dry-van and intermodal solutions. This division operates 44 remote sales offices or branches, as well as on-site logistics personnel working directly with customers as needed.

The firm offers medical, dental, vision, life, disability, auto and home insurance; a 401(k) plan; and healthcare and dependent care reimbursement accounts.

FINANCIAL DATA:
Note: Data for latest year may not have been available at press time.

In U.S. $	2018	2017	2016	2015	2014	2013
Revenue	8,614,874,000	7,189,568,000	6,555,459,000	6,187,646,000	6,165,441,000	5,584,571,000
R&D Expense						
Operating Income	681,021,000	623,789,000	721,020,000	715,694,000	631,542,000	576,708,000
Operating Margin %		.09%	.11%	.12%	.10%	.10%
SGA Expense	323,587,000	273,440,000	185,436,000	166,799,000	152,469,000	119,769,000
Net Income	489,585,000	686,263,000	432,090,000	427,235,000	374,792,000	342,382,000
Operating Cash Flow	1,087,841,000	855,153,000	854,143,000	873,308,000	646,779,000	574,351,000
Capital Expenditure	995,650,000	526,928,000	638,430,000	725,122,000	808,569,000	493,431,000
EBITDA	1,117,138,000	1,007,542,000	1,082,601,000	1,055,393,000	926,125,000	830,157,000
Return on Assets %		.17%	.12%	.12%	.12%	.13%
Return on Equity %		.42%	.32%	.34%	.34%	.38%
Debt to Equity		0.59	0.697	0.773	0.567	0.453

CONTACT INFORMATION:
Phone: 479 820-0000 Fax:
Toll-Free: 800-643-3622
Address: 615 J.B. Hunt Corporate Dr., Lowell, AR 72745-0130 United States

STOCK TICKER/OTHER:
Stock Ticker: JBHT
Employees: 22,190
Parent Company:

Exchange: NAS
Fiscal Year Ends: 12/31

SALARIES/BONUSES:
Top Exec. Salary: $845,298 Bonus: $
Second Exec. Salary: $500,630 Bonus: $

OTHER THOUGHTS:
Estimated Female Officers or Directors: 4
Hot Spot for Advancement for Women/Minorities: Y

JetBlue Airways Corporation

NAIC Code: 481111

www.jetblue.com

TYPES OF BUSINESS:
Airline
In-Flight Entertainment

BRANDS/DIVISIONS/AFFILIATES:
Fly-Fi
JetBlue Technology Ventures
JetSuite X
TWO Flight Center Hotel
JetBlue Travel Products

CONTACTS:
Note: Officers with more than one job title may be intentionally listed here more than once.

Robin Hayes, CEO
Stephen Priest, CFO
Joel Peterson, Chairman of the Board
Alexander Chatkewitz, Chief Accounting Officer
Eash Sundaram, Chief Technology Officer
Joanna Geraghty, COO
Frank Sica, Director
Martin St George, Executive VP
Brandon Nelson, General Counsel

GROWTH PLANS/SPECIAL FEATURES:

JetBlue Airways Corporation is a low-fare, low-cost passenger airline. The company primarily operates on point-to-point routes with its fleet of Airbus and Embraer aircraft. JetBlue serves 102 cities in the U.S., Caribbean and Latin America. Most of its 1000+ daily flights have an origin or destination with one of the company's six focus cities: Boston, Fort Lauderdale, Los Angeles/Long Beach, New York, Orlando and San Juan, Puerto Rico. In-flight entertainment options consist of gate-to-gate Fly-Fi service, offering more than 100 channels of DirecTV, Sirius XM Radio and movies, and on the Airbus A321, a 15-inch interactive video screen. The Fly-Fi network offers complementary in-flight WiFi on all flights, at speeds of 12-15 megabits per second. Subsidiaries and investment by JetBlue include: wholly-owned JetBlue Technology Ventures, which invests in and partners with early-stage startups in the travel, hospitality and transportation space; 10%-owned JetSuiteX, which invests in innovative ideas and aims to branch JetBlue further along the west coast; wholly-owned TWA Flight Center Hotel, which is located at JFK airport and offers more than 500 rooms; and wholly-owned JetBlue Travel Products, which sells travel insurance, car rentals and cruise line packages.

JetBlue offers employees medical, dental, vision and life insurance; short- and long-term disability insurance; 401(k); and various employee assistance programs.

FINANCIAL DATA:
Note: Data for latest year may not have been available at press time.

In U.S. $	2018	2017	2016	2015	2014	2013
Revenue	7,658,000,000	7,015,000,000	6,632,000,000	6,416,000,000	5,817,000,000	5,441,000,000
R&D Expense						
Operating Income	723,000,000	1,000,000,000	1,312,000,000	1,216,000,000	515,000,000	428,000,000
Operating Margin %		.14%	.20%	.19%	.09%	.08%
SGA Expense	294,000,000	267,000,000	259,000,000	264,000,000	231,000,000	223,000,000
Net Income	188,000,000	1,147,000,000	759,000,000	677,000,000	401,000,000	168,000,000
Operating Cash Flow	1,217,000,000	1,398,000,000	1,632,000,000	1,598,000,000	912,000,000	758,000,000
Capital Expenditure	1,114,000,000	1,202,000,000	1,011,000,000	941,000,000	857,000,000	637,000,000
EBITDA	792,000,000	1,452,000,000	1,712,000,000	1,562,000,000	1,082,000,000	733,000,000
Return on Assets %		.12%	.08%	.08%	.05%	.02%
Return on Equity %		.26%	.21%	.24%	.17%	.08%
Debt to Equity		0.207	0.298	0.435	0.778	0.992

CONTACT INFORMATION:
Phone: 718 286-7900   Fax: 718 709-3621
Toll-Free: 800-538-2583
Address: 27-01 Queens Plaza North, Long Island City, NY 11101 United States

STOCK TICKER/OTHER:
Stock Ticker: JBLU
Employees: 18,406
Parent Company:

Exchange: NAS
Fiscal Year Ends: 12/31

SALARIES/BONUSES:
Top Exec. Salary: $578,750   Bonus: $
Second Exec. Salary: $470,417   Bonus: $

OTHER THOUGHTS:
Estimated Female Officers or Directors: 5
Hot Spot for Advancement for Women/Minorities: Y

JM Family Enterprises Inc

www.jmfamily.com

NAIC Code: 423110

TYPES OF BUSINESS:
Automobile Distribution-Wholesale
Automobile Dealer
Parts Distribution
Financing & Insurance
Dealership Financing
Consulting Services

BRANDS/DIVISIONS/AFFILIATES:
Southeast Toyota Distributors LLC
Southeast Toyota Finance
JM Lexus
JM&A Group
Home Franchise Concepts
Budget Blinds
Concrete Craft
AdvantaClean

CONTACTS:
Note: Officers with more than one job title may be intentionally listed here more than once.

Brent Burns, Pres.
Ron Coombs, VP
Carmen Johnson, VP-Human Resources
Carmen Johnson, General Counsel
Frank Armstrong, Exec. VP
Ron Coombs, Sr. VP
Forrest Heathcott, Exec. VP
Ed Sheehy, Exec. VP
Colin Brown, Chmn.

GROWTH PLANS/SPECIAL FEATURES:

JM Family Enterprises, Inc. is a leading family-owned diversified automotive company. Through its subsidiaries, JM is a distributor of Toyotas, operates a Lexus dealership, provides finance and insurance products, and operates a franchise network in the home improvement goods and services space. Subsidiary Southeast Toyota Distributors, LLC is an independent distributor of Toyotas, distributing vehicles, parts and accessories to more than 175 independent Toyota dealers in Alabama, Florida, Georgia, North Carolina and South Carolina. JM Lexus is located in Margate, Florida, and is a Lexus Plus dealership which also maintains state-of-the-art service and parts departments as well as a Lexus Certified Collision Center. Southeast Toyota Finance is a finance company for JM's Toyota dealers, servicing more than 730,000 finance and lease accounts. The finance firm is part of World Omni Financial Corporation, a global leader in wholesale floorplan accounting and risk management systems. JM&A Group is an independent provider of finance and insurance products to more than 3,800 automobile dealerships, including protection programs for new and used vehicles. Last, Home Franchise Concepts is among the world's largest franchise businesses, encompassing four brands: Budget Blinds, a provider of custom window coverings; Tailored Living, providing whole-home organization solutions; Concrete Craft, offering decorative concrete products; and AdvantaClean, offering professional home cleaning services. Through these brands, Home Franchise Concepts has a total 1,700 franchises located in the U.S., Canada and Mexico.

JM offers its employees educational assistance and development programs; flextime; adoption assistance; an onsite fitness center and access to a cafeteria and credit union; massage therapy; health and dependent care spending accounts; and medical, dental, vision, prescription, life and disability insurance.

FINANCIAL DATA:
Note: Data for latest year may not have been available at press time.

In U.S. $	2018	2017	2016	2015	2014	2013
Revenue	16,300,000,000	15,100,000,000	14,900,000,000	14,500,000,000	13,750,000,000	12,500,000,000
R&D Expense						
Operating Income						
Operating Margin %						
SGA Expense						
Net Income						
Operating Cash Flow						
Capital Expenditure						
EBITDA						
Return on Assets %						
Return on Equity %						
Debt to Equity						

CONTACT INFORMATION:
Phone: 954-429-2000   Fax: 954-429-2300
Toll-Free:
Address: 100 Jim Moran Blvd., Deerfield Beach, FL 33442 United States

STOCK TICKER/OTHER:
Stock Ticker: Private
Employees: 4,300
Parent Company:

Exchange:
Fiscal Year Ends: 12/31

SALARIES/BONUSES:
Top Exec. Salary: $ Bonus: $
Second Exec. Salary: $ Bonus: $

OTHER THOUGHTS:
Estimated Female Officers or Directors: 1
Hot Spot for Advancement for Women/Minorities:

Sales, profits and employees may be estimates. Financial information, benefits and other data can change quickly and may vary from those stated here.

John Hancock Financial

NAIC Code: 524113

www.johnhancock.com

TYPES OF BUSINESS:
Life Insurance
Mortgages
Annuities
Retirement Products
Mutual Funds
Asset Management

BRANDS/DIVISIONS/AFFILIATES:
Manulife Financial Corporation
John Hancock Life Insurance

CONTACTS:
Note: Officers with more than one job title may be intentionally listed here more than once.

Marianne Harrison, CEO
Sebastian Pariath, COO
Martin Sheerin, CFO
Barbara Goose, CMO
Ellie Harrison, Dir.-Human Resources
James Gallagher, Chief Admin. Officer
James Gallagher, General Counsel
Andrew G. Arnott, CEO
Peter Gordon, Pres., John Hancock Retirement Plan Svcs.
Michael Doughty, Pres.

GROWTH PLANS/SPECIAL FEATURES:

John Hancock Financial, a subsidiary of Canada-based Manulife Financial Corporation, includes John Hancock Life Insurance, one of the largest life insurers in the U.S. Overall, the company offers a wide range of insurance products including annuities, individual and group long-term care insurance, 401(k) plans, multiple life insurance policies, securitized investments, benefit payment services, retiree health care solutions, 529 college savings plans and fixed income and equity services. The firm's core retail products include life insurance, long-term care insurance, annuities and mutual funds. John Hancock also specializes in institutional investment, providing opportunities for pension funds and endowments to invest. Corporate employers are among the firm's largest customers. The company's four operating business segments, serving its retail and institutional customers, are protection, which offers life and long-term care insurance; guaranteed and structural financial products, which provides a range of defined benefit and defined contribution retirement plan products; wealth management, which offers retirement services, annuities and institutional account management; and corporate and other, which provides investment advisory services for corporations.

The firm offers employees a 401(k) plan; a pension plan; flexible spending accounts; auto and home insurance; life insurance; medical, dental, vision and disability coverage; tuition reimbursement; an employee assistance program; legal services; mutual funds; onsite child care; a college savings plan; graduate programs; and eldercare benefits.

FINANCIAL DATA:
Note: Data for latest year may not have been available at press time.

In U.S. $	2018	2017	2016	2015	2014	2013
Revenue	8,599,500,000	8,190,000,000	7,800,000,000	7,780,000,000	7,500,000,000	
R&D Expense						
Operating Income						
Operating Margin %						
SGA Expense						
Net Income						
Operating Cash Flow						
Capital Expenditure						
EBITDA						
Return on Assets %						
Return on Equity %						
Debt to Equity						

CONTACT INFORMATION:
Phone: 617-663-3000 Fax: 617-572-6015
Toll-Free: 800-225-5291
Address: 601 Congress St., Boston, MA 02110 United States

SALARIES/BONUSES:
Top Exec. Salary: $ Bonus: $
Second Exec. Salary: $ Bonus: $

STOCK TICKER/OTHER:
Stock Ticker: Subsidiary Exchange:
Employees: 34,000 Fiscal Year Ends: 12/31
Parent Company: Manulife Financial Corporation

OTHER THOUGHTS:
Estimated Female Officers or Directors:
Hot Spot for Advancement for Women/Minorities: Y

Sales, profits and employees may be estimates. Financial information, benefits and other data can change quickly and may vary from those stated here.

Johnson & Johnson

NAIC Code: 325412

www.jnj.com

TYPES OF BUSINESS:
Personal Health Care & Hygiene Products
Sterilization Products
Surgical Products
Pharmaceuticals
Skin Care Products
Baby Care Products
Contact Lenses
Medical Equipment

BRANDS/DIVISIONS/AFFILIATES:
Motrin
Band-Aid
Listerine
Tylenol
Neosporin
Risperdal Consta
Remicade
Orthotaxy

CONTACTS:
Note: Officers with more than one job title may be intentionally listed here more than once.

Alex Gorsky, CEO
Joaquin Duato, Vice Chairman
Joseph Wolk, CFO
Jorge Mesquita, Chairman of the Board, Divisional
Ronald Kapusta, Chief Accounting Officer
Paulus Stoffels, Chief Scientific Officer
Thibaut Mongon, Executive VP, Divisional
Ashley McEvoy, Executive VP, Divisional
Jennifer Taubert, Executive VP, Divisional
Michael Sneed, Executive VP, Divisional
Kathy Wengel, Executive VP
Peter Fasolo, Executive VP
Michael Ullmann, General Counsel

GROWTH PLANS/SPECIAL FEATURES:

Johnson & Johnson, founded in 1886, is one of the world's most comprehensive and well-known researchers, developers and manufacturers of healthcare products. Johnson & Johnson's worldwide operations are divided into three segments: consumer, pharmaceuticals and medical devices. The company's principal consumer goods are personal care and hygiene products, including baby care, skin care, oral care, wound care and women's healthcare products as well as nutritional and over-the-counter pharmaceutical products. Major consumer brands include Motrin, Band-Aid, Listerine, Tylenol, Neosporin, Aveeno and Pepcid AC. The pharmaceutical segment covers a wide spectrum of health fields, including anti-infective, antipsychotic, contraceptive, dermatology, gastrointestinal, hematology, immunology, neurology, oncology, pain management and virology. Among its pharmaceutical products are Risperdal Consta, an antipsychotic used to treat schizophrenia, and Remicade for the treatment of immune mediated inflammatory diseases. In the medical devices segment, Johnson & Johnson makes a number of products including orthopedic joint reconstruction devices, surgical care, advanced sterilization products, blood glucose monitoring devices, diagnostic products and disposable contact lenses. The firm owns more than 260 companies in virtually all countries of the world, and is headquartered in New Brunswick, New Jersey. In 2018, Johnson & Johnson sold its LifeScan, Inc. business to Platinum Equity LLC for approximately $2.1 billion; acquired Orthotaxy, a developer of software-enabled surgery technology; agreed to acquire the assets of Medical Enterprises Distribution, LLC; and agreed to acquire the outstanding shares of Ci:z Holdings Co., Ltd., a Japanese company focused on the marketing, development and distribution of a broad range of dermocosmetic, cosmetic and skincare products.

FINANCIAL DATA:
Note: Data for latest year may not have been available at press time.

In U.S. $	2018	2017	2016	2015	2014	2013
Revenue	81,581,000,000	76,450,000,000	71,890,000,000	70,074,000,000	74,331,000,000	71,312,000,000
R&D Expense	11,901,000,000	10,962,000,000	9,124,000,000	9,270,000,000	8,672,000,000	8,763,000,000
Operating Income	20,049,000,000	18,714,000,000	21,136,000,000	18,065,000,000	20,959,000,000	18,377,000,000
Operating Margin %		.24%	.29%	.26%	.28%	.26%
SGA Expense	22,540,000,000	21,420,000,000	19,945,000,000	21,203,000,000	21,954,000,000	21,830,000,000
Net Income	15,297,000,000	1,300,000,000	16,540,000,000	15,409,000,000	16,323,000,000	13,831,000,000
Operating Cash Flow	22,201,000,000	21,056,000,000	18,767,000,000	19,279,000,000	18,471,000,000	17,414,000,000
Capital Expenditure	3,670,000,000	3,279,000,000	3,226,000,000	3,463,000,000	3,714,000,000	3,595,000,000
EBITDA	25,933,000,000	24,249,000,000	24,283,000,000	23,494,000,000	24,991,000,000	20,057,000,000
Return on Assets %		.01%	.12%	.12%	.12%	.11%
Return on Equity %		.02%	.23%	.22%	.23%	.20%
Debt to Equity		0.51	0.319	0.181	0.217	0.18

CONTACT INFORMATION:
Phone: 732 524-0400   Fax: 732 214-0332
Toll-Free:
Address: 1 Johnson & Johnson Plaza, New Brunswick, NJ 08933 United States

STOCK TICKER/OTHER:
Stock Ticker: JNJ
Employees: 134,000
Parent Company:

Exchange: NYS
Fiscal Year Ends: 12/31

SALARIES/BONUSES:
Top Exec. Salary: $1,642,308   Bonus: $
Second Exec. Salary: $1,178,300   Bonus: $

OTHER THOUGHTS:
Estimated Female Officers or Directors: 4
Hot Spot for Advancement for Women/Minorities: Y

Jones Lang LaSalle Incorporated

NAIC Code: 531120

www.us.jll.com

TYPES OF BUSINESS:
Real Estate Rental, Leasing & Management
Investment Management
Project Management
Consulting Services
Real Estate Investment Banking
Properties Brokerage

BRANDS/DIVISIONS/AFFILIATES:
LaSalle Investment Management

CONTACTS:
Note: Officers with more than one job title may be intentionally listed here more than once.

Gregory OBrien, CEO, Divisional
Grace Chang, Managing Director, Divisional
Anthony Couse, CEO, Divisional
Guy Grainger, CEO, Divisional
Richard Bloxam, CEO, Divisional
John Forrest, CEO, Divisional
Jeff Jacobson, CEO, Subsidiary
Christian Ulbrich, CEO
Stephanie Plaines, CFO
Sheila Penrose, Chairman of the Board
Louis Bowers, Chief Accounting Officer
Patricia Maxson, Chief Administrative Officer
Allan Frazier, Chief Information Officer
Alan Tse, Chief Legal Officer
Parikshat Suri, Executive VP
James Jasionowski, Executive VP
Judith Tempelman, Other Corporate Officer
Mary Bilbrey, Other Executive Officer
Bryan Duncan, Treasurer

GROWTH PLANS/SPECIAL FEATURES:
Jones Lang LaSalle Incorporated (JLL) is a leading professional services firm specializing in real estate and investment management. JLL is a Fortune 500 company with annual revenue of $16.3 billion (as of December 31, 2018) and operations in over 80 countries. The firm provides services for a broad range of clients active in a variety of industries and are based in markets throughout the world. JLL operates through four segments: the Americas; Europe, Middle East and Africa (EMEA); Asia Pacific; and LaSalle Investment Management. The Americas, EMEA and Asia Pacific segments provide a full range of leasing, capital markets, integrated property and facility management, as well as facility management, project management, advisory, consulting, valuations and digital solutions services locally, regionally and globally. The leasing division brokers transactions between tenants and landlords; capital markets is engaged in investment sales, debt placement and finance arrangements; the property and facility management division manages and outsources JLL's properties and portfolios; the project and development services division designs and manages real estate projects; the advisory, consulting and other business divisions offer workplace strategy, digital solutions, valuation and consulting/advisory services and solutions. Last, LaSalle Investment manages JLL's real estate investment business globally. JLL's services are offered to real estate owners, occupiers, investors and developers for a variety of property types, including critical environments, data centers, cultural facilities, educational facilities, government facilities, healthcare and laboratory facilities, hotels, industrial facilities, warehouses, infrastructure projects, military housing, office buildings, residential properties, retail/shopping malls, sort/fulfillment center, sports facilities and transportation centers.

FINANCIAL DATA:
Note: Data for latest year may not have been available at press time.

In U.S. $	2018	2017	2016	2015	2014	2013
Revenue	16,318,400,000	7,932,400,000	6,803,800,000	5,965,671,000	5,429,603,000	4,461,591,000
R&D Expense						
Operating Income	745,700,000	567,600,000	509,100,000	563,914,000	508,169,000	387,134,000
Operating Margin %		.07%	.07%	.09%	.09%	.09%
SGA Expense	8,157,700,000	7,197,600,000	6,152,900,000	5,293,615,000	4,827,097,000	3,994,604,000
Net Income	484,500,000	254,200,000	318,200,000	438,672,000	386,063,000	269,865,000
Operating Cash Flow	604,100,000	789,200,000	214,500,000	375,769,000	498,861,000	293,167,000
Capital Expenditure	161,900,000	151,400,000	216,200,000	149,076,000	156,927,000	110,684,000
EBITDA	931,800,000	734,800,000	650,900,000	672,056,000	602,506,000	466,987,000
Return on Assets %		.03%	.05%	.08%	.08%	.06%
Return on Equity %		.08%	.12%	.17%	.17%	.13%
Debt to Equity		0.208	0.422	0.197	0.115	0.197

CONTACT INFORMATION:
Phone: 312 782-5800   Fax: 312 782-4339
Toll-Free:
Address: 200 E. Randolph Dr., Chicago, IL 60601 United States

SALARIES/BONUSES:
Top Exec. Salary: $970,328   Bonus: $
Second Exec. Salary: $500,000   Bonus: $

STOCK TICKER/OTHER:
Stock Ticker: JLL   Exchange: NYS
Employees: 77,000   Fiscal Year Ends: 12/31
Parent Company:

OTHER THOUGHTS:
Estimated Female Officers or Directors: 2
Hot Spot for Advancement for Women/Minorities: Y

JP Morgan Chase & Co Inc

www.jpmorganchase.com

NAIC Code: 522110

TYPES OF BUSINESS:
Banking
Mortgages
Investment Banking
Stock Brokerage
Credit Cards
Business Finance
Mutual Funds
Annuities

BRANDS/DIVISIONS/AFFILIATES:
JPMorgan Chase Bank NA
Chase Bank USA NA
JP Morgan Securities LLC

CONTACTS: Note: Officers with more than one job title may be intentionally listed here more than once.
Mary Erdoes, CEO, Divisional
Douglas Petno, CEO, Divisional
Marianne Lake, CEO, Divisional
James Dimon, CEO
Jennifer Piepszak, CFO
Nicole Giles, Chief Accounting Officer
Lori Beer, Chief Information Officer
Ashley Bacon, Chief Risk Officer
Daniel Pinto, Co- President
Gordon Smith, Co- President
Stacey Friedman, General Counsel
Peter Scher, Other Corporate Officer
Robin Leopold, Other Corporate Officer

GROWTH PLANS/SPECIAL FEATURES:
J.P. Morgan Chase & Co., Inc. (JPM) is one of the largest banking institutions in the world, with operations in over 60 countries and $2.6 trillion in assets (as of October 2018). JPM's principal subsidiaries include JPMorgan Chase Bank, NA, a national banking association with operations in 23 U.S. states; Chase Bank USA, NA, a leading provider of retail banking services and credit cards; and J.P. Morgan Securities LLC, an investment banking firm. JPM operates its business through five segments: consumer and community banking (CCB), corporate and investment banking (CIB), commercial banking, asset management and corporate/private equity. The CCB segment serves consumers and businesses through personal service at bank branches and through ATMs, online, mobile and telephone banking. The CIB segment, comprised of banking and markets and investor services, offers a broad range of investment banking, market-making, prime brokerage, and treasury and securities products and services to a global client base. The commercial banking segment provides local expertise and service to U.S. and U.S. multinational clients, including corporations, municipalities, financial institutions and nonprofit entities with annual revenue generally ranging from $20 million to $2 billion. The asset management segment is a global leader in investment and wealth management. The corporate/private equity segment measures, monitors, reports and manages the firm's liquidity, funding and structural interest rate and foreign exchange risks. In July 2018, JPM announced that in September of the same year, BANK ONE Capital III would be liquidated, and its related securities cancelled.

The company offers benefits including medical, dental, vision, life, disability and accident insurance; 401(k) and retirement plans; and various employee assistance programs.

FINANCIAL DATA: Note: Data for latest year may not have been available at press time.

In U.S. $	2018	2017	2016	2015	2014	2013
Revenue	109,029,000,000	99,624,000,000	95,668,000,000	93,543,000,000	94,205,000,000	96,606,000,000
R&D Expense						
Operating Income						
Operating Margin %						
SGA Expense	45,209,000,000	41,615,000,000	39,722,000,000	38,651,000,000	38,514,000,000	38,735,000,000
Net Income	32,474,000,000	24,441,000,000	24,733,000,000	24,442,000,000	21,762,000,000	17,923,000,000
Operating Cash Flow	14,187,000,000	-2,501,000,000	20,196,000,000	73,466,000,000	36,593,000,000	107,953,000,000
Capital Expenditure						
EBITDA						
Return on Assets %		.01%	.01%	.01%	.01%	.01%
Return on Equity %		.10%	.10%	.10%	.10%	.08%
Debt to Equity		1.122	1.394	1.398	1.448	1.479

CONTACT INFORMATION:
Phone: 212 270-6000 Fax: 212 270-1648
Toll-Free: 877-242-7372
Address: 270 Park Ave., New York, NY 10017 United States

STOCK TICKER/OTHER:
Stock Ticker: JPM
Employees: 256,105
Parent Company:

Exchange: NYS
Fiscal Year Ends: 12/31

SALARIES/BONUSES:
Top Exec. Salary: $750,000 Bonus: $8,500,000
Second Exec. Salary: $750,000 Bonus: $7,900,000

OTHER THOUGHTS:
Estimated Female Officers or Directors: 3
Hot Spot for Advancement for Women/Minorities: Y

Juniper Networks Inc

NAIC Code: 0

www.juniper.net

TYPES OF BUSINESS:
Networking Equipment
IP Networking Systems
Internet Routers
Network Security Products
Internet Software
Intrusion Prevention
Application Acceleration

BRANDS/DIVISIONS/AFFILIATES:
ACX
MX
PTX
Cloud CPE
NorthStar
EX
QFX
Junos

CONTACTS:
Note: Officers with more than one job title may be intentionally listed here more than once.

Rami Rahim, CEO
Kenneth Miller, CFO
Scott Kriens, Chairman of the Board
Terrance Spidell, Chief Accounting Officer
Bikash Koley, Chief Technology Officer
Manoj Leelanivas, Executive VP
Anand Athreya, Executive VP
Brian Martin, Senior VP

GROWTH PLANS/SPECIAL FEATURES:
Juniper Networks, Inc. designs, develops and sells products and services for high-performance networks. These products help customers build highly scalable, reliable, secure and cost-effective networks for their businesses. Juniper sells its products in more than 150 countries across three geographic regions: Americas; Europe, Middle East and Africa (EMEA); and Asia Pacific. The company's offerings address high-performance network requirements for global service providers, cloud environments, enterprises, governments and research and public-sector organizations who view the network as critical to its business success. Routing products include the firm's ACX, MX and PTX, as well as its Cloud CPE end-to-end solution and NorthStar wide-area network controller. Switching products include the EX and QFX series, as well as the disaggregated version of Junos software, and the open networking switch designed to combine a cloud-optimized open compute project with the Junos operating system. Security products include the SRX series for data center gateway services, and for campus and branch gateway services; the vSRX virtual firewall; advanced malware protection; and the Sky ATP (advanced threat prevention), a cloud-based service designed to use both static and dynamic analysis with machine learning to find unknown threat signatures (zero-day attacks). Sky ATP is integrated with SRX firewalls and routers for automated enforcement. Other security products include the Cyphort software, offering security analytics for advanced threat defense. Juniper Networks owns over 3,300 issued or pending technology patents. In November 2018, Juniper announced its intent to acquire HTBASE, which has developed a unique and disruptive platform for software-defined enterprise multi-cloud.

Juniper Networks offers medical, dental, prescription and vision insurance; paid time off; and stock/savings plans.

FINANCIAL DATA:
Note: Data for latest year may not have been available at press time.

In U.S. $	2018	2017	2016	2015	2014	2013
Revenue	4,647,500,000	5,027,200,000	4,990,100,000	4,857,800,000	4,627,100,000	4,669,100,000
R&D Expense	1,003,200,000	980,700,000	1,013,700,000	994,500,000	1,006,200,000	1,043,200,000
Operating Income	579,500,000	913,700,000	893,000,000	911,400,000	597,300,000	605,000,000
Operating Margin %		.18%	.18%	.19%	.13%	.13%
SGA Expense	1,158,500,000	1,177,700,000	1,197,800,000	1,172,700,000	1,254,700,000	1,293,200,000
Net Income	566,900,000	306,200,000	592,700,000	633,700,000	-334,300,000	439,800,000
Operating Cash Flow	861,100,000	1,260,100,000	1,106,000,000	892,500,000	763,400,000	842,300,000
Capital Expenditure	147,400,000	151,200,000	214,700,000	210,300,000	192,900,000	243,100,000
EBITDA	846,400,000	1,138,600,000	1,131,800,000	1,112,000,000	166,700,000	773,800,000
Return on Assets %		.03%	.06%	.07%	-.04%	.04%
Return on Equity %		.06%	.12%	.13%	-.05%	.06%
Debt to Equity		0.456	0.43	0.36	0.274	0.137

CONTACT INFORMATION:
Phone: 408 745-2000 Fax: 408 745-2100
Toll-Free: 888-586-4737
Address: 1133 Innovation Way, Sunnyvale, CA 94089 United States

SALARIES/BONUSES:
Top Exec. Salary: $1,000,000 Bonus: $787,500
Second Exec. Salary: $460,000 Bonus: $737,000

STOCK TICKER/OTHER:
Stock Ticker: JNPR
Employees: 9,832
Parent Company:

Exchange: NYS
Fiscal Year Ends: 12/31

OTHER THOUGHTS:
Estimated Female Officers or Directors: 3
Hot Spot for Advancement for Women/Minorities: Y

Kaiser Permanente

NAIC Code: 622110

www.kaiserpermanente.org

TYPES OF BUSINESS:
General Medical and Surgical Hospitals
General & Specialty Hospitals
Outpatient Facilities
HMO
Health Insurance
Integrated Health Care System
Physician Networks
Clinical Record Management

BRANDS/DIVISIONS/AFFILIATES:
Kaiser Foundation Health Plan Inc
Kaiser Foundation Hospitals
Permanente Medical Groups
Kaiser Permanente Center for Health Research
KP HealthConnect

CONTACTS: Note: Officers with more than one job title may be intentionally listed here more than once.
Bernard J. Tyson, CEO
Gregory A. Adams, Pres.
Kathy Lancaster, CFO
Kathryn Beiser, Sr. VP
Raymond J. Baxter, Sr. VP-Community Benefit, Research & Health Policy
Richard D. Daniels, CIO
Mark S. Zemelman, General Counsel
Arthur M. Southam, Exec. VP-Health Plan Oper.
Chris Grant, Sr. VP-Corp. Dev. & Care Delivery Strategy
Diane Gage Lofgren, Sr. VP
Cynthia Powers Overmyer, Sr. VP-Internal Audit Svcs.
Daniel P. Garcia, Chief Compliance Officer
Anthony Barrueta, Sr. VP-Gov't Rel.
Amy Compton-Phillips, Associate Exec. Dir.-Quality, Permanente
Bernard J.Tyson, Chmn.

GROWTH PLANS/SPECIAL FEATURES:

Kaiser Permanente is a nonprofit company dedicated to providing integrated health care coverage. The firm operates in California, Colorado, Georgia, Hawaii, Maryland, Washington D.C., Oregon, Virginia and Washington. It serves 12.3 million members, most of which are in California (more than 8.9 million). Kaiser has three main operating divisions: Kaiser Foundation Health Plan, Inc., which contracts with individuals and groups to provide medical coverage; Kaiser Foundation Hospitals and their subsidiaries, operating community hospitals and outpatient facilities in several states; and Permanente Medical Groups, the company's network of physicians providing healthcare to its members. As of mid-2019, the company's resources include approximately 39 medical centers, including hospitals and outpatient facilities; 701 medical offices; and more than 22,910 physicians. Kaiser Permanente is one of the largest health plans serving the Medicare program. Kaiser Foundation Hospitals also fund medical- and health-related research. The Kaiser Permanente Center for Health Research, founded in 1964, is a single research center that spans two regions of Kaiser Permanente: Northwest and Hawaii. The center pursues a vigorous agenda of public health research within large, diverse populations, and specializes in the disciplines of biostatistics, clinical research support services, data resources, evidence-based practices and qualitative research. In addition, the company's KP HealthConnect platform integrates clinical records with appointments, registration and billing, thereby significantly improving care delivery and patient satisfaction.

Employees of the firm are offered medical, vision, dental and life insurance; a prescription plan; paid time off for vacations; designated holidays; sick leave; disability benefits; retirement plans; tuition reimbursement; employee assistance programs; and transit spending account options. Kaiser Permanente's employee health care coverage extends to spouses, domestic partners and unmarried children.

FINANCIAL DATA: Note: Data for latest year may not have been available at press time.

In U.S. $	2018	2017	2016	2015	2014	2013
Revenue	79,700,000,000	72,700,000,000	64,600,000,000	60,700,000,000	56,400,000,000	53,100,000,000
R&D Expense						
Operating Income						
Operating Margin %						
SGA Expense						
Net Income	2,500,000,000	3,800,000,000	3,100,000,000	1,900,000,000	3,100,000,000	2,700,000,000
Operating Cash Flow						
Capital Expenditure						
EBITDA						
Return on Assets %						
Return on Equity %						
Debt to Equity						

CONTACT INFORMATION:
Phone: 510-271-5910   Fax:
Toll-Free:
Address: 1 Kaiser Plaza, 19/Fl, Oakland, CA 94612 United States

STOCK TICKER/OTHER:
Stock Ticker: Nonprofit
Employees: 217,000
Parent Company:

Exchange:
Fiscal Year Ends: 12/31

SALARIES/BONUSES:
Top Exec. Salary: $ Bonus: $
Second Exec. Salary: $ Bonus: $

OTHER THOUGHTS:
Estimated Female Officers or Directors: 9
Hot Spot for Advancement for Women/Minorities: Y

KBR Inc

www.kbr.com

NAIC Code: 237000

TYPES OF BUSINESS:

Heavy Construction and Engineering
Energy & Petrochemical Projects
Program & Project Management
Consulting & Technology Services
Operations & Maintenance Services
Contract Staffing Services

BRANDS/DIVISIONS/AFFILIATES:

CONTACTS: *Note: Officers with more than one job title may be intentionally listed here more than once.*

Mark Sopp, CFO
Raymond Carney, Chief Accounting Officer
Eileen Akerson, Executive VP
Ian Mackey, Executive VP
Gregory Conlon, Other Executive Officer
William Bright, President, Divisional
John Derbyshire, President, Divisional
J. Ibrahim, President, Divisional
Farhan Mujib, President, Divisional
Stuart Bradie, President
Adam Kramer, Secretary

GROWTH PLANS/SPECIAL FEATURES:

KBR, Inc. is a global provider of differentiated professional services and technologies across the asset and program lifecycle within the government services and hydrocarbons sectors. The company has customers in over 75 countries, has operations in 40 countries and maintains offices throughout the U.S., Australia, Africa, the U.K., Asia and the Middle East. KBR operates in three segments: government services, technology and hydrocarbons services. The government services segment serves government customers globally, including capabilities that cover the full lifecycle of defense, space, aviation and other governmental programs and missions, from research and development to systems engineering to test and evaluation to program management to operations to maintenance and field logistics. The technology segment includes proprietary technology focused on the monetization of hydrocarbons (primarily natural gas and natural gas liquids) in ethylene and petrochemicals; ammonia, nitric acid and fertilizers; and oil refining and gasification. Last, the hydrocarbons services segment includes onshore oil and gas; liquefaction and regasification (LNG/GTL); oil refining; petrochemicals; chemicals; fertilizers; differentiated EPC; maintenance services (brown and root industrial services); offshore oil and gas (shallow water, deep water, subsea); floating solutions; and program management and related consulting services.

FINANCIAL DATA: *Note: Data for latest year may not have been available at press time.*

In U.S. $	2018	2017	2016	2015	2014	2013
Revenue	4,913,000,000	4,171,000,000	4,268,000,000	5,096,000,000	6,366,000,000	7,283,000,000
R&D Expense						
Operating Income	290,000,000	195,000,000	-31,000,000	170,000,000	-304,000,000	332,000,000
Operating Margin %		.05%	-.01%	.03%	-.05%	.05%
SGA Expense	166,000,000	147,000,000	143,000,000	155,000,000	239,000,000	249,000,000
Net Income	281,000,000	434,000,000	-61,000,000	203,000,000	-1,262,000,000	229,000,000
Operating Cash Flow	165,000,000	193,000,000	61,000,000	47,000,000	170,000,000	290,000,000
Capital Expenditure	17,000,000	8,000,000	11,000,000	10,000,000	53,000,000	78,000,000
EBITDA	527,000,000	318,000,000	14,000,000	209,000,000	-232,000,000	536,000,000
Return on Assets %		.11%	-.02%	.05%	-.26%	.04%
Return on Equity %		.44%	-.07%	.20%	-.71%	.09%
Debt to Equity		0.405	0.904	0.048	0.067	

CONTACT INFORMATION:

Phone: 713 753-3011 Fax: 713 753-5353
Toll-Free:
Address: 601 Jefferson St., Ste. 3400, Houston, TX 77002 United States

SALARIES/BONUSES:

Top Exec. Salary: $1,049,064 Bonus: $
Second Exec. Salary: $652,562 Bonus: $

STOCK TICKER/OTHER:

Stock Ticker: KBR Exchange: NYS
Employees: 27,500 Fiscal Year Ends: 12/31
Parent Company:

OTHER THOUGHTS:

Estimated Female Officers or Directors: 2
Hot Spot for Advancement for Women/Minorities: Y

Sales, profits and employees may be estimates. Financial information, benefits and other data can change quickly and may vary from those stated here.

Kelly Services Inc

www.kellyservices.com

NAIC Code: 561320

TYPES OF BUSINESS:
Staffing & Temporary Help
Human Resources Consulting
Outsourcing Solutions
Permanent Hiring Programs
Call Center Services
Benefits & Payroll Outsourcing

BRANDS/DIVISIONS/AFFILIATES:
Global Technology Associates LLC
NextGen Global Resources LLC

CONTACTS:
Note: Officers with more than one job title may be intentionally listed here more than once.

George Corona, CEO
Donald Parfet, Chairman of the Board
Laura Lockhart, Chief Accounting Officer
Hannah Lim-Johnson, Chief Legal Officer
Olivier Thirot, Executive VP
Teresa Carroll, Executive VP
Peter Quigley, Executive VP

GROWTH PLANS/SPECIAL FEATURES:

Kelly Services, Inc. is a staffing and services company that offers temporary staffing services, staff leasing, outsourcing and full-time placement. Kelly's workforce solutions are provided to customers through offices in three regions: the Americas; Europe, the Middle East and Africa (EMEA); and Asia Pacific (APAC). The operations of the firm are divided into three principal business segments: Americas staffing, global staffing solutions (GTS) and international staffing. The Americas staffing segment represents Kelly's branch-delivered staffing business in the U.S., Puerto Rico, Canada, Mexico and Brazil. This division delivers temporary staffing, as well as direct-hire placement services, in a number of specialty staffing services, including: office, education, marketing, electronic assembly, light industrial, engineering, information technology, creative services, finance/accounting, science and law. The GTS segment combines the delivery structure of Kelly's outsourcing and consulting group and centrally delivered staffing business. This division reflects the trend towards the adoption of holistic talent supply chain solutions which combine contingent labor, full-time hiring and outsourced services. It also provides executive placement, career transition/outplacement services and talent advisory services. The international staffing segment represents the firm's branch-delivered staffing business in the EMEA region. International staffing provides a similar range of staffing services as the Americas staffing segment, including: office, engineering, finance/accounting, healthcare, IT and science, as well as catering and hospitality and industrial. In January 2019, Kelly Services acquired: Global Technology Associates, LLC, a provider of engineering, technology and business consulting solutions; and NextGen Global Resources, LLC, a provider of telecommunications, wireless and connected technology staffing solutions.

FINANCIAL DATA:
Note: Data for latest year may not have been available at press time.

In U.S. $	2018	2017	2016	2015	2014	2013
Revenue	5,513,900,000	5,374,400,000	5,276,800,000	5,518,200,000	5,562,700,000	5,413,100,000
R&D Expense						
Operating Income	87,400,000	83,300,000	63,200,000	66,700,000	21,900,000	55,000,000
Operating Margin %		.02%	.01%	.01%	.00%	.01%
SGA Expense	884,800,000	870,800,000	843,100,000	853,600,000	886,500,000	834,500,000
Net Income	22,900,000	71,600,000	120,800,000	53,800,000	23,700,000	58,900,000
Operating Cash Flow	61,400,000	71,200,000	37,400,000	23,500,000	-70,000,000	115,300,000
Capital Expenditure	25,600,000	24,600,000	12,700,000	16,900,000	21,700,000	20,000,000
EBITDA	19,900,000	107,100,000	174,800,000	88,600,000	41,300,000	72,000,000
Return on Assets %		.03%	.06%	.03%	.01%	.03%
Return on Equity %		.07%	.13%	.06%	.03%	.08%
Debt to Equity						

CONTACT INFORMATION:
Phone: 248 362-4444 Fax: 248 362-2258
Toll-Free:
Address: 999 W. Big Beaver Rd., Troy, MI 48084 United States

SALARIES/BONUSES:
Top Exec. Salary: $1,000,000 Bonus: $
Second Exec. Salary: $575,000 Bonus: $

STOCK TICKER/OTHER:
Stock Ticker: KELYA
Employees: 507,500
Parent Company:

Exchange: NAS
Fiscal Year Ends: 12/31

OTHER THOUGHTS:
Estimated Female Officers or Directors: 11
Hot Spot for Advancement for Women/Minorities: Y

Kimpton Hotel & Restaurant Group LLC

www.kimptonhotels.com

NAIC Code: 721110

TYPES OF BUSINESS:
Hotels
Restaurants
Hotel Management Services

BRANDS/DIVISIONS/AFFILIATES:
InterContinental Hotels Group PLC
Hotel Vintage Plaza
Hotel Burnham
Cafe Pescatore
Area 31
Kimpton De Witt Amsterdam
Kimpton Saint George Hotel

CONTACTS:
Note: Officers with more than one job title may be intentionally listed here more than once.

Mike DeFrino, CEO
Judy Miles, General Counsel
Joe Long, Exec. VP-Dev.
Lisa Demoney, Sr. Dir.-Digital Mktg. & Media
Stephanie Moustirats, Dir.-Hotel Public Rel.
James Alderman, Sr. VP-Acquisitions & Dev.
James Lin, Sr. VP-Restaurant Oper.
Barry Pollard, Sr. VP-Hotel Oper.
Christine Lawson, Sr. VP-Hotel Sales & Catering

GROWTH PLANS/SPECIAL FEATURES:

Kimpton Hotel & Restaurant Group, LLC, based in San Francisco, owns more than 65 lifestyle boutique hotels primarily in the U.S., but also in other countries. Its holdings also consist of 80+ restaurants and bars next to or within its hotels. The firm specializes in renovating old, disused buildings to transform them into unique hotels as well as small, European-style restaurants. Its themed hotels include Hotel Vintage Plaza in Portland, Oregon, which has an Italian romance theme; Hotel Vintage in Seattle, highlighting local Washington wines; and Hotel Burnham in Chicago, which focuses on its significance in Chicago's history. Notable restaurants run by Kimpton include San Francisco bistros Cafe Pescatore, Scala's Bistro and Puccini & Pinetti; Sazerac in Seattle; Atwood Cafe in Chicago; Area 31 in Miami; Firefly in Washington, D.C.; Ruby Room in Boston; and Silverleaf Tavern in New York City. Internationally, the Kimpton De Witt Amsterdam hotel is close to Central Station, the Red Light district and other attractions; and the Kimpton Saint George Hotel is located in Toronto, Canada's annex area. The company also offers full service spas at some of its locations. Special services offered by its hotels include the Mind, Body, Spa Program, which offers in-room massage, yoga, Pilates and meditation; pet packages, which include pet-friendly amenities and services; and the Hosted Evening Wine Hour. The company is also engaged in comprehensive management services for other companies, offering everything from financial management to facilities renovation. Kimpton is owned by hotel giant InterContinental Hotels Group PLC. In March 2019, Kimpton announced its first property in the state of Montana, with a project of turning the National Guard Armory building in downtown Bozeman into a 122-room hotel with a signature restaurant.

The firm offers medical, dental, vision, life and disability coverage; and various employee assistance programs.

FINANCIAL DATA:
Note: Data for latest year may not have been available at press time.

In U.S. $	2018	2017	2016	2015	2014	2013
Revenue	1,300,000,000	1,100,000,000	1,300,000,000	1,200,000,000	1,049,880,000	1,000,000,000
R&D Expense						
Operating Income						
Operating Margin %						
SGA Expense						
Net Income						
Operating Cash Flow						
Capital Expenditure						
EBITDA						
Return on Assets %						
Return on Equity %						
Debt to Equity						

CONTACT INFORMATION:
Phone: 415-397-5572   Fax: 415-296-8031
Toll-Free: 800-546-7866
Address: 222 Kearny St., Ste. 200, San Francisco, CA 94108 United States

STOCK TICKER/OTHER:
Stock Ticker: Subsidiary   Exchange:
Employees: 7,754   Fiscal Year Ends: 12/31
Parent Company: InterContinental Hotels Group PLC

SALARIES/BONUSES:
Top Exec. Salary: $ Bonus: $
Second Exec. Salary: $ Bonus: $

OTHER THOUGHTS:
Estimated Female Officers or Directors: 9
Hot Spot for Advancement for Women/Minorities: Y

Kindred Healthcare LLC

NAIC Code: 623110

www.kindredhealthcare.com

TYPES OF BUSINESS:
Nursing Care Facilities
Nursing Centers
Contract Rehabilitation Services

BRANDS/DIVISIONS/AFFILIATES:
Humana Inc
TPG Capital
Welsh Carson Anderson & Stowe
Promise Hospital of East Los Angeles

GROWTH PLANS/SPECIAL FEATURES:
Kindred Healthcare, LLC is a healthcare services company based in Louisville, Kentucky. Through its subsidiaries, the firm provides healthcare services at 1,760 locations across 46 U.S. states. These locations include 71 long-term acute-care hospitals, 22 inpatient rehabilitation hospitals, 11 sub-acute units, 95 inpatient rehabilitation units (hospital-based) and contract rehabilitation service businesses that serve more than 1,560 non-affiliated sites of service. Kindred Healthcare is 40%-owned by Humana, Inc., and the remaining 60% is held by TPG Capital and Welsh, Carson, Anderson & Stowe (WCAS). In May 2019, Kindred Healthcare acquired Promise Hospital of East Los Angeles, a 177-bed hospital specializing in long-term acute care services, and also provides respiratory care, advanced wound care and rehabilitation therapies.

CONTACTS:
Note: Officers with more than one job title may be intentionally listed here more than once.

Benjamin A. Breier, CEO
Stephen Cunanan, Chief Administrative Officer
Phyllis Yale, Director
William Altman, Executive VP
David Causby, Executive VP
Joseph Landenwich, General Counsel
Pete Kalmey, President, Divisional
Jason Zachariah, President, Divisional
Benjamin Breier, President
John Lucchese, Senior VP
Paul Diaz, Vice Chairman of the Board

FINANCIAL DATA:
Note: Data for latest year may not have been available at press time.

In U.S. $	2018	2017	2016	2015	2014	2013
Revenue	6,335,828,890	6,034,122,752	6,292,529,000	6,119,218,000	4,110,991,000	3,908,814,000
R&D Expense						
Operating Income						
Operating Margin %						
SGA Expense						
Net Income		-698,352,000	-664,230,016	-93,384,000	-79,837,000	-168,492,000
Operating Cash Flow						
Capital Expenditure						
EBITDA						
Return on Assets %						
Return on Equity %						
Debt to Equity						

CONTACT INFORMATION:
Phone: 502 596-7300   Fax: 502 596-4170
Toll-Free: 800-545-0749
Address: 680 S. Fourth St., Louisville, KY 40202 United States

STOCK TICKER/OTHER:
Stock Ticker: Joint Venture
Employees: 36,000
Parent Company: Humana Inc

Exchange:
Fiscal Year Ends: 12/31

SALARIES/BONUSES:
Top Exec. Salary: $ Bonus: $
Second Exec. Salary: $ Bonus: $

OTHER THOUGHTS:
Estimated Female Officers or Directors: 4
Hot Spot for Advancement for Women/Minorities: Y

Koch Industries Inc

www.kochind.com

NAIC Code: 324110

TYPES OF BUSINESS:
Petroleum Refining
Chemicals
Textiles
Pipelines
Fertilizer Production
Chemical Equipment
Asphalt & Paving Supplies
Beef Production

BRANDS/DIVISIONS/AFFILIATES:
Flint Hills Resources LLC
Koch Minerals LLC
Koch Ag & Energy Solutions LLC
Koch Engineered Solutions
Koch Disruptive Technologies
Matador Cattle Company
INVISTA BV
Guardian Industries Corporation

CONTACTS: *Note: Officers with more than one job title may be intentionally listed here more than once.*

Charles G. Koch, CEO
David L. Robertson, COO
Steven J. Feilmeier, VP
Don Clay, Managing Dir.-Environmental & Regulatory Affairs
Michael William Hofmann, Chief Risk Officer
Charles G. Koch, Chmn.

GROWTH PLANS/SPECIAL FEATURES:

Koch Industries, Inc. is a diversified group of companies. Subsidiary Flint Hills Resources, LLC produces next-generation fuels and chemical components. Koch Minerals, LLC supplies coal and petroleum coke as well as cement, pulp and paper, sulfur and related products internationally. Koch Ag & Energy Solutions, LLC provides sustainable fertilizer products. Koch Engineered Solutions specializes in process and pollution control equipment for industrial facilities. Koch Disruptive Technologies invests in emerging high-growth technologies across a range of industries, with a focus on investments that improve Koch's core capabilities as well as those that create new platforms. Koch Equity Development is the acquisition and development arm of Koch Industries. The Matador Cattle Company, a division of the Koch Agriculture Company, operates three ranches in Kansas, Montana and Texas totaling 460,000 acres. INVISTA BV is a global producer and marketer of polymers and fibers, primarily for nylon, spandex and polyester applications. Georgia-Pacific, LLC manufactures and markets tissue, packaging, paper, building products, related chemicals and fluff, filter and market pulp under such brand names as Quilted Northern, Angel Soft, Brawny, Sparkle and Dixie. Guardian Industries Corporation is a diversified manufacturer of float, fabricated and value-added coated glass products and solutions for architectural, residential and technical glass applications. Molex Incorporated manufactures connecting components for electronics devices and systems in relation to communication, medical equipment, transportation, appliances and more. Koch Supply & Trading LP is a global trader of energy commodities and metals. Koch Industries is present in about 60 countries worldwide.

Employee benefits include: 401(k) and pension plans; and comprehensive health coverage.

FINANCIAL DATA:
Note: Data for latest year may not have been available at press time.

In U.S. $	2018	2017	2016	2015	2014	2013
Revenue	115,500,000,000	110,000,000,000	101,000,000,000	99,000,000,000	105,500,000,000	114,000,000,000
R&D Expense						
Operating Income						
Operating Margin %						
SGA Expense						
Net Income	105,000,000	1,040,000,000	1,030,000,000	10,000,000,000	10,600,000,000	10,500,000,000
Operating Cash Flow						
Capital Expenditure						
EBITDA						
Return on Assets %						
Return on Equity %						
Debt to Equity						

CONTACT INFORMATION:
Phone: 316-828-5500   Fax: 316-828-5739
Toll-Free:
Address: 4111 E. 37th St. N., Wichita, KS 67220 United States

SALARIES/BONUSES:
Top Exec. Salary: $ Bonus: $
Second Exec. Salary: $ Bonus: $

STOCK TICKER/OTHER:
Stock Ticker: Private   Exchange:
Employees: 120,000   Fiscal Year Ends: 12/31
Parent Company:

OTHER THOUGHTS:
Estimated Female Officers or Directors:
Hot Spot for Advancement for Women/Minorities:

Sales, profits and employees may be estimates. Financial information, benefits and other data can change quickly and may vary from those stated here.

Kohler Company

NAIC Code: 327110

www.corporate.kohler.com

TYPES OF BUSINESS:
Plumbing Fixtures
Resorts
Kitchen & Bath Products
Building Materials

BRANDS/DIVISIONS/AFFILIATES:
KOHLER Konnect
Sterling
Kallista
Kohler Engines
Kohler Power
Ann Sacks
Kallista
American Club Resort

CONTACTS:
Note: Officers with more than one job title may be intentionally listed here more than once.

K. David Kohler, CEO
Tom Adler, CFO
Laura Kohler, Sr. VP-Human Resources
Paul Ryan, CIO
Herbert V. Kohler, Jr., Chmn.

GROWTH PLANS/SPECIAL FEATURES:

Kohler Company, founded in 1873, is an American manufacturer that has more than 50 manufacturing locations on six continents worldwide. The firm's Internet of Things laboratory has development teams in the U.S. and China engaged in producing smart kitchen and bath products via highly-advanced technology. This KOHLER Konnect technology platform is creating intelligent toilets, bathtubs and faucets. For example, the bathroom lights and shower can be turned on and the toilet seat warmed via the bathroom mirror. Kohler has four divisions: kitchen and bath, power, decorative products and hospitality. The kitchen and bath division offers products under the Kohler, Sterling, Kallista, Ann Sacks and Robern brands. Products include fashionable sinks, faucets, toilets, bidets, vanities, medicine cabinets, accessories and commercial products. These products offer a number of features including luxury design, automated systems, stainless steel and touchless products. The power division is comprised of Kohler Engines, Lombardini, Kohler Power, Somo and Kohler Power Uninterruptible. Products include private and commercial agricultural equipment, including lawn mowers; maritime equipment, such as marine generators; home generators; and uninterruptible power solutions. The decorative products division includes the Ann Sacks, Kallista and Robern brands of furniture, lighting, home accessories, textiles, artesian stone design, plumbing products and high-end hospitality furnishings. Hospitality includes golf destinations and hospitality products. The hospitality division includes the American Club Resort (Kohler, Wisconsin) and Old Course Hotel (St. Andrews, Scotland), and offer spa services, golf, lodgings and high-end cuisine to their guests. Additional hospitality services include Kohler Original Chocolates and Kohler At Home, offering high-end bedding and spa-like products for home use.

Kohler offers its employees medical, dental, life and prescription insurance; dependent and health care spending accounts; a wellness program; a pension plan; a 401(k) plan with company matching; annual bonuses; paid time off; and employee discounts.

FINANCIAL DATA:
Note: Data for latest year may not have been available at press time.

In U.S. $	2018	2017	2016	2015	2014	2013
Revenue	7,000,000,000	6,500,000,000	6,350,000,000	6,000,000,000	5,210,000,000	5,000,000,000
R&D Expense						
Operating Income						
Operating Margin %						
SGA Expense						
Net Income						
Operating Cash Flow						
Capital Expenditure						
EBITDA						
Return on Assets %						
Return on Equity %						
Debt to Equity						

CONTACT INFORMATION:
Phone: 920-457-4441 Fax:
Toll-Free: 800-456-4537
Address: 444 Highland Dr., Kohler, WI 53044 United States

STOCK TICKER/OTHER:
Stock Ticker: Private
Employees: 37,000
Parent Company:

Exchange:
Fiscal Year Ends:

SALARIES/BONUSES:
Top Exec. Salary: $ Bonus: $
Second Exec. Salary: $ Bonus: $

OTHER THOUGHTS:
Estimated Female Officers or Directors:
Hot Spot for Advancement for Women/Minorities:

Sales, profits and employees may be estimates. Financial information, benefits and other data can change quickly and may vary from those stated here.

Kohls Corporation

NAIC Code: 452112

www.kohls.com

TYPES OF BUSINESS:
Discount Department Stores
Online Sales

BRANDS/DIVISIONS/AFFILIATES:
Kohl's
FILA
Off-Aisle
Kohls.com
Apt 9
Croft & Barrow
Jumping Beans
Sonoma Goods for Life

CONTACTS: Note: Officers with more than one job title may be intentionally listed here more than once.
Michelle Gass, CEO
Bruce Besanko, CFO
Frank Sica, Chairman of the Board
Greg Revelle, Chief Marketing Officer
Ratnakar Lavu, Chief Technology Officer
Douglas Howe, Other Executive Officer
Marc Chini, Other Executive Officer
Sona Chawla, President

GROWTH PLANS/SPECIAL FEATURES:

Kohl's Corporation operates family-oriented specialty department stores. The company comprises more than 1,100 Kohl's department stores, 12 FILA outlets and four Off-Aisle clearance centers throughout the U.S., as well as an eCommerce site Kohls.com. Together, these stores comprised 82.8 million selling square feet in 49 U.S. states. Kohl's stores offer apparel, shoes and accessories for women, children and men; soft home products, such as sheets and pillows; and other home products, such as small electronics and luggage. Brands sold include Kohl's proprietary Apt. 9, Croft & Barrow, Jumping Beans, SO and Sonoma Goods for Life, and exclusive brands developed and marketed through agreements such as Food Network, Jennifer Lopez, Marc Anthony, Simply Vera Want and Rock & Republic. Approximately 30% of Kohl's' merchandise is marketed towards women, 20% is marketed towards men, 19% is comprised of home furnishing products, 13% is designed for children, 9% is comprised of accessories and 9% is comprised of footwear. The firm maintains nine retail distribution centers located in Ohio, Texas, Virginia, Missouri, New York, California, Georgia and Illinois; and eCommerce fulfillment centers in Ohio, Maryland, Texas, Indiana and California.

The company offers its employees medical, dental and vision insurance; long-term disability and life insurance; a 401(k) plan; tuition reimbursement; onsite fitness classes, child care, dry cleaning and food service; adoption assistance; parental leave.

FINANCIAL DATA: Note: Data for latest year may not have been available at press time.

In U.S. $	2018	2017	2016	2015	2014	2013
Revenue	19,095,000,000	18,686,000,000	19,204,000,000	19,023,000,000	19,031,000,000	
R&D Expense						
Operating Income	1,416,000,000	1,369,000,000	1,553,000,000	1,689,000,000	1,742,000,000	
Operating Margin %	.07%	.07%	.08%	.09%	.09%	
SGA Expense	4,512,000,000	4,435,000,000	4,452,000,000	4,350,000,000	4,313,000,000	
Net Income	859,000,000	556,000,000	673,000,000	867,000,000	889,000,000	
Operating Cash Flow	1,691,000,000	2,148,000,000	1,474,000,000	2,024,000,000	1,884,000,000	
Capital Expenditure	672,000,000	768,000,000	690,000,000	682,000,000	643,000,000	
EBITDA	2,407,000,000	2,307,000,000	2,487,000,000	2,575,000,000	2,631,000,000	
Return on Assets %	.06%	.04%	.05%	.06%	.06%	
Return on Equity %	.16%	.10%	.12%	.14%	.15%	
Debt to Equity	0.809	0.865	0.834	0.776	0.79	

CONTACT INFORMATION:
Phone: 262 703-7000 Fax: 262 703-6373
Toll-Free:
Address: N56 W17000 Ridgewood Dr., Menomonee Falls, WI 53051 United States

STOCK TICKER/OTHER:
Stock Ticker: KSS
Employees: 129,000
Parent Company:

Exchange: NYS
Fiscal Year Ends: 01/31

SALARIES/BONUSES:
Top Exec. Salary: $1,400,000 Bonus: $
Second Exec. Salary: $1,200,000 Bonus: $

OTHER THOUGHTS:
Estimated Female Officers or Directors:
Hot Spot for Advancement for Women/Minorities: Y

KPMG LLP

NAIC Code: 541211

www.kpmg.com/US/en/Pages/default.aspx

TYPES OF BUSINESS:
Accounting Services
Human Resource Advisory Services
Accounting Technology
Publications
Risk Management

BRANDS/DIVISIONS/AFFILIATES:
KPMG International
Audit Committee Institute
KPMG TaxWatch

CONTACTS:
Note: Officers with more than one job title may be intentionally listed here more than once.

Lynne M. Doughtie, CEO
George Ledwith, Dir.-Global Comm.

GROWTH PLANS/SPECIAL FEATURES:

KPMG LLP, a subsidiary of global accounting cooperative KPMG International, is a leading provider of audit, advisory and tax services within the U.S. The firm's audit operations are based on a multidisciplinary approach focused on compliance tools, technological assistance and cultural values. KPMG founded and maintains the Audit Committee Institute, designed to educate audit committee members about governance, accounting, financial reporting and other audit issues. KPMG's tax services segment provides tax assistance in the following areas: economic and valuation services, exempt organizations tax, federal tax, inbound tax services, international corporate tax, international executive services, legislative and regulatory services, mergers and acquisitions, state and local tax and trade and customs. The company also provides tax-related news through its KPMG TaxWatch podcast series and tax-related newsletters and publications. The firm's advisory services division assists its clients in achieving strengthened governance, reporting and internal controls; early identification and assessment of risk and control issues; improved efficiency and effectiveness of key business processes; and informed responses to existing and proposed regulatory requirements. With offices across the country, KPMG serves companies and organizations in such major industry sectors as alternative investments, private capital, communications/media, consumer markets, energy, financial services, government, healthcare, life sciences, middle market and technology. The firm also maintains a special focus group that has industry experience with the issues Japanese companies face in the U.S., as well as both Japanese and U.S. business cultures, practices and standards.

KPMG offers employees medical, dental and vision coverage; short- and long-term disability; life and long-term care insurance; a 401(k) plan; a pension plan; flexible spending accounts; and discounts on cars, insurance, jewelry, retailers, transit passes and other programs.

FINANCIAL DATA: *Note: Data for latest year may not have been available at press time.*

In U.S. $	2018	2017	2016	2015	2014	2013
Revenue	11,100,000,000	10,480,000,000	9,100,000,000	7,890,000,000	6,870,000,000	6,140,000,000
R&D Expense						
Operating Income						
Operating Margin %						
SGA Expense						
Net Income						
Operating Cash Flow						
Capital Expenditure						
EBITDA						
Return on Assets %						
Return on Equity %						
Debt to Equity						

CONTACT INFORMATION:
Phone: 212-758-9700 Fax: 212-751-2109
Toll-Free:
Address: 345 Park Ave., New York, NY 10154-0102 United States

STOCK TICKER/OTHER:
Stock Ticker: Subsidiary
Employees: 57,000
Parent Company: KPMG International

Exchange:
Fiscal Year Ends: 09/30

SALARIES/BONUSES:
Top Exec. Salary: $ Bonus: $
Second Exec. Salary: $ Bonus: $

OTHER THOUGHTS:
Estimated Female Officers or Directors:
Hot Spot for Advancement for Women/Minorities:

Sales, profits and employees may be estimates. Financial information, benefits and other data can change quickly and may vary from those stated here.

Kroger Co (The)

NAIC Code: 445110

www.kroger.com

TYPES OF BUSINESS:
Grocery Stores
Convenience Stores
Jewelry Stores
Pharmacies
Food Processing
Gas Stations
Department Stores
Online Grocery Shopping

BRANDS/DIVISIONS/AFFILIATES:
Kroger
City Market
Dillons
Food 4 Less
Fred Meyer
Fry's
Home Chef
Ocado Group PLC

CONTACTS:
Note: Officers with more than one job title may be intentionally listed here more than once.

W. Mcmullen, CEO
Alessandro Tosolini, Senior VP, Divisional
J. Schlotman, CFO
Christopher Hjelm, Chief Information Officer
Yael Cosset, Chief Information Officer
Todd Foley, Controller
Michael Donnelly, Executive VP
Christine Wheatley, General Counsel
Mark Tuffin, Senior VP
Calvin Kaufman, Senior VP
Stuart Aitken, Senior VP
Stephen McKinney, Senior VP
Timothy Massa, Senior VP, Divisional
Robert Clark, Senior VP, Divisional
Carin Fike, Treasurer
Jessica Adelman, Vice President, Divisional

GROWTH PLANS/SPECIAL FEATURES:

The Kroger Co. is one of the largest supermarket operators in the U.S. The company operates 2,765 supermarkets under a variety of names such as Kroger, City Market, Dillons, JayC, Food 4 Less, Fred Meyer, Fry's and Smith's. More than 1,530 of these stores have fuel centers, and approximately 2,270 have pharmacies. Kroger's supermarkets operate under one of four store formats: combination food and drug stores, multi-department stores, marketplace stores and price impact warehouses. The combo stores are the primary food store format and typically draw customers from a 2- to 2.5-mile radius; multi-department stores are larger in size than combos and sell merchandise such as apparel, home furnishings, décor, outdoor living, electronics, automotive products, toys and fine jewelry; marketplace stores offer full-service grocery, pharmacy and beauty care departments, as well as general merchandise; and price impact warehouses offer low cost promotions for grocery, health and beauty items. Kroger's 263 fine jewelry stores operate under the Fred Meyer brand. Kroger manages many walk-in medical clinics located in its stores. The company operates 38 manufacturing plants, which supply approximately 40% of the corporate brand units sold in its retail outlets. These plants consist of 17 dairies, 10 deli or bakery plants, five grocery product plants, two beverage plants, two meat plants and two cheese plants. During 2018, the firm sold its convenience store business to the EG Group for $2.15 billion; acquired Illinois-based meal kit and food delivery company, Home Chef; and signed an eCommerce partnership with Ocado Group (in which Kroger holds a minority share) to build U.S. automated warehouse facilities for Kroger's online grocery business, with the first customer fulfillment center to be built in Ohio.

FINANCIAL DATA:
Note: Data for latest year may not have been available at press time.

In U.S. $	2018	2017	2016	2015	2014	2013
Revenue	122,662,000,000	115,337,000,000	109,830,000,000	108,465,000,000	98,375,000,000	
R&D Expense						
Operating Income	2,085,000,000	3,436,000,000	3,576,000,000	3,137,000,000	2,725,000,000	
Operating Margin %	.02%	.03%	.03%	.03%	.03%	
SGA Expense	22,479,000,000	20,059,000,000	18,669,000,000	17,868,000,000	15,809,000,000	
Net Income	1,907,000,000	1,975,000,000	2,039,000,000	1,728,000,000	1,519,000,000	
Operating Cash Flow	3,413,000,000	4,272,000,000	4,833,000,000	4,163,000,000	3,380,000,000	
Capital Expenditure	2,809,000,000	3,699,000,000	3,349,000,000	2,831,000,000	2,330,000,000	
EBITDA	4,521,000,000	5,776,000,000	5,665,000,000	5,085,000,000	4,428,000,000	
Return on Assets %	.05%	.06%	.06%	.06%	.06%	
Return on Equity %	.28%	.29%	.33%	.32%	.31%	
Debt to Equity	1.736	1.765	1.424	1.805	1.793	

CONTACT INFORMATION:
Phone: 513 762-4000 Fax: 513 762-1575
Toll-Free: 866-221-4141
Address: 1014 Vine St., Cincinnati, OH 45202 United States

SALARIES/BONUSES:
Top Exec. Salary: $1,311,984 Bonus: $
Second Exec. Salary: $907,292 Bonus: $

STOCK TICKER/OTHER:
Stock Ticker: KR
Employees: 443,000
Parent Company:

Exchange: NYS
Fiscal Year Ends: 01/31

OTHER THOUGHTS:
Estimated Female Officers or Directors: 5
Hot Spot for Advancement for Women/Minorities: Y

Laboratory Corporation of America Holdings   www.labcorp.com

NAIC Code: 621511

TYPES OF BUSINESS:
Clinical Laboratory Testing
Diagnostics
Urinalyses
Blood Cell Counts
Blood Chemistry Analysis
HIV Tests
Genetic Testing
Specialty & Niche Tests

BRANDS/DIVISIONS/AFFILIATES:
LabCorp
LabCorp Diagnositcs
Covance Drug Development
Medical Neurogenetics Laboratories

CONTACTS: Note: Officers with more than one job title may be intentionally listed here more than once.
John Ratliff, CEO, Divisional
David King, CEO
Glenn Eisenberg, CFO
Peter Wilkinson, Chief Accounting Officer
Sandra van der Vaart, Chief Compliance Officer
Lance Berberian, Chief Information Officer
Brian Caveney, Chief Medical Officer
Lisa Uthgenannt, Other Executive Officer

GROWTH PLANS/SPECIAL FEATURES:

Laboratory Corporation of America Holdings (LabCorp) is a global life sciences company deeply integrated in guiding patient care. LabCorp provides comprehensive clinical laboratory and end-to-end drug development services through LabCorp Diagnostics (LCD) and Covance Drug Development (CDD). The company provides diagnostic, drug development and technology-enabled solutions for more than 120 million patient encounters each year. The firm typically processes tests on more than 2.5 million patient specimens per week and supports clinical trial activity in about 100 countries through its central laboratory and preclinical development businesses. LCD is an independent clinical laboratory business, offering a comprehensive array of testing through an integrated network of primary and specialty laboratories across the U.S. This network is supported by an IT system, with more than 65,000 electronic interfaces to deliver test results, nimble and efficient logistics and local labs offering rapid response testing. LCD's online LabCorp patient portal and mobile app offer access to new and historical test results, information about tests and an option to receive information about clinical trials. CDD provides end-to-end drug development, medical devices and diagnostic development solutions from early-stage research to clinical development and commercial market access. CDD collaborated on 93% of the novel drugs approved by the U.S. Food and Drug Administration (FDA) in 2018, including 94% of the novel rare and orphan disease drugs and 94% of the novel oncology drugs. In addition, CDD has been involved in the development of all the current top 50 drugs on the market as measured by sales revenue. In March 2019, LabCorp acquired Medical Neurogenetics Laboratories (MNG), a clinical diagnostics company that specializes in next-generation sequencing and complex biochemical testing for neurology. MNG is based in Atlanta, Georgia.

Employee benefits include medical, dental, vision, life, AD&D, short/long-term disability coverage; 401(k) and stock purchase plans; and flexible spending accounts.

FINANCIAL DATA: Note: Data for latest year may not have been available at press time.

In U.S. $	2018	2017	2016	2015	2014	2013
Revenue	11,333,400,000	10,441,400,000	9,641,800,000	8,680,100,000	6,011,600,000	5,808,300,000
R&D Expense						
Operating Income	1,373,800,000	1,435,100,000	1,370,800,000	1,116,800,000	928,200,000	1,012,700,000
Operating Margin %		.14%	.14%	.13%	.15%	.17%
SGA Expense	1,570,900,000	1,812,400,000	1,630,200,000	1,622,000,000	1,198,200,000	1,128,800,000
Net Income	883,700,000	1,268,200,000	732,100,000	436,900,000	511,200,000	573,800,000
Operating Cash Flow	1,305,400,000	1,459,400,000	1,175,900,000	982,400,000	739,000,000	818,700,000
Capital Expenditure	379,800,000	315,400,000	278,900,000	255,800,000	203,500,000	202,200,000
EBITDA	2,064,600,000	1,903,200,000	1,823,800,000	1,464,800,000	1,181,700,000	1,242,200,000
Return on Assets %		.08%	.05%	.04%	.07%	.08%
Return on Equity %		.21%	.14%	.11%	.19%	.22%
Debt to Equity		0.929	0.963	1.212	0.951	1.16

CONTACT INFORMATION:
Phone: 336 229-1127   Fax: 336 229-7717
Toll-Free:
Address: 358 S. Main St., Burlington, NC 27215 United States

SALARIES/BONUSES:
Top Exec. Salary: $1,175,000   Bonus: $
Second Exec. Salary: $686,662   Bonus: $

STOCK TICKER/OTHER:
Stock Ticker: LH
Employees: 52,000
Parent Company:

Exchange: NYS
Fiscal Year Ends: 12/31

OTHER THOUGHTS:
Estimated Female Officers or Directors: 3
Hot Spot for Advancement for Women/Minorities: Y

Sales, profits and employees may be estimates. Financial information, benefits and other data can change quickly and may vary from those stated here.

Lam Research Corporation

NAIC Code: 333242

www.lamresearch.com

TYPES OF BUSINESS:
Semiconductor Manufacturing Equipment
Etch Processing Systems
Chemical Mechanical Planarization Systems
Wafer Cleaning Equipment & Services
Support Services

BRANDS/DIVISIONS/AFFILIATES:
Flex
Versys
Kiyo
Syndion
VECTOR
ALTUS
SABRE
SOLA

CONTACTS:
Note: Officers with more than one job title may be intentionally listed here more than once.

Timothy Archer, CEO
Douglas Bettinger, CFO
Stephen Newberry, Chairman of the Board
Richard Gottscho, Chief Technology Officer
Vahid Vahedi, General Manager, Divisional
Seshasayee Varadarajan, General Manager, Divisional
Patrick Lord, General Manager, Divisional
Sarah ODowd, Other Executive Officer
Kevin Jennings, Senior VP, Divisional
Scott Meikle, Senior VP, Divisional

GROWTH PLANS/SPECIAL FEATURES:

Lam Research Corporation supplies wafer fabrication equipment and services to semiconductor companies worldwide. The firm designs, manufactures, markets and services semiconductor processing equipment used in semiconductor device fabrication. The company's etch products are used to deposit special films on silicon wafers and to selectively etch away portions of these films utilizing plasma-based technologies, creating an integrated circuit (IC). Its products include the Flex product family for dielectric etch, the Versys metal and Kiyo product families for conductor etch and the Syndion product family for three-dimensional ICs. Lam's VECTOR family of plasma-enhanced chemical vapor deposition and atomic layer deposition systems delivers superior thin film quality, wafer-to-water uniformity, productivity and low cost of ownership. The firm also offers wafer cleaning services and equipment that employs proprietary technology and can be used throughout the semiconductor manufacturing process. Lam's ALTUS product family deposits a highly conformal atomic layer for advanced tungsten metallization applications. The patented multi-station sequential deposition architecture enables a layer to be formed using pulsed nucleation layer technology. The SABRE electrochemical deposition (ECD) product family is a system for copper damascene manufacturing. SABRE 3D addresses through-silicon via (TSV) and wafer-level packaging (WLP) applications, such as copper pillar, redistribution layers, high-density fanout, underbump metallization, bumping and microbumps used in post-TSV processing. The SPEED family of products are designed to provide void-free gapfill of high-quality dielectric films with throughput and reliability. And the SOLA product family is used for treatment of back-end-of-line low-k dielectric films and front-end-of-line silicon nitride strained films.

The firm offers employees life, disability, AD&D, medical, dental and vision insurance; flexible spending accounts; educational and employee assistance programs; adoption aid; and access to a credit union.

FINANCIAL DATA:
Note: Data for latest year may not have been available at press time.

In U.S. $	2018	2017	2016	2015	2014	2013
Revenue	11,077,000,000	8,013,620,000	5,885,893,000	5,259,312,000	4,607,309,000	3,598,916,000
R&D Expense	1,189,514,000	1,033,742,000	913,712,000	825,242,000	716,471,000	683,688,000
Operating Income	3,213,299,000	1,902,132,000	1,074,256,000	867,483,000	677,669,000	119,884,000
Operating Margin %		.24%	.18%	.16%	.15%	.03%
SGA Expense	762,219,000	667,485,000	630,954,000	591,611,000	613,341,000	599,487,000
Net Income	2,380,681,000	1,697,763,000	914,049,000	655,577,000	632,289,000	113,879,000
Operating Cash Flow	2,655,747,000	2,029,282,000	1,350,277,000	785,503,000	717,049,000	719,933,000
Capital Expenditure	273,469,000	157,419,000	175,330,000	198,265,000	145,503,000	160,795,000
EBITDA	3,575,571,000	2,236,312,000	1,385,918,000	1,092,452,000	1,077,309,000	431,182,000
Return on Assets %		.14%	.08%	.08%	.08%	.01%
Return on Equity %		.27%	.17%	.13%	.13%	.02%
Debt to Equity		0.287	0.609	0.244	0.199	0.217

CONTACT INFORMATION:
Phone: 510 572-0200 Fax: 510 572-6454
Toll-Free: 800-526-7678
Address: 4650 Cushing Pkwy., Fremont, CA 94538 United States

SALARIES/BONUSES:
Top Exec. Salary: $1,001,442 Bonus: $
Second Exec. Salary: $674,922 Bonus: $

STOCK TICKER/OTHER:
Stock Ticker: LRCX Exchange: NAS
Employees: 9,400 Fiscal Year Ends: 06/30
Parent Company:

OTHER THOUGHTS:
Estimated Female Officers or Directors: 3
Hot Spot for Advancement for Women/Minorities: Y

Larry H Miller Group of Companies

www.lhm.com

NAIC Code: 441110

TYPES OF BUSINESS:
Auto Dealers, Retail
Auto Financing & Service
Sports Arenas
Movie Theaters
Professional Sports Teams
TV Station
Sports Apparel Stores

BRANDS/DIVISIONS/AFFILIATES:
Larry H Miller Dealerships
Prestige Financial
Total Care Auto Powered by Lancar
Larry H Miller Megaplex Theaters
Vivint Smart Home Arena
Larry H Miller's Tour of Utah
Larry H Miller's Jordan Commons
Larry H Miller Real Estate

CONTACTS:
Note: Officers with more than one job title may be intentionally listed here more than once.

Steve Starks, CEO
Robert Tingey, General Counsel
Jay Francis, Exec. VP-Oper.
Clark Whitworth, CFO-Automotive
Robert Hyde, CFO-Sports & Entertainment
Steve Starks, Exec. VP-Oper.
Gail Miller, Owner

GROWTH PLANS/SPECIAL FEATURES:

Larry H Miller Group of Companies (LMG) is a holding firm that operates a large number of subsidiaries engaged in automotive dealerships, finance, insurance, sports, entertainment and retail. LMG has more than 80 businesses and properties located in 46 U.S. states. Larry H. Miller Dealerships sells a wide variety of automotive brands including Ford, Cadillac, Lexus, Toyota, Honda, Chevrolet and Jeep via 60 dealership locations under 20 different automotive brands in seven western states. Prestige Financial is a provider of consumer financial solutions for both franchised and independent automobile dealerships across America. Total Care Auto Powered by Landcar provides vehicle insurance coverage. The sports and entertainment and retail divisions include: Larry H. Miller Megaplex Theaters, which comprise more than 180 screens at 16 locations within Nevada and Utah; the Vivint Smart Home Arena, which seats more than 20,000 people for concerts, events and the Utah Jazz basketball games; the Larry H. Miller's Tour of Utah showcases professional cyclists for a week of racing during the month of August; the Salt Lake Bees are a triple-A affiliate of the Los Angeles Angels; the Salt Lake City Stars, NBA D-League team; Jazz Gaming, an NBA eSport team; the Saxton Horne advertising and communications agency, specializing in marketing and media buying services; and the Zone (1280 AM) and FOX Sports Radio (97.5 FM) are 50,000-watt sports radio stations in Utah. In addition, Larry H. Miller's Jordan Commons comprises restaurants, offices, a theatre and an event complex in Sandy, Utah; Larry H. Miller Management Corporation, which directs corporate governance, mergers/acquisitions, finance, human resource and related services; and Larry H. Miller Real Estate purchases, develops and manages properties for the firm's group of companies.

The company offers comprehensive benefits, 401(k) and retirement options, as well as a variety of employee assistance programs.

FINANCIAL DATA:
Note: Data for latest year may not have been available at press time.

In U.S. $	2018	2017	2016	2015	2014	2013
Revenue	5,159,425,257	4,913,738,335	4,679,750,795	3,933,621,552	4,565,000,000	4,300,000,000
R&D Expense						
Operating Income						
Operating Margin %						
SGA Expense						
Net Income						
Operating Cash Flow						
Capital Expenditure						
EBITDA						
Return on Assets %						
Return on Equity %						
Debt to Equity						

CONTACT INFORMATION:
Phone: 801-563-4100 Fax: 801-563-4198
Toll-Free:
Address: 9350 S.150 E., Ste. 1000, Sandy, UT 84070 United States

STOCK TICKER/OTHER:
Stock Ticker: Private
Employees: 10,000
Parent Company:

Exchange:
Fiscal Year Ends: 12/31

SALARIES/BONUSES:
Top Exec. Salary: $ Bonus: $
Second Exec. Salary: $ Bonus: $

OTHER THOUGHTS:
Estimated Female Officers or Directors:
Hot Spot for Advancement for Women/Minorities:

Las Vegas Sands Corp (The Venetian)

www.sands.com

NAIC Code: 721120

TYPES OF BUSINESS:
Hotel Casinos
Convention & Conference Centers
Shopping Center Development
Casino Property Development

BRANDS/DIVISIONS/AFFILIATES:
Palazzo Resort Hotel Casino (The)
Sands Expo and Convention Center (The)
Sands China Ltd
Sands Macao Casino (The)
Marina Bay Saynds Pte Ltd
Venetian Macao Resort Hotel (The)
Four Seasons Macao
Parisian Macao

CONTACTS:
Note: Officers with more than one job title may be intentionally listed here more than once.

Sheldon Adelson, CEO
Patrick Dumont, CFO
Randy Hyzak, Chief Accounting Officer
Robert Goldstein, COO
Lawrence Jacobs, Executive VP

GROWTH PLANS/SPECIAL FEATURES:

Las Vegas Sands Corp. (LVSC) is an international hotel, resort and casino firm. Its flagship property is The Venetian Resort Hotel Casino, which is connected to The Palazzo Resort Hotel Casino. Together, The Venetian and The Palazzo offer 225,000 square feet of gaming space, with 245 table games and 1,790 slot machines, as well as 7,092 hotel suites. LVSC also runs the 1.2 million square foot convention and trade show facility, The Sands Expo and Convention Center, and a supplemental event and conference center. Additionally, the firm operates the Sands Casino Resort Bethlehem in eastern Pennsylvania, which features 146,000 square feet of gaming space, a 282-room hotel, 150,000 square feet of retail space and other amenities. Outside the U.S., LVSC has operations in Macao, through majority-owned subsidiary Sands China Ltd., and Singapore, through Marina Bay Sands Pte. Ltd. The company's largest development project, the multi-billion-dollar Cotai Strip, is a collection of hotel properties, casinos and entertainment venues in Macao. Sands China runs The Sands Macao and The Venetian Macao Resort Hotel, the anchor property on the Cotai Strip. Other properties on the Cotai Strip include the Four Seasons Macao, the Plaza Casino and Parisian Macao. Its Singapore property, Marina Bay Sands features three 55-story hotel towers, gaming space, convention space, two state-of-the-art theaters and The Shoppes at Marina Bay Sands. The Parisian Macao is located on the Cotai Strip and features approximately 253,000 square feet of gaming space with approximately 385 table games and 1,560 slot machines, as well as approximately 3,000 rooms and suites and the Shoppes at Parisian, offering retail shopping. In March 2018, the firm agreed to sell the Sands Bethlehem property in Pennsylvania; as of March 2019, the transaction was still seeking regulatory approvals.

FINANCIAL DATA:
Note: Data for latest year may not have been available at press time.

In U.S. $	2018	2017	2016	2015	2014	2013
Revenue	13,729,000,000	12,882,000,000	11,410,000,000	11,688,460,000	14,583,850,000	13,769,880,000
R&D Expense	12,000,000	13,000,000	9,000,000	10,372,000	14,325,000	15,809,000
Operating Income	3,901,000,000	3,482,000,000	2,572,000,000	2,876,707,000	4,106,082,000	3,419,399,000
Operating Margin %		.27%	.23%	.25%	.28%	.25%
SGA Expense	1,483,000,000	1,415,000,000	1,284,000,000	1,267,415,000	1,258,133,000	1,329,740,000
Net Income	2,413,000,000	2,806,000,000	1,670,000,000	1,966,236,000	2,840,629,000	2,305,997,000
Operating Cash Flow	4,701,000,000	4,543,000,000	4,043,000,000	3,449,971,000	4,832,844,000	4,439,412,000
Capital Expenditure	949,000,000	837,000,000	1,445,000,000	1,528,642,000	1,178,656,000	943,982,000
EBITDA	4,918,000,000	4,587,000,000	3,678,000,000	3,924,666,000	5,179,079,000	4,462,543,000
Return on Assets %		.14%	.08%	.09%	.13%	.10%
Return on Equity %		.44%	.26%	.28%	.38%	.31%
Debt to Equity		1.439	1.526	1.375	1.371	1.224

CONTACT INFORMATION:
Phone: 702 414-1000 Fax: 702 414-4884
Toll-Free:
Address: 3355 Las Vegas Blvd. S., Las Vegas, NV 89109 United States

STOCK TICKER/OTHER:
Stock Ticker: LVS Exchange: NYS
Employees: 49,000 Fiscal Year Ends: 12/31
Parent Company:

SALARIES/BONUSES:
Top Exec. Salary: $5,000,000 Bonus: $
Second Exec. Salary: $3,400,000 Bonus: $

OTHER THOUGHTS:
Estimated Female Officers or Directors:
Hot Spot for Advancement for Women/Minorities:

Lear Corporation

www.lear.com

NAIC Code: 336300

TYPES OF BUSINESS:
Automobile Components
Automotive Interiors
Electrical Systems
Instrument Panels
Seat Systems
Flooring Systems
Entertainment & Wireless Systems
Keyless Entry Systems

BRANDS/DIVISIONS/AFFILIATES:

CONTACTS:
Note: Officers with more than one job title may be intentionally listed here more than once.

Raymond Scott, CEO
Jeffrey Vanneste, CFO
Henry Wallace, Chairman of the Board
Amy Doyle, Chief Accounting Officer
Thomas DiDonato, Chief Administrative Officer
Terrence Larkin, Executive VP, Divisional
Frank Orsini, President, Divisional
Shari Burgess, Treasurer

GROWTH PLANS/SPECIAL FEATURES:

Lear Corporation is one of the world's largest automotive interior systems suppliers. The firm serves every major automotive manufacturer, including General Motors, Ford, BMW, Fiat Chrysler and Daimler. The company currently operates 145 facilities in 22 countries. Its business is conducted through two segments: seating and e-systems. The seating segment consists of the design, engineering, just-in-time assembly and delivery of complete seat systems as well as the manufacture of all major seat components, including seat structures and mechanisms, seat covers, seat forms and headrests. The segment produces seat systems that are fully assembled and ready for installation in automobiles and light trucks. These include luxury and performance automotive seating required by premium automakers, including Alfa Romeo, Audi, Lamborghini, BMW, Cadillac, Ferrari, Jaguar Land Rover, Lincoln, Maserati, Mercedes-Benz and Porsche. The e-systems segment consists of the design, manufacture, assembly and supply of electrical distribution systems, electronic modules and related components and software for light vehicles globally. Its electrical distribution systems route electrical signals and manage electrical power within the vehicle for traditional vehicle architectures, as well as high power and hybrid electric systems. Electronics control various functions within the vehicle, and include body control modules, smart junction boxes, gateway modules, wireless control modules, lighting control modules and audio amplifiers. Connectivity capabilities facilitate secure, wireless communication between the vehicle's systems and external networks, as well as other vehicles. As of December 31, 2018, the company had 16 operating joint ventures located in five countries, of which 12 operated in Asia and four in North America. In April 2019, Lear agreed to acquire Seattle-based Xevo, Inc., an automotive software supplier that develops solutions for cloud, car and mobile devices.

FINANCIAL DATA:
Note: Data for latest year may not have been available at press time.

In U.S. $	2018	2017	2016	2015	2014	2013
Revenue	21,148,500,000	20,467,000,000	18,557,600,000	18,211,400,000	17,727,300,000	16,234,000,000
R&D Expense						
Operating Income	1,654,100,000	1,608,300,000	1,427,200,000	1,186,800,000	929,200,000	736,600,000
Operating Margin %		.08%	.08%	.07%	.05%	.05%
SGA Expense	612,800,000	635,200,000	621,900,000	580,500,000	529,900,000	528,700,000
Net Income	1,149,800,000	1,313,400,000	975,100,000	745,500,000	672,400,000	431,400,000
Operating Cash Flow	1,779,800,000	1,783,100,000	1,619,300,000	1,271,100,000	927,800,000	820,100,000
Capital Expenditure	677,000,000	594,500,000	528,300,000	485,800,000	424,700,000	460,600,000
EBITDA	2,106,900,000	2,040,100,000	1,799,000,000	1,466,000,000	1,165,800,000	964,000,000
Return on Assets %		.12%	.10%	.08%	.08%	.05%
Return on Equity %		.36%	.33%	.25%	.22%	.13%
Debt to Equity		0.47	0.621	0.66	0.499	0.347

CONTACT INFORMATION:
Phone: 248 447-1500 Fax:
Toll-Free: 800-413-5327
Address: 21557 Telegraph Rd., Southfield, MI 48033 United States

SALARIES/BONUSES:
Top Exec. Salary: $1,109,183 Bonus: $
Second Exec. Salary: $855,098 Bonus: $

STOCK TICKER/OTHER:
Stock Ticker: LEA
Employees: 161,000
Parent Company:

Exchange: NYS
Fiscal Year Ends: 12/31

OTHER THOUGHTS:
Estimated Female Officers or Directors: 1
Hot Spot for Advancement for Women/Minorities:

Legg Mason Inc

NAIC Code: 523110

www.leggmason.com

TYPES OF BUSINESS:
Stock Brokerage/Investment Banking
Mutual Funds

BRANDS/DIVISIONS/AFFILIATES:
Western Asset Management Company
ClearBridge Investments
Brandywine Global Investment Management
Clarion Partners
EnTrustPermal
RARE Infrastructure
Legg Mason Funds
Royce Funds

CONTACTS: *Note: Officers with more than one job title may be intentionally listed here more than once.*

Joseph Sullivan, CEO
Peter Nachtwey, CFO
Ursula Schliessler, Chief Administrative Officer
Thomas Merchant, Executive VP
Terence Johnson, Executive VP
John Kenney, Other Corporate Officer
Frances Cashman, Other Corporate Officer
Thomas Hoops, Other Corporate Officer
Patricia Lattin, Other Corporate Officer

GROWTH PLANS/SPECIAL FEATURES:

Legg Mason, Inc. is a global asset management company with more than $754 billion in consolidated assets under management. Operating through its subsidiaries, the firm provides investment management and related services to institutional and individual clients, company-sponsored mutual funds and other pooled investment vehicles. The company offers these products and services directly and through various financial intermediaries. The firm conducts its business primarily through several asset managers, housed in independent subsidiaries owned by Legg Mason. Asset managers provide a range of separate account investment management services to institutional clients, including pension and other retirement plans, corporations, insurance companies, endowments, foundations and governments as well as to high-net-worth individuals and families. They also sponsor and manage various groups of U.S. mutual funds and exchange-traded funds (ETFs), including equity, fixed income, liquidity and balanced funds. Asset managers include Western Asset Management Company, ClearBridge Investments, Brandywine Global Investment Management, Clarion Partners, EnTrustPermal, Royce & Associates, Martin Currie, QS Investors and RARE Infrastructure. U.S. funds primarily consist of proprietary mutual and closed-end funds, the Legg Mason Funds and the Royce Funds, totaling 127 mutual funds and 31 close-ended funds. Legg Mason Funds invest in a range of domestic and international equity and fixed income securities utilizing various investment styles; and the Royce Funds invest primarily in smaller-cap company stocks using a value investment approach. International funds include a broad range of cross border funds that are domiciled in Ireland and Luxembourg and are sold in a number of countries across Asia, Europe and Latin America. During 2017, the firm streamlined its business by divesting its interest in non-core asset managers and a joint venture.

The company offers employees paid time off, health care coverage, commuter discounts, a 401(k) plan, a profit sharing plan, a stock purchase plan, adoption assistance and tuition reimbursement.

FINANCIAL DATA: *Note: Data for latest year may not have been available at press time.*

In U.S. $	2018	2017	2016	2015	2014	2013
Revenue	3,140,322,000	2,886,902,000	2,660,844,000	2,819,106,000	2,741,757,000	
R&D Expense						
Operating Income	521,672,000	457,243,000	421,831,000	498,219,000	430,893,000	
Operating Margin %	.17%	.16%	.16%	.18%	.16%	
SGA Expense	313,558,000	322,599,000	320,467,000	292,146,000	273,106,000	
Net Income	285,075,000	227,256,000	-25,032,000	237,080,000	284,784,000	
Operating Cash Flow	492,936,000	539,772,000	454,451,000	568,118,000	437,324,000	
Capital Expenditure	37,346,000	39,977,000	40,330,000	45,773,000	40,452,000	
EBITDA	424,698,000	564,264,000	83,542,000	481,353,000	535,397,000	
Return on Assets %	.03%	.03%	.00%	.03%	.04%	
Return on Equity %	.07%	.05%	-.01%	.05%	.06%	
Debt to Equity	0.581	0.558	0.413	0.236	0.22	

CONTACT INFORMATION:
Phone: 410 539-0000   Fax: 410 454-4174
Toll-Free: 800-822-5544
Address: 100 International Dr., Baltimore, MD 21202 United States

SALARIES/BONUSES:
Top Exec. Salary: $500,000   Bonus: $3,400,000
Second Exec. Salary: $350,000   Bonus: $1,512,500

STOCK TICKER/OTHER:
Stock Ticker: LM   Exchange: NYS
Employees: 3,275   Fiscal Year Ends: 02/28
Parent Company:

OTHER THOUGHTS:
Estimated Female Officers or Directors: 2
Hot Spot for Advancement for Women/Minorities:

Sales, profits and employees may be estimates. Financial information, benefits and other data can change quickly and may vary from those stated here.

Lennar Corporation

NAIC Code: 236117

www.lennar.com

TYPES OF BUSINESS:
Construction, Home Building and Residential Mortgages
Title Insurance & Services

BRANDS/DIVISIONS/AFFILIATES:
Eagle Home Mortgage LLC
North American Title Insurance Company
North American Advantage Insurance Services LLC
Rialto Mortgage Finance
Lennar

CONTACTS:
Note: Officers with more than one job title may be intentionally listed here more than once.

Stuart Miller, Chairman of the Board
David Collins, Chief Accounting Officer
Richard Beckwitt, Director
Jonathan Jaffe, Director
Mark Sustana, Secretary
Jeffrey McCall, Senior VP
Diane Bessette, Vice President

GROWTH PLANS/SPECIAL FEATURES:

Lennar Corporation is a U.S. homebuilder and related financial services provider. The firm sells single-family attached and detached homes and, to a lesser extent, multi-level residential buildings primarily under the Lennar brand name in communities targeted to first-time, move-up and active adult homebuyers. The company also purchases, develops and sells residential land. Lennar divides its homebuilding operations into five segments: East (which includes Florida, New Jersey, North Carolina and South Carolina); Central (including Georgia, Illinois, Indiana, Maryland, Minnesota, Tennessee and Virginia); Texas; West (including Arizona, California, Colorado, Nevada, Oregon, Utah and Washington); and Other (including urban divisions and other homebuilding-related investments). Lennar's financial services are provided through subsidiary Eagle Home Mortgage, LLC, offering conforming conventional, FHA-insured and VA-guaranteed residential mortgage loan products and other home mortgage products to buyers of Lennar homes. More than 70% of Lennar homebuyers utilize its related mortgage services. Lennar's financial division also provides title and other insurance and closing services to its homebuyers. Title insurance policies are underwritten by subsidiary North American Title Insurance Company; and property and casualty insurance products are offered through subsidiary North American Advantage Insurance Services, LLC. In addition, subsidiary Rialto Mortgage Finance originates and sells into securitizations five-, seven- and ten-year mortgage loans. These loans are secured by income-producing commercial properties. In December 2018, Lennar sold its Rialto Investment and Asset Management business to investment funds managed by Stone Point Capital for $340 million. Rialto Mortgage Finance was subsequently placed within Lennar's financial services division.

The company offers employees medical, dental, vision, life and short-/long-term insurance; home and auto insurance; and mortgage and title perks.

FINANCIAL DATA:
Note: Data for latest year may not have been available at press time.

In U.S. $	2018	2017	2016	2015	2014	2013
Revenue	20,571,630,000	12,646,370,000	10,950,000,000	9,474,008,000	7,779,812,000	5,935,095,000
R&D Expense						
Operating Income	1,990,251,000	1,338,995,000	1,262,363,000	1,086,016,000	922,038,000	685,836,000
Operating Margin %		.11%	.12%	.11%	.12%	.12%
SGA Expense	343,934,000	285,889,000	232,562,000	216,244,000	177,161,000	146,060,000
Net Income	1,695,831,000	810,480,000	911,844,000	802,894,000	638,916,000	479,674,000
Operating Cash Flow	1,711,609,000	996,864,000	507,804,000	-419,646,000	-788,488,000	-807,714,000
Capital Expenditure	130,439,000	111,773,000	76,439,000	91,355,000	22,599,000	8,126,000
EBITDA	2,365,123,000	1,263,099,000	1,385,314,000	1,265,736,000	1,044,877,000	806,203,000
Return on Assets %		.05%	.06%	.06%	.05%	.04%
Return on Equity %		.11%	.14%	.15%	.14%	.13%
Debt to Equity		1.013	0.893	1.178	1.247	1.218

CONTACT INFORMATION:
Phone: 305 559-4000   Fax: 305 227-7115
Toll-Free: 800-741-4663
Address: 700 NW 107th Ave., Ste. 400, Miami, FL 33172 United States

SALARIES/BONUSES:
Top Exec. Salary: $750,000   Bonus: $2,400,037
Second Exec. Salary: $750,000   Bonus: $1,250,005

STOCK TICKER/OTHER:
Stock Ticker: LEN
Employees: 8,335
Parent Company:

Exchange: NYS
Fiscal Year Ends: 11/30

OTHER THOUGHTS:
Estimated Female Officers or Directors: 3
Hot Spot for Advancement for Women/Minorities: Y

Sales, profits and employees may be estimates. Financial information, benefits and other data can change quickly and may vary from those stated here.

LHC Group Inc

NAIC Code: 621610

www.lhcgroup.com

TYPES OF BUSINESS:
Home Health Care Services
Hospices
Long-Term Acute Care Hospitals

BRANDS/DIVISIONS/AFFILIATES:
Caregivers Health Network

GROWTH PLANS/SPECIAL FEATURES:
LHC Group, Inc. is a national provider of high-quality, affordable in-home healthcare services and innovations. The firm's services cover a wide range of healthcare needs for patients and families dealing with illness, injury or chronic conditions. LHC delivers home health, hospice, home- and community-based services, and facility-based care in 35 U.S. states and the District of Columbia, reaching 60% of the U.S. population aged 65 and older. In September 2019, LHC Group announced the formation of a new joint venture agreement with Norton Healthcare in Louisville, Kentucky, with the two organizations sharing ownership of Caregivers Health Network (CHN), a home health provider serving patients and families in Louisville and the surrounding region. Under the terms, Norton Healthcare will hold a minority interest in CHN.

CONTACTS:
Note: Officers with more than one job title may be intentionally listed here more than once.

Keith Myers, CEO
Joshua Proffitt, CFO
Collin McQuiddy, Chief Accounting Officer
Bruce Greenstein, Chief Strategy Officer
Donald Stelly, COO
Nicholas Gachassin, Executive VP

FINANCIAL DATA:
Note: Data for latest year may not have been available at press time.

In U.S. $	2018	2017	2016	2015	2014	2013
Revenue	1,809,963,000	1,072,086,000	914,823,000	816,366,000	733,632,000	658,283,000
R&D Expense						
Operating Income	115,690,000	76,253,000	71,761,000	67,616,000	49,132,000	46,757,000
Operating Margin %		.07%	.08%	.08%	.07%	.07%
SGA Expense	537,916,000	310,539,000	270,622,000	248,629,000	233,945,000	214,133,000
Net Income	63,574,000	50,112,000	36,583,000	32,335,000	21,837,000	22,342,000
Operating Cash Flow	108,585,000	32,326,000	67,472,000	59,934,000	38,657,000	45,915,000
Capital Expenditure	32,993,000	74,774,000	39,165,000	83,855,000	82,038,000	35,263,000
EBITDA	127,363,000	88,628,000	83,214,000	78,755,000	55,322,000	55,325,000
Return on Assets %		.07%	.06%	.06%	.05%	.06%
Return on Equity %		.12%	.10%	.10%	.07%	.08%
Debt to Equity		0.321	0.222	0.278	0.191	0.078

CONTACT INFORMATION:
Phone: 337 233-1307 Fax: 337 235-8037
Toll-Free:
Address: 901 Hugh Wallis Rd. S., Lafayette, LA 70508 United States

SALARIES/BONUSES:
Top Exec. Salary: $595,000   Bonus: $250,000
Second Exec. Salary: $500,000   Bonus: $250,000

STOCK TICKER/OTHER:
Stock Ticker: LHCG
Employees: 11,598
Parent Company:

Exchange: NAS
Fiscal Year Ends: 12/31

OTHER THOUGHTS:
Estimated Female Officers or Directors: 6
Hot Spot for Advancement for Women/Minorities: Y

Liberty Mutual Group Inc

NAIC Code: 524126

www.libertymutualgroup.com

TYPES OF BUSINESS:
Insurance, Direct Property & Casualty
Rehabilitation Services
Disability Care Management
Homeowners' Insurance
Auto Insurance
Group Life Insurance
Asset Management & Investment Products
Workers' Compensation

BRANDS/DIVISIONS/AFFILIATES:
Liberty Mutual Insurance Company
Liberty Mutual Fire Insurance Company
Employers Insurance of Wausau
Liberty Corporate Services LLC

CONTACTS: Note: Officers with more than one job title may be intentionally listed here more than once.
David H. Long, CEO
Christopher L. Peirce, CFO
Melanie M. Foley, Sr. VP-Human Resources
James M. McGlennon, CIO
Melanie M. Foley, Sr. VP-Admin.
James F. Kelleher, Sr. VP
Paul G. Alexander, Mgr.-Comm.
Laurance H.S. Yahia, Treas.
J. Paul Condrin III, Exec. VP
A. Alexander Fontanes, Exec. VP
Christopher L. Peirce, Exec. VP
Timothy M. Sweeney, Exec. VP
David H. Long, Chmn.
Luis Bonell, Exec. VP

GROWTH PLANS/SPECIAL FEATURES:
Liberty Mutual Group, Inc. offers a wide range of insurance products and services globally. The firm's global network provides personal automobile, homeowners, specialty lines, reinsurance, commercial multiple-peril, workers compensation, commercial automobile, general liability, surety and commercial property insurance. Liberty Mutual's principal stock insurance companies include: Liberty Mutual Insurance Company, Liberty Mutual Fire Insurance Company and Employers Insurance of Wausau. Its related service subsidiary is Liberty Corporate Services, LLC. Together the group operates from over 800 offices worldwide and conducts substantially all of its business through two units: global retail markets and global risk solutions. These units operate independently of the other in certain areas such as sales, underwriting and claims; but, as appropriate, collaborates in other areas such as actuarial and financial. The global retail markets business consists of four segments: U.S., offering personal and business insurance products; West, selling property and casualty, health and life insurance products and services to customers in Brazil, Colombia, Chile, Ecuador, Spain, Portugal and Ireland; East, selling property and casualty, health and life insurance products and services to customers in Thailand, Singapore, Hong Kong, Vietnam, Malaysia, India, China and Russia; and GRM Reinsurance, offering certain internal reinsurance programs. The global risk solutions business offers a wide range of property, casualty, specialty and reinsurance coverage distributed through brokers and independent agents globally. This business operates four segments: Liberty Specialty Markets, offering global risk solutions outside of North America, and global reinsurance; National Insurance, offering U.S. admitted and non-admitted property and casualty insurance in excess of $150,000 annual premium; North America Specialty, offering specialty lines and non-admitted property and casualty in North America; Global Surety, providing contract and commercial surety bonds to businesses of all sizes; and other global risk solutions, primarily consisting of internal reinsurance programs.

Comprehensive benefits, 401(k) and other employee benefits are offered.

FINANCIAL DATA: Note: Data for latest year may not have been available at press time.

In U.S. $	2018	2017	2016	2015	2014	2013
Revenue	41,568,000,000	39,409,000,000	38,308,000,000	37,617,000,000	37,721,000,000	36,556,000,000
R&D Expense						
Operating Income						
Operating Margin %						
SGA Expense						
Net Income	2,160,000,000	17,000,000	1,006,000,000	514,000,000	1,833,000,000	1,743,000,000
Operating Cash Flow						
Capital Expenditure						
EBITDA						
Return on Assets %						
Return on Equity %						
Debt to Equity						

CONTACT INFORMATION:
Phone: 617-357-9500 Fax: 617-350-7648
Toll-Free: 800-837-5254
Address: 175 Berkeley St., Boston, MA 02116 United States

STOCK TICKER/OTHER:
Stock Ticker: Mutual Company
Employees: 51,000
Parent Company:

Exchange:
Fiscal Year Ends: 12/31

SALARIES/BONUSES:
Top Exec. Salary: $ Bonus: $
Second Exec. Salary: $ Bonus: $

OTHER THOUGHTS:
Estimated Female Officers or Directors: 4
Hot Spot for Advancement for Women/Minorities: Y

Sales, profits and employees may be estimates. Financial information, benefits and other data can change quickly and may vary from those stated here.

LifePoint Health Inc

www.lifepointhealth.net

NAIC Code: 622110

TYPES OF BUSINESS:
General Medical and Surgical Hospitals

BRANDS/DIVISIONS/AFFILIATES:
Apollo Global Management LLC
Health Support Center

CONTACTS: Note: Officers with more than one job title may be intentionally listed here more than once.
David M. Dill, CEO
Michael Coggin, CFO
Michael S. Coggin, Exec. VP
Sonny Terrill, Exec. VP-Human Resources
David Dill, COO
Jennifer Peters, General Counsel
Jeffrey Seraphine, Other Executive Officer
Victor Giovanetti, President, Divisional
Melissa Waddey, President, Divisional
Robert Klein, President, Divisional
R. Raplee, President, Divisional

GROWTH PLANS/SPECIAL FEATURES:
LifePoint Health, Inc. is a holding company that operates through its subsidiaries, which own and operate hospitals or other healthcare providers in more than 80 communities throughout the U.S. LifePoint Health's facilities and practices are grouped into four geographic divisions (Eastern, Central, Mountain and Western), which each have their own leadership team. The group's Health Support Center (HSC) in Brentwood, Tennessee has expertise in every area of healthcare operations and provider services. HSC offers resources across the continuum of care, from before a patient accesses healthcare services to after they are sent home. HSC works with the group's local markets to help develop and implement proper strategies that ensure healthcare thrives in those communities. In November 2018, LifePoint Health, Inc. was acquired by Apollo Global Management, LLC and delisted from public trading.

The company offers its employees medical, dental, vision, life and disability insurance; adoption assistance; flexible spending accounts; a wellness program; a Wells Fargo Employee Home Mortgage Program; and a 401(k) plan.

FINANCIAL DATA: Note: Data for latest year may not have been available at press time.

In U.S. $	2018	2017	2016	2015	2014	2013
Revenue	7,400,000,000	7,263,099,904	7,273,600,000	6,014,400,000	5,300,899,840	4,428,700,160
R&D Expense						
Operating Income						
Operating Margin %						
SGA Expense						
Net Income		102,400,000	121,900,000	181,900,000	126,100,000	128,200,000
Operating Cash Flow						
Capital Expenditure						
EBITDA						
Return on Assets %						
Return on Equity %						
Debt to Equity						

CONTACT INFORMATION:
Phone: 615 920-7000 Fax:
Toll-Free:
Address: 330 Seven Springs Way, Brentwood, TN 37027 United States

STOCK TICKER/OTHER:
Stock Ticker: Subsidiary Exchange:
Employees: 47,000 Fiscal Year Ends: 12/31
Parent Company: Apollo Global Management LLC

SALARIES/BONUSES:
Top Exec. Salary: $ Bonus: $
Second Exec. Salary: $ Bonus: $

OTHER THOUGHTS:
Estimated Female Officers or Directors: 1
Hot Spot for Advancement for Women/Minorities: Y

Lincoln National Corporation

NAIC Code: 524113

www.lfg.com

TYPES OF BUSINESS:
Life Insurance
Investment Management
Retirement Plans
Mutual Funds
Financial Planning
Annuities

BRANDS/DIVISIONS/AFFILIATES:
Lincoln Financial Group

CONTACTS:
Note: Officers with more than one job title may be intentionally listed here more than once.

Wilford Fuller, CEO, Subsidiary
Dennis Glass, CEO
Randal Freitag, CFO
Christine Janofsky, Chief Accounting Officer
Kenneth Solon, Chief Information Officer
William Cunningham, Director
Leon Roday, Executive VP
Jamie Ohl, Executive VP
Ellen Cooper, Executive VP
Lisa Buckingham, Executive VP
Richard Mucci, Executive VP

GROWTH PLANS/SPECIAL FEATURES:

Lincoln National Corporation is a holding company operating multiple insurance and retirement businesses. The operations of the firm's subsidiaries, collectively known as Lincoln Financial Group, are divided into four operating businesses: retirement plan services, life insurance, annuities and group protection. Retirement plan services provides employers with retirement plan products and services, with a focus on defined contribution retirement plans. The life insurance segment offers life insurance products including term insurances, a linked-benefit product, indexed universal life (UL) insurance and both single and survivorship versions of UL and variable UL (VUL) products. In a UL contract, contract holders typically have flexibility in the timing and amount of premium payments and the amount of death benefit, provided there is sufficient account value to cover all policy charges. VUL products are UL products that provide a return on account values linked to an underlying investment portfolio of variable funds offered through the products. The annuities segment offers fixed and variable annuities to its clients. Group protection offers employers non-medical insurance products, principally term life, disability and dental. The company's other operations include financial data for operations that are not directly related to the business segments, investment income and its run-off institutional pension business. In addition, Lincoln National's retail and wholesale distributors include: Lincoln Financial Network, which offers the group's and non-proprietary products and advisory services through a national network of about 8,640 producers; and Lincoln Financial Distributors, which distributes the group's individual products and services, retirement plans, as well as corporate-owned UL insurance, corporate-owned VUL insurance, bank-owned UL insurance and bank-owned VUL insurance products and services. LFD has approximately 620 internal and external wholesalers.

Lincoln National offers medical, dental, vision, disability and life insurance; 401(k); and a variety of employee assistance programs.

FINANCIAL DATA:
Note: Data for latest year may not have been available at press time.

In U.S. $	2018	2017	2016	2015	2014	2013
Revenue	16,424,000,000	14,257,000,000	13,330,000,000	13,572,000,000	13,554,000,000	11,969,000,000
R&D Expense						
Operating Income						
Operating Margin %						
SGA Expense	1,953,000,000	1,766,000,000	1,687,000,000	1,730,000,000	1,700,000,000	1,692,000,000
Net Income	1,641,000,000	2,079,000,000	1,192,000,000	1,154,000,000	1,515,000,000	1,244,000,000
Operating Cash Flow	1,943,000,000	788,000,000	1,272,000,000	2,243,000,000	2,526,000,000	799,000,000
Capital Expenditure						
EBITDA						
Return on Assets %		.01%	.00%	.00%	.01%	.01%
Return on Equity %		.13%	.08%	.08%	.10%	.09%
Debt to Equity		0.283	0.369	0.41	0.335	0.395

CONTACT INFORMATION:
Phone: 484 583-1400 Fax: 215 448-3962
Toll-Free: 877-275-5462
Address: 150 N. Radnor Chester Rd., Ste. A305, Radnor, PA 19087 United States

SALARIES/BONUSES:
Top Exec. Salary: $1,299,000 Bonus: $
Second Exec. Salary: $774,292 Bonus: $

STOCK TICKER/OTHER:
Stock Ticker: LNC
Employees: 9,057
Parent Company:

Exchange: NYS
Fiscal Year Ends: 12/31

OTHER THOUGHTS:
Estimated Female Officers or Directors: 2
Hot Spot for Advancement for Women/Minorities: Y

LinkedIn Corporation

NAIC Code: 519130

www.linkedin.com

TYPES OF BUSINESS:
Business-Oriented Social Networking
Advertising Services
Recruiting Tools

BRANDS/DIVISIONS/AFFILIATES:
Microsoft Corporation
LinkedIn.com
Glint

CONTACTS:
Note: Officers with more than one job title may be intentionally listed here more than once.

Jeffrey Weiner, CEO
Reid Hoffman, Chairman of the Board
Steve Sordello, CFO
Shannon Brayton, CMO
Christina Hall, Sr. VP-Human Resources
Michael Gamson, Senior VP, Divisional
Patricia Wadors, Senior VP, Divisional
James Scott, Senior VP, Divisional
Shannon Stubo, Senior VP, Divisional
Steven Sordello, Senior VP
Michael Callahan, Senior VP

GROWTH PLANS/SPECIAL FEATURES:
LinkedIn Corporation operates an online social networking site targeting the business and professional community. On LinkedIn.com users can post profiles, connect with co-workers, post resumes and search for job openings. Other features on the site include company pages, which allows companies to showcase brands and products; and a suite of products for corporate recruitment initiatives, including sourcing and pipelining, a referral engine, career pages and recruitment ads. The site generates revenue through ad sales, user subscription fees on premium accounts and enterprise hiring software licensing fees. The company offers a range of solutions to its members, including free solutions, such as stay connected and informed, advance my career and ubiquitous access; and monetized solutions, such as talent, marketing and premium subscription. Its membership base has nearly 600 million users in over 200 countries and territories (as of December 2018), and is available in multiple languages including English, French, German, Italian, Portuguese, Spanish, Japanese, Korean, Russian, Arabic and Turkish. LinkedIn operates as a subsidiary of Microsoft Corporation. In November 2018, LinkedIn acquired Glint, a leader in employee engagement that helps people in organizations do their best work, develop their skills and improve business results.

FINANCIAL DATA:
Note: Data for latest year may not have been available at press time.

In U.S. $	2018	2017	2016	2015	2014	2013
Revenue	5,300,000,000	3,859,000,000	3,500,000,000	2,990,910,976	2,218,767,104	1,528,545,024
R&D Expense						
Operating Income						
Operating Margin %						
SGA Expense						
Net Income				-166,144,000	-15,747,000	26,769,000
Operating Cash Flow						
Capital Expenditure						
EBITDA						
Return on Assets %						
Return on Equity %						
Debt to Equity						

CONTACT INFORMATION:
Phone: 650 687-3600
Fax:
Toll-Free:
Address: 2029 Stierlin Ct., Mountain View, CA 94043 United States

STOCK TICKER/OTHER:
Stock Ticker: Subsidiary
Employees: 13,000
Parent Company: Microsoft Corporation
Exchange:
Fiscal Year Ends: 06/30

SALARIES/BONUSES:
Top Exec. Salary: $
Second Exec. Salary: $
Bonus: $
Bonus: $

OTHER THOUGHTS:
Estimated Female Officers or Directors: 4
Hot Spot for Advancement for Women/Minorities: Y

Lithia Motors Inc

www.lithia.com

NAIC Code: 441110

TYPES OF BUSINESS:
Auto Dealers
Automotive Repair & Maintenance
Insurance & Financing

BRANDS/DIVISIONS/AFFILIATES:

CONTACTS:
Note: Officers with more than one job title may be intentionally listed here more than once.

Bryan Deboer, CEO
Tina Miller, CFO
Sidney Deboer, Chairman of the Board
Thomas Dobry, Chief Marketing Officer
Christopher Holzshu, Executive VP
Erik Lewis, Other Executive Officer
Bryan Osterhout, Senior VP
Scott Hillier, Senior VP, Divisional
Chun-Wai Liang, Senior VP, Divisional

GROWTH PLANS/SPECIAL FEATURES:

Lithia Motors, Inc. is a leading operator of automotive dealerships, retailing both new and used vehicles through 182 U.S. locations and over the internet. California and Oregon represent the firm's two largest markets. Lithia sells new and used cars and light trucks; sells replacement parts; provides vehicle maintenance, warranty, paint and repair services; and arranges related financing, service contracts, protection products and credit insurance for its automotive customers. Lithia's dealerships offer new vehicles marketed under nearly 30 brands, and all brands of used vehicles. The locations and other facilities consist primarily of automobile showrooms, display lots, service facilities, collision repair and paint shops, supply facilities, vehicle storage lots, parking lots and offices. Lithia notifies owners of vehicles purchased at its franchises when their vehicles are due for periodic service. Other marketing services include direct-mail ads to previous customers as well as newspaper, television and radio ads. Lithia's various websites offers users several services, such as viewing new and used vehicle inventories and scheduling service appointments. Lithia lists its inventory on listing services such as cars.com, autotrader.com, cargurus.com, kbb.com, edmunds.com, craigslist and local webpages, as well as its own websites. The company also offers financing and insurance to customers that purchase new or used vehicles. In 2018, Lithia Motors sold approximately 184,600 new and 151,230 vehicles, with the average price of new vehicles selling for about $35,750 and the average selling price of used vehicles being $20,350.

Lithia offers employees medical, dental, vision, life and disability insurance; and employee stock and 401(k) plans.

FINANCIAL DATA:
Note: Data for latest year may not have been available at press time.

In U.S. $	2018	2017	2016	2015	2014	2013
Revenue	11,821,400,000	10,086,510,000	8,678,157,000	7,864,252,000	5,390,326,000	4,005,749,000
R&D Expense						
Operating Income	433,500,000	408,986,000	352,356,000	322,859,000	233,752,000	183,518,000
Operating Margin %		.04%	.04%	.04%	.04%	.05%
SGA Expense	1,196,100,000	993,565,000	855,707,000	771,437,000	529,445,000	402,957,000
Net Income	265,700,000	245,217,000	197,058,000	182,999,000	138,720,000	106,000,000
Operating Cash Flow	519,700,000	148,856,000	86,516,000	74,209,000	30,319,000	32,059,000
Capital Expenditure	158,000,000	105,378,000	100,761,000	83,244,000	85,983,000	50,025,000
EBITDA	531,200,000	478,903,000	381,630,000	343,329,000	261,461,000	206,546,000
Return on Assets %		.06%	.06%	.06%	.06%	.07%
Return on Equity %		.25%	.23%	.24%	.23%	.22%
Debt to Equity		0.949	0.845	0.732	0.905	0.459

CONTACT INFORMATION:
Phone: 541 776-6401 Fax: 541 776-6362
Toll-Free: 877-331-3084
Address: 150 N. Bartlett St., Medford, OR 97501 United States

SALARIES/BONUSES:
Top Exec. Salary: $1,020,000 Bonus: $
Second Exec. Salary: $600,000 Bonus: $

STOCK TICKER/OTHER:
Stock Ticker: LAD
Employees: 11,170
Parent Company:

Exchange: NYS
Fiscal Year Ends: 12/31

OTHER THOUGHTS:
Estimated Female Officers or Directors:
Hot Spot for Advancement for Women/Minorities:

Sales, profits and employees may be estimates. Financial information, benefits and other data can change quickly and may vary from those stated here.

Littelfuse Inc

www.littelfuse.com

NAIC Code: 335313

TYPES OF BUSINESS:
Electrical Switches, Sensors, Microelectronics, Optomechanicals

BRANDS/DIVISIONS/AFFILIATES:
Monolith Semiconductor Inc

CONTACTS:
Note: Officers with more than one job title may be intentionally listed here more than once.

Meenal Sethna, CFO
Gordon Hunter, Chairman of the Board
Jeffrey Gorski, Chief Accounting Officer
Ryan Stafford, Chief Legal Officer
Ian Highley, Chief Technology Officer
Deepak Nayar, General Manager, Divisional
Michael Rutz, General Manager, Divisional
David Heinzmann, President
Matthew Cole, Senior VP, Divisional
Alexander Conrad, Senior VP, Divisional

GROWTH PLANS/SPECIAL FEATURES:
Littelfuse, Inc. designs, manufactures and sells circuit-protection devices for the electronics, automotive and industrial markets. The firm operates through three segments: electronics, automotive and industrial. Electronics is the firm's largest segment, supplying manufacturers with circuit protection devices used in products such as mobile phones, computers and LCD (liquid crystal display) televisions. Some of the firm's customers in the electronics business include Cisco, Huawei, Samsung, Panasonic, IBM and Intel. The automotive segment supplies fuses for original equipment manufacturers (OEMs) and aftermarket customers. The segment's customers range from Ford and General Motors to O'Reilly Auto Parts and Pep Boys. Littelfuse's smallest segment, industrial, provides a broad range of low-voltage and medium-voltage circuit protection products to electrical distributors and their customers in the construction, OEM and industrial maintenance, repair and operating supplies markets. Common uses for the products are in mining and wet environments where power sources are exposed to water. The firm attempts to offer an array of circuit-protection solutions, rather than specializing in one product area. In November 2018, Littelfuse completed its acquisition of Monolith Semiconductor, Inc., a firm specializing in the development of silicon carbide power device technology.

FINANCIAL DATA:
Note: Data for latest year may not have been available at press time.

In U.S. $	2018	2017	2016	2015	2014	2013
Revenue	1,718,468,000	1,221,534,000	1,056,159,000	867,864,000	851,995,000	757,853,000
R&D Expense	87,301,000	50,489,000	42,198,000	30,802,000	31,122,000	24,415,000
Operating Income	225,049,000	218,511,000	145,453,000	104,157,000	133,830,000	129,881,000
Operating Margin %		.18%	.14%	.12%	.16%	.17%
SGA Expense	288,001,000	212,833,000	206,129,000	153,714,000	146,975,000	132,657,000
Net Income	164,565,000	119,519,000	104,488,000	82,466,000	99,418,000	88,784,000
Operating Cash Flow	331,828,000	269,170,000	180,133,000	165,826,000	153,141,000	117,367,000
Capital Expenditure	74,753,000	65,925,000	46,228,000	44,019,000	32,281,000	34,953,000
EBITDA	330,704,000	280,428,000	185,039,000	152,638,000	178,424,000	161,632,000
Return on Assets %		.07%	.08%	.08%	.09%	.10%
Return on Equity %		.14%	.13%	.11%	.14%	.14%
Debt to Equity		0.528	0.55	0.114	0.147	0.137

CONTACT INFORMATION:
Phone: 773 628-1000 Fax: 847 391-0434
Toll-Free:
Address: 8755 W. Higgins Rd, Chicago, IL 60631 United States

STOCK TICKER/OTHER:
Stock Ticker: LFUS
Employees: 10,300
Parent Company:

Exchange: NAS
Fiscal Year Ends: 12/31

SALARIES/BONUSES:
Top Exec. Salary: $763,000 Bonus: $
Second Exec. Salary: $487,834 Bonus: $

OTHER THOUGHTS:
Estimated Female Officers or Directors:
Hot Spot for Advancement for Women/Minorities:

Sales, profits and employees may be estimates. Financial information, benefits and other data can change quickly and may vary from those stated here.

LKQ Corporation

www.lkqcorp.com

NAIC Code: 336300

TYPES OF BUSINESS:
Remanufactured OEM Parts
Aftermarket Replacement Parts
Vehicle Salvage
Scrap/Bulk Automotive Parts
Refurbished Aluminum Wheels

BRANDS/DIVISIONS/AFFILIATES:

CONTACTS:
Note: Officers with more than one job title may be intentionally listed here more than once.
John Quinn, CEO, Geographical
Dominick Zarcone, CEO
Varun Laroyia, CFO
Ashley Brooks, Chief Information Officer
Michael Clark, Controller
Joseph Holsten, Director
Victor Casini, General Counsel
Walter Hanley, Senior VP, Divisional
Justin Jude, Senior VP, Divisional
Matthew McKay, Senior VP, Divisional

GROWTH PLANS/SPECIAL FEATURES:

LKQ Corporation is a global distributor of vehicle products, including replacement parts, components and systems used in the repair and maintenance of vehicles. The company also distributes specialty products and accessories that improve the performance, functionality and appearance of vehicles. LKQ operates through three segments: North America, Europe and specialty. The North America segment comprises the company's wholesale operations, which include aftermarket, recycled, remanufactured, refurbished and original equipment manufacturer (OEM) parts supplied to professional collision and mechanical automobile repair businesses throughout the U.S. and Canada. The Europe segment provides mechanical aftermarket parts for the repair of vehicles 3 to 15 years old. Top-selling products within this division include brake pads, discs, sensors, clutches, spark plugs, batteries, steering systems and components, suspension systems and components, filters, and oil/automotive fluids. Last, the specialty segment sells and distributes recreational vehicle appliances, vehicle air conditioners, tow hitches, truck bed covers, vehicle protection products, cargo management products, wheels, tires and suspension products. This division primarily supplies small- to medium-sized businesses that focus on a narrow product or market niche. In August 2019, LKQ divested AeroVision International, its recycled aviation parts business.

FINANCIAL DATA:
Note: Data for latest year may not have been available at press time.

In U.S. $	2018	2017	2016	2015	2014	2013
Revenue	11,876,670,000	9,736,909,000	8,584,031,000	7,192,633,000	6,740,064,000	5,062,528,000
R&D Expense						
Operating Income	947,913,000	866,990,000	801,160,000	724,138,000	664,674,000	540,353,000
Operating Margin %		.09%	.09%	.10%	.10%	.11%
SGA Expense	3,352,731,000	1,915,699,000	1,670,192,000	1,431,230,000	1,340,229,000	1,028,999,000
Net Income	480,118,000	533,744,000	463,975,000	423,223,000	381,519,000	311,623,000
Operating Cash Flow	710,739,000	518,900,000	635,014,000	529,837,000	370,897,000	428,056,000
Capital Expenditure	250,027,000	179,090,000	207,074,000	170,490,000	140,950,000	90,186,000
EBITDA	1,183,885,000	1,098,470,000	971,630,000	835,082,000	777,867,000	613,474,000
Return on Assets %		.06%	.07%	.08%	.08%	.08%
Return on Equity %		.14%	.14%	.15%	.15%	.14%
Debt to Equity		0.781	0.951	0.491	0.662	0.538

CONTACT INFORMATION:
Phone: 312 621-1950   Fax: 312 621-1969
Toll-Free: 877-557-2677
Address: 500 W. Madison St., Ste. 2800, Chicago, IL 60661 United States

STOCK TICKER/OTHER:
Stock Ticker: LKQ
Employees: 42,500
Parent Company:

Exchange: NAS
Fiscal Year Ends: 12/31

SALARIES/BONUSES:
Top Exec. Salary: $955,069   Bonus: $
Second Exec. Salary: $592,343   Bonus: $

OTHER THOUGHTS:
Estimated Female Officers or Directors:
Hot Spot for Advancement for Women/Minorities:

Lockheed Martin Corporation

NAIC Code: 336411

www.lockheedmartin.com

TYPES OF BUSINESS:
Aircraft Manufacturing
Military Aircraft
Defense Electronics
Systems Integration & Technology Services
Communications Satellites & Launch Services
Undersea, Shipboard, Land & Airborne Systems & Subsystems

BRANDS/DIVISIONS/AFFILIATES:

CONTACTS:
Note: Officers with more than one job title may be intentionally listed here more than once.

Marillyn Hewson, CEO
Kenneth Possenriede, CFO
Brian Colan, Chief Accounting Officer
Richard Edwards, Executive VP, Divisional
Dale Bennett, Executive VP, Divisional
Richard Ambrose, Executive VP, Divisional
Michele Evans, Executive VP, Divisional
Frank St John, Executive VP, Divisional
Maryanne Lavan, General Counsel
John Mollard, Treasurer

GROWTH PLANS/SPECIAL FEATURES:

Lockheed Martin Corporation is a global security and aerospace company engaged in the research, design, development, manufacture, integration and sustainment of advanced technology systems, products and services. It serves domestic and international customers with products and services that have defense, civil and commercial applications, with principal customers including agencies of the U.S. government (approximately 70% of annual sales). The company operates in four segments: aeronautics, missiles and fire control (MFC), rotary and mission systems (RMS) and space. The aeronautics segment, accounting for 39% of the firm's revenue, is engaged in the design, R&D, systems integration, production, sustainment, support and upgrade of advanced military aircraft, air and unmanned vehicles and related technologies. Major products include the F-35 Lightning strike fighter, the F-22 stealth fighter and the C-130 tactical airlifter. The MFC segment (14%) provides: air and missile defense systems; tactical missiles and air-to-ground precision strike weapon systems; logistics; fire control systems; mission operations support, readiness, engineering support and integration services; manned and unmanned ground vehicles; and energy management solutions. The RMS division (28%) provides: design, manufacture, service and support for a variety of military and commercial helicopters; ship and submarine mission and combat systems; mission systems and sensors for rotary and fixed-wing aircraft; sea and land-based missile defense systems; radar systems; the Littoral Combat Ship; simulation and training services; and unmanned systems and technologies. Last, the space segment (19%) is engaged in the R&D, design, engineering and production of satellites, strategic and defensive missile systems and space transportation systems.

FINANCIAL DATA:
Note: Data for latest year may not have been available at press time.

In U.S. $	2018	2017	2016	2015	2014	2013
Revenue	53,762,000,000	51,048,000,000	47,248,000,000	46,132,000,000	45,600,000,000	45,358,000,000
R&D Expense						
Operating Income	7,334,000,000	5,921,000,000	5,549,000,000	5,436,000,000	5,592,000,000	4,505,000,000
Operating Margin %		.12%	.12%	.12%	.12%	.10%
SGA Expense						
Net Income	5,046,000,000	2,002,000,000	5,302,000,000	3,605,000,000	3,614,000,000	2,981,000,000
Operating Cash Flow	3,138,000,000	6,476,000,000	5,189,000,000	5,101,000,000	3,866,000,000	4,546,000,000
Capital Expenditure	1,278,000,000	1,177,000,000	1,063,000,000	939,000,000	845,000,000	836,000,000
EBITDA	7,667,000,000	7,115,000,000	6,764,000,000	6,492,000,000	6,592,000,000	5,495,000,000
Return on Assets %		.04%	.11%	.08%	.10%	.08%
Return on Equity %		4.84%	2.30%	1.11%	.87%	1.20%
Debt to Equity			9.452	4.619	1.814	1.251

CONTACT INFORMATION:
Phone: 301 897-6000 Fax: 301 897-6083
Toll-Free:
Address: 6801 Rockledge Dr., Bethesda, MD 20817 United States

SALARIES/BONUSES:
Top Exec. Salary: $1,769,262 Bonus: $
Second Exec. Salary: $1,024,808 Bonus: $

STOCK TICKER/OTHER:
Stock Ticker: LMT
Employees: 97,000
Parent Company:

Exchange: NYS
Fiscal Year Ends: 12/31

OTHER THOUGHTS:
Estimated Female Officers or Directors: 5
Hot Spot for Advancement for Women/Minorities: Y

Sales, profits and employees may be estimates. Financial information, benefits and other data can change quickly and may vary from those stated here.

Loews Hotels Holding Corporation

www.loewshotels.com

NAIC Code: 721110

TYPES OF BUSINESS:
Hotels, Luxury
Hotel Management Services

BRANDS/DIVISIONS/AFFILIATES:
Loews Corporation
Loews Miami Beach Hotel
Loews Santa Monica Beach Hotel
Loews Royal Pacific Resort at Universal Orlando
Loews Portofino Bay Hotel at Universal Orlando
Loews Sapphire Falls Resort at Universal Orlando
Flavor by Loews Hotels
YouFirst Loyalty Program

CONTACTS:
Note: Officers with more than one job title may be intentionally listed here more than once.

Jonathan M. Tisch, CEO
Shawn Hauver, VP-Oper.
Lark-Marie Anton, Sr. VP-Public Rel. & Mktg. Comm.

GROWTH PLANS/SPECIAL FEATURES:
Loews Hotels Holding Corporation, a subsidiary of the Loews Corporation, currently has a portfolio of 29 owned and/or operated luxury hotels and resorts. Located in select cities throughout the U.S. and Canada, the firm's properties include the 790-room Loews Miami Beach Hotel in Florida, the 581-room Loews Philadelphia Hotel, the 347-room Loews Santa Monica Beach Hotel in Southern California and the 142-room Loews Hotel Vogue in Montreal. Loews Hotels operates joint venture hotels with Universal Studios in Orlando, Florida, including: Loews Royal Pacific Resort at Universal Orlando, one of its largest hotels with 1,000 rooms; the 750-room Loews Portofino Bay Hotel at Universal Orlando; and the 1,000-room Loews Sapphire Falls Resort at Universal Orlando Resort. Loews Hotels' business amenities include high-speed Internet access, a power breakfast with notable business leaders, notarization services, private dining rooms, boardrooms and concierge services. Flavor by Loews Hotels partners with neighborhood food and drink artisans to bring those flavors and culture into every Loews destination, allowing them to showcase their local specialties at various locations on the hotel property. For example, guests and Loews Miami Beach hotel can enjoy Floridian beers on tap at the hotel's restaurants, and Loews Ventana Canyon Resort offers tamales from Tucson Tamale Company. Loews' YouFirst Loyalty Program rewards guests based on number of stays and offers free Internet access, late checkout, guaranteed rooms and upgrades for guests who visit at least twice a year. Loews Hotels offers facilities for weddings, meetings and special events; and special programs and services designed for people traveling with pets, children and teenagers.

FINANCIAL DATA:
Note: Data for latest year may not have been available at press time.

In U.S. $	2018	2017	2016	2015	2014	2013
Revenue	1,422,750,000	1,355,000,000	1,293,000,000	604,000,000	472,659,000	380,000,000
R&D Expense						
Operating Income						
Operating Margin %						
SGA Expense						
Net Income			12,000,000	12,000,000	11,000,000	141,000,000
Operating Cash Flow						
Capital Expenditure						
EBITDA						
Return on Assets %						
Return on Equity %						
Debt to Equity						

CONTACT INFORMATION:
Phone: 212-521-2000 Fax: 212-521-2525
Toll-Free: 800-235-6397
Address: 667 Madison Ave., New York, NY 10021 United States

STOCK TICKER/OTHER:
Stock Ticker: Subsidiary
Employees: 9,348
Parent Company: Loews Corporation

Exchange:
Fiscal Year Ends: 12/31

SALARIES/BONUSES:
Top Exec. Salary: $ Bonus: $
Second Exec. Salary: $ Bonus: $

OTHER THOUGHTS:
Estimated Female Officers or Directors: 2
Hot Spot for Advancement for Women/Minorities: Y

Lowe's Companies Inc

www.lowes.com

NAIC Code: 444110

TYPES OF BUSINESS:
Home Centers, Retail
Home Improvement Products
Home Installation Services
Special Order Sales
Smarthome Products

BRANDS/DIVISIONS/AFFILIATES:
Orchard Supply Hardware

CONTACTS:
Note: Officers with more than one job title may be intentionally listed here more than once.

Marvin Ellison, CEO
David Denton, CFO
Richard Dreiling, Chairman of the Board
Seemantini Godbole, Chief Information Officer
Donald Frieson, Executive VP, Divisional
William Boltz, Executive VP, Divisional
Joseph Mcfarland, Executive VP, Divisional
Ross Mccanless, Executive VP
Jennifer Weber, Executive VP
Tiffany Mason, Senior VP, Divisional
Matthew Hollifield, Senior VP

GROWTH PLANS/SPECIAL FEATURES:

Lowe's Companies, Inc. is one of the largest home improvement retailers in the world. The company owns roughly 2,370 stores in 50 U.S. states, Mexico and Canada, each carrying approximately 37,000 products and 213 million square feet of retail space. The company also operates 87 stores under the Orchard Supply Hardware name in California, Oregon and Florida. Hundreds of thousands of items are also available through the firm's special-order system. Lowe's stores chiefly serve do-it-yourself (DIY) homeowners and commercial business customers, including contractors, landscapers, electricians, painters and plumbers. Its home improvement product categories include building materials, lighting, cabinets and countertops, seasonal living, millwork, lumber, flooring, lawn and landscaping items, hardware, fashion and rough plumbing, appliances, paint, tools, plants and plant pots, outdoor power equipment, rough electrical, home environment and organization and windows and walls. Each Lowe's store carries a wide selection of national brand name merchandise such as Samsung, Whirlpool, Stainmaster, GE, Valspar, Sylvania, Dewalt and Owens Corning; and exclusive brand names such as Kobalt, allen+roth, Blue Hawk, Utilitech and Aquasource. The company's Lowes.com web site facilitates customers researching, comparing and buying Lowe's products, and also allows customers to special order products not carried in its physical store locations. Lowe's entered the smarthome market with Iris, an affordable, cloud-based home management system, which allows users to interact and control their home's security cameras, thermostat, locks, lighting and appliances remotely from a smart phone or computer. In November 2018, Lowe's announced plans to close 20 underperforming U.S. stores and 31 Canadian stores.

Lowe's offers its employees life, short- and long-term disability, accident, auto, home, medical, dental and vision insurance; family assistance programs; stock purchase plan; tuition reimbursement; paid time off; 401(k); employee bonuses; and flexible spending accounts.

FINANCIAL DATA:
Note: Data for latest year may not have been available at press time.

In U.S. $	2018	2017	2016	2015	2014	2013
Revenue	68,619,000,000	65,017,000,000	59,074,000,000	56,223,000,000	53,417,000,000	
R&D Expense						
Operating Income	6,586,000,000	5,846,000,000	4,971,000,000	4,792,000,000	4,149,000,000	
Operating Margin %	.10%	.09%	.08%	.09%	.08%	
SGA Expense	15,376,000,000	15,129,000,000	14,115,000,000	13,281,000,000	12,865,000,000	
Net Income	3,447,000,000	3,091,000,000	2,546,000,000	2,698,000,000	2,286,000,000	
Operating Cash Flow	5,065,000,000	5,617,000,000	4,784,000,000	4,929,000,000	4,111,000,000	
Capital Expenditure	1,123,000,000	1,167,000,000	1,197,000,000	880,000,000	940,000,000	
EBITDA	7,678,000,000	7,448,000,000	6,562,000,000	6,384,000,000	5,715,000,000	
Return on Assets %	.10%	.09%	.08%	.08%	.07%	
Return on Equity %	.56%	.43%	.29%	.25%	.18%	
Debt to Equity	2.65	2.237	1.508	1.085	0.851	

CONTACT INFORMATION:
Phone: 704 758-1000   Fax: 336 658-4766
Toll-Free: 800-445-6937
Address: 1000 Lowe's Blvd., Mooresville, NC 28117 United States

SALARIES/BONUSES:
Top Exec. Salary: $864,423   Bonus: $1,712,912
Second Exec. Salary: $360,577   Bonus: $875,000

STOCK TICKER/OTHER:
Stock Ticker: LOW
Employees: 310,000
Parent Company:

Exchange: NYS
Fiscal Year Ends: 01/31

OTHER THOUGHTS:
Estimated Female Officers or Directors: 3
Hot Spot for Advancement for Women/Minorities: Y

Lubrizol Corporation (The)

NAIC Code: 325110

www.lubrizol.com

TYPES OF BUSINESS:
Manufacturing-Specialty Chemicals
Fuel & Lubricant Additives
Polymers
Performance Coatings, Resins & Additives
Plastic Plumbing, Automobile Molded Parts & Film
Rubber, Plastic & Lubricants Additives

BRANDS/DIVISIONS/AFFILIATES:
Berkshire Hathaway Inc
Lubrizol Additives
Lubrizol Advanced Materials

CONTACTS:
Note: Officers with more than one job title may be intentionally listed here more than once.

Eric R. Schnur, CEO
Eric R. Schnur, Chmn.

GROWTH PLANS/SPECIAL FEATURES:

The Lubrizol Corporation, a subsidiary of Berkshire Hathaway, Inc., is a manufacturer and marketer of specialty chemicals and additives for the transportation, consumer and industrial markets. The company maintains production facilities throughout the Americas, Europe, the Middle East & Africa and Asia Pacific. It operates through two segments: Lubrizol Additives and Lubrizol Advanced Materials. The Lubrizol Additives segment partners with customers and original equipment manufacturers to solve end-user challenges through additives for engine oils, driveline applications, gasoline and diesel fuel, and other transportation-related fluids and industrial applications. Engine oil additives are useful in heavy duty diesel vehicles, passenger cars, marine vehicles, motorcycles, recreational vehicles, power tools and stationary natural gas equipment. Driveline additives are useful in axle oil, transmission fluids, construction and mining fluids and agriculture processes. Industrial lubricant additives are useful in grease, metalworking, industrial gear oil, hydraulic fluids, emulsion explosives, turbine and circulating oils and compressor lubricants. Fuel additives are useful in diesel, home heating oil, gasoline, industrial, marine and biofuel processes and applications. The Lubrizol Advanced Materials segment (and subsidiary) provides formulations that enable the distinct characteristics in customer's products, such as enhanced durability, nourishment in products and better quality in digital printing. Products lines include: engineered polymers, personal and home care, performance coatings, CPVC (chlorinated polyvinyl chloride) piping systems (flexible and withstand temperatures) and life sciences (such as medical devices and pharmaceuticals).

Lubrizol employee benefits vary by country but include healthcare and disability coverage and retirement planning.

FINANCIAL DATA:
Note: Data for latest year may not have been available at press time.

In U.S. $	2018	2017	2016	2015	2014	2013
Revenue	6,800,000,000	6,300,000,000	6,100,000,000	6,300,000,000	6,600,000,000	6,300,000,000
R&D Expense						
Operating Income						
Operating Margin %						
SGA Expense						
Net Income						
Operating Cash Flow						
Capital Expenditure						
EBITDA						
Return on Assets %						
Return on Equity %						
Debt to Equity						

CONTACT INFORMATION:
Phone: 440-943-4200 Fax: 440-943-5337
Toll-Free:
Address: 29400 Lakeland Blvd., Wickliffe, OH 44092 United States

STOCK TICKER/OTHER:
Stock Ticker: Subsidiary   Exchange:
Employees: 8,700   Fiscal Year Ends: 12/31
Parent Company: Berkshire Hathaway Inc

SALARIES/BONUSES:
Top Exec. Salary: $ Bonus: $
Second Exec. Salary: $ Bonus: $

OTHER THOUGHTS:
Estimated Female Officers or Directors: 1
Hot Spot for Advancement for Women/Minorities:

Lyft Inc

NAIC Code: 561599

www.lyft.me

TYPES OF BUSINESS:
Car Ride Dispatch Service, Mobile App-Based
Bicycle Rental & Sharing Systems
Augmented Reality Technology

BRANDS/DIVISIONS/AFFILIATES:
Blue Vision Labs
Motivate International Inc

CONTACTS:
Note: Officers with more than one job title may be intentionally listed here more than once.

Logan Green, CEO
Brian Roberts, CFO
Prashant Aggarwal, Chairman of the Board
John Zimmer, Co-Founder
Jon McNeill, COO
Ran Makavy, Executive VP
Kristin Sverchek, General Counsel

GROWTH PLANS/SPECIAL FEATURES:

Lyft, Inc. is a smartphone-based ridesharing and peer-to-peer transportation company that designs, develops and develops a mobile app that matches drivers with passengers who requires rides. Riders turn on the app and locate nearby drivers that are available on-demand. Lyft drivers can be located in small or big cities throughout North America. Riders pay automatically through the app, which is processed from the passenger's saved credit card once the ride ends. In addition, users can schedule rides up to seven days in advance. Lyft provides additional insurance policies, at no cost to the driver. The firm works with leading insurance carriers to provide various coverages including, commercial auto liability insurance up to $1 million per occurrence, contingent comprehensive and collision insurance for drivers who carry comprehensive and collision coverage on their personal auto policy, and coverage for bodily injury caused by uninsured/underinsured motorists when engaged in a ride. Drivers rate passengers after each ride. Drivers get paid for every trip on a per-minute and mile basis. Money is deposited into the driver's account each week automatically, or can be cashed out instantly with Express Pay. Drivers must be 21 years of age and own an iPhone or Android phone; must undergo a DMV check, plus a national and county background check. Vehicles need to have four external door handles and at least five total seat belts. Drivers must be a covered party on the car's in-state insurance, and have in-state license plates. All of these are confirmed through the 19-point vehicle inspection process at the DMV. Cars have Lyft age requirements as well, which vary by state. During 2018, Lyft acquired Blue Vision Labs, a London-based augmented reality startup; and bike-sharing company, Motivate International, Inc. In March 2019, the firm successfully conducted an IPO.

FINANCIAL DATA:
Note: Data for latest year may not have been available at press time.

In U.S. $	2018	2017	2016	2015	2014	2013
Revenue	2,156,616,000	1,059,881,000	343,298,000			
R&D Expense	300,836,000	136,646,000	64,704,000			
Operating Income	-977,711,000	-708,272,000	-692,603,000			
Operating Margin %						
SGA Expense	1,251,689,000	788,461,000	594,306,000			
Net Income	-911,335,000	-688,301,000	-682,794,000			
Operating Cash Flow	-280,673,000	-393,526,000	-487,163,000			
Capital Expenditure	70,868,000	12,023,000	8,819,000			
EBITDA	-958,959,000	-705,661,000	-692,076,000			
Return on Assets %						
Return on Equity %						
Debt to Equity						

CONTACT INFORMATION:
Phone: 855-946-7433   Fax:
Toll-Free:
Address: 185 Berry St., Ste. 5000, San Francisco, CA 94107 United States

STOCK TICKER/OTHER:
Stock Ticker: LYFT
Employees: 4,791
Parent Company:

Exchange: NAS
Fiscal Year Ends:

SALARIES/BONUSES:
Top Exec. Salary: $419,231   Bonus: $420,000
Second Exec. Salary: $401,539   Bonus: $

OTHER THOUGHTS:
Estimated Female Officers or Directors: 2
Hot Spot for Advancement for Women/Minorities:

Sales, profits and employees may be estimates. Financial information, benefits and other data can change quickly and may vary from those stated here.

Magellan Health Inc

NAIC Code: 621999

www.magellanhealth.com

TYPES OF BUSINESS:
Specialty Managed Health Care Services
Psychiatric Hospitals
Residential Treatment Centers

BRANDS/DIVISIONS/AFFILIATES:
Magellan Complete Care

CONTACTS:
Note: Officers with more than one job title may be intentionally listed here more than once.
Mostafa Kamal, CEO, Subsidiary
Barry Smith, CEO
Jonathan Rubin, CFO
Caskie Lewis-Clapper, Other Executive Officer
Daniel Gregoire, Secretary
Jeffrey West, Senior VP

GROWTH PLANS/SPECIAL FEATURES:
Magellan Health, Inc. is engaged in the healthcare management business. Magellan develops innovative solutions that combine advanced analytics, agile technology and clinical excellence to promote best decision-making capabilities for its clients. The firm serves health plans, managed care organizations, employers, labor unions, various military and governmental agencies and third-party administrators. Magellan operates in two business segments: Magellan healthcare and Magellan Rx management. Magellan healthcare includes the firm's management of behavioral healthcare services and employee assistance program services; management of specialty areas such as diagnostic imaging and musculoskeletal management; and the integrated management of physical, behavioral and pharmaceutical health care for special populations delivered via Magellan Complete Care. Special populations include individuals with serious mental illness, dual eligible, long-term services and supports and other populations with unique and often complex health care needs. Magellan Rx management comprises products and solutions that provide clinical and financial management of pharmaceuticals paid under medical and pharmacy benefit programs. Its services include pharmacy benefit management, pharmacy benefit administration for state Medicaid and other government-sponsored programs, pharmaceutical dispensing operations, clinical and formulary management programs, medical pharmacy management programs, as well as programs for the integrated management of specialty drugs across both the medical and pharmacy benefit that treat complex conditions.

FINANCIAL DATA:
Note: Data for latest year may not have been available at press time.

In U.S. $	2018	2017	2016	2015	2014	2013
Revenue	7,314,151,000	5,838,583,000	4,836,884,000	4,597,400,000	3,760,118,000	3,546,317,000
R&D Expense						
Operating Income	64,522,000	155,314,000	152,892,000	75,532,000	124,006,000	166,200,000
Operating Margin %		.03%	.03%	.02%	.03%	.05%
SGA Expense						
Net Income	24,181,000	110,207,000	77,879,000	31,413,000	79,404,000	125,261,000
Operating Cash Flow	164,844,000	162,273,000	66,699,000	239,185,000	211,044,000	183,161,000
Capital Expenditure	68,275,000	57,232,000	60,881,000	71,584,000	62,337,000	64,542,000
EBITDA	211,250,000	276,907,000	261,756,000	180,541,000	216,377,000	240,179,000
Return on Assets %		.04%	.03%	.02%	.04%	.08%
Return on Equity %		.09%	.07%	.03%	.07%	.12%
Debt to Equity		0.58	0.195	0.224	0.226	0.021

CONTACT INFORMATION:
Phone: 602-572-6050 Fax:
Toll-Free: 800-410-8312
Address: 4800 Scottsdale Rd, Ste. 4000, Scottsdale, AZ 85251 United States

STOCK TICKER/OTHER:
Stock Ticker: MGLN
Employees: 9,700
Parent Company:

Exchange: NAS
Fiscal Year Ends: 12/31

SALARIES/BONUSES:
Top Exec. Salary: $1,200,002 Bonus: $
Second Exec. Salary: $646,049 Bonus: $

OTHER THOUGHTS:
Estimated Female Officers or Directors: 3
Hot Spot for Advancement for Women/Minorities: Y

Sales, profits and employees may be estimates. Financial information, benefits and other data can change quickly and may vary from those stated here.

Marathon Petroleum Corporation

www.marathonpetroleum.com

NAIC Code: 324110

TYPES OF BUSINESS:
Petroleum Refining
Gas Stations
Asphalt Production & Retail
Petrochemicals & Lubricants
Pipelines

BRANDS/DIVISIONS/AFFILIATES:
MPLX LP
Andeavor Logistics LP
Marathon
Speedway
ARCO

CONTACTS:
Note: Officers with more than one job title may be intentionally listed here more than once.

Gary Heminger, CEO
David Sauber, Senior VP, Divisional
Timothy Griffith, CFO
John Quaid, Chief Accounting Officer
Molly Benson, Chief Compliance Officer
Donald Wehrly, Chief Information Officer
Glenn Plumby, COO, Subsidiary
Gregory Goff, Director
Raymond Brooks, Executive VP, Divisional
Suzanne Gagle, General Counsel
Fiona Laird, Other Executive Officer
Donald Templin, President, Divisional
Anthony Kenney, President, Subsidiary
David Whikehart, Senior VP, Divisional
C. Case, Senior VP, Divisional
Brian Partee, Senior VP, Divisional
Richard Hernandez, Senior VP, Divisional

GROWTH PLANS/SPECIAL FEATURES:

Marathon Petroleum Corporation (MPC) is a leading integrated downstream energy company. The firm's refining system produces more than 3 million barrels per day of crude oil across 16 refineries. MPC also owns and operates retail convenience stores across the country. MPC's midstream operations are primarily conducted through MPLX LP and Andeavor Logistics LP, which own and operate crude oil and light product transportation and logistics infrastructure as well as gathering, processing and fractionation assets. MPC operates through three segments: refining and marketing, retail, and midstream. The refining and marketing segment refines crude oil and other feedstocks at the 16 refineries located in the West Coast, Gulf Coast and Mid-Continent regions of the U.S.; purchases refined products and ethanol for resale; and distributes refined products largely through transportation, storage, distribution and marketing services provided largely by the midstream segment. This division also sells refined products to wholesale marketing customers domestically and internationally, to buyers-on-the-spot market, to MPC's retail segment and to independent entrepreneurs who operate primarily Marathon-branded outlets. The retail segment sells transportation fuels and convenience products in the retail market via company-owned and -operated convenience stores, primarily under the Speedway brand, and long-term fuel supply contracts with direct dealers who operate locations mainly under the ARCO brand. Last, the midstream segment transports, stores, distributes and markets crude oil and refined products principally for the refining and marketing segment via refining logistics assets, pipelines, terminals, towboats and barges; gathers, processes and transports natural gas; and gathers, transports, fractionates, stores and markets natural gas liquids. In late-2018, MPC acquired rival Andeavor for $23 billion, creating the largest independent petroleum product refining, marketing, retail and midstream businesses in the U.S.

MPC offers employees health care benefits; 401(k) and pension plans; and various employee assistance programs.

FINANCIAL DATA:
Note: Data for latest year may not have been available at press time.

In U.S. $	2018	2017	2016	2015	2014	2013
Revenue	96,504,000,000	74,733,000,000	63,339,000,000	72,051,000,000	97,817,000,000	100,160,000,000
R&D Expense						
Operating Income	5,175,000,000	3,653,000,000	2,661,000,000	4,597,000,000	3,877,000,000	3,383,000,000
Operating Margin %		.05%	.04%	.06%	.04%	.03%
SGA Expense	2,418,000,000	1,743,000,000	1,605,000,000	1,576,000,000	1,375,000,000	1,248,000,000
Net Income	2,780,000,000	3,432,000,000	1,174,000,000	2,852,000,000	2,524,000,000	2,112,000,000
Operating Cash Flow	6,158,000,000	6,609,000,000	3,986,000,000	4,061,000,000	3,110,000,000	3,405,000,000
Capital Expenditure	3,578,000,000	2,732,000,000	2,892,000,000	1,998,000,000	1,480,000,000	1,206,000,000
EBITDA	8,004,000,000	6,083,000,000	4,361,000,000	6,308,000,000	5,363,000,000	4,633,000,000
Return on Assets %		.07%	.03%	.08%	.09%	.08%
Return on Equity %		.25%	.09%	.24%	.23%	.19%
Debt to Equity		0.878	0.778	0.899	0.615	0.309

CONTACT INFORMATION:
Phone: 419 422-2121 Fax:
Toll-Free:
Address: 539 S. Main St., Findlay, OH 45840 United States

STOCK TICKER/OTHER:
Stock Ticker: MPC
Employees: 44,460
Parent Company:

Exchange: NYS
Fiscal Year Ends: 12/31

SALARIES/BONUSES:
Top Exec. Salary: $1,687,500 Bonus: $
Second Exec. Salary: $937,500 Bonus: $

OTHER THOUGHTS:
Estimated Female Officers or Directors: 2
Hot Spot for Advancement for Women/Minorities:

Sales, profits and employees may be estimates. Financial information, benefits and other data can change quickly and may vary from those stated here.

Marriott International Inc

NAIC Code: 721110

www.marriott.com

TYPES OF BUSINESS:
Hotels & Resorts
Suites Hotels
Corporate Apartments
Extended Stay Lodging
Luxury Hotels
Business Hotels

BRANDS/DIVISIONS/AFFILIATES:
JW Marriott
Ritz-Carlton (The)
W Hotels
Marriott Hotels
Sheraton
Westin
Courtyard
Marriott Bonvoy

CONTACTS: Note: Officers with more than one job title may be intentionally listed here more than once.
Arne Sorenson, CEO
Craig Smith, Managing Director, Geographical
Kathleen Oberg, CFO
J. Marriott, Chairman of the Board
Bao Giang Val Bauduin, Controller
Sterling Colton, Director Emeritus
William Shaw, Director Emeritus
Rena Reiss, Executive VP
Stephanie Linnartz, Executive VP
David Rodriguez, Executive VP
Anthony Capuano, Executive VP
Argiris Kyriakidis, Managing Director, Geographical
Liam Brown, Managing Director, Geographical
David Grissen, President, Divisional
David Grissen, President, Divisional

GROWTH PLANS/SPECIAL FEATURES:

Marriott International, Inc. is a worldwide operator, franchisor and licensor of hotel, residential and timeshare properties in 130 countries and territories under 30 brand names. The company typically manages or franchises hotels, rather than owning them. Marriott operates through four business segments: North American full-service, North American limited-service, Asia Pacific and other international. The North American full-service segment comprises: 413 managed properties, with 184,541 rooms; 705 franchised/licensed properties, with 202,204 rooms; and nine owned/leased properties, with 5,275 rooms. The North American limited-service segment comprises: 408 managed properties, with 64,372 rooms; 3,432 franchised/licensed properties, with 395,522 rooms; and 20 owned/leased properties with 3,006 rooms. The Asia Pacific segment comprises: 612 managed properties, with 179,243 rooms; 98 franchised/licensed properties, with 27,258 rooms; and two owned/leased properties, with 410 rooms. The other international segment consists of Europe, Middle East, Africa, Caribbean and Latin America, and comprises: 524 managed properties, with 121,408 rooms; 411 franchised/licensed properties, with 82,243 rooms; 32 owned/leased properties, with 8,404 rooms; and 102 other types of properties, with 12,749 rooms. Timeshare properties consist of 89 franchised/licensed properties with 22,186 rooms. Brand names of the firm include JW Marriott, The Ritz-Carlton, W Hotels, Marriott Hotels, Sheraton, Westin, Courtyard, Residence Inn and Fairfield Inn & Suites. In February 2019, Marriott integrated its loyalty program, sales and marketing and reservation systems under one name, Marriott Bonvoy.

FINANCIAL DATA: Note: Data for latest year may not have been available at press time.

In U.S. $	2018	2017	2016	2015	2014	2013
Revenue	20,758,000,000	22,894,000,000	17,072,000,000	14,486,000,000	13,796,000,000	12,784,000,000
R&D Expense						
Operating Income	2,521,000,000	2,518,000,000	1,754,000,000	1,350,000,000	1,159,000,000	988,000,000
Operating Margin %		.11%	.10%	.09%	.08%	.08%
SGA Expense	927,000,000	894,000,000	704,000,000	634,000,000	659,000,000	726,000,000
Net Income	1,907,000,000	1,372,000,000	780,000,000	859,000,000	753,000,000	626,000,000
Operating Cash Flow	2,357,000,000	2,436,000,000	1,582,000,000	1,430,000,000	1,224,000,000	1,140,000,000
Capital Expenditure	556,000,000	429,000,000	279,000,000	426,000,000	476,000,000	465,000,000
EBITDA	2,969,000,000	3,414,000,000	1,586,000,000	1,561,000,000	1,351,000,000	1,144,000,000
Return on Assets %		.06%	.05%			
Return on Equity %		.30%	.88%	.13%	.11%	.10%
Debt to Equity		2.101	1.53			

CONTACT INFORMATION:
Phone: 301 380-3000 Fax: 301 380-3967
Toll-Free: 800-721-7033
Address: 10400 Fernwood Rd., Bethesda, MD 20817 United States

STOCK TICKER/OTHER:
Stock Ticker: MAR
Employees: 226,500
Parent Company:

Exchange: NAS
Fiscal Year Ends: 12/31

SALARIES/BONUSES:
Top Exec. Salary: $1,300,000 Bonus: $
Second Exec. Salary: $824,000 Bonus: $

OTHER THOUGHTS:
Estimated Female Officers or Directors: 7
Hot Spot for Advancement for Women/Minorities: Y

Mars Incorporated

NAIC Code: 311351

www.mars.com/global

TYPES OF BUSINESS:
Chocolate & Confectionery Manufacturing
Snack Foods & Candy Bars
Pet Nutrition
Drink Vending Systems
Prepared Foods
Information Technology Services

BRANDS/DIVISIONS/AFFILIATES:
Pedigree
M&Ms
Uncle Ben's

CONTACTS:
Note: Officers with more than one job title may be intentionally listed here more than once.

Grant F. Reid, CEO
Claus Aagaard, CFO
Eric Minvielle, VP-Human Resources
Richard Ware, VP-R&D
John Donofrio, General Counsel
David Kamenetzky, VP-Corp. Affairs
Frank Mars, Pres., Symbioscience
Martin Radvan, Pres., Wrigley
Grant Reid, Pres., Chocolate
Poul Weihrauch, Pres., Food
Richard Ware, VP-Supply & Procurement

GROWTH PLANS/SPECIAL FEATURES:
Mars Incorporated, founded in 1911, is a family-owned company that operates through five brands: Mars petcare, Mars Wrigley confectionery, Mars food, Mars drinks and Mars edge. Mars petcare is a diverse business present in more than 50 countries and comprises over 50 brands that serve the health and nutrition needs of pets. Brands include Pedigree, Whiskas, Royal Canin, Nutro, Greenies, Sheba, Cesar, IAMs and Eukanuba. The WALTHAM Centre for Pet Nutrition is engaged in advanced research for the nutrition and health of pets. Mars Wrigley confectionery is based in the U.S., and manufactures chocolate, confections, gum and mints. Its multi-billion-dollar portfolio of brands include M&M's, Snickers, Skittles, Starburst, Orbit and Altoids. Mars food is based in Brussels, Belgium and dedicated to providing ways to make everyday meals healthier, easier, more affordable and tastier. This division comprises 11 manufacturing sites and offers 12 leading food brands available in nearly 30 countries. Its Uncle Ben's rice brand is more than 70 years old, and other brands include Abu Siouf, Dolmio, Ebly, Kan Tong, MasterFoods, Miracoli, Pamesello and Raris, among others. Mars drinks solely supports the workplace by providing beverage products to businesses throughout North America, Europe and Asia. This division's products include: the Klix fully automatic in-cup drinks vending machine, Flavia single-serve hot drinks, Alterra coffees, The Bright Tea Co. teas, and Dove hot chocolates. Last, Mars edge partners with others to develop and deliver the latest in science, data and technology and offer seamless nutrition solutions. These include: Mars Symbioscience, which offers CocoaVia, a cocoa extract-based dietary supplement based on cocoa flavanols for cardiovascular benefits; mass-targeted nutrition, which focuses on helping close nutritional gaps worldwide; and personalized nutrition, which focuses on developing solutions regarding individual nutritional needs.

FINANCIAL DATA:
Note: Data for latest year may not have been available at press time.

In U.S. $	2018	2017	2016	2015	2014	2013
Revenue	37,931,250,000	36,125,000,000	36,000,000,000	35,500,000,000	34,000,000,000	33,200,000,000
R&D Expense						
Operating Income						
Operating Margin %						
SGA Expense						
Net Income						
Operating Cash Flow						
Capital Expenditure						
EBITDA						
Return on Assets %						
Return on Equity %						
Debt to Equity						

CONTACT INFORMATION:
Phone: 703-821-4900   Fax: 703-448-9678
Toll-Free: 800-627-7852
Address: 6885 Elm St., McLean, VA 22101 United States

STOCK TICKER/OTHER:
Stock Ticker: Private   Exchange:
Employees: 115,000   Fiscal Year Ends: 12/31
Parent Company:

SALARIES/BONUSES:
Top Exec. Salary: $ Bonus: $
Second Exec. Salary: $ Bonus: $

OTHER THOUGHTS:
Estimated Female Officers or Directors: 1
Hot Spot for Advancement for Women/Minorities:

Sales, profits and employees may be estimates. Financial information, benefits and other data can change quickly and may vary from those stated here.

Marsh & McLennan Companies Inc

www.mmc.com

NAIC Code: 524210

TYPES OF BUSINESS:
Insurance Brokerage
Consulting Services
Risk Management
Benefits Administration
Human Resources Services

BRANDS/DIVISIONS/AFFILIATES:
Marsh Inc
Guy Carpenter & Company LLC
Mercer Inc
Oliver Wyman Group
Lippincott
NERA Economic Consulting
Jardine Lloyd Thompson Group plc

CONTACTS:
Note: Officers with more than one job title may be intentionally listed here more than once.

John Doyle, CEO, Subsidiary
Julio Portalatin, CEO, Subsidiary
Scott McDonald, CEO, Subsidiary
Peter Hearn, CEO, Subsidiary
Martine Ferland, CEO, Subsidiary
Mark McGivney, CFO
E. Gilbert, Chief Information Officer
Stacy Mills, Controller
H. Hanway, Director
Daniel Glaser, Director
Peter Beshar, Executive VP
Laurie Ledford, Other Executive Officer

GROWTH PLANS/SPECIAL FEATURES:

Marsh & McLennan Companies, Inc. (MMC) is a global professional services firm. The company provides insurance as well management and consulting services in the areas of risk, strategy and human capital to clients in over 130 countries. MMC is the parent company of a number of leading risk experts and specialty consultants, including: Marsh, Inc., an insurance broker, intermediary and risk advisor; Guy Carpenter & Company, LLC, a risk and reinsurance specialist; Mercer, Inc., a provider of HR and related financial advice and services; and Oliver Wyman Group, a management consultancy. MMC operates in two divisions: risk and insurance services, and consulting. The risk and insurance services division generated 55% of the firm's total 2018 revenue and is primarily comprised of Marsh and Guy Carpenter. The consulting division generated 45% of total revenue and operates through Mercer and Oliver Wyman. The Mercer division offers investment consulting services and specialized management and economic consulting services as well as human resources consulting and related outsourcing. Oliver Wyman includes Lippincott, a consulting firm that helps clients with branding and corporate image; and NERA Economic Consulting, one of the world's largest consulting groups that focuses on economics and deploys professional economists. In April 2019, MMC completed the acquisition of Jardine Lloyd Thompson Group plc (JLT) for $5.6 billion, one of the most significant deals in the insurance sector. JLT's specialty business was merged within Marsh, its reinsurance business was merged within Guy Carpenter and its employee benefits business was merged within Mercer.

MMC offers comprehensive benefits, 401(k) and retirement plans, and a variety of employee assistance programs.

FINANCIAL DATA:
Note: Data for latest year may not have been available at press time.

In U.S. $	2018	2017	2016	2015	2014	2013
Revenue	14,950,000,000	14,024,000,000	13,211,000,000	12,893,000,000	12,951,000,000	12,261,000,000
R&D Expense						
Operating Income	2,761,000,000	2,856,000,000	2,664,000,000	2,419,000,000	2,301,000,000	2,077,000,000
Operating Margin %		.20%	.20%	.19%	.18%	.17%
SGA Expense						
Net Income	1,650,000,000	1,492,000,000	1,768,000,000	1,599,000,000	1,465,000,000	1,357,000,000
Operating Cash Flow	2,428,000,000	1,893,000,000	2,007,000,000	1,888,000,000	2,112,000,000	1,341,000,000
Capital Expenditure	314,000,000	302,000,000	253,000,000	325,000,000	368,000,000	401,000,000
EBITDA	3,028,000,000	3,361,000,000	3,107,000,000	2,893,000,000	2,610,000,000	2,498,000,000
Return on Assets %		.08%	.10%	.09%	.08%	.08%
Return on Equity %		.22%	.28%	.24%	.20%	.19%
Debt to Equity		0.71	0.726	0.676	0.479	0.332

CONTACT INFORMATION:
Phone: 212 345-5000 Fax: 212 345-4809
Toll-Free:
Address: 1166 Ave. of the Americas, New York, NY 10036 United States

STOCK TICKER/OTHER:
Stock Ticker: MMC
Employees: 60,000
Parent Company:

Exchange: NYS
Fiscal Year Ends: 12/31

SALARIES/BONUSES:
Top Exec. Salary: $1,475,000   Bonus: $
Second Exec. Salary: $1,000,000   Bonus: $

OTHER THOUGHTS:
Estimated Female Officers or Directors: 3
Hot Spot for Advancement for Women/Minorities: Y

Mary Kay Inc

www.marykay.com

NAIC Code: 454390

TYPES OF BUSINESS:
Cosmetics & Beauty Supplies, Direct Selling
Online Retail
Fragrances
Over-the-Counter Drugs
Cosmetics & Beauty Supplies, Manufacturing

BRANDS/DIVISIONS/AFFILIATES:
Cityscape
Forever Diamonds
Bella Belara
Thinking of You
Domain
MK High Intensity
Tribute
Mary Kay Museum

CONTACTS:
Note: Officers with more than one job title may be intentionally listed here more than once.

David B. Holl, CEO
Deborah Gibbins, CFO
Sheryl Adkins-Green, CMO
Melinda Foster Sellers, Chief People Officer
Kregg Jodie, CIO
Nathan Moore, Chief Legal Officer
Darrell Overcash, Pres., North America Region
Tara Eustace, Pres., European Region
Jose Smeke, Pres., Latin American Region
Richard R. Rogers, Exec. Chmn.
K.K. Chua, Pres., Asia Pacific Region
Dennis Greaney, Chief Supply Chain Officer

GROWTH PLANS/SPECIAL FEATURES:

Mary Kay, Inc. is one of the largest direct sellers of skin care products in the U.S., and has been in business for more than 55 years (established in 1963). The company's global portfolio includes more than 1,400 patents for products, technologies and packaging designs. Its more than 200 products span several categories, including skin care, color cosmetics, spa and body care and fragrances. Skin care includes anti-aging creams; cleansers; moisturizers; basic skin care for different skin types; products for specific needs, such as acne treatment and oil control; and lip and eye care. Color cosmetics products include lip, eyes, cheeks, nails, foundations and powder color enhancers as well as travel sets and applicators. The Mary Kay fragrance line has specialty scents for both men and women, including Cityscape, Forever Diamonds, Bella Belara and Thinking of You for women, and Domain, MK High Intensity and Tribute for men. Mary Kay develops, tests, manufactures and packages the majority of its products at its own plants. Most inventory is manufactured at the Dallas site, where the company headquarters and the Mary Kay Museum are located. An additional manufacturing facility is located in China. With FDA approval, the company also manufactures and distributes certain products classified as over-the-counter drugs, such as sunscreens and acne treatment products. Mary Kay independent beauty consultants serve customers in nearly 40 countries worldwide. About 40% of new sales recruits are relatively young, aged 18 to 30. A new recruit pays $100 for a basic starter kit in order to begin selling Mary Kay products. Independent beauty consultants may eventually become independent sales directors and/or independent national sales directors.

FINANCIAL DATA:
Note: Data for latest year may not have been available at press time.

In U.S. $	2018	2017	2016	2015	2014	2013
Revenue	3,250,000,000	3,450,000,000	3,500,000,000	3,700,000,000	3,200,000,000	3,100,000,000
R&D Expense						
Operating Income						
Operating Margin %						
SGA Expense						
Net Income						
Operating Cash Flow						
Capital Expenditure						
EBITDA						
Return on Assets %						
Return on Equity %						
Debt to Equity						

CONTACT INFORMATION:
Phone: 972-687-6300
Fax: 972-687-1611
Toll-Free: 800-627-9529
Address: 16251 Dallas Pkwy., Dallas, TX 75001 United States

SALARIES/BONUSES:
Top Exec. Salary: $
Bonus: $
Second Exec. Salary: $
Bonus: $

STOCK TICKER/OTHER:
Stock Ticker: Private
Employees: 5,000
Parent Company:
Exchange:
Fiscal Year Ends: 12/31

OTHER THOUGHTS:
Estimated Female Officers or Directors: 3
Hot Spot for Advancement for Women/Minorities: Y

Sales, profits and employees may be estimates. Financial information, benefits and other data can change quickly and may vary from those stated here.

MassMutual Financial Group

www.massmutual.com

NAIC Code: 524113

TYPES OF BUSINESS:
Life Insurance
Pension Products
Real Estate Equity Management
Disability Insurance
Investment Management Products
Mutual Fund Management
Investor Services

BRANDS/DIVISIONS/AFFILIATES:
Massachusetts Mutual Life Insurance Company
CM Life Insurance Company
MML Bay State Life Insurance Company
Oppenheimer Funds Inc
Barings LLC
MassMutual Ventures LLC

CONTACTS:
Note: Officers with more than one job title may be intentionally listed here more than once.

Roger Crandall, CEO
Mark Roellig, Chief Technology & Administration Officer
Susan Cicco, Chief Human Resources Officer
Timothy Corbett, Chief Investment Officer
Mark D. Roellig, General Counsel
Sharmaine Miller, VP-New Bus. Oper.
Douglas G. Russell, Sr. VP-Strategy & Corp. Dev.
Elizabeth A. Ward, Chief Enterprise Risk Officer
William F. Glavin, Jr., CEO
Elaine A. Sarsynski, Chmn.
Susan M. Cicco, VP
Roger Crandall, Chmn.
Elaine A. Sarsynski, CEO

GROWTH PLANS/SPECIAL FEATURES:
MassMutual Financial Group, a marketing name for Massachusetts Mutual Life Insurance Company and its affiliated companies, is a global, growth oriented, diversified financial services organization. Together, the group boasts more than 5 million customers and over $770 billion in managed assets (in 2017). The mutually-owned company offers financial protection, accumulation and income management by providing life insurance, annuities, disability income insurance, long-term care insurance, retirement planning products, income management and other products and services for individuals, business owners, corporations and institutions. It operates through several subsidiaries, including CM Life Insurance Company and MML Bay State Life Insurance Company. MassMutual's investment group provides investment management products, such as securities and real estate as well as mutual fund management primarily through Oppenheimer Funds, Inc. and Barings, LLC. MassMutual Ventures, LLC is a venture capital firm with the mandate to back startups and entrepreneurial businesses.

The firm offers employees life, health, dental, disability and vision insurance; flexible spending accounts; and a 401(k).

FINANCIAL DATA:
Note: Data for latest year may not have been available at press time.

In U.S. $	2018	2017	2016	2015	2014	2013
Revenue	32,484,000,000	26,113,000,000	29,560,000,000	29,488,000,000	26,400,000,000	27,560,000,000
R&D Expense						
Operating Income						
Operating Margin %						
SGA Expense						
Net Income	-716,000,000	137,000,000	70,000,000	546,000,000	799,000,000	-113,000,000
Operating Cash Flow						
Capital Expenditure						
EBITDA						
Return on Assets %						
Return on Equity %						
Debt to Equity						

CONTACT INFORMATION:
Phone: 413-744-1000 Fax: 413-744-6005
Toll-Free: 800-767-1000
Address: 1295 State St., Springfield, MA 01111 United States

SALARIES/BONUSES:
Top Exec. Salary: $ Bonus: $
Second Exec. Salary: $ Bonus: $

STOCK TICKER/OTHER:
Stock Ticker: Mutual Company
Employees: 9,500
Parent Company:

Exchange:
Fiscal Year Ends: 12/31

OTHER THOUGHTS:
Estimated Female Officers or Directors: 8
Hot Spot for Advancement for Women/Minorities: Y

MasterCard Inc

NAIC Code: 522320

www.mastercard.com

TYPES OF BUSINESS:
Credit Card Issuer
Transaction Processing Services

BRANDS/DIVISIONS/AFFILIATES:
MasterCard
Maestro
Cirrus
Masterpass
Vocalink

CONTACTS:
Note: Officers with more than one job title may be intentionally listed here more than once.

Ajay Banga, CEO
Michael Miebach, Other Executive Officer
Sachin Mehra, CFO
Sachin Mehra, CFO
Richard Haythornthwaite, Chairman of the Board
Sandra Arkell, Chief Accounting Officer
Raja Rajamannar, Chief Marketing Officer
Timothy Murphy, General Counsel
Michael Fraccaro, Other Executive Officer
Kevin Stanton, Other Executive Officer
Ajay Bhalla, President, Divisional
Gilberto Caldart, President, Divisional

GROWTH PLANS/SPECIAL FEATURES:

MasterCard, Inc. is a global payment solutions company that provides services to support the credit, debit and related payment programs of thousands of financial institutions. The company develops and markets payment solutions and processes payment transactions; it also provides consulting services to customers and merchants. MasterCard manages payment card brands including MasterCard, Maestro, Cirrus and Masterpass. A typical transaction processed over the MasterCard network involves four parties in addition to the firm: the cardholder, the merchant, the issuer (the cardholder's financial institution) and the acquirer (the merchant's financial institution). The company's customers are the financial institutions that act as issuers and acquirers. MasterCard generates revenues from the fees that it charges customers for providing these transaction processing and other payment-related services by assessing their customers based on their volume of dollar activity. The firm's credit and debit cards are accepted at more than 150 currencies in 210 countries and territories worldwide. During 2017, MasterCard acquired a controlling interest in Vocalink, which operates systems for automated clearing house (ACH) payments and ATM processing platforms in the U.K. and other countries.

The firm offers employees medical, dental and vision coverage; life, disability and AD&D insurance; child care options; flexible work hours; adoption assistance; financial wellness programs; and personal services and discounts.

FINANCIAL DATA:
Note: Data for latest year may not have been available at press time.

In U.S. $	2018	2017	2016	2015	2014	2013
Revenue	14,950,000,000	12,497,000,000	10,776,000,000	9,667,000,000	9,473,000,000	8,346,000,000
R&D Expense						
Operating Income	8,374,000,000	6,743,000,000	5,912,000,000	5,057,000,000	5,076,000,000	4,600,000,000
Operating Margin %		.54%	.54%	.52%	.54%	.54%
SGA Expense	6,117,000,000	5,318,000,000	4,491,000,000	4,244,000,000	4,076,000,000	3,488,000,000
Net Income	5,859,000,000	3,915,000,000	4,059,000,000	3,808,000,000	3,617,000,000	3,116,000,000
Operating Cash Flow	6,223,000,000	5,555,000,000	4,484,000,000	4,043,000,000	3,407,000,000	4,135,000,000
Capital Expenditure	504,000,000	423,000,000	382,000,000	342,000,000	334,000,000	299,000,000
EBITDA	7,849,000,000	7,113,000,000	6,114,000,000	5,385,000,000	5,448,000,000	4,772,000,000
Return on Assets %		.20%	.23%	.24%	.24%	.23%
Return on Equity %		.70%	.69%	.59%	.51%	.43%
Debt to Equity		0.992	0.916	0.545	0.22	

CONTACT INFORMATION:
Phone: 914 249-2000   Fax: 914 249-4206
Toll-Free: 800-627-8372
Address: 2000 Purchase St., Purchase, NY 10577 United States

STOCK TICKER/OTHER:
Stock Ticker: MA   Exchange: NYS
Employees: 11,300   Fiscal Year Ends: 12/31
Parent Company:

SALARIES/BONUSES:
Top Exec. Salary: $1,250,000   Bonus: $
Second Exec. Salary: $750,000 Bonus: $

OTHER THOUGHTS:
Estimated Female Officers or Directors: 2
Hot Spot for Advancement for Women/Minorities: Y

Match Group Inc

NAIC Code: 519130

www.match.com

TYPES OF BUSINESS:
Internet Dating Sites

BRANDS/DIVISIONS/AFFILIATES:
IAC/InterActiveCorp
Match
OkCupid
PlentyOfFish
Tinder
Twoo
LoveScout24
Pairs

CONTACTS:
Note: Officers with more than one job title may be intentionally listed here more than once.

Amanda Ginsberg, CEO
Gary Swidler, CFO
Philip Eigenmann, Chief Accounting Officer
Jared Sine, Chief Legal Officer
Joseph Levin, Director
Sharmistha Dubey, President

GROWTH PLANS/SPECIAL FEATURES:

Match Group, Inc., a subsidiary of IAC/InterActiveCorp, is a global provider of dating products. The company operates a portfolio of brands, including Match, OkCupid, PlentyOfFish, Tinder, Meetic, Twoo, OurTime, LoveScout24 and Pairs, each designed to increase user's likelihood of finding a romantic connection. Its target market includes all adults in North America, Western Europe and other select countries who are not in a committed relationship and who have access to the internet. Match Group currently offers its dating products in 42 languages across more than 190 countries. Match features include the ability to both search profiles, receive algorithmic matches and the ability to attend live events, promoted by Match, with other members. OkCupid attracts users through a mathematical and question/answer approach. PlentyofFish has the ability to search profiles and receive algorithmic matches. Tinder is a mobile-only offering with location-based features. Meetic serves users in France, Spain, Italy and the Netherlands and is similar to Match. Twoo is a dating product seeded through existing social networks, with its user base being primarily concentrated in Europe, Asia and South America. OurTime serves the needs of individuals for whom commonalities around age, religion, ethnicity or circumstance are of fundamental importance when making a romantic connection. LoveScout24 provides dating products in Germany, with a strong presence in Austria and Switzerland, and is characterized by its search-based offering rather than matching products. Pairs provides dating products in Japan.

FINANCIAL DATA:
Note: Data for latest year may not have been available at press time.

In U.S. $	2018	2017	2016	2015	2014	2013
Revenue	1,729,850,000	1,330,661,000	1,222,526,000	1,020,431,000	888,268,000	803,089,000
R&D Expense	132,030,000	101,150,000	83,065,000	67,348,000	49,738,000	42,973,000
Operating Income	553,294,000	360,517,000	305,908,000	193,556,000	228,567,000	221,333,000
Operating Margin %		.27%	.25%	.19%	.26%	.28%
SGA Expense	600,240,000	555,414,000	545,351,000	535,455,000	452,997,000	415,511,000
Net Income	477,939,000	350,148,000	171,451,000	120,383,000	147,764,000	125,003,000
Operating Cash Flow	603,455,000	321,091,000	234,106,000	209,082,000	173,615,000	174,797,000
Capital Expenditure	30,954,000	28,833,000	48,903,000	29,156,000	21,793,000	19,807,000
EBITDA	595,345,000	363,771,000	368,056,000	251,527,000	278,119,000	258,877,000
Return on Assets %		.17%	.09%	.07%	.11%	.10%
Return on Equity %		.70%	.44%	.22%	.18%	.15%
Debt to Equity		2.499		2.369	4.281	0.238	0.095

CONTACT INFORMATION:
Phone: 214-576-9352 Fax:
Toll-Free:
Address: 8750 N. Central Expressway, Ste. 1400, Dallas, TX 75231 United States

STOCK TICKER/OTHER:
Stock Ticker: MTCH
Employees: 5,100
Parent Company: IAC/InterActiveCorp

Exchange: NAS
Fiscal Year Ends:

SALARIES/BONUSES:
Top Exec. Salary: $750,000 Bonus: $1,750,000
Second Exec. Salary: $550,000 Bonus: $1,500,000

OTHER THOUGHTS:
Estimated Female Officers or Directors:
Hot Spot for Advancement for Women/Minorities:

Matthews International Corporation

www.matw.com

NAIC Code: 339995

TYPES OF BUSINESS:
Burial Caskets and Cases Manufacturing

BRANDS/DIVISIONS/AFFILIATES:
SGK Brand Solutions

CONTACTS:
Note: Officers with more than one job title may be intentionally listed here more than once.

Joseph Bartolacci, CEO
Steven Nicola, CFO
John Turner, Chairman of the Board
Edward Brady, Chief Information Officer
Gregory Babe, Chief Technology Officer
David Schawk, Director
Brian Dunn, Executive VP, Divisional
Brian Walters, General Counsel
Paul Rahill, President, Divisional
Steven Gackenbach, President, Divisional
Gary Kohl, President, Divisional
Paul Jensen, President, Divisional
Marcy Campbell, Senior VP, Divisional
Robert Marsh, Treasurer

GROWTH PLANS/SPECIAL FEATURES:
Matthews International Corporation is a designer, manufacturer and marketer of memorialization products and brand solutions. Memorialization products consist primarily of bronze memorials and other products, caskets and cremation equipment for the cemetery and funeral home industries. The company's products and operations are comprised of three business segments: SGK Brand Solutions, memorialization and industrial technologies. SGK Brand Solutions is comprised of the graphics imaging business, including wholly-owned Schawk, Inc., and Matthews' merchandising solutions operations. This segment provides brand development, brand management, pre-media services, printing plates and cylinders, embossing tools and creative design services to consumer packaged goods, retail and packaging industries. The memorialization segment manufactures and markets a full line of memorialization products used primarily in cemeteries, funeral homes and crematories. These products are sold primarily in the U.S., Europe, Canada and Australia, and include cast bronze memorials, granite memorials, caskets, cremation equipment and other memorialization products. This division also manufactures and markets architectural products used to identify or commemorate people, places, events and accomplishments. The industrial technologies segment designs, manufactures and distributes an array of marking, coding and industrial automation solutions, order fulfillment systems and related consumables. Manufacturers, suppliers and distributors worldwide rely on Matthews' integrated systems to identify, track, control and pick their products.

FINANCIAL DATA:
Note: Data for latest year may not have been available at press time.

In U.S. $	2018	2017	2016	2015	2014	2013
Revenue	1,602,580,000	1,515,608,000	1,480,464,000	1,426,068,000	1,106,597,000	985,357,000
R&D Expense						
Operating Income	132,834,000	112,603,000	118,815,000	105,023,000	82,891,000	95,792,000
Operating Margin %		.07%	.08%	.07%	.07%	.10%
SGA Expense	416,954,000	450,784,000	437,639,000	424,352,000	309,605,000	260,726,000
Net Income	107,371,000	74,368,000	66,749,000	63,449,000	43,674,000	54,888,000
Operating Cash Flow	147,574,000	149,299,000	140,274,000	141,064,000	92,399,000	109,326,000
Capital Expenditure	43,200,000	44,935,000	41,682,000	48,251,000	29,237,000	24,924,000
EBITDA	212,394,000	190,639,000	185,058,000	172,882,000	123,288,000	132,226,000
Return on Assets %		.03%	.03%	.03%	.03%	.05%
Return on Equity %		.10%	.09%	.08%	.07%	.11%
Debt to Equity		1.116	1.192	1.219	0.917	0.639

CONTACT INFORMATION:
Phone: 412-442-8200 Fax: 412-442-8290
Toll-Free:
Address: Two Northshore Center, Pittsburgh, PA 15212-5851 United States

STOCK TICKER/OTHER:
Stock Ticker: MATW
Employees: 10,300
Parent Company:

Exchange: NAS
Fiscal Year Ends: 09/30

SALARIES/BONUSES:
Top Exec. Salary: $874,285 Bonus: $
Second Exec. Salary: $646,623 Bonus: $

OTHER THOUGHTS:
Estimated Female Officers or Directors:
Hot Spot for Advancement for Women/Minorities:

Sales, profits and employees may be estimates. Financial information, benefits and other data can change quickly and may vary from those stated here.

MAXIMUS Inc

www.maximus.com

NAIC Code: 541512

TYPES OF BUSINESS:
Consulting-Government Agencies
Outsourced Program Management
IT Systems Management
Consulting

BRANDS/DIVISIONS/AFFILIATES:

CONTACTS:
Note: Officers with more than one job title may be intentionally listed here more than once.
Bruce Caswell, CEO
Richard Nadeau, CFO
Peter Pond, Chairman of the Board
Richard Montoni, Director
Raymond Ruddy, Director
David Francis, General Counsel
Mark Andrekovich, Other Executive Officer

GROWTH PLANS/SPECIAL FEATURES:

MAXIMUS, Inc. provides business process services (BPS) to government health and human services agencies. MAXIMUS is one of the largest pure-play health and human services BPS providers to governments in the U.S., the U.K., Australia, Canada, Saudi Arabia and Singapore. The company is divided into three segments: health services, accounting for 59% of 2018 revenue; human services, 21%; and U.S. federal services, 20%. Health services provides BPS and consulting services for state, provincial and federal government programs, such as Medicaid, CHIP (children's health insurance programs) and the Affordable Care Act, in the U.S.; Health Insurance BC (British Columbia), in Canada; and Health Assessment Advisory Service, in the U.K. Human services provides national, state and local human services agencies with a variety of BPS and related consulting services for government programs such as welfare-to-work, child support higher education and K-12 special education. The U.S. federal services segment provides BPS and program management for large government programs, independent health review and appeals services for both the U.S. federal government and similar state-based programs. This division also offers technology solutions for civilian federal programs. In November 2018, MAXIMUS acquired certain assets of General Dynamics Information Technology's large-scale, citizen engagement centers in the U.S. federal civilian market for $400 million.

The company offers its employees medical, dental, vision, life and AD&D insurance; flexible spending accounts; long-term care policies; legal services; employee assistance; 401(k); paid time off; discounts on childcare; and credit union accounts.

FINANCIAL DATA:
Note: Data for latest year may not have been available at press time.

In U.S. $	2018	2017	2016	2015	2014	2013
Revenue	2,392,236,000	2,450,961,000	2,403,360,000	2,099,821,000	1,700,912,000	1,331,279,000
R&D Expense						
Operating Income	298,836,000	315,187,000	280,555,000	264,577,000	225,308,000	188,376,000
Operating Margin %		.13%	.12%	.13%	.13%	.14%
SGA Expense	285,241,000	284,510,000	268,259,000	238,792,000	226,815,000	197,657,000
Net Income	220,751,000	209,426,000	178,362,000	157,772,000	145,440,000	116,731,000
Operating Cash Flow	323,525,000	337,200,000	180,026,000	206,217,000	213,600,000	120,938,000
Capital Expenditure	26,520,000	24,154,000	46,391,000	105,149,000	47,148,000	62,176,000
EBITDA	362,401,000	384,374,000	361,883,000	317,414,000	273,976,000	224,192,000
Return on Assets %		.16%	.14%	.14%	.17%	.15%
Return on Equity %		.25%	.26%	.27%	.27%	.24%
Debt to Equity		0.001	0.221	0.344		0.002

CONTACT INFORMATION:
Phone: 703 251-8500 Fax:
Toll-Free: 800-629-4687
Address: 1891 Metro Center Dr., Reston, VA 20190 United States

STOCK TICKER/OTHER:
Stock Ticker: MMS
Employees: 18,800
Parent Company:

Exchange: NYS
Fiscal Year Ends: 09/30

SALARIES/BONUSES:
Top Exec. Salary: $887,500 Bonus: $
Second Exec. Salary: $667,500 Bonus: $

OTHER THOUGHTS:
Estimated Female Officers or Directors: 3
Hot Spot for Advancement for Women/Minorities: Y

Sales, profits and employees may be estimates. Financial information, benefits and other data can change quickly and may vary from those stated here.

Mayo Clinic

NAIC Code: 622110

www.mayo.edu

TYPES OF BUSINESS:
General Medical and Surgical Hospitals
Physician Practice Management
Medical Research
Health Care Education

BRANDS/DIVISIONS/AFFILIATES:
Mayo Clinic
Mayo Clinic Hospital
Saint Marys Campus
Mayo Clinic Building
Samuel C Johnson Research
Mayo Clinic Collaborative Research
Mayo Clinic Specialty
Civica Rx

CONTACTS: Note: Officers with more than one job title may be intentionally listed here more than once.
Gianrico Farrugia, CEO
Steven F. Nicola, CFO
Shirley A. Weis, Chief Admin. Officer
Jonathan J. Oviatt, Chief Legal Officer
Harry N. Hoffman, Treas.
William C. Rupp, VP
Wyatt W. Decker, VP
Robert F. Brigham, Assistant Sec.
Sherry L. Hubert, Assistant Sec.
Samuel A. Di Piazza Jr., Chmn.

GROWTH PLANS/SPECIAL FEATURES:
Mayo Clinic is a nonprofit healthcare organization founded in 1864, and part of the Mayo Foundation for Medical Education and Research. Mayo Clinic provides medical treatment, physician management, healthcare education, research and other specialized medical services through a network of clinics and hospitals in Minnesota, Arizona and Florida. The organization's primary clinics are located in Rochester, Minnesota; Jacksonville, Florida; and Scottsdale and Phoenix, Arizona. The Rochester campus has been in business for more than 100 years, and includes the Mayo Clinic, the Mayo Clinic Hospital, Saint Mary's Campus and Mayo Clinic Hospital-Methodist Campus, which together provide comprehensive diagnosis and treatment in virtually every medical and surgical specialty. The Mayo Clinic Hospital, located on the Jacksonville campus, offers over 260 beds and represents more than 40 medical and surgical specialties. In Arizona, Mayo Clinic serves more than 100,000 patients every year, and focuses on adult specialty and surgical disciplines, supported by programs in medical education and research. The original Scottsdale campus opened in 1987, and includes the Mayo Clinic Building, the Samuel C. Johnson Research building and the Mayo Clinic Collaborative Research building. The Phoenix campus includes the Mayo Clinic Specialty building and Mayo Clinic Hospital. Mayo Clinic schools offer more than 400 educational programs across its campuses, which include five schools under the Mayo Clinic name. Mayo Clinic partnered with six other health organizations to create Civica Rx, a not-for-profit generic drug and pharmaceutical company founded in 2018 to combat life-saving drug shortages and affordability. In 2019, Mayo Clinic created an independent business subsidiary in London in partnership with Oxford University Clinic, to operate a clinic in the Harley Street medical area, with a focus on preventative healthcare.

Doctors are paid by salary, rather than fee for service. Employees are offered comprehensive benefits, retirement plans and employee assistance programs.

FINANCIAL DATA: Note: Data for latest year may not have been available at press time.

In U.S. $	2018	2017	2016	2015	2014	2013
Revenue	12,600,000,000	11,993,000,000	10,990,000,000	10,315,000,000	9,760,600,000	9,420,800,000
R&D Expense						
Operating Income						
Operating Margin %						
SGA Expense						
Net Income	706,000,000	707,000,000	475,000,000	526,000,000	834,800,000	612,100,000
Operating Cash Flow						
Capital Expenditure						
EBITDA						
Return on Assets %						
Return on Equity %						
Debt to Equity						

CONTACT INFORMATION:
Phone: 507-284-2511 Fax: 507-284-0161
Toll-Free: 800-660-4582
Address: 200 First St. SW, Rochester, MN 55905 United States

SALARIES/BONUSES:
Top Exec. Salary: $ Bonus: $
Second Exec. Salary: $ Bonus: $

STOCK TICKER/OTHER:
Stock Ticker: Nonprofit
Employees: 63,134
Parent Company:

Exchange:
Fiscal Year Ends: 12/31

OTHER THOUGHTS:
Estimated Female Officers or Directors: 5
Hot Spot for Advancement for Women/Minorities: Y

McAfee LLC

NAIC Code: 0

www.mcafee.com

TYPES OF BUSINESS:
Computer Software: Network Security, Managed Access, Digital ID, Cybersecurity & Anti-Virus
Virus Protection Software
Network Management Software

GROWTH PLANS/SPECIAL FEATURES:
McAfee, LLC is a cybersecurity company. The firm creates security solutions for consumer and business customers. Its solutions work with other companies' products and therefore helps businesses orchestrate cyber environments that are integrated and secure. McAfee's products enable the protection, detection and correction of threats on both sides of the spectrum: between McAfee and the business or consumer, simultaneously and collaboratively. Since McAfee products protect consumers across all connected devices, including mobile, homes and businesses can be monitored in real-time from anywhere. Moreover, McAfee works with other security players in an effort to unite against cybercriminal activities. McAfee is a joint venture between Thoma Bravo, LLC (51%) and Intel Corporation (49%).

BRANDS/DIVISIONS/AFFILIATES:
Thoma Bravo LLC
Intel Corporation

CONTACTS:
Note: Officers with more than one job title may be intentionally listed here more than once.

Christopher Young, CEO
John Giamatteo, Pres.
Michael Berry, CFO
Allison Cerra, CMO
Chatelle Lynch, Chief Human Resources Officer
Steven Grobman, CTO
Bryan Reed Barney, Exec. VP-Prod. Dev.
Ari Jaaksi, Sr. VP
Louis Riley, General Counsel
Tom Fountain, Sr. VP
Edward Hayden, Sr. VP-Finance & Acct.
Steve Redman, Exec. VP-Global Sales
Ken Levine, Sr. VP
Gert-Jan Schenk, Pres., EMEA
Barry McPherson, Exec. VP-Worldwide Delivery & Support Svcs.
Jean-Claude Broido, Pres., McAfee Japan
Barry McPherson, Exec. VP-Supply Chain & Facilities

FINANCIAL DATA:
Note: Data for latest year may not have been available at press time.

In U.S. $	2018	2017	2016	2015	2014	2013
Revenue	2,815,050,000	2,681,000,000	2,450,000,000	2,375,000,000	2,216,000,000	2,190,000,000
R&D Expense						
Operating Income						
Operating Margin %						
SGA Expense						
Net Income						
Operating Cash Flow						
Capital Expenditure						
EBITDA						
Return on Assets %						
Return on Equity %						
Debt to Equity						

CONTACT INFORMATION:
Phone: 972-963-8000   Fax:
Toll-Free: 855-380-6445
Address: 2821 Mission College Blvd., Santa Clara, CA 95054 United States

STOCK TICKER/OTHER:
Stock Ticker: Joint Venture
Employees: 7,600
Parent Company:

Exchange:
Fiscal Year Ends: 12/31

SALARIES/BONUSES:
Top Exec. Salary: $ Bonus: $
Second Exec. Salary: $ Bonus: $

OTHER THOUGHTS:
Estimated Female Officers or Directors: 3
Hot Spot for Advancement for Women/Minorities: Y

Sales, profits and employees may be estimates. Financial information, benefits and other data can change quickly and may vary from those stated here.

McCann Worldgroup

www.mccannworldgroup.com

NAIC Code: 541810

TYPES OF BUSINESS:
Advertising & Related Services
Direct Marketing
Customer Relationship Management
Brand Consulting, Analytics & Design
Promotions & Events
Health Care Communications Services
Public Relations
Media Planning & Buying

BRANDS/DIVISIONS/AFFILIATES:
Interpublic Group of Companies Inc
McCann Truth Central
McCann
MRM/McCann
Momentum Worldwide
McCann Health
CRAFT
PMK-BNC

CONTACTS:
Note: Officers with more than one job title may be intentionally listed here more than once.

Harris Diamond, CEO
Bill Kolb, Pres.
Gary Lee, CFO
Marjan M. Panah, Chief Talent Officer
Rob Reilly, Global Creative Chmn
Nicole Cramer, Global Chief Creativity Catalyst
Suzanne Powers, Chief Strategy Officer
Mike Parker, Chief Digital Officer
Jeremy Miller, Chief Comm. Officer
Rob Reilly, Global Creative Chmn.
Chris Macdonald, Pres., McCann New York
Laura Simpson, Global Dir.-McCann Truth Central
Harris Diamond, Chmn.
Charles Cadell, Pres., Asia Pacific

GROWTH PLANS/SPECIAL FEATURES:

McCann Worldgroup, a subsidiary of Interpublic Group of Companies, Inc., is a marketing firm dedicated to building customer and revenue growth. The company's McCann Truth Central service is the guiding concept in all its operations, created to conduct original research to inform and grow clients' businesses. McCann Worldgroup offers this extensive service through nine chief operating units: McCann, which is engaged in advertising; MRM/McCann, offering digital marketing and relationship management services and solutions; Momentum Worldwide, offering total brand experience services and solutions; McCann Health, offering professional and direct-to-consumer communications; CRAFT, offering global adaptation and production services and solutions; UM, offering medial management services and solutions; Weber Shandwick, offering public relations services and solutions; FutureBrand, providing consulting and design services and solutions; and PMK-BNC, providing entertainment, brand and popular culture services and solutions. McCann Worldgroup's current clients (as of March 2018) include L'Oreal, GM, MasterCard, ALDI, Cigna, Nestle, Coca-Cola, Microsoft, Reckitt Benckiser and Verizon.

FINANCIAL DATA: Note: Data for latest year may not have been available at press time.

In U.S. $	2018	2017	2016	2015	2014	2013
Revenue	5,500,000,000	5,000,000,000				
R&D Expense						
Operating Income						
Operating Margin %						
SGA Expense						
Net Income						
Operating Cash Flow						
Capital Expenditure						
EBITDA						
Return on Assets %						
Return on Equity %						
Debt to Equity						

CONTACT INFORMATION:
Phone: 646-865-2000 Fax: 646-487-9610
Toll-Free:
Address: 622 Third Ave., New York, NY 10017 United States

SALARIES/BONUSES:
Top Exec. Salary: $ Bonus: $
Second Exec. Salary: $ Bonus: $

STOCK TICKER/OTHER:
Stock Ticker: Subsidiary Exchange:
Employees: 22,000 Fiscal Year Ends: 12/31
Parent Company: Interpublic Group of Companies Inc

OTHER THOUGHTS:
Estimated Female Officers or Directors: 5
Hot Spot for Advancement for Women/Minorities: Y

Sales, profits and employees may be estimates. Financial information, benefits and other data can change quickly and may vary from those stated here.

McCormick & Company Incorporated

www.mccormick.com

NAIC Code: 311940

TYPES OF BUSINESS:
Herbs, Spices & Seasonings

BRANDS/DIVISIONS/AFFILIATES:
McCormick
French's
Frank's
RedHot
Lawry's
Club House
Gourmet Garden
OLD BAY

CONTACTS:
Note: Officers with more than one job title may be intentionally listed here more than once.

Lawrence Kurzius, CEO
Christina Mcmullen, Chief Accounting Officer
Michael Smith, Executive VP
Malcolm Swift, President, Divisional
Brendan Foley, President, Divisional
Lisa Manzone, Senior VP, Divisional
Nneka Rimmer, Senior VP, Divisional
Jeffery Schwartz, Vice President

GROWTH PLANS/SPECIAL FEATURES:

McCormick & Company, Incorporated is a global manufacturer, marketer and distributor of spices, seasonings and flavorings to the entire food industry, including retail outlets, food manufacturers and food service businesses. The firm operates in two segments: consumer and flavor solutions. The consumer segment consists of brands that reach consumers in approximately 150 countries and territories. Leading brands in the Americas include McCormick, French's, Frank's, RedHot, Lawry's and Club House, as well as Gourmet Garden and OLD BAY. Ethnic brands marketed by this division include Zatarain's, Stubbs, Thai Kitchen and Simply Asia. In the Europe, Middle East and Africa (EMEA) region, this division's major brands include Ducros, Schwartz, Kamis and Drogheria & Alimentari, as well as Vahine. In China the consumer segment markets products under the McCormick and DaQiao brands; in Australia, under the McCormick, Aeroplane and Gourmet Garden brands; in India, under the Kohinoor brand; and elsewhere in the Asia/Pacific region under the McCormick and other brands. Approximately half of this division's sales are derived from spices, herbs and seasonings. The flavor solutions segment provides a wide range of products to multinational food manufacturers and foodservice customers, which are supplied with branded, packaged products both directly and indirectly through distributors. Supplies include customized flavor solutions, including seasoning blends, spices, herbs, condiments, coating systems and compound flavors. This division continually engages in sensory testing, culinary research, food safety and flavor application.

McCormick offers its employees medical and dental insurance, life and disability insurance, adoption assistance, a profit sharing plan, an employee stock purchase plan, an employee assistance program and tuition assistance.

FINANCIAL DATA:
Note: Data for latest year may not have been available at press time.

In U.S. $	2018	2017	2016	2015	2014	2013
Revenue	5,408,900,000	4,834,100,000	4,411,500,000	4,296,300,000	4,243,200,000	4,123,400,000
R&D Expense						
Operating Income	942,100,000	765,400,000	656,700,000	609,900,000	608,200,000	575,500,000
Operating Margin %		.16%	.15%	.14%	.14%	.14%
SGA Expense	1,429,500,000	1,244,800,000	1,175,000,000	1,127,400,000	1,122,000,000	1,090,300,000
Net Income	933,400,000	477,400,000	472,300,000	401,600,000	437,900,000	389,000,000
Operating Cash Flow	821,200,000	815,300,000	658,100,000	590,000,000	503,600,000	465,200,000
Capital Expenditure	169,100,000	182,400,000	153,800,000	128,400,000	132,700,000	99,900,000
EBITDA	1,066,600,000	815,700,000	753,900,000	655,400,000	706,800,000	658,700,000
Return on Assets %		.06%	.10%	.09%	.10%	.09%
Return on Equity %		.23%	.29%	.23%	.24%	.22%
Debt to Equity		1.736	0.648	0.63	0.566	0.527

CONTACT INFORMATION:
Phone: 410-771-7301   Fax:
Toll-Free:
Address: 24 Schilling Rd., Ste. 1, Hunt Valley, MD 21031 United States

STOCK TICKER/OTHER:
Stock Ticker: MKC
Employees: 10,500
Parent Company:

Exchange: NYS
Fiscal Year Ends: 11/30

SALARIES/BONUSES:
Top Exec. Salary: $1,163,462   Bonus: $
Second Exec. Salary: $675,769   Bonus: $

OTHER THOUGHTS:
Estimated Female Officers or Directors: 1
Hot Spot for Advancement for Women/Minorities: Y

McDonald's Corporation

www.mcdonalds.com

NAIC Code: 722513

TYPES OF BUSINESS:
Fast Food Restaurants
Home-Meal Replacement Restaurants
Franchising

BRANDS/DIVISIONS/AFFILIATES:
Big Mac
Quarter Pounder
Filet O'Fish
Happy Meal
Egg McMuffin

CONTACTS: Note: Officers with more than one job title may be intentionally listed here more than once.
Kevin Ozan, CFO
Daniel Henry, Chief Information Officer
Enrique Hernandez, Director
Stephen Easterbrook, Director
Francesca DeBiase, Executive VP, Divisional
Silvia Lagnado, Executive VP
Jerome Krulewitch, Executive VP
David Fairhurst, Executive VP
Robert Gibbs, Executive VP
Joseph Erlinger, President, Divisional
Ian Borden, President, Divisional
Christopher Kempczinski, President, Geographical
Catherine Hoovel, Vice President

GROWTH PLANS/SPECIAL FEATURES:

McDonald's Corporation operates more than 37,555 fast-food restaurants in 120 countries, serving approximately 70 million customers per day. McDonald's has expanded through its franchising model, whereby independent businessmen and women provide capital by initially investing in equipment, signs, seating and restaurant decor and personally operating them. The company shares the investment by owning or leasing the land and buildings. Nearly 90% of McDonald's worldwide restaurants are franchises, the rest being operated directly by the company or under joint-venture agreements. The McDonald's menu includes items such as hamburgers, cheeseburgers, fish and chicken sandwiches, chicken nuggets, French fries, salads, milkshakes, desserts and soft drinks. McDonald's restaurants are also open during breakfast hours and offer egg sandwiches, hotcakes, biscuit and bagel sandwiches and muffins. Brand names include the Big Mac, Quarter Pounder, Filet O'Fish, Happy Meal and Egg McMuffin. As part of a multi-year beverage business strategy designed to take advantage of the significant and growing beverage category, the company offers hot specialty coffee offerings on a market-by-market basis, all of which serve as a platform for the recent introduction of smoothies, frappes and other beverage options in a number of markets. The company is continually working to provide nutritious additions to its menu, including salads, apple slices, oatmeal and low-fat yogurt. As of late-2018, McDonald's USA's classic burgers have no artificial preservatives, no artificial flavors and no added colors from artificial sources; the pickle contains an artificial preservative, which can be skipped if preferred. These ingredient changes affect all 14,000 U.S. restaurants, and classic burgers include the hamburger, cheeseburger, double cheeseburger, McDouble, Quarter Pounder with Cheese, double Quarter Pounder with Cheese and Big Mac.

The firm offers qualified employees medical, dental, vision and short/long-term disability insurance; short- and long-term disability; profit-sharing and other plans; and various employee assistance programs.

FINANCIAL DATA: Note: Data for latest year may not have been available at press time.

In U.S. $	2018	2017	2016	2015	2014	2013
Revenue	21,025,200,000	22,820,400,000	24,621,900,000	25,413,000,000	27,441,300,000	28,105,700,000
R&D Expense						
Operating Income	8,585,800,000	8,389,500,000	7,820,200,000	7,354,900,000	7,967,800,000	8,517,100,000
Operating Margin %		.37%	.32%	.29%	.29%	.30%
SGA Expense	2,200,200,000	2,231,300,000	2,384,500,000	2,434,300,000	2,487,900,000	2,385,600,000
Net Income	5,924,300,000	5,192,300,000	4,686,500,000	4,529,300,000	4,757,800,000	5,585,900,000
Operating Cash Flow	6,966,700,000	5,551,200,000	6,059,600,000	6,539,100,000	6,730,300,000	7,120,700,000
Capital Expenditure	2,741,700,000	1,853,700,000	1,821,100,000	1,813,900,000	2,583,400,000	2,824,700,000
EBITDA	10,279,300,000	10,858,200,000	9,267,300,000	8,749,700,000	9,587,000,000	10,311,500,000
Return on Assets %		.16%	.14%	.13%	.13%	.16%
Return on Equity %			1.92%	.45%	.33%	.36%
Debt to Equity				3.403	1.166	0.883

CONTACT INFORMATION:
Phone: 630 623-3000 Fax: 630 623-5700
Toll-Free: 800-244-6227
Address: 110 N. Carpenter St., Chicago, IL 60607 United States

STOCK TICKER/OTHER:
Stock Ticker: MCD
Employees: 375,000
Parent Company:

Exchange: NYS
Fiscal Year Ends: 12/31

SALARIES/BONUSES:
Top Exec. Salary: $1,341,667 Bonus: $
Second Exec. Salary: $791,667 Bonus: $

OTHER THOUGHTS:
Estimated Female Officers or Directors: 4
Hot Spot for Advancement for Women/Minorities: Y

Sales, profits and employees may be estimates. Financial information, benefits and other data can change quickly and may vary from those stated here.

McKesson Corporation

www.mckesson.com

NAIC Code: 424210

TYPES OF BUSINESS:
Pharmaceutical Distribution
Medical-Surgical Products Distribution
Health Care Management Software
Consulting
Outsourcing

BRANDS/DIVISIONS/AFFILIATES:
McKesson Canada
McKesson Prescription Technology Solutions
Change Healthcare

CONTACTS:
Note: Officers with more than one job title may be intentionally listed here more than once.

Brian Tyler, CEO
Britt Vitalone, CFO
Edward Mueller, Chairman of the Board
Sundeep Reddy, Chief Accounting Officer
Lori Schechter, Chief Compliance Officer
Kathleen McElligott, Chief Information Officer
Bansi Nagji, Executive VP, Divisional
Jorge Figueredo, Executive VP
Michele Lau, Secretary
Paul Smith, Senior VP, Divisional
Brian Moore, Senior VP

GROWTH PLANS/SPECIAL FEATURES:

McKesson Corporation provides healthcare management solutions, retail pharmacy, healthcare technology, community oncology and specialty care. The firm partners with life sciences companies, manufacturers, providers, pharmacies, governments and other healthcare organizations. McKesson operates through four business segments: U.S. pharmaceutical and specialty solutions, European pharmaceutical solutions, medical-surgical solutions and other. The U.S. pharmaceutical and specialty solutions segment distributes branded, generic, specialty, biosimilar and over-the-counter (OTC) pharmaceutical drugs and other healthcare-related products. It provides practice management, technology, clinical support and business solutions to community-based oncology and other specialty practices. This division also provides solutions for life sciences companies, including offering multiple distribution channels and clinical trials access to specific patient populations through McKesson's network of oncology physicians. The European pharmaceutical solutions segment provides distribution and related services to wholesale, institutional and retail customers, and serves patients and consumers in 13 European countries through McKesson's own pharmacies and participating pharmacies that operate under the brand partnership and franchise arrangements. The medical-surgical solutions segment distributes medical-surgical supplies and provides logistics and other services to healthcare providers in the U.S. Last, the other segment primarily consists of the following: McKesson Canada, a distributor of pharmaceutical and medical products, and an operator of Rexall Health retail pharmacies; McKesson Prescription Technology Solutions, a provider of innovative technologies that support retail pharmacies; and 70%-owned Change Healthcare, a provider of software and analytics, network solutions and technology-enabled services that delivers wide-ranging financial, operational and clinical benefits to payers, providers and consumers.

Employee benefits include medical, dental, vision, AD&D and dependent life insurance; an employee assistance program; and flexible spending accounts.

FINANCIAL DATA:
Note: Data for latest year may not have been available at press time.

In U.S. $	2018	2017	2016	2015	2014	2013
Revenue	208,357,000,000	198,533,000,000	190,884,000,000	179,045,000,000	137,609,000,000	
R&D Expense	125,000,000	341,000,000	392,000,000	392,000,000	456,000,000	
Operating Income	2,921,000,000	3,464,000,000	3,748,000,000	3,118,000,000	2,435,000,000	
Operating Margin %	.01%	.02%	.02%	.02%	.02%	
SGA Expense	8,138,000,000	7,466,000,000	7,276,000,000	7,901,000,000	5,418,000,000	
Net Income	67,000,000	5,070,000,000	2,258,000,000	1,476,000,000	1,263,000,000	
Operating Cash Flow	4,345,000,000	4,744,000,000	3,672,000,000	3,112,000,000	3,136,000,000	
Capital Expenditure	580,000,000	562,000,000	677,000,000	545,000,000	415,000,000	
EBITDA	1,473,000,000	8,109,000,000	4,488,000,000	4,048,000,000	3,103,000,000	
Return on Assets %	.00%	.09%	.04%	.03%	.03%	
Return on Equity %	.01%	.51%	.27%	.18%	.16%	
Debt to Equity	0.689	0.658	0.732	1.022	1.05	

CONTACT INFORMATION:
Phone: 972-446-4800 Fax:
Toll-Free: 800-826-9360
Address: 6555 State Hwy. 161, Irving, TX 75039 United States

SALARIES/BONUSES:
Top Exec. Salary: $1,680,000 Bonus: $
Second Exec. Salary: $929,375 Bonus: $

STOCK TICKER/OTHER:
Stock Ticker: MCK
Employees: 78,000
Parent Company:

Exchange: NYS
Fiscal Year Ends: 03/31

OTHER THOUGHTS:
Estimated Female Officers or Directors: 4
Hot Spot for Advancement for Women/Minorities: Y

Sales, profits and employees may be estimates. Financial information, benefits and other data can change quickly and may vary from those stated here.

McKinsey & Company Inc

NAIC Code: 541610

www.mckinsey.com

TYPES OF BUSINESS:
Management Consulting
Strategic & Logistics Consulting
Industry-Specific Consulting
Business Research
Business Publications

BRANDS/DIVISIONS/AFFILIATES:
McKinsey Global Institute
McKinsey Quarterly

CONTACTS:
Note: Officers with more than one job title may be intentionally listed here more than once.
Kevin Sneader, Managing Dir.

GROWTH PLANS/SPECIAL FEATURES:
McKinsey & Company, Inc. is a privately-held international management consulting firm established in 1926. Headquartered in New York, the firm maintains more than 120 offices in over 50 countries. McKinsey provides consulting services for leading businesses, governments, non-governmental organizations and non-profits. The company helps clients make improvements to their performance at every level of their organization. Business functions include analytics, diagnostics, business technology, digital technology, implementation, learning programs for clients, marketing and sales, operations, organization, recover and transformation services, risk, strategy and corporate finance, as well as sustainability and resource productivity. Industries served by McKinsey include advanced electronics, aerospace and defense, automotive and assembly, chemicals, consumer packaged goods, electric power and natural gas, financial services, healthcare systems and services, high tech, infrastructure, media and entertainment, metals and mining, oil and gas, paper and forest products, pharmaceuticals and medical products, private equity and principal investors, public sector, retail, semiconductors, social sector, telecommunications and travel/transport/logistics. The McKinsey Global Institute helps leaders in multiple sectors develop deeper understanding of the global economy. The firm's flagship business publication, McKinsey Quarterly, has been defining and informing the senior-management agenda since 1964.

FINANCIAL DATA:
Note: Data for latest year may not have been available at press time.

In U.S. $	2018	2017	2016	2015	2014	2013
Revenue	10,000,000,000	8,800,000,000	8,590,500,000	8,300,000,000	8,000,000,000	7,150,000,000
R&D Expense						
Operating Income						
Operating Margin %						
SGA Expense						
Net Income						
Operating Cash Flow						
Capital Expenditure						
EBITDA						
Return on Assets %						
Return on Equity %						
Debt to Equity						

CONTACT INFORMATION:
Phone: 212-446-7000   Fax: 212-446-8575
Toll-Free:
Address: 55 E. 52nd St., 21/Fl, New York, NY 10022 United States

STOCK TICKER/OTHER:
Stock Ticker: Private
Employees: 30,000
Parent Company:

Exchange:
Fiscal Year Ends: 12/31

SALARIES/BONUSES:
Top Exec. Salary: $ Bonus: $
Second Exec. Salary: $ Bonus: $

OTHER THOUGHTS:
Estimated Female Officers or Directors: 2
Hot Spot for Advancement for Women/Minorities: Y

Sales, profits and employees may be estimates. Financial information, benefits and other data can change quickly and may vary from those stated here.

MedStar Health

NAIC Code: 622110

www.medstarhealth.org

TYPES OF BUSINESS:
General Medical and Surgical Hospitals
Assisted Living Services
Home Health Services
Ambulatory Centers
Rehabilitation Centers
Nursing Homes
Physician Network Management
Research

BRANDS/DIVISIONS/AFFILIATES:
MedStar Franklin Square Medical Center
MedStar Good Samaritan Hospital
MedStar Harbor Hospital
MedStar Montgomery Medical Center
MedStar Southern Maryland Hospital Center
MedStar National Rehabilitation Hospital
MedStar Physician Partners
MedStar Health Research Institute

CONTACTS:
Note: Officers with more than one job title may be intentionally listed here more than once.

Kenneth A. Samet, CEO
Joy Drass, COO
Susan K. Nelson, CFO
Kevin P. Kowalski, Sr. VP-Mktg. & Strategy
Loretta Young Walker, VP-Chief Human Resources Officer
Stephen R.T. Evans, Chief Medical Officer
Michael J. Curran, Chief Admin. Officer
Oliver M. Johnson, II, General Counsel
Eric R. Wagner, Exec. VP-Diversified Oper. & External Affairs
Christine M. Swearingen, Exec. VP-Planning & Community Rel.
Jean Hitchcock, VP-Public Affairs & Mktg.
Susan K. Nelson, VP-Finance & Acct. Oper.
Carl Schindelar, Exec. VP-Oper., Baltimore Region
Jennie P. McConagha, Chief of Staff
Joel N. Bryan, Treas.
Pegeen Townsend, VP-Gov't Affairs
William J. Oetgen, Chmn.

GROWTH PLANS/SPECIAL FEATURES:

MedStar Health is a nonprofit, community-based health care organization primarily composed of several integrated businesses, including 10 major hospitals, with nearly 31,000 associates and 5,400 affiliated physicians (as of fiscal 2019). The hospitals are located within proximity of the Baltimore/Washington, D.C. area and include the following: MedStar Franklin Square Medical Center, MedStar Good Samaritan Hospital, MedStar Harbor Hospital, MedStar Montgomery Medical Center, MedStar Southern Maryland Hospital Center, MedStar St. Mary's Hospital, MedStar Union Memorial Hospital, MedStar Georgetown University Hospital, MedStar Washington Hospital Center and MedStar National Rehabilitation Hospital. The hospitals' services include primary, urgent and sub-acute care; behavioral health and psychiatric services; medical education; and research. MedStar also provides assisted living, home health, hospice and long-term care and operates nursing homes, senior housing, adult day care, rehabilitation and ambulatory centers. MedStar serves roughly 133,512 inpatients, over 4.92 million outpatients and conducts more than 301,850 home health visits annually. The organization manages MedStar Physician Partners, a comprehensive physician network serving in the region. Its MedStar Health Research Institute conducts research and clinical trials; and MedStar Health has one of the largest graduate medical education programs in the country, training more than 1,100 medical residents annually, and is the medical education and clinical partner of Georgetown University.

MedStar's employees are offered health, dental and vision insurance; flexible spending accounts; an employee assistance program; paid leave; a tax deferred retirement savings plan; life and disability insurance; and tuition assistance.

FINANCIAL DATA:
Note: Data for latest year may not have been available at press time.

In U.S. $	2018	2017	2016	2015	2014	2013
Revenue	5,800,000,000	5,530,000,000	5,125,000,000	5,030,000,000	4,628,100,000	4,200,000,000
R&D Expense						
Operating Income						
Operating Margin %						
SGA Expense						
Net Income				359,000,000	304,700,000	185,700,000
Operating Cash Flow						
Capital Expenditure						
EBITDA						
Return on Assets %						
Return on Equity %						
Debt to Equity						

CONTACT INFORMATION:
Phone: 410-772-6500 Fax: 410-715-3905
Toll-Free: 877-772-6505
Address: 10980 Grantchester Way, Columbia, MD 21044 United States

STOCK TICKER/OTHER:
Stock Ticker: Nonprofit   Exchange:
Employees: 32,000   Fiscal Year Ends: 06/30
Parent Company:

SALARIES/BONUSES:
Top Exec. Salary: $ Bonus: $
Second Exec. Salary: $ Bonus: $

OTHER THOUGHTS:
Estimated Female Officers or Directors: 15
Hot Spot for Advancement for Women/Minorities: Y

Sales, profits and employees may be estimates. Financial information, benefits and other data can change quickly and may vary from those stated here.

Menard Inc

www.menards.com

NAIC Code: 444110

TYPES OF BUSINESS:
Home Improvement Stores
Lumber
Housing Materials
Building Materials Manufacturing
Prefabricated Houses

BRANDS/DIVISIONS/AFFILIATES:
Menards
Midwest Manufacturing
MasterForce
MasterCraft
Menards Self Storage
Menards Transportation
Menard Real Estate
NailPlant.com

CONTACTS:
Note: Officers with more than one job title may be intentionally listed here more than once.

John R. Menard, Jr., Pres.

GROWTH PLANS/SPECIAL FEATURES:
Menard, Inc. is a family-owned company that began in 1960, which is headquartered in Eau Claire, Wisconsin and has 300 home improvement stores. The company's Menards-branded stores are located throughout the Midwest in a 14-state region: Illinois, Indiana, Iowa, Kansas, Kentucky, Michigan, Minnesota, Missouri, Nebraska, North Dakota, Ohio, South Dakota, Wisconsin and Wyoming. Menards operates five subsidiaries: Menard Real Estate, Midwest Manufacturing, Menards Transportation, NailPlant.com and Menards Self-storage. The firm's departments include appliances; bath; building materials; doors, windows and millwork; electrical; flooring and rugs; grocery and pet; heating and cooling; home and decor; kitchen; lighting and ceiling fans; maintenance, repair and operations; outdoors; paint; plumbing; home and patio; storage and organization; and tools and hardware. Menards provides a number of quality brands such as Midwest Manufacturing, Masterforce, Dakota, Mastercraft, Grip Fast, Tuscany, Tool Shop and Enchanted Garden/Enchanted Forest. Menard Real Estate is responsible for selling its properties. Midwest Manufacturing, operates a number of manufacturing facilities in Wisconsin, Illinois, Ohio, Nebraska, Iowa and Minnesota. Menards Transportation ships Menards products throughout its distribution area and has 13 locations. NailPlant.com is an e-commerce site that sells nails and other nail-like products and has a manufacturing plant in Rochester, Minnesota. Menards Self Storage has five locations, three in Wisconsin and two in Iowa. The firm has four distribution centers in Plato, Illinois; Shelby, Iowa; Holiday City, Ohio; and Eau Claire, Wisconsin.

The company offers employees medical, dental and disability insurance; a profit sharing program; advancement opportunities; a 401(k); store discounts; and bonuses.

FINANCIAL DATA:
Note: Data for latest year may not have been available at press time.

In U.S. $	2018	2017	2016	2015	2014	2013
Revenue	10,950,000,000	9,878,000,000	9,500,000,000	8,970,000,000	8,710,000,000	7,775,000,000
R&D Expense						
Operating Income						
Operating Margin %						
SGA Expense						
Net Income						
Operating Cash Flow						
Capital Expenditure						
EBITDA						
Return on Assets %						
Return on Equity %						
Debt to Equity						

CONTACT INFORMATION:
Phone: 715-876-5911 Fax: 715-876-2868
Toll-Free:
Address: 5101 Menard Dr., Eau Claire, WI 54703 United States

STOCK TICKER/OTHER:
Stock Ticker: Private Exchange:
Employees: 45,000 Fiscal Year Ends: 01/31
Parent Company:

SALARIES/BONUSES:
Top Exec. Salary: $ Bonus: $
Second Exec. Salary: $ Bonus: $

OTHER THOUGHTS:
Estimated Female Officers or Directors:
Hot Spot for Advancement for Women/Minorities:

Sales, profits and employees may be estimates. Financial information, benefits and other data can change quickly and may vary from those stated here.

Mercedes-Benz USA LLC

www.mbusa.com

NAIC Code: 336111

TYPES OF BUSINESS:
Automobile Manufacturing
Marketing & Sales Services
Dealership

BRANDS/DIVISIONS/AFFILIATES:
Daimler AG
Mercedex-Benz US International Inc
AMG Driving Academy

CONTACTS:
Note: Officers with more than one job title may be intentionally listed here more than once.
Dietmar Exler, CEO
Matthew E. Roy, VP-Admin.
Michelle D. Spreitzer, General Counsel
Donna Boland, Mgr.-Corp. Comm.

GROWTH PLANS/SPECIAL FEATURES:

Mercedes-Benz USA LLC (MBUSA), a wholly-owned subsidiary of Daimler AG, sells, services, distributes and markets Mercedes-Benz cars and light trucks and Maybach super-luxury sedans throughout the U.S. MBUSA's vehicles include the A-, C-, E- and S-Class and Maybach sedans; C-, E- and S-Class, CLA, CLS and AMG GT S coupes; G- and E-Class, GLA, GLC, GLE, GLE Coupe and GLS sport utility vehicles (SUVs) and wagons; SLC- and SL-Class roadsters; the C-, E- and S-Class Cabriolet convertibles; and the GLC hybrid and electric SUV. The firm sells these vehicles through a network of more than 300 independently owned dealerships in the U.S. MBUSA also provides sales, marketing and other services to Mercedes-Benz dealerships. Company certified collision centers are located in Alabama, Alaska, Arizona, California, Colorado, Connecticut, Delaware, District of Columbia, Florida, Georgia, Hawaii and Idaho. Mercedes-Benz U.S. International, Inc. (MBUSI), a division of Mercedes-Benz and a subsidiary of Daimler AG, operates a Mercedes-Benz automobile manufacturing plant near Vance, Alabama, which is approximately 5 million square feet in size and sits on a 966-acre plot. The factory produces more than 300,000 vehicles annually. In addition, the company operates the AMG Driving Academy, a teen driving school in Los Angeles; and a 71,000-square-foot research and development facility in Sunnyvale, California.

Employee benefits include medical, dental, vision, short- and long-term disability, life, AD&D, automobile, home and pet insurance; domestic partner benefits; flexible spending accounts; paid holidays; and a 401(k).

FINANCIAL DATA:
Note: Data for latest year may not have been available at press time.

In U.S. $	2018	2017	2016	2015	2014	2013
Revenue	48,171,422,250	45,877,545,000	43,692,900,000	43,260,000,000	41,197,513,000	38,394,700,000
R&D Expense						
Operating Income						
Operating Margin %						
SGA Expense						
Net Income			155,231,879	152,378,099	219,621,273	94,128,328
Operating Cash Flow						
Capital Expenditure						
EBITDA						
Return on Assets %						
Return on Equity %						
Debt to Equity						

CONTACT INFORMATION:
Phone: Fax:
Toll-Free: 800-367-6372
Address: 1 Mercedes-Benz Dr., Sandy Springs, GA 30328 United States

STOCK TICKER/OTHER:
Stock Ticker: Subsidiary
Employees: 23,750
Parent Company: Daimler AG

Exchange:
Fiscal Year Ends: 12/31

SALARIES/BONUSES:
Top Exec. Salary: $ Bonus: $
Second Exec. Salary: $ Bonus: $

OTHER THOUGHTS:
Estimated Female Officers or Directors: 2
Hot Spot for Advancement for Women/Minorities:

Sales, profits and employees may be estimates. Financial information, benefits and other data can change quickly and may vary from those stated here.

Mercer LLC

NAIC Code: 541612

www.mercer.com

TYPES OF BUSINESS:
Consulting-Human Resources
Investment/Financial Consulting
Health and Benefits Management
Human Capital Consulting
Outsourced Human Resources Services (BPO)
Investment Management
Retirement Plan Administration
Merger/Acquisition Consulting

BRANDS/DIVISIONS/AFFILIATES:
Marsh & McLennan Companies Inc

CONTACTS:
Note: Officers with more than one job title may be intentionally listed here more than once.

Martine Ferland, CEO
Bala Viswanathan, COO
Jackie Marks, CFO
Marcelo Modica, Chief People Officer
Gail Evans, Chief Digital Officer
Rian Miller, General Counsel
David Rahill, Pres., Health & Benefits
Phil de Cristo, Pres., Investments
Patricia Milligan, Pres., North America
Orlando Ashford, Pres., Talent
Simon O'Regan, Pres., EuroPac

GROWTH PLANS/SPECIAL FEATURES:

Mercer, LLC, a subsidiary of Marsh & McLennan Companies, Inc., offers a broad range of human resource advice and solutions to clients in 130 markets worldwide. The firm divides its services into four categories: health and benefits, wealth and investments, workforce and careers, and mergers and acquisitions. Health and benefits include private health exchange, employee benefits, global benefits, health benefits administration and affinity benefits. Wealth and investments include retirement plan administration, defined benefit pension plans, pension risk management, defined contribution plans, employee financial wellness, alternative investments, endowments and foundations and financial intermediary partnerships. Workforce and careers include talent strategy, executive compensation, workforce rewards, talent mobility, human resource transformation and employee communication. Mergers and acquisitions (MA) include M&A due diligence, M&A project management office, post-merger integration and private equity consulting and advisory. Mercer provides its solutions and services for those in business roles such as CEOs, boards, CFOs, talent leaders, benefits managers, financial advisors, trustees and fiduciaries and employees; for organizations such as corporations, multinational corporations, endowments and foundations, affinity, public sector, wealth management and private equity; and for industries such as energy, insurance, healthcare, financial services, higher education and retail. Based in New York, USA, the firm has offices throughout the world, including North America, Latin America, Europe, the Middle East, Africa, Asia-Pacific, Australia and New Zealand.

Employees of the firm receive benefits including medical, dental, life, disability and vision coverage; health club discounts; legal assistance; eldercare; continuing education programs; an employee stock purchase plan; paid vacations; tuition reimbursement; and family resource programs.

FINANCIAL DATA:
Note: Data for latest year may not have been available at press time.

In U.S. $	2018	2017	2016	2015	2014	2013
Revenue	4,745,300,000	4,487,680,000	4,359,630,000	4,313,000,000	4,350,000,000	4,241,000,000
R&D Expense						
Operating Income						
Operating Margin %						
SGA Expense						
Net Income						
Operating Cash Flow						
Capital Expenditure						
EBITDA						
Return on Assets %						
Return on Equity %						
Debt to Equity						

CONTACT INFORMATION:
Phone: 212-345-7000   Fax: 212-345-7414
Toll-Free:
Address: 1166 Ave. of the Americas, New York, NY 10036 United States

STOCK TICKER/OTHER:
Stock Ticker: Subsidiary   Exchange:
Employees: 23,000   Fiscal Year Ends: 12/31
Parent Company: Marsh & McLennan Companies Inc

SALARIES/BONUSES:
Top Exec. Salary: $ Bonus: $
Second Exec. Salary: $ Bonus: $

OTHER THOUGHTS:
Estimated Female Officers or Directors: 2
Hot Spot for Advancement for Women/Minorities: Y

Sales, profits and employees may be estimates. Financial information, benefits and other data can change quickly and may vary from those stated here.

Merck & Co Inc

www.merck.com

NAIC Code: 325412

TYPES OF BUSINESS:
Drugs-Diversified
Anti-Infective & Anti-Cancer Drugs
Dermatologicals
Cardiovascular Drugs
Animal Health Products

BRANDS/DIVISIONS/AFFILIATES:
MSD
Viralytics Limited
Antelliq Corporation
Immune Design

CONTACTS:
Note: Officers with more than one job title may be intentionally listed here more than once.

Kenneth Frazier, CEO
Robert Davis, CFO
Rita Karachun, Chief Accounting Officer
Jim Scholefield, Chief Information Officer
Michael Nally, Chief Marketing Officer
Jennifer Zachary, Executive VP
Frank Clyburn, Executive VP
Steven Mizell, Executive VP
Julie Gerberding, Executive VP
Sanat Chattopadhyay, Executive VP
Roger Perlmutter, Executive VP
Richard DeLuca, Executive VP

GROWTH PLANS/SPECIAL FEATURES:

Merck & Co., Inc., known as MSD outside of the U.S. and Canada, is a global healthcare company that develops and manufactures medicines, vaccines, biologic therapies and animal health products. The firm operates through four segments: pharmaceutical, animal health, healthcare services and alliances. Pharmaceutical, the company's primary segment, markets human health pharmaceutical and vaccine products either directly or through joint ventures. Merck & Co. markets and develops human health pharmaceutical products for the treatment of bone, respiratory, dermatology, immunology, cardiovascular, diabetes, obesity, infectious disease, neurological, ophthalmology and oncology conditions. These products are sold primarily to drug wholesalers and retailers, hospitals, government agencies and managed healthcare providers such as health maintenance organizations (HMOs), pharmacy benefit managers and other institutions. Vaccine products are primarily sold to physicians, wholesalers, physician distributors and government entities. This segment also offers certain women's health products, including contraceptives and fertility treatments. The animal health segment offers vaccine, anti-infective and anti-parasitic products for disease prevention, treatment and control in farm and companion animals. The healthcare services segment provides services and solutions that focus on engagement, health analytics and clinical services to improve the value of care delivered to patients. The alliances segment consists of revenue derived from the company's relationship with AstraZeneca LP. Merck continues to pursue opportunities for establishing external alliances to complement its internal research capabilities, including research collaborations as well as licensing preclinical and clinical compounds and technology platforms. During 2018, Merck & Co. acquired Viralytics Limited, an Australian public company focused on oncolytic immunotherapy treatments for a range of cancers. In April 2019, it acquired Antelliq Corporation, a provider of animal identification and tracking systems; and Immune Design, a clinical-stage immunotherapy company with next-generation in vivo approaches designed to enable the body's immune system to fight disease.

FINANCIAL DATA:
Note: Data for latest year may not have been available at press time.

In U.S. $	2018	2017	2016	2015	2014	2013
Revenue	42,294,000,000	40,122,000,000	39,807,000,000	39,498,000,000	42,237,000,000	44,033,000,000
R&D Expense	9,752,001,000	10,208,000,000	10,124,000,000	6,704,000,000	7,180,000,000	7,503,000,000
Operating Income	8,931,000,000	7,309,000,000	6,030,000,000	7,547,000,000	6,683,000,000	7,665,000,000
Operating Margin %		.18%	.15%	.19%	.16%	.17%
SGA Expense	10,102,000,000	9,830,000,000	9,762,000,000	10,313,000,000	11,606,000,000	11,911,000,000
Net Income	6,220,000,000	2,394,000,000	3,920,000,000	4,442,000,000	11,920,000,000	4,404,000,000
Operating Cash Flow	10,922,000,000	6,447,000,000	10,376,000,000	12,421,000,000	7,860,000,000	11,654,000,000
Capital Expenditure	2,615,000,000	1,888,000,000	1,614,000,000	1,283,000,000	2,317,000,000	1,548,000,000
EBITDA	13,992,000,000	11,912,000,000	10,793,000,000	12,448,000,000	24,706,000,000	13,334,000,000
Return on Assets %		.03%	.04%	.04%	.12%	.04%
Return on Equity %		.06%	.09%	.10%	.24%	.09%
Debt to Equity		0.622	0.606	0.536	0.384	0.413

CONTACT INFORMATION:
Phone: 908 423-1000   Fax: 908 735-1253
Toll-Free:
Address: 2000 Galloping Hill Rd., Kenilworth, NJ 07033 United States

STOCK TICKER/OTHER:
Stock Ticker: MRK
Employees: 68,000
Parent Company:

Exchange: NYS
Fiscal Year Ends: 12/31

SALARIES/BONUSES:
Top Exec. Salary: $1,610,577   Bonus: $
Second Exec. Salary: $553,846   Bonus: $750,000

OTHER THOUGHTS:
Estimated Female Officers or Directors: 4
Hot Spot for Advancement for Women/Minorities: Y

Sales, profits and employees may be estimates. Financial information, benefits and other data can change quickly and may vary from those stated here.

Merrill Lynch & Co Inc

NAIC Code: 523110

www.ml.com

TYPES OF BUSINESS:
Stock Brokerage & Investment Banking
Research Services
Financial Planning Services

BRANDS/DIVISIONS/AFFILIATES:
Bank of America Corporation

CONTACTS: *Note: Officers with more than one job title may be intentionally listed here more than once.*
Stephen I. Chazen, Exec.
Alexandre Bettamio, CEO-Brazilian Oper.
Manuel Ebner, CEO-Merrill Lynch Capital Markets AG

GROWTH PLANS/SPECIAL FEATURES:
Merrill Lynch & Co., Inc., a wholly owned subsidiary of Bank of America Corporation, is a wealth management, capital markets and advisory firm. The firm is one of the largest brokerages in the world, managing $1.4 trillion in client assets. Merrill Lynch provides banking, investing, asset management and other financial and risk management products and services to its clients. The company's services include corporate and investment banking services, such as commercial lending, high-yield debt, equity and mergers and acquisitions review; personal wealth management; private banking; and retail brokerage. It operates in three segments: global wealth and investment management (GWIM), global research and global banking and markets. GWIM primarily provides wealth management services to high-net-worth individuals and institutions, with a focus on retirement plans, philanthropic planning and asset management. This division utilizes a self-directing electronic platform that provides clients with access to Merrill Lynch investing and Bank of America banking. GWIM also comprises a fiduciary and special needs group to help caregivers of individuals with special needs ensure a lifetime of financial security. The global research segment informs and supports customer decisions by analyzing prospective companies, hedge funds, mutual funds, pension funds, wealth management funds and other investment targets. The global banking and markets segment services corporations, institutions and government entities with debt underwriting, financing and other banking services.

FINANCIAL DATA: *Note: Data for latest year may not have been available at press time.*

In U.S. $	2018	2017	2016	2015	2014	2013
Revenue	15,900,000,000	15,293,000,000	16,000,000,000	14,898,000,000	15,256,000,000	14,771,000,000
R&D Expense						
Operating Income						
Operating Margin %						
SGA Expense						
Net Income						
Operating Cash Flow						
Capital Expenditure						
EBITDA						
Return on Assets %						
Return on Equity %						
Debt to Equity						

CONTACT INFORMATION:
Phone: 212-449-1000 Fax: 212-449-9418
Toll-Free: 800-637-7455
Address: 250 Vesey St., 4 World Financial Center, New York, NY 10080 United States

STOCK TICKER/OTHER:
Stock Ticker: Subsidiary
Employees: 52,000
Parent Company: Bank of America Corporation

Exchange:
Fiscal Year Ends: 12/31

SALARIES/BONUSES:
Top Exec. Salary: $ Bonus: $
Second Exec. Salary: $ Bonus: $

OTHER THOUGHTS:
Estimated Female Officers or Directors: 2
Hot Spot for Advancement for Women/Minorities:

Sales, profits and employees may be estimates. Financial information, benefits and other data can change quickly and may vary from those stated here.

Microsoft Corporation

www.microsoft.com

NAIC Code: 0

TYPES OF BUSINESS:
Computer Software, Operating Systems, Languages & Development Tools
Enterprise Software
Game Consoles
Operating Systems
Software as a Service (SAAS)
Search Engine and Advertising
E-Mail Services
Instant Messaging

BRANDS/DIVISIONS/AFFILIATES:
Office 365
Dynamics
SQL
Windows
Visual Studio
Azure
Xbox
GitHub

CONTACTS:
Note: Officers with more than one job title may be intentionally listed here more than once.

Satya Nadella, CEO
Amy Hood, CFO
John Thompson, Chairman of the Board
Frank Brod, Chief Accounting Officer
Christopher Capossela, Chief Marketing Officer
William Gates, Co-Founder
Kathleen Hogan, Executive VP, Divisional
Margaret Johnson, Executive VP, Divisional
Jean-Philippe Courtois, Executive VP
Bradford Smith, Other Executive Officer

GROWTH PLANS/SPECIAL FEATURES:
Microsoft Corporation develops, license and supports software products, services and devices. It is a technology company that builds best-in-class platforms and productivity services for a mobile-first, cloud-first world. The firm's products include operating systems; cross-device productivity applications; server applications; business solution applications; desktop and server management tools; software development tools; video games; and training and certification of computer system integrators and developers. Microsoft also designs, manufactures and sells devices such as personal computers (PCs), tablets, gaming and entertainment consoles, phones, other intelligent devices and related accessories that integrate with its cloud-based offerings. It operates its business in three segments: productivity and business processes; intelligent cloud; and personal computing. Products offered through the productivity and business processes segment include Office 365 and Dynamics. Products offered through the intelligent cloud segment include SQL servers, Windows servers, Visual Studio, system centers and Azure, as well as enterprise and consulting services. The personal computing segment primarily consists of Windows, including Windows OEM licensing and other non-volume licensing of the Windows operating system; Devices, including Microsoft Surface, PC accessories, and other intelligent devices; Gaming, including Xbox hardware, software and services, comprising Xbox Live transactions, subscriptions and advertising, video games and third-party video game royalties; and search advertising. In October 2018, Microsoft completed its acquisition of GitHub, Inc., a web-based version control repository (Git) and internet hosting service, for $7.5 billion.

Microsoft offers its employees health, dental and vision coverage; onsite health screenings; adoption assistance; childcare service discounts; a 401(k) plan; an employee stock purchase plan; and tuition assistance.

FINANCIAL DATA:
Note: Data for latest year may not have been available at press time.

In U.S. $	2018	2017	2016	2015	2014	2013
Revenue	110,360,000,000	89,950,000,000	85,320,000,000	93,580,000,000	86,833,000,000	77,849,000,000
R&D Expense	14,726,000,000	13,037,000,000	11,988,000,000	12,046,000,000	11,381,000,000	10,411,000,000
Operating Income	35,058,000,000	22,632,000,000	21,292,000,000	28,172,000,000	27,886,000,000	26,764,000,000
Operating Margin %		.25%	.25%	.30%	.32%	.34%
SGA Expense	22,223,000,000	20,020,000,000	19,260,000,000	20,324,000,000	20,632,000,000	20,425,000,000
Net Income	16,571,000,000	21,204,000,000	16,798,000,000	12,193,000,000	22,074,000,000	21,863,000,000
Operating Cash Flow	43,884,000,000	39,507,000,000	33,325,000,000	29,080,000,000	32,231,000,000	28,833,000,000
Capital Expenditure	11,632,000,000	8,129,000,000	8,343,000,000	5,944,000,000	5,485,000,000	4,257,000,000
EBITDA	49,468,000,000	34,149,000,000	27,616,000,000	25,245,000,000	33,629,000,000	31,236,000,000
Return on Assets %		.10%	.09%	.07%	.14%	.17%
Return on Equity %		.29%	.22%	.14%	.26%	.30%
Debt to Equity		1.051	0.566	0.347	0.23	0.16

CONTACT INFORMATION:
Phone: 425 882-8080   Fax: 425 936-7329
Toll-Free: 800-642-7676
Address: One Microsoft Way, Redmond, WA 98052 United States

SALARIES/BONUSES:
Top Exec. Salary: $1,500,000   Bonus: $
Second Exec. Salary: $875,000   Bonus: $

STOCK TICKER/OTHER:
Stock Ticker: MSFT
Employees: 144,000
Parent Company:

Exchange: NAS
Fiscal Year Ends: 06/30

OTHER THOUGHTS:
Estimated Female Officers or Directors: 4
Hot Spot for Advancement for Women/Minorities: Y

Modine Manufacturing Company

www.modine.com

NAIC Code: 336300

TYPES OF BUSINESS:
Automobile Parts Manufacturer
Heat Exchangers & Systems
Oil Cores
Electronics Cooling
Heating & Air Conditioning Products
Radiator Cores
Fuel Cells

BRANDS/DIVISIONS/AFFILIATES:

CONTACTS:
Note: Officers with more than one job title may be intentionally listed here more than once.

Thomas Burke, CEO
Michael Lucareli, CFO
Scott Wollenberg, Chief Technology Officer
Scott Bowser, COO
Sylvia Stein, General Counsel
Matthew McBurney, Vice President, Divisional
Scott Miller, Vice President, Divisional
Dennis Appel, Vice President, Divisional
Brian Agen, Vice President, Divisional
Joel Casterton, Vice President, Divisional

GROWTH PLANS/SPECIAL FEATURES:

Modine Manufacturing Company is a worldwide leader in thermal management technology. The firm provides engineered heat transfer systems and heat transfer components for us in on- and off-highway original equipment manufacturer (OEM) vehicular applications. Modine also develops and markets thermal management technology and solutions for commercial, industrial and building, heating, ventilating, air conditioning and refrigeration markets. The company's primary product groups include: powertrain cooling and engine cooling; coils, coolers and coatings; and heating, ventilation and air conditioning. These products and systems help to solve heat transfer challenges requiring effective thermal management. Modine's top five customers are engaged in the automotive, commercial vehicle and off-highway markets, and its 10-largest customers accounted for 50% of fiscal 2019 sales. Nearly 60% of total sales are generated outside the U.S. During fiscal 2019, Modine sold its AIAC Air Conditioning South Africa Pty Ltd. business. In July 2019, the firm agreed to sell its 50% stake in its Nikkei Heat Exchanger Company, Ltd. joint venture to its JV partner, Nippon Light Metal Company, Ltd.

Modine offers employees medical benefits, educational assistance, retirement plans, life insurance and flexible spending accounts.

FINANCIAL DATA:
Note: Data for latest year may not have been available at press time.

In U.S. $	2018	2017	2016	2015	2014	2013
Revenue	2,103,100,000	1,503,000,000	1,352,500,000	1,496,400,000	1,477,600,000	
R&D Expense						
Operating Income	107,400,000	48,300,000	19,000,000	62,000,000	56,500,000	
Operating Margin %	.05%	.03%	.01%	.04%	.04%	
SGA Expense	249,100,000	205,000,000	204,500,000	184,500,000	181,700,000	
Net Income	22,200,000	14,200,000	-1,600,000	21,800,000	130,400,000	
Operating Cash Flow	123,800,000	41,600,000	72,400,000	63,500,000	104,500,000	
Capital Expenditure	71,000,000	65,400,000	104,500,000	75,000,000	57,300,000	
EBITDA	165,600,000	96,300,000	51,400,000	104,500,000	94,500,000	
Return on Assets %	.01%	.01%	.00%	.02%	.14%	
Return on Equity %	.05%	.04%	.00%	.06%	.38%	
Debt to Equity	0.788	0.98	0.334	0.364	0.309	

CONTACT INFORMATION:
Phone: 262 636-1200 Fax: 262 636-1424
Toll-Free:
Address: 1500 DeKoven Ave., Racine, WI 53403 United States

SALARIES/BONUSES:
Top Exec. Salary: $965,000 Bonus: $
Second Exec. Salary: $448,500 Bonus: $

STOCK TICKER/OTHER:
Stock Ticker: MOD Exchange: NYS
Employees: 11,200 Fiscal Year Ends: 02/28
Parent Company:

OTHER THOUGHTS:
Estimated Female Officers or Directors: 4
Hot Spot for Advancement for Women/Minorities: Y

Mohawk Industries Inc

NAIC Code: 314110

www.mohawkind.com

TYPES OF BUSINESS:
Floor Covering Stores
Tile & Stone Products
Extrusion
Laminate Flooring Technology
Roofing Systems

BRANDS/DIVISIONS/AFFILIATES:
Aladdin Commercial
Durkan
IVC
Mohawk
Daltile
Eliane
Marazzi
Xtratherm

CONTACTS:
Note: Officers with more than one job title may be intentionally listed here more than once.

Jeffrey Lorberbaum, CEO
Glenn Landau, CFO
James Brunk, Chief Accounting Officer
W. Wellborn, COO
Rodney Patton, General Counsel
Paul De Cock, President, Geographical
Bernard Thiers, President, Subsidiary

GROWTH PLANS/SPECIAL FEATURES:
Mohawk Industries, Inc. is a leading producer of floor-covering products for residential and commercial applications in the U.S., and residential applications in Europe. Mohawk's operating segments include: flooring NA (North America), global ceramic, and flooring ROW (rest of the world). The flooring NA segment designs, manufactures, sources, distributes and markets its carpet and rug product line in a broad range of colors, textures and patterns. It also markets and distributes ceramic tile, laminate, hardwood, resilient floor covering, carpet pad and flooring accessories. This division's brands include Aladdin Commercial, Durkan, IVC, Karastan, Mohawk, Pergo, Portico and Quick-Step. Flooring NA sells through independent floor covering retailers, home centers, mass merchandisers, department stores, shop at home, buying groups, commercial dealers and commercial end users. The global ceramic segment designs, manufactures, sources, distributes and markets a broad line of ceramic tile, porcelain tile and natural stone products. Its brands include American Olean, Daltile, Eliane, EmilGroup, KAI, Kaerama Marazzi, Marazzi and Ragno. The flooring ROW segment designs, manufactures, sources, licenses, distributes and markets laminate and hardwood flooring. This segment also licenses certain patents related to laminate flooring installation. Its brands include Balterio, Feltex, Godfrey Hirst, Hycraft, Itec, IVC, Leoline, Moduleo, Pergo and Quick-Step. This division also comprises the Unilin and Xtratherm brands of insulation boards, roof panels, medium-density fiberboard, chipboards and other wood products, which are marketed throughout Europe. During 2018, the firm acquired Godfrey Hirst Group, a leading flooring company in Australia and New Zealand; and acquired Eliane SA Revestimentos Ceramicos, a ceramic tile manufacturer in Brazil.

FINANCIAL DATA:
Note: Data for latest year may not have been available at press time.

In U.S. $	2018	2017	2016	2015	2014	2013
Revenue	9,983,634,000	9,491,290,000	8,959,087,000	8,071,563,000	7,803,446,000	7,348,754,000
R&D Expense						
Operating Income	1,095,326,000	1,354,173,000	1,279,943,000	837,566,000	772,796,000	546,931,000
Operating Margin %		.14%	.14%	.10%	.10%	.07%
SGA Expense	1,742,744,000	1,642,241,000	1,532,882,000	1,573,120,000	1,381,396,000	1,373,878,000
Net Income	861,704,000	971,638,000	930,362,000	615,302,000	531,965,000	348,786,000
Operating Cash Flow	1,181,344,000	1,193,595,000	1,327,553,000	911,873,000	662,188,000	525,163,000
Capital Expenditure	794,110,000	905,998,000	672,125,000	503,657,000	561,804,000	366,550,000
EBITDA	1,609,793,000	1,795,640,000	1,691,139,000	1,182,594,000	1,107,668,000	846,688,000
Return on Assets %		.09%	.09%	.07%	.06%	.05%
Return on Equity %		.15%	.18%	.13%	.12%	.09%
Debt to Equity		0.221	0.195	0.247	0.317	0.478

CONTACT INFORMATION:
Phone: 706 629-7721   Fax: 706 625-3851
Toll-Free: 800-241-4494
Address: 160 S. Industrial Blvd., Calhoun, GA 30701 United States

STOCK TICKER/OTHER:
Stock Ticker: MHK
Employees: 37,800
Parent Company:

Exchange: NYS
Fiscal Year Ends: 12/31

SALARIES/BONUSES:
Top Exec. Salary: $1,206,173   Bonus: $
Second Exec. Salary: $1,042,228   Bonus: $

OTHER THOUGHTS:
Estimated Female Officers or Directors: 1
Hot Spot for Advancement for Women/Minorities:

Sales, profits and employees may be estimates. Financial information, benefits and other data can change quickly and may vary from those stated here.

Molex LLC

NAIC Code: 334417

www.molex.com

TYPES OF BUSINESS:
Electronic Connector Manufacturing
Transportation Products
Commercial Products
Micro Products
Automation & Electrical Products
Integrated Products
Global Sales & Marketing Organization

BRANDS/DIVISIONS/AFFILIATES:
Koch Industries Inc
Molex

CONTACTS:
Note: Officers with more than one job title may be intentionally listed here more than once.

Martin P. Slark, CEO
Joseph William Nelligan, Jr., COO
K. Travis George, CFO
Gary J. Matula, CIO
Robert J. Zeitler, General Counsel
Tim Ruff, Sr. VP-Bus. Dev. & Corp. Strategy
David D. Johnson, Treas.
John H. Krehbiel, Jr., Co-Chmn.
Junichi Kaji, Pres., Global Mirco Prod. Div.
J. Michael Nauman, Pres., Global Integrated Prod. Div.
Joseph Nelligan, Pres., Commercial Prod. Division

GROWTH PLANS/SPECIAL FEATURES:

Molex, LLC, a subsidiary of Koch Industries, Inc., manufactures and supplies electronic components. The firm designs, manufactures and sells thousands of products, including 3D semiconductors, 3D custom circuitry, antennas, application tooling, audio-balanced armature, automation, cables, cable assemblies, capillary tubing, micro components, connectors, edgecards, sockets, electrical rubber solutions, power distribution electricals, grips, portable lighting, reels, test and control electronics, wiring devices, noise suppression sheets, flexible circuit solutions, FPGA computing systems, hoods, IT infrastructure solutions, lighting products, optical solutions, printed circuit board (PCB) assemblies, product traceability, sensor solutions, user interface and wireless solutions. Molex also provides manufacturing services to integrate specific components into a customer's product. The company's products are utilized across a wide range of industries, including data communications, consumer electronics, industrial, automotive, commercial vehicle, medical and other. Molex is a registered trademark of Molex, LLC in the U.S., and has 50 manufacturing locations in 18 countries worldwide.

FINANCIAL DATA:
Note: Data for latest year may not have been available at press time.

In U.S. $	2018	2017	2016	2015	2014	2013
Revenue	4,150,000,000	4,100,000,000	4,000,000,000	3,900,000,000	3,862,540,000	3,620,446,976
R&D Expense						
Operating Income						
Operating Margin %						
SGA Expense						
Net Income						
Operating Cash Flow						
Capital Expenditure						
EBITDA						
Return on Assets %						
Return on Equity %						
Debt to Equity						

CONTACT INFORMATION:
Phone: 630 969-4550   Fax: 630 969-1352
Toll-Free: 800-786-6539
Address: 2222 Wellington Ct., Lisle, IL 60532-1682 United States

SALARIES/BONUSES:
Top Exec. Salary: $ Bonus: $
Second Exec. Salary: $ Bonus: $

STOCK TICKER/OTHER:
Stock Ticker: Subsidiary   Exchange:
Employees: 40,200   Fiscal Year Ends: 06/30
Parent Company: Koch Industries Inc

OTHER THOUGHTS:
Estimated Female Officers or Directors: 2
Hot Spot for Advancement for Women/Minorities:

Sales, profits and employees may be estimates. Financial information, benefits and other data can change quickly and may vary from those stated here.

Molina Healthcare Inc

www.molinahealthcare.com

NAIC Code: 524114

TYPES OF BUSINESS:
HMO-Low Income Patients
Medicaid HMO
SCHIP HMO

BRANDS/DIVISIONS/AFFILIATES:
Molina Medicaid Solutions

CONTACTS: Note: Officers with more than one job title may be intentionally listed here more than once.
Thomas Tran, CFO
Dale Wolf, Chairman of the Board
Maurice Hebert, Chief Accounting Officer
Jeff Barlow, Chief Legal Officer
Ronna Romney, Director
Mark Keim, Executive VP, Divisional
Pamela Sedmak, Executive VP, Divisional
James Woys, Executive VP, Divisional
Joseph Zubretsky, President

GROWTH PLANS/SPECIAL FEATURES:
Molina Healthcare, Inc. is a multi-stage, managed care organization participating in government-sponsored health care programs for low-income persons, such as the Medicaid program and Children's Health Insurance Program (CHIP, including Perinatal). The company also focuses on a small number of persons who are dually eligible under the Medicaid and Medicare programs. Molina operates in two segments: health plans and other. Health plans consists of operational health plans in 14 states and Puerto Rico and Molina's direct delivery business. The health plans, serving approximately 3.8 million, are operated by the firm's wholly-owned subsidiaries in those states, each of which is licensed as a health maintenance organization (HMO). Molina manages the vast majority of its operations through the health plans segment. The other segment includes the historical results of the Pathways Health and Community Support, LLC (Pathways) behavioral health subsidiary, the historical results of the Molina Medicaid Solutions segment and certain corporate amounts not allocated to the health plans segment. In October 2018, the firm completed the sale of its Medicare management information business to DXC Technology Company for $231 million; additionally, the firm sold Pathways, a provider of home and community-based human services, to Atar Capital, LLC, a global private investment firm.

Molina offers employees medical, dental and vision plans; life insurance; disability; employee assistance; flexible spending accounts; 401(k); and an employee stock purchase plan.

FINANCIAL DATA: Note: Data for latest year may not have been available at press time.

In U.S. $	2018	2017	2016	2015	2014	2013
Revenue	18,765,000,000	19,813,000,000	17,744,000,000	14,160,000,000	9,658,508,000	6,582,044,000
R&D Expense						
Operating Income	1,067,000,000	79,000,000	268,000,000	369,000,000	184,824,000	129,670,000
Operating Margin %		.00%	.02%	.03%	.02%	.02%
SGA Expense	1,333,000,000	1,594,000,000	1,393,000,000	1,146,000,000	764,693,000	665,996,000
Net Income	707,000,000	-512,000,000	52,000,000	143,000,000	62,223,000	52,929,000
Operating Cash Flow	-314,000,000	804,000,000	673,000,000	1,125,000,000	1,060,257,000	190,083,000
Capital Expenditure	30,000,000	86,000,000	176,000,000	132,000,000	114,934,000	98,049,000
EBITDA	1,241,000,000	-316,000,000	488,000,000	514,000,000	326,519,000	227,083,000
Return on Assets %		-.06%	.01%	.03%	.02%	.02%
Return on Equity %		-.34%	.03%	.11%	.07%	.06%
Debt to Equity		1.134	0.711	0.745	0.896	0.675

CONTACT INFORMATION:
Phone: 562 435-3666   Fax: 562 499-0790
Toll-Free: 888-562-5442
Address: 200 Oceangate, Ste. 100, Long Beach, CA 90802 United States

STOCK TICKER/OTHER:
Stock Ticker: MOH
Employees: 21,000
Parent Company:

Exchange: NYS
Fiscal Year Ends: 12/31

SALARIES/BONUSES:
Top Exec. Salary: $507,692   Bonus: $1,844,542
Second Exec. Salary: $1,300,000   Bonus: $

OTHER THOUGHTS:
Estimated Female Officers or Directors: 2
Hot Spot for Advancement for Women/Minorities: Y

Monro Muffler Brake Inc

NAIC Code: 811100

www.monro.com

TYPES OF BUSINESS:
Automotive Repair & Maintenance
Under-Car Repair Services
Inspection Services
Tires

BRANDS/DIVISIONS/AFFILIATES:
Monro Service Corporation
Car-X LLC
Monro Muffler Brake & Service
Tread Quarters Discount tire
Mr Tire
Autotire Car Care Center
Ken Towery's Tire & Auto Care
Free Service Tire Company

CONTACTS:
Note: Officers with more than one job title may be intentionally listed here more than once.

Brett Ponton, CEO
Brian DAmbrosia, CFO
Robert Mellor, Chairman of the Board
Maureen Mulholland, General Counsel
Deborah Brundage, Senior VP, Divisional
Samuel Senuk, Vice President, Divisional
Raymond Pickens, Vice President, Divisional

GROWTH PLANS/SPECIAL FEATURES:

Monro Muffler Brake, Inc. operates through a chain of 1,248 company-operated stores, 98 franchised locations, eight wholesale locations, three retread facilities and two dealer-operated stores, providing automotive under-car repair and tire services in 30 U.S. states. These stores are typically located in high-visibility locations in suburban areas and small towns, and operate under the names Monro Muffler Brake & Service, Tread Quarters Discount Tire, Mr. Tire, Autotire Car Care Center, Tire Warehouse, Tire Barn Warehouse, Ken Towery's Tire & Auto Care, The Tire Choice, Car-X, McGee Tire, and Certified Tire. The firm's stores service more than 6.2 million vehicles annually (as of mid-2019). Monro provides a range of services on passenger cars, light trucks and vans for brakes; mufflers and exhaust systems; and steering, drive train, suspension and wheel alignment. Other products and services offered by the company include tires and routine maintenance services, such as state inspections. It specializes in the repair and replacement of parts that must be periodically replaced due to normal wear and tear. Typically, the firm does not perform under-the-hood repair, except for oil change services, heating and cooling system flush and fill services and some minor tune-ups. Monro operates through two wholly-owned subsidiaries: Monro Service Corporation, which provides purchasing, distribution, merchandising, advertising, accounting and other store support functions; and Car-X, LLC, which operates as a franchisor, with 101 Car-X franchised locations. In May 2019, Monro acquired 40 Certified Tire stores in California, entering its 30th state.

Monro offers its employees Automotive Service Excellence (ASE) certification reimbursement; recreational discounts; an employee assistance program; tool insurance; and medical, dental, life and disability insurance.

FINANCIAL DATA:
Note: Data for latest year may not have been available at press time.

In U.S. $	2018	2017	2016	2015	2014	2013
Revenue	1,127,815,000	1,021,511,000	943,651,000	894,492,000	831,432,000	
R&D Expense						
Operating Income	127,296,000	116,384,000	120,589,000	109,789,000	95,347,000	
Operating Margin %	.11%	.11%	.13%	.12%	.11%	
SGA Expense	308,278,000	280,505,000	265,114,000	243,561,000	224,627,000	
Net Income	63,935,000	61,526,000	66,805,000	61,799,000	54,459,000	
Operating Cash Flow	121,235,000	129,935,000	126,504,000	126,349,000	93,943,000	
Capital Expenditure	39,122,000	34,640,000	36,834,000	34,750,000	32,150,000	
EBITDA	176,631,000	161,013,000	160,358,000	145,510,000	127,035,000	
Return on Assets %	.05%	.06%	.07%	.07%	.07%	
Return on Equity %	.11%	.11%	.13%	.14%	.14%	
Debt to Equity	0.597	0.68	0.502	0.54	0.45	

CONTACT INFORMATION:
Phone: 585-647-6400 Fax: 585-647-0945
Toll-Free:
Address: 200 Holleder Pkwy., Rochester, NY 14615 United States

SALARIES/BONUSES:
Top Exec. Salary: $550,000   Bonus: $
Second Exec. Salary: $350,000   Bonus: $

STOCK TICKER/OTHER:
Stock Ticker: MNRO
Employees: 7,878
Parent Company:

Exchange: NAS
Fiscal Year Ends: 03/31

OTHER THOUGHTS:
Estimated Female Officers or Directors: 1
Hot Spot for Advancement for Women/Minorities:

Moody's Corporation

www.moodys.com

NAIC Code: 561450

TYPES OF BUSINESS:
Credit Bureau
Credit Risk Assessment Products & Services
Credit Processing Software
Credit Training Services

BRANDS/DIVISIONS/AFFILIATES:
Bureau van Dijk Electronic Publishing BV

CONTACTS:
Note: Officers with more than one job title may be intentionally listed here more than once.

Raymond Mcdaniel, CEO
Mark Kaye, CFO
Henry McKinnell, Chairman of the Board
Caroline Sullivan, Chief Accounting Officer
Richard Cantor, Chief Risk Officer
John Goggins, Executive VP
Melanie Hughes, Other Executive Officer
Mark Almeida, President, Subsidiary
Robert Fauber, President, Subsidiary

GROWTH PLANS/SPECIAL FEATURES:

Moody's Corporation is a provider of credit ratings; credit and economic related research, data and analytical tools; risk management software; quantitative credit risk measures, credit portfolio management solutions, training and financial credentialing and certification services; and outsourced research and analytical services to institutional customers. The company maintains offices worldwide. Moody's operates in two segments: Moody's investors service (MIS) and Moody's analytics (MA). MIS publishes rating opinions on a broad range of credit obligors and credit obligations issued in domestic and international markets, including various corporate and governmental obligations, structured finance securities and commercial paper programs. Ratings are distributed via press releases through a variety of print and electronic media, including the internet and other real-time information systems used by securities traders and investors. MIS has ratings relationships with approximately non-financial 4,700 corporate issuers, 4,100 financial institution issuers, approximately 18,000 public finance issuers and 1,000 infrastructure and project finance issuers. Additionally, the company has ratings relationships with approximately 11,000 structured finance transactions. MA offers a range of products that support the risk management activities of institutional participants in global financial markets. These products and services include in-depth research on major debt issuers, industry studies and commentary on topical credit related events as well as economic research, credit data and analytical tools such as quantitative credit risk scores. MA's customers represent more than 10,500 institutions worldwide operating in approximately 155 countries. During 2017, Moody's research website was accessed by over 252,000 individuals, including 36,000 client users. In August 2017, Moody's Corporation acquired Bureau van Dijk Electronic Publishing BV, a global provider of business intelligence and company information.

FINANCIAL DATA:
Note: Data for latest year may not have been available at press time.

In U.S. $	2018	2017	2016	2015	2014	2013
Revenue	4,442,700,000	4,204,100,000	3,604,200,000	3,484,500,000	3,334,300,000	2,972,500,000
R&D Expense						
Operating Income	1,925,200,000	1,831,600,000	1,516,100,000	1,479,800,000	1,445,500,000	1,253,800,000
Operating Margin %		.44%	.42%	.42%	.43%	.42%
SGA Expense	1,080,100,000	991,400,000	936,400,000	921,300,000	869,300,000	822,100,000
Net Income	1,309,600,000	1,000,600,000	266,600,000	941,300,000	988,700,000	804,500,000
Operating Cash Flow	1,461,100,000	747,500,000	1,226,100,000	1,153,600,000	1,018,600,000	926,800,000
Capital Expenditure	90,400,000	90,600,000	115,200,000	89,000,000	74,600,000	42,300,000
EBITDA	2,093,600,000	2,149,500,000	833,400,000	1,617,900,000	1,680,100,000	1,360,000,000
Return on Assets %		.14%	.05%	.19%	.22%	.19%
Return on Equity %					13.25%	2.23%
Debt to Equity						6.237

CONTACT INFORMATION:
Phone: 212 553-0300   Fax: 212 553-4820
Toll-Free:
Address: 250 Greenwich St., 7 World Trade Center, New York, NY 10007 United States

SALARIES/BONUSES:
Top Exec. Salary: $1,000,000   Bonus: $
Second Exec. Salary: $609,000   Bonus: $

STOCK TICKER/OTHER:
Stock Ticker: MCO
Employees: 10,600
Parent Company:

Exchange: NYS
Fiscal Year Ends: 12/31

OTHER THOUGHTS:
Estimated Female Officers or Directors: 2
Hot Spot for Advancement for Women/Minorities: Y

Morgan Stanley

NAIC Code: 523110

www.morganstanley.com

TYPES OF BUSINESS:
Stock Brokerage/Investment Banking
Institutional Securities
Wealth Management
Asset Management
Bank Holding Company

BRANDS/DIVISIONS/AFFILIATES:

CONTACTS: Note: Officers with more than one job title may be intentionally listed here more than once.
James Gorman, CEO
Jonathan Pruzan, CFO
Paul Wirth, Chief Accounting Officer
Keishi Hotsuki, Chief Risk Officer
Jeffrey Brodsky, Executive VP
Eric Grossman, Executive VP
Daniel Simkowitz, Other Corporate Officer
Thomas Kelleher, President

GROWTH PLANS/SPECIAL FEATURES:
Morgan Stanley is a global financial services firm with offices in 42 countries. Morgan Stanley provides a wide variety of products and services to a large and diversified group of clients, including corporations, governments, financial institutions and individuals. The firm operates in three business segments: institutional securities, investment management and wealth management. The institutional securities segment oversees activities such as capital raising; financial advisory services, including advice on mergers and acquisitions, restructurings, real estate and project finance; corporate lending; sales, trading, financing and market-making activities in equity and fixed income securities; risk management analytics; research; and investment activities. The investment management segment provides global asset management products and services in fixed income; alternative investments, including hedge funds and funds of funds; equity; and merchant banking, which includes real estate, private equity and infrastructure, to institutional clients through proprietary and third-party distribution channels. The wealth management segment provides comprehensive financial services to clients through a network of global representatives worldwide. This segment serves individual investors and small-to-medium sized businesses and institutions with an emphasis on ultra-high net worth, high net worth and affluent investors. Its advisory services cover equities, options, futures, foreign currencies, precious metals, fixed income securities, mutual funds, structured products, alternative investments, unit investment trusts, managed futures and mutual fund asset allocation programs. Wealth management also engages in fixed income principal trading. In March 2018, Morgan Stanley completed the acquisition of real estate credit platform Mesa West Capital LLC, which manages $48 billion of client assets. Morgan Stanley also launched Luma Financial Technologies in July 2018; Luma is a joint venture with Navian Capital and Merrill Lynch designed to automate workflow, monitor post-trade positions, and comprehensively educate, train and help with compliance management.

FINANCIAL DATA: Note: Data for latest year may not have been available at press time.

In U.S. $	2018	2017	2016	2015	2014	2013
Revenue	37,714,000,000	35,852,000,000	32,711,000,000	33,263,000,000	32,469,000,000	30,706,000,000
R&D Expense						
Operating Income						
Operating Margin %						
SGA Expense	20,339,000,000	19,566,000,000	18,252,000,000	18,464,000,000	20,117,000,000	18,683,000,000
Net Income	8,748,000,000	6,111,000,000	5,979,000,000	6,127,000,000	3,467,000,000	2,932,000,000
Operating Cash Flow	7,305,000,000	-4,505,000,000	2,447,000,000	3,674,000,000	1,131,000,000	35,553,000,000
Capital Expenditure	1,865,000,000	1,629,000,000	1,276,000,000	1,373,000,000	992,000,000	1,316,000,000
EBITDA						
Return on Assets %		.01%	.01%	.01%	.00%	.00%
Return on Equity %		.08%	.08%	.09%	.05%	.04%
Debt to Equity		2.796	2.404	2.273	2.355	2.449

CONTACT INFORMATION:
Phone: 212 761-4000 Fax: 212 761-0086
Toll-Free:
Address: 1585 Broadway, New York, NY 10036 United States

SALARIES/BONUSES:
Top Exec. Salary: $1,200,000 Bonus: $10,850,000
Second Exec. Salary: $1,000,000 Bonus: $8,670,000

STOCK TICKER/OTHER:
Stock Ticker: MS Exchange: NYS
Employees: 55,311 Fiscal Year Ends: 12/31
Parent Company:

OTHER THOUGHTS:
Estimated Female Officers or Directors: 3
Hot Spot for Advancement for Women/Minorities: Y

Mutual of Omaha Companies (The)

NAIC Code: 524113

www.mutualofomaha.com

TYPES OF BUSINESS:
Life Insurance
Asset Management
Annuities
Medical & Dental Insurance
Supplemental Health Insurance
IT Services & Consulting

BRANDS/DIVISIONS/AFFILIATES:
Mutual of Omaha Foundation
Mutual of Omaha Bank

CONTACTS:
Note: Officers with more than one job title may be intentionally listed here more than once.

James T. Blackledge, CEO
Richard C. Anderl, General Counsel
Stacy A. Scholtz, Exec. VP-Corp. Oper.
David A. Diamond, Treas.
Daniel P. Martin, Exec. VP-Group Benefit Svcs.
Michael C. Weekly, Exec. VP-Individual Financial Svcs.
Richard A. Witt, Chief Investment Officer
Kenneth R. Cook, Pres., East Campus Realty

GROWTH PLANS/SPECIAL FEATURES:

The Mutual of Omaha Companies provide insurance, Medicare and financial products and services through its subsidiaries. Insurance offered by Mutual of Omaha includes life, long-term care, disability, critical illness, and cancer/heart attack/stroke coverage. Medicare offerings include Medicare solutions, Medicare supplement insurance, a prescription drug plan and dental insurance. Financial services include a wide range of annuities, investments, banking and mortgage products. Mutual of Omaha serves nearly 4.8 million individual product customers, more than 11 million members and 39,000 employer groups. The firm employs associates in 43 U.S. states. The Mutual of Omaha Foundation supports programs that help break the cycle of poverty, placing emphasis on community service and charitable giving. During 2019, Mutual of Omaha agreed to sell its savings bank subsidiary, Mutual of Omaha Bank, to CIT Group, Inc. for $1 billion. The transaction would allow Mutual of Omaha to focus on its core insurance businesses.

The firm offers employees benefits including medical, dental, vision, life and disability insurance; flexible spending accounts; and a 401(k).

FINANCIAL DATA:
Note: Data for latest year may not have been available at press time.

In U.S. $	2018	2017	2016	2015	2014	2013
Revenue	9,347,200,000	8,731,940,000	7,898,472,000	7,235,734,000	6,878,021,000	6,602,152,000
R&D Expense						
Operating Income						
Operating Margin %						
SGA Expense						
Net Income	277,300,000	862,634,000	356,558,000	333,006,000	291,701,000	359,248,000
Operating Cash Flow						
Capital Expenditure						
EBITDA						
Return on Assets %						
Return on Equity %						
Debt to Equity						

CONTACT INFORMATION:
Phone: 402-342-7600   Fax: 402-351-2775
Toll-Free: 800-775-6000
Address: Mutual of Omaha Plz., Omaha, NE 68175 United States

STOCK TICKER/OTHER:
Stock Ticker: Mutual Company
Employees: 6,314
Parent Company:

Exchange:
Fiscal Year Ends: 12/31

SALARIES/BONUSES:
Top Exec. Salary: $ Bonus: $
Second Exec. Salary: $ Bonus: $

OTHER THOUGHTS:
Estimated Female Officers or Directors: 3
Hot Spot for Advancement for Women/Minorities: Y

Sales, profits and employees may be estimates. Financial information, benefits and other data can change quickly and may vary from those stated here.

National Instruments Corporation

www.ni.com

NAIC Code: 0

TYPES OF BUSINESS:
Software-Instrumentation
Virtual Instrumentation
Signal Conditioning Hardware
Test & Measurement Software
Motion Control Products
Analysis & Visualization Software
Automation Software
Image Acquisition Products

BRANDS/DIVISIONS/AFFILIATES:
LabVIEW
LabVIEW Real-Time
LabVIEW Communications System Design Suite
LabWindows/CVI and Measurement Studio
LabVIEW for LEGO MINDSTORMS

CONTACTS:
Note: Officers with more than one job title may be intentionally listed here more than once.

Karen Rapp, CFO
Michael McGrath, Chairman of the Board
John Roiko, Chief Accounting Officer
Jeffrey Kodosky, Co-Founder
Eric Starkloff, COO
Alexander Davern, Director
Royal Dixon, General Counsel
Scott Rust, Senior VP, Divisional

GROWTH PLANS/SPECIAL FEATURES:

National Instruments Corporation (NI) supplies test, measurement and automation products used by engineers and scientists from numerous industries. Its key markets range from the automotive, aerospace, electronics, semiconductors and defense sectors, to the education, government, medical research and telecommunications industries, among others. Products and services include system design software; programming tools; application software; hardware products and related driver software; the Ni education platform, including software and hardware products for teaching; NI services, including hardware services and maintenance; software maintenance services; and training and certification. The company's flagship product is LabVIEW, a system design software for measurement and control. With LabVIEW, users program graphically and can design custom virtual instruments by connecting icons with software wires to create block diagrams, which are natural design notations for scientists and engineers. Users can customize front panels with knobs, buttons, dials and graphs to emulate control panels of instruments or add custom graphics to visually represent the control and operation of processes. Add-ons LabVIEW Real-Time enables users to easily configure their application program to execute using a real-time operating system kernel instead of a general-purpose operating system. LabVIEW Communications System Design Suite is specifically for wireless prototyping, and also provides a plug-in architecture to offer productive starting points with open application frameworks for LTE, 802.11 and other key standards. LabWindows/CVI and Measurement Studio is designed for alternative programming environments. NI software products are complimentary to LabVIEW. The company's education platform combines software, hardware and courseware designed to create engaging, authentic learning experiences that prepare students for the next generation of innovation. LabVIEW for LEGO MINDSTORMS is used in the development of robotics projects in secondary school.

The company offers employees 401(k), stock purchase and profit sharing plans; health, dental and vision coverage; life and disability insurance; tuition assistance and more.

FINANCIAL DATA:
Note: Data for latest year may not have been available at press time.

In U.S. $	2018	2017	2016	2015	2014	2013
Revenue	1,359,132,000	1,289,386,000	1,228,179,000	1,225,456,000	1,243,862,000	1,172,558,000
R&D Expense	261,072,000	231,761,000	235,706,000	225,131,000	227,433,000	234,796,000
Operating Income	172,879,000	145,778,000	119,726,000	137,172,000	145,187,000	97,301,000
Operating Margin %		.11%	.10%	.11%	.12%	.08%
SGA Expense	591,454,000	583,523,000	559,626,000	546,197,000	553,110,000	535,218,000
Net Income	155,057,000	52,411,000	82,734,000	95,262,000	126,333,000	80,513,000
Operating Cash Flow	274,580,000	224,442,000	195,840,000	162,637,000	195,110,000	169,479,000
Capital Expenditure	54,266,000	74,302,000	78,626,000	68,154,000	73,559,000	67,861,000
EBITDA	243,546,000	218,473,000	193,116,000	210,501,000	215,393,000	165,275,000
Return on Assets %		.03%	.06%	.07%	.09%	.06%
Return on Equity %		.05%	.08%	.09%	.12%	.08%
Debt to Equity				0.022	0.034	

CONTACT INFORMATION:
Phone: 512 338-9119 Fax: 512 683-9300
Toll-Free: 800-433-3488
Address: 11500 N. Mopac Expressway, Austin, TX 78759-3504 United States

STOCK TICKER/OTHER:
Stock Ticker: NATI
Employees: 7,552
Parent Company:

Exchange: NAS
Fiscal Year Ends: 12/31

SALARIES/BONUSES:
Top Exec. Salary: $725,004 Bonus: $
Second Exec. Salary: $437,500 Bonus: $

OTHER THOUGHTS:
Estimated Female Officers or Directors: 1
Hot Spot for Advancement for Women/Minorities:

Sales, profits and employees may be estimates. Financial information, benefits and other data can change quickly and may vary from those stated here.

NBCUniversal Media LLC

NAIC Code: 515120

www.nbcuni.com

TYPES OF BUSINESS:
Television Broadcasting
Online News & Information
TV & Movie Production
Radio Broadcasting
Interactive Online Content
Cable Television Programming
Theme Parks
Film, TV & Home Video Distribution

BRANDS/DIVISIONS/AFFILIATES:
Comcast Corporation
Bravo Media
E! Entertainment
NBC Entertainment
NBC News
Hulu
Universal Pictures
Cozi

CONTACTS:
Note: Officers with more than one job title may be intentionally listed here more than once.

Steve Burke, CEO
Anand Kini, CFO
Jeff Shell, Chmn.-Universal Filmed Entertainment
Kimberley D. Harris, General Counsel
Maggie McLean Suniewick, Sr. VP-Strategic Integration
Cameron Blanchard, Exec. VP-Comm.
Patricia Fili-Krushel, Chmn.-NBCUniversal News Group
Robert Greenblatt, Chmn., NBC Entertainment
Bonnie Hammer, Chmn., NBCUniversal Cable Entertainment Group
Ted Harbert, Chmn., NBC Broadcasting
Mark Hoffman, Chmn.
Kevin MacLellan, Chmn., NBCUniversal Int'l
Matt Bond, Exec. VP-Content Dist.

GROWTH PLANS/SPECIAL FEATURES:

NBCUniversal Media, LLC is a world-leading entertainment and media company engaged in the development, production and marketing of news, entertainment and information. NBCU is a product of a 2004 merger of Vivendi Universal Entertainment and National Broadcasting Company (NBC). The firm now operates as a wholly-owned subsidiary of Comcast Corporation. NBCU operates in eight divisions: cable, broadcast, digital, film, parks, local media, TV studios production and international. The cable division includes Bravo Media, CNBC, E! Entertainment, Golf Channel, MSNBC, NBC Sports Network, Oxygen Media, SYFY, The Olympic Channel: Home of Team USA, Universal Kids, UNIVERSO and USA Network. The broadcast division includes NBC Entertainment, NBC News, NBC Olympics, NBC Sports and Telemundo. The digital division consists of Bluprint, Fandango, GolfNow, Hulu and SportsEngine. The film division includes DreamWorks Animation, Focus Features, Universal Brand Development, Universal Pictures, Universal Pictures Home Entertainment and Universal Pictures International. The parks division includes Universal Orlando Resort, Universal Studios Hollywood, Universal Studios Japan and Universal Studios Singapore. The local media division consists of Cozi TV, NBC Sports Regional Networks, NBCUniversal-owned television stations and TeleXitos. The international division includes CNBC International, hayu and global distribution. The TV studios production division consists of Telemundo Studios, Universal Cable Productions and Universal Television.

NBC Universal offers its employees medical, dental, vision and prescription drug coverage; a 401(k) plan; health club discounts; same-sex domestic partner benefits; life insurance; and flexible spending accounts.

FINANCIAL DATA:
Note: Data for latest year may not have been available at press time.

In U.S. $	2018	2017	2016	2015	2014	2013
Revenue	35,761,000,000	32,997,000,000	31,593,000,000	28,462,000,000	25,428,000,000	23,650,000,000
R&D Expense						
Operating Income						
Operating Margin %						
SGA Expense						
Net Income	5,279,000,000	5,218,000,000	4,546,000,000	3,624,000,000	3,297,000,000	2,122,000,000
Operating Cash Flow						
Capital Expenditure						
EBITDA						
Return on Assets %						
Return on Equity %						
Debt to Equity						

CONTACT INFORMATION:
Phone: 212-664-4444   Fax: 212-664-4085
Toll-Free:
Address: 30 Rockefeller Plaza, New York, NY 10112 United States

STOCK TICKER/OTHER:
Stock Ticker: Subsidiary
Employees: 62,500
Parent Company: Comcast Corporation

Exchange:
Fiscal Year Ends: 12/31

SALARIES/BONUSES:
Top Exec. Salary: $ Bonus: $
Second Exec. Salary: $ Bonus: $

OTHER THOUGHTS:
Estimated Female Officers or Directors: 12
Hot Spot for Advancement for Women/Minorities: Y

Sales, profits and employees may be estimates. Financial information, benefits and other data can change quickly and may vary from those stated here.

NCR Corporation

NAIC Code: 334118

www.ncr.com

TYPES OF BUSINESS:
Computer Manufacturing
Barcode Scanning Equipment
Automatic Teller Machines (ATMs)
Transaction Processing Equipment
Point-of-Sale & Store Automation
Data Warehousing
Printer Consumables

BRANDS/DIVISIONS/AFFILIATES:
BECPOS

CONTACTS: Note: Officers with more than one job title may be intentionally listed here more than once.
Andre Fernandez, CFO
William Nuti, Chairman Emeritus
Owen Sullivan, COO
Frank Martire, Director
Michael Hayford, Director
Daniel Campbell, Executive VP, Divisional
J. Ciminera, Executive VP, Divisional
Frank DAngelo, Executive VP, Divisional
James Bedore, Executive VP
Paul Langenbahn, Executive VP
Debra Bronder, Other Executive Officer
Adrian Button, Senior VP, Divisional

GROWTH PLANS/SPECIAL FEATURES:
NCR Corporation is a global technology company that provides information technology and related services to various industries, enabling client companies to interact more efficiently with customers. NCR offers financial-oriented self-service technologies, such as ATMs, cash dispensers, self-checkout kiosks and software solutions. Operations are divided into three operating segments: software, services and hardware. The software segment includes a portfolio of industry-based software applications and application suites for the financial services, retail, hospitality and small business industries. Moreover, this division offers other industry-oriented software applications including cash management software, video banking software, fraud and loss prevention applications, check and document imaging, remote-deposit capture and customer-facing digital banking applications for the financial services industry; and secure electronic and mobile payment solutions, sector-specific point of sale software applications, and back-office inventory and store and restaurant management applications for the retail and hospitality industries. The services segment provides global end-to-end services solutions including assessment and preparation, staging, installation, implementation, and maintenance and support for its hardware solutions. This division also provides systems management and complete managed services for its product offerings. In addition, it provides servicing for third-party networking products and computer hardware from select manufacturers. The hardware solutions segment includes its suite of financial-oriented self-service ATM-related hardware, and its retail- and hospitality-oriented point of sale terminal, self-checkout kiosk and related hardware. This division also offers other self-service kiosks, such as self-check in kiosks for airlines, and wayfinding solutions for buildings and campuses. In February 2019, NCR acquired BECPOS, a provider of hospitality point-of-sale technology based in Denver, Colorado.

FINANCIAL DATA: Note: Data for latest year may not have been available at press time.

In U.S. $	2018	2017	2016	2015	2014	2013
Revenue	6,405,000,000	6,516,000,000	6,543,000,000	6,373,000,000	6,591,000,000	6,123,000,000
R&D Expense	252,000,000	256,000,000	242,000,000	230,000,000	263,000,000	203,000,000
Operating Income	418,000,000	676,000,000	614,000,000	197,000,000	457,000,000	666,000,000
Operating Margin %		.10%	.09%	.03%	.07%	.11%
SGA Expense	1,005,000,000	932,000,000	926,000,000	1,042,000,000	1,012,000,000	871,000,000
Net Income	-88,000,000	232,000,000	270,000,000	-178,000,000	191,000,000	443,000,000
Operating Cash Flow	536,000,000	747,000,000	855,000,000	638,000,000	523,000,000	229,000,000
Capital Expenditure	313,000,000	294,000,000	227,000,000	229,000,000	258,000,000	226,000,000
EBITDA	537,000,000	999,000,000	893,000,000	386,000,000	602,000,000	865,000,000
Return on Assets %		.02%	.03%	-.02%	.02%	.06%
Return on Equity %		.17%	.31%	-.14%	.10%	.29%
Debt to Equity		4.088	4.318	4.499	1.856	1.877

CONTACT INFORMATION:
Phone: 937 445-5000 Fax: 937 445-5541
Toll-Free: 800-225-5627
Address: 864 Spring St. NW, Atlanta, GA 30308 United States

STOCK TICKER/OTHER:
Stock Ticker: NCR
Employees: 33,500
Parent Company:

Exchange: NYS
Fiscal Year Ends: 12/31

SALARIES/BONUSES:
Top Exec. Salary: $634,615 Bonus: $1,010,959
Second Exec. Salary: $409,616 Bonus: $662,671

OTHER THOUGHTS:
Estimated Female Officers or Directors: 3
Hot Spot for Advancement for Women/Minorities: Y

Plunkett Research, Ltd. 425

Netflix Inc
NAIC Code: 515210

www.netflix.com

TYPES OF BUSINESS:
Streaming Movies and TV Shows
DVD Rentals by Mail
Motion Picture Production

GROWTH PLANS/SPECIAL FEATURES:
Netflix, Inc. is one of the largest online movie rental subscription services, providing access to a library of movie, television and other filmed entertainment titles to nearly 130 million subscribers in over 190 countries. The company has three operating segments: domestic streaming, international streaming and domestic DVD. The domestic and international streaming segments derive revenues from monthly membership fees for services consisting solely of streaming content. Domestic streaming membership plans are priced at $7.99 per month (basic), $10.99 per month (standard) of which can be watched on two screens at the same time, and $13.99 per month (premium) of which can be watched on up to four devices concurrently. International streaming membership is priced at the equivalent of USD $7 to $14 per month. The domestic DVD segment derives revenues from monthly membership fees for services consisting solely of DVD-by-mail. The price per plan for DVD-by-mail varies from $7.99 to $14.99 per month according to the plan chosen by the member. DVD-by-mail plans differ by the number of DVDs a member may have out at any given point and the type of DVD, either a standard DVD or an HD Blu-ray disc. Netflix's streaming service allows subscribers to view a growing library of movies and television episodes over the internet or on Netflix-ready devices such as Blu-ray players, internet-connected TVs, digital video players, smartphones and game consoles. The Netflix streaming content library includes media acquired through deals with corporations. Additionally, through its Netflix Studios division, the company produces original content available exclusively on Netflix.

BRANDS/DIVISIONS/AFFILIATES:

CONTACTS: Note: Officers with more than one job title may be intentionally listed here more than once.
Reed Hastings, CEO
Spencer Neumann, CFO
Kelly Bennett, Chief Marketing Officer
David Hyman, General Counsel
Ted Sarandos, Other Executive Officer
Rachel Whetstone, Other Executive Officer
Jessica Neal, Other Executive Officer
Greg Peters, Other Executive Officer

FINANCIAL DATA: Note: Data for latest year may not have been available at press time.

In U.S. $	2018	2017	2016	2015	2014	2013
Revenue	15,794,340,000	11,692,710,000	8,830,669,000	6,779,511,000	5,504,656,000	4,374,562,000
R&D Expense	1,221,814,000	1,052,778,000	852,098,000	650,788,000	472,321,000	378,769,000
Operating Income	1,605,226,000	838,679,000	379,793,000	305,826,000	402,648,000	228,347,000
Operating Margin %		.07%	.04%	.05%	.07%	.05%
SGA Expense	2,999,763,000	2,141,590,000	1,568,877,000	1,231,421,000	876,927,000	684,190,000
Net Income	1,211,242,000	558,929,000	186,678,000	122,641,000	266,799,000	112,403,000
Operating Cash Flow	-2,680,479,000	-1,785,948,000	-1,473,984,000	-749,439,000	16,483,000	97,831,000
Capital Expenditure	212,532,000	227,022,000	184,830,000	169,206,000	144,516,000	120,070,000
EBITDA	9,303,408,000	7,053,910,000	5,335,599,000	3,821,646,000	3,181,386,000	2,441,896,000
Return on Assets %		.03%	.02%	.01%	.04%	.02%
Return on Equity %		.18%	.08%	.06%	.17%	.11%
Debt to Equity		1.814	1.255	1.067	0.484	0.375

CONTACT INFORMATION:
Phone: 408 540-3700 Fax: 408 540-3737
Toll-Free: 1-877-742-1480
Address: 100 Winchester Cir., Los Gatos, CA 95032 United States

STOCK TICKER/OTHER:
Stock Ticker: NFLX
Employees: 7,200
Parent Company:

Exchange: NAS
Fiscal Year Ends: 12/31

SALARIES/BONUSES:
Top Exec. Salary: $12,000,000 Bonus: $
Second Exec. Salary: $6,000,000 Bonus: $

OTHER THOUGHTS:
Estimated Female Officers or Directors: 3

Hot Spot for Advancement for Women/Minorities: Y

Sales, profits and employees may be estimates. Financial information, benefits and other data can change quickly and may vary from those stated here.

New York Life Insurance Company

www.newyorklife.com

NAIC Code: 524113

TYPES OF BUSINESS:
Life Insurance
Annuities
Mutual Funds
Asset Management
Life Insurance
Real Estate

BRANDS/DIVISIONS/AFFILIATES:
MainStay Investments

CONTACTS: Note: Officers with more than one job title may be intentionally listed here more than once.
Theodore A. Mathas, CEO
Craig L. De Santo, Exec. VP
Matthew M. Grove, Exec. VP
Carla T. rutigliano, Sr.VP-Human Resources
David J. Sactellani, Sr. VP
Frank M. Boccio, Chief Admin. Officer
Sheila K. Davidson, General Counsel
Barry Schub, Sr. VP-Strategy & Communications
George Nichols, III, Sr. VP-Office of Gov't Affairs
Christopher O. Blunt, Exec. VP
Mark W. Pfaff, Exec. VP
Susan A. Thrope, Deputy General Counsel
John T. Fleurant,

GROWTH PLANS/SPECIAL FEATURES:

New York Life Insurance Company provides life insurance, investments, retirement income and long-term care insurance. The firm operates through two segments: insurance products and investment products. Insurance products include life insurance and long-term care insurance. Types of life insurance includes term life, whole life, universal life, variable universal life, corporate sponsored plans and group membership associations. Long-term insurance helps provide for the cost of long-term care generally not covered by health insurance, Medicare or Medicaid. Investment products include retirement income, investment annuities and mutual funds. Retirement income offers several guaranteed income annuity products such as lifetime income annuities, future income annuities, lifetime mutual income annuities and future mutual income annuities. Investment annuities are types of savings plans that help prepare individuals for retirement and come in the form of variable annuities and fixed deferred annuities. Mutual funds are provided under New York Life's MainStay Investments registered service mark and name, offering a broad selection of mutual funds across multiple asset classes and investment styles. These investments include U.S./international/global stock funds; investment grade, high yield and municipal bond funds; and asset allocation funds that invest in a mix of asset classes and investment styles. In addition, New York Life offers premier services, helping premier clients and small business owners reach their retirement, estate planning and business goals. This division has professionals in law, taxation, accounting, business, insurance and philanthropic planning who can work with the clients' financial advisor.

FINANCIAL DATA: Note: Data for latest year may not have been available at press time.

In U.S. $	2018	2017	2016	2015	2014	2013
Revenue	43,425,300,000	30,328,000,000	27,908,000,000	26,127,000,000	27,451,000,000	24,781,000,000
R&D Expense						
Operating Income						
Operating Margin %						
SGA Expense						
Net Income	880,000,000	3,039,000,000	1,638,000,000	1,785,000,000	2,455,000,000	2,045,000,000
Operating Cash Flow						
Capital Expenditure						
EBITDA						
Return on Assets %						
Return on Equity %						
Debt to Equity						

CONTACT INFORMATION:
Phone: 212-576-7000 Fax: 212-576-8145
Toll-Free: 800-692-3086
Address: 51 Madison Ave., New York, NY 10010 United States

STOCK TICKER/OTHER:
Stock Ticker: Mutual Company
Employees: 11,388
Parent Company:
Exchange:
Fiscal Year Ends: 12/31

SALARIES/BONUSES:
Top Exec. Salary: $ Bonus: $
Second Exec. Salary: $ Bonus: $

OTHER THOUGHTS:
Estimated Female Officers or Directors: 4
Hot Spot for Advancement for Women/Minorities: Y

Sales, profits and employees may be estimates. Financial information, benefits and other data can change quickly and may vary from those stated here.

Nielsen Holdings plc

NAIC Code: 541910

www.nielsen.com

TYPES OF BUSINESS:
Market Research
Magazine Publishing
Media/Entertainment Audience Research
Trade Publications
Directories
Business Consulting
Internet Audience Research

BRANDS/DIVISIONS/AFFILIATES:
SuperData Research

CONTACTS:
Note: Officers with more than one job title may be intentionally listed here more than once.

David Kenny, CEO
David Anderson, CFO
George Callard, Chief Legal Officer
Giovanni Tavolieri, Chief Technology Officer
James Attwood, Director
Nancy Phillips, Other Executive Officer

GROWTH PLANS/SPECIAL FEATURES:

Nielsen Holdings plc is a leading global provider of marketing information, audience measurement and business media products and services with operations in over 100 countries and data measurements of millions of consumers worldwide. The firm has two major segments: what consumers watch (watch) and what consumers buy (buy). Accounting for about half (51% in 2017) of Nielsen's annual revenues, the watch segment provides viewership data and analytics primarily to the media industry, and advertising across three primary platforms that include mobile screens, online and television. Clients of this segment use Nielsen's data to plan and optimize their advertising spending and to better ensure that their advertisements reach the intended audience. The buy segment provides consumer behavior information and analytics primarily to businesses in the consumer packaged goods industry. Clients use the data to manage their brands, find new sources of demand, launch and grow new products, improve their marketing mix and establish more effective consumer relationships. In September 2018, Nielsen acquired SuperData Research, a provider of market intelligence on digital games, gaming video content and virtual/augmented reality across mobile, PC online, console and other digital platforms.

FINANCIAL DATA:
Note: Data for latest year may not have been available at press time.

In U.S. $	2018	2017	2016	2015	2014	2013
Revenue	6,515,000,000	6,572,000,000	6,309,000,000	6,172,000,000	6,288,000,000	5,703,000,000
R&D Expense						
Operating Income	1,077,000,000	1,305,000,000	1,248,000,000	1,144,000,000	1,178,000,000	980,000,000
Operating Margin %		.20%	.20%	.19%	.19%	.17%
SGA Expense	1,958,000,000	1,862,000,000	1,851,000,000	1,915,000,000	1,917,000,000	1,815,000,000
Net Income	-712,000,000	429,000,000	502,000,000	570,000,000	384,000,000	740,000,000
Operating Cash Flow	1,058,000,000	1,310,000,000	1,296,000,000	1,179,000,000	1,093,000,000	901,000,000
Capital Expenditure	520,000,000	489,000,000	433,000,000	408,000,000	412,000,000	374,000,000
EBITDA	187,000,000	1,842,000,000	1,752,000,000	1,846,000,000	1,494,000,000	1,350,000,000
Return on Assets %		.03%	.03%	.04%	.02%	.05%
Return on Equity %		.10%	.12%	.12%	.07%	.14%
Debt to Equity		1.969	1.886	1.585	1.279	1.133

CONTACT INFORMATION:
Phone: 646 654-5000 Fax:
Toll-Free: 800-864-1224
Address: 85 Broad St., New York, NY 10004 United States

STOCK TICKER/OTHER:
Stock Ticker: NLSN   Exchange: NYS
Employees: 43,000   Fiscal Year Ends: 12/31
Parent Company:

SALARIES/BONUSES:
Top Exec. Salary: $75,000   Bonus: $1,500,000
Second Exec. Salary: $1,000,000   Bonus: $

OTHER THOUGHTS:
Estimated Female Officers or Directors: 4
Hot Spot for Advancement for Women/Minorities: Y

Nike Inc

NAIC Code: 424340

www.nike.com

TYPES OF BUSINESS:
Footwear Distribution
Athletic Equipment
Sports Accessories
Retail Stores
Sports Apparel
Plastic Products
Hockey Products
Swimwear

BRANDS/DIVISIONS/AFFILIATES:
Converse Inc
Hurley International LLC
Jordan
NIKE IHM Inc (Air Manufacturing Innovation)
Chuck Taylor
All Star
One Star
Jack Purcell

CONTACTS:
Note: Officers with more than one job title may be intentionally listed here more than once.

Mark Parker, CEO
Chris Abston, Chief Accounting Officer
Hilary Krane, Chief Administrative Officer
Eric Sprunk, COO
Monique Matheson, Executive VP, Divisional
John Slusher, Executive VP, Divisional
Andrew Campion, Executive VP
Elliott Hill, President, Divisional

GROWTH PLANS/SPECIAL FEATURES:

Nike, Inc. designs, develops and markets footwear, apparel, equipment and accessories. It is one of the largest sellers of athletic footwear and athletic apparel in the world. The company's athletic footwear products are designed primarily for specific athletic use, although a large percentage of its products are worn for casual or leisure purposes. Running, training, basketball and soccer sport-inspired urban shoes and children's shoes are the firm's top-selling product categories. Nike also markets shoes designed for tennis, golf, baseball, football, lacrosse, walking, outdoor activities, skateboarding, bicycling, volleyball, wrestling, cheerleading, aquatic activities and other athletic and recreational uses. The firm maintains several wholly-owned subsidiaries: Converse, Inc., which distributes and licenses footwear, apparel and accessories through brand names Converse, All Star, One Star, Chuck Taylor, Star Chevron and Jack Purcell; Hurley International LLC, which is headquartered in the U.K. and designs/distributes a collection of action sports apparel sold under the Hurley brand; and Jordan, which sells a line of basketball shoes, clothing and gear for men. Another subsidiary, NIKE IHM, Inc. dba Air Manufacturing Innovation, sells small amounts of various plastic products to other manufacturers. Nike sells its products to retail accounts, through Nike-owned retail stores and through a mix of independent distributors and licensees worldwide. Within the U.S., the firm operates 392 Nike Brand and subsidiary retail stores: 251 Nike locations, 112 Converse stores including factory outlets and 29 Hurley locations. In the international market, which includes countries within Europe, Asia, South America and Africa, the firm maintains 790 retail stores (729 Nike and 61 Converse).

FINANCIAL DATA:
Note: Data for latest year may not have been available at press time.

In U.S. $	2018	2017	2016	2015	2014	2013
Revenue	36,397,000,000	34,350,000,000	32,376,000,000	30,601,000,000	27,799,000,000	
R&D Expense						
Operating Income	4,445,000,000	4,749,000,000	4,502,000,000	4,175,000,000	3,680,000,000	
Operating Margin %		.14%	.14%	.14%	.13%	
SGA Expense	11,511,000,000	10,563,000,000	10,469,000,000	9,892,000,000	8,766,000,000	
Net Income	1,933,000,000	4,240,000,000	3,760,000,000	3,273,000,000	2,693,000,000	
Operating Cash Flow	4,955,000,000	3,640,000,000	3,096,000,000	4,680,000,000	3,003,000,000	
Capital Expenditure	1,028,000,000	1,105,000,000	1,143,000,000	963,000,000	880,000,000	
EBITDA	5,219,000,000	5,465,000,000	5,164,000,000	4,824,000,000	4,312,000,000	
Return on Assets %		.19%	.17%	.16%	.15%	
Return on Equity %		.34%	.30%	.28%	.25%	
Debt to Equity		0.28	0.164	0.085	0.111	

CONTACT INFORMATION:
Phone: 503 671-6453 Fax: 503 671-6300
Toll-Free: 800-344-6453
Address: 1 Bowerman Dr., Beaverton, OR 97005 United States

STOCK TICKER/OTHER:
Stock Ticker: NKE
Employees: 73,100
Parent Company:

Exchange: NYS
Fiscal Year Ends: 05/31

SALARIES/BONUSES:
Top Exec. Salary: $1,676,923 Bonus: $
Second Exec. Salary: $1,142,308 Bonus: $

OTHER THOUGHTS:
Estimated Female Officers or Directors: 2
Hot Spot for Advancement for Women/Minorities: Y

Sales, profits and employees may be estimates. Financial information, benefits and other data can change quickly and may vary from those stated here.

Nordstrom Inc

www.nordstrom.com

NAIC Code: 452111

TYPES OF BUSINESS:
Department Stores
Outlet Stores
Online Retailing
Catalog Sales
Financial Services
Federal Savings Bank

BRANDS/DIVISIONS/AFFILIATES:
Nordstrom.com
Nordstronrack.com/HauteLook
TrunkClub.com
Nordstrom Rack
Jeffrey
Last Chance
Nordstrom fsb
Nordstrom Local

CONTACTS:
Note: Officers with more than one job title may be intentionally listed here more than once.

Erik Nordstrom, CEO
Anne Bramman, CFO
Bradley Tilden, Chairman of the Board
Kelley Hall, Chief Accounting Officer
Scott Meden, Chief Marketing Officer
Edmond Mesrobian, Chief Technology Officer
Peter Nordstrom, Co-President
Robert Sari, General Counsel
Christine Deputy Ott, Other Executive Officer
Ken Worzel, Other Executive Officer
Kenneth Worzel, Other Executive Officer
Geevy Thomas, President, Divisional
James Nordstrom, President, Divisional

GROWTH PLANS/SPECIAL FEATURES:

Nordstrom, Inc., founded in 1901, is an upscale fashion apparel and shoe retailer. Nordstrom operates a total of 380 stores in 40 U.S. states and Canada, as well as an e-commerce business through Nordstrom.com, Nordstromrack.com/HauteLook and TrunkClub.com. The retailer also operates five Nordstrom full-line stores in Canada. The company sells a wide selection of apparel, shoes and accessories for women, men and children. The west and east coasts of the U.S. are the areas where the company has its largest presence. Nordstrom operates through two segments: retail and credit. The retail segment includes 122 Nordstrom branded full-line stores in the U.S., Canada and Puerto Rico, 244 off-price Nordstrom Rack stores as well as other retail channels; six Trunk Club showrooms, three Jeffrey boutiques, three Nordstrom Local concepts and a clearance store that operates under the Last Chance name. The credit segment includes Nordstrom's wholly-owned federal savings bank, Nordstrom fsb, through which it offers a private label credit card, Nordstrom VISA credit cards and a debit card. It generates income through finance charges and fees on these cards and saves on interchange fees that the retail segment would incur when its customers use third-party cards. In April 2018, Nordstrom opened a flagship, full-line Nordstrom stand-alone men's store in New York City; the store is three levels and 47,000 square feet. Nordstrom announced in May 2018 an extended sizing expansion to include more zeroes, 2's, 14's, 16's and 18's. The expansion will span across 30 stores and include 100 brands. In July 2018 Nordstrom announced the opening of two more smaller-scale Nordstrom Local neighborhood hubs in Brentwood and Downtown Los Angeles; the stores opened in fall 2018.

Nordstrom offers employees benefits including medical, dental, vision, AD&D, life and short- and long-term disability insurance; wellness programs; 401(k) plan & profit sharing; employee stock purchase plan; access to the company bank and credit union; employee assistance programs; adoption financial assistance; and merchandise discounts.

FINANCIAL DATA:
Note: Data for latest year may not have been available at press time.

In U.S. $	2018	2017	2016	2015	2014	2013
Revenue	15,478,000,000	14,757,000,000	14,437,000,000	13,506,000,000	12,540,000,000	
R&D Expense						
Operating Income	926,000,000	1,002,000,000	1,101,000,000	1,323,000,000	1,350,000,000	
Operating Margin %	.06%	.07%	.08%	.10%	.11%	
SGA Expense	4,662,000,000	4,315,000,000	4,168,000,000	3,777,000,000	3,453,000,000	
Net Income	437,000,000	354,000,000	600,000,000	720,000,000	734,000,000	
Operating Cash Flow	1,400,000,000	1,648,000,000	2,451,000,000	1,220,000,000	1,320,000,000	
Capital Expenditure	731,000,000	846,000,000	1,082,000,000	861,000,000	803,000,000	
EBITDA	1,597,000,000	1,451,000,000	1,677,000,000	1,832,000,000	1,805,000,000	
Return on Assets %	.05%	.05%	.07%	.08%	.09%	
Return on Equity %	.47%	.41%	.36%	.32%	.37%	
Debt to Equity	2.744	3.176	3.209	1.28	1.493	

CONTACT INFORMATION:
Phone: 206 628-2111 Fax: 206 628-1795
Toll-Free: 888-282-6060
Address: 1617 Sixth Ave., Seattle, WA 98101 United States

SALARIES/BONUSES:
Top Exec. Salary: $768,889 Bonus: $150,000
Second Exec. Salary: $791,274 Bonus: $82,026

STOCK TICKER/OTHER:
Stock Ticker: JWN
Employees: 72,500
Parent Company:

Exchange: NYS
Fiscal Year Ends: 01/31

OTHER THOUGHTS:
Estimated Female Officers or Directors: 8
Hot Spot for Advancement for Women/Minorities: Y

Sales, profits and employees may be estimates. Financial information, benefits and other data can change quickly and may vary from those stated here.

Northrop Grumman Corporation

NAIC Code: 336411

www.northropgrumman.com

TYPES OF BUSINESS:
Aircraft Manufacturing
Shipbuilding & Engineering
Aircraft Manufacturing
Electronic Systems & Components
Hardware & Software Manufacturing
Design & Engineering Services
IT Systems & Services
Nuclear-Powered Aircraft Carriers & Submarines

BRANDS/DIVISIONS/AFFILIATES:
Northrop Grumman Innovation Systems
Orbital ATK Inc

CONTACTS:
Note: Officers with more than one job title may be intentionally listed here more than once.

Kathy Warden, CEO
Jennifer McGarey, Secretary
Kenneth Bedingfield, CFO
Wesley Bush, Chairman of the Board
Michael Hardesty, Chief Accounting Officer
Patrick Antkowiak, Chief Technology Officer
Sheila Cheston, General Counsel
Denise Peppard, Other Executive Officer
David Perry, Other Executive Officer
Christopher Jones, President, Divisional
Mark Caylor, President, Divisional
Janis Pamiljans, President, Divisional
Shawn Purvis, President, Divisional
Lesley Kalan, Vice President, Divisional
Lisa Davis, Vice President, Divisional

GROWTH PLANS/SPECIAL FEATURES:

Northrop Grumman Corporation (NGC) is a global aerospace and defense technology company. It has three primary segments: aerospace systems, mission systems, technology services and innovation systems. The aerospace systems segment designs, develops, integrates and produces manned aircraft, autonomous systems, spacecraft, high-energy laser systems, microelectronics and other systems/subsystems. This division's customers, primarily the Department of Defense (DoD) and other U.S. government agencies, use these systems in mission areas such as intelligence, surveillance and reconnaissance, strike operations, communications, earth observation, space science and space exploration. This division also produces autonomous aircraft systems for tactical and strategic intelligence, surveillance and reconnaissance (ISR) missions. The mission systems segment provides advanced end-to-end mission solutions and multifunction systems for DoD, intelligence community, international, federal civil and commercial customers. Its major products and services include C4ISR (command, control, communications and computer (C4)/ISR) systems; radar, electro-optical/infrared and acoustic sensors; electronic warfare systems; cyber solutions; space systems; intelligence processing systems; air and missile defense integration; navigation; and shipboard missile and encapsulated payload launch systems. Last, the technology services segment provides logistics solutions supporting the full life cycle of platforms and systems for global defense and federal-civil customers. Its offerings include software and system sustainment, modernization of platforms and associated subsystems, advanced training solutions and integrated logistics support. Northrop Grumman Innovation Systems designs, builds and delivers space, defense and aviation-related systems. The segments main products include launch vehicles, propulsion systems, missile products, defense electronics, armament systems and ammunition. In June 2018, Northrup acquired rocket motor and satellite firm Orbital ATK, Inc. for $7.8 billion; subsequently, Orbital ATK became a new business segment named Northrop Grumman Innovation Systems.

FINANCIAL DATA:
Note: Data for latest year may not have been available at press time.

In U.S. $	2018	2017	2016	2015	2014	2013
Revenue	30,095,000,000	25,803,000,000	24,508,000,000	23,526,000,000	23,979,000,000	24,661,000,000
R&D Expense						
Operating Income	3,780,000,000	3,299,000,000	3,193,000,000	3,076,000,000	3,196,000,000	3,123,000,000
Operating Margin %		.13%	.13%	.13%	.13%	.13%
SGA Expense	3,011,000,000	2,655,000,000	2,584,000,000	2,566,000,000	2,405,000,000	2,256,000,000
Net Income	3,229,000,000	2,015,000,000	2,200,000,000	1,990,000,000	2,069,000,000	1,952,000,000
Operating Cash Flow	3,827,000,000	2,613,000,000	2,813,000,000	2,162,000,000	2,593,000,000	2,483,000,000
Capital Expenditure	1,249,000,000	928,000,000	920,000,000	471,000,000	561,000,000	364,000,000
EBITDA	5,104,000,000	3,884,000,000	3,680,000,000	3,558,000,000	3,681,000,000	3,615,000,000
Return on Assets %		.07%	.09%	.08%	.08%	.07%
Return on Equity %		.33%	.41%	.31%	.23%	.19%
Debt to Equity		2.043	1.342	1.162	0.819	0.558

CONTACT INFORMATION:
Phone: 703 280-2900   Fax: 310 201-3023
Toll-Free:
Address: 2980 Fairview Park Dr., Falls Church, VA 22042 United States

SALARIES/BONUSES:
Top Exec. Salary: $1,578,039   Bonus: $
Second Exec. Salary: $963,462   Bonus: $

STOCK TICKER/OTHER:
Stock Ticker: NOC
Employees: 67,000
Parent Company:

Exchange: NYS
Fiscal Year Ends: 12/31

OTHER THOUGHTS:
Estimated Female Officers or Directors: 9
Hot Spot for Advancement for Women/Minorities: Y

Northwestern Mutual Life Insurance Company (The)

www.northwesternmutual.com
NAIC Code: 524113

TYPES OF BUSINESS:
Life Insurance
Disability Insurance
Employee Benefit Plans
Long-Term Care Insurance
Investment Products & Services
Financial Planning Services

BRANDS/DIVISIONS/AFFILIATES:
Northwestern Long Term Care Insurance Company
Northwestern Mutual Investment Services LLC
Northwestern Mutual Investment Management Co LLC
LearnVest Inc
Northwestern Mutual Wealth Management Company
Mason Street Advisors LLC

CONTACTS:
Note: Officers with more than one job title may be intentionally listed here more than once.

John E. Schlifske, CEO
Michael G. Carter, CFO
Aditi Javeri Gokhale, Exec. VP-Mktg. & Communications Officer
Joann M. Eisenhart, Exec. VP
Ronald P. Joelson, Chief Investment Officer
Jean M. Maier, Exec. VP-Tech.
Raymond J. Manista, General Counsel
Jean M. Maier, Exec. VP-Enterprise Oper.
Ronald P. Joelson, Exec. VP
Todd M. Schoon, Exec. VP-Agencies
John E. Schlifske, Chmn.

GROWTH PLANS/SPECIAL FEATURES:
Northwestern Mutual Life Insurance Company (NMLIC) is a financial network that, together with its subsidiaries, offers network services, insurance products, investment products and advisory services to more than 4.5 million policy owners. Its network services include asset and income protection, personal needs analysis, investment services, education funding and retirement products. NMLIC itself issues life and disability insurance, annuities, and life insurance with long-term care benefits. Subsidiary Northwestern Long Term Care Insurance Company issues long-term care insurance. Northwestern Mutual Investment Services, LLC is a broker-dealer and registered investment advisor that serves the investment planning and product needs of individuals and businesses. This company's special account services include electronic transfers, dividend reinvestment, a mutual fund purchase program, account protection, direct deposit, check writing privileges and online account access. It also offers a variety of individual investment services such as college education funding and IRA (individual retirement account) solutions. Northwestern Mutual Investment Management Company, LLC manages NMLIC's investments in publicly-traded debt and equity securities, privately-placed debt and equity securities, interests in private equity funds, mortgage loans and real estate equity. LearnVest, Inc. is a financial planning company which also sells personal finance software solutions. Northwestern Mutual Wealth Management Company is a limited purpose federal savings bank that also provides investment management, trust services and fee-based financial planning. This subsidiary is not a broker-dealer or insurance company. Mason Street Advisors, LLC is an investment advisor for Northwestern Mutual Series Fund variable annuity and variable life products.

NMLIC offers its employees flexible spending accounts, training programs, flexible work schedules, adoption assistance, an onsite fitness center, credit union membership, educational assistance and a business casual work environment.

FINANCIAL DATA:
Note: Data for latest year may not have been available at press time.

In U.S. $	2018	2017	2016	2015	2014	2013
Revenue	28,482,000,000	28,087,000,000	28,158,000,000	27,880,000,000	26,707,000,000	25,909,000,000
R&D Expense						
Operating Income						
Operating Margin %						
SGA Expense						
Net Income	783,000,000	1,017,000,000	818,000,000	815,000,000	679,000,000	802,000,000
Operating Cash Flow						
Capital Expenditure						
EBITDA						
Return on Assets %						
Return on Equity %						
Debt to Equity						

CONTACT INFORMATION:
Phone: 414-271-1444 Fax: 414-299-7022
Toll-Free:
Address: 720 E. Wisconsin Ave., Milwaukee, WI 53202 United States

STOCK TICKER/OTHER:
Stock Ticker: Mutual Company
Employees: 5,900
Parent Company:

Exchange:
Fiscal Year Ends: 12/31

SALARIES/BONUSES:
Top Exec. Salary: $ Bonus: $
Second Exec. Salary: $ Bonus: $

OTHER THOUGHTS:
Estimated Female Officers or Directors: 5
Hot Spot for Advancement for Women/Minorities: Y

Norwegian Cruise Line Holdings Ltd (NCL)

NAIC Code: 483112

www.ncl.com

TYPES OF BUSINESS:
Cruise Line
Luxury Cruise Lines

BRANDS/DIVISIONS/AFFILIATES:
Norwegian Cruise Line
Oceana Cruises
Regent Seven Seas Cruises

CONTACTS:
Note: Officers with more than one job title may be intentionally listed here more than once.

Daniel Farkas, Assistant Secretary
Andrew Stuart, CEO, Divisional
Jason Montague, CEO, Divisional
Robert Binder, CEO, Subsidiary
Frank Del Rio, CEO
Russell Galbut, Chairman of the Board
Faye Ashby, Chief Accounting Officer
T. Lindsay, Executive VP, Divisional
Mark Kempa, Executive VP
Harry Sommer, President, Divisional

GROWTH PLANS/SPECIAL FEATURES:
Norwegian Cruise Line Holdings Ltd. (NCLH) is one of the largest cruise line operators in the world. The firm operates the Norwegian Cruise Line, Oceana Cruises and Regent Seven Seas Cruises brands, comprising more than 25 ships. NCLH plans to introduce additional ships through 2025, with an option to introduce an additional two ships for delivery in 2026 and 2027. All of the company's brands offer an assortment of features, amenities and activities, including multiple dining venues, bars, lounges, spas, casinos and retail shopping areas, as well as a variety of entertainment choices. NCLH also offers a selection of shore excursions at each port of call, and hotel packages for stays before or after a voyage. The Norwegian line operates 17 ships, comprising a purpose-built format to offer guests the freedom and flexibility to design their ideal cruses vacation on their schedule. The Haven by Norwegian is a luxury ship with suites, private pools and dining, concierge services and personal butlers. Oceana Cruises offers fine cuisine at sea and immersive destination experiences worldwide. It operates a fleet of six mid-size ships. Regent Seven Seas is an all-inclusive cruise line which provides all-suite accommodations, round-trip air transportation, highly-personalized service, specialized cuisine, fine wines and spirits, unlimited internet access, sightseeing excursions in every port and other amenities.

FINANCIAL DATA:
Note: Data for latest year may not have been available at press time.

In U.S. $	2018	2017	2016	2015	2014	2013
Revenue	6,055,126,000	5,396,175,000	4,874,340,000	4,345,048,000	3,125,881,000	2,570,294,000
R&D Expense						
Operating Income	1,219,061,000	1,048,819,000	925,464,000	702,486,000	502,941,000	395,887,000
Operating Margin %		.19%	.19%	.16%	.16%	.15%
SGA Expense	897,929,000	773,755,000	666,156,000	554,999,000	403,169,000	301,155,000
Net Income	954,843,000	759,872,000	633,085,000	427,137,000	338,352,000	101,714,000
Operating Cash Flow	2,075,171,000	1,585,741,000	1,239,666,000	1,041,178,000	635,601,000	475,281,000
Capital Expenditure	1,566,796,000	1,372,214,000	1,092,091,000	1,122,734,000	1,051,974,000	894,851,000
EBITDA	1,786,033,000	1,570,303,000	1,371,099,000	1,152,821,000	807,818,000	640,998,000
Return on Assets %		.06%	.05%	.04%	.04%	.02%
Return on Equity %		.15%	.15%	.12%	.11%	.04%
Debt to Equity		0.989	1.287	1.525	1.593	1.089

CONTACT INFORMATION:
Phone: 305-436-4000 Fax: 305-436-4140
Toll-Free:
Address: 7665 Corporate Center Dr., Miami, FL 33126 United States

SALARIES/BONUSES:
Top Exec. Salary: $1,751,507 Bonus: $
Second Exec. Salary: $700,000 Bonus: $

STOCK TICKER/OTHER:
Stock Ticker: NCLH Exchange: NYS
Employees: 30,000 Fiscal Year Ends: 12/31
Parent Company:

OTHER THOUGHTS:
Estimated Female Officers or Directors: 4
Hot Spot for Advancement for Women/Minorities: Y

Sales, profits and employees may be estimates. Financial information, benefits and other data can change quickly and may vary from those stated here.

NVR Inc

NAIC Code: 236117

www.nvrinc.com

TYPES OF BUSINESS:
Construction, Home Building and Residential Mortgages
Townhouse Construction
Condominium Construction

BRANDS/DIVISIONS/AFFILIATES:
NVR Mortgage Finance Inc
Ryan Homes
NVHomes
Heartland Homes

CONTACTS:
Note: Officers with more than one job title may be intentionally listed here more than once.

Paul Saville, CEO
Daniel Malzahn, CFO
Dwight Schar, Chairman of the Board
Matthew Kelpy, Chief Accounting Officer
Paul Praylo, COO
Jeffrey Martchek, President, Divisional
Eugene Bredow, President, Subsidiary

GROWTH PLANS/SPECIAL FEATURES:
NVR, Inc. is primarily engaged in the construction and sale of single-family detached homes, townhomes and condominium buildings. Additionally, NVR offers mortgage banking services through its subsidiary NVR Mortgage Finance, Inc. (NVRM). NVRM originates mortgage loans for NVR's homebuilding customers and sells all mortgage loans it closes to investors in the secondary markets on a servicing released basis. The company operates in 14 states, with concentration in the Washington, D.C. and Baltimore, Maryland metropolitan areas, which accounted for 30% and 10% of its 2018 homebuilding revenues. NVR's homebuilding operations include the sale and construction of single-family detached homes, townhomes and condominium buildings under three brand names: Ryan Homes, NVHomes and Heartland Homes. The Ryan Homes products are moderately priced and marketed primarily to first-time homeowners and first-time move-up buyers. Ryan Homes are currently sold in 32 metropolitan areas located primarily in the eastern U.S. NVHomes and Heartland Homes are marketed primarily to move-up and upscale buyers. NVHomes are sold in Delaware, Washington, D.C., Baltimore and Philadelphia metropolitan areas. Heartland Homes are sold in Pittsburgh. The firm's houses range from approximately 1,000 to 9,500 square feet, typically including two to four bedrooms, and are priced between $130,000 and $1.5 million. NVR also provides mortgage-related services through its mortgage banking operations, which include subsidiaries that broker title insurance and perform title searches.

FINANCIAL DATA:
Note: Data for latest year may not have been available at press time.

In U.S. $	2018	2017	2016	2015	2014	2013
Revenue	7,175,267,000	6,313,690,000	5,830,113,000	5,165,493,000	4,449,508,000	4,216,250,000
R&D Expense						
Operating Income	983,768,000	869,948,000	682,318,000	626,130,000	476,137,000	440,536,000
Operating Margin %		.14%	.12%	.12%	.11%	.10%
SGA Expense	512,712,000	460,800,000	443,320,000	424,009,000	407,867,000	355,623,000
Net Income	797,197,000	537,521,000	425,262,000	382,927,000	281,630,000	266,477,000
Operating Cash Flow	723,126,000	568,904,000	384,465,000	203,391,000	184,549,000	270,222,000
Capital Expenditure	19,665,000	20,269,000	22,369,000	18,277,000	31,672,000	19,016,000
EBITDA	1,003,936,000	892,615,000	704,587,000	647,664,000	493,751,000	453,927,000
Return on Assets %		.19%	.16%	.16%	.12%	.10%
Return on Equity %		.37%	.33%	.32%	.24%	.19%
Debt to Equity		0.372	0.457	0.484	0.533	0.478

CONTACT INFORMATION:
Phone: 703 956-4000 Fax: 703 956-4750
Toll-Free:
Address: 11700 Plaza America Dr., Ste. 500, Reston, VA 20190 United States

STOCK TICKER/OTHER:
Stock Ticker: NVR
Employees: 4,900
Parent Company:

Exchange: NYS
Fiscal Year Ends: 12/31

SALARIES/BONUSES:
Top Exec. Salary: $1,919,000   Bonus: $
Second Exec. Salary: $580,000   Bonus: $

OTHER THOUGHTS:
Estimated Female Officers or Directors:
Hot Spot for Advancement for Women/Minorities:

O Reilly Automotive Inc

NAIC Code: 441310

www.oreillyauto.com

TYPES OF BUSINESS:
Auto Parts Stores
Tools
Auto Accessories

BRANDS/DIVISIONS/AFFILIATES:
O'Reilly Auto Parts
Power Torque
BrakeBest
Prestone
Master Pro
Omnispark
Super Start
Ultima

CONTACTS: *Note: Officers with more than one job title may be intentionally listed here more than once.*

Thomas McFall, CFO
Jonathan Andrews, Senior VP, Divisional
David OReilly, Chairman of the Board
Jeremy Fletcher, Controller
Gregory Johnson, Co-President
Jeff Shaw, Co-President
Lawrence OReilly, Co-Vice Chairman of the Board
Gregory Henslee, Co-Vice Chairman of the Board
Brad Beckham, Executive VP, Divisional
Jeffrey Lauro, Senior VP, Divisional
Scott Kraus, Senior VP, Divisional
Carl Wilbanks, Senior VP, Divisional
Robert Dumas, Senior VP, Divisional
Doug Bragg, Senior VP, Divisional
Richard Venosdel, Senior VP, Divisional
Jason Tarrant, Senior VP, Divisional
Larry Ellis, Senior VP, Divisional
Brent Kirby, Senior VP, Divisional
Jeffrey Groves, Senior VP, Divisional

GROWTH PLANS/SPECIAL FEATURES:

O'Reilly Automotive, Inc. is one of the largest specialty retailers of automotive aftermarket parts, tools, supplies, equipment and accessories in the U.S., selling products to both do-it-yourself (DIY) customers and professional installers. The company operates 5,344 stores under the O'Reilly Auto Parts name in 47 states across the U.S. Stores carry an average of 48,000 stock keeping units (SKUs) with an extensive product line consisting of new and remanufactured automotive hard parts, such as alternators, starters, brake system components, batteries, chassis parts and engine parts; maintenance items, such as oil, antifreeze, fluids, wiper blades, lighting, engine additives and appearance products; accessories, such as floor mats, truck accessories and seat covers; and a complete line of auto body paint and related materials, automotive tools and professional service equipment. Store merchandise generally consists of nationally recognized, well-advertised, name brand products such as AC Delco, Armor All, Bosch, BWD, Cardone, Castrol, Gates Rubber, Monroe, Moog, Pennzoil, Prestone, Quaker State, STP, Turtle Wax, Valvoline, Wagner and Wix. In addition to name-brand products, stores carry a wide variety of high-quality private-label products under the BestTest, BrakeBest, Import Direct, Master Pro, Micro-Gard, Murray, Omnispark, Precision, Power Torque, Super Start and Ultima brands. O'Reilly operates 27 distribution centers and 342 hub stores, each equipped with highly automated material handling equipment that expedites the movement of products to loading areas for shipment to individual stores on a nightly basis. In August 2019, O'Reilly agreed to acquire an auto parts company in Guadalajara, Mexico, called Mayoreo de Autopartes Y Aceites SA de CV.

O'Reilly offers its employees medical, dental, vision, pharmacy and life insurance; a credit union membership; a 401(k) plan with company match; a profit sharing plan; paid time off; a discount stock purchase plan; and an employee assistance program.

FINANCIAL DATA: *Note: Data for latest year may not have been available at press time.*

In U.S. $	2018	2017	2016	2015	2014	2013
Revenue	9,536,428,000	8,977,726,000	8,593,096,000	7,966,674,000	7,216,081,000	6,649,237,000
R&D Expense						
Operating Income	1,815,184,000	1,725,400,000	1,699,206,000	1,514,021,000	1,270,374,000	1,103,485,000
Operating Margin %		.19%	.20%	.19%	.18%	.17%
SGA Expense	3,224,782,000	2,995,283,000	2,809,805,000	2,648,622,000	2,438,527,000	2,265,516,000
Net Income	1,324,487,000	1,133,804,000	1,037,691,000	931,216,000	778,182,000	670,292,000
Operating Cash Flow	1,727,555,000	1,403,687,000	1,454,167,000	1,281,476,000	1,190,430,000	908,026,000
Capital Expenditure	504,268,000	465,940,000	476,344,000	414,020,000	429,987,000	395,881,000
EBITDA	2,075,153,000	1,962,998,000	1,925,988,000	1,727,751,000	1,469,677,000	1,291,196,000
Return on Assets %		.15%	.15%	.14%	.12%	.11%
Return on Equity %		.99%	.58%	.47%	.39%	.33%
Debt to Equity		4.561	1.16	0.709	0.692	0.71

CONTACT INFORMATION:
Phone: 417 862-6708 Fax: 417 863-2242
Toll-Free: 800-755-6759
Address: 233 S. Patterson Ave., Springfield, MO 65802 United States

SALARIES/BONUSES:
Top Exec. Salary: $803,846 Bonus: $
Second Exec. Salary: $771,154 Bonus: $

STOCK TICKER/OTHER:
Stock Ticker: ORLY Exchange: NAS
Employees: 74,580 Fiscal Year Ends: 12/31
Parent Company:

OTHER THOUGHTS:
Estimated Female Officers or Directors: 1
Hot Spot for Advancement for Women/Minorities: Y

Old Dominion Freight Line Inc

NAIC Code: 484122

www.odfl.com

TYPES OF BUSINESS:
Trucking
LTL Trucking
Freight Logistics

BRANDS/DIVISIONS/AFFILIATES:

CONTACTS: Note: Officers with more than one job title may be intentionally listed here more than once.
Adam Satterfield, Assistant Secretary
Greg Gantt, CEO
David Congdon, Chairman of the Board
Earl Congdon, Chairman of the Board
Kimberly Maready, Chief Accounting Officer
Kevin Freeman, COO
Ross Parr, General Counsel
Christopher Brooks, Senior VP, Divisional
Gregory Plemmons, Senior VP, Divisional
Cecil Overbey, Senior VP, Divisional
David Bates, Senior VP, Divisional

GROWTH PLANS/SPECIAL FEATURES:

Old Dominion Freight Line, Inc. is a less-than-truckload (LTL) carrier providing regional, inter-regional and national services. These services include ground and air expedited transportation, as well as consumer household pickup and delivery (P&D), through a single integrated organization. In addition to Old Dominion's core LTL services, the company offers a range of value-added services, including container drayage, truckload brokerage, supply chain consulting and warehousing. More than 97% of revenue is derived from transporting LTL shipments for customers. Old Dominion conducts its operations through approximately 235 U.S. service center locations across 48 states, with major break-bulk facilities in Atlanta, Georgia; Rialto, California; Indianapolis, Indiana; Greensboro, North Carolina; Columbus, Ohio; Harrisburg, Pennsylvania; Memphis and Morristown, Tennessee; Dallas and Houston, Texas; and Salt Lake City, Utah. The firm comprises about 45,000 tractors and trailers, with more than 25,000 trailers being 28 feet in length for line haul operations. These trailers are often combined into tractor-trailer-trailer combinations, allowing goods to be shipped with minimal unload/reload handling. Tractors are generally used in long-distance operations for roughly three to five years and are then transferred to less demanding pickup and delivery operations.

FINANCIAL DATA: Note: Data for latest year may not have been available at press time.

In U.S. $	2018	2017	2016	2015	2014	2013
Revenue	4,043,695,000	3,358,112,000	2,991,517,000	2,972,442,000	2,787,897,000	2,337,648,000
R&D Expense						
Operating Income	817,051,000	575,886,000	483,835,000	498,240,000	441,307,000	338,438,000
Operating Margin %		.17%	.16%	.17%	.16%	.14%
SGA Expense	75,188,000	69,472,000	65,765,000	64,281,000	61,652,000	54,052,000
Net Income	605,668,000	463,774,000	295,765,000	304,690,000	267,514,000	206,113,000
Operating Cash Flow	900,116,000	536,294,000	565,583,000	553,880,000	391,674,000	350,666,000
Capital Expenditure	588,292,000	382,125,000	417,941,000	462,059,000	367,680,000	295,606,000
EBITDA	1,046,059,000	783,749,000	671,786,000	660,570,000	585,590,000	465,378,000
Return on Assets %		.16%	.11%	.13%	.13%	.11%
Return on Equity %		.22%	.17%	.19%	.20%	.18%
Debt to Equity		0.02	0.057	0.064	0.08	0.126

CONTACT INFORMATION:
Phone: 336 889-5000   Fax: 336 822-5239
Toll-Free: 800-432-6335
Address: 500 Old Dominion Way, Thomasville, NC 27360 United States

SALARIES/BONUSES:
Top Exec. Salary: $611,833   Bonus: $
Second Exec. Salary: $611,833   Bonus: $

STOCK TICKER/OTHER:
Stock Ticker: ODFL   Exchange: NAS
Employees: 17,543   Fiscal Year Ends: 12/31
Parent Company:

OTHER THOUGHTS:
Estimated Female Officers or Directors:
Hot Spot for Advancement for Women/Minorities:

Sales, profits and employees may be estimates. Financial information, benefits and other data can change quickly and may vary from those stated here.

Oliver Wyman Group

www.oliverwyman.com/index.html

NAIC Code: 541610

TYPES OF BUSINESS:
Management Consulting
Business Strategy Consulting
Financial Services Consulting
Risk Management & Insurance Consulting

BRANDS/DIVISIONS/AFFILIATES:
Marsh & McLennan Companies Inc

CONTACTS: Note: Officers with more than one job title may be intentionally listed here more than once.
Scott McDonald, CEO
Matthew Cunningham, CFO
Paula McGlarry, General Counsel
Simon Harris, Chief Strategy & Corp. Dev. Officer
David Fishbaum, Actuarial
Rachel Kirsh, Chief Risk Officer

GROWTH PLANS/SPECIAL FEATURES:
Oliver Wyman Group, a subsidiary of Marsh & McLennan Companies, Inc., is a global consulting group with offices in 60 cities in nearly 30 countries. Oliver Wyman's expertise is grouped into three categories: industries, capabilities and insights. Industry expertise includes the following sectors: automotive, aviation, aerospace, business services, communications, consumer goods, defense, distribution, education, energy, financial services, health, industrial products, leisure, life sciences, media, public sector, retail, surface transportation, technology, travel and wholesale. Oliver Wyman's capabilities span actuarial, corporate finance, restructuring, digital, brand, innovation, operations, innovative approaches to technology, organizational effectiveness, payments, pricing, sales, marketing, risk management, strategy and sustainability. The firm's insights division offers expert perspectives on issues that are reshaping businesses, economies and societies, and include insights on areas such as biometrics, trends, operational resilience, banks and recession, millennials, smart investments, airline economic analysis, diversity, merchant payments and much more. Oliver Wyman is known for scheduling worldwide events, where industry leaders and experts gather to share experiences and spread knowledge. Upcoming events can be located on the firm's website.

FINANCIAL DATA: Note: Data for latest year may not have been available at press time.

In U.S. $	2018	2017	2016	2015	2014	2013
Revenue	2,033,700,000	1,963,360,000	1,803,530,000	1,751,000,000	1,710,000,000	1,483,000,000
R&D Expense						
Operating Income						
Operating Margin %						
SGA Expense						
Net Income						
Operating Cash Flow						
Capital Expenditure						
EBITDA						
Return on Assets %						
Return on Equity %						
Debt to Equity						

CONTACT INFORMATION:
Phone: 212-345-8000   Fax: 212-345-8075
Toll-Free:
Address: 1166 Ave. of the Americas, New York, NY 10036 United States

SALARIES/BONUSES:
Top Exec. Salary: $ Bonus: $
Second Exec. Salary: $ Bonus: $

STOCK TICKER/OTHER:
Stock Ticker: Subsidiary   Exchange:
Employees: 5,000   Fiscal Year Ends: 12/31
Parent Company: Marsh & McLennan Companies Inc

OTHER THOUGHTS:
Estimated Female Officers or Directors: 3
Hot Spot for Advancement for Women/Minorities: Y

Sales, profits and employees may be estimates. Financial information, benefits and other data can change quickly and may vary from those stated here.

Omnicom Group Inc

NAIC Code: 541810

www.omnicomgroup.com

TYPES OF BUSINESS:
Advertising Services
Public Relations
Market Research
Marketing & Brand Consulting
Interactive & Search Engine Marketing
Media Planning & Buying
Health Care Communications

BRANDS/DIVISIONS/AFFILIATES:
BBDO Worldwide Communications Group Inc
DDB Worldwide Inc
TBWA Worldwide Inc (Disruption Company (The))
DAS Group of Companies
Omnicom Media Group
Credera

CONTACTS:
Note: Officers with more than one job title may be intentionally listed here more than once.

Jonathan Nelson, CEO, Divisional
John Wren, CEO
Peter Swiecicki, Controller
Philip Angelastro, Executive VP
Michael OBrien, General Counsel
Andrew Castellaneta, Senior VP

GROWTH PLANS/SPECIAL FEATURES:

Omnicom Group, Inc. is a holding company that, through its subsidiaries, is a global provider of advertising, marketing and corporate communications services. The company's branded networks and agencies operate in all major global markets and provide a comprehensive range of services in the following disciplines: advertising, customer relationship management (CRM), public relations and healthcare. Omnicom's business is divided into two segments: CRM consumer experience, which includes Omnicom's digital/direct marketing agencies, branding agencies, shopper marketing agencies and experiential marketing agencies; and CRM execution and support, which includes field marketing, healthcare marketing, sales support, merchandising and point of sale, as well as specialized marketing and custom communications services. The firm's primary agency subsidiaries include: BBDO Worldwide Communications Group, Inc., specializing in creative marketing services, with approximately 300 offices in more than 80 countries; DDB Worldwide, Inc., an advertising and marketing network with more than 200 offices in over 90 countries, with its flagship office in New York, USA; TBWA Worldwide, Inc., also referred to as The Disruption Company, is a top-ten ranked brand advertising network, with offices in nearly 100 countries; and DAS Group of Companies, offering marketing services in the disciplines of specialty, public relations, healthcare, CRM, events, promotional marketing, branding and research. In addition, Omnicom Media Group is the media services division of Omnicom Group, serving over 5,000 clients in more than 100 countries. Omnicom Media provides full-service media capabilities, as well as data and analytics services. Omnicom Group's U.S. operations represent approximately 54% of annual revenue. Other geographical operations include Latin America, Europe, Asia, the Middle East, Africa, Australia and New Zealand. In August 2018, Omnicom acquired Credera, strengthening its management and IT consulting capabilities.

FINANCIAL DATA:
Note: Data for latest year may not have been available at press time.

In U.S. $	2018	2017	2016	2015	2014	2013
Revenue	15,290,200,000	15,273,600,000	15,416,900,000	15,134,400,000	15,317,800,000	14,584,500,000
R&D Expense						
Operating Income	2,133,500,000	2,059,700,000	2,008,900,000	1,920,100,000	1,944,100,000	1,866,700,000
Operating Margin %		.13%	.13%	.13%	.13%	.13%
SGA Expense	455,400,000	450,000,000	443,900,000	1,852,400,000	2,023,700,000	1,993,400,000
Net Income	1,326,400,000	1,088,400,000	1,148,600,000	1,093,900,000	1,104,000,000	991,100,000
Operating Cash Flow	1,722,300,000	2,023,900,000	1,931,200,000	2,172,300,000	1,476,500,000	1,809,000,000
Capital Expenditure	195,700,000	156,000,000	165,500,000	202,700,000	213,000,000	212,000,000
EBITDA	2,456,800,000	2,391,500,000	2,344,400,000	2,250,800,000	2,281,600,000	2,142,900,000
Return on Assets %		.05%	.05%	.05%	.05%	.04%
Return on Equity %		.46%	.50%	.41%	.34%	.27%
Debt to Equity		1.879	2.276	1.453	1.601	1.126

CONTACT INFORMATION:
Phone: 212 415-3600 Fax: 212 415-3393
Toll-Free:
Address: 437 Madison Ave., New York, NY 10022 United States

SALARIES/BONUSES:
Top Exec. Salary: $13,500,000 Bonus: $
Second Exec. Salary: $4,300,000 Bonus: $

STOCK TICKER/OTHER:
Stock Ticker: OMC
Employees: 78,500
Parent Company:

Exchange: NYS
Fiscal Year Ends: 12/31

OTHER THOUGHTS:
Estimated Female Officers or Directors: 6

Hot Spot for Advancement for Women/Minorities: Y

Oracle Corporation

www.oracle.com

NAIC Code: 0

TYPES OF BUSINESS:
Computer Software, Data Base & File Management
e-Business Applications Software
Internet-Based Software
Consulting Services
Human Resources Management Software
CRM Software
Middleware

BRANDS/DIVISIONS/AFFILIATES:
Zenedge
Aconex Limited
SparklineData
DataScience.com
goBalto
Talari Networks
Vocado
DataFox

CONTACTS:
Note: Officers with more than one job title may be intentionally listed here more than once.

Lawrence Ellison, Chairman of the Board
William West, Chief Accounting Officer
Mark Hurd, Co-CEO
Safra Catz, Co-CEO
Jeffrey Henley, Director
Dorian Daley, Executive VP
Edward Screven, Executive VP

GROWTH PLANS/SPECIAL FEATURES:

Oracle Corporation is a leading enterprise software company, providing hardware products and services to over 430,000 customers throughout the world. The firm markets its integrated hardware and software systems directly to corporations. Oracle's products can be categorized into three broad business categories: cloud and license, hardware and services. The cloud and license business category represents 82% of total 2018 fiscal revenues, and includes Oracle cloud services, cloud license and on-premise license offerings, as well as license support services. The hardware business (10%) is comprised of hardware products and related hardware support services for on-premise IT environments. Its Oracle engineered systems are core to the firm's on-premise and cloud-based infrastructure offerings, and are pre-integrated products designed to integrate multiple Oracle technology components in order to work together to deliver enhanced performance, availability, security and operational efficiency relative to the customer's products. The services business (8%) offers consulting services, enhanced support services and education services. During 2018, Oracle acquired: Zenedge, a server, storage and networking solutions provider; Aconex Limited, a provider of cloud-based collaboration software for construction projects; SparklineData and DataScience.com, both of which offer middleware software; goBalto, a provider of health sciences solutions; Talari Networks, offering communications and media solutions; and Vocado, Iridize, Grapeshot and DataFox, each of which are cloud- or AI-based applications that provide a variety of solutions.

Oracle offers employees a 401(k) plan; employee assistance and employee stock purchase plans; and a Live and Work Well program.

FINANCIAL DATA:
Note: Data for latest year may not have been available at press time.

In U.S. $	2018	2017	2016	2015	2014	2013
Revenue	39,831,000,000	37,728,000,000	37,047,000,000	38,226,000,000	38,275,000,000	
R&D Expense	6,091,000,000	6,159,000,000	5,787,000,000	5,524,000,000	5,151,000,000	
Operating Income	14,319,000,000	13,276,000,000	13,104,000,000	14,289,000,000	14,983,000,000	
Operating Margin %	.36%	.35%	.35%	.37%	.39%	
SGA Expense	9,720,001,000	9,373,000,000	9,039,000,000	8,732,000,000	8,605,000,000	
Net Income	3,825,000,000	9,335,000,000	8,901,000,000	9,938,000,000	10,955,000,000	
Operating Cash Flow	15,386,000,000	14,126,000,000	13,561,000,000	14,336,000,000	14,921,000,000	
Capital Expenditure	1,736,000,000	2,021,000,000	1,189,000,000	1,391,000,000	580,000,000	
EBITDA	17,701,000,000	15,766,000,000	15,418,000,000	16,838,000,000	17,526,000,000	
Return on Assets %	.03%	.08%	.08%	.10%	.13%	
Return on Equity %	.08%	.18%	.19%	.21%	.24%	
Debt to Equity	1.227	0.893	0.848	0.821	0.484	

CONTACT INFORMATION:
Phone: 650 506-7000 Fax: 650 506-7200
Toll-Free: 800-392-2999
Address: 500 Oracle Pkwy., Redwood City, CA 94065 United States

STOCK TICKER/OTHER:
Stock Ticker: ORCL
Employees: 138,500
Parent Company:

Exchange: NYS
Fiscal Year Ends: 05/31

SALARIES/BONUSES:
Top Exec. Salary: $950,000 Bonus: $
Second Exec. Salary: $950,000 Bonus: $

OTHER THOUGHTS:
Estimated Female Officers or Directors: 6
Hot Spot for Advancement for Women/Minorities: Y

Oracle NetSuite

NAIC Code: 0

www.netsuite.com

TYPES OF BUSINESS:
Business Management Application Suites
Enterprise Resource Planning
Customer Relationship Management
E-Commerce Capabilities

BRANDS/DIVISIONS/AFFILIATES:
Oracle Corporation
NetSuite OneWorld
NetSuite CRM
SuiteCommerce

CONTACTS: Note: Officers with more than one job title may be intentionally listed here more than once.
Jim McGeever, Exec. VP-Oper.
Marc Huffman, Sr. VP-Sales
Douglas Solomon, General Counsel
Marc Huffman, President, Divisional

GROWTH PLANS/SPECIAL FEATURES:
Oracle NetSuite is a global business unit of Oracle Corporation and a leading vendor of cloud-based financials, enterprise resource planning (ERP) and omnichannel commerce software. The firm's solutions run the business of more than 40,000 companies, organizations and subsidiaries in over 100 countries. Oracle NetSuite's cloud ERP, customer relationship management (CRM) and eCommerce products enable customers to manage their back-office, front-office and web operations in a single application. From comprehensive financial management capabilities to inventory, supply chain and warehouse management solutions, Oracle NetSuite empowers businesses of all sizes, across all industries. NetSuite OneWorld delivers a real-time, unified global business management platform for enterprises that manages multi-national and multi-subsidiary operations at a fraction of the cost of traditional on-premise ERP solutions. NetSuite CRM software delivers a real-time, 360-degree view of a business' customers. It provides a seamless flow of information across the entire customer lifecycle, from lead to sales order, fulfillment, upsell, cross-sell and support. NetSuite's professional services automation solutions meet the needs of fledgling startups to growing enterprises. SuiteCommerce unifies every step of the multichannel, multi-location business, from e-commerce, point of sale and order management, to marketing, merchandising, inventory, financials and support. Oracle NetSuite products offer a variety of management and procurement solutions, including financial, order, production, supply chain, warehouse/fulfillment and human capital management. Industries served by the company include software/internet companies, wholesale distribution, advertising/digital marketing, media/publishing, financial services, healthcare, non-profit, retail, manufacturing, IT services, professional services, consulting, energy and education.

FINANCIAL DATA: Note: Data for latest year may not have been available at press time.

In U.S. $	2018	2017	2016	2015	2014	2013
Revenue	914,550,000	871,000,000	855,000,000	741,148,992	556,284,032	414,508,000
R&D Expense						
Operating Income						
Operating Margin %						
SGA Expense						
Net Income				-124,743,000	-100,037,000	-70,409,000
Operating Cash Flow						
Capital Expenditure						
EBITDA						
Return on Assets %						
Return on Equity %						
Debt to Equity						

CONTACT INFORMATION:
Phone: 650 627-1000   Fax: 650 627-1001
Toll-Free: 877-638-7848
Address: 2955 Campus Dr., Ste. 100, San Mateo, CA 94403-2511 United States

STOCK TICKER/OTHER:
Stock Ticker: Subsidiary
Employees: 3,357
Parent Company: Oracle Corporation

Exchange:
Fiscal Year Ends: 12/31

SALARIES/BONUSES:
Top Exec. Salary: $ Bonus: $
Second Exec. Salary: $ Bonus: $

OTHER THOUGHTS:
Estimated Female Officers or Directors: 3
Hot Spot for Advancement for Women/Minorities: Y

Oshkosh Corporation

NAIC Code: 336120

www.oshkoshcorporation.com

TYPES OF BUSINESS:
Fire & Emergency Vehicles
Military Trucks
Truck Bodies
Specialty Trucks
Cement Mixers
Refuse Trucks

BRANDS/DIVISIONS/AFFILIATES:
JLG Industries Inc
Pierce Manufacturing Inc
Jerr-Dan

CONTACTS: Note: Officers with more than one job title may be intentionally listed here more than once.
William Jones, CEO
Tina Schoner, Other Executive Officer
David Sagehorn, CFO
Craig Omtvedt, Chairman of the Board
James Freeders, Chief Accounting Officer
Anupam Khare, Chief Information Officer
Bryan Brandt, Chief Marketing Officer
John Pfeifer, COO
Ignacio Cortina, Executive VP
Robert Sims, Executive VP
John Bryant, Executive VP
James Johnson, Executive VP
Frank Nerenhausen, Executive VP
Bradley Nelson, President, Divisional
Robert Messina, Senior VP, Divisional
Marek May, Senior VP, Divisional

GROWTH PLANS/SPECIAL FEATURES:

Oshkosh Corporation is a leading designer, manufacturer and marketer of specialty vehicles and vehicle bodies. The company operates in four segments: access equipment, defense, fire and emergency and commercial. The access equipment segment, accounting for 49% of the firm's sales, is formed through JLG Industries, Inc. a global manufacturer of aerial work platforms and telehandlers used in a wide variety of construction, agricultural, industrial, institutional and general maintenance applications to position workers and materials at elevated heights. This segment also manufactures towing and recovery equipment in the U.S. under the Jerr-Dan brand name. The defense segment, accounting for roughly 24% of the company's sales, supplies severe-duty, heavy-payload tactical trucks to the U.S. Department of Defense (DoD). The fire and emergency segment (14%), through subsidiary Pierce Manufacturing, Inc., is a leading domestic manufacturer of fire apparatus assembled on custom chassis. It also manufactures fire apparatus assembled on commercially-available chassis, snow removal vehicles and emergency vehicles, including pumpers; aerial and ladder trucks; tankers; light-, medium- and heavy-duty rescue vehicles; rough terrain response vehicles; mobile command and control centers; bomb squad vehicles; and hazardous materials control vehicles. The segment sells aircraft rescue and fire fighting (ARFF) vehicles to domestic and international airports. The commercial segment (13%), manufactures rear- and front-discharge concrete mixers, refuse collection vehicles, mobile and stationary compactors and waste transfer units, portable and stationary concrete batch plants and vehicle components. Oshkosh Corporation purchased part of the Lake Shore Municipal Golf Course in Oshkosh, Wisconsin to build its new headquarters on the property, with construction occurring through 2019. The city plans to redevelop the rest of the golf course into a new public space.

The firm offers employees medical, prescription, dental, vision, AD&D, disability and life insurance; 401(k), pension and stock purchase programs; and tuition reimbursement.

FINANCIAL DATA: Note: Data for latest year may not have been available at press time.

In U.S. $	2018	2017	2016	2015	2014	2013
Revenue	7,705,500,000	6,829,600,000	6,279,200,000	6,098,100,000	6,808,200,000	7,665,100,000
R&D Expense						
Operating Income	653,500,000	463,000,000	390,900,000	398,600,000	503,300,000	514,700,000
Operating Margin %		.07%	.06%	.07%	.07%	.07%
SGA Expense	663,900,000	665,600,000	612,400,000	587,400,000	624,100,000	620,500,000
Net Income	471,900,000	285,600,000	216,400,000	229,500,000	309,300,000	318,000,000
Operating Cash Flow	436,300,000	246,500,000	577,700,000	82,500,000	170,400,000	438,000,000
Capital Expenditure	100,100,000	113,200,000	127,300,000	158,000,000	124,900,000	59,900,000
EBITDA	786,000,000	601,400,000	496,200,000	520,700,000	630,100,000	637,800,000
Return on Assets %		.06%	.05%	.05%	.07%	.07%
Return on Equity %		.13%	.11%	.12%	.15%	.16%
Debt to Equity		0.35	0.418	0.447	0.441	0.422

CONTACT INFORMATION:
Phone: 920 235-9151   Fax:
Toll-Free:
Address: 2307 Oregon St., Oshkosh, WI 54902 United States

SALARIES/BONUSES:
Top Exec. Salary: $1,161,923   Bonus: $
Second Exec. Salary: $700,818   Bonus: $

STOCK TICKER/OTHER:
Stock Ticker: OSK
Employees: 13,800
Parent Company:

Exchange: NYS
Fiscal Year Ends: 09/30

OTHER THOUGHTS:
Estimated Female Officers or Directors: 5
Hot Spot for Advancement for Women/Minorities: Y

Sales, profits and employees may be estimates. Financial information, benefits and other data can change quickly and may vary from those stated here.

Owens Corning

www.owenscorning.com

NAIC Code: 326199

TYPES OF BUSINESS:
Building Materials (e.g., Fascia, Panels, Siding, Soffit), Plastics, Manufacturing
Glass Fiber Reinforcements
Manufactured Stone Veneer Products
Glass Fiber Fabrics
Construction Services

BRANDS/DIVISIONS/AFFILIATES:
Owens Corning PINK FIBERGLAS Insulation

CONTACTS:
Note: Officers with more than one job title may be intentionally listed here more than once.
Brian Chambers, CEO
Michael McMurray, CFO
Michael Thaman, Chairman of the Board
Kelly Schmidt, Controller
Ava Harter, General Counsel
Marcio Sandri, President, Divisional
Gunner Smith, President, Divisional
Julian Francis, President, Divisional
Daniel Smith, Senior VP, Divisional

GROWTH PLANS/SPECIAL FEATURES:

Owens Corning is a producer of residential and commercial building materials and glass fiber reinforcements and other similar materials for composite systems. The company operates through three business segments: composites, insulation and roofing. Composites includes the firm's reinforcements and downstream businesses, and accounted for 28% of total net sales in 2018. This division's glass fiber materials can be found in over 40,000 end-use applications within the following five markets: building and construction, transportation, consumer, industrial, and power and energy. End-use applications include pipe, roofing shingles, sporting goods, consumer electronics, telecommunications cables, boats, aviation, defense, automotive, industrial containers and wind-energy. Composites manufactures, fabricates and sells glass reinforcements in the form of fiber and of fabrics. Insulation comprises 38% net sales, and its products help customers conserve energy, provide improved acoustical performance and offer convenience of installation and use for new home construction and remodeling purposes. These products include thermal and acoustical batts, loosefill insulation, foam sheathing and accessories, and are sold under the brand and trademark name Owens Corning PINK FIBERGLASS Insulation. Roofing products (34%) include laminate and strip asphalt roofing shingles, as well as oxidized asphalt and roofing components and accessories. Owens Corning has operations in more than 30 countries.

The company offers employees medical, dental and vision insurance; a wellness program; short- and long-term disability coverage; health care and dependent care spending accounts; relocation assistance; life insurance; personal accident insurance; and auto and home insurance.

FINANCIAL DATA:
Note: Data for latest year may not have been available at press time.

In U.S. $	2018	2017	2016	2015	2014	2013
Revenue	7,057,000,000	6,384,000,000	5,677,000,000	5,350,000,000	5,276,000,000	5,295,000,000
R&D Expense	89,000,000	85,000,000	82,000,000	73,000,000	76,000,000	77,000,000
Operating Income	807,000,000	737,000,000	699,000,000	548,000,000	392,000,000	385,000,000
Operating Margin %		.12%	.12%	.10%	.07%	.07%
SGA Expense	700,000,000	620,000,000	584,000,000	525,000,000	487,000,000	530,000,000
Net Income	545,000,000	289,000,000	393,000,000	330,000,000	226,000,000	204,000,000
Operating Cash Flow	803,000,000	1,016,000,000	943,000,000	742,000,000	441,000,000	418,000,000
Capital Expenditure	537,000,000	337,000,000	373,000,000	393,000,000	363,000,000	353,000,000
EBITDA	1,254,000,000	1,037,000,000	1,041,000,000	853,000,000	650,000,000	717,000,000
Return on Assets %		.04%	.05%	.04%	.03%	.03%
Return on Equity %		.07%	.10%	.09%	.06%	.06%
Debt to Equity		0.578	0.545	0.455	0.539	0.534

CONTACT INFORMATION:
Phone: 419 248-8000 Fax: 419 248-8445
Toll-Free: 800-438-7465
Address: 1 Owens Corning Pkwy., Toledo, OH 43659 United States

STOCK TICKER/OTHER:
Stock Ticker: OC
Employees: 16,000
Parent Company:

Exchange: NYS
Fiscal Year Ends: 12/31

SALARIES/BONUSES:
Top Exec. Salary: $1,175,000 Bonus: $
Second Exec. Salary: $641,667 Bonus: $

OTHER THOUGHTS:
Estimated Female Officers or Directors: 2
Hot Spot for Advancement for Women/Minorities: Y

Sales, profits and employees may be estimates. Financial information, benefits and other data can change quickly and may vary from those stated here.

PAREXEL International Corporation

www.parexel.com

NAIC Code: 541711

TYPES OF BUSINESS:
Clinical Trial & Data Management
Biostatistical Analysis & Reporting
Medical Communications Services
Clinical Pharmacology Services
Consulting Services

BRANDS/DIVISIONS/AFFILIATES:
Pamplona Capital Management LLP
PAREXEL Biotech
PAREXEL Access

CONTACTS:
Note: Officers with more than one job title may be intentionally listed here more than once.

Jamie Macdonald, CFO
Sybrand Pretorius, Chief Scientific Officer
Greg Rush, Exec. VP
Michele Fournier, VP-Interim Human Resources
Josef Von Rickenbach, Founder
Michelle Graham, Other Executive Officer
Xavier Flinois, President, Divisional
Gadi Saarony, Senior VP, Divisional
Roland Andersson, Senior VP, Divisional
Joshua Schultz, Senior VP, Divisional
David Godwin, Senior VP, Divisional
Douglas Batt, Senior VP

GROWTH PLANS/SPECIAL FEATURES:
PAREXEL International Corporation is a leading biopharmaceutical outsourcing services company. The firm provides comprehensive drug development capabilities, including phase I-IV clinical research services, integrated eClinical technologies and advanced commercialization services. It helps to develop innovations and solutions by leveraging its comprehensive therapeutic, technical and functional expertise in more than 100 countries worldwide. PAREXEL has five business segments: PAREXEL Biotech, clinical research, informatics, consulting and PAREXEL Access. PAREXEL Biotech helps emerging biotech companies reach their goals via global clinical, regulatory, strategic consulting and commercial expertise. The clinical research segment offers the following solutions and services: early phase, phase I-IV, ForeSite clinical trial methodology, global data operations, medical writing, quantitative clinical development, clinical trial supplies/logistics, customer care services, genomic medicine and clinical adjudication. The informatics segment offers the following solutions and services: regulatory and clinical technology, patient technology, clinical trial supplies/logistics, Perceptive cloud, asset transfer, PAREXEL's education services and customer care services. The consulting segment offers: integrated product development, regulatory compliance, risk management, regulatory outsourcing, regulatory information management, IDMP (identification of medicinal products) solutions and market access consulting. Last, the PAREXEL Access segment provides a simplified and complete solution that can help identify, generate, evaluate and communicate the evidence of product value, which helps accelerate time to market, de-risk the reimbursement and market access process. Access' services include real world evidence, drug safety services, market access consulting, medical communications and outsourced field-based medical teams. PAREXEL is privately-owned by Pamplona Capital Management, LLP.

FINANCIAL DATA:
Note: Data for latest year may not have been available at press time.

In U.S. $	2018	2017	2016	2015	2014	2013
Revenue	2,221,000,000	2,117,600,000	2,094,300,000	2,016,000,000	1,939,400,000	1,995,965,952
R&D Expense						
Operating Income						
Operating Margin %						
SGA Expense						
Net Income		107,300,000	154,900,000	147,800,000	129,094,000	95,972,000
Operating Cash Flow						
Capital Expenditure						
EBITDA						
Return on Assets %						
Return on Equity %						
Debt to Equity						

CONTACT INFORMATION:
Phone: 781 487-9900   Fax: 781 487-0525
Toll-Free:
Address: 195 West St., Waltham, MA 02451 United States

STOCK TICKER/OTHER:
Stock Ticker: Private   Exchange:
Employees: 18,900   Fiscal Year Ends: 06/30
Parent Company: Pamplona Capital Management LLP

SALARIES/BONUSES:
Top Exec. Salary: $ Bonus: $
Second Exec. Salary: $ Bonus: $

OTHER THOUGHTS:
Estimated Female Officers or Directors: 1
Hot Spot for Advancement for Women/Minorities: Y

Patrick Industries Inc

NAIC Code: 321219

patrickind.com/

TYPES OF BUSINESS:
Reconstituted Wood Product Manufacturing

BRANDS/DIVISIONS/AFFILIATES:

CONTACTS: Note: Officers with more than one job title may be intentionally listed here more than once.
Todd Cleveland, CEO
Joshua Boone, CFO
Kip Ellis, Executive VP, Divisional
Jeff Rodino, Executive VP, Divisional
Courtney Blosser, Executive VP, Divisional
Andy Nemeth, President

GROWTH PLANS/SPECIAL FEATURES:
Patrick Industries, Inc. is a manufacturer of component products and a distributor of building products and materials, serving original equipment manufacturers (OEMs) primarily in the recreational vehicle (RV), manufactured housing and marine industries. The firm also supplies products to adjacent industrial markets, such as kitchen cabinet, office and household furniture, fixtures and commercial furnishings. Patrick Industries operates more than 105 manufacturing plants and 42 warehouses and distribution facilities in 22 U.S. states, China, Canada and the Netherlands. The company has two business segments: manufacturing and distribution, accounting for 77% and 23% of annual net sales. Manufactured products include laminated products, decorative vinyl products, solid surface countertops, fabricated aluminum products, custom cabinetry, electrical systems components, slide-out trim and fascia, hardwood furniture, fiberglass bath and tile products, boat covers and frames, softwood lumber, interior passage doors, wiring products, molds and composite parts, aluminum fuel tanks, shower surrounds, fiberglass and plastic components, air-handling products and more. These products are distributed to more than 2,400 active customers, the majority of which are in the RV industry, which derived 63% of the company's sales (by market/industry).

FINANCIAL DATA: Note: Data for latest year may not have been available at press time.

In U.S. $	2018	2017	2016	2015	2014	2013
Revenue	2,263,061,000	1,635,653,000	1,221,887,000	920,333,000	735,717,000	594,931,000
R&D Expense						
Operating Income	178,415,000	121,900,000	90,837,000	69,969,000	51,501,000	40,515,000
Operating Margin %		.07%	.07%	.08%	.07%	.07%
SGA Expense	203,238,000	137,641,000	98,264,000	73,523,000	62,525,000	48,137,000
Net Income	119,832,000	85,718,000	55,577,000	42,219,000	30,674,000	24,040,000
Operating Cash Flow	200,013,000	99,901,000	97,147,000	65,630,000	45,741,000	22,431,000
Capital Expenditure	34,486,000	22,497,000	15,406,000	7,958,000	6,542,000	8,669,000
EBITDA	233,467,000	155,441,000	115,199,000	86,744,000	61,934,000	47,812,000
Return on Assets %		.12%	.12%	.13%	.14%	.15%
Return on Equity %		.31%	.35%	.36%	.33%	.33%
Debt to Equity		0.912	1.385	1.507	0.983	0.668

CONTACT INFORMATION:
Phone: 574 294-7511 Fax: 574 522-5213
Toll-Free:
Address: 107 West Franklin St., Elkhart, IN 46515 United States

STOCK TICKER/OTHER:
Stock Ticker: PATK
Employees: 4,497
Parent Company:

Exchange: NAS
Fiscal Year Ends: 12/31

SALARIES/BONUSES:
Top Exec. Salary: $690,383 Bonus: $
Second Exec. Salary: $472,596 Bonus: $

OTHER THOUGHTS:
Estimated Female Officers or Directors:
Hot Spot for Advancement for Women/Minorities:

Paychex Inc

NAIC Code: 541214

www.paychex.com

TYPES OF BUSINESS:
Payroll Processing Services
Payroll & Tax Preparation
Internal Accounting Records
Human Resources Outsourcing
Employee Benefits Outsourcing
Regulatory Compliance
Workers' Compensation Insurance Services
Online Payroll Services

BRANDS/DIVISIONS/AFFILIATES:
Paychex Flex
Paychex Advance LLC
Paychex Insurance Agency Inc
Paychex Online Payroll
SurePayroll
Paychex Flex Enterprise
Oasis Outsourcing Acquisition Corporation

CONTACTS: Note: Officers with more than one job title may be intentionally listed here more than once.
Martin Mucci, CEO
Efrain Rivera, CFO
B. Golisano, Chairman of the Board
Jennifer Vossler, Controller
Stephanie Schaeffer, Other Executive Officer
Mark Bottini, Senior VP, Divisional
Michael Gioja, Senior VP, Divisional
John Gibson, Senior VP, Divisional
Laurie Zaucha, Vice President, Divisional

GROWTH PLANS/SPECIAL FEATURES:

Paychex, Inc. provides comprehensive payroll and integrated human resource and employee benefits outsourcing solutions for small- to medium-sized businesses. It serves more than 650,000 clients through 100 offices in the U.S. and Europe. Paychex primarily offers human capital management (HCM) services through Paychex Flex, a software-as-a-service (SaaS) platform that provides an integrated suite of solutions such as applicant tracking, employee onboarding, payroll, employee benefits and human resource administration, time and attendance, performance management and retirement services. Subsidiary Paychex Advance, LLC provides a range of services to the temporary staffing industry, including the purchasing of accounts receivable as a means of providing payroll funding to these clients. The firm's payroll processing services include the calculation, preparation and delivery of employee payroll checks; production of internal accounting records and management reports; preparation of federal, state and local payroll tax returns; and collection and remittance of clients' payroll obligations. Additionally, Paychex offers professional employer organization (PEO) services and insurance offerings through subsidiary Paychex Insurance Agency, Inc. For small businesses, products include Paychex Online Payroll, a suite of self-service and interactive services available twenty-four hours a day, seven days a week; and SurePayroll, do-it-yourself, self-service SaaS solution, as well as mobile applications. For mid-market businesses, products include Paychex Flex Enterprise solution set, which offers an integrated suite of HCM solutions tied together by the Paychex Flex platform. In December 2018, Paychex acquired Oasis Outsourcing Acquisition Corporation, a leading professional employer organization (PEO) and human resources outsourcing services provider.

Employees of Paychex receive medical, vision and dental coverage; a prescription drug plan; flexible spending accounts; child care and employee assistance programs; and tuition reimbursement.

FINANCIAL DATA: Note: Data for latest year may not have been available at press time.

In U.S. $	2018	2017	2016	2015	2014	2013
Revenue	3,380,900,000	3,151,300,000	2,951,900,000	2,739,600,000	2,518,900,000	
R&D Expense						
Operating Income	1,287,500,000	1,239,600,000	1,146,600,000	1,053,600,000	982,700,000	
Operating Margin %		.39%	.39%	.38%	.39%	
SGA Expense	1,075,600,000	992,100,000	948,200,000	878,000,000	803,700,000	
Net Income	933,700,000	817,300,000	756,800,000	674,900,000	627,500,000	
Operating Cash Flow	1,276,400,000	960,400,000	1,018,200,000	895,200,000	880,900,000	
Capital Expenditure	154,000,000	94,300,000	97,700,000	102,800,000	84,100,000	
EBITDA	1,438,000,000	1,374,200,000	1,267,300,000	1,167,300,000	1,094,200,000	
Return on Assets %		.12%	.12%	.11%	.10%	
Return on Equity %		.42%	.41%	.38%	.35%	
Debt to Equity						

CONTACT INFORMATION:
Phone: 585-385-6666　Fax: 585 383-3428
Toll-Free: 800-322-7292
Address: 911 Panorama Trail S., Rochester, NY 14625-0397 United States

SALARIES/BONUSES:
Top Exec. Salary: $950,000　Bonus: $
Second Exec. Salary: $500,000　Bonus: $

STOCK TICKER/OTHER:
Stock Ticker: PAYX
Employees: 14,300
Parent Company:

Exchange: NAS
Fiscal Year Ends: 05/31

OTHER THOUGHTS:
Estimated Female Officers or Directors: 6
Hot Spot for Advancement for Women/Minorities: Y

Sales, profits and employees may be estimates. Financial information, benefits and other data can change quickly and may vary from those stated here.

PayPal Holdings Inc

www.paypal.com

NAIC Code: 522320

TYPES OF BUSINESS:
Payment Processing-Intermediary
Online Payment Systems
Web-Enabled Payments
Online Auction Technology
Credit Cards
Debit Cards
Account Management
Money Transfer

BRANDS/DIVISIONS/AFFILIATES:
eBay Inc
PayPal
PayPal Credit
Braintree
Venmo
Xoom
iZettle
Paydiant

CONTACTS: Note: Officers with more than one job title may be intentionally listed here more than once.

Daniel Schulman, CEO
John Rainey, CFO
John Donahoe, Chairman of the Board
Aaron Karczmer, Chief Compliance Officer
Louise Pentland, Chief Legal Officer
Allison Johnson, Chief Marketing Officer
Jonathan Auerbach, Chief Strategy Officer
William Ready, COO
Mark Britto, Executive VP, Divisional
Brian Yamasaki, Secretary
Aaron Anderson, Vice President

GROWTH PLANS/SPECIAL FEATURES:

PayPal Holdings, Inc. is a leading technology platform and global online payment processing company. The firm's products allow businesses and consumers to cost-effectively send and receive payments within and between more than 200 markets and 100 currencies worldwide. The company has about 227 million active customer accounts worldwide. The PayPal system extends the existing financial infrastructure of bank accounts and credit cards, and can also be used to collect subscriptions, recurring payments and donations. Moreover, the firm is a leading payment processing provider for online auction services, with the bulk of the company's business coming from eBay. PayPal's combined payment solution capabilities are comprised of the PayPal, PayPal Credit, Braintree, Venmo, Xoom and Paydiant proprietary payments platform. These products make it safer and simpler for friends and family to transfer funds to each other, including cross border transfers. Merchants are provided an end-to-end payments solution that provides authorization and settlement capabilities, as well as instant access to funds. PayPal Credit provides the ability for consumers to receive a line of credit; Braintree specializes in mobile and web payment systems for eCommerce companies; Venmo is a mobile application which moves money between friends and family via mobile devices; Xoom enables consumers to send money, pay bills and send mobile phone reloads to family and friends around the world via mobile devices; and Paydiant provides cloud-based services for merchants, banks, and point-of-sale and ATM providers. During 2017, PayPal processed approximately 7.6 billion payment transactions, which translates to 33.6 payment transactions per active customer account. In June 2108, the firm announced it had agreed to acquire Simility, a fraud prevention and risk management platform, for $120 million. The following September, PayPal completed its acquisition of iZettle, a financial technology company, for $2.2 billion.

FINANCIAL DATA: Note: Data for latest year may not have been available at press time.

In U.S. $	2018	2017	2016	2015	2014	2013
Revenue	15,451,000,000	13,094,000,000	10,842,000,000	9,248,000,000	8,025,000,000	6,727,000,000
R&D Expense	1,071,000,000	953,000,000	834,000,000	947,000,000	890,000,000	727,000,000
Operating Income	2,503,000,000	2,259,000,000	1,586,000,000	1,509,000,000	1,268,000,000	1,091,000,000
Operating Margin %		.17%	.15%	.16%	.16%	.16%
SGA Expense	2,764,000,000	2,283,000,000	1,997,000,000	1,545,000,000	1,480,000,000	1,169,000,000
Net Income	2,057,000,000	1,795,000,000	1,401,000,000	1,228,000,000	419,000,000	955,000,000
Operating Cash Flow	5,483,000,000	2,531,000,000	3,158,000,000	2,546,000,000	2,220,000,000	1,993,000,000
Capital Expenditure	823,000,000	667,000,000	669,000,000	722,000,000	492,000,000	391,000,000
EBITDA	3,229,000,000	3,064,000,000	2,310,000,000	2,117,000,000	1,784,000,000	1,544,000,000
Return on Assets %		.05%	.05%	.05%	.02%	.05%
Return on Equity %		.12%	.10%	.11%	.05%	.13%
Debt to Equity					0.047	0.069

CONTACT INFORMATION:
Phone: 408-967-1000 Fax: 650-864-8001
Toll-Free:
Address: 2211 N. First St., San Jose, CA 95131 United States

SALARIES/BONUSES:
Top Exec. Salary: $1,000,000 Bonus: $
Second Exec. Salary: $721,154 Bonus: $

STOCK TICKER/OTHER:
Stock Ticker: PYPL
Employees: 21,000
Parent Company:

Exchange: NAS
Fiscal Year Ends: 12/31

OTHER THOUGHTS:
Estimated Female Officers or Directors: 1
Hot Spot for Advancement for Women/Minorities: Y

Sales, profits and employees may be estimates. Financial information, benefits and other data can change quickly and may vary from those stated here.

Penske Automotive Group Inc

www.penskeautomotive.com

NAIC Code: 441110

TYPES OF BUSINESS:
Auto Dealers
Automotive Leasing
Parts & Service

BRANDS/DIVISIONS/AFFILIATES:
CarSense
CarShop
Penske Commercial Vehicles Australia
Penske Power Systems
Penske Truck Leasing Co LP

CONTACTS: Note: Officers with more than one job title may be intentionally listed here more than once.
Roger Penske, CEO
J. Carlson, Chief Accounting Officer
Robert Kurnick, Director
Bud Denker, Executive VP, Divisional
Shane Spradlin, Executive VP

GROWTH PLANS/SPECIAL FEATURES:

Penske Automotive Group, Inc. (PAG) is an international transportation services company operating automotive and commercial truck dealerships primarily in the U.S., Canada and western Europe. PAG also distributes commercial vehicles, diesel engines, gas engines, power systems and related parts and services principally in Australia and New Zealand. As of December 31, 2018, PAG operated 345 automotive retail franchises, of which 154 are located in the U.S. and 191 outside of the U.S. The franchises outside the U.S. are located primarily in the U.K. This division also operates 14 stand-alone used vehicle supercenters in the U.S. and U.K., which retail and wholesale pre-owned vehicles under a one price, no haggle methodology. Through subsidiary CarSense operates five U.S. retail locations and five U.K. retail locations, as well as a vehicle preparation center under the CarShop name. In 2018, PAG company retailed and wholesaled more than 644,000 vehicles. The commercial vehicle is the exclusive importer and distributor of Western Star heavy-duty trucks (a Daimler brand), MAN heavy- and medium-duty trucks and buses (a Volkswagen brand), and Dennis Eagle refuse collection vehicles across Australia and New Zealand, as well as portions of the Pacific. This business is known as Penske Commercial Vehicles Australia, which distributes commercial vehicles and parts to more than 70 dealership locations, including nine company-owned retail commercial vehicle dealerships. The commercial vehicle segment also distributes engines and power systems for MTU, Detroit Diesel, Allison Transmission and Rolls Royce Power Systems. Penske Power Systems offers products across the on- and off-highway markets, construction, mining, marine and defense. Penske Truck Leasing Co., LP provides transportation and supply chain services.

Employee benefits include medical, dental, prescription, vision and life insurance; a 401(k) with company match; flexible spending accounts; an employee assistance program; and paid time off.

FINANCIAL DATA: Note: Data for latest year may not have been available at press time.

In U.S. $	2018	2017	2016	2015	2014	2013
Revenue	22,785,100,000	21,386,900,000	20,118,500,000	19,284,900,000	17,177,200,000	14,705,400,000
R&D Expense						
Operating Income	664,900,000	611,400,000	574,900,000	566,500,000	504,100,000	436,200,000
Operating Margin %		.03%	.03%	.03%	.03%	.03%
SGA Expense	2,646,300,000	2,516,000,000	2,302,000,000	2,223,000,000	1,999,600,000	1,761,900,000
Net Income	471,000,000	613,300,000	342,900,000	326,100,000	286,700,000	244,200,000
Operating Cash Flow	614,700,000	623,500,000	367,100,000	386,000,000	366,600,000	320,100,000
Capital Expenditure	305,600,000	247,000,000	203,100,000	199,500,000	174,800,000	169,900,000
EBITDA	903,400,000	814,100,000	734,100,000	683,800,000	630,900,000	528,600,000
Return on Assets %		.06%	.04%	.04%	.04%	.04%
Return on Equity %		.30%	.19%	.19%	.18%	.17%
Debt to Equity		0.873	1.044	0.701	0.796	0.687

CONTACT INFORMATION:
Phone: 248 648-2500 Fax: 248 648-2525
Toll-Free:
Address: 2555 Telegraph Rd., Bloomfield Hills, MI 48302 United States

SALARIES/BONUSES:
Top Exec. Salary: $1,400,000 Bonus: $
Second Exec. Salary: $547,917 Bonus: $350,000

STOCK TICKER/OTHER:
Stock Ticker: PAG
Employees: 24,000
Parent Company:

Exchange: NYS
Fiscal Year Ends: 12/31

OTHER THOUGHTS:
Estimated Female Officers or Directors: 2
Hot Spot for Advancement for Women/Minorities:

Sales, profits and employees may be estimates. Financial information, benefits and other data can change quickly and may vary from those stated here.

Penske Corporation

www.penske.com

NAIC Code: 532120

TYPES OF BUSINESS:
Truck Rental
Auto Racing
Auto Sales & Service
Supply Chain Solutions
Auto Accessories Manufacturing & Retail
Fuel Management Systems
Fleet Management Services
Vehicle Components & Systems

BRANDS/DIVISIONS/AFFILIATES:
Penske Automotive Group
Penske Motor Group
Penske Truck Leasing
Penske Logistics
Truck-Lite
Davco Technology LLC
Penske Racing
Ilmor Engineering Inc

CONTACTS:
Note: Officers with more than one job title may be intentionally listed here more than once.

Roger S. Penske, CEO
Robert H. Kurnick Jr., Pres.
Gregory J. Houfley, CFO
Robert H. Kurnick, Jr., Pres., Penske Automotive Group
Calvin C. Sharp, Exec. VP-Human Resources, Penske Automotive Group
David K. Jones, CFO
Shane M. Spradlin, General Counsel
Roger S. Penske, Chmn.
Marc Althen, Pres., Penske Logistics

GROWTH PLANS/SPECIAL FEATURES:

Penske Corporation is a diversified transportation company that participates in a variety of automotive markets through its network of subsidiaries. Its markets include auto sales and service, truck rental, supply chain solutions, vehicle headlight design and development, vehicle lighting and harness safety systems, fluid management and automobile racing. Penske Automotive Group is an international transportation services company that operates retail automotive dealerships, Hertz car rental franchises and commercial vehicle distribution. It operates primarily in the U.S., Western Europe, Australia and New Zealand. Penske Motor Group owns and operates automobile dealerships in California. Penske Truck Leasing operates over 240,000 vehicles, serving customers from more than 3,000 locations in North America, South America, Europe, Australia and Asia. This division comprises Penske Truck Rental, which offers fleet management services including service leasing, truck rentals, logistics, used trucks for sale and felt services for utility and transit companies with municipalities at more than 1,000 Penske facilities nationwide. Penske Logistics focuses on supply chain solutions, providing services designed to cut costs, reduce cycle time, improve service and integrate technology into the operations of its customers. Truck-Lite is responsible for creating vehicle lighting and harness safety systems for fleet vehicles through its affiliated subsidiaries: Truck-Lite Co., LLC and Truck-Lite Europe Limited. Davco Technology, LLC provides diesel fuel management with its line of filters, fuel/water separators and fuel warmers. Davco products include the Sea Pro for marine applications, Diesel Pro for medium trucks and the Industrial Pro for fuel filtration and water separation for industrial applications such as power generation, mining, oil and gas exploration. Penske Racing's operations include teams competing in NASCAR Sprint Cup Series, IndyCar Series, NASCAR Nationwide Series and American Le Mans Series. Other subsidiaries include Premier Truck Group, Penske Vehicle Service, Penske Logistics, and Ilmor Engineering, Inc.

FINANCIAL DATA:
Note: Data for latest year may not have been available at press time.

In U.S. $	2018	2017	2016	2015	2014	2013
Revenue	27,000,000,000	26,500,000,000	26,000,000,000	23,000,000,000	20,500,000,000	20,000,000,000
R&D Expense						
Operating Income						
Operating Margin %						
SGA Expense						
Net Income						
Operating Cash Flow						
Capital Expenditure						
EBITDA						
Return on Assets %						
Return on Equity %						
Debt to Equity						

CONTACT INFORMATION:
Phone: 248-648-2000 Fax: 248-648-2525
Toll-Free:
Address: 2555 Telegraph Rd., Bloomfield Hills, MI 48302 United States

SALARIES/BONUSES:
Top Exec. Salary: $ Bonus: $
Second Exec. Salary: $ Bonus: $

STOCK TICKER/OTHER:
Stock Ticker: Private
Employees: 52,000
Parent Company:

Exchange:
Fiscal Year Ends: 12/31

OTHER THOUGHTS:
Estimated Female Officers or Directors:
Hot Spot for Advancement for Women/Minorities:

Sales, profits and employees may be estimates. Financial information, benefits and other data can change quickly and may vary from those stated here.

PepsiCo Inc

NAIC Code: 312111

www.pepsico.com

TYPES OF BUSINESS:
- Soft Drink Manufacturing
- Snack Food Manufacturing
- Juice & Sports Drink Manufacturing
- Cereal Manufacturing
- Rice & Pasta Product Manufacturing
- Oatmeal Product Manufacturing
- Bottled Water Production
- Cereal Bar Manufacturing

BRANDS/DIVISIONS/AFFILIATES:
- Frito-Lay
- Quaker
- Doritos
- Pepsi
- Gamesa
- Walkers
- SodaStream
- Cheetos

CONTACTS:
Note: Officers with more than one job title may be intentionally listed here more than once.

- Vivek Sankaran, CEO, Divisional
- Paula Santilli, Pres., Geographical
- Kirk Tanner, CEO, Divisional
- Silviu Popovici, CEO, Geographical
- Mike Spanos, CEO, Geographical
- Laxman Narasimhan, CEO, Geographical
- Ramon Laguarta, CEO
- Hugh Johnston, CFO
- Marie Gallagher, Chief Accounting Officer
- Mehmood Khan, Chief Scientific Officer
- David Yawman, Executive VP, Divisional
- Ronald Schellekens, Executive VP

GROWTH PLANS/SPECIAL FEATURES:

PepsiCo, Inc. is a leading global food, snack and beverage company operating in six business units: Frito-Lay North America (FLNA); Quaker Foods North America (QFNA); North America Beverages (NAB); Latin America; Europe Sub-Saharan Africa (ESSA); and Asia, Middle East & North Africa (AMENA). FLNA manufactures markets, sells and distributes branded snacks including Lay's potato chips, Doritos, Cheetos, Fritos, Ruffles, Tostitos and Santitas. QFNA makes Aunt Jemima mixes and syrups, Quaker grits, Life cereal, and Rice-a-Roni side dishes. NAB makes, markets, distributes and sells beverage concentrates, fountain syrups and finished goods under various beverage brands including Pepsi, Gatorade, Mountain Dew, Diet Pepsi, Aquafina, Diet Mountain Dew, Tropicana Pure Premium, Mist Twst and Mug. Latin America offers several snack foods including Gamesa, Doritos, Cheetos, Ruffles, Lay's and Sabritas as well as Quaker brand cereals and snacks in Latin America. ESSA makes, markets, distributes and sells several leading snack food brands including Lay's, Walkers, Doritos, Cheetos and Ruffles, as well as many Quaker-branded cereals and snacks, through consolidated businesses as well as through noncontrolled affiliates. This division also manufactures and distributes sparkling water makers marketed under the SodaStream brand. AMENA makes, markets, distributes and sells a number of leading snack food brands including Lay's, Kurkure, Chipsy, Doritos, Cheetos and Crunchy through consolidated businesses, as well as through noncontrolled affiliates. In December 2018, PepsiCo acquired SodaStream International Ltd., a manufacturer and distributor of sparkling water makers.

PepsiCo offers employees medical, dental, vision, life, auto, home and disability insurance; 401(k) and retirement plans; and a variety of employee assistance programs.

FINANCIAL DATA:
Note: Data for latest year may not have been available at press time.

In U.S. $	2018	2017	2016	2015	2014	2013
Revenue	64,661,000,000	63,525,000,000	62,799,000,000	63,056,000,000	66,683,000,000	66,415,000,000
R&D Expense						
Operating Income	10,110,000,000	10,509,000,000	9,785,000,000	9,712,000,000	9,581,000,000	9,705,000,000
Operating Margin %		.17%	.16%	.15%	.14%	.15%
SGA Expense	25,170,000,000	24,231,000,000	24,735,000,000	24,885,000,000	26,126,000,000	25,357,000,000
Net Income	12,515,000,000	4,857,000,000	6,329,000,000	5,452,000,000	6,513,000,000	6,740,000,000
Operating Cash Flow	9,415,000,000	9,994,000,000	10,404,000,000	10,580,000,000	10,506,000,000	9,688,001,000
Capital Expenditure	3,282,000,000	2,969,000,000	3,040,000,000	2,758,000,000	2,859,000,000	2,795,000,000
EBITDA	13,113,000,000	13,122,000,000	12,263,000,000	10,828,000,000	12,291,000,000	12,465,000,000
Return on Assets %		.06%	.09%	.08%	.09%	.09%
Return on Equity %		.44%	.55%	.37%	.31%	.29%
Debt to Equity		3.115	2.719	2.459	1.369	1.004

CONTACT INFORMATION:
Phone: 914 253-2000 Fax:
Toll-Free:
Address: 700 Anderson Hill Rd., Purchase, NY 10577 United States

STOCK TICKER/OTHER:
Stock Ticker: PEP
Employees: 263,000
Parent Company:

Exchange: NAS
Fiscal Year Ends: 12/31

SALARIES/BONUSES:
Top Exec. Salary: $1,700,000 Bonus: $
Second Exec. Salary: $1,000,000 Bonus: $

OTHER THOUGHTS:
Estimated Female Officers or Directors: 10
Hot Spot for Advancement for Women/Minorities: Y

PerkinElmer Inc

www.perkinelmer.com

NAIC Code: 325413

TYPES OF BUSINESS:
Diagnostic Systems
Mechanical Components
Optoelectronics
Pharmaceutical Manufacturing
Life Science Systems
Environmental Safety Equipment

BRANDS/DIVISIONS/AFFILIATES:
AxION
Glutomatic
OilExpress
Supra-clean
DELFIA
VivoTag
ChemDraw
EnLite

CONTACTS:
Note: Officers with more than one job title may be intentionally listed here more than once.

Robert Friel, CEO
James Mock, CFO
Andrew Okun, Chief Accounting Officer
Prahlad Singh, COO
James Corbett, Executive VP
Joel Goldberg, General Counsel
Deborah Butters, Other Executive Officer
Daniel Tereau, Senior VP, Divisional
Tajinder Vohra, Senior VP, Divisional

GROWTH PLANS/SPECIAL FEATURES:
PerkinElmer, Inc. provides technology, services and solutions for the diagnostics, food, environmental, industrial, life sciences research and laboratory services markets. The company operates through two segments: discovery and analytical solutions, and diagnostics. The discovery and analytical solutions segment comprises a portfolio of technologies that help life sciences researchers better understand diseases and develop treatments. This division also helps the ability to detect, monitor and manage contaminants and toxic chemicals impacting the environment and food supply. Just a few of the many product, services and application solutions developed by this segment include: gas chromatographs, mass spectrometers, sample-handling equipment, advanced liquid chromatography systems, analyzers, quantitative pathology research solutions, radiometric detection solutions, screening systems and plate readers. The diagnostics segment offers instruments, reagents, assay platforms and software to hospitals, medical labs, clinicians and medical research professionals. This division focuses on reproductive health, emerging market diagnostics and applied genomics. Products, services and application solutions include screening platforms, in vitro diagnostic kits, blood analyzing kits, informatics data management, X-ray detectors, umbilical cord blood banking services, automated liquid handling platforms, next-generation sequencing automation and nucleic acid quantitation and automated small-scale purification. Brand names include AxION, Glutomatic, OilExpress, Supra-clean, DELFIA, VivoTag, ChemDraw, Asset Genius, EnLite, ViaCord and JANUS. PerkinElmer is headquartered in Waltham, Massachusetts, and markets its products and services in more than 150 countries.

FINANCIAL DATA:
Note: Data for latest year may not have been available at press time.

In U.S. $	2018	2017	2016	2015	2014	2013
Revenue	2,777,996,000	2,256,982,000	2,115,517,000	2,262,359,000	2,237,219,000	2,166,232,000
R&D Expense	193,998,000	139,404,000	124,278,000	125,928,000	121,141,000	133,023,000
Operating Income	335,028,000	317,460,000	288,190,000	299,724,000	224,132,000	258,101,000
Operating Margin %		.14%	.14%	.13%	.10%	.12%
SGA Expense	811,913,000	616,167,000	600,885,000	598,848,000	659,335,000	585,850,000
Net Income	237,927,000	292,633,000	234,299,000	212,425,000	157,778,000	167,212,000
Operating Cash Flow	311,038,000	288,453,000	350,615,000	287,098,000	281,597,000	158,591,000
Capital Expenditure	93,253,000	39,089,000	31,702,000	29,632,000	29,072,000	38,991,000
EBITDA	505,247,000	445,658,000	385,568,000	394,019,000	322,609,000	331,727,000
Return on Assets %		.06%	.06%	.05%	.04%	.04%
Return on Equity %		.13%	.11%	.10%	.08%	.09%
Debt to Equity		0.715	0.485	0.479	0.515	0.467

CONTACT INFORMATION:
Phone: 781 663-6900 Fax:
Toll-Free: 800-762-4000
Address: 940 Winter St., Waltham, MA 02451 United States

STOCK TICKER/OTHER:
Stock Ticker: PKI
Employees: 8,000
Parent Company:

Exchange: NYS
Fiscal Year Ends: 01/31

SALARIES/BONUSES:
Top Exec. Salary: $1,097,030 Bonus: $
Second Exec. Salary: $331,154 Bonus: $400,000

OTHER THOUGHTS:
Estimated Female Officers or Directors: 1
Hot Spot for Advancement for Women/Minorities: Y

PetSmart Inc

www.petsmart.com

NAIC Code: 453910

TYPES OF BUSINESS:
Pets & Pet Supplies, Retail
Online & Catalog Sales
Pet Training
In-Store Adoption Centers
Veterinary Services
Pet Boarding
Pet Grooming

BRANDS/DIVISIONS/AFFILIATES:
Argos Holdings Inc
PetSmart.com
PetPerks
Medical Management International Inc
Banfield Pet Hospital
PetSmart PetHotels
Chewy Inc
Chewy.com

CONTACTS: Note: Officers with more than one job title may be intentionally listed here more than once.
J.K. Symancyk, CEO
Alan Schnaid, CFO
Donald Beaver, Chief Information Officer
Paulette Dodson, General Counsel
Erick Goldberg, Senior VP, Divisional
Bruce Thorn, Senior VP, Divisional
Jaye Perricone, Senior VP, Divisional
Matthew McAdam, Senior VP, Divisional
Melvin Tucker, Senior VP, Divisional
Gene Burt, Senior VP, Divisional

GROWTH PLANS/SPECIAL FEATURES:

PetSmart, Inc. is a leading operator of superstores specializing in pet food, supplies and services. The company operates over 1,650 stores in the U.S., Puerto Rico and Canada, which offer an assortment of pet services and products. Its stores range in size from 12,000 to 27,500 square feet and carry roughly 11,000 distinct items in store and 9,000 additional items online through PetSmart.com. These items include nationally recognized brand names and a selection of proprietary or private label brands. PetSmart stores sell supplies for dogs, cats, fresh-water tropical fish, reptiles, birds and other small pets. The firm offers a PetPerks loyalty program to its customers. PetSmart stores also offer value-added pet services including grooming, training, boarding and day camp; and it operates full-service veterinary hospitals in many of its stores. Medical Management International, Inc., an operator of veterinary hospitals, operates more than 800 of PetSmart's hospitals under the name Banfield Pet Hospital. The remaining seven hospitals are located in Canada and operated by other third parties. PetSmart offers pet boarding in more than 200 stores through its PetSmart PetsHotels. PetsHotels provide boarding for dogs and cats, which includes 24-hour supervision by caregivers who are PetSmart-trained to provide personalized pet care, temperature-controlled rooms and suites and play time as well as day camp for dogs. The company also actively supports pet adoption through its in-store adoption centers. Independent subsidiary Chewy, Inc. operates an eCommerce pet platform at chewy.com, offering thousands of products and 24/7 support services. PetSmart is privately-owned by Argos Holdings, Inc.

PetSmart offers employees medical, dental and vision insurance; life and AD&D insurance; short- and long-term disability; a 401(k) plan; and various employee assistance programs.

FINANCIAL DATA: Note: Data for latest year may not have been available at press time.

In U.S. $	2018	2017	2016	2015	2014	2013
Revenue	9,912,500,000	7,125,000,000	7,050,000,000	7,000,000,000	6,916,626,944	6,758,237,184
R&D Expense						
Operating Income						
Operating Margin %						
SGA Expense						
Net Income						
Operating Cash Flow						
Capital Expenditure						
EBITDA						
Return on Assets %						
Return on Equity %						
Debt to Equity						

CONTACT INFORMATION:
Phone: 623 580-6100 Fax:
Toll-Free: 800-738-1385
Address: 19601 N. 27th Ave., Phoenix, AZ 85027 United States

SALARIES/BONUSES:
Top Exec. Salary: $ Bonus: $
Second Exec. Salary: $ Bonus: $

STOCK TICKER/OTHER:
Stock Ticker: Private Exchange:
Employees: 65,000 Fiscal Year Ends: 01/31
Parent Company: Argos Holdings Inc

OTHER THOUGHTS:
Estimated Female Officers or Directors: 3
Hot Spot for Advancement for Women/Minorities: Y

Sales, profits and employees may be estimates. Financial information, benefits and other data can change quickly and may vary from those stated here.

Pfizer Inc

www.pfizer.com

NAIC Code: 325412

TYPES OF BUSINESS:
Pharmaceuticals
Infusion Technologies

BRANDS/DIVISIONS/AFFILIATES:
Prevnar 13
Xeljanz
Eliquis
Lyrica
Enbrel
Lipitor
Celebrex

CONTACTS:
Note: Officers with more than one job title may be intentionally listed here more than once.

Albert Bourla, CEO
Michael Goettler, Pres., Divisional
Frank DAmelio, CFO
Ian Read, Chairman of the Board
Loretta Cangialosi, Chief Accounting Officer
Rady Johnson, Chief Risk Officer
Mikael Dolsten, Chief Scientific Officer
Lidia Fonseca, Chief Technology Officer
Sally Susman, Executive VP, Divisional
Douglas Lankler, Executive VP
Freda Lewis-Hall, Executive VP
Alexander Mackenzie, Executive VP
Dawn Rogers, Executive VP
John Young, Other Executive Officer
Margaret Madden, Other Executive Officer
Angela Hwang, President, Divisional

GROWTH PLANS/SPECIAL FEATURES:

Pfizer, Inc. is a research-based, global pharmaceutical company that discovers, develops, manufactures and markets healthcare products. Pfizer operates in two business segments: innovative health and essential health. The innovative health segment focuses on developing and commercializing novel, value-creating medicines and vaccines that significantly improve patients' lives, as well as products for consumer healthcare. Key therapeutic areas within this division include internal medicine, vaccines, oncology, inflammation/immunology, rare diseases and consumer healthcare. Leading brands within this segment include Prevnar 13, Xeljanz, Eliquis, Lyrica, Enbrel, Ibrance, Xtandi, Chantix/Champix and several over-the-counter (OTC) consumer products. The essential health segment comprises legacy brands that have lost or will soon lose market exclusivity in both developed and emerging markets. These branded products include generics, generic sterile injectable products and biosimilars. This division also includes a research and development organization, as well as the company's manufacturing business. Brands within this segment include Lipitor, Norvasc, Lyrica (within Europe, Russia, Turkey, Israel and Central Asia countries), Celebrex, Viagra, Inflectra/Remsima and Sulperazon, as well as several sterile injectable products. In December 2018, Pfizer and GlaxoSmithKline plc agreed to combine their consumer healthcare businesses into a new joint venture that will operate globally under the GSK Consumer Healthcare name; the transaction was expected to close mid-2019, and subject to shareholder and regulatory approvals. In July 2019, the firm agreed to merge its off-patent drug business, Upjohn, with Mylan NV, creating a new, yet to be named company. This new company, 57% controlled by Pfizer and 43% by Mylan, is expected to be among the world's sellers of generic and off-patent medicines. The deal is expected to close by mid 2020.

FINANCIAL DATA:
Note: Data for latest year may not have been available at press time.

In U.S. $	2018	2017	2016	2015	2014	2013
Revenue	53,647,000,000	52,546,000,000	52,824,000,000	48,851,000,000	49,605,000,000	51,584,000,000
R&D Expense	8,006,000,000	7,657,000,000	7,872,000,000	7,690,000,000	8,393,000,000	6,678,000,000
Operating Income	15,045,000,000	14,107,000,000	13,730,000,000	12,976,000,000	13,499,000,000	16,366,000,000
Operating Margin %		.27%	.26%	.27%	.27%	.32%
SGA Expense	14,455,000,000	14,784,000,000	14,837,000,000	14,809,000,000	14,097,000,000	14,355,000,000
Net Income	11,153,000,000	21,308,000,000	7,215,000,000	6,960,000,000	9,135,000,000	22,003,000,000
Operating Cash Flow	15,827,000,000	16,470,000,000	15,901,000,000	14,512,000,000	16,883,000,000	17,765,000,000
Capital Expenditure	2,196,000,000	2,217,000,000	1,999,000,000	1,496,000,000	1,583,000,000	1,465,000,000
EBITDA	19,585,000,000	19,844,000,000	15,294,000,000	15,321,000,000	19,137,000,000	23,540,000,000
Return on Assets %		.12%	.04%	.04%	.05%	.12%
Return on Equity %		.33%	.12%	.10%	.12%	.28%
Debt to Equity		0.47	0.528	0.445	0.443	0.399

CONTACT INFORMATION:
Phone: 212 733-2323   Fax: 212 573-7851
Toll-Free:
Address: 235 E. 42nd St., New York, NY 10017 United States

STOCK TICKER/OTHER:
Stock Ticker: PFE
Employees: 96,500
Parent Company:

Exchange: NYS
Fiscal Year Ends: 12/31

SALARIES/BONUSES:
Top Exec. Salary: $1,992,500   Bonus: $
Second Exec. Salary: $1,407,917   Bonus: $

OTHER THOUGHTS:
Estimated Female Officers or Directors: 7
Hot Spot for Advancement for Women/Minorities: Y

Pharmaceutical Product Development LLC

www.ppdi.com

NAIC Code: 541711

TYPES OF BUSINESS:
Contract Research
Drug Discovery & Development Services
Clinical Data Consulting Services
Medical Marketing & Information Support Services
Drug Discovery Services
Medical Device Development

BRANDS/DIVISIONS/AFFILIATES:
Carlyle Group (The)
Hellman & Friedman

CONTACTS:
Note: Officers with more than one job title may be intentionally listed here more than once.

David Simmons, CEO
Christine A. Dingivan, Chief Medical Officer
B. Judd Hartman, General Counsel
William W. Richardson, Sr. VP-Global Bus. Dev.
Randy Buckwalter, Head-Media
Luke Heagle, Head-Investor Rel.
Lee E. Babiss, Chief Science Officer
David Johnston, Exec. VP-Global Lab Svcs.
David Simmons, Chmn.
Paul Colvin, Exec. VP-Global Clinical Dev.

GROWTH PLANS/SPECIAL FEATURES:

Pharmaceutical Product Development, LLC (PPD), jointly owned by The Carlyle Group and Hellman & Friedman, provides drug discovery and development services to pharmaceutical, biotechnology, medical device, academic and government organizations. PPD's services are divided into eight segments: early development, which offers a range of early development services, phase 1 clinical trial services and non-clinical consulting; clinical development, which helps advance drug research and development for products; PPD Biotech, offering custom phase I-IV clinical development solutions for biotech and small-to-midsize pharmaceutical companies; PPD Laboratories, which provides comprehensive lab services; post-approval, which provides post-approval studies and late-stage clinical trials management; PPD Consulting, which acts as a consulting partner that assists companies with their biopharmaceutical product's success from pre-clinical through post-approval; functional service partnerships, provides customizable outsourcing solutions, including full-time equivalent models, units-based contracts and geographical-aligned agreements; and technology/innovation/performance, which helps companies deliver life-changing medicines, cutting-edge technologies, real-time analytics and customized training. Therapeutic areas of studies include cardiovascular, critical care, dermatology, dental pain research, endocrine and metabolics, gastroenterology, hematology and oncology, immunology, infectious diseases, neuroscience, ophthalmology, respiratory and urology. PPD is headquartered in North Carolina, USA, with more than 90 additional offices spanning 48 countries. In February 2019, PPD and Happy Lift Tech (of China) signed an agreement to develop a distinctive service offering for the China drug-development market, delivering data science-driven clinical trials and evidence of drug products' effectiveness, safety and value.

FINANCIAL DATA:
Note: Data for latest year may not have been available at press time.

In U.S. $	2018	2017	2016	2015	2014	2013
Revenue	1,400,000,000	1,350,000,000	1,300,000,000	1,200,000,000	1,222,000,000	1,023,100,000
R&D Expense						
Operating Income						
Operating Margin %						
SGA Expense						
Net Income						
Operating Cash Flow						
Capital Expenditure						
EBITDA						
Return on Assets %						
Return on Equity %						
Debt to Equity						

CONTACT INFORMATION:
Phone: 910-251-0081   Fax: 910-762-5820
Toll-Free:
Address: 929 N. Front St., Wilmington, NC 28401-3331 United States

STOCK TICKER/OTHER:
Stock Ticker: Private   Exchange:
Employees: 21,000   Fiscal Year Ends: 12/31
Parent Company: Carlyle Group (The)

SALARIES/BONUSES:
Top Exec. Salary: $ Bonus: $
Second Exec. Salary: $ Bonus: $

OTHER THOUGHTS:
Estimated Female Officers or Directors: 2
Hot Spot for Advancement for Women/Minorities:

Philips Healthcare

www.healthcare.philips.com

NAIC Code: 334510

TYPES OF BUSINESS:
Manufacturing-Medical Equipment
Diagnostic & Treatment Equipment
Imaging Equipment
Equipment Repair & Maintenance
Healthcare Consulting

BRANDS/DIVISIONS/AFFILIATES:
Koninklijke Philips NV
Medumo

CONTACTS:
Note: Officers with more than one job title may be intentionally listed here more than once.

Frans van Houten, CEO-Koninklijke Philips
Eric Silfen, Chief Medical Officer
Clement Revetti, Chief Legal Officer
Michael Dreher, Global Head-Oper. & Customer Svcs.
Diego Olego, Chief Strategy & Innovation Officer
Rachel Bloom-Baglin, Media Contact-Global
Frans van Houten, CEO-Royal Philips Electronics NV
Steve Laczynski, Pres., Americas
Desmond Thio, Pres., China
Brent Shafer, CEO-Home Health Care Solutions
Arjen Radder, Pres., Asia Pacific

GROWTH PLANS/SPECIAL FEATURES:
Philips Healthcare, a subsidiary of Koninklijke Philips NV, manufactures medical diagnostic and treatment solutions, distributing its products to more than 100 countries worldwide. The company's many products and services address advanced molecular imaging, breathing/respiratory care, clinical informatics, computed tomography machines/solutions, customer service solutions, diagnostic electrocardiogram (ECG), electroencephalogram (EEG) neuroimaging, emergency care and resuscitation solutions, enterprise telehealth, fluoroscopy, hospital respiratory care, image-guided therapy devices, interventional X-ray systems and solutions, medical parts and related supplies, mother/child care, magnetic resonance imaging (MRI) systems and solutions, pathology, patient monitoring, radiation oncology, radiography, refurbished systems, sleep and ultrasounds. Philips Healthcare provides integrated solutions across the health continuum, from healthy living and prevention to diagnosis, treatment and home care. In mid-2019, Philips Healthcare acquired Boston-based startup company, Medumo, which has developed a diagnostic patient management platform for healthcare providers to deliver patient engagement and education services.

FINANCIAL DATA:
Note: Data for latest year may not have been available at press time.

In U.S. $	2018	2017	2016	2015	2014	2013
Revenue	20,726,700,000	21,298,000,000	20,196,679,771	14,406,749,346	12,100,715,917	12,574,865,989
R&D Expense						
Operating Income						
Operating Margin %						
SGA Expense						
Net Income	1,254,740,000	2,240,000,000	1,570,860,000	697,041,000	748,736,000	976,696,340
Operating Cash Flow						
Capital Expenditure						
EBITDA						
Return on Assets %						
Return on Equity %						
Debt to Equity						

CONTACT INFORMATION:
Phone: 978-659-3000 Fax:
Toll-Free: 800-722-9377
Address: 3000 Minuteman Rd., Andover, MA 01810 United States

STOCK TICKER/OTHER:
Stock Ticker: Subsidiary
Employees: 77,400
Parent Company: Koninklijke Philips NV

Exchange:
Fiscal Year Ends: 12/31

SALARIES/BONUSES:
Top Exec. Salary: $ Bonus: $
Second Exec. Salary: $ Bonus: $

OTHER THOUGHTS:
Estimated Female Officers or Directors: 2
Hot Spot for Advancement for Women/Minorities:

Sales, profits and employees may be estimates. Financial information, benefits and other data can change quickly and may vary from those stated here.

Phillips 66

www.phillips66.com

NAIC Code: 324110

TYPES OF BUSINESS:
Petroleum Refineries
Natural Gas Gathering
Gasoline Marketing
Chemicals Interests

BRANDS/DIVISIONS/AFFILIATES:
DCP Midstream LLC
Phillips 66 Partners LP
Chevron Phillips Chemical Company LLC

CONTACTS:
Note: Officers with more than one job title may be intentionally listed here more than once.

Greg Garland, CEO
Kevin Mitchell, CFO
Robert Herman, Executive VP, Divisional
Timothy Roberts, Executive VP, Divisional
Paula Johnson, Executive VP, Divisional
Paula Johnson, Executive VP, Divisional
Brian Mandell, Senior VP, Divisional
Chukwuemeka Oyolu, Vice President

GROWTH PLANS/SPECIAL FEATURES:

Phillips 66 is a downstream energy company engaged in refining, marketing and distributing petroleum products as well as power generation. Previously a unit of ConocoPhillips, Phillips 66 is organized into four operating segments: refining, marketing & specialties (M&S), midstream and chemicals. The company's refining operations include 13 refineries with a net crude oil capacity of 2.18 million barrels per day (bpd). This segment buys, sells and refines crude oil and other feedstocks into petroleum products such as gasolines, distillates and aviation fuels. The M&S segment purchases refined petroleum products such as gasolines, distillates and aviation fuels for resale and markets, mainly in the U.S. and Europe. This segment includes the manufacturing and marketing of specialty products as well as power generation operations. The midstream segment comprises three business lines: transportation, which transports crude oil and other feedstocks to refineries and other locations, delivers refined and specialty products to market and provides storage services for crude oil and petroleum products; DCP Midstream LLC, which gathers, processes, transports and markets natural gas and transports, fractionates and markets natural gas liquids (NGL); and NGL, which transports, fractionates and markets NGL. The midstream segment also includes subsidiary Phillips 66 Partners LP, which owns, operates, develops and acquires fee-based crude oil, refined petroleum product and NGL pipelines and terminals as well as other transportation and midstream assets. The chemicals segment manufactures and markets petrochemicals and plastics on a worldwide basis. This segment includes its 50% interest in Chevron Phillips Chemical Company LLC, one of the world's top producers of olefins and polyolefins.

FINANCIAL DATA:
Note: Data for latest year may not have been available at press time.

In U.S. $	2018	2017	2016	2015	2014	2013
Revenue	111,461,000,000	102,354,000,000	84,279,000,000	98,975,000,000	161,212,000,000	171,596,000,000
R&D Expense						
Operating Income	5,209,000,000	1,838,000,000	1,098,000,000	4,548,000,000	3,430,000,000	2,666,000,000
Operating Margin %		.02%	.01%	.05%	.02%	.02%
SGA Expense	1,677,000,000	1,695,000,000	1,638,000,000	1,670,000,000	1,663,000,000	1,478,000,000
Net Income	5,595,000,000	5,106,000,000	1,555,000,000	4,227,000,000	4,762,000,000	3,726,000,000
Operating Cash Flow	7,573,000,000	3,648,000,000	2,963,000,000	5,713,000,000	3,529,000,000	6,027,000,000
Capital Expenditure	2,639,000,000	1,832,000,000	2,844,000,000	5,764,000,000	3,773,000,000	1,779,000,000
EBITDA	9,305,000,000	5,311,000,000	3,697,000,000	7,432,000,000	7,007,000,000	6,748,000,000
Return on Assets %		.10%	.03%	.09%	.10%	.08%
Return on Equity %		.22%	.07%	.19%	.22%	.17%
Debt to Equity		0.401	0.428	0.383	0.363	0.279

CONTACT INFORMATION:
Phone: 281-293-6600 Fax:
Toll-Free:
Address: 3010 Briarpark Dr., Houston, TX 77042 United States

SALARIES/BONUSES:
Top Exec. Salary: $1,675,008 Bonus: $
Second Exec. Salary: $826,696 Bonus: $

STOCK TICKER/OTHER:
Stock Ticker: PSX
Employees: 14,800
Parent Company:

Exchange: NYS
Fiscal Year Ends: 12/31

OTHER THOUGHTS:
Estimated Female Officers or Directors: 4
Hot Spot for Advancement for Women/Minorities: Y

PPG Industries Inc

NAIC Code: 325510

corporate.ppg.com

TYPES OF BUSINESS:
Automotive Paints
Coatings
Glass
Chemicals
Fiberglass
Industrial Products

BRANDS/DIVISIONS/AFFILIATES:
PPG
Glidden
Comex
Olympic
Dulux
Homax
SEM
RIPOLIN

CONTACTS: Note: Officers with more than one job title may be intentionally listed here more than once.
Michael McGarry, CEO
Vincent Morales, CFO
William Schaupp, Chief Accounting Officer
Anne Foulkes, General Counsel
Timothy Knavish, President, Geographical
Ramaparasad Vadlamannati, Senior VP, Divisional
Rebecca Liebert, Senior VP, Divisional
Amy Ericson, Senior VP, Divisional

GROWTH PLANS/SPECIAL FEATURES:
PPG Industries, Inc. is a global manufacturer of decorative and protective coatings that operates in three business segments: performance coatings and industrial coatings. The performance coatings and industrial coatings reportable segments supply coatings and specialty materials for customers in a wide array of end-use markets, including industrial equipment and components, packaging material; aircraft and marine equipment; automotive original equipment; as well as for other industrial and consumer products. In addition to supplying coatings to the automotive original equipment market, PPG supplies refinishes to the automotive aftermarket. PPG also serves commercial and residential new build and maintenance markets by supplying coatings to painting and maintenance contractors and directly to consumers for decoration and maintenance. These coatings are sold under the PPG, SEM, Glidden, Comex, Olympic, Dulux, Sikkens, Mulco, Flood, Liquid Nails, Sico, CIL, Renner, Taubman's, White Knight, Bristol and Homax brands in the U.S. and Asia Pacific. In the EMEA, these coatings are sold under IGMA, HISTOR, SEIGNEURIE, GUITTET, PEINTURES GAUTHIER, RIPOLIN, JOHNSTONE'S, LEYLAND, PRIMALEX, DEKORAL, TRILAK, PROMINENT PAINTS, GORI, BONDEX and DANKE! Brands

FINANCIAL DATA: Note: Data for latest year may not have been available at press time.

In U.S. $	2018	2017	2016	2015	2014	2013
Revenue	15,374,000,000	14,750,000,000	14,751,000,000	15,330,000,000	15,360,000,000	15,108,000,000
R&D Expense	441,000,000	453,000,000	466,000,000	486,000,000	492,000,000	488,000,000
Operating Income	1,872,000,000	2,074,000,000	2,113,000,000	2,118,000,000	1,893,000,000	1,858,000,000
Operating Margin %		.14%	.08%	.14%	.12%	.12%
SGA Expense	3,573,000,000	3,570,000,000	3,662,000,000	3,679,000,000	3,758,000,000	3,699,000,000
Net Income	1,341,000,000	1,591,000,000	877,000,000	1,406,000,000	2,102,000,000	3,231,000,000
Operating Cash Flow	1,467,000,000	1,568,000,000	1,325,000,000	1,837,000,000	1,528,000,000	1,791,000,000
Capital Expenditure	411,000,000	360,000,000	402,000,000	476,000,000	587,000,000	515,000,000
EBITDA	2,308,000,000	2,573,000,000	1,414,000,000	2,503,000,000	2,079,000,000	2,160,000,000
Return on Assets %		.10%	.05%	.08%	.13%	.20%
Return on Equity %		.31%	.18%	.28%	.42%	.72%
Debt to Equity		0.744	0.785	0.811	0.684	0.684

CONTACT INFORMATION:
Phone: 412 434-3131 Fax: 412 434-2571
Toll-Free:
Address: 1 PPG Pl., Pittsburgh, PA 15272 United States

SALARIES/BONUSES:
Top Exec. Salary: $1,258,333 Bonus: $
Second Exec. Salary: $569,167 Bonus: $

STOCK TICKER/OTHER:
Stock Ticker: PPG Exchange: NYS
Employees: 47,000 Fiscal Year Ends: 12/31
Parent Company:

OTHER THOUGHTS:
Estimated Female Officers or Directors: 6
Hot Spot for Advancement for Women/Minorities: Y

PRA Health Sciences Inc

NAIC Code: 541711

prahs.com

TYPES OF BUSINESS:
Clinical Research & Testing Services
Clinical Development Services
Clinical Trials
Data Management Services

BRANDS/DIVISIONS/AFFILIATES:

CONTACTS:
Note: Officers with more than one job title may be intentionally listed here more than once.
Colin Shannon, CEO
Michael Bonello, CFO

GROWTH PLANS/SPECIAL FEATURES:

PRA Health Sciences is a contract research organization (CRO) that provides clinical drug development and data solution services to pharmaceutical and biotechnology companies worldwide. The firm's therapeutic focus areas include oncology, immunology, central nervous system (CNS), inflammation, respiratory, cardiometabolic and infectious diseases. PRA's global clinical development platform encompasses more than 70 offices across North America, Europe, Asia, Latin America, South Africa, Australia and the Middle East. Since 2000, PRA has participated in more than 3,800 clinical trials, and conducted trials that led to U.S. Food and Drug Administration (FDA) or international regulatory approval of more than 85 drugs. The stages of clinical development span discovery, preclinical testing, Phase 1, 2 and 3, FDA review for approval, and Phase 4/post-marketing testing. The process from discovery through Phase 3 can take from four to nine years. PRA's data solutions division provides data, analytics, technology and consulting solutions to the life sciences market. It has proprietary sources of data about pharmaceutical transactions that it purchases from pharmaceutical retailers, prescribers, payers and institutional users. The data is anonymized and includes details on the patient, the location where they purchased the drug or therapy, and the payer. The details on the patient are tracked in such a way as to allow analysis of therapies and purchasing over a long term. The data is refreshed monthly. During 2016, 2017 and 2018, Kohlberg Kravis Roberts & Co. LP sold its shares in PRA Health, transitioning from wholly owning PRA to owning 10.2% of its stock as of December 31, 2018.

The firm offers employees comprehensive medical benefits, life insurance, retirement programs, holidays and paid time off, tuition advance payment programs and a scholarship program for employee dependents.

FINANCIAL DATA:
Note: Data for latest year may not have been available at press time.

In U.S. $	2018	2017	2016	2015	2014	2013
Revenue	2,871,922,000	2,259,389,000	1,811,711,000	1,613,883,000	1,459,586,000	
R&D Expense						
Operating Income	281,432,000	176,583,000	163,102,000	164,950,000	56,844,000	
Operating Margin %		.08%	.09%	.10%	.04%	.01%
SGA Expense	371,795,000	321,987,000	269,893,000	246,417,000	253,970,000	
Net Income	153,905,000	86,927,000	68,175,000	81,765,000	-35,742,000	
Operating Cash Flow	329,792,000	220,408,000	160,047,000	153,676,000	22,747,000	25,269,000
Capital Expenditure	55,880,000	61,318,000	33,143,000	32,814,000	27,323,000	19,716,000
EBITDA	393,679,000	254,810,000	232,608,000	242,902,000	153,408,000	
Return on Assets %		.03%	.03%	.04%	-.02%	-.04%
Return on Equity %		.10%	.10%	.12%	-.06%	-.19%
Debt to Equity		1.317	1.093	1.266	1.401	2.666

CONTACT INFORMATION:
Phone: 919-786-8200 Fax: 919-786-8201
Toll-Free:
Address: 4130 Park Lake Ave., Ste. 400, Raleigh, NC 27612 United States

STOCK TICKER/OTHER:
Stock Ticker: PRAH
Employees: 13,000
Parent Company:

Exchange: NAS
Fiscal Year Ends: 12/31

SALARIES/BONUSES:
Top Exec. Salary: $930,000 Bonus: $570,000
Second Exec. Salary: $390,000 Bonus: $250,000

OTHER THOUGHTS:
Estimated Female Officers or Directors: 2
Hot Spot for Advancement for Women/Minorities: Y

PriceSmart Inc

NAIC Code: 452910

www.pricesmart.com

TYPES OF BUSINESS:
Warehouse Clubs, Retail
Merchandise
Warehouse Club Membership

BRANDS/DIVISIONS/AFFILIATES:
Aeropost Inc

CONTACTS:
Note: Officers with more than one job title may be intentionally listed here more than once.

Sherry Bahrambeygui, CEO
Maarten Jager, CFO
Robert Price, Chairman of the Board
William Naylon, COO
Frank Diaz, Executive VP, Divisional
Rodrigo Calvo, Executive VP, Divisional
Brud Drachman, Executive VP, Divisional
John Hildebrandt, Executive VP, Divisional
Laura Santana, Executive VP, Divisional
Jesus Von Chong, Executive VP, Geographical
Francisco Velasco, Executive VP
Ana Bianchi, Executive VP

GROWTH PLANS/SPECIAL FEATURES:

PriceSmart, Inc. is one of the largest operators of warehouse membership clubs in Central America, the Caribbean and South America. The company serves over 3 million cardholders at 41 owned and operated warehouse clubs. PriceSmart's typical warehouse buildings range in sales floor size from 50,000 to 60,000 square feet, and are located primarily in and around the major cities of its markets. The firm also constructs smaller sales floor warehouse clubs so as to reach additional geographic areas. PriceSmart's membership club model is similar to U.S. clubs like Costco and Sam's, with some differences: smaller store size, lower membership fees (average $30), and merchandise is tailored to local preferences as well as for retail and wholesale customers. PriceSmart warehouse clubs can be found in Colombia, 7; Costa Rica, 7; Panama, 5; Trinidad and Tobago, 4; Dominican Republic, 4; Guatemala, 3; Honduras, 3; El Salvador, 2; Nicaragua, 2; and one each in Aruba, Barbados, Jamaica and the U.S. Virgin Islands. Online shopping is available to its members in all countries. Merchandise departments include electronics, computers, baby, automotive, restaurant/institutional, sporting goods, outdoor, hardware, toys and games, appliances, housewares, bed and bath, luggage, healthcare, furniture, office and fashion accessories. During 2018, PriceSmart acquired Aeropost, Inc., a cross-border freight forwarding business that also operates an online marketplace. It provides logistics, payment and eCommerce services in Latin America and the Caribbean, with Costa Rica, Trinidad and Jamaica being its largest markets.

FINANCIAL DATA:
Note: Data for latest year may not have been available at press time.

In U.S. $	2018	2017	2016	2015	2014	2013
Revenue	3,166,702,000	2,996,628,000	2,905,176,000	2,802,603,000	2,517,567,000	2,299,812,000
R&D Expense						
Operating Income	129,320,000	138,431,000	137,885,000	148,371,000	138,152,000	127,935,000
Operating Margin %		.05%	.05%	.05%	.05%	.06%
SGA Expense	88,461,000	69,772,000	64,344,000	56,371,000	49,944,000	46,784,000
Net Income	74,328,000	90,724,000	88,723,000	89,124,000	92,886,000	84,265,000
Operating Cash Flow	119,454,000	122,856,000	139,862,000	110,503,000	137,275,000	130,633,000
Capital Expenditure	98,109,000	135,294,000	77,700,000	89,185,000	118,101,000	69,927,000
EBITDA	180,299,000	185,812,000	176,925,000	177,481,000	167,019,000	151,871,000
Return on Assets %		.08%	.08%	.09%	.10%	.11%
Return on Equity %		.13%	.14%	.16%	.18%	.18%
Debt to Equity		0.124	0.115	0.129	0.145	0.125

CONTACT INFORMATION:
Phone: 858 404-8800   Fax: 858 404-8848
Toll-Free:
Address: 9740 Scranton Rd., San Diego, CA 92121 United States

SALARIES/BONUSES:
Top Exec. Salary: $762,654   Bonus: $
Second Exec. Salary: $543,526   Bonus: $

STOCK TICKER/OTHER:
Stock Ticker: PSMT
Employees: 8,680
Parent Company:

Exchange: NAS
Fiscal Year Ends: 08/31

OTHER THOUGHTS:
Estimated Female Officers or Directors: 4
Hot Spot for Advancement for Women/Minorities: Y

PricewaterhouseCoopers (PwC)

NAIC Code: 541211

www.pwc.com

TYPES OF BUSINESS:
Accounting Services
Business Advisory
Corporate Finance Services
Employee Benefits Services
Tax Services
Business Publications
Management Consulting

BRANDS/DIVISIONS/AFFILIATES:

CONTACTS: Note: Officers with more than one job title may be intentionally listed here more than once.
Martyn Curragh, CFO
Mike Fenlon, Chief People Officer
Gary Price, Chief Admin. Officer
Diana Weiss, General Counsel
Robert E. Moritz, Chmn.
Mitch Cohen, Vice Chmn.
Terri McClements, Head-U.S. Human Capital & Public Policy
Laura Cox Kaplan, Head-Regulation Affairs & Public Policy
Tim Ryan, Chmn.

GROWTH PLANS/SPECIAL FEATURES:

PricewaterhouseCoopers (PwC) is a global accounting firm with offices in more than 155 countries. PwC provides the following services: audit/assurance, consulting, entrepreneurial/private clients, family business, IFRS (a global financial reporting language), legal, people/organization, sustainability/climate change and tax. PwC covers such areas as cybersecurity and privacy, human resources, deals and forensics. The company serves a wide array of industry sectors, including aerospace/defense, asset and wealth management, automotive, banking/capital markets, capital projects, infrastructure, chemicals, communications, energy, utilities, mining, engineering, construction, entertainment/media, financial services, forest/paper/packaging, government services, public services, healthcare, hospitality/leisure, industrial manufacturing, insurance, metals, pharmaceuticals, life sciences, private equity, real estate, retail, consumer, sovereign wealth funds, technology and transportation and logistics. PwC is very active in the consulting business, including management consulting and technology consulting, representing a substantial portion of total revenues for the firm.

The company offers employees a formal work-life balance program; substantial sick leave and family care leave; flexible work arrangements that may include job-sharing, flex time, sabbaticals and a compressed work week; and access to training at the PwC Open University.

FINANCIAL DATA: Note: Data for latest year may not have been available at press time.

In U.S. $	2018	2017	2016	2015	2014	2013
Revenue	41,280,000,000	37,695,000,000	35,900,000,000	35,400,000,000	34,000,000,000	32,100,000,000
R&D Expense						
Operating Income						
Operating Margin %						
SGA Expense						
Net Income						
Operating Cash Flow						
Capital Expenditure						
EBITDA						
Return on Assets %						
Return on Equity %						
Debt to Equity						

CONTACT INFORMATION:
Phone: 646-471-3000   Fax: 813-286-6000
Toll-Free:
Address: 300 Madison Ave., New York, NY 10017-6204 United States

SALARIES/BONUSES:
Top Exec. Salary: $ Bonus: $
Second Exec. Salary: $ Bonus: $

STOCK TICKER/OTHER:
Stock Ticker: Private   Exchange:
Employees: 250,930   Fiscal Year Ends: 06/30
Parent Company:

OTHER THOUGHTS:
Estimated Female Officers or Directors: 5
Hot Spot for Advancement for Women/Minorities: Y

Sales, profits and employees may be estimates. Financial information, benefits and other data can change quickly and may vary from those stated here.

Principal Financial Group Inc

NAIC Code: 524113

www.principal.com

TYPES OF BUSINESS:
Asset Management
Life Insurance
Health Insurance
Annuities
Disability Insurance
Investment Services
Specialty Benefits Insurance

BRANDS/DIVISIONS/AFFILIATES:

CONTACTS: Note: Officers with more than one job title may be intentionally listed here more than once.
Patrick Halter, CEO, Subsidiary
Daniel Houston, CEO
Deanna Strable-Soethout, CFO
Gary Scholten, Chief Information Officer
Julia Lawler, Chief Risk Officer
Karen Shaff, Executive VP
Timothy Dunbar, Executive VP
Amy Friedrich, President, Divisional
Luis Valdes, President, Divisional
Nora Everett, President, Divisional

GROWTH PLANS/SPECIAL FEATURES:

The Principal Financial Group is a leading provider of retirement savings, investment and insurance products and services. It holds a total of $626.8 billion in assets and serves 24.2 million customers globally. The company is organized into four segments: retirement and income solutions, principal global investors, principal international and U.S. insurance solutions. The retirement and income solutions segment offers products and services for retirement savings and retirement income to small- and medium-sized businesses (companies with less than 1,000 employees), including 401(k) and 403(b) plans, benefit pension plans, non-qualified executive benefit plants, employee stock ownership plans, as well as SIMPLE individual retirement accounts (IRA) and payroll deduction plans. For large institutional clients, it offers investment-only products such as guaranteed investment contracts; and for employees of businesses and other individuals, it offers accumulate savings for retirement plans, as well as mutual funds, individual annuities and bank products. The principal global investors segment manages assets for sophisticated investors worldwide, including equity, fixed income, real estate and other alternative investments. This division maintains offices worldwide, including Australia, Belgium, Brazil, China, France, Germany, Hong Kong, Ireland, Japan, Luxembourg, the Netherlands, Portugal, Singapore, Spain, Switzerland, the UAE, the U.K. and the U.S. The principal international segment focuses on countries and territories with growing middle classes, favorable demographics and increasing long-term savings. This division has operations in Latin America and Asia. The U.S. insurance solutions segment offers group and individual insurance solutions, providing comprehensive insurance solutions for small- and medium-sized businesses and their owners and executives. These include both group and individual dental, vision, life and disability insurance; and both group and individual life insurance options. In mid-2019, The Principal Financial Group acquired Wells Fargo & Company's institutional retirement and trust business.

Employee benefits include medical, dental and vision coverage; and 401(k), employee stock and retirement plans.

FINANCIAL DATA: Note: Data for latest year may not have been available at press time.

In U.S. $	2018	2017	2016	2015	2014	2013
Revenue	14,237,200,000	14,093,200,000	12,394,100,000	11,964,400,000	10,477,600,000	9,289,500,000
R&D Expense						
Operating Income						
Operating Margin %						
SGA Expense	4,136,700,000	3,893,800,000	3,732,600,000	3,672,400,000	3,574,300,000	3,292,900,000
Net Income	1,546,500,000	2,310,400,000	1,316,500,000	1,234,000,000	1,144,100,000	912,700,000
Operating Cash Flow	5,156,500,000	4,188,000,000	3,857,800,000	4,377,100,000	3,102,900,000	2,221,200,000
Capital Expenditure	92,300,000	164,800,000	154,900,000	136,400,000	136,000,000	59,400,000
EBITDA						
Return on Assets %		.01%	.01%	.01%	.01%	.00%
Return on Equity %		.20%	.13%	.12%	.11%	.09%
Debt to Equity		0.247	0.306	0.353	0.249	0.269

CONTACT INFORMATION:
Phone: 515 247-5111   Fax:
Toll-Free: 800-986-3343
Address: 711 High St., Des Moines, IA 50392 United States

SALARIES/BONUSES:
Top Exec. Salary: $900,000   Bonus: $
Second Exec. Salary: $613,192   Bonus: $

STOCK TICKER/OTHER:
Stock Ticker: PFG
Employees: 14,854
Parent Company:

Exchange: NAS
Fiscal Year Ends: 12/31

OTHER THOUGHTS:
Estimated Female Officers or Directors: 10
Hot Spot for Advancement for Women/Minorities: Y

Sales, profits and employees may be estimates. Financial information, benefits and other data can change quickly and may vary from those stated here.

Procter & Gamble Company (The)

NAIC Code: 325620

www.pg.com

TYPES OF BUSINESS:
Personal Care Products
Beauty Products
Household Products and Cleansers
Personal Care Products
Fabric Care Products
Franchising, Dry Cleaners and Car Washes
Pet Products
Diapers and Toilet Paper

BRANDS/DIVISIONS/AFFILIATES:
Head & Shoulders
Olay
Braun
Crest
Metamucil
Downy
Swiffer
Pampers

CONTACTS: *Note: Officers with more than one job title may be intentionally listed here more than once.*

Jon Moeller, CFO
Mary Ferguson-McHugh, Pres., Divisional
Valarie Sheppard, Chief Accounting Officer
David Taylor, Director
Jeffrey Schomburger, Other Corporate Officer
Ioannis Skoufalos, Other Corporate Officer
M. Grabowski, Other Executive Officer
Kathleen Fish, Other Executive Officer
Marc Pritchard, Other Executive Officer
Deborah Majoras, Other Executive Officer
Gary Coombe, President, Divisional
Matthew Price, President, Divisional
Shailesh Jejurikar, President, Divisional
Fama Francisco, President, Divisional
Steven Bishop, President, Divisional
R. Keith, President, Divisional
Loic Tassel, President, Geographical

GROWTH PLANS/SPECIAL FEATURES:

The Procter & Gamble Company develops and manufactures a wide range of consumer packaged goods, which are marketed in more than 180 countries and territories. The firm operates in five reportable segments: beauty, grooming, health care, fabric and home care, and baby, feminine and family care. The beauty segment consists of two product categories: hair care such as conditioners, shampoo, styling aids and treatments; and skin and personal care such as antiperspirants, deodorants, personal cleansing and skin care. Major brands within this division include: (hair care) Head & Shoulders, Herbal Essences, Pantene and Rejoice; and (skin/personal care) Olay, Old Spice, Safeguard, SK-II and Secret. The grooming segment consists of shave products such as razors, blades, pre- and post-shave products, and related appliances. Brands include Braun, Gillette and Venus. The health care segment consists of: oral care such as toothbrushes, toothpaste and other oral care products; and personal health care such as gastrointestinal products, respiratory products, rapid diagnostics, vitamins/minerals/supplements, pain relievers and other personal health care products. Brands include: (oral care) Crest and Oral-B; and (personal health care) Metamucil, Neurobion, Pepto Bismol and Vicks. The fabric and home care segment consists of: fabric care such as fabric enhancers, laundry additives and laundry detergents; and home care such as air care, dish care, surface care and more. Brands include (fabric care) Airel, Downy, Gain and Tide; and (home care) Cascade, Dawn, Fairy, Febreeze, Mr. Clean and Swiffer. Last, the baby, feminine and family care segment consists of: baby care products such as wipes and diapers; feminine care products addressing adult incontinence and feminine care; and family care such as paper towels, tissues and toilet paper. Brands within this division include (baby care) Luvs and Pampers; (feminine care) Always, Always Discreet and Tampax; and (family care) Bounty, Charmin and Puffs.

FINANCIAL DATA: *Note: Data for latest year may not have been available at press time.*

In U.S. $	2018	2017	2016	2015	2014	2013
Revenue	66,832,000,000	65,058,000,000	65,299,000,000	76,279,000,000	83,062,000,000	84,167,000,000
R&D Expense						
Operating Income	13,711,000,000	13,955,000,000	13,441,000,000	13,818,000,000	15,288,000,000	14,789,000,000
Operating Margin %		.21%	.21%	.18%	.18%	.18%
SGA Expense	18,853,000,000	18,568,000,000	18,949,000,000	23,585,000,000	25,314,000,000	26,950,000,000
Net Income	9,750,000,000	15,326,000,000	10,508,000,000	7,036,000,000	11,643,000,000	11,312,000,000
Operating Cash Flow	14,867,000,000	12,753,000,000	15,435,000,000	14,608,000,000	13,958,000,000	14,873,000,000
Capital Expenditure	3,717,000,000	3,384,000,000	3,314,000,000	3,736,000,000	3,848,000,000	4,008,000,000
EBITDA	16,666,000,000	16,542,000,000	17,026,000,000	15,606,000,000	18,735,000,000	18,492,000,000
Return on Assets %		.12%	.08%	.05%	.08%	.08%
Return on Equity %		.27%	.17%	.10%	.17%	.17%
Debt to Equity		0.333	0.336	0.299	0.291	0.286

CONTACT INFORMATION:
Phone: 513 983-1100 Fax: 513 983-9369
Toll-Free:
Address: 1 Procter & Gamble Plz., Cincinnati, OH 45202 United States

SALARIES/BONUSES:
Top Exec. Salary: $1,600,000 Bonus: $2,736,000
Second Exec. Salary: $1,000,000 Bonus: $1,111,500

STOCK TICKER/OTHER:
Stock Ticker: PG Exchange: NYS
Employees: 92,000 Fiscal Year Ends: 06/30
Parent Company:

OTHER THOUGHTS:
Estimated Female Officers or Directors: 18
Hot Spot for Advancement for Women/Minorities: Y

Sales, profits and employees may be estimates. Financial information, benefits and other data can change quickly and may vary from those stated here.

Progressive Corporation (The)

www.progressive.com

NAIC Code: 524126

TYPES OF BUSINESS:
Insurance, Direct Property & Casualty
Automobile Insurance

BRANDS/DIVISIONS/AFFILIATES:
American Strategic Insurance Corp

CONTACTS:
Note: Officers with more than one job title may be intentionally listed here more than once.

Mariann Marshall, Assistant Secretary
Susan Griffith, Pres.
John Sauerland, CFO
Lawton Fitt, Chairman of the Board
Steven Broz, Chief Information Officer
William Cody, Chief Investment Officer
Daniel Mascaro, Chief Legal Officer
Jeffrey Charney, Chief Marketing Officer
Andrew Quigg, Chief Strategy Officer
Lori Niederst, Other Executive Officer
John Barbagallo, President, Divisional
Michael Sieger, President, Divisional
Patrick Callahan, President, Divisional
John Murphy, President, Divisional

GROWTH PLANS/SPECIAL FEATURES:

The Progressive Corporation is one of the largest auto insurers in the U.S. The firm is divided into seven business segments. The personal lines segment writes insurance for personal autos and recreational and other vehicles in all 50 states and the District of Columbia. The commercial lines segment primarily writes liability, physical damage and other auto-related insurance for automobiles and trucks owned and/or operated predominantly by small businesses as a part of the commercial auto market. This division offers its products in 50 states. The property segment, through American Strategic Insurance Corp. (ASI), is one of the 15 largest homeowners carriers in the U.S. ASI specializes in personal and commercial property insurance, personal umbrella insurance and primary and excess flood insurance. The other indemnity segment consists of managing The Progressive Corporation's run-off businesses, including the run-off of its professional liability business, with five professional liability policies currently in force. The service businesses segment includes the servicing of the company's commercial auto insurance procedures and plans, as well as the company's two commission-based service businesses: the direct business offers home, condo and renters insurance, among other products, written by Progressive or unaffiliated insurance companies in the U.S.; and the commercial lines business offers the ability to package auto coverage with other commercial coverages that are written by unaffiliated insurance companies or placed with additional companies through unaffiliated insurance agencies, offering general liability and business owners policies throughout most of the U.S. and workers' compensation coverage in 44 states. The reinsurance segment participates in mandatory state pools; acts as a servicing agent for state-mandated involuntary plans for commercial vehicles; and participates in federally regulated write-your-own plans for flood. Last, the claims segment manages the vehicle claims handling on a company-wide basis through approximately 260 stand-alone claims offices throughout the U.S.

Benefits offered!

FINANCIAL DATA:
Note: Data for latest year may not have been available at press time.

In U.S. $	2018	2017	2016	2015	2014	2013
Revenue	31,979,000,000	26,840,000,000	23,439,800,000	20,854,700,000	19,396,200,000	18,175,200,000
R&D Expense						
Operating Income						
Operating Margin %						
SGA Expense	134,100,000	109,500,000	92,000,000	77,500,000	50,900,000	38,800,000
Net Income	2,615,300,000	1,592,200,000	1,031,000,000	1,267,600,000	1,281,000,000	1,165,400,000
Operating Cash Flow	6,284,800,000	3,756,800,000	2,701,900,000	2,292,900,000	1,725,600,000	1,899,900,000
Capital Expenditure	266,000,000	155,700,000	215,000,000	130,700,000	108,100,000	140,400,000
EBITDA						
Return on Assets %		.04%	.03%	.05%	.05%	.05%
Return on Equity %		.18%	.14%	.18%	.20%	.19%
Debt to Equity		0.356	0.396	0.371	0.312	0.301

CONTACT INFORMATION:
Phone: 440 461-5000 Fax:
Toll-Free: 800-776-4737
Address: 6300 Wilson Mills Rd., Mayfield Village, OH 44143 United States

STOCK TICKER/OTHER:
Stock Ticker: PGR
Employees: 31,721
Parent Company:

Exchange: NYS
Fiscal Year Ends: 12/31

SALARIES/BONUSES:
Top Exec. Salary: $791,346 Bonus: $
Second Exec. Salary: $597,115 Bonus: $

OTHER THOUGHTS:
Estimated Female Officers or Directors: 2
Hot Spot for Advancement for Women/Minorities: Y

Sales, profits and employees may be estimates. Financial information, benefits and other data can change quickly and may vary from those stated here.

Providence St Joseph Health

www.psjhealth.org

NAIC Code: 622110

TYPES OF BUSINESS:
General Medical and Surgical Hospitals
Assisted Living Facilities
Low Income Living Facilities
Counseling

BRANDS/DIVISIONS/AFFILIATES:
Providence Health & Services
St. Joseph Health
Covenant Health
Facey Medical Foundation
Hoag Memorial Presbyterian
Kadlec
Pacific Medical Centers
Civica Rx

CONTACTS:
Note: Officers with more than one job title may be intentionally listed here more than once.

Rod Hochman, CEO
Mike Butler, Pres.-Operations
Venkat Bhamidipati, CFO
Myron Berdischewsky, Chief Medical & Quality Officer
Cindy Strauss, Sr. VP
David Brown, VP-Strategy & Bus. Dev.
Deborah Burton, VP
Jack Friedman, Sr. VP-Accountable Care & Payor Relations
Joel Gilbertson, VP-Gov't. & Public Affairs
John O. Mudd, Sr. VP-Mission leadership
Dave Hunter, VP-Supply Chain Mgmt.

GROWTH PLANS/SPECIAL FEATURES:

Providence St. Joseph Health comprises 51 hospitals, 829 clinics, 25,000 physicians, supportive housing facilities and 119,000 caregivers with the goal of improving the health of the communities it serves, especially the poor and the vulnerable. The faith-based firm provides a comprehensive range of services across Alaska, California, Montana, New Mexico, Oregon, Texas and Washington. The Providence St. Joseph Health family includes: Providence Health & Services (Alaska, Washington, Montana, Oregon and California), St. Joseph Health (California and Texas), Covenant Health (west Texas), Facey Medical Group (California), Hoag Memorial Presbyterian (California), Kadlec (southeast Washington), Pacific Medical Centers (Seattle, Washington), as well as Swedish Health Services (Seattle, Washington). The company established integrates mental health care into its primary care clinics to provide effective mental health services for those who struggle with mental health stigmatization, diagnosis and treatment. The funds derived by the foundation support research and startup operations regarding mental health awareness, diagnosis and treatment. Providence St. Joseph Health partnered with six other health organizations to create Civica Rx, a not-for-profit generic drug and pharmaceutical company founded in 2018 to combat life-saving drug shortages and affordability. In mid-2019, Providence St. Joseph agreed to acquire Bluetree, a consulting firm that specializes in managing Epic electronic health record systems; and announced a multi-year strategic alliance with Microsoft Corporation to use Microsoft's cloud, artificial intelligence (AI), research capabilities and collaboration tools with the clinical expertise and care environments of Providence St. Joseph Health, to improve health outcomes and reduce total cost of care.

FINANCIAL DATA:
Note: Data for latest year may not have been available at press time.

In U.S. $	2018	2017	2016	2015	2014	2013
Revenue	24,428,000,000	23,163,000,000	18,878,000,000	14,434,000,000	12,261,825,000	11,099,009,000
R&D Expense						
Operating Income						
Operating Margin %						
SGA Expense						
Net Income	-445,000,000	780,000,000	5,231,000,000	77,000,000	771,422,000	253,270,000
Operating Cash Flow						
Capital Expenditure						
EBITDA						
Return on Assets %						
Return on Equity %						
Debt to Equity						

CONTACT INFORMATION:
Phone: 425-525-3355 Fax:
Toll-Free:
Address: 1801 Lind Avenue SW, Renton, WA 98057 United States

SALARIES/BONUSES:
Top Exec. Salary: $ Bonus: $
Second Exec. Salary: $ Bonus: $

STOCK TICKER/OTHER:
Stock Ticker: Nonprofit Exchange:
Employees: 105,000 Fiscal Year Ends: 12/31
Parent Company:

OTHER THOUGHTS:
Estimated Female Officers or Directors: 5
Hot Spot for Advancement for Women/Minorities: Y

Sales, profits and employees may be estimates. Financial information, benefits and other data can change quickly and may vary from those stated here.

Prudential Financial Inc

www.prudential.com

NAIC Code: 524113

TYPES OF BUSINESS:
Insurance-Life
Property & Casualty Insurance
Asset Management
Life Insurance

BRANDS/DIVISIONS/AFFILIATES:

CONTACTS: Note: Officers with more than one job title may be intentionally listed here more than once.
Charles Lowrey, CEO
Robert Falzon, Vice Chairman
Kenneth Tanji, CFO
John Strangfeld, Chairman of the Board
Robert Axel, Chief Accounting Officer
Barbara Koster, Chief Information Officer
Timothy Schmidt, Chief Investment Officer
Nicholas Silitch, Chief Risk Officer
Scott Sleyster, COO, Divisional
Stephen Pelletier, COO, Geographical
Mark Grier, Director
Timothy Harris, Executive VP
Lucien Alziari, Other Executive Officer
Candace Woods, Other Executive Officer

GROWTH PLANS/SPECIAL FEATURES:
Prudential Financial, Inc. provides financial products and services, conducting business through five divisions, which together have seven segments. The PGIM division comprises the PGIM segment, which provides asset management services related to public and private fixed income, public equity, real estate, commercial mortgage origination and servicing, and mutual funds to institutional, private and sub-advisory clients, insurance company separate accounts, government-sponsored entities and Prudential's general account. The U.S. Workplace solutions division comprises the retirement and group insurance segments, which provide retirement investment and income products and services to retirement plan sponsors in the public, private and non-profit sectors; and provides group life, long- and short-term group disability and group corporate-, bank- and trust-owned life insurance in the U.S., primarily to institutional clients in connection with employee plans and affinity groups. The U.S. individual solutions division comprises the individual annuities and individual life segments, which develop and distribute individual variable and fixed annuity products to U.S. mass affluent ($100,000 annual income/investable assets) and affluent markets ($250,000+); and develop and distribute term life, variable life and universal life insurance products to the U.S. mass middle ($25,000+), mass affluent ($100,000+) and affluent ($250,000+). The international insurance division comprises the international insurance segment, which develops and distributes life insurance, retirement products and certain accident and health products with fixed benefits to the mass affluent and affluent markets through operations in Japan, Korea, Taiwan, Brazil, Argentina and Mexico. Last, the closed block division consists of the closed block segment, which is currently in run-off/divestiture status, but comprises a group of policyholders that hold domestic individual life insurance and annuity products under which they are eligible to receive dividends. In September 2019, Prudential Financial agreed to acquire online startup Assurance IQ, Inc. for $2.35 billion.

Prudential offers employees comprehensive benefits and retirement plans.

FINANCIAL DATA: Note: Data for latest year may not have been available at press time.

In U.S. $	2018	2017	2016	2015	2014	2013
Revenue	62,992,000,000	59,689,000,000	58,779,000,000	57,119,000,000	54,105,000,000	41,461,000,000
R&D Expense						
Operating Income						
Operating Margin %						
SGA Expense	11,949,000,000	11,915,000,000	11,779,000,000	10,912,000,000	11,807,000,000	11,011,000,000
Net Income	4,074,000,000	7,863,000,000	4,368,000,000	5,642,000,000	1,381,000,000	-667,000,000
Operating Cash Flow	21,664,000,000	13,445,000,000	14,778,000,000	13,895,000,000	19,396,000,000	8,445,000,000
Capital Expenditure						
EBITDA						
Return on Assets %		.01%	.01%	.01%	.00%	.00%
Return on Equity %		.16%	.10%	.13%	.04%	-.02%
Debt to Equity		0.346	0.44	0.676	0.62	0.761

CONTACT INFORMATION:
Phone: 973 802-6000 Fax: 973 367-6476
Toll-Free: 877-998-7625
Address: 751 Broad St., Newark, NJ 07102 United States

STOCK TICKER/OTHER:
Stock Ticker: PRU
Employees: 49,739
Parent Company:

Exchange: NYS
Fiscal Year Ends: 12/31

SALARIES/BONUSES:
Top Exec. Salary: $1,332,692 Bonus: $
Second Exec. Salary: $1,190,000 Bonus: $

OTHER THOUGHTS:
Estimated Female Officers or Directors: 6
Hot Spot for Advancement for Women/Minorities: Y

Sales, profits and employees may be estimates. Financial information, benefits and other data can change quickly and may vary from those stated here.

Publix Super Markets Inc

NAIC Code: 445110

www.publix.com

TYPES OF BUSINESS:
Grocery Stores
Dairy, Deli & Bakery Products
Convenience Stores
Liquor Stores
Restaurants

BRANDS/DIVISIONS/AFFILIATES:

CONTACTS:
Note: Officers with more than one job title may be intentionally listed here more than once.

Sharon Miller, Assistant Secretary
David Bornmann, VP
William Crenshaw, CEO
David Phillips, CFO
Laurie Zeitlin, Chief Information Officer
Charles Jenkins, Director
Hoyt Barnett, Director
Randall Jones, President
John Hrabusa, Senior VP
John Attaway, Senior VP
Linda Hall, Vice President
Dale Myers, Vice President
David Duncan, Vice President
David Bridges, Vice President
Michael Smith, Vice President
Thomas Mclaughlin, Vice President
William Fauerbach, Vice President
Alfred Ottolino, Vice President
Mark Irby, Vice President
John Frazier, Vice President
Marc Salm, Vice President

GROWTH PLANS/SPECIAL FEATURES:

Publix Super Markets, Inc. is a leading operator of supermarkets, with more than 1,200 locations in Alabama (70), Florida (799), Georgia (187), North Carolina (40), South Carolina (59), Tennessee (43) and Virginia (11). The firm's supermarkets sell groceries, dairy products, produce, deli foods, bakery items, meat, seafood, housewares and health and beauty merchandise. Many stores also feature pharmacies, floral departments, photo labs, liquor stores and in-store banking areas. It also owns several pharmacy and convenience store locations under various names. Publix's lines of merchandise include a variety of nationally advertised and private label brands as well as some unbranded merchandise, such as produce, meat and seafood. In addition to its retail operations, Publix manufactures dairy, bakery and deli products. Manufacturing facilities are located in: Florida, including Lakeland, Miami, Jacksonville, Sarasota, Orlando, Deerfield Beach and Boynton Beach; and Georgia, including Atlanta and Lawrenceville. The firm is one of the largest employee-owned grocery stores in the U.S.

Publix offers its employees health, dental and vision coverage; quarterly retail bonuses; an employee stock ownership plan; holiday bonuses; free hot lunches; prescription discounts; a 401(k) plan; a profit sharing plan; access to a credit union; tuition reimbursement; and an employee assistance plan.

FINANCIAL DATA:
Note: Data for latest year may not have been available at press time.

In U.S. $	2018	2017	2016	2015	2014	2013
Revenue	36,395,720,000	34,836,840,000	34,274,110,000	32,618,760,000	30,802,470,000	29,147,520,000
R&D Expense						
Operating Income	2,744,403,000	2,732,824,000	2,751,651,000	2,678,241,000	2,400,861,000	2,319,738,000
Operating Margin %		.08%	.08%	.08%	.08%	.08%
SGA Expense						
Net Income	2,381,167,000	2,291,894,000	2,025,688,000	1,965,048,000	1,735,308,000	1,653,954,000
Operating Cash Flow	3,631,926,000	3,580,281,000	3,252,955,000	2,941,365,000	2,777,232,000	2,567,303,000
Capital Expenditure	1,350,089,000	1,429,059,000	1,443,827,000	1,235,648,000	1,374,124,000	668,485,000
EBITDA	3,421,557,000	3,396,833,000	3,375,854,000	3,260,133,000	2,914,254,000	2,821,427,000
Return on Assets %		.13%	.12%	.12%	.12%	.13%
Return on Equity %		.17%	.16%	.17%	.16%	.17%
Debt to Equity		0.011	0.01	0.015	0.017	0.012

CONTACT INFORMATION:
Phone: 863 688-1188   Fax: 863 688-5532
Toll-Free: 800-242-1227
Address: 3300 Publix Corporate Pkwy., Lakeland, FL 33811 United States

STOCK TICKER/OTHER:
Stock Ticker: PUSH
Employees: 193,000
Parent Company:

Exchange: GREY
Fiscal Year Ends: 12/31

SALARIES/BONUSES:
Top Exec. Salary: $777,400   Bonus: $
Second Exec. Salary: $622,193   Bonus: $

OTHER THOUGHTS:
Estimated Female Officers or Directors: 5
Hot Spot for Advancement for Women/Minorities: Y

Sales, profits and employees may be estimates. Financial information, benefits and other data can change quickly and may vary from those stated here.

PulteGroup Inc

pultegroupinc.com

NAIC Code: 236117

TYPES OF BUSINESS:
Construction, Home Building and Residential
Financial Services
Mortgages
Land Development

BRANDS/DIVISIONS/AFFILIATES:
Pulte Mortgage LLC
Centex
Pulte Homes
Del Webb
DiVosta Homes
John Wieland Homes and Neighborhoods

CONTACTS:
Note: Officers with more than one job title may be intentionally listed here more than once.

Ryan Marshall, CEO
Robert OShaughnessy, CFO
James Ossowski, Chief Accounting Officer
Todd Sheldon, Executive VP
John Chadwick, President, Divisional
Stephen Schlageter, Senior VP, Divisional
Michelle Hairston, Senior VP, Divisional

GROWTH PLANS/SPECIAL FEATURES:

PulteGroup, Inc. is a leading homebuilder in the U.S. The firm's subsidiaries primarily engage in the homebuilding business, and Pulte Mortgage, LLC handles the mortgage banking and title operations of the group. PulteGroup builds a wide variety of homes targeted for first-time, first and second move-up and active adult home buyers, including detached units, townhouses, condominium apartments and duplexes, with varying prices, models, options and lot sizes. Homebuilding brands include Centex, Pulte Homes, Del Webb, DiVosta Homes and John Wieland Homes and Neighborhoods. The company operates in 44 homebuilding markets that span across 24 states, offering homes in about 815 active communities. During 2018, the firm closed 23,107 homes, with the average unit selling price of $425,000, compared with $395,000 in 2017. Sales prices range from $100,000 to more than $2,200,000, with 91% falling between $200,000 and $750,000. PulteGroup's homes are located six geographic segments: Northeast (Connecticut, Maryland, Massachusetts, New Jersey, New York, Pennsylvania and Virginia); Southeast (Georgia, North Carolina, South Carolina and Tennessee); Florida; Midwest (Illinois, Indiana, Kentucky, Michigan, Minnesota and Ohio); Texas; and West (Arizona, California, Nevada, New Mexico and Washington). The firm's strategy is based on extensive market research that reveals well-defined buying profiles, job demographics and lifestyle choices. In 2018, PulteGroup and Georgia Power announced a new partnership to develop Atlanta's first Smart NeighborhoodTM at Pulte's Altus. The state-of-the-art community will comprise technology-enhanced homes served by Georgia Power, with power supplemented by individual rooftop solar installations and in-home battery energy storage. The homes will also be equipped with advanced heating/cooling systems, light-emitting diode (LED) lighting, home automation smart thermostats, smart locks, voice control and more.

PulteGroup offers medical, dental, vision, life, AD&D and short/long-term disability insurance; 401(k); business travel accident insurance; and tuition reimbursement.

FINANCIAL DATA:
Note: Data for latest year may not have been available at press time.

In U.S. $	2018	2017	2016	2015	2014	2013
Revenue	10,188,330,000	8,573,250,000	7,668,476,000	5,981,964,000	5,822,363,000	5,679,595,000
R&D Expense						
Operating Income	1,347,589,000	952,979,000	968,864,000	820,486,000	703,279,000	590,662,000
Operating Margin %		.11%	.13%	.14%	.12%	.10%
SGA Expense	1,012,023,000	891,581,000	957,150,000	589,780,000	667,815,000	568,500,000
Net Income	1,022,023,000	447,221,000	602,703,000	494,090,000	474,338,000	2,620,116,000
Operating Cash Flow	1,449,744,000	663,077,000	68,270,000	-348,129,000	309,249,000	881,136,000
Capital Expenditure	59,039,000	32,051,000	39,295,000	45,440,000	48,790,000	28,899,000
EBITDA	1,397,587,000	990,329,000	988,543,000	863,033,000	730,471,000	560,121,000
Return on Assets %		.04%	.06%	.06%	.05%	.34%
Return on Equity %		.10%	.13%	.10%	.10%	.76%
Debt to Equity		0.829	0.743	0.502	0.412	0.465

CONTACT INFORMATION:
Phone: 404-978-6400   Fax:
Toll-Free: 866-785-8325
Address: 3350 Peachtree Rd. NE, Ste 150, Atlanta, GA 30326 United States

STOCK TICKER/OTHER:
Stock Ticker: PHM
Employees: 4,623
Parent Company:

Exchange: NYS
Fiscal Year Ends: 12/31

SALARIES/BONUSES:
Top Exec. Salary: $942,308   Bonus: $
Second Exec. Salary: $750,000   Bonus: $

OTHER THOUGHTS:
Estimated Female Officers or Directors: 4
Hot Spot for Advancement for Women/Minorities: Y

Sales, profits and employees may be estimates. Financial information, benefits and other data can change quickly and may vary from those stated here.

Qualcomm Incorporated

NAIC Code: 334413

www.qualcomm.com

TYPES OF BUSINESS:
Telecommunications Equipment
Digital Wireless Communications Products
Integrated Circuits
Mobile Communications Systems
Wireless Software & Services
E-Mail Software
Code Division Multiple Access

BRANDS/DIVISIONS/AFFILIATES:
RF360 Holdings Singapore Pte Ltd

CONTACTS: Note: Officers with more than one job title may be intentionally listed here more than once.
Steven Mollenkopf, CEO
David Wise, CFO
Jeffrey Henderson, Chairman of the Board
Erin Polek, Chief Accounting Officer
James Thompson, Chief Technology Officer
Michelle Sterling, Executive VP, Divisional
Brian Modoff, Executive VP, Divisional
Donald Rosenberg, Executive VP
Alexander Rogers, Executive VP
Cristiano Amon, President

GROWTH PLANS/SPECIAL FEATURES:

Qualcomm Incorporated provides digital wireless communications products, technologies and services. Its operations are divided into three segments: Qualcomm CDMA Technologies (QCT), Qualcomm Technology Licensing (QTL) and Qualcomm Strategic Initiatives (QSI). QCT designs application-specific integrated circuits based on Code Division Multiple Access (CDMA), Orthogonal Frequency-Division Multiple Access (OFDMA), Time Division Multiple Access (TDMA) and other technologies for use in voice and data communications, networking, application processing, multimedia functions and GPS products. QTL grants licenses and provides rights to use portions of Qualcomm's intellectual property portfolio to third-party manufacturers of wireless products and networking equipment. QSI makes strategic investments in various companies and technologies that Qualcomm believes will open new opportunities for its technologies. Joint venture (with TDK Corporation), RF360 Holdings Singapore Pte. Ltd., delivers radio frequency (RF) front-end modules and RF filters into fully integrated systems for mobile devices and fast-growing business segments such as the Internet of Things, drones, robotics, automotive applications and more. Qualcomm Incorporated has pioneered in 3G, 4G and 5G wireless technologies, not just for smartphones and mobile devices, but also for industries and applications including automotive, Internet of Things (IoT), networking, computing and artificial intelligence (AI). The company's non-reporting segments include cyber security solutions, mobile health, small cells and other wireless technology and service initiatives

U.S. employees of the company receive medical, dental and vision insurance; dependent/health care reimbursement accounts; tuition reimbursement; a 401(k); and an employee stock purchase plan.

FINANCIAL DATA: Note: Data for latest year may not have been available at press time.

In U.S. $	2018	2017	2016	2015	2014	2013
Revenue	22,732,000,000	22,291,000,000	23,554,000,000	25,281,000,000	26,487,000,000	24,866,000,000
R&D Expense	5,625,000,000	5,485,000,000	5,151,000,000	5,490,000,000	5,477,000,000	4,967,000,000
Operating Income	742,000,000	2,614,000,000	6,495,000,000	5,776,000,000	7,550,000,000	7,230,000,000
Operating Margin %		.20%	.27%	.28%	.30%	.30%
SGA Expense	2,986,000,000	2,658,000,000	2,385,000,000	2,344,000,000	2,290,000,000	2,518,000,000
Net Income	-4,864,000,000	2,466,000,000	5,705,000,000	5,271,000,000	7,967,000,000	6,853,000,000
Operating Cash Flow	3,895,000,000	4,693,000,000	7,400,000,000	5,506,000,000	8,887,000,000	8,778,000,000
Capital Expenditure	784,000,000	690,000,000	539,000,000	994,000,000	1,185,000,000	1,048,000,000
EBITDA	2,842,000,000	4,975,000,000	8,558,000,000	7,805,000,000	9,933,000,000	9,234,000,000
Return on Assets %		.04%	.11%	.11%	.17%	.15%
Return on Equity %		.08%	.18%	.15%	.21%	.20%
Debt to Equity		0.631	0.315	0.317		

CONTACT INFORMATION:
Phone: 858 587-1121 Fax: 858 658-2100
Toll-Free:
Address: 5775 Morehouse Dr., San Diego, CA 92121 United States

SALARIES/BONUSES:
Top Exec. Salary: $1,390,739 Bonus: $
Second Exec. Salary: $916,964 Bonus: $

STOCK TICKER/OTHER:
Stock Ticker: QCOM Exchange: NAS
Employees: 33,000 Fiscal Year Ends: 09/30
Parent Company:

OTHER THOUGHTS:
Estimated Female Officers or Directors: 2
Hot Spot for Advancement for Women/Minorities: Y

Sales, profits and employees may be estimates. Financial information, benefits and other data can change quickly and may vary from those stated here.

Quanta Services Inc

www.quantaservices.com

NAIC Code: 237130

TYPES OF BUSINESS:
Construction, Power & Communication Lines
Network Installation & Support Services
Network Design Services
Electric Power Transmission Systems
Gas Pipeline Systems

BRANDS/DIVISIONS/AFFILIATES:
Hallen Construction Co Inc

CONTACTS: Note: Officers with more than one job title may be intentionally listed here more than once.
Earl Austin, CEO
Derrick Jensen, CFO
David McClanahan, Chairman of the Board
Jerry Lemon, Chief Accounting Officer
Paul Gregory, Chief Strategy Officer
Jesse Morris, Executive VP, Divisional
Donald Wayne, Executive VP
James Probst, President, Divisional
Nicholas Grindstaff, Treasurer
Dorothy Upperman, Vice President, Divisional

GROWTH PLANS/SPECIAL FEATURES:
Quanta Services, Inc. is a specialty contract provider of infrastructure services. The company designs, installs and maintains networks for the electric power, energy and communications industries in the U.S., Canada, Australia, Latin America and other international markets. Quanta Services operates in two segments: electric power infrastructure services (EPIS) and pipeline and industrial infrastructure services (PIIS). EPIS provides comprehensive network solutions to customers in the electric power industry. Services generally cover electric power transmission and distribution infrastructure and substation facilities, along with other engineering and technical services. This division also provides emergency restoration services, such as the repair of infrastructure damaged by inclement weather, the energized installation, maintenance and upgrade of electric power infrastructure utilizing unique bare-hand and hot stick methods and Quanta's proprietary robotic arm technologies, and the installation of smart grid technologies on electric power networks. PIIS provides comprehensive infrastructure solutions to customers in the development, transportation, storage and processing of natural gas, oil and other products. Services generally span pipeline transmission and distribution systems, gathering systems, production systems, storage systems and compressor and pump stations, as well as related trenching, directional boring and mechanized welding services. This division also fabricates pipeline support systems and related structures, and provides high-pressure and critical-path turnaround services to the downstream and midstream energy markets. During 2019, Quanta Services acquired the following: The Hallen Construction Co., Inc.; two specialty utility foundation and pole-setting contractors serving the southeast U.S.; and a sizeable gas utility contractor serving key U.S. northeast markets.

FINANCIAL DATA: Note: Data for latest year may not have been available at press time.

In U.S. $	2018	2017	2016	2015	2014	2013
Revenue	11,171,420,000	9,466,478,000	7,651,319,000	7,572,436,000	7,851,250,000	6,522,842,000
R&D Expense						
Operating Income	589,644,000	436,906,000	328,777,000	295,954,000	475,575,000	526,928,000
Operating Margin %		.05%	.04%	.04%	.06%	.08%
SGA Expense	857,574,000	777,920,000	653,338,000	592,863,000	722,038,000	501,010,000
Net Income	293,346,000	314,978,000	198,383,000	310,907,000	296,714,000	401,921,000
Operating Cash Flow	358,789,000	372,475,000	380,141,000	640,525,000	310,824,000	446,592,000
Capital Expenditure	308,043,000	244,651,000	212,555,000	210,179,000	301,728,000	263,558,000
EBITDA	741,124,000	590,716,000	524,498,000	434,392,000	671,899,000	803,542,000
Return on Assets %		.05%	.04%	.05%	.05%	.07%
Return on Equity %		.09%	.06%	.08%	.07%	.10%
Debt to Equity		0.177	0.106	0.154	0.016	

CONTACT INFORMATION:
Phone: 713 629-7600 Fax: 713 629-7676
Toll-Free:
Address: 2800 Post Oak Blvd, Ste 2600, Houston, TX 77056 United States

STOCK TICKER/OTHER:
Stock Ticker: PWR
Employees: 28,100
Parent Company:

Exchange: NYS
Fiscal Year Ends: 12/31

SALARIES/BONUSES:
Top Exec. Salary: $1,100,002 Bonus: $
Second Exec. Salary: $850,001 Bonus: $

OTHER THOUGHTS:
Estimated Female Officers or Directors:
Hot Spot for Advancement for Women/Minorities:

Sales, profits and employees may be estimates. Financial information, benefits and other data can change quickly and may vary from those stated here.

Quest Diagnostics Incorporated

www.questdiagnostics.com

NAIC Code: 621511

TYPES OF BUSINESS:
Services-Testing & Diagnostics
Clinical Laboratory Testing
Clinical Trials Testing
Esoteric Testing Laboratories

BRANDS/DIVISIONS/AFFILIATES:
Quanum

CONTACTS:
Note: Officers with more than one job title may be intentionally listed here more than once.

Stephen Rusckowski, CEO
Mark Guinan, CFO
Michael Deppe, Chief Accounting Officer
James Davis, Executive VP, Divisional
Michael Prevoznik, General Counsel
Catherine Doherty, Other Corporate Officer
Everett Cunningham, Senior VP, Divisional
Carrie Eglinton Manner, Senior VP, Divisional

GROWTH PLANS/SPECIAL FEATURES:

Quest Diagnostics Incorporated is a world-leading provider of diagnostic information services. The firm's diagnostic insights reveal new avenues to identify and treat disease, inspire healthy behaviors and improve health care management. Diagnostic testing services range from routine blood tests (such as total cholesterol, Pap testing and white blood cell count) to complex, gene-based and molecular testing. These tests are grouped into two categories: general diagnostics, consisting of routine and non-routine testing; and advanced diagnostics, consisting of genetic and advanced molecular testing. These services enable healthcare partners to deliver health care more efficiently, and help support population health via data analytics and extended care services. Quest Diagnostics is also a global clinical trials laboratory services organization that helps biopharmaceutical, medical device and diagnostics customers improve human health through innovation that transforms science and data into medical insights. Quest Diagnostics also offers healthcare information technology (IT) solutions, with more than 200,000 physicians using its Quanum suite of technology and analytics solutions to order lab tests, receive test results, share clinical information quickly and securely, and prescribe drugs. Quanum is used to process over 1 million transactions every day and capable of electronic interconnectivity. Based in New Jersey, Quest Diagnostics' laboratories, patient service centers, offices and other facilities are located throughout the U.S., as well as select locations outside the U.S. In 2019, Quest Diagnostics became an in-network laboratory provider to UnitedHealthcare, providing access to 48 million plan members.

The firm offers employees medical, dental and life insurance; employee assistance program; and flexible spending accounts.

FINANCIAL DATA:
Note: Data for latest year may not have been available at press time.

In U.S. $	2018	2017	2016	2015	2014	2013
Revenue	7,531,000,000	7,709,000,000	7,515,000,000	7,493,000,000	7,435,000,000	7,146,000,000
R&D Expense						
Operating Income	1,105,000,000	1,165,000,000	1,159,000,000	1,065,000,000	983,000,000	1,001,000,000
Operating Margin %	.15%	.15%	.15%	.14%	.13%	.14%
SGA Expense	1,424,000,000	1,750,000,000	1,681,000,000	1,679,000,000	1,728,000,000	1,704,000,000
Net Income	736,000,000	772,000,000	645,000,000	709,000,000	556,000,000	849,000,000
Operating Cash Flow	1,200,000,000	1,175,000,000	1,069,000,000	810,000,000	938,000,000	652,000,000
Capital Expenditure	383,000,000	252,000,000	293,000,000	263,000,000	308,000,000	231,000,000
EBITDA	1,404,000,000	1,453,000,000	1,479,000,000	1,561,000,000	1,330,000,000	1,793,000,000
Return on Assets %		.07%	.06%	.07%	.06%	.09%
Return on Equity %		.16%	.14%	.16%	.13%	.21%
Debt to Equity		0.762	0.806	0.746	0.754	0.79

CONTACT INFORMATION:
Phone: 973 520-2700   Fax:
Toll-Free: 800-222-0446
Address: 500 Plaza Dr., Secaucus, NJ 07094 United States

SALARIES/BONUSES:
Top Exec. Salary: $1,100,000   Bonus: $
Second Exec. Salary: $613,077   Bonus: $

STOCK TICKER/OTHER:
Stock Ticker: DGX
Employees: 43,000
Parent Company:

Exchange: NYS
Fiscal Year Ends: 12/31

OTHER THOUGHTS:
Estimated Female Officers or Directors: 3
Hot Spot for Advancement for Women/Minorities: Y

Plunkett Research, Ltd.

Quicken Loans Inc

www.quickenloans.com

NAIC Code: 522310

TYPES OF BUSINESS:
Mortgages
Mortgage Products
Online Services
Consumer Loans
Title Services

BRANDS/DIVISIONS/AFFILIATES:
Rock Holdings Inc
Title Source Inc
In-House Realty LLC
One Reverse Mortgage LLC

CONTACTS:
Note: Officers with more than one job title may be intentionally listed here more than once.

Jay Farner, CEO
Robert Walters, Pres.
Jullie Booth, CFO
Linglong He, CIO
Robert Walters, Chief Economist
Daniel Gilbert, Chmn.

GROWTH PLANS/SPECIAL FEATURES:

Quicken Loans, Inc. is an online direct-to-consumer mortgage lender offering traditional FHA loans as well as settlement services and other real estate services. The firm is owned by Rock Holdings, Inc. The company is one of the largest online and traditional retail home lenders in the U.S., operating in all 50 states. Quicken offers conventional, home equity, jumbo and alternative residential loans. The company's information technology system allows consumers in all 50 states to shop and apply for residential mortgages online through its website or by telephone through its mortgage call center. This technology also allows the consumer to have immediate access to a real-time loan status and credit health evaluation. In addition, consumers are able to access the company's website to utilize several mortgage and financial calculators, get pre-approved online, request a free credit report, receive home financing information, receive information on first time homebuyer programs, receive free refinancing guideline information and print loan documents directly from the site. The company specializes in conventional, FHA and VA loan programs. Quicken includes three affiliate companies: Title Source, Inc., a provider of title insurance, property valuations and settlement services in the U.S.; In-House Realty, LLC, which connects people with real estate agents nationwide; and One Reverse Mortgage, LLC, a provider of retail home loans, as well as reverse mortgages to homeowners for their home financing needs. In September 2018, Quicken announced a long-term agreement with Universal McCann to oversee the company's media planning and buying.

The firm offers employees a 401(k); medical, dental and vision coverage; short- and long-term disability; and tuition assistance.

FINANCIAL DATA:
Note: Data for latest year may not have been available at press time.

In U.S. $	2018	2017	2016	2015	2014	2013
Revenue	4,305,000,000	4,100,000,000	4,000,000,000	3,700,000,000	3,600,000,000	
R&D Expense						
Operating Income						
Operating Margin %						
SGA Expense						
Net Income						
Operating Cash Flow						
Capital Expenditure						
EBITDA						
Return on Assets %						
Return on Equity %						
Debt to Equity						

CONTACT INFORMATION:
Phone: 734-805-5000 Fax: 734-805-8400
Toll-Free: 800-863-4332
Address: 1050 Woodward Ave., Detroit, MI 48226 United States

SALARIES/BONUSES:
Top Exec. Salary: $ Bonus: $
Second Exec. Salary: $ Bonus: $

STOCK TICKER/OTHER:
Stock Ticker: Private Exchange:
Employees: 15,000 Fiscal Year Ends: 07/31
Parent Company: Rock Holdings Inc

OTHER THOUGHTS:
Estimated Female Officers or Directors:
Hot Spot for Advancement for Women/Minorities:

Sales, profits and employees may be estimates. Financial information, benefits and other data can change quickly and may vary from those stated here.

Qurate Retail Inc

NAIC Code: 454111

www.qurateretailgroup.com

TYPES OF BUSINESS:
Online and Internet Businesses
e-Commerce

BRANDS/DIVISIONS/AFFILIATES:
QVC Inc
Zulily LLC
HSN Inc
HSN
Cornerstone
Liberty Interactive Corporation

CONTACTS: Note: Officers with more than one job title may be intentionally listed here more than once.
Michael George, CEO
Mark Carleton, CFO
Gregory Maffei, Chairman of the Board
Richard Baer, Chief Legal Officer
Albert Rosenthaler, Other Executive Officer

GROWTH PLANS/SPECIAL FEATURES:

Qurate Retail, Inc. (formerly Liberty Interactive Corporation) is primarily engaged in selling consumer products through video and eCommerce channels throughout North America, Europe and Asia. The firm's wholly-owned subsidiaries include: QVC, Inc.; Zulily LLC; and HSN, Inc., along with its catalog retail business called Cornerstone. QVC serves 13 million customers in the U.S. alone, with 93% of sales deriving from repeat/reactivate customers. Existing customers usually order 25 items per year, on average. Internationally, its video commerce, eCommerce (website) and social commerce channels earned $8.8 billion in 2017 revenue, and reached 370 million homes worldwide, including the U.S., the U.K., Europe and Asia. QVC has 14 television networks, more than 220 active social pages, and more than 1 billion visit its websites annually. Zulily is an American eCommerce company based in Washington. Through its website and mobile app, consumers can shop new sales daily beginning at 6am Pacific Time, which feature prices of up to 70% off regular prices. How Zulily works is once sales have ended, the firm places one large order to the brands presented that day. The brands ship the items to Zulily in about 8-10 days, and then Zulily ships them individually from its warehouse to its consumers. This process keeps prices low and selections fresh. HSN stands for Home Shopping Network, and is an American broadcast, basic cable and satellite television network based in Florida. HSN broadcasts reach approximately 90 million households via live programming 364 days per year, as well as through its website HSN.com. Mobile apps are offered through iPad, iPhone and Android devices. In March 2018, Liberty Interactive Corporation reorganized its business, reattributing certain assets and liabilities to QVC and selling others, and subsequently changed its corporate name to Qurate Retail, Inc.

FINANCIAL DATA: Note: Data for latest year may not have been available at press time.

In U.S. $	2018	2017	2016	2015	2014	2013
Revenue	14,070,000,000	10,381,000,000	10,219,000,000	9,169,000,000	10,028,000,000	10,307,000,000
R&D Expense						
Operating Income	1,357,000,000	1,135,000,000	1,011,000,000	1,170,000,000	1,213,000,000	1,164,000,000
Operating Margin %		.11%	.10%	.13%	.12%	.11%
SGA Expense	1,897,000,000	1,088,000,000	1,063,000,000	875,000,000	940,000,000	1,033,000,000
Net Income	916,000,000	1,208,000,000	473,000,000	640,000,000	520,000,000	438,000,000
Operating Cash Flow	1,273,000,000	1,222,000,000	1,273,000,000	981,000,000	1,204,000,000	972,000,000
Capital Expenditure	275,000,000	201,000,000	206,000,000	218,000,000	226,000,000	295,000,000
EBITDA	1,901,000,000	2,265,000,000	1,947,000,000	1,918,000,000	1,835,000,000	1,745,000,000
Return on Assets %		.08%	.03%	.05%	.04%	.03%
Return on Equity %		.21%	.09%	.14%	.10%	.07%
Debt to Equity		0.98	1.309	1.189	1.367	0.791

CONTACT INFORMATION:
Phone: 720 875-5300 Fax:
Toll-Free:
Address: 12300 Liberty Blvd, Englewood, CO 80112 United States

STOCK TICKER/OTHER:
Stock Ticker: QRTEA
Employees: 21,080
Parent Company:

Exchange: NAS
Fiscal Year Ends: 12/31

SALARIES/BONUSES:
Top Exec. Salary: $1,250,000 Bonus: $
Second Exec. Salary: $1,112,188 Bonus: $

OTHER THOUGHTS:
Estimated Female Officers or Directors: 1
Hot Spot for Advancement for Women/Minorities:

Sales, profits and employees may be estimates. Financial information, benefits and other data can change quickly and may vary from those stated here.

Rackspace Hosting Inc

www.rackspace.com

NAIC Code: 517110

TYPES OF BUSINESS:
Web Hosting Services
Data Centers
Cloud Computing Services
Server Farms

BRANDS/DIVISIONS/AFFILIATES:
Apollo Global Management LLC
RelationEdge

CONTACTS:
Note: Officers with more than one job title may be intentionally listed here more than once.

Joseph Eazor, CEO
David Meredith, COO
Louis Alterman, CFO
Mark Bunting, CMO
Laura Sue D'Annunzio, Chief People Officer

GROWTH PLANS/SPECIAL FEATURES:

Rackspace Hosting, Inc. provides managed cloud services in the business information technology (IT) market worldwide. The firm actively offers six service categories: managed hosting, managed cloud, colocation, application services, professional services and security and compliance. It delivers advice and integrated managed services across public and private clouds, managed hosting and enterprise applications. The company partners with leading technology platform providers, including VMware, Alibaba Cloud, Amazon Web Services, Google Cloud Platform, Microsoft, OpenStack, Pivotal Cloud Foundry, Oracle and SAP. Rackspace's solutions include application management, business intelligence, database management, eCommerce hosting, email hosting, enterprise resource planning (ERP), productivity and collaboration, web content management, website hosting and exiting the data center. Industries served by the firm include automotive, business services, education, energy, financial services, government, healthcare, manufacturing and retail. Rackspace is owned by private equity firm, Apollo Global Management, LLC. Based in Texas, the company serves approximately 150,000 business customers, including most of the Fortune 100, from data centers on five continents. During 2018, Rackspace acquired RelationEdge, a full-service Salesforce platinum consulting partner and digital agency.

The firm offers employees medical, dental and vision insurance; a 401(k) plan; profit sharing; employee training; and an onsite fitness facility.

FINANCIAL DATA:
Note: Data for latest year may not have been available at press time.

In U.S. $	2018	2017	2016	2015	2014	2013
Revenue	2,000,000,000	2,200,000,000	2,081,000,000	2,001,299,968	1,794,356,992	1,534,786,048
R&D Expense						
Operating Income						
Operating Margin %						
SGA Expense						
Net Income			135,200,000	126,200,000	110,553,000	86,737,000
Operating Cash Flow						
Capital Expenditure						
EBITDA						
Return on Assets %						
Return on Equity %						
Debt to Equity						

CONTACT INFORMATION:
Phone: 210 312-4000 Fax: 210 312-4300
Toll-Free: 800-961-2888
Address: 1 Fanatical Pl., City of Windcrest, San Antonio, TX 78218 United States

STOCK TICKER/OTHER:
Stock Ticker: Private
Employees: 6,184
Parent Company: Apollo Global Management LLC

Exchange:
Fiscal Year Ends: 12/31

SALARIES/BONUSES:
Top Exec. Salary: $ Bonus: $
Second Exec. Salary: $ Bonus: $

OTHER THOUGHTS:
Estimated Female Officers or Directors: 1
Hot Spot for Advancement for Women/Minorities:

Raymond James Financial Inc

www.raymondjames.com

NAIC Code: 523110

TYPES OF BUSINESS:
Stock Brokerage/Investment Banking
Trust Services
Asset Management
Banking

BRANDS/DIVISIONS/AFFILIATES:
Raymond James & Associates Inc
Raymond James Financial Services Inc
Raymond James Financial Services Advisors Inc
Raymond James Ltd
Eagle Asset Management Inc
Raymond James Bank NA
Raymond James Investment Services Limited
Raymond James Financial International Ltd

CONTACTS:
Note: Officers with more than one job title may be intentionally listed here more than once.

Paul Allison, CEO, Subsidiary
Scott Curtis, Pres., Divisional
Dennis Zank, CEO, Subsidiary
Steven Raney, CEO, Subsidiary
Tashtego Elwyn, CEO, Subsidiary
Paul Reilly, CEO
Jennifer Ackart, CFO, Subsidiary
Jeffrey Julien, CFO
Thomas James, Chairman Emeritus
Jeffrey Dowdle, Chief Administrative Officer
George Catanese, Chief Risk Officer
Francis Godbold, Director
Bella Allaire, Executive VP, Subsidiary
Jonathan Santelli, Executive VP
James Bunn, President, Subsidiary
Jodi Perry, President, Subsidiary
John Carson, President

GROWTH PLANS/SPECIAL FEATURES:

Raymond James Financial, Inc. (RJF) is a diversified financial services holding company with subsidiaries engaged in investment and financial planning primarily in the U.S. and Canada, but in overseas locations as well. The firm has more than 3,000 locations, with approximately $755 billion of total client assets under management. RJF's services include securities, brokerage, investment banking, asset management, banking and cash management and trust products. The firm's principal subsidiaries are: Raymond James & Associates, Inc. (RJ&A); Raymond James Financial Services, Inc. (RJFS); Raymond James Financial Services Advisors, Inc. (RJFSA); Raymond James, Ltd. (RJ Ltd); Eagle Asset Management, Inc. (Eagle); and Raymond James Bank, NA (RJ Bank). RJF operates through five segments: private client, capital markets, asset management, RJ Bank and other. The private client segment provides securities transaction and financial planning services to roughly 2.9 million client accounts through the branch office systems of RJ&A, RJFS, RJFSA, RJ Ltd., and in the U.K, through Raymond James Investment Services Limited. The capital markets segment offers equity and fixed income products and services in which institutional clients are serviced through the RJ&A fixed income department and its European offices, as well as through Raymond James Financial International Ltd. (headquartered in London) and through James European Securities, Inc. The asset management segment provides advisory and asset management services to individual and institutional investment portfolios. The division also sponsors the Eagle line of mutual funds; and provides services to the private client segment. RJ Bank is a federally-chartered bank that offers residential, consumer and commercial loans, as well as deposit accounts, to clients of the company's broker-dealer subsidiaries and to the general public. The other segment includes principal capital and private equity activities as well as various corporate overhead costs of RJF.

Raymond James offers its employees health and life insurance and other benefits.

FINANCIAL DATA:
Note: Data for latest year may not have been available at press time.

In U.S. $	2018	2017	2016	2015	2014	2013
Revenue	7,181,930,000	6,243,855,000	5,300,605,000	5,097,893,000	4,769,082,000	4,408,062,000
R&D Expense						
Operating Income						
Operating Margin %						
SGA Expense	5,342,724,000	4,694,274,000	4,052,906,000	3,950,740,000	3,705,001,000	3,435,780,000
Net Income	856,695,000	636,235,000	529,350,000	502,140,000	480,248,000	367,154,000
Operating Cash Flow	1,903,327,000	1,305,936,000	-518,324,000	899,177,000	507,587,000	659,805,000
Capital Expenditure	133,586,000	189,994,000	121,733,000	74,111,000	60,149,000	72,879,000
EBITDA						
Return on Assets %		.02%	.02%	.02%	.02%	.02%
Return on Equity %		.12%	.11%	.12%	.12%	.10%
Debt to Equity		0.439	0.468	0.39	0.419	0.343

CONTACT INFORMATION:
Phone: 727 567-1000 Fax:
Toll-Free: 800-248-8863
Address: 880 Carillon Pkwy., St. Petersburg, FL 33716 United States

STOCK TICKER/OTHER:
Stock Ticker: RJF Exchange: NYS
Employees: 11,900 Fiscal Year Ends: 09/30
Parent Company:

SALARIES/BONUSES:
Top Exec. Salary: $500,000 Bonus: $5,500,043
Second Exec. Salary: $281,250 Bonus: $2,825,052

OTHER THOUGHTS:
Estimated Female Officers or Directors: 1
Hot Spot for Advancement for Women/Minorities: Y

Raytheon Company

NAIC Code: 336414

www.raytheon.com

TYPES OF BUSINESS:
Guided Missile and Space Vehicle Manufacturing
Commercial Electronics
Technical Services
Communications & Information Systems
Sensors & Surveillance Equipment
Missile Systems
Software Engineering
Cybersecurity Solutions

BRANDS/DIVISIONS/AFFILIATES:
Forcepoint

CONTACTS: Note: Officers with more than one job title may be intentionally listed here more than once.
Thomas Kennedy, CEO
Frank Jimenez, VP
Anthony OBrien, CFO
Michael Wood, Controller
Ralph Acaba, President, Divisional
Wesley Kremer, President, Divisional
Rebecca Rhoads, President, Divisional
David Wajsgras, President, Divisional
Roy Azevedo, President, Divisional
Taylor Lawrence, Vice President
Randa Newsome, Vice President, Divisional

GROWTH PLANS/SPECIAL FEATURES:
Raytheon Company offers electronics, mission systems integration and mission support services to defense, homeland security and other government markets worldwide. Raytheon operates through five segments: integrated defense systems (IDS); intelligence, information and systems (IIS); missile systems (MS); space and airborne systems (SAS); and Forcepoint. IDS provides air and missile defense; radar solutions; naval combat and ship electronic systems; command, control, communications, computers and intelligence solutions; and Air Traffic Management systems. IIS specializes in global intelligence, surveillance and reconnaissance (ISR), navigation, Department of Defense space and weather solutions; cybersecurity, analytics, training, logistics, mission support and engineering and sustainment solutions. MS develops missile and combat systems, including weapon systems, projectiles, kinetic kill vehicles, directed energy effectors and advanced combat sensor solutions for the U.S. armed forces and other allied nations. SAS designs sensor and communication systems for advanced missions, including ISR, precision engagement, unmanned aerial operations and space. This segment provides electro-optical/infrared sensors, airborne radars for surveillance and fire control applications, lasers, precision guidance systems, signals intelligence systems, processors, electronic warfare systems, communication systems and space-qualified systems for civil and military applications. Forcepoint develops cybersecurity products serving commercial and government organizations, and include user and data security solutions, as well as cloud access and network security solutions. Its government organizations solutions include a suite of cross domain and insider threat technologies to access and transfer data, including streaming video, across multiple domains. In June 2019, the firm and United Technologies Corp announced plans to merge. The new firm would be named Raytheon Technologies Corp. The transaction is expected to close in the first half of 2020.

Employees receive medical, dental, drug and vision coverage; health care reimbursement accounts; life and AD&D insurance; disability; a retirement program; adoption assistance; and educational assistance.

FINANCIAL DATA: Note: Data for latest year may not have been available at press time.

In U.S. $	2018	2017	2016	2015	2014	2013
Revenue	27,058,000,000	25,348,000,000	24,069,000,000	23,247,000,000	22,826,000,000	23,706,000,000
R&D Expense	841,000,000	734,000,000	755,000,000	706,000,000	500,000,000	465,000,000
Operating Income	4,538,000,000	3,318,000,000	3,240,000,000	3,013,000,000	3,179,000,000	2,938,000,000
Operating Margin %		.13%	.13%	.13%	.14%	.12%
SGA Expense	2,106,000,000	2,220,000,000	2,127,000,000	1,954,000,000	1,852,000,000	1,771,000,000
Net Income	2,909,000,000	2,024,000,000	2,211,000,000	2,074,000,000	2,244,000,000	1,996,000,000
Operating Cash Flow	3,428,000,000	2,745,000,000	2,852,000,000	2,359,000,000	2,184,000,000	2,378,000,000
Capital Expenditure	821,000,000	611,000,000	625,000,000	457,000,000	380,000,000	329,000,000
EBITDA	3,899,000,000	3,868,000,000	3,777,000,000	3,509,000,000	3,635,000,000	3,412,000,000
Return on Assets %		.07%	.07%	.07%	.08%	.08%
Return on Equity %		.20%	.22%	.21%	.22%	.21%
Debt to Equity		0.477	0.53	0.526	0.56	0.429

CONTACT INFORMATION:
Phone: 788 522-3000 Fax: 781 522-3001
Toll-Free:
Address: 870 Winter St., Waltham, MA 02451 United States

STOCK TICKER/OTHER:
Stock Ticker: RTN
Employees: 63,000
Parent Company:

Exchange: NYS
Fiscal Year Ends: 12/31

SALARIES/BONUSES:
Top Exec. Salary: $1,511,559 Bonus: $
Second Exec. Salary: $977,101 Bonus: $19,542

OTHER THOUGHTS:
Estimated Female Officers or Directors: 4
Hot Spot for Advancement for Women/Minorities: Y

Sales, profits and employees may be estimates. Financial information, benefits and other data can change quickly and may vary from those stated here.

Red Hat Inc

NAIC Code: 0

www.redhat.com

TYPES OF BUSINESS:
Computer Software-Linux Operating Systems
Open-Source Software

BRANDS/DIVISIONS/AFFILIATES:
International Business Machines Corporation (IBM)
Red Hat Enterprise Linux
Red Hat JBoss Middleware
Red Hat Satellite
Red Hat Enterprise Linux
Red Hat Cloud
Red Had Mobile Application
Red Hat Storage

CONTACTS:
Note: Officers with more than one job title may be intentionally listed here more than once.

James Whitehurst, CEO
Eric Shander, CFO
Narendra Gupta, Chairman of the Board
Michael Kelly, Chief Information Officer
Arun Oberoi, Executive VP, Divisional
Michael Cunningham, Executive VP
DeLisa Alexander, Executive VP
Paul Cormier, President, Divisional

GROWTH PLANS/SPECIAL FEATURES:

Red Hat, Inc. is a provider of open-source software solutions. The firm's solutions include its core enterprise operating system platform Red Hat Enterprise Linux, the enterprise middleware platform Red Hat JBoss Middleware Suite, virtual solutions, cloud storage and other Red Hat enterprise technologies. The company offers a choice of operating system platforms for servers, work stations and desktops that support multiple application areas, including the data center, edge-of-the-network applications, IT infrastructure, corporate desktop and technical/developer workstation. Red Hat JBoss Middleware delivers a suite of middleware products for service-oriented architectures, permitting web-enabled applications to run on open source and other platforms. The software provides an application infrastructure for building and deploying distributed applications that are accessible via the internet, corporate intranets, extranets and virtual private networks. Applications deployed on JBoss include online e-business, hotel and airline reservations, online banking, credit card processing, securities trading, healthcare systems, customer and partner portals, retail and point of sale systems (POS), telecommunications network infrastructure and grid-based systems. The integrated management service, Red Hat Satellite, permit Red Hat enterprise technologies to be updated and configured as well as the performance of these and other technologies to be monitored and managed in an automated fashion. Red Hat Cloud software enables customers to build and manage various cloud computing environments, including the Red Hat OpenStack platform, Red Hat Cloud infrastructure and more. The Red Hat Mobile Application platform enables customers to develop, integrate, deploy and manage mobile applications for the enterprise. Last, Red Hat Storage software enables firms to manage large, unstructured or semi-structured data at large scale via commodity hardware in hybrid cloud environments. In July 2019, Red Hat was acquired by IBM, a multinational information technology company, for $35 billion.

FINANCIAL DATA:
Note: Data for latest year may not have been available at press time.

In U.S. $	2018	2017	2016	2015	2014	2013
Revenue	2,920,461,056	2,411,802,880	2,052,230,016	1,789,489,024	1,534,615,040	1,328,817,024
R&D Expense						
Operating Income						
Operating Margin %						
SGA Expense						
Net Income	258,803,008	253,703,008	199,364,992	180,200,992	178,292,000	150,204,000
Operating Cash Flow						
Capital Expenditure						
EBITDA						
Return on Assets %						
Return on Equity %						
Debt to Equity						

CONTACT INFORMATION:
Phone: 919 754-3700
Fax: 919 754-3701
Toll-Free: 888-733-4281
Address: 100 East Davie St., Raleigh, NC 27601 United States

SALARIES/BONUSES:
Top Exec. Salary: $
Bonus: $
Second Exec. Salary: $
Bonus: $

STOCK TICKER/OTHER:
Stock Ticker: Subsidiary
Exchange:
Employees: 10,500
Fiscal Year Ends: 02/28
Parent Company: International Business Machines Corporation (IBM)

OTHER THOUGHTS:
Estimated Female Officers or Directors: 3
Hot Spot for Advancement for Women/Minorities: Y

Sales, profits and employees may be estimates. Financial information, benefits and other data can change quickly and may vary from those stated here.

Regal-Beloit Corporation

NAIC Code: 335312

www.regal-beloit.com

TYPES OF BUSINESS:
Mechanical Products Manufacturing
HVAC Components

BRANDS/DIVISIONS/AFFILIATES:
Nicotra Gebhardt Spa

CONTACTS:
Note: Officers with more than one job title may be intentionally listed here more than once.

Louis Pinkham, CEO
Robert Rehard, CFO
Rakesh Sachdev, Chairman of the Board
Jason Longley, Chief Accounting Officer
Jonathan Schlemmer, COO
Thomas Valentyn, General Counsel
Timothy Oswald, Vice President, Divisional
John Avampato, Vice President

GROWTH PLANS/SPECIAL FEATURES:

Regal-Beloit Corporation is a U.S.-based multinational corporation that manufactures electric motors and motion controls, electric generators and power transmission products. The company operates through three segments: commercial & industrial systems (CIS), climate solutions and power transmission solutions. CIS designs, manufactures and sells fractional, integral and large horsepower AC and DC motors and controls for commercial and industrial applications. These motors are sold directly to original equipment manufacturer (OEM) and end-user customers through direct and independent sales representatives, as well as through regional and national distributors. Climate solutions designs, manufactures and sells fractional motors, electronic variable speed controls and blowers used in a variety of residential and light commercial air moving applications including HVAC systems and commercial refrigeration. Power transmission solutions designs, manufactures and markets standard, modified and highly engineered enclosed gear drives, gearmotors, transmissions and custom open gearing used for motion control within complex equipment systems. This gearing reduces the speed and increases the torque from an electric motor or other prime mover to meet the requirements of equipment such as a conveyor drive. Regal manufactures many the products that it sells at its facilities located in the U.S., Canada, Mexico, India, China, Thailand and Europe. During 2018, the firm acquired Nicotra Gebhardt SpA for $161.5 million, which manufactures, sells and services fans and blowers under the Nicotra and Gebhardt brands. Nicotra Gebhardt was merged into the CIS segment.

FINANCIAL DATA:
Note: Data for latest year may not have been available at press time.

In U.S. $	2018	2017	2016	2015	2014	2013
Revenue	3,645,600,000	3,360,300,000	3,224,500,000	3,509,700,000	3,257,100,000	3,095,700,000
R&D Expense						
Operating Income	365,200,000	330,100,000	320,600,000	332,700,000	281,000,000	289,000,000
Operating Margin %		.10%	.10%	.09%	.09%	.09%
SGA Expense						
Net Income	231,200,000	213,000,000	203,400,000	143,300,000	31,000,000	120,000,000
Operating Cash Flow	362,700,000	291,900,000	439,600,000	381,100,000	298,200,000	305,000,000
Capital Expenditure	77,600,000	65,200,000	65,200,000	92,200,000	88,200,000	91,000,000
EBITDA	489,800,000	470,500,000	480,500,000	416,500,000	268,100,000	341,400,000
Return on Assets %		.05%	.05%	.04%	.01%	.03%
Return on Equity %		.10%	.10%	.07%	.02%	.06%
Debt to Equity		0.447	0.643	0.886	0.323	0.296

CONTACT INFORMATION:
Phone: 608 364-8800　　Fax: 608 364-8818
Toll-Free:
Address: 200 State St., Beloit, WI 53511 United States

STOCK TICKER/OTHER:
Stock Ticker: RBC
Employees: 23,000
Parent Company:

Exchange: NYS
Fiscal Year Ends: 12/31

SALARIES/BONUSES:
Top Exec. Salary: $995,000　　Bonus: $
Second Exec. Salary: $612,500　　Bonus: $

OTHER THOUGHTS:
Estimated Female Officers or Directors:
Hot Spot for Advancement for Women/Minorities:

REI (Recreational Equipment Inc)

NAIC Code: 451110

www.rei.com

TYPES OF BUSINESS:
Outdoor Gear & Clothing, Retail
Sporting Equipment Retail & Rental
Adventure Travel Services
Catalog & Online Sales

BRANDS/DIVISIONS/AFFILIATES:
REI
REI Adventures
REI Gear and Apparel
Arizona Outback Adventures

CONTACTS:
Note: Officers with more than one job title may be intentionally listed here more than once.

Jerry Stritzke, CEO
Eric Artz, Exec. VP
Tracie Winbigler, CFO
Raquel Karls, Sr. VP-Human Resources
Chris Putur, CIO
Susan Viscon, VP-Merch.
Catherine Walker, General Counsel
Brad Brown, Sr. VP-e-Commerce & Direct Sales
Michael Collins, VP-Public Affairs
Sue Sallee, VP-Finance & Acct.
Tim Spangler, Sr. VP-Retail
Kathleen Peterson, VP-REI Private Brands
Steve Hooper, Chmn.
Rick Bingle, VP-Supply Chain

GROWTH PLANS/SPECIAL FEATURES:

Recreational Equipment, Inc. (REI) is one of the largest consumer cooperatives in the U.S. The firm offers quality outdoor gear, clothing and footwear selected for performance and durability in outdoor recreation, including hiking, climbing, camping, bicycling, paddling and winter sports. Today, REI has more than 17 million members served by over 150 retail stores across 35 U.S., as well as two online stores at REI.com and REI Outlet. Stores include a variety of facilities for testing equipment, including bike test trails, climbing pinnacles and camp stove demonstration tables. While anyone may shop at the stores, customers who pay a small fee to become members receive special discounts and a share in the company's profits through an annual patronage refund based on their purchases. REI's e-commerce site is one of the largest outdoor online stores, offering a comprehensive library of product information, expert gear advice and outdoor recreation information. In addition to nationally-recognized brands, the company sells private label apparel and accessories under the REI Gear and Apparel brand. It also offers mountain, road, specialty, hybrid, electric and kid's bikes under various brand names. Through REI Adventures, the company has been operating small group tours throughout the world for more than 20 years, avoiding standard tourist routes and emphasizing outdoor activities. Each year, REI Adventures plans domestic and international bicycling, trekking, kayaking, hiking, camping and mountaineering adventures. The firm invests millions of dollars on an annual basis to build trails, clean up the environment and teach children outdoor ethics. In February 2019, REI acquired its long-standing adventure travel partner, Arizona Outback Adventures.

The firm offers employees health, life and disability plans; tuition reimbursement; adoption and relocation assistance; an employee discount program; and a public transit subsidy.

FINANCIAL DATA:
Note: Data for latest year may not have been available at press time.

In U.S. $	2018	2017	2016	2015	2014	2013
Revenue	2,781,909,000	2,622,776,000	2,423,221,000	2,217,130,000	2,017,476,000	2,000,000,000
R&D Expense						
Operating Income						
Operating Margin %						
SGA Expense						
Net Income	46,753,000	30,525,000	38,275,000	44,183,000	19,031,000	153,300,000
Operating Cash Flow						
Capital Expenditure						
EBITDA						
Return on Assets %						
Return on Equity %						
Debt to Equity						

CONTACT INFORMATION:
Phone: 253-891-2500   Fax: 253-891-2523
Toll-Free: 800-426-4840
Address: 6750 S. 228th St., Kent, WA 98032 United States

STOCK TICKER/OTHER:
Stock Ticker: Private
Employees: 13,000
Parent Company:

Exchange:
Fiscal Year Ends: 01/02

SALARIES/BONUSES:
Top Exec. Salary: $ Bonus: $
Second Exec. Salary: $ Bonus: $

OTHER THOUGHTS:
Estimated Female Officers or Directors: 7
Hot Spot for Advancement for Women/Minorities: Y

Sales, profits and employees may be estimates. Financial information, benefits and other data can change quickly and may vary from those stated here.

Republic Services Inc

NAIC Code: 562111

www.republicservices.com

TYPES OF BUSINESS:
Solid Waste Collection
Recycling

BRANDS/DIVISIONS/AFFILIATES:

CONTACTS: Note: Officers with more than one job title may be intentionally listed here more than once.
Donald Slager, CEO
Charles Serianni, CFO
Brian Goebel, Chief Accounting Officer
Jeffrey Hughes, Chief Administrative Officer
Catharine Ellingsen, Chief Compliance Officer
Timothy Stuart, COO
Manuel Kadre, Director
Brian Bales, Executive VP
Jon Ark, President

GROWTH PLANS/SPECIAL FEATURES:
Republic Services, Inc. provides non-hazardous solid waste collection services for commercial, industrial, municipal and residential customers through 340 collection operations in 40 states and Puerto Rico. It owns or operates 201 transfer stations, 195 active landfills, 90 recycling centers, seven treatment/recovery/disposal facilities, 12 salt water disposal wells and 68 landfill gas and renewable energy projects. The company's operations primarily consist of providing collection, transfer station and disposal of non-hazardous solid waste and the recovery and recycling of certain materials. The firm provides solid waste collection services to commercial, industrial, municipal and residential customers through its collection operations. Republic Services generates approximately 74% of its revenue from collection services. Republic Services deposits waste at its transfer stations, as do other private haulers and municipal haulers. The waste is compacted and then transferred to trailers for transport to disposal sites or recycling facilities. The company's disposal and materials recovery activities generate revenue through the collection, processing and sale of corrugated cardboard, newspaper, aluminum, glass and other materials. Republic Services' facilities and operations are subject to a variety of federal, state and local requirements that regulate the environment, public health, safety, zoning and land use.

FINANCIAL DATA: Note: Data for latest year may not have been available at press time.

In U.S. $	2018	2017	2016	2015	2014	2013
Revenue	10,040,900,000	10,041,500,000	9,387,700,000	9,115,000,000	8,788,300,000	8,417,200,000
R&D Expense						
Operating Income	1,798,000,000	1,732,000,000	1,657,200,000	1,638,200,000	1,332,900,000	1,293,600,000
Operating Margin %		.17%	.18%	.18%	.15%	.15%
SGA Expense	1,024,700,000	1,028,000,000	955,000,000	964,900,000	897,800,000	995,400,000
Net Income	1,036,900,000	1,278,400,000	612,600,000	749,900,000	547,600,000	588,900,000
Operating Cash Flow	2,242,800,000	1,910,700,000	1,847,800,000	1,679,700,000	1,529,800,000	1,548,200,000
Capital Expenditure	1,071,800,000	989,800,000	927,800,000	945,600,000	862,500,000	880,800,000
EBITDA	2,818,800,000	2,716,500,000	2,354,000,000	2,563,700,000	2,174,100,000	2,117,700,000
Return on Assets %		.06%	.03%	.04%	.03%	.03%
Return on Equity %		.16%	.08%	.10%	.07%	.08%
Debt to Equity		0.94	0.995	0.974	0.91	0.886

CONTACT INFORMATION:
Phone: 480 627-2700   Fax:
Toll-Free:
Address: 18500 North Allied Way, Phoenix, AZ 85054 United States

STOCK TICKER/OTHER:
Stock Ticker: RSG
Employees: 33,000
Parent Company:

Exchange: NYS
Fiscal Year Ends: 12/31

SALARIES/BONUSES:
Top Exec. Salary: $1,134,327   Bonus: $
Second Exec. Salary: $623,077   Bonus: $

OTHER THOUGHTS:
Estimated Female Officers or Directors:
Hot Spot for Advancement for Women/Minorities:

ResMed Inc

NAIC Code: 334510

www.resmed.com

TYPES OF BUSINESS:
Sleep Disordered Breathing Medical Equipment
Diagnosis & Treatment Products

BRANDS/DIVISIONS/AFFILIATES:
AirSense 10
AirCurve 10
AirMini
Astral
Activox
Lumis
Mobi

CONTACTS:
Note: Officers with more than one job title may be intentionally listed here more than once.

Michael Farrell, CEO
Brett Sandercock, CFO
Peter Farrell, Chairman of the Board
David Pendarvis, Chief Administrative Officer
Robert Douglas, COO
James Hollingshead, President, Divisional
Rajwant Sodhi, President, Divisional
Richie McHale, President, Divisional

GROWTH PLANS/SPECIAL FEATURES:
ResMed, Inc. is an Australia-founded company that develops, manufactures, distributes and markets medical devices and cloud-based software applications for treating, diagnosing and managing sleep disordered breathing (SDB) and other respiratory disorders. SDB includes obstructive sleep apnea (OSA) and other related respiratory disorders that occur during sleep. Other respiratory disorders include chronic obstructive pulmonary disease (COPD) and neuromuscular disease. ResMed was originally founded to commercialize a continuous positive airway pressure (CPAP) treatment for OSA, which delivers pressurized air, typically through a nasal mask, to prevent collapse of the upper airway during sleep. Since the introduction of nasal CPAP, the firm has developed a number of innovative products, including related mask systems, headgear, airflow generators, diagnostic products and other accessories. The firm's recent CPAP products include AirSense 10 Elite and AirSense 10 CPAP. Its variable positive airway pressure (VPAP) products include the AirCurve 10S, AirCurve 10 V Auto, AirCurve 10 ST, AirCurve 10 ASV and the AirCurve 10 CS. Autoset products include the AirSense 10 Auto and the AirMini. Ventilation products include the Astral 100 and 150, Activox, Lumis 100 and 150, Lumis ST-A and Mobi. ResMed's business strategy includes expanding into new clinical applications by seeking to identify new uses for its technologies, as well as increasing consumer awareness of little-known conditions. The firm sells products in over 120 countries through wholly-owned subsidiaries and independent distributors. Through various subsidiaries, ResMed owns or has licensed rights to over 5,700 pending patents.

FINANCIAL DATA:
Note: Data for latest year may not have been available at press time.

In U.S. $	2018	2017	2016	2015	2014	2013
Revenue	2,340,196,000	2,066,737,000	1,838,713,000	1,678,912,000	1,554,973,000	1,514,457,000
R&D Expense	155,149,000	144,467,000	118,651,000	114,865,000	118,226,000	120,124,000
Operating Income	560,263,000	456,732,000	435,866,000	409,236,000	411,413,000	354,824,000
Operating Margin %	.22%	.22%	.24%	.24%	.26%	.23%
SGA Expense	600,369,000	553,968,000	488,057,000	478,627,000	450,414,000	430,802,000
Net Income	315,588,000	342,284,000	352,409,000	352,886,000	345,273,000	307,133,000
Operating Cash Flow	505,026,000	414,053,000	547,933,000	383,180,000	391,268,000	402,823,000
Capital Expenditure	71,457,000	71,476,000	67,829,000	71,944,000	81,156,000	71,782,000
EBITDA	669,627,000	559,136,000	537,621,000	514,750,000	510,661,000	469,786,000
Return on Assets %		.10%	.13%	.16%	.15%	.14%
Return on Equity %		.19%	.21%	.21%	.20%	.19%
Debt to Equity		0.55	0.516	0.189	0.171	0.00

CONTACT INFORMATION:
Phone: 858 836-5000   Fax: 858 746-2900
Toll-Free: 800-424-0737
Address: 9001 Spectrum Ctr. Blvd., San Diego, CA 92123 United States

STOCK TICKER/OTHER:
Stock Ticker: RMD
Employees: 5,940
Parent Company:

Exchange: NYS
Fiscal Year Ends: 06/30

SALARIES/BONUSES:
Top Exec. Salary: $934,154   Bonus: $
Second Exec. Salary: $813,385   Bonus: $

OTHER THOUGHTS:
Estimated Female Officers or Directors: 2
Hot Spot for Advancement for Women/Minorities:

Revlon Inc

NAIC Code: 325620

www.revlon.com

TYPES OF BUSINESS:
Cosmetics
Fragrances
Hair Care Products
Skin Care Products

BRANDS/DIVISIONS/AFFILIATES:
Revlon Consumer Products Corp
MacAndrews & Forbes Inc
Pure Ice
Revlon Professional
CND
American Crew
ColorSilk
Elizabeth Arden Inc

CONTACTS:
Note: Officers with more than one job title may be intentionally listed here more than once.

Victoria Dolan, CFO
Ronald Perelman, Chairman of the Board
Pamela Bucher, Chief Accounting Officer
Debra Perelman, Director
E. Beattie, Director

GROWTH PLANS/SPECIAL FEATURES:

Revlon, Inc., through its subsidiary Revlon Consumer Products Corporation, manufactures, markets and sells an extensive array of cosmetics, skin care, fragrances and personal care products. Revlon is one of the world's best-known names in cosmetics and is a leading mass-market brand. Revlon is an indirect majority-owned subsidiary of MacAndrews & Forbes, Inc., a corporation wholly-owned by Ronald O. Perelman. The firm's products are marketed under names including Almay, UniqOne, Charlie, Mitchum, Gatineau, Pure Ice, Revlon, Llongueras, Natural Honey, ColorSilk and Jean Nate. These products are sold in more than 150 countries worldwide. Revlon operates in four segments: consumer, professional, Elizabeth Arden and other. The consumer segment is comprised of products manufactured, marketed and sold primarily within the mass channel in the U.S. and internationally, as well as certain department stores and other specialty stores outside the U.S. The professional segment manufactures, markets and sells professional products primarily to hair and nail salons and distributors in the U.S., as well as internationally. Products in this division are marketed under such brands as Revlon Professional, for hair color, hair care and hair treatments; Creme of Nature for multi-cultural hair care; CND in nail polishes and enhancements such as CND Shellac and CND Vinylux nail polishes; and American Crew in men's grooming products. The Elizabeth Arden segment markets, distributes and sells fragrances, skin care and color cosmetics to prestige retailers, specialty stores, the mass retail channel, distributors, perfumeries, department stores, boutiques, travel retailers and other retailers in the U.S. and internationally. The other segment includes the operating results related to the development, marketing and distribution of certain licensed fragrances and other beauty products.

FINANCIAL DATA:
Note: Data for latest year may not have been available at press time.

In U.S. $	2018	2017	2016	2015	2014	2013
Revenue	2,564,500,000	2,693,700,000	2,334,000,000	1,914,300,000	1,941,000,000	1,494,700,000
R&D Expense						
Operating Income	-13,000,000	74,800,000	255,900,000	244,000,000	263,200,000	217,900,000
Operating Margin %		.03%	.11%	.13%	.14%	.15%
SGA Expense	1,460,500,000	1,467,600,000	1,161,000,000	1,002,500,000	1,009,500,000	731,700,000
Net Income	-294,200,000	-183,200,000	-21,900,000	56,100,000	40,900,000	-5,800,000
Operating Cash Flow	-170,800,000	-139,300,000	116,900,000	155,300,000	174,000,000	123,300,000
Capital Expenditure	57,200,000	108,300,000	59,300,000	48,300,000	55,500,000	28,600,000
EBITDA	61,900,000	142,100,000	236,900,000	297,200,000	304,400,000	226,100,000
Return on Assets %		-.06%	-.01%	.03%	.02%	.00%
Return on Equity %						
Debt to Equity						

CONTACT INFORMATION:
Phone: 212 527-4000 Fax: 212 527-4130
Toll-Free:
Address: 1 New York Plaza, New York, NY 10004 United States

STOCK TICKER/OTHER:
Stock Ticker: REV
Employees: 7,300
Parent Company: MacAndrews & Forbes Inc

Exchange: NYS
Fiscal Year Ends: 12/31

SALARIES/BONUSES:
Top Exec. Salary: $1,438,099 Bonus: $292,500
Second Exec. Salary: $484,615 Bonus: $450,000

OTHER THOUGHTS:
Estimated Female Officers or Directors: 6
Hot Spot for Advancement for Women/Minorities: Y

Ritz-Carlton Hotel Company LLC (The)

NAIC Code: 721110

www.ritzcarlton.com

TYPES OF BUSINESS:
Hotels, Luxury
Condominiums
Golf Courses
Spas
Time Share Units

BRANDS/DIVISIONS/AFFILIATES:
Marriott International Inc
Six Senses
La Prairie
ESPA
Ritz-Carlton Destination Club (The)
Residencies at the Ritz-Carlton (The)

CONTACTS: Note: Officers with more than one job title may be intentionally listed here more than once.
Herve Humler, Pres.
Bob Kharazmi, Global Officer

GROWTH PLANS/SPECIAL FEATURES:
The Ritz-Carlton Hotel Company, LLC, a subsidiary of Marriott International, Inc., is one of the world's best-known luxury hotel chains, operating 97 hotels in 30 countries and territories. The firm maintains international sales offices in locations such as Chicago, New York, Los Angeles, Dubai, Shanghai, Tokyo and London. To cater toward an upscale client base, full-service luxury spas are offered at most Ritz-Carlton resorts. Some spas operate under the brand names Six Senses, La Prairie and ESPA. Besides its hotels, the firm provides vacation properties and residential suites under The Ritz-Carlton Destination Club and The Residencies at the Ritz-Carlton. The Ritz-Carlton Destination Club is the firm's time-share ownership unit, offering a flexible alternative to a second home. Membership is currently available in locations such as Aspen Highlands, Bachelor Gulch and Vail, Colorado; St. Thomas, U.S. Virgin Islands; San Francisco and North Lake Tahoe, California; Jupiter, Florida; Abaco, Bahamas; and Kauai Lagoons and Maui, Hawaii. The Residencies at the Ritz-Carlton offer luxury condominiums and estate homes throughout the U.S. and in Canada, Thailand, Israel, the Bahamas and Malaysia. Ritz-Carlton also markets its 15 luxury golf courses (many designed by leading names in the golf world such as Greg Norman, Jack Nicklaus and Tom Fazio) and fitness facilities to both local residents and visitors, and hosts many PGA and Senior PGA tournaments. Partner hotels include Bulgari Hotels and Resorts, EDITION hotels and The Cosmopolitan (Las Vegas).

The Ritz-Carlton offers employees health, dental, vision and short-/long-term disability coverage; tuition reimbursement; credit union membership; and employee assistance programs.

FINANCIAL DATA: Note: Data for latest year may not have been available at press time.

In U.S. $	2018	2017	2016	2015	2014	2013
Revenue	2,415,000,000	2,300,000,000	2,200,000,000	2,400,000,000	2,355,320,000	2,222,213,400
R&D Expense						
Operating Income						
Operating Margin %						
SGA Expense						
Net Income						
Operating Cash Flow						
Capital Expenditure						
EBITDA						
Return on Assets %						
Return on Equity %						
Debt to Equity						

CONTACT INFORMATION:
Phone: 301-380-3000   Fax:
Toll-Free:
Address: 10400 Fernwood Rd., Bethesda, MD 20817 United States

STOCK TICKER/OTHER:
Stock Ticker: Subsidiary   Exchange:
Employees: 40,000   Fiscal Year Ends: 12/31
Parent Company: Marriott International Inc

SALARIES/BONUSES:
Top Exec. Salary: $ Bonus: $
Second Exec. Salary: $ Bonus: $

OTHER THOUGHTS:
Estimated Female Officers or Directors: 1
Hot Spot for Advancement for Women/Minorities:

Sales, profits and employees may be estimates. Financial information, benefits and other data can change quickly and may vary from those stated here.

Robert Half International Inc

www.rhi.com

NAIC Code: 561320

TYPES OF BUSINESS:
Staffing
Risk Consulting
Internal Audit Services
Litigation Consulting & Forensic Accounting

BRANDS/DIVISIONS/AFFILIATES:
Accountemps
Robert Half Finance & Accounting
Robert Half Management Resources
Robert Half Technology
OfficeTeam
Robert Half Legal
Creative Group (The)
Protiviti Inc

CONTACTS: Note: Officers with more than one job title may be intentionally listed here more than once.
Harold Messmer, CEO
M. Waddell, CFO
Michael Buckley, Chief Accounting Officer
Paul Gentzkow, COO, Divisional
Robert Glass, Executive VP, Divisional

GROWTH PLANS/SPECIAL FEATURES:

Robert Half International, Inc. (RHI) provides professional staffing and risk consulting services. RHI has more than 325 staffing locations around the world. It provides temporary, project and full-time workers to firms in areas such as accounting, finance, administrative and legal support, IT, advertising and marketing. RHI consists of specialized staffing divisions: Accountemps, for the staffing of accounting, tax and finance professionals; Robert Half Finance & Accounting and Robert Half Management Resources, for senior-level accounting and finance professionals; OfficeTeam, a division for highly skilled temporary administrative support staff; Robert Half Technology, for IT professionals; Robert Half Legal, which provides attorneys, paralegals and legal support personnel; and The Creative Group, for advertising, marketing and web design professionals. RHI has increased its focus on providing workers for small to mid-size businesses, and it has a growing number of highly-experienced, older workers on its list. Protiviti, Inc., the company's wholly-owned subsidiary, provides internal audit and risk consulting services by aiding clients in identifying, measuring and managing operational and technology-related risks in areas such as the media, hospitality, communications, energy, financial services, real estate, healthcare, government, education, non-profit, manufacturing, distribution and technology. Business risk consultations involve areas such as anti-money laundering, capital projects and construction, energy commodity risks, fraud investigation and forensic accounting. Technology risk consultations provide solutions for security and privacy, continuity, change management, IT assets and application effectiveness.

The firm offers employees medical, dental, vision and life insurance; a savings plan; short- and long-term disability coverage; an employee assistance program; and travel accident insurance.

FINANCIAL DATA: Note: Data for latest year may not have been available at press time.

In U.S. $	2018	2017	2016	2015	2014	2013
Revenue	5,800,271,000	5,266,789,000	5,250,399,000	5,094,933,000	4,695,014,000	4,245,895,000
R&D Expense						
Operating Income	587,220,000	515,717,000	553,222,000	580,480,000	496,625,000	396,577,000
Operating Margin %		.10%	.11%	.11%	.11%	.09%
SGA Expense	1,821,089,000	1,646,532,000	1,606,217,000	1,533,799,000	1,425,734,000	1,324,815,000
Net Income	434,288,000	290,584,000	343,389,000	357,796,000	305,928,000	252,195,000
Operating Cash Flow	572,322,000	452,991,000	442,081,000	438,236,000	340,698,000	309,217,000
Capital Expenditure	42,484,000	40,753,000	82,956,000	75,057,000	62,830,000	53,725,000
EBITDA	653,169,000	581,210,000	617,537,000	633,945,000	546,306,000	445,349,000
Return on Assets %		.16%	.20%	.21%	.20%	.18%
Return on Equity %		.27%	.33%	.36%	.32%	.29%
Debt to Equity		0.001	0.001	0.001	0.001	0.001

CONTACT INFORMATION:
Phone: 650 234-6000 Fax:
Toll-Free:
Address: 2884 Sand Hill Rd., Menlo Park, CA 94025 United States

STOCK TICKER/OTHER:
Stock Ticker: RHI
Employees: 16,400
Parent Company:

Exchange: NYS
Fiscal Year Ends: 12/31

SALARIES/BONUSES:
Top Exec. Salary: $525,000 Bonus: $
Second Exec. Salary: $265,000 Bonus: $

OTHER THOUGHTS:
Estimated Female Officers or Directors: 1
Hot Spot for Advancement for Women/Minorities:

Sales, profits and employees may be estimates. Financial information, benefits and other data can change quickly and may vary from those stated here.

Rockwell Automation Inc

www.rockwellautomation.com

NAIC Code: 334513

TYPES OF BUSINESS:
Architecture & Software Products
Control Products & Services

BRANDS/DIVISIONS/AFFILIATES:
FactoryTalk
A-B
Allen-Bradley
Rockwell Software
PTC Inc
Emulate3D

CONTACTS:
Note: Officers with more than one job title may be intentionally listed here more than once.

Blake Moret, CEO
Steven Etzel, VP
Patrick Goris, CFO
David Dorgan, Chief Accounting Officer
Christopher Nardecchia, Chief Information Officer
Sujeet Chand, Chief Technology Officer
Rebecca House, General Counsel
Fran Wlodarczyk, Senior VP
Frank Kulaszewicz, Senior VP
Elik Fooks, Senior VP
Michael Laszkiewicz, Senior VP, Divisional
Thomas Donato, Senior VP, Divisional
John Genovesi, Senior VP, Divisional
Robert Murphy, Senior VP, Divisional
John Miller, Vice President

GROWTH PLANS/SPECIAL FEATURES:
Rockwell Automation, Inc. is a global provider of industrial automation power, control and information products and services. It operates in two segments: architecture and software (A&S); and control products and solutions (CP&S). The A&S operating segment contains all elements of the company's integrated control and information architecture capable of connecting the customer's entire manufacturing enterprise. The division's integrated architecture and Logix controllers perform multiple types of control and monitoring applications, including discrete, batch, continuous process, drive system, motion and machine safety across various industrial machinery, plants and processes; and supply real time information to supervisory software and plant-wide information systems. Products include control platforms, software, I/O devices, communication networks, high performance rotary and linear motion control systems, electronic operator interface devices, condition based monitoring systems, sensors, industrial computers and machine safety components. These products are marketed primarily under the FactoryTalk, A-B, Allen-Bradley and Rockwell Software brand names. The CP&S segment's portfolio includes low voltage and medium voltage electro-mechanical and electronic motor starters, motor and circuit protection devices, AC/DC variable frequency drives, contractors, push buttons, signaling devices, termination and protection devices, relays and timers and condition sensors. The segment also offers value-added packaged solutions that range from configured drives and motor control centers to automation and information solutions where Rockwell provides design, integration and start-up services for custom-engineered hardware and software systems. Additionally, the CP&S segment provides life-cycle support services designed to help maximize a customer's automation investment, including multi-vendor customer technical support and repair, asset management, training and maintenance. During 2018, Rockwell Automation acquired a minority position (8.4%) in PTC, Inc., a computer software and services company based in Boston, Massachusetts. In January 2019, it acquired Emulate3D, an engineering software developer.

FINANCIAL DATA:
Note: Data for latest year may not have been available at press time.

In U.S. $	2018	2017	2016	2015	2014	2013
Revenue	6,666,000,000	6,311,300,000	5,879,500,000	6,307,900,000	6,623,500,000	6,351,900,000
R&D Expense						
Operating Income	1,273,200,000	1,032,700,000	1,008,100,000	1,196,700,000	1,183,800,000	1,036,100,000
Operating Margin %		.16%	.17%	.19%	.18%	.16%
SGA Expense	1,599,000,000	1,591,500,000	1,467,400,000	1,506,400,000	1,570,100,000	1,537,700,000
Net Income	535,500,000	825,700,000	729,700,000	827,600,000	826,800,000	756,300,000
Operating Cash Flow	1,300,000,000	1,034,000,000	947,300,000	1,187,700,000	1,033,300,000	1,014,800,000
Capital Expenditure	125,500,000	141,700,000	116,900,000	122,900,000	141,000,000	146,200,000
EBITDA	1,568,400,000	1,282,500,000	1,186,600,000	1,353,700,000	1,346,000,000	1,187,000,000
Return on Assets %		.12%	.11%	.13%	.14%	.13%
Return on Equity %		.35%	.34%	.34%	.31%	.34%
Debt to Equity		0.467	0.762	0.665	0.341	0.35

CONTACT INFORMATION:
Phone: 414 382-2000   Fax: 414 382-8520
Toll-Free:
Address: 1201 S. 2nd St., Milwaukee, WI 53204 United States

STOCK TICKER/OTHER:
Stock Ticker: ROK   Exchange: NYS
Employees: 22,000   Fiscal Year Ends: 09/30
Parent Company:

SALARIES/BONUSES:
Top Exec. Salary: $1,065,385   Bonus: $
Second Exec. Salary: $666,077   Bonus: $

OTHER THOUGHTS:
Estimated Female Officers or Directors: 1
Hot Spot for Advancement for Women/Minorities:

Sales, profits and employees may be estimates. Financial information, benefits and other data can change quickly and may vary from those stated here.

Roper Technologies Inc

www.ropertech.com

NAIC Code: 334513

TYPES OF BUSINESS:
Controls Manufacturing
Energy Controls
Medical Systems
Flow Controls

BRANDS/DIVISIONS/AFFILIATES:

CONTACTS:
Note: Officers with more than one job title may be intentionally listed here more than once.
L. Neil Hunn, CEO
Robert Crisci, CFO
Wilbur Prezzano, Chairman of the Board
Jason Conley, Chief Accounting Officer
John Stipancich, Executive VP
Paul Soni, Vice President

GROWTH PLANS/SPECIAL FEATURES:

Roper Technologies, Inc. is a diversified technology company that designs and develops software, as well as engineered products and solutions for a variety of niche and end markets. Roper operates through four segments: radio frequency (RF) technology, medical & scientific imaging, industrial technology, and energy systems & controls. The RF technology segment represented 41.8% of 2018 revenues, and provides RF identification (RFID) communication technology and software solutions. These offerings include application management software, software-as-a-service, card systems, integrated security solutions, toll/traffic systems, RFID card readers, metering and remote monitoring. The medical & scientific imaging segment (29.3%) is divided into two categories: products and software in medical applications; and high-performance digital imaging products. Medical products and software include diagnostic and laboratory software solutions for healthcare providers. This division's services and technologies support the needs of alternate site healthcare providers who deliver services outside of an acute care hospital setting. In addition, it provides a cloud-based financial analytics and performance software platform to healthcare providers; manufactures and sells patient positioning devices and related software for use in radiation oncology and 3D measurement technology in computer-assisted surgery; supplies diagnostic and therapeutic disposable products, and designs and manufactures a non-invasive instrument for portable ultrasound bladder volume measurement. The digital imaging products and software category manufactures and sells sensitive, high-performance electron filters, charged couple device (CCD) and complementary metal oxide semiconductor cameras, detectors and software for a variety of scientific and industrial uses. The industrial technology segment (17.3%) produces water meter and meter-reading technology, fluid handling pumps and materials analysis solutions. Last, the energy systems & controls segment (11.6%) produces control systems, testing equipment, valves and sensors. These are used for turbomachinery applications, as well as for oil and gas, pipeline, power generation, marine engine, global rubber, plastics, process and other industries.

FINANCIAL DATA:
Note: Data for latest year may not have been available at press time.

In U.S. $	2018	2017	2016	2015	2014	2013
Revenue	5,191,200,000	4,607,471,000	3,789,925,000	3,582,395,000	3,549,494,000	3,238,128,000
R&D Expense						
Operating Income	1,396,400,000	1,210,244,000	1,054,563,000	1,027,918,000	999,473,000	842,361,000
Operating Margin %		.26%	.28%	.29%	.28%	.26%
SGA Expense	1,883,100,000	1,654,552,000	1,277,847,000	1,136,728,000	1,102,426,000	1,040,567,000
Net Income	944,400,000	971,772,000	658,645,000	696,067,000	646,033,000	538,293,000
Operating Cash Flow	1,430,100,000	1,234,482,000	963,785,000	928,825,000	840,441,000	802,553,000
Capital Expenditure	58,600,000	59,536,000	40,106,000	36,260,000	37,644,000	42,528,000
EBITDA	1,763,400,000	1,555,209,000	1,295,016,000	1,232,179,000	1,196,757,000	1,031,551,000
Return on Assets %		.07%	.05%	.07%	.08%	.07%
Return on Equity %		.15%	.12%	.14%	.14%	.14%
Debt to Equity		0.634	1.003	0.616	0.463	0.582

CONTACT INFORMATION:
Phone: 941 556-2601 Fax: 941 556-2670
Toll-Free:
Address: 6901 Professional Parkway East, Sarasota, FL 34240 United States

STOCK TICKER/OTHER:
Stock Ticker: ROP
Employees: 14,155
Parent Company:

Exchange: NYS
Fiscal Year Ends: 12/31

SALARIES/BONUSES:
Top Exec. Salary: $1,030,115 Bonus: $
Second Exec. Salary: $900,000 Bonus: $

OTHER THOUGHTS:
Estimated Female Officers or Directors:
Hot Spot for Advancement for Women/Minorities:

Sales, profits and employees may be estimates. Financial information, benefits and other data can change quickly and may vary from those stated here.

Rosendin Electric Inc

www.rosendin.com

NAIC Code: 238210

TYPES OF BUSINESS:
Electrical Contractor

BRANDS/DIVISIONS/AFFILIATES:

CONTACTS: Note: Officers with more than one job title may be intentionally listed here more than once.
Tom Sorley, CEO
Larry Beltramo, Pres.
Sam Lamonica, CIO

GROWTH PLANS/SPECIAL FEATURES:

Rosendin Electric, Inc. is a San Jose, California-based employee-owned electrical contractor that has been operating since the early 1900s. Services provided by the firm include preconstruction services that assist general contractors and owners during the development phase of a project. These services include design-build engineering, prefabrication, 24-hour/seven-days-a-week service response, network services, electric utility work along highways, service and maintenance, as well as the construction of solar & wind farms. Rosendin's project portfolio includes services for the following industries: biotechnology, pharmaceuticals, data centers, education, healthcare, high tech, institutions, multi-family residences, solar power, transportation, commercial, design-build, entertainment, heavy industrial, hotels, power, telecom and wind energy. Rosendin is also experienced in meeting LEED regulations. Rosendin has additional offices throughout the U.S., including Arizona, Hawaii, Maryland, Nevada, North Carolina, Oregon, Texas and Virginia.

Rosendin offers employees an employee stock ownership plan, 401(k) matching program, health/life/disability insurance and various employee assistance program options.

FINANCIAL DATA: Note: Data for latest year may not have been available at press time.

In U.S. $	2018	2017	2016	2015	2014	2013
Revenue	2,000,000,000	2,000,000,000	1,400,000,000	1,300,000,000	1,100,000,000	935,000,000
R&D Expense						
Operating Income						
Operating Margin %						
SGA Expense						
Net Income						
Operating Cash Flow						
Capital Expenditure						
EBITDA						
Return on Assets %						
Return on Equity %						
Debt to Equity						

CONTACT INFORMATION:
Phone: 480-286-2800   Fax:
Toll-Free:
Address: 880 Mabury Rd., San Jose, CA 95133 United States

STOCK TICKER/OTHER:
Stock Ticker: Private   Exchange:
Employees: 6,000   Fiscal Year Ends:
Parent Company:

SALARIES/BONUSES:
Top Exec. Salary: $ Bonus: $
Second Exec. Salary: $ Bonus: $

OTHER THOUGHTS:
Estimated Female Officers or Directors:
Hot Spot for Advancement for Women/Minorities:

Sales, profits and employees may be estimates. Financial information, benefits and other data can change quickly and may vary from those stated here.

Ross Stores Inc

www.rossstores.com

NAIC Code: 448140

TYPES OF BUSINESS:
Discount Apparel Stores
Home Furnishings

BRANDS/DIVISIONS/AFFILIATES:
Ross Dress for Less
dd's DISCOUNTS

CONTACTS: Note: Officers with more than one job title may be intentionally listed here more than once.
Barbara Rentler, CEO
Michael Hartshorn, CFO
Norman Ferber, Chairman Emeritus
Michael Balmuth, Director
Brian Morrow, Other Executive Officer
James Fassio, Other Executive Officer
Lisa Panattoni, President, Divisional
Bernard Brautigan, President, Divisional

GROWTH PLANS/SPECIAL FEATURES:

Ross Stores, Inc. operates 1,483 off-price retail apparel and home accessories stores in 38 states, Washington, D.C. and Guam, most of which operate under the Ross Dress for Less brand. The company also operates 237 dd's DISCOUNTS locations in 18 states. Most of these stores are located in community and neighborhood strip shopping centers in heavily populated urban and suburban areas. The company's chains target value-conscious women and men ages 18-54. Ross offers new, in-season, name-brand and designer apparel, accessories, footwear and home merchandise at savings of 20%-60% off department and specialty store regular prices, while dd's DISCOUNTS, targeting lower-income customers, offers similar merchandise, but at savings of up to 70% off department and specialty store prices. The company's stores are supplied by four distribution processing facilities. Ross has combined a network of approximately 8,000 vendors and manufacturers, purchasing the vast majority of its merchandise directly from the manufacturer. By purchasing later in the merchandise buying cycle than department and specialty stores, Ross takes advantage of imbalances between retailers' demand for products and manufacturers' supply of those products. In addition, the company typically does not require that manufacturers provide promotional and markdown allowances, return privileges, split shipments, drop shipments to stores or delayed deliveries of merchandise, further enabling Ross to provide significant discounts on in-season merchandise. Sales of ladies products account for approximately 27% of the firm's revenues; home accents/bed and bath, 26%; men's products, 13%; accessories, lingerie, jewelry and fragrances, 13%; shoes, 13%; and children's products, 8%.

Ross offers its employees medical, dental, vision and life insurance; sick pay; health care spending accounts; holiday and personal days; a commuter reimbursement account; a 401(k) plan; and an employee stock purchasing plan.

FINANCIAL DATA: Note: Data for latest year may not have been available at press time.

In U.S. $	2018	2017	2016	2015	2014	2013
Revenue	14,134,730,000	12,866,760,000	11,940,000,000	11,041,680,000	10,230,350,000	
R&D Expense						
Operating Income	2,048,396,000	1,802,644,000	1,624,371,000	1,488,350,000	1,343,063,000	
Operating Margin %	.14%	.14%	.14%	.13%	.13%	
SGA Expense	2,043,698,000	1,890,408,000	1,738,755,000	1,615,371,000	1,526,366,000	
Net Income	1,362,753,000	1,117,654,000	1,020,661,000	924,724,000	837,304,000	
Operating Cash Flow	1,681,278,000	1,558,851,000	1,326,252,000	1,372,865,000	1,022,003,000	
Capital Expenditure	371,423,000	297,880,000	366,960,000	646,691,000	550,515,000	
EBITDA	2,372,730,000	2,108,240,000	1,899,877,000	1,721,720,000	1,549,721,000	
Return on Assets %	.25%	.22%	.21%	.22%	.22%	
Return on Equity %	.47%	.43%	.43%	.43%	.44%	
Debt to Equity	0.102	0.144	0.16	0.175	0.075	

CONTACT INFORMATION:
Phone: 925 965-4400 Fax:
Toll-Free:
Address: 5130 Hacienda Dr., Dublin, CA 94568-7579 United States

STOCK TICKER/OTHER:
Stock Ticker: ROST
Employees: 78,600
Parent Company:

Exchange: NAS
Fiscal Year Ends: 01/31

SALARIES/BONUSES:
Top Exec. Salary: $1,342,500 Bonus: $
Second Exec. Salary: $1,328,944 Bonus: $

OTHER THOUGHTS:
Estimated Female Officers or Directors: 4
Hot Spot for Advancement for Women/Minorities: Y

Sales, profits and employees may be estimates. Financial information, benefits and other data can change quickly and may vary from those stated here.

Royal Caribbean Cruises Ltd

www.royalcaribbean.com

NAIC Code: 483112

TYPES OF BUSINESS:
Cruise Line
Rail Tours
Online Travel Services
Academic Tours

BRANDS/DIVISIONS/AFFILIATES:
Royal Caribbean International
Celebrity Cruises
Azamara Club Cruises
Celebrity Xpedition
TUI Cruises
Pullmantur
SkySea Cruises
Silversea Cruises

CONTACTS:
Note: Officers with more than one job title may be intentionally listed here more than once.

Lawrence Pimentel, CEO, Divisional
Michael Bayley, CEO, Divisional
Lisa Lutoff-Perlo, CEO, Divisional
Richard Fain, CEO
Jason Liberty, CFO
Henry Pujol, Chief Accounting Officer
Bradley Stein, Chief Compliance Officer
Harri Kulovaara, Executive VP, Divisional

GROWTH PLANS/SPECIAL FEATURES:

Royal Caribbean Cruises, Ltd. is a global cruise vacation firm, serving the contemporary, premium and deluxe cruise markets, including the budget and luxury segments. With 50 ships offering more than 130,000 berths, the firm operates five brand names: Royal Caribbean International (RCI), Celebrity Cruises and Azamara Club Cruises. Royal Caribbean's ships have itineraries that call on approximately 535 destinations worldwide. RCI operates 26 ships with 78,150 berths, offering cruise itineraries that range from 2-24 nights. Its destinations include Alaska, Asia, Australia, Bahamas, Bermuda, Canada, the Caribbean, Europe, the Panama Canal, South America and New Zealand. Celebrity Cruises operates 15 ships with 23,170 berths targeted toward higher-end clientele. It also operates Celebrity Xpedition, a ship that travels to the Galapagos Islands and offers pre-cruise tours of Ecuador. This cruise line has four ships on order, offering a new generation known as Edge-class, with an capacity of 11,600 berths which are expected to enter service in late-2018 through 2022. Azamara Club Cruises serves the up-market and consists of two smaller ships, of about 1,400 passengers each, that focus on cruises to unique destinations, with an emphasis on on-board lectures and fine dining. Its ships sail in Asia, the Mediterranean, South America and less traveled Caribbean Islands. Partner brands are complemented by 50%-owned TUI Cruises, which is tailored for the German market; 49%-owned Pullmantur, which serves the Spanish, Portuguese and Latin American cruise markets; and 36%-owned SkySea Cruises, which offers a custom-tailored product for Chinese cruise guests. In April 2018, the firm's 230,000 ton Symphony of the Seas ship was completed, featuring a 6,780-passenger maximum (not counting the 2,175 crew). In June 2018, the firm purchased a 67% interest in luxury cruise line Silversea Cruises.

FINANCIAL DATA:
Note: Data for latest year may not have been available at press time.

In U.S. $	2018	2017	2016	2015	2014	2013
Revenue	9,493,849,000	8,777,845,000	8,496,401,000	8,299,074,000	8,073,855,000	7,959,894,000
R&D Expense						
Operating Income	1,894,801,000	1,744,056,000	1,485,657,000	1,286,169,000	946,177,000	855,094,000
Operating Margin %		.20%	.17%	.15%	.12%	.11%
SGA Expense	1,303,144,000	1,186,016,000	1,100,290,000	1,086,504,000	1,048,952,000	1,044,819,000
Net Income	1,811,042,000	1,625,133,000	1,283,388,000	665,783,000	764,146,000	473,692,000
Operating Cash Flow	3,479,139,000	2,874,566,000	2,516,690,000	1,946,366,000	1,743,759,000	1,412,068,000
Capital Expenditure	3,660,028,000	564,138,000	2,494,363,000	1,613,340,000	1,811,398,000	763,777,000
EBITDA	3,183,161,000	2,876,309,000	2,485,673,000	1,770,516,000	1,794,890,000	1,560,825,000
Return on Assets %		.07%	.06%	.03%	.04%	.02%
Return on Equity %		.16%	.15%	.08%	.09%	.06%
Debt to Equity		0.593	0.888	0.963	0.923	0.739

CONTACT INFORMATION:
Phone: 305 539-6000　　Fax: 305 539-0562
Toll-Free:
Address: 1050 Caribbean Way, Miami, FL 33132 United States

SALARIES/BONUSES:
Top Exec. Salary: $692,308　　Bonus: $450,000
Second Exec. Salary: $1,100,000　　Bonus: $

STOCK TICKER/OTHER:
Stock Ticker: RCL　　Exchange: NYS
Employees: 66,000　　Fiscal Year Ends: 12/31
Parent Company:

OTHER THOUGHTS:
Estimated Female Officers or Directors: 3
Hot Spot for Advancement for Women/Minorities: Y

RPM International Inc

NAIC Code: 325510

www.rpminc.com

TYPES OF BUSINESS:
Home & Industrial Maintenance Products
Specialty Paints
Protective Coatings
Roofing Systems
Sealants & Adhesives

BRANDS/DIVISIONS/AFFILIATES:
Tremco
Stonhard
Carboline
Dap
Rust-Oleum
Varathane
Day-Glo
Zinsser

CONTACTS:
Note: Officers with more than one job title may be intentionally listed here more than once.

Frank Sullivan, CEO
Russell Gordon, CFO
Keith Smiley, Chief Accounting Officer
Edward Moore, Chief Compliance Officer
Matthew Ratajczak, Treasurer
Janeen Kastner, Vice President, Divisional
Barry Slifstein, Vice President, Divisional

GROWTH PLANS/SPECIAL FEATURES:
RPM International, Inc., through its subsidiaries, manufactures, markets and sells specialty paints, protective coatings and roofing systems and sealants and adhesives. The firm focuses on maintenance and improvement needs of both the industrial, specialty and consumer markets. The industrial segment includes maintenance and protection products for roofing and waterproofing systems; flooring; corrosion control; and other specialty applications such as fluorescent pigments, industrial gratings and industrial sealants. These products are sold under brand names including Tremco, Stonhard, Carboline and Tremco illbruck. The specialty segment includes fluorescent colorants and pigments, fire and water damage restoration, wood treatment and fuel additives. Products in this segment are sold under the Day-Glo, Radiant, Unsmoke, Kop-Coat, Sapphire and NatureSeal brand names, among others. The consumer segment includes rust-preventative, special purpose and decorative paints, caulks, sealants, primers and other consumer products. This segment sells products under a variety of brand names, including Dap, Rust-Oleum, Varathane and Zinsser. The firm markets its products in roughly 166 countries and territories and operates manufacturing facilities in 145 locations in the U.S., Argentina, Belgium, Brazil Canada, Chile, Colombia, France, Germany, India, Italy, Malaysia, Mexico, the Netherlands, Norway, Poland, Saudi Arabia, South Africa, Spain, Sweden, Turkey, the UAE and the U.K. In 2018, RPM acquired Miracle Sealants Company, the Mean Green branded line of specialty cleaning products and the exclusive North American licensing for Roto-Rooter branded drain care products from CR Brands, Nudura Corporation, the leading manufacturer and distributor of insulated concrete forms (ICF) in North America; and Siamons International Inc. In June 2019, the fimrm acquired Schul International Co., LLC.

FINANCIAL DATA:
Note: Data for latest year may not have been available at press time.

In U.S. $	2018	2017	2016	2015	2014	2013
Revenue	5,321,643,000	4,958,175,000	4,813,649,000	4,594,550,000	4,376,353,000	
R&D Expense						
Operating Income	518,069,000	522,168,000	564,032,000	518,425,000	485,640,000	
Operating Margin %		.10%	.12%	.11%	.11%	
SGA Expense	1,663,143,000	1,643,520,000	1,520,977,000	1,422,944,000	1,390,128,000	
Net Income	337,770,000	181,823,000	354,725,000	239,484,000	291,660,000	
Operating Cash Flow	390,383,000	386,127,000	474,706,000	330,448,000	278,149,000	
Capital Expenditure	114,619,000	126,109,000	117,183,000	85,363,000	93,792,000	
EBITDA	650,094,000	458,060,000	686,188,000	640,044,000	595,507,000	
Return on Assets %		.04%	.07%	.05%	.07%	
Return on Equity %		.13%	.26%	.18%	.22%	
Debt to Equity		1.279	1.20	1.281	0.973	

CONTACT INFORMATION:
Phone: 330 273-5090   Fax: 330 225-8743
Toll-Free:
Address: 2628 Pearl Rd., Medina, OH 44258 United States

STOCK TICKER/OTHER:
Stock Ticker: RPM
Employees: 14,318
Parent Company:

Exchange: NYS
Fiscal Year Ends: 05/31

SALARIES/BONUSES:
Top Exec. Salary: $970,000   Bonus: $
Second Exec. Salary: $730,000   Bonus: $

OTHER THOUGHTS:
Estimated Female Officers or Directors: 2
Hot Spot for Advancement for Women/Minorities:

Ryder System Inc

NAIC Code: 532120

www.ryder.com

TYPES OF BUSINESS:
Truck Rental & Leasing
Trucking
Logistics & Consulting Services
Supply Chain Management
Dedicated Fleet Services
Fleet Management Services

BRANDS/DIVISIONS/AFFILIATES:

CONTACTS:
Note: Officers with more than one job title may be intentionally listed here more than once.

Robert Sanchez, CEO
Scott Parker, CFO
Frank Mullen, Chief Accounting Officer
Rajeev Ravindran, Chief Information Officer
Karen Jones, Chief Marketing Officer
John Gleason, Executive VP
Francisco Lopez, Executive VP
Robert Fatovic, Executive VP
Timothy Fiore, Other Executive Officer
Dennis Cooke, President, Divisional
John Diez, President, Divisional
John Sensing, President, Divisional

GROWTH PLANS/SPECIAL FEATURES:

Ryder System, Inc. is a global provider of transportation and supply chain management solutions. It operates in three segments: fleet management solutions (FMS), supply chain solutions (SCS) and dedicated transportation solutions (DTS). FMS, which accounts for 58% of Ryder's revenue, provides full service leasing, contract maintenance, contract-related maintenance and commercial rental of trucks, tractors and trailers to customers principally in the U.S., Canada and the U.K. The division also offers transaction fleet solutions, including commercial truck rental; maintenance services; and value-added fleet support services, such as insurance, vehicle administration and fuel services. In addition, it provides customers with access to a large selection of used trucks, tractors and trailers through its used vehicle sales program. SCS derives 27% of revenue, provides a broad range of innovative logistics management services designed to optimize a customer's supply chain and address its key business requirements. Supply chain solutions include distribution and transportation services for industry verticals such as automotive, technology, healthcare, consumer packaged goods, retail and industrial, which are primarily in located North America and Asia. DTS derives 15% of revenue, and provides vehicles and drivers as part of a dedicated transportation solution within the U.S. This segment combines the equipment, maintenance and administrative services of a full-service lease with drivers, along with other services, in order to offer solutions designed to increase Ryder customers' competitive position, improve risk management and integrate transportation needs with their overall supply chain. This division's additional services include routing and scheduling, fleet sizing, safety, regulatory compliance, risk management, technology and communications support and other technical support. DTS offers a high degree of specialization to meet customer needs. Ryder offers comprehensive health benefits and retirement/savings plans.

FINANCIAL DATA:
Note: Data for latest year may not have been available at press time.

In U.S. $	2018	2017	2016	2015	2014	2013
Revenue	8,409,215,000	7,329,599,000	6,786,984,000	6,571,893,000	6,638,774,000	6,419,285,000
R&D Expense						
Operating Income	601,421,000	476,278,000	545,258,000	505,909,000	342,574,000	394,074,000
Operating Margin %		.06%	.08%	.08%	.05%	.06%
SGA Expense	854,807,000	871,983,000	842,697,000	844,497,000	914,206,000	790,681,000
Net Income	273,298,000	790,558,000	262,477,000	304,768,000	218,575,000	237,792,000
Operating Cash Flow	1,635,095,000	1,547,986,000	1,601,022,000	1,441,788,000	1,369,991,000	1,217,289,000
Capital Expenditure	3,050,409,000	1,860,436,000	1,905,157,000	2,667,978,000	2,259,164,000	2,140,464,000
EBITDA	1,978,538,000	1,721,425,000	1,809,534,000	1,830,333,000	1,568,146,000	1,519,621,000
Return on Assets %		.07%	.02%	.03%	.02%	.03%
Return on Equity %		.32%	.13%	.16%	.12%	.14%
Debt to Equity		1.617	2.241	2.458	2.473	2.072

CONTACT INFORMATION:
Phone: 305 500-3726 Fax: 305 500-4129
Toll-Free:
Address: 11690 NW 105th St., Miami, FL 33178 United States

SALARIES/BONUSES:
Top Exec. Salary: $820,080 Bonus: $
Second Exec. Salary: $566,825 Bonus: $

STOCK TICKER/OTHER:
Stock Ticker: R Exchange: NYS
Employees: 34,500 Fiscal Year Ends: 12/31
Parent Company:

OTHER THOUGHTS:
Estimated Female Officers or Directors: 4
Hot Spot for Advancement for Women/Minorities: Y

Sabre Corporation

NAIC Code: 561510

www.sabre-holdings.com

TYPES OF BUSINESS:
Travel Reservations System for Airlines
Travel Marketing Solutions
Distribution & Technology Solutions
Consulting Services

BRANDS/DIVISIONS/AFFILIATES:
SabreSonic
Sabre AirVision Marketing & Planning
Sabre AirCentre Enterprise
SynXis
SynXis Property Manager Solutions

CONTACTS:
Note: Officers with more than one job title may be intentionally listed here more than once.

Sean Menke, CEO
Douglas Barnett, CFO
Jami Kindle, Chief Accounting Officer
Lawrence Kellner, Director
Kimberly Warmbier, Executive VP
Cem Tanyel, Executive VP
Dave Shirk, Executive VP
Wade Jones, Executive VP
Clinton Anderson, Executive VP
Richard Simonson, Other Corporate Officer

GROWTH PLANS/SPECIAL FEATURES:

Sabre Corporation is a provider of travel products and services through two business segments: travel network and airline and hospitality solutions. The travel network segment comprises Sabre's global business-to-business travel marketplace, consisting primarily of its global distribution system (GDS), new distribution capability (NDC) and related solutions that add value for travel suppliers and travel buyers. GDS/NDC facilitates travel via inventory, prices and availability from its travel suppliers, including airlines, hotels, car rental brands, rail carriers, cruise lines and tour operators, with travel buyers, including online travel agencies, offline travel agencies, travel management companies and corporate travel departments. The airline and hospitality solutions business offers a broad portfolio of software technology products, through a software-as-a-service (Saas) and hosted delivery model, to airlines, hotel properties and other travel suppliers. The airline solutions division provide software that helps Sabre's airline customers better market, sell, serve and operate. Its SabreSonic suite provides capabilities and managing sales and customer service across an airline's touch points. Sabre AirVision Marketing & Planning is a suite of airline commercial planning solutions that focus on helping Sabre airline customers improve profitability and develop their brand. Sabre AirCentre Enterprise is a suite of solutions that drive operational effectiveness through holistic planning and management of airline, airport and customer operations. The hospitality solutions division provides software and solutions to hotel properties worldwide. Solutions include distribution through Sabre's SynXis central reservation system, property management through SynXis Property Manager Solutions, marketing services and consulting services that optimize distribution and marketing. In November 2018, Sabre Corporation agreed to acquire Farelogix, an innovator in the travel industry specializing in NDC technology solutions.

FINANCIAL DATA:
Note: Data for latest year may not have been available at press time.

In U.S. $	2018	2017	2016	2015	2014	2013
Revenue	3,866,956,000	3,598,484,000	3,373,387,000	2,960,896,000	2,631,417,000	3,049,525,000
R&D Expense						
Operating Income	562,016,000	574,552,000	459,572,000	459,769,000	420,787,000	351,746,000
Operating Margin %	.16%	.16%	.14%	.16%	.16%	.12%
SGA Expense	513,526,000	510,075,000	626,153,000	557,077,000	468,152,000	792,929,000
Net Income	337,531,000	242,531,000	242,562,000	545,482,000	69,223,000	-100,494,000
Operating Cash Flow	722,902,000	673,185,000	679,922,000	529,443,000	181,671,000	143,092,000
Capital Expenditure	283,940,000	316,436,000	327,647,000	286,697,000	227,227,000	226,026,000
EBITDA	968,774,000	932,409,000	900,272,000	878,685,000	625,659,000	477,800,000
Return on Assets %		.04%	.04%	.11%	.01%	-.03%
Return on Equity %		.37%	.44%	1.93%		
Debt to Equity		4.902	5.259	6.566	36.549	

CONTACT INFORMATION:
Phone: 682-605-1000 Fax:
Toll-Free:
Address: 3150 Sabre Dr., Southlake, TX 76092 United States

STOCK TICKER/OTHER:
Stock Ticker: SABR
Employees: 10,000
Parent Company:

Exchange: NAS
Fiscal Year Ends: 12/31

SALARIES/BONUSES:
Top Exec. Salary: $943,269   Bonus: $
Second Exec. Salary: $291,923   Bonus: $500,000

OTHER THOUGHTS:
Estimated Female Officers or Directors: 1
Hot Spot for Advancement for Women/Minorities:

Sales, profits and employees may be estimates. Financial information, benefits and other data can change quickly and may vary from those stated here.

Safeco Insurance Company of America

www.safeco.com

NAIC Code: 524126

TYPES OF BUSINESS:
Direct Property & Casualty Insurance
Personal Insurance

BRANDS/DIVISIONS/AFFILIATES:
Liberty Mutual Group Inc

CONTACTS: *Note: Officers with more than one job title may be intentionally listed here more than once.*
Tyler Asher, Pres.
Donald J. DeShaw, General Counsel

GROWTH PLANS/SPECIAL FEATURES:
Safeco Insurance Company of America is a property and casualty insurance provider for homeowners and drivers. The company is a subsidiary of life, auto and home insurance provider Liberty Mutual Group, Inc. Safeco's personal insurance services include auto, homeowners, condo, rental and specialty insurance products for individuals. Specialty insurance products include umbrella, classic car, motorcycle, recreational vehicle and boat/watercraft owners' insurance coverage for individuals. The company also offers combined auto and home property insurance products. Safeco maintains regional offices in California, Texas, Indiana, Ohio, Colorado, Washington, New Hampshire and Georgia. It also has service offices in Missouri, Oregon, Illinois and Connecticut; and customer care centers in Indiana, Texas, Washington and Colorado. The firm's business insurance activities and other additional products and services are provided by Safeco's sister companies via Liberty Mutual.

Through Liberty Mutual Group, Safeco offers its employees comprehensive health benefits, 401(k) and retirement options and a variety of employee assistance programs.

FINANCIAL DATA: *Note: Data for latest year may not have been available at press time.*

In U.S. $	2018	2017	2016	2015	2014	2013
Revenue	1,840,000,000	1,764,000,000	1,680,000,000	1,650,000,000	1,595,200,000	1,461,447,245
R&D Expense						
Operating Income						
Operating Margin %						
SGA Expense						
Net Income						
Operating Cash Flow						
Capital Expenditure						
EBITDA						
Return on Assets %						
Return on Equity %						
Debt to Equity						

CONTACT INFORMATION:
Phone: 206-545-5000 Fax:
Toll-Free:
Address: 1001 Fourth Ave., Safeco Plz., Seattle, WA 98185 United States

STOCK TICKER/OTHER:
Stock Ticker: Subsidiary
Employees: 3,000
Parent Company: Liberty Mutual Group Inc
Exchange:
Fiscal Year Ends: 12/31

SALARIES/BONUSES:
Top Exec. Salary: $ Bonus: $
Second Exec. Salary: $ Bonus: $

OTHER THOUGHTS:
Estimated Female Officers or Directors:
Hot Spot for Advancement for Women/Minorities: Y

Sales, profits and employees may be estimates. Financial information, benefits and other data can change quickly and may vary from those stated here.

Safeway Inc

www.safeway.com

NAIC Code: 445110

TYPES OF BUSINESS:
Grocery Stores
Food Processing & Packaging
Online Grocery Sales & Home Delivery
Pharmacies
Gift Cards & Payment Processing Technology

BRANDS/DIVISIONS/AFFILIATES:
Albertsons Companies LLC
Safeway
Vons
Randalls
Tom Thumb
Carrs
GroceryWorks
Safeway SELECT

CONTACTS:
Note: Officers with more than one job title may be intentionally listed here more than once.

Robert G. Miller, CEO
Larree Renda, Executive VP
Kelly Griffith, Executive VP, Divisional
Diane Dietz, Executive VP
Melissa Plaisance, Senior VP, Divisional
David Stern, Senior VP, Divisional
Donald Wright, Senior VP, Divisional
Jerry Tidwell, Senior VP, Divisional
Russell Jackson, Senior VP, Divisional
Robert Gordon, Senior VP
Robert G. Miller, Chmn.

GROWTH PLANS/SPECIAL FEATURES:

Safeway, Inc. is one of the largest food retailers in the U.S., operating more than 2,200 Safeway stores throughout the U.S. These stores operate regionally under various names. For example, Safeway-branded stores are located in northern California and Hawaii; Vons stores are situated throughout southern California and Nevada; Randalls and Tom Thumb stores can be found in Texas; and Carrs 28 stores are in Alaska. All of the company's stores offer a wide selection of both food and general merchandise and feature a variety of special departments such as bakery, delicatessen, pharmacy and floral departments. In addition, Safeway offers online grocery shopping and home delivery through its wholly-owned subsidiary GroceryWorks. Safeway's own line of Safeway SELECT branded products range from packaged foods to laundry detergent. The firm's corporate-branded products include the O Organics, Eating Right, Bright Green and Open Nature brand names. Safeway is a wholly-owned subsidiary of Albertsons Companies, LLC.

Safeway offers its employees medical, prescription drug, vision and dental coverage; an employee assistance plan; flexible spending accounts; life insurance; short- and long-term disability; paid time off; a stock purchase plan; a retirement plan; and a 401(k) plan.

FINANCIAL DATA:
Note: Data for latest year may not have been available at press time.

In U.S. $	2018	2017	2016	2015	2014	2013
Revenue	37,600,000,000	37,500,000,000	36,000,000,000	36,980,000,000	36,330,200,000	35,064,900,000
R&D Expense						
Operating Income						
Operating Margin %						
SGA Expense						
Net Income						
Operating Cash Flow						
Capital Expenditure						
EBITDA						
Return on Assets %						
Return on Equity %						
Debt to Equity						

CONTACT INFORMATION:
Phone: 925 467-3000   Fax: 925 467-3323
Toll-Free: 877-723-3929
Address: 5918 Stoneridge Mall Rd., Pleasanton, CA 94588-3229 United States

STOCK TICKER/OTHER:
Stock Ticker: Private
Employees: 265,000
Parent Company: Albertsons Companies LLC

Exchange:
Fiscal Year Ends: 12/31

SALARIES/BONUSES:
Top Exec. Salary: $ Bonus: $
Second Exec. Salary: $ Bonus: $

OTHER THOUGHTS:
Estimated Female Officers or Directors: 4
Hot Spot for Advancement for Women/Minorities: Y

SalesForce.com Inc

www.salesforce.com

NAIC Code: 0

TYPES OF BUSINESS:
Software, Sales & Marketing Automation
Customer Relationship Management Software
Software Subscription Services

BRANDS/DIVISIONS/AFFILIATES:
Sales Cloud
Service Cloud
Marketing Cloud
Community Cloud
Industries
IoT Cloud
Salesforce Quip
Salesforce Platform

CONTACTS:
Note: Officers with more than one job title may be intentionally listed here more than once.

Mark Hawkins, CFO
Marc Benioff, Chairman of the Board
Joe Allanson, Chief Accounting Officer
Alexandre Dayon, Chief Strategy Officer
Parker Harris, Chief Technology Officer
Keith Block, Co-CEO
Amy Weaver, General Counsel
Cynthia Robbins, Other Executive Officer
Bret Taylor, Other Executive Officer
Srinivas Tallapragada, President, Divisional

GROWTH PLANS/SPECIAL FEATURES:
SalesForce.com, Inc. builds and delivers customer relationship management (CRM) applications through an on-demand web services platform. The firm's web-based services enable clients to track sales and marketing by delivering enterprise software as an online service, making software purchases like paying for a utility as opposed to a packaged product. The firm offers core cloud-based services such as sales force automation, customer service and support, marketing automation, community management, analytics, as well as a platform for building custom application. Products include Sales Cloud, Service Cloud, Marketing Cloud, Community Cloud, Industries, IoT (Internet of Things) Cloud, Commerce Cloud, Salesforce Quip and Salesforce Platform. Sales Cloud is a platform for sales force automation and solutions for partner relationship management; Service Cloud addresses customer service and support needs; Marketing Cloud is a digital marketing platform that manages customer interactions across email, mobile, social, web and connected products; Community Cloud creates destinations for customers, partners and employees to collaborate; Industries, offers cloud products that meet the specific needs of certain industries; IoT Cloud connects billions of events from devices, sensors, apps and more from the IoT to SalesForce; Commerce Cloud empowers brands to deliver a comprehensive digital commerce experience across web, mobile, social and store; Salesforce Quip is a next-generation productivity solution designed for teams with a mobile-first strategy; and Salesforce Platform is for building enterprise apps quickly via tools, frameworks and services. The Salesforce Platform also offers artificial intelligence, no-code, low-code and code development and integration services including Trailhead, Einstein, AI, Lightning, IoT, Heroku, analytics and the AppExchange. In June 2019, the firm agreed to acquire Tableau Software, Inc., a data-analytics platform, for more than $15 billion in stock.

SalesForce.com offers its employees paid time off, parental/family care, employee stock purchase plans, educational reimbursement, wellness allowances, volunteer time off and a 401(k) plan.

FINANCIAL DATA:
Note: Data for latest year may not have been available at press time.

In U.S. $	2018	2017	2016	2015	2014	2013
Revenue	10,480,010,000	8,391,984,000	6,667,216,000	5,373,586,000	4,071,003,000	
R&D Expense	1,553,073,000	1,208,127,000	946,300,000	792,917,000	623,798,000	
Operating Income	235,768,000	64,228,000	114,923,000	-145,633,000	-286,074,000	
Operating Margin %	.02%	.01%	.02%	-.03%	-.07%	
SGA Expense	5,917,649,000	4,885,590,000	3,951,445,000	3,437,032,000	2,764,851,000	
Net Income	127,478,000	179,632,000	-47,426,000	-262,688,000	-232,175,000	
Operating Cash Flow	2,737,965,000	2,162,198,000	1,612,585,000	1,173,714,000	875,469,000	
Capital Expenditure	534,027,000	463,958,000	709,852,000	416,889,000	299,110,000	
EBITDA	1,041,651,000	746,616,000	662,514,000	308,448,000	88,699,000	
Return on Assets %	.01%	.01%	.00%	-.03%	-.03%	
Return on Equity %	.02%	.03%	-.01%	-.07%	-.09%	
Debt to Equity	0.146	0.359	0.408	0.553	0.637	

CONTACT INFORMATION:
Phone: 415 901-7000 Fax: 415 901-7040
Toll-Free:
Address: Salesforce Tower, 415 Mission St., 3/Fl, San Francisco, CA 94105 United States

SALARIES/BONUSES:
Top Exec. Salary: $1,342,500 Bonus: $298,126
Second Exec. Salary: $1,550,000 Bonus: $

STOCK TICKER/OTHER:
Stock Ticker: CRM
Employees: 25,000
Parent Company:

Exchange: NYS
Fiscal Year Ends: 01/31

OTHER THOUGHTS:
Estimated Female Officers or Directors: 4
Hot Spot for Advancement for Women/Minorities: Y

Sanmina Corporation

www.sanmina.com

NAIC Code: 334418

TYPES OF BUSINESS:
Printed Circuit Assembly (Electronic Assembly) Manufacturing
Assembly & Testing
Logistics Services
Support Services
Product Design & Engineering
Repair & Maintenance Services

BRANDS/DIVISIONS/AFFILIATES:
Viking Technology
SCI Technology Inc

CONTACTS:
Note: Officers with more than one job title may be intentionally listed here more than once.

Michael Clarke, CEO
David Anderson, CFO
Jure Sola, Chairman of the Board
Brent Billinger, Chief Accounting Officer
Alan Reid, Executive VP, Divisional

GROWTH PLANS/SPECIAL FEATURES:

Sanmina Corporation is a global provider of customized, integrated electronics manufacturing services (EMS). With production facilities in 23 countries, the firm is one of the largest global EMS providers. The firm has two business segments: integrated manufacturing solutions (IMS) and components, products and services (CPS). The IMS includes printed circuit board assembly and test, which involves attaching electronic components such as integrated circuits, capacitors, microprocessors to printed circuit boards; final system assembly and test, which consists of combining assemblies and modules to form finished products; and direct-order-fulfillment, which involves receiving customer orders, configuring products and delivering the products either to the OEM, a distribution channel. This segment comprises 80% of the company's revenue. The CPS segment include product design and engineering, printed circuit boards, backplanes and backplane assemblies, case assemblies, plastic injection molded products and mechanical systems (enclosures, precision machining and plastic injection molding). This segment also includes the operations of Viking Technology, a manufacturer of flash memory and related storage products and SCI Technology, Inc.'s defense and aerospace products, as well as logistics and repair services. This segment comprises 20% of the company's annual revenue. The company caters to defense and aerospace, computing and storage, automotive, multi-media, clean technology, medical systems and communications network industries.

Employee benefits include a 401(k); tuition reimbursement; credit union membership; an employee assistance program; flexible spending accounts; and medical, prescription, dental, vision, life and AD&D insurance.

FINANCIAL DATA:
Note: Data for latest year may not have been available at press time.

In U.S. $	2018	2017	2016	2015	2014	2013
Revenue	7,110,130,000	6,868,619,000	6,481,181,000	6,374,541,000	6,215,106,000	5,917,124,000
R&D Expense	30,754,000	33,716,000	37,746,000	33,083,000	32,495,000	25,571,000
Operating Income	179,197,000	230,955,000	228,486,000	209,431,000	211,702,000	161,278,000
Operating Margin %		.03%	.04%	.03%	.03%	.03%
SGA Expense	250,924,000	251,568,000	244,604,000	239,288,000	242,288,000	238,072,000
Net Income	-95,533,000	138,833,000	187,838,000	377,261,000	197,165,000	79,351,000
Operating Cash Flow	156,424,000	250,961,000	390,116,000	174,896,000	307,382,000	317,889,000
Capital Expenditure	118,881,000	111,833,000	120,400,000	119,097,000	69,507,000	75,950,000
EBITDA	244,093,000	354,165,000	341,438,000	301,771,000	290,220,000	240,431,000
Return on Assets %		.04%	.05%	.11%	.06%	.03%
Return on Equity %		.09%	.12%	.27%	.17%	.08%
Debt to Equity		0.238	0.27	0.279	0.31	0.515

CONTACT INFORMATION:
Phone: 408-964-3500   Fax: 408-964-3636
Toll-Free:
Address: 2700 N. First St., San Jose, CA 95134 United States

STOCK TICKER/OTHER:
Stock Ticker: SANM
Employees: 45,397
Parent Company:

Exchange: NAS
Fiscal Year Ends: 09/30

SALARIES/BONUSES:
Top Exec. Salary: $937,500   Bonus: $
Second Exec. Salary: $925,000   Bonus: $

OTHER THOUGHTS:
Estimated Female Officers or Directors:
Hot Spot for Advancement for Women/Minorities:

Sales, profits and employees may be estimates. Financial information, benefits and other data can change quickly and may vary from those stated here.

Sapient Corporation

NAIC Code: 541512

publicis.sapient.com

TYPES OF BUSINESS:
IT Consulting
Internet Strategy Consulting
Interactive Marketing Software

BRANDS/DIVISIONS/AFFILIATES:
Publicis Groupe SA
Publicis.Sapient

CONTACTS:
Note: Officers with more than one job title may be intentionally listed here more than once.

Alan Wexler, CEO
Alan Wexler, Executive VP
J. Moore, Founder
Joseph LaSala, General Counsel
Harry Register, Managing Director, Divisional
Christian Oversohl, Managing Director, Geographical
Laurie MacLaren, Senior VP, Divisional

GROWTH PLANS/SPECIAL FEATURES:
Sapient Corporation, a subsidiary of Publicis Groupe SA, is a business consulting and technology services firm focused on digital transformation and the dynamics of an always-on world. The firm's Publicis.Sapient platform is designed to help clients reimagine core business activities via transformation in order to drive growth and improve operating efficiency. The platform's digital transformation technology helps businesses in three key ways: creates business opportunities by rapidly reaching, meeting and/or changing customer expectations and behavior; creates new value via ongoing technological advances in marketing, sales, service, supply chain, IT and more; and stays ahead of competitors through smart/connected products and an enterprise-wide open ecosystem. According to Sapient, digital is at the core of transformation because the entire business eventually needs to be wired for the digital world, primarily change-sensitive technology architectures and rapid development methods. The Publicis.Sapient platform's data and analytics on customers provide strategy and direction to Sapient Corporation's business consulting services to its clients. Therefore, Sapient combines these technology capabilities with consulting expertise for the best outcomes for its business clients. Sapient Corporation serves financial services, retail, technology, communications, consumer packaged goods, travel/leisure, automotive, energy services, government, health and education sectors, among others. Based in the USA, the firm has operations worldwide, including the Americas, Europe and Asia-Pacific.

FINANCIAL DATA:
Note: Data for latest year may not have been available at press time.

In U.S. $	2018	2017	2016	2015	2014	2013
Revenue	1,765,050,000	1,681,000,000	1,625,000,000	1,562,781,000	1,451,000,000	1,305,232,000
R&D Expense						
Operating Income						
Operating Margin %						
SGA Expense						
Net Income						
Operating Cash Flow						
Capital Expenditure						
EBITDA						
Return on Assets %						
Return on Equity %						
Debt to Equity						

CONTACT INFORMATION:
Phone: 617 621-0200 Fax: 617 621-1300
Toll-Free: 877-454-9860
Address: 131 Dartmouth St., Boston, MA 02116 United States

STOCK TICKER/OTHER:
Stock Ticker: Subsidiary
Employees: 20,000
Parent Company: Publicis Groupe SA
Exchange:
Fiscal Year Ends: 12/31

SALARIES/BONUSES:
Top Exec. Salary: $ Bonus: $
Second Exec. Salary: $ Bonus: $

OTHER THOUGHTS:
Estimated Female Officers or Directors: 2
Hot Spot for Advancement for Women/Minorities:

Sales, profits and employees may be estimates. Financial information, benefits and other data can change quickly and may vary from those stated here.

SAS Institute Inc

www.sas.com

NAIC Code: 0

TYPES OF BUSINESS:
Computer Software, Statistical Analysis
Business Intelligence Software
Data Warehousing
Online Bookstore
Consulting

BRANDS/DIVISIONS/AFFILIATES:

CONTACTS: Note: Officers with more than one job title may be intentionally listed here more than once.
James Goodnight, CEO
Oliver Schabenberger, COO
David Davis, VP
Randy Guard, VP
Jenn Mann, VP-Human Resources
Keith Collins, VP
John Boswell, Chief Legal Officer
Carl Farrell, Exec. VP-SAS Americas
John Sall, Exec. VP
Nick Lisi, Chief Sales Officer
Mikael Hagstrom, Exec. VP-EMEA & Asia Pacific

GROWTH PLANS/SPECIAL FEATURES:

SAS Institute, Inc. provides statistical analysis software. The company's products are designed to extract, manage and analyze large volumes of data, often assisting in financial reporting and credit analysis. Individual contracts can be tailored to specific global and local industries, such as banking, manufacturing and government. SAS' advanced analytics software is infused with cutting-edge, innovative algorithms that help its clients solve their most intractable problems, make the best decisions possible and capture new opportunities. The software comprises data mining, statistical analysis, forecasting, text analysis, optimization and stimulation features. Other products that provide enterprise solutions include business intelligence, cloud analytics, customer intelligence, data management, fraud and security intelligence, in-memory analytics, performance management, risk management, solutions for Hadoop and supply chain intelligence. Industries that utilize SAS products and solutions include automotive, banking, capital markets, casinos, communications, consumer goods, defense/security, government, healthcare, high-tech manufacturing, education, hotels, insurance, life science, manufacturing, media, oil and gas, retail, sports, travel, transportation and utilities. SAS serves more than 80,000 business, government and university sites in 144 different countries, including 96 of the top 100 companies on the 2017 Fortune Global 500 list.

SAS offers its employees life, disability, medical, dental, auto, home and vision insurance; flexible spending accounts; onsite health care and fitness centers; an employee assistance program; adoption assistance; scholarship programs; a 401(k); and a profit sharing plan.

FINANCIAL DATA: Note: Data for latest year may not have been available at press time.

In U.S. $	2018	2017	2016	2015	2014	2013
Revenue	3,300,000,000	3,240,000,000	3,200,000,000	3,160,000,000	3,090,000,000	3,020,000,000
R&D Expense						
Operating Income						
Operating Margin %						
SGA Expense						
Net Income						
Operating Cash Flow						
Capital Expenditure						
EBITDA						
Return on Assets %						
Return on Equity %						
Debt to Equity						

CONTACT INFORMATION:
Phone: 919-677-8000   Fax: 919-677-4444
Toll-Free: 800-727-0025
Address: 100 SAS Campus Dr., Cary, NC 27513 United States

STOCK TICKER/OTHER:
Stock Ticker: Private
Employees: 14,051
Parent Company:

Exchange:
Fiscal Year Ends: 12/31

SALARIES/BONUSES:
Top Exec. Salary: $ Bonus: $
Second Exec. Salary: $ Bonus: $

OTHER THOUGHTS:
Estimated Female Officers or Directors: 1
Hot Spot for Advancement for Women/Minorities: Y

Schlumberger Limited

NAIC Code: 213112

www.slb.com

TYPES OF BUSINESS:
Oil & Gas Field Services
Seismic Services
Reservoir Imaging
Data & IT Consulting Services
Outsourcing
Stimulation Services
Management Consulting
Project Management

BRANDS/DIVISIONS/AFFILIATES:
Cameron
M-I SWACO
WesternGeco
Sensia

CONTACTS: Note: Officers with more than one job title may be intentionally listed here more than once.
Paal Kibsgaard, CEO
Simon Farrant, VP, Divisional
Simon Ayat, CFO
Howard Guild, Chief Accounting Officer
Olivier Le Peuch, COO
Jean-Francois Poupeau, Executive VP, Divisional
Ashok Belani, Executive VP, Divisional
Patrick Schorn, Executive VP, Divisional
Alexander Juden, General Counsel
Vijay Kasibhatla, Other Corporate Officer
Saul Laureles, Other Corporate Officer
Pierre Chereque, Other Corporate Officer
Abdellah Merad, President, Divisional
Stephanie Cox, President, Divisional
Khaled Mogharbel, President, Divisional
Stephane Biguet, Vice President, Divisional
Hinda Gharbi, Vice President, Divisional
Guy Arrington, Vice President, Divisional

GROWTH PLANS/SPECIAL FEATURES:

Schlumberger Limited (SLB) is a leading oil field service company offering technology, project management and information solutions for customers in the international oil and gas industry. SLB operates in 85 countries throughout North America, Latin America, Europe, Africa, the Middle East and Asia. It also maintains a global network of research and engineering facilities. The SLB oilfield services segment is divided into four groups: reservoir characterization, which is involved in finding and defining hydrocarbon deposits; drilling, which includes the drilling and positioning of gas and oil wells; production, which includes the principal technologies associated with the lifetime production of gas and oil reservoirs; and Cameron, which consists of the technologies involved in pressure and flow control for drilling and intervention rigs, oil and gas wells and production facilities. The overall purpose of the oilfield services sector is to provide proper exploration with production services and technologies throughout the entire life cycle of a reservoir. Wholly-owned subsidiary, M-I SWACO, offers drilling and completion fluids to stabilize rock and minimize formation damage. Subsidiary WesternGeco is a geophysical services supplier, providing worldwide reservoir interpretation and data processing services. It provides a highly-efficient and scientifically-advanced imaging platform to its customers. During 2018, WesternGeco sold its onshore/offshore seismic acquisition business to Shearwater GeoServices Holding AS. In February 2019, SLB and Rockwell Automation entered a joint venture agreement to create Sensia, a fully-integrated digital oilfield automation solutions provider.

FINANCIAL DATA: Note: Data for latest year may not have been available at press time.

In U.S. $	2018	2017	2016	2015	2014	2013
Revenue	32,815,000,000	30,440,000,000	27,810,000,000	35,475,000,000	48,580,000,000	45,266,000,000
R&D Expense	702,000,000	787,000,000	1,012,000,000	1,094,000,000	1,217,000,000	1,174,000,000
Operating Income	3,191,000,000	2,678,000,000	2,285,000,000	5,566,000,000	9,490,000,000	8,345,000,000
Operating Margin %		.09%	.08%	.16%	.20%	.18%
SGA Expense	444,000,000	432,000,000	403,000,000	494,000,000	475,000,000	416,000,000
Net Income	2,138,000,000	-1,505,000,000	-1,687,000,000	2,072,000,000	5,438,000,000	6,732,000,000
Operating Cash Flow	5,713,000,000	5,663,000,000	6,261,000,000	8,572,000,000	11,219,000,000	9,786,000,000
Capital Expenditure	2,160,000,000	2,107,000,000	2,055,000,000	2,410,000,000	3,976,000,000	3,943,000,000
EBITDA	6,755,000,000	3,220,000,000	2,759,000,000	7,305,000,000	12,102,000,000	12,748,000,000
Return on Assets %		-.02%	-.02%	.03%	.08%	.10%
Return on Equity %		-.04%	-.04%	.06%	.14%	.18%
Debt to Equity		0.404	0.401	0.405	0.279	0.263

CONTACT INFORMATION:
Phone: 713 375-3400 Fax:
Toll-Free:
Address: 5599 San Felipe St., 17/Fl, Houston, TX 77056 United States

STOCK TICKER/OTHER:
Stock Ticker: SLB   Exchange: NYS
Employees: 95,000   Fiscal Year Ends: 12/31
Parent Company:

SALARIES/BONUSES:
Top Exec. Salary: $2,000,000   Bonus: $
Second Exec. Salary: $1,000,000   Bonus: $

OTHER THOUGHTS:
Estimated Female Officers or Directors: 3
Hot Spot for Advancement for Women/Minorities: Y

Sales, profits and employees may be estimates. Financial information, benefits and other data can change quickly and may vary from those stated here.

Science Applications International Corporation (SAIC)

www.saic.com
NAIC Code: 541512

TYPES OF BUSINESS:
IT Consulting
IT Infrastructure Management
Research & Development
Software Development
Engineering

BRANDS/DIVISIONS/AFFILIATES:

CONTACTS: Note: Officers with more than one job title may be intentionally listed here more than once.
Anthony Moraco, CEO
Charles Mathis, CFO
Donna Morea, Chairman of the Board
Nazzic Keene, COO
Steven Mahon, Executive VP
Karen Wheeler, Other Executive Officer

GROWTH PLANS/SPECIAL FEATURES:
Science Applications International Corporation (SAIC) provides technical, engineering and enterprise IT services to commercial operations and government agencies. The company's clients include all four branches of the U.S. military (Army, Air Force, Navy and Marines), the U.S. Defense Logistics Agency, the National Aeronautics and Space Administration, the U.S. Department of State and the U.S. Department of Homeland Security. In fiscal 2018, 98% of total revenues were derived from contracts with the U.S. government or from subcontracts with other contractors engaged in work for the U.S. government, all of which were entities located in the U.S. The firm's offerings include: engineering; technology and equipment platform integration; maintenance of ground and maritime systems; logistics; training and simulation; operation and program support services; and end-to-end services that span design, development, integration, deployment, management and operations, sustainment and security of customers' entire IT infrastructure. SAIC serves customers through approximately 1,300 active contracts and task orders via thousands of employees. In September 2018, SAIC agreed to acquire Engility Holdings, Inc., a provider of engineering and logistics services to several U.S. military and civilian agencies.

FINANCIAL DATA: Note: Data for latest year may not have been available at press time.

In U.S. $	2018	2017	2016	2015	2014	2013
Revenue	4,454,000,000	4,450,000,000	4,315,000,000	3,885,000,000	4,121,000,000	
R&D Expense						
Operating Income	256,000,000	281,000,000	253,000,000	240,000,000	241,000,000	
Operating Margin %	.06%	.06%	.06%	.06%	.06%	
SGA Expense	155,000,000	166,000,000	158,000,000	95,000,000	92,000,000	
Net Income	179,000,000	148,000,000	117,000,000	141,000,000	113,000,000	
Operating Cash Flow	217,000,000	273,000,000	226,000,000	277,000,000	183,000,000	
Capital Expenditure	22,000,000	15,000,000	20,000,000	22,000,000	16,000,000	
EBITDA	304,000,000	325,000,000	289,000,000	261,000,000	196,000,000	
Return on Assets %	.09%	.07%	.07%	.10%	.03%	
Return on Equity %	.53%	.40%	.32%	.39%	.08%	
Debt to Equity	3.006	2.887	2.666	1.325	1.297	

CONTACT INFORMATION:
Phone: 703 676-4300   Fax:
Toll-Free:
Address: 12010 Sunset Hills Rd., Reston, VA 20190 United States

STOCK TICKER/OTHER:
Stock Ticker: SAIC
Employees: 15,500
Parent Company:

Exchange: NYS
Fiscal Year Ends: 01/31

SALARIES/BONUSES:
Top Exec. Salary: $1,025,385   Bonus: $1,000,000
Second Exec. Salary: $734,616   Bonus: $

OTHER THOUGHTS:
Estimated Female Officers or Directors: 5
Hot Spot for Advancement for Women/Minorities: Y

Select Medical Holdings Corporation

www.selectmedicalcorp.com

NAIC Code: 622310

TYPES OF BUSINESS:
Extended Care Hospitals
Long-Term Acute Care
Outpatient Rehabilitation Clinics
Contract Therapy Services
Medical Equipment Distribution
Billing Services
Recruiting

BRANDS/DIVISIONS/AFFILIATES:
Select Medical Corporation
Concentra Inc
Dignity Health Rehabilitation Hospital

CONTACTS:
Note: Officers with more than one job title may be intentionally listed here more than once.

David Chernow, CEO
Martin Jackson, CFO
Robert Ortenzio, Chairman of the Board
Scott Romberger, Chief Accounting Officer
John Saich, Chief Administrative Officer
Rocco Ortenzio, Co-Founder
Michael Tarvin, Executive VP
Robert Breighner, Other Corporate Officer

GROWTH PLANS/SPECIAL FEATURES:

Select Medical Holdings Corporation, through its subsidiary Select Medical Corporation, operates critical illness recovery hospitals, rehabilitation hospitals, outpatient rehabilitation clinics and occupational health centers in the U.S. Critical illness recovery conditions include cardiac and heart failure, infectious disease, medically-complex illnesses, neurological, post trauma, pulmonary, ventilator weaning, renal and wound care. Inpatient rehabilitation conditions include brain injury, spinal cord injury, stroke, amputation, neurological disorders, orthopedic conditions, pediatric and cancer rehabilitation. Outpatient rehabilitation conditions include physical therapy, hand/occupational therapy, orthopedic rehabilitation, low back rehabilitation, work health, sports medicine, aquatic therapy, women's health, vestibular rehabilitation, cancer rehabilitation, pediatric therapy, prosthetics and orthotics. Select Medical's website offers information on caregivers, providing personal stories, making a referral, finding locations and requesting an appointment. The company operates nearly 100 critical illness recovery hospitals in 27 states, 26 rehabilitation hospitals in 11 states and 1,662 outpatient rehabilitation clinics in 37 states and the District of Columbia. In addition, joint venture Concentra, Inc. operates 524 occupational health centers in 41 states, and also provides contract services at employer worksites and Department of Veterans Affairs community-based outpatient clinics. During 2019, Select Medical opened Dignity Health Rehabilitation Hospital, a joint venture partnership with Dignity Health, offering a 60-bed hospital to serve the greater Las Vegas area.

Employee benefits include health, dental, vision and prescription coverage; life insurance; short- and long-term disability; tuition reimbursement; and a 401(k).

FINANCIAL DATA:
Note: Data for latest year may not have been available at press time.

In U.S. $	2018	2017	2016	2015	2014	2013
Revenue	5,081,258,000	4,443,603,000	4,286,021,000	3,742,736,000	3,065,017,000	2,975,648,000
R&D Expense						
Operating Income	417,279,000	435,369,000	368,940,000	334,162,000	329,076,000	338,859,000
Operating Margin %		.08%	.07%	.07%	.09%	.10%
SGA Expense	121,268,000	114,047,000	106,927,000	92,052,000	85,247,000	76,921,000
Net Income	137,840,000	177,184,000	115,411,000	130,736,000	120,627,000	114,390,000
Operating Cash Flow	494,194,000	238,131,000	346,603,000	208,415,000	170,642,000	192,523,000
Capital Expenditure	167,281,000	233,243,000	161,633,000	182,642,000	95,246,000	73,660,000
EBITDA	635,700,000	517,175,000	496,126,000	426,229,000	357,597,000	349,557,000
Return on Assets %		.03%	.02%	.03%	.04%	.04%
Return on Equity %		.21%	.13%	.16%	.15%	.15%
Debt to Equity		3.252	3.292	2.549	2.085	1.816

CONTACT INFORMATION:
Phone: 717 972-1100 Fax:
Toll-Free: 888-735-6332
Address: 4714 Old Gettysburg Rd., Mechanicsburg, PA 17055 United States

STOCK TICKER/OTHER:
Stock Ticker: SEM
Employees: 31,200
Parent Company:

Exchange: NYS
Fiscal Year Ends: 12/31

SALARIES/BONUSES:
Top Exec. Salary: $995,000 Bonus: $
Second Exec. Salary: $995,000 Bonus: $

OTHER THOUGHTS:
Estimated Female Officers or Directors: 1
Hot Spot for Advancement for Women/Minorities:

Service Corporation International Inc

www.sci-corp.com

NAIC Code: 812210

TYPES OF BUSINESS:
Funeral Homes and Funeral Services
Funeral Services
Cemetery Services

BRANDS/DIVISIONS/AFFILIATES:
Dignity Memorial
Dignity Planning
National Cremation Society
Advantage Funeral and Cremation Services
Funeraria del Angel
Making Everlasting Memories
Neptune Society
Trident Society

CONTACTS: Note: Officers with more than one job title may be intentionally listed here more than once.
Thomas Ryan, CEO
Tammy Moore, Chief Accounting Officer
Sumner Waring, COO
Robert Waltrip, Founder
Gregory Sangalis, General Counsel
Elisabeth Nash, Senior VP, Divisional
Steven Tidwell, Senior VP, Divisional
Eric Tanzberger, Senior VP

GROWTH PLANS/SPECIAL FEATURES:
Service Corporation International, Inc. is a provider of deathcare products and services in North America. The company is geographically diversified across 44 U.S. states, eight Canadian provinces, the District of Columbia and Puerto Rico. Service Corporation's funeral service and cemetery operations consist of more than 1,480 funeral service locations and 481 cemeteries, as well as crematoria and related businesses. The firm provides all professional services relating to funerals and cremations, including the use of funeral facilities and motor vehicles and preparation and embalming services. Funeral related merchandise, including caskets, burial vaults, cremation receptacles, flowers and other ancillary products and services are sold at funeral service locations. Service Corporation's cemeteries provide cemetery property interment rights, including mausoleum spaces, lots and lawn crypts, and sell cemetery related merchandise and services, including stone and bronze memorials, burial vaults, casket and cremation memorialization products, merchandise installations and burial openings and closings. Service Corporation has branded the company's funeral operations in North America under the name Dignity Memorial. Other brands include Dignity Planning, National Cremation Society, Advantage Funeral and Cremation Services, Funeraria del Angel, Making Everlasting Memories, Neptune Society and Trident Society.

FINANCIAL DATA: Note: Data for latest year may not have been available at press time.

In U.S. $	2018	2017	2016	2015	2014	2013
Revenue	3,190,174,000	3,095,031,000	3,031,137,000	2,986,380,000	2,994,012,000	2,556,382,000
R&D Expense						
Operating Income	614,823,000	567,766,000	538,704,000	543,757,000	490,936,000	394,433,000
Operating Margin %		.18%	.18%	.18%	.16%	.15%
SGA Expense	145,499,000	154,423,000	137,730,000	128,188,000	184,877,000	155,136,000
Net Income	447,208,000	546,663,000	177,038,000	233,772,000	172,469,000	143,848,000
Operating Cash Flow	615,830,000	502,340,000	463,595,000	472,186,000	317,355,000	384,709,000
Capital Expenditure	250,070,000	214,501,000	193,446,000	150,986,000	144,499,000	113,084,000
EBITDA	871,773,000	818,276,000	733,685,000	778,570,000	817,252,000	580,884,000
Return on Assets %		.04%	.01%	.02%	.01%	.01%
Return on Equity %		.44%	.16%	.18%	.12%	.10%
Debt to Equity		2.225	2.925	2.593	2.165	2.231

CONTACT INFORMATION:
Phone: 713 522-5141 Fax: 713 525-5586
Toll-Free:
Address: 1929 Allen Parkway, Houston, TX 77019 United States

SALARIES/BONUSES:
Top Exec. Salary: $1,200,000 Bonus: $
Second Exec. Salary: $750,000 Bonus: $

STOCK TICKER/OTHER:
Stock Ticker: SCI
Employees: 23,463
Parent Company:

Exchange: NYS
Fiscal Year Ends: 12/31

OTHER THOUGHTS:
Estimated Female Officers or Directors:
Hot Spot for Advancement for Women/Minorities:

Sales, profits and employees may be estimates. Financial information, benefits and other data can change quickly and may vary from those stated here.

ServiceMaster Company LLC (The)

NAIC Code: 561730

www.servicemaster.com

TYPES OF BUSINESS:
Lawn Care Services
Landscaping Services
Termite & Pest Control
Home Warranty
Disaster Restoration & Cleaning
Furniture Repair
Home Inspection

BRANDS/DIVISIONS/AFFILIATES:
ServiceMaster Global Holdings Inc
Merry Maids
AmeriSpec
Furniture Medic
ServiceMaster Clean
ServiceMaster Restore
Terminix

CONTACTS:
Note: Officers with more than one job title may be intentionally listed here more than once.

Nikhill Varty, CEO
Alan Haughie, CFO
Anthony DiLucente, Sr. VP
David Dart, Chief Human Resources Officer
Martin Wick, COO, Divisional
Robert Doty, CIO
James Lucke, General Counsel
William Derwin, President, Divisional
Timothy Haynes, President, Divisional
Mary Wegner, President, Subsidiary
Anthony DiLucente, Senior VP
Susan Hunsberger, Senior VP, Divisional
Mary Runyan, Senior VP, Divisional
Naren Gursahaney, Chmn.

GROWTH PLANS/SPECIAL FEATURES:

The ServiceMaster Company, LLC provides various cleaning, restoration and maintenance services to tens of thousands of homes and businesses every day. Its operations are divided into eight groups. The cleaning group offers the Merry Maids brand of residential cleaning services, as well as carpet cleaning, floor cleaning, tile/grout cleaning, upholstery cleaning, green cleaning, commercial cleaning, janitorial and hoarding clean-up services. The disaster restoration group provides disaster recovery, post-loss recovery and specialty damage recovery services. The fire damage restoration group provides fire damage restoration, smoke damage removal and pack-out services. The furniture and cabinet restoration group provides cabinet re-facing, residential furniture and woodwork repair, and commercial furniture and wood restoration services. The inspections group provides property inspections for home or commercial properties, and provides specialty inspections and services such as radon, water, mold, septic, carbon monoxide, lead-based paint, pool/spa, wood-destroying insects, energy assessments, new home construction reviews, well testing, gas leak detection, irrigation system inspections and infrared technology. The mold remediation group offers mold inspections and mold remediation services. The pest control group offers termite, pest, mosquito, bed bug, wildlife, commercial pest and industry-specific control and treatment services. Last, the water damage restoration group offers water damage restoration, flood damage restoration, basement flooding restoration and carpet drying services and solutions. Other brands by the company include AmeriSpec, Furniture Medic, ServiceMaster Clean, ServiceMaster Restore and Terminix. The ServiceMaster operates as a subsidiary of the publicly-traded ServiceMaster Global Holdings, Inc.

FINANCIAL DATA:
Note: Data for latest year may not have been available at press time.

In U.S. $	2018	2017	2016	2015	2014	2013
Revenue	1,900,000,000	2,912,000,000	2,745,999,872	2,593,999,872	2,456,999,936	2,292,999,936
R&D Expense						
Operating Income						
Operating Margin %						
SGA Expense						
Net Income	-41,000,000	510,000,000	155,000,000	160,000,000	-57,000,000	-507,000,000
Operating Cash Flow						
Capital Expenditure						
EBITDA						
Return on Assets %						
Return on Equity %						
Debt to Equity						

CONTACT INFORMATION:
Phone: 866-348-7672 Fax:
Toll-Free: 888-937-3783
Address: 860 Ridge Lake Blvd., Memphis, TN 38120 United States

STOCK TICKER/OTHER:
Stock Ticker: Subsidiary Exchange:
Employees: 13,000 Fiscal Year Ends: 12/31
Parent Company: ServiceMaster Global Holdings Inc

SALARIES/BONUSES:
Top Exec. Salary: $ Bonus: $
Second Exec. Salary: $ Bonus: $

OTHER THOUGHTS:
Estimated Female Officers or Directors: 2
Hot Spot for Advancement for Women/Minorities:

Sales, profits and employees may be estimates. Financial information, benefits and other data can change quickly and may vary from those stated here.

ServiceNow Inc

www.service-now.com

NAIC Code: 0

TYPES OF BUSINESS:
Computer Software: Network Management (IT), System Testing & Storage
Cloud-Based Workflow Software

BRANDS/DIVISIONS/AFFILIATES:
Parlo

CONTACTS:
Note: Officers with more than one job title may be intentionally listed here more than once.

Michael Scarpelli, CFO
Fay Goon, Chief Accounting Officer
Frederic Luddy, Director
John Donahoe, Director
Russell Elmer, General Counsel
Patricia Wadors, Other Executive Officer
Chirantan Desai, Other Executive Officer
David Schneider, President, Divisional

GROWTH PLANS/SPECIAL FEATURES:

ServiceNow, Inc. is a provider of cloud-based services that automate enterprise IT operations. The company's service includes a suite of applications built on its proprietary platform that automates workflow and provides integration between related business processes. The firm focuses on transforming enterprise IT by automating and standardizing business processes and consolidating IT across the global enterprise. Organizations deploy its service to create a single system of record for enterprise IT, lower operational costs and enhance efficiency. Additionally, customers use its extensible platform to build custom applications for automating activities unique to their business requirements. ServiceNow helps transform IT organizations from reactive, manual and task-oriented, to pro-active, automated and service-oriented organizations. The company's on-demand service enables organizations to define their IT strategy, design the systems and infrastructure that will support that strategy, and implement, manage and automate that infrastructure throughout its lifecycle while leveraging its self-service capability. The firm provides a broad set of integrated functionality that is highly configurable and extensible and can be efficiently implemented and upgraded. Its multi-instance architecture has proven scalability for global enterprises as well as having advantages in security, reliability and deployment location. The company offers its service under a Software-as-a-Service (SaaS) business model. Customers can rapidly deploy its service in a modular fashion, allowing them to solve immediate business needs and access, configure and build new applications as their requirements evolve. The firm's service, which is accessed through an intuitive web-based interface, can be easily configured to adapt to customer workflow and processes. ServiceNow serves more than 5,000 enterprise customers worldwide. During 2018, ServiceNow acquired: Parlo, an artificial intelligence (AT) workforce solution; and agreed to acquire the technology of FriendlyData, which makes it easy for non-technical users to ask quantitative questions and obtain fast answers directly or via data visualizations.

FINANCIAL DATA:
Note: Data for latest year may not have been available at press time.

In U.S. $	2018	2017	2016	2015	2014	2013
Revenue	2,608,816,000	1,933,026,000	1,390,513,000	1,005,480,000	682,563,000	424,650,000
R&D Expense	529,501,000	377,518,000	285,239,000	217,389,000	148,258,000	78,678,000
Operating Income	-42,426,000	-101,414,000	-152,808,000	-166,365,000	-151,835,000	-66,267,000
Operating Margin %		-.05%	-.30%	-.17%	-.22%	-.16%
SGA Expense	1,499,083,000	1,157,150,000	859,400,000	625,043,000	437,364,000	256,980,000
Net Income	-26,704,000	-149,130,000	-451,804,000	-198,426,000	-179,387,000	-73,708,000
Operating Cash Flow	811,089,000	642,825,000	159,921,000	315,091,000	138,900,000	81,746,000
Capital Expenditure	248,862,000	157,180,000	124,312,000	89,231,000	54,379,000	55,321,000
EBITDA	160,651,000	15,494,000	-335,476,000	-103,227,000	-105,980,000	-42,115,000
Return on Assets %		-.05%	-.24%	-.12%	-.14%	-.09%
Return on Equity %		-.31%	-.95%	-.40%	-.44%	-.23%
Debt to Equity			1.079	1.312		

CONTACT INFORMATION:
Phone: 408-501-8550 Fax:
Toll-Free:
Address: 2225 Lawson Lane, Santa Clara, CA 95054 United States

SALARIES/BONUSES:
Top Exec. Salary: $750,000 Bonus: $
Second Exec. Salary: $500,000 Bonus: $

STOCK TICKER/OTHER:
Stock Ticker: NOW
Employees: 4,801
Parent Company:

Exchange: NYS
Fiscal Year Ends: 12/31

OTHER THOUGHTS:
Estimated Female Officers or Directors:
Hot Spot for Advancement for Women/Minorities:

Sales, profits and employees may be estimates. Financial information, benefits and other data can change quickly and may vary from those stated here.

Shell Oil Company

NAIC Code: 211111

www.shell.us

TYPES OF BUSINESS:
Oil & Gas Exploration & Production
Chemicals
Power Generation
Nanocomposites
Nanocatalysts
Refineries
Pipelines & Shipping
Hydrogen Storage Technology

BRANDS/DIVISIONS/AFFILIATES:
Royal Dutch Shell plc

CONTACTS:
Note: Officers with more than one job title may be intentionally listed here more than once.
Bruce Culpepper, Pres.
Marvin E. Odum, Dir.-Upstream Americas-Royal Dutch Shell plc
Ben van Beurden, CEO-Royal Dutch Shell plc

GROWTH PLANS/SPECIAL FEATURES:

Shell Oil Company, a subsidiary of Royal Dutch Shell plc, is a natural gas, chemical and oil producer in the U.S. and internationally. Shell Oil's operations are divided into four businesses. The upstream business explores for new liquids and natural gas reserves, and develops major new projects where the company's technology and expertise adds value for resource holders. Within the integrated gas and new energies business, integrated gas focuses on LNG and converting gas to liquids so that it can be safely stores and shipped to markets worldwide; and new energies explores and invests in new low-carbon opportunities. The downstream business turns crude oil into a range of refined products, which are moved and marketed for domestic, industrial and transport use worldwide. It also produces and sells petrochemicals for industrial use; and oil sands North American mining activities are included this segment. Last, the projects and technology business is responsible for delivering new development projects, as well as the research and development that leads to innovative and low-cost investments for future use. Shell Oil's products and services include motor oils, lubricants, preventative maintenance services, chemicals, gasoline, diesel, heating oils and more. The firm also operates pipelines; trades natural gas, electrical power, crude oil, refined products, chemical feedstocks and environmental products; operates gasoline stations; provides commercial cards; and operates eCommerce sites for a range of Shell-branded items, including wearables, collectables and memorabilia.

The firm offers employees medical, vision and disability coverage; and pension and savings plans.

FINANCIAL DATA:
Note: Data for latest year may not have been available at press time.

In U.S. $	2018	2017	2016	2015	2014	2013
Revenue	9,000,000,000	8,400,000,000	8,000,000,000	8,800,000,000	10,981,000,000	10,648,000,000
R&D Expense						
Operating Income						
Operating Margin %						
SGA Expense						
Net Income						
Operating Cash Flow						
Capital Expenditure						
EBITDA						
Return on Assets %						
Return on Equity %						
Debt to Equity						

CONTACT INFORMATION:
Phone: 713-767-5300   Fax: 713-241-4044
Toll-Free:
Address: 1000 Main, 12/Fl, Houston, TX 77002 United States

SALARIES/BONUSES:
Top Exec. Salary: $ Bonus: $
Second Exec. Salary: $ Bonus: $

STOCK TICKER/OTHER:
Stock Ticker: Subsidiary   Exchange:
Employees: 35,000   Fiscal Year Ends: 12/31
Parent Company: Royal Dutch Shell plc

OTHER THOUGHTS:
Estimated Female Officers or Directors:
Hot Spot for Advancement for Women/Minorities:

Sales, profits and employees may be estimates. Financial information, benefits and other data can change quickly and may vary from those stated here.

Sherwin-Williams Company (The)

NAIC Code: 325510

www.sherwin-williams.com

TYPES OF BUSINESS:
Paints & Coatings Manufacturing
Retail Paint Stores
Wall Coverings
Automotive Finishing Products
Design Consulting

BRANDS/DIVISIONS/AFFILIATES:
Sherwin-Williams

CONTACTS:
Note: Officers with more than one job title may be intentionally listed here more than once.

John Morikis, CEO
Allen Mistysyn, CFO
Jane Cronin, Chief Accounting Officer
David Sewell, COO
Mary Garceau, General Counsel
Joel Baxter, General Manager, Divisional
Robert Lynch, President, Divisional
Aaron Erter, President, Divisional
Peter Ippolito, President, Divisional
Thomas Gilligan, Senior VP, Divisional
Robert Wells, Senior VP, Divisional

GROWTH PLANS/SPECIAL FEATURES:

The Sherwin-Williams Company is one of the largest international manufacturers, distributors and retailers of paint and related products to professional, industrial, commercial and retail customers. The company operates in three reportable segments: The Americas Group, Consumer Brands Group and Performance Coatings Group. The Americas Group consists of 4,696 company-operated stores in the U.S., Canada, Latin America and the Caribbean region. These company-operated stores sell Sherwin-Williams and other controlled brands architectural paint, coatings and other associated products and brands. The Americas Group consisted of operations from subsidiaries in 10 foreign countries. During 2018, the segment opened 91 new stores: 74 in the U.S., 16 in Canada and 1 in South America. The Consumer Brands Group supplies a broad portfolio of branded and private-label architectural paints, stains, varnishes, industrial products, wood finishes products, wood preservatives, applicators, corrosion inhibitors, aerosols, caulks and adhesives to retailers and distributors throughout North America, as well as in Australia, New Zealand, China and Europe. Additionally, this segment supports the other segments with new product research and development, manufacturing, distribution and logistics. The Consumer Brands Group consists of operations in the U.S. and subsidiaries in 6 foreign countries. The Performance Coatings Group develops and sells industrial coatings for wood finishing and general industrial (metal and plastic) applications, automotive refinish, protective and marine coatings, coil coatings, packaging coatings and performance-based resins and colorants worldwide. This segment consists of operations in the U.S. and subsidiaries in 45 foreign countries. Its products are distributed through the Americas Group and its 282 company-operated branches.

FINANCIAL DATA:
Note: Data for latest year may not have been available at press time.

In U.S. $	2018	2017	2016	2015	2014	2013
Revenue	17,534,490,000	14,983,790,000	11,855,600,000	11,339,300,000	11,129,530,000	10,185,530,000
R&D Expense						
Operating Income	1,890,373,000	1,773,589,000	1,719,898,000	1,614,637,000	1,305,472,000	1,151,636,000
Operating Margin %		.12%	.15%	.14%	.12%	.11%
SGA Expense	5,033,780,000	4,785,415,000	4,159,435,000	3,913,518,000	3,822,966,000	3,467,681,000
Net Income	1,108,746,000	1,772,262,000	1,132,703,000	1,053,849,000	865,887,000	752,561,000
Operating Cash Flow	1,943,700,000	1,883,968,000	1,308,572,000	1,447,463,000	1,081,528,000	1,083,766,000
Capital Expenditure	250,957,000	222,767,000	239,026,000	234,340,000	200,545,000	166,680,000
EBITDA	2,322,665,000	2,283,451,000	1,947,032,000	1,809,319,000	1,521,376,000	1,336,466,000
Return on Assets %		.13%	.18%	.18%	.14%	.12%
Return on Equity %		.64%	.82%	1.13%	.63%	.44%
Debt to Equity		2.677	0.645	2.212	1.127	0.647

CONTACT INFORMATION:
Phone: 216 566-2000 Fax:
Toll-Free: 800-474-3794
Address: 101 W. Prospect Ave., Cleveland, OH 44115 United States

STOCK TICKER/OTHER:
Stock Ticker: SHW
Employees: 42,550
Parent Company:

Exchange: NYS
Fiscal Year Ends: 12/31

SALARIES/BONUSES:
Top Exec. Salary: $1,276,924 Bonus: $
Second Exec. Salary: $513,756 Bonus: $228,800

OTHER THOUGHTS:
Estimated Female Officers or Directors: 2
Hot Spot for Advancement for Women/Minorities: Y

Sodexo Inc

NAIC Code: 722310

www.sodexousa.com

TYPES OF BUSINESS:
Food Service Outsourcing
Facilities Management
Laundry Services
Sports Arena Management
Plant Management
Grounds Keeping
Asset Management
Outsourced Procurement Services

BRANDS/DIVISIONS/AFFILIATES:
Sodexho Group
Sodexo Foundation

CONTACTS:
Note: Officers with more than one job title may be intentionally listed here more than once.

Lorna Donatone, CEO
Michael Norris, COO
Michel Landel, Pres.
Debbie White, CEO-Sodexo U.K. & Ireland

GROWTH PLANS/SPECIAL FEATURES:

Sodexo, Inc. is the North American subsidiary of French firm Sodexo Group, a global contract foodservice supplier. The company is one of the largest providers of contract food and facilities management services in the U.S., Mexico and Canada, with approximately 13,000 sites. In total, it serves 15 million consumers each day. Sodexo offers a wide variety of outsourcing solutions in food service, facilities management, business strategy, wellness, motivation solutions and corporate citizenship. The company provides these services to corporate, education, government, healthcare, senior living, sports and leisure, and energy and resources industries. Services to college stadiums and arenas involve concession stands, catering, physical plant management and sports field management. The firm also has a contract to manage the food operations for the U.S. Marine Corps, which includes meal preparation, operation of clean dining facilities and bringing national brands to Navy bases, Army bases and international locations. Moreover, the Sodexo Foundation is an independent charitable organization that supports initiatives addressing the problems of hunger in children and families, as well as offering economic, social and environmental development within the communities Sodexo operates.

The firm offers employees a pension plan; a 401(k) savings plan; health and family care spending accounts; employee assistance plans; tuition reimbursement; and medical, life, disability, dental and vision insurance.

FINANCIAL DATA:
Note: Data for latest year may not have been available at press time.

In U.S. $	2018	2017	2016	2015	2014	2013
Revenue	9,900,000,000	9,800,000,000	9,500,000,000	9,200,000,000	8,800,000,000	9,350,000,000
R&D Expense						
Operating Income						
Operating Margin %						
SGA Expense						
Net Income						
Operating Cash Flow						
Capital Expenditure						
EBITDA						
Return on Assets %						
Return on Equity %						
Debt to Equity						

CONTACT INFORMATION:
Phone: 301-987-4000   Fax: 301-987-4438
Toll-Free: 800-763-3946
Address: 9801 Washingtonian Blvd., Gaithersburg, MD 20878 United States

STOCK TICKER/OTHER:
Stock Ticker: Subsidiary
Employees: 150,000
Parent Company: Sodexo Group

Exchange:
Fiscal Year Ends: 08/31

SALARIES/BONUSES:
Top Exec. Salary: $ Bonus: $
Second Exec. Salary: $ Bonus: $

OTHER THOUGHTS:
Estimated Female Officers or Directors: 2
Hot Spot for Advancement for Women/Minorities: Y

Sales, profits and employees may be estimates. Financial information, benefits and other data can change quickly and may vary from those stated here.

Sonoco Products Company

www.sonoco.com

NAIC Code: 322220

TYPES OF BUSINESS:
Coated and Laminated Packaging Paper Manufacturing

BRANDS/DIVISIONS/AFFILIATES:
Corenso Holdings America Inc

CONTACTS:
Note: Officers with more than one job title may be intentionally listed here more than once.

Robert Tiede, CEO
Julie Albrecht, CFO
John Haley, Chairman of the Board
James Kirkland, Chief Accounting Officer
John Florence, General Counsel
R. Coker, Senior VP, Divisional
Rodger Fuller, Senior VP, Divisional
Kevin Mahoney, Senior VP, Divisional
Harold Cummings, Treasurer
Roger Schrum, Vice President, Divisional
James Harrell, Vice President, Divisional
Marcy Thompson, Vice President, Divisional
Adam Wood, Vice President, Divisional

GROWTH PLANS/SPECIAL FEATURES:
Sonoco Products Company manufactures industrial and consumer packaging products and provides various packaging services. The firm has 312 locations in 36 countries, and operates through four segments: consumer packaging, paper and industrial converted products (PICP), display and packaging, and protective solutions. Consumer packaging, which accounts for 44% of sales revenue, consists of 78 plants located worldwide which produces packaging solutions such as round composite cans, shaped rigid paperboard containers, fiber caulk/adhesive tubes, as well as aluminum, steel and peelable membrane easy-open closures for composite and metal cans; plastic bottles, jars, jugs, cups and trays; and printed flexible packaging and rotogravure cylinder engraving. PICP accounts for 35% of sales revenue and consists of 179 plants which provides the primary raw material for the company's fiber-based packaging. Sonoco uses approximately 62% of the paper this division manufactures and the remainder is sold to third parties. This vertical integration is supported by 23 paper mills with 33 paper machines and 23 recycling facilities throughout the world. Display and packaging accounts for 11% of sales revenue and consists of 23 plants which produce point-of-purchase displays, custom packaging, retail packaging and printed backer cards. This division also provides thermoformed blisters and heat-sealing equipment, as well as supply chain management and paperboard specialties. Protective solutions derives 10% of sales revenue and produces custom-engineered, paperboard-based and expanded foam protective packaging. This division also produces temperature-assured packaging for pharmaceutical and food products. In August 2019, Sonoco acquired Corenso Holdings America, Inc., a U.S. manufacturer of uncoated recycled paperboard and high-performance cores used in the paper, packing films, tape and specialty industries.

FINANCIAL DATA:
Note: Data for latest year may not have been available at press time.

In U.S. $	2018	2017	2016	2015	2014	2013
Revenue	5,390,938,000	5,036,650,000	4,782,877,000	4,964,369,000	5,014,534,000	4,848,092,000
R&D Expense						
Operating Income	477,700,000	405,718,000	431,425,000	433,181,000	414,303,000	386,333,000
Operating Margin %		.08%	.09%	.09%	.08%	.08%
SGA Expense	563,306,000	543,672,000	506,001,000	496,241,000	506,996,000	487,171,000
Net Income	313,560,000	175,345,000	286,434,000	250,136,000	239,165,000	219,113,000
Operating Cash Flow	589,898,000	349,358,000	398,679,000	452,930,000	417,915,000	538,027,000
Capital Expenditure	192,574,000	188,913,000	186,741,000	192,295,000	177,076,000	172,442,000
EBITDA	677,923,000	589,399,000	700,629,000	598,080,000	592,978,000	562,153,000
Return on Assets %		.04%	.07%	.06%	.06%	.05%
Return on Equity %		.11%	.19%	.17%	.15%	.14%
Debt to Equity		0.755	0.666	0.675	0.797	0.553

CONTACT INFORMATION:
Phone: 843 383-7000 Fax: 843 383-7008
Toll-Free:
Address: 1 N. 2nd St., Hartsville, SC 29550 United States

STOCK TICKER/OTHER:
Stock Ticker: SON
Employees: 20,000
Parent Company:

Exchange: NYS
Fiscal Year Ends: 12/31

SALARIES/BONUSES:
Top Exec. Salary: $814,077 Bonus: $
Second Exec. Salary: $579,356 Bonus: $

OTHER THOUGHTS:
Estimated Female Officers or Directors:
Hot Spot for Advancement for Women/Minorities:

Sales, profits and employees may be estimates. Financial information, benefits and other data can change quickly and may vary from those stated here.

Southwest Airlines Co

www.southwest.com

NAIC Code: 481111

TYPES OF BUSINESS:
Airline
Air Freight

BRANDS/DIVISIONS/AFFILIATES:
EarlyBird Check-In

CONTACTS:
Note: Officers with more than one job title may be intentionally listed here more than once.

Gary Kelly, CEO
Tammy Romo, CFO
Mark Shaw, Chief Legal Officer
Michael Van De Ven, COO
Robert Jordan, Executive VP, Divisional
Gregory Wells, Executive VP, Divisional
Andrew Watterson, Executive VP
Thomas Nealon, President
Ron Ricks, Vice Chairman of the Board

GROWTH PLANS/SPECIAL FEATURES:

Southwest Airlines Co. is one of the largest U.S. domestic air travel providers, primarily engaged in short haul, high-frequency airline services. At December 31, 2018, the firm operates an all-Boeing 737 fleet (750 total), serving 99 cities in 40 U.S. states, Washington, D.C. and Puerto Rico, as well as 10 near-international countries: Mexico, Jamaica, The Bahamas, Aruba, Dominican Republic, Costa Rica, Belize, Cuba, the Cayman Islands, and Turks and Caicos. About 77% of the company's customers flew nonstop in 2018, and Southwest's average aircraft trip length was 757 miles, with an average duration of approximately two hours. The busiest routes include roundtrips between Dallas and Houston, Burbank and Oakland, San Diego and San Jose, Denver and Chicago and Los Angeles and Las Vegas. Southwest primarily flies to conveniently-located, secondary or downtown airports such as Houston-Hobby, Dallas-Love Field and Chicago-Midway, which are typically less congested than other airlines' hub airports. Southwest employs a point-to-point route system, which allows for more direct nonstop routing, thereby minimizing connections, delays and total trip time. It also offers the EarlyBird Check-In service, which allows customers to reserve a boarding position prior to general check-in for a fee. Southwest expects to begin selling tickets for service to Hawaii in 2019.

Southwest's employee benefits include free, discounted and guest passes on Southwest Airlines flights; medical, vision, dental, life and long-term disability insurance; an employee assistance program; 401(K) plan; a profit-sharing plan; and an employee stock purchase plan.

FINANCIAL DATA:
Note: Data for latest year may not have been available at press time.

In U.S. $	2018	2017	2016	2015	2014	2013
Revenue	21,965,000,000	21,171,000,000	20,425,000,000	19,820,000,000	18,605,000,000	17,699,000,000
R&D Expense						
Operating Income	3,206,000,000	3,515,000,000	3,760,000,000	4,155,000,000	2,351,000,000	1,364,000,000
Operating Margin %		.17%	.18%	.21%	.13%	.08%
SGA Expense						
Net Income	2,465,000,000	3,488,000,000	2,244,000,000	2,181,000,000	1,136,000,000	754,000,000
Operating Cash Flow	4,893,000,000	3,929,000,000	4,293,000,000	3,238,000,000	2,902,000,000	2,477,000,000
Capital Expenditure	1,976,000,000	2,249,000,000	2,147,000,000	2,143,000,000	1,828,000,000	1,447,000,000
EBITDA	4,458,000,000	4,534,000,000	4,843,000,000	4,584,000,000	2,861,000,000	2,183,000,000
Return on Assets %		.14%	.10%	.11%	.06%	.04%
Return on Equity %		.37%	.28%	.31%	.16%	.11%
Debt to Equity		0.318	0.334	0.345	0.359	0.299

CONTACT INFORMATION:
Phone: 214 792-4000 Fax: 214 792-5015
Toll-Free:
Address: P.O. Box 36611, Dallas, TX 75235-1611 United States

STOCK TICKER/OTHER:
Stock Ticker: LUV
Employees: 53,500
Parent Company:
Exchange: NYS
Fiscal Year Ends: 12/31

SALARIES/BONUSES:
Top Exec. Salary: $750,000   Bonus: $300,000
Second Exec. Salary: $533,125   Bonus: $144,450

OTHER THOUGHTS:
Estimated Female Officers or Directors: 14
Hot Spot for Advancement for Women/Minorities: Y

Spectrum Brands Holdings Inc

www.spectrumbrands.com

NAIC Code: 335912

TYPES OF BUSINESS:
Primary Battery Manufacturing

BRANDS/DIVISIONS/AFFILIATES:
Kwikset
Weiser
Tetra
GloFish
Dingo
Spectracide
Black Flag
LiquidFence

CONTACTS: *Note: Officers with more than one job title may be intentionally listed here more than once.*
David Maura, CEO
Douglas Martin, CFO
Randal Lewis, COO
Ehsan Zargar, Executive VP

GROWTH PLANS/SPECIAL FEATURES:

Spectrum Brands Holdings, Inc. is a diversified branded consumer products company. The firm manufactures, markets and/or distributes its products in 160 countries throughout North America, Europe, the Middle East, Africa, Latin America and Asia-Pacific. Spectrum Brands' products are sold and distributed through retailers, wholesalers, distributors, original equipment manufacturers (OEMs), construction companies and hearing aid professionals. The company's products are divided into three groups: hardware & home improvement, global pet supplies, and home & garden. Hardware & home improvement products include residential and commercial locksets, door hardware, garage hardware, window hardware, floor protection, faucets and plumbing products. Products within the global pet supplies division include small animal food and treats, cleanup and training aid products, pet health and grooming products and aquarium and aquatic health supplies. Home & garden products include household insecticides, repellent products and weed control solutions. Brands of the firm include Kwikset, Weiser, Baldwin, Tell, Tetra, Marineland, Instant Ocean, GloFish, Dingo, FURminator, Nature's Miracle, Wild Harvest, IAMS, Spectracide, Black Flag, Garden Safe, EcoLogic and LiquidFence, among others. In early-2019, Spectrum Brands sold its global auto care business to Energizer Holdings, Inc. for $938.7 million.

FINANCIAL DATA: *Note: Data for latest year may not have been available at press time.*

In U.S. $	2018	2017	2016	2015	2014	2013
Revenue	3,145,900,000	5,008,500,000	5,215,400,000	5,815,900,000	5,963,000,000	5,543,400,000
R&D Expense	28,300,000					
Operating Income	309,100,000	516,300,000	655,100,000	447,500,000	650,500,000	791,700,000
Operating Margin %		.13%	.14%	.12%	.12%	.11%
SGA Expense	816,200,000	1,359,600,000	1,243,600,000	1,476,500,000	1,335,400,000	1,220,500,000
Net Income	768,300,000	106,000,000	-198,800,000	-556,800,000	-10,300,000	-45,800,000
Operating Cash Flow	343,100,000	840,100,000	913,300,000	283,600,000	607,900,000	522,300,000
Capital Expenditure	64,700,000	115,000,000	95,400,000	116,200,000	98,200,000	100,100,000
EBITDA	240,000,000	710,600,000	812,700,000	252,600,000	837,700,000	988,900,000
Return on Assets %		.04%	.05%	.02%	.04%	-.01%
Return on Equity %		.16%	.21%	.11%	.22%	-.06%
Debt to Equity		2.07	1.92	2.519	2.774	3.474

CONTACT INFORMATION:
Phone: 608 275-3340
Fax:
Toll-Free:
Address: 3001 Deming Way, Middleton, WI 53562 United States

SALARIES/BONUSES:
Top Exec. Salary: $315,384   Bonus: $5,000,000
Second Exec. Salary: $279,000   Bonus: $950,000

STOCK TICKER/OTHER:
Stock Ticker: SPB
Employees: 16,021
Parent Company:

Exchange: NYS
Fiscal Year Ends: 09/30

OTHER THOUGHTS:
Estimated Female Officers or Directors:
Hot Spot for Advancement for Women/Minorities:

Spectrum Health

www.spectrumhealth.org

NAIC Code: 622110

TYPES OF BUSINESS:
General Medical and Surgical Hospitals
Trauma Center
Neonatal Center
Burn Center
Poison Center
HMO
Long-Term Care
Children's Hospital

BRANDS/DIVISIONS/AFFILIATES:

CONTACTS:
Note: Officers with more than one job title may be intentionally listed here more than once.

Tina Freese Decker, CEO
Matthew Cox, CFO
Pamela Ries, Chief Human Resources Officer
Jason Joseph, CIO
Richard M. DeVos, Jr., Chmn.

GROWTH PLANS/SPECIAL FEATURES:

Spectrum Health is one of the largest health systems in western Michigan. The firm's not-for-profit system of care is dedicated to improving the health of families and individuals. As of fiscal 2019, Spectrum's organization includes 14 hospitals, 230 ambulatory sites (including integrated care campuses, urgent care centers, walk-in clinics and physician offices), 115 acute care hospitals, 4,200 physicians and advanced practice providers, 87,000 telehealth visits (available 24/7) and 3,200 active volunteers. Spectrum Health provides inpatient and outpatient services throughout Michigan and facilities are located in cities such as Grand Rapids, Holland, Zeeland, Belding, Reed City, Fremont, Kentwood, Rockford, Cutlerville, Greenville, Wyoming, Big Rapids, Canadian Lakes, East Grand Rapids, Allendale, Hastings, Lake Odessa, Grand Blanc, Grand Haven, Coopersville, Stanwood, Evart and many more. Spectrum Health's services include insurance, wellness products, state-of-the-art technology and medical treatments. Major services offered by the firm include cancer, continuing care, diabetes, endocrinology, digestive disease, heart and vascular, neurosciences, orthopedics, pediatrics, rehabilitation, transplant and women's health.

Employees of the company receive benefits including medical, dental, vision, life, disability and AD&D coverage; flexible spending accounts; retirement plans; employee assistance services; tuition assistance; and paid time off.

FINANCIAL DATA:
Note: Data for latest year may not have been available at press time.

In U.S. $	2018	2017	2016	2015	2014	2013
Revenue	6,004,223,000	5,681,000,000	5,220,515,000	4,625,176,000	4,107,828,000	3,937,360,000
R&D Expense						
Operating Income						
Operating Margin %						
SGA Expense						
Net Income	285,582,000	282,000,000	212,044,000	367,311,000	147,747,000	212,257,000
Operating Cash Flow						
Capital Expenditure						
EBITDA						
Return on Assets %						
Return on Equity %						
Debt to Equity						

CONTACT INFORMATION:
Phone: 616-391-1774 Fax: 616-391-2780
Toll-Free: 866-989-7999
Address: 100 Michigan St. NE, Grand Rapids, MI 49503 United States

SALARIES/BONUSES:
Top Exec. Salary: $ Bonus: $
Second Exec. Salary: $ Bonus: $

STOCK TICKER/OTHER:
Stock Ticker: Nonprofit Exchange:
Employees: 31,000 Fiscal Year Ends: 06/30
Parent Company:

OTHER THOUGHTS:
Estimated Female Officers or Directors:
Hot Spot for Advancement for Women/Minorities:

Spirit AeroSystems Holdings Inc

www.spiritaero.com

NAIC Code: 336413

TYPES OF BUSINESS:
Aircraft Fuselage Wing Tail and Similar Assemblies Manufacturing
Aerostructures
Fuselages
Wings & Flight Control Components
Engineering, Design & Materials Testing
Custom Tool Fabrication
Spare Parts & Maintenance Services
Supply Chain Management

BRANDS/DIVISIONS/AFFILIATES:
Onex Corporation

CONTACTS:
Note: Officers with more than one job title may be intentionally listed here more than once.

Thomas Gentile, CEO
Jose Garcia, CFO
Robert Johnson, Chairman of the Board
John Gilson, Chief Accounting Officer
Samantha Marnick, Chief Administrative Officer
John Pilla, Chief Technology Officer
Stacy Cozad, General Counsel
Ronald Rabe, Other Executive Officer
Duane Hawkins, Senior VP, Divisional
Kevin Matthies, Senior VP, Divisional
William Brown, Senior VP, Subsidiary

GROWTH PLANS/SPECIAL FEATURES:
Spirit AeroSystems Holdings, Inc. is an independent designer and manufacturer of aircraft parts and aerostructures for commercial and military aircraft. With its headquarters in Wichita, Kansas, the firm operates throughout the U.S., Europe and Asia. The firm operates through three principal segments: fuselage systems, propulsion systems and wing systems. The fuselage systems segment includes development, production and marketing of forward, mid and rear fuselage sections and systems, primarily to aircraft OEMs, as well as related spares. Additionally, it offers services that include numerical control programming, materials testing, onsite planning and global supply chain management. The propulsion systems segment offers production, development and marketing of struts, pylons, nacelles, thrust reversers and related engine structural components primarily to aircraft or engine OEMs, as well as related spares. The wing systems segment produces wings, wing components and flight control surfaces. Spirit Aerosystems is also engaged in tooling, the fabrication of custom tools and the manufacturing of structural components for military aircraft. The firm's tooling capabilities include tool design, computer numerical control (CNC) programming, machining, composite, aluminum and invar tooling. The company offers spare parts and components for all items of which it is the original production supplier and provides maintenance, repair and overhaul work for nacelles, fuselage doors, structural components and modification kits. Spirit Aerosystems is the largest independent supplier of aerostructures to Boeing and one of the largest to Airbus. The company is majority-controlled by Onex Corporation. During 2018, Spirit AeroSystems agreed to acquire Asco Industries NV, and received approval from the European Commission in March 2019, but the transaction was still subject to other conditions.

Employee benefits include a company profit sharing bonus; 401(k); relocation benefits; medical, vision and life insurance; healthcare spending accounts; disability coverage; and tuition assistance.

FINANCIAL DATA:
Note: Data for latest year may not have been available at press time.

In U.S. $	2018	2017	2016	2015	2014	2013
Revenue	7,222,000,000	6,983,000,000	6,792,900,000	6,643,900,000	6,799,200,000	5,961,000,000
R&D Expense	42,500,000	31,200,000	23,800,000	27,800,000	29,300,000	34,700,000
Operating Income	833,200,000	589,000,000	737,200,000	863,000,000	825,100,000	-334,000,000
Operating Margin %		.08%	.11%	.13%	.12%	-.06%
SGA Expense	210,400,000	200,300,000	228,300,000	220,800,000	233,800,000	200,800,000
Net Income	617,000,000	354,900,000	469,700,000	788,700,000	358,800,000	-621,400,000
Operating Cash Flow	769,900,000	573,700,000	716,900,000	1,289,700,000	361,600,000	260,600,000
Capital Expenditure	271,200,000	273,100,000	254,000,000	360,100,000	220,200,000	272,600,000
EBITDA	1,067,200,000	790,600,000	926,600,000	1,041,900,000	526,500,000	-199,400,000
Return on Assets %		.07%	.08%	.14%	.07%	-.12%
Return on Equity %		.19%	.23%	.42%	.23%	-.36%
Debt to Equity		0.622	0.55	0.518	0.706	0.777

CONTACT INFORMATION:
Phone: 316 526-9000   Fax:
Toll-Free: 800-501-7597
Address: 3801 S. Oliver St., Wichita, KS 67210 United States

SALARIES/BONUSES:
Top Exec. Salary: $1,241,233   Bonus: $
Second Exec. Salary: $650,000   Bonus: $

STOCK TICKER/OTHER:
Stock Ticker: SPR
Employees: 14,400
Parent Company: Onex Corporation

Exchange: NYS
Fiscal Year Ends: 12/31

OTHER THOUGHTS:
Estimated Female Officers or Directors: 2
Hot Spot for Advancement for Women/Minorities: Y

Sales, profits and employees may be estimates. Financial information, benefits and other data can change quickly and may vary from those stated here.

Spirit Airlines Inc

NAIC Code: 481111

www.spirit.com

TYPES OF BUSINESS:
Airline
Low-Fare Carrier

BRANDS/DIVISIONS/AFFILIATES:
FREE SPIRIT
$9 Fare Club

CONTACTS:
Note: Officers with more than one job title may be intentionally listed here more than once.

Edward Christie, CEO
Scott Haralson, CFO
H. Gardner, Chairman of the Board
Brian McMenamy, Chief Accounting Officer
John Bendoraitis, COO
Thomas Canfield, General Counsel
Martha Villa, Other Executive Officer
Matthew Klein, Other Executive Officer
Rocky Wiggins, Senior VP

GROWTH PLANS/SPECIAL FEATURES:

Spirit Airlines, Inc. is a leading ultra-low-fare airline based in Florida, USA. The company flies to more than 75 destinations and offers over 500 daily flight departures throughout the U.S., as well as in Latin America and the Caribbean. As of May 2019, its current fleet consists of 135 Airbus aircraft. Specifically, 31 A319s, 62 A320s, 12 A320neos and 30 A321s, all of which have an average age of 5.4 years. Spirit Airlines offers customers unbundled fares, with options to purchase checked and carry-on bags, advanced seat assignments, priority boarding and refreshments. The firm's targets underserved and/or overpriced markets, analyzes weekly and monthly profit reports, and performs near-term forecasting to remain competitive. Aircraft maintenance and repair consists of routine and non-routine maintenance, and work performed is divided into categories such as: line maintenance, encompassing daily and weekly aircraft checks; heavy maintenance, consisting of a series of complex tasks that can take from one to four weeks to accomplish and are required every 24 to 36 months; and component service. FREE SPIRIT is the company's affinity credit card program; and the $9 Fare Club is a low-fare subscription service in which members receive offers on exclusive deals on flights before promotions are offered to the public, and have access to reduced bag fee options. Spirit airlines also sells third-party travel insurance through its website.

FINANCIAL DATA:
Note: Data for latest year may not have been available at press time.

In U.S. $	2018	2017	2016	2015	2014	2013
Revenue	3,323,034,000	2,647,666,000	2,321,956,000	2,141,463,000	1,931,580,000	1,654,385,000
R&D Expense						
Operating Income	449,415,000	405,588,000	485,037,000	511,399,000	358,316,000	282,991,000
Operating Margin %		.15%	.21%	.24%	.19%	.17%
SGA Expense						
Net Income	155,749,000	420,606,000	264,879,000	317,220,000	225,464,000	176,918,000
Operating Cash Flow	506,463,000	425,240,000	473,678,000	472,985,000	260,512,000	195,376,000
Capital Expenditure	615,700,000	641,186,000	551,956,000	558,959,000	186,569,000	19,812,000
EBITDA	455,639,000	537,313,000	549,545,000	585,140,000	399,965,000	314,357,000
Return on Assets %		.12%	.09%	.15%	.16%	.17%
Return on Equity %		.27%	.20%	.28%	.25%	.26%
Debt to Equity		0.781	0.643	0.487	0.135	

CONTACT INFORMATION:
Phone: 954 447-7920
Fax: 248-727-2688
Toll-Free: 800-772-7117
Address: 2800 Executive Way, Miramar, FL 33025 United States

STOCK TICKER/OTHER:
Stock Ticker: SAVE
Employees: 5,742
Parent Company:
Exchange: NYS
Fiscal Year Ends: 12/31

SALARIES/BONUSES:
Top Exec. Salary: $647,917   Bonus: $
Second Exec. Salary: $543,750   Bonus: $

OTHER THOUGHTS:
Estimated Female Officers or Directors: 1
Hot Spot for Advancement for Women/Minorities:

Sales, profits and employees may be estimates. Financial information, benefits and other data can change quickly and may vary from those stated here.

Stanley Black & Decker Inc

www.stanleyblackanddecker.com

NAIC Code: 333991

TYPES OF BUSINESS:
Power Tools & Accessories Manufacturer
Security Solutions
Household Appliances
Home Improvement Products
Fastening & Assembly Systems
Plumbing Products
Automotive Machinery

BRANDS/DIVISIONS/AFFILIATES:
DeWALT
Porter-Cable
Bostitch
Guaranteed Tough
Mac Tools
LaBounty
Dubuis
WanderGuard

CONTACTS:
Note: Officers with more than one job title may be intentionally listed here more than once.

James Loree, CEO
Donald Allan, CFO
Jocelyn Belisle, Chief Accounting Officer
George Buckley, Director
Jeffery Ansell, Executive VP
Janet Link, General Counsel
Joseph Voelker, Other Executive Officer
John Wyatt, President, Divisional
Jaime Ramirez, President, Divisional

GROWTH PLANS/SPECIAL FEATURES:

Stanley Black & Decker, Inc. is a global manufacturer and marketer of hand tools, power tools and accessories, as well as hardware and home improvement products, security solutions and technology-based fastening systems. The firm is also a worldwide supplier of engineered fastening and assembly systems. Stanley Black & Decker products and services are marketed in hardware and home improvement stores around the globe. The firm operates in three reportable business segments: tools & storage, security and industrial. The tools & storage segment includes professional and consumer power tools and accessories, lawn and garden tools, consumer mechanics tools, storage systems and pneumatic tools and fasteners. The security segment provides both mechanical and electric access and security systems primarily for retailers; educational, financial and health care institutions; and commercial, government and industrial customers. The industrial segment manufactures and markets professional industrial and automotive mechanics tools and storage systems; metal and plastic fasteners and engineered fastening systems; hydraulic tools and accessories; plumbing, heating and air conditioning tools; assembly tools and systems; and specialty tools. The company sells these products to industrial clients in the automotive, transportation, aerospace, electronics and machine tool industries primarily through third-party distributors. Brand names include DeWALT, Porter-Cable, Bostitch, Proto, Powers, Guaranteed Tough, FatMax, Craftsman and Black & Decker as well as Mac Tools, CRC, LaBounty, Dubuis, Stanley, WanderGuard and many more. In mid-2019, Stanley Black & Decker sold its Sargent & Greenleaf mechanical locks business within the security segment to OpenGate Capital.

Employee benefits include medical, dental, life and disability insurance; and a 401(k).

FINANCIAL DATA:
Note: Data for latest year may not have been available at press time.

In U.S. $	2018	2017	2016	2015	2014	2013
Revenue	13,982,400,000	12,747,200,000	11,406,900,000	11,171,800,000	11,338,600,000	11,001,200,000
R&D Expense						
Operating Income	1,679,400,000	1,797,900,000	1,643,300,000	1,585,600,000	1,506,800,000	1,218,300,000
Operating Margin %		.14%	.14%	.14%	.13%	.11%
SGA Expense	3,143,700,000	2,965,700,000	2,602,000,000	2,459,100,000	2,575,000,000	2,700,900,000
Net Income	605,200,000	1,226,000,000	965,300,000	883,700,000	760,900,000	490,300,000
Operating Cash Flow	1,260,900,000	1,418,600,000	1,485,200,000	1,182,300,000	1,295,900,000	868,000,000
Capital Expenditure	492,100,000	442,400,000	347,000,000	311,400,000	291,000,000	365,600,000
EBITDA	1,806,500,000	2,209,400,000	1,828,600,000	1,745,200,000	1,711,800,000	1,188,300,000
Return on Assets %		.07%	.06%	.06%	.05%	.03%
Return on Equity %		.18%	.16%	.14%	.12%	.07%
Debt to Equity		0.377	0.599	0.66	0.597	0.559

CONTACT INFORMATION:
Phone: 860 225-5111   Fax: 860 827-3895
Toll-Free:
Address: 1000 Stanley Dr., New Britain, CT 06053 United States

STOCK TICKER/OTHER:
Stock Ticker: SWK
Employees: 54,023
Parent Company:

Exchange: NYS
Fiscal Year Ends: 12/31

SALARIES/BONUSES:
Top Exec. Salary: $1,250,000   Bonus: $
Second Exec. Salary: $725,000   Bonus: $

OTHER THOUGHTS:
Estimated Female Officers or Directors: 5
Hot Spot for Advancement for Women/Minorities: Y

Starbucks Corporation

NAIC Code: 722515

www.starbucks.com

TYPES OF BUSINESS:
Coffee Houses & Coffee Stores
Coffee-Related Accessories & Equipment
Wholesale Coffee Distribution
Tea and Accessories

BRANDS/DIVISIONS/AFFILIATES:
Starbucks Coffee Korea Co Ltd
President Starbucks Coffee Corporation
Tata Starbucks Limited (India)
Reserve Roastery & Tasting Room
Starbucks
Teavana
La Boulange
Ethos

CONTACTS:
Note: Officers with more than one job title may be intentionally listed here more than once.

Paul Mutty, Assistant Secretary
Patrick Grismer, CFO
Howard Schultz, Chairman Emeritus
Myron Ullman, Chairman of the Board
Jill Walker, Chief Accounting Officer
Rosalind Brewer, COO
Kevin Johnson, Director
Vivek Varma, Executive VP, Divisional
Rachel Gonzalez, Executive VP
Lucy Helm, Executive VP
Clifford Burrows, On Leave
John Culver, President, Divisional
Mellody Hobson, Vice Chairman of the Board

GROWTH PLANS/SPECIAL FEATURES:

Starbucks Corporation is a roaster, marketer and retailer of specialty coffee, with more than 15,300 retail stores worldwide (as of September 2018). The firm purchases and roasts high-quality coffees that it sells, along with handcrafted coffee, tea and other beverages and a variety of fresh food items, through company-operated stores. Starbucks also licenses its trademarks through other channels such as grocery stores and national foodservice accounts. In addition to its flagship Starbucks brand, the company's portfolio includes goods and services offered under the following brands: Teavana, Seattle's Best Coffee, Evolution Fresh, La Boulange, Ethos, Starbucks Reserve and Princi. The firm has four operating segments: Americas (the U.S., Canada and Latin America), accounting for 68% of total 2018 net revenues; Europe, Middle East and Africa (EMEA), 4%; China/Asia Pacific (CAP), 18%; and channel development, 9%; with all other corporate-related business accounting for the remaining 1%. The Americas, EMEA and CAP segments include both company-operated and licensed stores. The Americas and EMEA segments include certain food service accounts. Additionally, the Americas includes the company's La Boulange retail stores. Starbucks owns a 50% interest in each of the following companies: Starbucks Coffee Korea Co. Ltd., President Starbucks Coffee Corporation (Taiwan) Co. Ltd. and Tata Starbucks Limited (India). It also licenses the rights to produce and distribute Starbucks-branded products to its 50% joint venture with Pepsi-Cola Company, The North American Coffee Partnership, which develops and distributes bottled Starbucks beverages. Starbuck's Reserve Roastery & Tasting Room is the company's specialty store concept, where rare and exotic coffees are roasted and served at premium prices.

Starbucks offers employee health benefits, 401(k) and various assistance programs.

FINANCIAL DATA:
Note: Data for latest year may not have been available at press time.

In U.S. $	2018	2017	2016	2015	2014	2013
Revenue	24,719,500,000	22,386,800,000	21,315,900,000	19,162,700,000	16,447,800,000	14,892,200,000
R&D Expense						
Operating Income	3,806,500,000	3,896,800,000	3,853,700,000	3,351,100,000	2,792,600,000	2,207,300,000
Operating Margin %		.17%	.18%	.17%	.17%	.15%
SGA Expense	1,759,000,000	1,393,300,000	1,360,600,000	1,196,700,000	991,300,000	937,900,000
Net Income	4,518,300,000	2,884,700,000	2,817,700,000	2,757,400,000	2,068,100,000	8,300,000
Operating Cash Flow	11,937,800,000	4,174,300,000	4,575,100,000	3,749,100,000	607,800,000	2,908,300,000
Capital Expenditure	1,976,400,000	1,519,400,000	1,440,300,000	1,303,700,000	1,160,900,000	1,151,200,000
EBITDA	7,256,200,000	5,477,100,000	5,310,000,000	4,907,300,000	3,972,200,000	453,800,000
Return on Assets %		.20%	.21%	.24%	.19%	.00%
Return on Equity %		.51%	.48%	.50%	.42%	.00%
Debt to Equity		0.722	0.544	0.403	0.389	0.29

CONTACT INFORMATION:
Phone: 206 447-1575 Fax: 206 447-0828
Toll-Free: 800-782-7282
Address: 2401 Utah Ave. S., Seattle, WA 98134 United States

STOCK TICKER/OTHER:
Stock Ticker: SBUX
Employees: 291,000
Parent Company:

Exchange: NAS
Fiscal Year Ends: 09/30

SALARIES/BONUSES:
Top Exec. Salary: $1,461,533 Bonus: $
Second Exec. Salary: $961,540 Bonus: $334,000

OTHER THOUGHTS:
Estimated Female Officers or Directors: 5
Hot Spot for Advancement for Women/Minorities: Y

Sales, profits and employees may be estimates. Financial information, benefits and other data can change quickly and may vary from those stated here.

State Farm Insurance Companies

www.statefarm.com

NAIC Code: 524126

TYPES OF BUSINESS:

Insurance, Direct Property & Casualty
Accident Insurance
Health Insurance
Life Insurance
Annuities
Automobile Insurance
Banking/Savings Association
Mutual Funds

BRANDS/DIVISIONS/AFFILIATES:

CONTACTS: Note: Officers with more than one job title may be intentionally listed here more than once.

Michael L. Tipsord, CEO
Michael L. Tipsord, Chmn.

GROWTH PLANS/SPECIAL FEATURES:

State Farm Insurance Companies is a mutual company providing personal property and casualty insurance, as well as banking and investment products through State Farm agents located across the U.S. Insurance products include car, motorcycle, boat, off-road vehicles, motorhomes, home/property, life, health, disability, liability, identity restoration and small business. Home and property insurance encompasses home, condominium, renters insurance, rental property, personal articles and far and ranch. Life insurance spans term life, whole life and universal life. Health insurance includes supplemental health, Medicare supplement, individual medical and more. Disability insurance includes both short- and long-term coverage. Liability products include personal, business and professional. Banking products include vehicle loans, home loans, checking and savings accounts and credit cards. Investment products span retirement options, mutual funds, educational savings, estate planning and annuities. By the end of 2019, State Farm Insurance of Canada had been completely transferred and rebranded to Desjardins Insurance, which acquired the business in 2014.

Employee benefits include medical, dental and life coverage; a 401(k); a company retirement plan; and a wellness program.

FINANCIAL DATA: Note: Data for latest year may not have been available at press time.

In U.S. $	2018	2017	2016	2015	2014	2013
Revenue	81,700,000,000	78,300,000,000	76,100,000,000	75,700,000,000	71,200,000,000	68,291,000,000
R&D Expense						
Operating Income						
Operating Margin %						
SGA Expense						
Net Income	8,800,000,000	2,200,000,000	400,000,000	6,200,000,000	4,200,000,000	5,189,000,000
Operating Cash Flow						
Capital Expenditure						
EBITDA						
Return on Assets %						
Return on Equity %						
Debt to Equity						

CONTACT INFORMATION:

Phone: 309-766-2311 Fax: 309-766-3621
Toll-Free: 877-734-2265
Address: 1 State Farm Plaza, Bloomington, IL 61710 United States

SALARIES/BONUSES:

Top Exec. Salary: $ Bonus: $
Second Exec. Salary: $ Bonus: $

STOCK TICKER/OTHER:

Stock Ticker: Mutual Company
Employees: 70,000
Parent Company:

Exchange:
Fiscal Year Ends: 12/31

OTHER THOUGHTS:

Estimated Female Officers or Directors: 3
Hot Spot for Advancement for Women/Minorities: Y

Sales, profits and employees may be estimates. Financial information, benefits and other data can change quickly and may vary from those stated here.

Stericycle Inc

NAIC Code: 562112

www.stericycle.com

TYPES OF BUSINESS:
Medical Waste Treatment

BRANDS/DIVISIONS/AFFILIATES:
Bio-Systems
Steri-Safe
Shred-it

CONTACTS:
Note: Officers with more than one job title may be intentionally listed here more than once.

Cindy Miller, CEO
Daniel Ginnetti, Chief Accounting Officer
Richard Hoffman, Chief Accounting Officer
Michael Weisman, Chief Compliance Officer
David Stahl, Chief Information Officer
Robert Murley, Director
Stephen White, Executive VP, Divisional
Richard Moore, Executive VP, Divisional
Kurt Rogers, Executive VP
Dominic Culotta, Executive VP
William Seward, Executive VP
Joseph Reuter, Executive VP

GROWTH PLANS/SPECIAL FEATURES:

Stericycle, Inc. is engaged in the business of medical waste disposal. Through its national networks of 251 processing facilities, 307 transfer sites, 67 customer service or administration offices, 14 communication centers and two landfills, the firm serves all 50 U.S. states and 21 other countries. In order to dispose of medical waste, Stericycle utilizes various technologies, including autoclaving, an electro-thermal-deactivation system (ETD), chemical treatment and incineration. While Stericycle's customers are mainly hospitals, clinics, acute care facilities and dental offices, it also handles disposal of expired or surplus products from pharmacies and pharmaceutical manufacturers. The company generally provides its customers with its own waste containers, such as the plastic Bio-Systems containers, to avoid needle sticks and leakages. After treatment, the residual ash is passed on to a third-party landfill and the containers are returned to customers. Stericycle utilizes its own branded methodologies, which include Steri-Safe, a compliance program designed to familiarize clients with regulatory policies, mail-back programs, product recalls, returns and onsite waste disposal services. The company serves more than 1 million customers worldwide, including large-quantity generators such as hospitals, blood banks and pharmaceutical manufacturers; and small-quantity generators such as outpatient clinics, medical and dental offices, long-term and sub-acute care facilities and retail pharmacies. In addition, Stericycle owns Shred-it, a global leader in secure information destruction. Documents are cross-cut shredded and then baled to be sold as office paper for recycling.

Stericycle offers employees comprehensive benefits, retirement plans and a variety of employee assistance programs.

FINANCIAL DATA:
Note: Data for latest year may not have been available at press time.

In U.S. $	2018	2017	2016	2015	2014	2013
Revenue	3,485,900,000	3,580,700,000	3,562,342,000	2,985,908,000	2,555,601,000	2,142,807,000
R&D Expense						
Operating Income	197,600,000	-7,600,000	433,775,000	487,612,000	556,336,000	535,619,000
Operating Margin %		.00%	.12%	.16%	.22%	.25%
SGA Expense	1,178,400,000	1,470,100,000	904,179,000	712,803,000	489,937,000	390,610,000
Net Income	-244,700,000	42,400,000	206,359,000	267,046,000	326,456,000	311,372,000
Operating Cash Flow	165,700,000	508,600,000	547,249,000	390,328,000	448,500,000	403,467,000
Capital Expenditure	130,800,000	143,000,000	136,160,000	114,761,000	86,496,000	73,109,000
EBITDA	87,100,000	235,600,000	678,478,000	615,817,000	658,326,000	621,397,000
Return on Assets %		.00%	.03%	.04%	.08%	.08%
Return on Equity %		.01%	.06%	.11%	.18%	.19%
Debt to Equity		0.903	1.026	1.118	0.806	0.732

CONTACT INFORMATION:
Phone: 847 367-5910 Fax: 847 367-9493
Toll-Free: 800-643-0240
Address: 28161 N. Keith Dr., Lake Forest, IL 60045 United States

STOCK TICKER/OTHER:
Stock Ticker: SRCL
Employees: 25,000
Parent Company:

Exchange: NAS
Fiscal Year Ends: 12/31

SALARIES/BONUSES:
Top Exec. Salary: $1,000,000 Bonus: $
Second Exec. Salary: $370,000 Bonus: $327,541

OTHER THOUGHTS:
Estimated Female Officers or Directors:
Hot Spot for Advancement for Women/Minorities:

Sales, profits and employees may be estimates. Financial information, benefits and other data can change quickly and may vary from those stated here.

Stifel Financial Corp

NAIC Code: 523110

www.stifel.com

TYPES OF BUSINESS:
Stock Brokerage/Investment Banking
Underwriting
Broker-Dealer
Investment Advisory Services
Research
Insurance
Annuities

BRANDS/DIVISIONS/AFFILIATES:
Stifel Nicolaus & Company Inc
Keefe Bruyeete & Woods Inc
Miller Buckfire & Co LLC
Century Securities Associates Inc
Eaton Partners LLC
Stifel Nicolaus Europe Limited
Stifel Bank & Trust
Stifel Trust Company NA

CONTACTS:
Note: Officers with more than one job title may be intentionally listed here more than once.

Ronald Kruszewski, CEO
James Marischen, CFO
Thomas Weisel, Co-Chairman
David Sliney, COO
James Zemlyak, Co-President
Victor Nesi, Co-President
Richard Himelfarb, Executive VP, Subsidiary
Ben Plotkin, Executive VP, Subsidiary
Mark Fisher, General Counsel
Thomas Michaud, Senior VP

GROWTH PLANS/SPECIAL FEATURES:
Stifel Financial Corp. is a financial services holding company that operates through its subsidiaries, which offer banking, securities and financial services. Geographically, the firm's broker-dealer clients are served in the U.S. through: Stifel Nicolaus & Company, Inc.; Keefe Bruyette & Woods, Inc.; Miller Buckfire & Co., LLC; Century Securities Associates, Inc.; and Eaton Partners, LLC. In the U.K. and Europe, its clients are served through Stifel Nicolaus Europe Limited. The company's broker-dealer affiliates offer securities brokerage, investment banking, trading, investment advisory and related financial services to individual investors, professional money managers, businesses and municipalities. Stifel's institutional division offers research, equity and fixed income institutional sales and trading, as well as investment banking, public finance and syndicate solutions. In addition, Stifel Bank & Trust offers a comprehensive range of consumer and commercial lending solutions. Stifel Trust Company, NA and Stifel Trust Company Delaware, NA offer trust and related services. During 2018, Stifel acquired Ziegler Wealth Management, Business Bancshares, Inc. and Rand & Associates; and agreed to acquire First Empire Holding Corp. and MainFirst, including MainFirst Bank AG, MainFirst Schwiez AG and MainFirst Sec. US.

FINANCIAL DATA:
Note: Data for latest year may not have been available at press time.

In U.S. $	2018	2017	2016	2015	2014	2013
Revenue	2,982,914,000	2,882,300,000	2,531,181,000	2,289,076,000	2,171,869,000	1,936,221,000
R&D Expense						
Operating Income						
Operating Margin %						
SGA Expense	1,911,016,000	2,092,422,000	1,865,660,000	1,699,540,000	1,510,858,000	1,411,112,000
Net Income	393,968,000	182,871,000	81,520,000	92,336,000	176,067,000	162,013,000
Operating Cash Flow	529,526,000	662,349,000	-349,175,000	-326,829,000	250,269,000	702,219,000
Capital Expenditure	108,207,000	28,217,000	28,211,000	69,822,000	26,632,000	32,278,000
EBITDA						
Return on Assets %		.01%	.00%	.01%	.02%	.02%
Return on Equity %		.07%	.03%	.04%	.08%	.09%
Debt to Equity		0.768	0.672	0.334	0.305	0.199

CONTACT INFORMATION:
Phone: 314 342-2000 Fax: 314 342-1159
Toll-Free: 800-679-5446
Address: 501 N. Broadway, St. Louis, MO 63102 United States

STOCK TICKER/OTHER:
Stock Ticker: SF
Employees: 7,100
Parent Company:

Exchange: NYS
Fiscal Year Ends: 12/31

SALARIES/BONUSES:
Top Exec. Salary: $200,000 Bonus: $4,020,761
Second Exec. Salary: $250,000 Bonus: $2,942,500

OTHER THOUGHTS:
Estimated Female Officers or Directors:
Hot Spot for Advancement for Women/Minorities:

Strategy&

NAIC Code: 541610

www.strategyand.pwc.com

TYPES OF BUSINESS:
Management Consulting

BRANDS/DIVISIONS/AFFILIATES:
PricewaterhouseCoopers (PWC)

CONTACTS:
Note: Officers with more than one job title may be intentionally listed here more than once.

Joachim Rotergin, Global Leader
Mark Berlind, General Counsel
Jochim Rotering, Sr. Partner-Oper.
Peter B. Mensing, Managing Dir.-Europe
Mike Connolly, Sr. Partner-Health Svcs.
Leslie Moeller, Sr. Partner
Jay Davis, Global Dir.-Oper.
Ivan de Souza, Managing Dir.-Global Markets

GROWTH PLANS/SPECIAL FEATURES:

Strategy& is a management consulting firm that provides services to businesses and government institutions worldwide. Strategy& serves industries as diverse as aerospace, chemicals, consumer products, entertainment/media, financial services, health, industrials, oil & gas, power/utilities, public sector, steels/metals, technology, telecommunications and transportation. The firm's functional expertise span business strategy, customer strategy, operations strategy, organization strategy, product and service innovation and technology strategy. The company has offices in more than 40 countries, spanning Africa, Asia-Pacific, Europe, the Middle East and the Americas. Strategy& is owned by PricewaterhouseCoopers.

The firm offers employees a formal work-life balance program; substantial sick leave and family care leave; flexible work arrangements that may include job-sharing, flex time, sabbaticals and a compressed work week; and access to training at the PwC Open University.

FINANCIAL DATA:
Note: Data for latest year may not have been available at press time.

In U.S. $	2018	2017	2016	2015	2014	2013
Revenue	1,400,000,000	1,300,000,000	1,194,027,000	1,147,000,000	1,300,000,000	1,050,000,000
R&D Expense						
Operating Income						
Operating Margin %						
SGA Expense						
Net Income						
Operating Cash Flow						
Capital Expenditure						
EBITDA						
Return on Assets %						
Return on Equity %						
Debt to Equity						

CONTACT INFORMATION:
Phone: 212-697-1900 Fax: 212-551-6732
Toll-Free:
Address: 101 Park Ave., 18/Fl, New York, NY 10178 United States

SALARIES/BONUSES:
Top Exec. Salary: $ Bonus: $
Second Exec. Salary: $ Bonus: $

STOCK TICKER/OTHER:
Stock Ticker: Subsidiary Exchange:
Employees: 3,000 Fiscal Year Ends:
Parent Company: PricewaterhouseCoopers (PWC)

OTHER THOUGHTS:
Estimated Female Officers or Directors: 1
Hot Spot for Advancement for Women/Minorities:

Sales, profits and employees may be estimates. Financial information, benefits and other data can change quickly and may vary from those stated here.

Stryker Corporation

NAIC Code: 339100

www.stryker.com

TYPES OF BUSINESS:
Equipment-Orthopedic Implants
Powered Surgical Instruments
Endoscopic Systems
Patient Care & Handling Equipment
Imaging Software
Small Bone Innovations

BRANDS/DIVISIONS/AFFILIATES:
SafeAir AG
OrthoSpace Ltd

CONTACTS: Note: Officers with more than one job title may be intentionally listed here more than once.
Kevin Lobo, CEO
Glenn Boehnlein, CFO
William Berry, Chief Accounting Officer
Robert Fletcher, Chief Legal Officer
Timothy Scannell, COO
Michael Hutchinson, Other Corporate Officer
Bijoy Sagar, Other Executive Officer
M. Fink, Other Executive Officer
Viju Menon, President, Divisional
Yin Becker, Vice President, Divisional
Katherine Owen, Vice President, Divisional

GROWTH PLANS/SPECIAL FEATURES:

Stryker Corporation develops, manufactures and markets innovative products and services that help improve patient and hospital outcomes. The firm's products are sold in over 80 countries through company-owned subsidiaries and branches, as well as by third-party dealers and distributors. Stryker's products include implants used in joint replacement and trauma surgeries, surgical equipment, surgical navigation systems, endoscopic systems, communications systems, patient handling equipment, emergency medical equipment, intensive care disposable products, neurosurgical devices, spinal devices, neurovascular devices and other products used in a variety of medical specialties. These products are segregated within the three business segments of: MedSurg, deriving 44% of 2018 net sales; orthopedics, 37%; and neurotechnology and spine, 19%. Stryker owns approximately 3,068 U.S. patents and approximately 4,716 international patents. During 2019, Stryker completed its acquisition of SafeAir AG, a Swiss medical device company focused on the design, development and manufacture of innovative surgical smoke evacuation solutions. That March, Stryker acquired OrthoSpace, Ltd., a provider of highly differentiated technology for the treatment of massive irreparable rotator cuff tears.

Stryker offers employees health insurance, retirement programs, tuition reimbursement and wellness programs.

FINANCIAL DATA: Note: Data for latest year may not have been available at press time.

In U.S. $	2018	2017	2016	2015	2014	2013
Revenue	13,601,000,000	12,444,000,000	11,325,000,000	9,946,000,000	9,675,000,000	9,021,000,000
R&D Expense	862,000,000	787,000,000	715,000,000	625,000,000	614,000,000	536,000,000
Operating Income	2,560,000,000	2,463,000,000	2,324,000,000	2,157,000,000	2,007,000,000	1,304,000,000
Operating Margin %		.20%	.21%	.22%	.21%	.14%
SGA Expense	5,099,000,000	4,552,000,000	4,137,000,000	3,610,000,000	3,575,000,000	4,066,000,000
Net Income	3,553,000,000	1,020,000,000	1,647,000,000	1,439,000,000	515,000,000	1,006,000,000
Operating Cash Flow	2,610,000,000	1,559,000,000	1,812,000,000	899,000,000	1,782,000,000	1,886,000,000
Capital Expenditure	572,000,000	598,000,000	490,000,000	270,000,000	233,000,000	195,000,000
EBITDA	3,283,000,000	3,105,000,000	2,870,000,000	2,554,000,000	2,385,000,000	1,611,000,000
Return on Assets %		.05%	.09%	.08%	.03%	.07%
Return on Equity %		.10%	.18%	.17%	.06%	.11%
Debt to Equity		0.661	0.70	0.382	0.378	0.303

CONTACT INFORMATION:
Phone: 269 385-2600   Fax: 269 385-1062
Toll-Free:
Address: 2825 Airview Blvd., Kalamazoo, MI 49002 United States

STOCK TICKER/OTHER:
Stock Ticker: SYK
Employees: 33,000
Parent Company:

Exchange: NYS
Fiscal Year Ends: 12/31

SALARIES/BONUSES:
Top Exec. Salary: $1,194,833   Bonus: $
Second Exec. Salary: $691,250   Bonus: $

OTHER THOUGHTS:
Estimated Female Officers or Directors: 7
Hot Spot for Advancement for Women/Minorities: Y

Sutter Health Inc

NAIC Code: 622110

www.sutterhealth.org

TYPES OF BUSINESS:
General Medical and Surgical Hospitals
Neonatal Care
Pregnancy & Birth
Training Programs
Medical Research Facilities
Home Health Services
Hospice Networks
Long-Term Care

BRANDS/DIVISIONS/AFFILIATES:

GROWTH PLANS/SPECIAL FEATURES:
Sutter Health, Inc. is a non-profit healthcare network that delivers personalized care in more than 100 northern California communities. This network includes physician organizations, acute care hospitals, surgery centers, home health and hospice programs, medical research facilities, training programs and specialty services. As a non-profit, Sutter Health invests all of its earnings back into the communities it serves. There are more than 12,000 physicians within the network, 2,000 advanced practice clinicians, 14,500 nurses, 5,000 volunteers, 24 hospitals, 36 ambulatory surgery centers, seven cardiac centers, nine cancer centers, four acute rehabilitation centers, eight behavioral health centers, five trauma centers, 4,188 licensed general acute-care beds and eight neonatal intensive care units.

CONTACTS:
Note: Officers with more than one job title may be intentionally listed here more than once.

Sarah Krevans, CEO

FINANCIAL DATA:
Note: Data for latest year may not have been available at press time.

In U.S. $	2018	2017	2016	2015	2014	2013
Revenue	12,700,000,000	12,444,000,000	11,873,000,000	10,998,000,000	10,161,000,000	9,600,000,000
R&D Expense						
Operating Income						
Operating Margin %						
SGA Expense						
Net Income	-200,000,000	958,000,000	622,000,000	145,000,000	458,000,000	358,000,000
Operating Cash Flow						
Capital Expenditure						
EBITDA						
Return on Assets %						
Return on Equity %						
Debt to Equity						

CONTACT INFORMATION:
Phone: 916-733-8800 Fax:
Toll-Free:
Address: 2200 River Plaza Dr., Sacramento, CA 95833 United States

STOCK TICKER/OTHER:
Stock Ticker: Nonprofit
Employees: 67,000
Parent Company:

Exchange:
Fiscal Year Ends: 12/31

SALARIES/BONUSES:
Top Exec. Salary: $ Bonus: $
Second Exec. Salary: $ Bonus: $

OTHER THOUGHTS:
Estimated Female Officers or Directors: 3
Hot Spot for Advancement for Women/Minorities: Y

Sales, profits and employees may be estimates. Financial information, benefits and other data can change quickly and may vary from those stated here.

Plunkett Research, Ltd.

Symantec Corporation

www.symantec.com

NAIC Code: 0

TYPES OF BUSINESS:
Computer Software: Network Security, Managed Access, Digital ID, Cybersecurity & Anti-Virus
Remote Management Products
Consulting-Cyber Security
Information Protection Products

BRANDS/DIVISIONS/AFFILIATES:
Norton
Javelin Networks
Appthority

CONTACTS:
Note: Officers with more than one job title may be intentionally listed here more than once.

Richard Hill, CEO
Vincent Pilette, CFO
Daniel Schulman, Chairman of the Board
Matthew Brown, Chief Accounting Officer
Samir Kapuria, Executive VP, Divisional
Scott Taylor, Executive VP
Amy Cappellanti-Wolf, Senior VP

GROWTH PLANS/SPECIAL FEATURES:

Symantec Corporation provides a range of software, appliances and services designed to secure and manage information technology (IT) infrastructure. The company provides customers worldwide with software and services that protect, manage and control information risks related to security, data protection, storage, compliance and systems management. The firm has two operating segments: enterprise security and consumer security. The enterprise security segment protects organizations so they can securely conduct business while leveraging new platforms and data. This segment includes Symantec's threat protection products, information protection products, cyber security services, and website security offerings, previously named trust services. These products and services help secure information in transit and wherever it resides in the network path, from the user's device to the data's resting place. In addition, these products help to prevent the loss of confidential data by insiders, and help customers achieve and maintain compliance with laws and regulations. The consumer security focuses on making it simple for customers to be productive and protected at home and at work. The firm's Norton-branded services provide multi-layer security and identity protection on major desktop and mobile operating systems, to defend against increasingly complex online threats to individuals, families, and small businesses. Norton Security products help customers protect against increasingly complex threats and address the need for identity protection, while also managing the rapid increase in mobile and digital data, such as personal financial records, photos, music and videos. Symantec operates in over 40 countries. In November 2018, Symantec acquired Javelin Networks, which offers advanced software technology to defend enterprises against active director-based attacks; and acquired Appthority, which offers mobile application security analysis.

Symantec offers employees a 401(k) with company match, tuition reimbursement and adoption assistance.

FINANCIAL DATA:
Note: Data for latest year may not have been available at press time.

In U.S. $	2018	2017	2016	2015	2014	2013
Revenue	4,834,000,000	4,019,000,000	3,600,000,000	6,508,000,000	6,676,000,000	
R&D Expense	956,000,000	823,000,000	748,000,000	1,144,000,000	1,038,000,000	
Operating Income	459,000,000	173,000,000	593,000,000	1,401,000,000	1,453,000,000	
Operating Margin %		.04%	.16%	.22%	.22%	
SGA Expense	2,167,000,000	2,023,000,000	1,587,000,000	2,702,000,000	2,880,000,000	
Net Income	1,138,000,000	-106,000,000	2,488,000,000	878,000,000	898,000,000	
Operating Cash Flow	950,000,000	-220,000,000	796,000,000	1,312,000,000	1,281,000,000	
Capital Expenditure	142,000,000	70,000,000	272,000,000	381,000,000	260,000,000	
EBITDA	1,333,000,000	476,000,000	766,000,000	1,611,000,000	1,731,000,000	
Return on Assets %		-.01%	.20%	.07%	.06%	
Return on Equity %		-.03%	.52%	.15%	.16%	
Debt to Equity		1.972	0.60	0.294	0.361	

CONTACT INFORMATION:
Phone: 650 527-8000   Fax:
Toll-Free:
Address: 350 Ellis St., Mountain View, CA 94043 United States

SALARIES/BONUSES:
Top Exec. Salary: $1,000,000   Bonus: $
Second Exec. Salary: $865,000   Bonus: $

STOCK TICKER/OTHER:
Stock Ticker: SYMC   Exchange: NAS
Employees: 13,000   Fiscal Year Ends: 03/31
Parent Company:

OTHER THOUGHTS:
Estimated Female Officers or Directors: 3
Hot Spot for Advancement for Women/Minorities: Y

Sales, profits and employees may be estimates. Financial information, benefits and other data can change quickly and may vary from those stated here.

SYNNEX Corporation

NAIC Code: 423430

www.synnex.com

TYPES OF BUSINESS:
IT Supply Chain Services
Distribution Services
Contract Assembly Services
Outsourcing Services

BRANDS/DIVISIONS/AFFILIATES:
SYNNEX Infotec Corporation
SYNNEX Canada Limited
SYNNEX US
Westcon-Comstor Americas
Convergys Corporation

CONTACTS:
Note: Officers with more than one job title may be intentionally listed here more than once.

Dennis Polk, CEO
Marshall Witt, CFO
Matthew Miau, Chairman Emeritus
Kevin Murai, Chairman of the Board
Christopher Caldwell, Executive VP
Simon Leung, General Counsel
Peter Larocque, President, Divisional

GROWTH PLANS/SPECIAL FEATURES:

SYNNEX Corporation is a leading business process services company, serving resellers, retailers and original equipment manufacturers (OEMs) around the world. The firm operates in two segments: technology solutions and Concentrix. The technology solutions segment distributes computer systems and complimentary products to a variety of customers, including value-added resellers, system integrators and retailers. This segment also provides assembly services to OEMs, including integrated supply chain management; build-to-order and configure-to-order system configurations; materials; and management and logistics. Japanese subsidiary SYNNEX Infotec Corporation distributes IT equipment, electronic components and software in Japan. The Concentrix segment offers a range of services under the Concentrix trademark, including customer management, software development, web hosting, hosted software, domain name registration and back office processing. SYNNEX delivers these services through various methods, including voice, chat, web, email and digital print. The company purchases IT systems from OEM suppliers, with its primary OEM suppliers being Asus Tek Computer, Inc.; Dell, Inc.; HP, Inc.; Hewlett Packard Enterprise Company; Intel Corporation; Lenovo Group Ltd.; Microsoft Corporation; Panasonic Corporation; Samsung Semiconductor, Inc.; Seagate Technologies, LLC; and Xerox Corporation. SYNNEX then sells them to its reseller and retail customers. The firm currently distributes over 30,000 technology products from over 300 IT, consumer electronics and OEM suppliers to more than 25,000 resellers, system integrators and retailers. The firm operates approximately 40 distribution and administration facilities in the U.S., Canada, Japan, China and Mexico. Other subsidiaries of the firm include SYNNEX Canada Limited, SYNNEX U.S. and Westcon-Comstor Americas. In October 2018, SYNNEX acquired Convergys Corporation, a provider of customer management and information management products, primarily to large corporations.

SYNNEX employees receive medical, dental, vision, life and AD&D insurance; flexible spending accounts; 401(k); an employee assistance program; tuition reimbursement and more.

FINANCIAL DATA:
Note: Data for latest year may not have been available at press time.

In U.S. $	2018	2017	2016	2015	2014	2013
Revenue	20,053,760,000	17,045,700,000	14,061,840,000	13,338,400,000	13,839,590,000	10,845,160,000
R&D Expense						
Operating Income	551,035,000	508,965,000	379,596,000	354,552,000	308,507,000	240,828,000
Operating Margin %		.03%	.03%	.03%	.02%	.02%
SGA Expense	1,376,664,000	1,041,975,000	903,369,000	837,239,000	790,497,000	414,142,000
Net Income	300,598,000	301,173,000	234,946,000	208,525,000	180,034,000	152,237,000
Operating Cash Flow	100,706,000	176,764,000	326,951,000	643,609,000	-234,772,000	35,707,000
Capital Expenditure	125,305,000	97,546,000	123,233,000	100,106,000	57,377,000	28,965,000
EBITDA	776,322,000	668,851,000	500,889,000	458,062,000	400,206,000	265,290,000
Return on Assets %		.05%	.05%	.05%	.04%	.05%
Return on Equity %		.14%	.12%	.12%	.12%	.11%
Debt to Equity		0.497	0.305	0.355	0.16	0.046

CONTACT INFORMATION:
Phone: 510 656-3333 Fax: 510 668-3777
Toll-Free: 800-756-9888
Address: 44201 Nobel Dr., Fremont, CA 94538 United States

STOCK TICKER/OTHER:
Stock Ticker: SNX
Employees: 231,600
Parent Company:

Exchange: NYS
Fiscal Year Ends: 11/30

SALARIES/BONUSES:
Top Exec. Salary: $642,087 Bonus: $
Second Exec. Salary: $508,385 Bonus: $

OTHER THOUGHTS:
Estimated Female Officers or Directors: 2
Hot Spot for Advancement for Women/Minorities:

Sales, profits and employees may be estimates. Financial information, benefits and other data can change quickly and may vary from those stated here.

Synopsys Inc

NAIC Code: 0

www.synopsys.com

TYPES OF BUSINESS:
Computer Software-Electronic Design Automation
Consulting & Support Services

BRANDS/DIVISIONS/AFFILIATES:
DesignWare IP
Sentaurus
Proteus
CATS
Yield
Phoenix BV
Silicon and Beyond Private Limited

CONTACTS:
Note: Officers with more than one job title may be intentionally listed here more than once.

Trac Pham, CFO
Aart De Geus, Chairman of the Board
Sudhindra Kankanwadi, Chief Accounting Officer
Chi-Foon Chan, Co-CEO
John Runkel, General Counsel
Joseph Logan, Other Corporate Officer

GROWTH PLANS/SPECIAL FEATURES:

Synopsys, Inc. is a supplier of electronic design automation (EDA) software and related services for the design, creation and testing of integrated circuits (ICs). The company's products and services are divided into four groups: core EDA, intellectual property (IP), manufacturing solutions and professional services. Core EDA products and services include the company's digital and custom IC design software, its functional register transfer level verification products, and its field-programmable gate array design software. Designers use these core EDA products to automate the IC design process and to reduce errors. IP products and services include the company's DesignWare IP portfolio, system-level design products, as well as software quality and security testing solutions. Synopsys is a leading provider of high-quality, silicon-proven IP solutions for system-on-chips (SoCs), including wired and wireless interfaces, logic libraries, embedded memories, processor solutions, IP subsystems for audio/sensor/data fusion functionality and analog IP. Manufacturing solutions' software products and technologies enable semiconductor manufacturers to more quickly develop new fabrication processes that produce production-level yields. This group's solutions include Sentaurus technology computer-aided design device and process simulation products; Proteus mask synthesis tools; CATS mask data preparation software; and Yield Explorer Odyssey and Yield Manager management solutions. Last, professional services include consultation and design services that address all phases of the SoC development process. These services assist Synopsys customers with new tool and methodology adoption, chip architecture and specification development, functional and low-power design and verification, and physical implementation and signoff. This division also provides a range of training and workshops on the company's latest tools and methodologies. During 2018, Synopsys acquired PhoeniX BV, as well as Silicon and Beyond Private Limited.

Employee benefits include medical, dental and vision coverage; life, AD&D and disability insurance; an employee assistance program; educational assistance; adoption benefits; and a wellness program.

FINANCIAL DATA:
Note: Data for latest year may not have been available at press time.

In U.S. $	2018	2017	2016	2015	2014	2013
Revenue	3,121,058,000	2,724,880,000	2,422,532,000	2,242,211,000	2,057,472,000	1,962,214,000
R&D Expense	1,084,822,000	908,841,000	856,705,000	776,229,000	718,768,000	669,197,000
Operating Income	373,170,000	384,149,000	327,028,000	281,554,000	248,717,000	246,493,000
Operating Margin %		.14%	.13%	.13%	.12%	.13%
SGA Expense	885,538,000	746,092,000	668,330,000	639,504,000	608,294,000	569,773,000
Net Income	432,518,000	136,563,000	266,826,000	225,934,000	259,124,000	247,800,000
Operating Cash Flow	424,232,000	634,565,000	586,635,000	495,160,000	550,953,000	496,705,000
Capital Expenditure	101,926,000	73,554,000	71,040,000	90,647,000	106,913,000	69,068,000
EBITDA	588,357,000	579,843,000	540,351,000	496,245,000	466,863,000	464,766,000
Return on Assets %		.03%	.05%	.05%	.06%	.06%
Return on Equity %		.04%	.08%	.07%	.09%	.09%
Debt to Equity		0.041			0.015	0.027

CONTACT INFORMATION:
Phone: 650 584-5000   Fax: 650 965-8637
Toll-Free: 800-541-7737
Address: 690 E. Middlefield Rd., Mountain View, CA 94043 United States

STOCK TICKER/OTHER:
Stock Ticker: SNPS
Employees: 10,669
Parent Company:

Exchange: NAS
Fiscal Year Ends: 10/31

SALARIES/BONUSES:
Top Exec. Salary: $535,100   Bonus: $
Second Exec. Salary: $535,100   Bonus: $

OTHER THOUGHTS:
Estimated Female Officers or Directors: 3
Hot Spot for Advancement for Women/Minorities: Y

Sales, profits and employees may be estimates. Financial information, benefits and other data can change quickly and may vary from those stated here.

SYSCO Corporation

NAIC Code: 424410

www.sysco.com

TYPES OF BUSINESS:
Food-Wholesale Distribution
Restaurant Supplies Distribution
Medical & Surgical Supplies Distribution
Cleaning Supplies Distribution

BRANDS/DIVISIONS/AFFILIATES:
SYGMA Network Inc
Kent Frozen Foods

CONTACTS: Note: Officers with more than one job title may be intentionally listed here more than once.
Thomas Bene, CEO
Joel Grade, CFO
Anita Zielinski, Chief Accounting Officer
Wayne Shurts, Chief Technology Officer
Paul Moskowitz, Executive VP, Divisional
R. Charlton, Executive VP, Divisional
Greg Bertrand, Executive VP, Divisional
Russell Libby, Executive VP, Divisional
William Goetz, Senior VP, Divisional
Brian Todd, Senior VP, Divisional

GROWTH PLANS/SPECIAL FEATURES:

SYSCO Corporation, through its subsidiaries, is one of the largest distributors of food and food-related products to the foodservice industry in North America. The firm provides products and services to more than 600,000 customers, including restaurants, healthcare companies, educational facilities and lodging establishments. Restaurants account for approximately 62% of the company's sales; healthcare, 9%; education and government, 8%; travel, leisure and retail, 8%; and other sources, 13%. SYSCO distributes a wide variety of frozen and imported foods; fresh meats and seafood; dairy items; fresh produce; and nonfood items, including tableware, restaurant/kitchen equipment, medical/surgical supplies and cleaning supplies. Subsidiary SYGMA Network, Inc. distributes a full line of food products, non-food products and customer-specific proprietary products to certain chain restaurant customer locations. The company operates approximately 330 distribution facilities primarily located in the U.S., the U.K., France and Canada, with a fleet of approximately 14,000 delivery vehicles (consisting of tractor and trailer combinations, vans and panel trucks). More than 85% of these vehicles are owned by the firm, and the remainder are leased. During 2018, the firm acquired Kent Frozen Foods, a U.K.-based foodservice distributor. In January 2019, SYSCO agreed to acquire Waugh Foods, Inc., an Illinois-based broadline distributor.

The firm offers employees life, disability, medical, dental and vision insurance; annual performance incentives; an assistance program; tuition assistance; a stock purchase plan; matching charity gifts; a 401(k); direct deposit; and product discounts.

FINANCIAL DATA: Note: Data for latest year may not have been available at press time.

In U.S. $	2018	2017	2016	2015	2014	2013
Revenue	58,727,330,000	55,371,140,000	50,366,920,000	48,680,750,000	46,516,710,000	44,411,230,000
R&D Expense						
Operating Income	2,328,974,000	2,053,171,000	1,850,500,000	1,229,362,000	1,587,122,000	1,658,478,000
Operating Margin %		.04%	.04%	.03%	.03%	.04%
SGA Expense						
Net Income	1,430,766,000	1,142,503,000	949,622,000	686,773,000	931,533,000	992,427,000
Operating Cash Flow	2,158,632,000	2,176,425,000	1,933,142,000	1,555,484,000	1,492,815,000	1,511,594,000
Capital Expenditure	687,815,000	686,378,000	527,346,000	542,830,000	523,206,000	511,862,000
EBITDA	3,117,205,000	2,971,100,000	2,401,863,000	1,815,975,000	2,155,427,000	2,188,498,000
Return on Assets %		.07%	.05%	.04%	.07%	.08%
Return on Equity %		.39%	.22%	.13%	.18%	.20%
Debt to Equity		3.217	2.109	0.432	0.453	0.508

CONTACT INFORMATION:
Phone: 281 584-1390   Fax: 281 584-2880
Toll-Free:
Address: 1390 Enclave Pkwy., Houston, TX 77077 United States

SALARIES/BONUSES:
Top Exec. Salary: $1,250,000   Bonus: $
Second Exec. Salary: $1,000,000   Bonus: $

STOCK TICKER/OTHER:
Stock Ticker: SYY
Employees: 66,500
Parent Company:

Exchange: NYS
Fiscal Year Ends: 06/30

OTHER THOUGHTS:
Estimated Female Officers or Directors: 8
Hot Spot for Advancement for Women/Minorities: Y

T Rowe Price Group Inc

NAIC Code: 523920

www.troweprice.com

TYPES OF BUSINESS:
Investment Management & Mutual Funds
Retirement Accounts
Advisory Services

BRANDS/DIVISIONS/AFFILIATES:
T Rowe Price Associates Inc
T Rowe Price International Ltd
T Rowe Price Hong Kong Limited
T Rowe Price Singapore Private Ltd

CONTACTS:
Note: Officers with more than one job title may be intentionally listed here more than once.

Celine Dufetel, CFO
Jessica Hiebler, Chief Accounting Officer
Robert Sharps, Chief Investment Officer
William Stromberg, Director
Christopher Alderson, Other Corporate Officer
Andrew McCormick, Other Corporate Officer
Eric Veiel, Other Corporate Officer
Robert Higginbotham, Other Corporate Officer
Sebastien Page, Other Corporate Officer
Scott David, Other Corporate Officer
David Oestreicher, Other Executive Officer

GROWTH PLANS/SPECIAL FEATURES:

T. Rowe Price Group, Inc. is a financial services holding company. The firm derives revenue primarily from investment advisory services that it provides to individual and institutional investors. The firm manages approximately $1.02 trillion in assets (as of April 2018). T. Rowe Price operates its investment advisory business through subsidiaries T. Rowe Price Associates, Inc. and T. Rowe Price International, Ltd. In Hong Kong and Singapore, T. Rowe Price operates through T. Rowe Price Hong Kong Limited and T. Rowe Price Singapore Private Ltd., respectively. Products and services for the individual investor include mutual funds, retirement accounts, rollover individual retirement accounts (IRAs), college savings plans, private asset management, high-net-worth services, banking services and advisory services. In addition to investment services, T. Rowe Price offers institutional clients retirement plan services, including small business and corporate retirement plans as well as public sector plans for religious institutions, schools and hospitals. The company introduces new mutual funds and other investment portfolios in an attempt to complement and expand its investment offerings and respond to competitive developments in the marketplace. The firm manages a broad range of domestic and international stock, bonds and mutual funds and other investment portfolios. T. Rowe Price also offers administrative services to its clients, including mutual fund transferring, accounting and shareholder services, record keeping and transfer agent services for defined contribution retirement plans, discount brokerages and trust services. During 2018, T. Rowe Price announced plans to close its operations center in Tampa in mid-2019, consolidating it into other Florida sites.

The firm offers its employees medical, dental, prescription, vision, retiree, travel, life, AD&D, short- and long-term disability insurance; a nurse hotline; Lasik vision discount; fitness club reimbursement; a 401(k); flexible spending accounts; adoption assistance; tuition reimbursement; and community support programs.

FINANCIAL DATA:
Note: Data for latest year may not have been available at press time.

In U.S. $	2018	2017	2016	2015	2014	2013
Revenue	5,372,600,000	4,793,000,000	4,222,900,000	4,200,600,000	3,982,100,000	3,484,200,000
R&D Expense						
Operating Income	2,346,200,000	2,058,800,000	1,799,600,000	1,898,900,000	1,890,900,000	1,637,400,000
Operating Margin %		.44%	.41%	.45%	.47%	.47%
SGA Expense	779,500,000	286,900,000	252,700,000	238,900,000	219,900,000	224,500,000
Net Income	1,837,500,000	1,497,800,000	1,215,000,000	1,223,000,000	1,229,600,000	1,047,700,000
Operating Cash Flow	1,619,900,000	229,500,000	170,500,000	1,506,400,000	1,291,300,000	1,233,200,000
Capital Expenditure	168,500,000	186,100,000	148,300,000	151,300,000	126,200,000	105,800,000
EBITDA	2,505,700,000	2,202,400,000	1,933,600,000	2,025,200,000	2,002,600,000	1,728,400,000
Return on Assets %		.22%	.21%	.23%	.23%	.23%
Return on Equity %		.28%	.25%	.24%	.24%	.24%
Debt to Equity						

CONTACT INFORMATION:
Phone: 410 345-2000   Fax: 410 345-2394
Toll-Free: 800-638-7890
Address: 100 E. Pratt St., Baltimore, MD 21202 United States

SALARIES/BONUSES:
Top Exec. Salary: $350,000   Bonus: $
Second Exec. Salary: $350,000   Bonus: $

STOCK TICKER/OTHER:
Stock Ticker: TROW
Employees: 6,329
Parent Company:

Exchange: NAS
Fiscal Year Ends: 12/31

OTHER THOUGHTS:
Estimated Female Officers or Directors:
Hot Spot for Advancement for Women/Minorities:

TD Ameritrade Holding Corporation

www.amtd.com

NAIC Code: 523120

TYPES OF BUSINESS:
Discount Stock Brokerage
Online Brokerage
Financial Planning
Clearing Services

BRANDS/DIVISIONS/AFFILIATES:

CONTACTS: Note: Officers with more than one job title may be intentionally listed here more than once.
Bharat Masrani, CEO, Subsidiary
Stephen Boyle, CFO
Joseph Moglia, Chairman of the Board
Timothy Hockey, Director
Thomas Nally, Executive VP, Divisional
Steven Quirk, Executive VP, Divisional
Peter deSilva, Executive VP, Divisional
Ellen Koplow, Executive VP

GROWTH PLANS/SPECIAL FEATURES:

TD Ameritrade Holding Corporation and its subsidiaries provide securities brokerage services and technology-based financial services to retail investors and business partners. With $1.2 trillion in total client assets (as of October 2018), the company provides its services through online, telephone, branch and mobile channels. Products and services include: support, with licensed representatives available by phone and email 24/7, as well as online and in-person for one-on-one support; trading tools and platforms, designed for active traders and long-term investors, offering tools to research stocks, place trades, identify potential market opportunities and manage portfolios; investment products, with access to equities, exchange-traded funds (ETFs), bonds, CDs, options, non-proprietary mutual funds, futures and foreign exchange trading; research, offering independent investment research access from third parties such as Morningstar, S&P Capital IQ, Jaywalk and TheStreet; clear pricing, which includes flat-rate commission on all online equity trades, a variety of commission-free investments, no platform fees, no share limits, no trade requirements to access advanced features and no opening deposit minimums; and free investor education resources. In October 2018, TD Ameritrade announced that it had made a strategic investment in ErisX, a regulated derivatives exchange and clearing organization that will include digital asset futures and spot contracts on a single platform. Earlier that year, TD Ameritrade completed the conversion of Scottrade brokerage accounts to TD Ameritrade, just a few months after closing the acquisition of Scottrade's brokerage business.

The firm offers its employees a 401(k) and profit-sharing plan.

FINANCIAL DATA: Note: Data for latest year may not have been available at press time.

In U.S. $	2018	2017	2016	2015	2014	2013
Revenue	5,342,000,000	3,605,000,000	3,274,000,000	3,211,000,000	3,108,000,000	2,796,000,000
R&D Expense						
Operating Income						
Operating Margin %						
SGA Expense	2,216,000,000	1,496,000,000	1,372,000,000	1,328,000,000	1,260,000,000	1,153,000,000
Net Income	1,473,000,000	872,000,000	842,000,000	813,000,000	787,000,000	675,000,000
Operating Cash Flow	1,908,000,000	687,000,000	1,468,000,000	746,000,000	1,025,000,000	739,000,000
Capital Expenditure	229,000,000	197,000,000	105,000,000	71,000,000	144,000,000	144,000,000
EBITDA						
Return on Assets %		.03%	.03%	.03%	.03%	.03%
Return on Equity %		.14%	.17%	.17%	.17%	.15%
Debt to Equity		0.353	0.36	0.367	0.263	0.225

CONTACT INFORMATION:
Phone: 402 331-7856　　Fax:
Toll-Free: 800-237-8692
Address: 200 S. 108th Ave., Omaha, NE 68154 United States

STOCK TICKER/OTHER:
Stock Ticker: AMTD
Employees: 8,200
Parent Company:

Exchange: NAS
Fiscal Year Ends: 09/30

SALARIES/BONUSES:
Top Exec. Salary: $995,192　　Bonus: $
Second Exec. Salary: $650,000　　Bonus: $

OTHER THOUGHTS:
Estimated Female Officers or Directors: 4
Hot Spot for Advancement for Women/Minorities: Y

Team Health Holdings Inc

www.teamhealth.com

NAIC Code: 621111

TYPES OF BUSINESS:
Physicians and Hospital Staff Services
Hospital Administrative Services
Pediatrics
Radiology & Teleradiology Services
Urgent Care

BRANDS/DIVISIONS/AFFILIATES:
Blackstone Group LP (The)

GROWTH PLANS/SPECIAL FEATURES:
Team Health Holdings, Inc. is a physician-led company offering outsourced integrated care services. This 20,000-clinician-strong healthcare provider offers outsources staffing, with practice areas including emergency medicine, anesthesiology, hospital medicine, hospital medicine subspecialties, ambulatory care, post-acute care and behavioral health. Care is provided to ambulatory facilities, hospitals, post-acute care centers and in-home. Team Health's staff include residents, physicians, medical directors and advanced practice clinicians. Team Health is privately-held private The Blackstone Group LP.

CONTACTS:
Note: Officers with more than one job title may be intentionally listed here more than once.

Leif M. Murphy, CEO
Michael Wiechart, COO
H. Massingale, Chairman of the Board
David Jones, CFO
Oliver Rogers, Executive VP
Steven Clifton, Executive VP
Leif Murphy, President
Lynn Massingale, Chmn.

FINANCIAL DATA:
Note: Data for latest year may not have been available at press time.

In U.S. $	2018	2017	2016	2015	2014	2013
Revenue	4,500,000,000	4,200,000,000	3,900,000,000	3,597,246,976	2,819,642,880	2,383,595,008
R&D Expense						
Operating Income						
Operating Margin %						
SGA Expense						
Net Income				82,711,000	97,738,000	87,409,000
Operating Cash Flow						
Capital Expenditure						
EBITDA						
Return on Assets %						
Return on Equity %						
Debt to Equity						

CONTACT INFORMATION:
Phone: 865 693-1000   Fax:
Toll-Free: 800-818-1498
Address: 265 Brookview Ctr. Way, Ste. 400, Knoxville, TN 37919 United States

STOCK TICKER/OTHER:
Stock Ticker: Private   Exchange:
Employees: 20,000   Fiscal Year Ends: 12/31
Parent Company: Blackstone Group LP (The)

SALARIES/BONUSES:
Top Exec. Salary: $ Bonus: $
Second Exec. Salary: $ Bonus: $

OTHER THOUGHTS:
Estimated Female Officers or Directors: 3
Hot Spot for Advancement for Women/Minorities: Y

Sales, profits and employees may be estimates. Financial information, benefits and other data can change quickly and may vary from those stated here.

Tech Data Corporation

www.techdata.com

NAIC Code: 423430

TYPES OF BUSINESS:
Computer & Software Products, Distribution
Training
Assembly Services

BRANDS/DIVISIONS/AFFILIATES:

CONTACTS:
Note: Officers with more than one job title may be intentionally listed here more than once.

Richard Hume, CEO
Charles Dannewitz, CFO
Robert Dutkowsky, Chairman of the Board
Michael Rabinovitch, Chief Accounting Officer
John Tonnison, Chief Information Officer
David Vetter, Chief Legal Officer
Beth Simonetti, Executive VP
Joseph Quaglia, President, Geographical
Patrick Zammit, President, Geographical

GROWTH PLANS/SPECIAL FEATURES:

Tech Data Corporation is a worldwide distributor of information technology (IT) products, logistics management and other value-added services. The company serves more than 125,000 value-added resellers (VARs), direct marketers, retailers and corporate resellers in over 100 countries throughout North America, South America, Europe, the Middle East and Africa. Products are typically purchased directly from manufacturers or software publishers on a non-exclusive basis and then shipped to customers from one of Tech Data's 27 strategically-located logistics centers. The company's vendor agreements do not restrict it from selling similar products manufactured by competitors. The firm also provides resellers with extensive pre- and post-sale training, service and support as well as configuration and assembly services and e-commerce tools. Tech Data provides products and services to the online reseller channel and does business with thousands of resellers through its website. The firm's entire electronic catalog is available online, and its electronic software distribution initiative allows resellers and vendors to easily access software titles directly from a secure location on the website.

FINANCIAL DATA:
Note: Data for latest year may not have been available at press time.

In U.S. $	2018	2017	2016	2015	2014	2013
Revenue	36,775,010,000	26,234,880,000	26,379,780,000	27,670,630,000	26,821,900,000	
R&D Expense						
Operating Income	505,008,000	316,726,000	303,694,000	263,906,000	245,793,000	
Operating Margin %	.01%	.01%	.01%	.01%	.01%	
SGA Expense	1,608,961,000	984,152,000	991,763,000	1,136,277,000	1,116,553,000	
Net Income	116,641,000	195,095,000	265,736,000	175,172,000	179,932,000	
Operating Cash Flow	1,097,069,000	656,843,000	188,993,000	119,381,000	379,148,000	
Capital Expenditure	231,937,000	39,335,000	33,972,000	28,175,000	30,388,000	
EBITDA	561,337,000	348,008,000	454,159,000	334,478,000	303,894,000	
Return on Assets %	.01%	.03%	.04%	.03%	.03%	
Return on Equity %	.05%	.09%	.13%	.09%	.09%	
Debt to Equity	0.515	0.456	0.174	0.18	0.169	

CONTACT INFORMATION:
Phone: 727 539-7429 Fax: 727 538-7808
Toll-Free: 800-237-8931
Address: 5350 Tech Data Dr., Clearwater, FL 33760 United States

SALARIES/BONUSES:
Top Exec. Salary: $818,855 Bonus: $
Second Exec. Salary: $618,078 Bonus: $

STOCK TICKER/OTHER:
Stock Ticker: TECD
Employees: 9,500
Parent Company:

Exchange: NAS
Fiscal Year Ends: 01/31

OTHER THOUGHTS:
Estimated Female Officers or Directors: 1
Hot Spot for Advancement for Women/Minorities:

Plunkett Research, Ltd.

Tenneco Inc

www.tenneco.com

NAIC Code: 336300

TYPES OF BUSINESS:
Automotive Parts Manufacturer
Advanced Suspension Technologies
Ride Control Products
Emissions Systems
Performance Mufflers
Noise Control Systems

BRANDS/DIVISIONS/AFFILIATES:
Federal-Mogul LLC
Ohlinus Racing AB

CONTACTS: Note: Officers with more than one job title may be intentionally listed here more than once.
Jason Hollar, CFO
John Patouhas, Chief Accounting Officer
Benny Patel, Chief Technology Officer
Brian Kesseler, Co-CEO
Roger Wood, Co-CEO
Gregg Sherrill, Director
Rainer Jueckstock, Executive VP
Peng Guo, Executive VP
Bradley Norton, Executive VP
Brandon Smith, General Counsel
Kaled Awada, Other Executive Officer
Gregg Bolt, Senior VP, Divisional

GROWTH PLANS/SPECIAL FEATURES:
Tenneco, Inc. designs, manufactures and sells innovative products and services for light vehicle, commercial truck, off-highway, industrial and aftermarket customers. The firm serves both original equipment manufacturers (OEMs) and replacement markets worldwide. Tenneco is among the world's leading manufacturers of clean air, powertrain and ride performance systems and products. The clean air division invests in core sciences, including combustion and thermal management, materials science and thermoelectrical energy, all of which enables the development of creative solutions that help Tenneco better meet its customer's current and future emissions control needs. The powertrain division utilizes technology and expertise to help customers adopt hybrid and fully-electric powertrains, which offer enhanced vehicle ride performance via noise, vibration and harshness reduction capabilities for smoother rides. The ride performance division offers advanced suspension technologies that deliver performance, comfort and power to differentiate vehicles. Tenneco's 64 manufacturing plants are located throughout Asia Pacific (27), Europe (20) and North America (15), as well as in South America (2). In October 2018, Tenneco acquired Federal-Mogul LLC, a global supplier of technology and innovation in vehicle and industrial products for fuel economy, emissions reduction and safety systems. Subsequently, in mid-2019, Tenneco expects to separate its businesses to form two new independent, publicly-traded companies: an aftermarket and ride performance company and a powertrain technology company. In January 2019, Tenneco acquired Ohlinus Racing AB, which offers suspension systems and components to automotive and motorsport industries.

FINANCIAL DATA: Note: Data for latest year may not have been available at press time.

In U.S. $	2018	2017	2016	2015	2014	2013
Revenue	11,763,000,000	9,274,000,000	8,599,000,000	8,209,000,000	8,420,000,000	7,964,000,000
R&D Expense	204,000,000	158,000,000	154,000,000	146,000,000	169,000,000	144,000,000
Operating Income	349,000,000	432,000,000	533,000,000	524,000,000	499,000,000	428,000,000
Operating Margin %		.05%	.06%	.06%	.06%	.05%
SGA Expense	794,000,000	648,000,000	589,000,000	491,000,000	519,000,000	453,000,000
Net Income	55,000,000	207,000,000	363,000,000	247,000,000	226,000,000	183,000,000
Operating Cash Flow	439,000,000	629,000,000	489,000,000	517,000,000	341,000,000	503,000,000
Capital Expenditure	507,000,000	419,000,000	345,000,000	309,000,000	344,000,000	269,000,000
EBITDA	651,000,000	641,000,000	740,000,000	722,000,000	700,000,000	629,000,000
Return on Assets %		.05%	.09%	.06%	.06%	.05%
Return on Equity %		.32%	.71%	.53%	.49%	.54%
Debt to Equity		1.951	2.201	2.596	2.151	2.353

CONTACT INFORMATION:
Phone: 847 482-5000 Fax: 847 482-5940
Toll-Free:
Address: 500 N. Field Dr., Lake Forest, IL 60045 United States

STOCK TICKER/OTHER:
Stock Ticker: TEN
Employees: 31,000
Parent Company:

Exchange: NYS
Fiscal Year Ends: 12/31

SALARIES/BONUSES:
Top Exec. Salary: $1,050,000 Bonus: $
Second Exec. Salary: $670,000 Bonus: $

OTHER THOUGHTS:
Estimated Female Officers or Directors: 4
Hot Spot for Advancement for Women/Minorities: Y

Sales, profits and employees may be estimates. Financial information, benefits and other data can change quickly and may vary from those stated here.

Terex Corporation

NAIC Code: 333120

www.terex.com

TYPES OF BUSINESS:
Heavy Equipment
Cranes
Mining Equipment
Aerial Work Platforms
Road Building Equipment
Utility Products
Construction Equipment
Materials Handling Equipment

BRANDS/DIVISIONS/AFFILIATES:
Terex Financial Services

CONTACTS:
Note: Officers with more than one job title may be intentionally listed here more than once.

John Garrison, CEO
John Sheehan, CFO
Mark Clair, Chief Accounting Officer
Eric Cohen, General Counsel
Kieran Hegarty, President, Divisional
Matthew Fearon, President, Divisional
Stoyan Filipov, President, Divisional
Kevin Barr, Senior VP, Divisional
Brian Henry, Senior VP, Divisional

GROWTH PLANS/SPECIAL FEATURES:

Terex Corporation is a global manufacturer of lifting and materials processing products. The company operates through two business segments: aerial work platforms and materials processing. The aerial work platforms segment designs, manufactures, services and markets aerial work platform equipment, telehandlers, light towers and utility equipment, as well as their related components and replacement parts. Customers use these to: construct and maintain industrial, commercial and residential buildings and facilities; maintain utility and telecommunication lines, tree trimming, and certain construction and foundation drilling applications; and for other commercial and infrastructure projects. The materials processing segment designs, manufactures and markets materials processing and specialty equipment, including crushers, washing systems, screens, apron feeders, material handlers, pick and carry cranes, wood processing, biomass and recycling equipment, concrete mixer trucks, concrete pavers, conveyors, and their related components and replacement parts. Customers use these products in: construction, infrastructure and recycling projects; various quarrying and mining applications; landscaping and biomass production; material handling applications; maintenance applications to lift equipment and material; and building roads and bridges. In addition, subsidiary Terex Financial Services offers financial products and services to assist in the acquisition of Terex equipment. During 2019, Terex sold its Demag mobile cranes business to Tadano Ltd. for $215 million; and sold its boom truck, truck crane and crossover product lines to Custom Truck One Source LP.

FINANCIAL DATA:
Note: Data for latest year may not have been available at press time.

In U.S. $	2018	2017	2016	2015	2014	2013
Revenue	5,125,000,000	4,363,400,000	4,443,100,000	6,543,100,000	7,308,900,000	7,084,000,000
R&D Expense						
Operating Income	293,300,000	173,600,000	28,200,000	389,900,000	423,100,000	419,100,000
Operating Margin %		.04%	.01%	.06%	.06%	.06%
SGA Expense	673,500,000	642,400,000	684,200,000	918,600,000	1,030,400,000	1,020,400,000
Net Income	113,700,000	128,700,000	-176,100,000	145,900,000	319,000,000	226,000,000
Operating Cash Flow	94,200,000	153,000,000	367,000,000	212,900,000	410,700,000	188,500,000
Capital Expenditure	103,800,000	43,500,000	73,000,000	103,800,000	81,500,000	82,800,000
EBITDA	281,500,000	246,000,000	-72,000,000	459,400,000	572,000,000	569,700,000
Return on Assets %		.03%	-.03%	.03%	.05%	.03%
Return on Equity %		.10%	-.10%	.08%	.15%	.11%
Debt to Equity		0.802	1.052	0.933	0.816	0.863

CONTACT INFORMATION:
Phone: 203 222-7170   Fax: 203 222-7976
Toll-Free:
Address: 200 Nyala Farm Rd., Westport, CT 06880 United States

STOCK TICKER/OTHER:
Stock Ticker: TEX
Employees: 11,300
Parent Company:

Exchange: NYS
Fiscal Year Ends: 12/31

SALARIES/BONUSES:
Top Exec. Salary: $935,577   Bonus: $
Second Exec. Salary: $659,250   Bonus: $

OTHER THOUGHTS:
Estimated Female Officers or Directors: 1
Hot Spot for Advancement for Women/Minorities:

Texas Instruments Inc (TI)

NAIC Code: 334413

www.ti.com

TYPES OF BUSINESS:
Chips-Digital Signal Processors
Semiconductors
Calculators
Educational Software
Power Management Products
Broadband RF/IF & Digital Radio
MEMS
Microcontrollers (MCU)

BRANDS/DIVISIONS/AFFILIATES:

CONTACTS:
Note: Officers with more than one job title may be intentionally listed here more than once.

Richard Templeton, CEO
Rafael Lizardi, CFO
Ahmad Bahai, Senior VP
Hagop Kozanian, Senior VP
Kyle Flessner, Senior VP
Niels Anderskouv, Senior VP
Bing Xie, Senior VP
R. Delagi, Senior VP
Darla Whitaker, Senior VP
Julie Van Haren, Senior VP
Haviv Ilan, Senior VP
Ellen Barker, Senior VP
Cynthia Trochu, Senior VP

GROWTH PLANS/SPECIAL FEATURES:

Texas Instruments, Inc. (TI), founded in 1930, is a global designer and manufacturer of semiconductors with operations located in more than 30 countries, serving 90,000 customers worldwide. The firm operates in three segments: analog, embedded processing and other. Analog semiconductors change real-world signals, such as sound, temperature, pressure or images, by conditioning them, amplifying them and often converting them to a stream of digital data that can be processed by other semiconductors, such as embedded processors. Analog semiconductors are also used to manage power in every electronic device, whether plugged into a wall or running off a battery. Product lines include power supply controls, switches, interfaces, protection devices, high-voltage products, mobile lighting, display products, signal chain products, and high volume integrated analog and standard products. This segment comprises 66% of the firm's annual revenue. Embedded processors are designed to handle specific tasks and can be optimized for various combinations of performance, power and cost, depending on the application. The devices vary from simple, low-cost products used in electric toothbrushes to highly specialized, complex devices used in wireless base station communications infrastructure equipment. Products include processors, microcontrollers and connectivity. This segment comprises 23% of the firm's annual revenue. Last, the other division includes semiconductors such as the firm's proprietary DLP optical semiconductor products, which enable clear video and microprocessors that serve as the brains of everything from high-end computer servers to high definition televisions (HDTVs). This segment also includes educational products, such as handheld graphing calculators, business calculators and scientific calculators as well as a wide range of advanced classroom tools and professional development resources, including educational software.

TI offers its employees medical, dental, vision and life insurance; an employee assistance program; professional financial services; and product discounts on cars, appliances and software.

FINANCIAL DATA:
Note: Data for latest year may not have been available at press time.

In U.S. $	2018	2017	2016	2015	2014	2013
Revenue	15,784,000,000	14,961,000,000	13,370,000,000	13,000,000,000	13,045,000,000	12,205,000,000
R&D Expense	1,559,000,000	1,508,000,000	1,370,000,000	1,280,000,000	1,358,000,000	1,522,000,000
Operating Income	7,034,000,000	6,531,000,000	5,103,000,000	4,532,000,000	4,226,000,000	2,984,000,000
Operating Margin %		.43%	.38%	.35%	.32%	.24%
SGA Expense	1,684,000,000	1,694,000,000	1,767,000,000	1,748,000,000	1,843,000,000	1,858,000,000
Net Income	5,580,000,000	3,682,000,000	3,595,000,000	2,986,000,000	2,821,000,000	2,162,000,000
Operating Cash Flow	7,189,000,000	5,363,000,000	4,614,000,000	4,268,000,000	3,892,000,000	3,384,000,000
Capital Expenditure	1,131,000,000	695,000,000	531,000,000	551,000,000	385,000,000	412,000,000
EBITDA	7,765,000,000	7,062,000,000	5,965,000,000	5,439,000,000	5,198,000,000	4,146,000,000
Return on Assets %		.21%	.22%	.17%	.15%	.11%
Return on Equity %		.35%	.35%	.29%	.26%	.20%
Debt to Equity		0.346	0.284	0.314	0.35	0.385

CONTACT INFORMATION:
Phone: 972 995-3773   Fax: 972 995-4360
Toll-Free: 800-336-5236
Address: 12500 TI Blvd., Dallas, TX 75266-0199 United States

STOCK TICKER/OTHER:
Stock Ticker: TXN
Employees: 29,865
Parent Company:

Exchange: NAS
Fiscal Year Ends: 12/31

SALARIES/BONUSES:
Top Exec. Salary: $1,131,252   Bonus: $
Second Exec. Salary: $713,750   Bonus: $

OTHER THOUGHTS:
Estimated Female Officers or Directors: 3
Hot Spot for Advancement for Women/Minorities: Y

Sales, profits and employees may be estimates. Financial information, benefits and other data can change quickly and may vary from those stated here.

Textron Inc

www.textron.com

NAIC Code: 336411

TYPES OF BUSINESS:
Helicopters & General Aviation Aircraft Manufacturing
Aerospace
Electrical Test & Measurement Equipment
Fiber Optic Equipment
Off-Road Vehicles
Financing

BRANDS/DIVISIONS/AFFILIATES:
Bell Helicopter
Textron Systems
Textron Aviation
Textron Financial Corporation
E-Z-GO
Jacobsen
Kautex
Cushman

CONTACTS: Note: Officers with more than one job title may be intentionally listed here more than once.
Scott Donnelly, CEO
Frank Connor, CFO
Mark Bamford, Chief Accounting Officer
Julie Duffy, Executive VP, Divisional
Robert Lupone, Executive VP

GROWTH PLANS/SPECIAL FEATURES:

Textron, Inc. is a global multi-industry company active in the aircraft, defense, industrial and finance industries. The company divides its operations into five segments: Bell Helicopter, Textron Systems, Textron Aviation, industrial and finance. Bell Helicopter supplies helicopters, tilt rotor aircraft and helicopter-related spare parts and services for military and commercial applications. It also offers commercially-certified helicopters to corporate; offshore petroleum exploration; utility; charter; and police, fire, rescue and emergency medical helicopter operators. This segment also offers support and services for their vehicles. Textron Systems manufactures weapons systems and surveillance and intelligence products for the defense, aerospace, homeland security and general aviation markets. It sells most of its products to U.S. government customers, but also to customers outside the U.S. through foreign military sales sponsored by the U.S. government and directly through commercial sales channels. Textron Aviation is home to the Beechcraft and Cessna brands, which account for more than half of all general aviation aircraft flying. Its product portfolio includes five business lines: business jets, general aviation and special mission turboprop aircraft, high performance piston aircraft, military trainer and defense aircraft and a customer service organization. The industrial segment includes the business of E-Z-GO, Jacobsen, Kautex, Cushman, Textron Off Road, Douglas Equipment and TUG Technologies. These companies design, manufacture and sell diverse products such as golf carts, off-road utility vehicles, turf maintenance equipment, blow-molded fuel systems, electrical test and measurement instruments and fiber optic connectors. The finance segment consists of Textron Financial Corporation and its subsidiaries, which primarily support the company's other segments and has services in 80 countries. In July 2018, the firm sold its Tools and Test businesses to Emerson for $810 million.

Textron offers its employees medical, prescription, dental and vision coverage; flexible spending accounts; life, AD&D insurance; discounts on auto and home insurance; and educational assistance.

FINANCIAL DATA: Note: Data for latest year may not have been available at press time.

In U.S. $	2018	2017	2016	2015	2014	2013
Revenue	13,972,000,000	14,198,000,000	13,788,000,000	13,423,000,000	13,878,000,000	12,104,000,000
R&D Expense						
Operating Income	1,103,000,000	1,066,000,000	1,173,000,000	1,140,000,000	1,096,000,000	847,000,000
Operating Margin %		.08%	.08%	.08%	.07%	.07%
SGA Expense	1,275,000,000	1,337,000,000	1,304,000,000	1,304,000,000	1,361,000,000	1,126,000,000
Net Income	1,222,000,000	307,000,000	962,000,000	697,000,000	600,000,000	498,000,000
Operating Cash Flow	1,107,000,000	953,000,000	1,012,000,000	1,090,000,000	1,208,000,000	810,000,000
Capital Expenditure	369,000,000	423,000,000	446,000,000	420,000,000	429,000,000	444,000,000
EBITDA	1,987,000,000	1,383,000,000	1,499,000,000	1,601,000,000	1,503,000,000	1,236,000,000
Return on Assets %		.02%	.06%	.05%	.04%	.04%
Return on Equity %		.05%	.18%	.15%	.14%	.14%
Debt to Equity		0.69	0.595	0.674	0.905	0.725

CONTACT INFORMATION:
Phone: 401 421-2800 Fax: 401 421-2878
Toll-Free:
Address: 40 Westminster St., Providence, RI 02903 United States

SALARIES/BONUSES:
Top Exec. Salary: $1,229,077 Bonus: $
Second Exec. Salary: $1,000,000 Bonus: $

STOCK TICKER/OTHER:
Stock Ticker: TXT Exchange: NYS
Employees: 36,000 Fiscal Year Ends: 12/31
Parent Company:

OTHER THOUGHTS:
Estimated Female Officers or Directors: 10
Hot Spot for Advancement for Women/Minorities: Y

Sales, profits and employees may be estimates. Financial information, benefits and other data can change quickly and may vary from those stated here.

Thermo Fisher Scientific Inc

www.thermofisher.com

NAIC Code: 423450

TYPES OF BUSINESS:
Laboratory Equipment & Supplies Distribution
Contract Manufacturing
Equipment Calibration & Repair
Clinical Trial Services
Laboratory Workstations
Clinical Consumables
Diagnostic Reagents
Custom Chemical Synthesis

BRANDS/DIVISIONS/AFFILIATES:
Thermo Scientific
Applied Biosystems
Invitrogen
Fisher Scientific
Unity Lab Services
Brammer Bio

CONTACTS:
Note: Officers with more than one job title may be intentionally listed here more than once.

Marc Casper, CEO
Jim Manzi, Chairman of the Board
Mark Stevenson, COO
Michael Boxer, General Counsel
Gregory Herrema, President, Divisional
Patrick Durbin, President, Divisional
Michel Lagarde, President, Divisional
Stephen Williamson, Senior VP
Peter Hornstra, Vice President

GROWTH PLANS/SPECIAL FEATURES:
Thermo Fisher Scientific, Inc. is a distributor of products and services principally to the scientific-research and clinical laboratory markets. The firm serves over 400,000 customers including biotechnology and pharmaceutical companies; colleges and universities; medical-research institutions; hospitals; reference, quality control, process-control and research and development labs in various industries; and government agencies. It operates in four segments: life sciences solutions, analytical instruments, specialty diagnostics and laboratory products and services. Life sciences solutions provides a portfolio of reagents, instruments and consumables used in biological and medical research, discover and production of new drugs and vaccines. This division also provides diagnosis of disease. Analytical instruments provides a broad offering of instruments, consumables, software and services used for a range of applications in the laboratory, on the production line and in the field. These products are used by customers in pharmaceutical, biotechnology, academic, government, environmental, research, industrial markets, as well as clinical laboratories. Specialty diagnostics offers a range of diagnostic test kits, reagents, culture media, instruments and associated products in order to serve customers in healthcare, clinical, pharmaceutical, industrial and food safety laboratories. Laboratory products and services offers everything needed for the laboratory to enable customers to focus on core activities and become more efficient, productive and cost-effective. This segment's products are used primarily for drug discovery and development, as well as for life science research in order to advance the prevention and cure of diseases and enhance quality of life. The company's five primary brands include Thermo Scientific, Applied Biosystems, Invitrogen, Fisher Scientific and Unity Lab Services. In May 2019, Thermo Fisher acquired Brammer Bio for $1.7 billion, a viral vector manufacturer for gene and cell therapies. Brammer will become part of Thermo Fisher's pharma services business within the lab products segment.

Employees receive comprehensive benefits.

FINANCIAL DATA:
Note: Data for latest year may not have been available at press time.

In U.S. $	2018	2017	2016	2015	2014	2013
Revenue	24,358,000,000	20,918,000,000	18,274,100,000	16,965,400,000	16,889,600,000	13,090,300,000
R&D Expense	967,000,000	888,000,000	754,800,000	692,300,000	691,100,000	395,500,000
Operating Income	3,833,000,000	3,065,000,000	2,638,400,000	2,451,500,000	1,904,800,000	1,687,300,000
Operating Margin %		.15%	.14%	.14%	.11%	.13%
SGA Expense	6,057,000,000	5,492,000,000	4,975,900,000	4,612,100,000	4,896,100,000	3,446,300,000
Net Income	2,938,000,000	2,225,000,000	2,021,800,000	1,975,400,000	1,894,400,000	1,273,300,000
Operating Cash Flow	4,543,000,000	4,005,000,000	3,156,300,000	2,816,900,000	2,619,600,000	2,010,700,000
Capital Expenditure	758,000,000	508,000,000	444,400,000	422,900,000	427,600,000	282,400,000
EBITDA	6,196,000,000	5,054,000,000	4,251,500,000	4,039,500,000	4,251,900,000	2,581,500,000
Return on Assets %		.04%	.05%	.05%	.05%	.04%
Return on Equity %		.09%	.09%	.09%	.10%	.08%
Debt to Equity		0.743	0.714	0.537	0.601	0.564

CONTACT INFORMATION:
Phone: 781 622-1000 Fax: 781 933-4476
Toll-Free: 800-678-5599
Address: 168 Third Ave., Waltham, MA 02451 United States

SALARIES/BONUSES:
Top Exec. Salary: $1,482,740   Bonus: $
Second Exec. Salary: $1,005,025   Bonus: $

STOCK TICKER/OTHER:
Stock Ticker: TMO
Employees: 55,000
Parent Company:

Exchange: NYS
Fiscal Year Ends: 12/31

OTHER THOUGHTS:
Estimated Female Officers or Directors: 1
Hot Spot for Advancement for Women/Minorities: Y

Sales, profits and employees may be estimates. Financial information, benefits and other data can change quickly and may vary from those stated here.

Thor Industries Inc

NAIC Code: 336214

www.thorindustries.com

TYPES OF BUSINESS:
Recreational Vehicle Manufacturing
Motor Homes
Automotive Parts & Accessories
Buses

BRANDS/DIVISIONS/AFFILIATES:
Airstream Inc
Thor Motor Coach Inc
KZ Inc
Postle Operating LLC
Jayco Inc
Dutchman
Bison Coach
Erwin Hymer Group SE

CONTACTS:
Note: Officers with more than one job title may be intentionally listed here more than once.

Robert Martin, CEO
Colleen Zuhl, CFO
Peter Orthwein, Chairman of the Board
W. Woelfer, General Counsel
Kenneth Julian, Senior VP, Divisional

GROWTH PLANS/SPECIAL FEATURES:

Thor Industries, Inc. is a leading manufacturer of a wide range of recreational vehicles (RVs). The company's primary RV subsidiaries are Airstream, Inc.; Thor Motor Coach, Inc.; Keystone RV Company, which includes Crossroads and Dutchman; Heartland Recreational Vehicles LLC, which includes Bison Horse Trailers, LLC (dba Bison Coach), Cruiser RV, LLC and DRV, LLC; K.Z., Inc., which includes Venture RV; Postle Operating, LLC; and Jayco, Inc. (which includes Jayco, StarCraft, Highland Ridge and Entegra Coach). Together these businesses produce towable RVs, which account for 72.1% of annual net sales, as well as motorized RVs, which account for 25.8% of sales (3.7% goes toward other/related sales). Towable RVs include conventional travel trailers, fifth wheels and park models; truck and folding campers; and equestrian and other specialty towable vehicles. Park models are recreational dwellings towed to a permanent site such as a lake, woods or park, with the maximum size of park models in the U.S. being 400 square feet. Motorized RVs include Class A, B and C motorhomes, which are self-powered vehicles built on a chassis and self-contained with their own lighting, heating, cooking, refrigeration, sewage holding and water storage facilities. Thor also manufactures and sells related parts and accessories. During 2019, Thor acquired Germany RV manufacturer, Erwin Hymer Group SE, its first acquisition outside the U.S.

FINANCIAL DATA:
Note: Data for latest year may not have been available at press time.

In U.S. $	2018	2017	2016	2015	2014	2013
Revenue	8,328,909,000	7,246,952,000	4,582,112,000	4,006,819,000	3,525,456,000	3,241,795,000
R&D Expense						
Operating Income	632,104,000	559,811,000	392,094,000	290,639,000	248,764,000	219,429,000
Operating Margin %		.08%	.09%	.07%	.07%	.07%
SGA Expense	477,444,000	419,847,000	306,269,000	250,891,000	208,712,000	194,650,000
Net Income	430,151,000	374,254,000	256,519,000	199,385,000	179,002,000	152,862,000
Operating Cash Flow	466,508,000	419,333,000	341,209,000	247,860,000	149,261,000	145,066,000
Capital Expenditure	138,197,000	115,027,000	51,976,000	42,283,000	30,406,000	24,305,000
EBITDA	731,439,000	664,374,000	437,480,000	324,456,000	278,663,000	246,965,000
Return on Assets %		.15%	.13%	.14%	.13%	.12%
Return on Equity %		.26%	.22%	.20%	.19%	.18%
Debt to Equity		0.092	0.285			

CONTACT INFORMATION:
Phone: 574-970-7460   Fax:
Toll-Free:
Address: 601 E. Beardsley Ave., Elkhart, IN 46514-3305 United States

STOCK TICKER/OTHER:
Stock Ticker: THO
Employees: 17,800
Parent Company:

Exchange: NYS
Fiscal Year Ends: 07/31

SALARIES/BONUSES:
Top Exec. Salary: $750,000   Bonus: $
Second Exec. Salary: $600,000   Bonus: $

OTHER THOUGHTS:
Estimated Female Officers or Directors:
Hot Spot for Advancement for Women/Minorities:

Sales, profits and employees may be estimates. Financial information, benefits and other data can change quickly and may vary from those stated here.

TIAA

NAIC Code: 523920

www.tiaa-cref.org

TYPES OF BUSINESS:
Investment Management
Retirement & Supplemental Retirement Plans
College Savings Plans
Mutual Funds
Annuities & Pension Funds
Trust Services
Life Insurance

BRANDS/DIVISIONS/AFFILIATES:
TIAA Bank
TIAA FSB
TIAA-CREF Trust Company
Nuveen

CONTACTS:
Note: Officers with more than one job title may be intentionally listed here more than once.

Roger Ferguson, CEO
Gina Wilson, Sr. VP
Sean Woodroffe, Sr. VP
Rahul Merchant, Exec. VP
Brandon Becker, Chief Legal Officer
Doug Chittenden, Exec. VP-Individual Bus.
Carol Deckbar, Exec. VP
Stephen B. Gruppo, Exec. VP-Risk Mgmt.
Teresa Hassara, Exec. VP-Institutional Bus.

GROWTH PLANS/SPECIAL FEATURES:

TIAA (Teachers Insurance and Annuity Association) is a nonprofit private retirement system. In 2018, the firm celebrated 100 years in business. TIAA's products include investment, banking/loans and insurance. TIAA also offers advisory and performance data services, and its asset management services and solutions are provided through the Nuveen division and brand name. Investment products include retirement plans, individual retirement accounts (IRAs), mutual funds, retirement annuities, brokerage/trading, 529 education savings and managed investment accounts, as well as TIAA's personal portfolio. Banking and loan products and services include interest-building checking accounts, money market, certificates of deposit (CDs), mortgage loans and home loans. These products and services are provided through TIAA Bank, a division of TIAA, FSB. TIAA's insurance products are life insurance, offering both term and permanent options. Performance data and advisory services are provided through TIAA-CREF Trust Company, which presents performance data quotes and activities in relation to mutual funds, fixed annuities, variable annuities and FDIC-insured products. Asset classes include guaranteed, equities, real estate, fixed income, money market, multi-asset and more. Nuveen manages $973 billion in assets for over 1,500 institutional clients in 34 countries worldwide (as of June 2018). These assets include fixed income ($391 billion), equities ($320 billion), alternatives ($212 billion) and solutions-based strategies ($49 billion). Nuveen's clients include institutional investors such as corporations, public funds, insurance, Sovereign Wealth funds, endowments and foundations.

The firm offers its employees company-funded and employee-funded retirement plans; life insurance; flexible spending account; medical, dental and vision coverage; short- and long-term disability; retiree health care savings; long-term care insurance; and tuition and adoption assistance.

FINANCIAL DATA:
Note: Data for latest year may not have been available at press time.

In U.S. $	2018	2017	2016	2015	2014	2013
Revenue	41,052,100,000	32,000,000,000	30,797,000,000	26,857,000,000	26,197,000,000	33,817,000,000
R&D Expense						
Operating Income						
Operating Margin %						
SGA Expense						
Net Income			1,490,000,000	1,254,000,000	984,000,000	1,722,160,000
Operating Cash Flow						
Capital Expenditure						
EBITDA						
Return on Assets %						
Return on Equity %						
Debt to Equity						

CONTACT INFORMATION:
Phone: 212-490-9000 Fax: 212-916-4840
Toll-Free: 800-842-2252
Address: 730 Third Ave., New York, NY 10017 United States

STOCK TICKER/OTHER:
Stock Ticker: Private
Employees: 12,997
Parent Company:

Exchange:
Fiscal Year Ends: 12/31

SALARIES/BONUSES:
Top Exec. Salary: $ Bonus: $
Second Exec. Salary: $ Bonus: $

OTHER THOUGHTS:
Estimated Female Officers or Directors: 6
Hot Spot for Advancement for Women/Minorities: Y

Sales, profits and employees may be estimates. Financial information, benefits and other data can change quickly and may vary from those stated here.

TJX Companies Inc (T.J. Maxx)

NAIC Code: 448140

www.tjx.com

TYPES OF BUSINESS:
Discount Apparel Stores
Domestics
Footwear
Jewelry
Home Furnishings Stores
Accessories
Online Outdoor and Sporting Goods Sales

BRANDS/DIVISIONS/AFFILIATES:
Marmaxx
HomeGoods
TJX Canada
T.J. Maxx
Marshalls
Winners
HomeSense
Sierra Trading Post

CONTACTS: *Note: Officers with more than one job title may be intentionally listed here more than once.*

Scott Goldenberg, CFO
Carol Meyrowitz, Chairman of the Board
Douglas Mizzi, President, Divisional
Richard Sherr, President, Divisional
Kenneth Canestrari, President, Geographical
Ernie Herrman, President

GROWTH PLANS/SPECIAL FEATURES:

The TJX Companies, Inc. is a low-price apparel and home fashion retailer, operating over 3,800 stores in the U.S. and worldwide. TJX's stores offer merchandise sold at 20% to 60% below department and specialty store regular prices. The firm operates through four major divisions: Marmaxx, made up of T.J. Maxx and Marshalls; HomeGoods, made up of the HomeGoods retail chain; TJX Canada, comprised of Winners, HomeSense and Marshalls; and TJX international, operating T.K. Maxx and HomeSense. The Marmaxx group is the largest off-price retailer in the U.S., with 2,285 stores. T.J. Maxx and Marshalls stores offer brand-name family apparel, including footwear and accessories, and home fashions, including home basics, accent furniture and giftware. The chains are similar, although Marshalls features a full-line shoe department and larger men's and juniors' departments, while T.J. Maxx carries an extended line of jewelry and accessories. The HomeGoods segment offers discounted home fashions in 667 stores throughout the U.S. TJX Canada operates a total of 264 Winners, 111 HomeSense and 73 Marshalls locations throughout Canada. The TJX international segment operates 540 T.K. Maxx stores in the U.K., Ireland, Poland, Austria, the Netherlands and Germany, and 55 HomeSense locations in the U.K. In addition to its four main segments, the firm operates Sierra Trading Post, an off-price internet retailer (sierratradingpost.com) of brand name and quality outdoor gear, family apparel and footwear, sporting goods and home fashions. Sierra Trading Post also operates 27 retail stores in the U.S. The company purchases its inventory from over 20,000 vendors worldwide.

TJX offers its employees medical, dental, vision, disability and life insurance; 401(k) & profit sharing plans; auto/home insurance; savings & discount programs; paid vacation; and adoption assistance.

FINANCIAL DATA: *Note: Data for latest year may not have been available at press time.*

In U.S. $	2018	2017	2016	2015	2014	2013
Revenue	35,864,660,000	33,183,740,000	30,944,940,000	29,078,410,000	27,422,700,000	
R&D Expense						
Operating Income	3,987,426,000	3,849,523,000	3,704,700,000	3,606,501,000	3,350,570,000	
Operating Margin %	.11%	.12%	.12%	.12%	.12%	
SGA Expense	6,375,071,000	5,768,467,000	5,205,715,000	4,695,384,000	4,467,089,000	
Net Income	2,607,948,000	2,298,234,000	2,277,658,000	2,215,128,000	2,137,396,000	
Operating Cash Flow	3,025,624,000	3,601,894,000	2,937,343,000	3,008,369,000	2,590,329,000	
Capital Expenditure	1,057,617,000	1,024,747,000	889,380,000	911,522,000	946,678,000	
EBITDA	4,646,840,000	4,443,510,000	4,335,265,000	4,194,239,000	3,914,403,000	
Return on Assets %	.19%	.19%	.20%	.21%	.22%	
Return on Equity %	.54%	.52%	.53%	.52%	.54%	
Debt to Equity	0.476	0.533	0.397	0.395	0.301	

CONTACT INFORMATION:
Phone: 508 390-1000   Fax: 508 390-2091
Toll-Free:
Address: 770 Cochituate Rd., Framingham, MA 01701 United States

SALARIES/BONUSES:
Top Exec. Salary: $1,600,001   Bonus: $
Second Exec. Salary: $1,067,309   Bonus: $

STOCK TICKER/OTHER:
Stock Ticker: TJX   Exchange: NYS
Employees: 270,000   Fiscal Year Ends: 01/31
Parent Company:

OTHER THOUGHTS:
Estimated Female Officers or Directors: 4
Hot Spot for Advancement for Women/Minorities: Y

T-Mobile US Inc

www.t-mobile.com

NAIC Code: 517210

TYPES OF BUSINESS:
Mobile Phone and Wireless Services
Wireless Internet Services

BRANDS/DIVISIONS/AFFILIATES:
Deutsche Telekom AG
T-Mobile International AG
T-Mobile
MetroPCS

CONTACTS:
Note: Officers with more than one job title may be intentionally listed here more than once.

J. Carter, CFO
Timotheus Hottges, Chairman of the Board
Neville Ray, Chief Technology Officer
G. Sievert, COO
John Legere, Director
Peter Ewens, Executive VP, Divisional
Elizabeth McAuliffe, Executive VP, Divisional
David Carey, Executive VP, Divisional
David Miller, Executive VP
Thomas Keys, President, Subsidiary
Peter Osvaldik, Senior VP, Divisional

GROWTH PLANS/SPECIAL FEATURES:

T-Mobile US, Inc. (T-Mobile) is a national provider of wireless voice, messaging and data services, and is one of the largest cellular companies in America. The firm offers wireless service under both the T-Mobile and MetroPCS brands. T-Mobile uses GSM (global system for mobile communications) technology and is a member of the North American GSM Alliance, a group of U.S. and Canadian digital wireless carriers that provide seamless GSM wireless communications for its members in North America and internationally. Along with GSM, the firm uses technology platforms based on HSPA+ (high speed packet access plus), CDMA (code division multiple access) and LTE (long-term evolution) to service over 79.7 million customers in the postpaid, prepaid and wholesale markets (as of early-2019). The company's products include internet and e-mail; games and applications for mobile devices; messaging; voicemail; mobile device wallpapers; music and sounds; and handset protection services in case of loss, theft, malfunction or accidental damage to the product. In January 2019, T-Mobile actively started the launch of 5G in 30 cities, but the network will not be officially launched until 5G devices are available. The company plans for full nationwide 5G coverage by 2020. T-Mobile operates as a subsidiary of T-Mobile International AG, which itself is the mobile communications subsidiary of Deutsche Telekom AG. In mid-2018, Sprint Corporation and T-Mobile agreed to merge, potentially creating a third giant wireless network operator to compete against AT&T, Inc. and Verizon Communications, Inc. The transaction is expected to close mid-2019, but is subject to regulatory approval.

FINANCIAL DATA:
Note: Data for latest year may not have been available at press time.

In U.S. $	2018	2017	2016	2015	2014	2013
Revenue	43,310,000,000	40,604,000,000	37,242,000,000	32,053,000,000	29,564,000,000	
R&D Expense						
Operating Income	5,309,000,000	4,653,000,000	3,071,000,000	2,278,000,000	875,000,000	
Operating Margin %		.11%	.08%	.06%	.02%	
SGA Expense	13,161,000,000	12,259,000,000	11,378,000,000	10,189,000,000	8,863,000,000	
Net Income	2,888,000,000	4,536,000,000	1,460,000,000	733,000,000	247,000,000	
Operating Cash Flow	3,899,000,000	7,962,000,000	6,135,000,000	5,414,000,000	4,146,000,000	
Capital Expenditure	5,668,000,000	11,065,000,000	8,670,000,000	6,659,000,000	7,217,000,000	
EBITDA	11,760,000,000	10,816,000,000	10,300,000,000	7,162,000,000	6,176,000,000	
Return on Assets %		.07%	.02%	.01%	.00%	
Return on Equity %		.22%	.08%	.04%	.02%	
Debt to Equity		0.537	1.197	1.237	1.20	

CONTACT INFORMATION:
Phone: 425-378-4000   Fax: 425-378-4040
Toll-Free: 800-318-9270
Address: 12920 SE 38th St., Bellevue, WA 98006-1350 United States

SALARIES/BONUSES:
Top Exec. Salary: $1,878,205   Bonus: $
Second Exec. Salary: $1,108,654   Bonus: $

STOCK TICKER/OTHER:
Stock Ticker: TMUS
Employees: 50,000
Parent Company: Deutsche Telekom AG

Exchange: NAS
Fiscal Year Ends: 12/31

OTHER THOUGHTS:
Estimated Female Officers or Directors:
Hot Spot for Advancement for Women/Minorities:

Toll Brothers Inc

www.tollbrothers.com

NAIC Code: 236117

TYPES OF BUSINESS:
Construction, Home Building and Residential
Mortgages & Insurance
Property Management
Landscaping
Country Club Communities
Golf Courses
Security Monitoring
Lumber Distribution

BRANDS/DIVISIONS/AFFILIATES:

CONTACTS:
Note: Officers with more than one job title may be intentionally listed here more than once.

Douglas Yearley, CEO
Martin Connor, CFO
Robert Toll, Chairman Emeritus
Richard Hartman, COO
Michael Grubb, Senior VP

GROWTH PLANS/SPECIAL FEATURES:

Toll Brothers, Inc. designs, builds, markets and arranges financing for single-family detached and attached homes in luxury residential communities. The firm is also involved, both directly and through joint ventures, in building or converting existing rental apartment buildings into high-, mid- and low-rise luxury homes. Toll Brothers markets its services to move-up, empty-nester, active-adult, age-qualified and second-home buyers through its operations in 19 U.S. states. The company is present in major suburban and urban residential areas including the Philadelphia, Pennsylvania metropolitan area; Virginia and Maryland suburbs of Washington, D.C.; central and northern New Jersey; Boston, Massachusetts; Westchester and Dutchess Counties, New York; Los Angeles, San Diego and Palm Springs, California; the San Francisco Bay area; Phoenix, Arizona; Las Vegas and Reno, Nevada; and Chicago, Illinois. The average base sales price of the company's homes is roughly $864,300 (2018). Toll Brothers operates its own land development, architectural, engineering, mortgage, title, landscaping, lumber distribution, house component assembly and manufacturing operations. In addition, the company owns and operates golf courses in conjunction with several of its master planned communities. The company operates a portfolio of 638 communities with 53,400 homes sites.

The firm offers employees discounts on homes, mortgages, titles, home appliances and kitchen cabinets; life, medical, dental and long- and short-term disability coverage; a 401(k); and educational reimbursement. After two years of service, employees are able to use the company's furnished resort luxury guesthouses for their personal vacations.

FINANCIAL DATA:
Note: Data for latest year may not have been available at press time.

In U.S. $	2018	2017	2016	2015	2014	2013
Revenue	7,143,258,000	5,815,058,000	5,169,508,000	4,171,248,000	3,911,602,000	2,674,299,000
R&D Expense						
Operating Income	820,845,000	667,013,000	513,400,000	475,624,000	410,969,000	213,513,000
Operating Margin %		.11%	.09%	.11%	.10%	.08%
SGA Expense	684,035,000	607,819,000	535,382,000	455,108,000	432,516,000	339,932,000
Net Income	748,151,000	535,495,000	382,095,000	363,167,000	340,032,000	170,606,000
Operating Cash Flow	602,401,000	959,719,000	148,771,000	60,182,000	313,200,000	-568,963,000
Capital Expenditure	28,232,000	28,872,000	28,426,000	9,447,000	15,074,000	26,567,000
EBITDA	846,104,000	692,374,000	536,521,000	499,181,000	528,237,000	292,907,000
Return on Assets %		.06%	.04%	.04%	.04%	.03%
Return on Equity %		.12%	.09%	.09%	.09%	.05%
Debt to Equity		0.711	0.893	0.898	0.882	0.751

CONTACT INFORMATION:
Phone: 215 938-8000 Fax: 215 938-8023
Toll-Free:
Address: 250 Gibraltar Rd., Horsham, PA 19044 United States

STOCK TICKER/OTHER:
Stock Ticker: TOL
Employees: 3,500
Parent Company:

Exchange: NYS
Fiscal Year Ends: 10/31

SALARIES/BONUSES:
Top Exec. Salary: $1,000,000 Bonus: $
Second Exec. Salary: $1,000,000 Bonus: $

OTHER THOUGHTS:
Estimated Female Officers or Directors:
Hot Spot for Advancement for Women/Minorities:

Sales, profits and employees may be estimates. Financial information, benefits and other data can change quickly and may vary from those stated here.

Tractor Supply Company

NAIC Code: 444130

www.tractorsupplyco.com

TYPES OF BUSINESS:
Farming Supplies, Retail
Work Apparel
Light Truck Equipment
Footwear
Animal Care Products
Private Label Credit Cards

BRANDS/DIVISIONS/AFFILIATES:
Tractor Supply Company
Petsense
Del's Feed & Farm Supply
TractorSupply.com

CONTACTS:
Note: Officers with more than one job title may be intentionally listed here more than once.

Gregory Sandfort, CEO
Kurt Barton, CFO
Cynthia Jamison, Chairman of the Board
Robert Mills, Chief Technology Officer
Benjamin Parrish, Executive VP
Steve Barbarick, President
Chad Frazell, Senior VP, Divisional

GROWTH PLANS/SPECIAL FEATURES:

Tractor Supply Company (TSC) is one of the largest operators of retail farm and ranch stores in the U.S. and focuses on supplying the needs of recreational farmers and ranchers, tradesmen and small businesses. TSC also owns and operates Petsense, a pet supply and pet service chain retail outlet. Petsenses are found in outlet malls and rural markets across the country. TSC operates over 1,700 stores Tractor Supply Company and Del's Feed & Farm Supply in 49 states and 181 Petsense pet specialty stores in 27 states. These stores range from 15,000 to 20,000 square feet of inside selling space, along with additional outside selling space, and are primarily in towns outlying major metropolitan markets and in rural communities. TSC also operates two e-commerce sites: TractorSupply.com and petsense.com. The firm's market niche supplies the needs of recreational farmers and ranchers, as well as tradesmen, small businesses and those who enjoy the rural lifestyle. Types of merchandise in TSC's stores and online include equine, livestock, pet and small animal products, including items necessary for their health, growth and containment; hardware, truck towing and tool products; seasonal products such as heating, lawn and garden items, power equipment, gifts and toys; work/recreational clothing and footwear; and maintenance products for agricultural and rural use. Livestock and pet products account for 47% of company annual sales; hardware, tools, truck and towing, 22%; seasonal, gift and toy products, 19%; clothing and footwear, 8%; and agriculture, 4%. TSC's long term plan is to grow by about 120 new stores per year until it reaches a total of 2,500 stores.

The company offers employees benefits including medical, dental, vision, disability and life insurance; pet insurance; a 401(k) for both part- and full-time employees; stock purchase options; an adoption assistance program; tuition reimbursement; and merchandise discounts.

FINANCIAL DATA:
Note: Data for latest year may not have been available at press time.

In U.S. $	2018	2017	2016	2015	2014	2013
Revenue	7,911,046,000	7,256,382,000	6,779,579,000	6,226,507,000	5,711,715,000	5,164,784,000
R&D Expense						
Operating Income	701,737,000	686,382,000	694,080,000	650,508,000	589,472,000	514,650,000
Operating Margin %		.09%	.10%	.10%	.10%	.10%
SGA Expense	1,823,440,000	1,639,749,000	1,488,164,000	1,369,097,000	1,246,308,000	1,138,934,000
Net Income	532,357,000	422,599,000	437,120,000	410,395,000	370,885,000	328,234,000
Operating Cash Flow	694,394,000	631,450,000	639,040,000	429,180,000	409,178,000	333,681,000
Capital Expenditure	278,530,000	250,401,000	226,017,000	236,496,000	160,613,000	218,200,000
EBITDA	879,088,000	852,216,000	837,038,000	774,077,000	704,107,000	614,675,000
Return on Assets %		.15%	.17%	.19%	.19%	.18%
Return on Equity %		.29%	.31%	.31%	.29%	.29%
Debt to Equity		0.306	0.199	0.12	0.004	0.001

CONTACT INFORMATION:
Phone: 615 440-4000 Fax:
Toll-Free: 800-872-7721
Address: 5401 Virginia Way, Brentwood, TN 37027 United States

STOCK TICKER/OTHER:
Stock Ticker: TSCO
Employees: 26,000
Parent Company:

Exchange: NAS
Fiscal Year Ends: 12/31

SALARIES/BONUSES:
Top Exec. Salary: $1,090,769 Bonus: $
Second Exec. Salary: $806,923 Bonus: $

OTHER THOUGHTS:
Estimated Female Officers or Directors: 3
Hot Spot for Advancement for Women/Minorities: Y

Sales, profits and employees may be estimates. Financial information, benefits and other data can change quickly and may vary from those stated here.

Trader Joe's Company Inc

NAIC Code: 445110

www.traderjoes.com

TYPES OF BUSINESS:
Grocery Stores
Specialty Groceries
Vitamins & Dietary Supplements
Organic Foods

BRANDS/DIVISIONS/AFFILIATES:

CONTACTS:
Note: Officers with more than one job title may be intentionally listed here more than once.
Daniel T. Bane, CEO
Charles Pillitier, Sr. VP-Oper.
Brandt Sharrock, VP-Real Estate
Daniel T. Bane, Chmn.

GROWTH PLANS/SPECIAL FEATURES:
Trader Joe's Company, Inc. operates a chain of approximately 475 company-owned and -operated specialty grocery stores in 41 states and Washington, D.C., with about half of the stores located in California, where the company was founded. Although the stores sell some brand-name products, the vast majority of the selection is comprised of more than 3,000 Trader Joe's private-label products, including specialty vegetarian, kosher, organic food and vitamin supplement products as well as regional fare, such as Thai and Mexican foods. Prices tend to be comparable to or lower than traditional groceries, as a result of Trader Joe's efforts to buy many items and ingredients directly from suppliers and the chain's focus on its private label lines. The company also keeps costs down by eliminating service departments and using spaces of 15,000 square feet or less for its stores. Selections and inventory tend to vary from state to state and store to store because of the company's commitment to experimentation, regional and seasonal products and bringing variety to its customers. The firm is privately owned by a trust created by Theo Albrecht, co-founder of German supermarket chain ALDI Group.

Trader Joe's offers employees medical, dental and vision insurance; a company-paid retirement plan; a 10% employee discount; and paid time off. Medical, dental and vision coverage is available to both full and part-time employees of the firm.

FINANCIAL DATA:
Note: Data for latest year may not have been available at press time.

In U.S. $	2018	2017	2016	2015	2014	2013
Revenue	13,912,500,000	13,250,000,000	12,500,000,000	12,000,000,000	11,000,000,000	9,725,000,000
R&D Expense						
Operating Income						
Operating Margin %						
SGA Expense						
Net Income						
Operating Cash Flow						
Capital Expenditure						
EBITDA						
Return on Assets %						
Return on Equity %						
Debt to Equity						

CONTACT INFORMATION:
Phone: 626-599-3700   Fax: 626-301-4431
Toll-Free:
Address: 800 S. Shamrock Ave., Monrovia, CA 91016 United States

SALARIES/BONUSES:
Top Exec. Salary: $ Bonus: $
Second Exec. Salary: $ Bonus: $

STOCK TICKER/OTHER:
Stock Ticker: Private   Exchange:
Employees: 41,000   Fiscal Year Ends: 06/30
Parent Company:

OTHER THOUGHTS:
Estimated Female Officers or Directors: 2
Hot Spot for Advancement for Women/Minorities:

TransDigm Group Incorporated

www.transdigm.com

NAIC Code: 336413

TYPES OF BUSINESS:
Aircraft Control Surface Assemblies Manufacturing
Aftermarket Aircraft Parts

BRANDS/DIVISIONS/AFFILIATES:
Esterline Technologies Corporation

CONTACTS: Note: Officers with more than one job title may be intentionally listed here more than once.
Kevin Stein, CEO
Michael Lisman, CFO
W. Howley, Chairman of the Board
James Skulina, Chief Accounting Officer
Jorge Valladares, COO, Divisional
Bernt Iversen, Executive VP, Divisional
Halle Terrion, General Counsel
Robert Henderson, Vice Chairman

GROWTH PLANS/SPECIAL FEATURES:

TransDigm Group Incorporated designs, produces and supplies highly-engineered proprietary aerospace components and subsystems for use in both commercial and military aircraft. Its products are designed and manufactured through a network of subsidiaries and sold almost entirely to global aerospace customers. The company maintains approximately 60 manufacturing facilities. TransDigm operates through three business segments: power & control, airframe and non-aviation. The power & control segment primarily develops, produces and markets systems and components that provide power to or control power of the aircraft utilizing electronic, fluid, power and mechanical motion control technologies. This division's products include mechanical/electro-mechanical actuators and controls, ignition systems, engine technology, specialized pumps and valves, power conditioning devices, specialized AC/DC electric motors and generators, power controls, high-performance hoists, winches, lifting devices and cargo loading and handling systems. The airframe segment develops, produces and markets systems and components used in non-power airframe applications utilizing airframe and cabin structure technologies. This division's products include engineered latching and locking devices, rods, engineered connectors, elastomers, cockpit security components and systems, aircraft audio systems, specialized lavatory components, seat belts and safety restraints, engineered interior surfaces, lighting, control technology, military personnel parachutes and cargo delivery systems. Last, the non-aviation segment develops, produces and markets seat belts and safety restraints for ground transportation applications, mechanical/electro-mechanical actuators and controls for space applications, and refueling systems for heavy equipment used in mining, construction and other industries. In March 2019, TransDigm acquired Esterline Technologies Corporation for $4 billion. That August, the firm agreed to sell Esterline's interface technologies businesses to an affiliate of KPS Capital Partners, LP for approximately $190 million; these businesses include Advanced Input Systems, Gamesman and LRE Medical.

FINANCIAL DATA: Note: Data for latest year may not have been available at press time.

In U.S. $	2018	2017	2016	2015	2014	2013
Revenue	3,811,126,000	3,504,286,000	3,171,411,000	2,707,115,000	2,372,906,000	1,924,400,000
R&D Expense						
Operating Income	1,662,556,000	1,486,301,000	1,293,718,000	1,092,726,000	932,466,000	757,523,000
Operating Margin %		.42%	.41%	.40%	.39%	.39%
SGA Expense	442,500,000	409,100,000	356,900,000	302,900,000	271,800,000	246,400,000
Net Income	957,062,000	596,887,000	586,414,000	447,212,000	306,910,000	302,789,000
Operating Cash Flow	1,022,173,000	788,733,000	668,930,000	520,938,000	541,222,000	470,205,000
Capital Expenditure	73,341,000	71,013,000	43,982,000	54,871,000	34,146,000	35,535,000
EBITDA	1,792,400,000	1,627,326,000	1,415,388,000	1,186,389,000	1,028,851,000	831,038,000
Return on Assets %		.04%	.06%	.06%	.03%	.02%
Return on Equity %						.30%
Debt to Equity						

CONTACT INFORMATION:
Phone: 216 706-2960   Fax: 216 706-2937
Toll-Free:
Address: The Tower at Erieview, 1301 E. 9th St., Ste. 3000, Cleveland, OH 44114 United States

SALARIES/BONUSES:
Top Exec. Salary: $838,333   Bonus: $17,440
Second Exec. Salary: $567,500   Bonus: $1,688

STOCK TICKER/OTHER:
Stock Ticker: TDG
Employees: 9,200
Parent Company:

Exchange: NYS
Fiscal Year Ends: 09/30

OTHER THOUGHTS:
Estimated Female Officers or Directors:
Hot Spot for Advancement for Women/Minorities:

Sales, profits and employees may be estimates. Financial information, benefits and other data can change quickly and may vary from those stated here.

Travelers Companies Inc (The)

NAIC Code: 524126

www.travelers.com

TYPES OF BUSINESS:
Direct Property & Casualty Insurance
Reinsurance
Automobile & Homeowners' Insurance
General Liability & Commercial Multi-Peril Insurance
Marine Insurance
Risk Management Services

BRANDS/DIVISIONS/AFFILIATES:

CONTACTS:
Note: Officers with more than one job title may be intentionally listed here more than once.

Alan Schnitzer, CEO
Daniel Frey, CFO
Douglas Russell, Chief Accounting Officer
Andy Bessette, Chief Administrative Officer
Maria Olivo, Executive VP, Divisional
Christine Kalla, Executive VP
Diane Bengston, Executive VP
Mojgan Lefebvre, Executive VP
Gregory Toczydlowski, Executive VP
Michael Klein, Executive VP
Thomas Kunkel, Executive VP
Avrohom Kess, Other Executive Officer
William Heyman, Other Executive Officer
Jay Benet, Vice Chairman

GROWTH PLANS/SPECIAL FEATURES:

The Travelers Companies, Inc. is a holding company principally engaged in providing commercial and personal property and casualty (P&C) insurance products and services to businesses, government units, associations and individuals. The company operates in four segments: P&C insurance, business insurance, bond & specialty insurance and personal insurance. The P&C insurance segment offers coverage for cars, homes, renters, condos, landlords, boats/yachts, travel and weddings/events, as well as umbrella coverage and more. This division sells its P&C products in California, New York, Texas, Pennsylvania, Florida, New Jersey, Illinois, Georgia and Massachusetts, as well as other U.S.-based locations, and in Canada and other countries. The business insurance segment offers an array of P&C insurance and insurance-related services to customers primarily located in the U.S., but also in Canada, the U.K., Ireland, Brazil and other parts of the world. Business insurance products include commercial auto/trucking, cyber, general liability, management liability, professional liability, property, small business owners, surety bonds, workers' compensation and more. Industries served within the business segment include construction, energy, renewable energy, financial institutions, healthcare, manufacturing, real estate, technology, transportation, among others. The bond & specialty insurance segment provides surety, fidelity, management liability, professional liability and other P&C coverages and related risk management services to customers in the U.S., Canada, the U.K., Ireland and Brazil. Last, the personal insurance segment writes a broad range of P&C insurance covering individuals' personal risks, primarily in the U.S. and Canada. The primary products of automobile and homeowners insurance are complemented by a broad suite of related coverages.

FINANCIAL DATA:
Note: Data for latest year may not have been available at press time.

In U.S. $	2018	2017	2016	2015	2014	2013
Revenue	30,282,000,000	28,902,000,000	27,625,000,000	26,800,000,000	27,162,000,000	26,191,000,000
R&D Expense						
Operating Income						
Operating Margin %						
SGA Expense	4,297,000,000	4,170,000,000	4,154,000,000	4,079,000,000	3,952,000,000	3,757,000,000
Net Income	2,523,000,000	2,056,000,000	3,014,000,000	3,439,000,000	3,692,000,000	3,673,000,000
Operating Cash Flow	4,380,000,000	3,762,000,000	4,202,000,000	3,434,000,000	3,693,000,000	3,816,000,000
Capital Expenditure						
EBITDA						
Return on Assets %		.02%	.03%	.03%	.04%	.03%
Return on Equity %		.09%	.13%	.14%	.15%	.15%
Debt to Equity		0.252	0.254	0.248	0.236	0.252

CONTACT INFORMATION:
Phone: 917 778-6000 Fax:
Toll-Free: 800-328-2189
Address: 485 Lexington Ave., New York, NY 10017 United States

STOCK TICKER/OTHER:
Stock Ticker: TRV Exchange: NYS
Employees: 30,900 Fiscal Year Ends: 12/31
Parent Company:

SALARIES/BONUSES:
Top Exec. Salary: $1,000,000 Bonus: $
Second Exec. Salary: $850,000 Bonus: $

OTHER THOUGHTS:
Estimated Female Officers or Directors: 7
Hot Spot for Advancement for Women/Minorities: Y

Trimble Inc

www.trimble.com

NAIC Code: 334511

TYPES OF BUSINESS:
GPS Technologies
Surveying & Mapping Equipment
Navigation Tools
Autopilot Systems
Data Collection Products
Fleet Management Systems
Outdoor Recreation Information Service
Telecommunications & Automotive Components

BRANDS/DIVISIONS/AFFILIATES:
Trimble MAPS
AXIO-NET GmbH
Beena Vision Systems Inc
e-Builder
HHK Datentechnik GmbH
Innovative Software Engineering
MyTopo
Viewpoint

CONTACTS:
Note: Officers with more than one job title may be intentionally listed here more than once.

Steven Berglund, CEO
Robert Painter, CFO
Ulf Johansson, Chairman of the Board
Julie Shepard, Chief Accounting Officer
Darryl Matthews, Other Corporate Officer
Sachin Sankpal, Senior VP, Divisional
Bryn Fosburgh, Senior VP, Divisional
Michael Bank, Senior VP, Divisional
Ronald Bisio, Senior VP, Divisional
Rosalind Buick, Senior VP, Divisional
Thomas Fansler, Senior VP, Divisional
James Kirkland, Senior VP

GROWTH PLANS/SPECIAL FEATURES:

Trimble, Inc. provides technology solutions used in positioning, modeling, connectivity and data analytics to enable customers to improve productivity, quality, safety and sustainability. These products are sold in more than 100 countries, and include more than 2,000 patents. Trimble's global operations consist of offices and subsidiaries in nearly 40 countries. The company's subsidiaries include: Trimble MAPS (maps and applications for professional solutions), providing global map-centric technology dedicated to transforming journeys through innovative routing, scheduling, visualization and navigation solutions; AXIO-NET GmbH, a provider of reference networked services that deliver highly-accurate, satellite-based positioning and navigation information; Beena Vision Systems, Inc., a manufacturer of vision-based automatic wayside inspection systems for the railroad industry; e-Builder, a provider of integrated, cloud-based construction program management software for facility owners and the companies that act on their behalf; HHK Datentechnik GmbH; a developer and marketer of specialized office management, computer-aided design (CAD) and geographic information system (GIS) software solutions for municipal and cadastral offices, utility suppliers and engineering organizations; Innovative Software Engineering, an engineering and systems integration firm; MyTopo, a provider of navigation-ready mapping services, data and software; Muller-Elektronik GmbH & Co., KG, which develops, produces and sells electronic solutions for agricultural machinery; PeopleNet, a provider of internet-based and integrated onboard computing and mobile communications systems for the trucking fleet industry; Stabiplan, which develops and sells design software for MEP engineering in Europe; Trade Service, a provider of standardized product and price information to the mechanical, electrical, plumbing, industrial, automotive and office products industries; and Viewpoint, a global provider of integrated software solutions for the construction industry. In February 2019, Trimble announced the launch of a new division, Trimble MAPS (maps and applications for professional solutions), merging former ALK Technologies and TMW Appian Final Mile businesses into MAPS.

FINANCIAL DATA:
Note: Data for latest year may not have been available at press time.

In U.S. $	2018	2017	2016	2015	2014	2013
Revenue	3,108,400,000	2,654,200,000	2,362,200,000	2,290,400,000	2,395,546,000	2,288,124,000
R&D Expense	446,100,000	370,200,000	349,600,000	336,700,000	317,992,000	299,421,000
Operating Income	328,900,000	252,900,000	192,600,000	165,800,000	262,564,000	257,697,000
Operating Margin %		.10%	.08%	.07%	.11%	.11%
SGA Expense	829,600,000	706,500,000	633,600,000	629,900,000	634,689,000	564,982,000
Net Income	282,800,000	121,100,000	132,400,000	121,100,000	214,118,000	218,855,000
Operating Cash Flow	486,700,000	411,900,000	407,100,000	354,900,000	407,083,000	414,635,000
Capital Expenditure	67,600,000	43,700,000	26,300,000	44,000,000	54,945,000	70,877,000
EBITDA	566,400,000	467,500,000	390,400,000	376,500,000	476,337,000	460,023,000
Return on Assets %		.03%	.04%	.03%	.06%	.06%
Return on Equity %		.05%	.06%	.05%	.09%	.11%
Debt to Equity		0.332	0.212	0.275	0.286	0.294

CONTACT INFORMATION:
Phone: 408 481-8000   Fax: 408 481-2218
Toll-Free: 800-874-6253
Address: 935 Stewart Dr., Sunnyvale, CA 94085 United States

SALARIES/BONUSES:
Top Exec. Salary: $961,400   Bonus: $
Second Exec. Salary: $482,437   Bonus: $

STOCK TICKER/OTHER:
Stock Ticker: TRMB
Employees: 8,388
Parent Company:

Exchange: NAS
Fiscal Year Ends: 12/31

OTHER THOUGHTS:
Estimated Female Officers or Directors: 5
Hot Spot for Advancement for Women/Minorities: Y

Trinity Health

NAIC Code: 622110

www.trinity-health.org

TYPES OF BUSINESS:
General Medical and Surgical Hospitals
Assisted Living Facilities
Hospice Programs
Senior Housing Communities
Management & Consulting Services

BRANDS/DIVISIONS/AFFILIATES:
Senior Emergency Departments
Civica Rx

CONTACTS: Note: Officers with more than one job title may be intentionally listed here more than once.
Michael A. Slubowski, CEO
Cynthia A. Clemence, Sr. VP-Operations
Benjamin R. Carter, CFO
Edmund F. Hodge, Exec. VP-Human Resources
P. Terrence O'Rourke, Exec. VP-Clinical Transformation
Benjamin R. Carter, Exec. VP-Finance
James Bosscher, Chief Investment Officer
Paul Conlon, Sr. VP-Clinical Quality & Patient Safety
Rebecca Havlisch, Chief Nursing Officer
Louis Fierens, Sr. VP-Supply Chain & Capital Projects Mgmt.

GROWTH PLANS/SPECIAL FEATURES:

Trinity Health is one of the nation's largest multi-institutional Catholic healthcare delivery systems, serving patients and communities in 22 states. Trinity Health operates 92 acute care hospitals, 18 clinically-integrated continuing-care networks, 13 PACE center programs and 109 continuing care locations. The organization returns approximately $1 billion to its communities annually in the form of charity care and other community benefits programs. Trinity Health is known for its focus on the country's aging population, and is the innovator of Senior Emergency Departments, the largest non-profit provider of home healthcare services in the nation. The firm is a leading provider of PACE, which stands for Program of All-inclusive Care for the Elderly. Other services offered by the company include a military and veteran health program, research activities, population health management and supply chain management solutions. Trinity Health partnered with six other health organizations to create Civica Rx, a not-for-profit generic drug and pharmaceutical company founded in 2018 to combat life-saving drug shortages and affordability.

Trinity Health offers employees comprehensive health benefits, retirement plans and a variety of employee assistance programs.

FINANCIAL DATA: Note: Data for latest year may not have been available at press time.

In U.S. $	2018	2017	2016	2015	2014	2013
Revenue	18,345,405,000	17,627,845,000	16,339,047,000	14,388,150,000	13,600,000,000	13,293,723,000
R&D Expense						
Operating Income						
Operating Margin %						
SGA Expense						
Net Income	949,130,000	1,336,823,000	89,803,000	671,630,000	951,405,000	666,439,000
Operating Cash Flow						
Capital Expenditure						
EBITDA						
Return on Assets %						
Return on Equity %						
Debt to Equity						

CONTACT INFORMATION:
Phone: 734-343-1000 Fax:
Toll-Free:
Address: 20555 Victor Parkway, Livonia, MI 48152-7018 United States

SALARIES/BONUSES:
Top Exec. Salary: $ Bonus: $
Second Exec. Salary: $ Bonus: $

STOCK TICKER/OTHER:
Stock Ticker: Nonprofit
Employees: 129,000
Parent Company:

Exchange:
Fiscal Year Ends: 06/30

OTHER THOUGHTS:
Estimated Female Officers or Directors: 4
Hot Spot for Advancement for Women/Minorities: Y

Sales, profits and employees may be estimates. Financial information, benefits and other data can change quickly and may vary from those stated here.

Trinity Industries Inc

www.trin.net

NAIC Code: 336510

TYPES OF BUSINESS:
Railroad Car Manufacturing
Railroad Car Leasing & Management
Inland Barge Manufacturing & Services
Construction Materials Manufacturing
Highway Guardrails
Metal Containers
Steel Beams & Girders
Ready-Mix Concrete

BRANDS/DIVISIONS/AFFILIATES:
Trinity Rail Group LLC
Trinity Industries Leasing Company
TRIP Rail Holdings LLC
RIV 2013 Rail Holdings LLC
Arcosa Inc

CONTACTS:
Note: Officers with more than one job title may be intentionally listed here more than once.

Timothy Wallace, CEO
Melendy Lovett, CFO
Steven McDowell, Chief Accounting Officer
Sarah Teachout, Chief Legal Officer
Eric Marchetto, Other Executive Officer
Paul Mauer, President, Divisional
Brian Madison, President, Subsidiary

GROWTH PLANS/SPECIAL FEATURES:
Trinity Industries, Inc. is a holding company overseeing diversified leading industrial companies that manufacture various transportation, construction and industrial products. The company operates through two principal segments: rail, and railcar leasing and management services. The rail segment comprises wholly-owned subsidiary, Trinity Rail Group, LLC, one of the largest producers of freight and tank railcars in North America, manufactures railroad freight cars, principally pressure and non-pressure tank cars, hoppers and gondola cars used for transporting liquids, gases and dry cargo. Trinity's railcar leasing and management services segment, which operates primarily through subsidiary Trinity Industries Leasing Company, TRIP Rail Holdings, LLC and RIV 2013 Rail Holdings, LLC, provides comprehensive railcar fleet management services such as leasing and financing options; administration; regulatory compliance and tax preparation; and maintenance. In November 2018, Trinity completed the separation of its infrastructure-related business, Arcosa, Inc., a growth-oriented manufacturer of infrastructure-related products and services with leading positions in construction, energy, and transportation markets.

FINANCIAL DATA:
Note: Data for latest year may not have been available at press time.

In U.S. $	2018	2017	2016	2015	2014	2013
Revenue	2,509,100,000	3,662,800,000	4,588,300,000	6,392,700,000	6,170,000,000	4,365,300,000
R&D Expense						
Operating Income	273,700,000	462,500,000	724,800,000	1,260,100,000	1,146,600,000	751,700,000
Operating Margin %		.13%	.16%	.20%	.19%	.17%
SGA Expense	296,600,000	454,800,000	407,400,000	476,400,000	403,600,000	291,300,000
Net Income	159,300,000	702,500,000	343,600,000	796,500,000	678,200,000	375,500,000
Operating Cash Flow	379,100,000	761,600,000	1,090,200,000	939,700,000	819,200,000	662,200,000
Capital Expenditure	985,600,000	712,700,000	933,400,000	1,029,800,000	464,600,000	731,000,000
EBITDA	582,800,000	851,400,000	1,031,700,000	1,713,100,000	1,502,100,000	989,300,000
Return on Assets %		.07%	.04%	.09%	.08%	.05%
Return on Equity %		.16%	.09%	.24%	.25%	.17%
Debt to Equity		0.72	0.78	0.875	1.186	1.245

CONTACT INFORMATION:
Phone: 214 631-4420   Fax: 214 589-8501
Toll-Free:
Address: 2525 Stemmons Freeway, Dallas, TX 75207-2401 United States

STOCK TICKER/OTHER:
Stock Ticker: TRN
Employees: 17,680
Parent Company:

Exchange: NYS
Fiscal Year Ends: 12/31

SALARIES/BONUSES:
Top Exec. Salary: $1,050,000   Bonus: $
Second Exec. Salary: $489,250   Bonus: $345,000

OTHER THOUGHTS:
Estimated Female Officers or Directors: 2
Hot Spot for Advancement for Women/Minorities: Y

Tutor Perini Corporation

NAIC Code: 237310

www.tutorperini.com

TYPES OF BUSINESS:
Construction Services
Hospitality & Casino Construction
Construction Management Services
Civic & Infrastructure Construction
Design Services

BRANDS/DIVISIONS/AFFILIATES:

CONTACTS:
Note: Officers with more than one job title may be intentionally listed here more than once.

Leonard Rejcek, CEO, Divisional
Ronald Tutor, CEO
Gary Smalley, CFO
Ryan Soroka, Chief Accounting Officer
James Frost, COO
Michael Klein, Director
Wendy Hallgren, Executive VP
John Barrett, Secretary

GROWTH PLANS/SPECIAL FEATURES:

Tutor Perini Corporation and its subsidiaries provide general contracting, construction management and design-build services worldwide. It operates in three segments: building, civil and specialty contractors. The building segment focuses on large, complex projects in the hospitality and gaming, transportation, healthcare, municipal offices, sports and entertainment, education, correctional facilities, biotech, pharmaceutical, industrial and high-tech markets. The civil segment focuses on public works construction, including the new construction, repair, replacement and reconstruction of public infrastructure such as highways, bridges, mass transit systems and wastewater treatment facilities. The company's customers primarily award contracts through the public competitive bid, in which price is the major determining factor; or through a request for proposals, where contracts are awarded based on a combination of technical capability and price. The specialty contractors segment engages in electrical, mechanical, HVAC (heating, ventilation and air conditioning), plumbing and pneumatically paced concrete for construction projects in the commercial, industrial, hospitality, transportation and gaming markets.

The firm offers employees medical, dental, vision and life insurance; a flexible spending account; an employee assistance program; educational assistance; and reimbursement on health club memberships.

FINANCIAL DATA:
Note: Data for latest year may not have been available at press time.

In U.S. $	2018	2017	2016	2015	2014	2013
Revenue	4,454,662,000	4,757,208,000	4,973,076,000	4,920,472,000	4,492,309,000	4,175,672,000
R&D Expense						
Operating Income	191,876,000	179,477,000	201,920,000	105,413,000	241,690,000	203,822,000
Operating Margin %		.04%	.04%	.02%	.05%	.05%
SGA Expense	262,577,000	274,928,000	255,270,000	250,840,000	263,752,000	263,082,000
Net Income	83,436,000	148,382,000	95,822,000	45,292,000	107,936,000	87,296,000
Operating Cash Flow	21,402,000	163,550,000	113,336,000	14,072,000	-56,678,000	50,728,000
Capital Expenditure	77,069,000	30,280,000	15,743,000	35,912,000	75,013,000	42,360,000
EBITDA	243,399,000	275,289,000	276,199,000	161,595,000	288,126,000	244,657,000
Return on Assets %		.04%	.02%	.01%	.03%	.03%
Return on Equity %		.09%	.06%	.03%	.08%	.07%
Debt to Equity		0.412	0.434	0.517	0.574	0.496

CONTACT INFORMATION:
Phone: 818 362-8391 Fax:
Toll-Free:
Address: 15901 Olden St., Sylmar, CA 91342 United States

STOCK TICKER/OTHER:
Stock Ticker: TPC
Employees: 11,603
Parent Company:

Exchange: NYS
Fiscal Year Ends: 12/31

SALARIES/BONUSES:
Top Exec. Salary: $1,750,000   Bonus: $1,250,000
Second Exec. Salary: $725,000   Bonus: $302,083

OTHER THOUGHTS:
Estimated Female Officers or Directors:
Hot Spot for Advancement for Women/Minorities:

Sales, profits and employees may be estimates. Financial information, benefits and other data can change quickly and may vary from those stated here.

Tyson Foods Inc

NAIC Code: 311615

www.tyson.com

TYPES OF BUSINESS:
Poultry Processing
Beef & Pork Products
Ethnic Foods
Soups & Sauces
Frozen & Refrigerated Food

BRANDS/DIVISIONS/AFFILIATES:
Tyson Rizhao
Tyson Dalong
Tyson Nantong
Godrej Tyson Foods
Tyson Mexico Trading Company
Tovala
Keystone Foods LLC

CONTACTS:
Note: Officers with more than one job title may be intentionally listed here more than once.

Noel White, CEO
Stewart Glendinning, CFO
John Tyson, Chairman of the Board
Steve Gibbs, Chief Accounting Officer
Jay Spradley, Chief Technology Officer
Justin Whitmore, Executive VP, Divisional
Amy Tu, Executive VP
Scott Rouse, Executive VP
Mary Oleksiuk, Executive VP
Sally Grimes, President, Divisional
Douglas Ramsey, President, Divisional
Stephen Stouffer, President, Divisional
Curt Calaway, Senior VP, Divisional

GROWTH PLANS/SPECIAL FEATURES:

Tyson Foods, Inc. is a producer, distributor and marketer of chicken, beef, pork, prepared foods and related products. The company operates in four segments: chicken, beef, pork and prepared foods. The chicken operations include breeding and raising chickens as well as processing live chickens into fresh, frozen and value-added chicken products. This segment also includes logistics operations to move products through the supply chain. The beef operations include processing live cattle and fabricating dressed beef carcasses into primal and sub-primal meat cuts and case-ready products. This segment also includes sales from allied products, such as hides and variety meats. The pork operations include processing live market hogs and fabricating pork carcasses into primal and sub-primal cuts and case-ready products. This segment also includes the live swine group and related allied product processing activities. Prepared food operations include the manufacture and marketing of frozen and refrigerated food products. Products include pepperoni, bacon, beef and pork pizza toppings, pizza crusts, flour and corn tortilla products, appetizers, prepared meals, ethnic foods, soups, sauces, side dishes, meat dishes and processed meats. Products are marketed domestically to food retailers, foodservice distributors, restaurant operators and noncommercial foodservice establishments such as schools, hotel chains, healthcare facilities, the military and other food processors as well as to international markets. The company's international operations include Tyson Rizhao, Tyson Dalong, Tyson Nantong, Godrej Tyson Foods and Tyson Mexico Trading Company. These subsidiaries are engaged in the breading, production, processing and packaging of Tyson food products. Walmart Inc. accounts for 17.3% of the firm's annual revenue. In November 2018, Tyson acquired Keystone Foods LLC, a top supplier of meat to McDonald's Corp. and other chains, for $2.16 billion. In 2018, the firm sold its pizza crust business, the Sara Lee frozen bakery brand and Vans businesses.

FINANCIAL DATA:
Note: Data for latest year may not have been available at press time.

In U.S. $	2018	2017	2016	2015	2014	2013
Revenue	40,052,000,000	38,260,000,000	36,881,000,000	41,373,000,000	37,580,000,000	34,374,000,000
R&D Expense						
Operating Income	3,055,000,000	2,931,000,000	2,833,000,000	2,169,000,000	1,430,000,000	1,375,000,000
Operating Margin %		.08%	.08%	.05%	.04%	.04%
SGA Expense	2,071,000,000	2,152,000,000	1,864,000,000	1,748,000,000	1,255,000,000	983,000,000
Net Income	3,024,000,000	1,774,000,000	1,768,000,000	1,220,000,000	864,000,000	778,000,000
Operating Cash Flow	2,963,000,000	2,599,000,000	2,716,000,000	2,570,000,000	1,178,000,000	1,314,000,000
Capital Expenditure	1,200,000,000	1,069,000,000	695,000,000	854,000,000	632,000,000	558,000,000
EBITDA	4,038,000,000	3,668,000,000	3,552,000,000	2,925,000,000	1,914,000,000	1,921,000,000
Return on Assets %		.07%	.08%	.05%	.05%	.06%
Return on Equity %		.18%	.18%	.13%	.11%	.13%
Debt to Equity		0.882	0.645	0.62	0.848	0.306

CONTACT INFORMATION:
Phone: 479 290-4000 Fax: 479 290-7984
Toll-Free: 800-643-3410
Address: 2200 W. Don Tyson Pkwy., Springdale, AR 72762 United States

STOCK TICKER/OTHER:
Stock Ticker: TSN
Employees: 121,000
Parent Company:

Exchange: NYS
Fiscal Year Ends: 09/30

SALARIES/BONUSES:
Top Exec. Salary: $581,096 Bonus: $2,700,000
Second Exec. Salary: $1,208,442 Bonus: $

OTHER THOUGHTS:
Estimated Female Officers or Directors: 4
Hot Spot for Advancement for Women/Minorities: Y

Uber Technologies Inc

uber.com

NAIC Code: 561599

TYPES OF BUSINESS:
Car Ride Dispatch Service, Mobile App-Based
Freight Truck Dispatch Service
Restaurant Meal Delivery Service
Transportation Marketplace Technologies
Self-Driving Truck Technologies
Self-Driving Car Technologies

BRANDS/DIVISIONS/AFFILIATES:
UberEATS
Uber Freight
JUMP Bikes
Uber for Business
Uber Air

CONTACTS: Note: Officers with more than one job title may be intentionally listed here more than once.
Dara Khosrowshahi, CEO
Nelson Chai, CFO
Ronald Sugar, Chairman of the Board
Glen Ceremony, Chief Accounting Officer
Tony West, Chief Legal Officer
Thuan Pham, Chief Technology Officer
Travis Kalanick, Co-Founder
Manik Gupta, Other Executive Officer
Nikki Krishnamurthy, Other Executive Officer
Andrew Macdonald, Senior VP, Divisional
Jill Hazelbaker, Senior VP, Divisional
Jason Droege, Vice President, Divisional

GROWTH PLANS/SPECIAL FEATURES:
Uber, Inc. is a California-based creator of the Uber mobile app which connects drivers and ridesharing services with passengers. The application serves over 630 cities worldwide and is in cities in countries throughout the Americas, Europe, the Middle East, Africa and Asia Pacific. Upon receiving a ride request, Uber sends the closest drivers available to fulfill it. Riders can rate their experiences with drivers for other riders to view. The company retains a fee from each ride that it books and then passes the balance of the fare to the drivers. To begin their screening, drivers must upload their license, registration and proof of insurance, as well as other necessary information. Once approved, they can drive with Uber as an independent contractor and are provided everything needed to be a successful Uber driver. Uber has expanded very aggressively on a worldwide basis, although it merged its operations in China with local competitor Didi after incurring massive losses in China. This enabled the firm to concentrate expansion efforts and cash in on other markets, including the vast market in India. Uber has been purchasing cars in India, and leasing them out to local drivers who want to work with the firm. Uber is also expanding into delivery services of many types. Additional Uber divisions include: UberEATS, a restaurant-prepared meal delivery service available in dozens of cities worldwide; Uber Freight, connecting shippers with trucks; JUMP Bikes, featuring dockless bikes and e-assist; and Uber for Business, an all-in-one solution that simplifies how an organization gets around, whether it be a ride to the airport or a car for clients. As of late-2018 Uber was developing Uber Air, to enable shared, multimodal air transportation between suburbs, cities and ultimately within cities in 2023.

FINANCIAL DATA: Note: Data for latest year may not have been available at press time.

In U.S. $	2018	2017	2016	2015	2014	2013
Revenue	11,270,000,000	7,932,000,000	3,845,000,000			
R&D Expense	1,505,000,000	1,201,000,000	864,000,000			
Operating Income	-3,033,000,000	-4,080,000,000	-3,023,000,000			
Operating Margin %						
SGA Expense	5,233,000,000	4,787,000,000	2,575,000,000			
Net Income	997,000,000	-4,033,000,000	-370,000,000			
Operating Cash Flow	-1,541,000,000	-1,418,000,000	-2,913,000,000			
Capital Expenditure	558,000,000	829,000,000	1,635,000,000			
EBITDA	2,386,000,000	-3,586,000,000	-2,537,000,000			
Return on Assets %						
Return on Equity %						
Debt to Equity						

CONTACT INFORMATION:
Phone: 415-986-2715   Fax: 415-986-2104
Toll-Free:
Address: 1455 Market St., Ste. 400, San Francisco, CA 94103 United States

STOCK TICKER/OTHER:
Stock Ticker: UBER
Employees: 22,263
Parent Company:

Exchange: NYS
Fiscal Year Ends: 12/31

SALARIES/BONUSES:
Top Exec. Salary: $1,000,000   Bonus: $2,000,000
Second Exec. Salary: $500,000   Bonus: $1,000,000

OTHER THOUGHTS:
Estimated Female Officers or Directors: 1
Hot Spot for Advancement for Women/Minorities:

United Continental Holdings Inc

newsroom.united.com/corporate-fact-sheet

NAIC Code: 481111

TYPES OF BUSINESS:
Airline
Air Freight
Regional Airlines

BRANDS/DIVISIONS/AFFILIATES:
United Airlines Inc
United Express
MileagePlus

CONTACTS:
Note: Officers with more than one job title may be intentionally listed here more than once.

Oscar Munoz, CEO
Gerald Laderman, CFO
Jane Garvey, Chairman of the Board
Chris Kenny, Chief Accounting Officer
Brett Hart, Chief Administrative Officer
Gregory Hart, COO
Kate Gebo, Executive VP, Divisional
Linda Jojo, Executive VP, Divisional
Andrew Nocella, Executive VP
J. Kirby, President

GROWTH PLANS/SPECIAL FEATURES:

United Continental Holdings, Inc. is the holding company for United Airlines, Inc. The airline operates approximately 4,800 flights per day to 353 airports across five continents. Its route network includes U.S. mainland hubs in Chicago, Denver, Houston, Los Angeles, New York/Newark, San Francisco and Washington D.C. United and United Express operated more than 1.7 million flights carrying over 158 million customers during 2018. The company is a member of the Star Alliance, which offers more than 18,400 daily flights to 1,300 airports in 191 countries through its member airlines. United operates 770 mainline aircraft and the airline's United Express carriers operate 559 regional aircraft. The mainline fleet consists of Airbus A319, A320, Boeing 737 and 757 narrow-body aircraft, as well as Boeing 767, 777 and 787 wide-body aircraft. The regional fleet consists of Bombardier Q300, Canadair CRJ 200, CRJ 700, and Embraer 145 and E175 aircraft. United is a founding member of Star Alliance, which provides service to 193 countries via 28 member airlines. United's MileagePlus loyalty reward program enables members to earn elite travel benefits, including premier access airport services and merchandise redemption options.

United offers its employees travel passes; medical, dental, vision, life, personal and business accident insurance; flexible spending accounts; a 401(k) plan and profit sharing plans; a perfect attendance program; and on-time bonuses.

FINANCIAL DATA:
Note: Data for latest year may not have been available at press time.

In U.S. $	2018	2017	2016	2015	2014	2013
Revenue	41,303,000,000	37,736,000,000	36,556,000,000	37,864,000,000	38,901,000,000	38,279,000,000
R&D Expense						
Operating Income	3,779,000,000	3,674,000,000	4,976,000,000	5,492,000,000	2,816,000,000	1,769,000,000
Operating Margin %						
SGA Expense	1,558,000,000	1,349,000,000	1,303,000,000	1,342,000,000	1,373,000,000	1,390,000,000
Net Income	2,129,000,000	2,131,000,000	2,263,000,000	7,340,000,000	1,132,000,000	571,000,000
Operating Cash Flow	6,181,000,000	3,413,000,000	5,542,000,000	5,992,000,000	2,634,000,000	1,444,000,000
Capital Expenditure	4,177,000,000	3,998,000,000	3,223,000,000	2,747,000,000	2,005,000,000	2,164,000,000
EBITDA	5,557,000,000	5,707,000,000	6,338,000,000	6,658,000,000	3,490,000,000	2,962,000,000
Return on Assets %						
Return on Equity %						
Debt to Equity						

CONTACT INFORMATION:
Phone: 872-825-4000   Fax: 847 700-2214
Toll-Free:
Address: 233 South Wacker Dr., Chicago, IL 60606 United States

SALARIES/BONUSES:
Top Exec. Salary: $1,250,000   Bonus: $
Second Exec. Salary: $875,000   Bonus: $

STOCK TICKER/OTHER:
Stock Ticker: UAL
Employees: 92,000
Parent Company:

Exchange: NAS
Fiscal Year Ends: 12/31

OTHER THOUGHTS:
Estimated Female Officers or Directors: 2
Hot Spot for Advancement for Women/Minorities: Y

Sales, profits and employees may be estimates. Financial information, benefits and other data can change quickly and may vary from those stated here.

United Natural Foods Inc

NAIC Code: 424410

www.unfi.com

TYPES OF BUSINESS:
Food Distribution
Natural & Organic Foods Distribution
Nutritional Supplements Distribution
Personal Care Products Distribution
Retail Stores

BRANDS/DIVISIONS/AFFILIATES:
Tony's Fine Foods
Albert's Organics Inc
Nor-Cal Produce Inc
UNFI Canada, Inc
Select Nutrition
United Natural Trading Co
Woodstock Farms Manufacturing
Blue Marble Brands

CONTACTS:
Note: Officers with more than one job title may be intentionally listed here more than once.

Sean Griffin, CEO, Subsidiary
Michael Stigers, CEO, Subsidiary
Steven Spinner, CEO
Michael Zechmeister, CFO
Eric Dorne, Chief Administrative Officer
Christopher Testa, Chief Marketing Officer
Michael Funk, Co-Founder
Jill Sutton, General Counsel
Danielle Benedict, Other Executive Officer
Paul Green, Other Executive Officer

GROWTH PLANS/SPECIAL FEATURES:

United Natural Foods, Inc. (UNFI) is a national distributor of natural and organic foods and related products. The company, which is a Certified Organic Distributor, carries more than 100,000 natural and organic products. The firm offers six types of products: grocery and general merchandise; personal care items; produce; nutritional supplements; sports nutrition perishables; and frozen foods and bulk and food service products. UNFI serves over 43,000 customers, including supernatural chains (large chains of natural foods supermarkets), independently owned natural products retailers and conventional supermarkets located across the U.S. The firm's operations consist of two principal divisions: wholesale and manufacturing & branded products. The wholesale segment includes the operations of its distributors Tony's Fine Foods; Albert's Organics, Inc.; UNFI Canada, Inc.; and Select Nutrition. Tony's distributes specialty protein, cheese, deli, foodservice and bakery goods. Albert's, which includes the operations of Nor-Cal Produce, Inc., distributes organically grown produce and non-produce perishable items. UNFI Canada is a natural, organic and specialty distribution business in Canada. Select Nutrition distributes vitamins, minerals and supplements. The manufacturing & branded products segment is comprised of subsidiary United Natural Trading Co. (doing business as Woodstock Farms Manufacturing) and Blue Marble Brands. Woodstock Farms is an importer, processor, packager and wholesale distributor of natural and organic products, trail mixes, nuts, seeds, dried fruit and confections. The Blue Marble Brands portfolio is a collection of 17 organic, natural and specialty food brands representing more than 750 unique products. Field Day brand is primarily sold to customers in the independent natural products retailer channel. In October 2018, UNFI completed the acquisition of Supervalu, Inc., a publicly traded food wholesaler, for $2.9 billion.

UNFI offers employees medical, dental, life and disability insurance; an assistance program; and educational assistance.

FINANCIAL DATA:
Note: Data for latest year may not have been available at press time.

In U.S. $	2018	2017	2016	2015	2014	2013
Revenue	10,226,680,000	9,274,471,000	8,470,286,000	8,184,978,000	6,794,447,000	6,064,355,000
R&D Expense						
Operating Income	243,238,000	232,889,000	229,661,000	242,760,000	210,788,000	187,123,000
Operating Margin %						
SGA Expense						
Net Income	165,670,000	130,155,000	125,766,000	138,734,000	125,482,000	107,854,000
Operating Cash Flow	109,472,000	280,776,000	296,609,000	48,864,000	62,419,000	44,331,000
Capital Expenditure	44,608,000	56,112,000	41,375,000	129,134,000	147,303,000	66,554,000
EBITDA	316,847,000	317,588,000	295,487,000	308,067,000	263,919,000	222,411,000
Return on Assets %						
Return on Equity %						
Debt to Equity						

CONTACT INFORMATION:
Phone: 401 528-8634   Fax:
Toll-Free:
Address: 313 Iron Horse Way, Providence, RI 02908 United States

SALARIES/BONUSES:
Top Exec. Salary: $942,385   Bonus: $
Second Exec. Salary: $582,577   Bonus: $

STOCK TICKER/OTHER:
Stock Ticker: UNFI   Exchange: NYS
Employees: 9,700   Fiscal Year Ends: 07/31
Parent Company:

OTHER THOUGHTS:
Estimated Female Officers or Directors: 3
Hot Spot for Advancement for Women/Minorities: Y

Plunkett Research, Ltd.

United Parcel Service Inc (UPS)

NAIC Code: 492110

www.ups.com

TYPES OF BUSINESS:

Couriers and Express Delivery Services
Logistics Services
Supply Chain Services
International Products & Services
Ground & Air Delivery Services
Visibility & Technology Services

BRANDS/DIVISIONS/AFFILIATES:

UPS Hundredweight Services
UPS Next Day Air
UPS Freight
Mail Boxes Etc
UPS Supply Chain Solutions
UPS Capital

CONTACTS: Note: Officers with more than one job title may be intentionally listed here more than once.

David Abney, CEO
Richard Peretz, CFO
Juan Perez, Chief Information Officer
Kevin Warren, Chief Marketing Officer
James Barber, COO
Kate Gutmann, Other Executive Officer
Scott Price, Other Executive Officer
Teri Mcclure, Other Executive Officer
Nando Cesarone, President, Divisional
George Willis, President, Geographical
Norman Brothers, Senior VP

GROWTH PLANS/SPECIAL FEATURES:

United Parcel Service, Inc. (UPS) is one of the world's largest package delivery companies and a global provider of supply chain management. It delivers packages each business day to approximately 9 million receivers in over 220 countries and territories. The firm delivers an average of 20 million pieces per day worldwide. It is also a major provider of less-than-truckload (LTL) transportation services. Offerings include domestic and international package products and services and supply chain and freight services. The U.S. domestic package products and services business delivers packages traveling by ground or air transportation. In addition to the standard ground delivery products, UPS Hundredweight Services offers guaranteed, time-definite service to customers sending multiple package shipments. UPS Next Day Air offers several service options guaranteeing next business day delivery by 8:00AM, 10:30AM, noon, 3-4:30PM or by the end of the day in the 48 contiguous U.S. states and limited areas of Alaska. International services include guaranteed early morning, morning and noon delivery to major cities around the world as well as scheduled day-definite air and ground services. The supply chain and freight segment consists of its forwarding and logistics operations, UPS Freight and other related businesses. The division's worldwide services include supply chain design and management, freight distribution, customs brokerage, mail and consulting services. UPS Freight offers a variety of LTL/truckload services to customers in North America. Other business units within this segment include Mail Boxes Etc.; UPS Supply Chain Solutions; and UPS Capital.

U.S. employees at UPS receive benefits including tuition assistance; medical, prescription, dental, life and vision coverage; and health care spending accounts.

FINANCIAL DATA: Note: Data for latest year may not have been available at press time.

In U.S. $	2018	2017	2016	2015	2014	2013
Revenue	71,861,000,000	65,872,000,000	60,906,000,000	58,363,000,000	58,232,000,000	55,438,000,000
R&D Expense						
Operating Income	7,024,000,000	7,529,000,000	5,467,000,000	7,668,000,000	4,968,000,000	7,034,000,000
Operating Margin %		.11%	.09%	.13%	.09%	.13%
SGA Expense						
Net Income	4,791,000,000	4,910,000,000	3,431,000,000	4,844,000,000	3,032,000,000	4,372,000,000
Operating Cash Flow	12,711,000,000	1,479,000,000	6,473,000,000	7,430,000,000	5,726,000,000	7,304,000,000
Capital Expenditure	6,283,000,000	5,227,000,000	2,965,000,000	2,379,000,000	2,328,000,000	2,065,000,000
EBITDA	8,831,000,000	9,883,000,000	7,741,000,000	9,767,000,000	6,913,000,000	8,921,000,000
Return on Assets %		.11%	.09%	.13%	.08%	.12%
Return on Equity %		6.99%	2.39%	2.10%	.70%	.79%
Debt to Equity		20.278	30.602	4.581	4.607	1.672

CONTACT INFORMATION:

Phone: 404 828-6000 Fax: 404 828-6562
Toll-Free: 800-874-5877
Address: 55 Glenlake Parkway, NE, Atlanta, GA 30328 United States

STOCK TICKER/OTHER:

Stock Ticker: UPS
Employees: 453,000
Parent Company:

Exchange: NYS
Fiscal Year Ends: 12/31

SALARIES/BONUSES:

Top Exec. Salary: $350,000 Bonus: $950,000
Second Exec. Salary: $1,234,992 Bonus: $

OTHER THOUGHTS:

Estimated Female Officers or Directors: 4
Hot Spot for Advancement for Women/Minorities: Y

Sales, profits and employees may be estimates. Financial information, benefits and other data can change quickly and may vary from those stated here.

United States Cellular Corporation

www.uscellular.com

NAIC Code: 517210

TYPES OF BUSINESS:
Mobile Phone and Wireless Services

BRANDS/DIVISIONS/AFFILIATES:
Telephone and Data Systems Inc

CONTACTS:
Note: Officers with more than one job title may be intentionally listed here more than once.

Kenneth Meyers, CEO
Steven Campbell, CFO
Leroy Carlson, Chairman of the Board
Douglas Chambers, Chief Accounting Officer
Michael Irizarry, Chief Technology Officer
Paul-Henri Denuit, Director Emeritus
James Barr, Director Emeritus
Jay Ellison, Executive VP
Deirdre Drake, Executive VP

GROWTH PLANS/SPECIAL FEATURES:

United States Cellular Corporation (U.S. Cellular) is a leading U.S. wireless telecommunications firm, providing wireless voice and data services to 5 million customers nationwide. The company maintains interests in consolidated and investment wireless licenses that cover portions of 22 states and a total population of 31 million people. U.S. Cellular offers a range of wireless devices such as handsets, modems, mobile hotspots, home phone and tablets for use by its customers. The firm has also installed service repair programs at certain facilities, which assist customers with over-the-counter exchanges, Smartphone advance exchanges, loaner phones, device recycling and device returns. U.S. Cellular sells wireless devices to agents and other third-party distributors for resale. The wireless services segment provides a variety of packaged voice and data pricing plans. The company offers post-pay plans and prepaid plans. Moreover, U.S. Cellular services include connected home, a self-installed home security and automation system for home monitoring purposes. U.S. Cellular also offers data-services and app-like experiences to non-smartphone devices via a technology known as binary runtime environment for wireless (BREW). These enhanced data services include downloading news, weather, sports information, games, ring tones and other services. In addition, U.S. Cellular has recently engaged in VoLTE (voice over long-term evolution) trials, with plans to upgrade equipment in select markets to allow the trial processes to continue following the services official launch. Telephone and Data Systems, Inc. owns approximately 82% of the company.

Employee benefits include medical, dental and vision coverage; life insurance and AD&D; short- and long-term disability; a 401(k) and Roth IRA; a pension plan; and tuition reimbursement.

FINANCIAL DATA:
Note: Data for latest year may not have been available at press time.

In U.S. $	2018	2017	2016	2015	2014	2013
Revenue	3,967,000,000	3,890,000,000	3,939,000,000	3,996,853,000	3,892,747,000	3,918,836,000
R&D Expense						
Operating Income	150,000,000	60,000,000		68,816,000	-267,744,000	-324,775,000
Operating Margin %		.02%		.02%	-.07%	-.08%
SGA Expense	1,388,000,000	1,412,000,000	1,480,000,000	1,493,730,000	1,591,914,000	1,677,395,000
Net Income	150,000,000	12,000,000	48,000,000	241,347,000	-42,812,000	140,038,000
Operating Cash Flow	709,000,000	469,000,000	501,000,000	555,114,000	172,342,000	290,897,000
Capital Expenditure	520,000,000	654,000,000	496,000,000	866,400,000	643,233,000	734,402,000
EBITDA	971,000,000	456,000,000	813,000,000	1,096,278,000	604,679,000	1,105,400,000
Return on Assets %		.00%	.01%	.04%	-.01%	.02%
Return on Equity %		.00%	.01%	.07%	-.01%	.04%
Debt to Equity		0.441	0.445	0.457	0.349	0.259

CONTACT INFORMATION:
Phone: 773 399-8900 Fax: 773 399-8936
Toll-Free: 888-944-9400
Address: 8410 W. Bryn Mawr Ave., Ste. 700, Chicago, IL 60631 United States

STOCK TICKER/OTHER:
Stock Ticker: USM
Employees: 6,300
Parent Company: Telephone and Data Systems Inc
Exchange: NYS
Fiscal Year Ends: 12/31

SALARIES/BONUSES:
Top Exec. Salary: $1,051,000 Bonus: $1,280,400
Second Exec. Salary: $650,400 Bonus: $234,130

OTHER THOUGHTS:
Estimated Female Officers or Directors: 6
Hot Spot for Advancement for Women/Minorities: Y

United States Steel Corporation

www.ussteel.com

NAIC Code: 331110

TYPES OF BUSINESS:
Steel Manufacturing

BRANDS/DIVISIONS/AFFILIATES:
U.S. Steel Kosice

CONTACTS:
Note: Officers with more than one job title may be intentionally listed here more than once.

Kimberly Fast, Assistant Controller
David Burritt, CEO
Kevin Bradley, CFO
David Sutherland, Chairman of the Board
Duane Holloway, Chief Compliance Officer
Douglas Matthews, Other Corporate Officer
A. Melnkovic, Other Executive Officer
Christine Breves, Other Executive Officer
James Bruno, President, Geographical
Scott Buckiso, Senior VP, Divisional
Sara Greenstein, Senior VP, Divisional

GROWTH PLANS/SPECIAL FEATURES:

United States Steel Corporation is an integrated steel producer of flat-rolled and tubular products with major production operations in North America and Europe. The firm has an annual raw steel production capability of 22 million net tons (17 million tons in the U.S. and 5 million tons in Europe). United States Steel has three reportable operating segments: flat-rolled products (flat-rolled), United States Steel Europe (USSE) and tubular products (tubular). The flat-rolled segment includes the operating results of United States Steel's North American integrated steel mills and equity investees involved in the production of slabs, rounds, strip mill plates, sheets and tin mill products, as well as all iron ore and coke production facilities in the U.S. Flat-rolled has annual raw steel production capability of 17 million tons. The USSE segment, consisting solely of U.S. Steel Kosice in Slovakia, produced 5 million ton of raw steel, averaging 100% capacity in 2018. The tubular segment includes the operating results of United States Steel's tubular production facilities, primarily in the U.S., and equity investees in the U.S. and Brazil. These operations produce and sell seamless and electric resistance welded steel casing and tubing, standard and line pipe and mechanical tubing and primarily serve customers in the oil, gas and petrochemical markets. Tubular's annual production capability is approximately 1.6 million tons. As an integrated producer, United States Steel's primary raw materials are iron units in the form of iron ore pellets and sinter ore, carbon units in the form of coal and coke, and steel scrap.

United States Steel offers its employees health coverage, life insurance, a 401(k) plan, a pension and short- & long-term disability.

FINANCIAL DATA:
Note: Data for latest year may not have been available at press time.

In U.S. $	2018	2017	2016	2015	2014	2013
Revenue	14,178,000,000	12,250,000,000	10,261,000,000	11,574,000,000	17,507,000,000	17,424,000,000
R&D Expense						
Operating Income	1,019,000,000	518,000,000	-122,000,000	-528,000,000	914,000,000	114,000,000
Operating Margin %		.04%	-.01%	-.05%	.05%	.01%
SGA Expense	336,000,000	375,000,000	255,000,000	415,000,000	523,000,000	610,000,000
Net Income	1,115,000,000	387,000,000	-440,000,000	-1,642,000,000	102,000,000	-1,672,000,000
Operating Cash Flow	938,000,000	802,000,000	727,000,000	359,000,000	1,492,000,000	414,000,000
Capital Expenditure	1,001,000,000	505,000,000	306,000,000	500,000,000	419,000,000	489,000,000
EBITDA	1,501,000,000	1,028,000,000	321,000,000	-698,000,000	1,031,000,000	-1,282,000,000
Return on Assets %		.04%	-.05%	-.15%	.01%	-.12%
Return on Equity %		.14%	-.19%	-.53%	.03%	-.49%
Debt to Equity		0.813	1.311	1.279	0.821	1.08

CONTACT INFORMATION:
Phone: 412 433-1121 Fax: 412 433-1167
Toll-Free:
Address: 600 Grant St., Pittsburgh, PA 15219 United States

STOCK TICKER/OTHER:
Stock Ticker: X
Employees: 29,800
Parent Company:

Exchange: NYS
Fiscal Year Ends: 12/31

SALARIES/BONUSES:
Top Exec. Salary: $1,000,000 Bonus: $
Second Exec. Salary: $700,008 Bonus: $

OTHER THOUGHTS:
Estimated Female Officers or Directors: 2
Hot Spot for Advancement for Women/Minorities:

Sales, profits and employees may be estimates. Financial information, benefits and other data can change quickly and may vary from those stated here.

United Technologies Corporation

www.utc.com

NAIC Code: 336412

TYPES OF BUSINESS:
Aircraft Engine and Engine Parts Manufacturing
Aviation Technologies
Avionics and Instruments
Aircraft Parts & Maintenance

BRANDS/DIVISIONS/AFFILIATES:
Otis
Carrier
Pratt & Whitney
Collins Aerospace
Rockwell Collins Inc

CONTACTS:
Note: Officers with more than one job title may be intentionally listed here more than once.

Robert Ortberg, CEO, Divisional
David Whitehouse, Treasurer
David Gitlin, CEO, Divisional
Gregory Hayes, CEO
Akhil Johri, CFO
Robert Bailey, Chief Accounting Officer
Michael Dumais, Executive VP, Divisional
Charles Gill, Executive VP
Elizabeth Amato, Executive VP
Judith Marks, President, Divisional
Robert Mcdonough, President, Divisional
Robert Leduc, President, Divisional

GROWTH PLANS/SPECIAL FEATURES:

United Technologies Corporation (UTC) provides high technology products and services to building aerospace and defense industries worldwide. The company operates through four principle segments and brands: Otis, Carrier, Pratt & Whitney and Collins Aerospace. Otis manufactures, sells, installs and services a wide range of passenger and freight elevators for low-, medium-, and high-speed applications, as well as a broad line of escalators and moving walkways. Carrier provides fire safety, security, building automation, heating, ventilation, air conditioning and refrigeration systems and services, with a focus on promoting safe, smart and sustainable buildings. Pratt & Whitney is a global leader in aircraft propulsion, designing, manufacturing and servicing aircraft engines, auxiliary and ground power units, and small turbojet propulsion products. Last, Collins Aerospace supplies aircraft systems and components, as well as advanced aerospace and defense products, for business, military and international customers. In November 2018, UTC completed its acquisition of Rockwell Collins, Inc. Subsequently, the firm announced its intention to separate into three independent companies: United Technologies, which would include Collins Aerospace Systems and Pratt & Whitney, supplying systems to the aerospace and defense industry; Otis; and Carrier. The separations are expected to be complete in 2020. In June 2019, the firm and Raytheon Company announced plans to merge. The new firm would be named Raytheon Technologies Corp. The transaction is expected to close in the first half of 2020.

FINANCIAL DATA:
Note: Data for latest year may not have been available at press time.

In U.S. $	2018	2017	2016	2015	2014	2013
Revenue	66,501,000,000	59,837,000,000	57,244,000,000	56,098,000,000	65,100,000,000	62,626,000,000
R&D Expense	2,462,000,000	2,387,000,000	2,337,000,000	2,279,000,000	2,635,000,000	2,529,000,000
Operating Income	8,553,000,000	8,672,000,000	8,172,000,000	7,291,000,000	9,769,000,000	9,209,000,000
Operating Margin %		.14%	.14%	.13%	.15%	.15%
SGA Expense	7,066,000,000	6,183,000,000	6,060,000,000	5,886,000,000	6,500,000,000	6,718,000,000
Net Income	5,269,000,000	4,552,000,000	5,055,000,000	7,608,000,000	6,220,000,000	5,721,000,000
Operating Cash Flow	6,322,000,000	5,631,000,000	3,880,000,000	6,326,000,000	7,336,000,000	6,877,000,000
Capital Expenditure	2,302,000,000	2,394,000,000	2,087,000,000	2,089,000,000	2,304,000,000	2,410,000,000
EBITDA	11,938,000,000	10,920,000,000	10,256,000,000	9,275,000,000	11,894,000,000	11,167,000,000
Return on Assets %		.05%	.06%	.09%	.07%	.06%
Return on Equity %		.16%	.18%	.26%	.20%	.20%
Debt to Equity		0.844	0.787	0.706	0.573	0.62

CONTACT INFORMATION:
Phone: 860 728-7000 Fax: 860 728-7028
Toll-Free:
Address: 10 Farm Springs Rd., Farmington, CT 06032 United States

SALARIES/BONUSES:
Top Exec. Salary: $1,575,000 Bonus: $3,500,000
Second Exec. Salary: $868,750 Bonus: $1,400,000

STOCK TICKER/OTHER:
Stock Ticker: UTX Exchange: NYS
Employees: 202,000 Fiscal Year Ends: 12/31
Parent Company:

OTHER THOUGHTS:
Estimated Female Officers or Directors: 2
Hot Spot for Advancement for Women/Minorities: Y

Sales, profits and employees may be estimates. Financial information, benefits and other data can change quickly and may vary from those stated here.

UnitedHealth Group Inc

www.unitedhealthgroup.com

NAIC Code: 524114

TYPES OF BUSINESS:
Medical Insurance
Wellness Plans
Dental & Vision Insurance
Health Information Technology
Physician Practice Groups
Pharmacy Benefits Management
PBM

BRANDS/DIVISIONS/AFFILIATES:
United Healthcare
Optum
DaVita Medical Group
HealthCare Partners Nevada
Intermountain Healthcare

CONTACTS:
Note: Officers with more than one job title may be intentionally listed here more than once.

Steven Nelson, CEO, Subsidiary
Andrew Witty, CEO, Subsidiary
David Wichmann, CEO
John Rex, CFO
Stephen Hemsley, Chairman of the Board
Thomas Roos, Chief Accounting Officer
Marianne Short, Executive VP
D. Wilson, Executive VP

GROWTH PLANS/SPECIAL FEATURES:
UnitedHealth Group, Inc. offers health benefits and services in all 50 U.S. states and more than 130 other countries. The firm offers its products and services through two distinct businesses: UnitedHealthcare and Optum. UnitedHealthcare is the group's health benefits platform, offering state Medicaid and community programs, employer-sponsored and individual health benefits, health benefits for those eligible for Medicare and health benefits globally. Optum is the group's health services platform, offering information and technology-enabled health services for modernizing health systems and improving the health of members and communities. Health services by Optum include population health management, health care delivery, health care analytics, healthcare information, healthcare technology and pharmacy care services. In June 2019, UnitedHealth completed its acquisition of DaVita Medical Group, including HealthCare Partners Nevada, DaVita's primary care practice in southern Nevada, which will be renamed as Intermountain Healthcare.

UnitedHealth Group offers comprehensive benefits, retirement options, tuition reimbursement and a variety of employee assistance programs.

FINANCIAL DATA:
Note: Data for latest year may not have been available at press time.

In U.S. $	2018	2017	2016	2015	2014	2013
Revenue	224,871,000,000	200,136,000,000	184,012,000,000	156,397,000,000	129,695,000,000	121,744,000,000
R&D Expense						
Operating Income	15,968,000,000	14,186,000,000	12,102,000,000	10,311,000,000	9,495,000,000	8,878,000,000
Operating Margin %		.08%	.07%	.07%	.08%	.08%
SGA Expense						
Net Income	11,986,000,000	10,558,000,000	7,017,000,000	5,813,000,000	5,619,000,000	5,625,000,000
Operating Cash Flow	15,713,000,000	13,596,000,000	9,795,000,000	9,740,000,000	8,051,000,000	6,991,000,000
Capital Expenditure	2,063,000,000	2,023,000,000	1,705,000,000	1,556,000,000	1,525,000,000	1,307,000,000
EBITDA	19,772,000,000	17,454,000,000	14,985,000,000	12,714,000,000	11,752,000,000	10,998,000,000
Return on Assets %		.08%	.06%	.06%	.07%	.07%
Return on Equity %		.25%	.19%	.18%	.17%	.18%
Debt to Equity		0.604	0.673	0.753	0.493	0.463

CONTACT INFORMATION:
Phone: 952 936-1300 Fax: 952 936-0044
Toll-Free: 800-328-5979
Address: 9900 Bren Rd. E., Minnetonka, MN 55343 United States

SALARIES/BONUSES:
Top Exec. Salary: $1,300,000 Bonus: $
Second Exec. Salary: $1,000,000 Bonus: $

STOCK TICKER/OTHER:
Stock Ticker: UNH
Employees: 300,000
Parent Company:

Exchange: NYS
Fiscal Year Ends: 12/31

OTHER THOUGHTS:
Estimated Female Officers or Directors: 4
Hot Spot for Advancement for Women/Minorities: Y

Universal Health Services Inc

www.uhsinc.com

NAIC Code: 622110

TYPES OF BUSINESS:
General Medical and Surgical Hospitals
Radiation Oncology Centers
Behavioral Health Hospitals
Surgical Hospitals
Administrative Services
Physician Recruitment
Facilities Planning

BRANDS/DIVISIONS/AFFILIATES:

CONTACTS:
Note: Officers with more than one job title may be intentionally listed here more than once.
Alan Miller, CEO
Steve Filton, CFO
Marc Miller, Director
Marvin Pember, Executive VP

GROWTH PLANS/SPECIAL FEATURES:

Universal Health Services, Inc. (UHS), in business for more than 40 years, owns and operates through its subsidiaries acute care hospitals, outpatient facilities and behavioral healthcare facilities. UHS owns and/or operates more than 350 inpatient facilities and 37 outpatient and other facilities located in the U.S., the U.K. and Puerto Rico. Among the acute care facilities in the U.S., 26 are inpatient acute care hospitals, nine are free-standing emergency departments, six are outpatient centers and one is a surgical hospital. Among the behavioral healthcare facilities: the U.S. comprises 188 inpatient and 19 outpatient facilities; the U.K. comprises 133 inpatient and two outpatient facilities; and Puerto Rico comprises three inpatient facilities. During 2019, UHS received approval from the City of West Allis Common Council (in Wisconsin) to build a new state-of-the-art behavioral health hospital, and expects to break ground by the end of 2019 and open the facility in 2021.

The company offers its employees medical, dental, vision, life, AD&D and disability insurance; coverage availability for blended families; family and caregiving support; wellness support; a savings plan; an employee stock purchase plan; and flexible spending accounts.

FINANCIAL DATA:
Note: Data for latest year may not have been available at press time.

In U.S. $	2018	2017	2016	2015	2014	2013
Revenue	10,772,280,000	10,409,870,000	9,766,210,000	9,043,451,000	8,065,326,000	7,283,822,000
R&D Expense						
Operating Income	1,175,262,000	1,280,178,000	1,276,072,000	1,243,580,000	1,071,574,000	954,439,000
Operating Margin %		.12%	.13%	.14%	.13%	.13%
SGA Expense	106,094,000	103,127,000	97,324,000	94,973,000	93,993,000	97,758,000
Net Income	779,705,000	752,303,000	702,409,000	680,528,000	545,343,000	510,733,000
Operating Cash Flow	1,340,893,000	1,182,581,000	1,288,474,000	1,020,898,000	1,035,876,000	884,241,000
Capital Expenditure	775,426,000	580,384,000	1,133,742,000	912,976,000	822,536,000	371,129,000
EBITDA	1,641,671,000	1,716,807,000	1,681,473,000	1,640,952,000	1,405,003,000	1,317,607,000
Return on Assets %		.07%	.07%	.07%	.06%	.06%
Return on Equity %		.16%	.16%	.17%	.16%	.17%
Debt to Equity		0.70	0.889	0.797	0.859	0.988

CONTACT INFORMATION:
Phone: 610 768-3300 Fax: 610 768-3336
Toll-Free:
Address: 367 S. Gulph Rd., King Of Prussia, PA 19406 United States

SALARIES/BONUSES:
Top Exec. Salary: $1,665,064 Bonus: $1,000,000
Second Exec. Salary: $786,068 Bonus: $

STOCK TICKER/OTHER:
Stock Ticker: UHS
Employees: 62,230
Parent Company:

Exchange: NYS
Fiscal Year Ends: 12/31

OTHER THOUGHTS:
Estimated Female Officers or Directors: 2
Hot Spot for Advancement for Women/Minorities: Y

Sales, profits and employees may be estimates. Financial information, benefits and other data can change quickly and may vary from those stated here.

Unum Group

NAIC Code: 524114

www.unum.com

TYPES OF BUSINESS:
Supplemental Insurance
Short- & Long-Term Disability Insurance
Long-Term Care Insurance
Income Protection Insurance
Life Insurance

BRANDS/DIVISIONS/AFFILIATES:
Unum Life Insurance Company of America
Provident Life and Accident Insurance Company
Paul Revere Life Insurance Company (The)
Colonial Life & Accident Insurance Company
Starmount Life Insurance Company
Unum Limited
Unum Zycie TUiR SA

CONTACTS: Note: Officers with more than one job title may be intentionally listed here more than once.

Peter ODonnell, CEO, Divisional
Michael Simonds, CEO, Divisional
Timothy Arnold, CEO, Divisional
John McGarry, CFO
Kevin Kabat, Chairman of the Board
Daniel Waxenberg, Chief Accounting Officer
Puneet Bhasin, Chief Information Officer
Richard Mckenney, Director
Elizabeth Ahmed, Executive VP, Divisional
Breege Farrell, Executive VP
Lisa Iglesias, General Counsel
Danny Waxenber, Senior VP

GROWTH PLANS/SPECIAL FEATURES:

Unum Group operates through its insurance and non-insurance subsidiaries, serving the U.S., the U.K., Poland and, to a limited extent, certain other countries. Primary U.S. subsidiaries include Unum Life Insurance of America, Provident Life and Accident Insurance Company, The Paul Revere Life Insurance Company, Colonial Life & Accident Insurance Company, and Starmount Life Insurance Company. Unum Limited operates in the U.K.; and Unum Zycie TUiR SA operates in Poland. Unum Group also provides financial protection benefits in the U.S. and U.K. The group's products include disability, life, accident, critical illness, dental and vision, as well as related services. Unum markets its products primarily through the workplace.

Unum offers its employees medical, dental, vision and prescription drug insurance; long- and short-term disability coverage; life insurance; a pension plan; a 401(k) plan; tuition reimbursement; an adoption assistance program; and an employee assistance program.

FINANCIAL DATA: Note: Data for latest year may not have been available at press time.

In U.S. $	2018	2017	2016	2015	2014	2013
Revenue	11,598,500,000	11,286,800,000	11,046,500,000	10,731,300,000	10,509,700,000	10,353,800,000
R&D Expense						
Operating Income						
Operating Margin %						
SGA Expense	885,900,000	844,400,000	832,100,000	835,100,000	820,900,000	790,400,000
Net Income	523,400,000	994,200,000	931,400,000	867,100,000	413,400,000	858,100,000
Operating Cash Flow	1,536,500,000	1,149,400,000	1,116,100,000	1,292,100,000	1,223,600,000	1,031,500,000
Capital Expenditure	144,100,000	105,300,000	85,000,000	100,200,000	114,500,000	105,500,000
EBITDA						
Return on Assets %		.02%	.02%	.01%	.01%	.01%
Return on Equity %		.11%	.11%	.10%	.05%	.10%
Debt to Equity		0.286	0.334	0.286	0.307	0.31

CONTACT INFORMATION:
Phone: 423 294-1011   Fax:
Toll-Free: 800-887-2180
Address: 1 Fountain Sq., Chattanooga, TN 37402 United States

SALARIES/BONUSES:
Top Exec. Salary: $1,000,000   Bonus: $
Second Exec. Salary: $630,000   Bonus: $

STOCK TICKER/OTHER:
Stock Ticker: UNM   Exchange: NYS
Employees: 9,400   Fiscal Year Ends: 12/31
Parent Company:

OTHER THOUGHTS:
Estimated Female Officers or Directors:
Hot Spot for Advancement for Women/Minorities: Y

US Bancorp (US Bank)

NAIC Code: 522110

www.usbank.com

TYPES OF BUSINESS:
Banking
Lease Financing
Consumer Finance
Credit Cards
Discount Brokerage
Investment Advisory Services
Trust Services
Insurance

BRANDS/DIVISIONS/AFFILIATES:
US Bank NA
USBank
U.S. Bank

CONTACTS:
Note: Officers with more than one job title may be intentionally listed here more than once.

Andrew Cecere, CEO
Ismat Aziz, Exec. VP
Terrance Dolan, CFO
Craig Gifford, Chief Accounting Officer
Katherine Quinn, Chief Administrative Officer
Mark Runkel, Chief Credit Officer
Jodi Richard, Chief Risk Officer
James Chosy, Executive VP
Gunjan Kedia, Vice Chairman, Divisional
Leslie Godridge, Vice Chairman, Divisional
Shailesh Kotwal, Vice Chairman, Divisional

GROWTH PLANS/SPECIAL FEATURES:

U.S. Bancorp (USB), operating under the tradename US Bank, is a financial services holding company, with $357 billion in assets. USB operates more than 3,067 banking offices and 4,771 ATMs in the Midwest and Western regions of the U.S. Through U.S. Bank NA and other subsidiaries, the company is engaged in general banking, primarily in domestic markets, and serves individuals, businesses, institutional organizations, financial institutions and government entities. Lending services include traditional credit products, credit card services, financing, leasing, asset-backed lending and agricultural finance. Depository services include checking and savings accounts and time certificate contracts. Ancillary services include foreign exchange, treasury management and lock-box collection for corporate customers. A full range of asset management and fiduciary services are available for individuals, estates, business corporations, foundations and charitable organizations. USB's non-banking subsidiaries provide investment and insurance products as well as mutual fund processing services to a range of mutual funds. Mortgage services are available through the bank's offices, while consumer lending products are originated through banking offices, indirect correspondents and brokers.

The company offers employees benefits including medical, dental and vision insurance; flexible spending accounts; disability and life insurance; 401(k) and pension plans; an employee assistance plan; adoption benefits; and tuition reimbursement.

FINANCIAL DATA: Note: Data for latest year may not have been available at press time.

In U.S. $	2018	2017	2016	2015	2014	2013
Revenue	22,521,000,000	21,852,000,000	21,105,000,000	20,093,000,000	19,939,000,000	19,378,000,000
R&D Expense						
Operating Income						
Operating Margin %						
SGA Expense	9,124,000,000	8,774,000,000	8,032,000,000	7,524,000,000	7,137,000,000	7,026,000,000
Net Income	7,096,000,000	6,218,000,000	5,888,000,000	5,879,000,000	5,851,000,000	5,836,000,000
Operating Cash Flow	10,564,000,000	6,472,000,000	5,336,000,000	8,782,000,000	5,332,000,000	11,446,000,000
Capital Expenditure						
EBITDA						
Return on Assets %		.01%	.01%	.01%	.01%	.02%
Return on Equity %		.14%	.14%	.14%	.15%	.16%
Debt to Equity		0.74	0.797	0.79	0.833	0.551

CONTACT INFORMATION:
Phone: 651 466-3000   Fax:
Toll-Free:
Address: 800 Nicollet Mall, Minneapolis, MN 55402 United States

STOCK TICKER/OTHER:
Stock Ticker: USB   Exchange: NYS
Employees: 71,191   Fiscal Year Ends: 12/31
Parent Company:

SALARIES/BONUSES:
Top Exec. Salary: $1,100,000   Bonus: $
Second Exec. Salary: $675,000   Bonus: $

OTHER THOUGHTS:
Estimated Female Officers or Directors: 5
Hot Spot for Advancement for Women/Minorities: Y

USAA

NAIC Code: 524126

www.usaa.com

TYPES OF BUSINESS:
Insurance, Direct Property & Casualty
Banking
Life Insurance
Real Estate Development
Discount Brokerage
Investment Management
Mutual Funds

BRANDS/DIVISIONS/AFFILIATES:
United Services Automobile Association
USAA Casualty Insurance Company
USAA General Indemnity Company
Garrison Property and Casualty Insurance Company
USAA Limited
USAA Life Insurance Company
USAA Federal Savings Bank Member FDIC
USAA Mortgage Solutions

CONTACTS:
Note: Officers with more than one job title may be intentionally listed here more than once.

Stuart Parker, CEO
Shon Manasco, Chief Admin. Officer
Steven A. Bennett, General Counsel
Wendi E. Strong, Exec. VP-Enterprise Affairs
F. David Bohne, Pres., USAA Federal Savings Bank
Kevin J. Bergner, Pres., USAA Property & Casualty Insurance Group
Christopher W. Claus, Exec. VP-Enterprise Advice Group
Wayne Peacock, Pres., USAA Capital Corporation
Thomas B. Fargo, Chmn.

GROWTH PLANS/SPECIAL FEATURES:

USAA (United Services Automobile Association) is a diversified financial services group of companies. The association is a leading provider of financial planning, insurance, investments and banking products to members of the U.S. military and veterans. USAA offers property and casualty insurance, life insurance, annuities, investment products, investment advisory and related services, banking and a variety of discounts such as shopping. Just a few of the group's many companies include: USAA Casualty Insurance Company, USAA General Indemnity Company, Garrison Property and Casualty Insurance Company, USAA County Mutual Insurance Company, USAA Texas Lloyd's Company, USAA Limited, USAA Life Insurance Company, USAA Investment Management Company, USAA Financial Planning Services Insurance Agency Inc., USAA Federal Savings Bank Member FDIC, USAA Savings Bank (credit cards), USAA Mortgage Solutions and USAA Alliance Services. Among the companies, some are licensed in all 50 U.S. states, Puerto Rico, Guam and the U.S. Virgin Islands, some are licensed in select states and one is licensed in Europe.

Employee benefits include medical and dental coverage, a 401(k), military leave, an employee assistance program, educational assistance and adoption assistance.

FINANCIAL DATA:
Note: Data for latest year may not have been available at press time.

In U.S. $	2018	2017	2016	2015	2014	2013
Revenue	31,367,800,000	30,000,000,000	27,131,000,000	24,361,000,000	24,033,000,000	20,971,000,000
R&D Expense						
Operating Income						
Operating Margin %						
SGA Expense						
Net Income	2,291,900,000	2,400,000,000	1,779,000,000	2,266,000,000	3,317,000,000	2,726,000,000
Operating Cash Flow						
Capital Expenditure						
EBITDA						
Return on Assets %						
Return on Equity %						
Debt to Equity						

CONTACT INFORMATION:
Phone: 210-498-2211 Fax: 210-498-9940
Toll-Free: 800-531-8722
Address: 9800 Fredericksburg Rd., San Antonio, TX 78288 United States

STOCK TICKER/OTHER:
Stock Ticker: Mutual Company
Employees: 33,689
Parent Company:

Exchange:
Fiscal Year Ends: 12/31

SALARIES/BONUSES:
Top Exec. Salary: $ Bonus: $
Second Exec. Salary: $ Bonus: $

OTHER THOUGHTS:
Estimated Female Officers or Directors: 4
Hot Spot for Advancement for Women/Minorities: Y

Valassis Communications Inc

www.valassis.com

NAIC Code: 541800

TYPES OF BUSINESS:
Coupon Marketing Products & Services
Direct Mail
Newspaper Advertising
Sampling
Software

BRANDS/DIVISIONS/AFFILIATES:
MacAndrews & Forbes Inc
Harland Clarke Holdings Corp
RetailMeNot Everyday
Have You Seen Me?
NCH Marketing Services Inc
Clipper Magazine
Promotion Watch Inc
Valassis Digital

CONTACTS: *Note: Officers with more than one job title may be intentionally listed here more than once.*

Dan Singleton, CEO
Cali Tran, Pres.
Grant Fitz, CFO
Curtis Tingle, CMO
Cindy Walker, Sr. VP-Human Resources
Todd L. Wiseley, Exec. VP-Admin.
Todd L. Wiseley, General Counsel
Brian J. Husselbee, Pres.

GROWTH PLANS/SPECIAL FEATURES:

Valassis Communications, Inc. is a provider of intelligent media. The company integrates and optimizes campaigns such as direct mail, newspaper inserts and digital advertising to enhance its 63,000 local, regional and national clients' ROI (return on investment). Valassis' geography-based targeting enables its RetailMeNot Everyday trademarked media to reach nine out of 10 households with national or hyper-local print programs, and extend into nearly every neighborhood throughout the U.S. with digital advertising. The firm's signature Have You Seen Me? program, a joint venture effort with National Center for Missing & Exploited Children, features photos of missing children where there is the greatest opportunity for a recovery. Valassis provides insight-driven, measurable, multi-channel media solutions that engage and influence consumers wherever they plan, shop, buy and share. Industries supported by the firm include consumer packaged goods, grocery, retail, restaurant, telecommunications and financial. Other company's by Valassis include: NCH Marketing Services, Inc., providing coupon, audit and settlement services; Clipper Magazine, providing multichannel solutions to local businesses; Promotion Watch, Inc., providing protection to a brand's investment in sweepstakes, instant win games, contests and events with independent, third-party promotion security services; Valassis Digital, an advertising and marketing intelligence company that predicts customer behavior and builds off those insights; and Valassis Canada, Inc., the Canadian branch of Valassis. Valassis is a wholly-owned subsidiary of Harland Clarke Holdings Corporation, which itself is a subsidiary of MacAndrews & Forbes, Inc. In 2018, the firm acquired: One Brand Marketing, a postcard marketing solution firm; and Market Magazine, a Ohio-based magazine. In January 2019, the firm acquired GET1FREE Magazine, a direct mail company with a reach of more than 1 million.

Valassis Communications offers its employees medical, dental, life, vision and AD&D insurance; an employee assistance plan; a retirement plan and 401(k); adoption assistance; and short- and long-term disability.

FINANCIAL DATA: *Note: Data for latest year may not have been available at press time.*

In U.S. $	2018	2017	2016	2015	2014	2013
Revenue	2,341,000,000	2,310,000,000	2,300,000,000	2,285,000,000	2,225,000,000	2,200,000,000
R&D Expense						
Operating Income						
Operating Margin %						
SGA Expense						
Net Income						
Operating Cash Flow						
Capital Expenditure						
EBITDA						
Return on Assets %						
Return on Equity %						
Debt to Equity						

CONTACT INFORMATION:
Phone: 734 591-3000 Fax: 734 591-4503
Toll-Free: 800-437-0479
Address: 19975 Victor Pkwy., Livonia, MI 48152 United States

SALARIES/BONUSES:
Top Exec. Salary: $ Bonus: $
Second Exec. Salary: $ Bonus: $

STOCK TICKER/OTHER:
Stock Ticker: Subsidiary   Exchange:
Employees: 7,000   Fiscal Year Ends: 12/31
Parent Company: MacAndrews & Forbes Inc

OTHER THOUGHTS:
Estimated Female Officers or Directors: 4
Hot Spot for Advancement for Women/Minorities: Y

Sales, profits and employees may be estimates. Financial information, benefits and other data can change quickly and may vary from those stated here.

Valero Energy Corporation

www.valero.com

NAIC Code: 324110

TYPES OF BUSINESS:
Petroleum Refineries & Retail Marketing
Convenience Stores
Home Heating Fuels
Wholesale Fuel Marketing
Asphalt
Marine Transportation
Ethanol Production

BRANDS/DIVISIONS/AFFILIATES:

CONTACTS: Note: Officers with more than one job title may be intentionally listed here more than once.
Joseph Gorder, CEO
Donna Titzman, CFO
R. Riggs, COO
Jason Fraser, Executive VP
Gary Simmons, Senior VP, Divisional

GROWTH PLANS/SPECIAL FEATURES:

Valero Energy Corporation is a refiner and retailer of petroleum. Valero owns and operates 15 refineries in the U.S., Canada and the U.K., with a combined throughput capacity of approximately 3.1 million barrels per day (bpd). These refineries produce conventional gasolines, premium gasolines, gasoline meeting the specifications of the California Air Resources Board (CARB), diesel, low-sulfur diesel, ultra-low-sulfur diesel, CARB diesel, other distillates, jet fuel, asphalt, petrochemicals, lubricants, and other refined petroleum products. Valero sells its refined petroleum products in both the wholesale rack and bulk markets, and approximately 7,000 outlets carry the company's brand names in the U.S., Canada, the U.K. and Ireland. Valero also owns 14 ethanol plants in the U.S., with a combined production capacity of approximately 1.73 billion gallons per year. The ethanol plants are dry mill facilities that process corn to produce ethanol, distillers' grains and corn oil. The ethanol is primarily sold to refiners and gasoline blenders under term and spot contracts in bulk markets within the U.S. Valero also exports ethanol into the global markets. Valero's logistics assets encompass crude oil pipelines, refined petroleum product pipelines, terminals, tanks, marine docks, truck rack bays and more. In early-2019, the Valero corporation merged Valero Energy Partners LP into itself, with the logistics assets supporting the operations of the refining segment.

FINANCIAL DATA: Note: Data for latest year may not have been available at press time.

In U.S. $	2018	2017	2016	2015	2014	2013
Revenue	117,033,000,000	93,980,000,000	75,659,000,000	87,804,000,000	130,844,000,000	138,074,000,000
R&D Expense						
Operating Income	4,572,000,000	3,599,000,000	3,628,000,000	6,358,000,000	5,902,000,000	3,963,000,000
Operating Margin %		.04%	.05%	.07%	.05%	.03%
SGA Expense	925,000,000	835,000,000	715,000,000	710,000,000	724,000,000	758,000,000
Net Income	3,122,000,000	4,065,000,000	2,289,000,000	3,990,000,000	3,630,000,000	2,720,000,000
Operating Cash Flow	4,371,000,000	5,482,000,000	4,820,000,000	5,611,000,000	4,241,000,000	5,564,000,000
Capital Expenditure	1,752,000,000	1,379,000,000	1,278,000,000	1,618,000,000	2,153,000,000	2,121,000,000
EBITDA	6,771,000,000	5,661,000,000	5,522,000,000	8,246,000,000	7,639,000,000	6,067,000,000
Return on Assets %		.08%	.05%	.09%	.08%	.06%
Return on Equity %		.19%	.11%	.19%	.18%	.15%
Debt to Equity		0.398	0.394	0.353	0.28	0.322

CONTACT INFORMATION:
Phone: 210 370-2000 Fax:
Toll-Free: 800-871-4404
Address: 1 Valero Way, San Antonio, TX 78249 United States

SALARIES/BONUSES:
Top Exec. Salary: $800,000   Bonus: $2,200,997
Second Exec. Salary: $625,000   Bonus: $1,174,051

STOCK TICKER/OTHER:
Stock Ticker: VLO
Employees: 9,996
Parent Company:

Exchange: NYS
Fiscal Year Ends: 12/31

OTHER THOUGHTS:
Estimated Female Officers or Directors: 4
Hot Spot for Advancement for Women/Minorities: Y

Sales, profits and employees may be estimates. Financial information, benefits and other data can change quickly and may vary from those stated here.

Varian Medical Systems Inc

www.varian.com

NAIC Code: 334510

TYPES OF BUSINESS:
Radiation Oncology Systems
X-Ray Equipment
Software Systems
Security & Inspection Products

BRANDS/DIVISIONS/AFFILIATES:

CONTACTS:
Note: Officers with more than one job title may be intentionally listed here more than once.

Dow Wilson, CEO
Gary Bischoping, CFO
R. Eckert, Chairman of the Board
Magnus Momsen, Chief Accounting Officer
Timothy Guertin, Director
John Kuo, General Counsel
Kolleen Kennedy, Other Executive Officer
Christopher Toth, President, Divisional
Chris Toth, President, Divisional

GROWTH PLANS/SPECIAL FEATURES:

Varian Medical Systems, Inc. develops and manufactures medical devices and software for treating cancer and other medical conditions. Varian operates through two segments: oncology systems and proton systems. The oncology systems segment designs, manufactures, sells and services hardware and software products for treating cancer with conventional radiotherapy, and advanced treatments such as fixed field intensity-modulated radiation therapy (IMRT), image-guided radiation therapy (IGRT), volumetric modulated arc therapy (VMAT), stereotactic radiosurgery (SRS), stereotactic body radiotherapy (SBRT) and brachytherapy, as well as associated quality assurance equipment. This segment's software solutions also include informatics software for information management, clinical knowledge exchange, patient care management, practice management and decision-making support for comprehensive cancer clinics, radiotherapy centers and medical oncology practices. Hardware products include linear accelerators, brachytherapy after-loaders, treatment accessories and quality assurance software. The proton solutions segment develops, designs, manufactures, sells and services products and systems for delivering proton therapy, another form of external beam therapy using proton beams, for the treatment of cancer. Varian's current focus is bringing its expertise in X-ray beam radiation therapy to proton therapy to improve its clinical utility and to reduce its cost of treatment per patient. In mid-2019, Varian agreed to acquire the Boston Scientific portfolio of microsphere and bland embolic bead products for treating arteriovenous malformations and hyper-vascular tumors.

Varian offers employees medical, life, AD&D, disability, dental and vision plans; a 401(k); educational reimbursement; an employee assistance program; and a stock purchase plan.

FINANCIAL DATA:
Note: Data for latest year may not have been available at press time.

In U.S. $	2018	2017	2016	2015	2014	2013
Revenue	2,919,100,000	2,668,200,000	3,217,800,000	3,099,111,000	3,049,800,000	2,942,897,000
R&D Expense	233,900,000	210,000,000	253,500,000	245,211,000	234,840,000	208,208,000
Operating Income	500,400,000	393,300,000	567,700,000	548,967,000	596,285,000	608,890,000
Operating Margin %		.15%	.18%	.18%	.20%	.21%
SGA Expense	539,300,000	552,300,000	540,100,000	488,514,000	470,550,000	432,589,000
Net Income	149,900,000	249,600,000	402,300,000	411,485,000	403,703,000	438,248,000
Operating Cash Flow	454,900,000	399,100,000	356,300,000	469,556,000	448,986,000	455,185,000
Capital Expenditure	47,700,000	59,100,000	80,400,000	91,384,000	89,649,000	76,277,000
EBITDA	531,600,000	432,400,000	648,000,000	631,117,000	644,126,000	679,071,000
Return on Assets %		.07%	.11%	.12%	.12%	.14%
Return on Equity %		.15%	.23%	.25%	.24%	.27%
Debt to Equity			0.165	0.197	0.24	0.263

CONTACT INFORMATION:
Phone: 650 493-4000 Fax:
Toll-Free: 800-544-4636
Address: 3100 Hansen Way, Palo Alto, CA 94304 United States

SALARIES/BONUSES:
Top Exec. Salary: $1,000,000 Bonus: $
Second Exec. Salary: $684,899 Bonus: $

STOCK TICKER/OTHER:
Stock Ticker: VAR   Exchange: NYS
Employees: 7,800   Fiscal Year Ends: 09/30
Parent Company:

OTHER THOUGHTS:
Estimated Female Officers or Directors: 6
Hot Spot for Advancement for Women/Minorities: Y

VCA Inc

NAIC Code: 541940

www.vca.com

TYPES OF BUSINESS:
Animal Health Care Services
Veterinary Diagnostic Laboratories
Full-Service Animal Hospitals
Veterinary Equipment
Ultrasound Imaging

BRANDS/DIVISIONS/AFFILIATES:
Mars Incorporated
VCA Animal Hospital
VCA Canada
Companion Animal Practices of North America
Antech Diagnostics
South Technologies Inc
Camp Bow Wow

CONTACTS: Note: Officers with more than one job title may be intentionally listed here more than once.
Robert Antin, CEO
Arthur J. Antin, COO
Josh Drake, President, Subsidiary
Robert Antin, Chmn.

GROWTH PLANS/SPECIAL FEATURES:
VCA, Inc. is a leading animal healthcare company operating in the U.S. and Canada. The firm provides services and diagnostic testing to support veterinary care, and sells diagnostic equipment and other medical technology products to the veterinary market. VCA's hospitals offer a full range of general medical and surgical services for companion animals, as well as specialized treatments, including advanced diagnostic services, internal medicine, oncology, ophthalmology, dermatology and cardiology. In addition, the company provides pharmaceutical products and performs a variety of pet wellness programs such as health examinations, diagnostic testing, routine vaccinations, spaying, neutering and dental care. VCA's network of more than 900 animal hospitals provides service to over 10 million patients annually, which are located in 45 U.S. states and five Canadian provinces. In addition, VCA provides diagnostic services to more than 17,000 independent hospitals. Dog day care and boarding services are also offered at more than 130 locations. Brands and subsidiaries of VCA include: VCA Animal Hospital; VCA Canada; Companion Animal Practices of North America (CAPNA); Antech Diagnostics; South Technologies, Inc.; and Camp Bow Wow. VCA, Inc. operates as a distinct and separate business unit within Mars Incorporated's pet care segment. During 2019, VCA acquired CAPNA, adding another 82 practices to the VCA family.

FINANCIAL DATA: Note: Data for latest year may not have been available at press time.

In U.S. $	2018	2017	2016	2015	2014	2013
Revenue	3,000,000,000	2,700,000,000	2,516,863,000	2,133,675,008	1,918,482,944	1,803,368,960
R&D Expense						
Operating Income						
Operating Margin %						
SGA Expense						
Net Income			209,196,000	211,048,992	135,438,000	137,511,008
Operating Cash Flow						
Capital Expenditure						
EBITDA						
Return on Assets %						
Return on Equity %						
Debt to Equity						

CONTACT INFORMATION:
Phone: 310 571-6500   Fax: 310 571-6700
Toll-Free: 800-966-1822
Address: 12401 W. Olympic Blvd., Los Angeles, CA 90064 United States

STOCK TICKER/OTHER:
Stock Ticker: Subsidiary
Employees: 30,000
Parent Company: Mars Incorporated

Exchange:
Fiscal Year Ends: 12/31

SALARIES/BONUSES:
Top Exec. Salary: $ Bonus: $
Second Exec. Salary: $ Bonus: $

OTHER THOUGHTS:
Estimated Female Officers or Directors:
Hot Spot for Advancement for Women/Minorities:

Sales, profits and employees may be estimates. Financial information, benefits and other data can change quickly and may vary from those stated here.

Verizon Communications Inc

www.verizon.com

NAIC Code: 517110

TYPES OF BUSINESS:
Mobile Phone and Wireless Services
Telecommunications Services
Wireless Services
Long-Distance Services
High-Speed Internet Access
Video-on-Demand Services
e-Commerce & Online Services

BRANDS/DIVISIONS/AFFILIATES:
Verizon Wireless

CONTACTS:
Note: Officers with more than one job title may be intentionally listed here more than once.

Kumara Gowrappan, CEO, Divisional
Hans Vestberg, CEO
Matthew Ellis, CFO
Anthony Skiadas, Chief Accounting Officer
Marc Reed, Chief Administrative Officer
Kyle Malady, Chief Technology Officer
Craig Silliman, Executive VP, Divisional
Rima Qureshi, Executive VP
Ronan Dunne, Executive VP
Tami Erwin, Executive VP

GROWTH PLANS/SPECIAL FEATURES:

Verizon Communications, Inc. is a world-leading provider of communications services. The company operates through its subsidiaries, with products and services categorized into two primary segments: wireless and wireline. The wireless segment consists of wireless voice and data services and equipment sales, which are provided to consumer, business and government customers throughout the U.S. This division does business as Verizon Wireless, had 118 million retail connections in 2018 and represented approximately 70% of Verizon's aggregate revenues. Wireless' network technology platform is currently 4G LTE (long-term evolution), but the segment is engaged in 5G wireless technology development, with the ecosystems for fixed and mobile 5G wireless services. This division offers various post-paid account service plans, including unlimited plans, shared data plans, single connection plans and other plans tailored to the customer's need. Pre-paid connection plans are available, and feature domestic unlimited voice and unlimited domestic/international text. Access to the internet is available on all smartphones and nearly all basic phones; and network access needed to deliver various Internet of Things (IoT) products and services is also provided. The wireline segment (23%) consists of video and data services, corporate networking solutions, security and managed network services, and local and long-distance voice services. Wireline products and services are provided to consumers in the U.S., as well as to carriers, businesses and government customers both in the U.S. and worldwide. These products are built around a fiber-based network (as well as a copper-based one, to a lesser degree), supporting data, video and advanced business services in areas where high-speed connections is needed.

Verizon offers employees medical, dental, vision, disability, AD&D and life insurance; 401(k); and various employee, adoption and tuition assistance programs.

FINANCIAL DATA:
Note: Data for latest year may not have been available at press time.

In U.S. $	2018	2017	2016	2015	2014	2013
Revenue	130,863,000,000	126,034,000,000	125,980,000,000	131,620,000,000	127,079,000,000	120,550,000,000
R&D Expense						
Operating Income	26,869,000,000	29,188,000,000	27,059,000,000	33,060,000,000	19,599,000,000	31,968,000,000
Operating Margin %		.23%	.21%	.25%	.15%	.27%
SGA Expense	31,083,000,000	28,336,000,000	31,569,000,000	29,986,000,000	41,016,000,000	27,089,000,000
Net Income	15,528,000,000	30,101,000,000	13,127,000,000	17,879,000,000	9,625,000,000	11,497,000,000
Operating Cash Flow	34,339,000,000	25,305,000,000	22,715,000,000	38,930,000,000	30,631,000,000	38,818,000,000
Capital Expenditure	18,087,000,000	17,830,000,000	17,593,000,000	27,717,000,000	17,545,000,000	17,184,000,000
EBITDA	41,859,000,000	42,281,000,000	41,290,000,000	49,177,000,000	36,718,000,000	48,550,000,000
Return on Assets %		.12%	.05%	.07%	.04%	.05%
Return on Equity %		.92%	.67%	1.24%	.38%	.32%
Debt to Equity		2.637	4.681	6.313	8.988	2.309

CONTACT INFORMATION:
Phone: 212 395-1000   Fax:
Toll-Free: 800-837-4966
Address: 1095 Avenue of the Americas, New York, NY 10036 United States

STOCK TICKER/OTHER:
Stock Ticker: VZ
Employees: 160,900
Parent Company:

Exchange: NYS
Fiscal Year Ends: 12/31

SALARIES/BONUSES:
Top Exec. Salary: $603,448   Bonus: $1,999,998
Second Exec. Salary: $1,235,385   Bonus: $1,000,000

OTHER THOUGHTS:
Estimated Female Officers or Directors: 5
Hot Spot for Advancement for Women/Minorities: Y

Sales, profits and employees may be estimates. Financial information, benefits and other data can change quickly and may vary from those stated here.

Victoria's Secret

NAIC Code: 448120

www.victoriassecret.com

TYPES OF BUSINESS:
Intimate Apparel-Women's, Retail
Cosmetics
Fragrances
Personal Care Products
Online Sales
Sports Apparel

BRANDS/DIVISIONS/AFFILIATES:
L Brands Inc
PINK
Victorias Secret Beauty and Accessories
Very Sexy
Body by Victoria
VS Cotton
Dream Angels
Beauty Rush

CONTACTS: Note: Officers with more than one job title may be intentionally listed here more than once.
Stuart Burgdoefer, CEO
Brian VanOoyen, VP-Merch. Planning
Bridget Ryan-Berman, CEO-Victoria's Secret Direct
Sharen Jester Turney, CEO

GROWTH PLANS/SPECIAL FEATURES:

Victoria's Secret, a wholly-owned subsidiary of L Brands, Inc., purchases, distributes and sells lingerie, personal care products and women's sports apparel through over 950 retail stores throughout the United States. The stores offer branded merchandise such as PINK, Very Sexy, Body by Victoria, VS Cotton, Dream Angels, Beauty Rush, Angels and Victoria Sport. The firm also owns a number standalone PINK stores in the U.S., Canada and the UK, which sell intimate apparel, denim, casual apparel and body products targeted to young women ages 13-25, and standalone Victoria's Secret Beauty and Accessories stores, largely located in China. Victoria's Secret Beauty and Accessories stores offer a complete line of fragrance, cosmetics and body products for skin and hair, as well as backpacks, wristlets, bags and makeup cases. Once each year, Victoria's Secret conducts a televised fashion show featuring some of the world's top models and performances by acclaimed musicians such as Maroon 5 or Kanye West. During 2019, Victoria's Secret announced the closing of approximately 50 U.S. stores.

The company offers employees medical, dental, vision and prescription drug coverage; a 401(k) plan; a discount stock purchase plan; life insurance; discounts on products; tuition reimbursement; a commuter discount program; and an employee assistance program.

FINANCIAL DATA: Note: Data for latest year may not have been available at press time.

In U.S. $	2018	2017	2016	2015	2014	2013
Revenue	7,375,000,000	7,387,000,000	7,781,000,000	7,672,000,000	7,207,600,000	6,884,200,000
R&D Expense						
Operating Income						
Operating Margin %						
SGA Expense						
Net Income	462,000,000	932,000,000	1,173,000,000	1,391,000,000	1,271,000,000	903,000,000
Operating Cash Flow						
Capital Expenditure						
EBITDA						
Return on Assets %						
Return on Equity %						
Debt to Equity						

CONTACT INFORMATION:
Phone: 614-577-7111　　Fax:
Toll-Free: 800-411-5116
Address: 4 Limited Pkwy. E, Reynoldsburg, OH 43068 United States

STOCK TICKER/OTHER:
Stock Ticker: Subsidiary
Employees: 65,000
Parent Company: L Brands Inc

Exchange:
Fiscal Year Ends: 01/31

SALARIES/BONUSES:
Top Exec. Salary: $　　Bonus: $
Second Exec. Salary: $　　Bonus: $

OTHER THOUGHTS:
Estimated Female Officers or Directors: 3
Hot Spot for Advancement for Women/Minorities: Y

Visa Inc

www.visa.com

NAIC Code: 522320

TYPES OF BUSINESS:
Credit Cards
Debit Cards
Prepaid Cards

BRANDS/DIVISIONS/AFFILIATES:
Visa Canada Corporaiton
CyberSource Corporation
Visa USA Inc
Visa International Service Association
Inovant LLC
Visa Europe Ltd
VisaNet
Visa Checkout

CONTACTS: Note: Officers with more than one job title may be intentionally listed here more than once.
Alfred Kelly, CEO
Vasant Prabhu, CFO
Robert Matschullat, Chairman of the Board
James Hoffmeister, Chief Accounting Officer
Lynne Biggar, Chief Marketing Officer
Mary Richey, Chief Risk Officer
Rajat Taneja, Executive VP, Divisional
William Sheedy, Executive VP, Divisional
Kelly Tullier, Executive VP
Ryan McInerney, President

GROWTH PLANS/SPECIAL FEATURES:
Visa, Inc. is a global payments technology company that connects consumers, businesses, financial institutions and governments in over 200 countries. The company's processing network, VisaNet, facilitates authorization, clearing and settlement of payment transactions worldwide. It also offers fraud protection for account holders and rapid payment for merchants. Visa is not a bank and does not issue cards, extend credit or set rates and fees for account holders in Visa-branded cards and payment products. In most cases, account holder and merchant relationships belong to, and are managed by, Visa's financial institution clients. Visa's tokenization replaces account numbers with digital tokens for online and mobile payments, benefiting merchants and issuers by removing sensitive account information and reducing fraud risk. Visa's chip payment technology addresses fraud at the physical point-of-sale by working with merchants and Visa financial institution clients in the U.S. Visa Checkout is a fast, simple and intuitive payment experience that allows consumers to pay for goods online, on any device, in just a few clicks. The company's core products and services can be condensed into three divisions: debit, providing debit solutions that support issuers' payment products that draw on demand deposit accounts; prepaid, providing prepaid payment solutions that support issuer's products that access a pre-funded amount; and credit, providing credit payment solutions that support issuers' deferred payment and customized financing products. Subsidiaries of the company include Visa Canada Corporation; CyberSource Corporation; Visa U.S.A., Inc.; Visa International Service Association; and Inovant, LLC. In February 2018, Visa agreed to acquire Fraedom, a Software-as-a-Service technology company providing payments and transaction management solutions for financial institutions and their corporate customers.

FINANCIAL DATA: Note: Data for latest year may not have been available at press time.

In U.S. $	2018	2017	2016	2015	2014	2013
Revenue	20,609,000,000	18,358,000,000	15,082,000,000	13,880,000,000	12,702,000,000	11,778,000,000
R&D Expense						
Operating Income	12,954,000,000	12,144,000,000	9,760,000,000	9,063,999,000	7,697,000,000	7,239,000,000
Operating Margin %		.66%	.65%	.65%	.61%	.61%
SGA Expense	2,579,000,000	2,391,000,000	2,054,000,000	1,755,000,000	1,735,000,000	1,739,000,000
Net Income	10,301,000,000	6,699,000,000	5,991,000,000	6,328,000,000	5,438,000,000	4,980,000,000
Operating Cash Flow	12,713,000,000	9,208,001,000	5,574,000,000	6,584,000,000	7,205,000,000	3,022,000,000
Capital Expenditure	718,000,000	707,000,000	523,000,000	414,000,000	553,000,000	471,000,000
EBITDA	14,031,000,000	12,813,000,000	8,941,000,000	9,558,000,000	8,132,000,000	7,636,000,000
Return on Assets %		.10%	.11%	.16%	.15%	.13%
Return on Equity %		.25%	.21%	.22%	.20%	.18%
Debt to Equity		0.61	0.584			

CONTACT INFORMATION:
Phone: 650-432-3200 Fax:
Toll-Free: 800-847-2911
Address: P.O. Box 8999, San Francisco, CA 94128 United States

STOCK TICKER/OTHER:
Stock Ticker: V
Employees: 11,300
Parent Company:

Exchange: NYS
Fiscal Year Ends: 09/30

SALARIES/BONUSES:
Top Exec. Salary: $1,300,038 Bonus: $
Second Exec. Salary: $1,000,038 Bonus: $

OTHER THOUGHTS:
Estimated Female Officers or Directors: 6
Hot Spot for Advancement for Women/Minorities: Y

VMware Inc

www.vmware.com

NAIC Code: 0

TYPES OF BUSINESS:
Computer Software: Network Management (IT), System Testing & Storage
Virtual Infrastructure Automation
Virtual Infrastructure Management

BRANDS/DIVISIONS/AFFILIATES:
vSphere
VMware Horizon
VMware AirWatch
Workstation ONE
CloudCoreo
CloudHealth
E8 Security
Heptio

CONTACTS:
Note: Officers with more than one job title may be intentionally listed here more than once.

Patrick Gelsinger, CEO
Zane Rowe, CFO
Michael Dell, Chairman of the Board
Kevan Krysler, Chief Accounting Officer
Sanjay Poonen, COO, Divisional
Rangarajan Raghuram, COO, Divisional
Rajiv Ramaswami, COO, Divisional
Maurizio Carli, Executive VP, Divisional
Amy Olli, General Counsel

GROWTH PLANS/SPECIAL FEATURES:

VMware, Inc. is a leader in virtualization infrastructure software. The firm develops and markets its products through three areas: software-defined data center (SDDC), end-user computing and hybrid cloud computing. SDDC consists of four main product categories: compute, providing a hypervisor layer of software that enables compute virtualization through its flagship, vSphere; storage and availability, offering cost-effective holistic data storage and protection options to all applications running on vSphere; network and security, which abstracts physical networks and simplifies the provisioning and consumption of networking resources; and management and automation, which automates overarching IT processes involved in provisioning IT services and resources to users from initial deployment to retirement. The firm's end-user computing products enable IT organizations to deliver secure access to data, applications and devices to end-users. This segment's solutions include desktop streamlining applications through its VMware Horizon brand, which controls and delivers data, stores images, and provides cloud delivery and virtualization solutions; mobile solutions through VMware AirWatch, which offer enterprise mobile management and security solutions; and Workspace ONE, which integrates VMware's silos to streamline the delivery of new applications and experiences and is offered as both an on-premises installed platform or as-a-service. VMware's hybrid cloud computing cross-cloud architecture enables consistent deployment models, security policies, visibility and governance for all applications, running on-premises and off-premises, regardless of the underlying cloud, hardware platform or hypervisor. During 2018, VMware acquired CloudCoreo, CloudHealth, CloudVelox, Dell EMC, E8 Security, and Heptio.

FINANCIAL DATA:
Note: Data for latest year may not have been available at press time.

In U.S. $	2018	2017	2016	2015	2014	2013
Revenue	7,922,000,000		7,093,000,000	6,571,000,000	6,035,000,000	5,207,000,000
R&D Expense	1,755,000,000		1,503,000,000	1,300,000,000	1,239,000,000	1,082,000,000
Operating Income	1,779,000,000		1,491,000,000	1,220,000,000	1,043,000,000	1,161,000,000
Operating Margin %	.22%		.21%	.19%	.17%	.22%
SGA Expense	3,247,000,000		3,046,000,000	3,033,000,000	2,836,000,000	2,234,000,000
Net Income	570,000,000		1,186,000,000	997,000,000	886,000,000	1,014,000,000
Operating Cash Flow	3,211,000,000		2,381,000,000	1,899,000,000	2,180,000,000	2,535,000,000
Capital Expenditure	263,000,000		153,000,000	333,000,000	352,000,000	345,000,000
EBITDA	2,211,000,000		1,844,000,000	1,574,000,000	1,417,000,000	1,488,000,000
Return on Assets %	.03%		.07%	.06%	.06%	.09%
Return on Equity %	.07%		.15%	.13%	.12%	.16%
Debt to Equity	0.544		0.185	0.189	0.198	0.066

CONTACT INFORMATION:
Phone: 650 427-5000 Fax: 650 475-5005
Toll-Free: 877-486-9273
Address: 3401 Hillview Ave., Palo Alto, CA 94304 United States

SALARIES/BONUSES:
Top Exec. Salary: $1,000,000 Bonus: $
Second Exec. Salary: $823,213 Bonus: $

STOCK TICKER/OTHER:
Stock Ticker: VMW
Employees: 19,900
Parent Company:

Exchange: NYS
Fiscal Year Ends: 12/31

OTHER THOUGHTS:
Estimated Female Officers or Directors: 3
Hot Spot for Advancement for Women/Minorities: Y

Sales, profits and employees may be estimates. Financial information, benefits and other data can change quickly and may vary from those stated here.

W R Berkley Corporation

NAIC Code: 524126

www.wrberkley.com

TYPES OF BUSINESS:
Insurance, Direct Property & Casualty
Reinsurance
Regional Insurance
Specialty Insurance
Risk Management
Liability Insurance

BRANDS/DIVISIONS/AFFILIATES:
Acadia
Admiral
Berkley
Gemini Transportation
Midwest Employers Casualty
Union Standard
Vela Insurance
W/R/B Underwriting

CONTACTS: Note: Officers with more than one job title may be intentionally listed here more than once.
William Berkley, CEO
Richard Baio, CFO
William Berkley, Chairman of the Board
Lucille Sgaglione, Executive VP
James Shiel, Executive VP, Divisional
Philip Welt, Executive VP
Ira Lederman, Executive VP

GROWTH PLANS/SPECIAL FEATURES:
W.R. Berkley Corporation is an insurance holding company and among the largest commercial lines writers in the U.S. The firm, through its subsidiaries, operates worldwide in two segments of the property casualty insurance business: insurance and reinsurance. The insurance segment predominantly offers commercial insurance, including excess and surplus lines, admitted lines and specialty personal lines throughout the U.S.; and offers insurance products in the U.K., continental Europe, South America, Canada, Mexico, Scandinavia, Asia and Australia. The reinsurance segment operates on a facultative and treaty basis primarily in the U.S., the U.K., continental Europe, Australia, Asia-Pacific and South Africa. These two segments are composed of individual operating units that serve a market defined by geography, products, services or industry served. The insurance segment generates 92.5% of net premiums written, and reinsurance generates 7.5% of premiums written. Brands of the corporation include Acadia, Admiral, American Mining Insurance Group, Berkley, Continental Western Group, Gemini Transportation, Intrepid Direct, Key Risk, Midwest Employers Casualty, Nautilus Insurance Group, Preferred Employers Insurance, Union Standard, Vela Insurance, and W/R/B Underwriting.

FINANCIAL DATA: Note: Data for latest year may not have been available at press time.

In U.S. $	2018	2017	2016	2015	2014	2013
Revenue	7,718,718,000	7,343,332,000	7,666,088,000	6,784,955,000	6,718,933,000	6,011,031,000
R&D Expense						
Operating Income						
Operating Margin %						
SGA Expense	193,050,000	190,865,000	179,412,000	156,487,000	158,227,000	151,014,000
Net Income	640,749,000	549,094,000	601,916,000	503,694,000	648,884,000	499,925,000
Operating Cash Flow	620,199,000	710,883,000	848,376,000	881,304,000	734,847,000	819,798,000
Capital Expenditure	49,860,000	115,719,000	50,829,000	63,562,000	41,958,000	63,150,000
EBITDA						
Return on Assets %		.02%	.03%	.02%	.03%	.02%
Return on Equity %		.11%	.12%	.11%	.15%	.12%
Debt to Equity		0.461	0.493	0.475	0.535	0.469

CONTACT INFORMATION:
Phone: 203 629-3000 Fax:
Toll-Free:
Address: 475 Steamboat Rd., Greenwich, CT 06830 United States

SALARIES/BONUSES:
Top Exec. Salary: $650,000 Bonus: $500,000
Second Exec. Salary: $591,667 Bonus: $440,063

STOCK TICKER/OTHER:
Stock Ticker: WRB
Employees: 7,683
Parent Company:
Exchange: NYS
Fiscal Year Ends: 12/31

OTHER THOUGHTS:
Estimated Female Officers or Directors: 16
Hot Spot for Advancement for Women/Minorities: Y

Sales, profits and employees may be estimates. Financial information, benefits and other data can change quickly and may vary from those stated here.

WABCO Holdings Inc

www.wabco-auto.com

NAIC Code: 336340

TYPES OF BUSINESS:
Brake Systems Manufacturing
Suspension Systems

BRANDS/DIVISIONS/AFFILIATES:
Asset Trackr

CONTACTS:
Note: Officers with more than one job title may be intentionally listed here more than once.

Jacques Esculier, CEO
Sean Deason, CFO
Lisa Brown, Chief Legal Officer
Christian Brenneke, Chief Technology Officer
Mazen Mazraani, Other Executive Officer
Nicolas Bardot, Other Executive Officer
Nick Rens, President, Geographical

GROWTH PLANS/SPECIAL FEATURES:

WABCO Holdings, Inc. is a provider of electronic, mechanical, electro-mechanical and aerodynamic products for commercial truck, trailer, bus and passenger car manufacturers. The firm engineers, develops, manufactures and sells integrated systems controlling advanced braking, stability, suspension, steering, transmission automation, as well as air compression and processing. These systems improve vehicle safety, efficiency and performance while reducing overall vehicle operating costs. WABCO's largest-selling products are pneumatic anti-lock braking systems (ABS), electronic braking systems (EBS), electronic stability control (ESC) systems, brake controls, automated manual transmission systems, air disc brakes and a variety of conventional mechanical products such as actuators, air compressors and air control valves for medium- and heavy-duty trucks, buses and trailers. WABCO is also a global leader in hydraulic components, controls and brake systems for heavy-duty, off-highway vehicles used in agriculture, construction and mining. Aerodynamic products reduce the air drag of commercial trucks traveling long distance at highway speeds, thereby lowering consumption and CO_2 emissions. The company's advanced electronic suspension controls and vacuum pumps primarily serve the passenger car and SUV markets in Europe, North America and Asia. WABCO also supplies replacement parts, fleet management solutions, diagnostic tools, training and other services to commercial vehicle aftermarket distributors and service partners. The firm's global Asset Trackr fleet management solutions platform helps commercial fleets to track, analyze and optimize their transportation resources and assets in real-time via cloud-based solutions. In March 2019, WABCO agreed to be acquired by ZF Friedrichshafen AG for approximately $7 billion; the transaction is expected to close in 2020.

FINANCIAL DATA:
Note: Data for latest year may not have been available at press time.

In U.S. $	2018	2017	2016	2015	2014	2013
Revenue	3,831,000,000	3,304,200,000	2,810,000,000	2,627,500,000	2,851,000,000	2,720,500,000
R&D Expense	184,400,000	147,000,000	135,200,000	139,500,000	145,000,000	119,400,000
Operating Income	511,400,000	452,200,000	357,500,000	272,600,000	333,200,000	333,900,000
Operating Margin %		.13%	.13%	.10%	.12%	.12%
SGA Expense	476,000,000	411,200,000	377,700,000	368,400,000	386,800,000	352,800,000
Net Income	394,100,000	406,100,000	223,000,000	275,200,000	291,500,000	653,200,000
Operating Cash Flow	468,500,000	421,500,000	405,400,000	395,300,000	314,400,000	665,800,000
Capital Expenditure	132,100,000	110,500,000	114,000,000	100,600,000	135,900,000	121,500,000
EBITDA	636,100,000	559,300,000	455,500,000	369,300,000	434,800,000	419,100,000
Return on Assets %		.11%	.08%	.11%	.12%	.32%
Return on Equity %		.45%	.30%	.34%	.29%	.71%
Debt to Equity		0.913	1.367	0.634	0.365	0.041

CONTACT INFORMATION:
Phone: 248-260-9032   Fax:
Toll-Free:
Address: 1220 Pacific Dr., Auburn Hills, MI 48326-1589 United States

STOCK TICKER/OTHER:
Stock Ticker: WBC
Employees: 12,860
Parent Company:

Exchange: NYS
Fiscal Year Ends: 12/31

SALARIES/BONUSES:
Top Exec. Salary: $1,100,000   Bonus: $
Second Exec. Salary: $405,000   Bonus: $

OTHER THOUGHTS:
Estimated Female Officers or Directors: 2
Hot Spot for Advancement for Women/Minorities:

Walgreens Boots Alliance Inc

www.walgreens.com

NAIC Code: 446110

TYPES OF BUSINESS:
Drug Stores
Mail-Order Pharmacy Services
Pharmacy Benefit Management
Health Care Center Management
Online Pharmacy Services
Photo Printing Services
Specialty Pharmacy Services
Home Infusion Services

BRANDS/DIVISIONS/AFFILIATES:
Alliance Healthcare
Walgreens
Duane Reade
Boots
No7
Botanics
Sleek MakeUP
Soap & Glory

CONTACTS: *Note: Officers with more than one job title may be intentionally listed here more than once.*
Stefano Pessina, CEO
James Kehoe, CFO
James Skinner, Chairman of the Board
Heather Dixon, Chief Accounting Officer
Marco Pagni, Chief Administrative Officer
Ornella Barra, Co-COO
Alexander Gourlay, Co-COO
Kathleen Wilson-Thompson, Executive VP
Ken Murphy, Executive VP

GROWTH PLANS/SPECIAL FEATURES:
Walgreens Boots Alliance, Inc. is a global pharmacy-led health and wellbeing enterprise, with more than 18,500 stores worldwide. The company's pharmaceutical wholesale and distribution network is comprised of more than 390 distribution centers delivering to over 230,000 pharmacies, doctors, health centers and hospitals on an annual basis. The firm operates through three business segments: retail pharmacy USA, retail pharmacy international and pharmaceutical wholesale. Retail pharmacy USA oversees pharmacy-led health and beauty retail businesses in 50 states, the District of Columbia, Puerto Rico and the U.S. Virgin Islands. It operates more than 9,560 retail stores and fills over 823 million prescriptions (including immunizations) annually. The retail pharmacy international segment oversees pharmacy-led health and beauty retail businesses in eight countries, operating more than 4,767 retail stores across the U.K., Thailand, Norway, Ireland, the Netherlands, Mexico and Chile. The pharmaceutical wholesale segment operates primarily under the Alliance Healthcare brand, and supplies medicines and other healthcare products to more than 110,000 pharmacies, doctors, health centers and hospitals from 291 distribution centers in 11 countries, primarily in Europe. Walgreens' portfolio of retail and business global brands include Walgreens, Duane Reade, Boots and Alliance Healthcare, as well as global health and beauty product brands such as No7, Botanics, Sleek MakeUP, Liz Earle and Soap & Glory. In early-2019, Walgreens Boots Alliance and Microsoft Corp. formed a partnership to develop new health care delivery models, technology and retail innovations by combining Microsoft's Azure, cloud and artificial intelligence (AI) platform, health care investments and new retail solutions with Walgreens' customer reach, locations, outpatient health care services and industry expertise.

Walgreens offers medical, prescription, dental, life and accident insurance; and profit sharing and stock purchase plans.

FINANCIAL DATA: *Note: Data for latest year may not have been available at press time.*

In U.S. $	2018	2017	2016	2015	2014	2013
Revenue	131,537,000,000	118,214,000,000	117,351,000,000	103,444,000,000	76,392,000,000	72,217,000,000
R&D Expense						
Operating Income	6,223,000,000	5,422,000,000	5,964,000,000	4,353,000,000	3,577,000,000	3,576,000,000
Operating Margin %		.05%	.05%	.04%	.05%	.05%
SGA Expense	24,569,000,000	23,740,000,000	23,910,000,000	22,571,000,000	17,992,000,000	17,543,000,000
Net Income	5,024,000,000	4,078,000,000	4,173,000,000	4,220,000,000	1,932,000,000	2,450,000,000
Operating Cash Flow	8,265,000,000	7,251,000,000	7,847,000,000	5,664,000,000	3,893,000,000	4,301,000,000
Capital Expenditure	1,367,000,000	1,351,000,000	1,325,000,000	1,251,000,000	1,106,000,000	1,212,000,000
EBITDA	7,993,000,000	7,076,000,000	7,682,000,000	6,095,000,000	4,893,000,000	4,859,000,000
Return on Assets %		.06%	.06%	.08%	.05%	.07%
Return on Equity %		.14%	.14%	.16%	.10%	.13%
Debt to Equity		0.462	0.626	0.431	0.183	0.23

CONTACT INFORMATION:
Phone: 847 315-2500 Fax: 847 914-2804
Toll-Free: 800-925-4733
Address: 108 Wilmot Rd., Deerfield, IL 60015 United States

SALARIES/BONUSES:
Top Exec. Salary: $225,000   Bonus: $1,250,000
Second Exec. Salary: $963,756   Bonus: $

STOCK TICKER/OTHER:
Stock Ticker: WBA   Exchange: NAS
Employees: 345,000   Fiscal Year Ends: 08/31
Parent Company:

OTHER THOUGHTS:
Estimated Female Officers or Directors: 7
Hot Spot for Advancement for Women/Minorities: Y

Sales, profits and employees may be estimates. Financial information, benefits and other data can change quickly and may vary from those stated here.

Walmart Inc

www.walmartstores.com

NAIC Code: 452910

TYPES OF BUSINESS:
Discount Stores
Supermarkets
Warehouse Membership Clubs
Online Sales
Pharmacies
Vision Centers
Auto Repair Centers

BRANDS/DIVISIONS/AFFILIATES:
Walmart
Sams Club
Marketside
Walmart Neighborhood Market
walmart.com
Flipkart Pvt Ltd

CONTACTS: Note: Officers with more than one job title may be intentionally listed here more than once.
Gregory Foran, CEO, Divisional
Marc Lore, CEO, Divisional
John Furner, CEO, Subsidiary
C. McMillon, CEO
M. Biggs, CFO
Rachel Brand, Chief Legal Officer
David Chojnowski, Controller
Gregory Penner, Director
Jacqueline Canney, Executive VP, Divisional
Daniel Bartlett, Executive VP, Divisional
Judith McKenna, Executive VP

GROWTH PLANS/SPECIAL FEATURES:
Walmart, Inc. is one of the world's largest retailers, operating through a massive base of Walmart stores, supercenters, Sam's Clubs, Marketsides, Walmart Neighborhood Markets and eCommerce site, walmart.com. The company operates in three business segments: Walmart U.S., Walmart international and Sam's Club. Walmart U.S. is a mass merchandiser of consumer products, groceries and drugs, operating under the Walmart brand, as well as walmart.com. This segment operates retail stores in the U.S., including all 50 states, Washington D.C. and Puerto Rico, with supercenters in 49 states, Washington D.C. and Puerto Rico and Walmart discount stores in 41 states and Puerto Rico. Wal-Mart U.S. also operates a relatively small number Neighborhood Markets, which are about 42,000 square feet each. Its main line of business, the Walmart supercenters, average 178,000 square feet each. Walmart International consists of operations in 28 countries outside the U.S., and includes numerous formats divided into three major categories: retail, wholesale and other. These categories consist of formats such as supercenters, supermarkets, hypermarkets, warehouse clubs (including Sam's Clubs), cash & carry, home improvement, specialty electronics, restaurants, apparel stores, drug stores and convenience stores. Sam's Club operates membership-only warehouse clubs, as well as samsclub.com in the U.S. All memberships include a spouse/household card at no additional cost and Plus Members are eligible for cash rewards which provides $10 for every $500 in qualifying Sam's Club purchases up to a $500 cash reward annually. During 2018, Walmart announced plans to close 63 underperforming Sam's stores across the U.S.; planned to sell ASDA Stores Ltd., its British arm, to J Sainsbury, in a deal that would net Walmart a 42% stake in J Sainsbury; and invested about $16 billion in India eCommerce retailer, Flipkart Pvt. Ltd., taking a 77% majority holding in the firm.

FINANCIAL DATA: Note: Data for latest year may not have been available at press time.

In U.S. $	2018	2017	2016	2015	2014	2013
Revenue	500,343,000,000	485,873,000,000	482,130,000,000	485,651,000,000	476,294,000,000	
R&D Expense						
Operating Income	20,437,000,000	22,764,000,000	24,105,000,000	27,147,000,000	26,872,000,000	
Operating Margin %	.04%	.05%	.05%	.06%	.06%	
SGA Expense	106,510,000,000	101,853,000,000	97,041,000,000	93,418,000,000	91,353,000,000	
Net Income	9,862,000,000	13,643,000,000	14,694,000,000	16,363,000,000	16,022,000,000	
Operating Cash Flow	28,337,000,000	31,530,000,000	27,389,000,000	28,564,000,000	23,257,000,000	
Capital Expenditure	10,051,000,000	10,619,000,000	11,477,000,000	12,174,000,000	13,115,000,000	
EBITDA	27,982,000,000	32,944,000,000	33,640,000,000	36,433,000,000	35,861,000,000	
Return on Assets %	.05%	.07%	.07%	.08%	.08%	
Return on Equity %	.13%	.17%	.18%	.21%	.21%	
Debt to Equity	0.473	0.54	0.547	0.537	0.584	

CONTACT INFORMATION:
Phone: 479 273-4000   Fax: 479 273-1986
Toll-Free: 800-925-6278
Address: 702 SW 8th St., Bentonville, AR 72716 United States

STOCK TICKER/OTHER:
Stock Ticker: WMT
Employees: 2,200,000
Parent Company:

Exchange: NYS
Fiscal Year Ends: 01/31

SALARIES/BONUSES:
Top Exec. Salary: $1,276,892   Bonus: $
Second Exec. Salary: $1,104,201   Bonus: $

OTHER THOUGHTS:
Estimated Female Officers or Directors: 13
Hot Spot for Advancement for Women/Minorities: Y

Sales, profits and employees may be estimates. Financial information, benefits and other data can change quickly and may vary from those stated here.

Walt Disney Company (The)

NAIC Code: 515210

corporate.disney.go.com

TYPES OF BUSINESS:
Cable TV Networks, Broadcasting & Entertainment
Filmed Entertainment
Merchandising
Television Networks
Music & Book Publishing
Streaming Entertainment Subscriptions
Theme Parks, Resorts & Cruise Lines
Comic Book Publishing

BRANDS/DIVISIONS/AFFILIATES:
ESPN
LucasFilm
Star TV
Hulu
A+E
National Geographic Network
Disneyland Resort
Marvel

CONTACTS:
Note: Officers with more than one job title may be intentionally listed here more than once.

Roger Patterson, Assistant Secretary
Jolene Negre, Assistant Secretary
Gregory Belzer, Assistant Treasurer
Michael Salama, Assistant Treasurer
John Stowell, Assistant Treasurer
Robert Iger, CEO
Christine Mccarthy, CFO
James Kapenstein, Director
Brent Woodford, Executive VP, Divisional
Alan Braverman, General Counsel
Mary Parker, Other Executive Officer
Marsha Reed, Secretary
Zenia Mucha, Senior Executive VP, Divisional
Jonathan Headley, Treasurer
Daniel Grossman, Vice President

GROWTH PLANS/SPECIAL FEATURES:

The Walt Disney Company (Disney) is an international entertainment company operating in multiple business segments: media networks, studio entertainment, consumer products and interactive media, and parks and resorts. The media networks segment is comprised of cable and broadcast television networks, television production and distribution operations, television and radio networks, as well as television and radio broadcast stations. This division's primary cable networks include the ESPN, Disney and Freeform brands; A+E and Viceland. The studio entertainment segment produces and acquires live-action and animated motion pictures, direct-to-video content, musical recordings and live stage plays. This division distributes films primarily under the Walt Disney Pictures, Pixar, Marvel, Lucasfilm and Touchstone banners; and distributes Dreamworks Studios-produced live-action films that were released from 2010-2016. The consumer products and interactive media segment licenses the company's trade names, characters and visual and literary properties to various manufacturers, game developers, publishers and retailers worldwide. It also develops and publishes games, primarily for mobile platforms, and books, magazines and comic books. The parks and resorts business includes Disneyland Resort, Walt Disney World, Disneyland Paris, Tokyo Disney Resort, Hong Kong Disneyland, Disney Cruise Line, Disney Vacation Club, Aulani Disney Resort & Spa, Adventures by Disney and Walt Disney Imagineering. In March 2019, the acquisition by Disney of certain major Twenty-First Century Fox, Inc. (Fox) assets was completed for $71.3 billion. This included the Fox film production units, much of the Fox television businesses (except for Fox News and Fox Sports), the National Geographic Network on cable and a major stake in streaming media site Hulu. In 2019, Disney launched its Disney+ online streaming entertainment subscriptions platform, enabling it to compete directly with Netflix and Amazon Prime Video.

FINANCIAL DATA:
Note: Data for latest year may not have been available at press time.

In U.S. $	2018	2017	2016	2015	2014	2013
Revenue	59,434,000,000	55,137,000,000	55,632,000,000	52,465,000,000	48,813,000,000	45,041,000,000
R&D Expense						
Operating Income	14,837,000,000	13,873,000,000	14,358,000,000	13,224,000,000	11,540,000,000	9,450,000,000
Operating Margin %		.25%	.26%	.25%	.24%	.21%
SGA Expense	8,860,000,000	8,176,000,000	8,754,000,000	8,523,000,000	8,565,000,000	
Net Income	12,598,000,000	8,980,000,000	9,391,000,000	8,382,000,000	7,501,000,000	6,136,000,000
Operating Cash Flow	14,295,000,000	12,343,000,000	13,213,000,000	10,909,000,000	9,780,000,000	9,452,000,000
Capital Expenditure	4,465,000,000	3,623,000,000	4,773,000,000	4,265,000,000	3,311,000,000	2,796,000,000
EBITDA	18,422,000,000	17,077,000,000	17,749,000,000	16,487,000,000	14,828,000,000	12,161,000,000
Return on Assets %		.10%	.10%	.10%	.09%	.08%
Return on Equity %		.21%	.21%	.19%	.17%	.14%
Debt to Equity		0.463	0.381	0.287	0.282	0.287

CONTACT INFORMATION:
Phone: 818 5601000 Fax:
Toll-Free:
Address: 500 S. Buena Vista St., Burbank, CA 91521 United States

STOCK TICKER/OTHER:
Stock Ticker: DIS
Employees: 195,000
Parent Company:

Exchange: NYS
Fiscal Year Ends: 09/30

SALARIES/BONUSES:
Top Exec. Salary: $2,875,000 Bonus: $
Second Exec. Salary: $1,674,000 Bonus: $

OTHER THOUGHTS:
Estimated Female Officers or Directors: 7
Hot Spot for Advancement for Women/Minorities: Y

Walt Disney Studios (The)

NAIC Code: 512110

studioservices.go.com

TYPES OF BUSINESS:
Movie Production & Post-Production Services
Movie Distribution
Theatrical Productions
Music Production
Music Distribution

BRANDS/DIVISIONS/AFFILIATES:
Walt Disney Company (The)
Disney Digital Studio Services
Disney
Walt Disney Animation Studios
Pixar Animation Studios
Disneynature
Walt Disney Records
Disney Music Publishing

CONTACTS: *Note: Officers with more than one job title may be intentionally listed here more than once.*
Alan Horn, Chmn.

GROWTH PLANS/SPECIAL FEATURES:

The Walt Disney Studios, a division of The Walt Disney Company, acts as a central studio and production agency for its parent company's various television and cinema productions. The studio's production services include sound stages used for filming the live action sequences for films like Fantasia in 1940, and, more recently, for portions of Pearl Harbor, Pirates of the Caribbean and Armageddon. They have also been used to film TV shows such as the Mickey Mouse Club and Sports Night. The studio's business street features a 1950s facade, which has been featured in shows like Ellen, Alias, My Wife & Kids and commercials and print ads. Its backlot services include signs and graphics, a paint shop and craft services. The firm offers production services including costumes, set rentals and transportation services. Post-production services are offered through Disney Digital Studio Services and include dubbing and ADR (automated dialogue replacement) stages in the digital studio, all of which feature advanced sound editing tools and seating. Feature films are released under the following banners: Disney; Walt Disney Animation Studios; Pixar Animation Studios; Disneynature; Marvel Studios; and Touchstone Pictures, the banner under which live-action films from DreamWorks Studios are distributed. The Disney music division comprises the Walt Disney Records and Hollywood Records labels, as well as Disney Music Publishing. And the Disney theatrical division produces and licenses live events, including Disney on Broadway, Disney On Ice and Disney Live!

Employees of The Walt Disney Company receive benefits including medical, prescription, AD&D, long-term care, disability, life, dental and vision coverage; an employee assistance program; 401(k); an employee stock purchase program; education reimbursement; and employee discounts.

FINANCIAL DATA: *Note: Data for latest year may not have been available at press time.*

In U.S. $	2018	2017	2016	2015	2014	2013
Revenue	9,500,000,000	8,379,000,000	9,441,000,000	7,366,000,000	7,278,000,000	5,979,000,000
R&D Expense						
Operating Income						
Operating Margin %						
SGA Expense						
Net Income		2,355,000,000	2,703,000,000	1,973,000,000	1,549,000,000	661,000,000
Operating Cash Flow						
Capital Expenditure						
EBITDA						
Return on Assets %						
Return on Equity %						
Debt to Equity						

CONTACT INFORMATION:
Phone: 818-560-1000 Fax: 818-560-1930
Toll-Free:
Address: 500 S. Buena Vista St., Burbank, CA 91521 United States

STOCK TICKER/OTHER:
Stock Ticker: Subsidiary
Employees: 16,000
Parent Company: Walt Disney Company (The)
Exchange:
Fiscal Year Ends: 09/30

SALARIES/BONUSES:
Top Exec. Salary: $ Bonus: $
Second Exec. Salary: $ Bonus: $

OTHER THOUGHTS:
Estimated Female Officers or Directors:
Hot Spot for Advancement for Women/Minorities:

Sales, profits and employees may be estimates. Financial information, benefits and other data can change quickly and may vary from those stated here.

Waste Management Inc

www.wm.com

NAIC Code: 562000

TYPES OF BUSINESS:
Waste Disposal
Recycling Services
Landfill Operation
Hazardous Waste Management
Transfer Stations
Recycled Commodity Trading
Waste Methane Generation

BRANDS/DIVISIONS/AFFILIATES:
Think Green

CONTACTS:
Note: Officers with more than one job title may be intentionally listed here more than once.

James Fish, CEO
Devina Rankin, CFO
Thomas Weidemeyer, Chairman of the Board
Charles Boettcher, Chief Legal Officer
John Morris, COO
Michael Watson, Other Executive Officer
Tamla Oates-Forney, Other Executive Officer
Nikolaj Sjoqvist, Other Executive Officer
Tara Hemmer, Senior VP, Divisional
Steven Batchelor, Senior VP, Divisional
Leslie Nagy, Vice President

GROWTH PLANS/SPECIAL FEATURES:

Waste Management, Inc. provides comprehensive waste management services to municipal, commercial, industrial and residential customers throughout North America. Waste Management is the nation's largest collector of recyclables from businesses and households, collecting recyclable materials and depositing them at about a hundred local materials recovery facilities. The firm recycles several different materials including plastics, rubber, electronics and commodities. The company also has a pulp and paper trading group that reduces paper's overall long-term commodity price exposure. Waste Management owns or operates 249 landfill sites, as well as 305 transfer stations that consolidate, compact and transport waste. Its hazardous waste management services include geosynthetic manufacturing, radioactive waste services and landfill liner installation. Additionally, Waste Management promotes environmental initiatives such as Keep America Beautiful and Wildlife Habitat Council, as well as its own Think Green.

Waste Management offers its employees life, AD&D, medical, dental and vision insurance; prescription drug coverage; family assistance programs; flexible spending accounts; adoption assistance; education savings accounts; an employee stock purchase plan; and tuition reimbursement.

FINANCIAL DATA:
Note: Data for latest year may not have been available at press time.

In U.S. $	2018	2017	2016	2015	2014	2013
Revenue	14,914,000,000	14,485,000,000	13,609,000,000	12,961,000,000	13,996,000,000	13,983,000,000
R&D Expense						
Operating Income	2,735,000,000	2,620,000,000	2,412,000,000	2,142,000,000	2,221,000,000	2,070,000,000
Operating Margin %		.18%	.18%	.17%	.16%	.15%
SGA Expense	1,400,000,000	1,426,000,000	1,370,000,000	1,307,000,000	1,440,000,000	1,427,000,000
Net Income	1,925,000,000	1,949,000,000	1,182,000,000	753,000,000	1,298,000,000	98,000,000
Operating Cash Flow	3,570,000,000	3,180,000,000	2,960,000,000	2,498,000,000	2,331,000,000	2,455,000,000
Capital Expenditure	1,694,000,000	1,509,000,000	1,339,000,000	1,233,000,000	1,151,000,000	1,271,000,000
EBITDA	4,227,000,000	3,930,000,000	3,499,000,000	2,690,000,000	3,509,000,000	2,308,000,000
Return on Assets %		.09%	.06%	.04%	.06%	.00%
Return on Equity %		.34%	.22%	.13%	.22%	.02%
Debt to Equity		1.454	1.679	1.633	1.423	1.665

CONTACT INFORMATION:
Phone: 713 512-6200 Fax:
Toll-Free:
Address: 1001 Fannin St., Ste. 4000, Houston, TX 77002 United States

SALARIES/BONUSES:
Top Exec. Salary: $1,157,692 Bonus: $
Second Exec. Salary: $752,231 Bonus: $

STOCK TICKER/OTHER:
Stock Ticker: WM   Exchange: NYS
Employees: 41,200   Fiscal Year Ends: 12/31
Parent Company:

OTHER THOUGHTS:
Estimated Female Officers or Directors: 1
Hot Spot for Advancement for Women/Minorities: Y

Sales, profits and employees may be estimates. Financial information, benefits and other data can change quickly and may vary from those stated here.

Waters Corporation

www.waters.com

NAIC Code: 334516

TYPES OF BUSINESS:
Equipment-Liquid Chromatography Instruments
Mass Spectrometry Systems
Thermal Analyzers
Rheometry Equipment
Software Development
Food Safety Technology

BRANDS/DIVISIONS/AFFILIATES:

CONTACTS: Note: Officers with more than one job title may be intentionally listed here more than once.
Christopher O'Connell, CEO
Sherry Buck, CFO
Terrance Kelly, President, Divisional
Ian King, Senior VP, Divisional
Michael Harrington, Senior VP, Divisional
Robert Carson, Senior VP, Divisional
Francis Kim, Senior VP, Divisional
Elizabeth Rae, Senior VP, Divisional
Mark Beaudouin, Senior VP

GROWTH PLANS/SPECIAL FEATURES:
Waters Corporation is an analytical instrument manufacturer. The firm operates in two segments: waters and TA (thermal analysis). The waters segment designs, manufactures, sells and services liquid chromatography (LC) and mass spectrometry (MS) instrument systems, columns and other precision chemistry consumables that can be integrated and used along with other analytical instruments. The TA segment designs, manufactures, sells and services thermal analysis, rheometry and calorimetry instruments. These products are used by pharmaceutical, biochemical, industrial, nutritional safety, environmental, academic and governmental customers working in research and development, quality assurance and other laboratory applications. LC is a standard technique and is utilized in a broad range of industries to detect, identify, monitor and measure the chemical, physical and biological composition of materials, and to purify a full range of compounds. MS technology, principally in conjunction with chromatography, is employed in drug discovery and development, including clinical trial testing, the analysis of proteins in disease processes, nutritional safety analysis and environmental testing. LC-MS instruments combine a liquid phase sample introduction and separation system with mass spectrometric compound identification and quantification. Waters' thermal analysis, rheometry and calorimetry instruments are used in predicting the suitability and stability of fine chemicals, pharmaceuticals, water, polymers, metals and viscous liquids for various industrial, consumer goods and healthcare products, as well as for life science research.

Waters offers employees medical insurance, retirement planning programs, sickness/disability programs, life insurance and an employee assistance program.

FINANCIAL DATA: Note: Data for latest year may not have been available at press time.

In U.S. $	2018	2017	2016	2015	2014	2013
Revenue	2,419,929,000	2,309,078,000	2,167,423,000	2,042,332,000	1,989,344,000	1,904,218,000
R&D Expense	143,403,000	137,593,000	125,187,000	122,400,000	123,182,000	100,536,000
Operating Income	739,774,000	661,858,000	624,339,000	567,451,000	517,908,000	517,343,000
Operating Margin %	.29%	.29%	.29%	.28%	.26%	.27%
SGA Expense	536,902,000	544,703,000	513,031,000	495,747,000	512,707,000	492,965,000
Net Income	593,794,000	20,311,000	521,503,000	469,053,000	431,620,000	450,003,000
Operating Cash Flow	604,446,000	697,640,000	629,076,000	560,293,000	511,648,000	484,876,000
Capital Expenditure	96,079,000	90,473,000	94,967,000	103,012,000	106,248,000	118,450,000
EBITDA	839,195,000	803,938,000	741,474,000	668,149,000	619,162,000	599,850,000
Return on Assets %		.00%	.12%	.12%	.12%	.13%
Return on Equity %		.01%	.24%	.24%	.24%	.28%
Debt to Equity		0.849	0.739	0.725	0.654	0.675

CONTACT INFORMATION:
Phone: 508 478-2000   Fax: 508 872-1990
Toll-Free: 800-252-4752
Address: 34 Maple St., Milford, MA 01757 United States

SALARIES/BONUSES:
Top Exec. Salary: $943,269   Bonus: $
Second Exec. Salary: $325,769   Bonus: $400,000

STOCK TICKER/OTHER:
Stock Ticker: WAT
Employees: 6,899
Parent Company:

Exchange: NYS
Fiscal Year Ends: 12/31

OTHER THOUGHTS:
Estimated Female Officers or Directors: 3
Hot Spot for Advancement for Women/Minorities: Y

Sales, profits and employees may be estimates. Financial information, benefits and other data can change quickly and may vary from those stated here.

Wayfair LLC

NAIC Code: 454111

www.wayfair.com

TYPES OF BUSINESS:
Online Furniture Store

BRANDS/DIVISIONS/AFFILIATES:
CastleGate
Wayfair
Joss & Main
AllModern
Perigold
Birch Lane

CONTACTS:
Note: Officers with more than one job title may be intentionally listed here more than once.

Niraj Shah, CEO
Michael Fleisher, CFO
Edmond Macri, Chief Marketing Officer
John Mulliken, Chief Technology Officer
Steven Conine, Co-Chairman of the Board
James Savarese, COO
Steve Oblak, Other Executive Officer

GROWTH PLANS/SPECIAL FEATURES:

Wayfair, LLC is an eCommerce home furnishings company. The firm offers more than 10 million products from over 10,000 suppliers. These products include furniture, decor, decorative accents, housewares, seasonal decor and other home goods. Wayfair is able to offer this vast selection of products because it holds minimal inventory. Products are shipped to customers directly from the suppliers, or from Wayfair's CastleGate fulfillment network. The company's CastleGate solution enables suppliers to forward-position their inventory, allowing faster delivery to the customer with lower rates of damage and lowering Wayfair's cost per order over time. Wayfair offers five distinct sites, including websites, mobile websites and mobile applications, with each site comprising a unique brand identity that offers a tailored shopping experience. Sites and Brands include: Wayfair, offering home furnishings; Joss & Main, offering furniture; AllModern, offering modern home design merchandise; Perigold, offering fine home decor and furnishings; and Birch Lane, a collection of classic furnishings and timeless home decor. Based in the U.S., the firm operates internationally in Canada, the U.K., Ireland, Germany and the British Virgin Islands.

FINANCIAL DATA:
Note: Data for latest year may not have been available at press time.

In U.S. $	2018	2017	2016	2015	2014	2013
Revenue	6,779,174,000	4,720,895,000	3,380,360,000	2,249,885,000	1,318,951,000	915,843,000
R&D Expense						
Operating Income	-473,279,000	-235,453,000	-196,217,000	-81,350,000	-147,784,000	-16,019,000
Operating Margin %		-.05%	-.06%	-.03%	-.11%	-.02%
SGA Expense	2,060,002,000	1,354,276,000	1,004,028,000	621,183,000	457,902,000	239,721,000
Net Income	-504,080,000	-244,614,000	-194,375,000	-77,443,000	-148,098,000	-15,526,000
Operating Cash Flow	84,861,000	33,634,000	62,814,000	135,121,000	4,125,000	34,413,000
Capital Expenditure	221,955,000	146,879,000	128,086,000	62,184,000	45,985,000	15,779,000
EBITDA	-349,737,000	-148,433,000	-140,645,000	-48,904,000	-125,781,000	-2,928,000
Return on Assets %		-.25%	-.27%	-.12%	-.40%	-.23%
Return on Equity %		-15.75%	-1.21%	-.28%	-2.62%	
Debt to Equity			0.364	0.113		

CONTACT INFORMATION:
Phone: 866-263-8325 Fax:
Toll-Free: 877-929-3247
Address: 4 Copley Pl., 7/Fl, Boston, MA 02116 United States

SALARIES/BONUSES:
Top Exec. Salary: $200,000   Bonus: $50,000
Second Exec. Salary: $200,000   Bonus: $50,000

STOCK TICKER/OTHER:
Stock Ticker: W
Employees: 5,637
Parent Company:
Exchange: NYS
Fiscal Year Ends:

OTHER THOUGHTS:
Estimated Female Officers or Directors: 5
Hot Spot for Advancement for Women/Minorities: Y

Sales, profits and employees may be estimates. Financial information, benefits and other data can change quickly and may vary from those stated here.

WellCare Health Plans Inc

www.wellcare.com

NAIC Code: 524114

TYPES OF BUSINESS:
Insurance-Medical & Health, HMOs & PPOs

BRANDS/DIVISIONS/AFFILIATES:
WellCare of California
Ohana
Staywell
Care1st
Harmony
Meridian
Missouri Care
WellCare

CONTACTS:
Note: Officers with more than one job title may be intentionally listed here more than once.

Kenneth Burdick, CEO
Andrew Asher, CFO
Michael Meyer, Chief Accounting Officer
Michael Yount, Chief Compliance Officer
Darren Ghanayem, Chief Information Officer
Mark Leenay, Chief Medical Officer
Christian Michalik, Director
Michael Polen, Executive VP, Divisional
Kelly Munson, Executive VP, Divisional
Michael Radu, Executive VP, Divisional
Anat Hakim, Executive VP
Rhonda Mims, Executive VP
Timothy Trodden, Executive VP

GROWTH PLANS/SPECIAL FEATURES:

WellCare Health Plans, Inc. manages government-sponsored healthcare programs with a focus on Medicaid and Medicare programs. The firm offers a variety of managed care health plans for families, children and the aged, blind and disabled, as well as prescription drug plans. The company has served health plans and prescription drug plans for approximately 6.3 million members (as of June 2019). WellCare's Medicare plans have been offered under the WellCare name, except for its Hawaii and California coordinated care plans (CCPs), which are under the names Ohana and WellCare of California, respectively. For Medicaid plans, the brands depend on the state and consist of: Staywell, Care1st, Ohana, Harmony, Missouri Care, Meridian and WellCare. In September 2018, WellCare acquired three Meridian companies, collectively for $2.5 billion: Meridian Health Plan of Michigan, Inc.; Meridian Health Plan of Illinois, Inc.; and MeridianRx. In November 2018, WellCare acquired Aetna's Part D membership for $115.8 million. In March 2019, WellCare Health Plans agreed to be acquired by Centene Corporation, a multi-line healthcare plan firm operating in two segments: managed care and specialty services, for $15.3 billion. The transaction is expected to close by mid-2020.

WellCare offers employees several family benefit plans, wellness plans, dental and vision, prescription drug coverage, life insurance, AD&D, disability, 401(k), flexible spending accounts, tuition reimbursement and an employee assistance plan.

FINANCIAL DATA:
Note: Data for latest year may not have been available at press time.

In U.S. $	2018	2017	2016	2015	2014	2013
Revenue	20,414,100,000	17,007,200,000	14,237,100,000	13,890,200,000	12,959,900,000	9,527,900,000
R&D Expense						
Operating Income	785,800,000	537,500,000	588,600,000	384,200,000	211,800,000	293,000,000
Operating Margin %		.03%	.04%	.03%	.02%	.03%
SGA Expense	1,701,000,000	1,484,700,000	1,133,100,000	1,132,900,000	1,018,800,000	856,500,000
Net Income	439,800,000	373,700,000	242,100,000	118,600,000	63,700,000	175,300,000
Operating Cash Flow	279,000,000	1,050,000,000	748,300,000	712,600,000	299,300,000	178,900,000
Capital Expenditure	153,500,000	128,400,000	105,300,000	137,000,000	74,800,000	62,000,000
EBITDA	960,000,000	650,500,000	676,200,000	462,900,000	277,100,000	334,300,000
Return on Assets %		.05%	.04%	.02%	.02%	.06%
Return on Equity %		.17%	.13%	.07%	.04%	.12%
Debt to Equity		0.489	0.499	0.528	0.564	0.395

CONTACT INFORMATION:
Phone: 813 290-6200   Fax:
Toll-Free: 800-795-3432
Address: 8725 Henderson Rd., Renaissance 1, Tampa, FL 33634 United States

STOCK TICKER/OTHER:
Stock Ticker: WCG
Employees: 7,400
Parent Company:

Exchange: NYS
Fiscal Year Ends: 12/31

SALARIES/BONUSES:
Top Exec. Salary: $1,284,615   Bonus: $
Second Exec. Salary: $661,154   Bonus: $

OTHER THOUGHTS:
Estimated Female Officers or Directors: 3
Hot Spot for Advancement for Women/Minorities: Y

Sales, profits and employees may be estimates. Financial information, benefits and other data can change quickly and may vary from those stated here.

Westlake Chemical Corporation

www.westlake.com

NAIC Code: 325110

TYPES OF BUSINESS:
Plastics & Rubber, Manufacturing
PVC Piping
Vinyls
Olefins

BRANDS/DIVISIONS/AFFILIATES:
Westlake Chemical Partners LP
Suzhou Huasu Plastic Co Ltd
Westlake Chemical OpCo LP

CONTACTS:
Note: Officers with more than one job title may be intentionally listed here more than once.

Albert Chao, CEO
M. Bender, CFO
James Chao, Chairman of the Board
George Mangieri, Chief Accounting Officer
L. Ederington, Chief Administrative Officer
Robert Buesinger, Executive VP, Divisional
Lawrence Teel, Executive VP, Divisional
Roger Kearns, Executive VP, Divisional
Andrew Kenner, Senior VP, Divisional

GROWTH PLANS/SPECIAL FEATURES:
Westlake Chemical Corporation manufactures and markets vinyls, basic chemicals and fabricated products for use in the packaging, automotive, construction and coatings industries. The company operates in two business segments: olefins and vinyls. The olefins business provides ethylene, polyethylene, styrene and co-products. These olefins are used to create a variety of petrochemical products including packaging film, coatings, injection molding and complex chemicals. Principal products for the vinyls business include polyvinyl chloride (PVC), vinyl chloride monomer (VCM), chlorine, caustic soda and ethylene. Westlake manufactures and markets specialty pipe and fittings, water, sewer, irrigation and conduit pipe products under the North American Pipe and Royal Building Products brand names. Westlake maintains manufacturing facilities in North America, Europe and Asia, producing approximately 42.1 billion pounds of aggregate in fiscal 2018-19. Principal manufacturing facilities are located in Louisiana, Texas, Kentucky and West Virginia, USA; and Bavaria and North Rhine-Westphalia, Germany. Additionally, subsidiary Westlake Chemical Partners LP operates, acquires and develops facilities for the processing of natural gas liquids and related assets; Suzhou Huasu Plastic Co. Ltd. operates a PVC fabrication facility in China; and Westlake Chemical OpCo LP operates an olefins facility in Lake Charles, Louisiana and an ethylene production facility in Calvert City, Kentucky.

Westlake offers employees life, AD&D, medical, dental, vision and long-term disability insurance; a 401(k); paid time off; and an assistance program.

FINANCIAL DATA:
Note: Data for latest year may not have been available at press time.

In U.S. $	2018	2017	2016	2015	2014	2013
Revenue	8,635,000,000	8,041,000,000	5,075,456,000	4,463,336,000	4,415,350,000	3,759,484,000
R&D Expense						
Operating Income	1,441,000,000	1,262,000,000	685,126,000	959,827,000	1,123,991,000	952,576,000
Operating Margin %		.16%	.13%	.22%	.25%	.25%
SGA Expense	445,000,000	399,000,000	295,436,000	225,364,000	193,359,000	147,974,000
Net Income	996,000,000	1,304,000,000	398,859,000	646,010,000	678,523,000	610,425,000
Operating Cash Flow	1,409,000,000	1,538,000,000	833,852,000	1,078,836,000	1,032,376,000	752,729,000
Capital Expenditure	702,000,000	577,000,000	628,483,000	491,426,000	431,104,000	679,358,000
EBITDA	2,101,000,000	1,841,000,000	1,015,518,000	1,243,854,000	1,329,756,000	1,118,062,000
Return on Assets %		.11%	.05%	.12%	.15%	.16%
Return on Equity %		.31%	.12%	.21%	.25%	.28%
Debt to Equity		0.642	1.044	0.234	0.262	0.316

CONTACT INFORMATION:
Phone: 713 960-9111 Fax:
Toll-Free:
Address: 2801 Post Oak Blvd., Ste. 600, Houston, TX 77056 United States

STOCK TICKER/OTHER:
Stock Ticker: WLK
Employees: 8,870
Parent Company:

Exchange: NYS
Fiscal Year Ends: 12/31

SALARIES/BONUSES:
Top Exec. Salary: $413,661   Bonus: $2,000,000
Second Exec. Salary: $1,089,000   Bonus: $

OTHER THOUGHTS:
Estimated Female Officers or Directors:
Hot Spot for Advancement for Women/Minorities:

Sales, profits and employees may be estimates. Financial information, benefits and other data can change quickly and may vary from those stated here.

Weyerhaeuser Company

www.weyerhaeuser.com

NAIC Code: 321113

TYPES OF BUSINESS:
Timber Lands
Lumber & Wood Products
OSB Panels
Sheathing
Plywood
Building Materials Distribution

BRANDS/DIVISIONS/AFFILIATES:

CONTACTS:
Note: Officers with more than one job title may be intentionally listed here more than once.

Devin Stockfish, CEO
Russell Hagen, CFO
Rick Holley, Chairman of the Board
David Wold, Chief Accounting Officer
Denise Merle, Chief Administrative Officer
Kristy Harlan, General Counsel
Keith O'Rear, Senior VP, Divisional
James Kilberg, Senior VP, Divisional
Adrian Blocker, Senior VP, Divisional

GROWTH PLANS/SPECIAL FEATURES:

Weyerhaeuser Company is a real estate investment trust (REIT) that primarily owns timberlands and manufactures wood products from the trees. The firm owns or controls 12.2 million acres of timberlands in the U.S., and manages an additional 14 million acres of timberlands under long-term licenses in Canada. Weyerhaeuser plants seedlings to reforest harvested areas, manages the timberlands as the trees grow to maturity, harvests trees to be converted into lumber/wood products/pellets/pulp/paper, manages the health of the forests to sustainably maximize harvest volumes and offers recreational access. The company manufactures and distributes high-quality wood products such as structural lumber, oriented strand board (OSB), engineered wood products and other specialty products. These products are primarily supplied to the residential, multi-family, industrial, light commercial and repair and remodel markets. Weyerhaeuser operates 35 manufacturing facilities in the U.S. and Canada. In addition, Weyerhaeuser has investments in oil and natural gas production, construction aggregates, mineral extraction, wind and solar power, communication tower leases and transportation rights of way that exist in its ownership.

FINANCIAL DATA:
Note: Data for latest year may not have been available at press time.

In U.S. $	2018	2017	2016	2015	2014	2013
Revenue	7,476,000,000	7,196,000,000	6,365,000,000	7,082,000,000	7,403,000,000	8,529,000,000
R&D Expense	8,000,000	14,000,000	19,000,000	24,000,000	27,000,000	33,000,000
Operating Income	1,418,000,000	1,187,000,000	998,000,000	1,016,000,000	1,222,000,000	1,141,000,000
Operating Margin %		.16%	.16%	.14%	.17%	.13%
SGA Expense	406,000,000	397,000,000	421,000,000	402,000,000	450,000,000	675,000,000
Net Income	748,000,000	582,000,000	1,027,000,000	506,000,000	1,826,000,000	563,000,000
Operating Cash Flow	1,112,000,000	1,201,000,000	735,000,000	1,064,000,000	1,088,000,000	1,004,000,000
Capital Expenditure	427,000,000	419,000,000	510,000,000	443,000,000	354,000,000	261,000,000
EBITDA	1,668,000,000	1,630,000,000	1,500,000,000	1,329,000,000	1,857,000,000	1,277,000,000
Return on Assets %		.03%	.06%	.04%	.13%	.04%
Return on Equity %		.06%	.14%	.09%	.30%	.10%
Debt to Equity		0.70	0.745	1.113	1.021	0.797

CONTACT INFORMATION:
Phone: 206-539-3000 Fax:
Toll-Free:
Address: 220 Occidental Ave. South, Seattle, WA 98104-7800 United States

STOCK TICKER/OTHER:
Stock Ticker: WY
Employees: 10,400
Parent Company:

Exchange: NYS
Fiscal Year Ends: 12/31

SALARIES/BONUSES:
Top Exec. Salary: $1,000,000 Bonus: $
Second Exec. Salary: $570,000 Bonus: $

OTHER THOUGHTS:
Estimated Female Officers or Directors:
Hot Spot for Advancement for Women/Minorities:

Whole Foods Market Inc

NAIC Code: 445110

www.wholefoodsmarket.com

TYPES OF BUSINESS:
Natural Foods Grocery Stores
Nutritional Supplements
Seafood Processing
Coffee Roasting
Supermarkets
Bakeries
Prepared Meals to Go

BRANDS/DIVISIONS/AFFILIATES:
Amazon.com Inc
365-Whole Foods Market
365 Everyday Value
Whole Catch
Whole Foods Market
Allegro Coffee
Engine 2 Plant-Strong
Whole Paws

CONTACTS:
Note: Officers with more than one job title may be intentionally listed here more than once.

John Mackey, CEO
A.C. Gallo, Pres.
Gabrielle Sulzberger, Chairman of the Board
Keith Manbeck, CFO
Sonya Gafsi Oblisk, VP-Global Mktg.
Jason Buechel, CIO
Kenneth Meyer, Executive VP, Divisional
David Lannon, Executive VP, Divisional
James Sud, Executive VP, Divisional
Keith Manbeck, Executive VP

GROWTH PLANS/SPECIAL FEATURES:
Whole Foods Market, Inc. owns and operates a chain of natural organic food supermarkets in the U.S. and internationally, with 470 stores in the U.S., 13 in Canada and seven in the U.K. (as of September 2018). The firm's stores generally feature foods made from natural ingredients and free of chemical additives. Whole Foods' merchandise items include organically-grown and high-grade commercial produce; grocery products; environmentally safe household items; hormone- and antibiotic-free meats; bulk foods; fresh bakery goods; soups, salads, entrees and sandwiches; vitamins; cosmetics; and miscellaneous items. Merchandise is sold through its private-label brands such as 365 Everyday Value, Whole Catch and Whole Foods Market, which are chef quality, all-natural foods and products. Its stores, averaging 38,000 square feet in size, are supplemented by regional distribution centers, bakeries, commissary kitchens, seafood-processing facilities, produce procurement centers and a coffee roasting operation. Smaller, value-focused stores are branded under the 365-Whole Foods Market name, bringing fresh, healthy and affordable food as well as unique products in a fun and convenient retail format. In addition, the company operates a website that offers features such as online recipes, health information and environmental issue information. Other brands include Allegro Coffee, Engine 2 Plant-Strong and Whole Paws. The prepared foods and bakery department accounts for 19% of total sales, while other perishables accounts for 48%. During 2017, Amazon.com, Inc. acquired Whole Foods for $13.7 billion. Amazon immediately made significant retail price drops on a wide variety of merchandise.

FINANCIAL DATA:
Note: Data for latest year may not have been available at press time.

In U.S. $	2018	2017	2016	2015	2014	2013
Revenue	16,831,500,000	16,030,000,000	15,724,000,256	15,388,999,680	14,193,999,872	12,917,000,192
R&D Expense						
Operating Income						
Operating Margin %						
SGA Expense						
Net Income		245,000,000	507,000,000	536,000,000	579,000,000	551,000,000
Operating Cash Flow						
Capital Expenditure						
EBITDA						
Return on Assets %						
Return on Equity %						
Debt to Equity						

CONTACT INFORMATION:
Phone: 512 477-4455   Fax: 512 477-1069
Toll-Free:
Address: 550 Bowie St., Austin, TX 78703 United States

STOCK TICKER/OTHER:
Stock Ticker: Subsidiary
Employees: 60,000
Parent Company: Amazon.com Inc
Exchange:
Fiscal Year Ends: 09/30

SALARIES/BONUSES:
Top Exec. Salary: $ Bonus: $
Second Exec. Salary: $ Bonus: $

OTHER THOUGHTS:
Estimated Female Officers or Directors: 9
Hot Spot for Advancement for Women/Minorities: Y

Workday Inc

www.workday.com

NAIC Code: 0

TYPES OF BUSINESS:
Human Resources Software
Enterprise Financial Planning Software

BRANDS/DIVISIONS/AFFILIATES:
Adaptive Insights

CONTACTS: Note: Officers with more than one job title may be intentionally listed here more than once.
Aneel Bhusri, CEO
Philip Wilmington, Vice Chairman
Robynne Sisco, CFO
Sheri Rhodes, Chief Information Officer
Christine Cefalo, Chief Marketing Officer
David Clarke, Chief Technology Officer
David Duffield, Co-Founder
James Bozzini, COO
Chano Fernandez, Co-Pres.
Thomas Bogan, Executive VP, Divisional
Petros Dermetzis, Other Executive Officer
Ashley Goldsmith, Other Executive Officer
Sayan Chakraborty, Senior VP, Divisional
Emily McEvilly, Senior VP, Divisional
Doug Robinson, Senior VP, Divisional
James Shaughnessy, Senior VP
Michael Stankey, Vice Chairman of the Board

GROWTH PLANS/SPECIAL FEATURES:
Workday, Inc. provides enterprise cloud applications for finance and human resources. The company delivers financial management, human capital management and analytics applications designed for the world's largest companies, educational institutions and government agencies. Its software covers human capital management (HCM), payroll, financial management, grants management, time tracking, procurement, employee expense management and insight applications. HCM software helps enterprises organize and manage a global workforce, with tools addressing workforce lifecycle management, compensation, absences, employee benefits administration and career and development planning. Payroll solutions are intended to streamline an organization's payroll functions across a global workforce. Financial management tools allow organizations to track and analyze core finance tasks, such as accounting, cash management, governance and compliance; revenue management, such as contracts, billing and revenue recognition; and business assets, including tangible and intangible assets, lifecycle depreciation and reclaiming business assets. Grants management tool allows educational and government organizations to follow grant activity access information for grant reporting. Time tracking services work with the firm's HCM, payroll and financial management software to collect, process and distribute workforce time data. Procurement allows customers to configure procurement business processes and efficiently work with and manage suppliers and purchase orders. Employee expense management automates configurable expense management business processes and leverages workers, roles, organizations and security policies from the firm's HCM program. Insight applications leverage advanced date science and machine learning methods to help customers make smarter financial and workforce decisions. The firm maintains data centers across the U.S. as well as internationally in Ireland, Amsterdam, the Netherlands and Canada.

Employees receive health, vision and dental coverage; basic life and personal accident insurance; flexible spending accounts; disability coverage; and a 401(k).

FINANCIAL DATA: Note: Data for latest year may not have been available at press time.

In U.S. $	2018	2017	2016	2015	2014	2013
Revenue	2,143,050,000	1,569,407,000	1,162,346,000	787,860,000	468,938,000	
R&D Expense	910,584,000	680,531,000	469,944,000	316,868,000	182,116,000	
Operating Income	-303,223,000	-376,665,000	-264,659,000	-215,702,000	-153,282,000	
Operating Margin %	-.14%	-.24%	-.23%	-.27%	-.33%	
SGA Expense	906,276,000	781,996,000	582,634,000	421,891,000	263,294,000	
Net Income	-321,222,000	-408,278,000	-289,918,000	-247,982,000	-172,509,000	
Operating Cash Flow	465,727,000	348,655,000	258,637,000	102,003,000	46,263,000	
Capital Expenditure	152,536,000	120,813,000	133,667,000	103,646,000	75,725,000	
EBITDA	-133,263,000	-263,104,000	-171,030,000	-155,707,000	-116,518,000	
Return on Assets %	-.08%	-.14%	-.11%	-.11%	-.11%	
Return on Equity %	-.23%	-.36%	-.26%	-.21%	-.19%	
Debt to Equity	0.728	0.46	0.447	0.436	0.398	

CONTACT INFORMATION:
Phone: 925-951-9000 Fax:
Toll-Free: 877-967-5329
Address: 6230 Stoneridge Mall Rd., Ste. 200, Pleasanton, CA 94588 United States

STOCK TICKER/OTHER:
Stock Ticker: WDAY
Employees: 11,000
Parent Company:

Exchange: NAS
Fiscal Year Ends:

SALARIES/BONUSES:
Top Exec. Salary: $296,402 Bonus: $373,460
Second Exec. Salary: $339,231 Bonus: $200,000

OTHER THOUGHTS:
Estimated Female Officers or Directors: 2
Hot Spot for Advancement for Women/Minorities:

Sales, profits and employees may be estimates. Financial information, benefits and other data can change quickly and may vary from those stated here.

WW Grainger Inc

www.grainger.com

NAIC Code: 423830

TYPES OF BUSINESS:
Industrial Equipment & Products-Wholesale
Maintenance & Repair Products
Online Sales
Safety Products
Logistics Services

BRANDS/DIVISIONS/AFFILIATES:
Acklands-Grainger Inc
Zoro
Zoro.com
MonotaRO
DAYTON
SPEEDAIRE
AIR HANDLER
TOUGH GUY

CONTACTS:
Note: Officers with more than one job title may be intentionally listed here more than once.

Donald Macpherson, CEO
Thomas Okray, CFO
Eric Tapia, Chief Accounting Officer
John Howard, General Counsel
Kathleen Carroll, Other Executive Officer
Paige Robbins, Other Executive Officer
Deidra Merriwether, Senior VP, Divisional
Laura Brown, Senior VP, Divisional

GROWTH PLANS/SPECIAL FEATURES:

W. W. Grainger, Inc. offers facilities maintenance, repair and operating (MRO) products and services to more than 3.5 million customers such as businesses and institutions. The company is divided into two segments: U.S. and Canada. The U.S. segment offers a broad selection of MRO products and services. It purchases the products from approximately 3,000 suppliers, most of which are manufacturers, to fulfill the orders of its 1,100+ clients. This division operates and fulfills orders nationally through a network of 283 branches and 16 distribution centers, as well as an eCommerce platform and sales and service representatives. W.W. Grainger's customers represent a wide range of industries, including government, manufacturing, transportation, commercial and contractors. Products include material-handling equipment, safety and security supplies, lighting and electrical products, power and hand tools, pumps and plumbing supplies, cleaning and maintenance supplies and metalworking tools. W.W. Grainger's registered trademarks include DAYTON, SPEEDAIRE, AIR HANDLER, TOUGH GUY, WESTWARD and LUMAPRO. The Canada segment operates through Acklands-Grainger, Inc., has access to more than 194,000 stocked products, providing them to its Canadian customers through its branches, distribution centers and sales and service representatives. Other businesses of W. W. Grainger include: Zoro in the U.S., an online MRO distributor that primarily serves U.S. customers through its Zoro.com website, offering more than 2 million products; and MonotaRO in Japan and other Asian countries, which provides customers with access to approximately 20 million MRO products through its websites and catalogs.

Employee benefits include health, dental and prescription coverage; a profit sharing plan; an employee assistance program; adoption benefits; dependent care assistance; critical illness insurance; and a group legal plan.

FINANCIAL DATA:
Note: Data for latest year may not have been available at press time.

In U.S. $	2018	2017	2016	2015	2014	2013
Revenue	11,221,000,000	10,424,860,000	10,137,200,000	9,973,384,000	9,964,953,000	9,437,758,000
R&D Expense						
Operating Income	1,158,000,000	1,048,662,000	1,119,497,000	1,300,320,000	1,347,117,000	1,296,854,000
Operating Margin %	.10%	.10%	.11%	.13%	.14%	.14%
SGA Expense	3,190,000,000	3,048,895,000	2,995,060,000	2,931,108,000	2,967,125,000	2,839,629,000
Net Income	782,000,000	585,730,000	605,928,000	768,996,000	801,729,000	797,036,000
Operating Cash Flow	1,057,000,000	1,056,557,000	1,002,976,000	989,904,000	959,814,000	986,498,000
Capital Expenditure	239,000,000	237,283,000	284,249,000	373,868,000	387,390,000	272,145,000
EBITDA	1,426,000,000	1,279,846,000	1,334,247,000	1,512,243,000	1,552,805,000	1,481,437,000
Return on Assets %		.10%	.10%	.14%	.15%	.15%
Return on Equity %		.33%	.30%	.28%	.25%	.25%
Debt to Equity		1.33	1.024	0.613	0.126	0.137

CONTACT INFORMATION:
Phone: 847 535-1000   Fax:
Toll-Free: 800-323-0620
Address: 100 Grainger Pkwy., Lake Forest, IL 60045 United States

STOCK TICKER/OTHER:
Stock Ticker: GWW   Exchange: NYS
Employees: 25,600   Fiscal Year Ends: 12/31
Parent Company:

SALARIES/BONUSES:
Top Exec. Salary: $1,030,000   Bonus: $
Second Exec. Salary: $703,533   Bonus: $

OTHER THOUGHTS:
Estimated Female Officers or Directors:
Hot Spot for Advancement for Women/Minorities: Y

Wyndham Destinations Inc

NAIC Code: 721110

www.wyndhamdestinations.com

TYPES OF BUSINESS:
Hotels, Motels & Resorts
Property Management
Hotel Development
Vacation Property Exchange and Rental
Timeshare Resorts
Franchising
Vacation Ownership

BRANDS/DIVISIONS/AFFILIATES:
Club Wyndham
WorldMarkt by Wyndham
Margaritaville Vacation Club by Wyndham
RCI
Wyndham Worldwide Corporation
Wyndham Hotels & Resorts

GROWTH PLANS/SPECIAL FEATURES:
Wyndham Destinations, Inc. (formerly Wyndham Worldwide Corporation) operates more than 220 vacation ownership resorts and 4,300 affiliated exchange properties, with a global presence in 110 countries. The firm is a leading professionally-managed rental business in North America, offering over 20 brands. Vacation clubs within Wyndham's portfolio include Club Wyndham, WorldMark by Wyndham, and Margaritaville Vacation Club by Wyndham. Vacation ownerships can be exchanged for time at other resorts worldwide through the company's RCI exchange program. In mid-2018, Wyndham Worldwide Corporation spun off its Wyndham Hotels & Resorts subsidiary and changed its own corporate name to Wyndham Destinations, Inc. During February 2019, the firm announced plans to develop a new timeshare resort in Moab, Utah, and announced that it had started construction of new suites at its existing resort in Scottsdale, Arizona.

CONTACTS:
Note: Officers with more than one job title may be intentionally listed here more than once.

Michael Brown, CEO
Michael Hug, CFO
Stephen Holmes, Chairman of the Board
Elizabeth Dreyer, Chief Accounting Officer
James Savina, Chief Compliance Officer
Brad Dettmer, Chief Information Officer
Geoffrey Richards, COO, Divisional
Kimberly Marshall, Other Executive Officer
Jeffrey Myers, Other Executive Officer
Noah Brodsky, Other Executive Officer

FINANCIAL DATA:
Note: Data for latest year may not have been available at press time.

In U.S. $	2018	2017	2016	2015	2014	2013
Revenue	3,931,000,000	5,076,000,000	5,599,000,000	5,536,000,000	5,281,000,000	5,009,000,000
R&D Expense						
Operating Income	758,000,000	1,024,000,000	1,072,000,000	1,028,000,000	987,000,000	928,000,000
Operating Margin %		.20%	.19%	.19%	.19%	.19%
SGA Expense	1,122,000,000	1,421,000,000	1,543,000,000	1,574,000,000	1,557,000,000	1,471,000,000
Net Income	672,000,000	871,000,000	611,000,000	612,000,000	529,000,000	432,000,000
Operating Cash Flow	442,000,000	987,000,000	973,000,000	991,000,000	984,000,000	1,008,000,000
Capital Expenditure	99,000,000	153,000,000	191,000,000	222,000,000	235,000,000	238,000,000
EBITDA	704,000,000	959,000,000	1,328,000,000	1,275,000,000	1,191,000,000	1,030,000,000
Return on Assets %		.09%	.06%	.06%	.05%	.04%
Return on Equity %		1.09%	.73%	.56%	.37%	.24%
Debt to Equity		6.476	7.399	5.216	3.818	2.839

CONTACT INFORMATION:
Phone: 407-626-5200   Fax:
Toll-Free:
Address: 6277 Sea Harbor Dr., Orlando, FL 32821 United States

SALARIES/BONUSES:
Top Exec. Salary: $278,659   Bonus: $1,750,000
Second Exec. Salary: $223,371   Bonus: $1,010,000

STOCK TICKER/OTHER:
Stock Ticker: WYND
Employees: 37,800
Parent Company:

Exchange: NYS
Fiscal Year Ends: 12/31

OTHER THOUGHTS:
Estimated Female Officers or Directors: 2
Hot Spot for Advancement for Women/Minorities: Y

Sales, profits and employees may be estimates. Financial information, benefits and other data can change quickly and may vary from those stated here.

Wynn Resorts Limited

NAIC Code: 721120

www.wynnresorts.com

TYPES OF BUSINESS:
Hotel Casinos
Online Poker

BRANDS/DIVISIONS/AFFILIATES:
Wynn Las Vegas Resort & Country Club
Encore at Wynn Las Vegas
Wynn Macau Resort
Wynn Palace
Encore Theater
Encore at Wynn Macau
Wynn Boston Harbor

CONTACTS:
Note: Officers with more than one job title may be intentionally listed here more than once.

Matt Maddox, CEO
Craig Billings, CFO
Philip Satre, Chairman of the Board
Ellen Whittemore, Executive VP
Ian Coughlan, Other Corporate Officer
Linda Chen, Other Corporate Officer

GROWTH PLANS/SPECIAL FEATURES:

Wynn Resorts Limited is a developer, owner and operator of destination casino resorts. The firm owns and operates three destination casino resorts: Wynn Las Vegas Resort & Country Club in Las Vegas, Nevada, which includes Encore at Wynn Las Vegas; Wynn Macau Resort in the Macau Special Administrative Region of China; and Wynn Palace in the Cotai region of Macau. The Las Vegas operations offer 4,748 rooms and suites. The 192,000-square-foot casino features 247 table games, a poker room, 1,811 slot machines and a race and sports book. The resort also features 33 food and beverage outlets; three nightclubs; two spas and salons; a Ferrari and Maserati automobile dealership; wedding chapels; an 18-hole golf course; 290,000 square feet of meeting space; and a 160,000-square-foot retail promenade featuring boutiques from Alexander McQueen, Cartier, Chanel and Louis Vuitton. At the Encore Theater, the company offers headlining entertainment acts from personalities such as Beyonce. The company's Wynn Macau resort operations, including Encore at Wynn Macau, features 1,008 rooms and suites, approximately 273,000 square feet of casino gaming space with 810 slot machines and 317 table games, 11 food and beverage outlets, two health clubs, spas, 59,000 square feet of retail space and 31,000 square feet of meeting/convention space. Wynn Palace is a resort featuring 1,706 rooms and suites, 424,000 square feet of casino space with 320 table games and 1,041 slot machines, 13 food and beverage outlets, 106,000 square feet of high-end retail space, 37,000 square feet of meeting space and recreation/leisure facilities such as a gondola ride, health club, spa, salon and pool. The Wynn Boston Harbor is a new development under construction in Everett, Massachusetts (adjacent to Boston), and is scheduled to open in June 2019.

FINANCIAL DATA:
Note: Data for latest year may not have been available at press time.

In U.S. $	2018	2017	2016	2015	2014	2013
Revenue	6,717,660,000	6,306,368,000	4,466,297,000	4,075,883,000	5,433,661,000	5,620,936,000
R&D Expense						
Operating Income	1,259,357,000	1,085,141,000	576,484,000	669,349,000	1,276,715,000	1,307,229,000
Operating Margin %		.17%	.13%	.16%	.23%	.23%
SGA Expense	761,415,000	685,485,000	548,141,000	464,793,000	492,464,000	448,788,000
Net Income	572,430,000	747,181,000	241,975,000	195,290,000	731,554,000	728,652,000
Operating Cash Flow	961,489,000	1,876,577,000	970,546,000	572,813,000	1,098,317,000	1,676,642,000
Capital Expenditure	1,602,386,000	949,045,000	1,240,928,000	1,925,152,000	1,345,940,000	506,786,000
EBITDA	1,238,185,000	1,501,301,000	1,004,692,000	912,782,000	1,588,043,000	1,656,596,000
Return on Assets %		.06%	.02%	.02%	.08%	.09%
Return on Equity %		1.35%	10.53%			
Debt to Equity		10.092	64.105			

CONTACT INFORMATION:
Phone: 702 770-7555   Fax: 702 733-4681
Toll-Free:
Address: 3131 Las Vegas Blvd. South, Las Vegas, NV 89109 United States

SALARIES/BONUSES:
Top Exec. Salary: $1,901,923   Bonus: $
Second Exec. Salary: $849,519   Bonus: $

STOCK TICKER/OTHER:
Stock Ticker: WYNN
Employees: 24,600
Parent Company:

Exchange: NAS
Fiscal Year Ends: 12/31

OTHER THOUGHTS:
Estimated Female Officers or Directors: 3
Hot Spot for Advancement for Women/Minorities: Y

XPO Logistics Inc

www.xpologistics.com

NAIC Code: 488510

TYPES OF BUSINESS:
Freight Transportation Arrangement
Logistics
Supply Chain Solutions
Transportation Fleet

BRANDS/DIVISIONS/AFFILIATES:

CONTACTS:
Note: Officers with more than one job title may be intentionally listed here more than once.
Bradley Jacobs, CEO
Sarah Glickman, CFO
Lance Robinson, Chief Accounting Officer
Mario Harik, Chief Information Officer
AnnaMaria DeSalva, Director
Troy Cooper, President

GROWTH PLANS/SPECIAL FEATURES:

XPO Logistics, Inc. is a global logistics provider of supply chain solutions to companies worldwide, serving more than 50,000 customers via 1,535 locations in 32 countries. The U.S. derives approximately 59% of annual revenue (for 2018), France derives 13%, the U.K. derives 12% and other geographies, primarily across Europe and Asia, derive the remaining 16%. XPO operates its business in two segments: transportation and logistics. The transportation segment offers customers a network of multiple modes, flexible capacity and route density to swiftly and cost-effectively transport goods from origin to destination. This division provides freight brokerage, dedicated, non-dedicated, freight forwarding, last mile logistics, expedited shipment, truckload (TL), less-than-truckload (LTL) and intermodal services through its network of ocean, air, ground and cross-border capabilities. Globally, this segment's road fleet encompass approximately 16,000 tractors and 39,000 trailers, primarily related to its TL and LTL operations. The logistics segment, which is also referred to as supply chain or contract logistics by XPO, provides differentiated and data-intensive services, including highly-engineered and customized solutions, value-added warehousing and distribution, cold chain distribution and other inventory management solutions. This division performs eCommerce fulfillment, reverse logistics, recycling, storage, factory support, aftermarket support, manufacturing, distribution, packaging and labeling, as well as customized solutions. In addition, this segment offers supply chain optimization services such as production flow management and transportation management. Globally, XPO operates approximately 190 million square feet (18 million square meters) of contract logistics facility space, with about 91 million sf (8 million square meters) of that space located in the U.S.

FINANCIAL DATA:
Note: Data for latest year may not have been available at press time.

In U.S. $	2018	2017	2016	2015	2014	2013
Revenue	17,279,000,000	15,380,800,000	14,619,400,000	7,623,200,000	2,356,600,000	702,303,000
R&D Expense						
Operating Income	704,000,000	623,200,000	488,100,000	-28,600,000	-40,900,000	-52,325,000
Operating Margin %		.04%	.03%	.00%	-.02%	-.07%
SGA Expense	1,837,000,000	1,656,500,000	1,651,200,000	183,900,000	72,000,000	29,358,000
Net Income	422,000,000	340,200,000	69,000,000	-191,100,000	-63,600,000	-48,530,000
Operating Cash Flow	1,102,000,000	798,600,000	625,000,000	90,800,000	-21,300,000	-66,302,000
Capital Expenditure	551,000,000	503,800,000	483,400,000	249,000,000	44,600,000	11,585,000
EBITDA	1,499,000,000	1,203,400,000	1,111,300,000	299,100,000	56,600,000	-32,008,000
Return on Assets %		.03%	.01%	-.03%	-.06%	-.09%
Return on Equity %		.10%	.02%	-.11%	-.11%	-.17%
Debt to Equity		1.24	1.78	1.971	0.367	0.44

CONTACT INFORMATION:
Phone: 855-976-4636   Fax:
Toll-Free:
Address: Five american Lane, Greenwich, CT 06831 United States

STOCK TICKER/OTHER:
Stock Ticker: XPO
Employees: 98,000
Parent Company:

Exchange: NYS
Fiscal Year Ends: 12/31

SALARIES/BONUSES:
Top Exec. Salary: $425,000   Bonus: $276,300
Second Exec. Salary: $625,000   Bonus: $

OTHER THOUGHTS:
Estimated Female Officers or Directors: 2
Hot Spot for Advancement for Women/Minorities:

Sales, profits and employees may be estimates. Financial information, benefits and other data can change quickly and may vary from those stated here.

Zillow Inc

NAIC Code: 519130

www.zillow.com

TYPES OF BUSINESS:
Online Real Estate Information

BRANDS/DIVISIONS/AFFILIATES:
Zillow
Trulia
StreetEasy
HotPads
Naked Apartments
Zestimates
Mortech
dotloop

CONTACTS:
Note: Officers with more than one job title may be intentionally listed here more than once.

Richard Barton, CEO
Allen Parker, CFO
Lloyd Frink, Chairman of the Board
Jennifer Rock, Chief Accounting Officer
David Beitel, Chief Technology Officer
Arik Prawer, Other Corporate Officer
Dan Spaulding, Other Executive Officer
Stanley Humphries, Other Executive Officer
Errol Samuelson, Other Executive Officer
Greg Schwartz, President, Divisional
Jeremy Wacksman, President, Divisional

GROWTH PLANS/SPECIAL FEATURES:
Zillow, Inc. operates a real estate information marketplace dedicated to providing information about homes, real estate listings and mortgages and enabling homeowners, buyers, sellers and renters to connect with real estate and mortgage professionals. The company maintains a database of over 110 million homes in the U.S. that are either for sale, for rent or not currently on the market. Individuals and businesses that use Zillow have updated information on more than 68 million homes and added millions of home photos, creating exclusive home profiles that are available nowhere else. These profiles include detailed information about homes, such as property descriptions, listing information and purchase and sale histories. Zillow's real estate and rental marketplaces comprise consumer brands such as Zillow, Trulia, StreetEasy, HotPads, Naked Apartments, RealEstate.com and OutEast.com. In conjunction with the database, the firm offers users its proprietary automated valuation models, Zestimates and Rent Zestimates, on more than 100 million homes. Zillow also owns and operates a number of brands for real estate and mortgage professionals, including Mortech, dotloop, Bridge Interactive and New Home Feed.

FINANCIAL DATA:
Note: Data for latest year may not have been available at press time.

In U.S. $	2018	2017	2016	2015	2014	2013
Revenue	1,333,554,000	1,076,794,000	846,589,000	644,677,000	325,893,000	197,545,000
R&D Expense	410,818,000	319,985,000	273,066,000	198,565,000	86,406,000	48,498,000
Operating Income	-45,628,000	12,589,000	-192,682,000	-93,036,000	-23,202,000	-16,949,000
Operating Margin %		.01%	-.23%	-.14%	-.07%	-.09%
SGA Expense	814,774,000	659,017,000	694,614,000	477,534,000	233,228,000	147,186,000
Net Income	-119,858,000	-94,420,000	-220,438,000	-148,874,000	-43,610,000	-12,453,000
Operating Cash Flow	3,850,000	258,191,000	8,645,000	22,659,000	45,519,000	31,298,000
Capital Expenditure	78,535,000	78,635,000	71,722,000	68,108,000	44,242,000	25,972,000
EBITDA	-10,314,000	-46,334,000	-112,310,000	-72,644,000	12,422,000	6,305,000
Return on Assets %		-.03%	-.07%	-.08%	-.07%	-.03%
Return on Equity %		-.04%	-.08%	-.09%	-.08%	-.03%
Debt to Equity		0.145	0.145	0.086		

CONTACT INFORMATION:
Phone: 206 470-7000
Fax:
Toll-Free:
Address: 1301 Second Ave., Fl. 31, Seattle, WA 98101 United States

STOCK TICKER/OTHER:
Stock Ticker: Z
Employees: 4,300
Parent Company:
Exchange: NAS
Fiscal Year Ends: 12/31

SALARIES/BONUSES:
Top Exec. Salary: $423,225 Bonus: $500,000
Second Exec. Salary: $57,273 Bonus: $750,000

OTHER THOUGHTS:
Estimated Female Officers or Directors: 2
Hot Spot for Advancement for Women/Minorities: Y

Zimmer Biomet Holdings Inc

www.zimmerbiomet.com/

NAIC Code: 339100

TYPES OF BUSINESS:
Orthopedic Supplies
Human Bone Joint Replacement Systems
Orthopedic Support Devices
Operating Room Supplies
Powered Surgical Instruments
Dental Implants

BRANDS/DIVISIONS/AFFILIATES:
Persona
Zimmer
Taperloc
JuggerKnot
Gel-One
ALPS
3i T3
ROSA

CONTACTS: Note: Officers with more than one job title may be intentionally listed here more than once.
Bryan Hanson, CEO
Daniel Florin, CFO
Larry Glasscock, Director
Aure Bruneau, President, Divisional
Ivan Tornos, President, Divisional
Didier Deltort, President, Geographical
Sang Yi, President, Geographical
Chad Phipps, Senior VP

GROWTH PLANS/SPECIAL FEATURES:
Zimmer Biomet Holdings, Inc. designs, manufactures and markets musculoskeletal products for the healthcare industry. These include orthopedic reconstructive products; sports medicine, biologics, extremities and trauma products; spine, bone healing, craniomaxillofacial and thoracic products; dental implants; and related surgical products. Zimmer Biomet collaborates with healthcare professionals worldwide to advance the pace of innovation. The company's products and solutions help treat patients suffering from disorders of, or injuries to bones, joints or supporting soft tissues. Knee products include the Persona, NexGen, Vanguard and Oxford branded systems. Hip products include the Zimmer, Taperloc, Arcos, Continuum and G7 branded systems. Surgical, sports medicine, biologics, foot and ankle, extremities and trauma products include the A.T.S. automatic tourniquet systems, JuggerKnot soft anchor system, Gel-One cross-linked hyaluronate, Zimmer Trabecular Metal reverse shoulder system, Comprehensive shoulder system, Zimmer Natural Nail system and A.L.P.S. plating system. Dental products include the Tapered Screw-Vent and 3i T3 implant systems. Spine and craniomaxillofacial and thoracic products include the Polaris spinal system, Mobi-C cervical disc, and SternaLock closure and fixation systems brand lines. During 2019, Zimmer Biomet received FDA clearance of ROSA ONE spine system for robotically-assisted surgeries; and received FDA clearance for ROSA knee system for robotically-assisted surgeries.

FINANCIAL DATA: Note: Data for latest year may not have been available at press time.

In U.S. $	2018	2017	2016	2015	2014	2013
Revenue	7,932,900,000	7,824,100,000	7,683,900,000	5,997,800,000	4,673,300,000	4,623,400,000
R&D Expense	391,700,000	369,900,000	365,600,000	268,800,000	192,800,000	205,000,000
Operating Income	1,147,200,000	1,347,700,000	1,087,200,000	929,000,000	1,174,700,000	1,159,400,000
Operating Margin %		.17%	.14%	.15%	.25%	.24%
SGA Expense	3,526,200,000	3,369,700,000	3,283,400,000	2,660,500,000	2,050,000,000	1,966,900,000
Net Income	-379,200,000	1,813,800,000	305,900,000	147,000,000	720,100,000	761,000,000
Operating Cash Flow	1,747,400,000	1,582,300,000	1,632,200,000	816,700,000	1,052,800,000	963,100,000
Capital Expenditure	439,000,000	493,000,000	530,200,000	434,100,000	342,300,000	292,900,000
EBITDA	1,058,700,000	1,854,800,000	1,796,800,000	1,152,200,000	1,382,800,000	1,409,700,000
Return on Assets %		.07%	.01%	.01%	.07%	.08%
Return on Equity %		.17%	.03%	.02%	.11%	.13%
Debt to Equity		0.76	1.103	1.168	0.218	0.265

CONTACT INFORMATION:
Phone: 574-267-6639 Fax: 574-267-8137
Toll-Free: 800-613-6131
Address: 345 East Main St., Warsaw, IN 46580 United States

STOCK TICKER/OTHER:
Stock Ticker: ZBH
Employees: 18,500
Parent Company:

Exchange: NYS
Fiscal Year Ends: 05/31

SALARIES/BONUSES:
Top Exec. Salary: $1,050,000 Bonus: $
Second Exec. Salary: $113,077 Bonus: $763,000

OTHER THOUGHTS:
Estimated Female Officers or Directors: 3
Hot Spot for Advancement for Women/Minorities: Y

ADDITIONAL INDEXES

CONTENTS:

Index of Firms Noted as "Hot Spots for Advancement" for Women/Minorities	**588**
Index by Subsidiaries, Brand Names and Selected Affiliations	**590**

INDEX OF FIRMS NOTED AS HOT SPOTS FOR ADVANCEMENT FOR WOMEN & MINORITIES

3M Company
Abbott Laboratories
ABM Industries Incorporated
Accenture LLP
Acosta Inc
Adobe Systems Inc
Advance Auto Parts Inc
Advanced Micro Devices Inc (AMD)
AdventHealth
Advocate Aurora Health
AECOM
Aetna Inc
AFLAC Incorporated
Airbnb Inc
Alaska Air Group Inc
Alcoa Corporation
Alliance Data Systems Corporation
Allscripts Healthcare Solutions Inc
Alphabet Inc (Google)
Amazon.com Inc
American Airlines Group Inc
American Express Company
American Financial Group Inc
American International Group Inc (AIG)
American Tower Corporation (REIT)
Amerigroup Corporation
AmerisourceBergen Corporation
Amgen Inc
AMSURG Corporation
Anixter International Inc
Anthem Inc
Aon Hewitt
Applied Materials Inc
Archer-Daniels-Midland Company (ADM)
Arrow Electronics Inc
Arthur J Gallagher & Co
Ascena Retail Group Inc
Ascension
AT&T Inc
Automatic Data Processing Inc (ADP)
Avnet Inc
Ball Corporation
Bank of America Corporation
Bank of New York Mellon Corporation
Baxter International Inc
BB&T Corporation
Bechtel Group Inc
Becton, Dickinson and Company
Belden Inc
Best Buy Co Inc
Biogen Inc
Bio-Rad Laboratories Inc
BJC HealthCare
Black & Veatch Holding Company
BlackRock Inc
Bloomberg LP
Blue Shield of California
BMC Software Inc

Booking Holdings Inc
Booz Allen Hamilton Holding Corporation
BorgWarner Inc
Boston Consulting Group Inc (The, BCG)
Boston Scientific Corporation
Brinker International Inc
Bristol-Myers Squibb Company
Broadcom Inc
Brown & Brown Inc
Buffalo Wild Wings Inc
CACI International Inc
Capital One Financial Corporation
Cardinal Health Inc
Cargill Incorporated
CarMax Inc
Carnival Corporation
CBS Corporation
CDW Corporation
Celanese Corporation
Celgene Corporation
Centene Corporation
CenturyLink Inc
Cerner Corporation
CH Robinson Worldwide Inc
Charles River Laboratories International Inc
Charles Schwab Corporation (The)
Chemed Corporation
Chevron Corporation
Chevron Phillips Chemical Company LLC
Chick-fil-A Inc
Cigna Corporation
Cisco Systems Inc
Citigroup Inc
Cleveland Clinic Foundation (The)
Clorox Company (The)
Coca-Cola Bottling Co Consolidated
Comcast Corporation
Community Health Systems Inc
ConocoPhillips Company
Container Store Inc (The)
Cooper Companies Inc (The)
Corning Incorporated
CoStar Group Inc
Costco Wholesale Corporation
Cox Communications Inc
Cox Enterprises Inc
Crown Holdings Inc
Cullen-Frost Bankers Inc
Cummins Inc
CVS Health Corporation
Dana Incorporated
Darden Restaurants Inc
DaVita Healthcare Partners Inc
Deere & Company (John Deere)
Dell EMC
Dell Technologies Inc
Deloitte LLP
Delta Air Lines Inc
Discovery Inc
Disney Media Networks
DowDupont Inc
DTE Energy Company
Duke Energy Corporation
Edward D Jones & Co LP

Edwards Lifesciences Corporation
Eli Lilly and Company
EMCOR Group Inc
Emerson Electric Co
Enterprise Holdings Inc
Estee Lauder Companies Inc (The)
Exelon Corporation
Exxon Mobil Corporation (ExxonMobil)
ExxonMobil Chemical Company Inc
EY LLP
F5 Networks Inc
Facebook Inc
FactSet Research Systems Inc
Fairview Health Services
FedEx Corporation
FirstEnergy Corporation
Fluor Corporation
Ford Motor Company
Frito-Lay North America Inc
FTI Consulting Inc
Gartner Inc
Genentech Inc
General Dynamics Corporation
General Motors Company (GM)
GoDaddy Inc
Goldman Sachs Group Inc (The)
Group 1 Automotive Inc
HanesBrands Inc
Harris Corporation
Hartford Financial Services Group Inc (The)
Health Care Service Corporation (HCSC)
HEB Grocery Company LP
Henry Schein Inc
Hershey Company (The)
Hillenbrand Inc
Hill-Rom Holdings Inc
Hilton Worldwide Holdings Inc
Home Depot Inc (The)
Houston Methodist
Hub International Limited
Humana Inc
Hyatt Hotels Corporation
IAC/InterActiveCorp
IDEXX Laboratories Inc
Illinois Tool Works Inc
Ingram Micro Inc
Ingredion Incorporated
In-N-Out Burgers Inc
Intel Corporation
Interpublic Group of Companies Inc
Intuit Inc
IQVIA Holdings Inc
Jabil Inc
Jack Henry & Associates Inc
Jacobs Engineering Group Inc
JB Hunt Transport Services Inc
JetBlue Airways Corporation
John Hancock Financial
Johnson & Johnson
Jones Lang LaSalle Incorporated
JP Morgan Chase & Co Inc
Juniper Networks Inc
Kaiser Permanente
KBR Inc

Kelly Services Inc
Kimpton Hotel & Restaurant Group LLC
Kindred Healthcare LLC
Kohls Corporation
Kroger Co (The)
Laboratory Corporation of America Holdings
Lam Research Corporation
Lennar Corporation
LHC Group Inc
Liberty Mutual Group Inc
LifePoint Health Inc
Lincoln National Corporation
LinkedIn Corporation
Lockheed Martin Corporation
Loews Hotels Holding Corporation
Lowe's Companies Inc
Magellan Health Inc
Marriott International Inc
Marsh & McLennan Companies Inc
Mary Kay Inc
MassMutual Financial Group
MasterCard Inc
MAXIMUS Inc
Mayo Clinic
McAfee LLC
McCann Worldgroup
McCormick & Company Incorporated
McDonald's Corporation
McKesson Corporation
McKinsey & Company Inc
MedStar Health
Mercer LLC
Merck & Co Inc
Microsoft Corporation
Modine Manufacturing Company
Molina Healthcare Inc
Moody's Corporation
Morgan Stanley
Mutual of Omaha Companies (The)
NBCUniversal Media LLC
NCR Corporation
Netflix Inc
New York Life Insurance Company
Nielsen Holdings plc
Nike Inc
Nordstrom Inc
Northrop Grumman Corporation
Northwestern Mutual Life Insurance Company (The)
Norwegian Cruise Line Holdings Ltd (NCL)
O Reilly Automotive Inc
Oliver Wyman Group
Omnicom Group Inc
Oracle Corporation
Oracle NetSuite
Oshkosh Corporation
Owens Corning
PAREXEL International Corporation
Paychex Inc
PayPal Holdings Inc
PepsiCo Inc
PerkinElmer Inc
PetSmart Inc

Pfizer Inc
Phillips 66
PPG Industries Inc
PRA Health Sciences Inc
PriceSmart Inc
PricewaterhouseCoopers (PwC)
Principal Financial Group Inc
Procter & Gamble Company (The)
Progressive Corporation (The)
Providence St Joseph Health
Prudential Financial Inc
Publix Super Markets Inc
PulteGroup Inc
Qualcomm Incorporated
Quest Diagnostics Incorporated
Raymond James Financial Inc
Raytheon Company
Red Hat Inc
REI (Recreational Equipment Inc)
Revlon Inc
Ross Stores Inc
Royal Caribbean Cruises Ltd
Ryder System Inc
Safeco Insurance Company of America
Safeway Inc
SalesForce.com Inc
SAS Institute Inc
Schlumberger Limited
Science Applications International Corporation (SAIC)
Sherwin-Williams Company (The)
Sodexo Inc
Southwest Airlines Co
Spirit AeroSystems Holdings Inc
Stanley Black & Decker Inc
Starbucks Corporation
State Farm Insurance Companies
Stryker Corporation
Sutter Health Inc
Symantec Corporation
Synopsys Inc
SYSCO Corporation
TD Ameritrade Holding Corporation
Team Health Holdings Inc
Tenneco Inc
Texas Instruments Inc (TI)
Textron Inc
Thermo Fisher Scientific Inc
TIAA
TJX Companies Inc (T.J. Maxx)
Tractor Supply Company
Travelers Companies Inc (The)
Trimble Inc
Trinity Health
Trinity Industries Inc
Tyson Foods Inc
United Continental Holdings Inc
United Natural Foods Inc
United Parcel Service Inc (UPS)
United States Cellular Corporation
United Technologies Corporation
UnitedHealth Group Inc
Universal Health Services Inc
Unum Group
US Bancorp (US Bank)

USAA
Valassis Communications Inc
Valero Energy Corporation
Varian Medical Systems Inc
Verizon Communications Inc
Victoria's Secret
Visa Inc
VMware Inc
W R Berkley Corporation
Walgreens Boots Alliance Inc
Walmart Inc
Walt Disney Company (The)
Waste Management Inc
Waters Corporation
Wayfair LLC
WellCare Health Plans Inc
Whole Foods Market Inc
WW Grainger Inc
Wyndham Destinations Inc
Wynn Resorts Limited
Zillow Inc
Zimmer Biomet Holdings Inc

INDEX OF SUBSIDIARIES, BRAND NAMES AND AFFILIATIONS

$9 Fare Club; **Spirit Airlines Inc**
160over90; **Endeavor LLC**
2bPrecise; **Allscripts Healthcare Solutions Inc**
365 Everyday Value; **Whole Foods Market Inc**
365-Whole Foods Market; **Whole Foods Market Inc**
3i T3; **Zimmer Biomet Holdings Inc**
3M Purification Inc; **3M Company**
A+E; **Walt Disney Company (The)**
A+E Networks; **Disney Media Networks**
A-B; **Rockwell Automation Inc**
ABC Family Worldwide; **Disney Media Networks**
ABC Owned Television Stations Group; **Disney Media Networks**
ABC Television Network; **Disney Media Networks**
ABEL GmbH; **Hillenbrand Inc**
ABM; **ABM Industries Incorporated**
ABM Building Value; **ABM Industries Incorporated**
ABM Greencare; **ABM Industries Incorporated**
Abraxane; **Celgene Corporation**
Acadia; **W R Berkley Corporation**
Accenture plc; **Accenture LLP**
Accompany; **Cisco Systems Inc**
Accountemps; **Robert Half International Inc**
Acklands-Grainger Inc; **WW Grainger Inc**
Aconex Limited; **Oracle Corporation**
Acosta Marketing Group; **Acosta Inc**
Acosta Sales & Marketing; **Acosta Inc**
ActiveIRIS; **Gentex Corporation**
Activision Blizzard Distribution; **Activision Blizzard Inc**
Activision Blizzard Studios; **Activision Blizzard Inc**
Activision Publishing Inc; **Activision Blizzard Inc**
Activox; **ResMed Inc**
Acumen Hypotension Prediction Index; **Edwards Lifesciences Corporation**
ACX; **Juniper Networks Inc**
Adaptive Insights; **Workday Inc**
Adjusting Associates LLP; **Arthur J Gallagher & Co**
Admiral; **W R Berkley Corporation**
AdMob; **Alphabet Inc (Google)**
Adobe Connect; **Adobe Systems Inc**
Adobe Experience Cloud; **Adobe Systems Inc**
Adobe LiveCycle; **Adobe Systems Inc**
ADP GlobalView HCM; **Automatic Data Processing Inc (ADP)**
ADP TotalSource; **Automatic Data Processing Inc (ADP)**
ADP Vantage HCM; **Automatic Data Processing Inc (ADP)**
ADP Workforce Now; **Automatic Data Processing Inc (ADP)**
Advance Auto Parts; **Advance Auto Parts Inc**
Advanced Engineering Valves; **Emerson Electric Co**
AdvantaClean; **JM Family Enterprises Inc**
Advantage Funeral and Cremation Services; **Service Corporation International Inc**
Advocate BroMenn Medical Center; **Advocate Aurora Health**
Advocate Christ Medical Center; **Advocate Aurora Health**
Advocate Condell Medical Center; **Advocate Aurora Health**
Advocate Good Samaritan Hospital; **Advocate Aurora Health**
Advocate Good Shepherd Hospital; **Advocate Aurora Health**
Advocate Illinois Masonic Medical Center; **Advocate Aurora Health**
Advocate Lutheran General Hospital; **Advocate Aurora Health**
Advocate Trinity Hospital; **Advocate Aurora Health**
AdX; **Alphabet Inc (Google)**
Aeropost Inc; **PriceSmart Inc**
Aetna Inc; **CVS Health Corporation**
Aflac Life Insurance Japan; **AFLAC Incorporated**
Agent Alliance Reinsurance; **AmTrust Financial Services Inc**
AIG Europe Limited; **American International Group Inc (AIG)**
AIG General Insurance Company Ltd; **American International Group Inc (AIG)**
AIR HANDLER; **WW Grainger Inc**
AIR MILES; **Alliance Data Systems Corporation**
Airbnb Citizen; **Airbnb Inc**
Airbnb Experiences; **Airbnb Inc**
Airbnb for Business; **Airbnb Inc**
Airbnb Plus; **Airbnb Inc**
Airbnb.com; **Airbnb Inc**
AirCurve 10; **ResMed Inc**
AirMini; **ResMed Inc**
AirPods; **Apple Inc**
AirSense 10; **ResMed Inc**
Airstream Inc; **Thor Industries Inc**
Aladdin; **BlackRock Inc**
Aladdin Commercial; **Mohawk Industries Inc**
Alamo Rent A Car; **Enterprise Holdings Inc**
Alamo Title Insurance; **Fidelity National Financial Inc**
Alaska Airlines Inc; **Alaska Air Group Inc**
Albert's Organics Inc; **United Natural Foods Inc**
Albertsons Companies LLC; **Safeway Inc**
Alcoa World Alumina and Chemicals; **Alcoa Corporation**
Alera Lighting; **Hubbell Incorporated**
AlienVault Inc; **AT&T Inc**
Alimta; **Eli Lilly and Company**
All Star; **Nike Inc**
Allegro Coffee; **Whole Foods Market Inc**
Allen-Bradley; **Rockwell Automation Inc**
Alliance Healthcare; **Walgreens Boots Alliance Inc**
AllModern; **Wayfair LLC**
Allscripts CareInMotion; **Allscripts Healthcare Solutions Inc**
Allscripts Professional EHR; **Allscripts Healthcare Solutions Inc**
Allscripts TouchWorks EHR; **Allscripts Healthcare Solutions Inc**
ALMEA Insurance Inc; **Brown & Brown Inc**
Almidones Mexicanos SA; **Archer-Daniels-Midland Company (ADM)**
ALPS; **Zimmer Biomet Holdings Inc**
ALTUS; **Lam Research Corporation**
Amazon Go; **Amazon.com Inc**
Amazon Marketplace; **Amazon.com Inc**
Amazon Prime; **Amazon.com Inc**
Amazon Web Services (AWS); **Amazon.com Inc**
Amazon.com Inc; **Whole Foods Market Inc**
Amblin Partners; **Comcast Corporation**
AMD; **Advanced Micro Devices Inc (AMD)**
AMD Athlon; **Advanced Micro Devices Inc (AMD)**
AMD Geode; **Advanced Micro Devices Inc (AMD)**
Amerco Real Estate Company; **AMERCO (U-Haul)**
American; **AO Smith Corporation**
American Airlines Inc; **American Airlines Group Inc**
American Club Resort; **Kohler Company**
American Crew; **Revlon Inc**
American Eagle; **American Airlines Group Inc**
American Express Global Business Travel; **American Express Company**
American Express Travel Related Services Co Inc; **American Express Company**
American General Life Insurance Company; **American International Group Inc (AIG)**
American Home Assurance Company; **American International Group Inc (AIG)**
American Lumber Distributors; **Boise Cascade Company**
American Strategic Insurance Corp; **Progressive Corporation (The)**
American Tire Distributors Holdings Inc; **American Tire Distributors Inc**
American Tower International Inc; **American Tower Corporation (REIT)**

INDEX OF SUBSIDIARIES, BRAND NAMES AND AFFILIATIONS, CONT.

American Towers LLC; **American Tower Corporation (REIT)**
Americas 1st Choice; **Anthem Inc**
America's Tire Co; **Discount Tire Company**
AmerisourceBergen Consulting Services; **AmerisourceBergen Corporation**
AmeriSpec; **ServiceMaster Company LLC (The)**
AMG 520/CNP520; **Amgen Inc**
AMG Driving Academy; **Mercedes-Benz USA LLC**
Amplify Snack Brands Inc; **Hershey Company (The)**
AMSURG; **Envision Healthcare Corporation**
AmTrust E&S Insurance Services; **AmTrust Financial Services Inc**
AmTrust International; **AmTrust Financial Services Inc**
AmTrust Specialty Risk; **AmTrust Financial Services Inc**
AmTrust Title; **AmTrust Financial Services Inc**
Analytics 360; **Alphabet Inc (Google)**
Andaz; **Hyatt Hotels Corporation**
Andeavor Logistics LP; **Marathon Petroleum Corporation**
AndroGel; **AbbVie Inc**
Android; **Alphabet Inc (Google)**
ANGI Homeservices Inc; **IAC/InterActiveCorp**
Angie's List; **IAC/InterActiveCorp**
Animal Style; **In-N-Out Burgers Inc**
Ann Sacks; **Kohler Company**
Ann Taylor; **Ascena Retail Group Inc**
Annuity Investors Life Insurance Company; **American Financial Group Inc**
Antech Diagnostics; **VCA Inc**
Antelliq Corporation; **Merck & Co Inc**
Anthem Inc; **Amerigroup Corporation**
AO Smith; **AO Smith Corporation**
Aon plc; **Aon Hewitt**
Apalon; **IAC/InterActiveCorp**
Apartments.com; **CoStar Group Inc**
Apex; **Avis Budget Group Inc**
Apollo Global Management LLC; **LifePoint Health Inc**
Apollo Global Management LLC; **Rackspace Hosting Inc**
AppDynamics Inc; **Cisco Systems Inc**
Apple TV; **Apple Inc**
Apple Watch; **Apple Inc**
Applied Biosystems; **Thermo Fisher Scientific Inc**
Appthority; **Symantec Corporation**
Apt 9; **Kohls Corporation**
Aranesp; **Amgen Inc**
Arby's Restaurant Group Inc; **Buffalo Wild Wings Inc**
ARCO; **Marathon Petroleum Corporation**
Arcosa Inc; **Trinity Industries Inc**
Area 31; **Kimpton Hotel & Restaurant Group LLC**
Argos Holdings Inc; **PetSmart Inc**
Arizona Instrument; **Ametek Inc**
Arizona Outback Adventures; **REI (Recreational Equipment Inc)**
Aromax; **Chevron Phillips Chemical Company LLC**
Arris International plc; **CommScope Holding Company Inc**
art+commerce; **Endeavor LLC**
Artisanal Kitchen Supply; **Bed Bath & Beyond Inc**
Ascension At Home; **Ascension**
Ascension Care Management; **Ascension**
Ascension Global Mission; **Ascension**
Ascension Investment Management LLC; **Ascension**
Ascension Leader Institute; **Ascension**
Ascension Living; **Ascension**
Ascension Technologies; **Ascension**
Ascention Ventures; **Ascension**
Asset Trackr; **WABCO Holdings Inc**
Astral; **ResMed Inc**
AT&T Inc; **AT&T Mobility LLC**
ATDOnline; **American Tire Distributors Inc**
Ateva; **Celanese Corporation**
Atlantic City Electric Company; **Exelon Corporation**
Atonix Digital; **Black & Veatch Holding Company**
Audit Committee Institute; **KPMG LLP**
Autogrill SpA; **HMSHost Corporation**
Autopart International; **Advance Auto Parts Inc**
Autotire Car Care Center; **Monro Muffler Brake Inc**
Autotrader; **Cox Automotive Inc**
autotrader.com; **Cox Enterprises Inc**
Availity LLC; **Health Care Service Corporation (HCSC)**
Avis; **Avis Budget Group Inc**
AVONEX; **Biogen Inc**
AxION; **PerkinElmer Inc**
AXIO-NET GmbH; **Trimble Inc**
Ayudin; **Clorox Company (The)**
Azamara Club Cruises; **Royal Caribbean Cruises Ltd**
Azure; **Microsoft Corporation**
Bahama Breeze; **Darden Restaurants Inc**
Bain Media Lab; **Bain & Company Inc**
Bali; **HanesBrands Inc**
Baltimore Gas and Electric Company; **Exelon Corporation**
Band-Aid; **Johnson & Johnson**
Banfield Pet Hospital; **PetSmart Inc**
Bank of America Corporation; **Merrill Lynch & Co Inc**
Bank of New York Mellon (The); **Bank of New York Mellon Corporation**
Bank of New York Mellon Trust Company, NA (The); **Bank of New York Mellon Corporation**
Barings LLC; **MassMutual Financial Group**
BarnesCare; **BJC HealthCare**
Barnes-Jewish Hospital; **BJC HealthCare**
Batesville Casket Company; **Hillenbrand Inc**
Baylor Health Care System; **Baylor Scott & White Health**
BB&T Commercial Equipment Capital Corp; **BB&T Corporation**
BB&T Equipment Finance Corporation; **BB&T Corporation**
BB&T Insurance Services Inc; **BB&T Corporation**
BB&T Investment Services Inc; **BB&T Corporation**
BBDO Worldwide Communications Group Inc; **Omnicom Group Inc**
BD Interventional; **Becton, Dickinson and Company**
BD Life Sciences; **Becton, Dickinson and Company**
BD Medical; **Becton, Dickinson and Company**
BeadArray; **Illumina Inc**
Beauty Rush; **Victoria's Secret**
BECPOS; **NCR Corporation**
Bed Bath & Beyond; **Bed Bath & Beyond Inc**
Beena Vision Systems Inc; **Trimble Inc**
Bell Helicopter; **Textron Inc**
Bella Belara; **Mary Kay Inc**
Berkley; **W R Berkley Corporation**
Berkshire Hathaway Energy Company; **Berkshire Hathaway Inc (Holding Co)**
Berkshire Hathaway Inc; **Berkshire Hathaway Energy Company**
Berkshire Hathaway Inc; **Clayton Homes Inc**
Berkshire Hathaway Inc; **GEICO Corporation**
Berkshire Hathaway Inc; **Lubrizol Corporation (The)**
Berkshire Hathaway Primary Group; **Berkshire Hathaway Inc (Holding Co)**
Berkshire Hathaway Reinsurance Group; **Berkshire Hathaway Inc (Holding Co)**
Berry Global Inc; **Berry Global Group Inc**
Best Buy Direct; **Best Buy Co Inc**
Best Buy Express; **Best Buy Co Inc**
bestbuy.ca; **Best Buy Co Inc**
bestbuy.com; **Best Buy Co Inc**
bestbuy.com.mx; **Best Buy Co Inc**
Beyond by Airbnb; **Airbnb Inc**
BHE Renewables; **Berkshire Hathaway Energy Company**

INDEX OF SUBSIDIARIES, BRAND NAMES AND AFFILIATIONS, CONT.

Big Mac; **McDonald's Corporation**
BIG-IP; **F5 Networks Inc**
Bio-Systems; **Stericycle Inc**
Birch Lane; **Wayfair LLC**
BISAM Technologies SA; **FactSet Research Systems Inc**
Bison Coach; **Thor Industries Inc**
BizBuySell; **CoStar Group Inc**
BJC Community Health Services; **BJC HealthCare**
BJC Employee Assistance Program; **BJC HealthCare**
BJC Home Care Services; **BJC HealthCare**
BJC Hospice; **BJC HealthCare**
Black Box; **Constellation Brands Inc**
Black Flag; **Spectrum Brands Holdings Inc**
BlackRock Investment Institute; **BlackRock Inc**
BlackRock Solutions; **BlackRock Inc**
Blackstone Group LP (The); **Team Health Holdings Inc**
Blazin; **Buffalo Wild Wings Inc**
Blizzard Entertainment Inc; **Activision Blizzard Inc**
Bloomberg Briefs; **Bloomberg LP**
Bloomberg Business; **Bloomberg LP**
Bloomberg Government; **Bloomberg LP**
Bloomberg Indexes; **Bloomberg LP**
Bloomberg New Energy Finance Limited; **Bloomberg LP**
Bloomberg Terminal; **Bloomberg LP**
Bloomberg Tradebook; **Bloomberg LP**
Blue Cross and Blue Shield; **Health Care Service Corporation (HCSC)**
Blue Cross and Blue Shield Association; **Anthem Inc**
Blue Cross and Blue Shield Association; **Blue Shield of California**
Blue Marble Brands; **United Natural Foods Inc**
Blue Shield of California Foundation; **Blue Shield of California**
Blue Shield of California Life & Health Insurance; **Blue Shield of California**
Blue Vision Labs; **Lyft Inc**
BMC; **BMC Stock Holdings Inc**
BMC Design; **BMC Stock Holdings Inc**
BMC Timber Truss; **BMC Stock Holdings Inc**
BNY Mellon Investment Servicing Trust Co; **Bank of New York Mellon Corporation**
BNY Mellon National Association; **Bank of New York Mellon Corporation**
BNY Mellon Trust Company of Illinois; **Bank of New York Mellon Corporation**
BNY Mellon Trust of Delaware; **Bank of New York Mellon Corporation**
Body by Victoria; **Victoria's Secret**

Booking.com; **Booking Holdings Inc**
Boots; **Walgreens Boots Alliance Inc**
Bostitch; **Stanley Black & Decker Inc**
Botanics; **Walgreens Boots Alliance Inc**
BPS Direct LLC (Bass Pro Shops); **Cabela's Inc**
Braintree; **PayPal Holdings Inc**
BrakeBest; **O Reilly Automotive Inc**
Brammer Bio; **Thermo Fisher Scientific Inc**
Branch Bank and Trust Company; **BB&T Corporation**
BrandLoyalty Group BV; **Alliance Data Systems Corporation**
Brandywine Global Investment Management; **Legg Mason Inc**
Braun; **Procter & Gamble Company (The)**
Bravo Media; **NBCUniversal Media LLC**
Breathe Technologies inc; **Hill-Rom Holdings Inc**
Bridgecrest Acceptance Company; **DriveTime Automotive Group Inc**
Brightstar India; **Brightstar Corporation**
Brita; **Clorox Company (The)**
BroadSoft; **Cisco Systems Inc**
Budget; **Avis Budget Group Inc**
Budget Blinds; **JM Family Enterprises Inc**
Buffalito; **Buffalo Wild Wings Inc**
Buick; **General Motors Company (GM)**
Building Materials Holding Corp; **BMC Stock Holdings Inc**
Bureau van Dijk Electronic Publishing BV; **Moody's Corporation**
Burlington Northern Santa Fe; **Berkshire Hathaway Inc (Holding Co)**
buybuy BABY; **Bed Bath & Beyond Inc**
CA Technologies; **Broadcom Inc**
Cabela's CLUB VISA; **Cabela's Inc**
Cabelas.ca; **Cabela's Inc**
Cabelas.com; **Cabela's Inc**
CACI BV; **CACI International Inc**
CACI Limited; **CACI International Inc**
Cadillac; **General Motors Company (GM)**
Cafe Pescatore; **Kimpton Hotel & Restaurant Group LLC**
Call of Duty; **Activision Blizzard Inc**
Cambridge Global Payments; **FleetCor Technologies Inc**
Cameron; **Schlumberger Limited**
Camp Bow Wow; **VCA Inc**
Canopy by Hilton; **Hilton Worldwide Holdings Inc**
Capital Grille (The); **Darden Restaurants Inc**
Capital One Bank (USA) National Association; **Capital One Financial Corporation**

Capital One National Association; **Capital One Financial Corporation**
Carboline; **RPM International Inc**
Cardinal Health at-Home Solutions; **Cardinal Health Inc**
Cardinal.com; **Cardinal Health Inc**
Care1st; **WellCare Health Plans Inc**
Caregivers Health Network; **LHC Group Inc**
CareMore; **Anthem Inc**
Cargo Signal Solutions LLC; **Expeditors International of Washington Inc**
Carlyle Group (The); **Booz Allen Hamilton Holding Corporation**
Carlyle Group (The); **Pharmaceutical Product Development LLC**
CarMax Auto Finance; **CarMax Inc**
Carnival Cruise Lines; **Carnival Corporation**
Carnival Cruise plc; **Carnival Corporation**
Carpentier-Edwards PERIMOUNT; **Edwards Lifesciences Corporation**
Carquest; **Advance Auto Parts Inc**
CarRentals.com; **Expedia Group Inc**
Carrier; **United Technologies Corporation**
Carrs; **Safeway Inc**
CarSense; **Penske Automotive Group Inc**
CarShop; **Penske Automotive Group Inc**
Car-X LLC; **Monro Muffler Brake Inc**
Casa Noble; **Constellation Brands Inc**
CastleGate; **Wayfair LLC**
Catalyst Dx; **IDEXX Laboratories Inc**
Catherines; **Ascena Retail Group Inc**
CATS; **Synopsys Inc**
CBRE; **CBRE Group Inc**
CBRE Global Investors; **CBRE Group Inc**
CBS All Access; **CBS Corporation**
CBS Films; **CBS Corporation**
CBS Local Digital Media; **CBS Corporation**
CBS Television Network; **CBS Corporation**
CBS Television Stations; **CBS Corporation**
CDW Canada Inc; **CDW Corporation**
CDW Government LLC; **CDW Corporation**
CDW Ltd; **CDW Corporation**
CDW UK; **CDW Corporation**
Celaire; **Celanese Corporation**
Celanex; **Celanese Corporation**
Celebrex; **Pfizer Inc**
Celebrity Cruises; **Royal Caribbean Cruises Ltd**
Celebrity Xpedition; **Royal Caribbean Cruises Ltd**
CelFX; **Celanese Corporation**
CentAccount; **Centene Corporation**
Centex; **PulteGroup Inc**

INDEX OF SUBSIDIARIES, BRAND NAMES AND AFFILIATIONS, CONT.

Central Market; **HEB Grocery Company LP**
Century Securities Associates Inc; **Stifel Financial Corp**
Cephea Valve Technologies Inc; **Abbott Laboratories**
Cerberus Capital Management; **Albertsons Companies LLC**
Cerner Health Services; **Cerner Corporation**
Cerner Millennium; **Cerner Corporation**
CernerWorks; **Cerner Corporation**
Cestran; **Celanese Corporation**
Champion; **HanesBrands Inc**
Change Healthcare; **McKesson Corporation**
Charles Schwab & Co Inc; **Charles Schwab Corporation (The)**
Charles Schwab Bank; **Charles Schwab Corporation (The)**
Charles Schwab Investment Management Inc; **Charles Schwab Corporation (The)**
Chase Bank USA NA; **JP Morgan Chase & Co Inc**
Cheddar's Scratch Kitchen; **Darden Restaurants Inc**
Cheetos; **Frito-Lay North America Inc**
Cheetos; **PepsiCo Inc**
ChemDraw; **PerkinElmer Inc**
Chevrolet; **General Motors Company (GM)**
Chevron; **Chevron Corporation**
Chevron Corporation; **Chevron Phillips Chemical Company LLC**
Chevron Phillips Chemical Company LLC; **Chevron Corporation**
Chevron Phillips Chemical Company LLC; **Phillips 66**
Chewy Inc; **PetSmart Inc**
Chewy.com; **Chewy Inc (Chewy.com)**
Chewy.com; **PetSmart Inc**
Chewy.com Rescue and Shelter Network; **Chewy Inc (Chewy.com)**
Chicago Title Insurance Company; **Fidelity National Financial Inc**
Chick-fil-A Chicken Sandwich; **Chick-fil-A Inc**
Chick-fil-A Kid's Meal Program; **Chick-fil-A Inc**
Chick-fil-A One; **Chick-fil-A Inc**
Chili's Grill and Bar; **Brinker International Inc**
Christmas Tree Shops; **Bed Bath & Beyond Inc**
Chuck Taylor; **Nike Inc**
CIF 20/20; **Jack Henry & Associates Inc**
Cirrus; **MasterCard Inc**
Citi; **Citigroup Inc**
Citi Holdings; **Citigroup Inc**
Citibanamex; **Citigroup Inc**
Citibank; **Citigroup Inc**

Citicorp; **Citigroup Inc**
CitiMortgage; **Citigroup Inc**
Citoxlab; **Charles River Laboratories International Inc**
Citrix HDX Technologies; **Citrix Systems Inc**
Citrix Receiver; **Citrix Systems Inc**
Citrix Workspace Suite; **Citrix Systems Inc**
City Market; **Kroger Co (The)**
Cityscape; **Mary Kay Inc**
Civica Rx; **HCA Healthcare Inc**
Civica Rx; **Trinity Health**
Civica Rx; **Mayo Clinic**
Civica Rx; **Providence St Joseph Health**
Clarion Partners; **Legg Mason Inc**
Classic Builders; **DR Horton Inc**
Clayton Homes Inc; **Berkshire Hathaway Inc (Holding Co)**
ClearBridge Investments; **Legg Mason Inc**
ClearCurve; **Corning Incorporated**
ClearSight; **Edwards Lifesciences Corporation**
Cleveland Clinic Lerner College of Medicine; **Cleveland Clinic Foundation (The)**
Clifford/French; **Endeavor LLC**
Cliniclands; **Henry Schein Inc**
Clipper Magazine; **Valassis Communications Inc**
Clorox; **Clorox Company (The)**
Clorox 2; **Clorox Company (The)**
Cloud CPE; **Juniper Networks Inc**
CloudBlue; **Ingram Micro Inc**
CloudCoreo; **VMware Inc**
CloudHealth; **VMware Inc**
Club House; **McCormick & Company Incorporated**
Club Wyndham; **Wyndham Destinations Inc**
Clutch; **Cox Enterprises Inc**
Clutch Technologies; **Cox Automotive Inc**
CM Life Insurance Company; **MassMutual Financial Group**
CND; **Revlon Inc**
Coca-Cola Company (The); **Coca-Cola Bottling Co Consolidated**
Cognizant Consulting; **Cognizant Technology Solutions Corporation**
Cognizant Digital Business; **Cognizant Technology Solutions Corporation**
Cognizant Digital Operations; **Cognizant Technology Solutions Corporation**
Cognizant Digital Systems and Technology; **Cognizant Technology Solutions Corporation**
Colilert; **IDEXX Laboratories Inc**
Collins Aerospace; **United Technologies Corporation**
Colonial Life & Accident Insurance Company; **Unum Group**

ColorSilk; **Revlon Inc**
Comcast Corporation; **NBCUniversal Media LLC**
Comcast Spectator; **Comcast Corporation**
Comex; **PPG Industries Inc**
Command; **3M Company**
Commonwealth Edison Company; **Exelon Corporation**
Commonwealth Land Title Insurance Company; **Fidelity National Financial Inc**
CommScope Connectivity Solutions; **CommScope Holding Company Inc**
CommScope Inc; **CommScope Holding Company Inc**
CommScope Mobility Solutions; **CommScope Holding Company Inc**
Community Cloud; **SalesForce.com Inc**
Community Library Exchange; **Epic Systems Corporation**
Companion Animal Practices of North America; **VCA Inc**
Concentra Inc; **Select Medical Holdings Corporation**
Concrete Craft; **JM Family Enterprises Inc**
Conrad Hotels & Resorts; **Hilton Worldwide Holdings Inc**
Contained Home; **Container Store Inc (The)**
Container Store (The); **Container Store Inc (The)**
Convergys; **Concentrix Corporation**
Convergys Corporation; **SYNNEX Corporation**
Converse Inc; **Nike Inc**
Cooper-Atkins; **Emerson Electric Co**
CooperSurgical; **Cooper Companies Inc (The)**
CooperVision; **Cooper Companies Inc (The)**
Coperion Capital GmbH; **Hillenbrand Inc**
Core Director; **Jack Henry & Associates Inc**
Corenso Holdings America Inc; **Sonoco Products Company**
Cornerstone; **Qurate Retail Inc**
Corona; **Constellation Brands Inc**
Cost Plus World Market; **Bed Bath & Beyond Inc**
Costa Cruises; **Carnival Corporation**
CoStar; **CoStar Group Inc**
CoStar Property; **CoStar Group Inc**
Costco Wholesale Industries; **Costco Wholesale Corporation**
Courtyard; **Marriott International Inc**
Covance Drug Development; **Laboratory Corporation of America Holdings**
Covenant Health; **Providence St Joseph Health**
Cox Automotive; **Cox Enterprises Inc**

INDEX OF SUBSIDIARIES, BRAND NAMES AND AFFILIATIONS, CONT.

Cox Business Services; **Cox Communications Inc**
Cox Business Services; **Cox Enterprises Inc**
Cox Communications Inc; **Cox Enterprises Inc**
Cox Enterprises Inc; **Cox Automotive Inc**
Cox Enterprises Inc; **Cox Communications Inc**
Cox Media; **Cox Communications Inc**
Cox Media Group; **Cox Enterprises Inc**
Cozi; **NBCUniversal Media LLC**
Cozy Services Ltd; **CoStar Group Inc**
CRAFT; **McCann Worldgroup**
CRC Insurance Services Inc; **BB&T Corporation**
Creative Group (The); **Robert Half International Inc**
Creative Lodging Solutions; **FleetCor Technologies Inc**
Credera; **Omnicom Group Inc**
Crest; **Procter & Gamble Company (The)**
Croft & Barrow; **Kohls Corporation**
Crosswind Industries inc; **Archer-Daniels-Midland Company (ADM)**
Crown Castle USA Inc; **Crown Castle International Corp**
Crump Life Insurance Services Inc; **BB&T Corporation**
CSRA Inc; **General Dynamics Corporation**
Cullen-Frost Capital Trust; **Cullen-Frost Bankers Inc**
Cunard; **Carnival Corporation**
Curio Collection by Hilton; **Hilton Worldwide Holdings Inc**
Cushman; **Textron Inc**
Custom Closets; **Container Store Inc (The)**
CVS Health Corporation; **Aetna Inc**
CVS Pharmacy; **CVS Health Corporation**
CyberSource Corporation; **Visa Inc**
Cyramza; **Eli Lilly and Company**
Daimler AG; **Mercedes-Benz USA LLC**
Daltile; **Mohawk Industries Inc**
Dan Duncan LLC; **Enterprise Products Partners LP**
Dap; **RPM International Inc**
DAS Group of Companies; **Omnicom Group Inc**
Dasani; **Coca-Cola Bottling Co Consolidated**
DataFox; **Oracle Corporation**
DataScience.com; **Oracle Corporation**
Davco Technology LLC; **Penske Corporation**
DaVita Medical Group; **UnitedHealth Group Inc**
Day-Glo; **RPM International Inc**
DAYTON; **WW Grainger Inc**
DCP Midstream LLC; **Phillips 66**
DDB Worldwide Inc; **Omnicom Group Inc**
dd's DISCOUNTS; **Ross Stores Inc**
Dealertrack; **Cox Automotive Inc**
Dearborn National; **Health Care Service Corporation (HCSC)**
Del Webb; **PulteGroup Inc**
DELFIA; **PerkinElmer Inc**
Dell; **Dell Technologies Inc**
Dell EMC; **Dell Technologies Inc**
Dell Technologies Inc; **Dell EMC**
Delmarva Power & Light Company; **Exelon Corporation**
Deloitte Consulting; **Deloitte LLP**
Deloitte Touche Tohmatsu Lmited; **Deloitte LLP**
Del's Feed & Farm Supply; **Tractor Supply Company**
Demilec; **Huntsman Corporation**
Dental Network of America Inc; **Health Care Service Corporation (HCSC)**
Dentix; **Henry Schein Inc**
Dentsply Sirona Charlotte Academy; **Dentsply Sirona Inc**
Desert Heat; **Buffalo Wild Wings Inc**
DesignWare IP; **Synopsys Inc**
Deutsche Telekom AG; **T-Mobile US Inc**
DeWALT; **Stanley Black & Decker Inc**
DHI Mortgage; **DR Horton Inc**
Dignity Health Rehabilitation Hospital; **Select Medical Holdings Corporation**
Dignity Memorial; **Service Corporation International Inc**
Dignity Planning; **Service Corporation International Inc**
Dillons; **Kroger Co (The)**
Dingo; **Spectrum Brands Holdings Inc**
Diodes FabTech Inc; **Diodes Inc**
Diodes Hong Kong Holding Company Limited; **Diodes Inc**
Direct Vet Marketing Inc; **Henry Schein Inc**
Discount Tire; **Discount Tire Company**
Discount Tire Credit Card; **Discount Tire Company**
Discovery Channel; **Discovery Inc**
Disney; **Walt Disney Studios (The)**
Disney Consumer Products and Interactive Media; **Disney Parks, Experiences and Products (DPEP)**
Disney Digital Studio Services; **Walt Disney Studios (The)**
Disney Direct-to-consumer and International; **Disney Parks, Experiences and Products (DPEP)**
Disney Music Publishing; **Walt Disney Studios (The)**
Disney XD; **Disney Media Networks**
Disneyland Resort; **Walt Disney Company (The)**
Disneynature; **Walt Disney Studios (The)**
DiVosta Homes; **PulteGroup Inc**
dixon talent Inc; **Endeavor LLC**
DMAX; **Discovery Inc**
Dollar; **Dollar Thrifty Automotive Group Inc**
Domain; **Mary Kay Inc**
Doritos; **Frito-Lay North America Inc**
Doritos; **PepsiCo Inc**
Dotdash; **IAC/InterActiveCorp**
dotloop; **Zillow Inc**
DoubleClick; **Alphabet Inc (Google)**
DoubleTree by Hilton; **Hilton Worldwide Holdings Inc**
Downy; **Procter & Gamble Company (The)**
Dr Pepper; **Coca-Cola Bottling Co Consolidated**
Dream Angels; **Victoria's Secret**
DriveCare Powertrain Protection Plan; **DriveTime Automotive Group Inc**
DTE Electric; **DTE Energy Company**
DTE Gas; **DTE Energy Company**
Duane Reade; **Walgreens Boots Alliance Inc**
Dubuis; **Stanley Black & Decker Inc**
Duke Energy Carolinas; **Duke Energy Corporation**
Duke Energy Florida; **Duke Energy Corporation**
Duke Energy Indiana; **Duke Energy Corporation**
Duke Energy Ohio; **Duke Energy Corporation**
Duke Energy Progress; **Duke Energy Corporation**
Duke-American Transmission Co; **Duke Energy Corporation**
Dulux; **PPG Industries Inc**
Duo Security; **Cisco Systems Inc**
Duopa; **AbbVie Inc**
Durkan; **Mohawk Industries Inc**
Dutchman; **Thor Industries Inc**
DV 360; **Alphabet Inc (Google)**
Dwarf House; **Chick-fil-A Inc**
Dymaxium; **AmerisourceBergen Corporation**
Dynamics; **Microsoft Corporation**
E! Entertainment; **NBCUniversal Media LLC**
E8 Security; **VMware Inc**
Eagle Asset Management Inc; **Raymond James Financial Inc**
Eagle Home Mortgage LLC; **Lennar Corporation**
Eagle XG; **Corning Incorporated**
EarlyBird Check-In; **Southwest Airlines Co**
Easy Dental; **Henry Schein Inc**
Eaton Partners LLC; **Stifel Financial Corp**
eBay Inc; **PayPal Holdings Inc**
e-Builder; **Trimble Inc**

INDEX OF SUBSIDIARIES, BRAND NAMES AND AFFILIATIONS, CONT.

Echo; **Amazon.com Inc**
EchoStar Mobile Limited; **EchoStar Corporation**
Echostar Satellite Services; **EchoStar Corporation**
Eddie V's; **Darden Restaurants Inc**
Edibles Oils Limited; **Archer-Daniels-Midland Company (ADM)**
Edward Jones; **Edward D Jones & Co LP**
Edwards Intuity; **Edwards Lifesciences Corporation**
Edwards SAPIEN; **Edwards Lifesciences Corporation**
Effient; **Eli Lilly and Company**
Egg McMuffin; **McDonald's Corporation**
eInfochips; **Arrow Electronics Inc**
Elantra; **Hyundai Motor America**
element14; **Avnet Inc**
Elfa; **Container Store Inc (The)**
Elfa International AB; **Container Store Inc (The)**
Eliane; **Mohawk Industries Inc**
Eliquis; **Bristol-Myers Squibb Company**
Eliquis; **Pfizer Inc**
Elizabeth Arden Inc; **Revlon Inc**
Employers Insurance of Wausau; **Liberty Mutual Group Inc**
Emulate3D; **Rockwell Automation Inc**
Enable; **ExxonMobil Chemical Company Inc**
ENBREL; **Amgen Inc**
Enbrel; **Pfizer Inc**
Encore at Wynn Las Vegas; **Wynn Resorts Limited**
Encore at Wynn Macau; **Wynn Resorts Limited**
Encore Theater; **Wynn Resorts Limited**
Endeavor; **Endeavor LLC**
Endeavor Streaming; **Endeavor LLC**
Engine 2 Plant-Strong; **Whole Foods Market Inc**
EnLite; **PerkinElmer Inc**
Ensenta Corporation; **Jack Henry & Associates Inc**
Ensure; **Abbott Laboratories**
Enterprise Car Sales; **Enterprise Holdings Inc**
Enterprise CarShare; **Enterprise Holdings Inc**
Enterprise Products Holdings LLC; **Enterprise Products Partners LP**
Enterprise Products Operating LLC; **Enterprise Products Partners LP**
Enterprise Rent-A-Car; **Enterprise Holdings Inc**
Enterprise Truck Rental; **Enterprise Holdings Inc**
EnTrustPermal; **Legg Mason Inc**
Envision Healthcare Corporation; **AMSURG Corporation**

Envision Physician Services; **Envision Healthcare Corporation**
Envoy Aviation Group Inc; **American Airlines Group Inc**
EpicCare; **Epic Systems Corporation**
Epicenter; **Epic Systems Corporation**
Episys; **Jack Henry & Associates Inc**
EPOGEN; **Amgen Inc**
Epsilon; **Alliance Data Systems Corporation**
Erwin Hymer Group SE; **Thor Industries Inc**
ESPA; **Ritz-Carlton Hotel Company LLC (The)**
ESPN; **Walt Disney Company (The)**
ESPN Inc; **Disney Media Networks**
Esso; **Exxon Mobil Corporation (ExxonMobil)**
Esterline Technologies Corporation; **TransDigm Group Incorporated**
Ethos; **Starbucks Corporation**
Eurosport; **Discovery Inc**
EV1000; **Edwards Lifesciences Corporation**
Evergreen Coast Capital; **athenahealth Inc**
Evergreen Parent LP; **AmTrust Financial Services Inc**
Evolution Health; **Envision Healthcare Corporation**
EX; **Juniper Networks Inc**
EXACT; **Henry Schein Inc**
Exelon Generation Company LLC; **Exelon Corporation**
Exhale; **Hyatt Hotels Corporation**
Exotic Car Collection by Enterprise; **Enterprise Holdings Inc**
exp.o; **Expeditors International of Washington Inc**
exp.o Booking; **Expeditors International of Washington Inc**
exp.o ISF; **Expeditors International of Washington Inc**
Expedia Partner Solutions; **Expedia Group Inc**
Expedia.com; **Expedia Group Inc**
Expeditors Cargo Insurance Brokers; **Expeditors International of Washington Inc**
Expeditors Tradewin LLC; **Expeditors International of Washington Inc**
Express Scripts PBM; **Cigna Corporation**
Exxcore; **ExxonMobil Chemical Company Inc**
Exxon; **Exxon Mobil Corporation (ExxonMobil)**
Exxon Mobil Corporation; **ExxonMobil Chemical Company Inc**
ExxonMobil; **Exxon Mobil Corporation (ExxonMobil)**

ExxonMobil Chemical Technology Licensing LLC; **ExxonMobil Chemical Company Inc**
EY; **EY LLP**
E-Z-GO; **Textron Inc**
Facebook Platform; **Facebook Inc**
Facey Medical Foundation; **Providence St Joseph Health**
FactoryTalk; **Rockwell Automation Inc**
FareHarbor; **Booking Holdings Inc**
Fastenal; **Fastenal Company**
Federal Express Corporation; **FedEx Corporation**
Federal-Mogul LLC; **Tenneco Inc**
FedEx Corporate Services Inc; **FedEx Corporation**
FedEx Freight Corporation; **FedEx Corporation**
FedEx Freight Economy; **FedEx Corporation**
FedEx Freight Priority; **FedEx Corporation**
FedEx Ground Package System Inc; **FedEx Corporation**
FedEx Office and Print Services Inc; **FedEx Corporation**
FedEx SmartPost; **FedEx Corporation**
Fidelity Charitable; **Fidelity Investments Financial Services**
Fidelity Insitutional Asset Management; **Fidelity Investments Financial Services**
Fidelity National Title Insurance Company; **Fidelity National Financial Inc**
FILA; **Kohls Corporation**
Filet O'Fish; **McDonald's Corporation**
Filtrete; **3M Company**
FirePro; **Advanced Micro Devices Inc (AMD)**
First Data Corp; **Fiserv Inc**
FirstEnergy Solutions Corporation; **FirstEnergy Corporation**
Fisher Scientific; **Thermo Fisher Scientific Inc**
Flavor by Loews Hotels; **Loews Hotels Holding Corporation**
Flex; **Lam Research Corporation**
Flexdrive; **Cox Enterprises Inc**
Flint Hills Resources LLC; **Koch Industries Inc**
Flipkart Pvt Ltd; **Walmart Inc**
FloTrac; **Edwards Lifesciences Corporation**
Fluor Constructors International Inc; **Fluor Corporation**
Fly-Fi; **JetBlue Airways Corporation**
FMH Aerospace; **Ametek Inc**
FollowMyHealth; **Baylor Scott & White Health**
FollowMyHealth; **Allscripts Healthcare Solutions Inc**
Food 4 Less; **Kroger Co (The)**

INDEX OF SUBSIDIARIES, BRAND NAMES AND AFFILIATIONS, CONT.

Foot Con & Belding; **Interpublic Group of Companies Inc**
Forcepoint; **Raytheon Company**
Ford; **Ford Motor Company**
Ford Escape Hybrid SUV; **Ford Motor Company**
Ford F150; **Ford Motor Company**
Ford Focus; **Ford Motor Company**
Ford Motor Credit Co; **Ford Motor Company**
Ford Mustang; **Ford Motor Company**
Forever Diamonds; **Mary Kay Inc**
Formula 409; **Clorox Company (The)**
Forza Silicon; **Ametek Inc**
Four Seasons Macao; **Las Vegas Sands Corp (The Venetian)**
FranceCars; **Avis Budget Group Inc**
Frank's; **McCormick & Company Incorporated**
Fred Meyer; **Kroger Co (The)**
Free Service Tire Company; **Monro Muffler Brake Inc**
FREE SPIRIT; **Spirit Airlines Inc**
Freedom Health; **Anthem Inc**
Freego; **Abbott Laboratories**
French's; **McCormick & Company Incorporated**
Frito-Lay; **PepsiCo Inc**
Frost Bank; **Cullen-Frost Bankers Inc**
Frost Brokerage Services Inc; **Cullen-Frost Bankers Inc**
Frost Insurance Agency Inc; **Cullen-Frost Bankers Inc**
Frost Investment Advisors LLC; **Cullen-Frost Bankers Inc**
Fry's; **Kroger Co (The)**
Fullerton Health Corporate Services (Aus); **Arthur J Gallagher & Co**
FUMADERM; **Biogen Inc**
Funeraria del Angel; **Service Corporation International Inc**
Furniture Medic; **ServiceMaster Company LLC (The)**
Fusion Marketing; **Endeavor LLC**
FutureBrand; **Interpublic Group of Companies Inc**
G280; **Gulfstream Aerospace Corporation**
G500; **General Dynamics Corporation**
G500; **Gulfstream Aerospace Corporation**
G550; **Gulfstream Aerospace Corporation**
G600; **General Dynamics Corporation**
G600; **Gulfstream Aerospace Corporation**
G650; **Gulfstream Aerospace Corporation**
G650ER; **Gulfstream Aerospace Corporation**
Gamesa; **PepsiCo Inc**

Garrison Property and Casualty Insurance Company; **USAA**
GAZYVA; **Biogen Inc**
Geek Squad; **Best Buy Co Inc**
GEICO Advantage Insurance Company; **GEICO Corporation**
GEICO Casualty Company; **GEICO Corporation**
GEICO Choice Insurance Company; **GEICO Corporation**
GEICO Corporation; **Berkshire Hathaway Inc (Holding Co)**
GEICO County Mutual; **GEICO Corporation**
GEICO General Insurance Company; **GEICO Corporation**
GEICO Indemnity Company; **GEICO Corporation**
Gel-One; **Zimmer Biomet Holdings Inc**
Gemini Transportation; **W R Berkley Corporation**
General Dynamics Corporation; **Gulfstream Aerospace Corporation**
General Motors Financial Company Inc; **General Motors Company (GM)**
Genesis; **Hyundai Motor America**
Gillis Ellis & Baker Inc; **Arthur J Gallagher & Co**
GitHub; **Microsoft Corporation**
glaceau vitaminwater; **Coca-Cola Bottling Co Consolidated**
Glacier Bay; **Home Depot Inc (The)**
Glidden; **PPG Industries Inc**
Glint; **LinkedIn Corporation**
Global Business Policy Council; **AT Kearney Inc**
Global Payments Inc; **Heartland Payment Systems Inc**
Global Technology Associates LLC; **Kelly Services Inc**
GloFish; **Spectrum Brands Holdings Inc**
Glutomatic; **PerkinElmer Inc**
GM Cruise; **General Motors Company (GM)**
GMC; **General Motors Company (GM)**
goBalto; **Oracle Corporation**
Godrej Tyson Foods; **Tyson Foods Inc**
Golin; **Interpublic Group of Companies Inc**
Google Ad Manager; **Alphabet Inc (Google)**
Gorilla; **Corning Incorporated**
Gourmet Garden; **McCormick & Company Incorporated**
Grand Hyatt; **Hyatt Hotels Corporation**
Grandma's; **Frito-Lay North America Inc**
Grant Thornton International Ltd; **Grant Thornton LLP**
Great American Insurance Group; **American Financial Group Inc**

Great American Life Insrurance Company; **American Financial Group Inc**
GroceryWorks; **Safeway Inc**
GSW; **AO Smith Corporation**
Guaranteed Tough; **Stanley Black & Decker Inc**
Guardian Industries Corporation; **Koch Industries Inc**
Gulfstream Aerospace Corporation; **General Dynamics Corporation**
Gundlach; **Hillenbrand Inc**
Guy Carpenter & Company LLC; **Marsh & McLennan Companies Inc**
Hallen Construction Co Inc; **Quanta Services Inc**
Hampton Bay; **Home Depot Inc (The)**
Hanes; **HanesBrands Inc**
Hanes Beefy-T; **HanesBrands Inc**
Happy Meal; **McDonald's Corporation**
Harland Clarke Holdings Corp; **Valassis Communications Inc**
Harmony; **WellCare Health Plans Inc**
Harris Satellite (HSAT); **Harris Corporation**
Hartford Life Insurance Company; **Hartford Financial Services Group Inc (The)**
Have You Seen Me?; **Valassis Communications Inc**
Hawker Pacific; **General Dynamics Corporation**
HCA Holdings Inc; **HCA Healthcare Inc**
HCSC Insurance Service Company; **Health Care Service Corporation (HCSC)**
HDX; **Home Depot Inc (The)**
Head & Shoulders; **Procter & Gamble Company (The)**
Health Education Campus; **Cleveland Clinic Foundation (The)**
Health Support Center; **LifePoint Health Inc**
HealthCare Partners Nevada; **UnitedHealth Group Inc**
HealtheIntent; **Cerner Corporation**
HealthSun; **Anthem Inc**
Heartland Homes; **NVR Inc**
H-E-B; **HEB Grocery Company LP**
H-E-B Blooms; **HEB Grocery Company LP**
H-E-B plus!; **HEB Grocery Company LP**
Hellman & Friedman; **Pharmaceutical Product Development LLC**
Hellman & Friedman LLC; **Hub International Limited**
Hendrick Motorsports; **Hendrick Automotive Group**
Heptio; **VMware Inc**
Hershey Bars; **Hershey Company (The)**
Hershey Kisses; **Hershey Company (The)**
Hershey's Chocolate World; **Hershey Company (The)**

INDEX OF SUBSIDIARIES, BRAND NAMES AND AFFILIATIONS, CONT.

Hertz Global Holdings Inc; **Dollar Thrifty Automotive Group Inc**
HGN Group Co Ltd; **Ingram Micro Inc**
HHK Datentechnik GmbH; **Trimble Inc**
Hidden Valley; **Clorox Company (The)**
Hillrom; **Hill-Rom Holdings Inc**
Hilton Hotels & Resorts; **Hilton Worldwide Holdings Inc**
Hoag Memorial Presbyterian; **Providence St Joseph Health**
Holland America Line; **Carnival Corporation**
Homax; **PPG Industries Inc**
Home Box Office Inc (HBO); **AT&T Inc**
Home Chef; **Kroger Co (The)**
Home Depot Backyard (The); **Home Depot Inc (The)**
Home Franchise Concepts; **JM Family Enterprises Inc**
HomeAway; **Expedia Group Inc**
HomeGoods; **TJX Companies Inc (T.J. Maxx)**
HomeLink; **Gentex Corporation**
HomeLink Connect; **Gentex Corporation**
HomePod; **Apple Inc**
HomeSense; **TJX Companies Inc (T.J. Maxx)**
Horizon Air Industries Inc; **Alaska Air Group Inc**
Hotel Burnham; **Kimpton Hotel & Restaurant Group LLC**
Hotel Vintage Plaza; **Kimpton Hotel & Restaurant Group LLC**
Hotels.com; **Expedia Group Inc**
HotPads; **Zillow Inc**
Houston Methodist Baytown Hospital; **Houston Methodist**
Houston Methodist Clear Lake Hospital; **Houston Methodist**
Houston Methodist Continuing Care Hospital; **Houston Methodist**
Houston Methodist Hospital-Central; **Houston Methodist**
Houston Methodist Sugar Land Hospital; **Houston Methodist**
Houston Methodist The Woodlands Hospital; **Houston Methodist**
Houston Methodist West Hospital; **Houston Methodist**
Houston Methodist Willowbrook Hospital; **Houston Methodist**
HSN; **Qurate Retail Inc**
HSN Inc; **Qurate Retail Inc**
Hubbell; **Hubbell Incorporated**
Hubbell Outdoor Lighting; **Hubbell Incorporated**
Hughes Communications Inc; **EchoStar Corporation**
Hulu; **Walt Disney Company (The)**
Hulu; **NBCUniversal Media LLC**
Hulu; **Disney Media Networks**

Humana Inc; **Kindred Healthcare LLC**
HUMIRA; **AbbVie Inc**
Humulin; **Eli Lilly and Company**
Hungrana Ltd; **Archer-Daniels-Midland Company (ADM)**
Huntsman International LLC; **Huntsman Corporation**
Hurley International LLC; **Nike Inc**
Husky; **Home Depot Inc (The)**
Hyatt House; **Hyatt Hotels Corporation**
Hyatt Regency; **Hyatt Hotels Corporation**
Hyatt Ziva; **Hyatt Hotels Corporation**
Hyundai Motor Company; **Hyundai Motor America**
IAC Films; **IAC/InterActiveCorp**
IAC/InterActiveCorp; **Match Group Inc**
iApps; **F5 Networks Inc**
iCall; **F5 Networks Inc**
iControl; **F5 Networks Inc**
IDEXX VetLab; **IDEXX Laboratories Inc**
Ilmor Engineering Inc; **Penske Corporation**
IMBRUVICA; **AbbVie Inc**
Immune Design; **Merck & Co Inc**
Impact Biomedicines; **Celgene Corporation**
Industries; **SalesForce.com Inc**
InfiniCor; **Corning Incorporated**
In-House Realty LLC; **Quicken Loans Inc**
In-N-Out Burger; **In-N-Out Burgers Inc**
Innovative Risk Solutions Inc; **Brown & Brown Inc**
Innovative Software Engineering; **Trimble Inc**
Inovant LLC; **Visa Inc**
Inspire Brands Inc; **Buffalo Wild Wings Inc**
Instagram; **Facebook Inc**
Intel Corporation; **McAfee LLC**
Intel Neural Compute Stick 2; **Intel Corporation**
Intelligent Platforms; **Emerson Electric Co**
Interactive Data Managed Solutions; **FactSet Research Systems Inc**
InterContinental Hotels Group PLC; **Kimpton Hotel & Restaurant Group LLC**
Intermountain Healthcare; **UnitedHealth Group Inc**
International Business Machines Corporation (IBM); **Red Hat Inc**
Interpublic Group of Companies Inc; **McCann Worldgroup**
Intuit Tax Freedom Project; **Intuit Inc**
Investigation Discovery; **Discovery Inc**
INVISTA BV; **Koch Industries Inc**
Invitrogen; **Thermo Fisher Scientific Inc**
IOI Loders Croklaan; **Bunge Limited**
Ioniq; **Hyundai Motor America**
iOS; **Apple Inc**

IoT Cloud; **SalesForce.com Inc**
iPad; **Apple Inc**
iPhone; **Apple Inc**
IQVIA CORE; **IQVIA Holdings Inc**
Iris; **Corning Incorporated**
iRules; **F5 Networks Inc**
iRules LX; **F5 Networks Inc**
iShares; **BlackRock Inc**
IVC; **Mohawk Industries Inc**
iZettle; **PayPal Holdings Inc**
Jack Henry Banking; **Jack Henry & Associates Inc**
Jack Morton; **Interpublic Group of Companies Inc**
Jack Purcell; **Nike Inc**
Jacobsen; **Textron Inc**
Jammin Jalapeno; **Buffalo Wild Wings Inc**
Jardine Lloyd Thompson Group plc; **Marsh & McLennan Companies Inc**
Jasper; **Cisco Systems Inc**
Javelin Networks; **Symantec Corporation**
Jayco Inc; **Thor Industries Inc**
Jeffrey; **Nordstrom Inc**
Jerr-Dan; **Oshkosh Corporation**
JetBlue Technology Ventures; **JetBlue Airways Corporation**
JetBlue Travel Products; **JetBlue Airways Corporation**
JetSuite X; **JetBlue Airways Corporation**
Jevity; **Abbott Laboratories**
JLG Industries Inc; **Oshkosh Corporation**
JM Lexus; **JM Family Enterprises Inc**
JM&A Group; **JM Family Enterprises Inc**
JMS|Just My Size; **HanesBrands Inc**
Joe V's Smart Shop; **HEB Grocery Company LP**
John Deere; **Deere & Company (John Deere)**
John Hancock Life Insurance; **John Hancock Financial**
John Wieland Homes and Neighborhoods; **PulteGroup Inc**
Jones Financial Companies LLLP (The); **Edward D Jones & Co LP**
Jordan; **Nike Inc**
Joss & Main; **Wayfair LLC**
JP Morgan Securities LLC; **JP Morgan Chase & Co Inc**
JPMorgan Chase Bank NA; **JP Morgan Chase & Co Inc**
JuggerKnot; **Zimmer Biomet Holdings Inc**
JUMP Bikes; **Uber Technologies Inc**
Jumping Beans; **Kohls Corporation**
Juno Therapeutics Inc; **Celgene Corporation**
Junos; **Juniper Networks Inc**
Justice; **Ascena Retail Group Inc**
JW Marriott; **Marriott International Inc**
Kadlec; **Providence St Joseph Health**

INDEX OF SUBSIDIARIES, BRAND NAMES AND AFFILIATIONS, CONT.

Kaiser Foundation Health Plan Inc; **Kaiser Permanente**
Kaiser Foundation Hospitals; **Kaiser Permanente**
Kaiser Permanente Center for Health Research; **Kaiser Permanente**
KALETRA; **AbbVie Inc**
Kallista; **Kohler Company**
Kallista; **Kohler Company**
Kautex; **Textron Inc**
KAYAK; **Booking Holdings Inc**
Keefe Bruyeete & Woods Inc; **Stifel Financial Corp**
Kelley Blue Book; **Cox Enterprises Inc**
Kelly Blue Book; **Cox Automotive Inc**
Ken Towery's Tire & Auto Care; **Monro Muffler Brake Inc**
Kent Frozen Foods; **SYSCO Corporation**
Kern River Gas Transmission Company; **Berkshire Hathaway Energy Company**
Keystone Foods LLC; **Tyson Foods Inc**
Kim Lighting; **Hubbell Incorporated**
Kimco Realty; **Albertsons Companies LLC**
Kimpton De Witt Amsterdam; **Kimpton Hotel & Restaurant Group LLC**
Kimpton Saint George Hotel; **Kimpton Hotel & Restaurant Group LLC**
King Digital Entertainment; **Activision Blizzard Inc**
Kirkland Signature; **Costco Wholesale Corporation**
Kit Kat; **Hershey Company (The)**
Kiyo; **Lam Research Corporation**
KKR & Co Inc; **Envision Healthcare Corporation**
KKR & Co LP; **BMC Software Inc**
KKR & Co LP (Kohlberg Kravis Roberts & Co); **Academy Sports & Outdoors Ltd**
Knights Apparel; **HanesBrands Inc**
Koch Ag & Energy Solutions LLC; **Koch Industries Inc**
Koch Disruptive Technologies; **Koch Industries Inc**
Koch Engineered Solutions; **Koch Industries Inc**
Koch Industries Inc; **Molex LLC**
Koch Minerals LLC; **Koch Industries Inc**
Kohler Engines; **Kohler Company**
KOHLER Konnect; **Kohler Company**
Kohler Power; **Kohler Company**
Kohl's; **Kohls Corporation**
Kohls.com; **Kohls Corporation**
Kona; **Hyundai Motor America**
Koninklijke Philips NV; **Philips Healthcare**
KP HealthConnect; **Kaiser Permanente**
KPMG International; **KPMG LLP**
KPMG TaxWatch; **KPMG LLP**
Kroger; **Kroger Co (The)**
Kudzu.com; **Cox Communications Inc**

Kwikset; **Spectrum Brands Holdings Inc**
KZ Inc; **Thor Industries Inc**
L Brands Inc; **Victoria's Secret**
La Boulange; **Starbucks Corporation**
La Prairie; **Ritz-Carlton Hotel Company LLC (The)**
LabCorp; **Laboratory Corporation of America Holdings**
LabCorp Diagnositcs; **Laboratory Corporation of America Holdings**
LaBounty; **Stanley Black & Decker Inc**
LabVIEW; **National Instruments Corporation**
LabVIEW Communications System Design Suite; **National Instruments Corporation**
LabVIEW for LEGO MINDSTORMS; **National Instruments Corporation**
LabVIEW Real-Time; **National Instruments Corporation**
LabWindows/CVI and Measurement Studio; **National Instruments Corporation**
Lacerte; **Intuit Inc**
LandsofAmerica; **CoStar Group Inc**
Lane Bryant; **Ascena Retail Group Inc**
Larry H Miller Dealerships; **Larry H Miller Group of Companies**
Larry H Miller Megaplex Theaters; **Larry H Miller Group of Companies**
Larry H Miller Real Estate; **Larry H Miller Group of Companies**
Larry H Miller's Jordan Commons; **Larry H Miller Group of Companies**
Larry H Miller's Tour of Utah; **Larry H Miller Group of Companies**
LaSalle Investment Management; **Jones Lang LaSalle Incorporated**
Last Chance; **Nordstrom Inc**
LaunchPad; **Cognizant Technology Solutions Corporation**
Lawry's; **McCormick & Company Incorporated**
Lay's; **Frito-Lay North America Inc**
LEAF; **Corning Incorporated**
LearnVest Inc; **Northwestern Mutual Life Insurance Company (The)**
Legg Mason Funds; **Legg Mason Inc**
Lennar; **Lennar Corporation**
Leonard Green & Partners LP; **Container Store Inc (The)**
Lexington Insurance Company; **American International Group Inc (AIG)**
Liberty Corporate Services LLC; **Liberty Mutual Group Inc**
Liberty Interactive Corporation; **Qurate Retail Inc**
Liberty Mutual Fire Insurance Company; **Liberty Mutual Group Inc**
Liberty Mutual Group Inc; **Safeco Insurance Company of America**

Liberty Mutual Insurance Company; **Liberty Mutual Group Inc**
Linc Service; **ABM Industries Incorporated**
Lincoln; **Ford Motor Company**
Lincoln Financial Group; **Lincoln National Corporation**
Lincoln Navigator SUV; **Ford Motor Company**
LinkedIn.com; **LinkedIn Corporation**
Lipitor; **Pfizer Inc**
Lippincott; **Marsh & McLennan Companies Inc**
LiquidFence; **Spectrum Brands Holdings Inc**
Liquid-Plumr; **Clorox Company (The)**
LiquidVR; **Advanced Micro Devices Inc (AMD)**
Listerine; **Johnson & Johnson**
Loews Corporation; **Loews Hotels Holding Corporation**
Loews Miami Beach Hotel; **Loews Hotels Holding Corporation**
Loews Portofino Bay Hotel at Universal Orlando; **Loews Hotels Holding Corporation**
Loews Royal Pacific Resort at Universal Orlando; **Loews Hotels Holding Corporation**
Loews Santa Monica Beach Hotel; **Loews Hotels Holding Corporation**
Loews Sapphire Falls Resort at Universal Orlando; **Loews Hotels Holding Corporation**
LOFT; **Ascena Retail Group Inc**
LongHorn Steakhouse; **Darden Restaurants Inc**
LoopNet; **CoStar Group Inc**
LoveScout24; **Match Group Inc**
LoyaltyOne; **Alliance Data Systems Corporation**
LSI Lender Services LLC; **Brown & Brown Inc**
Lubrizol Additives; **Lubrizol Corporation (The)**
Lubrizol Advanced Materials; **Lubrizol Corporation (The)**
LucasFilm; **Walt Disney Company (The)**
Lucy; **Epic Systems Corporation**
Lumis; **ResMed Inc**
Lupron; **AbbVie Inc**
LXR Hotel & Resorts; **Hilton Worldwide Holdings Inc**
Lyrica; **Pfizer Inc**
M&Ms; **Mars Incorporated**
Mac Tools; **Stanley Black & Decker Inc**
MacAndrews & Forbes Inc; **Valassis Communications Inc**
MacAndrews & Forbes Inc; **Revlon Inc**
Maestro; **MasterCard Inc**

INDEX OF SUBSIDIARIES, BRAND NAMES AND AFFILIATIONS, CONT.

Magellan Complete Care; **Magellan Health Inc**
Maggiano's Little Italy; **Brinker International Inc**
Maggiore; **Avis Budget Group Inc**
Magnolia; **Best Buy Co Inc**
Maidenform; **HanesBrands Inc**
Mail Boxes Etc; **United Parcel Service Inc (UPS)**
Main Plaza Corporation; **Cullen-Frost Bankers Inc**
MainStay Investments; **New York Life Insurance Company**
Making Everlasting Memories; **Service Corporation International Inc**
Managed IP PBX; **Cox Communications Inc**
Manheim; **Cox Automotive Inc**
Manulife Financial Corporation; **John Hancock Financial**
Marathon; **Marathon Petroleum Corporation**
Marazzi; **Mohawk Industries Inc**
Marcus; **Goldman Sachs Group Inc (The)**
Margaritaville Vacation Club by Wyndham; **Wyndham Destinations Inc**
Marina Bay Saynds Pte Ltd; **Las Vegas Sands Corp (The Venetian)**
Marketing Cloud; **SalesForce.com Inc**
Marketo Inc; **Adobe Systems Inc**
Marketside; **Walmart Inc**
Marlex; **Chevron Phillips Chemical Company LLC**
Marmaxx; **TJX Companies Inc (T.J. Maxx)**
Marriott Bonvoy; **Marriott International Inc**
Marriott Hotels; **Marriott International Inc**
Marriott International Inc; **Ritz-Carlton Hotel Company LLC (The)**
Mars Incorporated; **VCA Inc**
Marsh & McLennan Companies Inc; **Mercer LLC**
Marsh & McLennan Companies Inc; **Oliver Wyman Group**
Marsh Inc; **Marsh & McLennan Companies Inc**
Marshalls; **TJX Companies Inc (T.J. Maxx)**
Marvel; **Walt Disney Company (The)**
Mary Kay Museum; **Mary Kay Inc**
Mason Street Advisors LLC; **Northwestern Mutual Life Insurance Company (The)**
Massachusetts Mutual Life Insurance Company; **MassMutual Financial Group**
MassMutual Ventures LLC; **MassMutual Financial Group**
Master Pro; **O Reilly Automotive Inc**
MasterCard; **MasterCard Inc**
MasterCraft; **Menard Inc**
MasterForce; **Menard Inc**
Masterpass; **MasterCard Inc**
Matador Cattle Company; **Koch Industries Inc**
Match; **Match Group Inc**
Match Group Inc; **IAC/InterActiveCorp**
maurices; **Ascena Retail Group Inc**
Maven; **General Motors Company (GM)**
Mayo Clinic; **Mayo Clinic**
Mayo Clinic Building; **Mayo Clinic**
Mayo Clinic Collaborative Research; **Mayo Clinic**
Mayo Clinic Hospital; **Mayo Clinic**
Mayo Clinic Specialty; **Mayo Clinic**
McCann; **McCann Worldgroup**
McCann Health; **McCann Worldgroup**
McCann Truth Central; **McCann Worldgroup**
McCann Worldgroup; **Interpublic Group of Companies Inc**
McCormick; **McCormick & Company Incorporated**
McGriff Seibels & Williams Inc; **BB&T Corporation**
McKesson Canada; **McKesson Corporation**
McKesson Prescription Technology Solutions; **McKesson Corporation**
McKinsey Global Institute; **McKinsey & Company Inc**
McKinsey Quarterly; **McKinsey & Company Inc**
McLane Company Inc; **Berkshire Hathaway Inc (Holding Co)**
Medecision Inc; **Health Care Service Corporation (HCSC)**
Medical Management International Inc; **PetSmart Inc**
Medical Neurogenetics Laboratories; **Laboratory Corporation of America Holdings**
MedStar Franklin Square Medical Center; **MedStar Health**
MedStar Good Samaritan Hospital; **MedStar Health**
MedStar Harbor Hospital; **MedStar Health**
MedStar Health Research Institute; **MedStar Health**
MedStar Montgomery Medical Center; **MedStar Health**
MedStar National Rehabilitation Hospital; **MedStar Health**
MedStar Physician Partners; **MedStar Health**
MedStar Southern Maryland Hospital Center; **MedStar Health**
Medumo; **Philips Healthcare**
MEDVAL LLC; **Brown & Brown Inc**
MemberConnections; **Centene Corporation**
Menard Real Estate; **Menard Inc**
Menards; **Menard Inc**
Menards Self Storage; **Menard Inc**
Menards Transportation; **Menard Inc**
Mercedex-Benz US International Inc; **Mercedes-Benz USA LLC**
Mercer Inc; **Marsh & McLennan Companies Inc**
Meridian; **WellCare Health Plans Inc**
Merry Maids; **ServiceMaster Company LLC (The)**
Messenger; **Facebook Inc**
Metamucil; **Procter & Gamble Company (The)**
MetroPCS; **T-Mobile US Inc**
M-I SWACO; **Schlumberger Limited**
Mi Tienda; **HEB Grocery Company LP**
MicroMD; **Henry Schein Inc**
Microsoft Corporation; **LinkedIn Corporation**
MidAmerican Energy Company; **Berkshire Hathaway Energy Company**
Midwest Employers Casualty; **W R Berkley Corporation**
Midwest Manufacturing; **Menard Inc**
MileagePlus; **United Continental Holdings Inc**
Miller Buckfire & Co LLC; **Stifel Financial Corp**
Millipede Inc; **Boston Scientific Corporation**
MindMeld; **Cisco Systems Inc**
Mint; **Intuit Inc**
Minute Maide; **Coca-Cola Bottling Co Consolidated**
MinuteClinic; **CVS Health Corporation**
Missouri Care; **WellCare Health Plans Inc**
MK High Intensity; **Mary Kay Inc**
MML Bay State Life Insurance Company; **MassMutual Financial Group**
Mobi; **ResMed Inc**
Mobil; **Exxon Mobil Corporation (ExxonMobil)**
Modelo; **Constellation Brands Inc**
Mohawk; **Mohawk Industries Inc**
Molex; **Molex LLC**
Molina Medicaid Solutions; **Molina Healthcare Inc**
Momentum Worldwide; **McCann Worldgroup**
Monolith Semiconductor Inc; **Littelfuse Inc**
MonotaRO; **WW Grainger Inc**
Monro Muffler Brake & Service; **Monro Muffler Brake Inc**
Monro Service Corporation; **Monro Muffler Brake Inc**

INDEX OF SUBSIDIARIES, BRAND NAMES AND AFFILIATIONS, CONT.

Monster Energy; **Coca-Cola Bottling Co Consolidated**
Mortech; **Zillow Inc**
Motec GmbH; **Ametek Inc**
Motivate International Inc; **Lyft Inc**
Motrin; **Johnson & Johnson**
Motto by Hilton; **Hilton Worldwide Holdings Inc**
MPLX LP; **Marathon Petroleum Corporation**
MPower; **ABM Industries Incorporated**
Mr Tire; **Monro Muffler Brake Inc**
MRM/McCann; **McCann Worldgroup**
mscripts; **Cardinal Health Inc**
MSD; **Merck & Co Inc**
MullenLowe Group; **Interpublic Group of Companies Inc**
Mungo Homes; **Clayton Homes Inc**
Mutual of Omaha Bank; **Mutual of Omaha Companies (The)**
Mutual of Omaha Foundation; **Mutual of Omaha Companies (The)**
MWI; **AmerisourceBergen Corporation**
MX; **Juniper Networks Inc**
MyBSWHealth; **Baylor Scott & White Health**
MyTopo; **Trimble Inc**
NailPlant.com; **Menard Inc**
Naked Apartments; **Zillow Inc**
Name Your Own Price; **Booking Holdings Inc**
National Amusements Inc; **CBS Corporation**
National Car Rental; **Enterprise Holdings Inc**
National Cremation Society; **Service Corporation International Inc**
National Geographic Network; **Walt Disney Company (The)**
National Indemnity Company; **GEICO Corporation**
National Title Insurance of New York Inc; **Fidelity National Financial Inc**
Navigators Group Inc; **Hartford Financial Services Group Inc (The)**
NBC Entertainment; **NBCUniversal Media LLC**
NBC News; **NBCUniversal Media LLC**
NBC Universal; **Comcast Corporation**
NCH Marketing Services Inc; **Valassis Communications Inc**
Neosporin; **Johnson & Johnson**
Neovia; **Archer-Daniels-Midland Company (ADM)**
Neptune Society; **Service Corporation International Inc**
NERA Economic Consulting; **Marsh & McLennan Companies Inc**
NETCONNECT; **CommScope Holding Company Inc**
NetScaler ADC; **Citrix Systems Inc**

NetSuite CRM; **Oracle NetSuite**
NetSuite OneWorld; **Oracle NetSuite**
Neulasta; **Amgen Inc**
NextGen Global Resources LLC; **Kelly Services Inc**
Nicotra Gebhardt Spa; **Regal-Beloit Corporation**
NIKE IHM Inc (Air Manufacturing Innovation); **Nike Inc**
No7; **Walgreens Boots Alliance Inc**
Nobilo; **Constellation Brands Inc**
Nor-Cal Produce Inc; **United Natural Foods Inc**
Nordstrom fsb; **Nordstrom Inc**
Nordstrom Local; **Nordstrom Inc**
Nordstrom Rack; **Nordstrom Inc**
Nordstrom.com; **Nordstrom Inc**
Nordstronrack.com/HauteLook; **Nordstrom Inc**
North American Advantage Insurance Services LLC; **Lennar Corporation**
North American Title Insurance Company; **Lennar Corporation**
Northern Natural Gas Company; **Berkshire Hathaway Energy Company**
Northern Powergrid; **Berkshire Hathaway Energy Company**
Northrop Grumman Innovation Systems; **Northrop Grumman Corporation**
NorthStar; **Juniper Networks Inc**
Northwestern Long Term Care Insurance Company; **Northwestern Mutual Life Insurance Company (The)**
Northwestern Mutual Investment Management Co LLC; **Northwestern Mutual Life Insurance Company (The)**
Northwestern Mutual Investment Services LLC; **Northwestern Mutual Life Insurance Company (The)**
Northwestern Mutual Wealth Management Company; **Northwestern Mutual Life Insurance Company (The)**
Norton; **Symantec Corporation**
Norwegian Cruise Line; **Norwegian Cruise Line Holdings Ltd (NCL)**
Novick Group Inc (The); **Arthur J Gallagher & Co**
Nuveen; **TIAA**
NV Energy Inc; **Berkshire Hathaway Energy Company**
NVHomes; **NVR Inc**
NVR Mortgage Finance Inc; **NVR Inc**
Oasis; **Henry Schein Inc**
Oasis Outsourcing Acquisition Corporation; **Paychex Inc**
Ocado Group PLC; **Kroger Co (The)**
Oceana Cruises; **Norwegian Cruise Line Holdings Ltd (NCL)**
OCREVUS; **Biogen Inc**
Octagon Worldwide; **Interpublic Group of Companies Inc**

Oculus; **Facebook Inc**
Off-Aisle; **Kohls Corporation**
Office 365; **Microsoft Corporation**
OfficeTeam; **Robert Half International Inc**
Ohana; **WellCare Health Plans Inc**
Ohio Brass; **Hubbell Incorporated**
Ohlinus Racing AB; **Tenneco Inc**
OilExpress; **PerkinElmer Inc**
OkCupid; **Match Group Inc**
Olay; **Procter & Gamble Company (The)**
OLD BAY; **McCormick & Company Incorporated**
Olive Garden; **Darden Restaurants Inc**
Oliver Wyman Group; **Marsh & McLennan Companies Inc**
Olympic; **PPG Industries Inc**
Omnicare; **CVS Health Corporation**
Omnicom Group Inc; **BBDO Worldwide**
Omnicom Media Group; **Omnicom Group Inc**
OmniServ; **ABM Industries Incorporated**
Omnispark; **O Reilly Automotive Inc**
One Day Pay; **AFLAC Incorporated**
One Kings Lane; **Bed Bath & Beyond Inc**
One Reverse Mortgage LLC; **Quicken Loans Inc**
One Star; **Nike Inc**
Onex Corporation; **Spirit AeroSystems Holdings Inc**
OnStar LLC; **General Motors Company (GM)**
Opdivo; **Bristol-Myers Squibb Company**
OpenTable; **Booking Holdings Inc**
Oppenheimer Funds Inc; **MassMutual Financial Group**
Oprah Winfrey Network (OWN, The); **Discovery Inc**
Optimum HealthCare; **Anthem Inc**
Optum; **UnitedHealth Group Inc**
Oracle Corporation; **Oracle NetSuite**
Orbital ATK Inc; **Northrop Grumman Corporation**
Orchard Supply Hardware; **Lowe's Companies Inc**
O'Reilly Auto Parts; **O Reilly Automotive Inc**
Orencia; **Bristol-Myers Squibb Company**
OrthoSpace Ltd; **Stryker Corporation**
Orthotaxy; **Johnson & Johnson**
Otezla; **Celgene Corporation**
Otis; **United Technologies Corporation**
Overwatch; **Activision Blizzard Inc**
Owens Corning PINK FIBERGLAS Insulation; **Owens Corning**
Oxford Life Insurance Company; **AMERCO (U-Haul)**
P&O Cruises; **Carnival Corporation**
Pacific Kitchen and Home; **Best Buy Co Inc**

INDEX OF SUBSIDIARIES, BRAND NAMES AND AFFILIATIONS, CONT.

Pacific Medical Centers; **Providence St Joseph Health**
Pacifico; **Constellation Brands Inc**
PacifiCorp; **Berkshire Hathaway Energy Company**
Pairs; **Match Group Inc**
Palazzo Resort Hotel Casino (The); **Las Vegas Sands Corp (The Venetian)**
Pampers; **Procter & Gamble Company (The)**
Pamplona Capital Management LLP; **PAREXEL International Corporation**
Paradigm; **Emerson Electric Co**
Paragon; **Allscripts Healthcare Solutions Inc**
PAREXEL Access; **PAREXEL International Corporation**
PAREXEL Biotech; **PAREXEL International Corporation**
Parisian Macao; **Las Vegas Sands Corp (The Venetian)**
Park Hyatt; **Hyatt Hotels Corporation**
Parlo; **ServiceNow Inc**
Partnerships in Care (PiC); **Acadia Healthcare Company Inc**
Paul Revere Life Insurance Company (The); **Unum Group**
Pavilions; **Albertsons Companies LLC**
Paychex Advance LLC; **Paychex Inc**
Paychex Flex; **Paychex Inc**
Paychex Flex Enterprise; **Paychex Inc**
Paychex Insurance Agency Inc; **Paychex Inc**
Paychex Online Payroll; **Paychex Inc**
Paydiant; **PayPal Holdings Inc**
Payless; **Avis Budget Group Inc**
PayPal; **PayPal Holdings Inc**
PayPal Credit; **PayPal Holdings Inc**
PECO Energy Company; **Exelon Corporation**
Pedialyte; **Abbott Laboratories**
Pedigree; **Mars Incorporated**
Pennsylvania Crusher; **Hillenbrand Inc**
Penske Automotive Group; **Penske Corporation**
Penske Commercial Vehicles Australia; **Penske Automotive Group Inc**
Penske Logistics; **Penske Corporation**
Penske Motor Group; **Penske Corporation**
Penske Power Systems; **Penske Automotive Group Inc**
Penske Racing; **Penske Corporation**
Penske Truck Leasing; **Penske Corporation**
Penske Truck Leasing Co LP; **Penske Automotive Group Inc**
Pepco Holdings LLC; **Exelon Corporation**
Pepsi; **PepsiCo Inc**
PepsiCo Inc; **Frito-Lay North America Inc**
Perigold; **Wayfair LLC**

Permanente Medical Groups; **Kaiser Permanente**
Pershing LLC; **Bank of New York Mellon Corporation**
Persona; **Zimmer Biomet Holdings Inc**
PersonalizationMall.com; **Bed Bath & Beyond Inc**
PetPerks; **PetSmart Inc**
Petsense; **Tractor Supply Company**
PetSmart Inc; **Chewy Inc (Chewy.com)**
PetSmart PetHotels; **PetSmart Inc**
PetSmart.com; **PetSmart Inc**
Philadelphia Flyers; **Comcast Corporation**
Phillips 66; **Chevron Phillips Chemical Company LLC**
Phillips 66 Partners LP; **Phillips 66**
Phoenix BV; **Synopsys Inc**
Phosphorylcholine (PC) Technology; **Cooper Companies Inc (The)**
Piedmont Airlines Inc; **American Airlines Group Inc**
Piedmont Natural Gas Company Inc; **Duke Energy Corporation**
Pierce Manufacturing Inc; **Oshkosh Corporation**
PINK; **Victoria's Secret**
Pirate Brands; **Hershey Company (The)**
Pivotal; **Dell Technologies Inc**
Pixar Animation Studios; **Walt Disney Studios (The)**
Playtex; **HanesBrands Inc**
PLEGRIDY; **Biogen Inc**
PlentyOfFish; **Match Group Inc**
PMK-BNC; **McCann Worldgroup**
Pomalyst/Imnovid; **Celgene Corporation**
Portal; **Facebook Inc**
Portal+; **Facebook Inc**
Porter-Cable; **Stanley Black & Decker Inc**
Portrazza; **Eli Lilly and Company**
Postle Operating LLC; **Thor Industries Inc**
Potomac Electric Power Company; **Exelon Corporation**
Power Torque; **O Reilly Automotive Inc**
POWERade; **Coca-Cola Bottling Co Consolidated**
PPG; **PPG Industries Inc**
Pratt & Whitney; **United Technologies Corporation**
Precision Castparts Corp; **Berkshire Hathaway Inc (Holding Co)**
Premier Farnell Ltd; **Avnet Inc**
President Starbucks Coffee Corporation; **Starbucks Corporation**
Prestige Financial; **Larry H Miller Group of Companies**
Prestone; **O Reilly Automotive Inc**
PREVELEAK; **Baxter International Inc**
Prevnar 13; **Pfizer Inc**
Priceline Group Inc; **Booking Holdings Inc**

Priceline.com; **Booking Holdings Inc**
PricewaterhouseCoopers (PWC); **Strategy&**
Prime Therapeutics LLC; **Health Care Service Corporation (HCSC)**
Princess Cruises; **Carnival Corporation**
Probiotics International Limited; **Archer-Daniels-Midland Company (ADM)**
Proclear; **Cooper Companies Inc (The)**
ProConnect Tax Online; **Intuit Inc**
ProfitStars; **Jack Henry & Associates Inc**
Prolia; **Amgen Inc**
Promise Hospital of East Los Angeles; **Kindred Healthcare LLC**
Promotion Watch Inc; **Valassis Communications Inc**
ProSeries; **Intuit Inc**
ProSys Inc; **Emerson Electric Co**
Proteus; **Synopsys Inc**
Protiviti Inc; **Robert Half International Inc**
Providence Health & Services; **Providence St Joseph Health**
Provident Life and Accident Insurance Company; **Unum Group**
Proximity Worldwide; **BBDO Worldwide**
PSA Airlines Inc; **American Airlines Group Inc**
PTC Inc; **Rockwell Automation Inc**
PTX; **Juniper Networks Inc**
Publicis Groupe SA; **Sapient Corporation**
Publicis.Sapient; **Sapient Corporation**
Pullmantur; **Royal Caribbean Cruises Ltd**
Pulte Homes; **PulteGroup Inc**
Pulte Mortgage LLC; **PulteGroup Inc**
Pure Ice; **Revlon Inc**
QFX; **Juniper Networks Inc**
Quaker; **PepsiCo Inc**
Quanum; **Quest Diagnostics Incorporated**
Quarter Pounder; **McDonald's Corporation**
Quazite; **Hubbell Incorporated**
QuickBooks Online; **Intuit Inc**
QVC Inc; **Qurate Retail Inc**
Raco; **Hubbell Incorporated**
Randalls; **Safeway Inc**
Randalls; **Albertsons Companies LLC**
RARE Infrastructure; **Legg Mason Inc**
Raymond James & Associates Inc; **Raymond James Financial Inc**
Raymond James Bank NA; **Raymond James Financial Inc**
Raymond James Financial International Ltd; **Raymond James Financial Inc**
Raymond James Financial Services Advisors Inc; **Raymond James Financial Inc**
Raymond James Financial Services Inc; **Raymond James Financial Inc**
Raymond James Investment Services Limited; **Raymond James Financial Inc**

INDEX OF SUBSIDIARIES, BRAND NAMES AND AFFILIATIONS, CONT.

Raymond James Ltd; **Raymond James Financial Inc**
RCI; **Wyndham Destinations Inc**
Ready-Frame; **BMC Stock Holdings Inc**
Realla; **CoStar Group Inc**
REC Solar; **Duke Energy Corporation**
RECOTHROM; **Baxter International Inc**
Red Had Mobile Application; **Red Hat Inc**
Red Hat Cloud; **Red Hat Inc**
Red Hat Enterprise Linux; **Red Hat Inc**
Red Hat Enterprise Linux; **Red Hat Inc**
Red Hat JBoss Middleware; **Red Hat Inc**
Red Hat Satellite; **Red Hat Inc**
Red Hat Storage; **Red Hat Inc**
Red Star Yeast Company LLC; **Archer-Daniels-Midland Company (ADM)**
Red Valve Company Inc; **Hillenbrand Inc**
RedHot; **McCormick & Company Incorporated**
Reese's; **Hershey Company (The)**
Regent Seven Seas Cruises; **Norwegian Cruise Line Holdings Ltd (NCL)**
RegTek.Solutions; **Bloomberg LP**
REI; **REI (Recreational Equipment Inc)**
REI Adventures; **REI (Recreational Equipment Inc)**
REI Gear and Apparel; **REI (Recreational Equipment Inc)**
RelationEdge; **Rackspace Hosting Inc**
Reliance; **AO Smith Corporation**
Remicade; **Johnson & Johnson**
RentalCars.com; **Booking Holdings Inc**
Republic Group; **AmTrust Financial Services Inc**
Repwest Insurance Company; **AMERCO (U-Haul)**
Reserve Roastery & Tasting Room; **Starbucks Corporation**
Residencies at the Ritz-Carlton (The); **Ritz-Carlton Hotel Company LLC (The)**
Results Delivery; **Bain & Company Inc**
RetailMeNot Everyday; **Valassis Communications Inc**
Revlimid; **Celgene Corporation**
Revlon Consumer Products Corp; **Revlon Inc**
Revlon Professional; **Revlon Inc**
RF360 Holdings Singapore Pte Ltd; **Qualcomm Incorporated**
RGA Group; **Arthur J Gallagher & Co**
Rialto Mortgage Finance; **Lennar Corporation**
Ribera Salud; **Centene Corporation**
RIDGID; **Home Depot Inc (The)**
RIPOLIN; **PPG Industries Inc**
Risperdal Consta; **Johnson & Johnson**
Riteflex; **Celanese Corporation**
RITUXAN; **Biogen Inc**
Ritz-Carlton (The); **Marriott International Inc**

Ritz-Carlton Destination Club (The); **Ritz-Carlton Hotel Company LLC (The)**
RIV 2013 Rail Holdings LLC; **Trinity Industries Inc**
Roark Capital Group; **Buffalo Wild Wings Inc**
Robert Half Finance & Accounting; **Robert Half International Inc**
Robert Half Legal; **Robert Half International Inc**
Robert Half Management Resources; **Robert Half International Inc**
Robert Half Technology; **Robert Half International Inc**
Robinson Fresh; **CH Robinson Worldwide Inc**
Roche Holding AG; **Genentech Inc**
Rock Holdings Inc; **Quicken Loans Inc**
Rockwell Collins Inc; **Collins Aerospace**
Rockwell Collins Inc; **United Technologies Corporation**
Rockwell Software; **Rockwell Automation Inc**
Rodelle Inc; **Archer-Daniels-Midland Company (ADM)**
Rold Gold; **Frito-Lay North America Inc**
ROSA; **Zimmer Biomet Holdings Inc**
Ross Dress for Less; **Ross Stores Inc**
Rotex Global LLC; **Hillenbrand Inc**
Roto-Rooter Corporation; **Chemed Corporation**
Royal Caribbean International; **Royal Caribbean Cruises Ltd**
Royal Dutch Shell plc; **Shell Oil Company**
Royce Funds; **Legg Mason Inc**
RSA; **Dell Technologies Inc**
RUN Powered by ADP; **Automatic Data Processing Inc (ADP)**
Rust-Oleum; **RPM International Inc**
Ryan Homes; **NVR Inc**
Ryobi; **Home Depot Inc (The)**
Ryzen; **Advanced Micro Devices Inc (AMD)**
SABRE; **Lam Research Corporation**
Sabre AirCentre Enterprise; **Sabre Corporation**
Sabre AirVision Marketing & Planning; **Sabre Corporation**
SabreSonic; **Sabre Corporation**
SafeAir AG; **Stryker Corporation**
Safemove; **AMERCO (U-Haul)**
Safestor; **AMERCO (U-Haul)**
Safetow; **AMERCO (U-Haul)**
Safeway; **Safeway Inc**
Safeway; **Albertsons Companies LLC**
Safeway SELECT; **Safeway Inc**
Saint Marys Campus; **Mayo Clinic**
Sales Cloud; **SalesForce.com Inc**
Salesforce Platform; **SalesForce.com Inc**
Salesforce Quip; **SalesForce.com Inc**
Sams Club; **Walmart Inc**

Samuel C Johnson Research; **Mayo Clinic**
Sands China Ltd; **Las Vegas Sands Corp (The Venetian)**
Sands Expo and Convention Center (The); **Las Vegas Sands Corp (The Venetian)**
Sands Macao Casino (The); **Las Vegas Sands Corp (The Venetian)**
SAP Concur; **Concur Technologies Inc**
SAP SE; **Concur Technologies Inc**
Scentinel; **Chevron Phillips Chemical Company LLC**
SCI Technology Inc; **Sanmina Corporation**
Scotch; **3M Company**
Scott & White Healthcare; **Baylor Scott & White Health**
Scott Safety; **3M Company**
Seabourn Cruise Line; **Carnival Corporation**
Seasons 52; **Darden Restaurants Inc**
Secureworks; **Dell Technologies Inc**
Select Medical Corporation; **Select Medical Holdings Corporation**
Select Nutrition; **United Natural Foods Inc**
SEM; **PPG Industries Inc**
Sempron; **Advanced Micro Devices Inc (AMD)**
Senior Emergency Departments; **Trinity Health**
Sensia; **Schlumberger Limited**
Sensipar; **Amgen Inc**
Sentaurus; **Synopsys Inc**
Serna Insurance Agency; **Arthur J Gallagher & Co**
Service Cloud; **SalesForce.com Inc**
ServiceLink Holdings LLC; **Fidelity National Financial Inc**
ServiceMaster Clean; **ServiceMaster Company LLC (The)**
ServiceMaster Global Holdings Inc; **ServiceMaster Company LLC (The)**
ServiceMaster Restore; **ServiceMaster Company LLC (The)**
Seventh-day Adventist Church; **AdventHealth**
SGK Brand Solutions; **Matthews International Corporation**
Shanghai Kaihong Technology Electronic Co Ltd; **Diodes Inc**
ShareFile; **Citrix Systems Inc**
Sheraton; **Marriott International Inc**
Sherwin-Williams; **Sherwin-Williams Company (The)**
Showtime Networks; **CBS Corporation**
Shred-it; **Stericycle Inc**
Sierra Trading Post; **TJX Companies Inc (T.J. Maxx)**
Silicon and Beyond Private Limited; **Synopsys Inc**
SilverLake; **Jack Henry & Associates Inc**

INDEX OF SUBSIDIARIES, BRAND NAMES AND AFFILIATIONS, CONT.

Silverline; **F5 Networks Inc**
SilverRail Technologies Inc; **Expedia Group Inc**
SilverScript Insurance Company; **CVS Health Corporation**
Silversea Cruises; **Royal Caribbean Cruises Ltd**
Similac; **Abbott Laboratories**
Simon & Schuster; **CBS Corporation**
Simply Healthcare; **Anthem Inc**
Six Senses; **Ritz-Carlton Hotel Company LLC (The)**
SkinnyPop; **Hershey Company (The)**
Sky plc; **Comcast Corporation**
SkySea Cruises; **Royal Caribbean Cruises Ltd**
Sleek MakeUP; **Walgreens Boots Alliance Inc**
SlimWare; **IAC/InterActiveCorp**
Smart For Your Baby; **Centene Corporation**
Smartfood; **Frito-Lay North America Inc**
SNAP Beta-Lactam; **IDEXX Laboratories Inc**
SNAP Lepto; **IDEXX Laboratories Inc**
SNAPshot DX; **IDEXX Laboratories Inc**
Soap & Glory; **Walgreens Boots Alliance Inc**
SodaStream; **PepsiCo Inc**
Sodexho Group; **Sodexo Inc**
Sodexo Foundation; **Sodexo Inc**
SoftBank Group Corp; **Brightstar Corporation**
Softvision; **Cognizant Technology Solutions Corporation**
SOLA; **Lam Research Corporation**
Soltex; **Chevron Phillips Chemical Company LLC**
Sonata; **Hyundai Motor America**
Sonoma Goods for Life; **Kohls Corporation**
SoundCom Systems; **Ametek Inc**
South Technologies Inc; **VCA Inc**
Southeast Toyota Distributors LLC; **JM Family Enterprises Inc**
Southeast Toyota Finance; **JM Family Enterprises Inc**
SparklineData; **Oracle Corporation**
Spectracide; **Spectrum Brands Holdings Inc**
SpectraSite Communications LLC; **American Tower Corporation (REIT)**
Spectro Scientific; **Ametek Inc**
Spectrum; **Charter Communications Inc**
Spectrum Business; **Charter Communications Inc**
Spectrum Community Solutions; **Charter Communications Inc**
Spectrum Enterprise Solutions; **Charter Communications Inc**

Spectrum Internet; **Charter Communications Inc**
Spectrum Reach; **Charter Communications Inc**
Spectrum TV; **Charter Communications Inc**
Spectrum Voice; **Charter Communications Inc**
SPEEDAIRE; **WW Grainger Inc**
Speedway; **Marathon Petroleum Corporation**
SPINRAZA; **Biogen Inc**
SQL; **Microsoft Corporation**
St Louis Children's Hospital; **BJC HealthCare**
St. Joseph Health; **Providence St Joseph Health**
Star TV; **Walt Disney Company (The)**
Starbucks; **Starbucks Corporation**
Starbucks Coffee Korea Co Ltd; **Starbucks Corporation**
Starmount Life Insurance Company; **Unum Group**
State; **AO Smith Corporation**
Staywell; **WellCare Health Plans Inc**
Stealthwatch Cloud; **Cisco Systems Inc**
Steri-Safe; **Stericycle Inc**
Sterling; **Kohler Company**
Stifel Bank & Trust; **Stifel Financial Corp**
Stifel Nicolaus & Company Inc; **Stifel Financial Corp**
Stifel Nicolaus Europe Limited; **Stifel Financial Corp**
Stifel Trust Company NA; **Stifel Financial Corp**
Stone Point Capital LLC; **AmTrust Financial Services Inc**
Stonhard; **RPM International Inc**
Stork Holding BV; **Fluor Corporation**
StreetEasy; **Zillow Inc**
SuiteCommerce; **Oracle NetSuite**
SunChips; **Frito-Lay North America Inc**
Sunett; **Celanese Corporation**
Sunrise; **Allscripts Healthcare Solutions Inc**
Super Start; **O Reilly Automotive Inc**
SuperData Research; **Nielsen Holdings plc**
SUPERVALU; **Albertsons Companies LLC**
Supra-clean; **PerkinElmer Inc**
SurePayroll; **Paychex Inc**
Suzhou Huasu Plastic Co Ltd; **Westlake Chemical Corporation**
SVEDKA; **Constellation Brands Inc**
Swan-Ganz; **Edwards Lifesciences Corporation**
Swiffer; **Procter & Gamble Company (The)**
SYGMA Network Inc; **SYSCO Corporation**
Symitar; **Jack Henry & Associates Inc**

Symposium/Itxpo; **Gartner Inc**
Syndion; **Lam Research Corporation**
SYNNEX Canada Limited; **SYNNEX Corporation**
SYNNEX Corporation; **Concentrix Corporation**
SYNNEX Infotec Corporation; **SYNNEX Corporation**
SYNNEX US; **SYNNEX Corporation**
SynXis; **Sabre Corporation**
SynXis Property Manager Solutions; **Sabre Corporation**
SYSTIMAX; **CommScope Holding Company Inc**
T Rowe Price Associates Inc; **T Rowe Price Group Inc**
T Rowe Price Hong Kong Limited; **T Rowe Price Group Inc**
T Rowe Price International Ltd; **T Rowe Price Group Inc**
T Rowe Price Singapore Private Ltd; **T Rowe Price Group Inc**
T.J. Maxx; **TJX Companies Inc (T.J. Maxx)**
Takagi; **AO Smith Corporation**
Talari Networks; **Oracle Corporation**
Taltz; **Eli Lilly and Company**
Taperloc; **Zimmer Biomet Holdings Inc**
Tata Starbucks Limited (India); **Starbucks Corporation**
TBWA Worldwide Inc (Disruption Company (The)); **Omnicom Group Inc**
Teavana; **Starbucks Corporation**
Tecentriq; **Genentech Inc**
TECFIDERA; **Biogen Inc**
TEGG; **ABM Industries Incorporated**
Telemundo; **Comcast Corporation**
Telephone and Data Systems Inc; **United States Cellular Corporation**
Telular; **Ametek Inc**
Temple Retail Support Center; **HEB Grocery Company LP**
Tenneco Inc; **Federal-Mogul LLC**
Terex Financial Services; **Terex Corporation**
Terminix; **ServiceMaster Company LLC (The)**
TerraSource Global; **Hillenbrand Inc**
Tetra; **Spectrum Brands Holdings Inc**
Texaco; **Chevron Corporation**
Textron; **Emerson Electric Co**
Textron Aviation; **Textron Inc**
Textron Financial Corporation; **Textron Inc**
Textron Systems; **Textron Inc**
Thai Curry; **Buffalo Wild Wings Inc**
The Collaboratory; **Cognizant Technology Solutions Corporation**
Thermo Scientific; **Thermo Fisher Scientific Inc**
Think Green; **Waste Management Inc**

INDEX OF SUBSIDIARIES, BRAND NAMES AND AFFILIATIONS, CONT.

Thinking of You; **Mary Kay Inc**
Thinsulate; **3M Company**
Thoma Bravo LLC; **McAfee LLC**
Thor Motor Coach Inc; **Thor Industries Inc**
Thrifty; **Dollar Thrifty Automotive Group Inc**
TIAA Bank; **TIAA**
TIAA FSB; **TIAA**
TIAA-CREF Trust Company; **TIAA**
Tianjin Tianhai Investment Co Ltd; **Ingram Micro Inc**
Tilex; **Clorox Company (The)**
Time Warner Inc; **AT&T Inc**
Tinder; **Match Group Inc**
TireBuyer.com; **American Tire Distributors Inc**
Title Source Inc; **Quicken Loans Inc**
TJX Canada; **TJX Companies Inc (T.J. Maxx)**
TLC; **Discovery Inc**
TM4 Inc; **Dana Incorporated**
T-Mobile; **T-Mobile US Inc**
T-Mobile International AG; **T-Mobile US Inc**
Tom Thumb; **Safeway Inc**
Tom Thumb; **Albertsons Companies LLC**
Tony's Fine Foods; **United Natural Foods Inc**
Total Care Auto Powered by Lancar; **Larry H Miller Group of Companies**
TOUGH GUY; **WW Grainger Inc**
Tovala; **Tyson Foods Inc**
TPG Capital; **Kindred Healthcare LLC**
Tractor Supply Company; **Tractor Supply Company**
TractorSupply.com; **Tractor Supply Company**
TradeFlow; **Expeditors International of Washington Inc**
Trajenta; **Eli Lilly and Company**
Trammell Crow Company; **CBRE Group Inc**
Travelocity; **Expedia Group Inc**
Tread Quarters Discount tire; **Monro Muffler Brake Inc**
Tremco; **RPM International Inc**
Tribute; **Mary Kay Inc**
Trident Society; **Service Corporation International Inc**
Tri-Frost Corporation; **Cullen-Frost Bankers Inc**
Trimble MAPS; **Trimble Inc**
Trinity Industries Leasing Company; **Trinity Industries Inc**
Trinity Rail Group LLC; **Trinity Industries Inc**
TRIP Rail Holdings LLC; **Trinity Industries Inc**
trivago; **Expedia Group Inc**

TriWest Healthcare Alliance; **Health Care Service Corporation (HCSC)**
Truck-Lite; **Penske Corporation**
Truett's Grill; **Chick-fil-A Inc**
Truett's Luau; **Chick-fil-A Inc**
Trulia; **Zillow Inc**
TrunkClub.com; **Nordstrom Inc**
Tucson; **Hyundai Motor America**
TUI Cruises; **Royal Caribbean Cruises Ltd**
Tum-E Yummies; **Coca-Cola Bottling Co Consolidated**
Turbo; **Intuit Inc**
Turbo Tax; **Intuit Inc**
Turion; **Advanced Micro Devices Inc (AMD)**
Turiscar Group; **Avis Budget Group Inc**
Turkish Airlines EuroLeague; **Endeavor LLC**
Turner Broadcasting System Inc; **AT&T Inc**
Twinbrook Insruance Brokerage Inc; **Brown & Brown Inc**
TWO Flight Center Hotel; **JetBlue Airways Corporation**
Twoo; **Match Group Inc**
Tylenol; **Johnson & Johnson**
Tyson Dalong; **Tyson Foods Inc**
Tyson Mexico Trading Company; **Tyson Foods Inc**
Tyson Nantong; **Tyson Foods Inc**
Tyson Rizhao; **Tyson Foods Inc**
U.S. Bank; **US Bancorp (US Bank)**
U.S. Steel Kosice; **United States Steel Corporation**
Uber Air; **Uber Technologies Inc**
Uber for Business; **Uber Technologies Inc**
Uber Freight; **Uber Technologies Inc**
UberEATS; **Uber Technologies Inc**
U-Haul International Inc; **AMERCO (U-Haul)**
Uhaul.com; **AMERCO (U-Haul)**
Ultima; **O Reilly Automotive Inc**
Uncle Ben's; **Mars Incorporated**
UNFI Canada, Inc; **United Natural Foods Inc**
UniCare; **Anthem Inc**
Union Standard; **W R Berkley Corporation**
Uniprise; **CommScope Holding Company Inc**
United Airlines Inc; **United Continental Holdings Inc**
United Development Systems Inc; **Brown & Brown Inc**
United Express; **United Continental Holdings Inc**
United Healthcare; **UnitedHealth Group Inc**
United Natural Trading Co; **United Natural Foods Inc**

United Services Automobile Association; **USAA**
United States Life Insurance Company (The); **American International Group Inc (AIG)**
United Technologies Corporation; **Collins Aerospace**
Unity Lab Services; **Thermo Fisher Scientific Inc**
Universal Pictures; **NBCUniversal Media LLC**
Unum Life Insurance Company of America; **Unum Group**
Unum Limited; **Unum Group**
Unum Zycie TUiR SA; **Unum Group**
UPS Capital; **United Parcel Service Inc (UPS)**
UPS Freight; **United Parcel Service Inc (UPS)**
UPS Hundredweight Services; **United Parcel Service Inc (UPS)**
UPS Next Day Air; **United Parcel Service Inc (UPS)**
UPS Supply Chain Solutions; **United Parcel Service Inc (UPS)**
US Bank NA; **US Bancorp (US Bank)**
US Craftmaster; **AO Smith Corporation**
USAA Casualty Insurance Company; **USAA**
USAA Federal Savings Bank Member FDIC; **USAA**
USAA General Indemnity Company; **USAA**
USAA Life Insurance Company; **USAA**
USAA Limited; **USAA**
USAA Mortgage Solutions; **USAA**
USBank; **US Bancorp (US Bank)**
UTC Aerospace Systems; **Collins Aerospace**
V Muller; **Becton, Dickinson and Company**
Valassis Digital; **Valassis Communications Inc**
Validus Holdings Ltd; **American International Group Inc (AIG)**
Vandar; **Celanese Corporation**
Vanderbilt Mortgage and Finance Inc; **Clayton Homes Inc**
Varathane; **RPM International Inc**
Variable Annuity Life Insurance Company (The); **American International Group Inc (AIG)**
Vascade; **Corning Incorporated**
vAuto; **Cox Automotive Inc**
VCA Animal Hospital; **VCA Inc**
VCA Canada; **VCA Inc**
VECTOR; **Lam Research Corporation**
Vela Insurance; **W R Berkley Corporation**
Velocity; **Discovery Inc**
Veloster; **Hyundai Motor America**

INDEX OF SUBSIDIARIES, BRAND NAMES AND AFFILIATIONS, CONT.

Venetian Macao Resort Hotel (The); **Las Vegas Sands Corp (The Venetian)**
Venmo; **PayPal Holdings Inc**
Veradigm; **Allscripts Healthcare Solutions Inc**
Veritas Capital; **athenahealth Inc**
Verizon Wireless; **Verizon Communications Inc**
Versys; **Lam Research Corporation**
Very Sexy; **Victoria's Secret**
Verzenio; **Eli Lilly and Company**
VetLyte; **IDEXX Laboratories Inc**
Vets First Choice; **Henry Schein Inc**
VetStat; **IDEXX Laboratories Inc**
Victoria; **Constellation Brands Inc**
Victorias Secret Beauty and Accessories; **Victoria's Secret**
Vidaza; **Celgene Corporation**
VIEKIRA PAK; **AbbVie Inc**
Viewpoint; **Trimble Inc**
Vigoro; **Home Depot Inc (The)**
Viking Technology; **Sanmina Corporation**
Vimeo; **IAC/InterActiveCorp**
VinSolutions; **Cox Automotive Inc**
VIPRION; **F5 Networks Inc**
Viralytics Limited; **Merck & Co Inc**
Virence Health Technologies; **athenahealth Inc**
VirtuStream; **Dell Technologies Inc**
Visa Canada Corporaiton; **Visa Inc**
Visa Checkout; **Visa Inc**
Visa Europe Ltd; **Visa Inc**
Visa International Service Association; **Visa Inc**
Visa USA Inc; **Visa Inc**
VisaNet; **Visa Inc**
Visual Studio; **Microsoft Corporation**
VITAS Healthcare Corporation; **Chemed Corporation**
Vivint Smart Home Arena; **Larry H Miller Group of Companies**
VivoTag; **PerkinElmer Inc**
Vmware; **Dell Technologies Inc**
VMware AirWatch; **VMware Inc**
VMware Horizon; **VMware Inc**
Vocado; **Oracle Corporation**
Vocalink; **MasterCard Inc**
Vons; **Safeway Inc**
Vons; **Albertsons Companies LLC**
VS Cotton; **Victoria's Secret**
vSphere; **VMware Inc**
W Hotels; **Marriott International Inc**
W/R/B Underwriting; **W R Berkley Corporation**
Waldorf Astoria Hotels & Resorts; **Hilton Worldwide Holdings Inc**
Walgreens; **Walgreens Boots Alliance Inc**
Walkers; **PepsiCo Inc**
Walmart; **Walmart Inc**
Walmart Neighborhood Market; **Walmart Inc**
walmart.com; **Walmart Inc**
Walt Disney Animation Studios; **Walt Disney Studios (The)**
Walt Disney Company (The); **Disney Media Networks**
Walt Disney Company (The); **Disney Parks, Experiences and Products (DPEP)**
Walt Disney Company (The); **Walt Disney Studios (The)**
Walt Disney Records; **Walt Disney Studios (The)**
Wamsutta; **Bed Bath & Beyond Inc**
WanderGuard; **Stanley Black & Decker Inc**
Warner Bros Entertainment Inc; **AT&T Inc**
watchOS; **Apple Inc**
Water-Right Inc; **AO Smith Corporation**
Wayfair; **Wayfair LLC**
WBR Insurance LLC; **Brown & Brown Inc**
Weber Shandwick; **Interpublic Group of Companies Inc**
Weiser; **Spectrum Brands Holdings Inc**
WellCare; **WellCare Health Plans Inc**
WellCare of California; **WellCare Health Plans Inc**
Wells Fargo Center; **Comcast Corporation**
Welsh Carson Anderson & Stowe; **Kindred Healthcare LLC**
Westcon-Comstor Americas; **SYNNEX Corporation**
Western Asset Management Company; **Legg Mason Inc**
WesternGeco; **Schlumberger Limited**
Westin; **Marriott International Inc**
Westlake Chemical OpCo LP; **Westlake Chemical Corporation**
Westlake Chemical Partners LP; **Westlake Chemical Corporation**
Westport Homes; **DR Horton Inc**
WhatsApp Messenger; **Facebook Inc**
Whole Catch; **Whole Foods Market Inc**
Whole Foods Market; **Amazon.com Inc**
Whole Foods Market; **Whole Foods Market Inc**
Whole Paws; **Whole Foods Market Inc**
Wiegmann; **Hubbell Incorporated**
Windows; **Microsoft Corporation**
Winners; **TJX Companies Inc (T.J. Maxx)**
WNB Capital Trust; **Cullen-Frost Bankers Inc**
Woodstock Farms Manufacturing; **United Natural Foods Inc**
Workstation ONE; **VMware Inc**
World Courier; **AmerisourceBergen Corporation**
World Financial Capital Bank; **Alliance Data Systems Corporation**
World Financial Network National Bank; **Alliance Data Systems Corporation**
World of Hyatt; **Hyatt Hotels Corporation**
World of Warcraft; **Activision Blizzard Inc**
WorldMarkt by Wyndham; **Wyndham Destinations Inc**
Worldpac; **Advance Auto Parts Inc**
World's Foremeost Bank; **Cabela's Inc**
www.fairview.org; **Fairview Health Services**
www.gene.com; **Genentech Inc**
Wyndham Hotels & Resorts; **Wyndham Destinations Inc**
Wyndham Worldwide Corporation; **Wyndham Destinations Inc**
Wynn Boston Harbor; **Wynn Resorts Limited**
Wynn Las Vegas Resort & Country Club; **Wynn Resorts Limited**
Wynn Macau Resort; **Wynn Resorts Limited**
Wynn Palace; **Wynn Resorts Limited**
Xbox; **Microsoft Corporation**
Xeljanz; **Pfizer Inc**
XenApp; **Citrix Systems Inc**
XenDesktop; **Citrix Systems Inc**
XenMobile; **Citrix Systems Inc**
XFINITY; **Comcast Corporation**
XGEVA; **Amgen Inc**
Xoom; **PayPal Holdings Inc**
XTO; **Exxon Mobil Corporation (ExxonMobil)**
Xtratherm; **Mohawk Industries Inc**
Yard House; **Darden Restaurants Inc**
Yield; **Synopsys Inc**
YouFirst Loyalty Program; **Loews Hotels Holding Corporation**
YouTube; **Alphabet Inc (Google)**
Yozell Associates; **Brown & Brown Inc**
Zenedge; **Oracle Corporation**
Zestimates; **Zillow Inc**
Zillow; **Zillow Inc**
Zimmer; **Zimmer Biomet Holdings Inc**
Zimride; **Enterprise Holdings Inc**
Zinsser; **RPM International Inc**
ZipCar; **Avis Budget Group Inc**
Zoro; **WW Grainger Inc**
Zoro.com; **WW Grainger Inc**
Zulily LLC; **Qurate Retail Inc**

INDEX OF SUBSIDIARIES, BRAND NAMES AND AFFILIATIONS, CONT.

CPSIA information can be obtained
at www.ICGtesting.com
Printed in the USA
FFHW010329190919
55065033-60765FF